dedicated to
Jacqueline T. Lewison
Selmer and Helen Lewison
Jean and Pete DeLozier

PREFACE

Courses in retailing have never been stronger offerings than they are now. The popularity of courses such as retailing can be attributed to several factors, not the least of which is the job-oriented student. With the sellers' market of the '60s and '70s turning into the buyers' market of the '80's, students today are primarily concerned with getting a good job. The need for courses that enhance their chances of finding entry-level management positions goes a long way to explain the increases in course offerings and enrollments in retailing courses.

With students' demands for more job-oriented subjects, basic courses such as retailing should continue to have a steady growth. Students as well as the business community view retailing as a practical, operations-oriented discipline. Accordingly, operations-oriented policies, methods, and procedures *must* be an integral part of the materials used in a retailing course. Academic credibility requires, however, that course materials be couched within a conceptual, theoretical framework. To meet these dual needs, we have set as our goal for *Retailing,* Second Edition, the task of striking a balance between academic credibility and the basic, operations-oriented needs of the job-seeking student.

To accomplish this goal we retained many of the features from the first edition and have added many new features. These are:

1. A complete coverage of basic retailing subjects within a new decision-making framework.
2. The addition of a chapter devoted to strategic retail management.
3. A bibliography of standard works in the retailing area, encompassing both academic and trade sources.
4. An author index and a subject index.
5. A set of exhibits (graphs, tables, pictures)

from authoritative works, as well as original exhibits created by the authors.
6. A set of cases that strengthen the students' decision-making capabilities.

The "plus" features of *Retailing,* Second Edition, are:

1. A new graphic treatment with full-color artwork and many color photographs, which enhance the textual presentation, as well as the use of color in the text design to highlight key concepts.
2. Each chapter begins with a chapter outline, followed by learning objectives.
3. Extensive subtitling enhances students' understanding of the text's organization and the subject matter.
4. Each chapter concludes with a summary. While each summary is short, it exposes the student to the basic chapter material for the third time.
5. At the end of each chapter is a set of key terms and concepts. This section includes both technical and nontechnical (jargon) terms.
6. Each chapter contains Review Questions that require the student to review the major concepts presented in each chapter.
7. Finally, each chapter concludes with an in-depth listing of Related Readings, which guide the student who may seek even more information.

This book is organized into six parts, which are further divided into 25 chapters that provide comprehensive yet brief learning modules to facilitate student learning. All major topics are contained in the book, including consumers; retail site location; designing, staffing, and organizing the retail store; developing the retail offering and getting the merchandise into the store; developing and controlling the merchandise plan; setting and adjusting retail prices; retail promotion activities; the importance of environmental influences on retail business; and retail financial statements and operations control. The basic topics serve the students' real needs for understanding the world of retailing.

The instructional-support package has been improved with this addition. The instructor's manual contains complete lecture outlines, answers to the discussion questions, and teaching notes for the cases. The package also contains transparency masters and a test bank of over 2000 true-false and multiple-choice questions.

In addition to these items, a new student guide prepared by the authors and George Prough and John Works, both of the University of Akron, is available to provide the student with additional examples and insights into retailing.

ACKNOWLEDGMENTS

This book, of course, could not have been possible without the valuable support of many people. Therefore, we wish to thank the following professors for reviewing the manuscript: George Lucas, Texas A&M University; L. Lynn Judd, Louisiana State University; Louis D. Canale, Genessee Community College; Anthony Urbaniak, Northern State College; and Larry Gresham, Texas A&M University.

Also, we wish to extend our appreciation to the helpful suggestions of reviewers in the earlier stages of manuscript preparation: Nathan Himelstein, Essex County College; John S. Berens, Indiana State University; Joseph Hrebenak, CCAC Allegheny Campus; Terryl S. Butwid, Rochester Institute of Technology; Frank McDaniels, Delaware County Community College; Glenn R. Barth, University of Montana; and Mary S. Andersen, Frostburg State College. With such qualitative input from so many knowledgeable people in the field of retailing, we believe this book can fulfill the needs students have for a basic understanding of both the theoretical and the practical applications of retailing.

For their support and encouragement, a special appreciation goes to James W. Dunlap, Dean of the College of Business Administration at the University of Akron, and to James F. Kane, Dean of the College of Business Administration at the University of South Carolina.

A special thanks goes to the staff of the Marketing Department at the University of Akron; to Betty Criss, who oversaw much of the original production of this revision; to Cheryl Nader, for her special typing skills; to my graduate assistants, Joseph McCafferty, Louis Stouch, James B. Works, and Sharon Neidert, for their research efforts; and to my student assistants, Yea Browning, Julie Mutschelknaus, Suzanna Simone, and Jonilon Evans, for their numerous contributions.

Additionally, we wish to thank editors Rex Davidson and Steve Smith of Merrill Publishing for their support in this project. Finally, we are indebted to our students who guide us through their questions and comments in the teaching of the basics of retailing.

Dale M. Lewison
M. Wayne DeLozier

BRIEF CONTENTS

CONTENTS

CASES

RETAILING

PART ONE
Discovering the World of Retail Marketing

Outline

WHAT IS RETAILING?

The Retailer
The Retail Level

THE IMPORTANCE OF RETAILING

THE PROBLEM OF RETAILING

The Marketing Concept

THE RIGHT MERCHANDISING BLEND

The Right Product
The Right Quantity
The Right Place
The Right Time
The Right Price
The Right Appeal

THE RIGHT PERFORMANCE STANDARDS

Operating Ratios
Financial Ratios

Objectives

- Appreciate the complexities of operating a retail business

- Distinguish retailers and their activities from other marketing institutions

- Describe the importance of retailing within our nation's economy

- Discuss the retailer's problem of striking a balance between the customer's merchandising needs and the retailer's performance needs

- Explain what merchandising factors are involved with offering the right product . . . in the right quantities . . . in the right place . . . at the right time . . . at the right price . . . by the right appeal

- Identify the role of operating and financial ratios in establishing performance standards for retailers

1
The Nature of Retailing

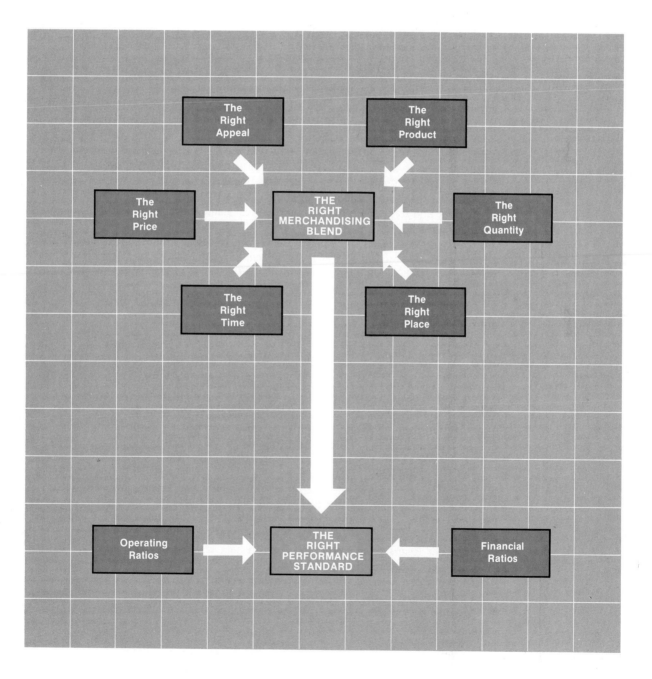

Successful retailing is a complex undertaking. "Over the years, the myth has grown that if you are not qualified or trained for any specific field you can 'make it' in retailing. After all, retailing is neither art nor science, it's sheer common sense."[1] While common sense is a definite asset to any retailer, common sense is not enough to survive in the competitive world of retailing. The days when "rules of thumb" were sufficient to run a successful retail business have long since disappeared.

In many respects, retailing requires greater skill for survival than most other business enterprises do. Successful retailers combine the creative aspects of art with the rigid requirements of science. Retailing activities such as advertising, personal selling, merchandising, and interior store design are as much an art as a science. Other activities such as inventory control, market research, and financial accounting demand the discipline of a science.

One reason the myth of retailing has existed for so long is the misguided perception of the ease with which a person can enter the field. A retailer is not required by law to have any formal education or other qualifications to open a business. The only requirement is that an owner have a business license. Also, since the initial capital investment for starting a limited retail operation can be relatively small (compared to that for some manufacturers and wholesalers), virtually anyone can enter some form of retail operation. As a result, most business start-ups each year are retail stores. In reality, a number of formidable entry barriers restrict one from starting a retail business, including (1) stiff competition from large, integrated retail organizations, (2) sophisticated management skills needed to solve complex and dynamic problems, and (3) escalating costs of physical, human, and financial resources.

The real challenge of retailing, however, is not entering the field, but knowing how to *stay* in business—this is the critical task. The failure rate among retailers is extremely high. While figures vary, Dun & Bradstreet estimates that approximately two out of every four retailers fail within the first year. To avoid such fate, the would-be J. C. Penney or F. W. Woolworth needs formal training in the art and science of retailing.

The Retailer

The many definitions of retailing all share the same basic thought: **retailing** is *the business activity of selling goods or services to the final consumer.* A **retailer** is *any business establishment that directs its marketing efforts toward the final consumer for the purpose of selling goods or services.* The key words in this definition are "the final consumer." A business selling the same product to two different buyers may in one instance perform a retailing activity, but in the other instance *not* perform a retailing activity. As an example, assume that you buy a chandelier to hang in your living room. In this case, the lighting company has made a retail sale. On the other hand, assume that a home builder walks into the *same* store, purchases the *same* chandelier, and installs it in a home he is building. In this case, the lighting company did *not* make a retail sale since the chandelier was not sold to the final consumer (user) of the product. Thus, a sale is a retail sale when the ultimate consumer purchases the product. What distinguishes a retail sale from other types of sales is the buyer's *reason* for buying. If the buyer purchases the product for personal use, the sale is considered a retail sale. If the buyer purchases the product for resale at a profit or to use in a business, the sale is *not* a retail sale. Instead, it is a business sale.

In the preceding example, is the lighting company a retailer? The answer depends upon the amount of business the company does with *final* consumers. According to the United States Bureau of the Census in its *Census of Retailing*, a retailer is any business establishment whose retail store can make both retail and business (nonretail) sales, but is classified as a retailer when its retail sales exceed 50 percent of its total sales.

The Retail Level

Retailers are referred to as "middlemen" or "intermediaries." Both references suggest that retailers occupy a position "in the middle of" or "between" two other levels. In fact, retailers do occupy a middle position. They purchase, receive, and store products from producers and wholesalers to provide consumers with convenient locations for buying products. As shown in Figure 1–1, retailers are part of a chain or channel that enables the movement of products from producer markets to local customers. This chain of business is called a marketing channel. A **marketing**

Will this retailer survive the competitive world of retailing?

FIGURE 1–1
The marketing channel

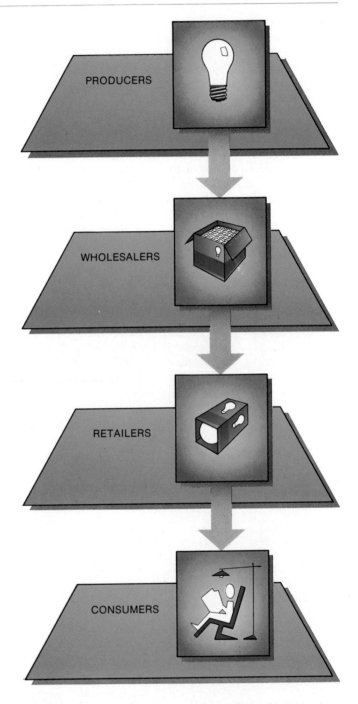

channel is *a team of marketing institutions that directs a flow of goods or services from the producer to the final consumer.* Generally, the team consists of a producer, one or more wholesalers, and many retailers.

While the retailer's role within the marketing channel team will be covered more extensively in Chapter 3, at this point it is instructive to point out some different operating characteristics distinguishing the retailers from other members of the channel team (producers and wholesalers):

(a)   (b)

Retailers place greater emphasis on internal atmospherics than do wholesalers

1. Retailers sell in smaller quantities (individual units) on a more frequent basis while the less frequent typical order quantity sold by wholesalers and producers is much larger (case and truck load lots).
2. Retailers' place of business is open to the general consuming public while producers and wholesalers do not normally make over-the-counter sales to the general public (factory and wholesaler outlets are exceptions).
3. Retailers charge higher per-unit prices than those commonly associated with producers and wholesalers (loss leaders are a notable exception).
4. Retailers tend to utilize a one-price policy while producers and wholesalers make more extensive use of variable prices based on some form of discounting structure.
5. Retailers rely on consumers to make the initial contact by visiting the store or placing mail or telephone orders, whereas producers and wholesalers employ outside sales representatives to make initial sales contacts (at-home retailing is a notable exception).
6. Retailers place greater emphasis on the external and internal atmospherics of their physical facilities and fixtures as major merchandising tools.

Retailing has a profound effect on our society and the people it comprises. The large number of establishments engaging in retail activities, the number of people those establishments employ, and the tremendous sales volume they generate indicate the importance of retailing within our society.

Retail establishments (individual operating units) outnumber the combined total of the other two major members of the distribution channel, manufacturers and wholesalers. As Figure 1–2 shows, 1.285 million retail establishments operate within the U.S. economy, compared with 329,000 manufacturers and 404,000 wholesalers. In relative terms, there are approximately 3.9 retail establishments for each manufacturing establishment and 3.1 retailers for every wholesaler.

Retailing's significance for the nation's economic welfare is reflected by the status of the retail industry as an employer of U.S. workers. Table 1–1 portrays 1983 employment figures for nonagricultural industries. Retailing is the third largest employer, exceeded only by the manufacturing and service sectors. Retailers provide employment for approximately one of every seven nonagricultural workers in the private sector. If past trends continue, retail employment is expected to exceed 20 million persons by the end of the decade.

Total retail sales, as well as per capita retail sales, have netted steady gains over the last 17 years (see Table 1–2). Total retail sales in 1983 were about $1,174

THE IMPORTANCE OF RETAILING

(a)

*Retailing: the **art** and **science** of selling **goods** and **services** to the final consumer*

(b)

(c)

FIGURE 1–2
Number of establish-
ments within the chan-
nel of distribution
(source: U.S. Depart-
ment of Commerce,
*Statistical Abstract of
the United States,*
105th ed. [Washington,
D.C.: U.S. Department
of Commerce, 1985],
518)

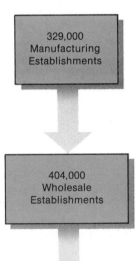

329,000
Manufacturing
Establishments

404,000
Wholesale
Establishments

1,285,000 Retail Establishments

Industry	Number Employed (thousands)
Mining	921
Construction	6,149
Manufacturing	19,946
Transportation, public utilities	6,988
Wholesaling	4,314
Retailing	16,832
Finance, insurance, real estate	6,510
Services	30,922
Public administration	4,710

TABLE 1–1

Employment: nonagri-
cultural industries
(1983)

CHAPTER 1
THE NATURE OF
RETAILING

Source: U.S. Department of Commerce, *Statistical Abstract of the United States,* 105th ed. (Washington, D.C.: U.S. Government Printing Office, 1985), 404.

Year	Total Retail Sales (billions)	Annual Percentage Change (%)	Per Capita Retail Sales (dollars)
1967	293.0	—	1,484
1968	324.4	10.7	1,627
1969	346.7	6.9	1,722
1970	368.4	6.3	1,806
1971	406.2	10.3	1,964
1972	449.1	10.6	2,146
1973	509.5	13.4	2,411
1974	541.0	6.2	2,536
1975	588.1	8.7	2,729
1976	657.4	11.8	3,022
1977	725.2	10.3	3,300
1978	806.9	11.3	3,633
1979	899.4	11.5	4,005
1980	960.8	6.8	4,228
1981	1,043.5	8.6	4,546
1982	1,074.6	3.0	4,636
1983	1,174.0	9.3	5,018

TABLE 1–2

Retail sales, 1967–
1983 (in current
dollars)

Source: U.S. Department of Commerce, *Statistical Abstract of the United States,* 105th ed. (Washington, D.C.: U.S. Government Printing Office, 1985), 782.

billion, compared to total retail sales of $293 billion in 1967. Per capita retail sales increased from $1,484 to $5,018 during the same time period. These figures increase in significance when one considers that retail sales account for approximately 45 percent of personal income.

Retail store sales by type of business are shown in Figure 1–3. The dominance of our stomachs and our love of the automobile are readily apparent in our spending. Combined food and drink sales are approaching $350 billion while automotive-related expenditures exceeded $275 billion in 1983.

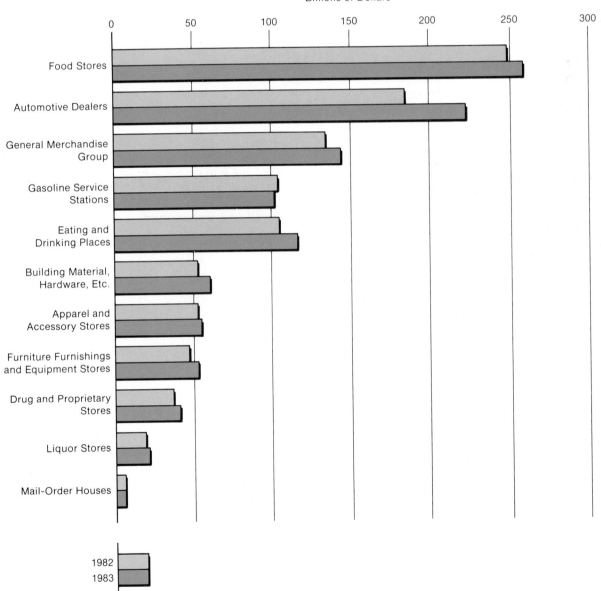

FIGURE 1–3
Retail store sales, by kind of business, 1982–1983 (source: U.S. Department of Commerce, *Statistical Abstract of the United States,* 105th ed. [Washington, D.C.: U.S. Government Printing Office, 1985], 778)

The retailer's problem is how to maintain a proper balance between the ability of the firm's merchandising programs to meet the needs of targeted consumers in a satisfactory manner and the ability of the firm's administrative plans to meet the retailer's need to operate effectively and efficiently. Just as the scales of justice must judge the rights and responsibilities of two disputing parties, the "scale of retailing" must weigh the product and service needs of the customer against the operational and financial needs of the retailer. A successful retail business strikes a balance between the customer's merchandising needs and the retailer's performance standards (see Figure 1–4). In other words, a successful retail management team consists of both "out front" merchandisers and "behind the scenes" operations managers, a problem that is at the heart of the marketing concept.

The Marketing Concept

The **marketing concept** is *the philosophy that the overall goal of every business organization is to satisfy consumer needs at a profit.*

Before the general acceptance of the marketing concept, the role of marketing in most businesses was either "to sell what we have produced" or "to sell what we have bought." A firm adopting the marketing concept, however, strives to sell what the customer wants. The marketing concept, then, stresses keying supply to demand rather than keying demand to supply. The equally important objective besides customer satisfaction, of course, is profit. Without profit, the firm cannot stay in business to satisfy anybody's needs.

For the retailer, more so than any other marketing institution, adoption of the marketing concept is an immediate problem.[2] Since the retailer deals with consumers on a day-to-day basis, it is more directly affected than wholesalers and producers by the need to deliver consumer satisfaction at a profit. The retailer is the first to reap the benefits of consumer satisfaction but also the first to bear the brunt of consumer dissatisfaction. Research indicates that "96 percent of dissatisfied customers never complain to the company."[3] Instead, 60 percent to 90 percent of them simply switch stores or brands. Insofar as it costs five times as much to attract a new customer as it does to retain an existing one, it makes sense for a store to try to ensure customer satisfaction.

Satisfying the customer at a profit is not a simple task, however. By definition, the solution to the marketing concept—and to the problem of retailing—demands

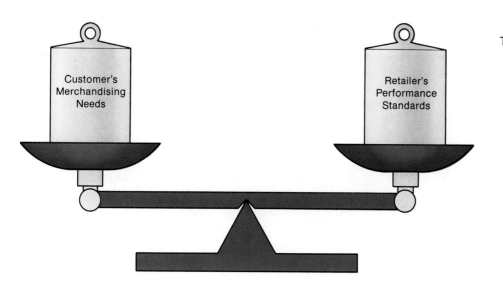

FIGURE 1–4
The scales of retailing

the solution of two other problems: the right merchandising blend and the right performance standards.

THE RIGHT MERCHANDISING BLEND

The right merchandising blend matches the ingredients of the retailer's merchandising program with the decisions the consumer faces in making the right choice. Figure 1–5 illustrates this problem. The right blend includes the following six ingredients:

> offering the right product
>> in the right quantities
>>> in the right place
>>>> at the right time
>>>>> at the right price
>>>>>> by the right appeal.

The right blend is thus the one that satisfies both customer and retailer. The right choice is the set of decisions that best satisfies the consumer's needs before, during, and after the purchase decision.

The Right Product

What makes a product "right" is a unique composite of three product elements—merchandising utilities, intrinsic qualities, and augmenting extras. Figure 1–6 shows the relationship between these three product elements.

Merchandising Utilities

The merchandising utilities associated with each product provide the foundation for building the right product offering. A product's **merchandising utilities** are *benefits*

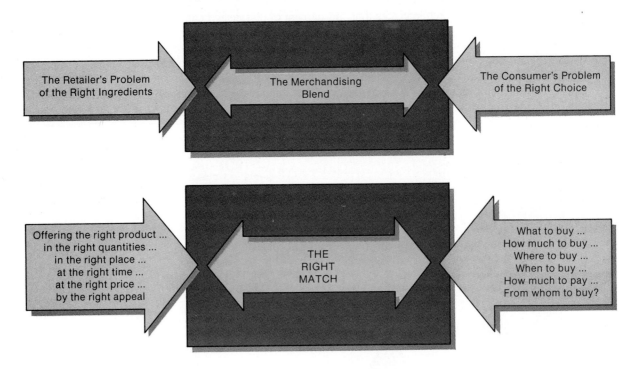

FIGURE 1–5
The problem of the right merchandising blend

12

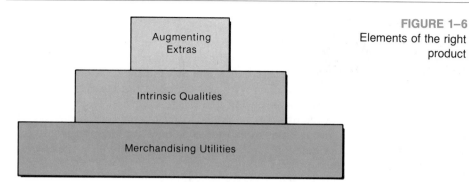

FIGURE 1–6
Elements of the right
product

CHAPTER 1
THE NATURE OF
RETAILING

the consumer seeks in buying, using, and possessing the product. Stated differently, a product's merchandising utilities are satisfactions that are either *perceived* (a woman feels her new suit makes her look more distinguished), *real* (other people think she looks more distinguished in her new suit), *functional* (a woman's new suit is a comfortable fit), or *psychological* (she believes the new suit makes her look thinner). We must then ask what the retailer is really selling. Is it deodorant or security, cosmetics or hope, club membership or acceptance? From the merchandising utilities perspective it is the expected benefits of security, hope, and acceptance.

Intrinsic Qualities

The tangible aspects of a product are also important in the consumer's evaluation of what makes a product right. **Intrinsic qualities** are *the inherent physical attributes such as product form, features, materials, and workmanship that satisfy consumer needs.* The intrinsic qualities of a product are important because they determine whether the product is capable of doing what it is supposed to do, looking the way it is supposed to look. Intrinsic qualities strongly influence the consumer's perception of a product's quality, suitability, and durability. Some aspects that determine a product's intrinsic qualities are style, design, shape, weight, color, and material.

Home delivery is an augmenting extra that provides supplemental benefits to the customer

Augmenting Extras

Augmenting extras are *auxiliary product dimensions that provide supplementary benefits to the customer.* Warranties, delivery, installation, packaging, instructions, and alterations are some of the major extras that can greatly enhance the customer's satisfaction with the product. The type and extent of the benefits such extras provide depend on the customer's buying and usage behavior. For example, the additional benefit of convenience can be provided by offering home delivery and packages with handles. A customer's need for additional security and reassurance when making a purchase decision can be augmented by warranties, maintenance contracts, and liberal return policies.

All three elements—merchandising utilities, intrinsic qualities, and augmenting extras—are needed to ensure buyer acceptance of a product. Therefore, each element is a necessary component of the "right product."

The Right Quantity

The right quantity is the exact match between the consumer's buying and using needs and the retailer's buying and selling needs. Factors the retailer must consider in determining the right quantity are (1) the number of units, (2) the size of units, (3) the unit measurements, and (4) the unit needs.

Number of Units

For some consumers, a single unit is the right quantity: one tube of toothpaste, one pack of cigarettes, one can of Coke, or one box of bandages. For other consumers, multiple-unit quantities are the right quantity: two tubes of toothpaste, a carton of cigarettes, a six-pack of Coke, or a home first-aid kit.

A single tube of toothpaste might be the right quantity if the retailer knows that consumers either are not concerned about price, are unmarried, have only one bathroom, or shop frequently. However, a retailer whose customers are price sensitive, married, have more than one bathroom, or shop infrequently should offer larger quantities at a price savings per unit. For example, the retailer could offer two tubes of toothpaste for $1.39 instead of one tube for $.75.

Sizes of Units

Products come in many sizes: small, medium, large, and extra-large; short, regular, and long; king, queen, and regular; super, jumbo, and superjumbo; individual and family. Retailers know that the "size" labels they carry affect the kind of clientele they attract and the sales they make. A shrewd clothing retailer, for example, knows that the right size for Bill is "extra large," but the right size for Mary is one for the "full-figured woman." The right size, then, is the size that fits the customer's needs, both physically and psychologically. And even though the sizes consumers desire are usually predictable, without proper inventory control, retailers can lose many sales by stocking the wrong sizes.

Unit Measurement

Quantities are expressed in various units of measurement: inches, feet, yards, and miles; centimeters, decimeters, meters, and kilometers; ounces, pounds, and English tons; grams, kilograms, and metric tons; pints, quarters, and gallons; liters and dekaliters. Retailers realize, at least for the present, that most Americans think the inch, pound, and quart are the right quantities and the centimeter, kilogram, and liter are the wrong quantities. Recent government efforts at metric education, however, could soon make metric measurements acceptable quantity expressions.

Unit Need

Unit need refers to the purchase-quantity decisions that both retailers and consumers must make. In the consumer's purchase decision process, buying too few units of a particular product means personal or family dissatisfaction, while buying too many units results in waste or leftovers. Buying just enough, however, provides personal and family satisfaction.

The retailer's decision about quantity is in many ways more critical than the consumer's. A retailer that does not purchase enough risks stockouts and therefore lost sales. Purchasing too much causes overstocking and subsequently higher inventory carrying costs and very likely reduced profit margins if markdowns are necessary. Therefore, buying the proper quantity leads to customer satisfaction and higher retail profits.

The Right Place

A retailer trying to determine the right place should consider the following place factors in making the decision: (1) market area, (2) market coverage, and (3) store layout and design.

A **market** is *a geographic area where buyers and sellers meet to exchange money for products and services.* The "right" marketplace for retailers is the area containing enough people to allow them to satisfy consumer needs at a profit. The retailer's marketplace can range from one block to several hundred miles, and it can range from thousands of miles, even countries, to a corner in a small rural crossroad town. To find the "right" market area, the retailer must consider (1) regional markets, (2) local markets, (3) trading areas, and (4) site.

Market Areas

Regional markets. For the retailer, the regional market is the right part of the country. That decision already has been made for many retailers. A woman who has inherited her father's furniture store in Little Rock, Arkansas, for example, probably has little concern about regional markets. Chain retailers, however, must evaluate different parts of the country to determine where to locate new stores. Many chain retailers face the decision of whether to expand into, or increase their representation within, parts of the rapidly growing sunbelt region of the United States. For some snowbelt retailers, the sunbelt offers numerous possibilities for expansion; for others—furriers, for instance—it offers very little opportunity.

Local markets. At the local level, retailers must determine the right town and the right part of town. For some retailers, the right town is one with a minimum population of 100,000. Large general merchandise and variety discount stores such as K Mart need a large population base to develop the sales volume they need to operate their stores profitably. On the other hand, smaller retailers are less concerned with total population, but rather with the size and demographic composition of a *segment* of the population. A children's shoe store chain, for example, would not fare well in a retirement community.

The right part of town for some retailers is the central city; for others, the suburbs. An office supply store probably would not succeed in a residential suburb, and a nursery probably would not flourish downtown. Some retailers cater to

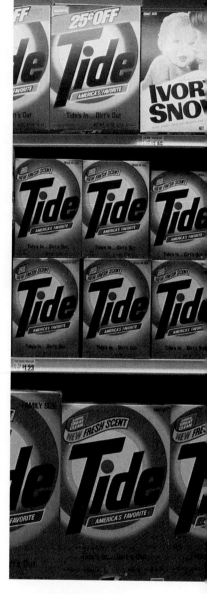

The right quantity: individual, regular, or family size?

In selecting the right place, some retailers choose the greater customer drawing power of a shopping center

upper- and middle-income consumers who often cluster in suburbs; others cater to lower-income consumers who often live in or near the inner city.

Trading areas. Once the right local market has been chosen, the retailer must then determine the right shopping area or the right shopping center. Some retailers go it alone, relying on their own abilities to draw customers. A convenience food store located near a residential neighborhood is an example. Other retailers rely on the drawing power of a cluster of stores. They believe that by grouping together in shopping centers or associating with anchor stores (such as department stores, discount houses, and supermarkets), they can create the "right" place. It would be difficult, for instance, for a bow-tie boutique to draw customers on the power of its own magnetism. However, it could attract considerable patronage from customers who pass the store in a shopping mall.

Site. For the freestanding retailer, the right site allows the store to intercept customers on their way to work or on their way home, is readily accessible to consumers from the standpoints of approaching, entering, and exiting, and is visible to passing consumer traffic. Within a shopping mall, the right site may be on the ground floor or at one end of the mall, or it may avoid customers who are incompatible with the operation (i.e., with complementary neighboring retailers). A pet shop, for example, might discourage potential patrons of a bridal boutique, and "head shop" patrons might repel potential customers of a classical record store. In summary, the right site is consistent with the customer's shopping needs and the retailer's image needs.

Market Coverage

The right place may be every place, a few places, or a single place. As part of the "right place" decision, retailers must decide whether they want intensive market coverage, selective market coverage, or exclusive market coverage (refer to Figure 1–7).

Intensive market coverage. With an intensive strategy, the retailer selects and utilizes as many retail outlets as are justified to obtain "blanket" coverage of an entire market area. Generally, convenience-goods retailers use an intensive market strategy. (Convenience goods are products and services consumers want to purchase with a minimum of effort; examples are snack foods and soft drinks.)

The number of outlets a retailer includes in an intensive market strategy depends on two factors—the type of business and the area it can serve from a single

FIGURE 1–7
Market area coverage and the right place

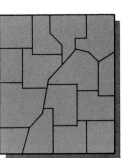

Intensive Coverage:
"Everyplace"

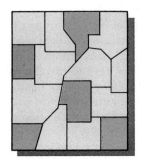

Selective Coverage:
"A Few Places"

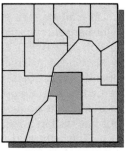

Exclusive Coverage:
"A Place"

16

outlet. A good strategy for a convenience food chain (such as 7-Eleven stores) might be to locate a store on every major traffic artery leading into each important residential area in town. A strategy for a record store, however, might be to place a store in each major shopping center in town. Since the retailer that employs an intensive coverage strategy must try to serve *all* customers within a given market area, the right place is *everyplace*.

Selective market coverage. When a retailer sells shopping goods, the logical strategy is to cover selective markets. (Shopping goods are products that consumers want to compare for style, price, or quality before making a purchase decision; examples are clothing, furniture, and appliances.) For these products, a retailer should choose enough locations to ensure adequate coverage of selected target markets.

The number of outlets the retailer establishes in the selective coverage strategy should equal the number of market segments served. The number of segments depends upon (1) how many market segments contain the type of customer the retailer is trying to reach, (2) the sales level expected for each potential market segment, and (3) the degree of representation the retailer wants in the total market to create a desired image and exposure level.

Generally speaking, chain retailers such as apparel stores, department stores, hardware stores, discount-department stores, auto repair shops, and drug stores follow a selective market coverage strategy. In this case, the right place is the *select* place.

Exclusive market coverage. In an exclusive market coverage strategy, the retailer elects to use one location to serve either an entire market area or some major segment of that market. An exclusive strategy is ideal for retailers who sell specialty goods. (Specialty goods are those that consumers are willing to put forth considerable effort to obtain.) Specialty-goods manufacturers often enter into exclusive arrangements with certain retailers. The advantages to manufacturers are more intense selling efforts on the part of their retailers and an exclusive, high-quality image for their products. By the same token, the exclusive retailer enjoys several advantages. Among the advantages are (1) the retailer's store image is enhanced because of the exclusive merchandise and (2) no *direct* competition exists for the *brands* of merchandise carried. For these retailers the right place is *a* place.

Many specialty stores dealing in well-known, prestigious products such as Mercedes-Benz, Jaguar, and Steuben Glass use this form of market coverage. An ethnic restaurant in an ethnic neighborhood provides another example of an exclusive market strategy.

In sum, market coverage is related to the nature of the retailer's product mix. As shown in Figure 1–8, retailers attempt to achieve intensive coverage when their product mix is convenience-oriented. At the other end of the continuum, using one outlet (exclusive coverage) is most appropriate when merchandising specialty goods. An intermediate strategy (selective coverage) is used when shopping goods predominate the product mix.

Store Layout and Design

Store layout and design are two essential elements to consider in creating the right shopping atmosphere for the target market. The retailer should consider both vertical and horizontal dimensions in determining store layout. Floor location and shelf position are the two major vertical places a retailer must evaluate.

17

FIGURE 1–8

The relationship be-
tween market coverage
and product mix

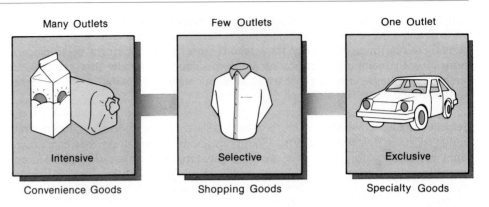

Many Outlets	Few Outlets	One Outlet
Intensive	Selective	Exclusive
Convenience Goods	Shopping Goods	Specialty Goods

Floor location. In some department stores, the right place in a store for a product, department, display, event, or activity may be either the basement, the first floor, or the top floor. Customers often think of the basement as the "bargain basement," the first floor as the "main floor," and the top floor as the "exclusive floor." The right floor is the one most consistent with where customers think things ought to be and where the retailer can provide the level of service consumers expect.

Shelf position. Retail merchandisers and marketers generally agree that the best place to shelve merchandise is at **eye level**. Placing merchandise at eye level is especially important when the retailer wants to attract new or additional sales. For example, in a supermarket, Campbell often will place several popular varieties of its soups such as tomato, chicken noodle, and vegetable beef at *non eye level* positions. These soups are in great demand and customers will seek them out. New varieties and slower-selling varieties, however, often are positioned at eye level to generate additional sales.

Two of the primary *horizontal* places that a retailer should consider are in-store locations and display locations.

In-store location. The right place within a store for a product, a customer service, or a display could be either in front, in back, along the sides, or in the center. The in-store layout of most supermarkets, for example, is based on the "ring of perishables" principle. Food retailers know that consumers purchase their perishables (eggs, milk, butter, meat, vegetables, etc.) every week. By placing perishables in a ring around the store (sides and back), supermarket retailers have learned that they can draw customers into other sections of the store. Supermarkets using this technique greatly increase the chances that customers will pass by and purchase other products in the store's total merchandise offering. Supermarket managers believe that the result of their strategy is additional impulse sales—purchases the consumer did not plan to make.

Another strategy some retailers use is the attractors and interceptors strategy. Many department stores place merchandise such as men's suits, better women's wear, furniture, appliances, and other big-ticket items in the back of the store to act as attractors, drawing customers through the entire length of the store. In the process, customers are intercepted by departments carrying complementary product lines, such as shirts, scarves, jewelry, and other possible impulse products. Since the interceptor items normally produce a higher percentage of profit per unit for the store, this layout strategy contributes to the store's overall profit rate.

Display location. Retailers use displays to draw attention to their product offerings. The right place must be found for them. Whether at end-of-aisle, at the checkout stand, or a freestanding location near high traffic areas, the right place is the "visible" place for these special displays. For example, supermarkets often place their weekly features of cakes, cookies, and pies at highly visible, end-of-the-aisle sites where frequently purchased items such as breads, buns, and rolls are located.

Within the display itself, "right is also right": the best position within a display is the right side. The right-side bias is based on the belief that most consumers view a display from right to left. So right is "right," because it is the first place consumers look.

The Right Time

The "right" timing is critical in athletics, war, politics, business, and other human endeavors. In business, retailers realize that there are good times and bad times to sell certain merchandise and services. The right time to sell is when consumers are willing to buy. Since time affects consumers in different ways, retailers must develop retailing strategies that coincide with consumer buying times.[4] Some particular times that retailers consider in developing time strategies are (1) calendar times, (2) seasonal times, (3) life times, and (4) personal times.

Calendar Times

In this category, consider times of the day, times of the week, times of the month, and times of the year. Since consumers' behavior is largely geared to these times, any one of these times can be an opportune time for the retailer.

Times of the day. Whether morning, noon, afternoon, or evening, many retailers have businesses with daily peak periods. Restaurants, for example, have definite "right times" of the day: breakfast, lunch, and dinner times. For most restaurants, these are the only times for sales and profits. Evenings are "most times" for motion pictures theaters. By reducing prices for the afternoon matinee, however, the theater

The right place for special displays is a highly visible one

19

manager can make afternoons a "sometimes" for some moviegoers. Morning and afternoon rush hours are the right times for some retailers who want to intercept consumers going to and from work. And the late hours, after supermarkets close, are the right times for convenience food stores.

Times of the week.   Certain days of the week are better times to sell some products than other days. Sunday is the right time of the week for some consumers since they have free time to shop. On the other hand, Sunday might not be the right time for other consumers because it is "God's time" or it is an illegal time (where Sunday closing laws are in effect).

Blue Monday is often a poor time for a retailer, since the consumer's mood usually is bad at the start of a new work week; however, the innovative retailer can convert a slow time into a fast time by convincing consumers that the answer to a blue Monday is a dollar-green Tuesday. For the cocktail lounge, it's TGIF (thank goodness it's Friday), since Friday afternoon is cocktail time for many consumers who have completed their work week.

Times of the month.   Paydays and bill-paying day are two examples of times of the month of which every retailer should be aware. Paydays are usually once, twice, or four times a month and they could very well be the most important times for the retailer regardless of when they occur. With money in their pockets, consumers are most susceptible to advertising, new merchandise, and old merchandise clearance sales. Bill-paying days are the right time to collect on past credit sales. However, they usually are poor times for making sales. Many homeowners have to make house payments, for example, at the beginning of the month, so unless they are paid monthly, they are likely to have hard times until the next payday.

Times of the year.   Holiday seasons often represent the "best times" of the year for retailers. Christmas, Easter, Thanksgiving, Memorial Day, Labor Day, and New Year's Eve are "special times" for consumers and provide special opportunities to retailers. For many retailers, back-to-school time is second only to Christmas in its potential to generate sales.

Seasonal Times

Consumers' buying patterns change with the seasons of the year. These are not only spring, summer, fall, and winter; but perhaps football, basketball, and baseball seasons; or planting, growing, and harvesting seasons; or even opera, social, and theater seasons. Depending upon geographic and cultural regions of the country, most retailers know which times are best for selling seasonal goods. Retailers also know that the best part of the season is the beginning of the season when they can sell goods at full markup. They also know that during the middle and latter part of the season, consumers are thinking about the next season, and therefore the retailer must mark down the prices on certain merchandise.

Life Times

In everyone's life there are special times—births, weddings, graduations, first dates, the first party, and many more—that are rare times for the retailer to make a special

(Opposite page)   Back to school is the right time of year for many retailers. (Courtesy of Gold Circle Stores)

effort to sell merchandise. They are also the right time for the retailer because consumers are in one of their most susceptible buying moods. At these times, the retailer can generate additional sales by "trading up" the consumer, that is, inducing the customer to buy a higher-quality, higher-price/markup product or to add features and extras to the selection.

Personal Times

Every consumer experiences working times, leisure times, and maintenance times. Every retailer should be sensitive to the merchandising times of the weekday, the weekend, the workday, and the day off. A building materials firm that caters to the home handyman, for example, makes most sales on Friday and Saturday. A company that produces many sporting goods, AMF, advertises that "we make weekends."

For the retailer, all of the times just discussed can be either good or bad times, fast or slow times, profitable or unprofitable times. In summary, *a right time is any time that helps the retailer either avoid losing sales or create new sales that ordinarily would not have been made.*

The Right Price

The right price is the amount consumers are willing to pay and retailers are willing to accept in exchange for merchandise and services. Consumers experience various forms of prices in the marketplace. They encounter odd prices, even prices, prices with coupons, sticker prices, bid prices, bargain prices, status prices, sales prices, manufacturers' suggested list prices, and retailers' prices, among many other price forms. Like consumers, retailers also face different forms of prices. There are markup prices, markdown prices, price lines, base prices, unit prices, package prices, promotional prices, regular prices, loss-leader prices, illegal prices, and prices that include accessories. These are only a few of the price forms that retailers deal with every day.

In developing a pricing strategy, the retailer must price merchandise low enough to generate sales, but high enough to cover costs and make a fair profit. At the same time, the retailer must consider pricing products in a manner consistent with consumers' expectations. For example, $25 may be the subjective value a consumer places on a pair of tire chains in July, but in January that same person may agree that $40 is okay. On the other hand, many consumers would rather be stuck in the snow than pay $75 for the chains.

The right price is one that is not only satisfactory to the customer before the sale, but after the sale as well. A consumer who is willing to pay a "premium" price for a product generally expects premium performance. If the product does not display this expected level of performance, the customer might not ever buy products from the same retailer again. Since retailers depend heavily upon repeat business, not meeting consumers' performance expectations would be disastrous for most retailers. Even worse, the dissatisfied customer is very likely to communicate that bad experience to friends and others and discourage their patronage at the store.

Finally, the right price must be competitive—if not with all competitors, then at least with those in the same trading area or with those who have similar operations. In a large city, for example, one record store might price albums 50 cents higher than another record store across town. Although competitors in the sense that both stores sell records, these two retailers are not in *direct* competition since they are in *different trading areas* within the same city. With the soaring price of gasoline and the value people place on their time, very few consumers would travel across town to "save" 50 cents. Additionally, two stores that sell the same basic product such as men's clothing and are located three doors apart in a shopping mall may not be in *direct* competition. One might be a "high fashion" men's store, whereas the other is a men's "value clothing" store. Thus, competitive pricing means setting a price that is about the same as that found in similar stores within the same trading area.

The Right Appeal

The right appeal is one that represents the *right message* to the *right audience* through the *right media.* Though the product, place, and price are right, the retailer will not be successful unless it can communicate its offering effectively to its target market. The retailer must inform and persuade consumers that its product mix precisely meets their particular needs. In making the right appeals, the retailer's problem is how to identify the target audience, create the appropriate message, and select the best medium of communication.

The Right Message

The right message is the right thing to say (the right message *content*) presented in the right *manner.* The right message content emphasizes what consumers are most concerned about and explains how the retailer's offerings can satisfy those concerns. For example, homemakers deciding among supermarkets may be more concerned with what they buy and how much they pay than from whom, where, and when they buy. In this case the best message emphasizes the *what* and *how much.* When deciding among furriers, however, the same individuals may be more concerned with what and from whom they buy, and less concerned with where and when they buy and how much they pay. In this situation, the retailer should emphasize the *what* and *from whom.*

The retailer must determine which purchase factors are most important to the consumer's buying decision and emphasize those appeals in the message. After gathering consumer information, a retailer may decide to make a **product appeal,** *emphasizing the rightness of its products for consumers;* a **patronage appeal,** *emphasizing the rightness of the store, location, and hours;* or a **price appeal.** Or, the retailer may make a combined appeal if it thinks several "right choice" elements are important to the consumer.

In structuring the message content, the retailer must also choose between direct action and indirect action. **Direct-action messages** *urge the consumer to come to the store now either to take advantage of a sale or to redeem a coupon.* **Indirect-action messages,** on the other hand, *have long-run goals. They attempt to change consumers' attitudes toward the retailer by cultivating its image as the "right" place for the consumer to buy* (e.g., "When you think of fine furniture, think of us"). Both types of messages have advantages and disadvantages. Direct-action messages usually result in immediate sales, but normally do not encourage regular patronage. Indirect-action messages encourage regular patronage, but the retailer must invest considerable time and money to develop it.

The retailer must not only present the right message content, but also present it in the right manner, by choosing either a logical or an emotional approach. Using the **logical approach,** *a retailer makes a factual presentation about its offering and then shows consumers why buying from that source is the "right" choice.* For example, a retailer might say, "Compare prices, and you'll see why you should shop with us." A retailer that uses an **emotional approach** *speaks not to what consumers think, but to what they feel* (pride, fear, etc.). Retailers that create emotional appeals in their messages try to incite consumers'

1. sense of loyalty ("Shop your local hometown merchants.")
2. sense of security ("We'll sell only brand-name merchandise.")
3. sense of fair play ("Please, before you buy, check our . . .")
4. sense of tradition and stability ("Serving you from the same location for 25 years.")
5. sense of adventure ("A new shopping experience . . .")
6. sense of success (". . . the largest dealer in the state.")
7. sense of belongingness ("Shop with us, where only the discriminating shop."), among other target emotions

The Right Audience

The right message must be directed to the right audience. In seeking to determine the right audience, the retailer can make one of two choices—either pursue the mass-market audience or pursue one or more target-market audiences.

Mass-market audience. A retailer that decides to appeal to all of the consumers within a market area should use a broad appeal to the mass market. By using a broad appeal, the retailer hopes to attract a few customers from all segments of the market. The message must be general enough to appeal to a wide range of consumers and their needs, but specific enough to stimulate consumers to action.

Target-market audience. The retailer may decide to appeal to a select group of customers within a market area. The process of dividing a market into smaller subsets is called "market segmentation," and the market segment to which the retailer directs its appeal is the "target market." Any market can be segmented along the lines of various characteristics. The three most common of these are demographic characteristics, patronage motives, and psychographic profiles.

Demographic characteristics include age, sex, income, race, occupation, family structure, and social class. A record store targeting upper-income teenagers is an example of a retailer segmenting the market by demographic characteristics (in this case, age and income). Patronage motives describe consumers' shopping and buying habits. How much they buy, when, where, what, and why they buy are all patronage market dimensions. A retailer catering to working mothers who buy after work is an example of a target market selected on the basis of patronage characteristics.

Psychographic profiles are composite "pictures" of different consumer life styles. To illustrate, one local tavern might appeal to politically inactive sedentary gentlemen who believe a woman's place is in the home and that hunting and fishing are adventurous men's activities. However, another local tavern might cater to men who actively participate in rugged athletic sports such as football, who feel that women should have equal opportunities and responsibilities, and who are politically active. Regardless of which target market the retailer selects, the right message is one that appeals to the needs and desires of its chosen market segment. However, the best appeal cannot be effective without the right media.

(Opposite page) Product appeal emphasizes the "rightness" of a retailer's product. (Courtesy of WESTIES, a Division of Fisher Camuto Corporation. Photograph by M. Alonzo)

WESTIES

The right shoe
at the right time...

Because timing is everything.

The Right Media

The means by which a retailer communicates its product offering to consumers is just as important as the content. Typically, a retailer has several choices in reaching an audience: newspapers, television, radio, magazines, telephone, direct mail, window displays, outdoor signs, instore demonstrations, and personal sales representatives. The right medium for the retailer is the one that effectively and economically reaches the largest portion of the mass or target audience.

Having discussed those elements of the right merchandising blend, let us now examine the other half of the equation for a successful retail organization—the right performance standards.

THE RIGHT PERFORMANCE STANDARDS

Retailers must have some means by which to judge both the operational and financial performance of their firms. Several operating and financial ratios can aid their judgment. These ratios concisely express the relationship between elements in the income statement and the balance sheet. Because these ratios have gained wide acceptance within the general business community as well as within specific retail trades, they have become trade standards by which retailers can judge their individual performances against national and trade norms. These standard ratios are published annually (or more frequently) by private firms such as Dun & Bradstreet, by trade organizations such as the National Retail Merchants Association, and by public agencies such as the Small Business Administration. Within individual retail organizations, historical comparisons can be made between current ratios and past ratios. The availability of these external and internal standards helps each retailer to make meaningful judgments on the firm's operating efficiency and financial ability. Ratio analysis provides a "snapshot" of the relative health of the retailer's operating and financial condition and serves as a control to identify conditions deviating from established norms.

Operating Ratios

Retailers compute some ratios to gain insight into the firm's operating performance. Retailers use **operating ratios** *to compute relationships between elements in the income statement.* Ratio computations simply divide one element of the income statement (e.g., operating profit) by another element (e.g., net sales). A standard practice is to convert ratios into percentages by multiplying the results by 100. Of particular concern to most retailers are operating ratios involving net sales (i.e., operating profit divided by net sales). Operating ratios are discussed in Chapter 7.

Financial Ratios

Financial ratios *identify relationships among elements of a balance sheet or between a balance sheet element and an element in the income statement.* The most widely used financial ratios are those reported by Dun & Bradstreet. These key performance measurements help the retailer make meaningful comparisons between the firm's financial performance and the national median performance of similar retailers. These ratios are also useful in establishing realistic financial objectives. In evaluating the firm's performance against these national norms, however,

(Opposite page)   A logical price appeal support by an emotional message that appeals to the customer's sense of tradition and stability. (Courtesy of Marshalls)

tradition
quality and value for 30 years

Famous maker sport shirts
comparable in quality at $25

A stock-up price on long sleeve, patterned sport shirts from two prestigious names. Polyester/cotton, sizes S-M-L-XL. First quality.

marshalls price
9⁹⁹

Famous maker twill pants
comparable in quality at $40

From a leading sportswear name, belted slacks for dress or casual. Assorted colors, in polyester/cotton twill. Sizes 32 to 40. First quality.

marshalls price
16⁹⁹

Famous maker dress shirts
comparable in quality at $20

Terrific value on these long sleeve, machine wash-and-dry polyester/cotton dress shirts. Assorted patterns. Sizes 14½ to 17. First quality.

marshalls price
9⁹⁹

Famous maker dress pants
comparable in quality at $35

A collection of famous maker gabardines in polyester/wool. Plain or pleated fronts. Assorted colors. Sizes 30 to 40. First quality.

marshalls price
16⁹⁹

Designer and famous maker ties. First quality. Pre-ticketed by the famous makers at 8.50 to $20 ...... **marshalls price 4.99 to 8.99**

the retailer must recognize that the firm's individual circumstances might prohibit direct comparison. The ratios of retailing are used as basic reference points and not as absolute guidelines for judging financial performance levels for a given retail firm. Chapter 7 provides more in-depth coverage of financial ratios in the discussion of managing the firm's resources.

SUMMARY

While at first glance retailing might appear to be a simple task, the successful operation of a retail store is, in fact, a very complex and difficult undertaking—a truth vividly illustrated by the number of retail enterprises that fail each year.

A retailer is a business organization within a marketing channel of distribution that makes most of its sales to final consumers. Retailers differ from other marketing institutions in that they (1) sell in small quantities on a more frequent basis, (2) open their place of business to the general public, (3) charge higher per-unit prices, (4) utilize a one-price policy, (5) rely on consumers to make the initial contact, and (6) use store atmospherics as a major merchandise tool. Evidence of their importance lies in the number of retail establishments and the many people they employ.

The basic task of retailing is to balance the product/service needs of the consuming public with the operational/financial needs of the retail organization: in other words, find the right merchandising blend to ensure the right performance standards. Elements of the retailer's right blend are offering the right products, in the right quantities, in the right place, at the right time, at the right price, by the right appeal. Performance standards can be expressed in terms of operating ratios and financial ratios.

KEY TERMS AND CONCEPTS

retailing	regional market	product appeal
retailer	local market	patronage appeal
marketing channel	trading area	price appeal
marketing concept	site	direct-action message
merchandising blend	intensive market coverage	indirect-action message
the right product	selective market coverage	logical approach
merchandising utilities	exclusive market coverage	emotional approach
intrinsic qualities	eye-level merchandisinng	the right audience
augmenting extras	the right time	the right media
the right quantity	the right price	performance standards
the right place	the right appeal	operating ratios
market	the right message	financial ratios

REVIEW QUESTIONS

1. Why is the retailing myth a myth?
2. What is retailing?
3. What is the marketing channel of distribution and where does the retailer fit into this organization?
4. How do retailers differ from other members of the marketing channel of distribution?
5. How does the number of retail establishments compare with other members of the marketing channel?
6. What is the problem of retailing?
7. Define the marketing concept and discuss how it relates to the problem of retailing.
8. What are the six ingredients of the right merchandising blend?
9. What makes a product right? Describe each element.
10. What are the consequences the retailer faces in misjudging unit need?
11. What is the "right place" in terms of regional and local markets, trading areas, and site?
12. Compare and contrast intensive, selective, and exclusive market coverage.
13. Why is eye-level merchandising an important concept in making display decisions?
14. Why is "right is right" in positioning products within a display?
15. What are the opportune times on a retailer's calendar?
16. What is the right price?
17. What are the three types of message appeals used in creating the right appeal?
18. How do direct-action messages differ from indirect-action messages?
19. Which characteristics are used to segment markets to target the retailer's promotional appeals?
20. How do operating ratios differ from financial ratios?

ENDNOTES

1. Ruth A. Keyes and Ronald A. Cushman, *Essentials of Retailing* (New York: Fairchild, 1977), 6.
2. E. M. Fram, "Application of the Marketing Concept to Retailing," *Journal of Retailing* 41 (Summer 1965): 19.
3. Dale R. Harley, "Customer Satisfaction Tracking Improves Sales Productivity, Morale of Retail Chains," *Marketing News,* 22 June 1984, 15.
4. Leonard L. Berry, "The Time-Buying Consumer," *Journal of Retailing* 55 (Winter 1979): 58–69.

RELATED READINGS

Arndt, Johan. "How Broad Should the Marketing Concept Be?" *Journal of Marketing* 42 (January 1978), 101–3.

Barksdale, Hiram C., and Darden, Bill. "Marketers' Attitudes toward the Marketing Concept." *Journal of Marketing* 35 (October 1971), 29–36.

Bell, Martin L., and Emory, C. William. "The Faltering Marketing Concept." *Journal of Marketing* 35 (October 1971), 37–42.

Cronin, J. Joseph, Jr., and Joyce, Mary L. "An Investigation between Marketing and Financial Strategies in Retail Firms." *Developments in Marketing Science, Proceedings.* J. D. Lindquist, ed. (Academy of Marketing Science 1984), 288–93.

Dickinson, Roger. "Innovations in Retailing." *Retail Control* (June - July 1983), 30–54.

Greensmith, Denis S. "New Retail Strategies for a Changing World Business Environment." *Retail Control* (June - July 1984), 2–17.

Hinnefeld, Edwin. "Competing in a Changing Retail Marketplace." *Retail Control* (September 1983), 9–19.

Hirschman, Elizabeth C. "Aesthetics, Ideologies, and the Limits of the Marketing Concept." *Journal of Marketing* 47 (Summer 1983), 45–55.

"Kolter: Rethink the Marketing Concept." *Marketing News* (September 14, 1984), 1, 22, 24.

Korgaonkar, Pradeep K., and Bellenger, Danny. "Nonstore Retailers and Consumer Characteristics." *Akron Business and Economic Review* 14 (Winter 1983), 29–34.

Kornblum, Warren. "Survival Tactics for Retailers." *Retail Control* (August 1984), 29–41.

Lazer, William, and Kelley, Eugene J. "The Retailing Mix: Planning and Management." *Journal of Retailing* 45 (Spring 1969), 34–41.

Marcus, Stanley. "Retailing's Urgent Need for Creativity as Viewed by Stanley Marcus." *Retail Control* (February 1984), 19–27.

Nason, Robert W., and Bitta, Albert J. Della. "The Incidence and Consumer Perceptions of Quantity Surcharges." *Journal of Retailing* 59 (Summer 1983), 40–54.

O'Neal, Larry R., and Tinsley, Dillard B. "Channel Implications of the Marketing Concept." *1984 Proceedings.* J. R. Lumpkin and J. C. Crawford, eds. (Southwestern Marketing Association 1984), 89–94.

Patlon, W. E., III; Greenwood, M. Craig; and Long, J. Mark. "Retail Performance in a Decade of Change." *Marketing: Theories and Concepts for an Era of Change, Proceedings.* J. Summey, R. Viswanathan, R. Taylor, and K. Glynn, eds. (Southern Marketing Association 1983), 113–16.

Schulz, David P. "Top 100 Stores." *Stores* (July 1985), 21–30.

————. "The Top 100 Specialty Store Chains." *Stores* (August 1985), 31–40.

Sharma, Subhash, and Mahajan, Vijay. "Early Warning Indicators of Business Failure." *Journal of Marketing* 44 (Fall 1980), 80–89.

Sheth, Jagdish N. "Emerging Trends for the Retailing Industry." *Journal of Retailing* 59 (Fall 1983), 6–18.

Turpin, Miles. "In Search of Retail Marketing Excellence." *Retail Control* (August 1984), 11–26.

Wilson, Cyrus C. "Changing Universe of Retailing." *Retail Control* (October 1983), 40–63.

Outline

STRATEGIC RETAIL MANAGEMENT

THE STRATEGIC PLAN

Organizational Mission
Organizational Objectives
Organizational Portfolio
Organizational Opportunities

THE RETAILING PLAN

Environmental Scan
Resource Assessment
Market Selection
Retailing Mix Management

Objectives

- Appreciate the need for strategic retail management and planning

- Develop an organizational mission statement that can serve as a focus for the firm's current and future activities

- Construct the organizational objectives for achieving the organization's mission

- Conduct a portfolio analysis and classify different business units on the basis of their market and cash flow positions

- Identify the various types of growth and performance opportunities and evaluate the appropriate strategies associated with each type of opportunity

- Discuss the basic components of the retailing plan

Strategic Retail Management

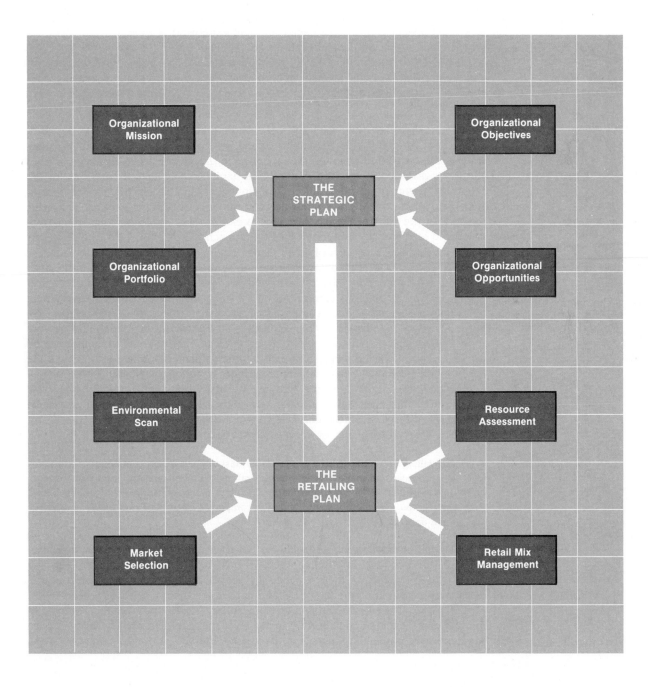

ome retail organizations have been slow to adopt strategic planning as part
of their management effort. Retailers are traditionally action oriented and
more concerned with short-run problems and results. Their resistance to and
skepticism of the long-run character of strategic planning are based on a number of
factors that differentiate retailing from other business enterprises. Some of the more
commonly cited factors are (1) rapid and unpredictable changes in the retail market,
(2) intense and diverse competition, (3) shorter retail institutional life cycles, (4)
unstable economic climate, and (5) the need for flexibility in the face of the changing
retailing scene.[1] As Rosenbloom points out, however, "Careful analysis and planning over a relatively long period are the necessary requisites for the development
of successful long-term strategies—even in the fast-paced and rapidly changing
world of retailing."[2] Strategies based on rapid expansion of branch store networks,
which were successful for many firms in the 1960s and 1970s, have been less
attractive in the 1980s. As a result, retail strategies for the near future will have to
put greater emphasis on diversification and on more selective management of established business operations.[3]

STRATEGIC RETAIL MANAGEMENT

Planning is essential if the retail organization is to survive and prosper in the competitive environment associated with consumer markets. **Strategic retail management** is *the process of planning the organization, implementation, and control of all
the firm's activities.* It involves making both strategic and tactical decisions for different levels within an organization. The strategic management process consists of
two major components: the strategic plan and the retailing plan. The schematic
diagram at the start of this chapter illustrates the relationship between these two
plans and identifies the major activities under each plan.

Before discussing each of these plans, it is instructive to examine the issue of
strategic versus tactical planning as it relates to the various levels (corporate, strategic business unit, store, department, and product line) within the retail organization. *Corporate planning* is carried out by the corporate headquarters management
team and is directed at developing an overall plan for the entire organization. The
corporate planning process is strategic because it establishes the general framework
for the firm's actions over an extended period of time. As a broad statement based
on experience, intuition, and analytical judgment, the corporate plan outlines the
organization's general business intent. *Business planning* involves developing a
course of action for each of the strategic business units (SBUs) within the retail
organization; this plan identifies what role each SBU has in the overall corporate
strategy. A **strategic business unit** is *a business division with "a clear market focus,
an identifiable strategy, and an identifiable set of competitors."*[4]

> In retailing enterprise, SBU's are probably best defined in terms of types of stores or
> store formats and market areas. For general merchandise retailers, it may be desir-
> able to define SBU's even more narrowly in terms of merchandise categories within
> their stores . . . the object of dividing a company's operations into SBU's is to per-
> mit a detailed strategic appraisal of such unit.[5]

The planning process continues with the development of plans for each store, department, and product line within each SBU. *Store, department, and product line
planning* is more tactical than strategic. It focuses more on current problems and
decisions faced in implementing SBU and corporate strategy.

Figure 2–1 presents planning levels for a large retail organization. Planning at
the corporate level is conducted by upper-level management for The May Department Stores Company in their corporate headquarters in St. Louis. Corporate plans

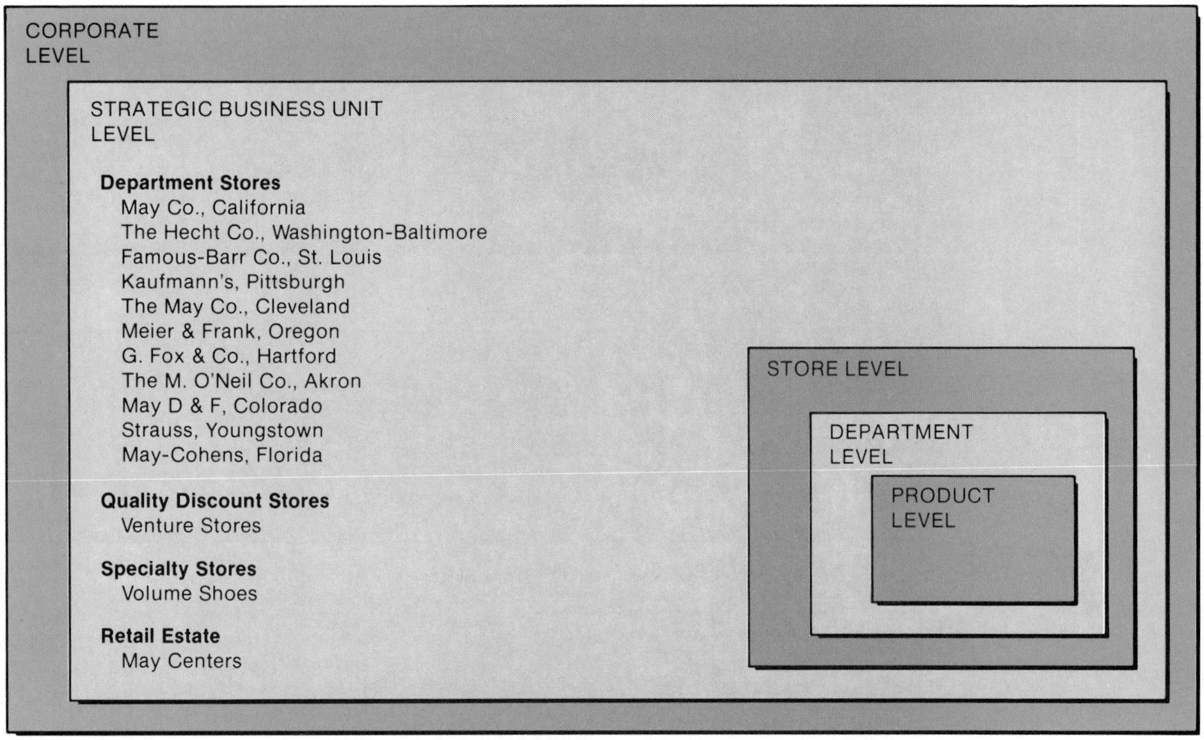

CORPORATE
LEVEL

STRATEGIC BUSINESS UNIT
LEVEL

Department Stores
May Co., California
The Hecht Co., Washington-Baltimore
Famous-Barr Co., St. Louis
Kaufmann's, Pittsburgh
The May Co., Cleveland
Meier & Frank, Oregon
G. Fox & Co., Hartford
The M. O'Neil Co., Akron
May D & F, Colorado
Strauss, Youngstown
May-Cohens, Florida

Quality Discount Stores
Venture Stores

Specialty Stores
Volume Shoes

Retail Estate
May Centers

STORE LEVEL

DEPARTMENT
LEVEL

PRODUCT
LEVEL

FIGURE 2–1
Business planning levels: The May Department Stores Co.

set the parameters for the business plans developed by each of the firm's SBUs (business segments and operating divisions). Using the corporate and business plans as guidelines, store, merchandise, and department managers develop tactical plans for each store, department, and product line. In a small retail organization such as a local chain or independent retail operator, the entire planning process may be conducted by one or a small group of individuals in a single location.

Keeping in mind that planning can be both strategic and tactical in nature and occurs at several levels within the organization, we now turn our attention to a more comprehensive examination of the strategic plan and the retailing plan. The discussion of the strategic plan will emphasize the large, diversified retail organization; the retailing plan is more applicable to a single retail business or any strategic business unit regardless of size and composition.

Strategic planning aims to develop a long-term course of action that will provide an overall sense of direction for a retail organization's business activities. The **strategic plan** is *a grand design or blueprint for ensuring success in all of the organization's business endeavors.* A strategic plan is directed at achieving a strategic fit between the organization's capabilities (present and future) and its environmental opportunities (present and future). A good fit positions the organization to enable it to sustain competitive assets and overcome competitive liabilities, as well as to anticipate external environmental changes and identify needed internal organizational adjustments. In other words, strategic planning is essential if the organization is to survive and prosper.

THE STRATEGIC PLAN

35

FIGURE 2–2
The strategic plan

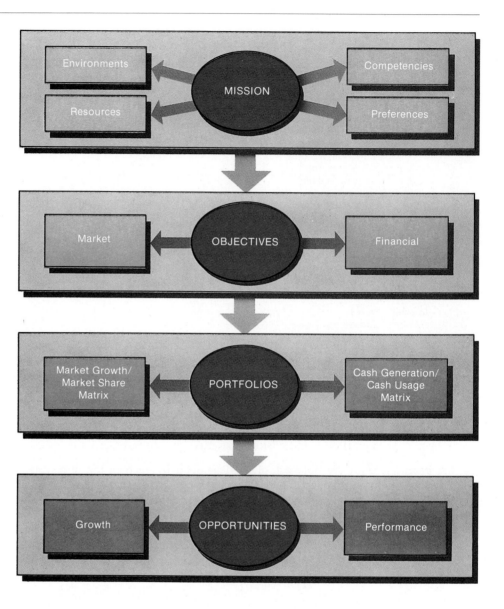

The development of an organization's strategic plan is a process that consists of (1) establishing the organization's mission, (2) identifying the organization's objectives, (3) evaluating the organization's portfolio of SBUs, and (4) assessing the organization's opportunities. Figure 2–2 illustrates the process of developing a strategic plan.

Organizational Mission

The **mission statement** is *a generalized yet meaningful expression of the organization's future direction.* It is a commitment to future actions. As a statement of intended future actions, the organizational mission has a number of tasks to perform.

First, a mission statement identifies both the business and customer domains wherein the organization operates or plans to operate. A well-defined mission will answer such business domain questions as "What *is* our business?" "What *will* our business be?" and "What *should* our business be?" Corresponding questions in the

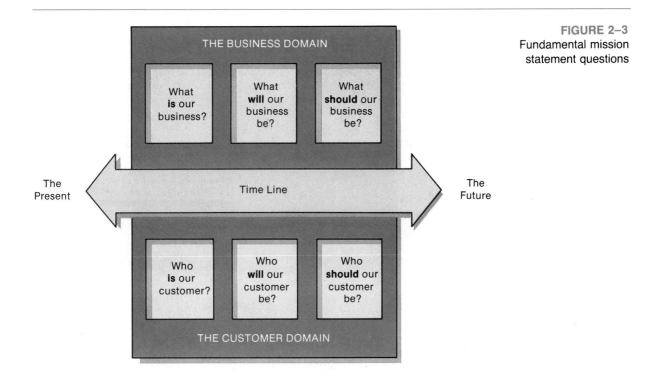

FIGURE 2–3
Fundamental mission
statement questions

THE BUSINESS DOMAIN

What **is** our business?

What **will** our business be?

What **should** our business be?

The Present

Time Line

The Future

Who **is** our customer?

Who **will** our customer be?

Who **should** our customer be?

THE CUSTOMER DOMAIN

customer domain are "Who *is* our customer?" "Who *will* our customer be?" and "Who *should* our customer be?" As Figure 2–3 illustrates, strategic gaps grow between each of these business and customer domain questions as one moves from the present to the future. These gaps represent the difference between current, expected, and desired performances, and as such, they indicate the possible need for changing the strategic plan of the organization. Later in the chapter, we will discuss this concept in more depth.

Second, a mission statement identifies the organization's responsibilities toward the people with which it interacts. Retailing has been described as a people business, and the mission statement should recognize this orientation. In its 1980 mission statement, the Dayton Hudson Department Store Co. reaffirmed its commitment to people through (1) serving *customers* by offering better service than competitors, (2) serving *communities* by contributing to a strong, healthy environment, (3) serving *shareholders* by providing a superior return on their investment, and (4) serving *employees* by offering rewarding careers.

Third, a mission statement provides a general blueprint for accomplishing the organizational mission. The May Department Stores Co.'s mission statement used a symbol for communicating its mission of excellence in retailing by meeting its general objective: "top quartile performance" as measured by "return on common stockholders' investment." The May mission symbol is a *pyramid* whose base is formed by the associates comprised by the organization. The May Co. said it plans to achieve its general mission and objective by "building a strong organization and setting clear strategy."[6] The organizational foundation of the firm's pyramid is directed at developing a superior general management, cultivating an innovative corporate culture, and securing the best talent in retailing. The strategy focus of the firm will be on productivity, merchandise impact, genuine customer service, sound pricing practices, vital sales promotions, visually exciting stores, and efficient systems (see Figure 2–4).

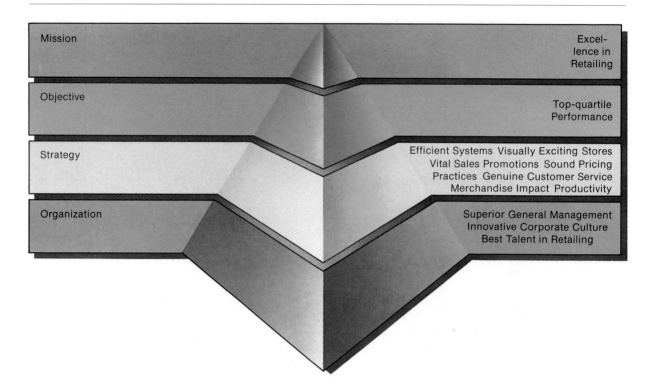

FIGURE 2–4

The mission pyramid of The May Department Stores Co. (source: The May Department Stores Co. annual report, 1983)

The statement of the organizational mission is developed taking several factors into account. These factors include environmental considerations, resource considerations, distinctive competencies, and managerial preferences.

Environmental Considerations

The retail organization must accommodate and react to several different environments that present both opportunities and threats. Some of the major components of an organization's environment are suppliers, marketing intermediaries, customers, competitors, and publics (see Figure 2–5).

As a marketing intermediary, the retail organization has an internal environment within which the daily operation of the firm must be successfully completed. The strengths and weaknesses of the organization's structure and personnel must be accounted for when developing mission statements. The planning process should involve all levels of the organization to ensure a full commitment from all affected parties.

As a team member in the marketing channel of distribution, the mission statement must also address the needs of suppliers and customers. The retailer's mission should recognize the need for a "coordinated effort" and a "cooperative spirit" in conducting channel affairs. Retail organizations that have adopted the marketing concept—customer satisfaction at a profit—will, as a matter of course, consider the expectations of their targeted markets and make provisions within the mission statement for gaining buyer acceptance of the firm's programs.

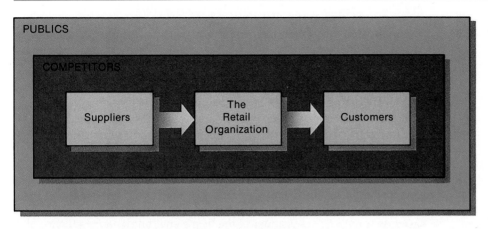

Retailing activities are not conducted within a vacuum; hence, the mission statement must recognize the existence of competitors and the expectations of the general public. The strategic planning process must devote considerable attention to positioning the retail organization relative to competitors. The general public's perception of the retail organization is also vital to acceptance of the firm's activities. The goal of serving the public need by being a responsive corporate citizen meeting its social responsibilities also needs addressing within the mission statement.

Resource Considerations

The mission statement must be realistic. The extent of that realism depends on the resources available to the retail organization. Since resources are essential to implement the firm's current and future strategies, the mission statement should recognize the problems associated with acquiring, maintaining, and using resources. The resource base to consider in developing the mission statement consists of (1) the financial assets and liabilities of the firm, (2) the organizational composition and structure of the management team, (3) the human resource component in terms of supporting personnel, and (4) the physical plant—store facilities, fixtures, and equipment.

Distinctive Competencies

A careful assessment of practically any retail organization will reveal certain merchandising and operating capabilities that distinguish it from competing organizations. Distinctive competencies are the comparative advantages one organization has over another. Distinctive competencies might occur in such areas as visual merchandising, exclusive supplier relationships, customer communications and sales promotions, unique store imagery, inventory planning and control systems, organization integration, product assortments, market coverage, or store atmospheres. The list of possible distinctive competencies is almost endless. In any case, distinctive competencies are solid foundations for suggesting future strategies in a mission statement.

Managerial Preferences

Additional considerations in developing a mission statement include the merchandising and operating preferences of the organization's cadre of managers. The type and extent of managerial expertise (e.g., mass merchandise vs. specialty retailing) will vary among retail organizations; hence, it is both logical and practical to consider management strengths when planning the organization's future directions. In addition, managerial intuition should not be overlooked when plotting a new and innovative course of action and finding unique methods of strategy implementation.

Organizational Objectives

An **organizational objective** can be defined as *a strategic position to be attained or a purpose to be achieved by the retail organization and/or one of its strategic business units.* It is an aim or end-of-action statement toward which the retail organization's efforts are directed. As such, organizational objectives need to be stated in quantitative, realistic, and consistent terms.[7] By stating objectives in *quantitative* terms (e.g., increase total sales volume by 12 percent next year), these expressions provide a specific measurement or target for judging performance. Performance must be based on a *realistic* assessment of the firm's environments, resources, and markets. For example, it would be wishful thinking to set an objective of a 50 percent increase in annual sales volume for a retail enterprise in a mature market. Finally, organizational objectives need to be *consistent.* A retailer simply cannot expect to minimize costs while maximizing sales volume.

Chapter 1 introduced the concept of the "scales of retailing"—the desirability of striking a balance between satisfying the customer's merchandising needs and meeting the retailer's need of a satisfactory financial performance. The two major categories of organizational objectives reflect this balance: the market objectives of customer patronage and competitive position and the financial objectives of profitability and productivity. Figure 2–6 presents a typology of organizational objectives.

Market Objectives

Market objectives are aimed at securing customer patronage and achieving competitive positions within the general marketplace. Market objectives are realized by carefully planned merchandising programs that can satisfy the consumer's psychological, social, and personal needs.

Sales volume. Sales volume increases are a commonly identified objective. A sales growth objective is typically expressed as a certain percentage increase (e.g., 15 percent) for a particular strategic business unit (e.g., store) over a defined time period (e.g., next year). It is an expansion objective that involves additional commitment of the organization's resources and the foregoing of short-term profits for long-term gains. Increases in total sales volume might be achieved by (1) adding new operating units, (2) increasing advertising expenditures, (3) improving a product/service offering, (4) lowering prices, or (5) making other merchandising adjustments (e.g., added convenience) that can increase customer satisfaction.

Another type of sales volume objective is to increase the average customer sale. Increasing the total amount spent by each customer during a store visit should have a direct and positive effect on total sales. Personal selling and various sales promotion methods are used to increase the amount of the average sale.

Customer traffic. Many retailers believe that if they can attract customers into the store, then they can obtain desired sales through customer exposure to the direct-merchandising efforts of the organization. Their objectives are thus to increase (1) the total number of customers visiting the store during a specific time period, (2) the total complement of various types of customers attracted into the store (e.g., low-, middle-, and upper-income consumers), and/or (3) the magnitude of specific

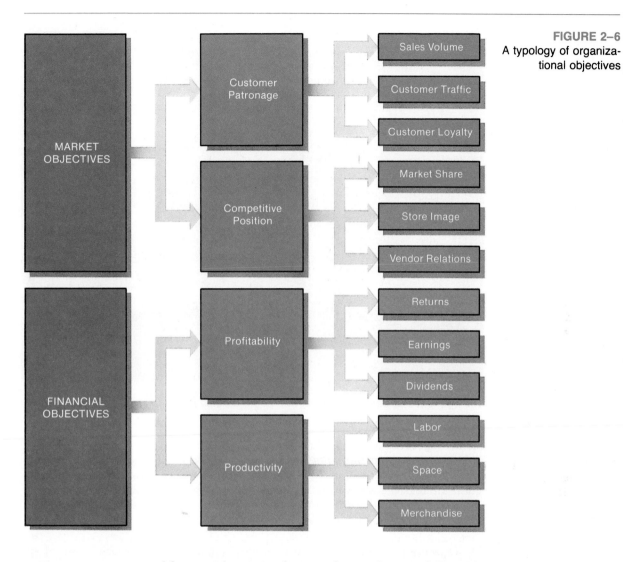

FIGURE 2–6
A typology of organiza-
tional objectives

customer groups targeted for special attention (e.g., professional women). Possible strategies to increase the total number of customer visits include additional mass advertising, sales promotions, and special-event merchandising. Offering a range of pricing points and a wider selection of merchandise are two means by which the firm can expand its appeal to a more extensive customer base. Offering unique services, specialty merchandise lines, and personal selling from sales representatives who have appropriate expertise can increase the traffic of targeted customer groups.

Customer loyalty.   A customer loyalty objective is aimed at improving return trade. Repeat business is essential to almost any retail operation since for many it represents store loyalty. The average number of store visits or purchases during a defined time period is one means of measuring return trade. Ideally, a worthy objective is to develop a high preference level for the organization and its merchandising programs. Obviously, the key to store loyalty is customer satisfaction.

The type and quality of services provided the customer are important strategic considerations in developing customer loyalty. A retail organization often develops

41

The right price appeal might be an odd price, bargain price, sales price, or warehouse price

strategies based on the *completeness* of the service offering: essential services (basic to the retailer's operation) and expected services ("extras" that help distinguish the retailer's service mix). Service quality is generally expressed in terms of the service levels offered by competitors—better transactional efficiency, better service availability, and less trouble in service execution.

Market share. Market share objectives are the most commonly used form of expressing competitive position. **Market share** is *a measure of a retail organization's sales position relative to all competitors within the same market.* It is calculated by dividing a retail organization's total sales by total market sales for a defined business type or product line category. In expanding market areas, *market share growth* could well be an appropriate objective (e.g., increase market share by 6 percent over the duration of this planning period). On the other hand, retail organizations operating in mature and stable market areas generally call for the more moderate objective of *market share maintenance* (e.g., protect our current market share against the aggressive actions of all competitors). In sum, the use of market share growth and maintenance objectives must consider market area conditions and the organization's resource capabilities.

Store image. An *image* is the mental conception of something held in common by members of a group. **Store image** is *the mental picture of a retail organization as viewed by customers and the general public.* Because we are using the term "store" in its most generalized meaning, to the consumer, store image is a symbolic representation of the basic attributes, orientations, and activities of the organization. Retailers establish image objectives because they realize that consumers tend to

(a)

(b)

(c)

Store image is a symbolic representation of a retailer's basic attributes. Which attributes would you assign to each of these restaurants?

categorize people, places, and things in relative terms (e.g., bigger, better, faster, easier, and sooner). By offering wider product selections, higher quality products, better price values, more convenient locations, easier credit terms, and faster service, retailers can competitively position themselves in the minds of consumers. By careful planning it is possible to position the organization in an imagery niche that clearly distinguishes it from its competitors.

Vendor relations. Carving out a viable competitive position includes a supply side that a retail organization's statement of objectives should also recognize. Prudent retail organizations strive to ensure that they are well positioned with respect to both established vendors (e.g., to be considered a preferred account by desired vendors) and new emerging sources (e.g., to engage in a systematic search for suppliers of new and innovative products). Retailers also must cooperate and coordinate their activities with other members of the marketing channel of distribution. To maintain a good working relationship (e.g., ordering, shipping, receiving, etc.) with other channel participants should be an important objective in any retailer's competitive positioning strategy.

Financial Objectives

Financial objectives are directed at ensuring that the retail organization operates profitably and productively. Financial objectives provide quantifiable standards by which the organization's performance will be judged.

Returns. The monetary return the retail organization desires can be stated in terms of return on sales or assets. These profit-based objectives reflect what management expects in return for its efforts. A *return on sales* (net profit divided by net sales) objective identifies what percentage of the average sales dollars should be profit. For example, an objective of 20 percent could be the targeted net profit return on net sales. To realize a fair return on the organization's asset investment, a *return on assets* (net profit divided by total assets) objective is frequently included in the organization's statement of objectives.

Earnings. Objectives should also reflect the performance of the organization relative to stockholders' interests. A targeted *earnings per share* of common stock can be established as an objective to show the amount of earnings available to the owners of common stock. A desired objective of $4 per share of common stock could be the targeted earnings-per-share ratio.

Dividends. A designated proportion of the earnings that will actually be allocated to stockholders can also serve as an objective. *Dividends* are a measure of the return to common stock owners representing the return on their investment (this statement does not reflect any increase or decrease in the market value of the common stock). For example, a retailer could set as its objective a $2 dividend yield on each share of common stock. In other words, it may establish an objective of distributing 50 percent of the organization's earnings per share in the form of dividends.

Labor. The productivity of the organization's labor pool can be measured by dividing net sales by the total number of employees or by dividing net sales by the total number of worker hours of labor; the latter measure would take into account the productivity of both full- and part-time employees. Retailing can be a labor-intensive business; hence, the contribution of human resources must be recognized and productivity performance standards established. Many retailers also recognize that turnover adversely affects labor productivity and therefore strive to reduce this phenomenon by setting employee satisfaction objectives aimed at increasing employee retention.

Space. One of the retailer's most important resources is the merchandising and operating space available. Most retail organizations attempt in their plans to maximize their selling space and its productivity. Sales-productivity ratios are established for stores as well as for individual department and product line areas. Space productivity is measured by dividing net sales or gross margin by the most appropriate expression of area. Some examples of sales/space or margin/space productivity ratios are (1) net sales per square foot of floor space, (2) net sales per cubic foot of display area, (3) net sales per linear foot of shelf space, and (4) gross margin dollars per square foot.

Merchandise. *Inventory turnover* is the most widely used criterion for measuring the productivity of merchandise; it can be defined as the number of times (e.g., eight times) during a specific time period (e.g., a year) that the average stock on hand is sold. The desired objective is to achieve the highest possible inventory turnover rate for the type of merchandise being sold and the additional resources that must be used to improve turnover rates. Obviously, convenience goods are going to have higher stock turns than specialty goods; hence, an annual turnover objective of 5 turns for specialty goods could be considered as productive as 40 yearly turns for convenience goods. An objective of increasing the turnover rate by increasing advertising or adding more sales personnel may prove productive if increased expenditures do not exceed the additional profits derived from such a strategy.

Other Objectives

In addition to market and financial objectives, retail organizations often identify a number of objectives that relate to their social responsibilities. Such social objectives include supporting charitable causes, providing educational opportunities, assuming an equitable tax burden, and participating in professional and social organizations and events.

Organizational Portfolio

The third stage in developing a strategic plan is to review the organization's portfolio of strategic business units. An **organizational portfolio** is *the collection of strategic business units held and managed by a retail organization.* The portfolio approach to retail planning is becoming an increasingly important method used by the diversified retail organization. Portfolio analysis is appealing because it suggests but does not dictate specific courses of action to achieve a balanced mix of businesses that will provide the maximum long-run benefits from scarce cash and managerial resources.[8] As Hall observed, "the total portfolio of businesses is managed by allocating capital and managerial resources to serve the interests of the firm as a whole in order to achieve balanced growth in sales, earnings, and asset mix with an acceptable and controlled level of risk."[9] Portfolio analysis is not in and of itself a strategy, however; rather, it is an analytical tool to provide perspective on the organization's current situation (where it is now) and suggesting possible courses of action for the future (where it wants to be).[10]

A commonly used portfolio approach is the growth/share matrix developed by the Boston Consulting Group (BCG). Let's examine this approach as it applies to the diversified retail organization.

BCG Portfolio Approach

The BCG portfolio approach is best illustrated by the use of two matrices: the market growth/market share matrix (see Figure 2–7) and the cash generation/cash usage matrix (see Figure 2–8). The former is used to illustrate current market positions of each strategic business unit while the latter identifies each SBU's net cash flow position.

Market growth/market share matrix. In Figure 2–7, the vertical axis identifies the annual growth rate (percentage) of each SBU's operating market. The logic of in-

FIGURE 2–7
Market growth/market
share matrix

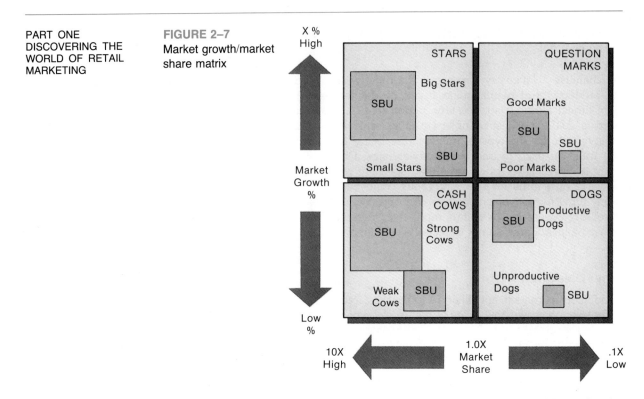

cluding market growth rate in such an analysis is based on the benefits to be derived from the experience curve: as the organization gains more experience it can reduce costs and realize greater business unit profits. The sales growth rate ranges from a low of zero percent to a high of whatever percentage is appropriate (e.g., 25 percent). A rate of 8 to 12 percent is generally considered to be quite good in most industries.

The horizontal axis indicates the relative market share of the SBU, a ratio of SBU share of the market to that of the largest competitor. Market share is considered important based on research indicating that profitability of an SBU is directly related to its market share. A "logarithmic scale is used for market share that goes from 1/10 the size of the competition to 10 times that of the largest competitor. Thus, business units located to the right of the value 1.0 are smaller than competition and those to the left are larger."[11] The size of each square in the matrix shows each SBU's dollar sales while the location of each SBU square indicates its competitive market share position with respect to various growth rate markets. The size and location of each SBU square simply suggest different financial and marketing needs.

To facilitate analysis of the growth/share matrix, it is arbitrarily divided into four quadrants classifying SBUs as one of four different types of businesses—stars, cash cows, question marks, or dogs. **Stars** are *SBUs having a high market share within a high-growth market.* These businesses are market leaders within their respective industries. As Figure 2–7 shows, stars can be big or small depending on the sales volume and share of the market. **Cash cows** are *SBUs having a high market share within a low-growth market.* Like stars, cash cows also have a dominant or leader position; unfortunately, this position occurs in a less desirable market. Some cows are stronger than others based on the sales volume, market share, and the growth characteristics of their market (see Figure 2–7). *SBUs with a low market share in a high-growth market* are classified as **question marks** (also known as *problem children*). These business enterprises are often called problem children because they offer considerable promise if given the attention they need. Depending on the amount of promise it shows, an SBU might be considered a good mark (reasonable chance for increasing market share and sales volume with an acceptable resource investment) or a poor mark (market share and sales volume increases are unlikely within acceptable resources commitments). **Dogs** are *SBUs that have a low market share within a low-growth market.* Their prospects for the future are dim; nevertheless, dogs can be productive if they find a market niche and produce an acceptable profit level.

We now turn our attention to cash flow characteristics of each of the SBU types.

Cash generation/cash usage matrix. The net cash flow situation for stars, cash cows, question marks, and dogs is shown in Figure 2–8. The vertical axis shows cash usage (low to high) while the horizontal axis portrays cash generation (low to high). *Stars* are both high users and generators of cash, but their net cash flow tends to be negative because they require considerable cash to expand with their growing market and maintain or improve their market share. *Cash cows* are the key to the organization's cash flow problems. Given the low market growth rate, fewer expenditures are needed to maintain market position; hence, cash cows tend to be net cash generators. The SBU cash cow provides the bulk of the cash to finance stars' and question marks' marketing operations. *Question marks* typically use more cash than they produce. If the organization decides that a question mark is capable of becoming a star, then it must provide the cash needed to capture additional market share. *Dogs* can produce either a positive or negative net cash flow. Properly niched within a secure market segment, some dogs are capable of providing some cash that can be used to finance stars and question marks. Other dogs are unproductive due to their vulnerable position in no-growth markets; in

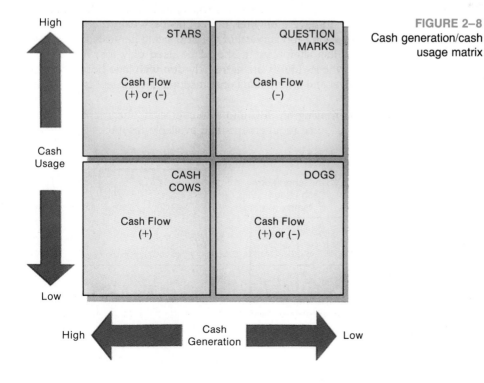

FIGURE 2–8
Cash generation/cash usage matrix

such cases, they can become "cash traps" and a lost cause. Day described an overall strategy for this type of portfolio analysis:

> The long-run health of the corporation depends on having some businesses that *generate* cash (and provide acceptable reported profits), and others that *use* cash to support growth. Among the indicators of overall health are the size and vulnerability of the "Cash Cows" (and the prospects for the "Stars," if any), and the number of "Problem Children" and "Dogs." Particular attention must be paid to those businesses with large cash appetites. Unless the company has abundant cash flow, it cannot afford to sponsor many such businesses at one time. If resources (including debt capacity) are spread too thin, the company simply will wind up with too many marginal businesses and suffer a reduced capacity to finance promising new business entries or acquisitions in the future.[12]

Resource allocation matrix. The combined information provided in the market growth/share matrix and the cash generation/usage matrix suggests ways to allocate financial resources. As Figure 2–9 illustrates, for each different category of SBU (stars, cash cows, question marks, and dogs), two or more of five possible allocation alternatives are suggested:

1. *Building* involves increasing an SBU's market share. The decision to build an SBU typically requires a cash infusion. The building alternative is used to expand smaller stars into bigger stars and to transform promising question marks into stars.
2. *Holding* involves maintaining an SBU's market share. The decision to hold is a defensive posture wherein the organization will protect and reinforce its current market share. The goal is to make big stars productive in terms of positive net cash flow and to keep strong cash cows producing a large cash flow.
3. *Harvesting* involves milking an SBU of its cash to finance other SBU alternatives that seem to have a brighter future. This cash extraction is often at the expense of the long-run survival of the SBU being harvested. Given the drastic nature of this alternative, it should be used only for weaker cash cows and dogs whose futures are extremely dim with little hope of maintenance or survival and where additional resource investment is unjustifiable.
4. *Niching* involves moving an SBU into a market niche (segment) in which the fit between resource requirements and available resources is more ac-

FIGURE 2–9
Strategies for allocating organizational resources

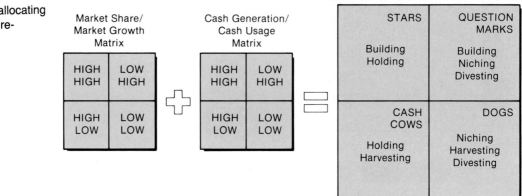

ceptable. The goal is to find a market niche wherein the SBU is reasonably protected from the actions of competitors while allowing it to generate sufficient long-term sales volumes and profits to justify the repositioning costs. Niching is used for some question marks and dogs that demonstrate the potential for a unique and limited market appeal.

5. *Divesting* involves disposing of SBUs that offer little or no hope of improving either their market share or cash flow position. Divestment can be accomplished by selling or liquidating the SBU. Unproductive dogs and poor question marks are both candidates for divestiture.

Organizational Opportunities

Portfolio analysis allows the retail organization to assess its current situation (what its business is) and to identify possible future courses of action (what its business should be) for various strategic business units. After completion of the portfolio analysis, the decision to target some SBUs for extinction (harvesting) or replacement (divesting) while others are targeted for maintenance (holding) and growth (building) often leaves a strategic gap between the current and desired performance of the retail organization; in other words, projected sales will fall short of desired sales (see Figure 2–10). To fill this strategic gap, retail management must take advantage of any opportunities for better growth and/or improved performance.

Growth Opportunities

Kotler identified three types of growth opportunities—intensive, integrative, and diversification.[13] Figure 2–11 illustrates these opportunities and identifies the appropriate strategies to be used in pursuing a particular type of opportunity.

Intensive growth.   Opportunities found within the organization's current portfolio of businesses are referred to as intensive growth opportunities. As shown in Figure 2–11, three possible strategies can improve the performance of existing SBUs: market penetration, market development, and product development. Table 2–1 (p. 51) outlines the objective for each of these intensive growth strategies and identifies some of the tactics and methods retailers use in implementing these strategies.

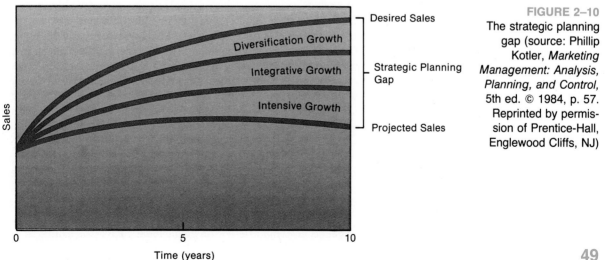

FIGURE 2–10

The strategic planning gap (source: Phillip Kotler, *Marketing Management: Analysis, Planning, and Control,* 5th ed. © 1984, p. 57. Reprinted by permission of Prentice-Hall, Englewood Cliffs, NJ)

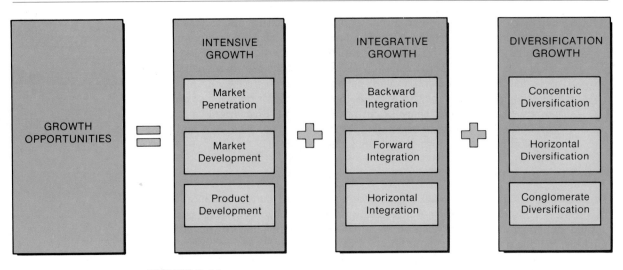

FIGURE 2–11
Types of growth opportunities

Integrative growth.   Opportunities can take the form of backward, forward, and horizontal integration. In this case, the organization's efforts focus on building or acquiring SBUs related to the organization's current portfolio of SBUs. An integration strategy aims to increase sales by incorporating one or more levels of the marketing channel of distribution into the organization's operations. *Backward integration* involves seeking ownership and/or control of supply systems (e.g., a retailer acquiring a wholesaler or manufacturer). *Horizontal integration* is achieved by seeking ownership and/or control of competitors at the same level within the marketing channel. Department store ownership groups such as Federated Department Stores (Bloomingdale's, Lazarus, Foley's, Rich's, etc.) and May Department Stores Co. (Hecht, Famous-Barr, Kaufman's, O'Neil's, G. Fox, etc.) have engaged extensively in horizontal integration. Many manufacturers (Sherwin-Williams) and wholesalers (True Value Hardware) have engaged in *forward integration* by developing or acquiring retail businesses and operating them as part of their strategic marketing efforts.

Diversification growth.   When the retail organization adds attractive SBUs whose business nature and format are dissimilar to current SBUs, the company is engaged in diversification growth. Concentric, horizontal, and conglomerate diversification are three different diversifying strategies for increasing sales. *Concentric diversification* tries to attract new customers by adding businesses having technological or marketing similarities with existing businesses. Wendy's, a retailer in the hamburger segment of the fast-food market, added Sisters' International to enter the chicken segment. The objective of *horizontal diversification* is to increase sales by adding SBUs that appeal to the organization's current customers even though they are not technologically related to its current businesses. A department store organization might decide to begin a catalog retailing operation by offering its current customers a line of specialty merchandise not found in its store merchandise lines. Finally, the retail organization can diversify by adding new businesses that are totally unrelated to its current SBUs in hopes of appealing to entirely new markets. Both Sears and J. C. Penney have engaged in *conglomerate diversification.* Sears, for example, has

TABLE 2–1

Intensive growth strategies

Strategy	Objective	Tactics	Methods
Market penetration	To increase the sales productivity of current SBU stores within existing markets	Increase patronage level of current customers by increasing the frequency of store visits and the amount of the average sale per customer visit Stimulate trial visits among nonpatrons who reside in existing trading areas Entice customers who currently patronize competing outlets with existing trading areas	Increase advertising and sales promotion activities Expand product and service mix Use suggestive selling techniques Engage in trade-up selling techniques Develop special event merchandising programs Offer lower prices
Market development	To increase sales by expanding existing store operations into new markets	Open new geographic markets Appeal to new market segments Expand into new market levels	Locate and develop new store sites within new trading areas Develop new product, service, price, and image programs that appeal to different consumer groups Offer products and services to wholesaling and manufacturing organizations
Product development	To increase sales within existing markets by developing new product/service mixes	Increase sales by replacing old product lines with new product lines Increase sales by adding new product lines and items	Adjust product variety and assortment to create a more differentiated product mix Add the more desirable product items that are normally associated with another type of retailer Develop general-purpose product mix by combining two or more broad product lines

diversified extensively into the area of financial services with insurance (Allstate), real estate (Coldwell Banker), and stock brokerage (Dean Witter Reynolds).

Performance Opportunities

A number of opportunities exist for improving the organization's profits and productivity through more efficient usage of organizational resources—financial, human, and facilities. The previous discussion on organizational objectives identified the need to achieve acceptable performance in (1) return on sales and assets, (2) earnings per share, (3) labor and space productivity, and (4) inventory turnover. Improved operational and managerial efficiencies are the key to achieving desired performance standards (see Chapters 7 through 11).

The value of strategic planning is that it provides a systematic method for analyzing the economic and competitive prospects for the retail organization and for charting a long-term course of action. The following statement by the chairman of Avon Products, Inc., suggests the importance of strategic thinking: "Those who succeed in thinking strategically and executing strategically are the people who are going to move ahead at this company."[14] The retail organization, however, must guard against having the strategic planning process become "less of a creative thinking exercise and more of a bureaucratic process," and retail management should not "confuse strategy with planning and implementation."[15] Without safeguards, the strategic planning process can lose contact with the external world of customers and competitors and the internal world of line managers who must implement designated strategies. In sum, a strategic plan "should be a device to integrate business units and enable the parent company to capitalize on synergies so that the whole of the corporation is more than just the sum of its units."[16] The key to a successful strategic plan is the implementation of the retailing plan.

THE RETAILING PLAN

The **retailing plan** is *an organized framework of activities directed at implementing the strategies identified in the strategic plan.* It addresses the operational questions of why, what, when, where, and how specific retail business activities are to be accomplished. The retailing plan tends to be more tactical than the strategic plan

Wendy's engaged in concentric diversification when they added Sisters' International to their business portfolio

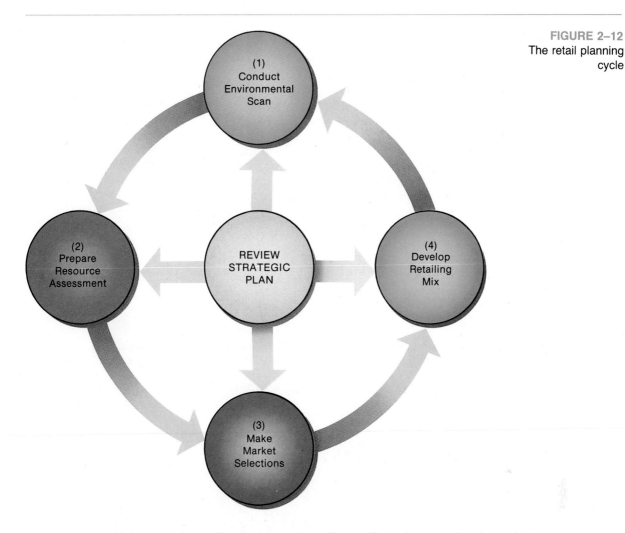

FIGURE 2–12
The retail planning
cycle

(1)
Conduct
Environmental
Scan

(2)
Prepare
Resource
Assessment

REVIEW
STRATEGIC
PLAN

(4)
Develop
Retailing
Mix

(3)
Make
Market
Selections

due to its limited scope and specific character. Typically, retailing plans are developed for each SBU and its stores, departments, and product lines.

The process of retail planning is a cyclical activity involving four stages: (1) conducting environmental scans, (2) preparing resource assessments, (3) making market selections, and (4) developing retailing mixes. As Figure 2–12 illustrates, the retail planning cycle depends on a review of the strategic plan; at each stage of the retail planning process the retail planner must review the guidelines in the strategic plan to ensure congruency with those guidelines.

The remainder of this text is devoted to the issues and concerns associated with implementing and controlling the activities that a retailing plan comprises. Figure 2–13 shows a model of the retailing plan that will be used as the general organizational framework for the discussion of retailing throughout this text. It identifies the major areas of concern at each stage of the retail planning cycle.

In Part II, the Environmental Scan, the uncontrollable environments of retailing are analyzed with respect to the competitive behavior of retail institutions (Chapter 3), the buying behavior of consumers (Chapter 4), and the protective and prohibitive nature of the regulatory environment (Chapter 5). Part II concludes with a discussion on the retail information system (Chapter 6), the methodology used in gathering and analyzing information about the environments of retailing.

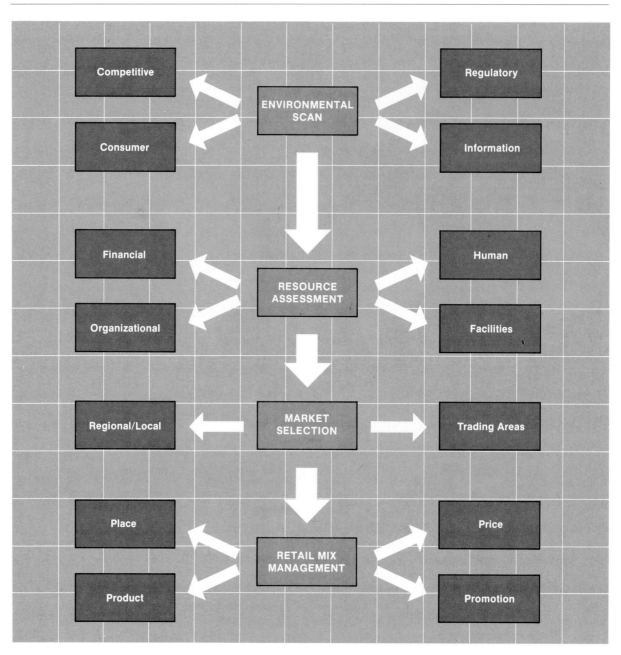

FIGURE 2–13
The retailing plan

Part III focuses on appraising the retailer's resources. Effective, efficient utilization of the organization's financial (Chapter 7), organizational (Chapter 8), human (Chapter 9), and facilities (Chapters 10 and 11) resources are highlighted in this topical coverage on resource assessments.

Identification, evaluation, and selection of retail markets are covered in Part IV. Analyzing regional and local markets (Chapter 12) and assessing retail trading areas (Chapter 13) are part of the general issue of market segmentation and the need to target selected market segments.

Part V discusses the management of the retailing mix—place, product, price, and promotion. The retailer's place of business—the retail site—is the focus of Chapter 14. The product dimension of the retailing mix is covered in Chapters 15 through 20. Discussions of the product mix (Chapter 15) and service mix (Chapter 16) are supported by an examination of the buying (Chapter 17), procuring (Chapter 18), planning (Chapter 19), and controlling (Chapter 20) processes. The pricing dimension is covered in the discussion of setting and adjusting retail prices (Chapter 21). The last dimension of the retailing mix is promotion, including retail advertising (Chapter 22), personal selling (Chapter 23), and retail displays, sales promotions, and publicity (Chapter 24).

Evaluating retail employment opportunities is the topic for discussion in Part VI. The pluses and minuses of a retail career are examined in Chapter 25.

SUMMARY

Strategic retail management is the process of planning the organization's survival and growth. Planning is conducted at corporate, SBU, store, department, and product-line levels of the organization. The retail organization's strategic plan is an overall business plan developed for the entire firm that involves (1) identifying the organizational mission, (2) establishing organizational objectives, (3) conducting an organizational portfolio analysis, and (4) evaluating organizational opportunities.

The mission statement is a generalized yet meaningful expression of the organization's future direction. Its three tasks are to identify (1) the business and customer domains within which the organization operates, (2) the organization's responsibilities toward the people with which it interacts, and (3) the blueprint for accomplishing the organizational mission. Mission statements are developed according to environmental and resource considerations, distinctive competencies, and managerial preferences.

Organizational objectives identify the specific purposes to be achieved by the firm. They need to be stated in quantitative, realistic, and consistent terms. Most retail organizations identify two general sets of objectives, market and financial. Market objectives aim at securing customer patronage (sales volume, customer traffic, and customer service objectives) and achieving competitive positions within the general marketplace (market share, store image, and vendor relations objectives). Financial objectives establish goals for profitability (returns, earnings, and dividends) and productivity (labor, space, and merchandise).

Organizational portfolio analysis involves reviewing the SBUs that the total business interest of a diversified retail organization comprises. The most commonly used portfolio approach is the market growth/market share matrix developed by the Boston Consulting Group. A portfolio analysis allows the retail organization to assess its current situation (what its business is) and to identify possible future courses of action (what the business should be).

The final step in developing a strategic plan is to identify and evaluate potential opportunities for continued organizational growth and improved organizational performance. Growth opportunities can be identified as intensive (market penetration, market development, and product development), integrative (backward, forward, and horizontal integration), and diversificative (concentric, horizontal, and conglomerate diversification). Performance opportunities include more efficient use of financial, human, and facility resources.

The retailing plan is an organizational framework of activities directed at implementing the strategies identified in the strategic plan. It is a cyclical process involving environment scans, resource assessments, market selections, and retailing mix management.

KEY TERMS AND CONCEPTS

strategic retail management	stars	forward integration
strategic business unit	cash cows	diversification growth
strategic plan	question marks	concentric diversification
mission statement	dogs	horizontal diversification
organizational objectives	intensive growth	conglomerate diversification
market objectives	market penetration	retailing plan
market share	market development	environmental scan
store image	product development	resource assessment
financial objectives	integrative growth	market selection
organizational portfolio	backward integration	retailing mix management
BCG portfolio approach	horizontal integration	

REVIEW QUESTIONS

1. Why have many retailers exhibited resistance to and skepticism about strategic planning?
2. What is strategic retail management? What are its two major components? Define each.
3. At what level does strategic and tactical planning occur? How is each planning level different from the others?
4. What is a strategic plan? What are its purposes?
5. What are the four elements of the strategic planning process? Define each.
6. Describe the three tasks of an organizational mission.
7. What factors should be considered in developing an organizational mission? Briefly describe each factor.
8. How should organizational objectives be stated?
9. Why should a retailer consider developing both market and financial objectives?
10. What are the six types of market objectives? Provide a brief description and example of each.
11. What are the six types of financial objectives? Provide a brief description and example of each.
12. What is the appeal of the portfolio approach to retail planning?
13. Describe the BCG market growth/market share matrix approach to portfolio analysis.
14. What are the five possible alternatives for the allocation of financial resources as identified in the BCG portfolio approach?
15. What three strategies are associated with integrative growth opportunities? Briefly describe each.
16. How does concentric diversification differ from horizontal and conglomerate diversification?
17. What specific questions does the retailing plan address?

ENDNOTES

1. Bert Rosenbloom, "Strategic Planning in Retailing: Prospects and Problems," *Journal of Retailing* 56 (Spring 1980): 110.
2. Ibid., 108.
3. Robert D. Buzzell and Marc K. Drew, "Strategic Management Helps Retailers Plan for the Future," *Marketing News,* 7 March 1980, 1.
4. Derek Abell and John S. Hammond, *Strategic Market Planning* (Englewood Cliffs, NJ: Prentice-Hall, 1979), 10.
5. *Marketing News,* 7 September 1980, 1.
6. The May Department Stores Co., Annual Report, 1982, 1.
7. Phillip Kotler, *Marketing Management,* 5th ed. (Englewood Cliffs, NJ: Prentice-Hall, 1984), 49.
8. George S. Day, "Diagnosing the Product Portfolio," *Journal of Marketing* 41 (April 1977): 29.
9. William K. Hull, "SBU's: Hot New Topic in the Management of Diversification," *Business Horizons* (February 1978): 18.
10. "The New Breed of Strategic Planners," *Business Week,* 17 September 1984, 66.
11. Douglas J. Dalrymple and Leonard J. Parsons, *Marketing Management: Strategy and Cases,* 3rd ed. (New York: John Wiley and Sons, 1983), 35.
12. Day, "Diagnosing the Product Portfolio," 31.
13. Kotler, *Marketing Management,* 58.
14. "The New Breed of Strategic Planners," 62.
15. Ibid., 66.
16. Ibid., 68.

RELATED READINGS

Achrol, Ravi Singh, and Appel, David L. "News Developments in Corporate Strategy Planning." *AMA Educators' Proceedings.* P. E. Murphy et al, eds. (American Marketing Association 1983), 305–10.

Barmash, Isadore. "Retail Pie." *Stores* (March 1982), 9–13.

Berens, John S. "The Marketing Mix, the Retailing Mix, and the Use of Retail Strategy Continue." *Developments in Marketing Science, Proceedings.* J. C. Rogers, III, ed. (Academy of Marketing Science 1983), 323–27.

Bivins, Jacquelyn. "Diversification: Retailers Reach Out." *Chain Store Age Executive* (March 1985), 25, 28, 31–32.

Cronin, J. Joseph, Jr., and Skinner, Steven J. "The Marketing-Finance Interface: The Impact of Marketing Objectives and Financial Conditions on Retail Profitability." *Developments in Marketing Science, Proceedings.* N. K. Malhotra, ed. (Academy of Marketing Science 1985), 182–86.

Feinberg, Richard A.; Koscica, Donna; and Recobs, Stephen J. "Strategic Planning: What the Top 100 Stores Say." *Retail Control* (October 1983), 9–21.

Horr, David A. "How the Independent Store Can Benefit from Strategic Planning." *Retail Control* (March 1984), 40–48.

Ingene, Charles A. "Productivity and Functional Shifting in Spatial Retailing: Private and Social Perspectives. *Journal of Retailing* 60 (Fall 1984), 15–36.

Kelly, J. Patrick, and George, William R. "Strategic Management Issues for the Retailing of Services." *Journal of Retailing* 58 (Summer 1982), 26–43.

Klokis, Holly. "Retailing's Grande Dame: Cloaked in New Strategies." *Chain Store Age Executive* (March 1985), 18–20.

Lovelock, Christopher H., and Weinberg, Charles B. "Retailing Strategies for Public and Nonprofit Organizations." *Journal of Retailing* 59 (Fall 1983), 93–115.

Lusch, Robert F., and Moon, Soo Young. "An Exploratory Analysis of the Correlates of Labor Productivity in Retailing." *Journal of Retailing* 60 (Fall 1984), 37–61.

Mason, Todd. "That Neiman-Marcus Mystique Isn't Traveling Well." *Business Week* (July 8, 1985), 44–45.

Ring, Lawrence J. "Retail Positioning: A Multiple Discriminant Analysis Approach." *Journal of Retailing* 55 (Spring 1979), 25–36.

Russell, Lloyd J. "Strategic Planning: What's Wrong with Retailer Strategies?" *Retail Control* (September 1983), 2–8.

Sager, Jeffrey K. "Four Areas of Organizational Considerations in Implementing a Strategic Market Plan." *Marketing: Theories and Concepts for an Era of Change, Proceedings.* J. Summey, R. Viswanathan, R. Taylor, and K. Glynn, eds. (Southern Marketing Association 1983), 54–58.

Schulz, David P. "Retail Expansion." *Stores* (August 1985), 19–24.

Sheth, Jagdish N., and Frazier, Gary L. "A Margin Return Model for Strategic Market Planning." *Journal of Marketing* 47 (Spring 1983), 100–109.

Soldner, Helmut. "Conceptual Models for Retail Strategy Formulation." *Journal of Marketing* 44 (Fall 1976), 47–56.

Spekman, Robert E., and Gronhaug, Kjell. "Insights on Implementation: A Conceptual Framework for Better Understanding the Strategic Marketing Planning Process." *AMA Educators' Proceedings.* P. E. Murphy et al, eds. (American Marketing Association 1983), 311–15.

Trombella, William L. "An Empirical Approach to Marketing Strategy for the Small Retailer." *Journal of Small Business* (October 1976), 55–58.

PART TWO
Environmental Scan: Analyzing the Environments of Retailing

Outline

THE NATURE OF MARKETING CHANNELS

Channel Levels
Channel Teams
Channel Interactions
Channel Flows
Channel Teamwork

THE NATURE OF RETAIL COMPETITION

THE NATURE OF RETAIL INSTITUTIONS

THE COMPETITIVE STRATEGIES OF RETAILERS

Specialty Store Retailing
Department Store Retailing
Chain Store Retailing
Discount Store Retailing
Off-Price Retailing
Supermarket Retailing
Convenience Store Retailing
Contractual Retailing
Warehouse Retailing
At-Home Retailing
Mail-Order Retailing
Telephone Retailing
Electronic Retailing
Vending Machine Retailing

RETAIL INSTITUTIONAL CHANGE

Wheel of Retailing
Dialectic Process

Objectives

■ Describe the marketing channel of distribution and understand the role of the retailer within this organizational system

■ Identify and discuss the four major types of retail competition

■ Recognize the different types of retailing institutions that the retailing community comprises

■ Identify the organizational and operational traits that characterize each type of retailer

■ Discuss the principal product, price, place, and promotional strategies each type of retailer employs

■ Discern the relative advantages and disadvantages that accrue to each type of retailer

■ Identify and discuss the theories of retail institutional change that are used to explain past evolution and predict future developments in retailing

3
The Competitive Behavior of Retail Institutions

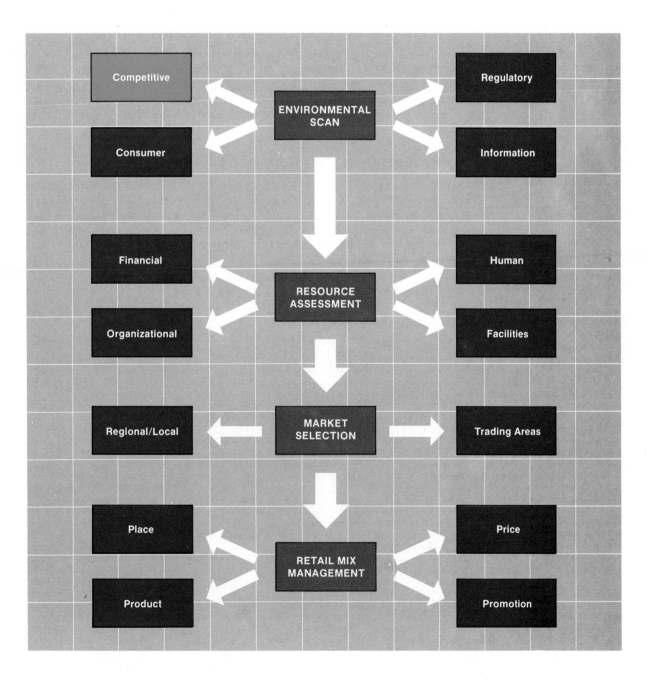

A
s consumers, all of us have shopped at specialty and department stores, discount and chain stores, stores that use the supermarket method of operations, and stores that operate by the warehouse method. Also, many of us have made retail purchases over the telephone, by mail, and through catalogs. All these experiences provide us with a good foundation for understanding the organizational and operational structures of retail institutions. In this chapter, we extend understanding beyond personal experiences with retailing institutions by reviewing the various types of retail institutions and examining their respective competitive, operational, and merchandising (product, price, place, and promotion) strategies. Understanding the competitive behavior of retail institutions first requires a basic knowledge of marketing channels, retail competition, and retail classifications.

THE NATURE OF MARKETING CHANNELS

The goal of a marketing channel of distribution is to have the right product . . . in the right quantities . . . in the right place . . . at the right time. The marketing channel's actions are directed at bringing together producers and their respective customers. The **marketing channel** can be described as *a multilevel structure made up of channel teams whose interactions coordinate channel flows through channel teamwork.*

Channel Levels

Marketing channels can be characterized by a number of different structural designs defined by the inclusion or exclusion of various intermediaries. The producer has a number of alternative channel structures to reach consumers. As Figure 3–1 illustrates, there are three basic alternative channel structures: extended, limited, and direct. The first alternative is to use an **extended channel** by *marketing through both wholesalers and retailers.* In this case, producers rely on wholesalers to reach retailers that, in turn, will stock their products and sell them to final consumers. Since there usually are fewer wholesalers than retailers in a marketing channel, this option allows the producer to spend less time and money cultivating the necessary channel contacts to reach the ultimate consumers.

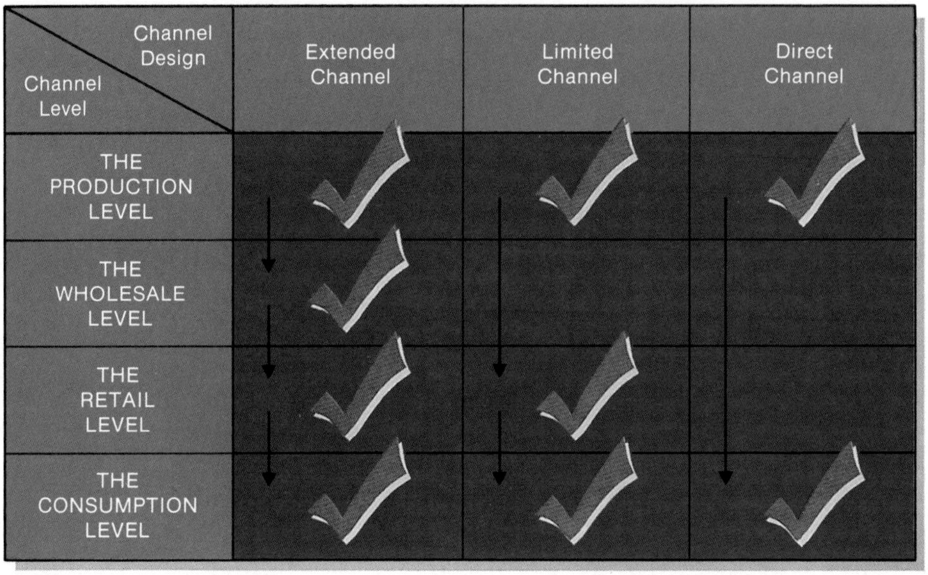

FIGURE 3–1
Alternative channel structures

Channel Level \ Channel Design	Extended Channel	Limited Channel	Direct Channel
THE PRODUCTION LEVEL	✓	✓	✓
THE WHOLESALE LEVEL	✓		
THE RETAIL LEVEL	✓	✓	
THE CONSUMPTION LEVEL	✓	✓	✓

The second alternative for a producer is the **limited channel**; that is, *to use only retailers, thereby eliminating the wholesaler.* A growing number of producers of such products as automobiles, furniture, appliances, and other big-ticket items are using the limited channel. Also, manufacturers of "perishable" products such as clothing (which goes out of style quickly) and fresh and frozen foods (which spoil rapidly) frequently utilize a limited channel.

The third alternative is the **direct channel**. In this case, *the producer eliminates both the retailer and the wholesaler.* By using door-to-door, television, magazine, or direct-mail selling techniques, these producers market directly to final consumers. Examples of products distributed that way include Electrolux Vacuum Cleaners, Avon Cosmetics, and Fuller Brushes.

Although a producer may choose not to use another team member in the channel, it can never eliminate the functions that must be performed at each channel level. In other words, *it can eliminate the retailer, but not the retail level and the retail functions.* Thus, producers who sell directly to consumers have taken over, but not eliminated, retailer operations at the retail level. Such producers become both wholesalers and retailers.

Channel Teams

Channel teams include both full- and limited-member institutions supported by facilitating nonmember institutions. Membership in the marketing channel team is based on the nature of an institution's transactional involvements and whether members assume title to the goods involved in the transaction. A **full-member institution** is *a wholesaler or retailer directly involved in the purchase and/or sale of products and that takes title to the products involved in the transaction.* Merchant wholesalers and nearly all retailers have full membership in the channel team. **Limited-member institutions** are *marketing intermediaries with a direct involvement in purchase/sales transactions that do not take title to the involved product.* Agent wholesalers hold limited team membership, as do retailers when they engage in consignment selling. A number of organizations provide a wide range of support functions; these **nonmember facilitating institutions** *assist the team effort by providing specialized advertising, research, transportation, storage, financial, risk-taking, and/or consulting services.* These facilitators neither take title to goods involved in a transaction nor become directly involved in sales/purchase of those goods.

Channel Interactions

Interactions between participants within the marketing channel of distribution can take several forms. As intermediaries, wholesalers and retailers must successfully complete a number of tasks for each other and their clientele for distribution and transactional functions to be accomplished most efficiently and effectively. These interactive tasks include buying, selling, breaking bulk, creating assortments, stocking, delivering, extending credit, informing, consulting, and transferring titles and payments (see Figure 3–2).

Channel Flows

A marketing channel can be likened to a pipeline or conduit that guides the movement of entire marketing programs between channel participants. While the flow of physical goods is the channel flow most commonly recognized by the general public, other types of flows are equally important to delivering a successful marketing

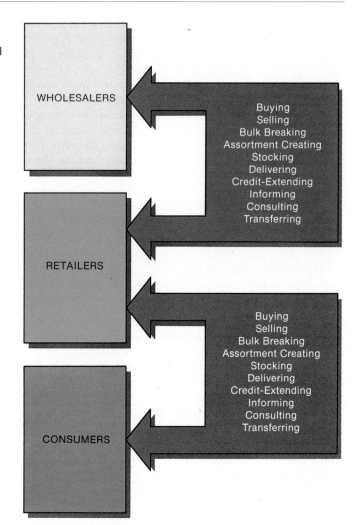

FIGURE 3–2

Interactive tasks performed by the channel team

effort. The five major types of channel flows are

1. *physical flow*—the actual movement of a physical product from one channel participant to another
2. *ownership flow*—transferring title (right of ownership and usage) from one channel participant to another
3. *information flow*—the two-way communication of useful data between channel participants
4. *payment flow*—the transfer of monies from one channel participant to another as compensation for services rendered and/or goods delivered
5. *promotion flow*—the flow of persuasive communication directed at influencing the decisions of consumers (consumer promotion) and other channel participants (trade promotion)

The nature and degree of involvement with each of these flows for any given channel participant will vary depending on the structure of the channel. In most channel structures, however, retailers have a direct involvement in each of these flows and play a key role in successful channel flow management.

Channel Teamwork

As a social interactive system, the marketing channel is subject to the behavioral processes inherent in all such systems. The behavior of each channel participant affects all other participants; hence, the need for channel teamwork. Good teamwork results in a cooperative spirit and a coordinated effort; poor teamwork nets channel disruptions and conflict. To ensure good teamwork the channel of distribution needs to be integrated. **Channel integration** is *the process of incorporating all channel members into one channel system and uniting them under one leadership and one set of goals.* As Chapter 2 showed, channel integration can be accomplished through backward integration of retailers and wholesalers, forward integration of producers and wholesalers, and horizontal integration of each channel member within its respective channel level.

Channel integration ends the segregation of intermediary operations and their functional tasks. As Figure 3–3 shows, channel integration can take the form of a highly integrated vertical marketing system or a modestly integrated conventional marketing channel. A **vertical marketing system** is *"a professionally managed and centrally programmed network, pre-engineered to achieve operating economies and maximum market impact."*[1] The advantage of this type of system is that it allows the channel team to achieve technological, managerial, and promotional leverages through integrating and synchronizing the five channel flows.[2] A vertical marketing system can be established using persuasive administrative powers, legally binding contractual agreements, and partial or total ownership of channel members.

In a vertical marketing system, each channel member assumes the functions and tasks that will best support the entire channel system. As a team member, the retailer operates within the retail level of distribution and provides most of the teamwork at that level. Some, however, engage in operations at the wholesale and even

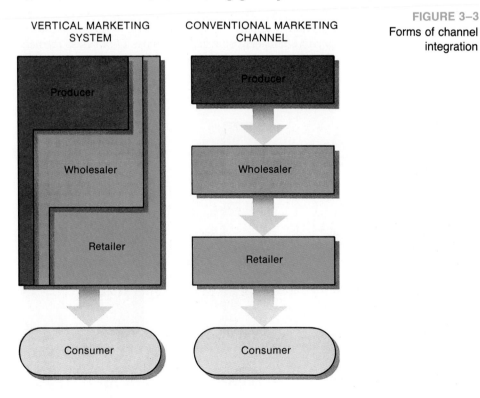

VERTICAL MARKETING SYSTEM

CONVENTIONAL MARKETING CHANNEL

Producer

Wholesaler

Retailer

Consumer

FIGURE 3–3

Forms of channel integration

65

the production levels of the marketing channel. Sears, Roebuck & Co., for example, conducts extensive operations at both the wholesale and production levels of the channel. Sears buys a large portion of its products from manufacturers in which it has part ownership. Also, individual stores obtain most of their merchandise from Sears' wholesale distribution facilities.

A **conventional marketing channel** is *a loosely aligned, independently owned and operated channel team.* The chief advantage of this type of an arrangement is the freedom each member has in conducting business. The disadvantages of conventional channels include (1) the failure to achieve economies of scale, (2) the instability of the arrangement due to the ease of channel entry and exit, and (3) the limited levels of cooperation and coordination as a result of the greater autonomy of participating members. In short, the conventional marketing channel is becoming an outdated mode of operation for most retailers. The exceptions are the smaller, more specialized retailers that need their freedom of action to target specialty markets.

Now that we have an appreciation for the complexities faced by the retailer in developing channel relationships and arrangements, we can proceed with our discussion of the complex nature of retail competition.

THE NATURE OF RETAIL COMPETITION

Retailers compete with one another on the basis of their product, place, price, and promotion strategies. These strategies are directed at securing the attention and patronage of ultimate consumers and serve as the focus for retail competitive actions; however, retail competition is more complex than just two similar stores competing against each other. Figure 3–4 shows the four different types of retail competition: intratype, intertype, vertical, and systems competition. **Intratype competition** *involves the competition between two or more retailers using the same type of business format.* For example, in a regional shopping mall we often see several small independent women's apparel shops competing with one another. *Competition between two or more retailers using different types of business formats to sell the same type of merchandise is referred to as* **intertype competition.** A

FIGURE 3–4
Types of competition

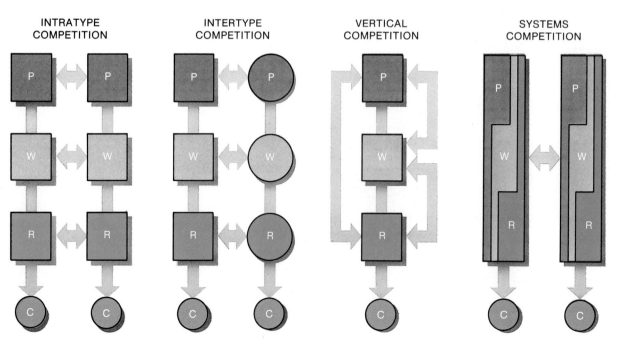

INTRATYPE COMPETITION	INTERTYPE COMPETITION	VERTICAL COMPETITION	SYSTEMS COMPETITION

supermarket and a discount store attempting to sell Crest toothpaste to the same customer are engaging in intertype competition. **Vertical competition** is *the competition between a retailer and a wholesaler or producer that is attempting to make retail sales to the retailer's customers.* For example, if a retailer were to stock and sell a product line that the manufacturer was also offering through a catalog operation, the retailer and manufacturer would be engaged in vertical competition. The final type of competition occurs between entire marketing channel systems. **Systems competition** is *the competition between two or more vertical marketing systems.* The competition between McDonald's, Burger King, and Wendy's is between three highly integrated marketing systems at all levels of the distribution channel.

Retailers can be classified on the basis of their ownership, merchandise, size, affiliation, contractual, location, service, organizational, and operational characteristics. The diversity and complexity of business formats found within the retailing industry preclude developing a mutually exclusive classification that clearly distinguishes each type of retailer from all other types. For example, specialty and department stores can be distinguished on the basis of their respective merchandise mix; however, each might also be classified as a chain, affiliated, or integrated operation. Table 3–1 outlines the multiplicity of characteristics that classify retail institutions.

The next section discusses the competitive strategies of various retail institutions from the perspective of 12 general types of retail operations. In reading that discussion, you should keep in mind the variety and complexity of retail characteristics as shown in Table 3–1 on page 69.

One of the most dramatic developments in today's world of retailing is the number of alternative types of stores available to consumers. "By and large, people have a wide repertoire of stores that they patronize. And they are open to all kinds of retail alternatives. So a store is not simply competing with other stores in its own retail category. It's competing with retailers across the board."[3]

Specialty Store Retailing

As the name implies, **specialty store retailers** *"specialize" in the merchandise or service they offer a consumer.* Specialty stores vary significantly in their degree of merchandise specialization.

Types of Specialty Retailers

There are two types of specialty retailers: the single-line specialty retailer and the limited-line specialty retailer. **Single-line specialty stores** *offer only one or a very few closely related product lines.* For example, retailers that specialize in either jewelry, shoes, hardware, furniture, or apparel are single-line specialty retailers. In each example, the specialized product line is due either to retail selling requirements or consumer usage behavior.

Limited-line specialty stores *specialize more than single-line specialty stores— within a single line of merchandise.* For example, the retailer that specializes in either men's, women's, or children's shoes is a limited-line specialty store. Some retailers create still more limited merchandise lines. An example is a retailer that specializes only in "better" women's formal wear and sportswear, excluding even "moderate" offerings in these product lines. Some retailers even limit their merchandise line to one manufacturer's brand, such as The Levi's Place, Kristopher's Keepsake Diamonds, and the Lazy Boy Shop. Within any given merchandise line, retailers can specialize on the basis of price (e.g., discount), size (e.g., tall or big men's), quality (e.g., exclusive), style (e.g., early American), or fashion (e.g., new wave).

The diverse and complex world of retailing precludes a mutually exclusive classification of retailers

Merchandising Strategies

A key tactic in the specialty retailer's product strategy is merchandise assortment. Although specialty stores carry only a limited variety of products, they do offer con-

(a)

(b)

(c)

(d)

(e)

TABLE 3–1
Classifying retail institutions

A. By ownership of establishment
  1. Single-unit independent stores
  2. Multiunit retail organizations
    a) chain stores
    b) branch stores
  3. Manufacturer-owned retail outlets
  4. Consumers' cooperative stores
  5. Farmer-owned establishments
  6. Company-owned stores (industrial stores) or commissaries
  7. Government operated stores (post exchanges, state liquor stores)
  8. Public utility company stores (for sale of major appliances)

B. By kind of business (merchandise handled)
  1. General merchandise group
    a) department stores
    b) dry goods, general merchandise stores
    c) general stores
    d) variety stores
  2. Single-line stores (e.g., grocery, apparel, furniture)
  3. Specialty stores (e.g., meat markets, lingerie shops, floor coverings stores)

C. By size of establishment
  1. By number of employees
  2. By annual sales volume

D. By degree of vertical integration
  1. Nonintegrated (retailing functions only)
  2. Integrated with wholesaling functions
  3. Integrated with manufacturing or other form-utility creation

E. By type of relationship with other business organizations
  1. Unaffiliated
  2. Voluntarily affiliated with other retailers
    a) through wholesaler-sponsored voluntary chains
    b) through retailer cooperation
  3. Affiliated with manufacturers by dealers franchises

F. By method of consumer contact
  1. Regular store
    a) leased department
  2. Mail order
    a) by catalog selling
    b) by advertising in regular media
    c) by membership club plans
  3. Household contacts
    a) by house-to-house canvassing
    b) by regular delivery route service
    c) by party plan selling

G. By type of location
  1. Urban
    a) central business district
    b) secondary business district
    c) string street location
    d) neighborhood location
    e) controlled (planned) shopping center
    f) public market calls
  2. Small city
    a) downtown
    b) neighborhood
  3. Rural stores
  4. Roadside stands

H. By type of service rendered
  1. Full service
  2. Limited service (cash-and-carry)
  3. Self-service

I. By legal form of organization
  1. Proprietorship
  2. Partnership
  3. Corporation
  4. Special types

J. By management organization or operational technique
  1. Undifferentiated
  2. Departmentalized

Source: T. N. Beckman, W. R. Davidson, and W. W. Talarzyk, *Marketing,* 9th ed. (New York: Ronald Press Co., 1973), 239.

sumers the opportunity to choose from a deep assortment within each line. The large number of brands, models, styles, sizes, and colors within each product line is the principal means by which specialty retailers attract customers. In general, the more specialized the retailer, the greater the depth of the product assortment. A specialty store might stock national brands, designer labels, private labels, or some combination of these products. In recent years, the desirability of store labels and brands has increased as the distribution of national and designer labels has become more commonplace (see Figure 3–5).

FIGURE 3–5
Private labels are no
secret anymore

> The search for uniqueness and better profit margins has led many specialty stores, department stores and mass merchandisers to reconsider the value of a private label. Not only can retailers impose higher markups on their signature appeal, but they can also exercise quality control over the manufacture of those garments.
>
> A private label helps reinforce corporate identity even as it represents a particular fashion statement. What better exposure for a store than its own name or trademark positioned prominently in a silk dress or cashmere sweater? And, as any retailer will tell you, it's nice to have at least one brand on the selling floor that's not traded all over town.

Source: Frances Dunne, "Private Labels Are No Secret Anymore," *Advertising Age,* 25 July 1983, M30.

Specialty retailers usually are high-margin operations. The prices specialty retailers charge are customarily at or above market prices. A few specialty retailers, however, emphasize lower-than-market prices.

Specialty retailers normally operate in comparatively small facilities with decor and layouts complementing the nature of their merchandise. Although specialty retailers are found in a variety of locations, in recent years they have tended to favor large shopping centers and downtown malls.

Specialty stores' promotions stress the uniqueness and distinctiveness of their product offerings and the depth of selection they offer the consumer.

In final analysis, the product, price, place, and promotional strategies of the specialist are directed at serving the needs of a limited but homogeneous market segment. Unlike the mass merchandiser that attempts to serve some consumers in many markets, the specialty retailer attempts to serve all consumers in one or a limited number of markets. As Kenderdine and McCammon note,

> As consumer markets become more segmented, specialty stores will become increasingly important. This trend is already well advanced in a variety of product categories. Consider, for example, the explosive growth of such firms as Aaron Brothers (artist's supplies and picture frames), Hickory Farms (specialty foods), The Limited (junior apparel), and Mervin's (family apparel). In addition to these established chains, a new wave of "super" specialists has emerged. Included in this latter movement are such companies as Athlete's Food, County Seat, Calculators, Inc. and The Gap. In short, specialty store retailing has become a high-growth sector of the economy.[4]

Department Store Retailing

Department stores are *large retailing institutions that carry a wide variety of merchandise lines with a reasonably good selection within each line.* What distinguishes the department store from other general-line merchandisers is its organizational structure, specifically the high degree of "departmentalization." From an operational standpoint, most of the basic functions of buying, selling, promoting, and servicing are conducted entirely or at least in part at the department level. Also, accounting and control procedures are organized on a departmental basis. The advantages of this type of organization are that it allows both *functional* (buying, selling, etc.) and *merchandise* (apparel, shoes, etc.) specialization, while at the same time gaining the economies of scale associated with a large retailing operation.

Types of Department Store Retailers

Although all department stores share the common characteristic of departmentalization, they differ in terms of ownership and operational characteristics. The four basic types of department stores are independent, chain, ownership group, and branch.[5]

The **independent department store** is *one that has no ownership affiliation with other department stores or retailing organizations.* Usually they represent an "established department store operation within either a single urban or regional market. Today, the independent department store is almost an endangered species, they are finding it very difficult to compete in today's fast-paced retailing industry. Few are expected to survive."[6]

The **department store chain** is *a multiunit retailing organization that operates under central ownership, management, and control.* Examples of department store chains are Sears, Roebuck & Co., the J. C. Penney Co., and Montgomery Ward. Because the chain store organization encompasses such an important segment of the retailing business, it will be discussed separately later in this chapter.

A special type of multiunit department store organization is the **ownership group,** *one that forms through the acquisition activities of a central retailing organization.* Department stores that are part of an ownership group differ from department store chains because each "acquired" store retains considerable local identity. Some of the largest U.S. ownership groups are shown in Table 3–2.

The fourth type of department store is the **branch department store,** *usually a scaled-down operation of a main or parent store.* Typically, the branch has fewer departments with a more restricted selection in most merchandise lines. Frequently, they are convenient to a particular market segment and are tailored to meet the needs of that market.

Merchandising Strategies

The number of merchandise departments within a department store varies with the size of the store; with the degree of specialization needed in buying, promoting, and selling the merchandise; and with management's general merchandising philosophy. Some department stores limit their departmentalization to a few (less than 20) broad merchandise lines, whereas others departmentalize into many (more than 100) very limited merchandise groups. Whatever the degree of departmentalization, department stores commonly divide merchandise into "hard" and "soft" line departments. Home furnishings is an example of a broad, hard-line department that could be further departmentalized into consumer electronics, floor coverings, furniture, major appliances, and decorative furnishings. The women's department is a soft line that can be further departmentalized by creating separate departments for dresses, footwear, hosiery, lingerie, jewelry, and ladies' accessories.

Several inherent advantages to departmental organization aid the retailer in developing and implementing a product strategy. First, department managers are in a good position to supervise and control each individual product line closely. Second, sales personnel operating at the departmental level are directly in touch with consumers' needs, buying problems, and special concerns. Third, a departmental organization allows the retailer to segment the consumer market. Figure 3–6 (p. 74) illustrates how retailers can use store departmentalization to satisfy a particular market segment's needs. Referring to that figure, we can see that with more departments the retailer can appeal to several market segments by orient-

TABLE 3–2
Major department store
"ownership groups"

Chain and Division	Sales Volume (millions)	Number of Units
Federated Department Stores		
Bloomingdales	788	14
Abraham and Straus	732	15
Foley's	626	15
Burdine's	630	25
Bullock's	589	28
Rich's	509	17
Lazarus	420	17
Sanger Harris	362	14
Shillito/Rikes	360	14
Filene's	293	14
Goldsmith's	148	6
Boston Stores	131	8
Levy's	38	2
Dayton Hudson		
Hudson's	728	20
Dayton's	514	16
Diamond's	160	6
John A. Brown	82	6
May Department Stores		
May Co. (CA)	725	34
Hecht Co.	477	23
Famous-Barr	419	16
Kaufman's	302	11
May Co. (Cleveland)	212	10
Meier & Frank	204	7
G. Fox & Co.	174	8
M. O'Neil Co.	156	10
May D&F	148	11
Strouss	104	8
May-Cohens	68	6
Associated Dry Goods		
Lord & Taylor	630	40
J. W. Robinson (CA)	470	21
L. S. Ayres	275	18
Sibley, Lindsay & Curr	172	14
Joseph Horne	170	13
Denver Dry Goods	128	12
Hahne	112	8
Goldwaters	102	9
Robinson's (FL)	84	7
Stewart's Dry Goods	70	7

ing its product strategy to meet a combination of consumers' needs, such as life-style and price/quality needs. Chicago's Carson Pirie Scott & Co. has made a major statement of its targeting strategy by creating Corporate Level, a separate department tailored to the needs and wants of executive and professional women. Not just any working women will be targeted, only those with individual incomes of at least $25,000.[7]

TABLE 3-2,
continued

Chain and Division	Sales Volume (millions)	Number of Units
H. & S. Pouge	67	5
Powers Dry Goods	48	7
Allied Stores		
Jordan Marsh (NE)	470	16
The Bon	430	36
Joske's	400	28
Sterns	350	16
Maas Bros.	300	19
Jordan Marsh (FL)	260	15
Brooks Bros.	210	38
Pomeroy's	130	14
Bonwit Teller	125	14
Miller & Rhoads	120	22
Donaldson's	110	9
Garfinckel's	100	10
Miller's	90	12
Read's	75	6
Block's	75	9
Carter Hawley Hale		
The Broadway (CA)	815	40
Emporium Capwell	570	21
Neiman-Marcus	510	20
John Wanamaker	415	16
Weinstock's	215	12
Thalheimer's	220	26
Holt-Renfrew	180	17
Broadway-Southwest	145	10
R. H. Macy & Co.		
Bamberger's	1,055	23
Macy's New York	1,045	17
Macy's California	880	22
Davidson's	270	13
Macy's Midwest	215	18
Batus (retail group)		
Saks Fifth Avenue	836	34
Marshall Field's	675	21
Gimbels East	470	20
Frederick & Nelson	228	15
Kohl's	211	31
Gimbels Midwest	200	11
Gimbels Pittsburgh	160	7

Source: Reprinted by permission from *Chain Store Age Executive*, August 1984, pp. 42, 44. Copyright © Lebhar-Friedman, Inc. 425 Park Avenue, New York, NY 10022.

Department stores usually are high-margin operations. Because of the high operating expenses (30–33 percent of sales) stemming from the store's organizational structure, service offering, physical facilities, and high-risk merchandise, margins between merchandise costs and retail selling prices must be substantial to ensure a fair profit.

FIGURE 3–6
Market segmentation
through store depart-
mentalization

LIFESTYLE DIMENSION

Formal ⬌ Informal

	Moderate Dresses Department	Moderate Sportswear Department
Women's Department	Better Dresses Department	Better Sportswear Department

Price/Quality Dimension — Economy / Prestigious

LIMITED DEPARTMENTALIZATION ⬌ EXTENSIVE DEPARTMENTALIZATION

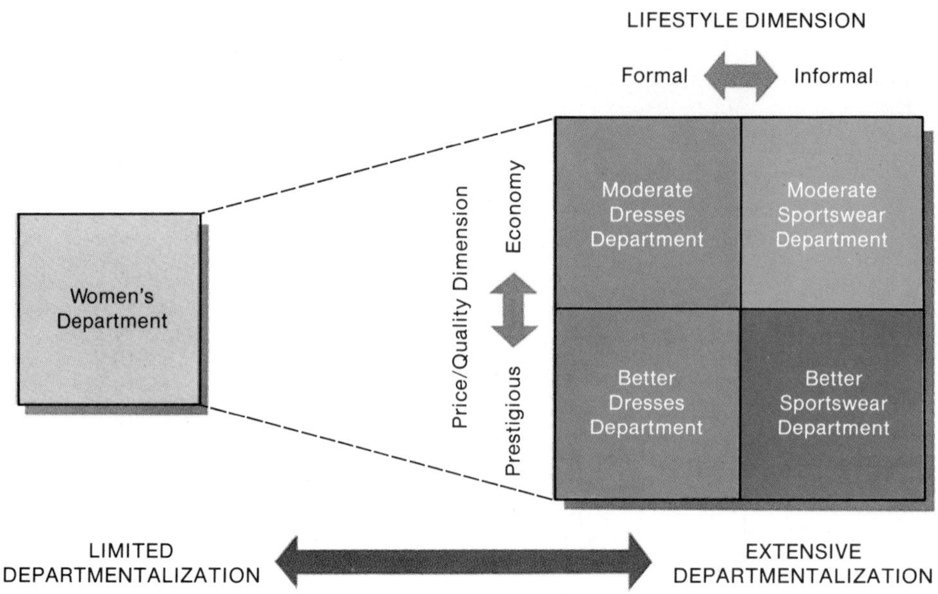

Department stores normally appeal to middle- and upper-income consumers. To appeal to such a diverse group of consumers, most department stores have at least three pricing points. "Low or economy" prices are directed at the lower- to middle-income consumer; "midline" prices appeal to those who want neither the lowest nor the highest priced merchandise; "prestige" prices are aimed at the upper-income consumer who desires the best. These good, better, and best price lines not only allow the department store to project a broad price appeal, but also help consumers to make price/quality comparisons.

Department stores typically occupy high-rent locations within major commercial centers. In their early stages of development, department stores were located exclusively in the central business districts (CBD) of major urban areas. In recent years, the place strategy of most department stores has been to locate in an "anchor" (end) position at one or more major suburban shopping centers. In many parts of the country, department stores have become synonymous with regional shopping centers.

The exterior and interior motifs of the average department store are designed to create a prestige image. Externally, the architectural form might communicate either bigness, success, uniqueness, strength, security, elegance, or any number of store images. Internally, the store's layout, fixtures, and decor create consumer buying moods by appealing to all the customers' sensory modes of sight, sound, smell, taste, and touch.

The department store's principal promotional appeals are product selection and quality, service offerings, and shopping atmosphere. Each of these appeals is directed toward enhancing the prestige image of the department store. Both product and institutional advertising are an integral part of the department store's strategy to favorably influence potential consumers. While advertisements feature several carefully selected products, every department store advertising campaign subtly communicates the message that "this is the place to shop." In addition to media advertising, the typical department store relies heavily on in-store promotion. Once people have been attracted into the store, considerable attention is given to capitalizing on customer traffic by creating buyer excitement through attractive displays, special effects, promotional demonstrations, and seasonal entertainment. Department stores like to create the "big event" by developing shopping themes consistent with the customer's moods and needs, the seasons or current events, the merchandise, and the store's environment. For example, Bloomingdale's likes to stage multimillion-dollar extravanganzas honoring individual countries' crafts.

Chain Store Retailing

In retailing, the term "chain" is used in a variety of ways. As commonly used, a **chain** is *any retail organization that operates multiple outlets*. To be properly classified as a chain, however, a retail organization must meet several additional criteria. What distinguishes chain operations from similar types of operations are the number of units (stores), the merchandise mix, and the form of ownership and control.

Types of Chain Store Retailers

Technically, any retail organization that operates more than one unit can be classified as chain. However, many retailing and government officials prefer to use the classification categories established by the *Census of Business,* which considers chains as retail organizations that operate 11 or more units. A workable compromise is to discuss chain organizations as *small chains* (2–10 units) and *large chains* (11 or more units). Small chains are local and regional market operations that enjoy some, but not necessarily all, of the advantages of large chain organizations. Large chains are either regional or national in scope and can take full advantage of the economies of scale of operating multiple outlets.

Another criterion for classifying a conglomeration of stores as a chain is that each unit in the chain must *sell similar lines of merchandise.* So long as the product is basically the same, a chain store organization could be a multiunit operation of specialty stores, discount stores, department stores, or food stores. If, however, a retail firm were to operate a supermarket, a variety store, and a drug store, it would not by definition be considered a chain.

The third criterion used to determine if a group of stores is a chain is whether there is a *central form of ownership and control.* With central ownership, one governing body has "full control over its retail units, assumes full financial responsibility for them, bears all losses, and retains all profits made by the store."[8] Central ownership is the key variable distinguishing chain stores from other chainlike operations. For example, franchise organizations operate multiple retailing units. In most cases, however, the individual franchisee retains store ownership.

Highly centralized control is the principal organizational characteristic of the chain store. Product, place, price, and promotion decisions are made at the home office by central managers who specialize in each functional area. The entire marketing strategy for the chain organization and its operating units is directed from a central control center.

Merchandising Strategies

Chain stores offer highly standardized merchandise. Frequently, the home office establishes two merchandise lists—a standard stock list and an optional stock list. The **standard stock list** is *an enumeration of the standard lines of merchandise that each individual unit of the chain must stock.* These standard items are typically staple merchandise that has a relatively high market demand and turnover rate. The merchandise items included in the standard stock list are the most popular brands, styles, models, sizes, and colors. Although a standardized line of products increases operating efficiency, it does not allow each store the necessary flexibility to adjust to local market demands. Because of this limitation many chains also use the more flexible optional stock list approach. The **optional stock list** *permits local store managers to select additional items from a stock list that they believe are appropriate to the needs of their customers.* However, while local store managers can tailor their merchandise offering to local markets within the constraints of the optional stock list, rarely are they allowed to add products to that list.

In recent years, many of the larger chain organizations have engaged in "private label" branding (the retailer's brand) as part of their overall product strategy. In some cases, a few of the private brands of very large chains have become, in effect, national brands. For example, most consumers think of Sears' "Craftsman" and "Kenmore" brands as high-quality, national brands. By virtue of the fact that Sears' operations are national in scope, many more of their private labels are viewed in the same perspective (see Figure 3–7).

Economies of scale are an important part of the chain's central buying policies. By buying in large quantities, often directly from the manufacturer, chain stores receive substantial quantity discounts. Large quantity purchases also reduce the cost of merchandise, since the chains can take advantage of lower transportation rates on carload and truckload shipments. Additional benefits associated with large-scale purchases are the favorable relationships that chains develop with suppliers. Because of these relationships, chains can gain *promotional allowances* (payments that chains receive from suppliers to help defray the cost of advertising the suppliers' products) and *cash discounts* (reductions in the suppliers' prices if the cash payment is received within a prescribed period of time). The net result of the chain's centralized buying policies is that it can acquire merchandise at the lowest costs in the retailing industry.

Several advantages accrue to chain store operations. First, by operating a large number of stores within a particular market, chains can exert substantial control over their stores and achieve economies of scale through a centralized distribution system. The result is high turnover rates and few stockouts and overstocks.

Second, chains can spread risk over many different stores in many different markets. For example, if a new market offers potential future profits, initial store opening and operating losses can be absorbed by existing stores until the new store can generate those potential profits. Likewise, losses resulting from poor economic conditions in one local market can be covered by profits from stores operating in markets with favorable economic conditions.

Third, chain organizations obtain benefits from vertically integrating their channels of distribution. Sears, for example, obtains approximately 50 percent of its merchandise from manufacturers in which it has equity interest. Finally, chain operations enjoy the advantage of a high level of consumer recognition. The use of a standardized sign and architectural motif reinforces consumers' awareness of the chain and what it has to offer. Assuming that the consumer's prior shopping experience was satisfactory, chains then benefit from both return trade to the same store and additional trade to other stores in the same chain.

Promotional strategies vary considerably from one chain to another; certain common practices do exist, however. Chain stores usually promote both their store image and their individual products. Generally, chains promote the standardized nature of their operations and therefore the consistency (product quality, customer service, etc.) of their product offerings from store to store. Chains also commonly promote their convenience and large number of locations available to their customers. Finally, many chains stress the reliability of buying from a large national or regional firm.

Strategically, the most important advantage chain retailers have over most of their competitors is their ability to spread promotional expenses over multiple out-

FIGURE 3–7
Just who or what is
Sears?

THEN—1978

Sears is a family store for middle-class, home-owning America . . . We are the premier distributor of durable goods for these families, their homes and their automobiles. We are the premier distributor of nondurable goods that have their acceptance based in function rather than fashion and, as a result of this, have increased our market share in nondurables over the past decade, reflective of an increased proportion of selling space devoted to them. We are valued by middle-class America for our integrity, our reputation, for fair-dealing and our guarantee . . . We are not a fashion store. We are not a store for the whimsical, nor the affluent. We are not a discounter, nor an avantgarde department store. We are not, by the standards of the trade press or any other group of bored observers, an exciting store. We are not a store that anticipates. We reflect the world of Middle America, and all of its desires and concerns and problems and faults. And we must all look on what we are, and pronounce it good! And seek to extend it. And not be swayed from it by the attraction of other markets, no matter how enticing they might be.

Source: "Sears' New 5-Year Plan: To Serve Middle America," Reprinted with permission from the December 4, 1978, issue of *Advertising Age,* pp. 3, 18. Copyright © by Crain Communications, Inc.

NOW—1984

Forget Sears, Roebuck. Nowdays Sears, Tiegs might be more appropriate. In 12 million American homes, the first image Sears customers are seeing as they flip through the new fall-winter catalog is the cover picture of Model Cheryl Tiegs . . . Sears has taken a fancy to Tiegs, embracing her in its catalog and TV commercials and identifying itself with her wholesome all-American looks . . . some people would say that Sears has become downright sassy . . . the "catalog of the future," as Sears now calls it . . . appeals to the upwardly mobile young women of the '80s, with sexy models sporting slightly punk hairdos and clad in leather skirts, silk dresses, and wool blazers. "Come share the excitement," teases the copy . . . Change is also sweeping the aisles of Sears' 806 retail stores in all 50 states . . . By October [1984] Sears will have 107 "stores of the future," which will depart sharply from its traditional selling places. They have a friendlier, more welcoming look than the Sears stores of old, with more aisles, lower ceilings and merchandise displayed with flair and style at eye level. Fashion labels with big names—Arnold Palmer, Joe Namath, Diane von Furstenberg, Johnny Carson, and Evonne Goolagong—stare back at the customer.

Source: "Sears' Sizzling New Vitality," Copyright 1983 Time Inc. All rights reserved. Reprinted by permission from TIME.

lets. With multiple locations within a given market, chain stores can effectively use the most expensive media (television) and exposure time (prime time) while most small, single-unit retailers simply cannot justify the costs of such promotional vehicles.

Discount Store Retailing

The **discount store** is *a retailing institution that sells a wide variety of merchandise at less than traditional retail prices.* Targeted to meet the needs of the economy-minded consumer, the discount store utilizes mass merchandising techniques that enable it to offer discount prices as its major consumer appeal. However, discount operations vary with respect to the size of the discount and the nature of the merchandise offered for sale. Two general types of discounters are the distressed discount store and the conventional discount store.

Types of Discount Store Retailers

A store that sells merchandise substantially below the market price is a **distressed discount store.** Often referred to as "discount barns" or "salvage stores," they offer merchandise usually classified as either damaged, discontinued, seconds, irregulars, or used. Low-quality foreign goods and surplus merchandise also are commonly included in the merchandise offering. Appealing primarily to lower-income consumers, distressed discounters can maintain low prices not only because of the type of merchandise they sell but also because of their method of operation. The distressed discount store operates at the lowest possible overhead to maintain the lowest possible margins. Spartan facilities located in isolated low-rent areas are operated as cash-and-carry self-service stores offering a bare minimum of customer services.

The **conventional discount store** *sells name-brand (national or manufacturers' brands) merchandise at prices that consumers easily recognize as below traditional prices* (see Figure 3–8). While price is the main marketing appeal of the conventional discount store, shopping convenience, broad product assortment, and an adequate customer service offering are all services designed to appeal to a wider range of shoppers than simply the economy-minded consumer.

Merchandising Strategies

The conventional discount store carries a fairly complete variety of hard and soft goods. In its drive for high turnover, the typical discounter stocks only the most popular brands, styles, models, sizes, and colors, along with its own private labels. In general, the product strategy of the discount store is to carry many different product lines but limit the amount of selection within each line.

Nationally well-known brands are an integral part of the discounter's product strategy. In selling national brands, the discounter takes advantage of the fact that consumers know the going price for various products. Thus, it sells most of its merchandise to the price-conscious and price-comparing shopper. Also, selling national brands below suggested manufacturer's retail price greatly enhances the

FIGURE 3–8
Selected examples of conventional discount stores (source: Reprinted by permission from *Chain Store Age*, General Merchandise Edition, June 1978, pp. 49–55 and *Chain Store Age Executive*, August 1984. Copyright © Lebhar-Friedman, Inc. 425 Park Ave., New York, New York 10022)

Discount Chain	Parent Organization
K Mart	S. S. Kresge
T.G. & Y.	Household Merchandising
Wal-Mart	Wal-Mart
Rose's	Rose's Department Stores
Dollar General	Dollar General Corporation
Magic Mart	Sterling Stores
Gold Circle	Federated Department Stores
Richway	Federated Department Stores
Jefferson Stores	Montgomery Ward
Venture Stores	May Department Stores
Target	Dayton-Hudson Corporations
Zayre	Zayre Corporation
Caldor	Associated Dry Goods

store's discount image. This image helps the discounter convince the general public that its private labels are also a good value. Moreover, by offering nationally branded merchandise for sale, the discounter has the further advantage of the product's preselling by the manufacturer through its national advertising, eliminating the need for personal selling. In addition to merchandising lines common to all discount stores, many discounters have added specialty lines. Specialty lines include drug, camera, jewelry, shoe, electronics, and automotive departments.

The discounter's service offering is limited to services necessary to run the operation. Traditionally cash-and-carry businesses, most major discount chains now offer limited credit services. Sales personnel are used in departments (jewelry, camera, etc.) that absolutely need them. Offering presold, prepackaged, self-selecting, and standardized merchandise from national manufacturers limits the number of store personnel needed for customer services to those who staff information booths, return and credit approval counters, and checkouts.

The pricing strategy of the conventional discount store promotes the highest possible turnover rate. A high rate of stock turns is the key to success and profitability for the discount retailer. While the amount of the discount varies greatly from one product line to another, it is large enough for the majority of the consuming public to recognize it as a discount. One rule of thumb that some discounters use is to discount prices at least 10 percent from the "going" market prices since this cut is usually enough for consumers to recognize savings. Whether this percentage is right is not the point. More important is that consumers must perceive the discount price as noticeably below the "established" or manufacturer's suggested retail price.

One strategy that conventional discounters use in an attempt to enhance their discount image is to price certain products that consumers purchase on a regular, frequent basis at substantially lower prices. This *leader pricing* strategy is geared toward attracting consumers into the store where, it is hoped, they will purchase additional products that have higher profit margins.

Traditionally, conventional discount stores were located as isolated units in lower rent areas. In recent years the conventional discounter has selected suburban locations convenient to the large, middle-class consumer market. Today, discount houses frequently serve as anchors for community shopping centers and, in some cases, as the major anchors of a regional shopping center.

The typical, conventional discounter operates out of a modest but modern one-story building ranging in area from 20,000 to 150,000 square feet. The store size depends upon the local market size. Although the interior decor is plain, it generally has a bright, cheerful atmosphere. Many discount stores create a carnival-like environment through their store decor and special sales events. Tile floors, plain pipe racks, bargain tables and bins, and rows of shelving are the primary ways for these discounters to display their merchandise.

Centralized checkout areas are a prominent part of all discount operations. Some leased departments and high-ticket item departments have localized checkouts.

Most conventional discount stores are aggressive advertisers. Discounters use a broad message appeal highlighting variety, selection, and especially price. Newspapers have been and still are the discounter's principal medium, but television and radio advertising are increasing.

Another key promotional strategy discounters use to inform and persuade the consumer is the point-of-purchase display. Bargain tables, bins, and stacks greet consumers as they enter, check out, and exit. End-of-aisle and main-aisle displays intercept shoppers as they travel through the store. In-store loudspeaker announcements of unadvertised specials are used to draw customers throughout the store.

Off-Price Retailing

Off-price retailers are *specialty retailers that sell mainly fashion apparel and other soft goods at discount prices significantly (20 to 60 percent) below regular retail prices.* This new price-oriented retail channel is able to make such deep reductions due to buying and merchandising practices. In buying, off-price retailers tend to pay promptly and do not ask for such extras as advertising allowances, return privileges, and markdown adjustments. Hence, they buy for less because these extras are not built into the seller's price structure. On the selling side, off-price retailers strive to keep expense structures low to maintain low margin structures. Modest facilities, limited advertising, and self-service selling are three key factors in maintaining low costs. As Buff observes,

> Two conflicting forces are shaping the evolution of this new channel: the customer's desire for currency and continuity, on the one hand, the customer's attraction to keep price discounts, on the other. The two largest factors in the business, Marshalls . . . and T. J. Maxx . . . are closest to the "pure" form of off-price retailer. They handle a relatively wide range of price lines, from good to better to best, and carry a wide range of merchandise, including men's, women's, and children's apparel in addition to domestics. The average price discount is significant—about 40 percent. The age of their merchandise varies from highly current to pack-aways from last season. Buying is opportunistic, and thus there is less emphasis on continuity.
>
> At the other end of the spectrum are off-price retailers that place great emphasis on currency and continuity. This mix includes items bought at regular wholesale prices and sold at shorter markups, "unbundled" purchases (those bought without any extras) sold at 20 percent off, opportunistic purchases for women's apparel, and some of them tend to be more upscale in ambiance than the full-time off-price supermarts. Examples of these retailing hybrids are T. H. Mandy . . . Hit or Miss . . . and Plum's.[9]

Table 3–3 lists some of the major U.S. off-price retailers.

Supermarket Retailing

Supermarket retailing as we know it began in the early 1900s when Piggly Wiggly experimented with the self-service method of food retailing. No commonly accepted definition of a supermarket exists because of the wide range of business formulas used in this industry. One commonly used definitional classification of supermarkets is as follows:

- *conventional supermarkets:* a self-service grocery store that offers a full line of groceries, meat, and produce with at least $2 million in annual sales
- *superstore:* a modern, upgraded version of the conventional supermarket with at least 30,000 square feet in total area and more than $8 million in annual sales; offers an expanded selection of nonfoods and service departments (e.g., deli, bakery, seafood)
- *food and drug combo:* combination of superstore and drug store under a single roof and common checkout; drug store merchandise represents at least one-third of the selling area and a minimum of 15% of store sales
- *warehouse store:* a low-margin grocery store that combines reduced variety, lower service levels, simpler decor, streamlined merchandising presentation, and aggressive prices
- *super warehouse store:* a high-volume hybrid of the superstore and the warehouse store offering full variety, quality perishables, and low prices

TABLE 3-3

The big names in bargain clothes: a profile of the leading off-price clothing chains

Chain (Parent Company)	Sales (millions)		Number of Outlets	
	1982	1983 (est.)	1982	1983 (est.)
Marshall's (Melville Corp.)	$830	$1,100 —	137	175
T. J. Maxx, Hit or Miss (Zayre Corp.)	525	755	353	471
Loehmann's Inc. (Associated Dry Goods)	260	275	61	70
Pic-A-Dilly (Lucky Stores)	165	210	250	271
Syms Inc.	147	185	8	11
Burlington Coat Factory	128	200	31	46
J. Brannam (F. W. Woolworth)	85	75	30	38
T. H. Mandy et al (U.S. Shoe)	80	200	52	122
Dress Barn Inc.	32	44	49	70
Ross Stores*	15	80	6	26

*Began operations in June 1982.
Note: Some sales figures are analysts' estimates.

Source: Isodora Barmash, "A Revolution in American Shopping," *New York Times,* 23 October 1983, sec. 3. Copyright © 1983 by The New York Times Company. Reprinted by permission.

■ *limited-assortment store:* a very "bare bones," low-price grocery store that eliminates services and carries fewer than 1,000 items with few, if any, perishables[10]

The products offered by a supermarket include a relatively broad variety and complete assortment of dry groceries, fresh meats, produce, and dairy products. In recent years, the basic food lines have been supplemented by a variety of prepared food lines (the deli department) and nonfood lines. By adding prepared foods, the supermarkets hoped to negate the threat posed by fast-food restaurants. The addition of "carry out services" and "eating in areas" for such foods as deli products, fresh bakery products, and fast-food restaurant lines (e.g., hamburgers, hot dogs, chicken, tacos, and fish) represents a direct effort to obtain a large share of this eating-out business.

By broadening their merchandise lines to include nonfood products, supermarkets have successfully increased sales and profits. With large numbers of customers moving through their stores each week, this product strategy has resulted in numerous sales of convenience and shopping goods. This nonfood item strategy began with the addition of health and beauty aids, limited lines of housewares, and family-oriented magazines. Today, supermarkets include such nonfood lines as prescription drugs, small appliances, linens, auto accessories, and housewares. If the "scrambling" process continues, the supermarket of the future could well become the modern version of the "general store."

Supermarkets are low-margin operations that depend on very high stock turn-over rates to sustain profits. Operating out of clean, modern facilities (an extremely important patronage motive for most food shoppers), the supermarket is basically a self-service operation offering few free services with the exception of parking and bagging. While some supermarkets accept credit cards, and most do offer tote services to automobiles, cash and carry is the preferred method of doing business. The most distinguishing promotional characteristic of supermarkets is the weekly advertising of loss or low-price leaders (products sold below or at cost). Leader pricing is aimed at attracting consumers into the store where it is hoped they will purchase the rest of their weekly shopping list at full markup prices.

Convenience Store Retailing

The modern-day version of the corner "mom and pop" grocery store is the **convenience store**. As its name suggests, *the convenience store offers customers a convenient place to shop*. In particular, it offers time convenience by being open longer and during the inconvenient early morning and late night hours, and place convenience by being a small, compact, fast-service operation that is close to consumers' homes and places of business. Their time and place convenience appeals are suggested in their trade names—7-Eleven, Stop-N-Go, Majik Markets, Quik-Pik, Minit Markets, and Jiffy.

The basic premise of the convenience store is capturing fill-in or emergency trade—after the consumer has forgotten to purchase a needed product during the planned weekly trips to the supermarket or has unexpectedly run out of a needed product before the next planned supermarket trip. Because they are frequently located between the consumer's home and the nearest supermarket, they serve as effective "interceptors" of fill-in and emergency trade.

Convenience stores carry both food and nonfood merchandise lines. Like supermarkets, convenience stores have broadened their basic product mix to include items such as motor oil, toys, prepared foods (7-Eleven's Hot-To-Go), firewood, ice drinks, and self-service gasoline.

Product assortment within each line is very limited. In such lines as cigarettes and candy, however, the assortment is quite extensive. Major national brands dominate the product line, although some of the major chain organizations offer private labels in beverages and some canned goods. In essence, the convenience store sells a limited offering of the high-volume products found in supermarkets.

Because they provide time and place utilities, convenience stores charge appreciably higher prices than other stores. From a promotional viewpoint, the store's sign and location are the most important weapons in the war to attract consumers. The convenience store's facilities include buildings that range from 1,000 to 3,200 square feet and parking areas that accommodate 5 to 15 cars. Store layouts are designed to draw customers through the store to increase impulse purchasing. To accomplish this, convenience store managers place high-volume items at or near the back of the store.

Contractual Retailing

Independent retailers often attempt to achieve "systematic economies and an increased market impact" by integrating their operations with other retailers and wholesalers.[11] By entering contractual arrangements, retailers can formalize their rights and obligations of each party in the contract. The terms of the contract can, and often do, cover all aspects of the retailer's product, place, price, and promotional activities. Contractual retailing exists in several forms, but the four most common forms are retailer-sponsored cooperative groups, wholesaler-sponsored voluntary chains, franchised retailers, and leased departments.

Retailer-Sponsored Cooperative Group

The **retailer-sponsored cooperative group** is *a contractual organization formed by many small independent retailers and usually involves the common ownership of a wholesaler.* Originally formed to combat competition from large chain organizations, this type of contractual system allows the small independent to realize economies of scale by making large-quantity group purchases. The contractual agreement usually requires individual members to concentrate their purchases of products from the cooperative wholesaler and, in turn, receive some form of patronage refund. The amount of the refund often is based on the amount of merchandise purchased from the cooperative. Individual cooperative members may or may not identify themselves as part of the cooperative and they may or may not use common advertising and marketing programs. Associated Grocers and Certified Grocers are two large food wholesalers having cooperative contractual arrangements with independent food retailers.

Wholesaler-Sponsored Voluntary Chain

The **wholesaler-sponsored voluntary chain** is *a contractual arrangement in which a wholesaler develops a merchandising program that independent retailers voluntarily join.* By agreeing to purchase a certain amount of merchandise from the wholesaler, the retailer is assured of lower prices. These lower prices are possible because the wholesaling organization can buy in larger quantities with the knowledge that it has an established market. With some of the quantity savings passed on to the retailer, both parties are able to compete more effectively with large, centralized chains. The Independent Grocers Alliance (IGA) and Super Valu Stores, Inc., are both food wholesalers that sponsor voluntary chains. Other examples include Western Auto in the automotive and household-accessories market and Ben Franklin in the variety store market.

Franchise Retailer

Franchising is a contractual form of retailing agreed upon by a franchisor and franchisee. More specifically,

> The parent company is termed the franchisor, the receiver of the privilege the franchisee; and the right, or privilege itself, the franchise. The privilege may be quite varied. It may be the right to sell the parent company's products, to use its name, to adopt its methods, and to copy its symbols, trademarks, or architecture, or the franchise may include all of these rights. The time period and the size of the area of business operations, which are specified, may also vary greatly. The rights that are granted and the duties and obligations of the respective parties, the franchisor and the franchisee, are usually, but not always, spelled out in a written contract.[12]

In total, what the franchisor offers the franchisee is a patterned way of doing business that includes *product, price, place, and promotional strategies,* as well as numerous *initial and continuous services.* In establishing a franchised outlet, the franchisor initially provides such services as (1) market surveys, (2) site evaluation and selection advice, (3) plans for store design and layout, (4) advice on negotiating leases, (5) financing advice, (6) an operations manual, and (7) training programs for managers and employees. Once the franchised outlet has been established, the

83

franchisor offers such continous services as field supervision, retraining programs for managers and employees, sales promotion material, national advertising campaigns, accounting management and control, and analysis of market trends.[13]

Franchisors expect franchisees to conform to a particular business pattern and also provide them with some form of compensation for their right to use the franchise. Franchisor compensation usually involves either one or a combination of the following:

1. *initial franchise fee*—a fee that the franchisor charges up front for the franchisee's right to own the business and to receive initial services
2. *royalties*—an operating fee imposed on the franchisee's gross sales
3. *sales of products*—profits the franchisors make from sales to franchisees of raw and finished products, operating supplies, furnishings, and equipment
4. *rental and lease fees*—fees that franchisors charge for the use of their facilities and equipment
5. *management fee*—a fee that franchisors charge for some of the continuous services they provide the franchisee[14]

The number of franchised retailing systems that exist is difficult to determine because of the lack of a clear definition of franchising. Three definable categories have emerged for classifying franchising arrangements: manufacturer-sponsored retailers, wholesaler-sponsored retailers, and service firm-sponsored retailers.

The **manufacturer-sponsored retailer** is *a franchising organization in which the manufacturer is the franchisor and the retailer is the franchisee.* When manufacturers want to *maintain a high level of control* over distribution and merchandising of their products, they often choose a franchise system. While automobile dealerships and gasoline service stations represent the most common form of manufacturer-sponsored retailers, manufacturers of shoes, auto parts and accessories, paints, and wearing apparel also use this franchising arrangement.

The **wholesaler-sponsored retailer** franchise organization is *established by the wholesaler (the franchisor) for the same reasons that manufacturers establish franchises.* Besides controlling channels of distribution, the wholesaler can reasonably ensure a market for its products. Rexall Drug Stores and Sentry Drug Centers are examples of this kind of franchise system.

Service firm-sponsored retailers are *franchising arrangements whereby a service firm positions itself between the retail and wholesale distribution levels.* The service firm is the franchisor and the retailer is the franchisee. The growth of these franchising systems seems to be limited only by service firms' ability to create a unique pattern or format for conducting business.

The franchising industry as a whole has experienced phenomenal growth during the last two decades. For the near future, the growth prospects in franchising appear to be in the areas of equipment-rental services, business aids and services, home-improvement services, and recreational and leisure-time services. Fast-food franchising is also expected to continue expanding into new, developing areas and small cities.

The advantages of franchising are numerous for both the franchisor and the franchisee. For the small entrepreneur with limited retailing experience, the franchise offers a proven method for entry into the retailing field. Like most forms of business, however, franchising organizations vary greatly in what they can offer and what they expect in return.

Leased Departments

Leased departments are *retailers that operate departments (usually in specialized lines of merchandise) under contractual arrangements with conventional retail stores.* Many supermarkets and department stores, for example, lease space to outside organizations to sell magazines (as in supermarkets) and auto supplies and shoes (as in many department and discount stores). The lessor usually furnishes space, utilities, and basic in-store services necessary to the lessee's operation. In turn, the lessee agrees to provide the personnel, management, and capital necessary to stock and operate a department with carefully defined merchandise. Generally, the contract calls for the lessee to pay the lessor either a flat monthly fee, a percentage of gross sales, or some combination of the two.

Warehouse Retailing

In the last decade, one of the major trends in the institutional development of retailing has been the application of warehouse operating principles to retailing activities. The typical **warehouse retailing operation** *involves some combination of warehouse and showroom facilities.* In some cases these facilities are located in separate but adjacent areas. In some cases both warehouse and showroom facilities are combined into one large physical structure. Generally, the warehouse retailer can use warehouse principles to reduce operating expenses and thereby offer discount prices as a primary customer appeal. Four types of warehouse retailers can be identified: warehouse showroom, catalog showroom, home center, and hypermarket.

Warehouse Showroom

The **warehouse showroom** is generally *a single-line hard-goods retailer that stocks merchandise such as furniture, appliances, or carpeting.* To help the consumer make price comparisons with conventional home-furnishing retailers, the warehouse showroom typically stocks only well-known, nationally advertised brands. These retailers set up sample merchandise displays in showrooms so potential consumers can get an idea of what the products will look like in their homes. For example, Levitz Furniture outlets partition "rooms" of furniture in their warehouse outlets. Instead of seeing a single piece of furniture, such as a bed, consumers view a "package" of bedroom furniture complete with chest of drawers, bed, night table, lamps, bedspread, and even curtains. After making a selection, consumers immediately receive the merchandise in shipping cartons from the completely stocked adjacent warehouse. Although they prefer the "cash-and-carry" mode of operation, many warehouse retailers realize that consumers' buying habits for these products dictate a policy of offering credit, delivery, and installation services. Many consumers need these services because of the high cost of these products (credit), the weight and size of these products (delivery), and the lack of knowledge of how to set up the product in the home (installation). Hence, many warehouse retailers provide these services at an additional fee over the selling price.

Due to space and delivery requirements, plus the need to attract consumers from a large market area, warehouse showroom locations usually are freestanding sites near major traffic intersections such as interstate highway systems. Where states permit it, warehouse showrooms usually operate 12 hours a day (9 A.M. to 9 P.M.) seven days a week. Levitz Furniture and Wickes are two of the country's leading warehouse showroom operations.

Catalog Showroom

The **catalog showroom** is *a warehouse retailer featuring hard goods such as housewares, small appliances, jewelry, watches, toys, sporting goods, lawn and garden equipment, luggage, stereos, televisions, and other electronic equipment at a discount.* The distinguishing feature of the catalog showroom is that a merchandise catalog is combined with the showroom and an adjacent warehouse as part of the retailer's operation. By adding a catalog of products to showroom products, the retailer expands product offerings without tying up additional showroom space and inventory. Further, this approach provides consumers with both an in-store and at-home method of buying merchandise.

Catalogs, which are generally issued biannually, sometimes incorporate a unique method of illustrating the discounted price. List prices appear in plain bold numerals while the actual discounted prices are the last several digits of a code. This method often accentuates the discount nature of the price by forcing the customer to calculate the difference. The price tags on the sample merchandise on display in the showroom incorporate the same pricing method. As with the warehouse showroom, the catalog showroom features nationally branded merchandise that facilitates consumer price comparisons with conventional hard-goods retailers.

For consumers, the typical shopping trip to a catalog showroom involves (1) filling out an order form using the merchandise/price code found on either the showroom price tag or in the catalog, (2) ordering and paying for merchandise at a cashier's desk, and (3) picking up the merchandise at a pick-up desk. The pick-up desk is directly connected to an adjacent warehouse containing a complete stock of merchandise. In the final analysis, the basic merchandising strategy of catalog showrooms such as Service Merchandise, Inc., Best, and H. T. Wilson is to achieve a level of operating efficiencies that will permit selling at 15–20 percent below the going market price.

Home Center

The modern **home center** *combines the traditional hardware store and lumber yard with a self-service home-improvement center.* The typical merchandise mix includes a wide variety and deep assortment of building materials, hardware, paints, plumbing and heating equipment, electrical supplies, power tools, garden and yard equipment, and other home-maintenance supplies. Some home centers have also expanded their merchandise offerings to include household appliances and home furnishings. Home centers usually have large showrooms that display sample merchandise (large, bulky items) and complete stock (small, standardized items). Consumers purchase showroom sample merchandise by placing an order at the order desk, and clerks pull the order from adjacent warehouse stocks. Customers simply serve themselves with showroom stock.

While appealing to all home owners, the home center has been particularly successful in appealing to the "do it yourselfer." By providing customers with information on materials and equipment and by offering "how to" services, home centers have developed a strong customer following. Such firms as Republic Lumber, Wickes, and Handy Man have experienced considerable success with this type of warehouse/showroom operation.

Hypermarket

The **hypermarket** is *a general-merchandise warehouse retailer that stocks and sells food products and a wide variety of both hard and soft goods.* Operating out of a spartan warehouse, the hypermarket displays offerings in wire baskets, metal racks, wooden bins, and simple stacks of merchandise that often reach heights of 12–15 feet. A self-service retailer with central checkouts and a sophisticated system of materials handling, the hypermarket attempts to underprice traditional retailers by as much as 15–20 precent. A European innovation, the hypermarket has not made major inroads into U.S. retailing. One exception is the 245,000-square-foot hypermarket that Meijer, Inc., built near Detroit.

At-Home Retailing

At-home retailing is *the market approach of making personal contacts and sales in the consumers' homes.* This form of retailing offers the consumer the ultimate in *place convenience* and, with some planning on the part of the salesperson (such as making an appointment), can provide an equal amount of *time convenience.* At-home retailing provides several other advantages to the consumer. First, it is a highly personalized service because of the one-on-one relationship between the customer and salesperson. Second, at-home retailing aids consumers in making a product evaluation before the purchase by letting them try the product in a home setting. Next, it saves the consumer the time and effort of going to the store, searching for needed merchandise, and waiting in checkout lines. Finally, this type of retailing usually includes home delivery, which appeals to most customers, especially the elderly.

At-home retailing also offers the seller certain advantages, including (1) no direct competition since the seller presents its products in "isolation" in the home, where consumers cannot make direct comparisons with similar products; (2) avoidance of uncontrollable intermediaries, and (3) elimination of investments in stores and other facilities, since sales representatives are compensated on a commission basis and pay their own expenses.

The at-home method of retailing, also referred to as "door-to-door" and "house-to-house" selling, exists in several forms. The three principal forms are the cold-canvass, the established territory or route, and the party plan.

Cold-Canvass Method

The **cold-canvass method** involves *soliciting sales door-to-door without either advanced selection of homes or prior notice to potential consumers of an intended sales call.* Usually cold canvassing is not done in completely random fashion. Residential areas are selected that contain homes of potential customers who are most likely to afford the merchandise and make a purchase. For example, firewood is sold door-to-door on a cold-canvassing basis, but only in residential areas (usually middle- and upper-class neighborhoods) containing homes with fireplaces. Vacuum cleaners, magazines, and books are some of the more common products sold by the cold-canvass method.

Established Territory Method

The **established territory method** *assigns salespeople to prescribed geographical areas, in which they must make their door-to-door sales and delivery calls at regular, predetermined time intervals.* Two factors that influence a company's decision to use this method are the product's characteristics and the salespersons' effectiveness. Highly perishable, frequently used products are well adapted to at-home sales within an established territorial approach (e.g., dairy and bakery products). Door-to-door effectiveness is substantially improved if territories are served frequently and regularly by the same person. Homemakers may be understandably reluctant to purchase an unknown brand from an unknown salesperson at an unexpected time. Established routes and familiar salespersons help to overcome this reluctance.

Some of the best known users of the established territory method are Avon (cosmetics), Fuller Brush (household products), Stanley Home Products (household products), and Sarah Coventry (jewelry).

Party Plan Method

The **party plan method** of at-home retailing *requires a salesperson to make sales presentations in the home of a host or hostess who has invited potential customers to a "party."* Usually the party plan includes various games and other entertainment activities in which participants receive small, inexpensive gifts. Closing the sale occurs when the salesperson takes orders from the people attending the party. As a reward for holding the party, the host or hostess receives either cash or gifts from the salesperson. The amount or value of the "gift" is determined by the amount of sales resulting from the party.

Several advantages accrue to the retailer that uses the party plan. First, it can make multiple sales to customers at the same time under informal, personalized conditions. Second, because most of the party goers are friends of the host or hostess, they are predisposed to buy something. Finally, the host or hostess frequently serves as distribution agent by delivering the orders to the homes of the participants. Tupperware and Wearever Aluminum Products make extensive use of the party method. Toys, books, home-decorating products, household goods, jewelry, health and beauty aids, and apparel are just a few of the products sold in this manner.

Mail-Order Retailing

Originally, mail-order retailers served the scattered populations of the rural United States by offering them specialty goods that were not available in their local general stores. Mail-order retailers contacted prospective customers by mail, received their orders by mail, and made their deliveries by mail. The modern mail-order operation varies significantly from the original mail-order business because of changes in merchandise lines and operations (i.e., methods of customer contact, order placement, and delivery arrangements). As we shall see, "mail order" probably is a misnomer for the modern mail-order retailer.

Mail-order operations differ tremendously in the variety and assortment of merchandise lines they offer the mail-order customer. Three important types of mail-order operations have been identified. The **general merchandise mail-order house** is *a mail-order retailer offering a wide variety of merchandise lines.* The depth of the assortment within each merchandise line varies among houses and among lines. Sears, J. C. Penney, and Spiegel of Chicago all operate general merchandise mail-order operations.

The second type of mail-order operation is the **novelty mail-order retailer** *whose lines are often limited to unusual products not normally carried by conventional retailers.* Frequently, the novelty operator directs merchandise appeals to a small market segment. For example, intimate wearing apparel, unusual reading materials, specialized sporting equipment, exotic foods, unusual hobby equipment, and novel gifts are the kind of merchandise that novelty mail-order retailers sell. Because potential customers are scattered throughout the country and market demand is limited to these customers, mail-order retailing is the only feasible means of reaching this dispersed market on a continuing basis.

The third type of mail-order retailing is the **supplementary mail-order operations** of department and specialty stores. Some conventional department and specialty stores offer mail-order service for the convenience of their customers. In some cases, they use this form of mail-order operation to complement their telephone ordering buiness; in other cases, they use it either to merchandise specialty product lines or to promote special events. The Neiman-Marcus Christmas catalog best exemplifies this type of mail-order retailing.

Because of different operating characteristics, three forms of mail-order retailing have emerged. They are catalogs, brochures, and coupons. Any given mail-order retailer can use one or any combination of these three forms.

Catalog operations *involve the use of specially prepared catalogs that present the retailer's merchandise both visually and verbally.* Basic product assortment (sizes, colors, materials, styles, models, etc.) and pricing information are included along with directions stating how to order on the order blanks provided. Several types of catalogs exist. *General merchandise catalogs* offer a wide variety and a somewhat limited assortment of merchandise on either an annual or seasonal (e.g., Sears' fall/winter catalog) basis. *Specialty catalogs* are either customer (e.g., Sears' big and tall men's sizes catalog) or product (e.g., Sears' power tool catalog) oriented. Both of these catalogs exhibit an extensive assortment of products within their specialties. *Promotional catalogs* are used to promote special sales and seasonal merchandise, but are limited offerings in terms of time (one to four weeks) and assortment (individual product items generally are featured). Modern catalog operations allow the customer to place orders by mail, telephone, or in person at a catalog desk. In addition, catalog operations offer a variety of delivery arrangements such as mail, parcel post, express service, customer pickup, and store delivery.

Some retailers utilize a **brochure form** of mail-order retailing by *preparing a small booklet or leaflet that they mail to potential consumers.* The distinguishing feature of this type of brochure is that it usually displays only a limited number of product items. Items included in the brochure are those that can attract consumer attention and interest. These interesting and attention-getting displays usually emphasize either the innovative nature or the good value of the product.

Traditionally, brochures were mailed to consumers likely to be interested in products the brochure featured. The brochure was "targeted" by carefully constructed mailing lists. Recent developments in the brochure mail-order business, however, involve mass mailings of brochures to consumers on a standard mailing list without the benefit of any form of market segmentation. This "scattering" approach is best exemplified by the brochures most MasterCard and Visa customers find in their monthly statements. This merchandising strategy has two advantages. First, brochures can be included in these standard mailings at a minimal cost. Second, the convenience of simply charging it to a credit card makes the purchase easy. Mass brochure mail-order retailing is also employed by Sears, J. C. Penney, and other major retailers.

The **coupon form** of mail-order retailing *involves using magazine and newspaper advertisements.* Advertisements featuring special merchandise and mail-order coupons are placed in magazines and newspapers that appeal to specific market segments. For example, a mail-order retailer that offers personal accounting materials, income tax booklets, and books on personal finance can best contact interested consumers by coupon advertising in such publications as *Money* magazine and *Changing Times.* To some extent, most magazines and newspapers segment their markets either geographically (regional or local editions) or psychographically (subscribers to specialty publications usually have certain common activities, interests, and opinions).

Telephone Retailing

In recent years, the telephone has helped some retailers increase service satisfaction by providing greater customer convenience. For customers who want to avoid traffic congestion and parking problems, telephone shopping is a desirable alternative. This form of retailing also can be of service to shut-ins, the elderly, parents with babysitting problems, working people who do not have time to shop, and consumers who do not like to shop.

Retailers' major reasons for using telephone retailing are that it (1) provides customers with information on new merchandise and upcoming sales events, (2) allows customers to order merchandise that retailers are willing to deliver to the customers' homes, and (3) gives consumers a convenient way to hold merchandise that they can pick up at a later date.

Electronic Retailing

Retailing via electronic and video systems is in the innovation stage of the retail life cycle. While a large number of potential electronic retailing options exist and the number of options are expected to expand as new technologies are brought on line, retailers are currently focusing their attention on videotex and electronic catalogs.

Videotex

Videotex is *"an interactive electronic system in which data and graphics are transmitted from a computer network over telephone or cable lines and displayed on a subscriber's TV or computer-terminal screen."*[15] The basic components and interactions of a videotex system appear in Figure 3–9.

Shopping with a videotex system consists of selecting from a series of choices, called menus, that are displayed on the screen. For example, a shopper narrows down the choice by selecting from a menu of product lines and product items (brands, styles, sizes, colors, prices, and so on). In addition to at-home shopping, videotex systems can provide subscribers a wide selection of services—news, weather, sports, financial, and consumer information; at-home banking, reservations, and travel information; electronic encyclopedias and magazines, videocoupons and educational/instructional games; directories; real-estate/employment listings; home energy management; security-medical-fire monitoring; and electronic mail/messaging. Given this combined products/services mix, together with the demand for more leisure time and the desire for more convenience, the likelihood of electronic retailing entering the accelerated growth stage of the retail life cycle is great. Table 3–4 profiles the "teleshopping-prone" consumer and the "ideal product" for teleshopping.

Electronic Catalog

A wide variety of electronic catalog retailing systems are curently being developed and tested. Two systems currently being introduced are the electronic multi-catalogue retail shopping system by Catalogia, Inc., of Tuxedo Park, New York (see Figure 3–10), and the "Electronic Bed and Bath Fashion Center" developed by the J. P. Stevens Co. Stevens' system is an in-store video disk, text, and printer information system that allows consumers to see and purchase virtually the entire product line. "A printout from the Stevens unit gives a record of the entire order for the customer . . . the customer is helped at the console by a store salesperson specially trained by Stevens. After she punches all her keypad buttons, she is given the order printout, which must be taken to a cashier for completion of the sale."[17]

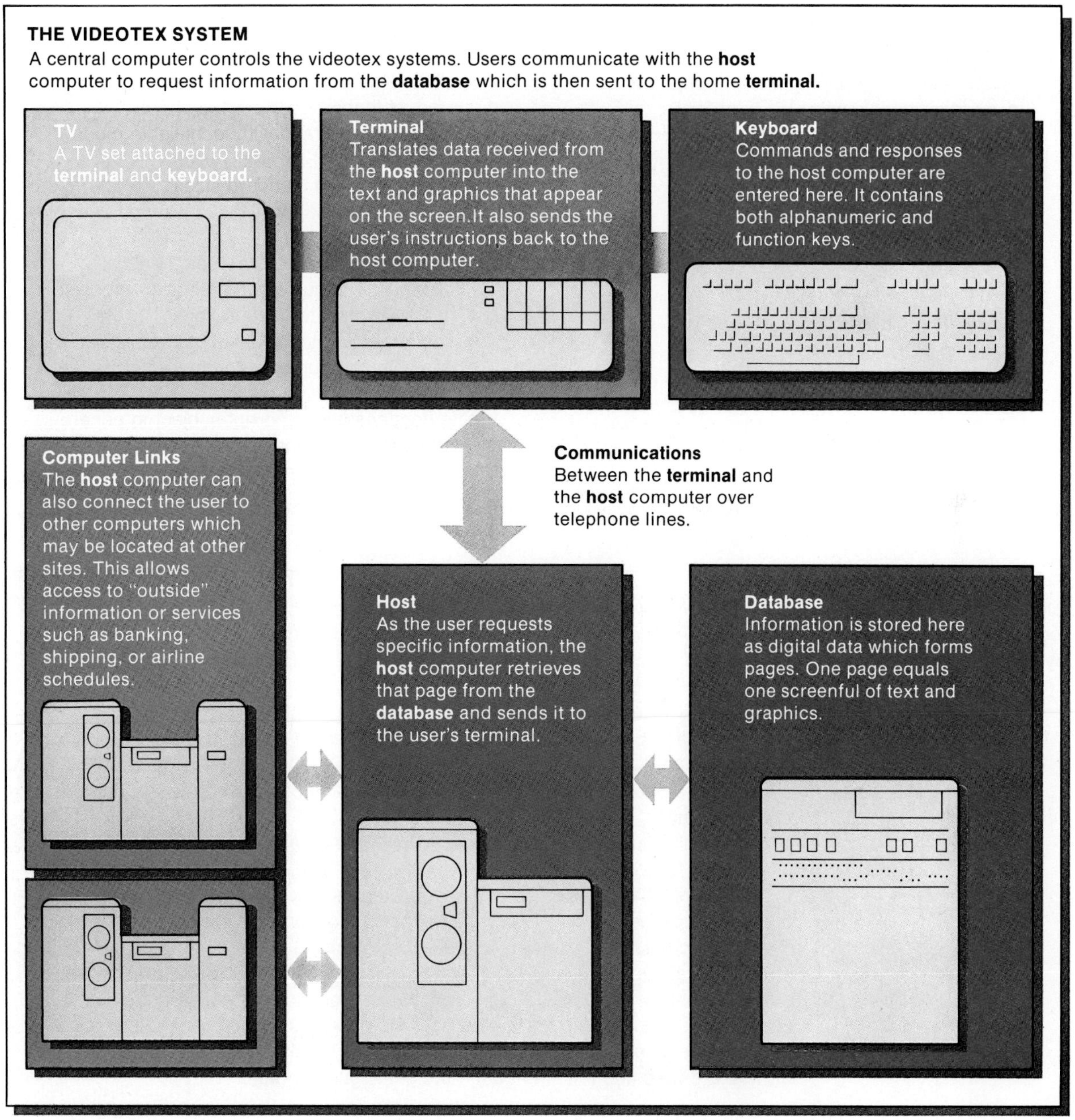

THE VIDEOTEX SYSTEM

A central computer controls the videotex systems. Users communicate with the **host** computer to request information from the **database** which is then sent to the home **terminal.**

TV
A TV set attached to the **terminal** and **keyboard**.

Terminal
Translates data received from the **host** computer into the text and graphics that appear on the screen. It also sends the user's instructions back to the host computer.

Keyboard
Commands and responses to the host computer are entered here. It contains both alphanumeric and function keys.

Computer Links
The **host** computer can also connect the user to other computers which may be located at other sites. This allows access to "outside" information or services such as banking, shipping, or airline schedules.

Communications
Between the **terminal** and the **host** computer over telephone lines.

Host
As the user requests specific information, the **host** computer retrieves that page from the **database** and sends it to the user's terminal.

Database
Information is stored here as digital data which forms pages. One page equals one screenful of text and graphics.

FIGURE 3–9

Basic components and interactions of a videotex system (source: Tom Mach, "High-Tech Opportunities Getting Closer to Home," Reprinted with permission of *Advertising Age,* 16 April 1984, Copyright Crain Communications Inc.)

Vending Machine Retailing

Consumer demand for greater time and place convenience and concurrent technological developments spurred the successful introduction and market expansion of the self-contained, automatic vending machine in the late 1940s. These mechanical,

91

TABLE 3–4
Teleshopping profiles

Profile of the "teleshopping-prone" consumer	Profile of the "ideal product" for teleshopping

• younger female who:
   • is part of a two-career household
   • has heavy demands on her time
   • is affluent
   • has above-average education
   • takes risks
   • seeks information
   • uses direct mail
   • is technology-fluent
	• a product that:
	   • has a strong brand with identifiable model number
	   • comes in a few standard sizes
	   • does not need special customization and prepurchase service
	   • does not involve considerable sensual experience in customer evaluation process
	   • has a low bulk to value ratio
	   • has a medium-to-low level of complexity
	   • has a limited number of attributes important to consumer decision making
	   • is nonperishable and not subject to price negotiation at point-of-sale
	   • is a planned-purchase-type product

Source: "Videotex to Curtail Canada In-Store Retailing; Study Predicts 15% Home Penetration by 1990," *Marketing News,* 25 November 1983, 20.

FIGURE 3–10
Electronic multicatalogue retail shopping system

Here is how the system works: A shopper enters a Catalogia outlet and tells the clerk he is looking for a goosedown jacket. The clerk enters the request on the keyboard of a video-display terminal linked to Catalogia's central computer memory bank, which contains all items listed in some 270 mail-order catalogues.

Within seconds the shopper is handed a computer printout which lists the catalogues and page numbers on which such a jacket is located. The shopper then moves to a section of the store which stocks the catalogues and has tables, chairs, and a photocopy machine. Each catalogue is bound and includes order pad, note paper, and pen.

After the customer comparison-shops in the catalogues (not on a video screen), he fills out the order form and hands it to the clerk along with payment by approved check, credit card, or cash. The order is placed immediately by phone or, in some cases, via on-line computer communication with the catalogue warehouse. Merchandise availability also can be confirmed on the spot.

The catalogue house then ships the selected merchandise to the shopper or designated party (Catalogia stores don't have inventory). Catalogia does not charge the shopper a fee for this service; the catalogue houses pay Catalogia 20% of each purchase. The average order is about $47. Customers who simply want to browse are welcome to look through the catalogue libraries.

Source: "Plan Network of Electronic Multicatalogue Retail Shopping Systems," *Marketing News,* 26 November 1982, 10.

coin-operated machines became an important retailing method for making products available where and when store retailing was not feasible. Rather than competing with store retailing, vending machines became a complement of the store's operations by vending products that are usually a nuisance to handle within conventional store operations. On a much smaller scale, vending machines are similar to convenience store retailing in that they usually serve to meet the "fill-in," "emergency," and "after- or off-hour" needs of consumers.

Products that vending machines dispense have several characteristics in common. They typically are small, branded, and standardized products of low-unit value. Candies, soft drinks, hot beverages, and cigarettes are the most popular vending machine items. Among other food products commonly sold in vending machines are milk, snack foods, bakery products, and sandwiches. Nonfood products frequently sold by vending machines include life insurance policies for air travel, postage stamps, newspapers, ice, health and beauty aids, and some novelty items. One of the most significant developments in the use of vending machines is in the field of entertainment. Jukeboxes, pinball machines, and electronic games have greatly expanded the sales potential of vending operations.

The high per-unit price associated with vending machine operations is directly related to the industry's high cost of doing business. Companies that own and operate vending machines experience high costs due to the need to rent space in expensive high-traffic areas, the large investment costs of the machines themselves, exorbitant distribution costs (many scattered outlets), high pilferage rates, and additional maintenance costs. The net result is a relatively low per-unit dollar profit, but sufficient *total* profits generated through a substantial turnover rate.

Retailing and the institutions of retailing are still undergoing numerous changes in response to a number of environmental trends in today's world.[18] Innovative merchandising strategies and operational methods are constantly being developed to meet these environmental challenges. What the future will bring to the ever-changing retailing world is a matter of speculation. Given that "the past is the key to the future," however, some retailing experts have identified patterns of change that they express as theories of retail institutional change. Of the many theories, two of the more commonly accepted are the wheel of retailing and the dialetic process.

Wheel of Retailing

One of the most widely recognized theories of retail institutional change is the wheel of retailing. First hypothesized by Malcolm P. McNair, the **wheel of retailing** states that *the dynamics of institutional change are a "more or less definite cycle"; the cycle "begins with the bold new concept, the innovation" and ends with "eventual vulnerability . . . to the next fellow who has a bright idea."*[19] A careful examination of the wheel theory reveals three distinct phases to each cycle and that a pattern of cycles will develop over a period of time. Figures 3–11 and 3–12 illustrate the three phases of entry, trading up, and vulnerability and how each cycle might be repeated to form a wavelike pattern.

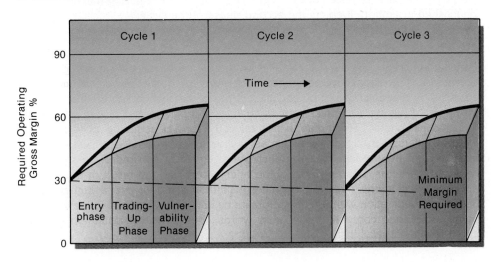

FIGURE 3–11
The wheel of retailing

FIGURE 3–12
The retailer and the
wheel of retailing

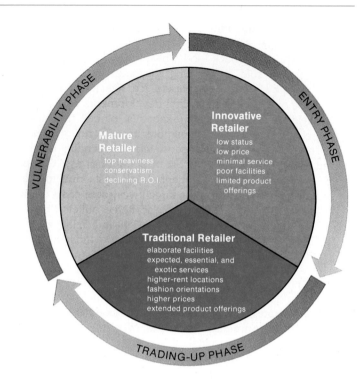

Entry Phase

In the first phase of the cycle an innovative retailing institution enters the market as a low-status, low-price operation. By reducing operating expenses to a minimum, the new institution can operate at a gross margin substantially below (e.g., 30 percent as opposed to 50 percent) the required gross margins of the more established retailers in the market. Operating expenses usually are maintained at low levels by (1) offering minimal customer services, (2) providing a modest shopping atmosphere in terms of exterior and interior facilities, (3) occupying low-rent locations, and (4) offering limited product mixes. Generally, market entry is easier for retailers selling low-margin, high-turnover products. Although consumers and competitors consider the innovative institution low-status, it does gain market penetration primarily on the basis of price appeals. Once the new form of retailing has become an established institution, it enters the second phase of the cycle.

Trading-Up Phase

Emulators quickly copy the successful innovation because of its success and market acceptance. The competitive actions of these emulators force the original innovative business to differentiate itself by engaging in the process of trading up. The trading-up phase of the cycle involves various changes to upgrade and distinguish the innovative institution.[20] Trading up usually takes the form of acquiring more elaborate facilities, offering expected and exotic as well as essential services, and locating in high-rent neighborhoods. Also, product lines frequently are traded up to include high markup items, often with a fashion orientation. The end result of the trading-up phase is that the original innovative institution matures into a higher-status, higher-price operation with a required operating gross margin comparable to that of many established competitors. In other words, the innovative institution matures into a traditional retail institution.

Vulnerability Phase

With maturity, the now-established innovative institution enters a phase "characterized by top-heaviness, conservatism, and a decline in the rate of return on investments."[21] Eventually, the original innovator becomes vulnerable "to the next fellow who has a bright idea and who starts his business on a low-cost basis, slipping in under the (price) umbrella that the old-line institutions have hoisted."[22] The entry of a new low-price innovator into the retail market signals the end of one cycle and the beginning of a new cycle.

In practice, the theory of the wheel of retailing has been used to explain numerous changes in the institutional structure of U.S. retailing. In the food industry, the independent corner grocery store was replaced to a large extent by the chain grocery store which, in turn, became vulnerable to the competition of the supermarket operation. A second commonly cited example of the "wheel" concept is the emergence of the department store innovation as an alternative to the small specialty retailer, and its subsequent vulnerability to discount retailers. Recently, some discount retailers have progressed far enough into the trading-up phase that they, in turn, are becoming vulnerable to discount warehouses, showroom operations, and off-price retailers.

Dialectic Process

The dialectic process is a "melting pot" theory of retail institutional change in which two substantially different forms of retailing merge together into a new retailing institution, a composite of the original two forms. Figure 3–13 (p. 96) illustrates the dialectic process, involving a thesis (the established institutional form), an antithesis (the innovative institutional form), and a synthesis (the new form drawn from the other two). The dynamics of the dialectic process, as outlined by Maronick and Walker, are as follows:

> In terms of retail institutions, the dialectic model implies that retailers mutually adapt in the face of competition from "opposites." Thus, when challenged by a competitor with a differential advantage, an established institution will adopt strategies and tactics in the direction of that advantage, thereby negating some of the innovator's attraction. The innovator, meanwhile, does not remain unchanged. Rather, as McNair noted, the innovator over time tends to upgrade or otherwise modify products and institutions. In doing so, he moves toward the "negated" institution. As a result of the mutual adaptions, the two retailers gradually move together in terms of offerings, facilities, supplementary services, and prices. They thus become indistinguishable or at least quite similar and constitute a new retail institution, termed the synthesis. This new institution is then vulnerable to "negation" by new competitors as the dialetic process begins anew.[23]

SUMMARY

The retailer is a member of a marketing channel of distribution whose actions are directed at bringing producers and their respective customers together. The marketing channel is a multilevel structure (extended, limited, and direct channels) made up of channel teams (full, limited, and nonmember institutions) whose interactions (buying, selling, etc.) coordinate channel flows (physical, ownership, information, payment, and promotion) through channel teamwork.

The retailer must operate in a very complex competitive environment. Retail competition can take one of several forms: intratype, intertype, vertical, and systems.

The various types of retailing institutions are distinguishable on the basis of product-line variety, organizational structure, price appeals, customer convenience,

FIGURE 3–13
The dialectic process

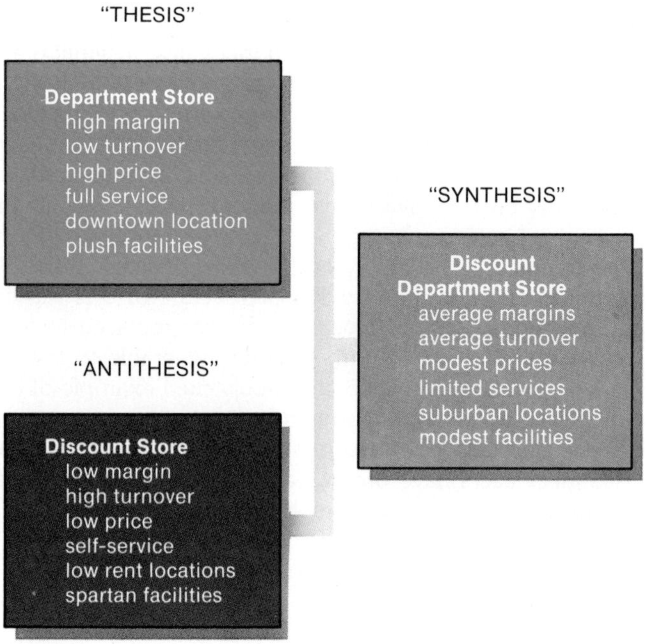

"THESIS"

Department Store
  high margin
  low turnover
  high price
  full service
  downtown location
  plush facilities

"SYNTHESIS"

**Discount
Department Store**
  average margins
  average turnover
  modest prices
  limited services
  suburban locations
  modest facilities

"ANTITHESIS"

Discount Store
  low margin
  high turnover
  low price
  self-service
  low rent locations
  spartan facilities

and many other criteria. Based on the variety of product lines offered and their organizational structure, retailers are classified as either specialty or department stores. Chain stores are multiunit retailers that use a high degree of centralization in their operations. The discounter and off-price retailer emphasize price by offering nationally branded and designer merchandise at below market prices. A major development in food retailing has been the supermarket with its emphasis on a complete, self-serve product offering. Time and place convenience distinguish the convenience store in its efforts to provide the "fill-in" and "emergency" needs of consumers. Some retailers try to formalize their relationships with suppliers and other retailers by entering a contractual arrangement. The retailer-sponsored cooperative group, the wholesaler-sponsored voluntary chain, the franchising organization, and the leased department are all examples of contractual retailing. Other retailers tend to stress a certain method of operation. Warehouse showrooms, catalog showrooms, home centers, and hypermarket retailers employ warehouse methods of operation. At-home, mail-order, telephone, electronic, and vending machine retailing are nonstore retailers that attempt to serve potential consumers where they live, work, and play.

Theoretically, retail institutional change exhibits certain patterns over time. Two theories that help to explain these patterned changes are the wheel of retailing and the dialectic process.

KEY TERMS AND CONCEPTS

marketing channel

extended channel

limited channel

direct channel

full-member institutions

limited-member institutions

nonmember facilitating
institutions

physical flow

ownership flow

information flow

payment flow

promotion flow

channel integration

vertical marketing system

conventional marketing channel

intratype competition

intertype competition

vertical competition

systems competition

specialty store retailer

single-line specialty retailer

limited-line specialty retailer

department store

independent department store

department store chain

department store ownership
group

branch department store

chain store

standard stock list

optional stock list

vertical integration

discount store

distressed discount store

conventional discount store

off-price retailer

supermarket

convenience store

contractual retailing

retailer-sponsored cooperative
group

wholesaler-sponsored voluntary
chain

franchise retailer

manufacturer-sponsored retailer

wholesaler-sponsored retailer

service firm—sponsored retailer

leased department

warehouse retailing

warehouse showroom

catalog showroom

home center

hypermarket

at-home retailing

cold-canvass method

established territory method

party plan method

mail-order retailing

general merchandise mail-order
retailer

novelty mail-order retailer

supplementary mail-order
retailer

catalog mail-order retailing

general merchandise catalogs

specialty catalogs

promotional catalogs

brochure mail-order retailing

coupon mail-order retailing

teleshopping

REVIEW QUESTIONS

1. What are the three basic alternative channel structures? Describe each.
2. How is membership in the marketing channel team determined? Discuss the three channel membership classes.
3. What are the five major types of channel flows? Define each.
4. How is good channel teamwork accomplished?
5. What are the four types of retail competition? Diagram each.
6. Identify the various ways by which retailers can be classified.
7. What is the most distinguishing characteristic of specialty store retailing? Describe the key merchandising strategies employed by the specialty retailer.
8. How does the department store distinguish its operations from other retailing institutions? Identify the four types of department stores.
9. What are the principal merchandising strategies employed by the department store in its efforts to attract customers?
10. List the three criteria used to determine whether or not a retail operation can be classified as a chain store retailer.
11. How can a distressed discount store be distinguished from a conventional discount store?
12. What are the distinguishing merchandising strategies employed by a conventional discount store?
13. What is an off-price retailer? What buying and selling strategies do they use?
14. How are supermarkets attempting to negate the competitive threat posed by the fast-food industry?
15. What is the basic marketing premise of a convenience store operation?
16. What is contractual retailing? Identify and define the four types of contractual retailers.
17. How are franchisors compensated?
18. Identify and define the four types of warehouse retailers.
19. Compare and contrast the three forms of at-home retailing.
20. Compare and contrast the three types of mail-order retailing.
21. What are the three forms of mail-order retailing? Describe each form.
22. Why do retailers use telephone retailing?
23. Discuss the videotex system of electronic retailing.
24. Describe the three phases of the wheel of retailing.
25. What does the dialectic model of retail institutional change imply?

ENDNOTES

1. Bert C. McCammon, Jr., "Perspectives for Distribution Programming," in *Vertical Marketing Systems,* ed. Louis P. Bucklin (Glenview, IL: Scott, Foresman, and Co., 1970), 43.
2. Ibid.
3. Belinda Hulin-Sakin. "Value Heads Up the New Shopper List," *Advertising Age,* 25 July 1983, M33.
4. James M. Kenderine and Bert C. McCammon, Jr., "Structures and Strategy in Retailing," *Proceedings: Southern Marketing Association,* ed. Henry W. Nash and Donald P. Robin, 1973, 119.
5. Theodore N. Beckman, William R. Davidson, and W. Wayne Talarzyk, *Marketing,* 9th ed. (New York: Ronald, 1973), 255.
6. Roy Reed, "A Family Store Takes Stock," *The New York Times Magazine,* 21 November 1983.
7. Joanne Cleaver, "New Leader Directs Carson's Rebuilding," *Advertising Age,* 9 August 1984, 16.
8. Beckman, Davidson, and Talarzyk, *Marketing,* 261–62.
9. Jerome Buff, "The New Environment for Branded Apparel," *Conference on Off-Price Retailing* (New York: New York University, Institute of Retail Management and the Retail Research Society, 21 June 1983, 10.
10. "There's One for All," *Advertising Age,* 10 October 1983, M11; *Competitive Edge* (Barrington, IL: Willard Bishop Consulting Economists, June 1983).
11. Donald N. Thompson, "Contractual Marketing Systems: An Overview," in *Contractual Marketing Systems,* ed. D. N. Thompson (Lexington, MA: Heath Lexington, 1971), 5.
12. Charles L. Vaughn, *Franchising* (Lexington, MA: Heath Lexington, 1974), 2.
13. Louis W. Stern and Adel I. El-Ansary, *Marketing Channels* (Englewood Cliffs, NJ: Prentice-Hall, 1977), 401.
14. Ibid., 415–16.
15. "Videotex: What It's All About," *Marketing News,* 25 November 1983, 16.

16. Ibid.
17. JoAn Paganetti, "High-Tech Ads Gleam to Service with a Smile," *Advertising Age,* 25 July 1983, M24.
18. Donald D. Michman, "Changing Patterns in Retailing," *Business Horizons* 22 (October 1979): 33–40.
19. Malcolm P. McNair, "Significant Trends and Development in the Post War Period," in *Competitive Distribution in a Free, High-Level Economy and Its Implications for the Universities,* ed. A. B. Smith (Pittsburgh: University of Pittsburgh Press, 1958), 18.
20. Arieh Goldman, "The Role of Trading-Up in the Development of the Retailing System," *Journal of Marketing* 39 (January 1975): 54–62.

21. Arieh Goldman, "Institutional Changes in Retailing: An Updated 'Wheel of Retailing' Theory," in *Foundations of Marketing Channels,* ed. A. G. Woodside, J. T. Sims, D. M. Lewison, and I. F. Wilkinson (Austin, TX: Lone Star, 1978), 193.
22. McNair, "Significant Trends and Development in the Post War Period," 18.
23. Thomas J. Maronick and Bruce J. Walker, "The Dialectic Evolution of Retailing," *Proceedings: Southern Marketing Association,* ed. Burnett Greenburg, 1974, 147.

RELATED READINGS

Barmash, Isadore. "DD: Deep Discounting." *Stores* (March 1985), 22–26.

Berkowitz, Eric N.; Walton, John R.; and Walker, Orville C., Jr. "In-Home Shoppers: The Market for Innovative Distribution Systems." *Journal of Retailing* 55 (Summer 1979), 15–33.

Bucklin, Louis P. "Technological Change and Store Operations: The Supermarket Case." *Journal of Retailing* 56 (Spring 1980), 3–15.

Carpenter, Kimberley. "Catalog Showrooms Revamp to Keep Their Identity." *Business Week* (June 10, 1985), 117, 120.

"Combos Take the Lead in Performance Race." *Chain Store Age Executives,* (June 1985), 10–26.

Deiderick, Terry E., and Dodge, H. Robert. "The Wheel of Retailing Rotates and Moves." *Marketing: Theories and Concepts for an Era of Change, Proceedings.* J. Summey, R. Viswanathan, R. Taylor, and K. Glynn, eds. (Southern Marketing Association 1983), 149–52.

English, Wilke, and Foster, J. Robert. "Assessing the Impact of Electronic Retailing upon Competition: A Buyer Perspective." *Marketing: Theories and Concepts for an Era of Change, Proceedings.* J. Summey, R. Viswanathan, R. Taylor, and K. Glynn, eds. (Southern Marketing Association 1983), 153–55.

Goldstucker, Jac L.; Stanley, Thomas J.; and Moschis, George P. "How Consumer Acceptance of Videotex Services Might Affect Consumer Marketing." *AMA Educators' Proceedings.* R. W. Belk et al, eds. (American Marketing Association 1984), 200–204.

Goodrich, J. N., and Hoffman, Jo Ann. "Warehouse Retailing: The Trend of the Future?" *Business Horizons* 22 (April 1979), 45–50.

Greene, Robert C., Jr. "The Convenience Store—A Retail Institution in Transition: The Image Contrasted with the User Public's Needs." *Developments in Marketing Science, Proceedings.* N. K. Malhotra, ed. (Academy of Marketing Science 1985), 222–25.

Henderson, Bruce D. "The Anatomy of Competition." *Journal of Marketing* 47 (Spring 1983), 7–11.

Hirschman, Elizabeth C. "Intertype Competition among Department Stores." *Journal of Retailing* 55 (Winter 1979), 20–34.

Ingene, Charles A. "Intertype Competition: Restaurants versus Grocery Stores." *Journal of Retailing* 59 (Fall 1983), 49–75.

_____. "Structural Determinants of Competition in Food Retailing." *AMA Educator's Proceedings.* P. E. Murphy et al, eds. (American Marketing Association 1983), 251–58.

Klokis, Holly. "Catalog Options: Mail-Order or Store Traffic?" *Chain Store Age Executive* (May 1985), 31–33.

Koenig, Harold F.; Kroeten, Terrence T.; and Brown, James R. "The Bases of Power: Their Effects upon Retailer's Perception of Uncertainty." *AMA Educators' Proceedings.* R. W. Belk et al, eds. (American Marketing Association 1984), 266–70.

Kotler, Phillip. "Not-So-Sweet Key to Mail Selling: Marketing." *Marketing Times* 27 (November - December 1980), 7–10.

Korgaonkar, Pradeep K. "Consumer Preferences for Catalog Showrooms and Discount Stores." *Journal of Retailing* 58 (Fall 1982), 76–88.

Lemon, Katherine N., and Daley, James M. "The Off-Price Retailer: Customer Service Strategies." *Developments in *Marketing Science, Proceedings*. J. D. Lindquist, ed. (Academy of Marketing Science 1984), 283–87.

O'Brien, Donald. "Jordan Marsh: Metamorphosis of a Legend." *Retail Control* (February 1984), 8–18.

Patton, Charles R., and DeLozier, M. Wayne. "The Wheel of Retailing Keeps Spinning: Supermarkets Continue to (R)Evolve." *Developments in Marketing Science, Proceedings*. J. D. Lindquist, ed. (Academy of Marketing Science 1984), 349–52.

Robbins, John E.; Speh, Thomas W.; and Mayer, Morris L. "Retailers' Perceptions of Channel Conflict Issues." *Journal of Retailing* 58 (Winter 1982), 46–67.

Rosenberg, Larry J., and Hirschman, Elizabeth C. "Retailing without Stores." *Harvard Business Review* 58 (July - August 1980), 103–12.

Schul, Patrick L.; Pride, M. William; and Little, Taylor L. "The Impact of Channel Leadership Behavior on Intrachannel Conflict." *Journal of Marketing* 47 (Summer 1983), 21–34.

Sharma, Subhash; Bearden, William O.; and Teel, Jesse E. "Differential Effects of In-Home Shopping Methods" *Journal of Retailing* 59 (Winter 1983), 29–52.

Sibley, Stanley D., and Michie, Donald A. "An Exploratory Investigation of Cooperation in a Franchise Channel." *Journal of Retailing* 58 (Winter 1982), 23–45.

Urbany, Joel E., and Talarzyk, W. Wayne. "Videotex: Implications for Retailing." *Journal of Retailing* 59 (Fall 1983), 76–92.

Wintzer, Fred W., Jr. "The Future of Off-Price Retailing." *Retail Control* (January 1985), 21–26.

Outline

THE CONSUMER BUYING BEHAVIOR PROCESS

WHY CONSUMERS BUY: PSYCHOLOGICAL INFLUENCES

Motivation Learning
Perception Attitudes

WHY CONSUMERS BUY: PERSONAL INFLUENCES

Self-Concept Life Cycle
Life-Style

WHY CONSUMERS BUY: SOCIOLOGICAL INFLUENCES

Culture Reference Groups
Subcultures The Family
Social Class

WHAT CONSUMERS BUY: PRODUCTS AND SERVICES

Product Life Expectancy Shopping Effort
Product Type

HOW CONSUMERS BUY: THE BUYING PROCESS

Problem-Solving Situations
Problem-Solving Process
Service Expectations

WHEN CONSUMERS BUY: BUYING RHYTHMS

Time of Purchase
Regularity and Frequency of Purchase
Patronage Motives

WHERE CONSUMERS BUY: BUYING SCENES

Buying Scenes Patronage Motives

Objectives

- Explain the interaction of psychological, personal, and sociological influences on the buying behavior of consumers

- Understand the concepts of motivation, perception, learning, and attitude formation and explain how each influences buyer behavior

- Discuss why consumers buy from the perspective of the individual consumer's self-concept, life-style, and life cycle

- Evaluate the role of cultures, subcultures, social classes, reference groups, and the family in the consumer purchase decision process

- Describe and assess what consumers buy

- Understand the criteria and procedures consumers use in different purchase problem situations

- Appreciate the fact that timing is critical to retail selling and differentiate consumer buying rhythms

- Describe where consumers actually buy and where consumers think they buy

The Buying Behavior of Consumers

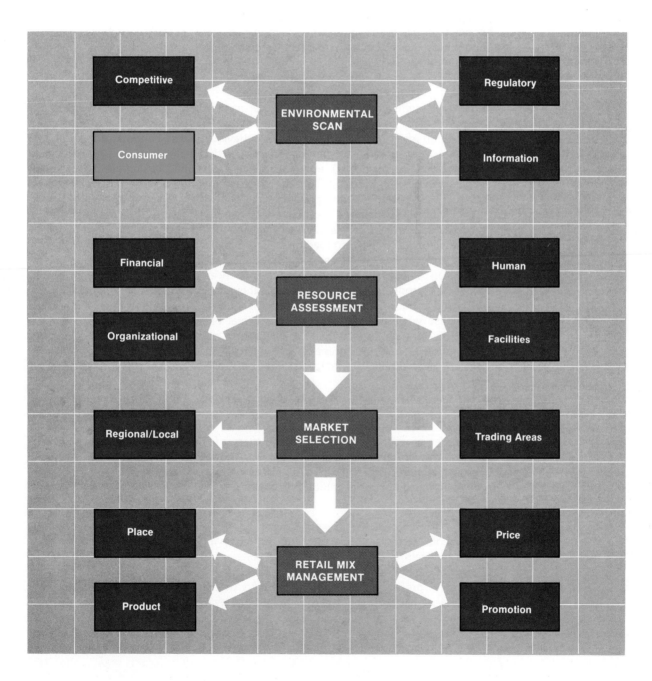

P ractically all retailers consciously or unconsciously base their marketing efforts on some underlying theory of consumer behavior. That is, their merchandising strategies are directed at what they think the consumer needs, wants, and desires. If these strategies succeed in delivering customer satisfaction, and therefore sales, the retailer's theory of consumer behavior is most likely accurate. A misguided theory of consumer behavior, though, can lead to serious errors in developing retailing strategies. Thus, retailers need to have a working knowledge of consumer behavior—why, what, how, when, and where consumers buy.

The choices a consumer has of where to buy anything from branded jeans to food have increased sharply over the last decade. This proliferation means that people have choices on levels of service, type, and quality of goods. They can select goods that will enable them to save money or time, or they can choose products and outlets that will help them preserve a standard of quality even when their purchasing power is declining.[1]

THE CONSUMER BUYING BEHAVIOR PROCESS

Consumer buying behavior is *the manner in which consumers act, function, and react to various situations involving the purchase of a good or service or the acceptance of an idea.* The consumer buying behavior process consists of a number of activities (acts, subprocesses, and social relationships) involving people (individuals, groups, and organizations) and experiences (obtaining, using, and possessing goods, services, and ideas).[2] This chapter examines the activities, people, and experiences associated with the act of buying.

Figure 4–1 illustrates the major elements in the consumer buying behavior process. Consumers' behavior, the purchases they make, and the stores they patronize are ultimately determined by the interactions of various influences from both within and without the consumer's psyche. This chapter examines some of the psychological, personal, and sociological influences that determine *why* consumers choose the products, services, and stores they do. But understanding only the *why*s of buying is not enough. As illustrated in Figure 4–1, the retailer must understand how these whys affect the consumer's actual buying behavior. Consumers want many different products (whats), buy them in different ways (hows), at different times (whens), and in different places (wheres). These outcomes, in turn, affect the retailer's merchandising strategy, selling-space allocation, store layout and design, store hours, buying policies, employee scheduling, financing requirements, and many other facets of retail management.

WHY CONSUMERS BUY: PSYCHOLOGICAL INFLUENCES

A number of important clues to the mystery of the whys of consumer behavior have come from the field of psychology. The most commonly discussed psychological factors that affect why consumers buy include the processes of motivation, perception, learning, and attitude formation.

Motivation

The mental processes preceding the act of buying are part of a general process called **motivation,** *the process by which consumers are moved or incited to action.* The process of consumer motivation is illustrated in Figure 4–2. As shown, the motivation process starts within a *stimulus* that acts upon a *need* resulting in a *motive* that activates a *drive* that impels *behavior.* Let's examine each of these motivational elements.

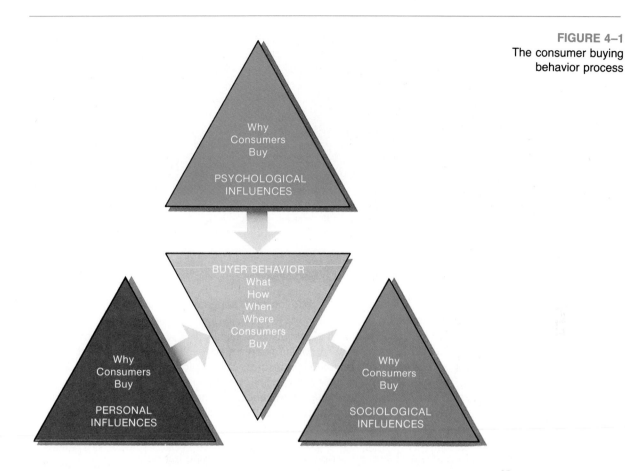

FIGURE 4–1
The consumer buying
behavior process

Stimulus

A **stimulus** may be either *an internal force coming from inside the consumer, such as a hunger pang or a headache, or an external cue from outside the consumer, such as a restaurant sign or an advertisement for aspirin.* Because external cues can be created by the retailer and they help the consumer select from among alternative responses, we will focus our discussion on this type of stimulus.

Cues direct consumers toward specific objects that can satisfy their basic needs and reduce their drives. Elements of the retailer's entire marketing mix serve

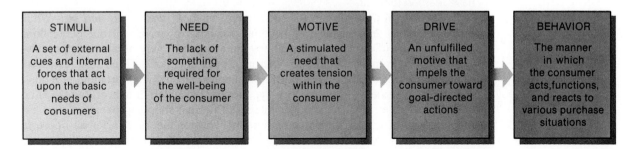

FIGURE 4–2
The motivational process

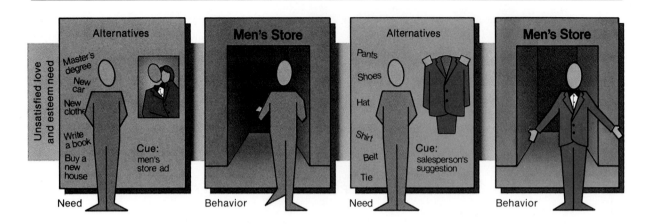

FIGURE 4–3
The role of cues in consumer buying behavior

as cues for consumers. The store's location, appearance, advertising, merchandise, and prices are all cues.

The part cues play in the consumer decision-making process is shown in Figure 4–3. In this illustration, a consumer recognizes that he is unsatisfied with his social acceptability and status. He considers and explores several possible alternatives to alleviate this unsatisfied need. The men's store ad in the newspaper, however, triggers a drive for a better appearance, and he visits the store with no particular desires in mind (he might tell the salesclerk he is "just looking"). All the items of merchandise in the store, their prices, and everything the salesclerk says serve as cues. In this illustration, he ultimately buys the three-piece suit that the clerk says "all the businessmen are going back to this year" (another cue).

Needs

Needs are the basic source of consumer behavior. Once consumers become aware of an unsatisfied need, they are driven to action. The psychologist Abraham H. Maslow suggested that human needs could be classified into a hierarchy, or rank ordering, based on their strengths as motivators.[3] This hierarchy is shown in Figure 4–4. The most basic needs, physiological (or bodily) needs and safety needs, are innate. They are called primary needs. The remaining three classes of needs are called secondary or learned needs. These needs represent things that most humans have *learned* to want.

Physiological needs are for such things as *food, water, air, and sex.* When these needs go unsatisfied, they become powerful organizers of our perceptions and motivators of our behavior until they are satisfied. A very hungry shopper driving down a commercial street, for example, pays attention to food and restaurant signs almost exclusively, and is much less interested in clothing, furniture, and other merchandise available for sale. Once the shopper has eaten, however, hunger is no longer a motivator and the shopper returns to normal shopping behavior. This example suggests a basic principle of human behavior that is true for all needs in Maslow's hierarchy. *Satisfied needs do not motivate behavior, but unsatisfied needs do.*

Safety needs include *the need for protection and the need to feel free from physical harm or danger.* In our advanced society, consumers rarely feel in imminent danger unless some crisis occurs. Yet, some retailers have effectively aroused

safety needs by promoting home smoke- or burglar-alarm systems, second-story escape ladders, and blowout-proof tires. Safety needs, once aroused, are powerful motivators.

Love needs, *sometimes called belongingness needs, are people's desires to have affectionate relationships with other people and groups* (such as the family). Since most people's primary needs are largely satisfied in an affluent society, love needs and other secondary needs present the major opportunities for retailers in developing promotion and merchandising strategies. The love need, for example, can be a strong motivator for a consumer acting as a purchasing agent for the rest of the family. A homemaker buying food, clothing, and home furnishings for other members of the family is very concerned with their preferences. Shrewd retailers will question the consumer to discern the preferences of other family members and show the consumer how these preferences might be satisfied through a certain purchase.

Esteem needs *go beyond the desire to "fit in." Consumers also wish to "stand out," to have others think of them as special.* The respect and admiration of others satisfy the esteem need. From a practical viewpoint, consumers probably are most concerned with their esteem when buying conspicuous merchandise such as automobiles, home furnishings, clothing, and houses. A retailer that observes a customer rejecting "popular" merchandise should guide the customer to the more "distinctive" merchandise that will "set the customer apart from others." The recent success of designer labels and "limited edition" merchandise in apparel, art prints,

107

and collectibles illustrates many consumers' desire to own merchandise allowing them to stand out rather than to fit in.

Retailers that target upper-income customers as their primary market should recognize that their lower-order needs probably are already very well satisfied. Thus, these consumers are strongly motivated to satisfy their esteem needs. Through careful merchandising and promotions, retailers should emphasize that their stores and merchandise are not for the masses, but instead are for the discriminating buyer. Moreover, customers who value esteem are likely to be willing to pay for it, so the retailer can take higher markups on exclusive merchandise. Mass promotion such as newspaper advertising should be oriented toward developing store image rather than promoting specific products.

Self-actualization, *the highest-order need, reflects a person's desire to achieve one's own potential as an individual.* "What you can be, you must be" best describes the need for self-actualization. "A musician must make music, an artist must paint, a poet must write."[4] The self-actualization need can play an important role in the retailer's strategy formulation. For example, retailers of fur and jewelry products have successfully promoted their merchandise as symbols that the wearer has "arrived" socially.

Motives, Drives, and Behavior

An aroused or stimulated need becomes a motive. A motive manifests itself in the form of an inner force or feelings of tension within the consumer. For example, the consumer may have feelings of hunger, loneliness, anger, and inadequacy, or feel unwanted, unrecognized, or not appreciated. When the tensions become strong enough the consumer is impelled to take action to reduce these uncomfortable feelings. In other words, the consumer is driven toward goal-direction actions that will satisfy an unfulfilled motive. The resulting behavior may or may not involve the purchase of a product. A student who is feeling unrecognized may choose to purchase an eye-catching ensemble, join a professional club, talk with the school counselor, or engage in some attention-getting behavior.

Perception

Consumers form images of stores, products, advertisements, themselves, and other people. The foundation of image formation is the perceptual process. **Perception** is *the human process of forming mental pictures of objects, people, and places.* It is accomplished through the five senses of sight, sound, touch, taste, and smell. The perceptual process is completed when the consumer attaches *meaning* to something sensed. The meaning is defined when the consumer compares what has been sensed to concepts learned and stored in memory. For example, when viewing a row of buildings fronted by a parking lot, a baby might see only a group of rectangular shapes, a child might perceive a group of buildings, but an adult would perceive a shopping center. The differences in the meanings that each person ascribed to the view is due not to what they saw (which was the same), but to the sophistication of the memory to which the scene was compared.

Besides providing a quick means of understanding the external world, perceptual processes simplify the consumer's world through a screening process called

(Opposite page)   Love and belongingness needs are important psychological influences affecting store patronage behavior. (Courtesy of Chess King. Jan Schoenbrun, art director)

selective perception. The selectivity of perception affects the receiving (selective exposure), organizing (selective retention), and interpreting (selective distortion) of stimuli. **Selective exposure** is *the act of limiting the type and amount of stimuli received and admitted to awareness.* **Selective retention** is *the act of remembering only information the individual wants to remember.* **Selective distortion** is *the act of misinterpreting incoming stimuli to make them consistent with the individual's beliefs and attitudes.*

Selective perception helps consumers satisfy their needs and protect their self-images in an efficient manner. This concept suggests that retailers should demonstrate through their advertising that shopping in their stores and buying their merchandise will enhance consumers' self-concepts. Consumers notice advertisements about stores and merchandise that will protect and enhance their self-concept and ignore messages from sources that will not.

Before consumers can perceive a stimulus, they must first attend to it. Consumers' attention is drawn more easily to some stimuli than to others. By using one or more principles of attention, retailers can increase the amount of attention that consumers pay to their signs, displays, advertisements, and prices. Some of these principles follow.[5]

1. *Size.* In general, larger objects attract more attention than smaller ones. For the retailer, larger advertisements, larger signs, and larger promotional displays attract more attention than smaller ones.
2. *Novelty.* People's perceptual processes adapt to their environment by blocking out commonplace objects. Something unusual, however, tends to attract people's attention.
3. *Color.* Color is one of the surest methods of attracting and holding attention. Color advertisements almost always attract more attention than competing black and white advertisements. In addition, color can add prestige to the store's image and its merchandise.
4. *Motion.* Everyone has noticed flashing neon signs while driving at night. This example illustrates the attention-getting power of motion. Some retailers have success with point-of-purchase and window displays that use moving parts.

Learning

Learning is the logical extension of the motivation and perception processes. **Learning** can be defined as *the process of acquiring knowledge through past experiences or the acquisition of information.* In buying, the consumer learns by comparing the actual results of buying behavior with the anticipated results. The outcome of this comparison, in turn, affects future behavior. To continue the example in Figure 4–3, if the consumer does feel more secure socially in his new suit, as he had hoped, he experiences satisfaction. When he again becomes aware of an unsatisfied esteem need, he is more likely than before to return to the same store to make a similar purchase such as another new suit, new shoes, a tie, or a shirt. If he again experiences satisfaction, *reinforcement occurs and learning takes place.* As repeated, positive reinforcement occurs, the probability that he will continue to repeat the same pattern of behavior increases. That is, he is more and more likely to return to the same store when similar circumstances arise.

The learning process also can work against the retailer. If the consumer's comparison of expectations to actual results is unfavorable, he learns that the response (the suit bought from the store) failed to satisfy his need. He is then *less* likely to repeat the behavior (visiting the same store) when the situation arises again. There-fore, retailers need to create realistic expectations, since they have a strong impact on whether satisfaction and reinforcement takes place.

The wise retailer is aware that consumers are constantly seeking reinforce-ment—assurance that their decisions are correct. Therefore, the retailer's promo-tional effort should be directed as much toward present and past customers as toward potential customers. A program of regular follow-ups after the sale to deter-mine whether alterations, adjustments, and so forth are required will go a long way toward developing satisfied, regular customers.

Attitudes

Some authorities suggest that one of the principal results of learning is its effect on consumers' attitudes. **Attitudes** may be thought of as *evaluative mental orientations that provide a predisposition to respond in a certain manner.*[6] Attitudes are evalua-tive in the sense that people use them to analyze and judge things as good or bad, right or wrong, helpful or harmful, and so forth. Attitudes are orientations in the sense that they focus one's judgments on particular objects, states, persons, or groups, such as stores, products, and brands. Attitudes also provide customers with a preset way to respond to the object of the attitude. For example, if Kathy thinks that Joe's Super Value is a "cheap" store with "shoddy" merchandise, she avoids shopping there (see Figure 4–5). Thus, attitudes perform an important simplification function for consumers. And obviously, retailers want favorable consumer attitudes toward their stores and merchandise so that people will shop there on a regular basis.

Practitioners and academicians generally agree that consumers' behavior is consistent with their attitudes. Thus, the retailer's major marketing task is to either create or change consumers' attitudes in a manner favorable to the store and its merchandise. Attitude formation and change is a complex subject, and a detailed discussion of it is beyond the scope of this book; however, some general principles of attitude change are presented here.[7]

1. *Stronger attitudes are more difficult to change than less intense ones.* Therefore, it is easier to change a consumer's attitude from unfavorable to favorable than from extremely unfavorable to favorable.

2. *Central attitudes are difficult to change.* Centrality means that the object of the attitude is of great importance to the consumer. Attitudes about reli-gion, the nature of the world, and basic human relationships are central to a person's attitude structure.

3. *Attitudes are easier to change when little is known about the object of the attitude.* A new store, for example, will have an easier time establishing a store image than will an established store striving to change its image.

4. *Repetition generally helps to change attitudes.* A retailer that wants to change consumers' attitudes about its store, merchandise, and prices should be prepared to repeat its promotion continuously over a substantial period of time.

5. *In a promotional message designed to persuade consumers to change their attitudes, a two-sided argument is more effective if the target consum-ers either are well-educated or have an initially unfavorable attitude toward the store and its merchandise.* In presenting a two-sided message, the re-tailer acknowledges the consumer's present attitude, but presents infor-mation to refute it.

111

FIGURE 4–5

What an attitude might
"look" like

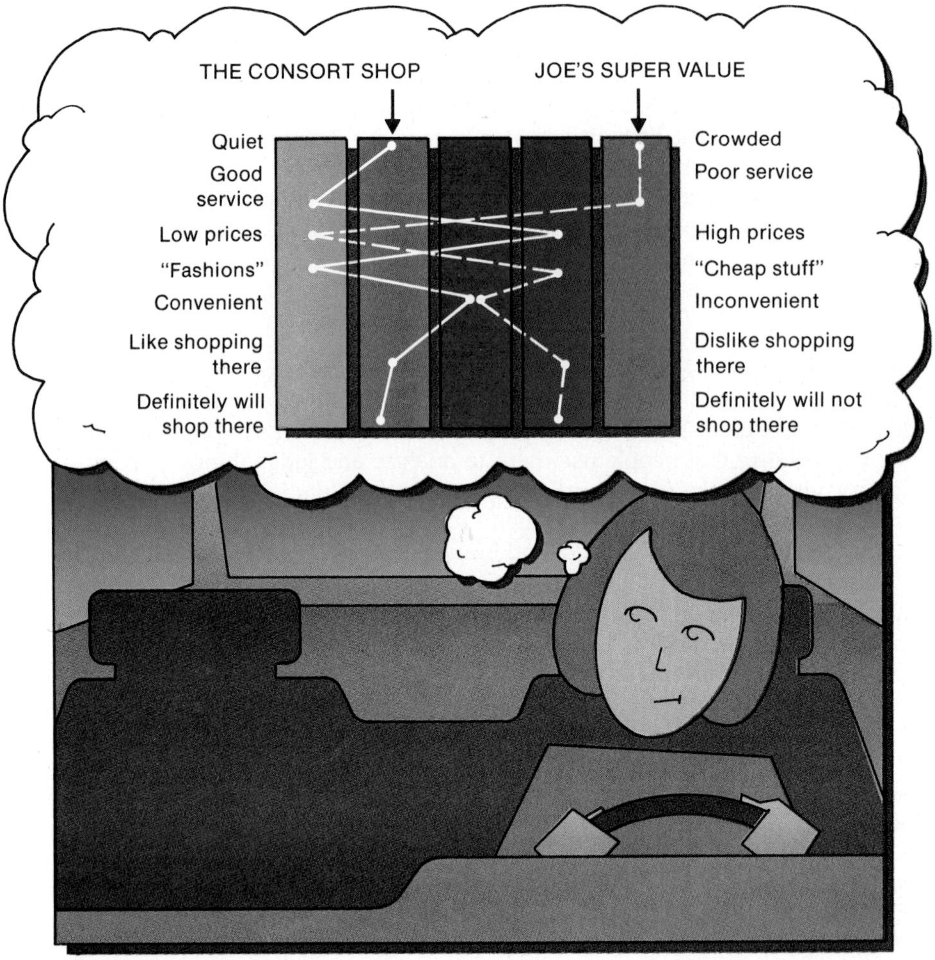

THE CONSORT SHOP   JOE'S SUPER VALUE

Quiet	Crowded
Good service	Poor service
Low prices	High prices
"Fashions"	"Cheap stuff"
Convenient	Inconvenient
Like shopping there	Dislike shopping there
Definitely will shop there	Definitely will not shop there

WHY CONSUMERS BUY: PERSONAL INFLUENCES

Buying behavior is influenced by a number of factors relating to the individual affairs of the consumer. Three of the more important personal buying behavior influences are self-concept, life-styles, and life cycles.

Self-Concept

Who are we? **Self-concept** is *the set of perceptions that a person has of himself or herself within a social context.* More simply, it is our conscious notion of "who we are" and what our characteristics and capabilities are in relation to other people and the world.[8] The self-concept consists of four parts—the *real self* (the way we actually are), the *ideal self* (how we would like to be), the *looking-glass self* (how we think others see us), and the *self-image* (how we see ourselves). This set of "ideals," then, serves as goals for the consumer to attain through conscious behavior. Most researchers in the field of self-concept believe that consumers will never consciously purchase products that are incompatible with their self-concepts.

A "good provider," for example, buys large amounts of life insurance, purchases inexpensive clothing, drives a used car to work, and indulges only in inexpensive hobbies such as gardening, meanwhile providing expensive clothing, autos, and orthodontal and dermatological services for the children and sending them on a luxury cruise to the Bahamas because "all the kids are going."

A "budding scholar" foregoes conspicuously expensive clothing, automobiles, and homes, and instead buys the means of mental enhancement: education, books, travel, concerts, lectures, and works of art.

The "swinging bachelor" buys expensive clothing, automobiles, and furnishings for his apartment, spends copiously on dates and entertainment, saves very little, and would never be caught dead in a station wagon.

Some authorities believe that the study of consumers' self-concepts is futile since the self-concept cannot be observed. However, the "real" and "ideal" selves are defined in terms of *other people's* perceptions. Thus, the consumer must communicate these selves to other people. This communication is often done through nonverbal symbols, including products bought in retail stores.

For example, say a junior executive dresses only in natural-shoulder, three-piece suits of solids, pinstripes, or muted glen plaid; he wears only wing-tip shoes, button-down collar shirts, and striped, solid, or foulard ties. He is consciously communicating to others his self-concept of the dignified, mature, conservative executive. A retailer probably could not interest him in a continental shaped suit with flared trousers since this apparel communicates a showy, perhaps immature, image that is the opposite of the self-concept this consumer wishes to communicate. A wise retailer, on the other hand, can learn much about customers by observing their symbolic communications. The consumers' clothing, mannerisms, and even speech patterns serve in part to alert the smart retailer to customers' self-concepts.

Life-Style

An important influence on what, when, how, and where consumers buy is the way consumers live. **Life-style** is *a pattern of living shaped by psychological influences and social experiences.* Consumer life-style profiles can be developed by examining the consumer's activities (A), interests (I), and opinions (O), together with their demographic makeup. Life-style research is conducted by asking customers to respond to AIO statements, then analyzing the responses to find customer groupings with similar activities, interests, and opinions. AIO questions are of two types: general life-style and product-specific. Examples of general AIO statements are

- Exercise is crucial to good health.
- A woman's place is in the home.
- I will probably have more money next year than I have now.
- People should not need the government to help them.
- Children are the most important thing in a marriage.

Examples of specific AIO statements are

- I jog at least three times a week.
- I do almost all my baking from scratch.
- I frequently use a bank credit card.
- I always vote Republican.
- Children should develop a musical talent.[9]

Marketing research has produced a large number of different life-style profiles designed for a specific product, brand, or company. A more universal life-style typology was developed by SRI International, a nonprofit think tank. They developed the VALS system, which groups individuals into three major categories and nine subcategories based on their values (V) and life-styles (LS). The VALS system is presented in Table 4–1.

TABLE 4–1

A typology of consumer values and life-styles

Percentage of Population	Consumer Type	Values and Life-Styles	Demographics	Buying Patterns
	Need-driven consumers			
6	Survivors	Struggle for survival Socially misfit Ruled by appetites	Poverty-level income Many minority members Live in city slums	Price dominant Focused on basics Buy for immediate needs
10	Sustainers	Concern with safety, security Insecure, compulsive Dependent, following Want law and order	Low-income Low education Much unemployment Live in country as well as cities	Price important Want warranty Cautious buyers
	Outer-directed consumers			
32	Belongers	Conforming, conventional Unexperimental Traditional, formal Nostalgic	Low to middle income Low to average education Blue collar jobs Tend toward noncity living	Family Home Fads Middle and lower mass markets
10	Emulators	Ambitious, show-off Status conscious Upwardly mobile Macho, competitive	Good to excellent income Youngish Highly urban Traditionally male, but changing	Conspicuous consumption "In" items Imitative Popular fashion
28	Achievers	Achievement success, fame Materialism Leadership, efficiency Comfort	Excellent incomes Leaders in business, politics, etc. Good education Suburban and city living	Give evidence of success Top of the line Luxury and gift markets "New and improved" products

Life Cycle

The **life cycle** concept is *a series of stages of marital status and child raising through which most people move in the course of their lives.* A consumer's buying behavior is often determined by the practical considerations of whether they are: single or married, working or retired, and whether the household includes children. The nine stages of the family life cycle are as follows:[10]

1. *bachelor stage.* This stage consists of young, single people living alone. These people have few financial burdens, spending sparingly on basic

TABLE 4–1,
continued

Percentage of Population	Consumer Type	Values and Life-Styles	Demographics	Buying Patterns
	Inner-directed consumers			
3	I-am-me	Fiercely individualistic Dramatic, impulsive Experimental Volatile	Young Many single Student or starting job Affluent backgrounds	Display one's taste Experimental fads Source of far-out fads Clique buying
5	Experiential	Drive to direct experience Active, participative Person-centered Artistic	Bimodal incomes Mostly under 40 Many young families Good education	Process over product Vigorous, outdoor sports "Making" home pursuits Crafts and introspection
4	Societally conscious	Societal responsibility Simple living Smallness of scale Inner growth	Bimodal low and high incomes Excellent education Diverse ages and places of residence Largely white	Conservation emphasis Simplicity Frugality Environmental concerns
2	Integrated	Psychological maturity Sense of fittingness Tolerant, self-actualizing World perspective	Good to excellent incomes Bimodal in age Excellent education Diverse jobs and residential patterns	Varied self-expression Esthetically oriented Ecologically aware One-of-a-kind items

Source: Raymond L. Horton, *Buyer Behavior—A Decision Making Approach* (Columbus: Charles E. Merrill Publishing Co., 1984), 314–15. Assembled from data presented in Arnold Mitchell, *Consumer Values: A Typology.* Menlo Park, Ca.: SRI International, 1978.

household goods, but spend more heavily on clothing, automobiles, and recreation.

2. *young married couples with no children.* Since both partners usually work and since there are no children, these couples are better off financially than they will be in the near future. They have the highest purchase rate and the highest average purchases of consumer durable goods such as automobiles, furniture, and appliances.

3. *full nest I: youngest child under six.* In this stage, both partners are less likely to be working, since one must take care of children not yet in school. Expenditures for housing and household operations are at a peak during this stage, while expenditures for toys, medical care and medicines, and baby food also are substantial. The family has fewer liquid assets at this stage and little to spend on luxuries.

4. *full nest II: youngest child over six.* At this point, most husbands' salaries have increased, and many wives have returned to work since their children are of school age. Because their financial situation is better, the family spends more on recreation, clothing, and other goods; however, it spends less on housing and household furnishings.

5. *full nest III: older married couples with dependent children.* In this stage, even more wives work than in the last stage, and the family is in a better financial position. Although the percentage of income they spend for housing declines, their percentage-of-income expenditures for home furnishings and equipment remain roughly constant as the family upgrades its living standards by buying more "tasteful" home furnishings and nonnecessary appliances. Also, expenditures for education increase.

6. *empty nest I: older married couples with no dependent children; head of household in labor force.* In this stage, most families are as comfortable financially as they ever have been or ever will be. The couple is interested in travel, education, and recreation; expenditures for these services increase accordingly.

7. *empty nest II: older married couples with no dependent children; head of household retired.* In this stage, family income declines drastically, and expenditures for medical care and personal comfort increase.

8. *solitary survivor I: in labor force.* Income is good in this stage, but the one survivor is likely to sell the home and begin to rent. Expenditures for travel, recreation, and education usually increase.

9. *solitary survivor II: retired.* This survivor experiences a decline in income, but most expenditures also decline, except for medical and personal care.

WHY CONSUMERS BUY: SOCIOLOGICAL INFLUENCES

All individuals' needs, motives, preferences, attitudes, and behavior are heavily shaped by many kinds of groups. As Figure 4–6 (p. 118) illustrates, the largest group affecting the consumer is the general society. Within the society, consumers' subcultures exert tremendous influence on their behavior. The social class to which consumers belong also affects their behavior, as do reference groups. The smallest, most immediate, and perhaps most important group affecting a consumer's behavior is the family. This section discusses the nature of group effects on consumer behavior.

Culture

For our purposes, **culture** is defined as *the sum total of knowledge, attitudes, symbols, and patterns of behavior shared by a group of people and transmitted from one generation to the next.*[11] A **society** is *a group of people bound by a common culture.* Cultural traits include profound *beliefs,* such as religion and the ways humans should react toward each other; fundamental *values,* such as achievements and independence; and *customs* and *manners,* such as "ladies first" and not belching at the dinner table.

Cultural traits highly valued by a society, such as the sanctity of human life, are usually codified into law with formal punishment for violation, such as execution for murder. Less important values are more likely to be enforced by social approval and disapproval.

(Opposite page)   How does this advertisement appeal to the consumer's self-concept? (Courtesy of Chess King. Jan Schoenbrun, art director)

FIGURE 4–6
Sociological influences
on consumer buying
behavior

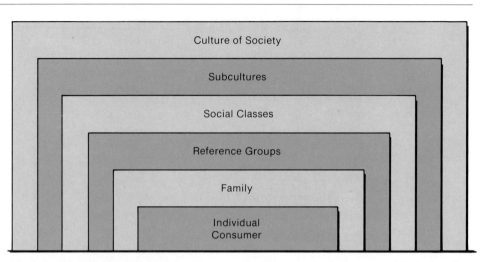

The individual consumer is a member of many groups — some large, some small, but all having a significant effect on his or her behavior.

The basic "core" of U.S. culture affecting retailers includes religiousness, achievement, security, sociability, and conformity, leisure, youthfulness, and the role of women.[12] Retailers can reflect these cultural dimensions in their advertising messages to appeal to the U.S. consumer.

Religiousness. Most Americans adhere to either Christian or Jewish faiths, both of which emphasize the value of the individual and the subordination of the self to a supreme being. The Puritan ethic, still adhered to by many, emphasizes hard work and thrift, while condemning conspicuous or frivolous consumption.

Achievement. The U.S. culture is competitive, and success in any endeavor is highly valued. Professional and business success in the competitive economic system is often measured in terms of accumulated wealth and income. Since bank accounts and tax returns are not visible, many consumers express their achievements by buying goods and services that show the wealth they have amassed and that symbolize their achievements.

Security. Perhaps due to fear of failure in competition, U.S. consumers also value security. The desire for security makes consumers cautious in buying high-risk, big-ticket items such as homes, automobiles, appliances, and furniture. For these purchases, consumers tend to seek dependable retailers, with established reputations, that sell well-known brands with good warranties.

Sociability and conformity. Because U.S. consumers have many face-to-face interactions with one another, they highly value social acceptability. Consumers' tastes and preferences are greatly influenced—almost conditioned—by other people. Moreover, social acceptability is best gained through conformity—accepting the tastes and preferences, and mirroring behavior, of others. Retailers that stress in their promotion that other people accept their stores and merchandise are able to capitalize upon this cultural characteristic.

Leisure. A trend contrary to the Puritan ethic is Americans' increasing desire for leisure. This trend has caused a booming demand for sports and recreational equipment and services, time-saving products, and convenience foods. In addition, con-

118

sumers appear to be less willing to commit leisure time to shopping—they are less willing to seek out the retailer. Thus, for some products, the retailer must stress leisure and occupy convenient locations to attract customers.

Youthfulness. Although many cultures revere age, U.S. culture values youthfulness. We consider youthfulness a highly desirable cultural trait representing vigor, athletic and sexual prowess, and attractiveness. The widespread interest in dieting, health foods, exercise, cosmetics, and cosmetic surgery is evidence of consumers' desires to prolong youth and forestall aging.

Role of women. The arrival of the dual-income home brings many changes to retailing. Among these changes are buyers with higher incomes, less time to shop, a desire to shop during the evening and other "nonworking" hours, and a greater demand for convenience food and other time-saving products.[13]

The retailer must be aware that cultural values change. Exposure to other cultures coupled with mass communications means that people are increasingly exposed to alternative values. Such exposure inevitably causes change in consumer tastes and buyer behavior. The retailer should take time to monitor cultural changes and to assess their impact upon the business.

Subcultures

A culture holds many subcultures. **Subcultures** are *smaller, more homogeneous societies within a culture that have their own distinct set of attitudes, values, symbols, and patterns of behavior.* Subcultures can be based upon ethnic background (blacks, American Indian tribes, the Cajun subculture of Louisiana), national origin (Poles, Cubans, Lithuanians, Puerto Ricans), and other bases such as religion (Mormons), geography (southerners), and value systems (environmentalists). Although blacks constitute the largest U.S. subculture, many other subcultures are significant in size and have identifiable consumption patterns that retailers should seriously consider when making retail decisions. These subcultures generally live in concentrated geographic areas, speak their own language, and have their own newspapers and radio stations. Retailers targeting a subcultural group should study it to determine its members' merchandise preferences, locate within their geographic area, promote in their language when possible, and hire a staff including members of that subculture.

A vivid example of how a retailer can adapt and thrive in a particular subculture was seen recently in the state of Hawaii. Hawaii is like a "country unto itself." Its population consists primarily of Asian and South Pacific peoples. Their dress, customs, and food preferences are distinctly different from the mainland United States. Recognizing these differences, McDonald's adapted its restaurants to seat people in an open, "breezeway" shelter, included foods on its menu that would appeal to Hawaiians, and tailored its advertising and other promotions to the local subculture. McDonald's is now a thriving business in Hawaii, while the future of other, less adaptable retailers there is uncertain.

Social Class

Social classes are *societal, rank-ordered groupings within which individuals or families are placed.* Members of higher social classes receive more status and esteem than members of lower social classes. Many characteristics determine an individual's or family's social class. Among them are occupation, education, place of residence (prestige of neighborhood), income, and wealth.

Retailers need to understand social classes. Members of the same social class tend to behave similarly, have similar tastes and preferences, patronize the same stores, have similar outlooks on life, and live in similar neighborhoods. For these reasons, a given social class can serve as a target market for a retailer.

Sociologists have developed several classification schemes for social classes in this country. One of the most widely used is the system developed by W. Lloyd Warner.[14]

Warner's Social Class System

Warner divides social class into six levels. Knowledge of each class is essential to retailers.

The *upper-upper class* (1.5 percent of the population) is society's "aristocracy," the social elite. Money alone is not enough for membership; wealth must be inherited. Upper-uppers generally live in older, fashionable neighborhoods, often maintain two homes, belong to their city's most prestigious country club, and educate their children at the most elite private preparatory schools and colleges.

The *lower-upper class* (1.5 percent) contains society's "new rich"—successful professionals, high-level business executives, and successful entrepreneurs who often earn more money than upper-upper class members. Lower-uppers were often educated at public universities, but send their own children to the elite universities of the upper-upper class. Lower-uppers may have all the material possessions of the upper-upper class and more, and are often in civic affairs.

The U.S. *upper-middle class* (10 percent) consists of career-oriented professionals such as physicians, lawyers, engineers, and college professors. They generally are the best-educated social class. Upper-middles are typically status-conscious and communicate their status through material symbols such as location in prestigious neighborhoods, swank automobiles, and expensive clothing.

White-collar workers such as office workers, clerks, teachers, technicians, and sales representatives comprise the *lower-middle class* (about 30 percent). Many people think of this class as "typical" America. Generally they are the most conforming, hard-working, religious, and home-and-family oriented of the social classes.

The *upper-lower class* (about 33 percent) is the largest in the social system, consisting largely of blue-collar factory workers and some skilled tradesworkers. Upper-lower class members typically live a routine day-to-day existence and are not particularly status conscious. Most do not expect to rise above their present social station.

The *lower-lower class* (25 percent) consists of unskilled, often chronically unemployed, poorly educated slum dwellers, who usually belong to unassimilated, ethnic minority groups, and the rural poor. The lower-lower class member generally rejects middle-class values.

Social Class Differences

Different social classes exhibit significant differences in life-styles and purchase behavior. Middle- and lower-class consumers have considerably different outlooks on life.

Upper-middle class consumers search for "quality" and are fashion conscious. Their likings depend strongly on both the tastes of their class and the class above

(Opposite page)   Targeting the black consumer. (Courtesy of McDonald's Corporation)

"McDonald's® is music to my ears."

"I started out as a freelance arranger-composer and one of the first national spots I ever produced was for McDonald's. Then I formed my own company and they gave me enough work to get me over the hump and establish myself in the business. At the time, McDonald's was one of the first advertisers to produce commercials directed to the Black consumer on such a large scale. As a result, I was able to open the door for a lot of talented Black musicians and singers who had never worked professionally before. So McDonald's really opened up the business for many people in this town. And we're all still working for McDonald's. And that's great."

McDonald's continues to support Black-owned businesses and individuals in communications. Morris "Butch" Stewart and his Joy-Art Productions is one of them. And his work is music to our ears.

Morris "Butch" Stewart
Joy Art Music Production
Chicago, IL.

WE'RE INVOLVED. McDonald's

them. Since many of their purchases are used to communicate a notion of "who they are" to others, the upper-middle class is an important market to retailers.

Retailers must be aware that "tastefulness" is important to upper-middle class consumers. Refinement and elegance should characterize store layout and promotion. Although upper-middle class consumers are willing to pay a premium price for prestigious products, they purchase carefully and are unlikely to pay that premium for commonplace merchandise. If media are selected carefully, advertisers can easily reach the upper-middle class market since members of this class are well-educated and receptive to the mass media.

By using the proper promotional theme and media, retailers can lure upper-middle class shoppers into the store, since they are the most venturesome class of shoppers, seeking out new places to shop.

Because lower-middle class consumers are more concerned with fitting in than with standing out, they expect the retailer to provide them help in fashion expressiveness. For example, they are more likely than the upper-middle class to buy "coordinated combinations" both in clothing and furniture. Also, lower-middle class families are the most price-sensitive social class and will visit several stores to find the best value.

Most upper-lower class consumers earn good incomes, but avoid spending their money on status items, such as expensive clothing. In general, they buy products for personal enjoyment rather than to impress others. Though spending a low proportion of their incomes on housing in low status neighborhoods, they spend proportionally more than other groups for inside-the-house goods such as modern appliances that make living easier. In the retail store, the upper-lower class shopper tends to be an impulsive buyer, yet remains loyal to previously bought brands, particularly well-known national brands. Also, this class is hesitant to try new stores, but will shop at places that offer convenience, face-to-face service, well-known brands, and services such as delivery and credit. Retailers that target this market typically use broadcast media since the lower-lower classes are the least literate segment of society.

Reference Groups

Reference groups have a powerful influence on consumers' purchase behavior. A **reference group** is *a group that provides a model or standard for an individual's behavior and attitudes.* Consumers have several reference groups. They include the family, coworkers, friends, personalities, or groups a person would like to join (such as a country club). Consumers use reference groups as a frame of reference to decide what they should buy and where they should buy it. If their reference group approves of a product, brand, or store, then that is the product and brand they purchase, and the store at which they buy.

Reference groups have tremendous influence over some consumer purchases, but none over others. In general, reference groups exert influence on the purchase of conspicuous, highly visible products and brands. Clothing, furniture, and automobiles are examples of highly conspicuous products. However, the *brand* of furniture or clothing is often not conspicuous and thus the consumer may give little thought to what others think in deciding among brands. When the brand also is visible (say, for jeans), reference group influence is substantial for both product and brand.

Many "invisible," privately consumed products, such as basic food items, toiletries, health and beauty aids, and small appliances, are bought by consumers with little thought given to reference groups. Instead, consumers evaluate the intrinsic characteristics of the product and its price. A retailer should gauge the potential reference group influence on its merchandise assortment by analyzing its conspic-uousness. If either the products or brands are conspicuous, the retailer should stress the social acceptability of the item and take a higher margin. If the product is incon-spicuous, the retailer should expect the consumer to carefully consider product characteristics and prices.

The Family

The family exerts the strongest influence on consumer behavior. In fact, retailers should think of their consumers not as individuals, but as a family represented by an individual. The average U.S. household consists of four persons. Some goods and services are bought for personal consumption, others are bought for one family member by another, and still others are bought for the entire family by one mem-ber. In some cases, two or more members of the family participate in buying a family good or service.

Retailers must understand that each family member plays a different role in the buying process. Family buying assumes five specific roles:

1. *initiator*—the family member who first recognizes the problem
2. *user*—the family member who will actually use or consume the product or service
3. *decision maker*—the member who decides what will be bought and at what time, place, and source
4. *decision influencer*—the family member who has input or affects the choice of the decision maker
5. *purchasing agent*—the family member who actually visits the store and makes the purchase

The retailer must tailor marketing efforts toward different members of the family, depending on their roles.

In the purchase of a child's bedroom suite, for example, a mother (initiator) recognizes that her daughter needs a new bedroom suite, and asks the father if they can afford a new one. Father says that they can, and sets a price limit (decision influencer). Mother reads advertising and shops in furniture stores, always consid-ering the needs and desires of her child (the user). Finally, she narrows the range of choice down to three and asks the child (decision influencer) which she likes best. Since the child's selection is also acceptable to the mother, she buys the suite (decision maker and purchasing agent).

A retailer must use knowledge of *what* consumers buy to develop a merchandising strategy, plan a buying budget, allocate selling space, lay out the store, and devise competitive tactics. Retailers view the goods and services consumers buy from three perspectives: (1) product life expectancy, (2) product type, and (3) degree of shop-ping effort consumers expend.

WHAT CONSUMERS BUY: PRODUCTS AND SERVICES

Product Life Expectancy

Consumers buy products and services that have varying life expectancies. Product life expectancies affect consumers' perceptions of what the total product offering should be.

Durable goods *last a long time and survive many uses.* Examples are furni-ture, appliances, and automobiles. Retailers of durable goods, especially those that perform continuous functions such as automobiles and dishwashers, should be aware that consumers are not only buying a "thing" but also satisfying a need over a long period of time. Because of this, such factors as warranty, maintenance, repair service, and easy credit terms are extremely important.

Nondurable goods are *products that people consume in one or a few uses.* Examples are food, liquor, tobacco, and personal-care items such as medicine and cosmetics. Whereas durable goods are bought infrequently, nondurable goods are purchased regularly and often routinely. Retailers should provide consumers of non-durable goods with convenient locations and quick service.

Services are *the intangible functions performed for consumers.* Although services have a short life, their results may linger. Examples are automobile and appliance repairs, barber and beautician services, pest-control services, and health-care services.

Product Type

Another way to view consumer goods and services is by product type. In this system, goods are classified as food, alcoholic beverages, tobacco, house furnishings and equipment, transportation (automobiles, gasoline, accessories, and service), personal-care items, recreational equipment, reading and educational materials, and all other goods. Consumers' expenditures for these goods vary according to their incomes and their stages in the family life cycle.

Families' incomes and expenditures have been studied and grouped into a set of relationships known as Engel's Laws. Briefly, these laws state that

1. As a family's income *increases,* the percentage of income spent on food *decreases.*
2. As a family's income *increases,* the percentage of income spent on clothing is *roughly constant.*
3. As a family's income *increases,* the percentage of income spent on housing and household operations remains *roughly constant.*
4. As a family's income *increases,* the percentage of income spent on all other goods *increases.*

It should be noted that the percentages of income, not the amounts, change. Generally, as a family's income increases, the actual dollars spent for all goods increases. Consumers' expenditures also vary according to their stages in the family life cycle.

Shopping Effort

What consumers buy is directly related to their willingness to spend time, money, and effort in securing the good or service. Hence, a useful method of classifying goods is to group products on the basis of the *degree of effort* consumers are willing to exert to buy a product. One such system is the shopping-effort classification system. In this system, goods are classified as either convenience goods, shopping goods, or specialty goods.[15] Figure 4–7 illustrates the shopping effort continuum.

Convenience Goods

Convenience goods are *products that consumers want but are not willing to spend a great deal of time, effort, or money for.* Products such as bread, cigarettes, razor blades, and burn ointments are convenience goods for most people. Convenience goods usually are low-price, low-markup, high-turnover products. Convenience goods are further classified into staples, impulse goods, and emergency goods.

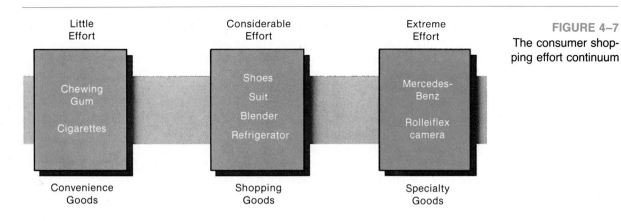

FIGURE 4–7
The consumer shopping effort continuum

Staples are *products that consumers buy very frequently and that they believe are daily and weekly necessities*. Examples are cigarettes, bread, milk, eggs, personal-care items (such as toothpaste, soap, and aspirin), and household products such as laundry detergent and paper towels. Most consumers buy staples on a routine basis at supermarkets and discount houses. Since consumers buy their staples during a single shopping trip, they often patronize one store for these items. Thus, consumers buy from the store that offers them the greatest *total* satisfaction (preferred products and brands, total price, and buying convenience) rather than the greatest satisfaction for any one product or brand.

Impulse goods are *products that consumers buy the moment they see them.* Impulse goods include snack foods, panty hose, magazines, records, rose bushes, batteries, toys, and costume jewelry. Consumers buy impulse goods because of an immediate desire that sight of the product arouses. If the consumer does not see the product, the desire is never aroused and the sale is never made. Hence, eye-catching end-of-aisle, freestanding, and check-out displays are the key to merchandising impulse goods.

Emergency goods are *purchased when a severe need arises.* But unlike impulse goods, some *event,* rather than sight of the product, evokes the need. Bandages, umbrellas, and tire chains are examples of emergency goods. Since the buyer urgently needs the product, neither price nor brand is important. Therefore, retailers can reduce the variety of common emergency goods they stock and take higher markups on what they do sell.

Shopping Goods

Shopping goods are *products that consumers are willing to expend considerable time and effort in evaluating.* Two classes of shopping goods are homogeneous and heterogeneous.

Homogeneous shopping goods are *brands of products that consumers perceive as similar.* As a result, they compare prices among the various brand alternatives and generally select the brands with the lowest price. Homogeneous shopping goods usually are relatively high-price, big-ticket items that perform substantially similar functions. Examples are dishwashers, washers and dryers, and refrigerators.

To succeed in selling homogeneous shopping goods, retailers must develop their marketing mix to meet the needs of their consumers. First, their prices should be the lowest or nearly the lowest in their trading area, since customers for homogeneous shopping goods compare prices. Second, their advertising approach should establish an *identity* for their stores so that customers will consider them

125

when looking for homogeneous shopping goods. Third, retailers should promote regular "sales" and sales promotions to generate a store traffic of shoppers who can either buy what is advertised or trade up to more expensive merchandise. And, finally, the sales staff must be well-trained in techniques on how to "close" a sale and how to discourage shoppers from looking elsewhere.

Heterogeneous shopping goods are *products that consumers perceive as different and want to examine for quality, suitability, and style.* Examples of heterogeneous shopping goods are major clothing items, furniture, automobiles, wallpaper, nursery products, and hair-styling services.

As with homogeneous shopping goods, retailers must tailor their marketing mix to the distinctive buying behavior consumers exhibit for heterogeneous shopping goods. Retailers must know their target market's preferences and offer merchandise that satisfies those preferences. Since the product's characteristics are the customer's most important consideration, the retailer's product and brand mixes should be determined by consumers' preferences within the retailer's trading area.

For heterogeneous shopping goods, brand loyalty is difficult to establish since consumers will not buy even well-known brands if they are not suited to their needs. Not even the most status-conscious shopper, for example, would buy the most famous designer label dress if she consciously believed it was unflattering. Moreover, the *brand* of a heterogeneous shopping good often is not visible or apparent to others, as is true of clothing and furniture. Thus, price is much less important to consumers in buying heterogeneous shopping goods than it is for homogeneous shopping goods. If a product is unsuitable to a customer, a low price is unlikely to induce a purchase. If the product is suitable, a consumer is much more willing to pay a higher price.

Specialty Goods

Specialty goods are *products on which consumers are willing to expend an extremely large amount of shopping effort, time, and money.* Consumers, in fact, insist on one brand and will accept no substitute. Specialty goods are not a type of product but specific, branded products, such as Florsheim shoes and Mercedes-Benz automobiles or "one of a kind" products such as a rare painting.

Since consumers usually go to great lengths to obtain specialty goods, manufacturers often restrict distribution to one particular exclusive retailer per geographic area. Retailers usually go to elaborate lengths to obtain the rights to sell certain specialty goods; but once obtained, the right is well worth the effort and cost, because the target market is willing to pay a premium price for the product. Location is less important to specialty goods retailers since consumers are willing to exert extra effort to obtain the product. Also, promotion can be limited simply to informing the appropriate market of where and when the product is available.

HOW CONSUMERS BUY: THE BUYING PROCESS

By knowing *how* consumers buy, the retailer can allocate a marketing budget and direct efforts to the stages in the process that affect consumers' buying decisions. Buyer behavior can be thought of as a problem-solving process. Hunger, cold, loneliness, and insecurity are problems that consumers attempt to solve in part through the buying process. This section discusses the problem-solving situations faced by the consumer and the process used by consumers in solving buying problems.

Problem-Solving Situations

Three types of problem-solving situations exist: extensive problem solving, limited problem solving, and routinized buying behavior.[16]

Extensive problem-solving *occurs when consumers consider buying a product that is important, relatively costly, and with which they have no knowledge or experience.* A young couple buying its first washer/dryer is an example. **Limited problem solving** *occurs when a buyer has some knowledge or experience with the purchase.* This knowledge allows a narrowing of the range of choices. A man buying his tenth set of tires, for example, may have decided that steel-belted radials are too expensive and that name-brand tires are no better than the brands at discount stores, chain department stores, and service stations. His buying decision is thus simplified, since he searches only among those stores for the best price on either glass fiber-belted tires or four-ply polyesters.

Routinized buying behavior *occurs when the consumer has decided which decision is most satisfactory in a certain situation and simply makes the same purchase decision each time the need arises.* Homemakers routinely buy their family's favorite brand of toothpaste when the supply runs low and the same cold remedy each time a member of the family catches a cold. This form of purchase behavior is habitual.

Retailers should estimate the problem-solving situation their consumers are in since that determines how much information the latter need to make a purchase decision. Two principles can guide retailers:

1. In general, younger, less affluent buyers have less buying experience and are, therefore, apt to be in limited or extensive problem-solving situations.
2. All consumers have less experience in buying durable goods than nondurable goods because durable goods are bought less frequently.

Problem-Solving Process

A large part of consumer behavior is conscious problem solving. The conscious problem-solving process generally follows these steps:

1. The consumer becomes aware of a problem and wants to solve it.
2. The consumer outlines various alternative solutions to the problem.
3. The consumer gathers information about the alternatives. This process consists of reviewing information already stored in memory, talking with friends and acquaintances, actively reading advertisements, making shopping visits to stores, and talking to salespeople.
4. The consumer evaluates and selects the most appropriate alternative.
5. The consumer makes the purchase.
6. The consumer evaluates the appropriateness of the purchase decision.[17]

The retailer that understands this process can gain an advantage over competitors. By playing an active rather than a passive role, the retailer can "guide" the consumer through the decision-making process. This time-honored prescription for effective selling also works for retailers.

The following example illustrates the process. By late summer or early fall, most homeowners' interest in lawn and garden maintenance has waned, and nursery sales fall. An aggressive nursery, however, can *evoke* consumers' needs by prompting their memories of winter kill, lush spring weeds, and tough summer crabgrass. By offering consultation, soil tests, and a preventive winterizing lawn treatment, the retailer presents a doubly attractive alternative to "do nothing at all or do it yourself." By promising an early spring follow-up with whatever treatment is necessary, the retailer can increase spring sales and deliver postsale satisfaction.

127

Service Expectations

A final aspect of "how" consumers buy is the level of services customers expect when they buy from a retailer. The kinds of customer services a store might offer include sales help, permitting returns and allowances, credit, delivery, wrapping, repair, alteration, installation, advice on use of merchandise, and others—limited only by the amount the retailer is able and willing to spend. Customer services generally are labor-intensive activities, and since employees are the retailer's major expense, customer services increase total retailer costs and are usually recovered in the form of higher prices.

Being human, most consumers want many services *and* lower prices, but the retailer that tries to offer both will quickly go bankrupt. Therefore, the retailer must decide which service/price level to offer. Retailers can offer a level of services ranging from no service/low prices ("self service") to full service/high prices.

WHEN CONSUMERS BUY: BUYING RHYTHMS

In sports, comedy, politics, or retailing, *timing* is critical to success. For retailers, knowing *when* consumers buy can make the difference between profit and loss. Two important benefits for retailers that understand when consumers buy are avoiding missed sales and creating unexpected sales. First, by having merchandise available when buyers are looking, the retailer avoids missed sales. Second, the retailer can create sales by making merchandise available at a time when it can stimulate consumers' desires and cause them to buy. One way to examine when consumers buy is to analyze their buying rhythms.

People have many built-in rhythms: most work five days and relax two, work in the daytime and rest in the evening, and enjoy themselves outdoors in warm weather and indoors in cool weather. These life rhythms also cause rhythms in consumers' buying patterns; that is, they buy sometimes, abstain sometimes, and buy more at one time and less at another. Retailers should study buyers' rhythms to create sales and avoid missed sales. Consumers' buying rhythms are discussed here according to (1) time of purchase and (2) regularity and frequency of purchase.

Time of Purchase

Figure 4–8, a matrix of possible times of purchase, shows that people's buying rhythms have two dimensions: (1) time of day, week, year, or life, and (2) specific times or anytime. The matrix shows eight different products classified according to whether consumers buy them at specific times or at any time of the day, week, year, or life. As the matrix illustrates, consumers buy most newspapers during early morning hours, go to the movies most on weekends, buy most of their fashions in early spring and fall, and purchase most wedding gowns only before the wedding. On the other hand, they might buy cigarettes at any time of the day, groceries at any time of the week, underwear at any time of the year, and photographs at any time in their lives.

In general, merchandise, sales, advertising, sales promotion, and pricing activities should be geared to these rhythms. If a product is bought at a particular time, the retailer must have it available at that time to avoid losing sales. If the product is bought anytime, then the retailer must have it available at *all* times.

Although a retailer must adapt its marketing efforts to consumers' times of purchase, it can choose to alter consumers' buying patterns to increase sales. There are many examples. Taverns often promote a reduced "happy hour" price from 5 P.M. to 7 P.M. Theaters can reduce prices on weekdays and afternoons to create

FIGURE 4–8
CHAPTER 4
THE BUYING BEHAVIOR
OF CONSUMERS

TIME PERIOD	Specific Time	Any Time
Day	newspapers	cigarettes
Week	movies	most food items
Year	fashions	underwear
Life	wedding gowns	photographs

Time of purchase matrix (source: based on discussion by Bud Wilson, *Principles of Merchandising: A Key to Profitable Marketing* [New York: Fairchild Publications, 1976], 62–63)

sales. Fashion merchandisers gear their promotional activities to the beginnings of the fall and spring seasons, when customers are most interested in buying.

Regularity and Frequency of Purchase

A more subtle aspect of "when" consumers buy is their regularity and frequency of purchase. **Regularity** refers to *the consistent recurrence of consumer purchases.* Consumers buying cigarettes once a day, soft drinks once a week, birth control pills once a month, and automobiles once every five years are examples of regular purchase behavior. An irregular buying pattern has no predictable time lapse between purchases. One example is the purchase of auto engine replacement parts, bought only when part of an engine wears out. A driver might buy a new fan belt six months after buying a car and not buy another for three years.

    Frequency refers to *the number of purchases a person makes over some time period.* U.S. consumers usually buy toothpaste frequently and dentures infrequently; gasoline frequently, but motor oil less frequently; and automobile tune-ups frequently, but automobiles less frequently. Retailers must detect these buying patterns and adjust their stock accordingly.

    A retailer's store can be thought of as a "plant" where the retailer uses limited space to display and sell goods, stock merchandise, and manage operations. The more merchandise "shown," other things being equal, the more the retailer can sell. Thus, the retailer should allocate as much space as possible to attractive display of merchandise and minimal space to storage. The best allocation of space is possible only if customers' frequency and regularity of purchase are correctly predicted.

    Given our understanding of consumer regularity and frequency in buying merchandise, we can classify the when of customers' buying into four categories. Figure 4–9, a matrix of products classified according to consumers' degree of purchase frequency and regularity, shows four different customer time patterns of purchase: (1) frequent and regular, (2) infrequent and regular, (3) frequent and irregular, and (4) infrequent and irregular.

Where consumers buy determines the selling approach a smart retailer uses. Some people buy products such as pots and pans, cosmetics, encyclopedias, and vacuum cleaners in their homes. Others purchase these same products in a retail store. Still others purchase these products at their places of work. This section describes where

**WHERE
CONSUMERS
BUY: BUYING
SCENES**

FIGURE 4–9

Purchase frequency and regularity matrix (source: based on discussion by Bud Wilson, *Principles of Merchandising: A Key to Profitable Marketing* [New York: Fairchild Publications, 1976], 64–65)

REGULARITY OF PURCHASE	FREQUENCY OF PURCHASE	
	Frequent	Infrequent

Regular	newspapers
	cigarettes
	milk
	meat
	other staple
	  foods
	household
	  products
		insurance payments
		magazine
		  subscriptions
		dental services
		tires
		regular automobiles
		pest control services

Irregular	gasoline
	over-the-counter
	  drugs
	snack foods
	"fast" foods
	panty hose
		luxury
		  automobiles
		jewelry
		furs
		medicine

consumers buy from two different perspectives—where consumers *actually* buy (buying scenes) and where consumers *think* they buy (patronage motives).

Buying Scenes

A **buying scene** is *the place where consumers complete a purchase transaction.* Consumers buy at one of four scenes: (1) retail stores, (2) their homes, (3) their places of work, and (4) afield (i.e., the point of consumption). Retailers can offer their merchandise at one, several, or all of these scenes, each having its own advantages and disadvantages.

The Retail Store

Due to custom or general preferences, U.S. consumers choose to make the majority of their purchases at the retail store. About 97 percent of all retail sales occur at this scene, indicating that customers see many advantages to buying at stores.

The main advantage that retail stores have is their wide selections of merchandise. Customers generally enter stores with their buying needs only partly specified. Inside the store, they hope to see and be reminded to buy. The merchandise and sales aids serve as a form of communication that helps consumers to crystallize their desires.

Stores also offer other advantages to customers. Because they can make several purchases at a single store, consumers shop at stores to save time and effort. The large "scrambled merchandising" stores that have developed over the last several years offer buyers satisfaction for practically every household need in a single shopping trip. For many people, shopping in stores is not just a way to obtain products and services, but a form of recreation.

Shopping at retail stores has its disadvantages. To get to a store, consumers must expend time, effort, and money. Once there, they must compete with other customers to get sales attention and to check out. Also, because many people think of buying as a private matter for some products, they are uncomfortable shopping in the presence of stores' salespeople and other shoppers.

The Consumer's Home

A growing volume of products is sold to consumers in their homes, either through direct house-to-house sales or catalog sales. Catalog sales are made through the mail, over the telephone, and through the catalog stores of large mail-order retailers such as Sears. The major advantage to mail, telephone, and catalog approaches is that consumers do not feel pressure from a salesperson to purchase the product. Further, the customer is more relaxed and has more time to make a leisurely decision. One disadvantage for consumers is their inability to see, feel, and try out the merchandise. (This disadvantage is partly overcome when retailers offer "free" trials and money-back guarantees.) Another disadvantage is the length of time between the customers' decision to purchase the product and the time they receive it.

The Consumer's Place of Work

This buying scene offers consumers both some of the advantages and some of the disadvantages of home retailing. The primary disadvantage is that a place of work is a place of production, not consumption. As a result, many businesses forbid retail solicitation on their premises. Nonetheless, some retailers achieve considerable success at this scene. Life insurance sales representatives, canteen operators, and charitable organizations are examples of retailers that operate at the consumer's place of work.

The Point of Consumption

Many consumers buy products and services for immediate consumption. Hot dogs and soft drinks at ball games, magazines at airports, and newspapers at restaurants are examples. Consumers normally buy these products incidental to other activities. For this reason, this form of retailing is often called "parasite" retailing. Retailers whose business depends upon other businesses or activities often pay a franchise fee for the right to sell at this buying scene. If an appropriate scene can be located, however, the fee is well worth the money.

An important buying scene is the point of consumption

Patronage Motives

Another aspect of where consumers buy is where they *think* they buy; that is, how they perceive the store they shop in and why they patronize it. Consumers shop and buy at certain stores for specific reasons—**patronage motives.** The major patronage motives are (1) store prices and values, (2) merchandise selection, (3) buying convenience, (4) store services, (5) merchandise quality, (6) buyer treatment, and (7) store reputation or status.[18]

Just as consumers view products as either convenience, shopping, or specialty goods, so do they view stores as convenience stores, shopping stores, and specialty stores. Consumers patronize convenience stores because they are easy to get to and easy to buy from. Consumers patronize shopping stores because of their wide selection of merchandise. And consumers shop at specialty stores when they insist upon buying particular merchandise.

Retailers must base their marketing policies on how their target markets or potential target markets perceive not only their merchandise but their stores. Figure 4–10 shows a matrix of nine possible combinations of product-patronage motives and the consumer's expected behavior for each combination. Retailers that analyze their markets according to this matrix can position themselves in market areas to which no appeal has yet been made.

131

FIGURE 4–10
The product-patronage matrix (source: adapted from Louis P. Bucklin, "Retail Strategy and the Classification of Consumer Goods," *Journal of Marketing* 27 [January 1963]: 53–54)

PRODUCT			
	Convenience Goods	Shopping Goods	Specialty Goods
Convenience Store	Consumer will accept any available brand of product at the most convenient store	Consumer shops among selection offered by most convenient store	Consumer buys preferred brand of product from the most convenient store that stocks it
Shopping Store	Consumer will accept any brand of product but compares stores for best prices/service combination	Consumer compares characteristics of both brands of products and price/service levels of stores	Consumer prefers certain brand of product, but compares price/service levels of stores
Specialty Store	Consumer will accept any brand available at a particular store	Consumer shops for best product and brand available at a preferred store	Consumer insists upon a specific brand at a particular store

(PATRONAGE — row label for the left column)

To illustrate, assume a businessman wants to open a men's clothing store. Upon investigation he determines that no men's store in the market area offers a complete selection of men's clothing together with a wide variety of styles and prices. That is, no store offers consumers the opportunity for complete one-stop shopping. If the retailer found that a substantial number of men wish to buy clothing in this manner, he could monopolize this market by adopting the specialty-store/shopping-goods profile. Thus, an understanding of this matrix can help retailers identify retail opportunities and increase the likelihood of successful operations.

SUMMARY

Retailers cannot merchandise or promote their products effectively unless they first understand why, what, how, when, and where consumers buy. In deciding which products and services to buy and which stores to patronize, consumers are affected by psychological, personal, and sociological influences.

Psychological influences that help explain why consumers buy include the processes of motivation, perception, learning, and attitude formation. Motivation is the process by which consumers are incited to satisfy their basic needs. Perception is the human process of forming mental pictures of objects, people, and places. Perception is selective; the selectivity of perception affects receiving (selective exposure), organizing (selective retention), and interpreting (selective distortion) of stimuli. Learning is the process of acquiring knowledge through past experiences or the acquisition of information. Much of consumers' buying behavior is learned behavior; if the consumer experiences a satisfactory buying experience, reinforcement occurs and learning takes place. Attitudes are evaluative mental orientations that provide a predisposition to respond in a certain manner. Most experts agree that a consumer's buying behavior is consistent with attitudes toward the retailer, the store, and the merchandise.

A consumer's self-concept, life-style, and life cycle all have important personal influences on an individual's buying behavior. Self-concept is the set of perceptions that people have of themselves within a social context. Consumers rarely, if ever, purchase products or patronize stores that are incompatible with their perception of themselves. The way consumers live—their life-style—has an important impact on what, when, how, and where they buy. The practical considerations of marriage, children, and work all have an impact on buying behavior. The family life cycle concept helps to explain the whys of buying behavior in terms of a series of stages of marital status and child raising through which people move in the course of their lives.

Cultures and subcultures, social classes and reference groups, and the individual's family are all important sociological influences on buying behavior. Of these social influencers, the family is thought to be the strongest influence.

Successful retailers must base their marketing efforts on their target market's buying patterns: they must look at what, how, when, and where consumers buy. In analyzing what consumers buy, they should consider product life expectancies (durable and nondurable products), product type (food, apparel, furniture, etc.), and the amount of shopping effort the consumer is willing to expend (convenience, shopping, and specialty goods).

How consumers buy depends upon how they perceive their problem-solving situation, the buying process they use, and the customer service level they expect. Three types of problem-solving situations exist: extensive, limited, and routinized. The consumer buying process consists of the following steps: (1) problem identification, (2) alternative identification, (3) information search, (4) information evaluation, (5) alternative selection, (6) purchase, and (7) postpurchase evaluation.

When consumers buy depends upon their buying rhythms. Buying rhythms are the times that consumers purchase together with the frequency and regularity with which they purchase. Successful retailers match the quantity of the merchandise they carry with the times consumers demand that merchandise.

Where consumers buy is a function of where they actually buy (buying scenes) and where they think they buy (patronage motives). Buying scenes include the retail store, the consumer's home, the consumer's place of work, and the point of consumption. Patronage motives are the reasons people shop at certain stores. They include store prices, convenience, services, merchandise quality, buyer treatment, and store reputation.

KEY TERMS AND CONCEPTS

consumer buying behavior	drives	sociological influences
psychological influences	perception	society
motivation	selective exposure	culture
stimulus	selective retention	subcultures
needs	selective distortion	social classes
physiological needs	learning	reference groups
safety needs	attitudes	the family
love needs	personal influences	durable goods
esteem needs	self-concept	nondurable goods
self-actualization needs	life-style	services
motives	life cycle	convenience goods

staples   specialty goods   purchase regularity

impulse goods   extensive problem-solving   purchase frequency

emergency goods   limited problem-solving   buying scene

shopping goods   routinized problem-solving   patronage motives

homogeneous shopping goods   buying rhythms

heterogeneous shopping goods   purchase times

REVIEW QUESTIONS

1. What is consumer buying behavior?
2. What are the major components of the consumer buying behavior process? Describe the relationship between influences and buyer behavior.
3. How does the consumer motivation process operate?
4. How are human needs classified? Identify and describe the five basic needs.
5. What is perception and how is it accomplished?
6. Describe the selectivity of perception in terms of how it affects the receiving, organizing, and interpreting of stimuli.
7. Explain how the consumer learning process works.
8. What is an attitude? How do consumers use attitudes in their buying behavior?
9. Who are we? Answer this question using the concept of self-concept.
10. What is life-style? How are consumer life-styles developed?
11. What factors determine which stage in the family life cycle a consumer occupies?
12. Identify and describe the nine stages of the family life cycle.
13. How does a consumer's culture affect buying behavior?
14. What is a social class? Briefly describe Warner's six social class categories.
15. How does the buying behavior of the upper-middle class differ from the buying behavior of the lower-middle class consumer?
16. What is a reference group? How might a reference group influence an individual's buying behavior?
17. What roles can a family member assume in the family buying process?
18. From the perspective of product life expectancy, what do consumers buy?
19. Briefly describe Engel's Laws of family expenditures.
20. Compare and contrast the three types of consumer products as defined by the degree of effort consumers are willing to exert in buying them.
21. What are the three types of consumer problem-solving situations? Describe each.
22. Describe the consumer problem-solving process.
23. Which factors should be considered in determining consumer buying rhythms?
24. Where do consumers buy?

ENDNOTES

1. Belinda Hulin-Sakin, "Value Heads Up the New Shopping List," *Advertising Age,* 25 July 1983, M33.
2. See Gerald Zaltman and Melanie Wallendorf, *Consumer Behavior,* 2d ed. (New York: John Wiley and Sons, 1983), 6.
3. See A. H. Maslow, *Motivation and Personality* (New York: Harper and Row, 1984).
4. M. Wayne Delozier, *The Marketing Communication Process* (New York: McGraw-Hill, 1976), 230.
5. See James F. Engel and Roger D. Blackwell, *Consumer Behavior,* 4th ed. (New York: The Dryden Press, 1982), 292–94.
6. Kenneth E. Runyon, *Consumer Behavior,* 2d ed. (Columbus: Charles E. Merrill Publishing Co., 1980), 191.
7. Engel and Blackwell, *Consumer Behavior,* 461–90.
8. Runyon, *Consumer Behavior,* 266–86.
9. Raymond L. Horton, *Buying Behavior* (Columbus: Charles E. Merrill Publishing Co., 1984), 319–23.
10. See William D. Wells and George Gubar, "Life Cycle

Concept in Marketing Research," *Journal of Market Research* 3 (November 1966): 362.

11. Leon G. Schiffman and Leslie L. Kanuk, *Consumer Behavior*, 2d ed. (Englewood Cliffs, NJ: Prentice-Hall, 1983), 388.

12. Runyon, *Consumer Behavior*, 96–98.

13. Suzanne McCall, "Meet the Workwife," *Journal of Marketing* 41 (July 1977): 55–65.

14. W. Lloyd Warner, *American Life, Dream and Reality* (Chicago: University of Chicago Press, 1953).

15. See E. Jerome McCarthy and William D. Perreault, Jr., *Basic Marketing*, 8th ed. (Homewood, IL: Richard D. Irwin, 1984), 291–95.

16. John A. Howard and Jagdish N. Sheth, *The Theory of Buying Behavior* (New York: John Wiley and Sons, 1969), 27–28.

17. McCarthy and Perreault, *Basic Marketing*, 214.

18. Louis P. Bucklin, "Retail Strategy and the Classification of Consumer Goods," *Journal of Marketing* 22 (January 1963): 53–54.

RELATED READINGS

Bartos, Rena. "Over 49: The Invisible Consumer Market." *Harvard Business Review* 58 (January - February 1980), 140–49.

Bellenger, Danny N., and Korgaonkar, Pradeep K. "Profiling the Recreational Shopper." *Journal of Retailing* 56 (Fall 1980), 77–92.

Bivins, Jacquelyn. "Adult Boom: The Aging of the Wundergeneration." *Chain Store Age Executive* (May 1985), 27–30.

Blackwell, Roger D., and Talarzyk, W. Wayne. "Lifestyle Retailing: Competitive Strategies for the 1980s." *Journal of Retailing* 59 (Winter 1983), 7–28.

Claxton, John D., and Ritchie, J. R. Brent. "Consumer Prepurchase Shopping Problems: A Focus on the Retailing Component." *Journal of Retailing* 55 (Fall 1979), 24–43.

Downs, Phillip E., and Haynes, Joel B. "Examining Retail Image before and after a Repositioning Strategy." *Journal of the Academy of Marketing Science* 12 (Fall 1984), 1–24.

Gutman, Jonathan, and Mills, Michael K. "Fashion Life-Style, Self-Concept, Shopping Orientation and Store Patronage." *Journal of Retailing* 58 (Summer 1982), 64–86.

Hirschman, Elizabeth C., and Wallendorf, Melanie R. "Characteristics of the Cultural Continuum: Implications for Retailing." *Journal of Retailing* 58 (Spring 1982), 5–21.

Hornik, Jacob, and Feldman, Laurence P. "Retailing Implications for the Do-It-Yourself Consumer Movement." *Journal of Retailing* 58 (Summer 1982), 44–63.

Jensen, Donald M., and Granzin, Kent L. "Consumer Logistics: The Transportation Subsystem." *Developments in Marketing Science, Proceedings.* N. K. Malhotra, ed. (Academy of Marketing Science 1985), 26–30.

Jensen, Thomas D., and Fields, Mike. "Store Image: When and Where Consumers Shop." *1984 Proceedings.* J. R. Lumpkin and J. C. Crawford, eds. (Southwestern Marketing Association 1984), 84–88.

Korgaonkar, Pradeep K. "Consumer Shopping Orientations, Non-Store Retailers, and Consumer's Patronage Intentions: A Multivariate Investigation." *Journal of the Academy of Marketing Science* 12 (Winter - Spring 1984), 11–22.

Lavin, Marilyn. "Husband-Wife Decision Making: A Theory-Based, Process Model." *1985 AMA Educators' Proceedings.* R. F. Lusch et al, eds. (American Marketing Association 1985), 21–25.

Lumpkin, James R., and Greenberg, Barnett A. "Apparel-Shopping Patterns of the Elderly Consumer." *Journal of Retailing* 58 (Winter 1982), 68–89.

Malhotra, Naresh K. "A Threshold Model of Store Choice." *Journal of Retailing* 59 (Summer 1983), 3–21.

McNeal, James U., and McKee, Daryl. "The Case of Anti-Shoppers." *1985 AMA Educators' Proceedings.* R. F. Lusch et al, eds. (American Marketing Association 1985), 65–68.

Onkuisit, Sak, and Shaw, John J. "Personality as a Predictor Variable: Problems and Implications." *Developments in Marketing Science, Proceedings.* J. C. Rogers, III, ed. (Academy of Marketing Science 1983), 104–9.

Oumlil, A. Ben, and Rao, C. P. "Income Effects on Consumer Store Choice Behavior under Changed Environmental Conditions." *1985 Proceedings.* J. C. Crawford and B. C. Garland, eds. (Southwestern Marketing Association 1985), 54–57.

Palmer, Art. "Retail Image Dimensions and Consumer Preferences." *Developments in Marketing Science, Proceedings.* N. K. Malhotra, ed. (Academy of Marketing Science 1985), 2–6.

Palmer, Art, and Gray, Tammy K. "Five Retail Image Attributes: An Empirical Analysis." *1984 Proceedings.* J. R. Lumpkin and J. C. Crawford, eds. (Southwestern Marketing Association 1984), 64–67.

Randall, E. James; Howard, Hubert, Jr.; and George, Jaymi. "Low Involvement and High Involvement Products: An Analysis of Where College Students Buy and Implications for Retailers." *Marketing: Theories and Concepts for an Era of Change, Proceedings.* J. Summey, R. Viswanathan, R. Taylor, and K. Glynn, eds. (Southern Marketing Association 1983), 76–79.

Shuptrine, F. Kelly. "Store-Switching Attributes for Department Stores, Discount Stores, and Supermarkets: An Exploratory Study." *Marketing: Theories and Concepts for an Era of Change, Proceedings.* J. Summey, R. Viswanathan, R. Taylor, and K. Glynn, eds. (Southern Marketing Association 1983), 144–47.

Sirgy, M. Joseph; Samli, A. Coskun; Bahn, Kenneth; and Varvoglis, T. G. "Self-Concept and Retailing Strategy." *Developments in Marketing Science, Proceedings.* N. K. Malhotra, ed. (Academy of Marketing Science 1985), 2–6.

Tatzel, Miriam. "Skill and Motivation in Clothes Shopping: Fashion-Conscious, Independent, and Apathetic Consumers." *Journal of Retailing* 58 (Winter 1982), 90–97.

Unger, Lynette S.; Stearns, James M.; and Lesser, Jack A. "Sources of Consumer Satisfaction with Retail Outlets: Issues and Evidence." *Developments in Marketing Science, Proceedings.* J. C. Rogers, III, ed. (Academy of Marketing Science 1983), 34–37.

Outline

THE LEGAL ENVIRONMENT

THE LEGAL ASPECTS OF RETAIL COMPETITION

Present Restraints on Trade
Probable Restraints on Trade
Unfair Trade Practices

THE LEGAL ASPECTS OF STORE OPERATIONS

Store Organization and the Law
Personnel Management and the Law
Store Facilities and the Law

THE LEGAL ASPECTS OF RETAIL MERCHANDISING

Product Legalities
Price Legalities
Promotion Legalities
Distribution Legalities

Objectives

- Respect the legal complexities under which the retailer must operate

- Understand the legal framework establishing the lawful limits within which retailing activities must be conducted

- Identify and discuss the legal aspects of retail competition

- Distinguish the legal aspects of retail store operations

- Describe the legal aspects of retail merchandising

5

The Regulatory Aspects of Retailing

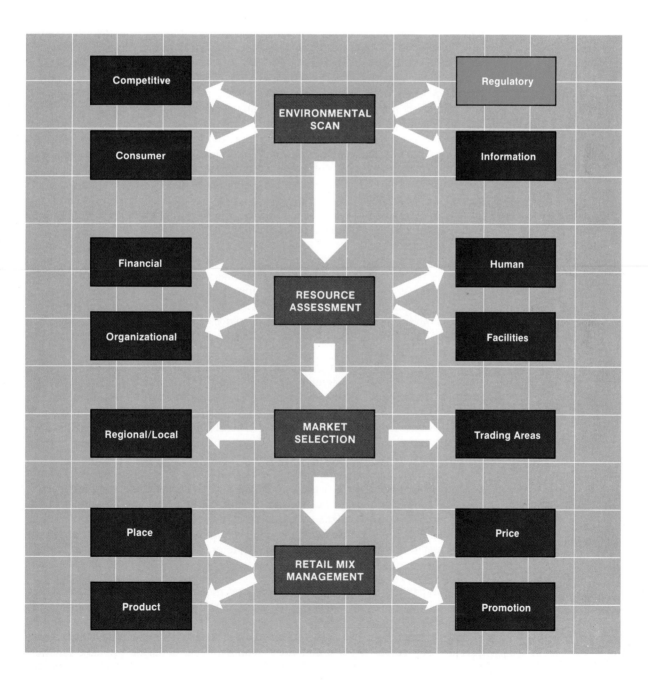

T he legal aspects of retailing are an integral part of store operations. Legal considerations affect almost all aspects of the retailer's daily operations. To the retailer, these legal constraints are largely uncontrollable, at least in the short run. Equally noteworthy is the fact that the law constantly changes as a result of the political activities (lobbying, lawsuits, referenda, and negotiations) of a large number of concerned interest groups. To operate successfully *and* legally, the retailer must both understand and appreciate the legal environment.

THE LEGAL ENVIRONMENT

The legal environment is the framework that establishes the lawful limits within which retailing and other business activities must be conducted. It is the attempt by various governmental bodies to modify or control the retailer's behavior and activities through various statutory measures and regulatory instruments. The legal environment and the need for a legal framework are the result of the ever-increasing complexity of the business and social climate. This complexity is the natural outgrowth of the numerous and diverse relationships (with customers, suppliers, and competitors) that retailers must establish and maintain.

Conflicts are bound to emerge from increased economic and social interdependence. Sources of conflict include disputes over competitive business practices; priorities regarding the use of scarce human, raw-material, and financial resources; controls on environmental pollution and energy consumption; and rights and responsibilities of various members within a channel of distribution. Regardless of the sources of conflict, some "rules of conduct" must be established to settle conflicting issues and to guide future behavior. Creation and continual modification of the legal environment are ways to referee these conflicts.

The legal environment is often viewed as restrictive and prohibitive of business activities. In many respects the legal environment *is* restrictive. In some cases, it restricts how the retailer can conduct business, and in other cases, it prohibits certain business practices. The legal environment is also protective, however. It protects the retailer, the employee, the stockholder, the community, and the retailer's suppliers and competitors from unfair dealings. In total, the legal environment should be viewed in terms of how well it balances the needs of the retailer with the needs of the public at large.

The legal environment is defined by the actions of the legislative, executive, and judicial branches of federal, state, and local governments. As illustrated in Figure 5–1, the principal legal measures and regulatory instruments used in defining the environment are statutes, ordinances, administrative regulations, contracts, certificates, licenses, taxes, and emergency controls. In addition, governments have other means of influencing the general legal environment. Subsidies and government ownership are two examples.

In retailing, the legal environment has a direct bearing on the two basic components of any enterprise—store operations and store merchandising activities. It also directly affects the type and degree of retail competition. The remainder of this chapter examines the retailer's concerns with the legal aspects of retail competition, store operations, and retail merchandising. Figure 5–2 (page 142) summarizes the major legal issues to be addressed in this chapter.

THE LEGAL ASPECTS OF RETAIL COMPETITION

Retail competition *involves the actions of one retailer against other retailers in securing resources and the patronage of consumers.* Such competitive actions include both the actual operation of the store and retailers' merchandising strategies and tactics. Governments make laws to ensure that these competitive actions are conducted under equitable rules and circumstances. What is fair or equitable naturally is open to interpretation; generally the court system and various governmental reg-

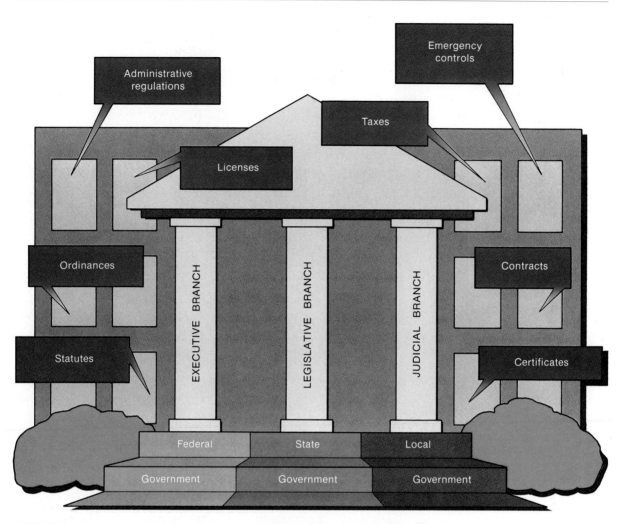

FIGURE 5–1
The legal environment

ulatory agencies make such interpretations. One effort to create and maintain a competitive business environment has taken the form of antitrust legislation.

Antitrust legislation is *a set of laws directed at preventing unreasonable "restraints on trade" and "unfair trade practices" in order to foster a competitive environment.* According to "what" exactly it is preventing and "when" it seeks to prevent it, government's antitrust legislation aims to protect consumers and business from (1) present restraints on trade, (2) probable restraints on trade, and (3) unfair trade practices.[1] Figure 5–3 identifies the principal legislative measures (laws) associated with each classification.

Present Restraints on Trade

The federal government, in an attempt to control big business' control or restraint of free trade, passed the **Sherman Antitrust Act** in 1890. The existence of cartels, pools, and trade associations during the post-Civil War years led to fear that big business might control prices and supplies of products in the marketplace. In passing the Sherman Antitrust Act, the federal government restricted the size and eco-

FIGURE 5–2
The retailer and the law

RETAILER'S LEGAL CONCERNS

RETAIL COMPETITION

Present restraints on trade

Probable restraints on trade

Unfair trade practices

STORE OPERATIONS

Store Organization
  legal forms
  vertical integration

Personnel Management
  job discrimination
  working conditions

Store Facilities
  zoning ordinances
  building codes
  licensing
  operating

RETAIL MERCHANDISING

Product Legalities
  product guarantees
  product warranties
  product liability

Price Legalities
  price discrimination
  price maintenance

Promotion Legalities
  price advertising
  product advertising
  sales practices

Distribution Legalities
  exclusive dealings
  leasing arrangements
  typing contracts
  exclusive territories

FIGURE 5–3
Principal federal anti-trust legislation (source: adapted from Larry J. Rosenberg, *Marketing* [Englewood Cliffs, NJ: Prentice-Hall, 1977], 59)

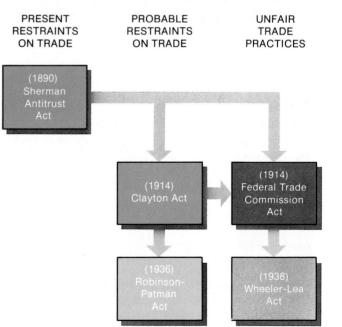

PRESENT RESTRAINTS ON TRADE

PROBABLE RESTRAINTS ON TRADE

UNFAIR TRADE PRACTICES

(1890) Sherman Antitrust Act

(1914) Clayton Act

(1914) Federal Trade Commission Act

(1936) Robinson-Patman Act

(1938) Wheeler-Lea Act

nomic power of any given organization, with the purpose of correcting existing—and preventing future—unreasonable restraints on trade. Sections 1 and 2, the key provisions of the act, state that every contract, combination, or conspiracy in restraint of trade is illegal, and that all monopolies or attempts to monopolize are also illegal. However, because of the vague language of the Sherman Antitrust Act, the Supreme Court ruled that the company's act must constitute an *unreasonable* restraint of trade to be unlawful. This court's ruling has become known as the "rule of reason," making the Sherman Antitrust Act ineffective since each case had to be tried against the rule of reason. Later legislation filled the gaps in the Sherman Act.

Probable Restraints on Trade

To overcome the shortcomings of the Sherman Antitrust Act, several pieces of federal legislation were passed to curtail competitive actions that *might* lead to restraints on trade if allowed to continue. In essence, these legislative amendments were enacted to prevent rather than correct restraints of trade. The first of these legislative amendments was the Clayton Act passed by Congress in 1914. The **Clayton Act** *dealt with several specific anticompetitive actions such as price discrimination, tying contracts, exclusive dealings, and interlocking boards of directors* (each of these actions will be discussed later in the chapter). It declared such actions illegal where the effect may be to "substantially lessen competition" or "tend to create a monopoly." With passage of the Clayton Act, the government no longer had to prove that either a restraint of trade or a monopoly existed. Instead, it was sufficient to show that a *probable* restraint of trade or monopoly *might* result if certain competitive actions were allowed to continue.

The **Robinson-Patman Act** of 1936 *amended the Clayton Act by broadening the scope and clarifying the meaning of unlawful competition.* Under the Robinson-Patman Act, unlawful competition included any competitive action that would tend "to injure, destroy, or prevent competition." Subsequent interpretation extended the intent of the law: ". . . although the law was supposedly concerned with avoiding injury to 'competition,' it was often interpreted by the FTC (Federal Trade Commission) and the courts to mean prohibiting injury to 'competitors,' especially small retailers."[2] The major thrust of the Robinson-Patman Act was directed at various means of price discrimination.

Unfair Trade Practices

In 1914, Congress passed the **Federal Trade Commission Act**, *prohibiting unfair trade practices that could be injurious to either competition or competitors.* To determine what constitutes fair and unfair trade practices, the FTC was established as a quasi-judicial agency having limited judicial powers. In 1938, Congress amended the 1914 act by passing the **Wheeler-Lea Act**, *banning unfair and deceptive business acts or practices.* The significance of this amendment is that it outlaws unfair and deceptive activities regardless of their effects on competition or competitors. Armed with this amendment, the FTC has become, for most retailers, the single most important regulatory agency. The rules and regulations the FTC administers affect primarily deceptive advertising and sales practices.

The procedures the FTC uses to enforce these rules and regulations include (1) individual-firm or industry-wide conferences to secure voluntary compliance, (2) consent orders whereby the firm or industry agrees to abandon an unfair trade practice, and (3) formal court action to force the firm or industry to comply with FTC decisions.[3] The first two procedures have been so successful in preventing and correcting unfair or deceptive trade practices that reliance on formal legal action has been significantly reduced.

Government regulations and controls extend to all aspects of the physical operations of the store. In "running" the store, the retailer must follow laws pertaining to its organizational structure, store personnel, physical facilities, and other aspects of the operation.

Store Organization and the Law

In establishing, expanding, contracting, and discontinuing a retail business, the law imposes certain restrictions and controls. The influence of the law plays an especially important role in store organization.

Legal Forms of Retail Organization

Three basic forms of business organization are recognized by law: the sole proprietorship, the partnership, and the corporation. The **sole proprietorship** is a *business owned and managed by a single individual.* Having its origins in common law, the sole proprietorship is the simplest legal form of organization. The principal legal advantages of this form of organization are that it has

1. no formal legal requirement—except for a business license—so the retailer does not have to obtain authorization from state or federal governments to form the business
2. greater flexibility in operations—the retailer is not expected to meet the maze of state regulations imposed on corporations
3. single taxation—all profits taxed at once as personal income

Unlimited liability is the major legal limitation of a sole proprietorship. Unlimited liability means that the sole proprietor assumes total responsibility for all debts stemming from the business and that that responsibility extends to current and future *personal as well as business assets.* In other words, not only is the proprietor's business in jeopardy should the business fail in some way, personal assets can also be seized to cover bad debts. Some sole proprietors attempt to protect their personal assets by placing them in their spouses' names.

When two or more persons form a business without incorporating, the business is a **partnership.** Partnerships can consist of any number of partners whose share and control of the business is determined at the time the organization is formed. In a **general partnership,** *all partners take part in the control and operation of the partnership;* hence, all partners can be held jointly and severally liable for the debts of the partnership. The unlimited liability of all general partners represents substantial personal risk, since each partner is legally liable for the actions of all other partners. When one partner makes a business commitment, it is legally binding on all of the other partners. Hence, not only are commonly owned business assets subject to legal judgments, but also each of the other partners' personal assets can be used to pay off the business liabilities of another partner.

An alternative partnership arrangement is the **limited partnership.** *This is a legal form of organization wherein one or more members of the partnership contribute captial to the formation and running of the partnership, but limited partners do not take part in managing the firm's retail operations.* The main advantage of the limited partnership is that the personal assets of limited partners may not be reached by creditors to the partnership. In exchange for this limited liability, the limited partner foregoes control over the running of the partnership.

A **corporation** is *a legal business entity authorized by state law to operate as a single person even though it may consist of many persons. Limited liability* is the principal legal advantage of this type of organization. The liability of any given owner (shareholder) is limited to equity money, or the amount of stock owned. The nonlegal advantages of being able to raise investment capital and to engage in a greater degree of operational and managerial specialization are equally important incentives that lead many retailers to utilize a corporate form of organization. Corporations, however, are subject to a greater number of legal controls (e.g., public financial accountability, public stockholders' meetings, certificates of incorporation) and possibly double taxation (the corporation pays a corporate income tax and stockholders pay personal income tax on any dividends they receive). In some cases, smaller retail corporations can overcome the latter disadvantage by simply setting the owners' salaries so that no corporate profit exists. In this situation, the owners must work for the corporation and no nonworking owners can expect dividends.

In choosing the legal form of organization, the retailer should consider both the legal and nonlegal advantages and disadvantages of each form. Additional factors influencing the choice are (1) the size of the organization, (2) the number and nature of the people involved, (3) the expected growth rate of the firm, (4) the need for operating flexibility, and (5) the need for capital investment.

Limitations on Vertical Integration

The law places certain limitations on any retailer's attempts to integrate vertically. **Vertical integration** is *the merger of two organizations from different levels within a channel of distribution.* Examples of vertical integration are the merger of a retailer and a wholesaler or a retailer and a producer. **Mergers** occur when *one firm acquires the stocks or assets of another firm.* Mergers are regulated by Section 7 of the Clayton Act (1914) as amended by the Celler-Kefauver Act (1950). These acts prohibit any company from acquiring the stocks or assets of other firms in any line of commerce in any part of the country if the effect is to substantially reduce competition or tend to create a monopoly. The federal government views mergers as monopolistic when they tend to either close out other retailers from a source of supply or close out other suppliers from a market area. For example, the "merger of the Brown Shoe Company and the G. R. Kinney Company, the largest independent chain of shoe stores, was declared illegal by the Supreme Court because it was believed that the merger would foreclose other manufacturers from selling through Kinney."[4]

Although the legality of vertical integration is more likely to affect the organizational arrangements of large chain retailers, small- and medium-size retailers also can be affected when the courts choose to define "market areas" in very narrow terms. Even the merger activities of a small retailer can substantially reduce competition if the market area is small enough.

Personnel Management and the Law

The law protects the retail employee in a variety of ways. Because of this, a store's personnel manager must be acquainted with the legal environment surrounding job discrimination, working conditions, and various compensation requirements.

Job Discrimination

Equal employment opportunity is a civil right. The **Civil Rights Act** of 1964 makes job discrimination illegal if it is based on the applicant's or employee's sex, race, color, creed, age, or national origin. Essentially, the intent of the Civil Rights Act is to eliminate both intentional and inadvertent discriminatory employment practices. It charges the Equal Employment Opportunity Commission (EEOC) with administering the act, and it charges each employer with the implicit obligation to discover discriminatory pratices and to eliminate them.

The two most prevalent forms of employment discrimination are personal and systematic. *Personal discrimination* occurs when the personal biases of an individual in authority enter the decision-making process in employment matters to the detriment of applicants or employees. *Systematic discrimination* is the unintentional and inadvertent discrimination resulting from policies, practices, and decision-making criteria that negatively affect protected classes. In all areas of staffing (job description and specification, recruitment and selection, training and supervision, evaluation and compensation), the retailer must take every precaution to ensure compliance with the intent of the law.

To eliminate discriminatory employment criteria and measurements (age, sex, race, etc.), the retailer should follow two basic guidelines to help ensure compliance with the law: consistency and supportability. Consistency means treating all employees and job applicants in a uniformly fair and equitable manner. Any deviation from this policy could be grounds for a job discrimination suit against the employer. Also, all actions taken by the retailer for or against an employee should be carefully *documented and supported* on the basis of legally defensible economic and/or social terms. If an employer can show due cause through documentation for firing an employee, promoting an employee, or creating a new position for an employee, then the employer probably has reasonably safe ground for actions and employees are likely to be protected from bias and job discrimination. Compiling the proper statistics using reliable and valid personnel tests helps protect the retailer from unwanted lawsuits and employees from unfair treatment.

Figure 5–4 illustrates the complexity of the equal employment opportunity issue. The legalities of preemployment questions alone clearly indicate that the retailer must proceed with great caution to ensure full compliance with the various laws, administration rulings, and judicial interpretations of the laws concerning equal employment opportunity.

FIGURE 5–4
Legal and illegal preemployment questions

Here is a series of questions that the New York State Division of Human Rights has compiled as being lawful and unlawful preemployment inquiries. As New York appears to be stricter than most states and the federal government, by following these recommendations, lawyers suggest that a company may be less likely to find itself in difficulty with the authorities because of preemployment inquiries.

Subject	Lawful*	Unlawful
Race or Color:		Inquiry into complexion or color of skin Coloring
Religion or Creed:		Inquiry into applicant's religious denomination, religious affiliations, church parish, pastor, or religious holidays observed
		Applicant may not be told "This is a (Catholic, Protestant, or Jewish) organization"

(continued)

Subject	Lawful*	Unlawful
National Origin:		Inquiry into applicant's lineage, ancestry, national origin, descent, parentage, or nationality Nationality of applicant's parents or spouse What is your mother tongue?
Sex:		Inquiry as to sex Do you wish to be addressed as Mr.? Mrs.? Miss? or Ms.?
Marital Status:		Are you married? Are you single? Divorced? Separated? Name or other information about spouse Where does your spouse work? What are the ages of your children, if any?
Birth Control:		Inquiry as to capacity to reproduce, advocacy of any form of birth control or family planning
Age:	Are you between 18 and 70 years of age? If not, state your age.	How old are you? What is your date of birth?
Disability:	Do you have any impairments, physical, mental, or medical, that would interfere with your ability to perform the job for which you have applied? If there are any positions or types of positions for which you should not be considered, or job duties you cannot perform because of physical, mental, or medical disability, please describe.	Do you have a disability? Have you ever been treated for any of the following diseases . . . ?
Arrest Record:	Have you ever been convicted of a crime? Give details	Have you ever been arrested?
Name:	Have you ever worked for this company under a different name? Is any additional information relative to change of name, use of an assumed name, or nickname necessary to enable a check on your work record? If yes, explain.	Original name of an applicant whose name has been changed by court order or otherwise Maiden name of a married woman If you have ever worked under another name, state name and dates.
Address or Duration of Residence:	Applicant's place of residence How long a resident of this state or city?	
Birthplace:		Birthplace of applicant Birthplace of applicant's parents, spouse, or other close relatives

(continued)

147

Subject	Lawful*	Unlawful
Birthdate:		Requirement that applicant submit birth certificate, naturalization, or baptismal record Requirement that applicant produce proof of age in the form of a birth certificate or baptismal record
Photograph:		Requirement or option that applicant affix a photograph to employment form at any time before hiring
Citizenship:	Are you a citizen of the United States? If not a citizen of the United States, do you intend to become a citizen of the United States? If you are not a United States citizen, have you the legal right to remain permanently in the United States? Do you intend to remain permanently in the United States?	Of what country are you a citizen? Whether an applicant is naturalized or a native-born citizen; the date when the applicant acquired citizenship Requirement that applicant produce naturalization papers or first papers Whether applicant's spouse or parents are naturalized or native-born citizens of the United States; the date when such parents or spouse acquired citizenship
Language:	Inquiry into languages applicant speaks and writes fluently	What is your native language? Inquiry into how applicant acquired ability to read, write, or speak a foreign language
Education:	Inquiry into applicant's academic, vocational, or professional education and the public and private schools attended	
Experience:	Inquiry into work experience	
Relatives:	Name of applicant's relatives, other than a spouse, already employed by this company	Names, addresses, ages, numbers, or other information concerning applicant's spouse, children, or other relatives not employed by the company
Notice in Case of Emergency:		Name and address of person to be notified in case of accident or emergency
Military Experience:	Inquiry into applicant's military experience in the Armed Forces of the United States or in a State Militia Inquiry into applicant's service in United States Army, Navy, etc.	Inquiry into applicant's general military experience
Organizations:	Inquiry into applicant's membership in organizations the applicant considers relevant to his or her ability to perform the job	List all clubs, societies, and lodges to which you belong.
Driver's License:	Do you possess a valid driver's license?	Requirement that applicant produce a driver's license prior to employment

Source: The New York State Division of Human Rights, January 1982.

Working Conditions and Compensation

Numerous legal requirements govern the conditions under which retail employees work. Of importance to the retailer are wage and hour requirements, restrictions on the use of child labor, provisions regarding equal pay, workers' compensation, and unemployment benefits.

The **Fair Labor Standards Act** (FLSA) of 1938 *sets the legal requirements for minimum wages and maximum working hours.* It also governs the use of child labor and contains an equal-pay provision. Initially, the act did not affect retail businesses; however, later amendments (1966) established a minimum hourly wage for all retail organizations with annual sales of $250,000 and above. The FLSA also established a 40-hour work week. Employees working in excess of this maximum are entitled to overtime benefits (extra compensation). While more retailers are increasingly feeling the impact of the FLSA, there are several exceptions. For example, executive, administrative, and professional employees, family-owned and -operated retail stores, and in some cases the employees of certain types of retailing establishments (restaurants, motion picture theaters, auto dealerships, among others) can be exempt from the provisions of the FLSA. Retailers can apply for and receive a certificate from the Department of Labor that allows them to pay full-time students 85 percent of the hourly minimum wage.

The use of child labor is also restricted by the FLSA. The law determines at what age minors can work, at what type of job (hazardous versus nonhazardous occupations), and when they can work (hours, days, etc.). Also, the FLSA equal-pay provision prohibits wage differentials for doing work requiring equal skill, effort, and responsibility. Legal wage differentials are justified on the basis of training, education, and experience. However, even these justifications are now being questioned when a company cannot prove that these factors have direct bearing on job performance.

The **Williams-Steiger Occupational Safety and Health Act** of 1970 *established the Occupational Safety and Health Administration (OSHA).* This agency is charged with enforcing the provisions of the act—to have each employer "furnish . . . a place of employment which is free from recognized hazards that cause or are likely to cause death or serious physical harm to employees." Compliance officers from OSHA make unannounced workplace inspections to ensure compliance. Any citations issued after an inspection identify the nature of the alleged violations and the time set for abatement. In addition to requiring corrective actions, OSHA may issue monetary penalties depending on the seriousness of the violation. Employee deaths, accidents, and complaints are three of the more prominent reasons for a compliance officer to visit a store.

Workers' compensation is *an employee accident and disability insurance program required under various state laws.* It covers the employee who is accidentally injured while working or who is unable to work as a result of a disease associated with a particular occupation. While these programs vary between states, they generally provide for medical expenses and basic subsistence during the disabling period. Both public (state operated) and private (insurance company) programs are available to companies and employees in most states. The insurance premiums that retailers pay for these programs represent a substantial operating expense, so they must be planned for and managed with considerable care.

Unemployment compensation is *a tax levied by the state on each retailer's payroll.* The state uses the revenue to create an unemployment fund for the retailer. Qualified former employees of the retailer can draw unemployment benefits from the fund, the amount and duration of which are prescribed by state law. Employees who are either laid off or fired usually qualify for benefits; employees who simply quit usually do not qualify. Unemployment tax usually ranges from 3 to 5 percent of the retailer's payroll, but under some circumstances it can be less if the employer has a low rate of firings and layoffs.

Store Facilities and the Law

A number of local regulations have direct bearing on the retailer's facilities. Zoning ordinances, building codes, licensing requirements, and operating requirements are the most common forms of local controls on the retailer's facilities and operations.

Zoning Ordinances

Zoning ordinances are controls that local governments place on land use by regulating the type of activities and buildings located in certain areas. Land is zoned according to residential, commercial, and industrial uses. By controlling the use of land, local governments offer the retailer (1) protection against undesirable neighbors by ensuring that land users are properly situated in relation to one another, (2) assurance that an orderly growth of business will occur in only those areas zoned for business activities, and (3) certainty that adequate government services, such as trash removal, street maintenance, and police protection, will be available to businesses.

Sometimes, however, ordinances can unduly restrict new business development. In an attempt to limit competition and to gain or preserve a competitive advantage, some local governments pass anti-new-business zoning ordinances, protecting already established, and sometimes influential, local businesses. At times, small, independent local retailers can restrict some of the activities of large, national chain store operations.

Building Codes

Local governments enact numerous regulations affecting the design and construction of retail facilities. Design regulations include local authority over the (1) size of the building relative to the size of the site; (2) height of the building; (3) number of entrances and exits; (4) architectural style of building (some communities, such as Sante Fe, New Mexico, require businesses to conform to a particular style); and (5) safety features of buildings, such as plumbing, electricity, and fire protection.

Construction regulations control both the methods and the materials used in construction. Public safety and convenience, such as access for the handicapped, are two major guidelines local governments use in developing construction regulations. Associated with building codes are inspection requirements that retailers must meet before they can open the facility to the public.

Licensing Requirements

Retailers usually must meet two types of local licensing requirements before they can begin operations. Many local communities require retailers to obtain a **general business license** before they can operate a business. In most cases, it is nothing more than a registration fee to operate a business. A major purpose of the general business license is to generate a source of revenue for a community. A **special business license** applies to either the sale of certain types of products (e.g., guns, prepared foods, drugs, gasoline) or the operation of a particular type of retail organization (e.g., vending machines, door-to-door selling, telephone selling, various types of personal services). Depending upon the community, some retailers might have to procure several special licenses as well as a general business license.

Operating Requirements

Many of the retailer's day-to-day operations also are controlled by state and local regulations. In some states and communities, a host of **"blue laws"** regulate everything from operating hours (such as "sundown laws" that prohibit the sale of liquor after sundown) and days (Sunday closing laws that limit the types of goods consumers can purchase on Sunday) to operating locations (prohibiting the sale of certain products such as liquor and beer within a prescribed distance of a church, school, or some other community facility). Retailers should learn which blue laws affect their business, the legal and social implications of such laws on the business, and where and when they can operate successfully and legally. In addition, local ordinances regulate trash pickup, snow removal, sign placement, the number and width of entrances and exits (curb cuts), customers' minimum age (e.g., for liquor), and many others.

Legal requirements govern all aspects of the retailer's merchandising efforts. Strategies in pricing, promoting, and distributing products must fall within certain legal limits.

THE LEGAL ASPECTS OF RETAIL MERCHANDISING

Product Legalities

As a reseller of products, the retailer assumes three major responsibilities in the areas of product guarantees, product warranties, and product liability. Because of these responsibilities, retailers incur additional operating expenses; however, sales volume can offset these expenses and help a retailer establish a reliable and dependable reputation.

Product Guarantees

Product guarantees are *policy statements by retailers expressing their general responsibility for the products they sell.* Some retailers offer very broad guarantees, such as "complete satisfaction or your money back." Other retailers limit their guarantee statements to certain aspects of the product (e.g., six months from date of purchase). The retailer is legally responsible to fulfill the general intent of any guarantee made.

Product Warranties

A **warranty** is *a specific statement by the seller of the quality or performance capabilities of the product and the exact terms under which the seller will take action to correct product deficiencies.* There are two basic types of warranties—expressed and implied. **Expressed warranties** are *written and oral statements that the seller makes to consumers about a product and performance and that the retailer is legally obligated to honor.* While written statements of fact are expressed in fairly specific terms and subject to precise interpretation, oral statements of fact and promises are more difficult to interpret. A fine line distinguishes oral promises from mere sales talk. Often the distinction is made on the basis of whether the statements made during a sale are an expression of opinion or of fact. Courts have recognized the difference between "puffing" and promise. To avoid being charged with engaging in unfair competitive acts, the retailer must be careful that its sales "puffery" is not construed as a legally binding promise of product performance. The same care must be applied to all of the retailer's advertisements.

Implied warranties are *the seller's implied or "intended" promises of product performance, even though they were not actually expressed in either written or oral form.* Under the Uniform Commercial Code, every sale is subject to a warranty of merchantability and a warranty of title.[5] The "warranty of merchantability" implies that all merchandise that retailers offer for sale is fit for the purpose for which it was sold.[6] A clothes dryer that scorches clothes is not fit for its intended purpose, for example. The "warranty of title" implies that the seller has offered the buyer a free and clear title to the product. Consumers have the right to assume that they own the product and have full use of it without fear of repossession. That assumption is not valid, however, when the consumer elects to purchase an item from a questionable source (e.g., a car from "Midnight Auto Sales.")

The most significant piece of federal legislation concerning warranties in recent years is the Magnuson-Moss Warranty Act of 1975. This act greatly strengthens consumers' rights by substantially increasing the responsibilities of retailers and other sellers of products under warranty.[7] Of importance to retailers are the first three regulations the FTC issued under this act. They require retailers to (1) provide consumers with warranty information before they buy the product, (2) disclose terms of the product warranty in "simple and readily understood language," and (3) establish and maintain procedures for handling customer complaints.[8]

Product Liability

The retailer, as well as the manufacturer, can be held liable for an unsafe product. The retailer's **product liability** can result from either failing to inform the customer of the dangers associated with using the product; misrepresenting the product as to how, when, and where it should be used; or selling a product that results in injury due to its failure to meet warranty standards. Much confusion exists over the exact nature of the retailer's product liability. The retailer's best protection is to provide the consumer with adequate product safety information, to correctly represent the product, and to obtain adequate liability insurance.

Price Legalities

The most regulated aspect of a retailer's merchandising program is pricing. Government regulations influence prices that the retailer pays the supplier, prices the retailer charges customers, the conditions under which prices are set or adjusted, and the impact of the retailer's prices on the competitive structure of the marketplace.

Price Discrimination

In a very broad sense, **price discrimination** covers a number of situations involving pricing arrangements under various buying and selling circumstances. The law recognizes both illegal and legal price discrimination. Illegal pricing *potentially* exists when *different prices* are offered or received under *similar circumstances,* or when *similar prices* are offered or received under *different circumstances.* Price discrimination can be legally justified when *different prices* are offered or received under *different circumstances.* Obviously, the degree of the price differential, the exact nature of the circumstances, and their effects on all parties involved determine the precise legalities of the situation. Retailers become involved with price discrimination in a number of ways. As illustrated in Figure 5–5, the retailer can be both a victim and a perpetrator of price discrimination as a result of both buying activities with

FIGURE 5–5
The retailer's involve-
ment with price dis-
crimination

PRICE DISCRIMINATION AGAINST	THE RETAILER'S ROLE IN PRICE DISCRIMINATION	
	Victim	Perpetrator
Buying Activities Supplier Interactions	product discrimination quantity discrimination allowance discrimination service discrimination	coercive buying dummy brokerage
Selling Activities Customer Interactions		predatory pricing price fixing

suppliers and selling activities with consumers. Each of these circumstances will be examined individually.

When a supplier treats one retailer unequally or differently from the way it treats other retailers, the one retailer becomes a potential victim of price discrimination. As defined by Section 2 of the Robinson-Patman Act, unequal treatment or price discrimination is illegal when its effect "may be to substantially lessen competition or tend to create a monopoly . . . or to injure, destroy, or prevent competition." Price discrimination against retailers can result when a supplier treats one retailer differently from others with respect to product characteristics, quantity discounts, special allowances, and special services.

Product characteristics. It is unlawful for any business to discriminate directly or indirectly in price among different purchasers of commodities of like grade and quality. *Competing retailers are entitled to pay the same price for the same type of merchandise.* While the meaning of "like grade and quality" is ambiguous, courts have generally interpreted the phrase to mean that there must be clearly distinguishable differences in either materials or workmanship. Courts have generally found products with minor differences in materials and workmanship to be of "like grade and quality." Thus, where minor differences exist, sellers run the risk of price discrimination if they sell to different buyers at different prices under similar circumstances.

Quantity discounts. The general principle is that *all competing retailers are entitled to pay the same price for the same quantity of "like" merchandise.* Suppliers often try to encourage volume buying by offering their customers (retailers) discount prices for large-quantity orders. However, even this form of seller inducement is illegal unless the seller can show that the lower prices for volume buyers result from a cost savings from producing and selling the larger quantity.

Sellers offer quantity discounts in two ways—cumulative and noncumulative. *Cumulative* quantity discounts apply to customers' purchases over an extended time. For example, if a buyer purchases a certain quantity of merchandise over a 12-month period, the seller will give the buyer a discount on any additional purchases. *Noncumulative* quantity discounts apply only to a single large-volume purchase. Recent court rulings have clarified the legalities of noncumulative and cumulative discounts. Because cumulative discounts do not represent cost savings equal to those of noncumulative discounts, the courts ruled that cumulative dis-

153

counts cannot be as large. The Federal Trade Commission also can place quantity discount limits on certain commodities "if it can be determined that only a few very large buyers (retailers) can qualify for the largest discount category in a seller's pricing schedule."[9]

Special allowances. The Robinson-Patman Act makes it unlawful for a seller to grant payment of any special allowances for any services that a retailer might provide to attempt to sell, advertise, or distribute a product, unless those allowance payments are also made available to all competing retailers on proportionately equal terms. Therefore, *all competing retailers are entitled to the same opportunities to receive the same allowance payments for providing the same special services.* Of special interest to the retailer is the "push money" that various suppliers provide. Push money is money that suppliers pay the retailer's sales personnel for making a special selling effort on their brands. Push money is legal if the same incentives are available to all competing retailers, if the retailer gives its consent, and if it does not reduce competition or severely affect competitive products.

Special services. It is unlawful for a supplier to provide retailers with services and facilities that aid them in selling merchandise unless those same favors are made available to all competing retailers on proportionately equal terms. Thus, *all competing retailers are entitled to receive the same support in services and facilities to sell the same goods.* Regulatory agencies have permitted the use of substitute services or facilities. When the original service or facility offer is impractical for competing retailers, regulatory agencies have allowed sellers to substitute different, but equal, services or facilities more suitable to their operations.

Price-discrimination defenses. Although each of the seller activities discussed could lead to price-discrimination suits, the Robinson-Patman Act contains provisions for a legal defense for price differentials. Cost justification and good faith are two of the common defenses.

The *cost-justification defense* makes it lawful to charge retailers different prices if the supplier can justify those price differences on the basis of its cost of doing business with each competing retailer. If it costs a supplier more to do business with one retailer than another, then the supplier can legally charge that retailer a higher price. The courts have placed the burden of proof on the seller, however, and have been quite particular about which costs (e.g., overhead) the seller can include in estimates and how cost calculations can be made.

The *good-faith defense* makes it lawful for a seller to discriminate in price if such action is done in good faith to meet an equally low price of a competitor. The essential factor in using the good-faith defense is whether the discriminatory price was necessary to meet competition rather than an offensive move to beat competition. Defensive price discrimination is legal; offensive price discrimination is illegal.

Price discrimination may be legal under several additional circumstances. For example, price differences may be allowed "when a product is sold for different uses, when separate markets are involved, when sales of the product(s) take place at different times, and when sales are made to government agencies."[10]

The retailer assumes the role of a perpetrator of illegal price discrimination when it uses coercive buying techniques or deceptive brokerage practices to obtain a lower price than that available to competing retailers. **Coercive buying** is *the retailer's use of financial, distribution, marketing, and other powers to gain lower prices from sellers.* Since some retailing organizations are larger than their suppliers, they are in a position to force favorable but unfair price treatment. However, under Section 2(f) of the Robinson-Patman Act, it is unlawful for a retailer to knowingly receive or induce a discriminatory price or special allowance and service. Thus, a "giant" retailer making a supplier sell merchandise at unfairly low prices is breaking a law and could cause legal action to be taken against the retailer.

Deceptive brokerage activities involve *the establishment and use of "dummy" brokerage firms to secure a brokerage allowance from suppliers, giving retailers an unfair purchase-price advantage.* A dummy brokerage firm is a brokerage company owned and operated by a retailer but that represents itself as an independent operation. As such, the brokerage firm does not charge its parent retailing firm a brokerage fee for bringing the buyer and seller together and such "savings" in brokerage fees are passed on to the the retailer. In this situation, the retailer with a dummy brokerage firm pays less for merchandise and therefore can sell products at a lower price, thus creating an unfair competitive advantage. Section 2(c) of the Robinson-Patman Act makes it unlawful for a company to receive brokerage allowances (fees and/or discounts) unless the broker is completely independent of both the supplier and retailer.

Retailers can also run the risk of price discrimination in selling activities by engaging in predatory pricing and price fixing. **Predatory pricing** is *a pricing tactic whereby the retailer charges customers different prices for the same merchandise in different markets to eliminate competition in one or more of those markets.* Such pricing practices are illegal except when the firm can show a cost justification. **Price fixing** is *an illegal pricing activity in which several retailers establish a fixed retail selling price for a particular product line within a market area.* The illegality of price fixing is established by both the Sherman Antitrust Act and the Federal Trade Commission Act.

Resale Price Maintenance

Resale price maintenance legislation, commonly referred to as "fair-trade laws," was designed to permit manufacturers and wholesalers to set retail prices by requiring retailers to sign contracts agreeing to sell their products at the "suggested" prices. The primary purpose of these laws was to protect the small, independent retailer who could not compete effectively on a price basis with the large chains and discount operations.

With the changing economic environment and the rampant inflation of the 1970s, however, Congress removed the enabling legislation, wiping out the fair trade laws that still existed in 21 states. The question of "fair trade" has resurfaced in recent years. At issue is whether some degree of resale price maintenance should be allowed. One survey indicated that most business executives support free-market principles over a fair-trade doctrine (see Figure 5–6).

Although resale price maintenance is no longer legal, *a limited type of resale price maintenance exists in some states in the form of* **unfair trade practice acts**. These state laws regulate the right of retailers to sell either below cost or at cost plus some minimum markup (e.g., cost plus 5 percent). The intent of these laws is to preserve competition by eliminating predatory price cutting and loss-leader selling (the use of a below-cost price on a popular item to attract customers into the store). These laws vary from state to state, depending upon the definition of costs, the minimum required markups, if any, and the products covered by such laws. As a rule, unfair trade practice laws have been ineffective due to enforcement problems and the large number of exceptions. Typical exemptions permitting sales below cost include clearance sales, closeout sales, business liquidation sales, sales to relief

155

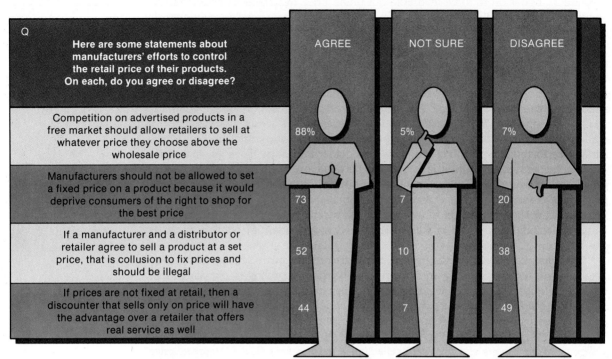

FIGURE 5–6

How business views fair trade (source: "Resounding Support for Price Competition," Reprinted from the November 14, 1983 issue of *Business Week* by special permission, © 1983 by McGraw-Hill, Inc.)

agencies or for charitable purposes, and sales of products with deteriorating marketability (such as seasonal, damaged, and perishable goods). It is hard to conceive of a situation when a retailer could not qualify for one of these exemptions.

Promotion Legalities

Freedom of speech for the retailer is not without its limitations. Numerous laws govern what retailers may communicate to their customers and how they may communicate it. Legal restrictions influence all aspects of the retailer's promotional efforts—advertising, sales promotions, and personal selling. The principal legal vehicles through which the federal government regulates promotional activities are the Federal Trade Commission Act (1914) and the Wheeler-Lea Amendment to that act. Together these laws make it illegal for a retailer to engage in any unfair method of competition or unfair or deceptive act or practice in commerce. If retailers are caught using either deceptive price advertising, deceptive product advertising, or misleading personal sales information, the FTC can take legal action against them.

Deceptive Price Advertising

Retailers can express price information in a number of confusing and misleading ways. For example, prices expressed as the "suggested retail price," the "original price," the "regular price," "our price and our competitor's price," "two for the price of one," "buy one and get one free," "50 percent off," and "reduced one-half" can all be used to mislead consumers into believing that they are receiving a better price

156

or a larger discount than is actually being offered. The FTC has established several guidelines for the use of such pricing terms.

Former-price comparisons. The retailer that uses such pricing terms as "originally," "usually," or "regularly" is using a former-price comparison that suggests an item is selling at a price lower than its former price. To avoid charges of deceptive price advertising, the retailer should determine whether the former price was well established as the original, usual, or regular selling price. When the former price is established, the retailer's advertisements can inform consumers that the "new" price is a discount price. If the former price was not established, the retailer cannot make a former-price comparison. Also, for a sale price to be legal, the price reduction should be for a specific and reasonable period of time and be accompanied by a price increase at the end of the sales period.

Competitive-price comparisons. When making an advertising claim that its prices are lower than its competitors', the retailer must establish that the competitors' prices are, in fact, ones that they regularly and typically charge. In addition, under FTC guidelines, the competitive-price comparison must be made on identical products. If the retailer wishes to make competitive-price comparisons on similar but not identical products, then the advertisement must make it clear to the consumer that the price comparison is being made on "comparable" and not "identical" products. FTC guidelines allow the retailer to make price comparisons on comparable products of "like grade and quality" as long as it clearly states that different products of essentially the same quality and quantity are being compared. Hence, a retailer can make price comparisons between a private-label brand and a nationally advertised brand if they are of the same quality and quantity.

Free merchandise. Advertisements offering free merchandise represent a price reduction, since the offer usually depends upon the consumer meeting certain conditions (e.g., "buy one, get one free"). These promotional pricing practices are not considered deceptive if the advertisement clearly states the conditions under which the merchandise is "free."

Cents-off pricing. When a retailer's advertisement contains a cents-off coupon, it should be based on the regular price. If the retailer raises the product's price to inflate the coupon value, then the FTC will consider this kind of promotional effort deceptive.

Another deceptive act is the retailer's failure to stock sufficient quantities of the coupon product to meet the normal demand associated with such a sale. The FTC does consider "rain checks" (for the same or comparable product at a later date at the same price) as an adequate substitute when an unusual demand or out-of-stock problem unexpectedly arises; however, if retailers use rain checks in conjunction with planned shortages of advertised products hoping that only a small percentage of the rain checks will be redeemed, they are engaging in a deceptive practice. As with free merchandise offerings, any conditional aspects of the cents-off offering (e.g., quantity limitations) must be clearly stated in the advertisement.

Deceptive Product Advertising

Deceptive product advertising involves making a false or misleading claim about the physical makeup of the product, the appropriate uses for the product, or the benefits from using the product, as well as using packages and labels that tend to mislead the customer about the exact contents, quality, or quantity of the package. Several laws have been enacted to control the various claims about the physical makeup of the product. Among these laws are the Wool Products Labeling Act (1941), the Fur Products Labeling Act (1952), the Flammable Fabrics Act (1953), and the Textile Fiber Products Identification Act (1960).

Other legislation has been directed at identifying appropriate product usage. For example, the Child Protection and Toy Safety Act of 1965 instructs manufacturers to identify the appropriate age group for a particular toy. Armed with the Wheeler-Lea Amendment (known as the Truth in Advertising Act), the FTC has taken an active role in correcting false claims concerning product benefits. The agency's major weapon has been "the concept of corrective advertising where companies using deceptive advertising are required to use promotional messages correcting these previous claims."[11]

Finally, the Fair Package and Labeling Act of 1966 was drafted to prevent companies from using deceptive packaging and labeling methods. Companies must properly label the contents, ingredients, net quantity, and name and address of the manufacturer on the package. Also, the act contains guidelines regarding deceptive package sizes and shapes as well as the misleading use of printed material on packages.

Deceptive Sales Practices

The law also places restrictions on several kinds of personal selling practices. One such practice is called **bait and switch**. The "bait" is an advertised low price on a product that the retailer does not really intend to sell. The "switch" involves personal selling techniques that induce the customer to buy a higher-priced product that will provide the retailer with greater profits. These selling techniques involve (1) making disparaging remarks about the product, (2) either failing to stock the product or planning a stockout, (3) refusing to show or demonstrate the product to the consumer on some false pretense, or (4) denying credit arrangements in conjunction with the sale of the product. Although "bait and switch" selling techniques are common among local small retailers of major durable products, the FTC still considers these practices deceptive. To date, the FTC has directed most of its watchdog activities at large retail chain organizations with extensive interstate operations. To protect the consumer, the FTC can require any retailer to make good any "bait" offer extended to consumers.

A legal issue related to sales transactions involves **deceptive credit contracts**. In 1960, Congress passed the **Truth-in-Lending Act**, requiring full disclosure of credit terms. Retailers must give borrowers a disclosure statement detailing the exact terms of their contract. Terms such as the loan amount, finance charges, annual percentage rate, miscellaneous charges, number of payments and the amount of each payment, and description of any property held by the lender as security must be clearly stated in the disclosure statement. Additional legal requirements of retail lenders have been enacted through amendments to protect the consumer further. These amendments state that

1. monthly statements (bills) must include information (address and telephone number) about where inquiries about them can be made
2. consumers have 60 days to lodge complaints concerning billing errors; retailers have 30 days to reply to the complaint and must make a reasonable effort to resolve each complaint
3. all credit arrangements containing a "free period" provision require retailers to mail monthly statements 14 days prior to assessment of finance charges

4. credit payments must be credited to the customer's account on the day that they are received
5. issuers of credit cards cannot restrict the retailer from offering the final consumer a cash discount.[12]

In 1980, Congress passed the *Truth in Lending Simplification and Reform Act.* In adopting the act, Congress sought to simplify for both creditors and consumers the complex provisions surrounding the Truth-in-Lending Act. The later act simplified both the disclosure forms and the regulations governing the extension of credit.[13]

Distribution Legalities

Retailers often enter into agreements with suppliers that might give them a competitive edge in the marketplace. These agreements are legal under some circumstances but illegal under others. Some of these competitively advantageous, but potentially illegal, arrangements are exclusive dealings, anticompetitive leasing arrangements, tying contracts, and exclusive territories.

Exclusive Dealings

Exclusive dealings are *arrangements between retailers and suppliers in which the retailer agrees to handle only the supplier's products or no other products that pose direct competition.* Such agreements are not illegal per se; however, Section 3 of the Clayton Act declares exclusive dealings to be illegal where the effect of such arrangements may be to substantially lessen competition or to create a monopoly. The courts have generally viewed exclusive dealings as illegal when they exclude competitive products from a large share of the market and when they represent a large share of the total sales volume for a particular product type.

Anticompetitive Leasing Arrangements

A variation of exclusive dealings involves various forms of **anticompetitive leasing arrangements.** *The purpose of the contracts is to limit the type and amount of competition a particular retailer faces within a given area.* Generally associated with shopping centers, anticompetitive leasing arrangements grant some retailers certain rights such as "(1) the right to be the only retailer of its kind, (2) the right to reject or accept the opportunity to operate an additional outlet in a shopping center where it already has one, (3) the right to prohibit or control the entrance of tenants into shopping centers, and (4) the right to restrict the business operations of other tenants in shopping centers."[14] Under Section 5 of the Federal Trade Commission Act, the FTC has the power to enforce rules prohibiting one retailer in a shopping center from limiting the competitive activities of another retailer.

Tying Contracts

Tying contracts are *conditional selling arrangements between retailers and suppliers in which a supplier agrees to sell a retailer a highly sought-after line of products if the retailer will agree to buy additional product lines in return (usually those not frequently sought) from the same supplier.* An extended version of the tying contract concept is **full-line forcing** *whereby the supplier requires the retailer to carry the supplier's full line of products if the retailer wishes to carry any part of that line.* The FTC views both tying contracts and full-line forcing as illegal when the supplier possesses sufficient coercive powers to force compliance.

The most serious problems involving tying arrangements are those associated with franchise retailing. Quite often, franchise agreements contain provisions whereby the franchisee must purchase all raw materials and supplies from the franchisor. The courts generally consider tying provisions of a franchise agreement legal as long as there is sufficient proof that these arrangements are necessary to maintain quality control. Otherwise, they are viewed as unwarranted restraints of competition.

Exclusive Territories

Exclusive territories are *agreements under which a supplier grants a retailer the exclusive right to sell its products within a defined geographic area.* In return, the retailer agrees not to sell the product anywhere except within the agreed-upon area. In essence, a geographic monopoly is created for a particular product line. For obvious reasons, these territorial arrangements are generally viewed as unlawful systems of distribution. The law does not, however, prevent suppliers and retailers from establishing territorial responsibilities as long as they are not exclusive and do not restrict the resale of products.

SUMMARY

Legal considerations are an integral part of the retailer's daily operations. The retailer must consider the legal aspects of retail competition, store operations, and retail merchandising within the legal environment created by federal, state, and local legislative, executive, and judicial branches of government.

The legal aspects of competition deal with attempts by various governmental bodies to correct present restraints on trade and to prevent probable trade restraints and unfair trade practices. The major laws dealing with maintaining a competitive environment are the Sherman Antitrust Act, the Clayton Act, the Robinson-Patman Act, the Federal Trade Commission Act, and the Wheeler-Lea Act.

The legal forms of store organization (sole proprietorship, partnership, and corporation), the limitations of vertical integration, the laws governing personnel management (job discrimination, working conditions, and compensation requirements), the restrictions on store facilities (zoning ordinances, building codes, licensing requirements, and operating requirements) all are central legal issues in store operations.

The legal aspects of merchandising require the retailer to carefully consider the legalities of its product, price, promotion, and distribution mix. Guarantees, warranties, and liability are three of the more important legalities associated with the product. Price discrimination in terms of product characteristics, quantity discounts, and special allowances or services, together with resale price maintenance activities, are the retailer's chief legal concerns regarding price. Deceptive price and product advertising and deceptive sales practices are illegalities of promotion that retailers must avoid. Finally, the laws pertaining to distribution call for careful consideration of exclusive dealings, anticompetitive leasing arrangements, tying contracts, and the use of exclusive territories.

KEY TERMS AND CONCEPTS

retail competition

antitrust legislation

Sherman Antitrust Act

Clayton Act

Robinson-Patman Act

Federal Trade Commission Act

Wheeler-Lea Act

sole proprietorship

partnership

general partnership

limited partnership

corporation

vertical integration

mergers

Civil Rights Act

Fair Labor Standards Act

Williams-Steiger Occupational Safety and Health Act

workers' compensation

unemployment compensation

general business license

special business license

blue laws

product guarantees

product warranties

expressed warranties

implied warranties

product liability

price discrimination

coercive buying

deceptive brokerage activities

predatory pricing

price fixing

resale price maintenance

unfair trade practice acts

deceptive price advertising

deceptive product advertising

deceptive sales practices

bait and switch

deceptive credit contracts

Truth-in-Lending Act

exclusive dealings

anticompetitive leasing arrangements

tying contracts

full-line forcing

exclusive territories

REVIEW QUESTIONS

1. Whose actions define the retailer's legal environment?
2. What is antitrust legislation?
3. What action was taken to overcome the shortcomings of the Sherman Antitrust Act? Be specific.
4. Compare and contrast the legal and operational advantages and disadvantages of sole proprietorship, partnership, and corporate forms of retail organization.
5. What are the two most prevalent forms of employment discrimination? Describe each.
6. Which two basic guidelines should a retailer follow to ensure compliance with the provisions of the Civil Rights Act?
7. What is OSHA? Describe the primary responsibility of this governmental agency.
8. What is workers' compensation? Whom does it cover?
9. Who qualifies for unemployment compensation?
10. Why do local governments enact zoning ordinances? What are the benefits and limitations for the retailer?
11. What two types of local licensing requirements do retailers usually have to meet before they can begin operations? Define each.

12. Compare and contrast product guarantees with product warranties.
13. What are the two basic types of warranties? Describe each type.
14. Under what conditions can the retailer be held liable for an unsafe product?
15. What is price discrimination?
16. When is price discrimination illegal?
17. Describe the two legal defenses for price discrimination.
18. What techniques or practices constitute illegal price discrimination? Describe each technique or practice.
19. To avoid charges of deceptive price advertising when using former- and competitive-price comparisons, the retailer should follow which practices?
20. What is deceptive product advertising?
21. What is the major weapon the FTC uses in correcting false claims concerning product benefits? Explain.
22. Describe the sales practice of bait and switch. When is it illegal?
23. Identify the requirements of the Truth-in-Lending Act.
24. Compare and contrast the distribution arrangements of exclusive dealings, tying contracts, and exclusive territories. When are they illegal?

ENDNOTES

1. See Maurice I. Mandell and Larry J. Rosenberg, *Marketing,* 2d ed. (Englewood Cliffs, NJ: Prentice-Hall, 1981), 55–58.
2. E. Jerome McCarthy, *Basic Marketing,* 6th ed. (Homewood, IL: Richard D. Irwin, 1978), 101.
3. See David L. Kurtz and Louis E. Boone, *Marketing,* 2d ed. (New York: The Dryden Press, 1984), 33.
4. Louis W. Stern and Adel I. El-Ansary, *Marketing Channels,* 2d ed. (Englewood Cliffs, NJ: Prentice-Hall, 1982), 393.
5. R. Ted Will and Ronald W. Hasty, *Retailing,* 2d ed. (San Francisco: Canfield, 1977), 337.
6. Ibid.
7. C. L. Kendell and Frederick A. Russ, "Warranty and Complaint Policies: An Opportunity for Marketing Management," *Journal of Marketing* 39 (April 1975): 37.
8. See Laurence P. Feldman, "New Legislation and the Prospects for Real Warranty Reform," *Journal of Marketing* 40 (July 1976): 41–47.
9. See Joseph B. Mason and Morris L. Mayer, *Modern Retailing—Theory and Practice* (Dallas: Business Publications, 1981), 728.
10. Stern and El-Ansary, *Marketing Channels,* 386.
11. Kurtz and Boone, *Marketing,* 33.
12. See Sheldon Feldman, *Compliance with Simplified Truth in Lending by Retailers—Review of 1981 Changes in the Act and Regulation 2* (New York: National Retail Merchants Association, 1981), 1–41; *Fair Credit Billing Act—Summary of Federal Reserve Board Regulation* (New York: National Retail Merchants Association, 1981), 1–19.
13. Ibid.
14. Stern and El-Ansary, *Marketing Channels,* 368.

RELATED READINGS

Adams, Ronald J. "FTC-Ordered Consumer Arbitration in Cases Involving Retail Furniture and Appliance Firms." *Evolving Marketing Thought for 1980, Proceedings.* J. H. Summey and R. D. Taylor, eds. (Southern Marketing Association 1980), 363–66.

"Antitrusters Revive 'Fair Trade'." *Chain Store Age, General Merchandise Edition* (February 1982), 35–36.

Boedecker, Karl A., and Morgan, Fred W. "The Channel Implications of Product Liability Developments." *Journal of Retailing* 56 (Winter 1980), 59–72.

Crawford, Carol T. "The Federal Trade Commission and Consumer Protection." *Retail Control* (November 1984), 43–57.

Cromartie, Jane. "New Trends in Robinson-Patman Enforcement: Implications for the Marketing Manager." *Marketing: Theories and Concepts for an Era of Change, Proceedings.* J. Summey, R. Viswanathan, R. Taylor, and K. Glynn, eds. (Southern Marketing Association 1983), 64–66.

Davis, Jennifer, and Renforth, William. "Consumer Product Warranties: Has the Magnuson-Moss Act Affected Their Readability?" *Marketing: Theories and Concepts for an Era of Change, Proceedings.* J. Summey, R. Viswanathan, R. Taylor, and K. Glynn, eds. (Southern Marketing Association 1983), 194–97.

Emamalizadeh, Hossein. "Bait-and-Switch Advertising: A Conceptual Approach." *Developments in Marketing Science, Proceedings.* J. C. Rogers, III, ed. (Academy of Marketing Science 1983), 470–72.

Houston, Michael J. "Minimum Markup Laws: An Empirical Assessment." *Journal of Retailing* 57 (Winter 1981), 98–113.

Hunt, Shelby O., and Nevin, John R. "Tying Agreements in Franchising." *Journal of Marketing* 39 (July 1975), 20–26.

Lambert, Zarrel V. "Consumer Alienation, General Dissatisfaction, and Consumerism Issues: Conceptual and Managerial Perspectives." *Journal of Retailing* 56 (Summer 1980), 3–24.

"The Liability Explosion." *Chain Store Age Executive* (April 1981), 54–56.

Mason, J. B. "Power and Channel Conflict in Shopping Center Development." *Journal of Marketing* 39 (April 1975), 28–35.

Nevin, John R., and Churchill, Gilbert A., Jr. "The Equal Credit Opportunity Act: An Evaluation." *Journal of Marketing* 43 (Spring 1979), 95–104.

"Recall Tactics." *Stores* (January 1981), 76–78.

Seesel, John H. "Off-Price Retailing: Regulatory Issues." *Retail Control* (November 1983), 55–61.

Turk, Michael A., and Cooke, Ernest F. "What Is False, Deceptive, or Misleading Advertising?" *Developments in Marketing Science, Proceedings.* J. D. Lindquist, ed. (Academy of Marketing Science 1984), 249–53.

Welch, Joe L. *Marketing Law.* (Tulsa: Petroleum Publishing Company, 1980)

Wiener, Joshua L. "The Inferences Consumers Draw from a Warranty: Did They Become More Accurate after the Magnuson-Moss Act?" *1985 AMA Educators' Proceedings.* R. F. Lusch et al, eds. (American Marketing Association 1985), 309–12.

Outline

THE RETAILER'S NEED TO KNOW

THE RETAILING INFORMATION SYSTEM

Locating Information
Gathering Information
Processing Information
Utilizing Information

RETAIL INTELLIGENCE

Library Sources of Retail Intelligence
Government Sources of Retail Intelligence
Association Sources of Retail Intelligence
Commercial Sources of Retail Intelligence

RETAIL RESEARCH

The Scientific Method
Collecting Primary Information
Analyzing Primary Information

ELECTRONIC DATA PROCESSING SYSTEM

The Input
The Computer
The Output
Computer Applications in Retailing

Objectives

- Describe how to reduce the risks of doing business through an adequate retailing information system

- Determine what information is available, what information is needed, how information is gathered and processed, and where information is obtained

- Productively use information in retail problem-solving and decision-making situations

- Recognize the key considerations in effective management of the retailing information system

- Design, implement, and manage a retail research project

- Understand and appreciate the role of the electronic data processing system within the retailing information system

6
The Retailing Information System

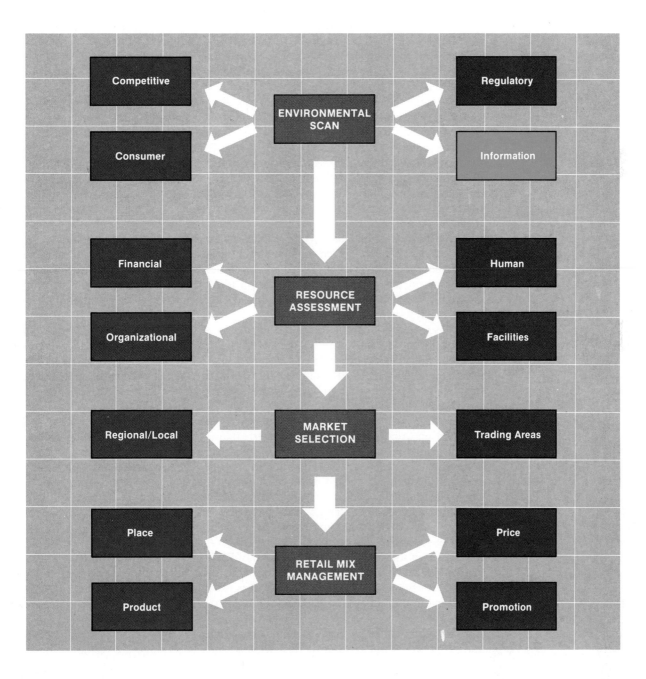

The retailer must learn how to reduce the risks of doing business to succeed in today's complex dynamic retailing environment. Basing decisions on reliable information is perhaps the single most effective way to reduce business risks. Because good information is the precursor to effective decision making and problem solving, we have placed this chapter early in the text. In this chapter we examine the retailer's need to know and the information systems that serve that need.

"No organization, retailing included, can be effectively managed without some type of information system. Decisions based on an absence of information are decisions for disaster."[1] Retailers need to know what information is available, what information is needed, how and where information can be obtained, and how to use productively the information received. The kinds of information in which the retailer is interested are those that can make problem solving and decision making as effective as possible.

In *Future Shock*, Alvin Toffler develops the thesis that society and technology are changing so rapidly that the reverberations disorient and confuse all members of society.[2] This constant state of environmental flux continually tests the retailer's ability to manage a retailing information system. Successful information systems are future oriented by necessity. A major function of any information system is to predict today what is going to happen tomorrow. Equally important is the capability of the information system to reduce the time span required to make a decision. The adage "He who hesitates is lost" is all too true in retailing where fast adaptation to new market opportunities is necessary.

As diagnosed by Toffler, one of the major causes of "future shock" is the *information explosion,* which is the mind-boggling rate at which the amount of information and its availability is expanding. Much of this information, however, is of little or no use to a particular retailer. Thus, a major function of any retailing information system should be to determine the information needed to make a particular retail decision.

Associated with the information explosion is the "data syndrome," the idea that the more data we have, the better off we are. This notion is false, however: data are not information; instead, data are bits and pieces of facts that become information when they "take on *meaning* for an individual."[3] Thus, another major function of a retailing information system is to process *useless data* into *useful information.*

Several environmental factors also virtually force most retailers to develop and maintain an adequate information system. Many of these environmental factors have emerged in the 1980s. Scarcity, for example, adversely affects both the retailer's buying and selling activities. On the buying side, certain product lines have been in short supply due to limited resources such as oil, natural gas, wood, and so forth. On the selling side, consumers are deemphasizing the purchase of nonessentials and the accumulation of "things" as a result of inflation, high interst rates, and social presssures to conserve and to protect the environment.

Consumerism is another factor requiring retailer information. The consumer movement produced the "Consumer's Bill of Rights," with two rights directly affecting the retailer's information system: the right to be heard and the right to be informed. For the retailer to remain in business, an information system must not only keep it informed, but also be capable of providing consumers with information they want and need.

Government intervention requires the retailer to be informed about existing and proposed legislation and rulings. Without such knowledge the retailer risks violating new laws affecting the business. With new technology and computerization, however, the retailer's ability to store and process vast amounts of information on the changing environments of economic resources, consumerism, government legislation, and consumer buying behaviors has provided the means to cope with the information explosion. Thus, with the aid of modern technology and the computer, an important function of the retailing information system is to monitor and analyze the social, political, legal, technological, and economic environments.

THE RETAILING INFORMATION SYSTEM

Because successful retailing starts with the possession and proper use of business information, many retailers have developed and implemented some form of retailing information system (RIS). An **RIS** is *an interacting organization of people, machines, and methods designed to produce a regular, continuous, and orderly flow of information necessary for the retailer's problem-solving and decision-making activities.* The RIS is a planned, sequential flow of information tailored to the needs of a particular retail operation. As shown in Figure 6–1, the four basic activities of the RIS are locating, gathering, processing, and utilizing pertinent retailing information.

Locating Information

The fundamental purpose of the RIS is to provide a framework for gathering input (information) from both the retailer's external and internal environments so that the retailer can develop the best possible output ("correct" decisions). In the first stage the decision maker must locate information relevant to its business. Before activating the first stage of an RIS, however, the retailer must understand the two basic *types* of information and the two *sources* from which this information can be derived. The two types of information are secondary and primary information, and the two sources of information are external and internal information.

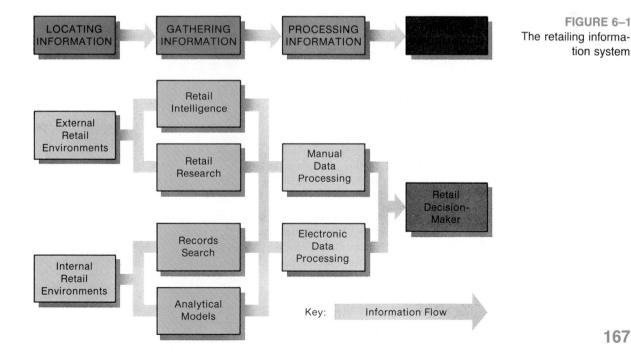

FIGURE 6–1
The retailing information system

Types of Information

Secondary information is *existing information that has been collected for another purpose and that is often published.* Although secondary information is collected for some other purpose, a retailer often can adapt this information to its own needs. Given the tremendous wealth of secondary information collected and published by government agencies, trade associations, and other research groups, the chance of finding useful information for other purposes is very high. Even though secondary information might not fit the retailer's *precise needs,* a major function of the RIS is to convert this information into a reservoir of useful knowledge. As is true with any type of information, secondary information has advantages and disadvantages (see Figure 6–2).

Primary information is *new information the retailer collects for a specific purpose tailored to its needs.* Original data are collected using various survey, panel, laboratory, and statistical techniques. Sometimes the retailer collects primary information because it can find no secondary sources to help make an important decision. At other times, the retailer obtains primary information to corroborate the secondary information gathered.

By using primary information, the retailer overcomes most of the disadvantages associated with secondary information. Primary information is generally more accurate, more current, and more suitable to the retailer's problem at hand. Unfortunately, primary information is usually more costly and time-consuming to obtain. Additionally, to gain the advantages of primary information, a retailer normally must be willing to invest in specialized equipment and personnel to gather the information.

Sources of Information

The retailer has two sources of information—external and internal. **External information** is *information obtained from outside the firm.* It originates from formal (library, government, trade, and commercial) organizations and from informal (supplier, competitor, and consumer) sources. With the great variety of outside sources, the task of locating and collecting external information often is very tedious and time-consuming.

Internal information is *information found within the firm.* For example, various departments and divisions generate a wide range of useful information in the normal course of their operations. It comes from a variety of sources such as operating statements, sales records, expense records, purchasing and inventory records, accounts receivable and payable records, and prior written reports. Additional information can be obtained from employee surveys and employment records. By applying certain statistical and analytical procedures, the retailer can generate additional information.

Gathering Information

Once the information has been located, the second stage is to gather it. Figure 6–3 represents a taxonomy of information-gathering methods including retail intelligence, retail research, records search, and analytical models. At this point we shall briefly define and describe each of the methods. Later in the chapter, retail intelligence and retail research will be discussed in more depth.

Retail intelligence is *any method or combination of methods used to obtain external secondary information.* To keep the firm's decision makers current, the retailing information system must be capable of monitoring on a day-to-day basis the developments of the marketplace. Retail intelligence involves search procedures

FIGURE 6–2
The advantages and disadvantages of secondary information

DISADVANTAGES

Lack of Suitability

Suitability is the "match" between pertinent secondary information and the information needs of the retailer. Where there is a lack of suitability, there is a poor match between the secondary information and the retailer's information needs. Lack of suitability can be the result of either geographic or class conformity. Geographic conformity is concerned with whether the information is broken down by geographic units (census areas, cities, counties, states, etc.) which are consistent with the retailer's needs. Class conformity is concerned with how information is classified and defined, as well as what units of measurements are used in measuring each class. Sales, for example, can be defined as gross *or* net sales per square *or* linear foot.

Lack of Accuracy

Secondary data can be inaccurate for a number of reasons: (1) a considerable amount of secondary information is reported without sufficient comment on how, when, and under what circumstances the information was collected and tabulated; (2) some secondary sources get their information from other sources, with the result being third-hand information for the retailer, for whom the problems of accuracy are substantially increased; and (3) secondary information was collected for a specific purpose and frequently that purpose was to promote a particular idea, position, or organization. By definition and design, such information is biased and often inaccurate.

Obsolescence

The usefulness of secondary information is sometimes limited by its obsolescence. In the time it takes to collect, tabulate, and publish secondary information, it can become quite dated. Census information, for example, is collected at 5-, 7-, and 10-year intervals, depending on the particular type of census.

ADVANTAGES

Less Costly

Secondary information generally costs less to obtain than primary information. By using published sources of information, the very expensive collecting, editing, and tabulating phases can be avoided. The use of unpublished secondary information requires a more extensive search process; however, such information usually can be obtained at costs below primary information. Many governmental agencies and trade associations provide vast amounts of information either free of charge or at some minimal charge. Private commercial sources normally charge substantial fees; nevertheless, due to their operating economies and efficiencies, they frequently can provide secondary information at rates lower than the costs of the retailer doing it.

Greater Speed and Availability

Secondary information often can be obtained immediately or in a matter of days, whereas the collection of primary information can take several weeks or months. When the firms's decision makers require at least some information, secondary information may be the only feasible alternative.

Greater Familiarity

Since the firm's managers have been exposed at one time or another to many of the standard types of secondary information, they tend to be more comfortable with that information because they are more aware of its uses and its limitations.

Possible Greater Credibility

Secondary information has greater credibility when the original source is highly credible. Sources with questionable reputations are usually perceived as having less credible information.

FIGURE 6–3

A taxonomy of information-gathering methods

DIMENSIONS OF INFORMATION		Types of Information	
		Secondary	Primary
Sources of Information	External	retail intelligence	retail research
	Internal	records search	analytical models

to comb libraries and government and trade sources for pertinent information on a regular and systematic basis. For a fee, additional retail intelligence can be secured from various commercial organizations that specialize in monitoring certain aspects of the marketplace.

Retail research *involves the use of a set of scientific procedures to gather external primary information from consumers, suppliers, and competitors.* Typically, retail research is project oriented and directed at a particular decision-making or problem-solving situation. Two major characteristics of retail research are: (1) it is conducted in a fragmented, intermittent fashion, and (2) a computer usually processes the data. Surveys, panels, and laboratory experiments are the most common information-gathering techniques used in retail research.

Records search *includes all methods used in gathering internal secondary information.* The firm's internal accounting system and its various operational control subsystems are capable of providing a wealth of information on all aspects of the retailer's operations. A records search can generate information on both past and current performances and activities. Such internal records contain information on sales, expenses, inventories, purchases, potential vendors, and a host of other factors. They also indicate a great deal about the relationship between these factors and the retailer's products, prices, promotions, facilities, and personnel. Sources and uses of internal records are identified and discussed throughout the remainder of the text.

Analytical models are *various statistical and quantitative methods that researchers use internally to generate primary information.* Used mostly by large retailers, analytical models employ mathematical techniques to find the best solution to a particular problem. Retailers use analytical models to estimate a trading area's sales potential, to evaluate an advertising campaign, to predict operating expense under various circumstances, and to analyze stocking and handling procedures. Essentially, analytical models generate primary information from secondary information using a complex set of quantitative procedures. Numerous analytical merchandising and operational models will be presented throughout the text.

Processing Information

After locating and gathering information, the RIS must be able to process the information effectively. The information-processing system consists of (1) selecting and preparing input; (2) evaluating, storing, and retrieving processed information; and (3) preparing and disseminating output. As shown in Figure 6–1, the information-processing system can be either manual or electronic.

Manual data processing *uses human labor to process information.* The typical hardware of such a system usually consists of typewriters, calculators, filing cabinets, and hand-carried files. The software typically consists of written instructions on how each of the processing functions should be conducted. For small retailers, manual data processing is practical and can be effective if the system is carefully developed and maintained.

Electronic data processing is *a computer-based system of processing information.* The computer is the principal piece of hardware used in preparing, evaluating, storing, retrieving, and disseminating information. It has three major components—an input system, a central processing unit, and an output system. The software consists of the instructional procedures for programming the computer. Traditionally, only large retailing organizations could afford a computer-based electronic data processing system. With the recent development of the minicomputer and the increasing number of time-sharing programs associated with larger units, however, electronic data processing is becoming a more viable option for the medium and small retailer.

Utilizing Information

No matter how well the RIS accomplishes the tasks of locating, gathering, and processing information, the total system is a failure if the decision maker does not fully utilize the information. Information, the principal input into every decision-making and problem-solving situation, is crucial to the retailer in establishing goals and objectives, identifying and analyzing alternatives, developing plans, and making recommendations and decisions. To avoid "muddling through" problems and making decisions with crude rules of thumb and rough approximations, reliable and pertinent information must be available and must be used.

Gathering retail intelligence from library, government, association, and commercial sources provides the retailer with information about the legal, political, social, economic, and technological environments. For any one of these sources, the information can be published or reported in the form of books, monographs, reports, periodicals, bulletins, tapes, films, or several types of special publications. Additionally, unpublished retail intelligence can be secured if the researcher knows what to look for and how to find it. The prudent strategy in this case is to seek help from someone familiar with unpublished sources of information.

RETAIL INTELLIGENCE

Library Sources of Retail Intelligence

The library is not only a source of information on a wide variety of subjects, but it also frequently serves as a means for locating other sources of retail intelligence. For the retailer seeking external secondary information, the library is a good starting point. Library research skills are developed by using the library and becoming familiar with its information retrieval systems (e.g., card catalogs and visual display terminals). A number of excellent reference guides contain potential sources of retail intelligence (see Figure 6–4). Also, many libraries have specialized personnel (e.g., government documents librarian) trained in finding specific information.

FIGURE 6–4
Selected reference
guides

Business Periodicals Index
> A cumulative subject index to English-language periodicals in the fields of accounting, advertising and public relations, automation, banking, communications, economics, finance and investment, insurance, labor, management, marketing, taxation, and specific businesses, industries, and trades.

Wall Street Journal Index
> A monthly index with annual cumulations prepared by M. Dow Jones and Company from the final eastern edition of the *Wall Street Journal.* The index consists of two parts: corporate news and general news.

New York Times Index:
> A semimonthly subject index with annual cumulations covering every subject reported in the final late city edition of the *New York Times.* Contains brief abstracts of news stories classified by subject, geographic, association, institution, and company headings.

Monthly Catalog of U.S. Government Publications
> A monthly subject index to publications of the various branches of government. A condensed biweekly version, *Selected U.S. Government Publications,* contains a list of business-related publications that have general application to most businesses.

Reader's Guide to Periodical Literature
> A semimonthly author, subject, and title index of approximately 130 general, nontechnical U.S. publications.

Government Sources of Retail Intelligence

The most prolific compilers of external secondary information are federal, state, and local governments. While government sources collect and disseminate an enormous amount of information on a wide variety of subjects, the type of information retailers use most often is census and registration data.

Census Information

The U.S. Bureau of the Census of the Department of Commerce regularly conducts nine different censuses. These constitute the most important sources of external secondary information for most businesses. In addition to the volume of information they contain, Census Bureau reports are quite accurate, particularly in light of the monumental work involved in collecting data from so many sectors of the U.S. economy.

The nine censuses produced by the federal government are

- Census of Population
- Census of Housing
- Census of Governments
- Census of Agriculture
- Census of Construction
- Census of Business
- Census of Manufacturing
- Census of Mineral Industries
- Census of Transportation

The frequency and timing of each census vary. The population and housing censuses are taken every 10 years in years ending with 0. All other censuses, except the *Census of Agriculture,* are taken every five years in years ending with 2 and 7. The *Census of Agriculture* is taken every five years in years ending with 4 and 9.

The *Census of Population* and the *Census of Housing* contain a vast amount of detailed information broken down according to predefined geographical reporting units. Information for both censuses is reported by states, counties, cities, and various urban area classifications. Within urban areas, population and housing characteristics are available on a very localized level. Urban areas are subdivided into census tracts, enumeration districts, and census blocks for reporting purposes. In addition to population, housing counts, and density measurements (persons or units per area), each census contains an extensive amount of information concerning each person or unit. For example, the *Census of Population* provides statistics on the demographic makeup of a given reporting area, such as statistics on age, sex, race, education, occupation, income, marital status, living arrangements, and family structure of the population. The *Census of Housing* gives additional information on the occupancy status and the financial and structural characteristics of the housing stock.

The *Census of Governments* describes the operating characteristics of all levels of government—federal, state, and local. Employment, payroll, revenue, and expenditure statistics, as well as information on school districts, forms of government, and other fiscal characteristics, are presented in this census report.

The economic censuses of agriculture, construction, business, manufacturers, mineral industries, and transportation are presented by geographical areas and by Standard Industrial Classification (SIC) system codes. States, counties, and cities (in some cases) are the most common reporting units for the economic censuses. The SIC is a standardized code that categorizes industries into major groups and subclassifies them into highly descriptive groups. Each of the economic censuses enumerates the number of establishments as well as information on their sales, expenditures, number of employees, size of operation, and types of facilities and equipment they use in their operations. The most important economic census for the retailer is the *Census of Business,* consisting of three parts: "Retail Trade," "Wholesaler Trade," and "Selected Services." These are sources that every retailer should become very familiar with. The remaining chapters will illustrate the use of data from these sources as they apply to the subject of the chapter.

Registration Information

All levels of government at various times require individuals and organizations to register and report activities in which they are engaged. This routinely collected data can provide the retailer with a tremendous amount of useful information if the retailer knows how and where to secure it. Some of the more commonly used forms of registration include public records on (1) births, (2) deaths, (3) marriages, (4) school enrollments, (5) income, (6) sales tax payments, (7) automobile and recreational vehicle registration, and (8) general and special business licenses and crime statistics.[4] This list of registration information is far from comprehensive; it merely illustrates the kinds of information that retailers can get from public records.

Additional Information

At all levels of government, various departments and agencies produce a mountain of information pertaining to their areas of responsibility. The *County and City Data Book* provides information on a variety of topics of interest to the retailer. This source contains economic and social facts on local areas such as counties, cities, metropolitan areas, urbanized areas, and unincorporated places of 25,000 or more inhabitants in the United States.

The Small Business Administration (SBA) is the federal government agency most concerned with the activities of retailers, especially small, independent retailers. The SBA offers several services ranging from financial assistance to management consulting. It also publishes a number of aids directed at specific problems retailers frequently encounter. These aids take one of several forms: (1) Small Marketer's Aids, (2) Management Aids, (3) Small Business Bibliographies, (4) Small Business Management Series, (5) Starting and Managing Series, and (6) nonseries publications.

Association Sources of Retail Intelligence

A third major source of external secondary information is the large group of trade and professional associations that collect and publish highly specialized information. It would be difficult to find a subject that one or more of these groups or associations could not provide information on. Their charges for information range from free to various organization membership fees and publication subscription rates. To contact these organizations, the retailer can consult the *World Almanac* (which lists more than 1,100 associations in the United States), the *Encyclopedia of Associations* (with more than 16,000 names), or the *Writer's Guide* (which lists the names and addresses of literally thousands of magazines).

Most associations publish either a magazine, a journal, or a newsletter; they usually issue special reports, maintain files of information, and send out promotional literature as well. Figure 6–5 lists some of the more important trade and professional associations and publications of particular interest to retailers. In using information from these associations, the retailer should remember that some of these sources are promoting special interests and therefore have certain biases.

Commercial Sources of Retail Intelligence

The need for marketing information has led many firms into the business of providing it commercially. Commercial sources make a business out of collecting, tabulating, analyzing, and reporting information. *Bradford's Directory* lists more than 350 firms engaged in the commercial gathering and selling of information. Typically, commercial information sources provide either a standardized information service or a service tailored to the informational needs of a particular customer.

Standardized information services provide a prescribed type of information continuously and regularly. Figure 6–6 (p. 176) illustrates several examples of standardized information sources and the types of information they provide. *Tailored information services* provide customized information for the specific needs of the retailer. These services are typically performed on either a single occasion or an irregular, contractual basis.

Generally, commercial sources of information produce reliable information, if for no other reason than their business reputations depend on it. The information they provide usually specifies certain limitations they experienced in collecting and analyzing the data and also gives ranges of possible error. In the final analysis, the best way to evaluate the reliability of information from commercial sources is to investigate the reliability of the company itself.

RETAIL RESEARCH

Retail research is *the systematic process of gathering and analyzing primary, external information about consumers, suppliers, and competitors.* It is conducted on a project-by-project basis and directed at a particular problem-solving or decision-making situation. The main purpose of research is to obtain specific information to help reduce the risks of making a decision. Conducting research can be an expen-

Trade and Professional Associations

American Booksellers Association
American Management Association
American Marketing Association
American Retail Federation
Automotive Parts and Accessories Association
Better Business Bureau
Chamber of Commerce
International Franchise Association
Mass Retailing Institute
Menswear Retailers of America
National Appliance and Radio-TV Dealers Association
National Association of Retail Druggists
National Association of Retail Grocers
National Association of Variety Stores
National Home Furnishing Association
National Industrial Conference Board
National Jewelers of America
National Lumber and Building Materials Association
National Retail Furniture Association
National Retail Hardware Association
National Retail Merchants Association
National Shoe Retailers Association
National Sporting Goods Association
Sales and Marketing Executives
Urban Land Institute

Trade and Professional Publications

Advertising Age
American Fabrics and Fashions
Auto Merchandising News
Business Week
California Apparel News
Chain Store Age
Clothes
Curtain, Drapery and Bedspread Magazine
Dealerscope (Appliances)
Discount Merchandiser
Drug Topics
Earnshaw's Infants, Girls, and Boyswear Review
Floor Covering Weekly
Florist
Fortune
Furniture News
Hardware Age
Hardware Merchandiser
Harvard Business Review
Home and Auto
Journal of Advertising Research
Journal of Marketing
Journal of Marketing Research
Journal of Retailing
Juvenile Merchandising
Luggage and Leather Goods
Mart Magazine
Merchandising Week
Modern Jeweler
Office Products News
Progressive Grocer
Publishers Weekly
Retail Advertising Week
Sales and Marketing Management
Sports Merchandiser
Sporting Goods Business
Stores
Visual Merchandising
Volume Retail Merchandising
Women's Wear Daily

FIGURE 6–5
Association sources of retail intelligence

sive and time-consuming venture, so each research project must be selected carefully on the basis of its potential for providing meaningful, useful information.

Research projects that have proven to be productive ventures for the retailer in the past include studies on (1) consumer attitudes toward the retailer and its merchandising efforts, (2) consumer purchase motives and preferences, (3) demographic and psychographic profiles of both customers and noncustomers, (4) buyer-behavior patterns and their relationships to the retailer's mode of operations, (5) service and performance records of suppliers, (6) price and cost comparisons between suppliers, (7) merchandising and operational strengths and weaknesses of competitors, (8) comparative advantages that the retailer has over competitors, (9) consumer perceptions of competitors, and (10) employee perceptions of the company and its dealings with them. Retail research also provides information on the

FIGURE 6–6
Selected examples of
standardized informa-
tion sources

Survey of Buying Power .... Sales and Marketing Executives	Information on population, retail sales by store group, and effective buying income.
Market Survey .... The Editor and Publisher Market Guide	Information on the number of retail stores and their sales, population, disposable personal income, number of households, and household income.
Retail Index .... A. C. Nielsen Co.	Information on retail sales by product class and brand, purchases by retailers, retail inventories and stock turn, and retail and wholesale prices.
Consumer Panel .... Market Research Corporation of America	Information on product and brand sales by type of consumer, type of household, and type of retailer.
Supermarket Audit .... Market Research Corporation of America	Information on in-store type and amount of stock, prices of products, and shelf space assignments.
Channel Survey .... Selling Areas-Marketing, Inc.	Information on movements of products from suppliers to retailers.
Television Index .... A. C. Nielsen Co.	Information on size of television audience, viewing habits, flow of audience, and cost per 1,000 homes reached.
Media Survey .... Audit Bureau of Circulation	Information on readership of newspaper and magazine ads.
Media Survey .... Standard Rate and Data Service	Information on advertising rates for various media.

sales potential and customer acceptance of product lines, advertisng and personal selling effectiveness, locational attributes of the retailer's outlets, and consumer service and price perceptions. To conduct research, a basic understanding of the scientific method is useful.

The Scientific Method

The **scientific method** is *a set of procedures that allows the retailer to gather and analyze data in a systematic, controlled fashion.* It is perhaps the most commonly used method of producing *defensible results* and drawing *reliable conclusions.* The commonly accepted stages of the scientific method are

- identifying the problem
- developing a hypothesis
- collecting information
- analyzing information
- drawing conclusions

Its objectivity in the midst of creative and mechanical processes gives the scientific method its unusual level of acceptance.

The Creative Process

The creative aspect of the scientific method consists of identifying problems and developing hypotheses, the most critical part of any research project. The *problem-identification process* requires the retailer to clearly identify the problem and then state it in precise terms. Problem statements are made in the form of a declarative sentence: "The problem is to determine the relationship. . . . " or expressed as a question: "What is the relationship between . . . ?" Perhaps the importance of the problem-identification process is best expressed by the old saying "A problem well defined is a problem half solved." Problem identification demands more than just basic knowledge and skills. It demands creative perception and insight and the ability to look beyond the "symptoms" of a problem in an effort to find its causes.

The *hypothesis-development* process is the most important stage in the scientific method. It is the stage that characterizes the whole process of scientific investigation by focusing that investigation. In developing a hypothesis, the researcher formulates a definite position that will be either accepted or rejected in the analysis stage. In essence, the hypothesis is nothing more than a statement of the researcher's tentative solution to the identified problem. A hypothesis takes what we know to be fact and proposes a relationship one step beyond existing knowledge. Once the hypothesis has been developed, it is considered "cast in concrete." Based upon the outcome of the analysis, the researcher's decision is automatic: either to accept or to reject the hypothesis. The hypothesis can be expressed in statistical terms or verbal terms. The important factor in developing any hypothesis is to express explicitly the researcher's objectives, whether statistical or verbal. Moreover, once the hypothesis has been stated, the rest of the research process becomes largely mechanical.

The Mechanical Process

Compared to the creative stages of the scientific method, the last three stages (collection, analysis, and conclusion) are largely mechanical. In the *information-collection process,* the researcher must select and use one or more research methods, such as survey, observation, or experimental, in association with a research instrument such as a questionnaire. This process also involves the use of some form of scientific sampling. While collecting information is a laborious mechanical task, it does produce highly visible results that satisfy the basic human desire to have something to show for one's efforts. Information collection will be discussed more fully later in this chapter.

The *information-analysis process* consists of several mechanical activities. The first is to prepare the information for analysis. Examples are editing and tabulating raw data. The second step is to calculate statistical expressions such as percentages, averages, and measures of central tendency. The third activity is to observe the relationships between these statistical expressions. For example, the researcher might want to observe similarities and differences between the statistics. The fourth step is testing the degree of relationship between the statistical expressions. The degree of relationship can be determined through a variety of statistical tests that measure how significant the differences are and how strongly data are associated. These four steps in information analysis should be followed in sequence.

Drawing conclusions is the final stage of the scientific method and should evolve naturally from the problem-identification, hypothesis-development, information-collection, and analysis stages. Conclusions usually state whether the hypothesis was accepted or rejected, together with an operational interpretation of the results. Because the retailer's decisions are based on the final conclusions of the research, the research analyst should take considerable care to present the results clearly, concisely, and professionally.

Collecting Primary Information

Various methods and instruments are used to collect information in retail research. The following discussion identifies and examines the most commonly used methods and instruments.

Research Methods

Retail analysts use three basic methods in collecting external primary information: surveys, observation, and experimentation. The method they use depends on the nature of the research problem. In some cases, they might employ all three of the methods in one single project. We describe these research methods with their advantages and disadvantages.

The survey method. The **survey method** is *one in which the researcher systematically gathers information directly from the appropriate respondents.* Generally, in the survey method the researcher uses a questionnaire administered either in person, over the telephone, or by mail. The *personal interview* is a face-to-face question-and-answer session between the interviewer and the respondent. Interviewers can contact respondents either at their homes or places of employment or at public places (street corners, shopping centers, retail stores). Typically, the personal interview consists of the following steps:

1. identification—a statement of who is conducting the interview, what the survey is about, for whom the survey is being conducted, and why the survey is being conducted
2. permission—a request of the respondents to be interviewed
3. administration—a time interval when the interviewer asks a predetermined list of questions and records the respondent's answers
4. closure—the terminating step in which the interviewer thanks the respondent for his or her cooperation

Two other survey methods retailers use are the telephone survey and the mail survey. With the *telephone survey,* retailers phone potential respondents at their homes. Successful telephone interviews take no more than three or four minutes of the respondent's time. The basic survey steps of identification, permission, administration, and closure are essentially the same for telephone surveys as they are for personal surveys.

Mail surveys differ somewhat from personal interviews and telephone surveys in that the questionnaire is administered in written as opposed to oral form. The potential respondent in a mail survey receives and returns the questionnaire by mail. Other ways in which the survey director can administer the survey are by attaching questionnaires to products or packages, passing them out in a store or on the street, or placing them in newspapers. In these cases, respondents are asked to return the questionnaire in a self-addressed, postage-paid envelope. Because the questionnaire is in written form and the interviewer is not available to ask or answer questions, the questionnaire should be short and simple and have complete instructions.

In determining which survey method to use, the retailer must select the method most appropriate to the problem under investigation. To aid the retailer in

TABLE 6–1

Determining which survey method to use

Selection Criteria	Survey Method		
	Personal Interview	Telephone Survey	Mail Survey
Cost:[1] What is the most expensive method of collecting information?	Most expensive	Intermediate	Least expensive
Speed: What is the fastest method of collecting information?	Slowest method	Fastest method	Intermediate
Accuracy: What is the most accurate method of collecting information?	Most accurate	Intermediate	Least accurate
Volume: Which method is capable of collecting the most information?	Most information	Least information	Intermediate
Response rate: Which method results in the highest number of completed interviews?	Highest response	Intermediate	Lowest response
Flexibility: What method is most capable of adjusting to changing interviewing conditions?	Most flexible	Intermediate	Least flexible
Sample control:[2] Which method is capable of securing the best representative sample of the total population?	Intermediate	Worst representation	Best representation
Interview control: What method provides the interviewer the greatest amount of control over the interview situation?	Greatest control	Intermediate	Least control
Administrative control: Which method provides the retailer the greatest amount of control over the actions of the interviewer?	Least control	Intermediate	Greatest control

[1]Where the sample is scattered over a wide geographic area.
[2]Assumes an accurate mailing list.
Source: Adapted from K. L. McGown, *Marketing Research: Text and Cases* (Cambridge, MA: Winthrop Publishers, 1979), 135.

selecting the best survey method, Table 6–1 summarizes the relative strengths and weaknesses of each method.

The observation method. Researchers can obtain significant amounts of primary information simply by observing consumers' behavior. **Observation** is *a method of recording some aspect of consumers' overt behavior by either personal or mechanical means.* What the consumer does, not says, is the principal focus of the observation method. The advantages of this method are that it (1) eliminates any interviewer bias associated with the survey method, and (2) does not require the respondent's cooperation. The major disadvantage of the observation method is that the retailer cannot investigate the consumer's motives, attitudes, beliefs, and feelings. If the retailer uses this method, it must decide on the observation and recording techniques to use, the setting in which to make the observation, and whether to inform consumers that they are being observed. Each of these decisions is outlined in Table 6–2. In some situations, the retailer might find it beneficial to

TABLE 6–2

Using the observation method

Decision	Description	Example
Observation methods:		
1. Direct	Observing current behavior	Watching the number of consumers who stop to inspect a store display
2. Indirect	Observing past behavior	Counting the number of store-branded products (e.g. Sears) found in the consumer's home
Recording methods:		
1. Personal	Recording observations by hand	Logging customer reactions to a sales presentation by visually observing and manually recording the process
2. Nonpersonal	Recording observations mechanically or electronically (counters, cameras, sensors)	Measuring television viewing habits using an "audiometer," measuring pupil dilation while an advertisement is viewed as an indication of interest using a "perceptoscope," and using an "eye camera" to measure eye movement of a consumer as he or she views a display
Observation setting:		
1. Natural	Observing behavior in an unplanned and real setting	Observing the customer's natural and unobstructive trip behavior through the store
2. Artificial	Observing behavior in a planned and contrived setting	Observing sales personnel reaction to various customer "plants" who dress in a different fashion (e.g. well-dressed or shabbily dressed)
Observation organization:		
1. Structured	Observing specific behavior patterns	Observing the actions of only female customers who purchase a particular product
2. Unstructured	Observing general behavior patterns	Observing all of the actions of all customers regardless of who they are or what they buy
Observation situation:		
1. Disguised	Observing behavior without the person being aware that he or she is being observed	Using a two-way mirror to observe how customers inspect a display
2. Nondisguised	Observing behavior in an open fashion, thereby allowing the person to be aware that he or she is being observed	Following the customer around the store to observe shopping patterns

combine the observation method with the survey method. For example, by first observing the consumers' behavior patterns the retailer might obtain a more objective assessment of what actions the consumer actually took and then, through a follow-up survey, learn why the consumer took those actions.

The experimentation method. An **experiment** is *a technique that researchers use to determine a cause-and-effect relationship between two or more factors.* Generally, an experiment is conducted under controlled conditions; that is, the factors under study are manipulated while all other factors are held constant. For example, a retailer might increase the price of a product by $5.00 to see what effect the price change had on sales and profits, while holding all other factors, such as location, amount of shelf space, advertisements, and in-store displays, constant. A number of experimental designs are illustrated in Figure 6–7.

The before-after design *without* a control group measures the dependent factor (sales volume) before and after the factor has been manipulated (e.g., change

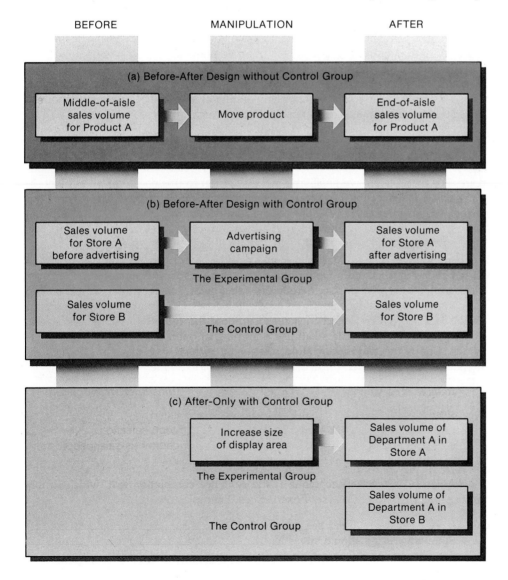

FIGURE 6–7
Experimental research designs

BEFORE   MANIPULATION   AFTER

(a) Before-After Design without Control Group

Middle-of-aisle sales volume for Product A → Move product → End-of-aisle sales volume for Product A

(b) Before-After Design with Control Group

Sales volume for Store A before advertising → Advertising campaign → Sales volume for Store A after advertising

The Experimental Group

Sales volume for Store B → Sales volume for Store B

The Control Group

(c) After-Only with Control Group

Increase size of display area → Sales volume of Department A in Store A

The Experimental Group

Sales volume of Department A in Store B

The Control Group

from a middle- to end-of-aisle display). The researcher assumes that the difference in sales volume is caused by the change in location, since all other factors affecting the sale of the product were held constant (see Figure 6–7a).

The before-after design *with* control group is essentially the same as the design just described except that a control group is used to determine if any changes in sales volume would have occurred regardless of any manipulation. For example, in Figure 6–7b, Store A's sales volume is measured before and after an advertising compaign to determine the effects of advertising. To prove that all changes in sales volume are the result of advertising, any changes in the sales volume of control Store B, which is unaffected by the advertising campaign, are also measured over the same period of time. If control Store B experienced no change in sales volume, then the researcher can more comfortably state that changes in sales volume for Store A are the result of the advertising campaign, everything else being equal.

The after-only *with* control group design is the most widely used design because of its simplicity and ease of implementation. As shown in Figure 6–7c, it involves measuring the dependent factor (sales volume of Department A in Store A) for one group that has been manipulated (increased size of display area) and comparing it with the same dependent factor (sales volume of Department A in Store B) for the control group that was not manipulated.

In general, the major advantage of using the experimentation method is that it systematically demonstrates cause-and-effect relationships. High costs, artificial settings, and the difficulties of controlling all of the factors that might influence the results of the experiment are its principal limitations.

Research Instruments

By far the most widely used research instrument in retail research is the questionnaire. For that reason, we shall limit our discussion to this particular instrument. In this section we describe how to construct a good questionnaire. The four major factors a researcher must carefully consider are structuring, wording, and sequencing questions and scaling answers in the questionnaire.

Structuring questions. Questions can be either open-ended (unstructured) or closed-ended (structured). Open-ended questions allow respondents to answer questions in their own words, thereby providing greater freedom in communicating their responses. Used extensively in motivation research, the open-ended question allows respondents to project their feelings about the retailer's merchandising and operational activities. Retailers can use a number of open-ended or projective techniques. One is the **word-association test**—*a set of words or phrases to which respondents must give their immediate reactions.* For example:

Retailer (interviewer):	*Consumer (respondent):*
store	clean
products	good selection
services	courteous salespeople
prices	low

A second projective technique is the **sentence-completion test,** which simply *asks respondents to finish a set of sentences.* Examples are

Store personnel should be _____.
Store advertising should stress _____.
Store convenience is a matter of _____.

A third open-ended questionnaire is the **narrative projection test** in which *the researcher provides respondents with a descriptive situation and asks them to write a paragraph in response.* An example of a descriptive situation the researcher might give respondents is the following:

> A neighbor asks you what is the best store in town for buying draperies and why you think it is best. What would you tell her?

Respondents would then write their reactions to this description.

The fourth projection technique is the **thematic apperception test.** In this test, *respondents are shown a cartoon, drawing, or picture and then asked to put themselves into the situation and tell a story about what is happening or what they would do.* For example:

> A picture showing one customer observing a poorly dressed elderly woman placing merchandise into a pocket.

A typical response to this picture might be, "She lives on welfare, has very little money, and must resort to shoplifting."

The major purpose of most open-ended questionnaires is to *explore and identify potential problems* and to obtain information that could be included in a structured research study. Because of the numerous difficulties in classifying and interpreting the results of open-ended questions, many retailers prefer to use structured questioning. The closed-ended questionnaire meets this need.

The closed-ended questionnaire is a highly structured format giving respondents a set of answers from which to choose. The three most common closed-ended questionnaires are dichotomous, multiple-choice, and rank-ordered questions.

Dichotomous questions *limit a respondent's answer to only one of two choices.* Examples of dichotomous questions are

Is our store the closest food store to your home?
_____ Yes
_____ No
Is price the most important factor in comparing products?
_____ True
_____ False

Multiple-choice questions *provide several possible answers from which the respondent can select the best answer.* For example,

What is your favorite type of television program?
_____ Sports
_____ News
_____ Comedy
_____ Mystery
_____ Drama
_____ Variety
_____ Other
What is your approximate income?
_____ Under $15,000
_____ $15,000–$24,999
_____ $25,000–$34,999
_____ Above $35,000

The third type of structured question is the **rank-ordered question,** in which *the respondent is asked to rank a list of factors in order of their importance.* An example of a rank-ordered question is the following:

> Please rank the following store services in terms of their importance in attracting you as a customer. Let 1 be the most important service, 2 the second most important service, and so on until each service has been ranked.
>
> _____ Easy credit terms
> _____ Liberal return policy
> _____ Free home delivery
> _____ Free layaway service
> _____ Good repair service
> _____ Long store hours

Many researchers prefer structured questions because they are easier to tabulate and analyze and because they eliminate the ambiguity of answers and the interpretation problems of unstructured questions. The major disadvantage of using structured questions is that they limit the amount and type of answers the respondent can make.

Scaling answers. To overcome the high cost and interpretation problems associated with unstructured questions and to gain more information than structured questions provide, many researchers prefer to use questions whose answers reflect the relative degree of the respondent's attitudes and opinions on a subject. The two most commonly used scales in retail research are Likert's summated ratings scale and Osgood's semantic differential.

Likert's summated rating scale *measures attitudes and opinions by asking respondents to indicate their extent of agreement or disagreement with a list of statements concerning the issue being studied.*[5] The answers to several statements concerning a clothing store's merchandise offering could be scaled as follows:

	Strongly Agree	Agree	Undecided	Disagree	Strongly Disagree
The Castle Shop:					
Stocks a wide assortment of products	(+2)	(+1)	(0)	(−1)	(−2)
Stocks only high quality products	(+2)	(+1)	(0)	(−1)	(−2)

The responses for each statement are given a numerical weight of either +2, +1, 0, −1, and −2, or 5, 4, 3, 2, and 1. An overall measure of opinion and attitudes is determined either by summing all subjects' responses to a particular statement or by summing one subject's responses for all statements.

One of the most popular scaling instruments in recent years is the semantic differential. The **semantic differential** is *a set of seven-point, bipolar scales that measures the meanings and attitudes that people have regarding some object.*[6] The respondent is asked to mark one of seven positions on a scale with ends identified by opposite descriptive terms. For example, the retailer that wants to obtain information concerning the appearance of its store might use the following scale:

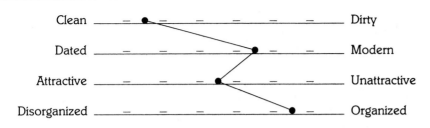

Each position of the semantic scale is assigned a numerical value that can be used to calculate arithmetic means for all respondents' answers to each scale. These figures can be used to profile a store's image, as illustrated by the connected lines in the preceding example.

Wording of questions. If questions are leading, ambiguous, worded poorly, or use a vocabulary with which respondents are unfamiliar, then the resulting answers will be of low quality and perhaps even meaningless. To help the researcher avoid wording problems, the following guidelines should be observed:

1. Keep each question as short as possible.
2. Limit each question to one idea.
3. Use simple, concise language.
4. Avoid technical or "buzz" words.
5. Ask questions with answers that the respondent can be expected to know and remember.
6. Ask personal questions in a generalized manner.

These guidelines along with common sense will help the researcher avoid many pitfalls in wording questions.

Sequencing of questions. Once the researcher has carefully worded the questionnaire, the next step is to place the questions in some order. In sequencing questions the following three guidelines are suggested:

1. Use an attention getter and an interest grabber for the opening question.
2. Ask general questions first, specific questions last.
3. Place personal questions at the end of the questionnaire.

Order is an important aspect of developing any questionnaire since the sequence can affect the final results.

Sampling Procedures

After selecting the type of research method and the instrument, the retailer must decide on the sampling procedure to use in collecting information. That is, once the retailer has decided on "what" information is needed and "how" it is to be obtained, it then must determine "who" it will ask to obtain the desired information. The "who" in this case is a **sample,** or *some portion of a predefined population.* A **population** is *the total membership of a defined group of individuals or items.* For example, a population could be defined as either all potential consumers or all actual consumers of a particular product. The reason researchers use samples instead of an entire population is that it is too costly and time-consuming to observe or survey an entire population. If proper sampling procedures are used, the researcher can draw valid conclusions about the attitudes, opinions, makeup, or behavior of the total population without contacting its entire membership. The retailer's sampling procedures follow three essential steps: (1) identifying the sampling frame, (2) determining the size of the sample, and (3) selecting the sample items.

Identifying the sample frame.   The first step in sampling is to either create or find a list of individuals included in the defined population being investigated. From this list the sample will be drawn. For example, the list could be the names of retail businesses listed in the phone book, the names and addresses of all adults (age 18 and over) living within a defined trading area, or a list of a store's credit card holders. The sample frame must be carefully identified to obtain meaningful and appropriate information.

Determining the sample size.   Sample size is the number of people the researcher wants to survey. A large sample normally results in greater accuracy and more reliable information; however, as the size of the sample increases, so do the costs of obtaining the sample. If scientific sampling procedures are followed carefully, small samples such as 400 or 500 people can provide satisfactory results and reliable information. Almost any marketing research text provides the necessary procedures for calculating the required sample size for a predetermined level of reliability, but these procedures are beyond the scope of this text.

Selecting the sample item.   The last sampling procedure is to select the sample, determining how the sample items or individuals are to be chosen. There are two general types of samples—probability and nonprobability. A **probability sample** is *one in which each individual in the total population has a known chance of being selected.* A **nonprobability sample** is *one in which each individual in the total population does not have a known and equal chance of being selected, but the researcher controls selection.* Whenever possible, the researcher should use a probability sample, since it provides more reliable results and permits the use of more sophisticated analytical techniques. Figure 6–8 identifies and briefly defines the various types of probability and nonprobability samples.

Analyzing Primary Information

The retailer's second major concern in conducting retail research is to analyze the collected information. While a complete discussion of all of the techniques that have been developed for analyzing information is impossible in this text, Figure 6–9 identifies the basic approaches researchers use to analyze information.

Researchers use summarization procedures to simplify and organize information into meaningful descriptive measurements. **Statistical inferences** are *used to make interpretations from a sample about the total population under study.* **Bayesian analysis** *"attempts to combine managerial judgment and objective information to assess dollars-and-cents consequences of alternative decisions."*[7] **Mathematical programming** *involves the use of mathematics to find optimal solutions to problems,* while **simulation** *uses mathematics to develop models of retailing situations and to provide solutions "by inserting various values of parameters and observing results."*[8] A more complete description of each of these approaches together with their respective techniques can be found in most marketing research textbooks.

FIGURE 6–8
Types of probability
and nonprobability
samples

Probability Samples	Nonprobability Samples
1. *Simple random:* A sampling procedure in which one sample is drawn from the entire population, with each individual or item having an equal probability of being selected.	1. *Convenience:* A sampling procedure in which each sample individual or item is selected at the convenience of the researcher (e.g., whoever walks in the store).
2. *Stratified random:* A sampling procedure in which the population is first subdivided into groups based on some known and meaningful criteria (e.g., sex, age). Then a simple random sample is drawn for each subgroup.	2. *Judgment:* A sampling procedure in which each sample individual or item is selected by the researcher based on an idea of what constitutes a representative sample (e.g., every seventh person who walks past the display counter).
3. *Cluster or area:* A sampling procedure in which geographical areas (e.g., census tracts or blocks) are randomly selected. Then a simple random sample is used to select a certain number of individuals or items (e.g., houses) from each of the selected geographical areas.	3. *Quota:* A sampling procedure in which the researcher divides the total population into several segments based on some factor believed to be important (e.g., sex and age). Then the researcher arbitrarily selects a certain number (quota) from each segment (e.g., selects five females over age 40, five females under age 40, five males over age 40, and five males under age 40).
4. *Systematic:* A sampling procedure in which the first individual or item of a sampling frame is selected randomly. Then each subsequent individual or item is selected at every *n*th interval (e.g., every fifth item on the list).	

FIGURE 6–9
Processing techniques
for information analysis

1. Summarization procedures
   Percentages
   Measures of central tendency
   Trend analysis (time series)

2. Statistical inference
   Estimation
   Hypothesis testing
   Analysis of associative data

3. Bayesian analysis
   Prior
   Preposterior
   Posterior

4. Mathematical programming
   Linear programming
   Nonlinear programming
   Critical path scheduling

5. Simulation
   Micro models
   Organization models
   System models

Source: Keith K. Cox and Ben M. Enis, *The Marketing Research Process* (Pacific Palisades, CA: Goodyear Publishing, 1972), 351.

Processing information is the third basic activity of the retailing information system. An integral part of this processing activity is the electronic data processing system (EDPS). **Electronic data processing** is *that part of the information processing system built around a computer.* As illustrated in Figure 6–10, the EDPS consists of three basic elements: the input, the computer, and the output. The computer's ability to process large volumes of data with incredible speed and accuracy makes it such a valuable tool. If properly utilized, electronic data processing can be extremely efficient for many retail operations.

The Input

Any system must have the right input in the right form with the right directions if it is to produce the desired results. This is especially true when inputting data into the computer. The input element of an EDPS requires that the retailer carefully select and prepare the data and provide the computer with instructions on exactly what to do with the data.

The data selected as input will depend upon the retailer's needs. Before inputting any data into the computer, the retailer must clearly identify what information is needed, for what purpose, when, and in what form. If the retailer has clearly identified the problem, data selection has already been predetermined. The actual data to be inputted into the EDPS can come from any of the previously discussed sources—retail intelligence, retail research, internal records, or analytical models. Once the right data have been selected, they must be prepared to meet the input requirements of the computer.

The computer is fussy. It will accept only data in its own machine language. The basic machine languages of the computer consist of binary numbers—various combinations of ones and zeros. To communicate with the computer, several binary arrangements are substituted for numbers, letters, and other special characters. After the data are transformed into machine language, the next step is to feed the data into the computer. The data can be fed into the computer in batches or in a continuous fashion (real-time). In **batch processing** *the retailer waits until considerable amounts of data have been collected and then processes the entire batch at one time* (e.g., at the end of the day or week). **Real-time processing** *involves continuous inputting of data from input devices that are directly connected to the computer.* It allows the immediate processing of all data.

Regardless of which processing method is used, all input must be accompanied by instructions to the computer about what to do with the data. In many cases these instructions simply ask the computer to recall earlier, more detailed instruc-

FIGURE 6–10
The electronic data processing system (EDPS)

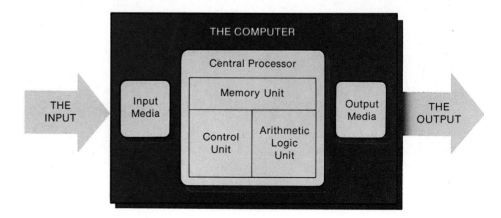

tions. Instructions to the computer are in the form of computer programs that the retailer can write or obtain as part of a "software package" from either the manufacturer of the computer or various software firms. Computer programs are written in a number of languages. Figure 6–11 describes some of the more commonly used languages.

Small computers have been multiplying like frenzied gerbils in recent years, and so have computer languages, the stuff from which all computer programs are built. Lest you sound ignorant next time the cocktail-hour conversation turns to the latest in software, here's a brief rundown on some of the most popular languages.

ALGOL. ALGOrithmic Language. Granddaddy of 'em all, ALGOL has been around for years and is said to be particularly well suited to number-type applications. Numerous "improvements" on this program have been written over the years, some of them of dubious utility. However, one computer jock referred to ALGOL 60 (written in 1960, in case you wonder) as "a great improvement on all its successors."

APL. A Programming Language. APL was designed for mathematical applications. It uses a lot of symbols that permit complex instructions to be economically expressed. Statements that might take dozens of lines in other languages can be squeezed into one in APL. Widely available on mainframe computers, it is seldom used on microcomputers.

BASIC. Beginners' All-purpose Symbolic Instructional Code. BASIC, originally developed at Dartmouth College for instructional purposes, has become the language most widely used on microcomputers.

COBOL. COmmon Business Oriented Language. Originally developed by the Department of Defense, COBOL is used around the world for business applications such as accounting, bookkeeping and inventory control.

In itself an admirably no-nonsense language, COBOL unfortunately inspired would-be computer comedians to come up with numerous lame puns as names for their own languages, such as CUBOL (Computer Usage Business Oriented Language) and the unbelievably tortured SNOBOL (StriNg Oriented symBOlic Language). These in turn gave rise to such gems as LISP (LISt Processing), PRONTO (PROgram for Numerical Tool Operation) and MUMPS (Multi-User Multi-Processing System).

FORTRAN. FORmula TRANslator. One of the earliest computer languages, FORTRAN was originally developed to make it easier to program complex scientific and engineering equations, although it's been used at one time or another for just about everything. Considered a bit old-fashioned by the avant-garde of the computer world, FORTRAN nonetheless has the advantage of being the closest thing the data processing biz has to a universal language.

PASCAL. Named for Blaise Pascal, the famous mathematician and philosopher. The comer among computer languages. Pascal may soon become more popular than BASIC. Powerful and versatile, it is said to be extremely easy to learn, although you'd never know it from looking at a program.

In a quote from a book on Pascal, it read: "FORTRAN has the rugged simplicity of a Model T Ford, and BASIC displays a childlike naivete, but Pascal exhibits the elegant simplicity that derives from economy and rightness of concept." Uh-huh.

PL/1. Programming Language 1 is a name universally regarded as an example of typical IBM arrogance, inasmuch as hundreds of languages preceded it. It must be admitted, however, that something called Programming Language 143 lacks something in the way of snappiness. PL/1 is IBM's attempt to combine the business capabilities of COBOL with the mathematical finesse of FORTRAN.

Source: Ed Zohi, "Let's Get Down to BASICs." Reprinted with permission of *Advertising Age*, 14 Nov. 1983. Copyright Crain Communications Inc.

FIGURE 6–11
Commonly used computer languages

The Computer

The heart of the electronic data processing system is the computer, an information processing machine. As illustrated in Figure 6–10, for a computer to be functional it must consist of three "hardware" components: an *input medium* for feeding information into a *central processor* that stores and manipulates information and an *output medium* for delivering the results.

Based on the number of input and output devices that can be handled simultaneously, the amount of storage or memory, and the speed of processing, computers fall into three categories.

1. **Mainframe computers** are large machines with large CPUs and vast amounts of memory. They can handle a large number of terminals simultaneously and have incredibly fast processing speeds.
2. **Microcomputers** are small personal computers with self-contained CPUs and a single, attached input terminal. While these home computers have limited memory and processing speeds, they nevertheless have many of the processing capabilities associated with mainframes. Use ranges from sophisticated desktop computers to portable typewriter-size models.
3. **Minicomputers** are medium-size computers designed for business use. They are capable of handling several terminals. Minis have memory and processing speeds sufficient for most small business systems.[9]

Computers are capable of accepting data via punched cards, punched paper tapes, magnetic tapes, teletypes, and optical scanners. Thus, the input medium can be any one or combination of the following: card readers, tape readers, teletypewriters, and wand readers.

The central processor consists of three basic units: a memory unit for internal storage of data and instruction, an arithmetic logic unit for making the necessary mathematical computations, and a control unit for guiding the operations of the other two units. The principal output media available to the retailer are those that produce printouts and visual displays. Output in the form of punched cards and magnetic tapes also is available for storing data for future use.

The Output

The output from the EDPS should be meaningful information. The whole purpose of an EDPS is to process raw data into useful information. The application of electronic data processing to the retailer's merchandising and operating activities can be quite extensive, depending upon the retailer's willingness to invest in the equipment, facilities, and personnel necessary for its operation.

Computer Applications in Retailing

"The computer has been used to improve retailers' inventory control, payroll, general ledger, merchandise reporting, purchase order management and accounts payable."[10] In addition to these conventional uses of the computer in retailing operations, "there are numerous innovative applications that can help the retail manager exploit market opportunities." Some of the more innovative applications include

- **electronic point-of-sale** systems involving cash registers that allow the retailer to quickly transcribe, validate, and collect sales information that ties specific purchases to certain consumers, thereby improving its segmentation strategies

- **electronic funds-transfer** systems that allow customers to use a bank card in making purchases by electronically transfering funds from their account to the store's account;[11] these transactions (size and nature) can be linked to demographic and psychographic information and used by the retailer in developing target market strategies
- **electronic pushbutton questionnaire** systems involving the use of a computer to conduct in-store customer surveys; one such system is TELLUS, which allows the retailer to conduct surveys on performance levels, store image, and other consumer perceptions

Retailing opportunities created by innovative computer-based technologies include

- advanced teleshopping systems that will enable consumers to sit at home and use their video screens and keypads to select merchandise, arrange for payment, and express satisfaction/dissatisfaction to channel members after purchase
- centralized retail establishments that will allow consumers to shop at home or in electronic malls and receive overnight delivery
- buyers in centralized offices that will be able to randomly ask consumers about their opinions on new fashions and other trendy merchandise
- complete customer profiles, both demographic and psychographic, could be keyed with major purchasing habits by product class and brand to provide the ultimate in direct marketing promotion
- the delivery of retail repair services will become more productive when electronic and mechanical products are diagnosed in the home over phone lines connected to retailers' diagnostic computers
- with the proliferation of electronic media, retailers will be excluded from mass market advertising blitzes; consumers could request and prescreen product information from a "retailer service bureau" that will rate each retailer
- retailers will service customers 24 hours a day, thereby eliminating the "hours of operation" limitation; retailers will provide consumers with the ability to shop at their leisure
- shopping motives will change as electronic technology eliminates or equalizes certain retail attributes; consumers' perceived images of retailers will be based on product assortment and price[12]

The preceding discussion has attempted to outline the basic elements of electronic data processing and some of its uses. Discussions throughout the remainder of the text will more fully consider the various applications of the EDPS.

SUMMARY

Information is the key to reducing the risks associated with retail decision making and problem solving. Retailers need to know what information is needed, what information is available, how to gather information, where to obtain information, and how to use information once it has been obtained.

The retailing information system consists of four basic activities: locating, gathering, processing, and utilizing information. Locating information requires the retailer to be acquainted with the various types (primary and secondary) and sources (external and internal) of information. In gathering information, the retailer engages in the four basic activities of retail intelligence, retail research, records search, and constructing analytical models. Having located and gathered the necessary information, the retailer then processes it, using either manual or electronic data processing techniques. Each of the three preceding steps is useless unless the retailer utilizes the information in day-to-day operations.

Retail intelligence is any method or combination of methods used to obtain external secondary information. The principal sources of retail intelligence are libraries, government publications (e.g., census and registration information), association information (trade and professional organizations), and commercial providers (those that make a business out of collecting, analyzing, and reporting information).

Retail research uses a set of scientific procedures to gather external primary information from consumers, suppliers, and competitors. These scientific procedures are best described in the five stages of the scientific method—identifying problems, developing hypotheses, collecting information, analyzing information, and drawing conclusions. Collection of primary information is accomplished using such research methods as surveys, observations, and experiments. Sampling procedures are crucial in conducting primary retail research. The retailer must develop the skills for identifying the sample frame, determining the sample size, and selecting the sample item. The last issue in retail research is analyzing primary information; summarization procedures, statistical inferences, Bayesian analysis, mathematical programming, and simulation all are used in the analysis process.

Electronic data processing systems are computer-based procedures for analyzing information. The retailer requires sound input, computer, and output systems to process information effectively.

KEY TERMS AND CONCEPTS

RIS	experimentation	statistical inferences
secondary information	word-association test	Bayesian analysis
primary information	sentence-completion test	mathematical programming
external information	narrative projection test	simulation
internal information	thematic apperception test	batch processing
retail intelligence	dichotomous question	real-time processing
retail research	multiple-choice question	mainframe computer
records search	rank-ordered question	microcomputer
analytical models	Likert's summated rating scale	minicomputer
manual data processing	semantic differential rating sale	electronic point-of-sale
electronic data processing	sample	electronic funds-transfer
scientific method	population	electronic pushbutton questionnaire
survey	probability sample	
observation	nonprobability sample	

REVIEW QUESTIONS

1. How does the data syndrome affect the retailing information system?
2. Why do scarcity, consumerism, and government intervention encourage retailers to develop and maintain information systems?
3. Define RIS. What are the four basic activities of an RIS?
4. Compare and contrast secondary and primary information. What are their relative advantages and disadvantages?
5. Compare and contrast external and internal sources of information.
6. Identify and define the four information-gathering methods.
7. What are the two types of systems used in processing information? Briefly describe each.
8. What are the nine censuses produced by the federal government? Briefly characterize each census.
9. How do the two general forms of commercial sources of retail intelligence differ?
10. What are the five stages of the scientific method? Describe the major task to be accomplished in each stage.
11. What are the three basic methods of collecting external primary information? Define each method.
12. Characterize the personal interview process. How should a personal interview be conducted?
13. How do mail surveys differ from personal and telephone surveys?
14. How are mail surveys administered?
15. Develop a graphic presentation of the three experimental designs used by researchers.
16. Describe the four open-ended or projective techniques used in collecting primary information.
17. Develop a questionnaire that explores why a consumer has selected a particular product brand. Use each of the three types of closed-ended questions in developing your questionnaire.
18. What guidelines should be followed to avoid the many pitfalls in wording questionnaire items?
19. How should questions be sequenced?
20. What is a sample frame?
21. Describe briefly the various types of probability and nonprobability samples.
22. In an EDPS, what is the difference between batch and real-time processing?
23. Compare and contrast the mainframe computer, microcomputer, and minicomputer.
24. What is TELLUS?

ENDNOTES

1. Robert F. Lusch, "Recent Retailing Texts: A Comparative Review," *Journal of Marketing* 43 (Fall 1979): 152.
2. Alvin Toffler, *Future Shock* (New York: Random House, 1970).
3. Charles D. Schewe and Reuben M. Smith, *Marketing: Concepts and Applications* (New York: McGraw-Hill, 1980), 79.
4. See Harper W. Boyd, Jr., Ralph Westfall, and Stanley F. Stasch, *Marketing Research: Text and Cases,* 4th ed. (Homewood, IL: Richard D. Irwin, 1977), 152.
5. See R. A. Likert, "A Technique for the Measurement of Attitudes," *Archives of Psychology* 140 (1932).
6. See C. E. Osgood, C. J. Suci, and P. H. Tannenbaum, *The Measurement of Meaning* (Urbana, IL: University of Illinois Press, 1957); William Mindak, "Fitting the Semantic Differential to the Marketing Problem," *Journal of Marketing* 25 (April 1981): 28–33.
7. Keith D. Cox and Ben M. Enis, *The Marketing Research Process* (Pacific Palisades, CA: Goodyear Publishing, 1972), 350.
8. Ibid.
9. See Antonia Stone, "Getting Out of the Maze— A Basic Primer Cuts through the Jargon," *Advertising Age,* 11 April 1983, M42; "A Glossary of Computer Terms," *Advertising Age,* 11 April 1983, M42.
10. Duane L. Davis and Mary Joyce, "Some Retailers Snooze, While Others Use New Technologies to Gain Marketing Edge," *Marketing News,* 22 November 1981, 1.
11. See Paul A. Suneson and Ernest R. Cadotte, "Research Suggests Automated Polling Machines Yield Reliable and Valid Data," *Marketing News,* 6 January 1984, 8.
12. Davis and Joyce, "Some Readers Snooze," 17.

RELATED READINGS

Abend, Jules. "Mainframe." *Stores* (May 1982), 72–77.

Bolger, Joseph P. "Dealing with the Micro Computer Revolution at J. C. Penney." *Retail Control* (October 1984), 40–49.

"Electronicstore Debuts." *Marketing News* (May 24, 1985), 1, 42.

Hansen, Robert A., and Deutscher, Terry. "Measurement Issues in Retail Image Research." *Proceedings*. H. W. Nash and D. P. Robin, eds. (Southern Marketing Association 1977), 152–55.

Hawes, Jon M.; Varble, Dale L.; and d'Amico, Michael F. "Increasing Mail Survey Response Rates." *Developments in Marketing Science, Proceedings*. N. K. Malhotra, ed. (Academy of Marketing Science 1985), 394–98.

Holbrook, Morris B. "On the Importance of Using Real Products in Research on Merchandising Strategy." *Journal of Retailing* 59 (Spring 1983), 4–20.

Horr, David A., and Barker, William E. "Choosing Your First Computer System." *Retail Control* (March 1984), 46–54.

Joseph, Anthony M. "EPP Strategies: New Options, New Challenges." *Retail Control* (August 1983), 44–64.

Prasad, V. Kanti; Casper, Wayne R.; and Schieffer, Robert J. "Alternatives to the Traditional Retail Store Audit: A Field Study." *Journal of Marketing* 48 (Winter 1984), 54–61.

Schulz, David P. "EFTS Status Report." *Stores* (March 1985), 61–63.

Seiberling, Steve; Taylor, Steve; and Ursic, Michael. "Open Ended Question V. Rating Scale: An Empirical Comparison." *Developments in Marketing Science, Proceedings*. J. C. Rogers, III, ed. (Academy of Marketing Science 1983), 440–45.

"Toffler on Marketing." *Marketing News* (March 15, 1985), 1, 30–31.

Tse, David K. C. "Retail Store Image Research—A Critical Review." *Developments in Marketing Science, Proceedings*. J. C. Rogers, III, ed. (Academy of Marketing Science 1983), 28–33.

Tyebjee, Tyzoon. "Telephone Survey Methods: The State of the Art." *Journal of Marketing* 43 (Summer 1979), 68–78.

Zikmund, William G. *Exploring Marketing Research*, 2nd ed. (New York: The Dryden Press, 1985)

PART THREE
Appraising the Retailer's Resources

Outline

THE RETAILER'S FINANCIAL RECORDS

THE RETAILER'S FINANCIAL STATEMENTS

The Income Statement
The Balance Sheet
The Financial Status Checklist

PERFORMANCE ANALYSIS

Operating Ratios
Financial Ratios

CAPITAL MANAGEMENT

Capital Requirements
Types of Financing
Sources of Funding

EXPENSE MANAGEMENT

Expense Classification
Expense Allocation
Expense Budgeting

Objectives

- Defend the need for fiscal control as an essential ingredient in any successful retail operation

- Identify and define the basic financial records required to accomplish fiscal control

- Discuss the concept of profit and its impact on retailing activities

- Prepare a basic income statement for a retailing enterprise

- Prepare a basic balance sheet for a retailing enterprise

- Analyze and evaluate the operational and financial performance of a retail firm

- Explain how to generate and maintain sufficient capital to conduct a retail business

- Describe the procedures for managing the retailer's operating expenses

7
Managing the Firm's Finances

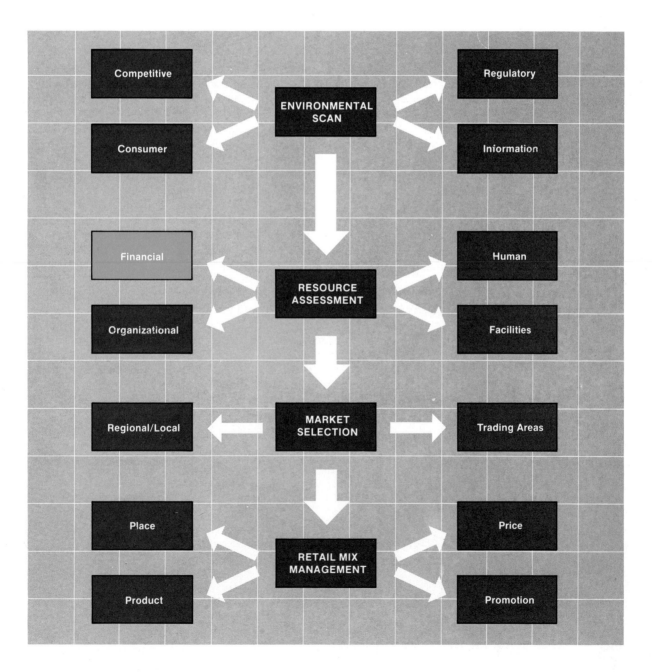

Fiscal control is an essential ingredient to success of any retail operation. To develop and maintain a viable retail enterprise, the retailer must control the financial health of the firm. Many retailers encounter financial trouble in spite of respectable sales volumes. A common cause of such trouble is insufficient planning and control of the firm's financial affairs. Before the retailer can improve operations, it must be fully aware of the present state of operations. In this chapter, we examine the retailer's financial system. As Figure 7–1 illustrates, the retailer's financial system consists of (1) developing and maintaining good financial records, (2) preparing and analyzing financial statements, (3) constructing and evaluating financial performance ratios, and (4) obtaining and managing capital funds and planning and controlling operating expenses. Each of these tasks is examined in this chapter.

THE RETAILER'S FINANCIAL RECORDS

The retailer's financial records begin with bits and pieces of paper—saleschecks, credit memos, cash register tapes, written receipts, check stubs, petty cash slips, bank statements, and a host of other forms and statements.[1] The papers are essential, for they are the foundation upon which record keeping procedures are built. To organize the facts and figures contained on each of these papers, the retailer must establish some type of record keeping system. A good record keeping system is simple to use, easy to understand, reliable, accurate, consistent, and designed to provide information on a timely basis.[2] Size and operational complexities of the retail firm determine the type and level of sophistication of the record keeping system the retailer uses. Most retailers, however, maintain a number of ledger accounts. "An **account** is *a record of the increases and decreases in one type of asset, liability, capital, income, or expense. A book or file in which a number of accounts are kept together is a* **ledger**."[3] The following basic ledger accounts or records are fairly standard:

- cash receipts—used to record the cash received
- cash disbursements—used to record the firm's expenditures
- sales—used to record and summarize monthly income
- purchases—used to record the purchases of merchandise bought for processing or resale
- payroll—used to record the wages of employees and their deductions, such as income tax and social security
- equipment—used to record the firm's capital assets, such as equipment, office furniture, and motor vehicles

FIGURE 7–1
The retailer's financial system

- inventory—used to record the firm's investment in stock, needed to arrive at a true profit on financial statements and for income tax purposes
- accounts receivable—used to record the balances that customers owe to the firm
- accounts payable—used to record what the firm owes its creditors and suppliers[4]

As one accountant found, "A set of books is like a roll of exposed film. The latter must be developed before you can see the picture. Similarly, your books contain facts and figures which make up a picture of your business. They have to be arranged into an order before you see the picture."[5]

To gain a clear picture of the firm's financial position, the retailer must prepare two standard financial statements—the income statement and the balance sheet. The **income statement** (also referred to as the profit and loss statement, operating statement, or earnings statement) is *a picture of the retailer's profits or losses over a period of time;* it summarizes the firm's income and expenses. The **balance sheet** is *a picture of the firm's assets, liabilities, and net worth on a given date;* it summarizes the basic accounting equation of assets equal liabilities plus net worth.

THE RETAILER'S FINANCIAL STATEMENTS

The Income Statement

To understand fully the many dimensions of profit, the retailer must have some procedure for organizing these dimensions. The retail accounting procedure known as the income statement is an excellent means by which to organize and understand the many facets of profit. The income statement is a summary of the retailer's financial activity for a given period of time. The principal objective of the income statement is to show whether the retailer had a profit or a loss. Before examining the various considerations in preparing an income statement, we shall first review the basic profit concept.

The Profit Concept

Customer satisfaction at a profit has previously been identified as the overriding objective of every retailer. Both elements (customer satisfaction and profit) are essential to operating a successful retailing enterprise. The successful retailer cannot have one element without the other, at least not over an extended period of time. Dissatisfied customers will soon turn profits to losses, and unsatisfactory profits—or losses—will soon force the retailer out of business. Therefore, every retailer needs to understand the concept of "profit": what it is, how to determine it, and how to evaluate it.

It has often been said that "profit will take care of itself if the retailer will take care of sales and expenses." In essence, this statement expresses the basic relationship in the profit concept—profit or loss is the *difference* between the retailer's sales volume and the total of all expenses. The retailer realizes a profit when sales revenues exceed both the cost of the goods sold and all the direct and indirect expenses incurred in selling those goods. When sales revenues are not sufficient to cover the cost of goods sold and all operating expenses, the retailer suffers a loss. To be profitable, the retailer must obtain goods (suitable to the target market) at the lowest possible price, maintain strict control over all operating expenses, and increase sales revenues at the same time.

The concept of profit is viewed in many different ways. It can be thought of as (1) the money the retailer gains over time as the result of buying and selling activities; (2) the retailer's reward or return for ideas, work, and investment; (3) the means of assuring the long-term continuation of the retailer's business; (4) the measure of the retailer's success; (5) what the retailer must pay income tax on; and (6) the performance criterion by which the retailer can be judged or evaluated.

The term "profit" is a relative word that can be determined and expressed in a variety of ways, depending upon the context in which it is used. For example, we can express profit as either operating or net profit, dollar or percentage profit, or before- or after-tax profit. Also, profit can be expressed in relation to sales, selling space, number of transactions, net worth, and average inventory investment.

Preparation of the Income Statement

Time, unit, and usage are three important variables retailers must consider in preparing the income statement. *Time* considerations concern when income statements are prepared. Depending upon the individual retailer and the type of operation, income statements can be (and often are) prepared annually, semiannually, quarterly, monthly, or over any other time frame the retailer deems necessary. Federal and state income tax regulations require that the retailer prepare at least an annual income statement. However, by preparing the income statement on a more frequent basis, the retailer can maintain closer control over operations.

Unit considerations influence how many income statements and at what organization level income statements are prepared. Both the size and the organizational structure of the retail firm have direct impact on these two questions. For the small, independent retailer, a single income statement should suffice for the entire store. A department store typically would prepare an income statement for each department as well as for the store as a whole. For a departmentalized chain store operation, income statements are prepared for the department and store unit as well as for the entire chain organization. As with greater frequency of preparation, greater control of operations is the primary advantage gained by preparing income statements for each of the retailer's operating units.

Usage considerations involve the type of format to use in preparing income statements. Because retailing organizations vary in size, type, and organizational structure, no single or standardized income statement format is appropriate for all firms. Thus, the retailer must adjust the income statement format to accommodate its individual needs. Nevertheless, a retailer should select an appropriate standardized format, since standardization will allow the retailer to (1) compare current income statements with previous statements and (2) analyze trends in sales, expenses, profits, and losses.

Elements of the Income Statement

Whether the retailer prepares its own statement or has an accountant prepare it, each retailer should understand the basic elements of the income statement and the relationships among them. Every income statement has at least nine basic elements, regardless of the size, type, or organizational structure of the retail enterprise. Figure 7–2 illustrates the nine elements and the relationships that exist among them, and it shows that the elements of an income statement can be divided into two major groups: income measurements and income modifications.

Income measurements are *different expressions of the monetary gain the retailer realizes from retailing activities.* The exact nature of each income measurement depends on where it appears in the income statement and the income modifications that have been applied in calculating it. Figure 7–2 shows five income measurements—gross sales, net sales, gross margin, operating profit, and net

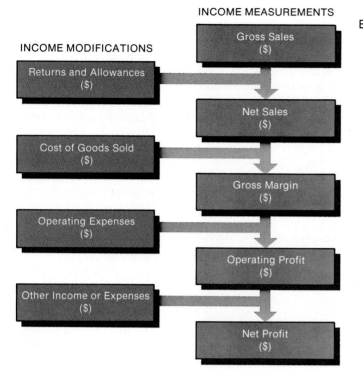

FIGURE 7–2
Elements of the income
statement

profit. In essence, each income expression represents the monetary gain the retailer realizes before making certain adjustments.

Income modifications are *monetary additions or reductions applied to one income measurement to calculate another measurement of income.* These income modifications simply reflect normal adjustments required by the operating characteristics of the retailer. Most income modifications are reductions; they represent the various costs the retailer incurs in conducting the business, and they are necessary to arrive at the retailer's true income—the bottom line of the income statement or net profit before taxes. In one case, an income modification represents an addition to a measurement of income. This "other income" usually represents income the retailer generates outside normal retailing activities. As illustrated in Figure 7–2, there are four general income modifications—returns and allowances, cost of goods sold, operating expenses, and other income or expenses.

The basic format for the income statement is shown in Figure 7–3. The retailer must carefully follow the format to maintain the correct relationships between the basic statement elements.

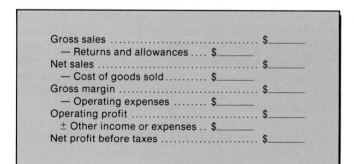

FIGURE 7–3
Format of the income
statement

201

Gross sales.   Gross sales can be defined as *the total dollar revenues the retailer receives from the sale of merchandise and services.* The gross sales figure, which includes both cash and credit sales, is obtained by first posting in a sales ledger all cash and credit sales at the price actually charged customers, then totaling those sales for the appropriate accounting period. The gross sales figure is the starting point from which all other income measurements are calculated. This figure is important because it reflects the total dollar amount that must not only cover all of the retailer's costs of doing business but also provide a reward (profit) for conducting that business.

To better understand the gross sales figure, many retailers calculate a number of ratios and make a number of comparisons. The relationship of gross sales to different operating characteristics can greatly enhance the retailer's understanding of its sales picture and the operation's efficiency. Some of the more commonly computed relationships are

$$\frac{\text{gross sales per square}}{\text{foot of selling space}} = \frac{\text{gross sales dollars}}{\text{square feet of selling space}}$$

$$\text{average gross sales size} = \frac{\text{gross sales dollars}}{\text{total number of sales transactions}}$$

$$\text{gross sales per employee} = \frac{\text{gross sales dollars}}{\text{total number of employees}}$$

To gain a measurement of the effectiveness of the retailer's sales force, total number of salespersons can be substituted for total number of employees.

While gross sales relationships provide insight into the retailer's operations, these insights can be greatly enhanced by comparing the gross sales figure with both internal and external records. For example, by comparing current gross sales figures with the same figures for previous accounting periods, the retailer can identify sales gains or losses as well as any emerging sales patterns or trends. By examining trade data, the retailer can also make comparisons between gross sales performance and that of similar retail operations. Most trade associations periodically publish various averages for their particular industry (e.g., food, hardware, clothing). In summary, gross sales comparisons enable the retailer to evaluate sales-performance levels according to company and industry standards.

Returns and allowances.   Not all customer purchases are finalized with the initial sale. Some customers will become dissatisfied with their purchases and will expect the retailer to make some sort of adjustment. **Returns from customers** and **allowances to customers,** *two means by which retailers adjust for customer dissatisfaction, represent cancellation of sales;* therefore, the gross sales figure must be adjusted to reflect these cancellations. While some returns and allowances are expected, excessive returns and allowances can be a major problem. A control procedure should be established to analyze the causes of returns and allowances (see the discussion on customer complaints in Chapter 16) and to determine whether they are excessive, relative to industry norms.

Returns and allowances can be expressed in percentage terms and compared with previous years or with industry-wide averages. The retailer can use the following formula to compute the return and allowance percentage:

$$\text{return and allowance percentage} = \frac{\text{returns and allowances in dollars}}{\text{net sales dollars}}$$

Analyzing returns and allowances is important because it helps the retailer to identify areas of customer dissatisfaction and to prevent additional expenses associated with those returns and allowances.

Net sales. Net sales, *the income measurement that results when returns and allowances are subtracted from gross sales,* represent the amount of merchandise the retailer actually sold during the accounting period. Most retailers perform the same type of analysis on net sales as they do on gross sales; they calculate net sales per square foot, average net sales, and net sales per employee group. In addition, they make both internal comparisons with past accounting periods and external comparisons with trade averages.

Cost of goods sold. *The value of the merchandise the retailer sells during any given accounting period* is the **cost of goods sold.** The cost of goods sold is a function of six factors: beginning inventory, net purchases, transportation charges, ending inventory, cash discounts earned, and alteration and workroom costs. The format for calculating cost of goods sold is illustrated in Figure 7–4. As shown, the calculating procedures consist of four steps: determining (1) total goods handled, (2) gross cost of goods sold, (3) net cost of goods sold, and (4) total cost of goods sold.

The first step in calculating cost of goods sold is to determine the total amount of goods that were handled during the accounting period. **Total goods handled** is *the value of the beginning inventory plus net purchases and transportation charges during the accounting period.* **Beginning inventory** is *the dollar value of the inventory the retailer has on hand at the beginning of the accounting period (usually the value of the ending inventory for the previous period).*

Net purchases are *calculated by subtracting from gross purchases the returns to and allowances from suppliers.* **Gross purchases** are *expressed in terms of "billed costs" to the retailer, and they represent the invoice cost minus any trade and/or quantity discounts granted by the supplier.* **Returns to vendors** occur *when the retailer returns merchandise to the supplier,* and **allowances from vendors** occur *when the retailer receives a downward price adjustment from the supplier.* **Transportation charges** are *costs the retailer incurs in getting the merchandise to the store from the supplier's place of business.* In addition to the actual transit charges, handling costs and insurance in transit must be included if the retailer is responsible for these charges.

FIGURE 7–4

Calculating cost of goods sold

```
Opening inventory ....................... ($)
     + Net purchases .................... ($)
     + Transportation charges............ ($)

Total goods handled .................... ($)
     − Ending inventory ................ ($)

Gross cost of goods sold ............... ($)
     − Cash discounts earned ........... ($)

Net cost of goods sold ................. ($)
     + Alteration and workroom costs .... ($)

Total cost of goods sold ............... ($)
```

The second step in calculating cost of goods sold is determining **gross cost of goods sold.** *Total goods handled (computed in the first step) minus ending inventory equals gross cost of goods sold* (see Figure 7–4). **Ending inventory** is *the value of the goods the retailer has on hand at the end of the accounting period;* however, the value of the ending inventory may not be worth what the retailer originally paid for it. The value of the ending inventory may have increased or decreased, depending on general marketplace conditions and the retailer's individual operating conditions. For example, increases or decreases in the value of the retailer's inventory will occur as a result of increases and decreases in wholesale prices.

Ending inventory must be examined to determine its true worth. Incorrect inventory valuation can result in a number of adverse effects. An undervalued ending inventory understates profits for the current accounting period but overstates profits for the next accounting period. An overvalued ending inventory overstates profits for the current accounting period but understates profits of the next accounting period. Incorrect inventory also leads to overpaying or underpaying taxes during a given accounting period.

Several different methods can determine the value of an ending inventory (e.g., cost and retail methods); each of these methods will be discussed in detail in Chapter 20. For present purposes, the objective of any valuation of inventory is to obtain a conservative estimate. Original cost or current market value, whichever is lower, provides the best conservative estimate of inventory. For example, if the ending inventory had cost the retailer $9,000 and the current market value of that inventory is appraised at $11,000, the retailer values it at the lower cost of $9,000. On the other hand, if the current market value has declined to $7,000, then the market value of $7,000 is used.

If *cash discounts earned by the retailer are subtracted from gross cost of goods sold, the remainder* is **net cost of goods sold** (see Figure 7–4). The retailer earns **cash discounts** *if it makes full payment of the invoice within a prescribed period of time.* (Chapter 17 discusses cash discounts in detail.) Because cash discounts represent a reduction in the cost of goods sold, they must be deducted from gross cost of goods sold to arrive at the net cost of goods sold.

By *adding alteration and workroom costs to net costs of goods sold,* the retailer can arrive at the **total cost of goods sold.** Frequently, merchandise must be altered to meet the needs of the consumer. This creation of "form utility" by the retailer adds to the cost of the merchandise, and this cost must be included in the calculation of the total cost of goods sold. Alteration and workroom costs include not only materials and labor costs, but also operating supplies and expenses directly involved.

Gross margin. Gross margin is defined as *the dollar difference between the retailer's net sales and the total cost of goods sold* (see Figure 7–3). It represents the funds available for covering operating expenses and generating a profit. Gross margin is sometimes referred to as gross profit. The gross profit term is misleading since gross margin dollars might not be sufficient to cover expenses, let alone provide a profit.

Operating expenses. Every retailer incurs certain expenses (payroll, rent, utilities, supplies, etc.) in operating a business. To realize a profit, the retailer's **operating expenses** must be less than the gross margin figure identified in the previous discussion. Therefore, every retailer must fully understand the management of operating expenses. Later in this chapter we shall look at expense management in terms of expense classification, expense allocation, and expense budgeting.

Operating profit. *The difference between gross margin and operating expenses is the retailer's* **operating profit** (see Figure 7–3). It is what remains after the retailer has covered the cost of goods sold and the cost of doing business. For any given operating unit within the retailer's organization (e.g., a department within a store), operating profit represents the final expression of profit. However, operating profit is not the figure that determines the retailer's tax liability; net profit must be determined by considering other income and expenses associated with the operation.

Other income and/or expenses. The final modification to the income statement is considering other income the retailer receives and other expenses incurred in conducting the business. **Other income** can be defined as *additional revenues that result from retailing activities other than the buying and selling of goods and services.* Rent from a leased department, interest on installment credit, and interest on deposited bank funds are all examples of other income that must be added to operating profit to obtain the retailer's net profit. Before the retailer can compute the final net sales figure, however, some additional expenses must be deducted from the operating profit figure. *Interest paid by the retailer on borrowed funds is an example of* **other expenses.**

Net profit. Net profit is *operating profit plus other income and minus other expenses* (see Figure 7–3). Net profit is the figure upon which the retailer pays income tax, and it is usually referred to either in terms of "net profit before taxes" or "net profit after taxes."

The Balance Sheet

The second accounting statement used in reporting financial information is the balance sheet—a statement of the retailer's financial condition as of a given date. In its most basic form, the balance sheet summarizes the relationship among the retailer's assets, liabilities, and net worth. The following equation shows this basic balance sheet relationship:

$$\text{assets} = \text{liabilities} + \text{net worth}$$

The balance sheet is prepared to show what the retailer owns (the amount and distribution of assets), what the retailer owes (the amount and distribution of liabilities), and what the retailer is worth (the difference between assets and liabilities). By comparing the current year's balance sheet with those of previous years, the retailer can identify any changes in the firm's financial position and determine whether any operational improvements are possible. Later in this chapter, we will examine a number of ratios computed from information contained in the balance sheet; these standard ratios serve as measurements for making useful comparisons.

A typical balance sheet format, illustrated in Figure 7–5, consists of two major parts. The first part is a listing of assets, while the second part lists the retailer's liabilities and states the equity position (the net worth of the owners). As Figure 7–5 shows, the total assets figure always equals the sum of total liabilities plus net worth. We shall examine these major elements to better understand the composition of the balance sheet.

The Retailer's Assets

The first part of the balance sheet reports the retailer's asset position. An **asset** is *anything of value owned by the retail firm.* Assets are categorized into two groups, current assets and fixed assets.

FIGURE 7–5
Balance sheet format

Assets		
Current assets		
Cash	$10,000	
Accounts	15,000	
Merchandise inventory	90,000	
Supply inventory	5,000	
Total current assets		$120,000
Fixed assets		
Building (less depreciation)	75,000	
Fixtures and equipment	25,000	
(less depreciation)		
Total fixed assets		100,000
Total assets		220,000
Liabilities and net worth		
Current liabilities		
Accounts payable	$25,000	
Payroll payable	10,000	
Taxes payable	5,000	
Notes payable	15,000	
Total current liabilities		$55,000
Fixed liabilities		
Mortgage payable	50,000	
Notes payable	20,000	
Total fixed liabilities		70,000
Net worth		
Capital surplus	85,000	
Retained earnings	10,000	
Total net worth		95,000
Total liabilities and net worth		$220,000

Current assets *include all items of value that the retailer can easily convert into cash within a relatively short time, usually within one year or less.* In addition to cash on hand, current assets include accounts receivable, merchandise inventory, and supply inventory. Accounts receivable are amounts that customers *owe* the retailer for goods and services. Frequently, the retailer reduces the accounts receivable figure by some fixed percentage (based on past experience) to take into account customers that will eventually default on their payments. The retailer makes this adjustment to avoid overstating assets. The value of the merchandise on hand at the time of preparing the balance sheet is a part of the retailer's current assets. Stating the merchandise inventory in terms of "cost or current market value, whichever is lower" is a more conservative approach that helps the retailer avoid overstating its assets. Supply inventory reflects operating supplies on hand that have been paid for but not used; in effect, they represent prepaid expenses. The retailer arrives at the total current asset figure by totaling cash on hand, accounts receivable, merchandise inventory, and supply inventory (see Figure 7–5).

Fixed assets *are those that require a significant length of time to convert into cash* (more than one year). These long-term assets including buildings, fixtures (e.g., display racks), and equipment (e.g., delivery trucks). The value of fixed assets is expressed in terms of their cost to the retailer minus an assigned depreciation. This depreciation is necessary because fixed assets have a limited useful life; therefore, it provides a better reflection of their true value. The depreciation also helps to avoid overstating the retailer's total assets. Although not shown in Figure 7–5, some retailers include a fixed asset value for such intangibles as goodwill or the store loyalty the retailer has developed. Usually the value assigned to intangible assets is minimal.

Total assets equal *current assets plus fixed assets* (see Figure 7–5). Now let's look at the other half of the balance sheet.

The Retailer's Liabilities

Part two of the balance sheet reflects the retailer's liabilities and net worth. A **liability** is *a debt owed to someone.* On the balance sheet, liabilities represent a legitimate claim against the retailer's assets. Liabilities are classified as either current or long-term.

Current liabilities are *short-term debts that must be paid during the current fiscal year.* Included in the current liabilities column are accounts payable, payroll payable, and notes payable that are due within one year. Accounts payable is money owed suppliers for goods and services they have provided the retailer. Payroll payable is money owed store employees for labor performed for the retailer. Principal and interest the retailer owes on a bank loan (notes payable) and taxes the retailer owes local, state, and federal governments (taxes payable) are classified as current liabilities.

Long-term liabilities are *long-term indebtedness.* Mortgages and long-term notes and bonds not due during the current fiscal year are the most common long-term liabilities. Another category sometimes treated as a long-term liability is a reserve account to provide the retailer with funds for emergencies. The total liability figure is computed by combining the current and long-term liabilities.

The Retailer's Net Worth

Net worth represents *the owner's equity in the retail business and is defined by the following equation:*

$$\text{net worth} = \text{total assets} - \text{total liabilities}$$

Another way to look at net worth is to view it as the owner's share of the firm's total assets.

The Financial Status Checklist

To achieve sound fiscal control over the retail operation, the retailer must maintain accurate and timely records and statements. Figure 7–6 illustrates a financial status checklist of the kinds of financial information retailers need and how frequently (daily, weekly, and monthly) they should compile this information. By carefully checking the status of each financial record on a frequent, regular basis, retailers can identify problem situations and take the necessary action to correct or eliminate those problems. Examples of problems retailers can identify and correct include wasteful spending, unreasonable shortages, incorrect tax reporting, improper buying procedures, unnecessary labor costs, and excessive bad-debt losses.

FIGURE 7–6
Financial status check-
list for retailers

Daily
1. cash on hand
2. bank balance (business and personal funds kept separate)
3. daily summary of sales and cash receipts
4. all errors in recording collections on accounts corrected
5. a record maintained of all monies paid out, by cash or check

Weekly
1. accounts receivable (action taken on slow payers)
2. accounts payable (advantage taken of discounts)
3. payroll (records include name and address of employee, social security number, number of exemptions, date ending the pay period, hours worked, rate of pay, total wages, deductions, net pay, check number)
4. taxes (sales, withholding, social security, etc.) paid and reports to state and federal government completed on time

Monthly
1. all journal entries classified according to like elements (these should be generally accepted and standard for both income and expense) and posted to general ledger
2. income statement for the month available within a reasonable time—usually 10 to 15 days following the close of the month
3. balance sheet accompanying the income statement, showing assets (what the business has), liabilities (what the business owes), and the investment of the owner
4. bank statement reconciled (that is, the owner's books are in agreement with the bank's record of the cash balance)
5. petty cash account in balance (that is, the actual cash in the petty cash box, plus the total of the paid-out slips that have not been charged to expense, total the amount set aside as petty cash)
6. all federal tax deposits, withheld income and FICA taxes, and state taxes made
7. accounts receivable aged—i.e., 30, 60, 90 days, etc., past due (all bad and slow accounts pursued)
8. inventory control worked to remove dead stock and order new stock (What moves slowly? Reduce. What moves fast? Increase.)

Source: Adapted from John Cotlon, *Keeping Records in Small Business,* Small Marketers Aids No. 155 (Washington, D.C.: Small Business Administration, May, 1974), 8.

PERFORMANCE ANALYSIS

The income statement and balance sheet provide the retailer with a wealth of data. To convert these data into meaningful information, retailers rely on **ratio analysis**—*an examination of the relationship between elements in the income statement and/or the balance sheet.* A number of different ratios and relationships can assist retailers in their appraisal of the firm's past and present performances as well as provide some insight into the firm's future performance. By making comparisons among the firm's past ratios and the ratios of similar national and local firms, the retailer can make a constructive evaluation of the firm's performance. Past performance and trade standards provide the necessary reference points for making valid judgments on how well the firm is achieving its financial goals. Ratios can be grouped into two general categories: operating ratios and financial ratios.

Operating Ratios

Operating ratios *express relationships between elements of the income statement.* They are used to judge how efficient the retailer is in generating sales and in managing expenses. To obtain operating ratios, one element of the retailer's income statement must be divided by another element and multiplied by 100. To illustrate the use of operating ratios, we use Figure 7–7. This figure uses information from an income statement (see Figure 7–7a) to calculate several operating ratios (see Figure 7–7b) that show the basic relationship between net sales and (1) gross sales, (2) cost of goods sold, (3) gross margin, (4) operating expenses, (5) operating profit, and (6) net profit. By making historical comparisons with past years, the

FIGURE 7–7

The use of operating
ratios

(a) 1986 Income Statement:
The Smart Shop

Gross sales............................		$220,000
− Returns and allowances	$ 4,000	
Net sales		$216,000
− Cost of goods sold	$104,000	
Gross margin		$112,000
− Operating expenses..........	$ 80,000	
Operating profit		$ 32,000
+ Other income..............	$ 1,000	
− Other expenses	$ 3,000	
Net profit..............................		$ 30,000

(b) 1986 Operating Ratios
The Smart Shop

Ratio	Calculation	Interpretation
$\dfrac{\text{Gross sales}}{\text{Net sales}}$	$\dfrac{\$220,000}{\$216,000} \times 100$	Gross sales equal 102 percent of net sales.
$\dfrac{\text{Cost of goods sold}}{\text{Net sales}}$	$\dfrac{\$104,000}{\$216,000} \times 100$	Cost of goods sold equals 48.1 percent of net sales.
$\dfrac{\text{Gross margin}}{\text{Net sales}}$	$\dfrac{\$112,000}{\$216,000} \times 100$	Gross margin equals 51.9 percent of net sales.
$\dfrac{\text{Operating expenses}}{\text{Net sales}}$	$\dfrac{\$ 80,000}{\$216,000} \times 100$	Operating expenses equal 37 percent of net sales.
$\dfrac{\text{Operating profit}}{\text{Net sales}}$	$\dfrac{\$ 32,000}{\$216,000} \times 100$	Operating profit equals 14.8 percent of net sales.
$\dfrac{\text{Net profit}}{\text{Net sales}}$	$\dfrac{\$ 30,000}{\$216,000} \times 100$	Net profit equals 13.9 percent of net sales.

retailer can detect any positive or negative changes that might be significant in judging operating efficiency. Comparisons with trade data allow the retailer to determine whether significant differences exist between its operation and national operating norms.

Financial Ratios

Financial ratios *express relationships between the elements of a balance sheet or between a balance sheet element and an element in the income statement.* These ratios are used to identify relative strengths and weaknesses in the retailer's financial status and to discover trends that will affect the firm's future performance capabilities. Liquidity, leverage, and profitability ratios are the three key financial areas of concern.

Liquidity Ratios

Liquidity determines whether the retailer can meet its payment obligations as they mature. It is the state of possessing sufficient liquid assets that can be quickly and easily converted to cash to meet scheduled payments or to take advantage of special merchandising opportunities. Liquidity ratios answer the question of "how solvent is the retailer?" The current ratio and the quick ratio are the two most commonly used measures of the solvency or insolvency of a retailing enterprise.

The **current ratio** *represents the retailer's ability to meet current debts with current assets; it is computed by dividing current assets by current liabilities* (see previous definitions of current assets and liabilities). While the desired current ratio will depend on the nature of the retailer's operation (i.e., high volume, high turnover operations do not require as high a ratio as low volume, low turnover retailers), a current ratio of 2 to 1, two dollars of current assets to one dollar of current liabilities, is the most commonly used benchmark in retailing. Low current ratios suggest liquidity problems; high ratios indicate good long-term solvency. If a retailer's current ratio is too high, however, it might indicate that management is not using its assets to their fullest potential.

The **quick ratio** *is a more severe measure of the retailer's liquidity position.* It measures the retailer's ability to meet current payments with assets that can be immediately converted to cash. To calculate the quick ratio (also referred to as the acid test), simply divide the firm's quick assets by its current liabilities. Quick assets include cash, readily marketable securities, notes receivable, and accounts receivable.[6] Typically, a quick ratio of 1.1 is deemed satisfactory for most retailing organizations.

Leverage Ratios

Owner financing versus creditor financing is addressed by leverage ratios. A **leverage ratio** *measures the relative contributions of owners and creditors in the financing of the firm's operations.* One type of leverage ratio is the **debt ratio**—*total debt (current plus long-term liabilities) divided by total assets (current plus fixed assets).* The higher the ratio, the greater the role of creditors in the firm's total financing. Within reason, owners like to limit their own financial investment; hence they prefer high debt ratios while creditors prefer the lower risks associated with more moderate debt ratios.

To compare what the retail firm owes to what it owns, management can compute the **debt to net worth ratio**—*a measure of the retailer's ability to cover both creditor and owner obligations in case of liquidation.* Total debt divided by tangible net worth equals the debt to net worth ratio (i.e., current liabilities plus long-term liabilities minus capital plus capital stock plus earnings surplus plus retained earnings minus intangible assets).[7] Higher debt to net worth ratios result in greater risk to creditors and greater difficulty for owners in securing credit. A high ratio suggests a possible undercapitalization of the firm and an overextension in terms of credit.

Profitability Ratios

An overall assessment of a retailer's performance in terms of profit can be obtained from the Strategic Profit Model (SPM). The SPM is

$$\frac{\text{profit}}{\text{margin}} \times \frac{\text{asset}}{\text{turnover}} = \frac{\text{return on}}{\text{assets}} \times \frac{\text{financial}}{\text{leverage}} = \frac{\text{return on}}{\text{net worth}}$$

where

Profit margin is net profit (after taxes) divided by net sales. This ratio measures the after-tax profit per dollar of sales.

Asset turnover is net sales divided by total assets. This ratio measures the productivity of the firm with respect to asset utilization.

Return on assets is net profit (after taxes) divided by total assets. This ratio measures the return on all funds invested in the firm by both owners and creditors.

Financial leverage is total assets divided by net worth. This ratio is a measure of the relative owner/creditor contributions in the firm's capital structure.

Return on net worth is net profit (after taxes) divided by net worth. This ratio measures the return on funds invested in the firm by its owners.

Profitability goals can be established by setting a target rate of return on net worth. Profit performance can be judged by how well the firm achieves its targeted return. What constituted a high performer in the retail industry has varied considerably over the last few decades; the definition of high performance increased from 4.4 percent return on net worth in 1960 to 10.0 percent in 1980.[8] To improve its return on net worth ratio, a retailer can strive to improve profit margins, increase its asset turnover rate, or seek higher leverage ratios.

The most widely used financial ratios are those reported by Dun & Bradstreet in its publication *Industry Norms and Key Business Ratios.* An example of these ratios is shown in Figure 7–8. These key performance measurements aid the retailer in making meaningful comparisons between the firm's financial performance and the national median performance of similar retailers. These ratios are also useful in establishing realistic financial objectives. In evaluating the firm's performance against these national norms, however, the retailer must recognize that the firm's individual circumstances might prohibit direct comparisons. The ratios of retailing are used as basic reference points and not as absolute guidelines for judging financial performance levels for a given retail firm.

CAPITAL MANAGEMENT

A major concern of every retailer is how to create and maintain sufficient capital to conduct business. Careful financial planning and control are means to alleviate this concern. Few retailers, if any, have enough money available at all times to finance daily business operations and meet long-term investment requirements. Hence, the retailer's ability to *obtain* money and to secure *credit* is essential to sustaining a healthy financial situation.

	SIC 5271 Mobile Home Dealers (no breakdown)		SIC 5311 Department Stores (no breakdown)		SIC 5331 Variety Stores (no breakdown)		SIC 5399 Misc Genl Mdse Stores (no breakdown)	
	1982 (826 Estab)		1982 (1072 Estab)		1982 (747 Estab)		1982 (1962 Estab)	
	$	%	$	%	$	%	$	%
Cash	35,420	9.0	82,323	8.2	16,045	10.2	21,585	11.2
Accounts receivable	20,071	5.1	162,638	16.2	2,360	1.5	12,912	6.7
Notes receivable	6,690	1.7	10,039	1.0	472	0.3	964	0.5
Inventory	186,153	47.3	448,762	44.7	93,911	59.7	95,783	49.7
Other current	19,678	5.0	45,177	4.5	4,876	3.1	7,323	3.8
Total current	268,013	68.1	748,940	74.6	117,664	74.8	138,568	71.9
Fixed assets	56,279	14.3	129,508	12.9	25,641	16.3	32,185	16.7
Other non-current	69,266	17.6	125,493	12.5	14,000	8.9	21,970	11.4
Total assets	393,558	100.0	1,003,941	100.0	157,305	100.0	192,723	100.0
Accounts payable	16,136	4.1	106,418	10.6	16,202	10.3	17,923	9.3
Bank loans	11,413	2.9	24,095	2.4	5,820	3.7	4,047	2.1
Notes payable	33,059	8.4	25,099	2.5	5,506	3.5	4,818	2.5
Other current	127,513	32.4	106,418	10.6	14,629	9.3	14,069	7.3
Total current	188,121	47.8	262,029	26.1	42,158	26.8	40,857	21.2
Other long term	48,408	12.3	139,548	13.9	19,191	12.2	19,850	10.3
Deferred credits	1,181	0.3	2,008	0.2				
Net worth	155,849	39.6	600,357	59.8	95,956	61.0	132,015	68.5
Total liab & net worth	393,558	100.0	1,003,941	100.0	157,305	100.0	192,723	100.0
Net sales	943,404	100.0	1,729,833	100.0	319,826	100.0	334,147	100.0
Gross profit	187,737	19.9	572,575	33.1	98,506	30.8	98,573	29.5
Net profit after tax	25,472	2.7	44,976	2.6	15,991	5.0	20,383	6.1
Working capital	79,892	—	486,911	—	75,506	—	97,711	—

Ratios	UQ	MED	LQ	UQ	MED	LQ	UQ	MED	LQ	UQ	MED	LQ
Solvency												
Quick ratio (times)	0.5	0.2	0.1	2.2	1.1	0.4	1.3	0.4	0.2	2.4	0.9	0.3
Current ratio (times)	1.9	1.3	1.1	5.4	3.1	2.0	7.3	3.3	1.8	8.9	3.9	2.0
Curr liab to NW (%)	53.0	153.4	362.3	16.6	41.1	83.9	12.7	37.7	101.1	8.7	25.7	65.8
Curr liab to INV (%)	79.9	101.1	121.3	32.3	54.9	83.1	17.9	37.2	68.2	17.2	36.7	69.1
Total liab to NW (%)	79.2	209.4	437.4	20.7	64.5	147.8	20.1	59.8	151.7	13.3	38.7	107.3
Fixed assets to NW (%)	14.6	41.6	85.3	7.1	19.9	51.0	10.5	25.4	54.7	7.5	21.2	53.2
Efficiency												
Coll period (days)	2.5	6.9	16.0	5.4	24.8	55.4	1.0	3.2	7.6	4.0	11.3	26.2
Sales to INV (times)	6.8	4.6	3.2	6.6	4.8	3.4	4.8	3.5	2.6	6.9	3.9	2.6
Assets to sales (%)	27.8	42.8	69.7	35.4	47.8	64.4	33.2	44.5	67.6	31.7	49.5	84.8
Sales to NWC (times)	29.5	12.7	5.8	7.2	4.3	2.9	7.3	4.2	2.8	7.5	4.0	2.3
Acct pay 10 sales (%)	0.5	1.0	2.6	2.6	5.2	7.7	2.2	4.2	7.2	1.9	3.9	7.6
Profitability												
Return on sales (%)	6.4	2.6	0.5	5.0	2.0	0.4	9.8	4.7	1.4	10.7	4.4	1.6
Return on assets (%)	10.2	4.1	0.4	9.0	4.0	0.8	16.3	8.3	2.6	16.1	8.1	3.2
Return on NW (%)	33.3	14.1	1.6	16.0	8.2	1.8	29.1	14.4	5.7	25.0	12.1	5.2

FIGURE 7–8

The ratios of retailing (source: 1982–83 Industry Norms and Key Business Ratios. © Dun and Bradstreet Inc., 1982)

Capital management involves planning and controlling the retailer's **equity capital** *(what the retailer owns)* and **borrowed capital** *(money the retailer has obtained from outside sources)*. The following discussion examines the retailer's capital requirements, types of retail financing, and various sources of funds.

Capital Requirements

A retailer needs money for a variety of purposes.[9] **Fixed capital** is *money needed to purchase such physical facilities as buildings, fixtures, and equipment.* This type of capital requirement represents long-term investments that tie up capital for extended periods. **Working capital** is *money needed to meet day-to-day operating costs.* It is used to pay the rent and utility bills, to purchase inventories, and to cover payroll expenses. **Liquid capital** is *money held in reserve for emergency situations.* It usually takes the form of cash or disposable securities (e.g., stocks, bonds, certificates of deposit).

The amount of fixed, working, and liquid capital required by a particular retail operation is a function of the size and nature of that operation. Capital requirements for larger retailers are greater than those for smaller retailers, all other things being equal. Upscale retail operations featuring complete product assortments, plush facilities, personal selling, and many services have a greater need for capital than retailers offering limited product assortments, spartan facilities, and limited services.

In planning capital requirements for *existing* operations, a retailer can consult past company records and adjust for anticipated additional needs for capital. Capital requirement estimates should also include a safety factor for unexpected needs.

For the *new* retail establishment, estimating capital requirements presents greater problems. Given the lack of any previous company records, the new retailer must rely on outside sources of information. Local financial institutions (e.g., banks and other commercial lending institutions) can often provide information on average capital requirements for similar retail operations. Trade associations frequently maintain similar data for their fields by various size categories and operational characteristics. Small retailers just starting can secure reliable information and financial advice from the Small Business Administration. Whether the retailer is a new or an existing business, careful enumeration of the firm's capital requirements is absolutely necessary for securing financing from most outside sources.

Types of Financing

The first step a retailer takes in securing capital funds is determining what kind of money is needed. The retailer's purpose for the money (e.g., for use as fixed, working, or liquid capital) determines the type of financing. There are three types of financing: short-, intermediate-, and long-term credit. **Short-term credit** is *money the retailer can borrow for less than one year.* Lending institutions provide retailers with short-term loans primarily for working capital. For example, banks extend short-term credit to retailers to purchase next season's inventory. In such cases, the loans are self-liquidating because they generate sales dollars.[10] **Intermediate-term credit** is *usually offered for periods longer than one year but less than five years.* Retailers secure such loans to finance smaller, fixed-capital expenditures (e.g., fixtures and equipment). **Long-term credit** *takes the form of loans that retailers secure for periods greater than five years.* Typically, retailers use long-term financing to purchase major fixed capital investments such as buildings and land. For both intermediate- and long-term credit, the retailer must make periodic installment payments (monthly, quarterly, or annually) from earnings.

Sources of Funding

To obtain funds, retailers can turn to a number of sources, including equity, vendors, lending institutions, and the government. Determining which source to use depends on the type of financing the retailer needs, the nature and size of the business, and the retailer's particular financial condition. Most retailers find it necessary to tap several sources of funds.

Equity sources of funds are obtained by selling part ownership in the business. Equity sales allow the retailer to raise funds without borrowing money or having to pay interest and repay a loan. Investors in a retail business are individuals willing to accept a certain amount of risk (i.e., the amount of their investment) for potential long-term gains. Before selling equity shares, however, the retailer should determine how much control over the business would be relinquished by making the sale.

Vendors, who supply retailers with merchandise, are frequently used as sources for short-term credit. This form of "trade credit" is made available by vendors when they extend dating terms—the amount of time the retailer has to pay the net invoice price for a shipment of merchandise. By extending dating terms to 60, 90, and even 120 days, the vendor is effectively financing the retailer's inventory for that period. Favorable dating terms often give the retailer time to sell the merchandise before having to pay for it. While vendor credit can be a valuable source of funds, the retailer must keep in mind that by utilizing the fully allowable period for paying invoices, it foregoes the opportunity to take advantage of the vendor's cash discount terms. When favorable cash discount terms are offered (e.g. 2 percent), the retailer is well advised to find alternative sources of funds and to take advantage of cash discounts.

Lending institutions are sources of short- and long-term retail financing. Commercial banks, credit associations, and insurance companies are the most common lending institutions willing to make loans to credit-worthy retailers. When lending institutions make short-term working capital loans, they expect repayment immediately after they have served the purpose for which the loan was made. For example, a seasonal inventory loan must be repaid at the end of the season. Repayment and other terms associated with fixed capital loans are carefully spelled out by the lender in written contractual agreements.

Commercial lending institutions make both secured and unsecured loans. Retailers with good credit ratings can often get loans on their signature alone. That is, they can obtain unsecured loans whereby no liens are placed on any of their property or possessions. When loans are for large amounts, or extended time periods, or to retailers with questionable credit ratings, commercial lending institutions require that the loan be secured by a pledge of the retailer's assets. Figure 7–9 identifies the various methods by which a loan can be secured.

Government sources of funds are usually the only viable alternative for the small retailer whose credit rating is either uncertain or not established. The Small Business Administration (SBA) was established to provide consulting services for small business enterprises on a number of business activities. SBA is also entrusted with the responsibility of making available financial resources for small businesses, including retailers, have exhausted all other avenues (e.g., traditional sources such as banks) for financing. SBA provides financing by acting as a (1) "guarantor"—guaranteeing a loan made by a bank to a retailer—or (2) "lender"—directly lending money to retailers when local banks will not. In addition to SBA, other government agencies are empowered to lend money to qualified retailers (e.g., to minority businesses). Commercial lending institutions and SBA can direct interested individuals to these sources.

Endorser	A third party signs a note to bolster the retailer's credit. If the retailer fails to pay the note, the bank expects the endorser to make the payments.
Comaker	A third party creates an obligation jointly with the retailer. The bank can collect directly from either the retailer or the comaker.
Guarantor	A third party guarantees the payment of a note by signing a guaranty commitment.
Assignment of leases	An arrangement in which the bank automatically receives the rent payments from a leasing agreement made between a retailer and a third party. Used in franchising to finance buildings.
Warehouse receipts	An arrangement in which the bank accepts commodities as security by lending money on a warehouse receipt. Such loans are generally made on staple merchandise that can be readily marketed.
Floor-planning	An arrangement in which banks accept a trust receipt for display merchandise as collateral. Used for securing loans on serial-numbered merchandise (automobiles, appliances, boats). When the retailer signs a trust receipt, it (1) acknowledges receipt of the merchandise, (2) agrees to keep the merchandise in trust for the bank, and (3) promises to pay the bank as soon as the merchandise is sold.
Chattel mortgage	An arrangement in which the bank accepts a lien on a piece of new equipment as security for the loan needed to buy the equipment.
Real estate	An arrangement in which the bank accepts a mortgage on real estate as collateral for a loan.
Accounts receivable	An arrangement in which the bank accepts accounts receivable (money owed the retailer) as collateral for a loan. Under the *notification plan* the retailer's customers are informed by the bank that their accounts have been assigned to the bank and all payments are made to the bank. Under the *nonnotification plan,* the retailer's customers are not informed of the assignment to the bank. The customer continues to pay the retailer who, in turn, pays the bank.
Savings accounts or life insurance	An arrangement in which the bank extends a loan to a retailer that assigns to the bank a savings account or the cash value of a life insurance policy as collateral.
Stocks and bonds	An arrangement in which the bank accepts as collateral marketable stocks and bonds. Usually the bank will accept as collateral only a certain percentage of the current market value of the stock or bond.

Source: Adapted from *ABCs of Borrowing,* Management Aids No. 170 (Washington, D.C.: Small Business Administration, April, 1977) 2–3.

FIGURE 7–9
Methods for securing a retail loan

Expense management is the planning and control of operating expenses. To ensure an operating profit, operating expenses must be less than the retailer's gross margin. With an inflationary economy and its impact on costs, coupled with increased competition, expense management is essential to any successful retail enterprise. The retailer that fails to plan and control operating expenses risks losing financial control over an important segment of the business. Expense management entails three basic planning and control activities: classifying expenses, allocating expenses, and budgeting expenses.

Expense Classification

All planning and control activities require careful identification and classification of every relevant factor. Hence, the first step in expense management is to recognize the various costs of doing business and to classify these costs into logical groupings based on some common feature. In retailing, four fundamental perspectives on operating expenses will lead to different classifications. They are sales, control, allocation, and accounting perspectives.

Sales Perspective

One way to look at operating expenses is to see how such expenses are affected by sales. From a sales perspective, operating expenses are classified as fixed and variable. **Fixed expenses** are *usually fixed for a given period of time* (e.g., the life of a contract, or a planning or operating period). Expenses are classified as fixed when they remain the same regardless of the sales volume. As sales increase or decrease, fixed expenses remain constant.

Expenses that vary with the volume of sales are called **variable expenses.** As sales increase or decrease, variable expenses also increase or decrease. While the relationship between sales and expenses is not always directly proportional, they are sufficiently related that the retailer can reasonably predict changes in operating expenses. By being attentive to specific relationships between a variable expense and sales, the retailer can identify opportunities for increasing profits. For example, initial increases in advertising expenditures could increase sales to such a degree that profit increases are greater than the incurred advertising expense. However, the retailer would want to continue monitoring the original relationship to determine the point at which additional advertising expenditures are no longer profitable.

Control Perspective

The second way to look at operating expenses is to see whether a particular expense is controllable. As the name implies, **controllable expenses** are those over which the retailer has direct control. Retailers can adjust these expenses as warranted by operating conditions. For example, part-time help can be reduced during slack sales periods.

Uncontrollable expenses are outlays over which retailers have no control and that, in the short run, they cannot adjust to current operating needs. Expenses incurred as a result of long-term contractual arrangements are uncontrollable over the short run. Given their adaptability, controllable expenses should be the focus of the retailer's attention. Daily or weekly monitoring of these expenses aids the retailer in maintaining operating expenses at acceptable levels.

Allocation Perspective

In using the allocation perspective, the retailer looks at operating expenses to see if they can be directly attributed to some operating unit. Many retailers find it useful for purposes of analysis and control to allocate operating expenses to various operating units, such as store units or departmental units.

Under this approach, retailers classify operating expenses as either direct or indirect expenses. **Direct expenses** are *those directly attributable to the operations of a department or some other defined operating unit.* If the retailer eliminated a department or unit, then the direct expenses associated with that department would also be eliminated. Salaries and commissions of departmental sales personnel are examples of direct expenses. Expenses *not directly attributable to the operations of a department* are classified as **indirect expenses.** These costs cannot be eliminated if a particular department is dropped. Indirect expenses are general business expenses a retailer incurs in running the entire operation.

Accounting Perspective

A final way to look at operating expenses is to classify them into well-defined groups that the retailer can use to identify year-to-year trends for each expense class and to make comparisons with trade averages of similar retailers. This expense classification system helps the retailer to identify, analyze, and initiate controls for expenses that are out of line with either last year's figures or those of similar retailers. Using the accounting approach, the retailer can classify operating expenses using either a natural division of expenses or expense-center accounting.

Using the **natural division of expenses,** *the retailer classifies expenses on the basis of the kind of expense each is,* without regard for (1) which store functions (e.g., selling, buying, or receiving) incurred the expense, or (2) where (e.g., store or department) the expense was incurred. The natural division method of expense classification is used primarily by small- and medium-sized retailers looking for simple yet acceptable means of classifying expenses. The natural classification of expenses as recommended by the National Retail Merchants Association appears in Figure 7–10.

The second accounting method for classifying operating expenses is **expense-center accounting.** An expense center is a functional center within the store's operation or a center of a certain store activity. The center incurs expenses in the process of providing its assigned functions or performing its required activities. Expense-center accounting is *a system of classifying operating expenses into such functional or activity classes as management, direct selling, customer services, and so on.* The National Retail Merchants Association has identified 44 major expense centers, shown in Figure 7–11. Expense-center accounting is used most frequently by large, departmentalized retailers.

In using the expense-center accounting system, the retailer follows a two-step procedure. The first step is to classify operating expenses according to natural divisions. The second step is to cross-classify each of the natural expenses with each of the 23 expense centers. As illustrated in Figure 7–12 (p. 220), the retailer can use expense-center accounting to identify, analyze, and control operating expenses either by the kind or type of expense (i.e., natural divisions) or by the function or activity that incurred the expense (i.e., expense center). Typically, the expense-center accounting system provides greater detail in classifying operating expenses than do other methods. Once operating expenses have been classified, the retailer's second task is to allocate expenses to each of the operating units, such as departments within a store or stores within a chain organization.

Expense Allocation

The small retailer views operating expenses from the standpoint of the entire store; therefore, it gives little thought to the problem of allocating operating expenses to

Natural Division 01—*Payroll*

Includes all items of compensation for services actually rendered by employees of a company—wages, salaries, commissions, promotion money, bonuses, prizes, and vacation, sick, and holiday payments.

Natural Division 02—*Allocated Fringe Benefits*

Includes a transfer account to allocate fringe benefits out of their appropriate expense centers to all other expense centers with a payroll natural division.

Natural Division 03—*Media Costs*

Includes all cost of media—the cost of newspaper, periodical, program, streetcar and billboard space, the cost of radio and television time, and the cost of direct mail advertising.

Natural Division 04—*Taxes*

Includes all state and local taxes (excluding taxes based on income), unemployment, social security and disability taxes, and government license fees.

Natural Division 06—*Supplies*

Includes the cost of items consumed in the operation of the business—stationery and related items, wrapping, packaging, cleaning, and repairing materials, and heating, cooling, lighting, and other power expenses.

Natural Division 07—*Services Purchased*

Includes charges for all nonprofessional services rendered by outsiders that aid, supplement, or substitute for the normal routine activity of the store—cleaning, delivery, shopping, detective, alarm, armored car, statistical, typing, and collection services.

Natural Division 08—*Unclassified*

Includes all expenses not otherwise classified as chargeable to another natural division.

Natural Division 09—*Travel*

Includes all expenses resulting from domestic (local or out of town) and foreign travel of all employees of the company for business purposes—transportation, hotel bills, meals, tips, and incidentals.

Natural Division 10—*Communications*

Includes all expenses relative to the cost of store and central organization communications—local and long distance telephone services and postage.

Natural Division 11—*Pensions*

Includes all expenses relating to pensions, retirement allowances, pension funds, insured and trusteed plans, and direct payments to retired employees.

Natural Division 12—*Insurance*

Includes the cost of all insurance.

Natural Division 13—*Depreciation*

Includes depreciation of the original cost of the capital assets employed in the operation of the business—building, leasehold improvements, equipment, furniture, and fixtures.

Natural Division 14—*Professional Services*

Includes the cost of any serivce of a highly specialized and professional character furnished by outside organizations—legal, accounting, appraisal, management service, architectural, and survey fees.

Natural Division 16—*Bad Debts*

Includes actual bad debts written off or the provision relating to an allowance for doubtful accounts; it also includes losses due to bad checks and fraudulent purchases, less recoveries.

Natural Division 17—*Equipment Rentals*

Includes the costs of all equipment rented or leased and is restricted to expense centers where equipment represents a significant investment in the center's operations.

Natural Division 18—*Outside Maintenance and Equipment Service Contracts*

Includes the costs of outside contractual arrangements for servicing and maintaining equipment.

Natural Division 20—*Real Property Rentals*

Includes expenses incurred or rent paid for real estate used in the operation of the business.

Natural Division 90—*Expense Transfers In*
Natural Division 91—*Expense Transfers Out*
Natural Division 92—*Credits and Outside Revenues*

Source: Adapted from *Retail Accounting Manual, Revised* (New York: Financial Executives Division, National Retail Merchants Association, 1978), III-3.

FIGURE 7–10

Natural division of expenses

FIGURE 7–11
Major expense centers

010　Property and equipment
　020　Real estate, buildings, and building equipment
　030　Furniture, fixtures, and nonbuilding equipment
100　Company management
　110　Executive office
　130　Branch management
　140　Internal audit
　150　Legal and consumer activities
200　Accounting and management information
　210　Control management, general accounting, and statistical
　220　Sales audit
　230　Accounts payable
　240　Payroll and time-keeping department
　280　Data processing
300　Credit and accounts receivable
　310　Credit management
　330　Collection
　340　Accounts receivable and bill adjustment
　350　Cash office
　360　Branch/store selling location offices
400　Sales promotion
　410　Sales promotion management
　420　Advertising
　430　Shows, special events, and exhibits
　440　Display
500　Service and operations
　510　Service and operations management
　530　Security
　550　Telephones and communications
　560　Utilities
　570　Housekeeping
　580　Maintenance and repairs
600　Personnel
　610　Personnel management
　620　Employment
　640　Training
　660　Medical and other employee services
　670　Supplementary benefits
700　Merchandise receiving, storage, and distribution
　710　Management of merchandise receiving, storage, and distribution
　720　Receiving and marking
　730　Reserve stock storage
　750　Shuttle services
800　Selling and supporting services
　810　Selling supervision
　820　Direct selling
　830　Customer services
　840　Selling support services
　860　Central wrapping and packing
　880　Delivery
900　Merchandising
　910　Merchandising management
　920　Buying
　930　Merchandise control

219

Source: *Retail Accounting Manual, Revised* (New York: Financial Executives Division, National Retail Merchants Association, 1978), III-3.

FIGURE 7–12
Expense-center accounting system

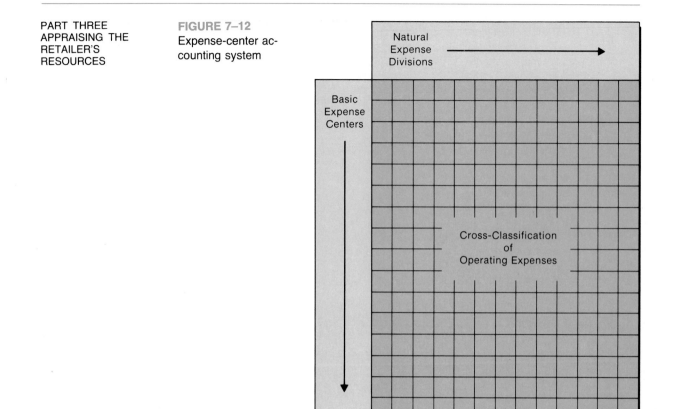

various operating units. Since most small retailers operate their businesses as a whole rather than as several individual operating units, the need for expense allocation generally is absent. On the other hand, large retailers that are either departmentalized or multiunit (chain) operations have great need for examining the operating expenses of individual operating units.

Three methods retailers commonly use to allocate operating expenses to operating units are (1) the net profit plan, (2) the contribution plan, and (3) the net profit/contribution plan. Figure 7–13 illustrates each of the three expense allocation plans. In reviewing this figure, several points should be noted. First, the bottom line for a departmental income statement is its operating profit. However, this profit expression is often referred to as the department net profit. Second, each of the allocation methods is quite similar. The principal differences between the methods are the ways indirect expenses are treated and the calculation criteria for the operating unit.

Net Profit Plan

When employing the **net profit plan,** *the retailer allocates all direct and indirect expenses.* Direct expenses are directly attributed to the particular department that incurred them. Indirect expenses are not *directly* attributed to a particular department, but instead are allocated to departments based on a prejudged set of criteria. Figure 7–14 lists common criteria for retailers. To illustrate, the salary of a department manager would be considered a direct expense that could be directly allocated to the department. However, the salary of the store manager would be an indirect

FIGURE 7–13
Allocating operating
expenses

```
Net profit plan
    Department gross margin ..................................... ($)
      – Direct expenses of the department .......................... ($)
      – Indirect expenses charged to department ................... ($)
    Department net profit ........................................ ($)*

Contribution plan
    Department gross margin ..................................... ($)
      – Direct expenses of the department .......................... ($)
    Contribution of the department ............................... ($)*

Net profit contribution plan
    Department gross margin ..................................... ($)
      – Direct expenses of the department ........................ ($)
    Contribution of the department ............................... ($)*
      – Indirect expenses charged to department ................... ($)
    Department net profit ........................................ ($)*
```
*Measurement used to evaluate departmental performance.

FIGURE 7–14
Selected expense-
center allocation criteria

Type of Expense	Allocation Criteria
Property and equipment	Weighted floor space
Company management	Net sales
Accounting and management information	Gross sales
Credit and accounts receivable	Number of transactions
Sales promotion	Number of displays
Personnel	Number of employees
Merchandise receiving storage and distribution	Number of invoices
Selling and supporting services	Number of units
Merchandising	Net sales

expense to any given department. Therefore, the store manager's salary could be allocated to various departments based on each department's percentage of total net sales.

As shown in Figure 7–13, the department's gross margin minus both the department's direct and indirect expenses equals the department's net profit. The treatment of each department as a profit-producing center has the advantage of providing a "hard figure" (net profit) evaluation of departmental operations and encourages each department to be expense-control conscious. On the other hand, unfair or questionable allocations of indirect expenses to the department can distort the department's profit picture and create considerable dissatisfaction among departmental managers whose careers are on the line.

Contribution Plan

The **contribution plan** *can be characterized as follows: (1) direct expenses are allocated to the departments that incurred them, while (2) indirect expenses are not allocated to departments—instead, they are allocated to a general expense account.* The department's *contribution* is defined as the department's gross margin minus its direct expenses. Again referring to Figure 7–13, we see that each department is judged on the basis of its contribution to the store. The sum of the contributions from each department is treated as a "reservoir" used to cover the indirect expenses in the general expense account and to provide an operating profit for the store. While most department managers prefer the contribution plan, it has its limitations. The contribution plan may give the department manager a false impression of the department's performance, since the department will almost always show a positive contribution. However, the question of whether the department's contribution is large enough to cover the department's fair share of indirect expenses and to contribute to the store's profit is not answered. Some retailers prefer to combine the two plans to balance these shortcomings.

Net Profit/Contribution Plan

Using the **net profit/contribution plan,** *the retailer calculates both the department's net profit and its contribution* (see Figure 7–13). This plan involves a two-step procedure. First, the department's contribution is calculated by subtracting the department's direct expenses from its gross margin. Second, the department's net profit is calculated by subtracting the department's indirect expenses from its contribution. The combination net profit/contribution plan allows examination of departmental performance from both the contribution and net profit perspectives.

Expense Budgeting

An **expense budget** is *a plan or a set of guidelines that a retailer uses to control operating expenses.* It is an estimate or a forecast of the amount of money needed during a given accounting period to operate the business. Essentially, the expense budget is a continuation of the retailer's total budgetary process. Just as merchandise budgets are developed to plan and control expenditures for merchandise items, the major purpose of expense budgets is to plan and control the amount of money the retailer spends in merchandising those items.

An annual expense budget for the entire store is the normal starting point in expense control. The annual budget is then broken down into monthly and weekly expense plans. While small retailers typically operate on a store-wide expense budget, larger departmentalized retailers usually find it necessary to prepare departmental expense budgets separately from the store budget.

Proponents of tight budgetary control over expenses cite the following as its advantages: (1) it forces the retailer to establish expense objectives; (2) it assigns an individual responsibility to achieve expense objectives; (3) it motivates management to reach expense objectives; (4) it identifies expenditures that deviate too far from expected norms; (5) it promotes a review of past expense performances; and (6) it encourages the firm's management to plan ahead for future expense needs. Opponents of expense budgets that require strict adherence believe that overbudgeting can lead to a cumbersome rigidity that prevents the freedom and flexibility a retailer needs to adapt to the continuous changes that occur in the firm's external and internal operating environments. Opponents are also quick to point out that expense budgets are a product of various estimates (e.g., sales) that may or may not be totally accurate. To demand strict adherence to such questionable budgetary requirements would, in their opinions, be unrealistic and in some cases meaningless.

In practice, expense budgets should act as a general game plan, not as a straitjacket of unbreakable rules. As a plan of action, it must be flexible enough for management to adjust as conditions warrant it, but rigid enough to provide meaningful guidance.

One of the first steps in preparing an expense budget is to determine an overall expense figure for the prescribed operating period. This figure is a general estimate of the amount of money that the retailer will have available to cover operating expenses. The estimate can be figured in a simple way by following these two steps: (1) secure a net sales estimate for the forthcoming period (obtained from the merchandising budget) and (2) make a gross margin estimate by subtracting a cost of goods sold estimate from the net sales estimate. This estimated gross margin represents the amount of money available to cover operating expenses plus achieve an operating profit. By subtracting the desired level of operating profit from gross margin, the retailer has an estimate of money that should be available to cover both fixed and variable expenses. In some cases, retailers take the process one step further. Because fixed expenses are generally known and fairly constant, they are deducted to determine the amount of money that can be allocated to variable expenses.

Several specific budgetary procedures have been developed for expense planning and control. The retailer can elect to use any one of the following three approaches to expense budgeting: zero-based budgeting, fixed-based budgeting, and productivity-based budgeting.

Zero-Based Budgeting

As the name implies, under **zero-based budgeting,** *each operating department or unit starts with no allocated operating expenses.* To secure operating funds, each operating department must justify its need for each expense item on the budget. While past expenditures may be considered supporting evidence, management does not accept past expenditures as total justification for future expense allocations. To obtain operating funds, department personnel must use justifications based on current merchandising plans, market conditions, competitive atmospheres, and operating requirements. Although zero-based budgeting is generally time consuming and costly, it does force each operating department to reevaluate its expenses and to define the needs and benefits that should be derived from each expenditure. Zero-based budgeting is the most appropriate way to establish an expense budget for a new retailer or a new department.

Fixed-Based Budgeting

In the **fixed-based budgeting** process, *each expense* (e.g., payroll, supplies,) *is budgeted at a specific dollar amount.* The predetermined amount is based on past experience as well as on an evaluation of the need for incurring the expense in the forthcoming budgeting period. A fixed-based budgeting form is illustrated in Figure 7–15. To facilitate control, the retailer should fill in the form for both the budgeted and the actual expenditure in the current budget period, as well as complete a year-to-date summary.

The form also provides space for the retailer to report variances between actual and budgeted amounts in both dollars and percentages. Management carefully scrutinizes these variances; when they exceed either a predetermined dollar or percentage amount, the manager of the operating department should examine and correct the situation and submit either a written or oral report to the supervisor. In the example provided in Figure 7–15, the manager of the receiving department appears to be controlling the department's expenses adequately. Although the current period shows that the department is slightly over budget, the year-to-date expenses are slightly below the amount budgeted for the department.

Period: Third Quarter			Store: 12			Expense Center:	721-Receiving		
Natural Division			Current Period				Year-to-Date		
			Amount		Variance		Amount		Variance	

Natural Division		Current Period				Year-to-Date			
		Amount		Variance		Amount		Variance	
No.	Expense	Actual	Budget	Dollar	Percent	Actual	Budget	Dollar	Percent
01	Payroll	4,000	4,000	00	00	12,000	12,000	00	0.0
06	Supplies	1,000	800	(200)	(25)	2,600	2,400	(200)	(8.3)
07	Services Purchased	500	600	100	16.7	1,400	1,800	400	22.2
10	Communications	100	100	00	00	270	300	30	10.0
	Total	5,600	5,500	(100)	1.8	16,270	16,500	230	1.4

FIGURE 7–15
Fixed-based budgeting form

Productivity-Based Budgeting

Expense budgets based on levels of productivity provide a high degree of flexibility in the budgetary process. Under a **productivity-based budget,** *the retailer prepares a series of expense budgets to correspond to various sales levels* (or some other productivity measure). As illustrated in Figure 7–16, an increase in unit sales automatically increases the amount budgeted for each item in the department's expense budget. Given that numerous operating expenses are either directly or indirectly related to sales, a budget based on sales productivity should help the retailer make operational adjustments to meet changing market conditions. Some retailers think that a productivity-based budget is the most appropriate approach to expense bud-

Natural Division		Period: April		Store: 12		Expense Center: 410—		Sales Promotion	
		Unit Sales							
No.	Expense	500	1000	1500	2000	2500	3000	3500	4000
01	Payroll	$2,000	$2,000	$2,500	$2,500	$3,000	$3,500	$4,000	$4,500
03	Advertising	500	1,000	1,500	2,000	2,500	3,000	3,500	4,000
06	Supplies	500	550	600	700	800	1,000	1,200	1,400
	Total	$3,000	$3,550	$4,600	$5,200	$6,300	$7,500	$8,700	$9,900

FIGURE 7–16

Productivity-based budgeting form

geting, expecially when reliable sales estimates are difficult to make or when there is a high likelihood for extreme sales variations. Essentially, this budget approach allows the retailer to allocate limited financial resources based on actual need, as opposed to anticipated requirements.

SUMMARY

A key means of gaining retailing success is fiscal control. To ensure an adequate degree of control over financial affairs, the retailer must develop and maintain a set of financial records that provide a broad picture of the firm's financial condition. A typical set of records includes a separate record for each of the following: sales, cash receipts, cash disbursements, purchases, payroll, equipment, inventory, accounts receivable, and accounts payable. The retailer then uses these records to prepare two essential financial statements: the income statement and the balance sheet.

The income statement summarizes the retailer's financial activity for a stated accounting period. It is prepared to show the profit (or loss) a retailer has made during an accounting period. The income statement is a systematic set of procedures that helps the retailer identify five income measurements—gross sales, net sales, gross margin, operating profit, and net profit.

The balance sheet is a statement of the retailer's financial condition on a given date. It summarizes the basic relationship among the retailer's assets, liabilities, and net worth. The balance sheet gets its name from its principal objective of showing how the sides of the accounting equation (assets = liabilities + net worth) are balanced.

The financial status checklist provides a means for retailers to check the status of each financial record or statement and identify financial problems requiring corrective action.

In performance analysis, the retailer must make judgments on the operating and financial performance of the firm. By using several standardized operating and financial ratios, the retailer can compare the performance of the firm either on a historical basis or on a trade basis with national norms.

Capital management involves planning and controlling the retailer's equity capital (what the retailer owns) and borrowed capital (what the retailer owes). A retailer needs money for a variety of reasons, including funds for fixed, working, and liquid capital requirements. The type of financing a retailer needs depends on its capital requirements. Short-term credit is used when the retailer needs working capital, whereas intermediate- and long-term credit are used to meet fixed capital requirements. Equity sales, vendor credit, and loans from lending institutions and government agencies are the major sources of funds for the retailer.

Expense management entails three basic planning and control activities: classifying, allocating, and budgeting expenses. Logical groupings of operating expenses are essential to planning and control. Expenses can be classified on the basis of sales (variable or fixed), control (controllable or uncontrollable), or allocation (direct or indirect) characteristics, and according to accounting procedures (natural division of expenses or expense-center accounting). In departmentalized or chain store organizations, operating expenses must be allocated to various operating units. Expense allocation is accomplished by using the net profit plan, the contribution plan, and the net profit/contribution plan. An expense budget is used to plan and control operating expenditures. The retailer can elect to use one of several budgeting procedures: zero-based, fixed-based, or productivity-based.

KEY TERMS AND CONCEPTS

account	operating profit	return on assets
ledger	other income	return on net worth
income statement	other expenses	equity capital
balance sheet	net profit	borrowed capital
income measurements	asset	fixed capital
income modifications	current asset	working capital
gross sales	fixed asset	liquid capital
returns from customers	total assets	short-term credit
allowances to customers	liability	intermediate-term credit
net sales	current liability	long-term credit
cost of goods sold	long-term liability	fixed expenses
total goods handled	net worth	variable expenses
beginning inventory	financial status checklist	controllable expenses
net purchases	ratio analysis	uncontrollable expenses
gross purchases	operating ratios	direct expenses
returns to vendors	financial ratios	indirect expenses
allowances from vendors	liquidity ratios	natural division of expenses
transportation charges	current ratio	expense-center accounting
gross cost of goods sold	quick ratio	net profit plan
ending inventory	leverage ratios	contribution plan
net cost of goods sold	debt ratio	net profit/contribution plan
cash discounts	debt to net worth ratio	expense budget
total cost of goods sold	Strategic Profit Model	zero-based budgeting
gross margin	profit margin	fixed-based budgeting
operating expenses	asset turnover	productivity-based budgeting

REVIEW QUESTIONS

1. What are the characteristics of a good record-keeping system?
2. Identify the nine basic ledger accounts.
3. What is the purpose of an income statement? How does a balance sheet differ from an income statement?
4. Briefly describe the time, unit, and usage considerations in preparing an income statement.
5. What are the nine elements of an income statement? Define each element.
6. Outline the steps used in calculating cost of goods sold.
7. Why is a balance sheet prepared?
8. How do current assets differ from fixed assets?
9. How do current liabilities differ from long-term liabilities? Cite examples of each type of liability.
10. Define net worth.
11. What is ratio analysis?
12. What relationships are expressed by operating ratios and financial ratios?
13. How does the current ratio differ from the quick ratio?
14. What does a leverage ratio measure?
15. Describe the strategic profit model.
16. What are fixed, working, and liquid capital needed for?
17. Briefly describe the three types of financing.
18. What are the retailer's primary sources of financing?
19. How can expenses be classified? Identify and define the eight expense classifications.
20. How can the large retailer allocate operating expenses to operating units?
21. What are the three approaches to expense budgeting? Briefly describe each approach.

ENDNOTES

1. Robert C. Ragan, *Financial Recordkeeping for Small Stores,* Small Business Management Series No. 32 (Washington: Small Business Administration, 1976), 5.
2. John Cotlon, *Keeping Records in Small Business,* Small Marketers Aids No. 155 (Washington: Small Business Administration, May 1974), 2.
3. Ragan, *Financial Recordkeeping for Small Stores,* 5–6.
4. Irving M. Cooper, *Accounting Services for Small Service Firms,* Small Marketers Aids No. 126 (Washington: Small Business Administration, March 1977), 3.
5. Ibid.
6. See Norman M. Scarborough and Thomas W. Zimmerer, *Effective Small Business Management* (Columbus: Charles E. Merrill Publishing Co., 1984), 215.
7. Ibid., 216–17.
8. Robert F. Lusch, *Management of Retail Enterprises* (Boston: Kent Publishing Co., 1982), 25.
9. See Harold Shaffer and Herbert Greenwald, *Independent Retailing: A Money-Making Manual* (Englewood Cliffs, NJ: Prentice-Hall, Inc., 1976), 293.
10. See John F. Murphy, *Sound Cash Management and Borrowing,* Small Marketers Aids No. 147 (Washington: Small Business Administration, July 1977), 3.

RELATED READINGS

Abend, Jules. "Increasing Profitability." *Stores* (June 1985), 22–32.

Achabal, Dale D.; Heineke, John M.; and McIntyre, Shelby H. "Issues and Perspectives on Retail Productivity." *Journal of Retailing* 60 (Fall 1984), 107–27.

Christensen, Kenneth. "Expense Budgeting and Control for Productivity." *Retail Control* (August 1983), 26–37.

Cronin, J. Joseph, Jr.; Ingram, Thomas N.; and Skinner, Steven J. "The Impact of Financial Conditions on the Relationship between Margin-Turnover and Profit Performance." *Marketing Comes of Age, Proceedings.* David M. Klein and Allen E. Smith, eds. (Southern Marketing Association 1984), 138–41.

Cronin, J. Joseph, Jr.; and Skinner, Steven J. "Marketing Outcome, Financial Conditions, and Retail Profit Performance." *Journal of Retailing* 60 (Winter 1984), 9–22.

Curhan, Ronald C.; Salmon, Walter J.; and Buzzell, Robert D. "Sales and Profitability of Health and Beauty Aids and General Merchandise in Supermarkets." *Journal of Retailing* 57 (Spring 1983), 77–99.

Higgins, Robert C., and Kerin, Roger A. "Managing the Growth—Financial Policy Nexus in Retailing." *Journal of Retailing* 59 (Fall 1983), 19–48.

Hise, Richard T.; Kelly, J. Patrick; Gable, Myron; and McDonald, James B. "Factors Affecting the Performance of Individual Chain Store Units." *Journal of Retailing* 59 (Summer 1983), 22–39.

Ingene, Charles A. "Labor Productivity in Retailing." *Journal of Marketing* 46 (Fall 1982), 75–90.

Kelly, William D. "An Approach to Expense Control." *Retail Control* (December 1982), 2–8.

Little, Michael W.; Wijnholds, H. B.; and Doudna, Donald. "One-Step Financial Shopping by Independent Retailers: A Pilot Project." *Developments in Marketing Science, Proceedings.* J. D. Lindquist, ed. (Academy of Marketing Science 1984), 408–11.

Ratchford, Brian T. "The Flow of Capital Services and Productivity of Capital of Retail Food Stores." *1985 AMA Educators' Proceedings.* R. F. Lusch et al, eds. (American Marketing Association 1985), 223–28.

Rizzi, Joseph. "Return on Investment as a Measure of Asset Management." *Retail Control* (September 1983), 20–26.

Siegel, Joel G., and Akel, Anthony. "Monitoring the Financial Health of Independent Stores." *Retail Control* (November 1984), 35–42.

Steven, Michael T. "Methods of Analyzing and Improving Store Profitability." *Retail Control* (March 1985), 49–55.

Stevens, Robert E. "Using Accounting Data to Make Decisions." *Journal of Retailing* 51 (Fall 1975), 23–28.

Waybright, George. "GMROI: Get More Return on Investments." *Retail Control* (October 1984), 2–10.

Outline

ELEMENTS OF RETAIL ORGANIZATION

Organizational Objectives
Organizational Tasks

PRINCIPLES OF RETAIL ORGANIZATION

Specialization and Departmentalization
Authority and Responsibility
Unity of Command
Span of Control

FORMS OF RETAIL ORGANIZATION

Number of Organizational Levels
Job and Task Organization

PATTERNS OF RETAIL ORGANIZATION

Small Store Organization
Department Store Organization
Chain Store Organization

Objectives

- Understand factors that determine the best organizational structure for meeting the retailer's operational needs

- Develop organizational objectives that can provide focus for the structure and activities of the retail firm

- Identify the organizational tasks necessary to realize the firm's organizational objectives

- Explain the basic principles of organization that are an inherent part of any effective retail structure

- Prepare an organizational chart capable of expressing the formal relationships among various parts of the retail organization

- Distinguish among the organizational patterns of various types of retailers

8
Organizing the Retail Firm

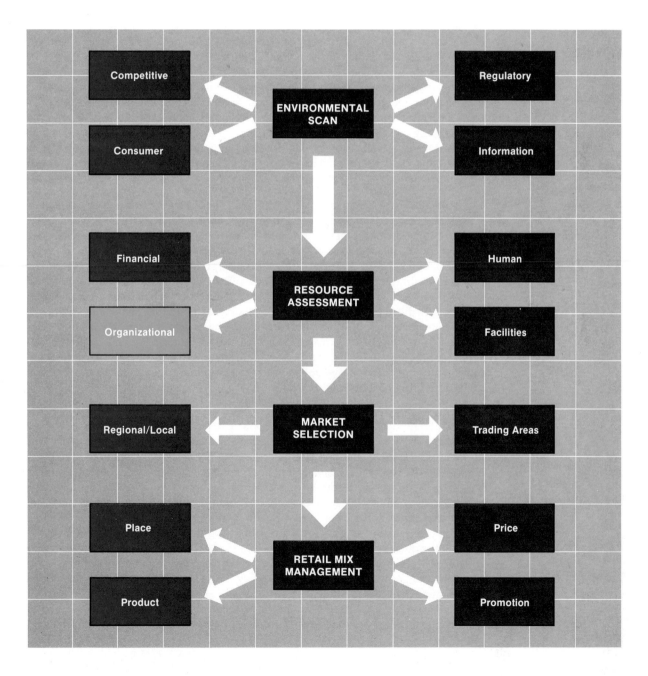

O rganization is essential to any group of people having a common purpose or goal. Whether the group is an army, a church, a football team, or a retail business, organization is the binding force that coordinates, channels, and propels the group toward its stated mission.

Within any organizational structure, each person's responsibilities and authority are defined as they pertain to the functions necessary to accomplish the group's goals. A head football coach has the authority to hire and fire assistant coaches, to say who will play and who will not, and to call the offensive and defensive plays. He also has certain reponsibilities for his players' physical and academic health, for keeping the fans and alumni informed, and for reporting income and expenditures to the university administration. The coach's authority and responsibilities properly pertain to his functions within the organizational framework. Similarly, in a business, each person's authority and responsibilities are an outgrowth of a position and the functions assigned to that position within the organization.

As with any organized group of people, retailers can use a vast number of different organizational structures to organize their people. However, all retailing organizations incorporate certain common organizational "elements" and "principles" structured around one of several basic organizational forms. This chapter examines these organizational elements, principles, and forms, as well as presents the general organizational patterns that small independent retailers, department store retailers, and chain store retailers use in organizing groups of people.

ELEMENTS OF RETAIL ORGANIZATION

The particular organizational foundation a retail firm adopts depends on several factors. Although custom and tradition have been the basis for retail organizational structure for particular types of retailing activities in the past, modern retailers are taking a more objective look at the factors that should determine the best possible organizational structure to meet their particular operating needs. Some of these factors are (1) the type of merchandise to be offered, (2) the variety and assortment of the merchandise stocked, (3) the type and number of customer services performed, (4) the type and number of locations used, (5) the type and degree of promotional activities, (6) the nature of pricing levels and margin requirements obtained, (7) the type of store image projected, (8) the availability and quality of personnel employed, (9) the amount of capital invested, and (10) the legal requirements and/or restrictions. Given this vast array of influential factors, the organization of the firm must center around specific organization objectives and tasks.

Organizational Objectives

In retailing, the firm's organizational foundation focuses on achieving the objectives of the firm. Therefore, the first step in organizing the retail business is to identify its organizational objectives. Establishing well-defined organizational objectives is an important step because it forces the retailer to think through what the firm is trying to accomplish, where the firm is going, and how the firm intends to get there. In addition, organizational objectives provide a realistic orientation to the retailer's planning process as well as a means of evaluating the firm's past performance and its current status.

Three levels of organizational objectives correspond to the three general levels of retail management (see Figure 8–1). They are (1) strategic objectives developed by top managers at the strategic level of management, (2) operational objectives identified by middle managers within the administrative level of management, and (3) functional objectives that direct front-line managers at the operational management level.

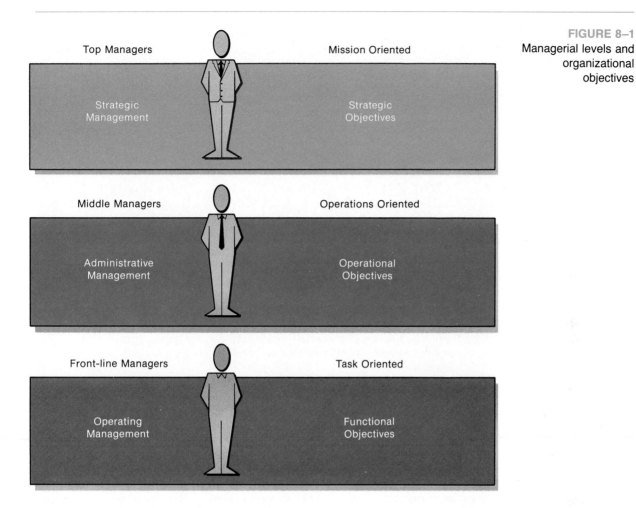

FIGURE 8–1
Managerial levels and
organizational
objectives

Top Managers	Mission Oriented
Strategic Management	Strategic Objectives

Middle Managers	Operations Oriented
Administrative Management	Operational Objectives

Front-line Managers	Task Oriented
Operating Management	Functional Objectives

Strategic objectives are *general, long-term goals that the retail firm intends to pursue.* Essentially, a strategic objective identifies an overall mission that the firm's management wishes to realize. **Operational objectives** are *general, long-term operational requirements necessary to achieve a strategic objective.* Operational objectives establish the general framework within which a particular merchandising or operating function can be identified. **Functional objectives** are *specific task objectives that identify a specific function and how it is to be accomplished.* The unique value of functional objectives is their quantifiability, which makes them especially useful in planning, executing, and controlling a particular retailing activity. Figure 8–2 provides examples of strategic, operational, and functional objectives for an upscale specialty retailer of women's apparel. The objectives in Figure 8–2 identify not only the target markets, but also how to serve them in terms of product offering and assortment.

Organizational Tasks

In developing the retail organization, the retailer must identify and assign the various tasks necessary to realize the firm's stated organizational objectives. The number of organizational tasks that can be identified is large. Figure 8–3 lists the basic organizational tasks inherent to any retail organization.

233

Strategic Objectives	Operational Objectives	Functional Objectives
To appeal to the "perfectionist," the "updated," the "traditionalist," and the "establishment" consumer	To offer the "perfectionist" consumer the most advanced fashion apparel	To ensure the "perfectionist" consumer a new and fresh selection of fashionables by stocking only one garment in each size category (e.g., Misses 4–14) and by timing new arrivals every week
	To offer the "updated" consumer new styles that have gained wide acceptance	To ensure the "updated" consumer stylish yet not extreme fashion apparel by stocking a limited selection of last season's perfectionist styles in Misses sizes 4–16
	To offer the "traditionalist" and the "establishment" consumer well-established yet fashionable apparel	To ensure the "traditionalist" and "establishment" consumer a complete selection of stylish yet dignified fashion apparel by stocking a representative offering of well-established designer labels in Misses sizes 8–20

FIGURE 8–2
Examples of organizational objectives

Although the list of tasks in Figure 8–3 can help a retailer develop a general organizational structure, a more detailed description of tasks must be made in assigning responsibilities and authority to each position in the organization. Additionally, the retailer should develop written job descriptions for each job classification. These detailed and specific written statements of authority, responsibility, and job duties promote an efficient organization with fewer conflicts among employees, less confusion, greater harmony and understanding among employees of their roles, and better coordination among activities within the store.

PRINCIPLES OF RETAIL ORGANIZATION

There are several basic principles of organization that every retailer should consider in establishing a retail organization. Organizational principles that are particularly appropriate to the retail firm are the principles of specialization and departmentalization, of lines of authority and responsibility, of unity of command, and of span of control. By applying these principles, retailers can avoid managerial confusion and employee discontent.

Specialization and Departmentalization

Specialization and departmentalization are inherent parts of any efficient retail organizational structure. With job **specialization,** *employees concentrate their efforts on a limited number of tasks.* Retailers have learned that specialization improves the speed and quality of employee performance.

FIGURE 8–3
Basic organizational
tasks

1. **Operating the store**
   a. Recruiting store personnel
   b. Training store personnel
   c. Supervising store personnel
   d. Planning information systems
   e. Meeting legal obligations
   f. Designing store facilities
   g. Maintaining store facilities
   h. Ensuring store security

2. **Finding the best location**
   a. Analyzing regional markets
   b. Assessing trading areas
   c. Appraising site locations

3. **Developing the merchandise mix**
   a. Determining consumer product needs
   b. Evaluating product alternatives
   c. Planning product-mix strategies
   d. Determining consumer-service requirements
   e. Evaluating service alternatives
   f. Planning service-mix levels

4. **Buying the merchandise**
   a. Identifying sources of supply
   b. Contacting sources of supply
   c. Evaluating sources of supply
   d. Negotiating with sources of supply

5. **Procuring the merchandise**
   a. Ordering merchandise
   b. Receiving merchandise
   c. Checking merchandise
   d. Marking merchandise
   e. Stocking merchandise

6. **Controlling the merchandise**
   a. Planning sales
   b. Planning stocks
   c. Planning reductions
   d. Planning purchases
   e. Planning markups
   f. Planning margins
   g. Controlling inventories
   h. Taking inventory
   i. Valuating inventory
   j. Evaluating inventory

7. **Pricing the merchandise**
   a. Setting prices
   b. Adjusting prices

8. **Promoting the merchandise**
   a. Planning advertising strategies
   b. Selecting advertising media
   c. Preparing advertisements
   d. Designing promotional displays
   e. Planning promotional events
   f. Gaining favorable publicity
   g. Managing the personal-selling effort

Departmentalization, an extension of the specialization principle, *occurs when tasks and employees are grouped together into departments to achieve the operating efficiencies of specialization for a group performing similar tasks.* Specialization and departmentalization can be based on *product type* (such as apparel, home furnishings, and appliances), *activity* (such as buying, selling, and stocking), *activity location* (such as main store, branch store, and warehouse) and *consumer type* (such as household consumer and business customers). In choosing which of these bases to use in departmentalizing the store, a retailer should select the one providing management with the best level of control and producing the highest employee efficiency.

Authority and Responsibility

Lines of authority and responsibility are *the organizational principles that each store employee (managerial and nonmanagerial) should be given the authority to accomplish whatever responsibilities have been assigned to that individual.* Figure 8–4 demonstrates the relationship between the responsibilities and the authority of a

235

Department Sales Manager's Responsibilities	Equals	Department Sales Manager's Authority
1. to ensure that the store's customer service standards and policies are maintained		1. to direct customer service standards and procedures; make customer adjustments
2. to provide (ensure) adequate floor coverage while controlling personnel budgets		2. to assign personnel within area; prepare weekly personnel schedule; request additional personnel
3. to ensure that the physical appearance of the area is visually appealing and orderly		3. to determine the merchandising set-up of area; request the removal or addition of fixtures; request and followup maintenance services
4. to communicate selling trends and other merchandise information to merchants and associates		4. to request sales and merchandising information; analyze current reports and information
5. to supervise the receipt, movement, maintenace, and display of merchandise on the selling floor and in the stockroom area		5. to determine merchandising set-up of selling-floor area; coordinate merchandising set-up of stockroom area; maintain a merchandise-movement information file
6. to ensure that advertised merchandise is available and properly priced, ticketed, and displayed		6. to communicate information about advertised merchandise to Central Stock, Receiving, and/or the merchandising staff; make necessary price and/or ticket changes
7. to shop the competition		7. to visit the competition to determine competitive pricing; communicate and/or adjust price changes for competition
8. to lead, delegate, control, discipline, and train associate employees		8. to establish, monitor, and appraise selling personnel on standards of performance; enforce store policies and procedures; communicate all information pertinent to the department operation
9. to maintain inventory control		9. to inspect and approve all paperwork within area; ensure that adjustments are properly recorded

FIGURE 8–4
Authority should equal responsibility

sales manager whose general charge is to direct the customer service, personnel, sales, merchandising, and operations activities of a department to achieve sales goals and to maximize profit. To assume certain responsibilities and accomplish them in the most efficient manner, an employee must be given the necessary authority to call upon whatever resources are necessary to complete the task.

An equally important aspect of this principle is that all members of the organization know and respect the established lines of authority and responsibility. A retailer's "chain of command" comprises lines of authority that link together the various managerial levels of the organization. Line and staff relationships are the linkages that join management levels and create organizational hierarchies. **Line relationships** are *affiliations among managers at different organizational levels or* between a manager and a subordinate within the same level who are directly responsible for achieving the firm's strategic, operational, and/or functional objectives. In a line relationship the manager has direct authority over the subordinate. On an organizational chart, line relationships are typically shown as solid lines. **Staff relationships** are *advisory or supportive and appear on organizational charts as broken lines.* Staff employees are typically specialists with expertise in a particular area of concern (e.g., legal affairs, taxation, or market analysis) and their primary function is to assist line managers to realize their objectives. To avoid confusion, duplication of effort, and territorial disputes, an organization needs to distinguish clearly the responsibilities and authority of each line manager and supportive staff.

Unity of Command

The principle of **unity of command** states that *the organizational structure of the retail firm should ensure that each store employee should be directly accountable to only one immediate supervisor at any one time for any given task.* Most employees find it difficult if not impossible to satisfy several superiors at the same time. It is not unusual for different supervisors to want subordinates to accomplish a particular task in a different way at a different time. The store employee who must serve several masters at one time is often confused, inefficient, and frustrated. A well-planned organizational structure ensures that unity of command will exist from the top of the retail organization to the bottom for all of its personnel.

Span of Control

Every organization must determine how many subordinates one person can manage. According to authorities on management, the ideal number of subordinates ranges from 4 at the highest levels to 12 at the lowest levels of organization.[1] The principle of **span of control** *sets guidelines for the number of subordinates a superior should control, depending upon the level within the organization and the nature of the tasks being performed.* Three of the guidelines follow.

1. As employees' tasks become more complex and unstandardized, their supervisor's span of control should narrow.
2. Where supervisors and employees are highly competent and well-trained, the supervisor's span of control can be broader.
3. Where tasks are highly centralized in one location, a person can supervise more subordinates than if the tasks are scattered throughout a location.

These guidelines suggest the latitudes within which organizers vary the "4–12" rule for supervisors. In retailing, these guidelines can help determine the size of the various merchandising and operating departments and divisions.

The organizational structure of the retail firm can assume many different forms. To help employees understand the organizational structure, the retailer prepares organizational charts that show the formal relationships existing between various parts of the organization. Organizational charts also describe the hierarchy of authority, the areas of responsibility, the span of control, the type and degree of specialization and departmentalization, and the reporting relationships among employees at different levels.

In planning an organizational structure, the retailer must ask two critical questions. The first is how many organizational *levels* are needed for effective and efficient operation of the firm; the second, how the various tasks should be organized into *areas of responsibility* (jobs) and how many of these areas should be designated. Some answers to these questions are given in the following sections.

Number of Organizational Levels

The number of levels separating the firm's top manager from its lowest-level employee can be viewed as a hierarchy of organizational levels. *Firms that limit the number of organizational levels to one or two levels* are using a **flat organizational structure** as illustrated in Figure 8–5a. Small, independent retailers and low-margin retailers attempting to keep their operating expenses at the lowest possible level typically use a flat organizational structure. In addition to lower operating expenses, the flat organizational structure allows direct communications with employees, higher employee morale, and quicker reaction time to problems that may arise. A flat organizational structure is often a wide organizational structure, however, which means the supervisor might have too many people to manage at one time.

Vertical or tall organizational structures *have many layers of supervisor-subordinate relationships.* As illustrated in Figure 8–5b, a large number of levels separates top management from employees at the bottom of the organization. Large retailers (e.g., department stores) and multiunit retailers (e.g., chain stores) typically

FIGURE 8–5
The number of organizational levels

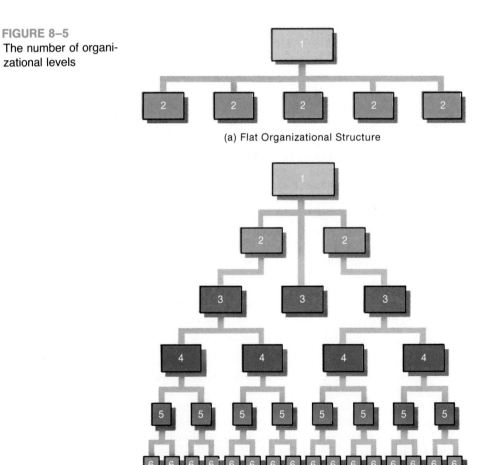

(a) Flat Organizational Structure

(b) Vertical or Tall Organizational Structure

use a taller organizational structure. The impersonal nature, lack of direct communications, and rigidness associated with a large number of organizational levels are the primary limitations of such organizations. These limitations may be offset by the benefits of having well-defined areas of responsibility and gaining increased supervision over employees and their assigned tasks.

Job and Task Organization

The exact form of organizational structure of any retailer depends upon how the retailer classifies jobs that employees must perform. A retailer can classify jobs on the basis of their functional nature, geographic location, product involvement, or some combination of the three. Using the **functional approach** to retail organizational structure, *the retailer groups tasks and classifies jobs according to such functional areas as store operations, the buying and selling of merchandise, promotional activities, or the recruiting and training of store personnel.* In essence, the functional approach is one of task and job specialization in one or more general functions. The degree of specialization and the resulting number of functional divisions vary with the type and size of the retail firm.

Small, independent retailers usually have a two-function organizational structure, thereby limiting specialization. As illustrated in Figure 8–6a, merchandising and store operations are the first two functional divisions that retailers usually create. As their firms become larger and more complex, retailers will create additional functional divisions. In the three-function organizational structure, shown in Figure 8–6b, retailers add a third division to the basic merchandising and operating divisions, typically one of the following: a financial controls division, a sales promotion division, or a personnel division. Although Figure 8–6 illustrates only the two- and three-function organizations, it is not unusual for the retailer to create four, five, or more functional divisions. The number of divisions depends upon such factors as

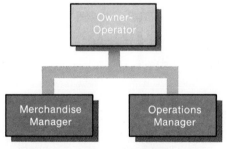

(a) The Two-Functional Organization

FIGURE 8–6
Functional organization
structures

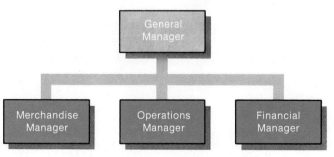

(b) The Three-Functional Organization

239

(1) the type of customer to whom the retailer wants to appeal, (2) the number and nature of the retailer's product lines, (3) the level of service the target consumer expects, (4) the type and number of facilities the retailer uses, and (5) the availability of qualified personnel. Four- and five-function organizations are illustrated and discussed under department store organizational patterns.

The **geographic approach** to organizational structure is one in which *the retailer organizes tasks and assigns jobs on the basis of where those tasks and jobs are performed.* Multiunit retailers (such as chain stores) frequently use the geographic approach. The geographic size of the retailer's market influences both the number of organizational levels and the degree of market specialization at each level. A multiunit retailer with a limited number of stores within a concentrated geographic market usually has only two levels (the main store with several branch stores) and a local market specialization (neighborhood or community). On the other hand, large chain organizations with many stores operating all over the country typically form organizational structures with several levels and various degrees of market specialization. Figure 8–7 illustrates a national retail firm that uses the geographic approach of organization.

In the **product approach** to retail organizational structure, *the retailer organizes the store by product line.* This organizational form centers around task and job specialization to meet the buying needs that consumers have for certain products. For many shopping and specialty goods, for example, consumers think, shop, and buy in terms of product groupings. Figure 8–8 illustrates a family apparel store organized around the general product lines of men's, women's, and children's apparel and accessories.

In varying degrees, most large retailing firms use all three approaches to develop their organizational structure. By creating various combinations of task and job specializations based on functions, geography, and products, the large retailer forms an organizational structure tailored to the consumption needs of its markets

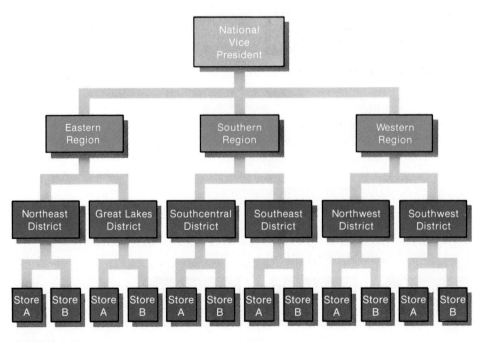

FIGURE 8–7
Geographic organization structure

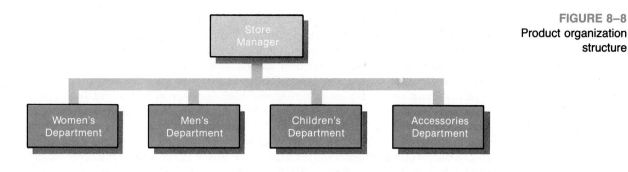

FIGURE 8–8
Product organization
structure

and to its own operational style. Several organizational combinations using functional, geographic, and product specialties are possible.

Over the years various retail organizational patterns have emerged as the result of the diverse sizes and natures of firms. To characterize these patterns, we shall look at the organizational structures of small, independent retailers, department store retailers, and chain store retailers.

PATTERNS OF RETAIL ORGANIZATION

Small Store Organization

Many retailers began business as a one-person, owner-operated shop. In these cases, the owner-operator was the organization. As such, the individual had the responsibility and authority for all organizational tasks. As the firm grew, the owner-operator hired additional store personnel to handle the increasing number of complex tasks that accompany a larger, more formal organizational structure.

The typical organizational structure of the small, independent retailer has previously been characterized as flat, typically with two levels and a general organization and a limited amount of specialization. As illustrated in Figure 8–9, the owner-manager develops store and personnel policies; administers expense, sales, and merchandising budgets; and oversees accounting and other control procedures. In most small retail firms, however, it is common for the owner-manager to become directly involved with many of the routine merchandising tasks and day-to-day operations.

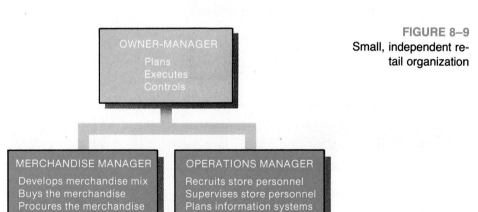

FIGURE 8–9
Small, independent retail organization

Also illustrated in Figure 8–9 are the two most common functional divisions that small retailers use: the merchandising and operations divisions. The merchandise manager usually is a salesperson with considerable experience in merchandising and has been an employee for a long time. Typically, this person is assigned responsibilities for buying and selling the firm's merchandise. The operations manager is an employee who assumes the responsibilities for recruiting and supervising store personnel; for planning, securing, and maintaining store facilities, equipment, and supplies; and for many of the back-room activities of receiving and stocking merchandise and overseeing the activities of the office staff. A principal concern of all small retail organizations is span of control. Many small retail firms outgrow the owner-manager's ability to directly supervise the activities of store personnel and their tasks. At some point, the owner-manager must be willing to develop the degree of specialization necessary to operate a growing store more efficiently.

Department Store Organization

Department store organizations are more formal and complex than small retailers'. As mentioned earlier, the organizational structure of department stores is taller and more specialized than small retail stores. To understand department store organization, we shall examine the Mazur Plan of retail organization and its functional and geographic modifications.

The Mazur Plan

Most retailing experts date modern retail organizational structures from 1927 when Paul Mazur, an investment banker, introduced his ideas on how to structure a retail store.[2] The **Mazur Plan** *divides the retail organization into four functional divisions—finance, merchandising, promotion, and operations.* Each of these division managers has specific responsibilities (see Figure 8–10).

The *finance manager's* chief responsibilities are to control the firm's assets and to ensure that sufficient working capital is available for each of the firm's functional divisions. In particular, the finance manager has responsibility for (1) developing

FIGURE 8–10
The Mazur Plan for department store organization

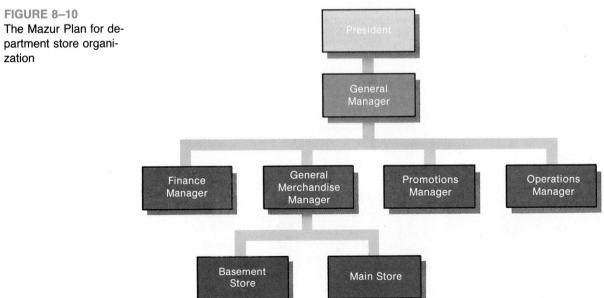

and maintaining accounting and other record-keeping systems; (2) planning and controlling physical inventory, merchandise budgets, and expense budgets; and (3) preparing financial reports for the firm's general management, government agencies, and trade organizations.

The *general merchandising manager* is responsible primarily for supervising the firm's buying and selling activities. An equally important responsibility is to coordinate these activities with those of the finance, promotions, and operations managers. Given the consumer orientation of retailing, the general merchandise division is usually the most important functional area within the organization. Figure 8–11 presents the organizational structure of the typical general merchandise division. As shown, line managers and personnel include divisional merchandising managers (e.g., women's wear), department managers (e.g., coats, dresses, lingerie, sportswear), assistant department managers, heads of stock and sales, and stock personnel. Line managers have direct authority over and responsibility for their operations. Staff personnel, on the other hand, have no authority but instead serve in an advisory or support capacity. Staff organizations include fashion bureaus, comparison shopping units, and merchandise testing and research groups.

The *promotions manager* is responsible for directing the firm's persuasive communications to consumers. Specifically, the promotions manager oversees all advertising, sales promotional activities (e.g., fashion shows, demonstrations), interior and window displays, public relations, and publicity. In addition, the promotions manager handles consumer feedback and directs advertising research in companies that conduct these activities.

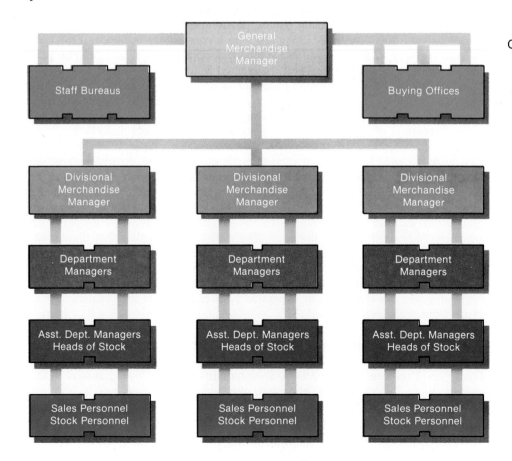

FIGURE 8–11
Organizational structure for the general merchandising division

The *operations manager* is generally responsible for all the physical operations of the store that are not directly assigned to one of the other divisions. Major tasks assigned to the store operations division are facilities development and maintenance; customer services and assistance; receiving, checking, marking, and stocking of incoming merchandise; store security; and general store housekeeping. Recruiting, training, and evaluating store personnel also are responsibilities assigned to the operations manager in a four-function organization.

Functional modifications. The two most common functional modifications in the Mazur Plan are (1) changing the number of functional divisions and (2) separating the buying and selling functions. In changing the Mazur Plan, department stores most often create a five-function organization by establishing a personnel division, equal in status to the other four divisions. Since recruiting and training good store personnel have become extremely important in recent years because of increased unionization, wage and salary demands, security expectations, and government regulations in the area of personnel, many retailers have elevated the status of the personnel function. Also, because payroll expenses are the costliest item for most retail organizations, the need for a separate personnel division has taken on greater significance. Other functional activities that retailers might consider for separate divisional status are distribution, real estate and construction, and catalog operations.

According to the Mazur Plan, the buying and selling functions both fall under the direct supervision of the general merchandise manager. Some retailing experts argue, however, that these functions should be separated. Proponents of separation believe that (1) buying and selling require different skills, talents, and training; (2) selling activities suffer because buying takes up a considerable amount of the buyer's time spent away from the store; (3) feedback on consumer needs can be handled better by a well-developed and maintained merchandise-control system; (4) greater flexibility in the use of sales and buying personnel is possible when these individuals specialize in either selling or buying activities; and (5) in-store grouping of merchandise should be based on selling, not buying, activities. Those arguing against separation of buying and selling activities, however, hold that (1) the buyer must have direct contact with customers to determine their needs; (2) the individual who buys the merchandise is responsible for selling it and therefore exercises greater care in buying activities; and (3) it is easier to assign responsibility for the department's profit performance if buying and selling are conducted by the same person, since the buyer cannot blame the seller for not putting out the necessary selling effort, and the seller cannot blame the lack of a good profit performance on buying mistakes. Both sides of the issue offer valid arguments. Whether the department store owner chooses to combine these functions or separate them depends upon the number of stores, variations in local customer preferences, and the organizational preferences of top management. How buying and selling activities in department stores are combined or separated is discussed later in conjunction with branch store organizations.

Geographic modifications. When department stores began to "branch out" into other geographic areas, they necessitated several additional changes in the basic Mazur Plan. These new organizational arrangements, based on geographical modifications, were the main-store approach, the separate-store approach, and the equal-store approach.

The **main-store approach** to branch organization *has the parent organization (the main store) exercise control over branch stores.* As illustrated in Figure 8–12,

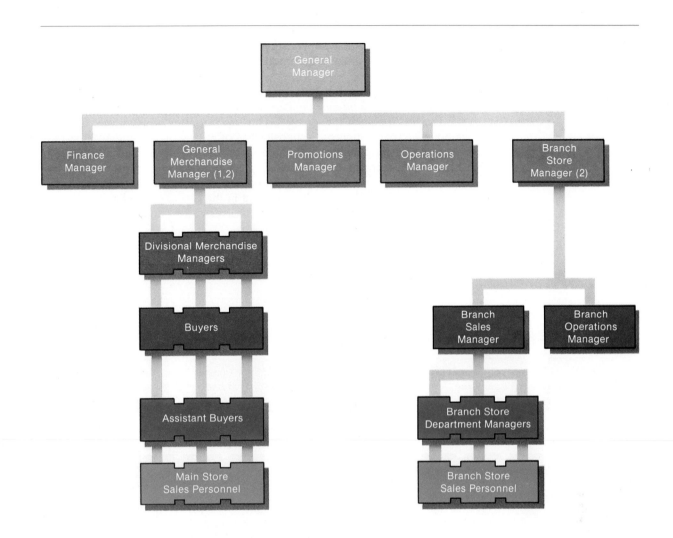

FIGURE 8–12

The main-store approach to branch department-store organization

main-store managers of finance, general merchandise, promotion, and operations are responsible for supervising the same functions in the branch stores as they are at the main store. Under this organizational plan, main-store buyers and their assistants are responsible for securing merchandise for the main store and all branches. Sales activities in the main store are under the direct supervision of buyers, whereas sales activities in all branch stores are the responsibility of branch sales managers. In essence, those who use the main-store approach treat branch stores as sales organizations, performing merchandise and operation functions from within the main store.

Used by department stores in the initial stages of expansion, the main-store approach is most appropriate when (1) there are only a few branches; (2) customer preferences and the merchandise mix are fairly similar for the main and branch stores; (3) branch stores are located near the main store; and (4) main-store management and supporting staff can comfortably supervise branches without overextending themselves. The main-store approach with its degree of centralization becomes inappropriate, however, when the number of branch stores increases to

245

the point at which considerable supervisory strain is placed on central management and staff. To relieve this strain, a common remedy is to decentralize the organizational structure.

The **separate-store approach** to branch department-store organization *treats each branch as an independent operation with its own organizational structure of managers, buyers, and sales personnel.* Under this plan, branch store management assumes both the merchandising responsibilities of buying and selling and the routine responsibilities of operating the branch store. As shown in Figure 8–13, each branch has its own store manager as well as personnel, merchandise, and operations managers who operate separately from the parent organization. Although the parent organization has little direct involvement in the day-to-day operations of the branch store, it does have the general responsibilities of serving in an advisory and policy-making capacity.

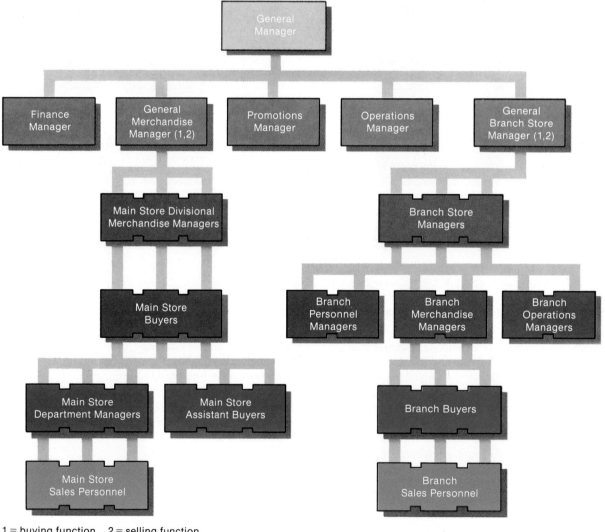

1 = buying function   2 = selling function

FIGURE 8–13
Separate-store approach to branch department-store organization

The separate-store approach is generally used by department stores that have four to seven branches approximately the size of the main store. The major advantage of this approach is that each branch has great flexibility in tailoring its merchandise and operations to meet the needs of its local clientele. The principal disadvantages are (1) a loss in economies of scale in buying; (2) an increase in operating costs because of additional management and staff needs; (3) increased difficulties in maintaining a consistent image from store to store; and (4) increased problems of coordination (e.g., stock transfers, promotion activities,).

In response to the increasing number of branch stores, retailers have developed an alternative strategy to the separate-store approach. Instead of the decentralized authority and responsibility used in the separate-store approach, the **equal-store approach** *emphasizes centralization of authority and responsibility.* Under the equal-store plan, all major managerial functions are controlled from a central headquarters. The finance, merchandise, promotions, and operations functions are under the direct supervision of headquarters managers. This approach has two unique features. First, the buying and selling functions are separated—the buying function remains a centralized activity under the general merchandise manager, while the selling function becomes a decentralized activity under the manager of stores. Second, all stores (main and branches) are treated equally as basic sales units (see Figure 8–14, p. 248). The equal-store plan attempts to combine the advantages of centralized buying (economies of scale) with the advantages of localized selling (target market selling). To gain these two advantages, the information feedback system from sellers to buyers must be well developed and maintained. The equal-store approach incorporates many of the organizational principles used by chain store organizations. In recent years the equal-store plan has gained wide acceptance from department store retailers.

Chain Store Organization

Chain store organizations vary considerably in size, geographic spread, local markets, product mix, and number of operating units. Although all of these factors influence how a chain store will organize, three distinctive elements characterize all chain store organizations: centralization, specialization, and standardization.

Centralization is *the concentration of policy and decision making in one location, either called central headquarters or the home office.* Within the chain-store organizational structure, the authority and responsibilities for most operating and merchandising functions are assigned to home office management personnel. The primary exception is sales, which are under the decentralized control of local management. In recent years chain store organizations have tended to adopt limited decentralization. Thus, more and more functional authority and responsibility are being given to regional and divisional levels of the organization. The main reason behind this change is the gigantic size of many chain store retailers (see Figure 8–15).

A high degree of **specialization** is another distinguishing feature of chain store organizations. Typically, the chain store incorporates a greater number of functional divisions in its organizational structure. In addition to the four basic functional divisions of finance, merchandising, operations, and promotions, many chain stores include one or more of the following functional divisions: distribution (traffic and warehousing), marketing, real estate and construction, personnel, and industrial relations. Some large chains also specialize geographically.

The third distinguishing feature of chain organizations is a high degree of **standardization**, or *similarities between the operating and merchandising operations of the business.* To support standardization, chain store management establishes an

247

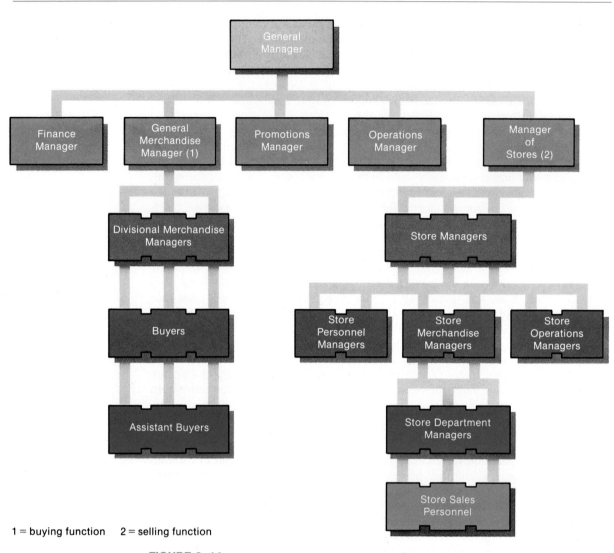

1 = buying function   2 = selling function

FIGURE 8–14
Equal-store approach to branch department-store organization

elaborate system of supervision and control mechanisms to keep fully informed. Through standardization, the chain projects a consistent company image and minimizes total costs of doing business.

SUMMARY

Retailers use a number of different structures to organize their people, tasks, and operations. In retailing, the firm's organization is directed at accomplishing certain strategy objectives (general, long-term goals); operational objectives (long-term operational requirements to obtain strategy objectives); and functional objectives (specific task-oriented objectives). Also, retailers must organize in such a manner that the basic operational tasks of planning and controlling the product, price, promotion, and place can be readily facilitated.

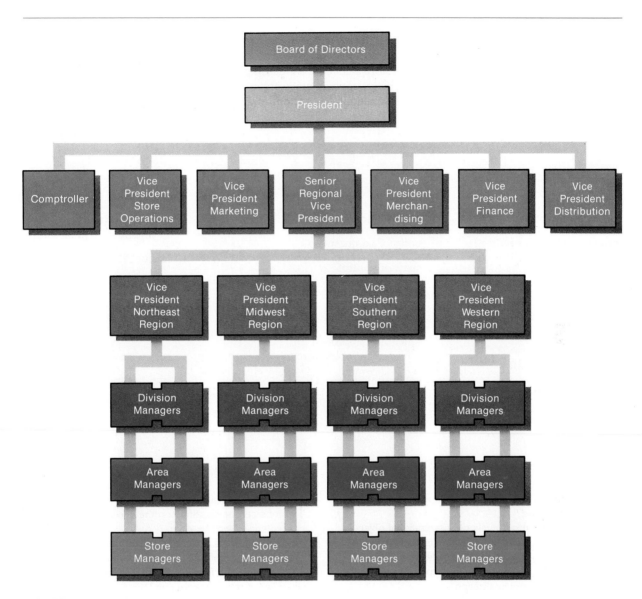

FIGURE 8–15
Chain store organization

The retailer should consider several basic principles of organization in developing the structure of the firm. Of particular interest are the organizational principles of specialization and departmentalization, lines of authority and areas of responsibility, unity of command, and span of control.

Many retailers prepare charts to illustrate their form of retail organization. Some retail organizational structures are characterized by a limited number of levels (flat organizations), while others incorporate many levels of organization (vertical structures). Organizational forms are strongly influenced by how retailers classify jobs and tasks. Depending on the firm, jobs and tasks can be classified on the basis of their functional, geographic, or product relationships; also, a combination of these three factors can be used in job and task classification.

249

Patterns of retail organization vary considerably between the simple structures of the small, independent retailer and the often complex organization of the department and chain store retailer. Centralization, specialization, and standardization are the key characteristics of chain store organizational structures, while the Mazur Plan, together with its variations, characterizes department store organizations.

KEY TERMS AND CONCEPTS

strategic objectives

operational objectives

functional objectives

specialization

departmentalization

lines of authority

lines of responsibility

line relationships

staff relationships

unity of command

span of control

flat organizational structure

vertical organizational structure

functional approach to
organizational structure

geographic approach to
organizational structure

product approach to
organizational structure

Mazur Plan

main-store organization

separate-store organization

equal-store organization

centralization

standardization

REVIEW QUESTIONS

1. What factors influence the selection of an organizational structure?
2. What are the three levels of organizational objectives? Define each and describe its relationship to the general levels of retail management.
3. Describe the organizational principles of specialization and departmentalization.
4. How can specialization and departmentalization be accomplished?
5. Distinguish between line and staff relationships.
6. What is the principle of unity of command?
7. What is the ideal span of control?
8. What determines the number of subordinates a superior should control?
9. Why use a flat organizational structure?

10. What organizations use a vertical structure?
11. Jobs can be classified on the basis of which three criteria? Describe each.
12. Which factors determine the number of functional divisions within a retail organization?
13. What are the four functional divisions in the Mazur Plan of retail organization?
14. Why should the buying and selling functions be separated?
15. Compare and contrast the main-store, separate-store, and equal-store approaches to branch department-store organization.
16. What distinguishes chain store operations? Discuss each distinctive element.

ENDNOTES

1. Lyndall Urwick, "Axioms of Organization," *Public Administration,* October 1955, 348–49.

2. Paul M. Mazur, *Principles of Organization Applied to Modern Retailing* (New York: Harper & Row, 1927).

RELATED READINGS

Brief, Arthur P. *Managing Human Resources in Retail Organizations.* (Lexington, Mass.: Lexington Books, 1984)

Fink, Stephen L.; Jenks, R. Stephen; and Willits, Robin D. *Designing and Managing Organizations.* (Homewood, Ill.: Richard D. Irwin, 1983)

Gable, Myron, and Hollon, Charles. "Employee Turnover of Managerial Trainees in a Department Store Chain." *Retail Control* (January 1984), 54–61.

Gray, Jerry L., and Starke, Frederick A. *Organizational Behavior: Concepts and Applications,* 3rd ed. (Columbus: Charles E. Merrill Publishing Co., 1984)

Griffin, Ricky W. *Task Design.* (Glenview, Ill.: Scott, Foresman & Company, 1982)

Hansen, Stephen W. "Restructuring for Organizational Efficiency." *Retail Control* (August 1983), 20–25.

Horney, Bryan. "Implementing a Management Control System." *Retail Control* (March 1984), 18–32.

Johns, Gary. *Organizational Behavior—Understanding Life at Work.* (Glenview, Ill.: Scott, Foresman & Company, 1983)

Kanuk, Leslie. "Leadership Effectiveness of Department Managers in a Department Store Chain: A Contingency Analysis." *Journal of Retailing* 52 (Spring 1976), 9–16.

Larsson, Kent. "Retail Management Will Shift Focus from Merchandising to Marketing." *Marketing News* (May 30, 1980), 5.

Miller, John D., and Wilson, George. "An Evolving Department Store Structure: A Case Study for the 90's." *Retail Control* (February 1984), 46–55.

Randolph, W. Alan. *Understanding and Managing Organizational Behavior.* (Homewood, Ill.: Richard D. Irwin, 1985)

Steers, Richard M. *Introduction to Organization Behavior,* 2nd ed. (Glenview, Ill.: Scott, Foresman & Company, 1984)

"Teamwork Pays Off at Penney's." *Business Week* (April 12, 1982), 107–8.

Outline

Objectives

- Conduct a job analysis to determine the specific objectives, tasks, and skills required of the employee

- Write a job description and develop specifications for each position

- Identify potential sources of store employees and describe the criteria and methods for screening job applicants

- Understand and use the basic techniques for matching job requirements with employee attributes

- Specify the different procedures used in training and supervising store personnel

- Discuss when to evaluate, what to evaluate, and how to evaluate employees and their performances

- Evaluate the various methods used in compensating store personnel

9
Staffing the Retail Store

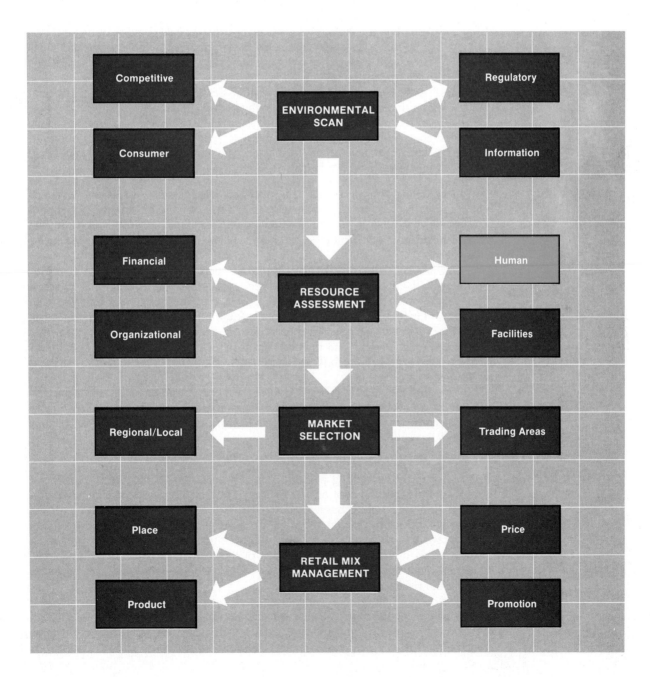

P eople make a successful business! Regardless of the number and quality of machines, product lines carried, floor and shelf space, and other material aspects of a business, people make the difference. Therefore, staffing the retail store may be one of the most difficult and certainly most important tasks facing the retailer. Problems in finding and keeping good store personnel are largely the result of two factors: working conditions surrounding a retail job and the characteristics of the labor pool from which retailers can choose. Retail working conditions generally have the following undesirable aspects:

1. *Long hours*—the typical retail manager often devotes 50 to 60 hours a week to the job.
2. *Wrong hours*—most retail employees are expected to work during evening hours and over weekends. Also, many employees must work split shifts (morning, a break, then evening) and irregular schedules (8 to 5 one day, 1 to 9 the next).
3. *Part-time employment*—many employees are needed only on a part-time basis during peak demand periods (such as Christmas).
4. *Low compensation*—retail wages and benefits at lower-level positions have traditionally been lower than those in other fields of business; however, wages and benefits at the higher-level positions are generally equal to those found in other industries.

The labor pool from which the retail firm obtains many of its employees is characterized by groups that, historically, lacked training and experience. Many part-time employees work in retailing to supplement their family income, so their loyalty to and need for the job may be marginal. Hence, their productivity may also be marginal.

The impact of these difficulties on retail operations has been high turnover. Some retailers experience annual employee turnover rates in excess of 50 percent. Generally, employee turnover rates are highest in lower-level positions. With high employee turnover rates, the retailer incurs large recruiting and training expenses, lower labor productivity, and disruptions in store operations. Given these problems, the retailer must develop and maintain an effective employee staffing process, particularly since employee compensation generally accounts for more than 50 percent of the retailer's expenses.

The retailer's staffing process involves not only finding capable store personnel, but also developing working environments that will enable the retailer to keep productive employees. Specifically, the staffing process consists of the eight steps shown in Figure 9–1.

DESCRIBING THE JOB

The first step in the staffing process is to develop a well-defined and clearly expressed **job description**. Not only does this step force the retailer to carefully determine its personnel needs, but it also provides the potential employee with a means of evaluating the job. Prior to writing a job description, the retailer should conduct a job analysis to determine (1) specific job-performance objectives and standards; (2) the tasks, duties, and responsibilities of the job; and (3) the skills, aptitudes, experience, education, and physical stature that potential employees must possess to meet the minimum job requirements.

Job-content information can be obtained through observation, interviews, or questionnaires. Hourly and machine-paced kinds of jobs are assessed best through observation. The questionnaire approach is well suited for obtaining information concerning clerical, sales, and lower-level supervisory positions. Middle- and upper-

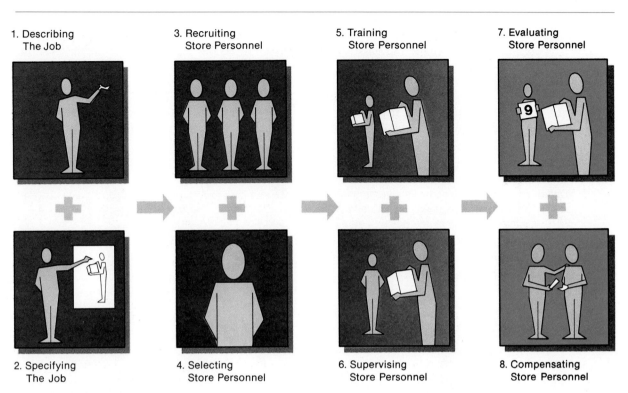

1. Describing
   The Job

3. Recruiting
   Store Personnel

5. Training
   Store Personnel

7. Evaluating
   Store Personnel

2. Specifying
   The Job

4. Selecting
   Store Personnel

6. Supervising
   Store Personnel

8. Compensating
   Store Personnel

FIGURE 9–1
The retail staffing process

management job content is best obtained using one-on-one interviews between the job analyst and job incumbent.[1] Figure 9–2 illustrates a job-analysis questionnaire for a retail salesperson.

Once the job analysis is completed, the retailer can write a job description containing the following items: (1) the job title (e.g., salesclerk, assistant store manager); (2) the job location (e.g., store, department); (3) the job position and relationships with the firm's organizational structure (e.g., identify superiors and subordinates, if any); and (4) job description (i.e., duties and responsibilities). Figure 9–3 presents a typical job description for a sales manager position.

Job descriptions have been criticized for a number of reasons. Perhaps the most valid criticism is that they often define the job in narrow terms, thereby stifling the employee's initiative and creativity. To overcome this criticism, some retailers write job descriptions in the form of job "objectives." This description gives the employee greater latitude in job interpretation and performance. It should be noted that Figure 9–3 includes job objectives within the job description.

To meet federal, state, and local regulations on hiring practices, many retailers provide potential employees with a written job specification.[2] A **job specification** *clearly states the minimum qualifications a person must have to obtain the job applied for.* Qualification criteria include education and training requirements and/or basic knowledge and skill requirements. Because of recent legislation, retailers need to recognize that they might be asked to prove that their qualifying criteria are directly related to successful performance in the positions outlined in their job descriptions. To avoid costly lawsuits, they must establish the validity of the relationship between

SPECIFYING THE
JOB

255

Salesperson

Job Title: _____   Store Name _____

Supervisor's Position: _____   Location: _____

Store Department: _____   Approvals: _____ (Incumbent)

                                                     _____ (Supervisor)

1. *Major Function:* (Write a brief statement on the reason for the job's existence).
2. *Dimensions:* (This section should give pertinent statistics about the job. What is the individual sales volume? What are the department and store sales volumes? What are the numbers of sales people on the floor, on average, during store-opening time?)
3. *Merchandise:* (List here the lines sold—number and/or types of merchandise.)
4. How is the department merchandised?
5. Does merchandise need fitting or alterations?
6. Are deliveries involved?
7. List specific duties:
   a.
   b.
   c.
   etc.
8. Who assigns, reviews, and/or approves work?
9. What responsibility or decision-making authority have you?
10. Do you prepare reports and, if so, what are they and what are they used for?
11. Do you operate or service any equipment, fixtures or machinery?
12. What is the hardest part of the job?
13. What experience is necessary to perform the job adequately?
14. How long does it take to learn the job adequately?
15. How would you describe the working conditions in which you perform?
16. Additional useful information.

Source: Jon Laking and Robin Roark, *Retailing Job Analysis and Job Evaluation* (New York: Personnel Division, National Retail Merchants Association, 1975), 6–7

FIGURE 9–2
Job-analysis questionnaire

job success and the stated job qualifications. Before filling any position, the retailer should protect itself by gathering evidence that the job qualifications actually enable an employee to meet job expectations. The retailer must avoid certain illegal conditions for employment in writing job qualifications, such as any requirement related either directly or indirectly to the applicant's race, age, creed, color, sex, religion, or national origin.

RECRUITING STORE PERSONNEL

Recruiting is the active search for qualified employees. The astute manager recruits personnel by aggressively *seeking* lists of qualified prospects, *screening* large numbers of applicants, and *maintaining* a pool of prospective employees. Successful recruiting is the process of knowing where to look, what to look for, and how to find qualified people.

Job title:	Sales manager
Job location:	Men's shoe department Walnut Valley Branch Selmer's Department Stores
Job position:	Reports to assistant store manager
Job description:	To achieve sales goals by setting and maintaining customer service standards, training and motivating a professional sales staff, and maintaining merchandise presentation standards.
Job objectives:	1. To work as a partner with the merchandise analyst to develop sales plans and to reach sales goals within the area of responsibility.
	2. To ensure that the store's customer service standards and policies are maintained.
	3. To train, develop, motivate, and appraise the sales associates working within the area of responsibility.
	4. To work as a partner with the merchandise analyst and assistant store manager in developing stock assortments and quantities.
	5. To verify that the appearance and presentation of merchandise on the selling floor adhere to the visual merchandising guidelines.
	6. To ensure that selling services provide appropriate floor coverage to meet or exceed productivity goals.
	7. To communicate with the branch store coordinator, assistant store manager, and merchandise analyst concerning floor presentation.
	8. To ensure that advertised merchandise is properly priced, ticketed, and displayed and to ensure that sales associates are aware of this merchandise.
	9. To control merchandise inventories, including but not limited to receiving, pricing, transfers, price changes, security, and damages.
	10. To conduct all stock counts.
	11. To supervise the control of sales register media and cash register shortage.
	12. To shop the competition.
	13. To input information into major sale resumes.
	14. To disseminate all pertinent information to all sales associates including night contingents.
	15. To ensure the correct documentation of time sheets within the area.
	16. To implement credit promotions and other programs in the area.

FIGURE 9–3

A typical job description

Finding Employees

Several internal and external sources can provide the names and general backgrounds of prospective employees. Internal sources include lists of current and past employees as well as employee recommendations. *Current employees* should not be overlooked if they possess the necessary qualifications for the job. Promotions and transfers are not only a means of finding qualified persons, but also a way to improve employee morale by demonstrating that advancement is possible within the firm. The fact that current employees represent known quantities and are familiar with the firm and its marketing effort are additional pluses for this recruiting method.

Past employees with satisfactory service records make up an internal source of employees that retailers often overlook. By maintaining files on past employees (full- and part-time), the personnel manager has access to prospective employees who could be productive immediately with minimal training.

The third internal source is *employee recommendations.* Frequently, the firm's employees know of friends, relatives, and acquaintances who are in the job market and have the necessary skills and training to fill a position. While the value of the recommendation will vary with the individual employee, it is nevertheless an inside track to potentially viable prospects.

External sources of prospective employees are provided by advertisements, employment agencies, educational institutions, and unsolicited applications. *Advertisements* in newspapers, trade publications, and professional papers and journals are common methods of attracting applicants. Each of these printed media frequently devotes sections to employment opportunities at certain times or within particular issues. Examples are the Tuesday edition of the *Wall Street Journal* and the Sunday edition of many major metropolitan newspapers. Although advertisements usually generate more applications than do other recruiting sources, the qualifications of most of these applicants are generally low.

Private and public *employment agencies* are also sources of prospective employees. Two advantages of using employment agencies are that they provide initial screening for a large number of prospects and that they maintain the retailer's anonymity during the initial stages of the recruiting process. Before using the services of a private or government employment agency, the retailer should determine the agency's fee structure and which party is responsible for paying the fee—the employer or the employee. Like most organizations, employment agencies differ in the type and level of services provided. Retailers should take time to check the agency's reputation and the services it offers. For lower-echelon employees, government employment agencies are good sources of potential employees. For top management positions, retailers can use executive search firms to find qualified prospects.

The third external source of prospective employees consists of *educational institutions.* Career counselors at most high schools often can provide a list of suitable prospects for part-time and entry-level positions. Placement offices at junior colleges and four-year colleges and universities are always eager to supply retailers and other businesses with the names and qualifications of prospective employees for low- and middle-management positions. And, directors of MBA (Masters of Business Administration) programs are willing to help retailers match their middle- and upper-management needs with interested, competent students.

Walk-ins and mail-ins represent *unsolicited applications* that retailers should keep on file and periodically review when a job becomes available. Although unsolicited applications usually come from individuals who are more likely qualified for part-time and lower-level positions, they can contribute to the list of potential candidates during the initial recruitment process.

One additional external source of employees is *pirating*—hiring an employee who works for a noncompeting retailer. The major advantage of pirating is the retailing experience the prospective employee undoubtedly has. However, the retailer should proceed cautiously when hiring another retailer's employee. First, it should determine whether the employee is really interested in the position or is simply trying to obtain leverage for a salary increase or promotion with the current employer. Second, to avoid retaliation and unpleasant relationships, some retailers make it a hiring practice to extend an offer at or about the same salary the employee is currently receiving with the stipulation that a substantial increase will be forthcoming within a short period of time if the employee performs satisfactorily.

Screening Applicants

In the screening process retailers examine the qualifications of an applicant to determine whether the person has the requisite background and capabilities to perform the job. The most common criteria retailers use in the initial screening process are the person's educational background, ability to communicate in oral and written form, experience in working with people, and knowledge, experience, or skills to perform a particular activity (e.g., typing). Other screening criteria retailers use indirectly and subjectively are personal appearance, general attitude, motivation, and personality. After the recruiting list has been trimmed through the initial screening process, the retailer can then proceed to the fourth stage of the staffing process, selecting employees.

From the list of qualified applicants the retailer must select the individual best suited to the job.[3] Matching job requirements to employee attributes is the point of the selection step of the staffing process. In finding the best match, the retailer has available several methods of generating additional information on the prospective employee before deciding to make an offer. These methods include application forms, personal interviews, reference checks, testing instruments, and physical examinations.[4] The particular methods retailers use in gathering applicant information depend on the size of the firm, the preferences of its personnel division, and the nature and level of the job to be filled. Small firms typically rely on application forms and personal interviews in selecting employees, whereas large retail firms often use all or nearly all of these methods.

SELECTING STORE PERSONNEL

Application Forms

All retailers should require each prospective employee to complete an application form as a prerequisite for further processing. Application forms provide the retailer with preliminary information on each applicant and (1) serve as a means of checking minimum qualifications during initial screening; (2) provide basic information to guide the interviewer during the personal interview process; (3) allow a preliminary check on the applicant's ability to follow instructions; and (4) provide background information for a permanent record if the applicant is hired.[5] The typical application form provides space for the applicant's name, address, telephone number, employment history (when and where the applicant has previously worked, levels of compensation, and reasons for leaving previous jobs), formal education and training, personal health history, and demographic information allowed by state and federal regulations (see Chapter 5). Also, the application form usually includes space for a list of personal references. Although the retailer should carefully review all the information on the application form, special attention should be given to *omissions* and *job changes*. What is *not* on the application form could be as important as what *is* on it. The retailer should seek clarification of all omissions on application forms. A careless or deceptive omission can tell the retailer a great deal about the character of the prospective employee. Frequent job changes without good cause can also reveal something about the applicant's character. As a supplement to the application form, some retailers find it helpful to have the applicant attach a transcript of high school and college work.

Reference Checks

Once the retailer has initially screened prospective employees' application forms and eliminated those who are unqualified, it should then contact the references of the remaining prospects. Although most references that the applicants list are favorably biased, they do give the retailer a way to verify the accuracy and completeness of the applicant's form. Telephone calls to references normally provide more complete and honest evaluations of the applicant's form than do letters, mainly due to the immediate and personal two-way communications telephone conversations allow. Telephone contact allows the retailer a chance to question the reference about issues of particular concern. To reinforce reference checks, many retailers contact former employers, teachers, and other individuals who might have specific knowledge of the applicant's character and abilities. Some retailers even check applicants' credit by calling local credit bureaus.

Personal Interviews

Retailers use personal interviews to question and observe applicants in a face-to-face situation. Several factors retailers should consider are the degree of formality and structure of interviews, the number of people to be interviewed, where the interviews are to take place, the length of each interview, the number of interviews per applicant, and the type of questions to be asked of each applicant. Formal, highly structured interviews have the advantage of establishing the relative roles of each party in the interview, permitting a controlled interviewing environment, and facilitating complete, effective information gathering. Informal and unstructured interviews help the applicant to relax, to talk freely, and to act naturally—thereby allowing the interviewer to view the applicant in an unguarded state. Most retailers prefer to compromise by injecting enough formality and structure into the interview to promote efficiency, but not enough to create undue tension in the applicant. The number of interviews usually depends on the level of the position to be filled. When retailers are trying to fill upper-level managerial positions, they normally interview each applicant several times. For entry-level positions, one interview generally suffices. An exception occurs when two or more highly qualified people are applying for the same job.

The location of any interview should be private and in pleasant surroundings. Both of these factors help to relax the prospective employee and give the retailer a chance to see the applicant in a natural setting. The length of an interview may be from a few minutes for low-echelon, part-time employees to several days for the applicant who is interviewing for a high-level management position. Many retailers find it advantageous to have the applicant interview with several of the firm's managers so they can elicit several opinions of the applicant's qualifications. This approach significantly increases the likelihood of finding the best person for the position.

The personal interviewing process should fully comply with state and federal equal employment opportunity regulations. Questions asked in the interview must be job-related and necessary to judging the applicant's qualifications and abilities. To avoid charges of discrimination, the retailer should construct a list of questions to use in the interviewing process and have the store's legal department review it for any possible discriminatory inquiries. Figure 9–4 indentifies several questions concerning past job experiences, current job expectations, and personal goals and ambitions that could be legally asked in an interview.

Testing Instruments

In the hiring process, some retailers use testing instruments to evaluate prospective employees. These instruments are pencil-and-paper tests that applicants take to demonstrate their abilities to handle a job. Although the validity and usefulness of

About past job experiences

- Can you give me an example of your abilities to manage or supervise others?
- What are some things you would like to avoid in a job? Why?
- What are some of the things on your job you feel you have done particularly well or in which you have achieved the greatest success?
- What were some of the things about your last job that you found difficult to do?
- In what ways do you feel your present job has developed you to take on even greater responsibilities?
- What do you feel has been your greatest frustration or disappointment on your present job and why do you feel this way?
- What are some of the reasons that are prompting you to consider leaving your present job?
- What are some of the things about which you and your supervisor might occasionally disagree?

About current job expectations

- What do you see in this job that makes it appealing to you that you do not have in your present job?
- How do you evaluate our company as a place to build your future?
- What would you say there is about this job that is particularly appealing to you?
- What aspects of this job do you find undesirable?
- What are some of the first things you need to know about before you could really step in and do your assignment justice?

About personal goals and ambitions

- Where do you see yourself going from here?
- What are your long-term career objectives?
- What is it you have going for you that might make you successful on the job?
- Who or what in your life would you say influenced you most with regard to your career objectives?
- What would you say are some of the basic factors that motivate you?
- How would you describe yourself as a person?
- What things give you the greatest satisfaction?

FIGURE 9–4
What an interviewer can ask

these instruments have been debated, many retailers believe they provide valuable insights into a person's qualifications for employment. Regardless of the value of testing instruments, retailers should not use them as the sole basis for a final employment decision, but rather as additional inputs.

Retailers use two general types of instruments to evaluate their applicants: psychological tests and achievement tests. **Psychological tests** are *instruments designed to measure an applicant's personality, intelligence, aptitudes, interests, and supervisory skills.* Regardless of which tests are used, the retailer needs trained personnel to administer and interpret the results.

Achievement tests are *questionnaires designed to measure a person's basic knowledge and skills.* Tests that measure an applicant's ability to do basic arithmetic computations or to operate mechanical devices, such as cash registers, typewriters, and calculators, are examples. Generally, retailers prefer achievement tests to psychological tests because they are easier to administer and interpret. Also, most retailers believe that achievement tests are more valid than psychological tests since the statistical relationship between the skills they measure and job success is

261

stronger—a particularly important consideration in light of recent court rulings regarding equal employment opportunities.

Physical Examinations

Some retailers require applicants to undergo a physical examination. Usually this examination is requested only after the applicant has been judged the most qualified person for the job. Some states have laws requiring a physical examination for employees handling food and drug products. In addition, some firms' health, life, and disability insurance programs require exams.

Final Selection

Ultimately, the retailer must make a final selection among the qualified applicants. No absolute, totally objective method can determine the most qualified person; rather, the final selection is largely a subjective choice based on all available information. An experienced personnel manager with good intuition is perhaps one of the most valuable assets a firm can have for selecting employees who will make a significant contribution over an extended period. Objective tests, experience, and good personal judgment are the tools a personnel manager needs to make the final selection.

TRAINING STORE PERSONNEL

The fifth step in the staffing process is employee training. Training programs are needed not only for new employees, but also for existing employees to update their knowledge and skills. Although the personnel manager in large stores and the owner-manager in small stores are responsible for developing training programs, all of the company's employees should take an active role in creating and participating in such programs. Training programs are designed to help both the employer and employee reach mutually beneficial goals.

The employer's goals in instituting training programs are (1) to increase employee productivity, thereby reducing wage costs per sale and increasing profits; (2) to reduce the level of supervision needed to ensure a smooth operation; (3) to promote greater conformity and standardization of operations, thus enhancing efficiency; and (4) to provide a higher customer-service level and thereby a higher degree of customer satisfaction. Training goals for employees are (1) to develop job skills and knowledge; (2) to help them understand the company's policies, rules, regulations, benefits, and privileges; (3) to increase their earnings and productivity; and (4) to improve their morale, job security, and job satisfaction.

Retail training programs vary according to the size and complexity of the retail organization, the number of employees, the type and complexity of the job, the abilities and experience of the individual employee, and the program goals. Regardless of the retailer's individual situation, however, every sound retail training program should address three basic questions. These elements are *what type* of training the employee should have, *where* the training should take place, and *how* the training should be done. Figure 9–5 identifies these basic elements.

What Training to Give

Two basic kinds of training that both new and old employees need are organization orientation and functional training. **Organization orientation** is *a program that either initiates new employees or updates old employees on the general organizational structure of the firm and its policies, rules, and regulations.* It also acquaints employees with the company's history, objectives, and future expectations. Essentially,

FIGURE 9–5

Elements of a retail
training program

CHAPTER 9
STAFFING THE RETAIL
STORE

WHAT	Organizational orientation
	Functional training
WHERE	On the job—decentralized training
	Off the job—centralized training
HOW	Individual methods
	"on your own"
	programmed learning
	Sponsor method
	Group methods
	lectures
	demonstrations
	case studies
	role playing
	Executive training programs

an organization orientation program makes employees aware of what the firm is trying to accomplish and how it plans to accomplish it. One aim of this program is to improve employees' morale and to make them feel they are members of the "team."

Functional training is *a program that develops and expands the basic skills and knowledge employees need to perform their jobs successfully.* Training sessions on selling techniques and inventory control are two examples of functional training directed at improving basic employee skills. Increasing employees' knowledge of the company's product lines and helping them to understand customer purchase motives are examples of knowledge-oriented, functional training. An integral part of employee functional training is to teach workers not only *how* they should perform their jobs, but also *why* they should perform them in that specific way. When employees understand why particular tasks should be done in a certain manner, they more easily accept and adopt the prescribed methods.

Where to Train

The second element of the training program concerns where training is to take place and under whose supervision. Normally, training takes place either on the job during regular working hours, off the job during scheduled training periods, or in some combination of both. **On-the-job training** is *a decentralized approach that occurs on the sales floor, in the stockroom, or in some other work environment where employees are performing their jobs.* The trainee usually is under the direct supervision of the department manager or some other designated person responsible for handling the training program. **Off-the-job training** is *conducted in centralized training classrooms away from the employee's work environment.* In centralized classrooms, the trainer can use various learning aids (e.g., films, demonstrations, and role playing) under controlled conditions, allowing the employee to focus on the learning experience without interruption. Also, in off-the-job training, many retailers use specialized personnel who are "trained to train," and who usually are very objective in their instruction since they are not as closely involved in company matters as management and employees. Finally, many retailers prefer to use a combination of these two methods. For example, a retailer may decide to use on-the-job instruction for functional training and off-the-job training for organizational orientation.

How to Train

The third element in the retailer's training program is how each employee should be instructed; that is, which methods the retailer should use in the training process. As Figure 9–5 outlines, there are four general training methods: individual, sponsor, group, and executive. In the **individual training method,** *employees "train" themselves.* One individual training method is the "on your own" approach. In this training situation the employee is put on the job and expected to learn by trial and error, observation, and asking questions. In essence, this sink-or-swim approach includes no formal training. Although the retailer bears no training costs in the short run, the total costs in the long run could be substantial because of potential low employee productivity, high employee turnover, employee errors, and dissatisfied customers due to improper service.

An alternative method retailers use is programmed learning, which uses a highly structured format. First, employees study a unit of material. Second, they respond to a series of questions (true/false, multiple-choice, fill-in-the-blank, etc.) on the material they have read. Third, they receive immediate feedback on their performance in answering the questions. Fourth, the continue to repeat the first three steps until they master the material. Once the employees achieve an acceptable competence level on a unit of material, they move on to the next level of instruction. Repetition is the key to programmed learning. Equally important, programmed learning is geared to the employee's learning pace and work schedule. These training devices are available in both written and machine form. Written programs are more commonly used because of their low costs. Although programmed learning methods are excellent tools for teaching employees specific bits of knowl-

On-the-job training is the preferred method of teaching functional tasks

edge, they are of limited value in teaching mechanical skills and personal interrelationships.

The **sponsor method** of training *uses an experienced employee to assume part or all of the responsibility for training a new employee*. Most retailers believe that this one-on-one approach is the best method for teaching new employees the basic skills of selling, buying, promotion, and so forth. The responsibilities of the sponsor also extend to introducing the employee to fellow workers, evaluating the employee's progress, and providing advice on the employee's problems and concerns. To establish a successful sponsor training program, the retailer must select sponsors carefully. The sponsor must possess (1) basic retailing knowledge and skills, (2) the patience and skills to teach, and (3) the willingness to assume the responsibilities of sponsorship. Successful sponsor training programs involve sponsors who volunteer for the assignment and who are compensated for their efforts (e.g., with money or time off).

Group training methods involve *the simultaneous training of several employees through the use of lectures (or discussion, films, or slides), demonstrations (on sales or marking and stock presentations), case studies (e.g., oral and written problem-solving situations), and role-playing activities (e.g., a sales or customer complaint situation)*. Large retailers use group training in centralized training facilities with specialized personnel. Group training sessions may last from five to ten minutes to update existing employees on new policies to as long as several days of classes on a wide variety of subjects. The advantage of group training is the low cost of training several employees at one time. The principal drawback is the lack of individual attention.

Executive training programs (ETPs) are *eductional sessions directed at supervisors, managers, and executives*. Common among large department store and chain organizations, ETPs are designed to recruit personnel who have executive potential and to provide them with the opportunity to gain management experience. The typical ETP is a step-by-step training procedure whereby the executive trainee gains practical management experience by progressing from low- to higher-level management positions. Figure 9–6 illustrates a typical ETP for a retailer. This example shows several alternative routes that a trainee might follow. An executive trainee is first promoted to either an assistant buyer or an area sales manager position. The progression from that point varies according to the individual and the company needs. The amount of time one spends at any position depends on individual ability, the type and complexity of the position, and the number of positions open at any given time. Lower-level positions usually involve several months of training, whereas middle- and upper-level positions frequently necessitate several years' experience. By moving potential executives from one position to another, the retailer gives them complete exposure to all or most of the firm's operations, policies, and procedures.

Many large retail organizations also have special executive development programs for new and existing employees having extensive educational backgrounds and experience. These programs normally include orientation programs, project assignments, executive seminars, and sponsorship programs with one of the firm's top executives. Many companies also encourage a wide range of self-development activities.

Supervision is *the process of directing, coordinating, and inspecting the efforts of store employees to attain both company and individual goals*. Effective supervisors can successfully satisfy the needs of the retailer (such as quality job performance, company loyalty, satisfactory profits) and the needs of the employee (such as fair

**SUPERVISING
STORE
PERSONNEL**

FIGURE 9–6
An executive training program

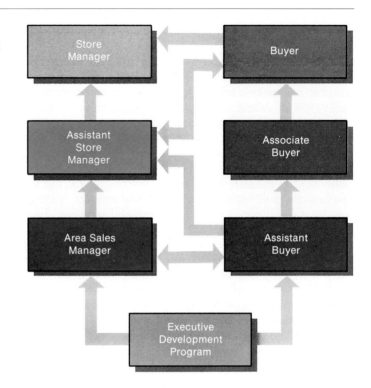

treatment, a decent standard of living, a chance for advancement). The key to good supervision is knowing how to motivate employees. **Motivation** is *the drive that moves people to act.* Employees are driven to excel in a variety of ways. Some employees are motivated by money, others by praise, and still others possibly by the promise of free time to spend with their families. The supervisor must discover the key that motivates each employee.

How to Motivate

Frederick Herzberg offered one method of motivation in his theory of satisfiers and dissatisfiers.[6] **Satisfiers** are *employment factors that produce pleasurable reactions within people's work lives.* Herzberg found that the primary employment satisfiers were a challenging job, recognition of achievement, a responsible position, a chance for advancement, and professional and personal growth. In essence, motivation factors are conditions that enhance the employee's personal needs for esteem and self-actualization.

Dissatisfiers are *employment factors that make workers unhappy with their job, leading to high turnover and weak performance.* Oversupervision, poorly developed work rules, undesirable working conditions, restrictive company policies, and inadequate wages and fringe benefits are common examples of dissatisfiers. In general, dissatisfiers are closely associated with an individual's physiological and security needs. Given Herzberg's findings, the answer to the question "How to motivate?" is to eliminate conditions that generate dissatisfiers and initiate programs and policies that promote satisfiers.

How to Supervise

The optimal level of employee supervision depends largely upon how motivated employees are. Two opposing schools of thought on the amount of supervision that employers should exercise are the "heavy-handed" approach and the "light-handed" approach. Those who support the **heavy-handed** approach *assume that employees are lazy, passive, self-centered, and irresponsible.* With these assumptions, they maintain that employers must closely supervise and control their employees to motivate them to work toward company goals and to assume responsibilities. Retailers that subscribe to this school of thought view economic inducements as the primary means of motivation (McGregor's Theory X).[7] In particular, some retailers consider the heavy-handed approach the only way to motivate people in the lower-level positions of their stores. In modern society, however, the heavy-handed approach may not apply.

A more contemporary view of motivation and supervision is the **light-handed** approach. Retailers that support this view believe that *providing employees with a favorable work environment can create a situation in which employees will obtain job satisfaction and their personal goals by directing their efforts toward the firm's needs* (McGregor's Theory Y). Retailers that use the light-handed approach think that close supervision and control are unnecessary. Employees, they feel, will assume their responsibilities and, in part, supervise themselves if a desirable social and psychological environment is present. The previously discussed satisfiers are the keys to creating this desirable social and psychological condition. Within this kind of working environment, less supervision produces better job performance.

A summary of Douglas McGregor's two contrasting models of motivation, Theory X and Theory Y, appears in Figure 9–7 (p. 268).

EVALUATING STORE PERSONNEL

The seventh step in the store staffing process is the development of personnel evaluation procedures. Each store employee, regardless of position or level, should be periodically evaluated. The purpose of personnel evaluations are to (1) determine compensation, (2) recommend or deny promotions and transfers, and (3) justify demotions and terminations. If conducted constructively, a retailer's personnel evaluations can be used to motivate employees, improve store morale, generate information for planning purposes, encourage employee self-development, and improve communications between the employee and employer. In developing the store's personnel evaluation methods and procedures, the retailer should decide when to evaluate, what to evaluate, and how to evaluate.

When to Evaluate

A smart retailer evaluates personnel continuously. It would be unfair to judge an employee's contribution and performance at the end of an arbitrary time period, such as the end of the fiscal year. Instead, retailers should provide their employees with immediate feedback on their progress. This form of informal feedback, however, should also be accompanied by an established, formal evaluation in which employees receive a detailed account of their job performance. Formal evaluations tell employees exactly what their status is. It is not unusual for new employees to be evaluated weekly or monthly. Established lower-level employees, however, are typically evaluated on a formal basis every six months, while annual evaluations for upper-level management and executive personnel are the norm.

What to Evaluate

Retailers have learned that the most important employee factors to evaluate are performance and personal attributes. These factors appear to be most related to employee success. Examples of such characteristics appear in Figure 9–8.

Theory X states that efficiency will be high when:	Theory X assumes that:
■ Authority flows down a hierarchical chain in which each subordinate has but one supervisor or manager.	■ Most people prefer to be directed and have little desire for responsibility and creativity.
■ Work is divided into the smallest number of sets of similar functions.	■ Motivation occurs only at an economic level. The worker is resistant to change.
■ Span of management is kept small, but balanced against the number of levels of management.	■ People must be closely supervised. They have a short time span of responsibility. People are by nature indolent.
■ Jobs are carefully defined and the worker is hired to fit the job.	■ People can be considered alike as units of production. No differentiation of jobs to utilize different interests and capacities is desirable. The worker is self-centered and indifferent to organizational needs.

Theory Y states that efficiency will be high when:	Theory Y assumes that:
■ Authority and communication flow in all directions in both formal and informal systems.	■ Workers are social beings who can work together for organizational and personal goals.
■ Work is varied and enriched.	■ Capacity for creativity is present to some degree in everybody. Needs at the level above the economic level are powerful motivators.
■ Span of management is as broad as possible as long as major objectives can be achieved.	■ People desire self-fulfillment through directing their own activities and participating in setting their own objectives.
■ Tasks are grouped into different meaningful jobs to accommodate individual talents and capacities.	■ Workers achieve their fullest potential when their aspirations and job challenges are matched to their capabilities.

Source: Norman M. Scarborough and Thomas W. Zimmerer, *Effective Small Business Management* (Columbus: Charles E. Merrill Publishing Co., 1984), 503

FIGURE 9–7
McGregor's Theory X and Theory Y models of motivation

FIGURE 9–8
Employee evaluation factors

Performance characteristics	Personal attributes
Job knowledge	Enthusiasm
Quality of work	Loyalty
Quantity of work	Dependability
Organizing capabilities	Leadership
Supervision requirements	Maturity
Promptness	Stability
Peer relationships	Creativity
Customer relations	Honesty
Analytic abilities	Initiative

In selecting evaluation criteria and their respective measuring instruments, the retailer must consider the legal ramifications of each decision and the influence of any labor union that might be involved. It often is a good policy to seek advice regarding the legality of the employee evaluation system and to consult with appropriate union representatives in formulating evaluation methods and procedures.

Degree of Formality \ Degree of Objectivity	Objective	Subjective
Formal	performance records MBO (management by objectives)	rating scales checklists
Informal	professional shoppers	intuition

FIGURE 9–9
Store personnel evaluation methods

How to Evaluate

Retailers use a variety of methods for evaluating store personnel; the method used depends on the degree of objectivity and formality that the retailer wants. Figure 9–9 identifies several objective employee evaluation methods—which are based largely on factual and measurable criteria—and subjective methods—which are based on the evaluator's perceptions, feelings, and prejudices. Formal methods are regularly scheduled evaluations; informal methods follow no set schedule and the criteria and procedures may or may not be known to the employee.

Formal Objective Evaluation Methods

Formal objective employee evaluation procedures *include performance records and management by objectives (MBO) procedures.* Performance records are quantitative measures of the employee's performance and include such varied statistics as (1) total sales dollars, (2) total number of sales transactions, (3) number of customer complaints, (4) number of merchandise returns and their dollar value, (5) number of times an employee is absent or late for work, and (6) net sales per working hour or per hourly wage. By comparing the employee's performance against the store average for any one of the above criteria, the retailer can identify above-, at-, and below-average performers. MBO procedures set measurable performance objectives for employees that should match their job descriptions. Employees are then evaluated on how well they achieved their objectives. MBO procedures have the advantage of drawing the employee into the evaluation process and thereby encouraging self-development and self-evaluation. In utilizing MBO procedures, the employee is asked to (1) set objectives in specific terms, (2) determine the method of accomplishment, (3) set an accomplishment time frame, and (4) determine the measure of accomplishment.

Formal Subjective Evaluation Methods

Rating scales and checklists constitute two of the more common **formal subjective evaluation methods.** The typical procedure is to identify and list several criteria in checklist form. The evaluator may weight the individual criteria according to their importance (see Figure 9–10). Typical scales are (1) satisfactory or unsatisfactory; (2) below average, average, or above average; and (3) poor, fair, average, good, and excellent. Given the subjective character of these ratings, many retailers prefer to have several supervisors rate each employee. The average of these ratings forms the basis for the employee's evaluation. To obtain additional viewpoints, some retailers ask fellow employees to rate one another. In using rating scales, retailers should recognize the central tendency effect—the tendency of evaluators to rate everyone at or near the midpoint of the scale.

269

FIGURE 9–10
A formal subjective employee evaluation form

Employee's name _____   Date _____

Employee's title _____   Supervisor _____

Instructions: Please review the performance of the employee whose name is listed above on each of the following items. In order to guide you in your rating, the five determinants of performance have been defined.

Rating Points

5 OUTSTANDING
A truly outstanding employee whose achievements are far above acceptable. Has consistently performed far beyond established objectives and has made significant contributions beyond current position. Requires minimal direction and supervision. (Relatively few employees would be expected to achieve at this level.)

4 SUPERIOR
An above-average employee whose performance is clearly above acceptable. Has usually performed beyond established objectives and, at times, has made contributions beyond responsibilities of present position. Requires less than normally expected degree of direction and supervision.

3 AVERAGE
A fully acceptable employee who consistently meets all requirements of position. Has consistently met established objectives in a satisfactory and adequate manner. Performance requires normal degree of supervision and direction. (The majority of employees should be at this level.)

2 BELOW AVERAGE
A somewhat below-average employee whose performance, while not unsatisfactory, cannot be considered fully acceptable. Generally meets established objectives and expectations, but definite areas exist where achievement is substandard. Performance requires somewhat more than normal degree of direction and supervision.

1 UNACCEPTABLE
A far-below-average employee whose performance is barely adequate to meet the requirements of the position. Generally performs at a level below established objectives with the result that overall contribution is marginal. Performance requires an unusually high degree of supervision. (This level is considered acceptable only for employees new to the job.)

JOB CRITERIA   **POINTS**

1. Amount of work. Consider here only the **quantity** of the employee's output.   _____
   Supervisor's comments:

2. Quality of work. Consider how well the employee does each job assigned. Include your   _____
   appraisal of such items as accuracy, thoroughness, and orderliness.
   Supervisor's comments:

3. Cooperation. How well does this employee work and interact with you and coworkers   _____
   for the accomplishment of organization goals?
   Supervisor's comments:

4. Judgment. Consider this employee's ability to reach sound and logical conclusions.   _____
   Supervisor's comments:

FIGURE 9–10, *continued*

5. Initiative. The energy or aptitude to originate action toward organization goals.   _____
   Supervisor's comments:

6. Job knowledge. How well does the employee demonstrate an understanding of the   _____
   basic fundamentals, techniques, and procedures on the job?
   Supervisor's comments:

7. Interest in job. Does the employee demonstrate a real interest in the job and the orga-   _____
   nization?
   Supervisor's comments:

8. Ability to communicate. How well does this employee exchange needed information   _____
   with others in the work group and with supervisors?
   Supervisor's comments:

9. Dependability. Consider the employee's absences, tardiness, punctuality, timeliness in   _____
   completing job assignments, and the amount of supervision required.
   Supervisor's comments:

10. Adaptability. Consider the degree to which this employee demonstrates adjustment to   _____
    the varying requirements of the job.
    Supervisor's comments:

                                                            TOTAL POINTS   _____

   Supervisor's general comments:

Instructions: After you have rated the employee and made whatever comments you feel are pertinent to each criterion and the overall evaluation, schedule a meeting to review each item with the employee. An employee wishing to make comments about the evaluation should be asked to do so in the following space.

Employee's comment:

Date: _____

Supervisor present (Name): _____

Employee's signature: _____   Date: _____

Notice to employee: Signing the form does not imply that you either agree or disagree with the evaluation.

Source: Norman M. Scarborough and Thomas M. Zimmerer, *Effective Small Business Management* (Columbus: Charles E. Merrill Publishing Co., 1984), 521–23.

Informal Objective Evaluation Methods

The most common **informal objective evaluation method** that retailers use is *to employ professional shoppers.* Professional shoppers are people who wander into a store to "shop" for merchandise in a "typical" way. Actually, they are professional investigators who attempt to learn how a retailer's employees behave toward them. This method is informal since these professionals interact with the retailer's employees in the same way that any other shopper would interact with them. But it is objective because these people are from outside of the organization. This evaluation method should not be the *basis* of employee evaluation, but a *supplement* to the retailer's assessment of employees' job performance.

Informal Subjective Evaluation Methods

Informal subjective evaluation methods *have no structure and rely heavily on the supervisor's intuition.* While the feelings and perceptions of a supervisor might represent a correct evaluation of an employee, the lack of objectivity and formality leaves such a method open to criticism by both employees and outside concerns (e.g., the Fair Labor Standards Law). A constant danger in using intuition as an evaluative method is the "halo effect" or the "good old boy syndrome." An employee who is a good person is not necessarily making a contribution to the firm's efforts. In fact, such considerations often lead to other employees' accusations of favoritism.

Regardless of the method used in evaluating store personnel, the employees should be made aware of the method (its criteria, measurements, and procedures), provided feedback after each evaluation, and permitted to appeal the evaluation.

COMPENSATING STORE PERSONNEL

Equitable compensation is an integral part of the retailer's staffing process. Compensation methods include the straight-salary plan, the straight-commission plan, the salary plus commission plan, and the salary plus bonus plan.

Straight-Salary Plan

The **straight-salary plan** is *a fixed amount of compensation for a specified work period such as a day, week, month, or year.* For example, an employee's salary might be set at $200 per week or $4 per hour. For the retailer, the straight-salary plan offers the advantages of easy administration and a high level of employer control. Under the straight-salary plan the retailer can expect employees to engage in nonselling activities such as stocking and housekeeping. For the employee, the straight-salary plan has a known level of financial security and stability. The disadvantages of this plan for the retailer are (1) limited incentives to increase employee performance, (2) fixed costs that result in a high wage-cost-to-sales ratio, and (3) lack of downward salary adjustments during periods of sales decline. Retailers typically use straight-salary plans when a job involves a considerable amount of customer service and nonselling time, such as stocking, receiving, clerking, and checking out.

Straight-Commission Plan

Under a **straight-commission plan,** *a store employee receives a percentage of what he or she sells.* The commission percentage is either fixed (e.g., 5 percent on all sales) or variable (e.g., 6 percent on high-margin lines and 3 percent on low-margin lines). In some cases, the time of year determines the commission (e.g., 4 percent during the Christmas season or the annual clearance sale). Retailers calculate an employee's commission on the basis of *net sales* (gross sales dollars minus dollar value of returned merchandise). Retailers that use straight-commission plans are those that sell big-ticket items such as automobiles, furniture, appliances, and jewelry. It also is the common method for compensating door-to-door salespersons.

The major advantage of a straight-commission plan is the monetary incentive it creates for employees; however, this incentive often causes several problems. Salespeople on commission often become overly aggressive in trying to make a sale. Commissioned salespeople sometimes pursue only customers who are interested in high-commission products and ignore customers who are seeking inexpensive items or who are just looking around. Open hostility can occur between commisioned salespersons who are vying for the attention of a potential customer. To overcome this problem, some stores have initiated a "call system," whereby customers are assigned to salespeople on a rotating basis.

High-pressure selling is also a temptation when commission sales are involved. By exerting undue pressure on the customer to buy now (as opposed to later, when a different salesperson might be serving the customer), the sale could be lost to the retailer forever. Also, commission sales tempt many salespeople to practice trading up the customer to more expensive merchandise. However, when trading up leads to a large number of returns, not only does the salesperson lose the commission, but the retailer also loses a sale and very likely the goodwill of the store's clientele.

For the commissioned salesperson, the straight-commission plan has the weaknesses of financial insecurity and instability. To overcome these limitations, many retailers have established "drawing accounts" that allow employees to draw a fixed sum of money at regular intervals against future commissions. Of all the compensation plans, straight commission is the least preferred by salespeople due to the high risk involved.

Salary Plus Commission Plan

As the name implies, the **salary plus commission plan** *provides employees with a salary and a commission.* There are a number of variations to this plan. The *straight salary/single commission* variation uses a base salary (e.g., $200 per week) plus (1) a single commission (e.g., 1/2 percent) on all net sales up to the sales quota and a larger commission (e.g., 2 percent) on all sales in excess of the sales quota, *or* (2) a commission only on net sales that exceed the quota. As a general rule, the base salary constitutes the greatest share of the employee's total compensation. To offer greater sales incentive, however, a retailer can increase the commission rate to make commission income a significantly higher proportion of the employee's total income.

The strengths of this plan are that it provides employees with financial security and stability while helping the retailer to control and motivate personnel. While the combination plan is more difficult to administer, its benefits generally outweigh its costs.

Salary Plus Bonus Plan

A popular method for compensating middle-management personnel (such as department managers, store managers, and buyers) is the **salary plus bonus plan**, which involves *a straight monthly salary supplemented by either semiannual or annual bonuses for exceeding performance goals.* Performance goals and related bonuses are usually set by upper management for each operating unit and are

A physical fitness center is an important benefit for both employee and employer

usually expressed in the form of increased sales or profits, decreased operating costs, or some other measure of the operating unit's productivity. The most common problems associated with the salary plus bonus plan are employees' difficulty understanding such plans and administrators' difficulty setting up the performance criteria and measurement instruments to make the system work.

Fringe Benefits

The employee's total compensation package also includes fringe benefits, which vary greatly from one retail firm to another. In recent years, fringe benefits have become more important in the retailer's efforts to attract and keep qualified personnel. Fringe benefits are much more important for middle- and upper-level positions than for entry-level positions. As unionization of lower-level personnel becomes more common, however, benefit packages at that level will become more significant.

Among the most popular fringe benefits are (1) insurance programs covering life, health, accident, and disability, (2) sick leave, (3) personal leave time, (4) holiday leave and paid vacations, (5) pension plans, (6) profit sharing, (7) employee discounts, (8) recreation facilities, (9) coffee breaks, (10) employee parties, and (11) team sponsorships. Fringe benefits are becoming a more important form of compensation in today's leisure-oriented society, with the goal of making employees happy, content, and loyal to the store.

SUMMARY

A key ingredient in any successful retail operation is its personnel. Merchandising and operational plans are of limited value without loyal, productive employees. All retailers face the problem of finding and keeping good people.

The staffing process consists of eight steps. First, describing the job includes developing job descriptions and conducting job analyses. Second, specifying the job involves writing job classifications that not only outline the responsibilities of the position, but also avoid charges of unfair employment practices. Third, recruiting store personnel includes both finding and screening potential employee candidates. The fourth step in the staffing process is selection. From the list of qualified applicants, the retailer selects individuals best suited to the job by carefully reviewing application forms, personal interviews, reference checks, testing instruments, and physical examinations.

Training store personnel is the fifth step in the staffing process. It requires the retailer to know what to train (organization orientation and functional or task training), where to train (on the job or off the job), and how to train (individual training method, programmed learning, sponsor or group training methods). Executive training programs are sessions directed at store supervisors, managers, and executives. The sixth step is supervision. An important supervising task is motivation. One method of motivating employees is to eliminate conditions that generate job dissatisfaction and to initiate programs that promote satisfaction. Supervising can be approached in a heavy-handed manner (close supervision) or in a light-handed fashion (limited supervision).

Evaluating store employees constitutes the seventh step in the staffing process. The retailer must address such issues as when to evaluate, what to evaluate, and how to evaluate personnel. Finally, the retailer must determine the type of compensation system to use. Alternatives are the straight-salary plan, straight-commission plan, salary plus commission plan, and salary plus bonus plan, all of which might involve various fringe benefits.

KEY TERMS AND CONCEPTS

job description

job specification

psychological tests

achievement tests

organization orientation

functional training

on-the-job training

off-the-job training

individual training method

programmed learning

sponsor training method

group training method

executive training programs

supervision

motivation

satisfier

dissatisfier

heavy-handed supervision

light-handed supervision

formal objective employee evaluations

formal subjective employee evaluations

informal objective employee evaluations

informal subjective employee evaluations

straight-salary plan

straight-commission plan

salary plus commission plan

salary plus bonus plan

REVIEW QUESTIONS

1. What are the undersirable aspects of retail working conditions?
2. What specific information should be obtained in a job analysis?
3. Why should a written job specification be given to a potential employee?
4. Identify the internal and external sources of prospective employees.
5. What is the most effective way to check an applicant's references?
6. What advantages are there to using a formal, highly structured interviewing process?
7. What two general types of testing instruments are used to evaluate applicants? Describe each type.
8. Compare and contrast employer and employee training goals.
9. Describe the two types of training needed by both old and new employees.
10. How do on-the-job and off-the-job training differ?
11. What methods are available to the retailer for training employees? Briefly describe each method.
12. What are satisfiers and dissatisfiers? How do they affect employee motivation?
13. Compare and contrast McGregor's Theory X and Theory Y.
14. How are formal objective employee evaluations conducted? Describe the two methods.
15. Professional shoppers are used to conduct which type of employee evaluation?
16. What are the disadvantages of the straight-salary compensation plan?
17. What problems result from the monetary incentive created by the straight-commission plan?
18. How does the straight salary/single commission plan differ from the straight salary/quota commission plan?

ENDNOTES

1. See Jon Laking and Robin Roark, *Retailing Job Analysis and Job Evaluation* (New York: Personnel Division, National Retail Merchants Association, 1975), 4.
2. See "Uniform Guidelines on Employee Selection Procedures," *Federal Register* 43 (25 August 1978).
3. W. Austin Spivey, J. Michael Munson, and William B. Locander, "Meeting Retail Staffing Needs Via Improved Selection," *Journal of Retailing* 55 (Winter 1979): 3–19.
4. Charles J. Hollon and Myron Gable, "Information Sources in Retail Employment Decision-Making Process," *Journal of Retailing* 55 (Fall 1979): 58–74.
5. Robert F. Hartley, "The Weighted Application Blank," *Journal of Retailing* 46 (Spring 1970): 32–40.
6. Frederick Herzberg, "One More Time: How Do You Motivate Employees?" *Harvard Business Review* 46 (January-February 1968): 53–62.
7. See Douglas McGregor, "The Human Side of Enterprise," in *Leadership and Motivation: Essays of Douglas McGregor*, ed. W. G. Bennis and E. Schein (Cambridge, MA: MIT Press, 1966).

RELATED READINGS

Allmon, Dean E., and Garrott, Stephen. "Retail Personnel Turnover: A Predictive Demographic Model." *1984 Proceedings*. J. R. Lumpkin and J. C. Crawford, eds. (Southwestern Marketing Association 1984), 50–52.

Burstiner, Irving. "Current Personnel Practices in Department Stores." *Journal of Retailing* 51 (Winter 1975), 3–14.

Cayer, Maurice. "Common Sense Ways for Selecting Better People." *Retail Control* (February 1985), 13–36.

Donnelly, Jack, Jr., and Etzel, Michael J. "Retail Store Performance and Job Satisfaction: A Study of Anxiety, Stress, and Propensity to Leave among Retail Employees." *Journal of Retailing* 53 (Summer 1977), 23–28.

Dreher, George F., and Sackett, Paul R. *Perspectives on Employee Staffing and Selection*. (Homewood, Ill.: Richard D. Irwin, 1983)

Dubinsky, Alan J., and Skinner, Steven J. "Impact of Job Characteristics on Retail Salespeople's Reactions to Their Jobs." *Journal of Retailing* 60 (Summer 1984), 35–62.

_____. "Turnover Tendencies among Retail Salespeople: Relationships with Job Satisfaction and Demographic Characteristics." *AMA Educators' Proceedings*. R. W. Belk et al, eds. (American Marketing Association 1984), 153–57.

Gable, Myron; Hollon, Charles J.; and D'angello, Frank. "Predicting Voluntary Managerial Trainee Turnover in a Large Retailing Organization from Information on Employment Application Blank." *Journal of Retailing* 60 (Winter 1984), 43–63.

Ingene, Charles A. "The Effect of Scale, Localization, and Urbanization Economies on Productivity in Retailing." *AMA Educators' Proceedings*. R. W. Belk et al, eds. (American Marketing Association 1984), 190–94.

Judd, L. Lynn. "Owner/Manager's Age and Retailing Experience: Do They Influence Business Strategies and Success?" *Developments in Marketing Science, Proceedings*. J. C. Rogers, III, ed. (Academy of Marketing Science 1983), 12–16.

Kesavan, Ram, and Rowe, Clair D. "Does Your Sales Job Influence Your Job Satisfaction?" *Evolving Marketing Thought for 1980, Proceedings*. J. H. Summey and R. D. Taylor, eds. (Southern Marketing Association 1980), 37–40.

Klatt, Lawrence; Murdick, Robert G.; and Schuster, Frederick. *Human Resource Management*. (Columbus: Charles E. Merrill Publishing Co., 1985)

Lake, Marjorie A. "Recruiting." *Stores* (April 1982), 63–71.

Mangiafico, Edgar S. "The Effective Management of Internal and External Expertise." *Retail Control* (December 1984), 14–20.

Mosely, Donald C., and Pietri, Paul H. *Supervisory Management*. (Cincinnati: South-Western Publishing Co., 1985)

Muczyk, Jan; Schwartz, Eleanor B.; and Smith, Ephraim. *Principles of Supervision: First and Second Level Management*. (Columbus: Charles E. Merrill Publishing Co., 1984)

Ringel, Lance. "Buyer Training." *Stores* (April 1981), 47–48.

Skinner, Steven J.; Dubinsky, Alan J.; and Cronin, J. Joseph, Jr. "Sex Differences in Retail Salespeople's Attitudinal and Behavioral Responses." *Marketing Comes of Age, Proceedings*. David M. Klein and Allen E. Smith, eds. (Southern Marketing Association 1984), 131–33.

Still, Leonie V. "Part-Time versus Full-Time Salespeople: Individual Attributes, Organizational Commitment, and Work Attitudes." *Journal of Retailing* 59 (Summer 1983), 55–79.

Teas, R. Kenneth. "Performance-Reward Instrumentalities and the Motivation of Retail Salespeople." *Journal of Retailing* 58 (Fall 1982), 4–26.

Outline

THE STORE'S ENVIRONMENT

Creating a Store Image
Creating a Buying Atmosphere

THE STORE'S EXTERIOR

The Store's Position
The Store's Architecture
The Store's Sign
The Store's Front

THE STORE'S INTERIOR

The Store's Space
The Store's Layout

Objectives

- Appreciate the physical and psychological impact that store facilities have on customer attraction, employee morale, and store operations

- Distinguish design features vital in creating a desirable store image, in targeting the appropriate consumer group, and in communicating the right impression

- Understand design features necessary to create a store atmosphere conducive to buying

- Identify and explain the major considerations in planning store exteriors capable of stopping and attracting customers

- Specify and discuss the key features of the store's interior and their role in creating an inviting, comfortable, and convenient facility

10
Designing Store Facilities

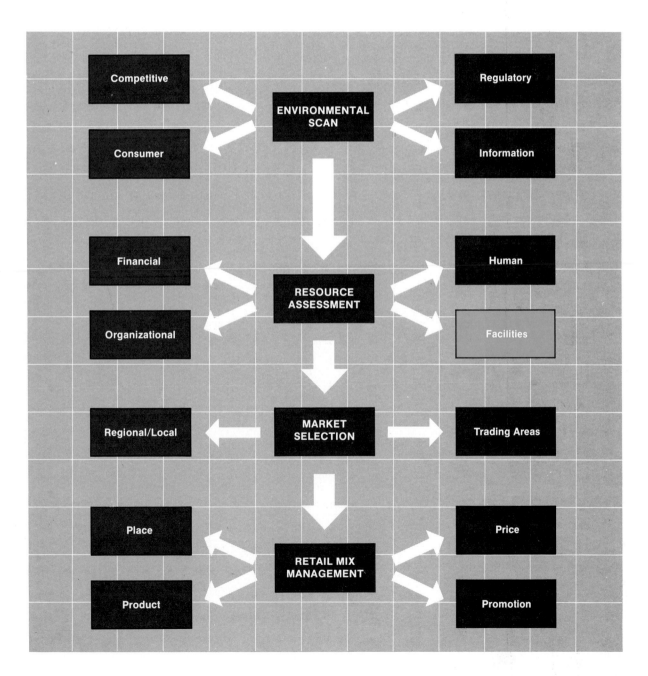

A store and its immediate area create the environment within which a retailer must operate. It is an environment that either attracts or repels potential customers. Accordingly, the retailer must make a concentrated effort to ensure that the store's environment is conducive both to retail operations and to consumers' shopping needs. The elements of store design are shown in Figure 10–1. The bulk of this chapter discusses the physical aspects of the store's exterior and interior design. First, however, we shall examine the psychological aspects of the retailer's facilities and the environment they create.

THE STORE'S ENVIRONMENT

In selecting and developing a store's environment, the retailer must consider its *physical* and *psychological* impacts on customer attraction, employee morale, and store operations. Store operations and customer shopping are both enhanced by a well planned and designed setting. A store's physical environment is a composite of the tangible elements of form reflected in the way land, building, equipment, and fixtures are assembled for the convenience and comfort of both customers and retailer. Equally important is the store's psychological environment—the perceived

FIGURE 10–1
The elements of store design

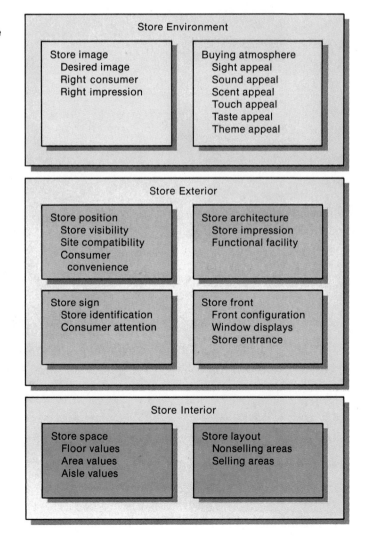

Store Environment

Store image
  Desired image
  Right consumer
  Right impression

Buying atmosphere
  Sight appeal
  Sound appeal
  Scent appeal
  Touch appeal
  Taste appeal
  Theme appeal

Store Exterior

Store position
  Store visibility
  Site compatibility
  Consumer
    convenience

Store architecture
  Store impression
  Functional facility

Store sign
  Store identification
  Consumer attention

Store front
  Front configuration
  Window displays
  Store entrance

Store Interior

Store space
  Floor values
  Area values
  Aisle values

Store layout
  Nonselling areas
  Selling areas

280

atmosphere the retailer creates. In essence, a store's psychological environment is the mental image of the store produced in customers' minds. A store's effectiveness and uniqueness lie in the retailer's ability to plan, create, and control both the store's physical and psychological setting. The psychological impressions a store makes on consumers depend on the store's image and buying atmosphere.

Creating a Store Image

Creating a **store image** should be one of the retailer's principal concerns. The fact that it *represents to the consumer a composite picture of the retailer* makes image one of the most powerful tools in attracting and satisfying consumers. Creating an image, however, is a very difficult task. An image is a mental picture that forms in the human mind as a result of many different stimuli. These stimuli include the retailer's physical facilities, the store's location, product lines, service offering, pricing policies, and promotional activities.

Identifying the Desired Image

A store's image is its personality. It is how the consumer *sees* the store as well as what the consumer *feels* about the store. It is important, therefore, that retailers know and plan what they want the consumer to see and feel. A retailer can choose from among many different images, some of the more common being

- prestigious or economical
- contemporary or traditional
- swinging or subdued
- family or singles
- formal or informal
- friendly or reserved
- restful or active

Store images also vary in complexity. Some retailers choose to focus on a unidimensional image, whereas others strive for something multidimensional. In identifying itself as "the savings place," K Mart is focusing on an economical image. Generally, K Mart's physical facilities support this impression. Sears, on the other hand, identifies itself as the place "where America shops." In trying to appeal to a broader cross section of shoppers, Sears' image increases in complexity. Each consumer's concept of what constitutes America determines to some extent that shopper's image of Sears. Whatever image the retailer wishes to project, it should be clearly identifiable to both the retailer and the desired consumer group, since a store image that is not clearly identified cannot be effectively communicated.

The store's exterior and interior are key factors in the retailer's image-creating efforts. *Externally,* the position of the store on the site, its architectural design, its store front, and the placement of signs, entrances, and display windows all contribute to the store's image. *Internally,* a store's image can be created, in part, by the layout of departments and traffic aisles, the use of store displays, and the selection of store fixtures and equipment. No standard combinations of external and internal store factors are capable of producing a given image. The number of possible combinations of physical facilities and their image-creating abilities are virtually limitless.

Targeting the Right Consumer

In designing the image-creating features of the store's physical facilities, the retailer must work with a particular target consumer in mind. Neither the retailer nor the store can be all things to all people. Likewise, neither can a single image be created that will appeal to *all* consumers. Therefore, a store's facilities should be tailored to the psychological and physical needs of a selected customer group. One shopper typology, for example, identifies four types of customers based on their shopping personalities. Each type is attracted to a store for different reasons. These four types are (1) the economic shopper, (2) the personalized shopper, (3) the apathetic shopper, and (4) the ethical shopper.[1]

The **economic shopper** *is extremely sensitive to the price and quality of the retailer's merchandise.* Therefore, physical facilities should portray a simple yet quality image. Too-plush facilities could create a high-price image; too-spartan facilities might lead the shopper to conclude that the store's merchandise is not of good quality. In designing store layouts and displays for the economic shopper, the retailer should try to facilitate the consumer's price/quality comparisons. In total, store facilities with a clean, modern look are consistent with the psychological needs of the economic shopper.

The **personalized shopper** *looks for a store offering a lot of individual treatment from sales personnel and little interference from other shoppers.* Desirable store layouts might have areas set aside for easy, comfortable, personal interaction between the shopper and the store's selling personnel.

"Getting it over with" is the principal shopping motive of the **apathetic shopper,** for whom shopping is an unpleasant task. Facilities designed with convenience and efficiency in mind appeal to this shopper. From the parking lot to the store's entrance and from the display counter to the checkout stand, the retailer's facilities must be designed to allow this shopper to get in and out in a hurry.

The **ethical shopper** *feels the need to "help out the little person."* Physical facilities that appeal to the ethical shopper are difficult to identify, except they may have limited space and facilities and/or be a local operation. A friendly, hometown atmosphere with a decor that reflects the local community appeals to the ethical shopper.

Communicating the Right Impression

The physical facilities of a retail store can be an important vehicle for nonverbal communication. "A store's uniqueness and effectiveness lie in management's ability to imbue its appeal to customers with a memorable verbal theme reinforced by such nonverbal elements as . . . interior and exterior design."[2] The importance of communicating the right impression assumes that the store's personality helps "position" one retailer against other retailers, thereby facilitating the store-selection process for consumers. One author describes the role of the store personality as follows:

> It is probably safe to say that all stores project a personality or image to consumers. Furthermore, the same store can have different images to different consumers. To the low- and middle-income groups a high fashion store may communicate extravagance, waste, and snobbishness. It might evoke feelings of uneasiness for them to shop in this kind of store. In contrast, a high-income group may perceive the same store as elegant, prestigious, and high-styled.[3]

Of course, a high-fashion image is the right impression if the retailer has decided to position the store's personality to well-to-do shoppers.

Communicating the right impression, then, is a problem of how best to use physical facilities to convey to consumers what the retailer wants them to see and feel. "The greater the number of messages and signals received by the consumer, the more lasting the impression."[4] Retailers must remember in designing these non-verbal messages and signals that they do not necessarily "see" and "feel" exactly as consumers do. Therefore, they should conduct research to learn which communication cues to use in their physical facilities "message" to evoke the desired response from their target audience.

Creating a Buying Atmosphere

To create an atmosphere conducive to buying, a retailer should establish in the consumer a frame of mind that promotes a buying spirit. Even the economy-minded consumer wants something more than a shopping atmosphere with only the bare essentials. Today's shoppers, regardless of their principal shopping motives, are drawn to safe, attractive, and comfortable shopping environments. The store's atmosphere should be an agreeable environment for both the consumer and the retailer. Such a environment "is one that provides congenial, yet stimulating, surroundings for customers and salespeople through appropriate layout, fixturization, illumination, color, and space utilization."[5] Some congenial yet stimulating atmospheres might include

- quiet and plush for the prestige shopper
- safe but exciting for the elderly shopper
- friendly and loud for the youthful shopper
- clean and cheerful for the family shopper
- formal and pleasant for the professional shopper

The retailer wants to influence the consumer's mood by creating an atmosphere that will positively influence buying behavior. An appealing buying atmosphere uses cues that appeal to the consumer's five senses of sight, hearing, smell, touch, and taste. These sensory cues can be strongly reinforced if they are structured around shopping themes that unify and organize the store's atmosphere. The following sections discuss how a retailer can use sensory appeals to effect a favorable store image and pleasant shopping environment.

Sight Appeal

The sense of sight provides people with more information than any other sense mode and therefore must be classified as the most important means by which retailers can appeal to consumers. For present purposes, and for the sake of simplicity, sight appeal can be viewed as the process of imparting stimuli, resulting in perceived visual relationships. Size, shape, and color are three primary visual stimuli that a retailer can use in planning store facilities to arouse the consumer's attention. Visual relationships are interpretations made by the "mind's eye" from visual stimuli consisting of harmony, contrast, and clash. *Harmony* is "visual agreement"; *contrast,* "visual diversity"; and *clash,* "visual conflict" that can occur among the many parts of any display, layout, or physical arrangement. In any given situation, either harmony, contrast, or clash may be the best means of creating an appealing shopping atmosphere. Harmonious visual relationships are generally associated with a quieter, plusher, and more formal shopping setting, whereas contrasting and clashing visual relationships can promote an exciting, cheerful, or informal atmosphere. In seeking to control these environmental impressions, the retailer must understand the basics of visual stimuli. While no single formula for effectively using visual stimuli exists, there are some commonly agreed-upon beliefs about how the majority of consumers perceive these stimuli.

What feelings are aroused by these various lines and shapes?

Size perceptions. The sheer physical size of a store, a display, a sign, or a department can communicate many things to many people. Size can communicate relative importance, success, strength, power, and security. Some consumers feel more secure when they buy from large stores because they believe that large stores are more capable and more willing to fix, adjust, or replace faulty merchandise. Other consumers prefer larger stores because of the prestige they associate with such operations. A smaller store, display, or department may not be perceived as being as important, successful, or powerful as its larger counterparts, but it could be viewed as more personal, intimate, or friendly.

Size is a key element in creating harmony, contrast, and clash. To achieve a harmonious atmosphere in a store department or display, the retailer should maintain a consistent size relationship among its various elements. Using *moderately* different size elements can create contrast among different departments within the store or different displays within the department. Clashing relationships can be created by using *substantially* different size elements. Unless the store designer consciously tries to reduce the atmospheric influence of some element within the store, department, or display, proportions should be maintained among the various elements.

Shape perceptions. Shapes arouse certain emotions within buyers. In planning store layouts and in designing store displays, the retailer should recognize that the horizontal line "suggests restfulness and quiet and evokes feelings of tranquility . . . The vertical line evokes feelings of strength, confidence and even pride. The slanted line suggests upward movement to most people . . . round curving lines connote femininity, whereas sharp, angular objects suggest masculinity."[6] Equally important in facilities planning is the similarity or dissimilarity of shapes. "For the creation of perfect harmony in a display, shapes that correspond exactly to one another are used exclusively. Inharmonious or dissimilar shapes may be used in a display to create contrast and, in some instances, a point of emphasis."[7] Combined with size, shape can be a powerful tool in the facility designer's efforts to devise an atmosphere that appeals to a particular class of shoppers.

(a)

(b)

(c)

(a)   (b)

Which display represents harmony (visual agreement) and which represents visual conflict?

Color perceptions. Color makes the first impression on a person looking at an object. Color is often what catches customers' eyes, keeps their attention, and stimulates them to buy. The U.S. consumer is becoming increasingly color conscious. For most customers, if the color is wrong, all is wrong.

The psychological impact of color is the result of the three color properties of hue, value, and intensity. *Hue* is the name of the color. *Value* is the lightness or darkness of a hue. Darker values are referred to as "shades," while lighter values are called "tints." The brightness or dullness of a hue is its *intensity*. For the retailer, color psychology is important not only in selling merchandise but also in creating the proper atmosphere for selling that merchandise. Let's examine each of these color properties and its potential impact on facilities design.

The impact of color psychology becomes apparent as soon as we classify *hues* into "warm" and "cool" tones. The warm colors of red, yellow, and orange and the cool colors of blue, green, and violet symbolize different things to different consumer groups. Table 10–1 identifies some of the associations and symbols consumers attach to colors. Warm colors give the impression of a comfortable, informal atmosphere. Cool colors, on the other hand, project a formal, aloof, icy impression. When used properly, however, both warm and cool colors can create a relaxing yet stimulating atmosphere in which to shop.

Red is one of the most stimulating colors and should be used with considerable care. Too much red can be overpowering; it should thus be used as an accent color rather than a basic background color. To attract attention and to stimulate buyer action, red frequently appears in building signs, fixtures, and displays. Two exceptions to using red as an accent color are restaurants and cocktail lounges, where red is thought to stimulate people's appetites. Christmas and Valentine's Day are two holiday seasons in which red is an appropriate display color. Shades of red are also appropriate for certain decorative themes, such as carnivals and sports. The red in many nationalistic themes is still another frequent and appropriate use of the color.

285

TABLE 10–1

Perceptions of colors

Warm Colors				Cool Colors		
Red	Yellow	Orange		Blue	Green	Violet
Love	Sunlight	Sunlight		Coolness	Coolness	Coolness
Romance	Warmth	Warmth		Aloofness	Restful	Retiring
Sex	Cowardice	Openness		Fidelity	Peace	Dignity
Courage	Openness	Friendliness		Calmness	Freshness	Rich
Danger	Friendliness	Gaiety		Piety	Growth	
Fire	Gaiety	Glory		Masculine	Softness	
Sinful	Glory			Assurance	Richness	
Warmth	Brightness			Sadness	Go	
Excitement	Caution					
Vigor						
Cheerfulness						
Enthusiasm						
Stop						

Which color is most visible?

Yellow, like red, is a very stimulating color that must be used with caution. Yellow's principal asset is its visibility at long distances, which makes shades of yellow a logical color selection for signs, walls, and poorly lit areas. The time to use yellow is in the spring, particularly around Easter. Yellow is also considered a color for children, so it is appropriate for decorating infants', children's, and toy departments.

How do the store atmospherics differ for the two retailers shown below?

(a)

(b)

Orange is used sparingly due to its high intensity and its tendency to clash with other colors. Orange is most often thought of as a fall color (fall foliage, harvest, and Halloween). It is used largely for accent purposes and not as a basic decorative color. Orange, like yellow, is a children's color and livens up a children's department by evoking warm, cheerful surroundings.

Blues are associated with the cool, blue sky and the calm, blue sea. As a result, retailers use blues to create a calm, relaxing shopping atmosphere. Shades of blue are often a part of the men's departments since this color also connotes masculinity. In addition, blue works well as a trim and as a basic background.

Like blue, *green* suggests many pleasant associations—the newness and freshness of spring and the peace and restfulness of the great outdoors. Many experts believe that green is probably the single most popular and accepted color. Its soft and relaxing qualities make green an ideal choice for many uses. Green is perceived as a spacious color and is therefore very useful for retailers that want to make small areas appear larger. Its softness also helps accentuate displayed merchandise.

Violet is little used in retail displays, except to achieve special effects. Too-extensive use of this hue is thought to dampen shoppers' spirits.

Are these colors the most appropriate for the children's department?

The lightness and darkness of colors create optical illusions that retailers can use to modify the physical characteristics of the store. Generally, lighter colors make a room or an object appear larger, while darker colors create an illusion of smallness. "A long narrow store can be made to appear shorter and wider by the use of a deep warm tone (such as brown) on the narrow distant walls and a light cool tone on the long side walls."[8] Light neutral tones (e.g., beige) are popular as fixture colors because they are perceived as warm and soft and do not detract from the displayed merchandise. On the other hand, darker colors have attention-grabbing ability that retailers can use to gain the consumer's attention. For example, through the use of darker colors at the back of a store, a retailer can draw consumers' attention to that area and increase the flow of customer traffic throughout the store.

The brightness and dullness of different physical facilities also affect the buying atmosphere. As with color value, color intensity can be used to create illusions. Bright colors make the retailer's facilities appear larger than do duller colors. A bright color tends to create an illusion of hardness, however, whereas a dull color appears softer. As a rule, children react more favorably to brighter colors; hence, their widespread use in children's departments. Adults, on the other hand, prefer softer tones, which might help to explain why so many retailers use pastels.

Sound Appeal

Sound can either enhance or hinder a store's buying atmosphere. In planning store facilities, it is as important to avoid undesirable sounds as it is to create desirable ones. Disturbing noises detract from a store's appeal, whereas pleasant sounds can attract customers. This section discusses the functions of sound avoidance and sound creation.

Sound avoidance. Obtrusive sounds distract consumers, interrupting the buying process. Whether these sounds originate inside or outside of the store, they must be either controlled or eliminated. The clicking of heels on a hard floor surface, the humming of an air conditioner, the rattling of a jackhammer in the street outside, or the blaring music of the record shop next door may represent sound "pollution" to a retailer's selling efforts. Certain buying decisions require considerable thought, and disruptive noises during this thought process are irritating, possibly causing the loss of a sale or a long-term customer. In a private study conducted to determine the reasons for patronage loss at a local restaurant, the researchers learned that most of the established customers were driven away by noise emanating from the kitchen. Sounds of pots and pans banging together distrated from what should have been a pleasant evening.

Noise avoidance is a problem tailor-made for physical facilities planning. Careful use of architectural design, construction materials, equipment, and interior decors can eliminate or at least substantially reduce most obtrusive sounds. For example, clicking heels can be eliminated by heavy, durable carpeting, humming air conditioners can be strategically positioned away from selling areas, and rattling jackhammers and undesirable external music can be neutralized by proper insulation. Lower ceilings and sound-absorbing partitions and fixtures can reduce unwanted sounds even further.

Sound creation. To create an atmosphere that encourages buying, the retailer can use sound in a variety of ways. Sound can be a mood setter, an attention getter, and an informer. Music can relax the customer, promote a buying spirit, set the stage for a particular shopping theme (e.g., a Mexican fiesta), or remind the customer of a special season or holiday (particularly Christmas), as well as generally provide the customer with a pleasant background of familiar sounds. Music must complement the selling scene, though, not detract from it. The type (rock, classical, soul, etc.) and volume of music must be suitable to the retailer's consuming public.

Sound has been employed as an attention getter under a variety of circumstances. Attention-getting sound can draw customers to a particular display or department. Noise-making toys are very effective in attracting both children and adults to the toy department. A principal attention-getting device of stereo departments is the quality of sound emanating from the area. Attention-getting sound is also used to announce special (advertised or unadvertised) bargains. K Mart stores draw attention to their "blue light specials" by loud announcements: "Attention K Mart shoppers." Finally, fast, convenient, and pleasurable shopping requires that the customer have sufficient information about the store and its operations. Frequently, the retailer must inform the consumer about where to go, when to go, and how to get there. Verbal instructions are one of the most effective means of providing basic knowledge of store operations. Because this basic information is a prerequisite to the buying process, the *informer* role of sound is a key element in creating a buying atmosphere.

Scent Appeal

The creation of scent appeal is a problem similar in scope to the sound-appeal problem—how to avoid unpleasant odors and how to create pleasant scents. Stale, musty, and foul odors offend everyone and are sure to create negative impressions. Inadequate ventilation, insufficient humidity control, and poorly placed and maintained sanitation facilities are frequent causes of undesirable odors. Store facilities should be designed to minimize these problems or eliminate them entirely. Pleasurable scents, on the other hand, are key ingredients in creating atmospheric conditions that induce the customer to buy. A well-placed fan in a bakery shop, candy store, or delicatessen attracts the passerby to these almost unavoidable pleasurable scents of products frequently bought on impulse. Retailers of foods, tobacco, flowers, perfumes, and other scented products know the value of exposing their customers' noses to the scents. For some products, scent appeal is a purchase prerequisite. In the case of perfumes, for example, displays must be well placed to encourage the consumer to sample the various fragrances.

A store should smell like it is supposed to smell. Some retailers, such as a drug store, should smell clean and antiseptic. For others, such as an antique store, a dusty, musty smell could enhance the buying atmosphere.

Touch Appeal

At one point in the history of retailing, the vending machine was considered the retailing store of the future. Today, while the vending machine is admittedly an important retailer of some standardized products, it is still an unacceptable way of selling most goods. The vending machine's lack of acceptance is, to a large extent, the direct result of its inability to provide touch appeal. For most products, personal inspection—handling, squeezing, and cuddling—is a prerequisite to buying. Consider the Charmin example: "It's so squeezably soft." Before buying a product, the average consumer must at least hold it, even if it cannot be removed from its package. Many consumers have become upset because supermarkets now prepackage so many of their fruits, vegetables, and meats in hopes of reducing product damage inflicted by "the squeezers." In general, however, store layouts, fixtures, equipment, and displays must be planned to encourage and facilitate the consumer's sense of touch. While most consumers never expect to experience their own "touch of mink," they don't mind "trying it on" or "trying it out." The chances of a sale increase substantially when the consumer handles the product. The expression

"I just couldn't put it down" underscores the importance of getting the consumer to pick up a product.

Good facilities planning not only encourages the consumer to pick up the product, it also helps protect the product. Displays and fixtures should be designed to (1) provide consumers with samples to handle, thereby protecting products for sale from unnecessary handling, while at the same time they (2) provide product protection from normal store dust and dirt.

Taste Appeal

For some food retailers, providing the consumer with a taste might be a necessary condition for buying. This is often the case with specialty foods such as meats, cheeses, and bakery and dairy products. Hickory Farms and Baskin Robbins are two specialty food retailers that use taste appeal as part of their selling operations. In designing in-store displays, such retailers provide potential customers with a sample of the product under clean and sanitary conditions.

Theme Appeal

Many retailers find that a *shopping theme* helps provide a focus in planning physical facilities. Themes are useful vehicles around which the five sensory appeals can best be organized. Any number of themes can be employed. Some of the more common themes center around natural and holiday seasons, historical periods, current issues (energy, environment), and special events (anniversaries). Shopping themes can be organized either on a store-wide, department, or product-line basis. Later in this chapter we discuss the use of themes in connection with the elements of a retailer's physical facilities.

How does this display appeal to the consumer's physical senses?

(a)

(b)

(c)

What are the strengths and limitations of these shopping themes? How do they appeal to your physical senses?

First impressions are so important they are often the swing factor in a consumer's decision to stop at one store or another. Frequently, a consumer's first impression about a store is produced by the store's exterior. The store's exterior is a key factor in stopping and attracting new customers and retaining existing customers. The major considerations in planning store exteriors are the store's position, architecture, sign, and front.

The Store's Position

How and where the store is positioned on the site affect the retailer's ability to attract customers. In evaluating existing store facilities or planning future site layouts, the retailer should consider at least the following three questions: (1) How visible is the store? (2) Is the store compatible with its surroundings? and (3) Are store facilities placed for consumer convenience?

Ensuring Store Visibility

For the physical exterior of the store to accomplish its goals of stopping, attracting, and inviting customers to shop, customers must see it. A visible store becomes part of the consumer's mental map of where to shop for a given product or service. Visual awareness of a store's existence has the short-run benefit of alluring impulse shoppers and the long-run benefit of attracting customers in the future who develop a particular need for the retailer's products. Simply put, *people shop more frequently at stores they are aware of, and* **store visibility** *is an important factor in developing that awareness.* Ideally, a store should be positioned so that it is clearly visible from the major traffic arteries (foot and/or vehicle) adjacent to the site. The retailer improves the store's visibility by using the three interacting factors of setback, angle, and elevation to advantage.

Setback. Reduced visibility can result either from setting the store too far back from a traffic artery or from positioning it too close to the street. A store set too far back on a site might have its visibility impaired by adjacent stores, or it might simply be missed by fast-moving traffic. Stores set too close to a traffic artery may not allow passersby the opportunity to gain any visual perspective of the facility. If consumers see only a blank wall, they will never form a favorable impression of the store or its activities. Ideally, a store should be set back far enough to give passersby a broad perspective of the entire store, but close enough to let them read major signs and see any window displays.

Angle. Visual impressions also can be enhanced or hindered by the angle of the store relative to a traffic artery. In positioning the store, a retailer should place the building at an angle to the traffic artery that maximizes exposure. Since the store's front is designed to stop and attract potential customers, it should face the major traffic artery. When a store's back or sides are visible to passersby, they too should be attractive and informative. In an attempt to maximize land usage, some retailers have made the mistake of positioning the front of their stores perpendicular to the traffic artery. While this practice might make better use of the land, it often reduces the store's visibility and impairs its attractiveness.

Elevation. The elevation of a site can place the retailer's store above or below the main traffic artery level. Roofs and basement walls do little to attract and inform consumers. Elevation problems can be partially overcome by landscaping and the use of signs; however, such problems always translate into visibility problems for retailers that need exposure. Most consumers do not see stores that are too high or too low. These stores are also perceived as having accessibility problems.

Designing Site Compatibility

Fitting the store to the natural lay of the land and the natural habitat can reap substantial benefits for the retailer in terms of visual impressions. Pleasant shopping environments are becoming increasingly important for the typical U.S. family, which wants an entertainment trip as well as a shopping trip. **Site compatability** is also an important concern for the retailer that wants to satisfy the environmental concerns of some consumer groups and the environmental-impact requirements of local and state governments. In designing for site compatibility, the retailer should consider a number of issues. First, the size of the facility should be appropriate to the size of the site. Placing an oversized building on a small site produces a distorted sense of proportion that is visually disturbing to customers and noncustomers alike. It also reduces the contractor's ability to landscape the site properly. Second, the type of facility should be as consistent with the surrounding area as possible. The architectural design and the construction materials used should demonstrate a harmonious relationship with the immediate environment. And, finally, a certain amount of open space greatly enhances the appearance of an attractive store.

Planning Consumer Convenience

In planning the on-site position of the store, the retailer should consider how the business's position affects consumer convenience. The retailer might ask a number of questions. Does the store's position allow a sufficient number of parking spaces and permit easy access to them? Can cars and trucks turn around in the parking lot? Does the position of the store permit safe, convenient pedestrian traffic? Does the store's position enhance or does it hinder pedestrian access to the store?

The Store's Architecture

A store's architecture is a major factor both in making the right impression on the consumer and in developing an efficient retail operation. In most cases the store's architecture is a compromise between these two objectives.

Making an Impression

The architectural motif of a store can convey any number of different impressions as well as communicate a considerable amount of information. A certain architectural style can indicate the size and prestige of the retailer's operation, the nature of the retailer's principal product line (e.g., Taco Bell), and the retailer's affiliation (standard store designs used by chain operations, such as McDonald's). In addition, the store's architectural design can support a central theme or focal point for the retailer's merchandising activities. A *marketplace* theme can be architecturally suggested by the use of open space—open store fronts, central squares, and shopping stalls standing out in the open. A *period* theme can be created by adhering to a common architectural form (e.g., Colonial Shopping Center). A *naturals* theme is reinforced by using only natural building materials. In today's all-too-common "me too" retailing environment, a store's architecture can provide some much-needed individuality and identity.

Designing a Functional Facility

The impression-creating elements of the store's architecture must be balanced against the functional needs of retailer and consumer. Functional considerations that are paramount in the store's design are *costs, energy efficiency, security, operational efficiency,* and *customer convenience.*

Rapidly rising land, construction, and materials costs have made the retailer's attempt to differentiate a store from the competition increasingly difficult. Additionally, architectural freedom is limited by the costs associated with maintenance; conversely, architectural designs that reduce maintenance costs often limit customer convenience and store attractiveness.

With soaring energy prices, the retailer has an overriding obligation to minimize energy costs. In recent years energy-saving equipment, materials, and construction methods have been developed; these often are costly, however, and can interfere with desired architectural designs. These energy-saving methods include lower ceilings, less window space, proper air circulation, controlled entrances and exits, and proper insulation.

Because of the rising crime rate, modern retailers have had to design facilities that increase store security. In their architectural plans, retailers have included such security features as reduced window space, elimination of unexposed areas, controlled entrances and exits, proper lighting, limited exposure of high-value products, and security devices such as television monitors, two-way mirrors, and observation areas.

293

Another architectural design consideration is operational efficiency. The best allocation of store space for operational activities is where there is easy movement for customers, sales personnel, and merchandise, and where the retailer can gain maximum product exposure. Of the objectives in architectural design, maximizing selling areas and creating the highest level of product exposure are the architect's chief concerns.

With new government regulations and public pressure, the retailer must ensure that all possible physical barriers to handicapped consumers are removed. Physical barriers can also present problems for the elderly and the consumer with small children. Eliminating physical barriers is equally important to unhindered movement of all consumers: a few steps, a narrow aisle, or a hard-to-open door can substantially reduce consumer traffic.

The Store's Sign

A store's sign (marquee) is often the first "mark" of the retailer seen by a potential customer. It serves the two key purposes of identifying the store and attracting the consumer's attention.

Identifying the Store

Signs provide the potential customer with the "who, what, where, and when" of the retailer's offering. Signs identify *who* the retailer is by a name, logo, or some other symbol. Sears, Safeway, and Holiday Inn are immediately recognized by most consumers. Equally recognizable are McDonald's golden arches and Kentucky Fried Chicken's big bucket. Signs can also convey something more to the consumer about who the retailer is. Consider the different impressions that a sign reading "Joe's Bar and Grill" communicates as opposed to one for the "Olde English Pub." Additionally, signs inform consumers about *what* the retailer's operation is. They transmit information concerning the type of retail operation (department store, supermarket, catalog showroom), the nature of the product line (food, hardware, clothing, gifts), the extent of the service offering (full-service bank, self-service gasoline station), and the character of the pricing strategy (discount prices, family prices). Signs inform the consumer *where* the retailer is located and in some cases how to get there (e.g.,

Does this sign explain "who, what, where, and when"?

"Located at 5th and Main," or "Take the next right and follow Washington Avenue for one block"). Finally, some retailers use signs to inform the consumer *when* they are willing to provide service or when they are open (e.g., 24 hours). As we can see, a store's sign says many things about the retailer.

Attracting Consumer Attention

Distinctiveness in sign design is essential in achieving store recognition. The store's sign should create awareness, generate interest, and invite the consumer to try the store. The size, shape, color, lighting, and materials all contribute to the sign's distinctiveness and its abilities to create awareness and interest. The special design of McDonald's golden arches has helped it to become one of the most highly recognized signs in the United States. An equally important factor in a sign's ability to attract consumer attention is placement. Within setback and size limitations dictated by local regulations, the sign should be put in the most visible location consistent with good on-site positioning and planning.

The Store's Front

A store's front is the first major impression that consumers have of a store. The three primary design elements in a facade are storefront configuration, window displays, and store entrances.

Storefront Configurations

The three basic storefront configurations are the straight, angled, and arcade fronts. As illustrated in Figure 10–2, the **straight front** is *a store configuration that runs parallel to the sidewalk, street, mall, or parking lot.* Usually the only break in the front is a small recess for an entrance. This storefront design is operationally efficient since it does not reduce interior selling space. It lacks consumer appeal, however, because it is monotonous and less attractive than either of the other two configurations. Window shoppers can inspect only a small part of any display from any one position when retailers use the straight-front configuration. Reflective glare from windows can inhibit window shopping, while heavy foot traffic and little privacy deter in-store shopping.

The **angled-front** configuration *overcomes the monotony of the straight front by positioning the store's front at a slight angle to the traffic arteries.* To create a more attractive and interesting front, retailers that use the angled-front approach place windows and entrances off-center or at one end of the store's front. Angled

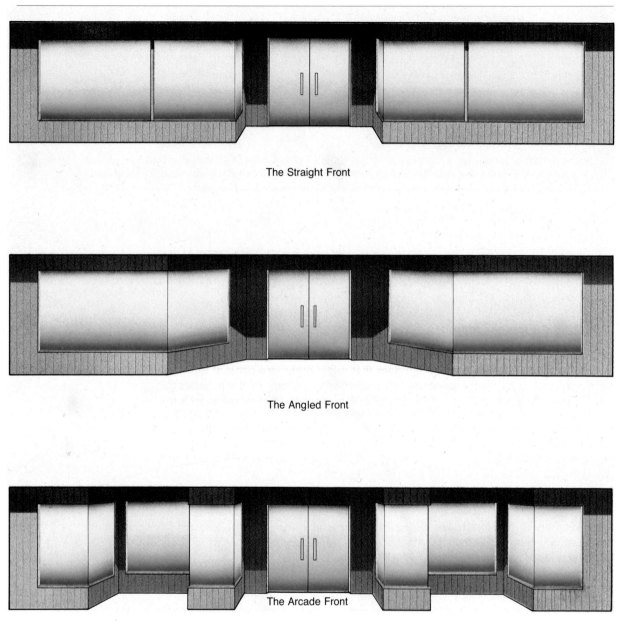

The Straight Front

The Angled Front

The Arcade Front

FIGURE 10–2
Types of storefront configurations

fronts also give the window shopper a better viewing angle of the merchandise in the window and reduce window glare. Retailers that use angled fronts locate their entrances at the most recessed part of the front to funnel and direct consumers into the store. Although its design provides more protection for the consumer than the straight front, the angled front does not provide the privacy and protection of the arcade front. The main limitation of the angled front is that it reduces the interior space the retailer can devote to selling.

The **arcade front** is *characterized by several recessed windows and/or entrances.* Its advantages are that it (1) increases the store's frontage exposure and display areas, (2) provides the shopper with several protected areas for window shopping, (3) increases the privacy under which the shopper can inspect window displays, (4) creates an attractive, relaxing atmosphere for the shopper, and (5) reduces glare for a substantial part of the store front. Its disadvantages are that it considerably reduces interior space for selling and displaying merchandise; it requires a substantial investment in construction and materials; and it requires a professional display staff to make full use of the arcade concept of window settings.

Window Displays

The number, size, depth, and type of windows a store has can substantially alter its exterior appearance and the general impression it produces on consumers. To create the desired impression, the retailer can use one or a combination of the elevated, ramped, shadow box, or island displays.

Elevated windows are *display windows with floors of varying heights.* These floor elevations range from 12 to 36 inches above sidewalk level. The floor height the retailer chooses depends upon the kind of merchandise it displays and the elevation necessary to place the display at the eye level of the typical shopper. Small merchandise such as shoes, jewelry, books, and cosmetics are normally displayed in windows with a floor elevation of 36 inches, whereas large merchandise such as furniture, appliances, and clothing displayed on mannequins usually appears in windows with a floor elevation of 12, 18, or 24 inches. Elevated windows provide consumers with an excellent visual perspective of the retailer's merchandise and also protect the glass window from damages that might otherwise occur at sidewalk levels. In planning elevated windows, the retailer can use one of three backings: open-backed display windows, which permit the consumer to view the store's interior; closed-back display windows, which prevent that view; and partial-back display windows, which allow the consumer to see only part of the store's interior.

Ramped windows are *standard display windows having a display floor higher in back than in front.* The floor ramp either is a wedge or is tiered, while the backing may be either open, partially opened, or closed. The principal advantage of the ramped display window is the greater visual impact of merchandise displayed in the rear.

Shadow box windows are *small, box-like display windows set at eye-level heights.* They are usually completely enclosed and are used to focus the shopper's attention on a selected line of merchandise. Jewelry stores use this type of window display extensively.

Island windows are *four-sided display windows isolated from the rest of the store.* Used in conjunction with the arcade storefront configuration, the island window can effectively highlight merchandise lines from all angles. However, this display advantage can become a disadvantage if the retailer does not carefully select and position merchandise. Island windows can appear cluttered or uncoordinated without good display planning.

Store Entrance

Retailers should design store entrances for the customer's *safety, comfort, and convenience,* as well as for guiding the customer into the store. Design considerations for store entrances should include (1) good lighting, (2) flat entry surfaces (no steps), (3) nonskid materials, (4) easy-to-open doors (slide away or air curtains), (5) little or no entrance clutter, such as merchandise tables, and (6) doors wide enough for people carrying large parcels. In addition, store entrances must meet all access regulations for the handicapped.

Is this window display effective?

The store's interior must contribute to the retailer's basic objectives of minimizing operating expenses while maximizing sales and customer satisfaction. To accomplish these goals, the store's interior not only must be inviting, comfortable, and convenient for the customer, it must also permit the retailer to use interior space efficiently and effectively. For the customer, a good interior store design has wide, uncluttered aisles, easy-to-find merchandise, logical merchandise groupings, and attractive surroundings. For the retailer, a well-designed store interior (1) enhances employee productivity by reducing the amount of time and effort they must spend to complete sales transactions; (2) provides maximum product exposure and encourages impulse buying by permitting the customer ease of movement and a broad view of the store's interior from anyplace within the store; (3) keeps product-handling requirements to a minimum by facilitating a smooth, orderly flow of goods from the time the retailer receives them to the time it sells them to the customer; (4) discourages employee and customer theft by promoting an open, yet controlled, environment; and (5) enhances the physical and psychological well-being of employees by creating a desirable working environment.

The Store's Space

Not all of the store's interior space is of equal value when judged against its revenue-producing capabilities. The consumer's in-store shopping responses to different interior store arrangements vary substantially. In general, greater consumer response (sales) is expected near major, in-store shopping focal points, so the further a given unit of space lies from these focal points, the less valuable it is in generating sales. Specifically, the value of any unit of store space will vary with the floor location, with the area position within each floor, and with its location relative to various types of traffic aisles. Many retailers recognize these variations in the value of store space and allocate total store rent to sales departments according to where they are located and how valuable each space is.

Floor Values

For multilevel stores, the value of space decreases the further it is from the main or entry-level floor. Although experts have different opinions on exactly how to allocate rental costs to each floor, they all agree that sales areas on the main floor should be charged a higher rent than sales areas located in the basement or on the second, third, and higher floors (see Figure 10–3). The additional customer exposure associated with entry-level floors justifies both the greater sales expectations (value of space) and the higher rent allocation of total store rent by floors.

Area Values

The value of space also varies depending upon where customers enter and how they traverse the store. In assigning value to interior store areas (and in making rent allocations), the retailer should take the following three factors into consideration. First, the most exposed area of any floor is the immediate area surrounding the entrance. Second, most consumers tend to turn right when entering the store or floor. Third, a general rule of thumb is that only one-quarter of the store's customers will go more than halfway into the store. Based on these three considerations, Figure 10–4 provides one of several variations that might be used in allocating store rents to a floor area. Another commonly used rule of thumb in assigning rent allocations is the **4-3-2-1 rule** (see Figure 10–5, p. 300).

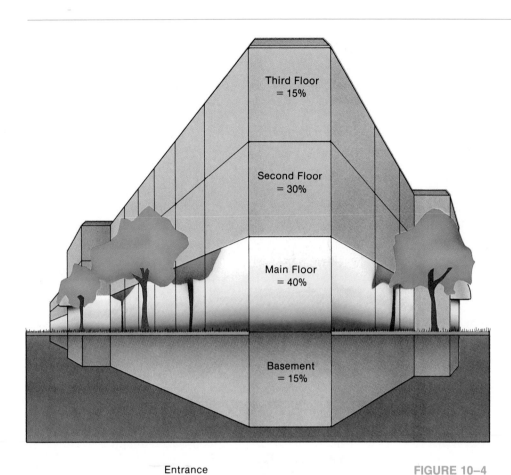

FIGURE 10–3
Rent allocation by
floors

Third Floor
= 15%

Second Floor
= 30%

Main Floor
= 40%

Basement
= 15%

Entrance

FIGURE 10–4
Rent allocations by
areas

Window

Window

18%	18%	12%
14%	12%	10%
5%	6%	5%

299

FIGURE 10–5
The 4-3-2-1 rule

The decline in value of store space from front to back of the shop is expressed in the 4-3-2-1 rule. This rule assigns 40 percent of a store's rental cost to the front quarter of the shop, 30 percent to the second quarter, 20 percent to the third quarter, and 10 percent to the final quarter. Similarly, each quarter of the store should contribute the same percentage of sales revenue.

For example, suppose that a small department store anticipates $120,000 in sales this year. Each quarter of the store should generate the following sales volume:

Front quarter	$120,000 · .40 =	$ 48,000
Second quarter	120,000 · .30 =	36,000
Third quarter	120,000 · .20 =	24,000
Fourth quarter	120,000 · .10 =	12,000
Total		$120,000

Source: Norman M. Scarborough and Thomas W. Zimmerer, *Effective Small Business Management* (Columbus: Charles E. Merrill Publishing Co., 1984), 339.

Aisle Values

Because merchandise located on primary traffic aisles greatly benefits from increased customer exposure, the retailer should assign a higher value and a higher rent to space along these aisles than to that along secondary aisles. To illustrate, Figure 10–6 classifies interior store space into high-, medium-, and low-rent areas based on their position relative to primary and secondary traffic aisles. As illustrated,

FIGURE 10–6
Rent allocations based
on traffic aisles

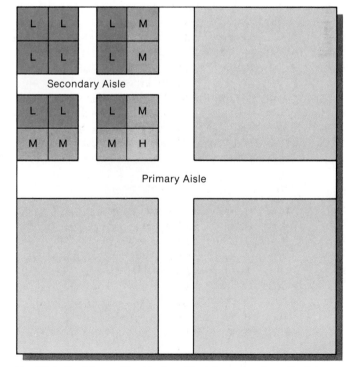

H = High-Rent Area   M = Medium-Rent Area   L = Low-Rent Area

a high-rent area is one exposed to two primary traffic aisles, while a low-rent area is exposed only to secondary aisles. Medium-rent areas are exposed to one primary and one secondary aisle. The classification of high-, medium-, and low-rent areas would, however, change with modifications in the layout configuration.

The Store's Layout

Nonselling Areas

A store's interior can be divided into two general areas according to usage: nonselling areas and selling areas. A nonselling area is space devoted to customer services, merchandise processing, and management and staff activities. Figure 10–7 identifies some of the more common nonselling areas. Small retailers that devote only about 10 percent of the store's interior space to nonselling areas will combine and/or eliminate several of the areas shown in Figure 10–7. In contrast, large department and specialty stores may devote up to 50 percent of the store's interior to nonselling areas and will designate separate areas for most of the activities outlined in Figure 10–7.

An important consideration in planning a store's interior is where to locate nonselling areas. While nonselling areas are of secondary importance compared to selling areas, they nevertheless must be located to facilitate *customer convenience* (a customer with a minor complaint who cannot find the complaint desk may turn out to be a customer with a major complaint) and *employee productivity* (a salesperson who has to spend more time running to and from various customer- and merchandise-service areas will simply be less productive in generating sales).

FIGURE 10–7
Selected examples of
nonselling areas

```
CUSTOMER SERVICE AREAS

     Checkout areas
     Dressing rooms
     Wrapping desk
     Complaint desk
     Credit desk
     Catalog desk
     Repair counter
     Return desk
     Rest rooms
     Restaurants


MERCHANDISE SERVICE AREAS

     Receiving areas
     Checking areas
     Marking areas
     Stocking areas
     Merchandise control areas
     Alteration and work rooms

MANAGEMENT/STAFF AREAS

     Offices
     Lounges
     Locker rooms
     Conference rooms
     Classrooms
     Training areas
```

The four general approaches to locating nonselling areas capable of satisfying both customer-convenience and employee-productivity needs are the sandwich, core, peripheral, and annex approaches.[9] The **sandwich approach** involves *using one floor of a multilevel store for nonselling activities* (see Figure 10–8a). By sandwiching a nonselling floor between selling floors, the retailer can concentrate all nonselling activities in one area and can realize certain economies of scale in handling customer- and merchandise-service activities. The principal limitation of this plan is the inconvenience for both customers and employees of needing to go to a separate floor to obtain a particular service.

The **core approach** is *the concept of locating all nonselling areas within a central core area surrounded by selling areas* (see Figure 10–8b). Because this ap-

FIGURE 10–8
General approaches to locating nonselling areas

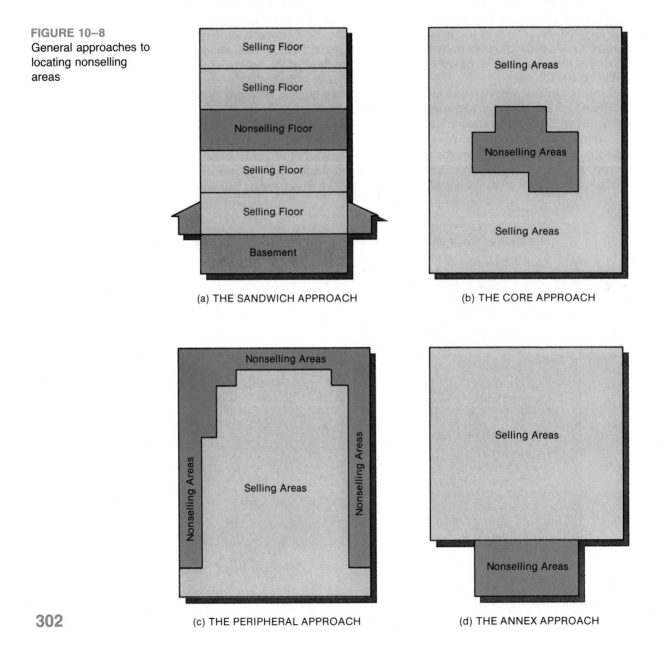

(a) THE SANDWICH APPROACH

(b) THE CORE APPROACH

(c) THE PERIPHERAL APPROACH

(d) THE ANNEX APPROACH

proach concentrates nonselling activities in one area, it helps the retailer achieve some economies of scale. Also, customer and salesperson convenience improves since neither is very far away from the nonselling area. The most serious disadvantages of the core approach are the problems associated with the merchandise-service activities of receiving and checking. By locating these activities in the central core, the flow of incoming merchandise interferes with the flow of customers within the selling areas.

The **peripheral approach** is perhaps the most widely used method of locating nonselling areas. As illustrated in Figure 10–8c, the peripheral approach *locates nonselling areas around the exterior of the store or floor.* The peripheral layout satisfies the convenience needs of both customers and sales personnel. Furthermore, it facilitates merchandise handling without interfering with customer movement.

The fourth approach to locating nonselling areas is the **annex approach.** To avoid any interference with selling activities, *some retailers locate all nonselling activities away from the sales floor in a nonselling annex.* Usually, the annex is an appendage to the back of the store where all merchandise-service and management/staff activities are concentrated. With the exception of checkout stands, dressing rooms, and wrapping and packaging areas, most consumer services are also located in the annex (see Figure 10–8d).

Selling Areas

Selling space is the area of the store devoted to the display of merchandise and the interaction between customers and store personnel. In planning the store's interior selling areas, the designer must organize merchandise into logical selling groups and allocate space, locate merchandise, and design layouts that are conducive to both the selling function and efficient overall operations.

Grouping merchandise. Better merchandise *planning,* greater merchandise *control,* and a more *personalized shopping atmosphere* are three important reasons for assembling merchandise into some type of natural grouping. A logical grouping of merchandise also helps customers find, compare, and select merchandise suited to their needs. Merchandise groupings can be either formal or informal; for either, the retailer must use certain criteria in grouping merchandise. The most common criteria the retailer uses are (1) functional (footwear, underwear, outerwear), (2) storage and display (racks, bins, shelves or dry, refrigerated, frozen), and (3) target-market consumer criteria (men's, women's, children's or economy-minded, prestige-oriented, convenience-directed). The key points retailers must ensure in grouping merchandise are that the customer understands and appreciates the organization and that merchandise groupings are consistent with efficient operating principles.

Allocating space. Once a retailer has grouped merchandise according to some logical criteria, selling space must be allocated to each merchandise group. Given that each store has a limited amount of space, the retailer must select some method to allocate selling space. One method is the *model stock method* whereby the retailer determines the amount of floor space needed to stock a desired assortment of merchandise for each grouping. For the more important merchandise groupings, the retailer allocates a sufficient amount of space to achieve the desired assortment. Merchandise groupings of lesser importance are allocated space based on their assortment needs and the remaining available space. Apparel retailers frequently employ the model stock method.

303

A second method retailers use in allocating selling space is the *sales-productivity ratio*. This method allocates selling space on the basis of sales per square foot for each merchandise group. Some retailers use profit per square foot as the basis of space allocation. Merchandise groups with lower sales or profit productivity are assigned space on an availability and needs basis. Hardware and food retailers commonly use this method.

Locating merchandise. Where on the sales floor to put each merchandise group is the third factor in planning the sales floor. Criteria that retailers consider are rent-paying ability, consumer buying behavior, merchandise compatibility, seasonality of demand, space requirements, and display requirements.[10] *Rent-paying ability* is the contribution that a merchandise group can generate in sales to pay the rent for the area to which it is assigned within the store. As discussed previously, the value of selling space varies substantially from one part of the store to another. Other things being equal, merchandise groups with the highest rent-paying ability are located in the most valuable space.

Consumer buying behavior criteria are based on the recognition that consumers are willing to spend different amounts of time and effort in searching for merchandise. For example, the retailer should place impulse and convenience goods in areas with high exposure (major aisles, checkout stands, etc.) since customers will not exert much effort in searching for them. In contrast, the retailer should locate shopping and specialty goods in less accessible areas, since consumers' purchase intent is well established and they will exert the necessary effort to find them. As a matter of policy, some retailers locate shopping and specialty goods at the rear of the store in an attempt to draw the customer throughout the selling area.

The degree of relationship between various merchandise groups is termed *merchandise compatibility*. This concept states that closely related merchandise should be located together to promote complementary purchases. For example, the sale of a man's suit will increase the chances of selling men's ties and shirts if those products are located close to and are visible from the men's suit department.

Merchandise characterized by *seasonality of demand* is often accorded highly valuable, visible space during the appropriate season. In addition, merchandise groups with different seasonal selling peaks are often placed together to allow the retailer to expand or contract these lines without major changes in the store's layout. Examples are Christmas toys, lawn and garden equipment, women's coats, and women's dresses.

Space requirements for each merchandise group must also be considered in making in-store location decisions. For example, merchandise groups that require large amounts of floor space (e.g., a department store's furniture department) use less valuable space either at the rear of the store, on an upper floor or in the basement, or in an annex. Normally, the bulky nature of such products cannot justify their placement in higher-rent locations.

Display requirements also influence where the retailer will locate a particular group of merchandise. For example, merchandise such as clothing which must be hung to display it probably is located along the sides of walls or at the rear of the store where it will not interfere with the customer's needs for convenience and comparison shopping, and the selling and operating needs of the retailer.

Designing layouts. In designing the layouts of the sales floors, the retailer must consider the arrangement of merchandise, fixtures, displays, and traffic aisles so that they accommodate the spatial and locational requirements of different merchandise groups. Selling floor layouts are extremely important because they strongly influence in-store traffic patterns, shopping atmosphere, shopping behavior, and operational efficiency. Some of the factors the retailer must consider in designing the sales floor layout include

- the *type of displays* (shelves, tables, counters) and *fixtures* (stands, easels, forms, platforms)
- the *size* and *shape* of fixtures
- the *permanence* of displays and fixtures
- the *arrangement* (formal or informal balance) of displays and fixtures
- the *width* and *length* of traffic aisles
- the *positioning* of merchandise groups, customer services, and other customer attractions

Three basic layout patterns are the grid, free-form, and boutique layout. The **grid layout** is *a rectangular arrangement of displays and aisles that generally run parallel to one another.* As illustrated in Figure 10–9, the grid layout represents a formal arrangement in which the size and shape of display areas and the length and width of the traffic aisles are homogeneous throughout the store. Although the retailer can develop various modifications in this layout to create variety and to respond to the operational needs of the store, this grid pattern essentially retains its formal arrangement. Used most frequently by supermarkets and convenience, variety, and discount stores, the grid layout offers several advantages. First, it allows the most efficient use of selling space of any of the layout patterns. Second, it simplifies shopping by creating clear, distinct traffic aisles. Third, it promotes the image of a clean, efficient shopping atmosphere. Fourth, it facilitates routine and planned shopping behavior as well as self-service and self-selection by creating a well-organized environment. And, finally, it allows more efficient operations by simplifying the stocking, marking, and housekeeping tasks, and reduces some of the problems concerned with inventory and security control. The major disadvantage of the grid layout is the sterile shopping atmosphere it creates. For this reason, the grid pattern is simply inappropriate for most shopping- and specialty-goods retailers.

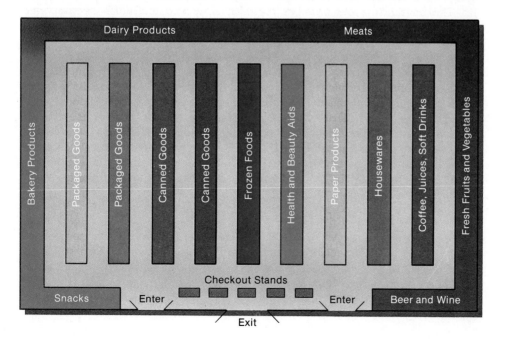

FIGURE 10–9
The grid layout

FIGURE 10–10
The free-form layout

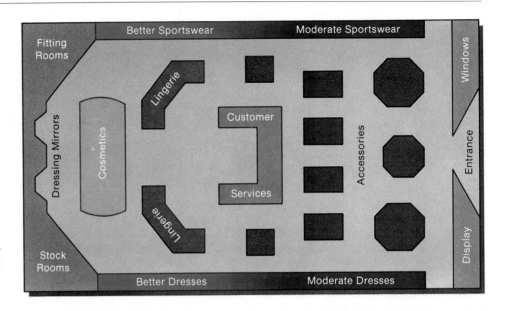

The **free-form layout,** on the other hand, *arranges displays and aisles in a free-flowing pattern* (see Figure 10–10). This layout employs a variety of different sizes, shapes, and styles of displays, together with fixtures positioned in an informal, unbalanced arrangement. The main benefit retailers derive from the free-form layout is the pleasant atmosphere it produces—an easy-going environment that promotes window shopping and browsing. This comfortable environment increases the time the customer is willing to spend in the store and results in an increase in both planned and unplanned purchases. These benefits of a superior shopping atmosphere are partially offset by the increased cost of displays and fixtures, high labor requirements, additional inventory and security control problems, and the wasted selling space that normally accompany a free-form layout.

The **boutique layout** *arranges the sales floor into individual, semiseparate areas, each built around a particular shopping theme.* The boutique layout illustrated in Figure 10–11 shows the sales floor divided into several small specialty shops. By using displays and fixtures appropriate to a particular shopping theme and by stocking the boutique according to this theme, the retailer can create an unusual and interesting shopping experience. For example, the "Leisure World" boutique might include such an unconventional merchandise assortment as sporting goods, exercise equipment, home electronics (computer games, stereos, televisions), and art and music supplies. The "Naturals Shop" could feature apparel and food products along with home furnishings, all made from natural materials. To reinforce the theme, the fixtures could be constructed out of natural, unfinished woods. Boutique layouts have essentially the same advantages and disadvantages as free-form layouts.

SUMMARY

One of the most valuable ways the retailer can attract customers is by appearance of the store and its immediate surroundings. The environment of each store has both physical and psychological repercussions in the battle for the customer's attention and for efficient operations. By identifying the desired image, targeting the right consumer, and communicating the right impression, the retailer creates a store image that is right for shopping and working. Appeals to the five senses promote a

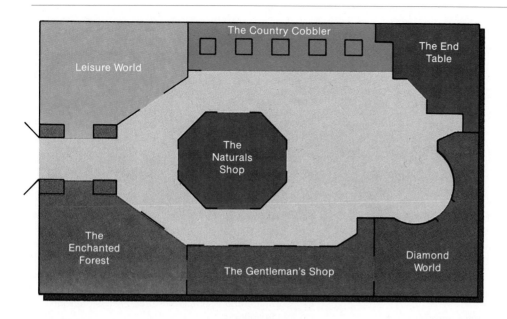

FIGURE 10–11
The boutique layout

favorable buying atmosphere. Sight, sound, smell, touch, and taste appeals have an obvious influence on the consumer's buying behavior.

Communication with the consumer is facilitated by the store's exterior. How and where the store is positioned on the site affect the retailer's ability to attract customers. The store should be positioned so that it is visible to the consumer, compatible with the natural environment, and convenient for on-site movement of people and vehicles. The store's architecture should incorporate features that make a good impression while remaining functionally efficient. The store's sign serves two purposes: identifying the store and attracting consumer attention. Because the facade of the store often is the first impression consumers have of the retailer, the appropriate configuration, attractive window displays, and accessible store entrances are essential.

The store's interior should minimize operating expenses while maximizing sales activities and customer satisfaction. In planning store layouts, the retailer must consider that all space is not equal in sales-producing potential. Also, wise use of nonselling space is needed for the retailer to meet consumers' needs for services.

KEY TERMS AND CONCEPTS

store image	sound appeal	site compatibility
economic shopper	scent appeal	straight-front configuration
personalized shopper	touch appeal	angled-front configuration
apathetic shopper	taste appeal	arcade-front configuration
ethical shopper	theme appeal	elevated windows
sight appeal	store visibility	ramped windows

shadow box windows   core approach   grid layout

island windows   peripheral approach   free-form layout

4-3-2-1 rule   annex approach   boutique layout

sandwich approach   merchandise compatibility

REVIEW QUESTIONS

1. What is store image?
2. How does the economic shopper differ from the personalized shopper? Which store design features are appropriate for each type of shopper?
3. Why is it important for the store to communicate the right impression?
4. What are the three types of visual relationships? Briefly describe each type.
5. How are large and small sizes perceived?
6. What emotions or feelings do consumers associate with horizontal lines, vertical lines, and slanted lines?
7. What determines the psychological impact of color? Explain.
8. How should the color red be used in interior store design?
9. What color has the greatest visibility from long distances?
10. What illusions are created by bright colors?
11. Who prefers softer tones?
12. What are the three uses for sound in creating a buying atmosphere?
13. What is site compatibility? How is it achieved?
14. What three factors determine a store's visibility? Explain.
15. What should the retailer consider in designing a functional facility? Explain.
16. Describe the who, what, where, and when functions of a retail store sign.
17. Compare and contrast the three basic storefront configurations.
18. Which features should the retailer take into consideration when designing store entrances?
19. Which floor of a multilevel store should be charged a higher rent?
20. What is the 4-3-2-1 rule?
21. What are the four general approaches to locating nonselling areas? Describe each approach.
22. Compare and contrast the model stock and sales-productivity methods of allocating selling space.
23. How can seasonality of demand affect the in-store location of merchandise?
24. Describe the three basic layout patterns. What are the strengths and weaknesses of each pattern?

ENDNOTES

1. Adapted from Gregory P. Store, "City Shoppers and Urban Identification: Observations on the Social Psychology of City Life," *The American Journal of Sociology* (July 1954): 36–45.
2. John E. Mertes, "The Retail Store as an Instrument of Nonverbal Communications," *Oklahoma Business Bulletin* (March 1970): 3.
3. M. Wayne DeLozier, *The Marketing Communications Process* (New York: McGraw-Hill, 1976), 201.
4. Mertes, "The Retail Store as an Instrument of Nonverbal Communications," 3.
5. Rom J. Markin, Jr., *Retailing Management* (New York: Macmillan, 1977), 193.
6. DeLozier, *The Marketing Communications Process,* 179.
7. Kenneth H. Mills and Judith E. Paul, *Create Distinctive Displays* (Englewood Cliffs, NJ: Prentice-Hall, 1974), 61.
8. DeLozier, *The Marketing Communications Process,* 204.
9. See Markin, *Retailing Management,* 204.
10. See William R. Davidson, Alton F. Doody, and Daniel J. Sweeney, *Retailing Management* (New York: Ronald Press, 1975), 534–35.

RELATED READINGS

Abend, Jules. "Reasserting Store (and Human) Identity by Design." *Stores* (February 1982), 27–28.

Barmash, Isadore. "Spaced Out!" *Stores* (July 1982), 26–28.

Bellizzi, Joseph A.; Crowley, Ayn E.; and Hasty, Ronald W. "The Effects of Color in Store Design." *Journal of Retailing* 59 (Spring 1983), 21–45.

Curham, Ronald C. "Shelf Space Allocation and Profit Maximization in Mass Retailing." *Journal of Marketing* 37 (July 1973), 54–60.

Dawson, Lyndon E., and Bettinger, Charles O., III. "On the Relationship of Consumer Behavior and the Sense of Touch." *Contemporary Marketing Thought, 1977 Educators' Proceedings.* B. A. Greenberg and D. N. Bellenger, eds. (American Marketing Association 1977), 27–30.

Donovan, Robert J., and Rossiter, John R. "Store Atmosphere: An Environmental Psychology Approach." *Journal of Retailing* 58 (Spring 1982), 34–57.

Harris, Mark. "Evaluate Lighting Systems as a Marketing Device, Not Overhead." *Marketing News* (October 26, 1984), 1, 10.

Jewell, Thomas R. "Excess Space: J. C. Penney's Solution." *Retail Control* (January 1984), 28–33.

Markin, Rom J.; Lillis, Charles M.; and Narayana, Chem L. "Social-Psychological Significance of Store Space." *Journal of Retailing* 52 (Spring 1976), 43–54.

Milliman, Ronald E. "Using Background Music to Affect Behavior of Supermarket Shoppers." *Journal of Marketing* 46 (Summer 1982), 86–91.

Novak, Adolph, and Toman, James. *Store Planning and Design.* (New York: Lebhan Griedman Books, 1977)

Ruess, Jim. "In 1980's, Redoing Retail Facilities Requires Analytical Framework, Options, Master Plan." *Marketing News* (March 7, 1980), 10.

Schaninger, Charles M. "The Emotional Value of Different Color Combinations." *Contemporary Marketing Thought, 1977 Educators' Proceedings.* B. A. Greenberg and D. N. Bellenger, eds. (American Marketing Association 1977), 27–30.

Schulz, David P. "Computer-Aided Design." *Stores* (March 1985), 47–48, 74.

Spalding, Lewis A. "New Store Planning." *Stores* 64 (March 1979), 24–29.

"Supermarket Design Takes Bold Strides." *Chain Store Age Executive* (May 1985), 37, 40, 43.

Outline

CUSTOMER THEFT

Shoplifter Types and Reasons
Shoplifting Devices and Techniques
Shoplifting Detection and Prevention
Shoplifter Apprehension and Prosecution

EMPLOYEE PILFERAGE

Pilferers: Types and Reasons
Pilferers: Devices and Techniques
Pilferage: Detection and Prevention
Pilferers: Apprehension and Prosecution

SUPPLIER PILFERAGE

BAD CHECKS

Bad Checks: Types and Reasons
Bad Checks: Detection and Prevention

BAD CREDIT CARDS

BURGLARY AND ROBBERY

Preventing Burglary
Handling Robbery

Objectives

- Appreciate the need for an aggressive security program

- Identify the various types of security problems and recognize their causes

- Distinguish between various devices and techniques employed by thieves

- Outline the methods used by retailers in detecting and preventing criminal activities

- Discuss the procedures used in apprehending and prosecuting criminals

11
Ensuring Store Security

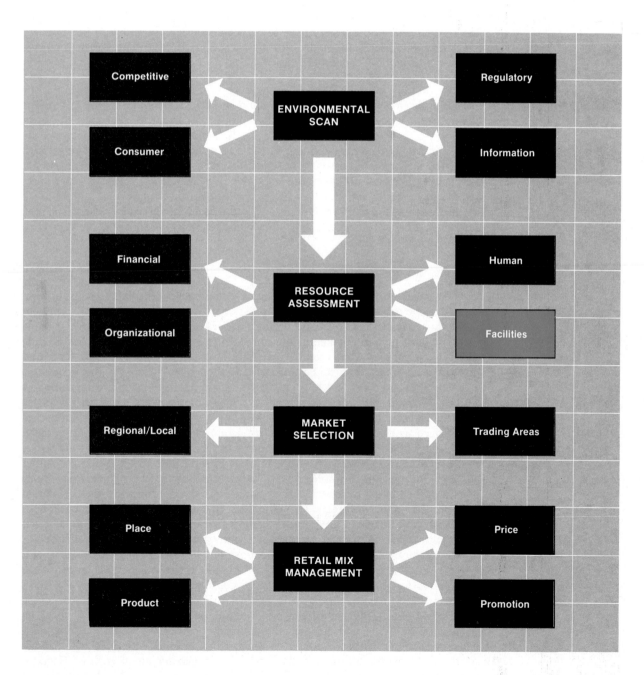

Customer theft, employee pilferage, burglary, and robbery are everyday facts of life that every retailer must face and protect against. Collectively, these protective measures are called store security. In developing a store security program, the retailer must protect not only the store and its merchandise, but also its customers and employees. This chapter describes how a retailer can detect and prevent many of the losses that might result from such criminal activities as shoplifting by customers, pilferage by employees and suppliers, passing of bad checks and credit cards, and thefts by burglary and robbery. While estimates vary greatly, about five cents out of every dollar spent in a retail store goes to cover the losses resulting from these criminal activities and the security measures used to prevent them. Retailers also experience a number of losses as a result of noncriminal activities or day-to-day operations of the store, for example, losses due to mismarking, misplacing, and accidental breakage of merchandise. These losses and their control will be discussed in Chapters 18, 19, and 20.

CUSTOMER THEFT

Shoplifting is *the act of pilfering merchandise from a store display by customers and individuals posing as customers.* To pilfer is to commit or practice petty theft. This form of petty thievery can account for 30 to 40 percent of all stock losses the retailer suffers. Unfortunately for the store's customers, retail prices must be set high enough to cover these losses. Shoplifting occurs in three basic ways: (1) outright theft of merchandise, (2) alteration of the retailer's price tag to reflect a lower price, and (3) switching or substituting a lower price tag for the original tag. In the following discussion we review what a retailer should do about shoplifting and shoplifters, who they are, why they are, why they shoplift, how they shoplift, and how to control shoplifting.

Shoplifter Types and Reasons

Shoplifters fall into two general categories: the amateur who steals to satisfy physical or psychological needs and the professional who steals for a living. **Amateur shoplifters** *may be anyone.* Usually they neither look nor act the part. They range from juveniles to homemakers, kleptomaniacs to vagrants, and alcoholics to drug addicts. *Juvenile shoplifters* make up about "50 percent of all shoplifters"; they steal "for kicks, on dares, and to be accepted by their peer groups."[1] The *occasional shoplifter* is inclined to yield to temptation. This type steals to relieve tension or is hit by a "sense he can get away with it."[2] *Kleptomaniacs* are individuals from all walks of life who have a neurotic impulse to steal. They steal to satisfy a psychological need as opposed to making some economic or personal gain. Frequently, the objects kleptomaniacs steal have some symbolic significance to them. *Vagrants, alcoholics, and drug addicts* steal merchandise to resell it so that they can buy either food, liquor, or drugs. Vagrants and alcoholics "are probably the most clumsy shoplifters and the easiest to detect."[3] Drug addicts are usually the most desperate and therefore the most dangerous. They should be handled by the police or other specially trained personnel. These groups are not the only amateur shoplifters. If given an opportunity or an excuse, people from nearly any customer group will shoplift.

Professional shoplifters *are in the business for the money.* By stealing and then reselling the merchandise, professionals make their livelihood. They cause serious losses for the retailer because they focus their activities on high-value merchandise that is easily fenced but difficult to trace and recover. The "low-class" professional often uses various devices and equipment to facilitate shoplifting. The "high-class" professionals avoid using shoplifting devices and equipment because, if they are caught, it could be used in court as evidence of intent to steal. Professional shoplifters are difficult to detect and to deter with security measures. Because they are professional with specialized shoplifting techniques and methods, however, they develop definite patterns of stealing in the process of trying to perfect their full-time craft.[4] These patterns can be useful in the retailer's shoplifting detection and prevention measures if store personnel are trained to recognize them.

Shoplifting Devices and Techniques

The amateur and the professional use a variety of devices in their attempts at shoplifting. The main purpose of shoplifting devices is to conceal both the actual act of stealing and the merchandise once it has been stolen. Shoplifting devices include various types of clothing (e.g., coats, booster panties, wide-top boots, and other loose-fitting garments) and parcels (e.g., booster boxes, purses, umbrellas, newspapers, magazines, and shopping, school, and knitting bags). The shoplifter might also hide stolen merchandise (e.g., jewelry) in merchandise actually purchased (e.g., box of candy).

Shoplifters use a number of techniques in their pilfering activities. Shoplifters who employ these techniques can be characterized as the booster, the diverter, the blocker, the sweeper, the walker, and the wearer.

The Booster

The **booster** is a shoplifter who *shoves merchandise into concealed areas of parcels and/or clothing.* Booster boxes are carefully constructed boxes that appear to be authentic, tightly wrapped packages, but that contain trap doors that allow the shoplifter to slip merchandise into the box quickly and easily. Another variation is the false-bottom booster box that the shoplifter simply places over merchandise on a counter and by manipulating it traps the merchandise inside the box.

Other booster devices are *booster hooks* and *bags* securely fastened to the inside of a large, bulky coat. Using this equipment, the shoplifter simply slips merchandise onto the hooks or into the bags and walks away. Some shoplifters use *booster coats* constructed to conceal merchandise. For example, a coat with large, baggy sleeves or pockets can be used to transport a large amount of merchandise out of the store. Still others wear *booster panties,* loose-fitting bloomers that are tightly fastened around the knees and worn under bulky clothing. The shoplifter simply drops merchandise into them at the waist. In general, the booster tends to use a number of boostering devices to first conceal the merchandise, then transport it out of the store.

The Diverter

The **diverter** is one member of a team of shoplifters who *attempts to divert the attention of the store's personnel while a partner shoplifts.* Diverters use several techniques to attract store personnel's attention. They include (1) engaging the salesperson in conversation, (2) acting suspicious, (3) creating an attention-grabbing disturbance of fainting, falling, or fighting, (4) requesting merchandise that requires the salesperson to go to the stockroom, and (5) purchasing merchandise that requires the salesclerk to make change and then accidentally dropping the change on the floor behind the counter. If the diverter manages to draw attention, the shoplifter partner can secure the merchandise and be out of the store before anyone realizes what has happened.

The Blocker

Obstructing the vision of store personnel while they or a partner shoplift is the principal technique of **blockers**. In a team effort the blocker simply stands between the salesperson and a shoplifting partner. Working as a single, the blocker might employ a topcoat draped over the arm and use it to shield the shoplifting activities of the other hand. The blocker might also wear a topcoat with inside pocket slits. Although the blocker's hands appear to be harmlessly tucked into pockets, they are in fact free to engage in shoplifting activities behind the shield of the coat.

The Sweeper

The **sweeper** *simply brushes merchandise off the counter into a shopping bag or some other type of container.* Typically sweepers reach over a counter apparently to examine a piece of merchandise, but in the process of bringing their arm back they sweep merchandise off the counter and into the container. While this technique may sound clumsy, the nature, grace, and speed of the professional sweeper who has refined the technique make it an effective shoplifting approach.

The Walker

Some shoplifters have perfected the technique of *walking naturally while carrying concealed merchandise between their legs.* The **walker** is usually a woman. Shoplifters who have developed this skill are capable of carrying, in a completely natural way, both small items such as jewelry and large items such as small appliances. If you do not believe this method is difficult, try walking naturally with this text between your legs.

The Wearer

The **wearer** *tries on merchandise, then wears it out of the store.* The *open-wearer* is a bold shoplifter who tries on a hat, coat, or some other piece of clothing, removes the tags, and then openly wears it while shopping and exiting the store. It is the boldness of this technique that makes it successful. Most people, including store personnel, simply would not be willing to take such risks and find it hard to believe that others are. *Under-wearers* steal clothing items by wearing them under their own loose outerwear. The most common technique is to take several items into the fitting room, but return fewer to the racks.

Other Techniques

Several other shoplifting techniques are also used by both amateur and professional shoplifters. The **carrier** *walks in, picks up a large piece of merchandise, removes the tags, affixes a fake sales slip, and walks out.* **Self-wrappers** *use their own wrapping paper to wrap store merchandise before removing it from the store.* And, the **price changer** *pays for the merchandise, but only after taking a shoplifters' reduction by altering the store's price tag, switching store price tags, or removing the store's price tag and substituting realistic fakes.*

Shoplifting Detection and Prevention

The retailer's security program should include both shoplifting detection and shoplifting prevention measures. Detection of shoplifters is largely a matter of good observation. Successful detection involves knowing what to look for and where to look. By training store employees to be better observers, the retailer not only increases the chances of detecting actual shoplifting activities, but also increases the likelihood that potential shoplifters will be discouraged by the employees' skilled observation powers. Some basic observation rules should be followed to spot shoplifting activities.

1. Watch the eyes.   Professional shoplifters avoid looking at the merchandise they are about to steal. Their eyes are searching for possible observers of their shoplifting activities. Amateur shoplifters, on the other hand, often focus undue attention on the merchandise they are about to steal.

2. Watch the hands.   "Shoplifters and magicians have one thing in common. Both rely on sleight-of-hand. However, amusement turns to anguish when individuals who pretend to be customers come into a small store and prove that 'the hand is quicker than the eye.' "[5] Equally important is to watch *both* hands. While one hand may be visibly handling merchandise on top of the counter, the other hand may be busily engaged in shoplifting activities.

3. Watch the body.   "Quick movements and shoulder jerks often give away shoplifters as they go through the motions of concealing or juggling the merchandise."[6] Unnatural body movements are more common with amateur shoplifters than with professionals who have been trained to use smooth, fluid body movements.

4. Watch the clothing.   Loose and bulky clothing are trademarks of a potential shoplifter. Therefore, store personnel should be on the lookout for customers dressed in this way. When such clothing is out of season (e.g., winter clothing in the summer), when it appears to be inconsistent with the individual wearing it (e.g., large, bulky clothing on a small person), and when it is inconsistent with the weather (e.g., a raincoat on a bright sunny day), the likelihood that the customer is a potential shoplifter is substantially increased.

5. Watch for devices.   As previously discussed, the shoplifter uses numerous concealment devices. Anything that the customer carries is a potential concealment device. Here again, if the object the shopper is carrying appears out of place, such as an umbrella on a sunny day or gloves on a warm day, store personnel should pay special attention to that individual.

6. Watch for groups.   Amateur teenage shoplifters often travel in groups or gangs. While two or three members divert attention, the other members shoplift. It usually requires more than one employee to keep track of these multimember groups. Security personnel should be notified immediately when such groups enter the department and/or store.

7. Watch for loiterers.   Many amateur shoplifters must work up the nerve to steal. In doing so, they frequently loiter around the area containing the merchandise that they target for the theft. Professionals also must wait for the opportunity to shoplift. Undue time spent in inspecting exposed merchandise is a good telltale sign of potential shoplifting activities. Equally suspicious are individuals who loiter in places where they should not be, such as behind the checkout counter, in the stockroom, or in the bathroom.

8. Watch for switches.   Shoplifters often work in pairs: one shoplifts the merchandise and then passes it on to a partner. Telephone booths, restrooms, and restaurants are favorite switching places for this team effort, so they should be scrutinized.

   To facilitate observation and detection, many retailers use a number of devices, such as mirrors, observation towers, closed-circuit television, and electronic bugs (see Figure 11–1).

315

FIGURE 11–1

Observation methods (source: Adapted from M. E. Williams, "Theft: Stores Fight Back: For Retailers, 'tis the Season to Be Wary," Copyright 1984, *USA Today*. Reprinted with permission.)

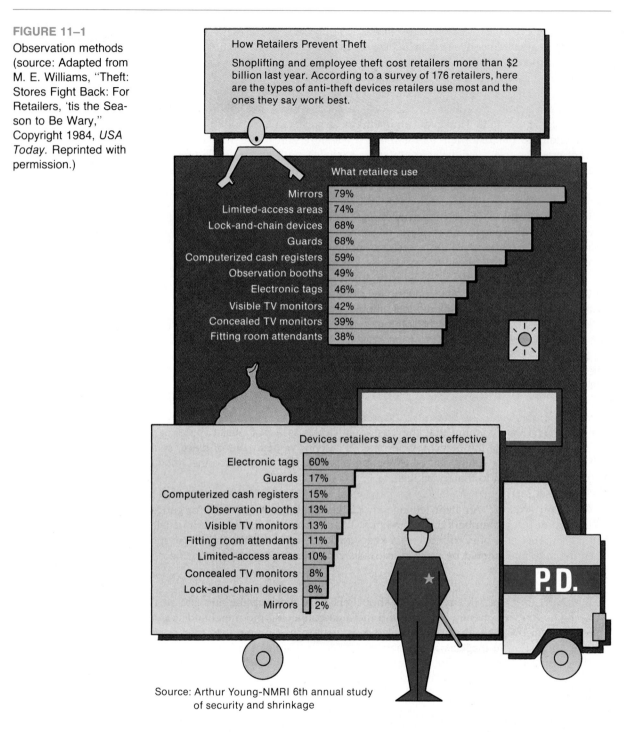

How Retailers Prevent Theft

Shoplifting and employee theft cost retailers more than $2 billion last year. According to a survey of 176 retailers, here are the types of anti-theft devices retailers use most and the ones they say work best.

What retailers use

Mirrors	79%
Limited-access areas	74%
Lock-and-chain devices	68%
Guards	68%
Computerized cash registers	59%
Observation booths	49%
Electronic tags	46%
Visible TV monitors	42%
Concealed TV monitors	39%
Fitting room attendants	38%

Devices retailers say are most effective

Electronic tags	60%
Guards	17%
Computerized cash registers	15%
Observation booths	13%
Visible TV monitors	13%
Fitting room attendants	11%
Limited-access areas	10%
Concealed TV monitors	8%
Lock-and-chain devices	8%
Mirrors	2%

Source: Arthur Young-NMRI 6th annual study of security and shrinkage

Convex mirrors that are strategically located throughout the store allow a limited number of employees to observe all areas of the store. They also serve as a psychological deterrent to most amateur shoplifters. On the other hand, these same mirrors could help the professional shoplifter to observe store personnel. *One-way mirrors* are also used to observe customers without their being aware of it. Their principal limitation is that they generally permit only a small part of the store to be observed from any one vantage point. *Observation towers* (which frequently double as office space) are elevated areas in either the middle or back of the store from which personnel can view the entire sales floor. While they facilitate general detection of potential shoplifters, their effectiveness is somewhat reduced since the observer is not right on the scene for close observation and apprehension should a theft occur.

Closed-circuit television is an expensive yet effective method of observation. Through strategic placement of cameras, the retailer can observe all areas of the store on a central monitor. In addition, television cameras act as psychological deterrents to shoplifting. In fact, some retailers install fake cameras as a psychological deterrent, a strategy that can be effective if the shoplifter is convinced that the cameras are operational. Professional shoplifters soon recognize dirty and stationary cameras as fakes and therefore ignore them as a threat. All of these security devices are truly effective only if the retailer is willing to absorb the additional payroll expenses associated with trained observers.

Finally, some retailers employ *electronic bugs* or *pellets* which, when attached to expensive lines of merchandise, set off alarms positioned at the exit if they are not removed or desensitized. The removal and/or desensitization process requires specialized equipment, and to remove the "bug" without this equipment damages the merchandise.

Prevention measures are the best means available to the retailer for controlling losses due to shoplifting. Without good prevention, the retailer's reputation as "easy pickings" travels fast. While some retailers employ door guards, floor walkers, and mechanical detection devices, the best prevention measures are well-trained, observant employees. By training store employees in the following basic security measures, retailers create the best arsenal to combat shoplifting.

1. Be aware. Store employees should be aware of all individuals in their areas of responsibility. Anonymity is the shoplifter's friend. Suspicious individuals should be reported to the appropriate security personnel.

2. Be visible. Store employees should attempt to maintain a high profile in terms of visibility. Shoplifting opportunities are notably reduced in the shoplifter's mind when store personnel are readily visible.

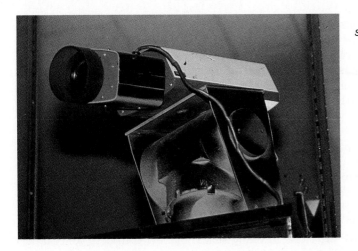

How is this type of security device used?

317

3. Be alert. Store employees should be watchful at all times for possible shoplifting activities. Regardless of their activities (selling, stocking, housekeeping), store employees should be alert to the actions of others in the department. The store employee who appears to be "on the lookout" will discourage all but the boldest of shoplifters.

4. Be available. Store employees should endeavor to serve all customers as promptly as possible. In situations where the store employee is busy with a customer and another customer is examining merchandise, the latter's presence should be acknowledged by saying, "I'll be with you in a minute." This acknowledgment will tend to discourage the shoplifter, while a customer interprets it as courteous and efficient service.[7]

5. Be organized. Store employees can reduce shoplifting opportunities and increase detection of shoplifting by being well organized. Shoplifting opportunities can be reduced by keeping a minimum amount of merchandise on open counters, returning all merchandise to its proper place after showing it to customers, keeping all high-value merchandise in secured display cases when not showing it, removing all merchandise from fitting rooms, and using a check-in and check-out system for all merchandise taken into a fitting room. Detecting shoplifting activities is easier when displays are neatly organized; then the likelihood of detecting missing merchandise is substantially increased. Messy, disorganized displays greatly hinder detection of missing items.

Shoplifter Apprehension and Prosecution

Approaching, apprehending, and prosecuting an individual for shoplifting is a tricky business. State and local laws differ concerning the apprehension and prosecution of shoplifters. A number of general rules are appropriate in dealing with any shoplifting situation.

Rule 1: Be absolutely certain. Before approaching or accusing an individual of shoplifting, the retailer should be as certain as possible that the individual has pilfered merchandise. "Be certain or risk a false arrest suit is a good rule to follow when catching a shoplifter."[8] Ideally, the person observing the pilferage should be able to identify both the pilfered items and where they were concealed.

Rule 2: Use trained personnel. Only trained personnel (e.g., security personnel or store manager) who are familiar with the legalities and techniques of apprehension should attempt to apprehend shoplifters. Store employees who observe actual pilferage of merchandise should notify the proper store security people and should keep the shoplifter in sight at all times to ensure that the pilfered merchandise is not paid for or discarded between the time of the theft and the apprehension by security personnel.[9]

Rule 3: Pick the right place. Good judgment is needed to know where to apprehend the shoplifter. In some cases it is best to wait until the shoplifter has left the store because (1) it can improve the store's legal case in prosecuting the shoplifter, and (2) it may avoid a scene or commotion in front of the store's legitimate customers who might misunderstand what is happening. In other cases, in-store apprehension is preferred when high-value merchandise is involved or when the shoplifter might successfully leave the store. In many states, the law considers concealment of merchandise an illegal act of shoplifting.

Rule 4: Make a positive approach.   Suspected shoplifters should be approached in a positive and firm manner; however, strong-arm tactics should be avoided. The Super Market Institute recommends the following approach:

> One of the common problems in confronting shoplifters is getting them to admit the theft. In most cases approaching the person with "Pardon me, but haven't you got an item you haven't reported?" will get good results. The customer may profess innocence, but if the manager can point out exactly where the item is hidden the guilty person will usually admit it and produce the item. Take advantage of the surprise element and act quickly and positively. If that doesn't work, asking whether the shoplifter would rather deal with the police will usually get results. Never let the customer you apprehend feel that there is a shadow of a doubt about the theft. Most shoplifters are scared to death when apprehended. Many of them are so embarrassed they will do what you ask to get out of there as fast as they can. Although a firm attitude at the start usually helps bring offenders to terms much more effectively than gentle talk, remember that your approach may call for extreme care as well as good judgment. Occasionally a shoplifter who is "cornered" will create an unpleasant disturbance in the presence of other customers, or may even have a heart attack.[10]

Rule 5: Observe legal rights.   In apprehending shoplifters the retailer must observe the suspect's legal rights. Undue harassment or force will eliminate any chance of successful prosecution. In fact, it might leave the retailer open to a lawsuit. Whenever possible, every aspect of the detection and apprehension should be witnessed by a third party.

Rule 6: Call the police.   The police, not the retailer, are duly authorized agents of the law. If the retailer decides to detain the suspect for any reason, the police should be called immediately. They have both the authority and experience to judge the legal ramifications of the situation.

Rule 7: Prosecute when warranted.   Opinions vary greatly as to when, who, and how often to prosecute. Most retailers agree that professional shoplifters should be fully prosecuted at every opportunity where evidence is sufficient for a reasonable chance of conviction. The prosecution of amateur shoplifters presents a more difficult decision. Many retailers like to examine the individual circumstances surrounding each case of amateur shoplifting. Other retailers feel that failure to prosecute amateur shoplifters simply encourages other amateurs to shoplift. In any case, the retailer should establish definite policies regarding when, who, and how often to prosecute.

EMPLOYEE PILFERAGE

Employee pilferage represents serious losses for many retailers. Employee theft accounts for approximately 44 percent of retail shrinkage.[11] It is not unusual for employee theft to result in losses exceeding those from all other forms of theft. Perhaps the single most important factor contributing to these losses is the retailer's belief that trusted employees do not and will not steal.

Recognizing the problem exists and understanding why and how employees pilfer are the first steps in developing a security program to detect and prevent losses from employee pilferage.

Pilferers: Types and Reasons

Employee pilferage takes one of two forms: the theft of merchandise and the theft of money. Both forms of pilferage are likely to occur in a variety of ways by any or all of the retailer's employees. Opportunity and need are the two most commonly cited factors responsible for the honesty or dishonesty of employees. If provided easy and continuous opportunities to pilfer, just about any employee could be expected to take advantage of the situation. What might start out as an occasional "bonus" candy bar could well turn into supplementary income programs of regular and systematic pilferage. By reducing the opportunity to pilfer, the retailer can go a long way to help keep honest employees honest. Some employees may think they need to steal to meet their basic financial obligations. Employees who are intentionally or unintentionally underpaid are prime candidates for "making up the difference" through a self-help program of pilfering. By assuring each full-time employee a "living" wage, the retailer can reduce, but not eliminate, the need factor in employee theft.

Employees usually can find some justification for their pilferage activities. Some employees justify their thefts by reasoning that "They can afford it," "It's a big outfit," "Everyone else does it," and "They'll never miss it." Other employees steal for personal reasons—"to get even" for what they believe to be unfair treatment, or "They owe me for all I have done for them." For the retailer, there are no good justifications, only costly ones. While the retailer can attempt to create a working atmosphere conducive to the well-being of both the employee and the firm, it cannot eliminate all of the potential employer/employee conflicts that might be used as justification for pilferage of either money or merchandise.

Pilferers: Devices and Techniques

Like most thieves, the employee who pilfers money and/or merchandise develops definite patterns or modes of operation (MOs). Based on these MOs, profiles can be developed that characterize the typical methods of employee pilferage. The most common profiles include the eater, the smuggler, the discounter, the dipper, the embezzler, the partner, and the stasher.

The Eater

The **eater** is *the employee who samples the retailer's food and beverage lines or supplements lunch with a soft drink or dessert.* Unfortunately, what starts out as a free snack often leads to a six-course feast. For the food store, restaurant, and cocktail lounge, the eater (or drinker) can literally eat up the profits. If the retailer permits employees to consume food and drink on the store's premises, it should only be allowed under clearly stated and highly restrictive policies (times, places, etc.). The retailer should never tolerate the occasional "freebie." The only "free lunch" should be one the retailer grants employees under specific and strict guidelines.

The Smuggler

The **smuggler** is *the employee who takes merchandise out of the store by whatever means are available.* Many retailers might be surprised to learn how much merchandise is carried out the back door in trash cans and bags. The smuggler also uses coats, lunch boxes, purses, and various other types of bags and packages to conceal and transport merchandise from the store's premises. Employees, like shoplifters, can prove to be quite innovative in their smuggling activities. One supermarket employee used hollowed-out pumpkins to smuggle expensive merchandise out of the store.

The Discounter

The **discounter** *feels entitled to give unauthorized discounts to friends and relatives.* By charging $10 for a $16 pair of slacks, the employee may satisfy a "special" customer but certainly not at a profit for the retailer. Other employees give their friends and relatives unauthorized discounts with free merchandise or "two for one" sales. The friend or relative who receives two for the price of one is sure to spread the word among other friends and relatives. Before long, the employee is in a very compromising position with few alternatives other than to quit the job. Unfortunately, before these employees realize their predicament, they may have cost the retailer a considerable amount of money as well as the goodwill of friends and relatives who were former customers.

The Dipper

The **dipper** is the store employee who *steals cash money by dipping into the cash register or mishandles cash in some other way,* such as making short rings, fraudulent refunds, or false employee discounts. A *short ring* occurs when the employee fails to ring a sale on the cash register or rings less than the purchase amount. In either case the employee pockets whatever money is left over from the transaction. An employee who engages in short rings is faced with two problems. The first is the bookkeeping problem of keeping track of how much money has been stolen. The second is how to conceal the money until it can be transported out of the store. Bookkeeping devices include keeping a mental record, using pen and paper, and counting various objects such as hairpins, matches, and pennies. The most common method of concealing the stolen money is to leave it in the cash register until it can be safely transferred to either a pocket, purse, shoe, or an accomplice. Regular occurrences of either shortages or overages are perhaps the best clue to possible short rings and the employee's inability to keep track of what has been pilfered.

Fraudulent refunds is the second method the dipper uses to steal money. By writing up refund tickets for merchandise that has not been returned, the dipper can pocket the entire amount of the refund. To use this method the dipper must have access to refund slips and the authority to issue refunds. *False employee discounts* also allow the dipper to pilfer cash. Using this method, the employee simply rings up a regular customer sale as an employee discount sale and pockets the difference. If employees are allowed a 10 percent discount, a $10 false employee-discount sale would net the dipper one dollar.

The Embezzler

The **embezzler** is *most often a highly trusted employee who takes advantage of that trust to divert the retailer's funds for either permanent or temporary use.* Obviously, a permanent diversion of funds is an outright theft; equally dishonest, and illegal, however, is the temporary diversion of funds for personal use. The employee who diverts either large sums of money for a short period of time or small sums of money for a long period of time can realize substantial gains (e.g., interest) from such activities. The retailer loses not only the income from these funds but also the opportunity to use them as capital for daily operations.

While listing all the numerous and sophisticated embezzlement schemes that bilk retailers is beyond the scope of this discussion, it should be noted that any employee who has access to the retailer's books and records has the opportunity to juggle them. Some of the simpler embezzlement schemes are (1) adding the names of relatives and fictitious employees to the payroll and collecting "their" multiple paychecks; (2) creating dummy suppliers and falsifying purchase orders, then collecting for fictitious shipments; (3) accepting kickbacks from suppliers for inflated purchases; (4) padding expense accounts; (5) falsifying overtime records; and (6) using company supplies and facilities (postage stamps, long distance calls, etc.) for personal use.

The Partner

The **partner** is a store employee who *does not actually pilfer the merchandise or money, but who supplies outside individuals with information (such as security procedures) or devices (such as keys) that increase the likelihood of successful theft.* In return, the store employee receives a cut of the pilfered merchandise. As previously mentioned, the store employee can become a partner in a number of different shoplifting schemes. There are times, for example, when a store employee can become an unintentional partner simply by engaging in loose talk about the store and its security. While such talk is not illegal, it can substantially reduce the security of the retail store.

The Stasher

The **stasher** is the store employee who hides merchandise in a secure place within the store. Later in the selling season when the merchandise is marked down for clearance, the employee removes the stashed merchandise from its hiding place and purchases it at the discount price. Essentially, the store employee has pilfered the difference between the original price of the merchandise and the discounted price.

Pilferage: Detection and Prevention

To combat employee pilferage, the retailer's security program should include (1) creating a security atmosphere, (2) using security personnel, and (3) establishing security policies.

Creating a Security Atmosphere

One of the most effective methods of controlling employee theft is to create a general store atmosphere in which not even the slightest degree of dishonesty is tolerated and where honesty and integrity are rewarded. The first step in creating a security atmosphere is to stop employee theft before it starts. By carefully screening employees before they are hired and by properly training them after they are employed, the retailer can reduce the number of dishonest employees in the store. Some retailers require each prospective employee to take a polygraph (lie-detector) test as a prerequisite to being hired. Such tests are subject to various state laws regarding their use, while in some states they are prohibited altogether or their use is severely restricted.

The second step in creating a security atmosphere is for management to set the example. By engaging in dishonest or questionable behavior, the manager sets the tone for an atmosphere that can lead to employee pilferage. If the manager can munch a lunch on the house, why can't the employee? And if the manager is not subject to various security measures, why should employees tolerate them?

A third step in creating a security atmosphere is to create a work environment free of unnecessary temptation. By establishing and enforcing good security policies, opportunities for employee theft can be substantially reduced. Many retailers hold awareness-raising seminars for managers to assist them in identifying theft opportunities.

Finally, an important step toward creating a security atmosphere is to establish an environment that makes employees think they are trusted and respected members of a team. By being aware and interested in employees' problems, needs, and aspirations, the retailer can develop a personal relationship that encourages the employees' honesty and loyalty.

Using Security Personnel

To detect, discourage, and prevent employees from pilfering, some retailers use several types of security personnel. Stationing *uniformed guards* at employee entrances/exits and requiring employees to check in and out of the store reduce opportunities for removing merchandise from the store. The threat of search on a random basis can serve as a major deterrent to employee theft. Retailers also use **undercover shoppers** to check on the honesty of employees. *Posing as a legitimate customer, an undercover shopper can often detect the activities of the eater, the discounter, and the dipper.* By informing store employees that such undercover security personnel are present in the store, the retailer has activated an effective preventive measure.

Additional security measures include **silent witness programs** that *reward employees with cash for anonymous tips on theft activities of other employees.* Tips are transmitted to a third party, who relays the information to the employer.

Establishing Security Policies

Retailers have established a number of store security policies to control employee theft. The following list of policies is aimed at controlling the activities of employee pilferers.

1. All packages, bags, trash cans, and other devices for concealing merchandise are subject to unannounced random inspection.
2. All store employees (including management personnel) will enter and leave the store by designated entrances and exits.
3. All customers' discounts must be specifically approved by the store manager.
4. All sales must be registered and each customer must be given a sales receipt.
5. All customer returns and refunds must be approved by the department or store manager. Each refund slip must be cosigned by both the store employee making the refund and the department or store manager.
6. All sales involving employee discounts must be approved by the store manager.
7. All cash registers and cash boxes are subject to regularly scheduled checks as well as random unscheduled checks.
8. All records (sales, purchase, expense, etc.) are audited on a regular and random basis.
9. All sales personnel are assigned individual cash draws and are responsible for their security.
10. All refund slips, sales slips, price tags, and other recording instruments are sequentially numbered and assigned to the store employee who, in turn, is responsible for their proper use.
11. All employee purchases must be made during regular working hours.

12. All locks are changed periodically and new keys issued only to authorized personnel.
13. All employee purses, handbags, lunch boxes, packages, and coats will be kept off the sales floor and out of the stockroom. Central locker facilities will be provided for their security.
14. All store facilities, supplies, and equipment are to be used for store business only. Personal use of such facilities, equipment, and supplies is forbidden.
15. All employees are forbidden to accept any favor, gift, or other unauthorized consideration for any reason from any supplier.
16. All employees are responsible for keeping accurate records on all transactions.
17. All payments above a specific limit require a countersignature.
18. All employees caught pilfering will be fired and prosecuted.

While not all these policies are appropriate as stated to all retailers, each retailer should somehow deal with each of the issues they address.

Pilferers: Apprehension and Prosecution

The same rules apply in approaching, apprehending, and prosecuting employee pilferers as apply for shoplifters. These rules include: (1) be absolutely certain, (2) use trained personnel, (3) pick the right place, (4) make a positive approach, (5) observe legal rights, (6) call the police, and (7) prosecute when warranted. Many security experts strongly recommend, as a store policy, the prosecution of employee pilferers.[12]

SUPPLIER PILFERAGE

In developing a store security program, the retailer should remember that suppliers have some of the same security problems with dishonest employees as the retailer does. Therefore, it is prudent to take security precautions against pilfering by supplier representatives. The retailer is very vulnerable to pilfering activities of delivery personnel. These activities include (1) **short counts**—*delivering fewer items than were listed on the purchase order and signed for on the invoice*—and (2) **merchandise removal**—*stealing merchandise from receiving, checking, stocking, and selling areas*. In the latter case, dishonest delivery personnel have readily accessible concealment devices, such as empty boxes, delivery carts, and bulky work clothes. Retailers can use numerous security requirements and procedures to reduce and eliminate pilferage by supplier personnel, some of which are listed here.

1. Establish a receiving area (preferably in the rear of the store) for accepting all incoming merchandise.
2. Supervise all deliveries made directly to the sales floor and/or stockroom.
3. Limit the number of entrances to the receiving area and secure them with locks, alarms, surveillance equipment, etc.
4. Control entry and exit to the receiving area by restricting the area to authorized store personnel only or to individuals who are under the direct supervision of authorized employees.
5. Inform all delivery personnel that they and their equipment are subject to random inspection while they are on the store's premises.
6. Check all incoming shipments using one of the many available checking procedures (to be discussed in Chapter 18).

7. Document all incoming shipments as to contents, weight, size, condition of shipment, and any other information pertaining to the supplier, the shipment, and conditions of acceptance.
8. Accept only shipments from suppliers that agree to make necessary adjustments resulting from inaccurate, damaged, or otherwise unacceptable merchandise (in cases where the shipment cannot be immediately checked and inspected).
9. Avoid collusion between supplier personnel and store personnel by developing adequate auditing procedures.

All of these security measures can help the retailer reduce supplier pilferage.

BAD CHECKS

Accepting checks in exchange for merchandise has become an essential part of most retailers' service offering. Accepting bad checks, however, is not part of that service. A bad check is, of course, not honored for payment when the retailer presents it to the designated bank. The retailer's security program must include safeguards against accepting worthless checks and appropriate procedures for recovering losses resulting from such exchanges.

Bad Checks: Types and Reasons

In exchange for merchandise, the customer may present a number of different kinds of checks: personal, two-party, payroll, government, blank, counter, and travelers'. A *personal check* is one drawn on the customer's personal account, made out to the store, and written and signed by the customer. A *two-party check* is a check issued by one person to a second person (the store's customer), who presents it to the retailer (by endorsing it) as payment for merchandise. A check issued by an employer to an employee for services rendered constitutes a *payroll check.* Various federal, state, and local government agencies issue checks for a variety of reasons. *Government checks* are issued to government employees and recipients of tax refunds, pensions, welfare payments, and veterans' benefits. A *blank check* is, as the name implies, a blank form that provides space for the customer to fill in the name and address of the bank, the account number, the amount and date of the check, and the customer's signature. *Counter checks* are checks banks issue to depositors for funds withdrawn from their accounts. Banks also issue (sell) *travelers' checks* for predetermined amounts that the customer must sign at the time of purchase and countersign when cashing them at the store.

Any of these checks can represent a bad check. Bad checks can be stolen and falsely endorsed, written on bank accounts with insufficient funds, and written on nonexistent or closed bank accounts. Also, a check can be bad if the customer stops payment on the check, or intentionally or unintentionally fills it out incorrectly, or the bank simply does not accept a particular type of check (e.g., a blank check). Given this number of possibilities for accepting a bad check, the retailer must carefully develop detection and prevention measures.[13]

Bad Checks: Detection and Prevention

It is virtually impossible to avoid some bad checks. By initiating proper detection and prevention measures, however, the retailer can keep bad check losses at a minimum. This section discusses three ways the retailer can detect and prevent bad checks.

Inspect Checks

Clues to worthless checks are often contained on the checks themselves. By carefully examining each check not only for fraudulent information but for simple, honest mistakes in writing, the retailer can help avoid accepting checks that are intentionally or unintentionally bad. For most retailers, the following guidelines should be observed in accepting and cashing checks:

1. Do not accept checks on nonlocal banks unless clear identification of the customer can be made. Then use extreme caution.
2. Do not accept nondated checks.
3. Do not accept postdated checks.
4. Do not accept checks with a date more than 30 days old.
5. Do not accept two-party checks.
6. Do not accept checks on which the numerical amount does not agree with the written amount.
7. Do not accept checks that are not written legibly.
8. Do not accept checks with written-over amounts.
9. Do not accept counter checks.
10. Do not accept checks in excess of the amount of the purchase.
11. Do not accept payroll checks on which the company's name is stamped or typed. It should be a printed check.
12. Do not accept payroll checks on an unknown company.
13. Do not accept payroll checks unless they are endorsed exactly as the name appearing on the face of the check.
14. Do not accept checks over an established maximum amount unless you can positively identify the customer.

When the customer is well known, strict adherence to these guidelines may not be necessary, though only the store manager should make exceptions. Once the retailer has determined that the check is okay, it is then necessary to determine whether the customer offering the check is the right person (see Figure 11–2).

Require Identification

No check should be accepted without proper identification. Many retailers require at least two pieces of acceptable identification. Driver's licenses, automobile registration cards, credit cards, and employment identification cards are most accepted by retailers. In some cases, retailers will not cash checks unless the customer has at least one piece of identification with a current photograph. While no identification is foolproof, certain pieces of identification are especially suspect because they are easy to forge or to obtain under false pretenses. Business cards, library cards, and club or organization cards are especially poor identification documents. It is important not only to require identification, but to *record* pertinent information from the identification *on the check itself.* Many retailers use a rubber stamp to imprint a form on the back of the check. As a final step, the authorized personnel should carefully compare the signature on the check with that appearing on the identification documents.

Establish a System

The retailer should establish a system that clearly states check-cashing policies. Employees and customers alike should be informed of the types of checks that are acceptable and the conditions under which the retailer will accept them. Some retailers have created check-cashing systems that employ various recording devices

FIGURE 11–2
Spotting the bad check
artist

- Does the age of the customer match with the identification? Birthdate on ID seem correct for the customer? Is customer with a driver's license old enough to drive?

- Does the sex shown on the ID match the customer? Does the name on check and identification match the sex of the presenter?

- If photo identification is shown, does the picture look reasonably like the customer, allowing for aging and cosmetic changes, such as hair coloring?

- Is the customer nervous? Or appear to be in a rush? Does the customer hesitate when signing the check or when asked to verbally repeat the address or phone number?

- Is the customer shopping in a "high risk" merchandise department? These might include: jewelry; consumer electronics; appliances; and other merchandise categories where goods can be sold quickly for cash. Your own store's experiences will help you determine where you are most at risk.

- Is the transaction too rapid for the type of merchandise selected? For example, does the customer fail to ask about warranty, delivery, layaway, or other questions which frequently arise in connection with the merchandise being purchased?

Source: *Check Acceptance Policies and Procedures,* Credit Management Division, National Retail Merchants Association, New York, 1984, 9.

and registration methods. Some retailers, such as Richway, use *camera systems* to take a simultaneous photograph of the check-cashing customer, the identification, and the check. Other retailers use the *thumbprint system,* which imprints a customer's thumb on the back of the check. If the check is bad, later identification is possible. With the *registration system,* retailers request that their customers register identification information at some prior time with the store's credit or customer-service office. Once registered, the customer receives a check-cashing ID card. All pertinent information concerning the customer is gathered at the time of registration and verified by the central office. When paying by check, the customer simply shows the ID to the salesclerk who records the ID number on the check and compares the check signature with the ID signature.

BAD CREDIT CARDS

Sales charged to stolen, fictitious, cancelled, and expired credit cards cause substantial losses for retailers each year. To reduce these costs, a good policy for retailers is to exercise as much care in accepting credit cards as in cashing checks. In accepting both third-party credit cards (bank cards, entertainment cards, etc.) and the store's own credit cards, the following procedures are recommended:

1. Check credit card against "stolen card" list.
2. Check credit card against "cancelled card" list.
3. Check credit card expiration date.
4. Compare signature on credit card with that on credit slip.
5. Obtain approval of all credit card sales above a specific amount.
6. Fill in all required information on each credit slip (date of purchase, itemized list and amounts of purchases, sales tax charges, and total amount of purchases).
7. Submit all credit card sales for immediate processing.

A more detailed discussion of credit sales and the procedures for handling them is presented in Chapter 16—The Service Mix.

Retail stores are prime targets for burglary and robbery because they are less secure than most other businesses.[14] This lack of security results from carelessness on the part of some retailers as well as from the general nature of the retailing business (which literally requires some isolated locations, evening hours, exposed cash in registers, etc.). While retailers can do little to alter the nature of their business, they can initiate security measures to make their stores a less desirable target for burglary and robbery and reduce their harmful impact. **Burglary** is *defined as "any unlawful entry to commit a felony or a theft, even though no force is used to gain entrance."*[15] **Robbery** is *"stealing or taking anything of value by force, or violence, or by use of fear."*[16] Given the steady increase in the number of burglaries and robberies in recent times, the retailer's security program must incorporate careful measures to prevent such crimes.

Preventing Burglary

Burglars usually operate under the cover of darkness after the store is closed. They gain entry to the store by picking locks, forcing doors or windows open, using duplicate keys, or by hiding in the store until it closes. Most security measures are directed at (1) preventing the burglar from gaining entry to the store, (2) securing all high-value merchandise, and (3) informing police and other security personnel of all successful and unsuccessful attempts at entry. Most retailers use locks and lights to discourage attempts at entry, safes to secure valuables, and alarms to warn police.

Security Locks

Good security locks offer protection in a number of ways. First, they discourage the less-skilled burglar from attempting entry. Second, they are generally "pick proof," thereby requiring the burglar to make a forced entry, which is more risky because of the time it takes, the noise it makes, and the evidence it leaves. Third, by making it necessary for the burglar to use force in entering the store, the retailer is protected by insurance since most burglary insurance policies require evidence of forced entry.

The retailer can use several types of security locks. The pin-tumbler cylinder lock has three to seven pins that make it very difficult to force open. Most experts believe that it offers the best protection when it has five or more pins. Dead-bolt locks are pick-proof locks in which a rod slides into a hole in the door jamb. It has no spring and can be opened only from the inside by sliding the bolt out of its hole in the door jamb with a key. Double-cylinder dead locks are door locks that require a key to open from both sides. They are most often used with glass doors since they prevent the burglar from breaking the glass and reaching inside to unlock the door. The double-cylinder dead lock aids in detecting "break outs"—the burglar who hides inside the store until after closing time, and then attempts to break out with stolen merchandise. Not being able to unlock the door from the inside without the key, the burglar must make a forced exit, increasing the chances of detection and apprehension. It is not enough to use good security locks; they must be installed by a professional locksmith, and the keys to each lock must be safely guarded against duplication and theft.

Security Safes

Some skilled burglars can gain undetected entry to the store regardless of the preventive measures the retailer uses. However, these highly skilled burglars are usually interested only in high-value merchandise or cash. By using a burglar-resistant safe, the retailer can create another major obstacle to the burglar's attempted theft. The safe should be well lighted, usually near the front of the store, and located where it is visible from the outside. To boost security, the retailer can bolt the safe to the floor or set it in concrete. Even when the retailer has a reasonably secure building and safe, it can further discourage burglary attempts by "keeping the cupboard bare." All excess cash should be banked every day and only the bare minimum of operating cash for opening the store on the following day should be kept in the safe overnight. The "word" on the bareness or fullness of the retailer's safe will get around. A bare cupboard is not worth the burglar's efforts and the associated risks.

Security Alarms

Security alarms serve a number of purposes. They discourage some burglars from attempting entry, they detect the entry of those who do not know they are there or who do not know how to circumvent them, and they notify the police or a private security agency that an illegal entry has been made. The silent, central-station burglary alarm system gives the retailer the best protection. As opposed to the local bell alarm, the silent alarm alerts the police or security service without alerting the burglar. By using a silent alarm, the retailer increases the likelihood of apprehending the burglar and retrieving the stolen merchandise, since the burglar is not alerted and the police have time to react. Retailers can choose from several alarm sensing devices: (1) radar motion detectors, (2) invisible photo beams, (3) ultrasonic sound detectors, and (4) vibration detectors.

In addition to locks, safes, and alarms, retailers located in high-crime areas might also consider the use of heavy window screens (removable metal grating),

What is the purpose of this ultrasonic sound detector?

burglar-resistant glass (shatterproof), watchdogs, private security patrols, and security lights. Savings from fewer thefts and reduced insurance premiums could more than offset the additional cost of these security measures.

Handling Robbery

While burglary can result in substantial losses of money and merchandise, robbery is far more serious since it always holds the potential of loss of life as well as property. By definition, robbery is a violent crime in which one person uses force, or the threat of it, against another individual. Perhaps the most disturbing aspect of robbery is that many robberies are committed for very small sums of cash or merchandise, often by individuals who are extremely unstable (e.g., drug addicts). By training employees to cope with robbers and by limiting the opportunities for robbery, the retailer can help to ensure the well-being of store personnel and to reduce property losses.

Training Employees

The retailer's first concern in developing any robbery security program is to train store employees to handle the actual robbery situation. The following procedures and instructions can help:

1. Remain as calm as possible.
2. Make no sudden moves.
3. Reassure robbers that they can expect full cooperation in every way.
4. Make no attempt to be a hero by trying to apprehend the robber.
5. Give robbers whatever they want when they want it.
6. Attempt to make mental notes on the robber's description (height, weight, hair and eye color, complexion, voice, clothing, and any other distinguishing characteristics).
7. Remain stationary until the robber has completely exited the store's premises. Then call the police and the store's management.
8. Talk only to the police and store manager regarding the robbery situation and the robber.

Using these recommendations may save an employee's life.

Reducing Risks

Several preventive measures might well reduce the number of robbery attempts as well as losses suffered from robberies. To reduce the risk of robbery, the retailer should heed the following guidelines:

1. Keep as little cash in each cash register as possible and remove excess cash from the register frequently.
2. Maintain a minimum level of operating cash in the store. Bank all excess cash.
3. Use armored-car service for making bank deposits. If impractical, vary bank trip routes and times.
4. Keep store safes locked at all times. Do not leave a safe open during operating hours.
5. Use two persons to open and close the store—one for the actual opening and closing of the store and the other as an outside security lookout.

6. Exercise extreme caution when someone asks you to make an emergency opening during hours the store is closed. Before going to the store, call the police and make sure they will be there for the unscheduled opening.

These measures can help to reduce the potential loss of an employee's life and the loss of cash and merchandise.

Establish the Defense

Antirobbery defense systems are directed at discouraging and apprehending the robber. Some of the more common robbery-protection systems include panic buttons, till traps, video systems, and cash-control devices.[17] Panic buttons are hidden alarm devices that silently alert the police or security company that a robbery is in progress. Most security experts recommend that buttons be placed in several locations to increase the chances of their being activated. Till traps are devices installed in cash register drawers that trigger a silent alarm when the last dollar bill is removed from the till. In-house video systems are highly visible closed-circuit TV monitors trained on the cash register. They serve the dual purpose of discouraging potential robbers and providing police with pictures of an actual robbery. "Where there is money, there are robberies."[18] To correct this situation, retailers can install cash-control devices that accept currency deposits and dispense cash on an irregular basis. By keeping small amounts of cash in the till, robbery is discouraged.

SUMMARY

Store security calls for developing the necessary safeguards for the store and its merchandise by initiating programs for detecting and preventing losses resulting from shoplifting by customers, pilfering by employees and suppliers, passing of bad checks and credit cards, and burglary and robbery.

Shoplifting is the theft of merchandise by customers or individuals posing as customers. Basically, two types of shoplifters exist: those who steal from need and for psychological reasons (amateurs) and those who steal for a living (professionals). Several shoplifting devices and techniques can be enumerated: the booster, the diverter, the blocker, the sweeper, the walker, and the wearer. The best means of detecting shoplifters is good observation—knowing what to look for and where to look. In addition to well-trained personnel, retailers use convex mirrors, one-way mirrors, observation towers, closed-circuit television, and electronic "bugs" to aid in the detection process. Retailers should apprehend shoplifters in full compliance with the law and prosecute shoplifters when conditions warrant it.

Store employees do steal; losses from employee pilferage exceed those from shoplifting. Opportunity and need are the two most critical causes for this type of theft. The eater, the smuggler, the discounter, the dipper, the embezzler, the partner, and the stasher all are types of dishonest employees who pilfer merchandise and money. The retailer can reduce this form of theft by creating an atmosphere of honesty, by using security personnel, and by establishing strict security policies.

The retailer's security program must also extend to procedures for controlling pilferage by suppliers, for guarding against bad checks and credit cards, and for reducing opportunities for burglary and robbery.

KEY TERMS AND CONCEPTS

shoplifting	the carrier	the partner
amateur shoplifters	the self-wrapper	the stasher
professional shoplifters	the price changer	undercover shoppers
the booster	pilferers	silent witness programs
the diverter	the eater	short counts
the blocker	the smuggler	merchandise removal
the sweeper	the discounter	burglary
the walker	the dipper	robbery
the wearer	the embezzler	

REVIEW QUESTIONS

1. What are the three basic ways by which shoplifting is accomplished?
2. How does a juvenile shoplifter differ from an occasional shoplifter?
3. Why do kleptomaniacs steal?
4. What distinguishes a low-class professional shoplifter from a high-class professional?
5. Describe the shoplifting devices used by the booster.
6. How does the diverter distract the attention of sales personnel?
7. Who are walkers?
8. How does the price changer secure unauthorized price reductions?
9. What are the eight basic rules for spotting shoplifting activities?
10. What are the major devices retailers use in observing and detecting shoplifters?
11. Where should shoplifters typically be apprehended?
12. When should retailers prosecute shoplifters?
13. What are the two most commonly cited factors for explaining the dishonesty of employees?
14. Who is the discounter?
15. How does the dipper dip? Discuss the three types of dipping.
16. What are the three types of security personnel used in detecting and preventing employee theft?
17. What are the two most common methods of supplier pilferage?
18. Which types of check-cashing systems might the retailer use to record or register check cashers?
19. How does burglary differ from robbery?
20. How do good security locks offer protection against burglary?
21. What antirobbery defense system might the retailer use to help discourage or apprehend robbers?

ENDNOTES

1. Addison H. Verrill, *Reducing Shoplifting Losses,* Small Marketers Aids No. 129 (Washington: Small Business Administration, 1967), 3.
2. M. E. Williams, "For Retailers, 'tis the Season to Be Wary," *USA Today,* 16 November 1984, 1B.
3. Verrill, *Reducing Shoplifting Losses,* 4.
4. Mercantile Stores Department Manager *Training Manual* (New York: Mercantile Stores Company, Inc.), 104.
5. Verrill, *Reducing Shoplifting Losses,* 2.
6. Mercantile Stores, *Training Manual,* 104.
7. Ibid., 108.

8. Verrill, *Reducing Shoplifting Losses,* 7.
9. Super Market Institute, *How to Control Pilferage and Bad Check Losses* (Chicago: Super Market Institute), 5.
10. Ibid.
11. Larry Hansen, "Thwarting the In-House Thief," *USA Today,* 16 November 1984, 1B.
12. National Retail Merchants Association, *Apprehending and Prosecuting Shoplifters and Dishonest Employees* (New York: National Retail Merchants Association), 29.
13. Discussion based on Leonard Kolodny, *Outwitting the Bad Check Passer,* Small Marketers Aids No.

137 (Washington: Small Business Administration, 1969).
14. Discussion based on S. J. Curtis, *Preventing Burglary and Robbery Loss,* Small Marketers Aids No. 134, (Washington: Small Business Administration, 1968).
15. Ibid., 2.
16. Ibid.
17. See David Rowe, "Robbery," *Video Store* 5 (July 1983), 32–33.
18. Ibid., 32.

RELATED READINGS

Abend, Jules. "Shortages." *Stores* (June 1982), 48–57.
——————. "Why, What, and How Some Steal." *Stores* (January 1982), 71–77.

Budden, Michael C., and Miller, Joseph H., Jr. "District Attorneys Look at Shoplifting: An Empirical Analysis." *Marketing Comes of Age, Proceedings.* David M. Klein and Allen E. Smith, eds. (Southern Marketing Association, 1984), 190–94.

"Chains Fortifying Shrinkage Defenses." *Chain Store Age* (January 1981), 53–57.

Cooper, Donald; Clare, Donald; and Korgaonkar, Pradeep. "Retailers' Evaluation of Electronic Article Surveillance (EAS) System: An Exploratory Study." *Developments in Marketing Science, Proceedings.* N. K. Malhotra, ed. (Academy of Marketing Science 1985), 238–41.

Deevey, Robert J. "Modifying Store Layout to Minimize Shrinkage." *Retail Control* (January 1985), 10–20.

Evans, Brian A. "Preventing Internal Theft." *Retail Control* (September 1982), 21–29.

French, Warren A.; Crask, Melvin R.; and Mader, Fred H. "Retailers' Assessment of the Shoplifting Problem." *Journal of Retailing* 60 (Winter 1984), 108–15.

Fugate, Douglas L. "A View on the Use of Parental Influence to Prevent Juvenile Shoplifting." *Evolving Marketing Thought for 1980, Proceedings.* J. H. Summey and R. D. Taylor, eds. (Southern Marketing Association 1980), 76–79.

Goldfinger, Jack I. "Pilferage Loss Resulting in Short Shipments." *Retail Control* (November 1982), 31–32.

Grossman, John. "Fighting the Five-Finger Discount." *American Way* (November 1980), 72–76.

Guffey, Hugh J., Jr.; Harris, James, R.; and Laumer, J. Ford, Jr. "Shopper Attitudes toward Shoplifting and Shoplifting Preventive Devices." *Journal of Retailing* 55 (Fall 1979), 75–89.

Klokis, Holly. "Confessions of an Ex-Shoplifter." *Chain Store Age Executive* (February 1985), 15–18.

Lewison, Dale M.; DeLozier, M. Wayne; and Robbins, Ray B. "Retail Thieves: By Their Tricks Ye Shall Know Them." *Developments in Marketing Science, Proceedings.* V. V. Bellur, ed. (Academy of Marketing Science 1981), 313.

Miller, Joseph H., Jr., and Budden, Michael C. "Biorhythm and Shoplifting: An Empirical Investigation." *1985 Educators' Proceedings.* R. F. Lusch et al, eds. (American Marketing Association 1985), 56–58.

Rosen, Mark, and Zingman, Mitchell S. "Coping with Bad Checks: Legal Remedies." *Retail Control* (November 1983), 25–29.

Schulz, David. "How Much is Enough?" *Stores* (June 1985), 72–75.

Summey, John; Raveed, Sion; and Richardson, Neil. "Shoplifting; Why, Where, How Often, and Possible Deterrents: A Randomized Response Measurement Approach." *1979 Proceedings.* R. S. Franz et al, eds. (Southern Marketing Association 1979), 232–33.

"Taking the High-Tech Approach to Pilferage." *Chain Store Age Executive* (February 1985), 55–56.

Whalen, Bernie. "Threshold Messaging Touted as Antitheft Measure." *Marketing News* (March 15, 1985), 5–6.

Wilkes, Robert. "Fraudulent Behavior by Consumers." *Journal of Marketing* 42 (October 1978), 67–74.

PART FOUR
Market Selection: Evaluating Retail Markets

Outline

THE MARKET

THE MARKET-AREA IDENTIFICATION PROCESS

Selecting Identification Criteria
Identifying Market Areas

THE MARKET-AREA EVALUATION PROCESS

Standard Evaluation Sources
Standard Evaluation Methods

THE MARKET-AREA SELECTION PROCESS

Objectives

- Appreciate the considerable impact that the retail-location decision has on all other aspects of the retailer's business

- Characterize a market and describe its components

- Explain why retail location is a problem of market segmentation

- Employ standardized criteria to delineate and describe regional and local market areas

- Evaluate regional and local market areas by sales potential and operational suitability

- Select regional and local market areas capable of meeting the sales and operational needs of a particular retailing firm

12

Analyzing Regional and Local Markets

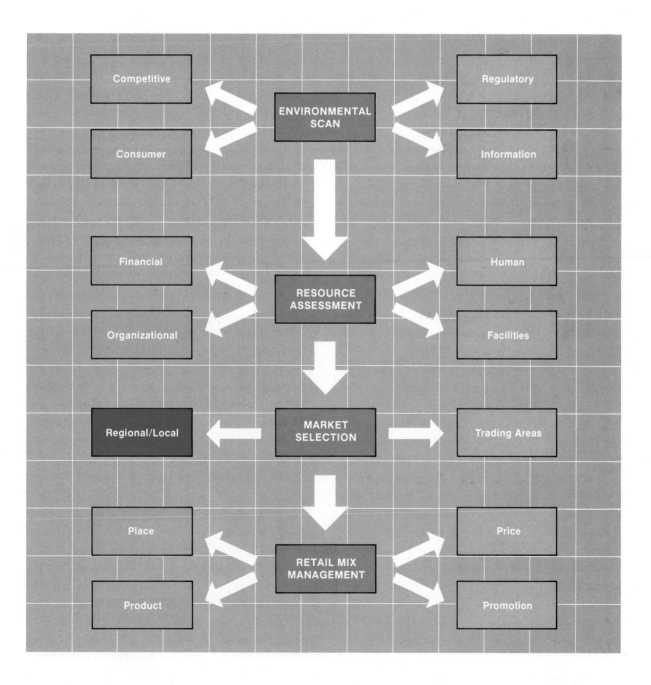

The importance of location decisions cannot be overstated. The location decision perhaps is the single most important operational decision a retailer makes because of its tremendous impact on virtually all other operational decisions. A retailer that selects a poor location will always be at a competitive disadvantage. To overcome a poor location (a struggle that is not always successful), the retailer must make substantial adjustments in the product, price, and promotional mixes. These adjustments usually are expensive to implement, though, and therefore adversely affect the firm's profits. On the other hand, if the retailer selects a good location, the chances of success are greater because it allows greater flexibility in developing the product, price, and promotional mix. Given the long-term commitment, the substantial financial investments, and the effects on the retailing mix, the retailer must consider the location problem extremely carefully.

This chapter discusses the nature of markets and how they can be subdivided into more meaningful and operational segments. It also covers how regional and local markets are identified, evaluated, and selected.

THE MARKET

Fundamental to an understanding of the market and its behavior is the definition of a market. In this discussion, the term market has a precise meaning and usage. As shown in Figure 12–1, a **market** is *a group of actual and potential buyers at a given time and place whose actions lead to an exchange of goods and services or create the potential for an exchange*. In essence, a market is a buying population and its behavior.

Buying populations can be classified into one of two groups: consumer markets or organizational markets. **Consumer markets** are *composed of individuals and/or households that are the ultimate consumers of goods and services*. Ultimate consumers are those who purchase goods and services for their own personal use or for use by members of their household; as such, ultimate consumers define the retail market and account for the bulk of sales made by retailers. **Organizational**

FIGURE 12–1
A market definition

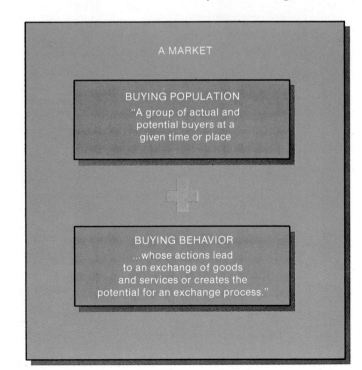

A MARKET

BUYING POPULATION
"A group of actual and potential buyers at a given time or place

BUYING BEHAVIOR
...whose actions lead to an exchange of goods and services or creates the potential for an exchange process."

FIGURE 12–2
The market segmenta-
tion view of the total
market

markets are *composed of industrial firms, resellers, and governments that represent intermediate consumers of goods and services.* This market accounts for the non-retail sales made by retailers. This discussion is limited to the consumer market and its impact on retail location.

Retail location is a problem of **market segmentation**—*the act of viewing the total market as a collection of heterogeneous consumers and the process of subdividing the total market into consumer market segments.* Market segmentation starts with the belief that identifiable differences exist among various consumers of a product and that these differences are relevant to their buying and store-patronage behavior. The goal of market segmentation is to identify smaller, homogeneous submarkets that exist within the larger, heterogeneous mass market (see Figure 12–2). Stated differently, the market segmenter views the market as consisting of several demand curves—one for each market segment or consumer subgroup.

The major tasks associated with segmenting markets appear in Figure 12–3. By identifying, evaluating, and selecting retail market and trading areas, the retailer is in fact segmenting the total mass market on the basis of geographic dimensions. This chapter examines the basic identification, evaluation, and selection methods for analyzing regional and local markets. Figure 12–4 outlines the basic procedures for analyzing regional and local markets. Identifying, evaluating, and selecting retail trade areas is discussed in the next chapter, Assessing Retail Trading Areas.

The market-area identification process involves delineating and describing general retail market areas. There are two major steps in this process: (1) selecting market-area identification criteria and (2) identifying regional and local markets.

**THE MARKET-
AREA
IDENTIFICATION
PROCESS**

FIGURE 12–3

Market-segmentation
tasks

IDENTIFYING MARKET SEGMENTS

Task 1: To disaggregate total market by
identifying significant differences
between consumers and their
buying behavior

Task 2: To regroup disaggregated consumers
into homogeneous submarkets by
identifying meaningful commonalities
between consumers and their buying
behavior

EVALUATING MARKET SEGMENTS

Task 3: To determine whether the identified
market segments are meaningful

Task 4: To determine whether the identified
market segments are serviceable

SELECTING MARKET SEGMENTS

Task 5: To determine which market segments
offer the most attractive opportunities

Task 6: To determine which market segments
offer the most feasible opportunities

Selecting Identification Criteria

Retailers use several criteria to identify retail market areas. Two of the more common criteria are market potential and retail operations. Using the **market potential approach,** *retailers select criteria that reflect the support (in sales, number of customers, etc.) that a geographic area will provide a given retail operation.* The **retail operations approach** is one in which *the retailer examines factors that might enhance or limit its operations.*

The Market Potential Approach

In using the market potential approach, the retailer identifies segmenting criteria specific to its class of goods (i.e., retailer-specific criteria). Whereas certain segmenting criteria are very useful to one retailer, the same criteria may be of no use to another retailer. The major areas from which retailer-specific criteria are drawn are (1) population, (2) housing, (3) buyer behavior, and (4) physical environment.

Population characteristics are the most often used segmenting criteria. As illustrated in Figure 12–5 (p. 342), a retailer can describe any geographic area (state, county, city, etc.) using any combination of population characteristics. Although total

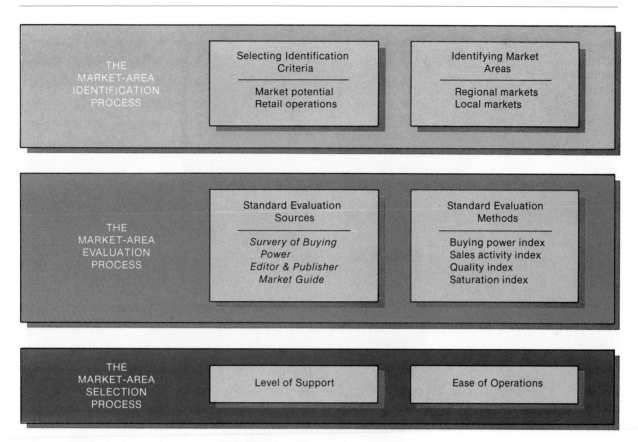

FIGURE 12–4

The basic procedure for analyzing regional and local markets

population figures and population densities are of primary importance to retailers, the retailer can get a more detailed profile of a market by examining education, age, income, sex, occupation, religion, race, nationality, and family characteristics data. The retailer's purpose is to match a market's population characteristics to the population characteristics of people who desire its goods and services.

Retailers can get population and demographic data from the *Census of Population* (already described in Chapter 6). For more current data, retailers can consult the *Current Population Survey,* which provides estimates and projections on a variety of population characteristics. Also, several federal agencies (such as the Labor Department), state and local governmental agencies, and private and trade organizations collect, analyze, and disseminate population information on a regular basis.

Housing characteristics are a very important criterion for some retailers in determining profitable markets. Hardware retailers, home-improvement centers, and home-furnishings stores are examples of retailers that rely on data on the housing market. Of particular interest to these retailers are figures on home ownership, housing quality, type of construction, number of rooms, and the nature of plumbing and heating facilities. Figure 12–6 (p. 343) illustrates some of the more important housing characteristics that retailers use to identify lucrative market areas. To locate these data, retailers turn to the *Census of Housing* and the *Annual Housing Survey.* Also, the Census Bureau produces several special publications, such as *Current Housing Reports* and *Current Construction Reports.* At the local level, retailers examine building permits to determine economic activity affecting their businesses.

FIGURE 12–5
Using population characteristics as criteria in identifying market areas

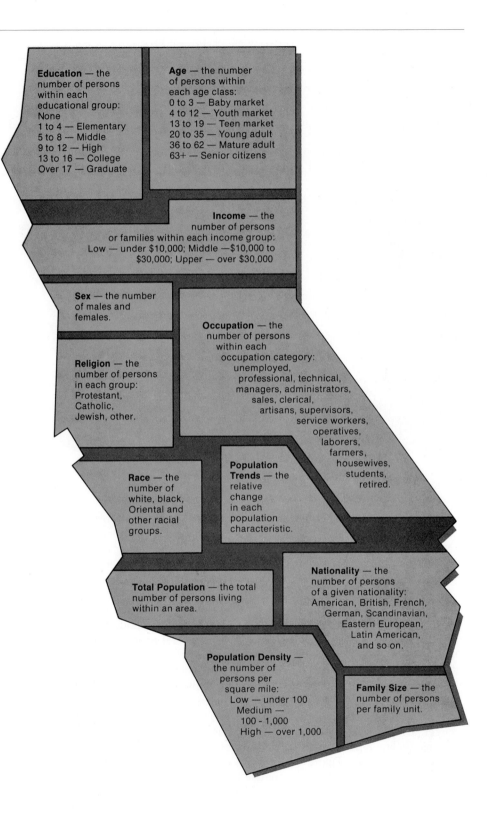

Education — the number of persons within each educational group:
None
1 to 4 — Elementary
5 to 8 — Middle
9 to 12 — High
13 to 16 — College
Over 17 — Graduate

Age — the number of persons within each age class:
0 to 3 — Baby market
4 to 12 — Youth market
13 to 19 — Teen market
20 to 35 — Young adult
36 to 62 — Mature adult
63+ — Senior citizens

Income — the number of persons or families within each income group: Low — under $10,000; Middle —$10,000 to $30,000; Upper — over $30,000

Sex — the number of males and females.

Occupation — the number of persons within each occupation category: unemployed, professional, technical, managers, administrators, sales, clerical, artisans, supervisors, service workers, operatives, laborers, farmers, housewives, students, retired.

Religion — the number of persons in each group: Protestant, Catholic, Jewish, other.

Race — the number of white, black, Oriental and other racial groups.

Population Trends — the relative change in each population characteristic.

Nationality — the number of persons of a given nationality: American, British, French, German, Scandinavian, Eastern European, Latin American, and so on.

Total Population — the total number of persons living within an area.

Population Density — the number of persons per square mile:
Low — under 100
Medium — 100 - 1,000
High — over 1,000

Family Size — the number of persons per family unit.

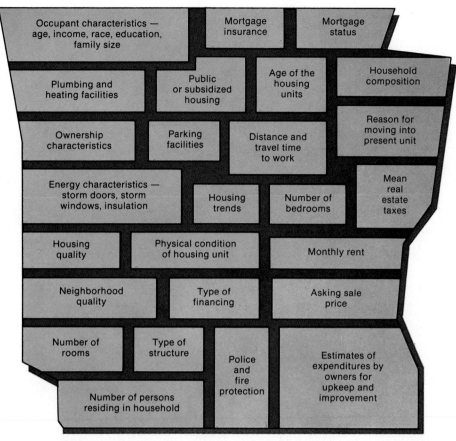

FIGURE 12–6
Using housing charac-
teristics as criteria in
identifying market
areas

The figure contains the following labeled boxes:

- Occupant characteristics — age, income, race, education, family size
- Mortgage insurance
- Mortgage status
- Plumbing and heating facilities
- Public or subsidized housing
- Age of the housing units
- Household composition
- Ownership characteristics
- Parking facilities
- Distance and travel time to work
- Reason for moving into present unit
- Energy characteristics — storm doors, storm windows, insulation
- Housing trends
- Number of bedrooms
- Mean real estate taxes
- Housing quality
- Physical condition of housing unit
- Monthly rent
- Neighborhood quality
- Type of financing
- Asking sale price
- Number of rooms
- Type of structure
- Police and fire protection
- Estimates of expenditures by owners for upkeep and improvement
- Number of persons residing in household

Buyer behavior characteristics also are extremely useful in identifying and segmenting retail markets, as Figure 12–7 illustrates. Among such characteristics are store loyalty, consumer psychographics, store-patronage reasons, usage rates, lifestyles, sought benefits, and purchase situations. Although buyer behavior characteristics provide retailers with the most useful information to make location decisions, the data are neither easily measured nor easily obtainable. The various dimensions of buyer behavior were discussed in detail in Chapter 4; a review of that chapter with a view toward the segmentation process would be most instructive.

Another way retailers measure market potential is to examine an area's physical environment. Some people live in the "snow belt," others in the "sun belt"; some live in the deserts of the west, others in the humid, subtropical areas of the southeast; some in the highlands of the Rocky Mountains, others in the flatlands of the Great Plains. Differing characteristics of these physical environments influence people's choices of clothing, housing, foods, and forms of recreation, as well as their preferences among many other products, services, and activities. Certainly, physical environment influences *when* consumers buy products or use services and thereby determines when markets occur—or at least when they are most profitable. Since *physical environment characteristics* are easily measured and obtained, they are excellent criteria for segmenting markets for many products such as skis, suntan lotion, lip balm, fertilizer, and so forth.

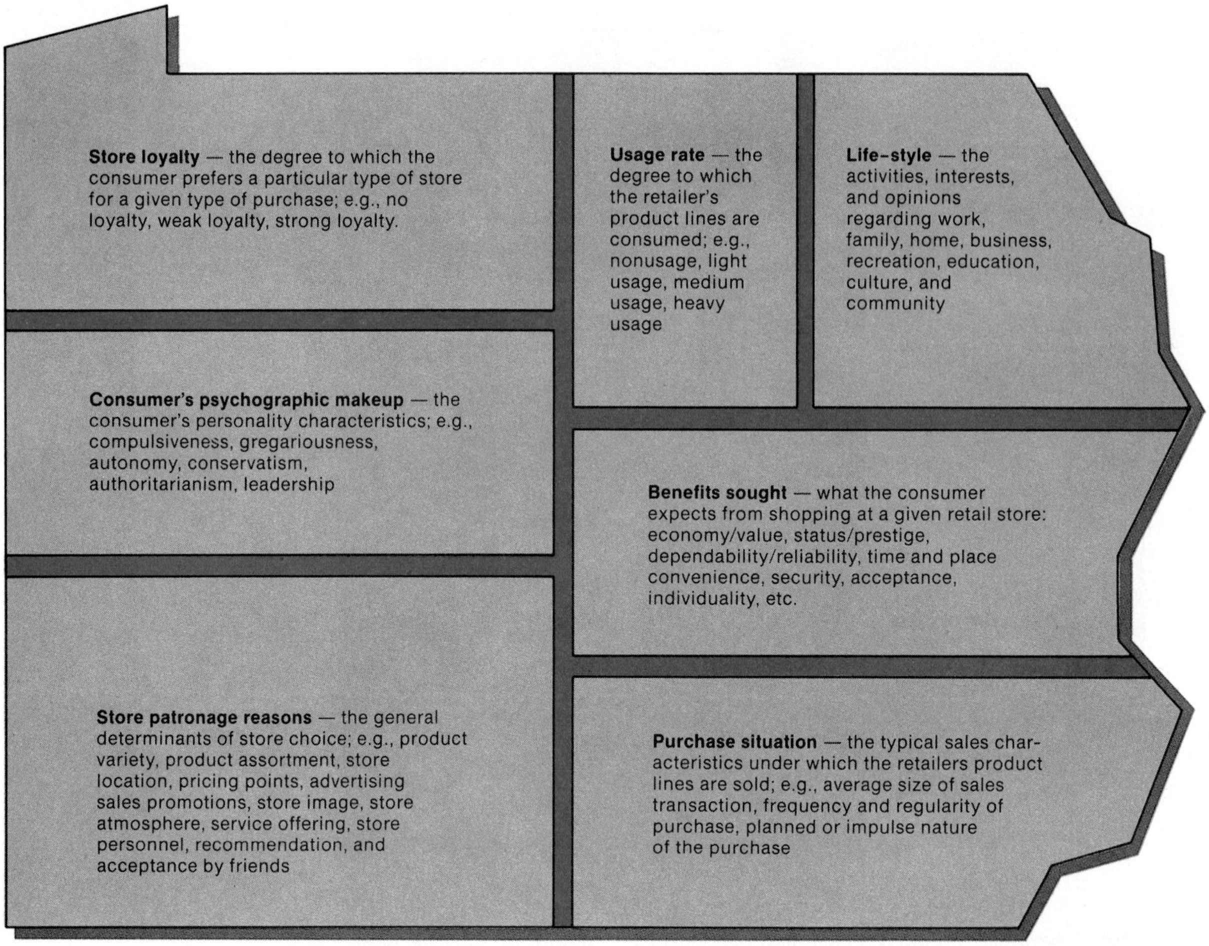

FIGURE 12–7
Using buyer behavior characteristics as criteria in identifying market areas

Store loyalty — the degree to which the consumer prefers a particular type of store for a given type of purchase; e.g., no loyalty, weak loyalty, strong loyalty.

Usage rate — the degree to which the retailer's product lines are consumed; e.g., nonusage, light usage, medium usage, heavy usage

Life–style — the activities, interests, and opinions regarding work, family, home, business, recreation, education, culture, and community

Consumer's psychographic makeup — the consumer's personality characteristics; e.g., compulsiveness, gregariousness, autonomy, conservatism, authoritarianism, leadership

Benefits sought — what the consumer expects from shopping at a given retail store: economy/value, status/prestige, dependability/reliability, time and place convenience, security, acceptance, individuality, etc.

Store patronage reasons — the general determinants of store choice; e.g., product variety, product assortment, store location, pricing points, advertising sales promotions, store image, store atmosphere, service offering, store personnel, recommendation, and acceptance by friends

Purchase situation — the typical sales characteristics under which the retailers product lines are sold; e.g., average size of sales transaction, frequency and regularity of purchase, planned or impulse nature of the purchase

The Retail Operations Approach

In identifying market areas, the location specialist must take into account the nature of the retailer's operations. A profitable retail store is one that not only serves a consumer market of high potential, but also operates in a market that allows for efficiency and competitiveness. Several realities that directly influence the retailer's chances to operate successfully are (1) distribution, (2) competition, (3) promotion, and (4) legal considerations.

Distribution factors. A crucial problem all retailers have is getting the product into the store. This problem area involves inventory control. As described in Chapter 1, overstocks increase carrying costs, whereas stockouts cause lost sales and customer ill will. The retailer must consider transportation and handling costs, delivery time, and reliability of delivery services. Information concerning these factors influences how the retailer identifies potential market areas.

To identify potential market areas, the retailer also must consider the location of suppliers, delivery practices of suppliers, and the market area's ability to support distribution facilities. For retailers, speed and reliability in getting merchandise are key factors in deciding upon a market area. Therefore, the *location* of suppliers is important in evaluating a market area.

Competitive factors. Competition is an operational reality for all market areas regardless of how they are identified. Therefore, it is imperative that the retailer take into account the reality of the competition when identifying market areas. Competition varies from one area to another according to the type, number, and size of competitors.

Retailers either directly or indirectly compete with each other. The type of competition is based on the retailer's product offering. **Direct competitors** *offer the same type of products under similar merchandising programs (price, place, service, promotion).* As an example, K Mart is a direct competitor of Venture. **Indirect competitors** *offer similar products, but under different merchandising conditions.* For example, a women's boutique selling women's apparel competes *directly* with other specialty retailers selling the same product lines; however, the same store competes *indirectly* with department, discount, variety, and catalog retailers. Thus, retailing analysts must determine types of competition in delineating a market area.

The **level of competition** a retailer faces in any market area, which also requires consideration, is *a function of the number and size of competitors within that area.* Generally, a good market area contains only a few small competitors, as opposed to an area affording either a large number of small competitors or a few large competitors. To determine the level of competition, the retailer can turn to several excellent government sources of information, such as *Census of Retail Trade, Census of Selected Services,* and *County Business Patterns.* Also, private trade sources such as *Chain Store Age* and *Progressive Grocer* provide information on the activities of specific types of retailers.

Promotional factors. A retailer that depends heavily upon promotional activities can identify market areas by analyzing the advertising media within each market area and the behavior of competitive retailers. Media selectivity and coverage are both important. With respect to **media selectivity,** the retailer should look at **geographic selectivity,** *"the ability of a medium to hit a specific geographic area such as a city or a region,"*[1] and **class selectivity,** *"the ability of a medium to reach specific kinds of people who possess certain common traits."*[2] In other words, most advertising media are "targeted" to serve certain geographical areas and to appeal to certain groups of consumers. For example, a radio station serves only the geographical area defined by its transmitting power, antenna system, frequency on the dial, and other local conditions. If the station happens to follow a "pop" format, certain listeners will be attracted by the format.

Media coverage is *the number of people an advertising medium reaches in a given market area.* More precisely, coverage is "the ability of a medium to reach a certain percentage of homes in a given area or persons within a particular market segment."[3] For example, a newspaper might provide excellent coverage in one county by reaching 90 percent of the homes, but cover only 30 percent of the homes in a distant county.

Perhaps the simplest way to identify retail market areas by broadcasting stations is to use data generated by a research firm. The Arbitron Co. has identified **areas of dominant influence** (ADIs), which it defines as

> a geographic market design which defines each market, exclusive of another, based on measurable viewing patterns. The ADI is an area that consists of all counties in which the home market stations receive a preponderance of viewing. Each county in

the U.S. (excluding Alaska) is allocated exclusively to only one ADI. There is no overlap.

A similar research firm, the A. C. Nielsen Co., has created **designated marketing areas** (DMAs). A DMA *represents a geographic area best served by selected broadcasting stations.* Both ADIs and DMAs are supported with a wealth of audience information from their respective research firms and the individual broadcasting stations.

Newspaper circulation is still another criterion by which retailers can identify market areas. Newspaper circulation falls into three categories. They are *city zone, retailing zone,* and *all others.* Frequently, the city and retailing trade zones are classified as a newspaper's primary circulation markets, whereas the "all others" category (usually small towns and rural areas) represents outside circulation or secondary markets.[4] While newspapers generally are considered local media, there is considerable flexibility in the circulation patterns relative to the geographic areas they cover. The zoned editions of some large metropolitan newspapers, together with many small local newspapers, allow the location specialist considerable freedom in identifying the market areas. This freedom is described by one retail advertising specialist:

> Small city newspapers, suburban weeklies, and community-centered newspapers everywhere tend to develop circulation patterns that closely approximate the natural trading area of individual stores. Large metropolitan papers spread over huge areas—central city plus the vast suburban fringe—and tend to price themselves out of the market for one-store retailers' advertising. To make advertising more economical for merchants whose pattern of store location does not justify use of the vast total circulation available, large papers may divide up their circulation into zones and offer zoned editions (often just on certain days of the week) targeted on a specified segment of their metropolitan area.[5]

Magazine circulation is yet another media characteristic that can be used to identify retail markets. Because magazines generally have a smaller impact than newspapers on the retailer's promotional program, their use in market-area identification is limited. Nevertheless, the geographic editions of many nationally circulated magazines provide a convenient means of identifying market areas. Retailers can buy circulation in whatever markets they wish by buying space in *sectional* or *regional* editions.[6]

Legal factors. The final group of criteria that retailers use to identify market areas are state and local legal requirements. Laws regulating the use of land and the conduct of business have become important factors in determining whether a particular geographical area is a potentially viable market. Land-use regulation in the form of *zoning restrictions, building codes,* and *signing requirements* has a direct bearing on the success of a retailer's operation. State and local taxes on the retail firm's *real estate, personal property,* and *inventory* can have an equally important impact on the retailer's cost of operation. Retailers must also meet certain *licensing requirements* to conduct a business. License availability and cost are necessary considerations. Additional limitations imposed on retailers can include legal constraints that affect *store hours, local minimum wage laws,* and *Sunday closing laws.* Information on legal/political constraints can be obtained from the appropriate state and local regulatory agencies.

Identifying Market Areas

Market areas come in all sizes, shapes, and descriptions. The dimensions of a market area depend upon several factors, such as population density and media coverage. This section discusses the two general problems facing the location specialist: (1) how to identify regional markets and (2) how to identify local markets. These two problems and their particular components are illustrated in Figure 12–8.

Identifying regional markets consists of determining the "right region" of the country and the "right part of the region." The geographic extent of a regional market is not fixed, and could include either one state or a multistate area. For many small, independent retailers, the regional market problem is not a concern. They often have narrowed their choice of regions to the ones in which they currently live or work. For the chain organization or for the retailer that intends to expand, however, the starting point in the location-decision process is identifying regional and subregional markets.

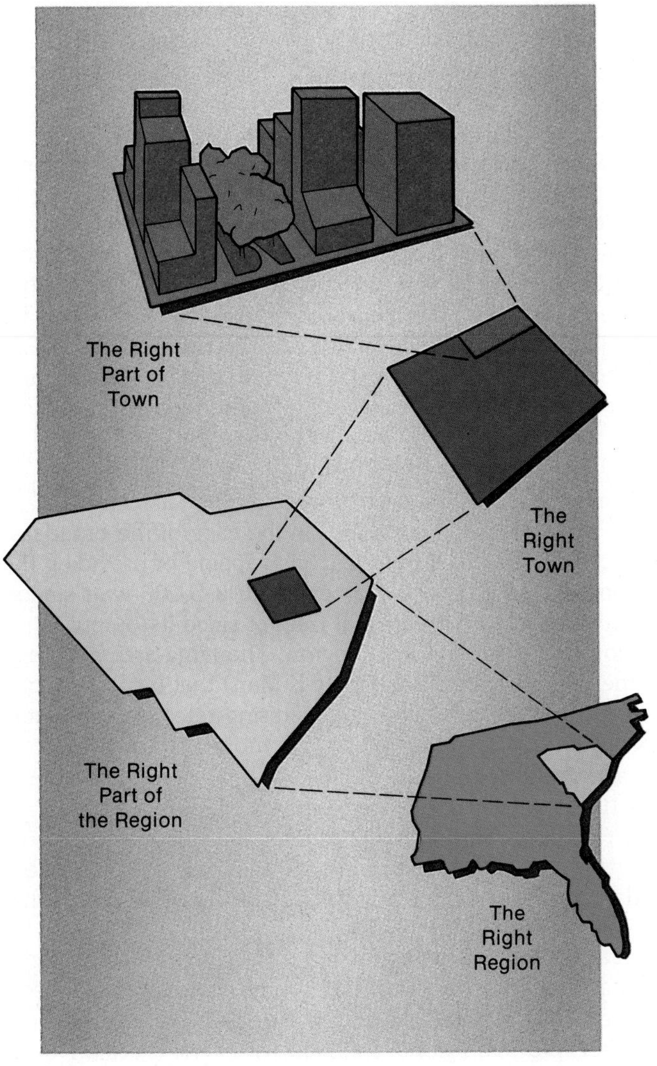

FIGURE 12–8

The identification of regional and local market areas

The Right
Part of
Town

The
Right
Town

The Right
Part of
the Region

The
Right
Region

347

As shown in Figure 12–8, the local market problem is how to find the "right town" and the "right part of town." For our purposes, "town" refers to any size urban center that can be associated with a particular regional or subregional market.

The following sections present several selected examples of regional and local market areas. In identifying regional and local market areas, the location specialist has the choice of either creating an original market-area classification or using one of the many standard classifications. By creating its own market-area classification scheme, the retailer can tailor the market area to the needs of the firm. By using a standard classification scheme, on the other hand, the retailer has the advantage of a lot of information already available about market areas.

Regional Markets

Most business organizations have regionalized the United States some way. One regional classification with which we are all familiar is the division of the United States into the New England, Mid-Atlantic, South Atlantic, East North Central, East South Central, West North Central, South West Central, Mountain, and Pacific states. This regional classification scheme suggests that people perceive social, cultural, and economic differences among various parts of the country. The retailer should try to identify and analyze these perceived differences.

Regional markets based on census areas. Perhaps the most widely used regional classification system is one developed by the U.S. Census Bureau. As shown in Figure 12–9, the Census Bureau divides the United States into nine census regions. The relative importance of this classification scheme is evident from the fact that many public and private organizations use this system as the organization framework for their information reporting and analyzing process. Two private organizations that use this classification are of particular interest to the retailer: *Sales and Marketing Management*'s annual publication of the *Survey of Buying Power,* and Standard Rate and Data Service's monthly rate and data publication, *Spot Television.*

Regional markets based on communication areas. Regional markets can be identified on the basis of various types of media coverage. In the case of the broadcast media, a 50,000-watt radio station like WGN in Chicago is capable of providing the retailer with multistate regional coverage. On the other hand, a 5,000-watt station like KVI in Seattle/Tacoma covers only a subregional market since its output is restricted to the western portion of the state of Washington. The large-area coverage by WGN is appropriate to the multiunit retailer (such as K Mart) that has operations in each of the states WGN covers. Assuming lower advertising rates, a small retail operation finds the less extensive coverage typified by KVI more appropriate.

Print media also provide good operational definitions of regional and subregional markets. Figure 12–10 shows the multistate regional coverage of the *New York News.* By dividing the total New York regional markets into 27 zones (a process referred to as "zoned insert marketing"), the regional market is effectively segmented into subregional markets. Figure 12–10 discusses some of the operational advantages of subregional market-area segmentation.

Magazines also recognize the value of regional and subregional classifications. *Newsweek,* for example, has segmented the U.S. market into five regions—Western, West Central, East Central, Eastern, and Southern—and three of these regional markets are segmented further into subregional markets—Western (Pacific Northwest, Pacific Southwest, and California), Southern (Southwest, Southeast, Texas, and Florida), and Eastern (Mid-Atlantic and New England). Regional and subregional

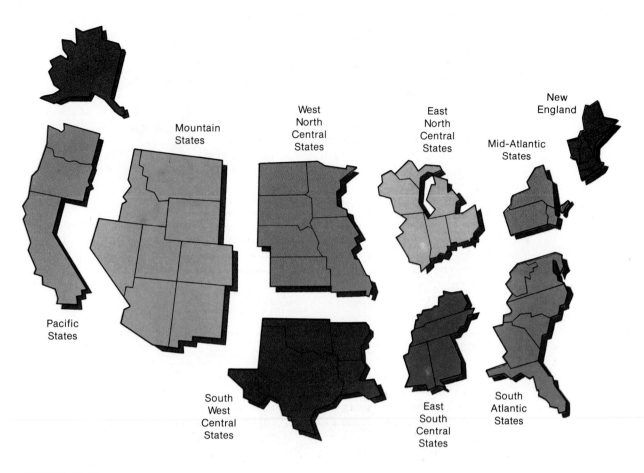

Census regions as defined by the Census Bureau

issues of magazines such as *Newsweek* provide regional and local retailers with an opportunity to advertise in prestigious publications to reach an upper-bracket audience within a selective geographic area.

Local Markets

Finding the "right town" and the "right part of town" constitutes the local market identification problem. Faced with an array of thousands of urban centers, the retail location specialist must utilize some organized method to identify local markets. Several methods of local market identification are discussed here.

Function markets: The right town.   Urban centers often are classified on the basis of the types of economic activities they support. While most urban centers are multifunctional, one or two functions (such as manufacturing and retailing) tend to dominate a local economy. Most cities have "acquired a distinction for the real or reputed dominance of one function or another."[7] Some examples of real and perceived dominance are Detroit for auto manufacturing, Miami for resort and retirement activities, Washington, D.C., for governmental functions, and Berkeley for educational activities. These urban centers are known as "functional" markets based

349

Introducing 27 small bites of the Big Apple.

For a small businessman, New York can be a big place. A little too big, perhaps. Even for a businessman who's not so small.

So, the New York News, New York's largest newspaper, has taken it upon itself to cut the New York market down to size.

More accurately, we've cut it down to sizes. 27 of them.

It's as if New York were made up of 27 small towns, each with its own demographic character. Now an advertiser can have a preprint inserted in The Sunday News and have that preprint delivered only to the market or markets vital to him.

We call this new marketing concept ZIM.

Who's ZIM?

ZIM stands for Zoned Insert Marketing. It marries the ever increasing power and popularity of inserts with the precision and flexibility of direct mail. So, while we may call it ZIM, we think you'll call it terrific.

ZIM vs. the P.O.

When you insert a message in an envelope and send it through the mail, you can hardly count on it reaching all your customers at virtually the same time. You can count on that with ZIM, however.

And you can count on spending less money too. For ZIM costs just a fraction of what direct mail costs.

You spend less, you waste less.

With ZIM you can buy the full run of The Sunday News. Any combination of zones, or just one zone. That's anywhere from a circulation of 2½ million to as little as 35,000.

You can match your distribution. And speak only to those New Yorkers who speak your language. So you're not throwing money away on people who'll throw your message away.

And you're not biting off more of the Big Apple than you can chew.

In other words, ZIM lets you be anything you want in the Big Apple. From small potatoes to a big cheese.

ZIM lets you test. Anything.

You can test copy with ZIM by running different strategies in similar zones.

You can test zones with ZIM. By running the same copy strategies in different zones.

You can also change copy according to local conditions and regulations.

Add all that to the couponing capabilities inherent in inserts and you have a testing device that truly makes the grade.

Us and ZIM.

It's appropriate that the newspaper that can give you more New Yorkers than anyone else can also give you as few as you want.

But that's not the whole News story.

We can give you the highest level of penetration in the city, the highest level of penetration in the suburbs. Or both.

And with our Instant Market Data service with its on-line computer facility, we can tell you an awful lot about our readers by income, occupation and product use.

What's more, we can particularize census data by zip code information for any zone or combination of zones.

So, not only do we offer you the use of ZIM, but we can also help you make even better use of it.

You and ZIM.

A phone call to your News sales rep or our research department (212-682-1234) can get you a specific breakdown for each zone by population, circulation and percent of household coverage.

A phone call to Jim (ZIM) Ruddy (212-682-1234) can get you information on the maximums, the minimums, the costs and the variety of insert sizes, from catalogs on down. Also, the uses, applications and combinations available with ZIM.

Maybe ZIM is just the thing to help keep you from getting chewed up in the Big Apple.

SUNDAY NEWS
NEW YORK'S PICTURE NEWSPAPER
Today... you really need it!

FIGURE 12–10

Regional and local markets as delineated by newspaper circulation (Courtesy of New York Daily News, Inc.)

on the functions they perform. By classifying urban centers, the location specialist can obtain a broad overview of each center as a potential retail market. Urban centers tend to take on a certain character or atmosphere reflected by how the population makes its living.

ABC markets: The right town. A second method of classifying urban centers is to group them according to sales volume potential. Many retailing operations employ population and demographic analysis to determine each market's sales potential for a particular line of merchandise or a given type of retail operation. Based on their sales volume potential, urban centers can be classified in descending order as either "A," "B," or "C" markets. The exact definition of what constitutes an A, B, or C market varies from one retailing organization to another, since each retailing organization uses different decision variables. Nevertheless, the purpose of identifying various-sized markets is to help the retailer adjust the business format to meet the consumption needs of a particular market. By identifying different-size markets, the retailer can tailor the product, place, price, and promotional strategies to satisfy customer needs and to increase the firm's profitability.

A markets are capable of providing the highest levels of support for retailers. Typically, A markets have the sales potential to support large operating units and/or a multiple number of operating units. J. C. Penney, for example, defines A markets as those "where the sales potential for 'department store type merchandise' exceeds $100 million in sales."[8] In an A market, the J. C. Penney organization often operates several large (100,000–200,000 + square feet), full-line department stores, as well as several smaller, limited-line soft-goods outlets. The former usually are located in regional shopping malls, whereas the latter are associated with community shopping centers and strip developments. Because of the tremendous potential of an A market, the retailer can develop a wide range of products from a broad assortment to a highly specialized one. In addition, A markets provide retailing environments that can support pricing, advertising, and personal-selling strategies that range from discount to prestige pricing, mass to direct advertising, and store to in-home selling.

From Baton Rouge, Louisiana, to Lancaster, Ohio, many medium-size cities offer adequate sales potential for a wide variety of retailing activities. While lacking the sales potential of the A market, the B market is still strong for most types and sizes of store operations. The J. C. Penney organization defines a B market as having the "potential of racking up 'department store type merchandise' sales of between $25 million and $100 million."[9] Typically, a B market would not warrant a full-line department store operation unless special circumstances prevailed in the market. Usually, a B market calls for an extensively stocked soft-goods operation with limited lines of hard goods.

The C market is basically the small-town market. The potential of these smaller C markets is considerable: many of the country's retailing giants in recent years have targeted these markets as major areas for expansion. This once-secure market domain of the small, independent retailer has felt the impact of entry by such large multiline chain retailers as K Mart, Wal-Mart, and TG&Y. Towns having potential sales of "department store type merchandise" of less than $25 million are classified by Penney's as C markets, but J. C. Penney management does not necessarily view C markets as small. According to the company, "J. C. Penney started out in small towns, is still in small towns, and is planning to go into more small towns."[10]

Intraurban markets: The right part of town. For most retailers, there are literally "right" and "wrong" parts of town. An urban center is not simply a homogeneous mass; rather, it is a heterogeneous grouping of people and activities that can have a profound effect on a retailer's operations. The location specialist must determine the internal structure of the local market and select areas within the city that increase the retailer's chances for success.

The internal structure of urban centers is composed of many recognizable areas, including the downtown and the suburbs; shopping centers and strip shopping developments; ethnic and racial areas; residential, commercial, and industrial areas; and low-, middle-, and high-income areas. To facilitate our understanding of the internal structure of cities, we shall examine several theories of urban structure based on *land-use patterns*. Over time, these patterns emerge as certain activities (such as commercial, industrial, and residential) tend to dominate the land use of particular areas in and around the urban center. To describe these patterns, retailing analysts have proposed several theories; of these, the three most recognized are (1) the concentric zone theory, (2) the sector theory, and (3) the multiple-nuclei theory.

Concentric zone theory *asserts that the internal structure of a city develops as a series of concentric zones, each characterized by a particular set of activities.* As illustrated in Figure 12–11a, there are five basic zones; each one "under conditions of normal city growth tends to extend its area by invading the next outer zone. The process has been likened to the outward movement of ripples when one tosses a stone into a still pond."[11]

The first zone, the *central business district (CBD),* is the center of a city's social and economic life. Typically, the zone is divided into the inner and outer CBD. The land-use pattern of the inner CBD usually consists of several identifiable districts, each supporting a predominant economic activity. Some of the more common districts are retail, financial, hotel and entertainment, government, and general office complex. The outer CBD is composed of commercial businesses that cannot afford

FIGURE 12–11
Theories of urban structure

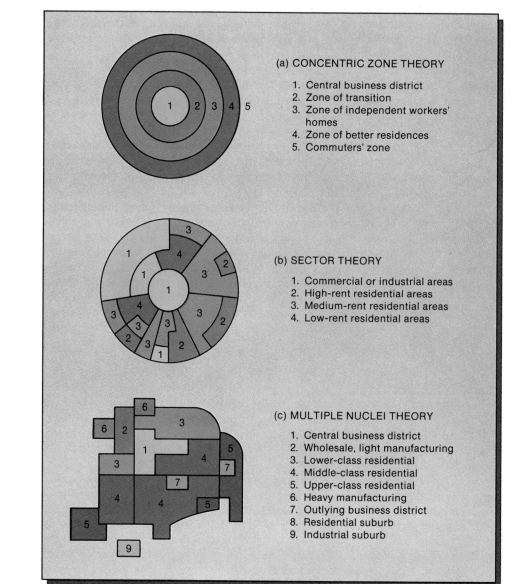

(a) CONCENTRIC ZONE THEORY

1. Central business district
2. Zone of transition
3. Zone of independent workers' homes
4. Zone of better residences
5. Commuters' zone

(b) SECTOR THEORY

1. Commercial or industrial areas
2. High-rent residential areas
3. Medium-rent residential areas
4. Low-rent residential areas

(c) MULTIPLE NUCLEI THEORY

1. Central business district
2. Wholesale, light manufacturing
3. Lower-class residential
4. Middle-class residential
5. Upper-class residential
6. Heavy manufacturing
7. Outlying business district
8. Residential suburb
9. Industrial suburb

the high rent associated with the inner CBD. Businesses typically in the outer CBD include wholesaling, "low rent" retailing, and transportation activities.

As the name implies, the *zone of transition* is in a state of transition, from residential to nonresidential land use. The encroachment of light and heavy industry results in deteriorated housing and the formation of slum areas. "The inner belt of the zone is likely to be a business and light manufacturing district, and the outer boundary a ring of retrogressing neighborhoods from which, as people become more prosperous, they escape into Zone 3."[12] Low incomes and high crime rates make this zone undesirable for most retailers.

The *zone of independent workers' homes,* a blue-collar, residential area, is populated by low- to middle-income groups that often cluster in ethnic neighborhoods. Although their housing is usually of the moderate, low, or tract type, these people have considerable local pride in maintaining a well-kept neighborhood. With few exceptions, commercial activities tend to be limited to neighborhood corner retailers and small retailing clusters.

Middle-class Americans dominate the *zone of better residences.* The population of this zone is likely to include white-collar workers (independent businesspeople, professional people, clerical staff, and salespersons). At strategic points, business clusters are interspersed with single- and multiple-family dwelling units. A major shopping mall is likely to be found at the intersection of primary traffic arteries.

The *commuters' zone* is composed of many small cities and towns that ring a central city. Often referred to as "bedroom" or "dormitory" cities, these small urban centers house largely middle- and higher-income people who commute to work in the central city. Spot development of commercial and industrial land use is found primarily along major traffic arteries.

A second theory of land-use patterns is the **sector theory,** which hypothesizes that *residential land-use patterns are essentially "wedges or sectors radiating from the center of the city along the lines of transportation."*[13] Whereas the theory deals primarily with residential land use, commercial and industrial land use also are incorporated into the sector concept. The wedge-shaped land-use patterns hypothesized in this theory result from rent patterns.

> The highest rent areas of a city tend to be located in one or more sectors of the city. There is a gradation of rentals downward from these high rental areas in all directions. Intermediate rental areas, or those ranking next to the highest rental areas, join the high rent area on one or more sides, and tend to be located in the same sectors as high rental areas. Low rent areas occupy other entire sectors of the city from the center to the periphery.[14]

Because people from different rent areas tend to migrate, a continually changing pattern of wedge-shaped areas occurs. The key to these changing patterns is the high-rent areas. As people from the high-rent areas move outward from the central city and away from industrial and commercial areas, the city is pulled in the same direction. The result of this migration is the evolution of residential areas from high- to middle- to low-rent areas, as shown in Figure 12–11b.

A third theory of land-use patterns is the **multiple-nuclei theory,** which *states that there are several identifiable centers of activities within a city, with each specializing in a given activity such as retailing, wholesaling, government, or education.* The development of these centers does not necessarily correspond to a set pattern. In fact, any number of land-use patterns can develop. Figure 12–11c illustrates one possible land-use pattern.

In summary, no single theory can fully explain the internal structure of urban centers, but studies have demonstrated that each of these theories has some validity in practice. By examining land-use maps of urban areas, the retailer should try to determine whether any one of these or possibly another theory applies to the cities under consideration. If so, the retailer can recognize land-use trends that should help in making a sound location decision.

THE MARKET-AREA EVALUATION PROCESS

Once the retail location specialist has identified potential market areas, each must be *evaluated*. The identification process itself should have provided considerable insight into the various capabilities of each area to support a given type of retail organization. The evaluation process involves collection and analysis of data pertinent to a particular retailer's operation. Although we could discuss many evaluation tools (such as averages, ratios, percentages, indexes), our discussion in the following sections is limited to some of the standard evaluation sources and methods.

Standard Evaluation Sources

In evaluating retail market areas, retailing analysts primarily use two major sources: the *Survey of Buying Power* and the *Editor & Publisher Market Guide*. Both contain vast amounts of data that retailers use to estimate a retail market's potential sales.

Survey of Buying Power

The ***Survey of Buying Power*** is an annual publication compiled by the editors of Sales and Marketing Management *magazine*. Surveys are divided into two parts. Part I consists of four sections: (1) survey highlights, (2) national and regional summaries, (3) metro area, county, and city data by states, and (4) the Canadian survey of buying power. Part II of the survey (1) provides an analysis of changes in metropolitan markets, (2) makes five-year projections for metropolitan markets, (3) evaluates newspaper and TV markets, and (4) discusses merchandise-line sales. While the survey contains a great deal of information that is useful to the retailer, three basic categories of information are of particular interest to the retail location specialist attempting to evaluate potential market areas. Those three categories are population, retail sales, and effective buying income. Each of the three categories is further divided into subcategories to provide additional, detailed information on smaller geographic units. These figures help the retailer to identify and evaluate all of the market-area problems previously discussed, with the exception of the "right part of town."

The survey contains information for all census regions, states, metro areas, counties, and cities. While the population and retail sales figures reported in the survey are self-explanatory, the expression "effective buying income" requires additional explanation. As used in the survey, effective buying income is all personal income (wages, salaries, rental income, dividends, interest, pension, welfare) less federal, state, and local personal taxes, contributions for social security insurance, and nontax payments (fines, fees, penalties). In essence, effective buying income is the rough equivalent of disposable personal income; that is, the spendable income available to the consumer.

The raw population, retail sales, and income figures provide the location specialist with a demographic overview of the *absolute* sales potential of various market areas. By comparing each identified market area with others, the location specialist can develop "relative" measures of each market's potential. In addition, the retailer can use this survey information to develop several relevant measures of a market's potential in terms of percentages, averages, ratios, and indices.

Editor & Publisher Market Guide

The second standard source of information for evaluating market areas is *Editor & Publisher Market Guide.* While it is similar in some aspects to the *Survey of Buying Power,* its yearly editions provide additional and different information about market areas. In addition to standard information on population, income, households, farm products, and retail sales for states, metro areas, counties, and cities, the guide provides specific features for each city.

Standard Evaluation Methods

The previous section described two major standard evaluation sources that retailers use to obtain market information. This section discusses several standard *methods* that retailers use to evaluate market areas: the buying power index, the sales activity index, the quality index, and the index of retail saturation.

Buying Power Index

The **buying power index,** published annually in the *Survey of Buying Power,* is "a measurement of a market's ability to buy."[15] The index is constructed using three criteria:

1. the market area's population expressed as a percentage of the total U.S. population
2. the market area's retail sales expressed as a percentage of total U.S. retail sales
3. the market area's effective buying income expressed as a percentage of the total U.S. effective buying income

The index does not equally weight each criterion as an indicator of a market area's ability to buy. Instead, each is weighted according to its perceived importance— population by 2, retail sales by 3, and effective buying income by 5. The buying power index (BPI) is calculated in the following way:

$$\text{BPI} = \frac{(\text{pop.} \times 2) + (\text{retail sales} \times 3) + (\text{effect. buying inc.} \times 5)}{10 \text{ (the sum of the weights)}}$$

The higher the index value, the greater the market area's ability to buy and therefore to support retailing activities. Although the BPI provides a good estimate of the spendable income within a market area, it does not indicate the area's "distribution of income," "stability of income," or "income trends." As described by the editors of *Survey of Buying Power,* the index "is most useful in estimating the potential for mass products sold at popular prices. The further a product is removed from the mass market, the greater is the need for a BPI to be modified by more discriminating factors—income, class, age, sex, etc."[16]

Sales Activity Index

The *Survey of Buying Power* also reports the standardized **sales activity index** (SAI), *"a measure of the per capita retail sales of an area compared with those of the nation."*[17] Although the SAI is reported for the nine census regions and for each state within those regions, it can be calculated for any geographic subdivision contained in the survey. The SAI is calculated in the following manner:

$$\text{SAI} = \frac{\text{a market area's percentage of U.S. retail sales}}{\text{a market area's percentage of U.S. population}}$$

Because the numerator (retail sales) reflects all sales made in an area regardless of where the consumer is from and the denominator (population) includes only those people who live in the area, the sales activity index does not specify whether a market area's sales activity is the result of the shopping activities of area residents, nonresidents, business concerns, or some combination. "A high index may, therefore, indicate a strong influx of nonresident shoppers, heavy buying by business concerns, heavy buying by residents, or all three."[18]

Quality Index

A third index prepared by *Sales and Marketing Management* and reported in the *Survey of Buying Power* is the **quality index** (QI). As described by the publishers, the quality index

> shows the extent to which the market's quality is above or below par (represented by 100). If a market's percent of the national population, which can be taken to represent par, is divided into the buying power index, it yields the quality index. A high index could reflect either above-average buying power or a strong influx of shoppers from outside the area, or both.[19]

Index of Retail Saturation

The **index of retail saturation** (IRS) is *a measure of the potential sales per square foot of store space for a given product line within a particular market area.* As a market-area evaluation tool, it incorporates both consumer demand and competitive supply. Essentially, the index is the ratio between a market area's capacity to consume and its capacity to retail. The formulation of the index of retail saturation is expressed as

$$IRS = \frac{(C)(RE)}{RF}$$

where

IRS = index of retail saturation for a given product line(s) within a particular market area

C = number of customers in a particular market area for a given product line

RE = retail expenditures—the average dollar expenditure for a given product line(s) within a particular market area

RF = retail facilities—the total square feet of selling space allocated to a given product line(s) within a particular market area[20]

To illustrate, assume that a retail operation needs sales of $45 per square foot of selling space for a given product line to operate profitably. Also assume that the retailer is currently examining three potential market areas (see Table 12–1). Market area A can be eliminated from further consideration because it does not meet the $45 minimum sales per square foot criterion. Both markets B and C meet the minimum sales criterion; however, if all other location considerations are equal, market B would be preferable to C because it offers the retailer more ($3.33 higher) sales potential per square foot of selling space.

The index of retail saturation allows the retailer to classify market areas on the basis of their competitive situation. Market areas can be described as either understored, overstored, or saturated.[21] **Understored market areas** are *those in which the capacity to consume exceeds the capacity to retail.* In other words, there are too

TABLE 12–1
Market-area evaluation
using the index of retail
saturation

	Market Area		
	A	B	C
Number of customers (C)	40,000	50,000	70,000
Retail expenditures (RE)	$10	$12	$10
Retail facilities (RF)	10,000	12,000	15,000
Index of retail saturation (IRS)	$40.00	$50.00	$46.67

few stores and/or too little selling space devoted to a product line to satisfy consumer needs. **Overstored market areas** occur *when the capacity to retail exceeds the capacity to consume.* In this situation, retailers have devoted too much space to a particular product line. Finally, a **saturated market area** is *one in which the capacity to retail equals the capacity of buyers to consume a product line.* In this case, the demand for and supply of a given product line are in equilibrium. The *understored* market area obviously offers the best retailing opportunity for the retailer seeking a new location.

Upon completing the market-area identification and evaluation processes, the retailer must select a regional and local market. There are no simple decision rules to aid the retailer in selection. The basis of the location decision will vary with various types of retailers, their operational characteristics, and their stated objectives. At this point, the retailer's *judgment* is the critical factor. Ultimately, the retailer should select the regional and local markets that provide sufficient levels of support (sales potential) that are conducive to the operational needs of the firm. Generally, the market area a retailer selects represents a compromise among several promising but different market situations.

A market consists of buying populations and their buying behavior. Consumer and organizational markets are the two market types from which retailers secure their business. Retail location is a problem of market segmentation—the process of dividing the total market into more meaningful and homogeneous market segments.

The retail-location problem is multidimensional. The retailer must identify, evaluate, and select a market area to support a particular operation. The market-area identification process involves two tasks. The first is determining which criteria to use in segmenting markets. Both market criteria (population, housing, buyer behavior, and physical environment characteristics) and retail operation criteria (distribution, competition, promotion, and legal characteristics) are useful in identifying retail market areas.

The second task is to identify market areas. Market areas can be delineated as regional markets ("the right region" and the "right part of the region") and local markets (the "right town" and the "right part of town"). Based on census areas, communication areas, functional markets, *ABC* markets, and intraurban markets, the retailer can identify several regional and local market areas.

The market-area evaluation process is an attempt to ascertain a market area's relative potential. Although the retailer is free to develop original sources and methods of evaluation, several standard sources (such as the *Survey of Buying Power* and the *Editor & Publisher Market Guide*) and standard methods (such as the buying power index, quality index, sales activity index, and index of retail saturation) are readily available.

**THE MARKET-
AREA
SELECTION
PROCESS**

SUMMARY

357

Finally, the market-area selection process requires the retailer to choose (1) regional and local markets that provide potential sales large enough to support a firm's operations and (2) retailing environments that will enhance the retailer's operations. In the selection process, the retailer has no magical "rules of thumb" to use in arriving at a final decision. Instead, the retailer must use judgment and experience to select a market area from the several alternatives that have been identified and evaluated.

KEY TERMS AND CONCEPTS

market	class selectivity	multiple-nuclei theory
consumer markets	media coverage	*Survey of Buying Power*
organizational markets	areas of dominant influence	*Editor & Publisher Market Guide*
market segmentation	designated marketing areas	buying power index
market potential approach	census markets	sales activity index
retail operations approach	communication markets	quality index
direct competitors	functional markets	index of retail saturation
indirect competitors	ABC markets	understored market area
level of competition	intraurban markets	overstored market area
media selectivity	concentric zone theory	saturated market area
geographic selectivity	sector theory	

REVIEW QUESTIONS

1. What is a market?
2. How do consumer markets differ from organizational markets?
3. Describe the market-segmentation process. What are the major tasks to be accomplished in segmenting markets?
4. What are the four criteria used to segment markets based on market potential?
5. Compare and contrast direct and indirect competitors.
6. How might geographic selectivity and class selectivity be used to identify promotional market areas?
7. What two standardized areas are used in identifying retail markets based on the coverage by broadcast stations?
8. What are the nine census regions that make up the U.S. market?

9. How are *ABC* markets defined? Briefly describe each *ABC* market.
10. Describe the concentric zone theory of intraurban markets.
11. Compare and contrast the sector and multiple-nuclei theories of intraurban structure.
12. What does the buying power index measure?
13. How is the sales activity index determined? What does it show?
14. Describe the quality index.
15. How is the formulation of the index of retail saturation expressed?
16. What are the three market-area classifications as defined by the index of retail saturation?
17. On what basis are regional and local markets selected?

ENDNOTES

1. John S. Wright, Daniel S. Warner, Willis L. Winter, Jr., and Sherilyn K. Zeigler, *Advertising*, 4th ed. (New York: McGraw-Hill, 1977), 193.
2. Ibid.
3. Ibid., 195.
4. Kenneth E. Runyon, *Advertising and the Practice of Marketing* (Columbus: Charles E. Merrill Publishing Co., 1979), 318.
5. William Haight, *Retail Advertising* (Morristown, NJ: General Learning Press, 1976), 256.
6. Otto Kleppner, *Advertising Procedure*, 7th ed. (Englewood Cliffs, NJ: Prentice-Hall, 1979), 190.
7. Raymond E. Murphy, *The American City—An Urban Geography* (New York: McGraw-Hill, 1966), 114.
8. "JCP/Stores—What Makes Penney Run," *Chain Store Age* December, 1977, 141.
9. Ibid., 155.
10. Ibid., 165.
11. Murphy, *The American City*, 209.
12. Ibid., 208.
13. Ibid., 211.
14. "The Structure and Growth of Residential Neighborhoods in American Cities" (Washington: U.S. Federal Housing Administration, 1976), 76.
15. *1978 Survey of Buying Power, Sales, and Marketing Management*, 121, 24 July 1978, A69.
16. Ibid.
17. Ibid., A72.
18. Ibid.
19. Ibid.
20. Adapted from Bernard J. LaLonde, "New Frontiers in Store Location," *Supermarket Merchandising*, February, 1963, 110.
21. Ibid.

RELATED READINGS

Bellenger, Danny; Robertson, Dan H.; and Hirschman, Elizabeth C. "Age and Education as Key Correlates of Store Selection for Female Shoppers." *Journal of Retailing* 52 (Winter 1976), 71–78.

Bush, Ronald H.; Tatham, Ronald L.; and Hair, Joseph F., Jr. "Community Location Decisions by Franchisors: A Comparative Analysis." *Journal of Retailing* 52 (Spring 1976), 33–42.

Cooke, Ernest F. "The Major (Largest? Best?) Consumer Markets—Where Are They?" *Developments in Marketing Science, Proceedings*. V. V. Bellur, ed. (Academy of Marketing Science 1981), 334–39.

Craig, C. Samuel, and Ghosh, Avijit. "Covering Approaches to Retail Facility Location." *AMA Educators' Proceedings*. R. W. Belk et al, eds. (American Marketing Association 1984), 195–99.

Garreau, Joel. *The Nine Nations of North American.* (New York: Avon Books, 1981)

Ghosh, Avijit, and Craig, C. Samuel. "Formulating Retail Location Strategy in a Changing Environment." *Journal of Retailing* 47 (Summer 1983), 56–68.

Ingene, Charles A. "Structural Determinants of Market Potential." *Journal of Retailing* 60 (Spring 1984), 5–36.

Joyce, Mary, and Guiltinan, Joseph. "The Professional Women: A Potential Market Segment for Retailers." *Journal of Retailing* 54 (Summer 1978), 59–70.

Kaufman, Carol J. "Occupational Status within the Household: An Approach to Segmentation." *Developments in Marketing Science, Proceedings*. N. K. Malhotra, ed. (Academy of Marketing Science 1985), 51–56.

Kramer, Jonathan M. "Benefits in the Use of Suburban Press for Large Metropolitan Buys." *Journal of Marketing* 41 (January 1977), 68–70.

Samli, A. Coskun; Riecken, Glen; and Yavas, Ugur, "Inter-Market Shopping Behavior and the Small Community: Problems and Prospect of a Widespread Phenomenon." *Journal of the Academy of Marketing Science* 11 (Winter - Spring 1983), 1–14.

Valentin, E. K. "Strategic Location Analysis: A Rudimentary Framework." *1985 Educators' Proceedings*. R. F. Lusch et al, eds. (American Marketing Association 1985), 233–37.

Zeithaml, Valarie A. "The New Demographics and Market Fragmentation." *Journal of Marketing* 49 (Summer 1985), 64–73.

Outline

THE RETAIL TRADING AREA

THE TRADING-AREA IDENTIFICATION PROCESS

The Dimensions of Retail Trading Areas
Techniques for Identifying Trading Areas

THE TRADING-AREA EVALUATION PROCESS

The Gross Adequacy of Trading Areas
The Net Adequacy of Trading Areas
The Growth Potential of Trading Areas

THE TRADING-AREA SELECTION PROCESS

Objectives

- Define a retail trading area in terms of its operational dimensions

- Describe the size, shape, and structural dimensions of retail trading areas

- Understand and use various techniques for trading-area identification

- Ascertain the gross and net adequacy of retail trading areas

- Evaluate and select retail trading areas in accordance with established minimum criteria

13
Assessing Retail Trading Areas

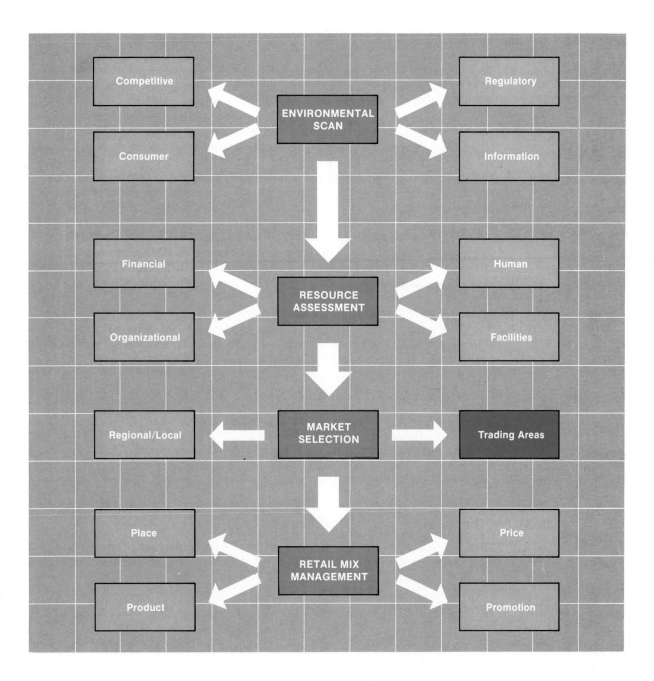

A critical element in determining a retailer's success is the ability to assess and acquire a good retail location. To achieve this objective, the retailer must *identify, evaluate,* and *select* retail trading areas to segment its consumer markets further. After the retailer has identified and evaluated its local markets, it must then segment them into *trading areas* (i.e., areas from which it attracts potential customers). This chapter explains how a retailer can define and evaluate the retail trading area to operate profitably.

THE RETAIL TRADING AREA

A **retail trading area** is broadly defined as *an area "from which a store gets its business within a given span of time."*[1] Depending upon the *kind* of retail operations, a retail trading area can be described more specifically in the following terms:

- *drawing power*—the area from which a *shopping center* could expect to derive as much as 85 percent of its total volume[2]
- *per capita sales*—the area from which a *general merchandise store* can derive a minimum annual per capita sale of one dollar[3]
- *patronage probability*—the area from which potential customers come who have a probability greater than zero of purchasing a given class of products or services that either a retailer or group of retailers offers for sale[4]
- *retail operations*—the area from which either a marketing unit or group can operate economically, depending upon volume and cost to operate and to sell and/or deliver a good or service[5]

Two characteristics common to these four definitions are (1) they identify an area from which a retailer or group of retailers *draws customers* over a specific period of time and (2) they identify a *single focal point* (such as a town, a shopping center, or a single retail outlet) around which the trading area develops. Essentially, then, retail trading areas are "gravity areas"—retail sites to which consumers will gravitate or be "pulled" from an identifiable area.

To assess a trading area, a retailer examines the area using a central-place/gravity persepctive, first locating a site (the central place) and then determining the capability of the proposed or existing site to attract customers (retail gravity).

The three purposes of any trading-area analysis are to determine the area from which the majority of the retailer's customers might come, to determine the potential sales level of the area of majority support, and to determine the source of support in terms of customers' needs.

Given these purposes, the three-fold problem of retailers is how to (1) identify several potential trading areas, (2) evaluate these trading areas, and (3) select a trading area. Retailers use several methods and criteria in assessing the trading-area problem (see Figure 13–1).

THE TRADING-AREA IDENTIFICATION PROCESS

The Dimensions of Retail Trading Areas

Retailers use three dimensions to describe a retail trading area: size, shape, and structure. Describing a retail trading area's dimensions is the first step in the retail trading-area identification process.

Trading-Area Size

Trading areas range in size from a few square blocks to a radius of many miles. The size of a trading area is a function of the cumulative effects of several *opera-*

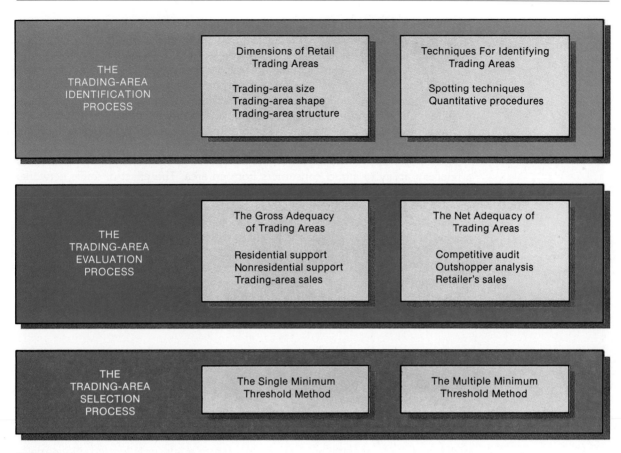

FIGURE 13–1
Assessing retail trading areas

tional and *environmental* factors. The two major operational factors are the type and size of retail operation. *Type of retail operation* means the kind of goods and services the retailer offers. Retailers that offer specialty and shopping goods will draw consumers from a wider geographic area than retailers that offer convenience goods. The reason is that consumers are willing to exert greater effort and to travel greater distances to buy specialty and shopping goods than to buy convenience goods.

The second operational factor, *store size*, is directly related to the retailer's trading-area size. That is, the larger the retail store and the greater its selection of merchandise, the larger its trading area will be. Because of their physical size and wide range of merchandise, Gimbel's of New York and Rich's of Atlanta are department stores with a very large trading area. On the other hand, a "Smith's Department Store" of considerably smaller physical size and fewer merchandise offerings would have a much smaller trading area.

The second set of factors that determine the size of a retailer's trading area are environmental, including (1) the number, size, and type of *neighboring stores;* (2) the nature and activity of *competing stores;* and (3) the character of the *transportation network.*

A retailer that locates near other retailers often finds that the combined trading area of all the *neighboring retailers* in the cluster is larger than if it were located in

363

an isolated location. Thus, a retailer that locates in a regional shopping mall shares more potential customers from a larger area than a retailer that locates either in a small, neighborhood shopping center or in an isolated, freestanding location.

The size of a retailer's trading area also depends on the location, size, and activity of *competing stores*. One large department store, for example, might locate next to another large department store to facilitate consumers' comparative shopping and thus draw from a larger geographic area. Consumers reason that by going to the geographic site of two similar stores, they probably will find what they are looking for.

The third environmental factor, the *transportation network,* strongly influences a retailer's ability to attract consumers from an area. The effect of traffic networks on the size of a retailer's trading area becomes apparent when we consider that stores located on major thoroughfares usually have larger trading areas than those located on secondary streets and roads. Roads with high traffic volume and faster speeds afford better site locations than those with less volume and lower speeds. A desirable site would be near the junction of two interstate highways, for example. Thus, the number of traffic lanes, the number and nature of intersections (controlled or uncontrolled), the speed limit, and the presence or absence of barriers to uncongested movement all affect the size of the area from which a retailer can attract consumers.

Trading-Area Shape

Trading areas assume many different shapes, a result of three distinct factors: (1) transportation networks; (2) physical, social, and political barriers; and (3) location of competitors.

Transportation networks. The shape of a trading area depends largely upon the makeup of the transportation network near which a retailer is located. Along major transportation routes, such as an interstate highway with minor routes spawning from it, trading areas tend to be elongated in the direction of the major transportation route. Because of the ease of movement along a major artery (such as an interstate) and the lack of physical barriers (such as traffic lights, traffic signs, and low speed limits), a retailer that locates its store along a major route should expect an elongated trading-area shape. Where two major arteries intersect, the shape of the trading area tends to be elongated along both major routes.

Physical, social, and political barriers. Although major transportation arteries extend a retailer's trading area, certain physical, social, and political barriers reduce these extensions. Figure 13–2 illustrates the influence of all three barriers on the shape of a retailer's trading area. First, the lake acts as a *physical* barrier to the retailer's trading area. Similar physical barriers include rivers, mountain sides, ocean, deserts, land formations, limited-access highways, and railroad tracks. Another kind of barrier that affects a trading area's shape is a *social* barrier. In this illustration, a high-crime area limits the retailer's trading area. Another example might be ethnic neighborhoods whose inhabitants would never think of going outside their neighborhoods to shop. Finally, *political* barriers can limit a retailer's trading area. A state line (perhaps because of higher and lower sales taxes), federal and state parks (a physical barrier due to political entities), and the borders of counties (one that limits or does not allow the sale of certain merchandise) might greatly influence the shape of a retailer's trading area.

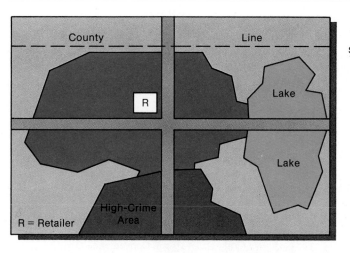

Location of competitors. Where competitors locate their stores influences the shape of a retailer's trading area. Figure 13–3 provides an example of how competitors can cut into a retailers's trading area. A competitor's location, size, and type of operation all alter the shape of another retailer's trading area.

Trading-Area Structure

The third and final dimension of a retail trading area is structure. Trading-area structure is the comparative ability of a retailer or a cluster of retailers to attract customers from various distances or from various customer regions. Three trading-area structures are general, composite, and proportional.[6]

General trading areas. These areas *provide the majority of a retailer's business.* This trading area includes any and all customers who do, or might, buy any product line that the retailer carries. Thus, a customer who purchases only perfume at the store would be included in the retailer's general trading area along with a customer who buys perfume, dresses, shoes, handbags, and several other products (see Figure 13–4a).

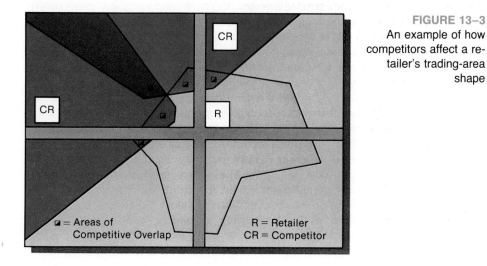

FIGURE 13–3
An example of how competitors affect a retailer's trading-area shape

365

FIGURE 13–4
Trading-area structure

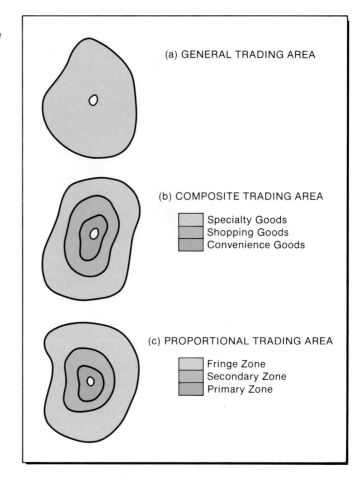

(a) GENERAL TRADING AREA

(b) COMPOSITE TRADING AREA

Specialty Goods
Shopping Goods
Convenience Goods

(c) PROPORTIONAL TRADING AREA

Fringe Zone
Secondary Zone
Primary Zone

Composite trading areas.   A **composite trading area** is *a set of trading areas, each of which is structured according to the type of goods the retailer sells.* Figure 13–4b illustrates the composite trading area for a store (or shopping center) selling convenience, shopping, and specialty goods. Because many retailers carry several lines of products, this representation is rather realistic. In this case, the retailer draws from a larger trading area for specialty goods than for shopping and convenience goods. The consumer's willingness to exert shopping effort, as described earlier, accounts for the composite-area boundary lines.

Proportional trading areas.   Whereas the composite trading area is based upon the types of products retailers carry and the degree of consumer willingness to search for a product, a **proportional trading area** *is based upon the distance customers are from the store.* The further customers are from the retail store, the less likely they are to patronize the store. The closer customers are to the retail store, the greater the likelihood they will patronize the store. These two statements define what retailers call the "distance decay function." That is, the number of customers attracted to a given store decreases as their distance from the store increases. As illustrated in Figure 13–4c, three distance zones—primary, secondary, and fringe—constitute the proportional trading area. The zone trading areas for a proportional trading area vary from one store to another, depending upon the nature of the retail operation and its neighboring activities.

The **primary zone** is *the area around which a retailer can expect to attract 50 to 70 percent of its business.* The primary trading area might be defined in one of the following three ways: (1) the area closest to the store, (2) the area in which the retailer has a competitive advantage, such as customer convenience and accessibility, and (3) the area from which the retailer produces the highest per capita sales.

The **secondary zone** *surrounds the primary zone and generally represents 20 to 30 percent of the retailer's total sales volume.* Whereas the retailer's secondary trading area is an important source of customers, the primary-zone advantages of convenience and accessibility are largely lost because of competitors' locations. In the retailer's secondary zone, consumers usually select the store as their second or third shopping choice.

The **fringe zone** is *that area from which the retailer occasionally draws customers* (5 to 10 percent of the business). Retailers generally attract customers from this zone either because "they just happened to be in the vicinity" or because they are extremely loyal to the store or its personnel. Generally, customers from the fringe zone are ones who either like to shop at large stores on major thoroughfares or stores with a high degree of specialization. Since customers in the fringe zone are generally a small proportion of the retailer's total business, they do not represent a significant target market.

Techniques for Identifying Trading Areas

Retailers can use several specific techniques to identify their trading areas. Two general research approaches are spotting techniques and quantitative procedures. Quantitative approaches are more appropriate for the new or expanding retailer, while spotting techniques are more commonly used by the existing retailer seeking to determine the extent of its present trading area. Most retailers use a combination of these approaches.

Spotting Techniques

Spotting techniques *include several methods by which the retailer attempts to "spot" customer origins on a map.* By carefully observing the magnitude and arrangement of these origins, the retailer can identify the dimensions of the trading area. Retailers normally define customer origins by home addresses, although customer places of employment also are important. For purposes of trading-area identification, the most successful spotting techniques not only obtain the customer's address but also provide information on the customer's buying habits. Some of the more commonly used spotting techniques include surveys of customer's license plates, customer surveys, analyses of customer records, and studies of customer activities.

License plate surveys. By recording the license plate numbers of automobiles in the store's parking lot, retailers can obtain customer home addresses. In their sampling procedure, retailers should observe license plates at different times of the day, different days of the week, and different weeks of the month to ensure a representative sample. The primary advantage of this technique is that it is relatively inexpensive to administer. License plate surveys have several limitations, including the following: (1) there is no way to determine who actually drove the car to the store, or whether that car represents a regular customer or someone who just happened to be in the neighborhood; (2) a survey of license plates reveals no information on the shopping behavior of customers, such as what they bought, how much they bought, where they bought, why they bought, or if they bought anything at all; (3)

367

the technique provides no customer demographic information, such as age, sex, occupation, and income; and (4) the number of purchasers in each car cannot be determined from the license plate. Nevertheless, the relatively low cost and minimal time requirements of license plate surveys make them an attractive method for providing general information about a trading area.

Customer surveys.   Either a personal interview, mail questionnaire, or telephone survey can provide information on who lives or works in a given area and who either current or potential customers are. Actual customers can be surveyed on premise (within a particular store or shopping mall) by either personal interviews or take-home/mail-back questionnaires. Good surveying techniques must be employed to ensure an unbiased, representative sample. Customer surveys can provide a significant amount of information such as demographics and shopping behavior. Limitations of customer surveys are cost, time, and the skill required to conduct them efficiently and effectively.

Customer records.   Retailers have several ways to obtain the addresses of their current customers as well as additional valuable information. Customer credit, service, and delivery records contain a great deal of information if properly developed and maintained. From their records, retailers can find customer addresses and places of employment, ages, sex, family status, telephone numbers, and types and amounts of purchases. While customer credit, service, and delivery records are a fast and inexpensive means of obtaining information, they are biased since cash customers, who require no services or delivery, are omitted from the analysis.

Customer activities.   Any method that asks or requires customers to provide their names and addresses can be used to identify an existing or proposed trading area. Promotional activities such as contests and sweepstakes can be effective in obtaining names and addresses. Unfortunately, they tend to be biased toward the consumer who is willing to participate (i.e., the high-income consumer frequently does not think it is worth the time). Cents-off coupons that require the consumer to provide minimal information also have been used in identifying trading areas.

Quantitative Procedures

Retailers have used several quantitative procedures to delineate retail trading areas. The one used by most retailers is the **retail gravitation concept,** *which provides a measure of the potential interaction between various locations by determining the relative drawing power of each location.* Based on the relative drawing power of a location within an area, each area can be identified as being part of a trading area (in some cases, areas can be shared by more than one location). Retailing analysts have developed several formulations of the gravitation concept, each of which uses a somewhat different procedure for identifying trading areas. Two of the more widely recognized formulations are Converse's break-even point and Huff's probability model.

Converse's break-even point.   Converse developed a formula that allows the retailer to calculate the **break-even point** in miles between competing retail centers (stores, shopping centers, or cities).[7] In essence, Converse computes the break-even point *as the point between the competing retailing centers where the probability of a consumer patronizing each retailing center is equal.* This break-even point identifies the trading-area boundary line between competing retail trade centers. By identifying the break-even point between one retail center and all competing centers, the retailer can determine the trading area. The break-even point formula is expressed as

$$BP = \frac{d}{1 + \dfrac{P_1}{P_2}}$$

where

BP = the break-even point between the competing retail centers in miles from the smaller center

d = the distance between the two competing retail centers

P_1 = the population of the larger retail center

P_2 = the population of the smaller retail center

Both the distance and population expressions require further explanation. Although distance is normally measured in miles, recent studies show that many people think of distance in terms of travel time. Retail analysts can use travel time to replace miles for the distance between competing retail centers. The cost of acquiring the travel-time data might impose a constraint on this approach, however.

The population expressions (P_1 and P_2) can be expressed in several different ways. First, the total population in each center is the most commonly used measurement. Another approach is to use the total number of retailers or the total retail square footage in the center as the population measurement. Any measurement that reflects a retail center's ability to attract customers can be used as an expression of population. Figure 13–5 (p. 370) illustrates the identification of shopping center trading areas using the break-even point method.

Huff's probability model. The consumer choice of a retail store or shopping cluster is a complex decision-making process. The number and importance of store and cluster attributes used in the selection process vary with each shopper. Huff's model "was the first to suggest that market areas were complex, continuous, and probabilistic rather than the nonoverlapping geometrical areas of central place theory."[8] The basic premise of Huff's "shopper attraction" model is based on the following empirical regularities:

1. The proportion of consumers patronizing a given shopping area [cluster] varies with distance from the shopping area.
2. The proportion of consumers patronizing various shopping areas [clusters] varies with the breadth and depth of merchandise offered by each shopping area.
3. The distance that consumers travel to various shopping areas [clusters] varies for different types of products purchased.
4. The "pull" of any given shopping area [cluster] is influenced by the proximity of competing shopping areas.[9]

The Huff model computation is shown in Figure 13–6 (p. 371).

The basic problem of any trading-area evaluation is to answer the following two questions: (1) what is the total amount of business that a trading area can generate now and in the future? and (2) what share of the total business can a retailer in a given location expect to attract? Although no standard trading-area evaluation process exists, most evaluation procedures use the concepts of trading-area adequacy

FIGURE 13–5

A problem using Converse's break-even point formula

The Problem:
Where are the break-even points between the following retail trade centers?

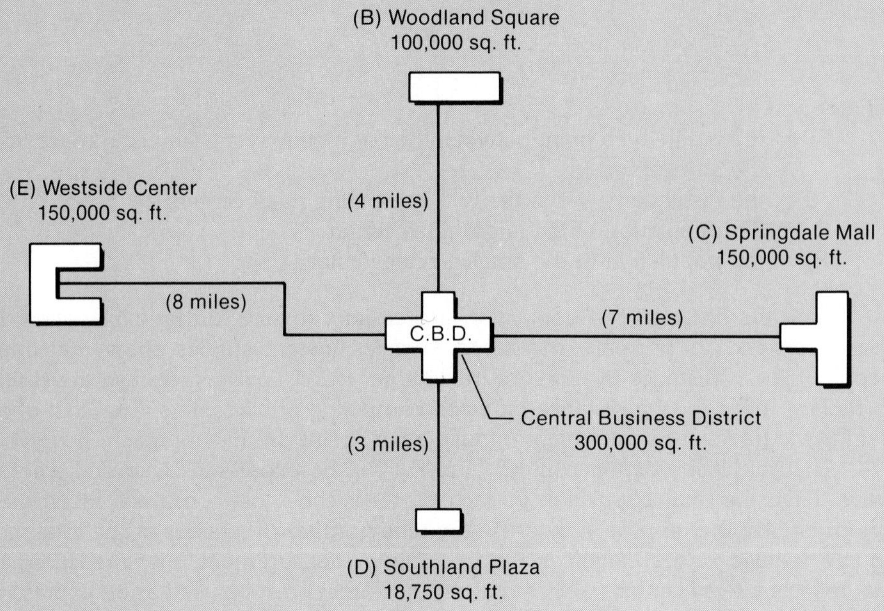

(B) Woodland Square
100,000 sq. ft.

(E) Westside Center
150,000 sq. ft.

(4 miles)

(C) Springdale Mall
150,000 sq. ft.

(8 miles)

C.B.D.

(7 miles)

Central Business District
300,000 sq. ft.

(3 miles)

(D) Southland Plaza
18,750 sq. ft.

The Calculation

$$BP_{AB} = \frac{4}{1 + \sqrt{\dfrac{300,000}{100,000}}} = \frac{4}{1 + \sqrt{3}} = \frac{4}{1 + 1.73} = \frac{4}{2.73} = 1.46$$

$$BP_{AC} = \frac{7}{1 + \sqrt{\dfrac{300,000}{150,000}}} = \frac{7}{1 + \sqrt{2}} = \frac{7}{1 + 1.41} = \frac{7}{2.41} = 2.90$$

$$BP_{AD} = \frac{3}{1 + \sqrt{\dfrac{300,000}{18,750}}} = \frac{3}{1 + \sqrt{16}} = \frac{3}{1 + 4} = \frac{3}{5} = .60$$

$$BP_{AE} = \frac{8}{1 + \sqrt{\dfrac{300,000}{300,000}}} = \frac{8}{1 + \sqrt{1}} = \frac{8}{1 + 1} = \frac{8}{2} = 4.00$$

The Interpretation
The break-even point between Central Business District and
(1) Woodland Square is 1.46 miles from Woodland Square
(2) Springdale Mall is 2.90 miles from Springdale Mall
(3) Southland Plaza is .60 miles from Southland Plaza
(4) Westside Center is 4.00 miles from either Center, i.e., halfway between

FIGURE 13–6
Huff's probability model
for defining and esti-
mating a trading area

CHAPTER 13
ASSESSING RETAIL
TRADING AREAS

The model developed by D. L. Huff to measure the probability of consumers expected to be attracted to a particular shopping cluster can be formally expressed as follows:

$$P_{ij}^k = \frac{\dfrac{S_j^k}{(T_{ij})^\lambda}}{\displaystyle\sum_{j=1}^{n} \dfrac{S_j^k}{(t_{ij})^\lambda}}$$

(1)

$i = 1, 2, \ldots , m$
$j = 1, 2, \ldots , n$
$k = 1, 2, \ldots , p$

where

P_{ij}^k = the probability of a consumer at a given origin i traveling to a particular shopping cluster j for a type k shopping trip

S_j^k = the size of the shopping cluster j devoted to shopping tip k (measured in square footage of retail selling area devoted to shopping trip k items)

T_{ij} = the travel time involved in getting from a consumer's point of origin i to a given shopping cluster j

λ = a parameter which is to be estimated empirically to reflect the effect of travel time on various kinds of shopping trips

m = the number of origins in the marketing area

n = the number of shopping clusters in the marketing area

P = the number of different types of shopping trips defined.

and trading-area potential to predict total trading-area business and the share of business a particular retailer can expect.

Trading-area adequacy is *the ability of a trading area to support proposed and existing retail operations.*[10] This support capability may be viewed in a gross as well as net form (see Figure 13–7).[11] **Gross adequacy** is *the ability of a trading area to support a retail operation without any consideration of retail competition.* That is, the gross adequacy measures the *total amount of business* available to all competing retailers within a defined trading area. On the other hand, **net adequacy** is *the ability of a trading area to provide support for a retailer after competition has been taken into account.*

Finally, **trading-area potential** is *the predicted ability of a trading area to provide acceptable support levels for a retailer in the future.*

The Gross Adequacy of Trading Areas

When a retailer measures gross adequacy, it determines a trading area's total *capacity to consume.* The capacity of a retail market to consume is a function of the total *number of consumers* within a trading area at any given time and their *need, willingness,* and *ability to purchase* a particular class of goods (see Figure 13–8). Unfortunately, it is not easy to determine consumers' need, willingness, and ability to buy a certain class of goods. To determine gross adequacy, the retailer must first

FIGURE 13–7

Elements of trading-area adequacy

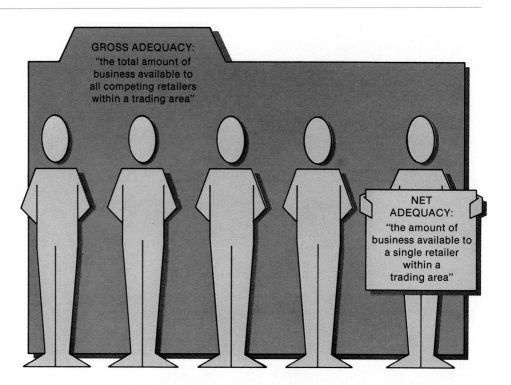

consider appropriate consumption units (such as people, homes, businesses, and so forth) to count for a general class of goods. Second, the retailer must find an appropriate measure of a consumption unit's need, willingness, and ability to buy. To feel confident in their analyses, retailers must use one or more indicators of their potential buyers' behavior. Finally, the support capabilities of a trading area depend to some extent on sources outside of the gross trading area.

Residential Support Levels

Once a retailer has sufficiently identified the gross trading area, it needs to concentrate on the most important source of business: the residents of the area. To measure a trading area's potential consumers, the retailer must analyze population/demographic and household/residential variables.

Population/demographic analysis. A trading area's total capacity to consume is, in part, a function of the total number of persons residing in that trading area. However, because population densities vary greatly from one city to another and between suburban and intracity areas, it is often quite difficult to obtain an accurate count of the total population residing in a localized trading area. The need to obtain an accurate population count is very important. Since the total population figure plays a part in several quantitative estimates of gross and net adequacy, the population figure must be accurate to produce reliable estimates. Also, because merchandise offerings appeal to broad segments of the area's consuming public, an accurate population count could be sufficient to obtain a reasonably reliable initial indication of the trading area's market opportunities. While total population figures are informative, many experts think these figures need to be qualified in terms of their demographic makeup.

The actual level of support for a given line of products or services that can be expected from persons living in the trading area may be, for example, for those

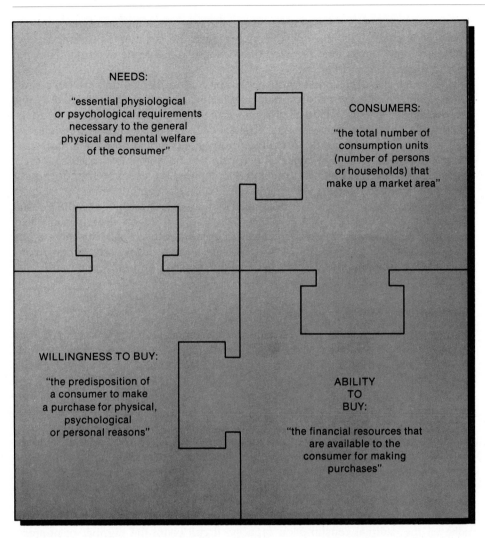

FIGURE 13-8
The market potential
puzzle: Determinants of
a market's capacity to
consume

NEEDS:

"essential physiological
or psychological requirements
necessary to the general
physical and mental welfare
of the consumer"

CONSUMERS:

"the total number of
consumption units
(number of persons
or households) that
make up a market area"

WILLINGNESS TO BUY:

"the predisposition of
a consumer to make
a purchase for physical,
psychological
or personal reasons"

**ABILITY
TO
BUY:**

"the financial resources that
are available to the
consumer for making
purchases"

persons who have an annual income of $15,000 or more and are between the ages of 20 and 35. That is, a trading area's capacity to consume may not be directly related to its total population. Instead, it may be a function of the number of persons who possess a certain demographic makeup such as age, sex, income, occupation, and family status. For example, such measurements as the number of children (bike store), the number of women (women's clothing store), or the number of high-income homeowners (expensive home furnishings) indicate a population count that should produce more reliable gross adequacy estimates.

The process of evaluating gross adequacy is a matter of identifying demographic characteristics that best indicate the consumer's need, willingness, and ability to buy, and of obtaining a reliable count of the number of persons who have the desired demographic makeup. At the local trading-area level, a good source of population and demographic information is the *Census of Population* (see Chapter 6).

Household/residential analysis. For some retailing operations, a trading area's capacity to consume is more directly related to the *number of households* or *residential units* than it is to the number of persons in the trading area. For example, a count of household or residential units probably is more indicative of the consump-

373

tion capacity of a trading area for hardware, furniture, and appliance goods than is a population count. This relationship simply reflects the fact that the household unit purchases many goods, and the consumer's home is the prime determinant of the need for certain product lines.

Although the definitions of household unit and residential unit are quite similar, the primary difference is the occupancy factor. *Households* are defined as private dwelling units that include all persons occupying a particular house or an apartment, while a *residential unit* is a housing unit occupied as separate living quarters, such as an apartment building. A count of households would produce a more reliable estimate of the existing capacity to consume, and a count of residential units might better reflect the potential consumption capacity, at least in terms of existing residential facilities. A household unit count can be obtained by tracts and blocks from the *Census of Population*. A residential unit count is available from the *Census of Housing* for either census tracts or blocks and can be checked through field observation and air photographs. To reflect their consumption capacity more accurately, each residential unit can be weighted by average value, size, type of construction, and the characteristics obtained from housing census reports and local building permits.

Nonresidential Support Levels

Although the vast majority of a trading area's consumption capacity comes from people who live in that area, some of the consumption support does not. Consumers who reside outside a trading area contribute significantly to that area's capacity to consume.[12]

Most trading areas are characterized by daily inward, outward, and through migration of consumers who are attracted into the trading area for work, recreation, and other reasons, such as the need for professional services. While these consumers might live many miles away, they do represent a significant portion of trade customers who visit the area. Some of these customers visit frequently and regularly (work trip); others visit infrequently and irregularly (recreation trip). Nevertheless, this external consumption capacity should be included in any assessment of the gross adequacy of a trading area.

It is impossible for a retailer to count accurately the number of consumers that make up the external consumption capacity. It *can* count the number of nonresidential units likely to attract consumers to the trading area (e.g., retailers, wholesalers, manufacturers, offices, schools, churches). Since not all nonresidential units have equal consumption-generating abilities, each must be weighted according to its ability to generate traffic. Because some nonresidential units are more compatible with a retail enterprise than others, the weights a retailer assigns to each nonresidential unit should reflect the degree of consumer-retailer compatibility.

Although a weighted nonresidential unit count does not fully describe or measure the impact of "outsiders" upon the volume of a trading area, it does provide the retailer with a reasonable estimate of this impact. At the very least, it forces the retailer to consider the effects of nonresidential consumers in calculating trade-area gross adequacy.

Estimating Trading-Area Sales

Several methods are available to estimate trading-area sales. The two most widely used techniques are the corollary data method and the per capita sales method.

Corollary data method. The **corollary data method** *assumes that an identifiable relationship exists between sales for a particular class of goods and one or more* *trading-area characteristics* (such as population, residential units, etc.). Knowledge of these relationships aids retailers in estimating total sales.

Per capita sales method. Retail sales figures by store groups and general merchandise categories are available from the *Survey of Buying Power* and *Editor & Publisher Market Guide,* respectively. Unfortunately, the localized nature of most retail trading areas makes is difficult to obtain sales data because identified trading areas rarely correspond to the reported geographical areas (states, metro areas, counties, and cities) found in these trade sources. However, retailers can get reasonably reliable estimates despite the lack of conformity in these secondary sources of information.

One method for estimating trading-area sales is the **per capita sales method.** The estimated trading-area sales for a general product line is a function of the *per capita expenditures for that product line times the total population of that trading area.*

As discussed in a previous section, retailers can obtain reliable population counts from census materials and per capita expenditure figures from consumer surveys and trade-source estimates.

In consumer surveys the researcher asks residents in a particular trading area how much they have spent on a given category of merchandise over a specified time period. In some cases, the researcher asks consumers to keep a diary of their expenditures. Later, these diaries are analyzed to determine consumer expenditure patterns for the trading area. Although consumer surveys can provide detailed data, most retailers cannot afford the considerable time and money it takes to conduct these surveys. Instead, they usually rely on trade-source estimates, which are much less expensive than consumer surveys, easier and faster in obtaining the desired data, and generally as accurate as most consumer surveys. Additionally, they include per capita expenditures for specific trading areas within local markets.

For example, by using the *Survey of Buying Power,* a retailer can find an estimate of retail sales for a particular store group (such as food) for a particular geographic unit (such as a city) and divide that figure by the city's population to yield a per capita expenditure for food. The retailer can use this figure as the average per capita expenditure on food for *all* trading areas within the city. The retailer then can make either upward or downward adjustments in this figure depending upon its knowledge of the particular trading area in which it is interested. This figure is called the gross adequacy of a trading area. Gross adequacy, remember, is the estimated total sales for a particular product line in a specified trading area. The question that the retailer must then answer is "What is my slice of the pie?"

The Net Adequacy of Trading Areas

To answer the preceding question, a retailer must estimate the net adequacy of the trading area. Net adequacy has been defined as the proportion of sales volume that a retailer can expect to receive from the total sales in a trading area. That is, net adequacy is the percentage of gross adequacy (or market share) that a retailer can expect to get. To determine net adequacy, a retailer must consider the trading area's *capacity to consume* and its *capacity to sell.*[13]

The capacity to consume is the gross adequacy measurement discussed previously. Having obtained a gross estimate of the trading area's sales volume capabilities, the retailer's problem is to find a method of allocating total sales volume to each of the existing and proposed competitors in the trading area. This allocation process consists of (1) analyzing the competitive environment and (2) making estimates of each retailer's sales and market share.

375

To determine the net adequacy of a trading area, a retailer must first identify the competitive environment. To analyze the competitive environment, the retailer must examine the types of competition, the number and size of competitors, and the marketing mix of competitors. These characteristics were discussed in Chapter 11 in the analysis of regional and local markets; however, to assess a trading area's net adequacy requires certain refinements. To gain a clearer picture of the competitive environment, a retailer can use two methods: (1) a competitive audit and (2) an outshopper analysis.

Competitive Audit

A **competitive audit** is *an arbitrary, composite rating of each competitor's product, service, price, place, and promotion mixes.* In using a competitive audit, a retailer assesses the ability of competitors to provide a marketing mix that consumers desire within the trading area. The sum of all audits is a measurement of total competition.

Retailers use a competitive audit in several ways. First, they use it to measure the total competition within the trading area (the sum of all competitors times their competitiveness rating). Second, they derive a measure of each competitor's expected share of total trading-area sales. Third, they gain a picture of an unfulfilled product position or "niche" in the trading area. The latter information can help the retailer develop its own marketing strategy.

Outshopper Analysis

Not all consumers living within a trading area shop exclusively in that area. A group of consumers known as "outshoppers" shop outside their local trading area on a frequent and regular basis. These consumers spend a considerable amount of time, money, and effort in making inter-trading-area shopping trips. One analyst characterizes outshoppers and their shopping behavior in this way:

> Some outshoppers are looking for economic gains resulting from lower prices in larger trading centers where assortments are better and the level of competition more intense. Some outshoppers simply seek the diversity of unfamiliar or more stimulating surroundings . . . demographically, outshoppers are younger (25–54 year age group), are relatively well educated (had some college), and the relative income is high . . . psychographically outshoppers are active, on the "go," urban-oriented housewives who are neither time-conscious nor store-loyal shoppers. They tend to manifest a distaste for local shopping and hence a strong preference for out-of-town shopping areas.[14]

To obtain an accurate estimate of total expected sales, the retailer must perform **outshopper analysis**, *subtracting outshopping sales, referred to as "sales leakage," from the trading area's gross sales to arrive at a more realistic total sales volume for the trading area* (see Figure 13–9).

To estimate sales leakage due to outshopping behavior, a retailer can either conduct consumer surveys or use standard adjustments. In using consumer surveys, the retailer asks trading-area consumers to estimate how much they spend locally on a particular class of goods as a percentage of their total expenditures for those goods. The retailer then can use this percentage to adjust the gross sales figure for the trading area. As noted earlier, however, consumer surveys are very costly and take considerable time.

A simple and less expensive method to use is standard adjustments. A standard adjustment figure depends upon prevailing trading-area conditions. For example, if the trading area contains a large number of consumers who are similar to

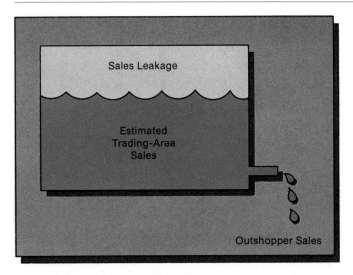

FIGURE 13–9
The effects on trading-
area sales volume as a
result of sales leakage
from outshopper be-
havior

CHAPTER 13
ASSESSING RETAIL
TRADING AREAS

the demographic and psychographic profile of outshoppers, the retailer should
make a standard downward adjustment (e.g., 5 percent) in gross sales. Other factors the retailer should consider in making standard adjustments are (1) the existence of major shopping centers outside the trading area that are within easy driving
distance, (2) the presence of major traffic arteries that facilitate outshopping, and (3)
the lack of a sufficient number of competing retailers to facilitate consumer's comparison shopping. While estimates of outshopping are not always accurate, the retailer must consider these factors in making a conservative estimate of trading-area
net adequacy.

Estimating the Retailer's Sales

Having completed the evaluation of the competitive environment, a retailer can estimate the sales of each competitor. To calculate net adequacy (i.e., the trading-area
market share) figure, the retailer can use either the "total sales method" or the
"sales per square foot method." Both methods use a ratio of trading-area capacity
to consume (gross adequacy) to trading area capacity to sell.

Total sales method.   In using the **total sales method,** *a retailer allocates an equal
share of the trading area's total sales for a specific product category to each competing retailer.* This calculation is shown in Figure 13–10. The advantage in using
this method is that it is simple and quick to calculate. A limitation, however, is the
assumption that all competing retailers are equal and can generate an equal share
of the trading-area sales. Because competing retailers devote different amounts of
time, money, space, and effort to sales, the analyst must make adjustments to the
"all are equal" assumption. The competitive audit, discussed earlier, can be used to
make this adjustment.

$$\frac{\text{Capacity to Consume}}{\text{Capacity to Retail (Sell)}} = \frac{\text{Total Sales for Product Category}}{\text{Number of Retailers Selling Product Category*}} = \frac{\text{Total Sales per Retailer for Product Category}}{}$$

*Includes proposed retail operations

FIGURE 13–10
Total sales method for
estimating a retailer's
sales

377

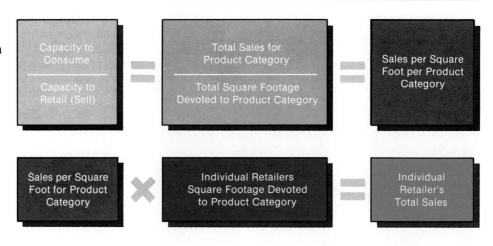

FIGURE 13–11

Sales per square foot method for estimating a retailer's sales

Sales per square foot method. Another method retailers use to allocate trading-area sales to competitors is the **sales per square foot method.** Using this method, *the retailer computes a ratio of each retailer's floor space devoted to a specific product category to the total of all retail floor space for the product category in the trading area.* The calculation procedure is illustrated in Figure 13–11. Employing this method, the retailer assumes that selling space is a good predictor of a retailer's competitiveness. Variations of this method substitute amount of shelf space (linear, square, or cubic feet), sales per employee, sales per checkout counter or/for sales per square foot.

The Growth Potential of Trading Areas

Before completing the trading-area evaluation process, the retailer must answer an additional question: What does the future hold for the trading area? Because marketing opportunities can change quickly, dynamically growing trading areas often become either static or declining markets. Without growth, the retailer either must fight to maintain present market share or be willing to survive on a smaller share. With growth, however, the retailer has an opportunity to expand sales and market share at a reasonable amount of cost and effort. Therefore, the final step in evaluating retail trading areas is to determine the area's future growth.

Because the future of a trading area is an outgrowth of past and current conditions, the retailer often can learn what to expect by examining those conditions. Visual observation of an area is a simple method of looking into the future. While lacking scientific methodology, a visual inspection of an area's current activities can produce a useful picture of the future. A retailer should consider several factors.

1. New and expanding residential areas combined with older, stable neighborhoods provide a solid base for future growth.
2. An expanding commercial or industrial base signals growth opportunities.
3. A good balance between items 1 and 2 reflects a stable growth rate that avoids overdependence on limited economic activity.
4. A well-developed transportation network as well as proposed future transportation networks in the trading area contribute to its growth.
5. An involved local government that takes an interest in residential and business development is a great asset.
6. A progressive social and cultural environment (theaters, museums, zoos, etc.) is a healthy climate for business.

FIGURE 13–12
A simple checklist to
evaluate a trading
area's potential growth

CHAPTER 13
ASSESSING RETAIL
TRADING AREAS

FACTORS[1]	RATING SCALE[2]				
	Excellent (5)	Good (4)	Fair (3)	Poor (2)	Very Poor (1)
1					
2					
3					
4					
5					
6					

[1]Factors may be added to or deleted from this checklist depending
upon local conditions.

[2]Total Rating Points   Trading Area Growth Potential

27 to 30	excellent
21 to 26	good
15 to 20	fair
10 to 14	poor
6 to 9	very poor

Figure 13–12 provides a checklist of these factors and how they might be used to
assess the growth potential of a trading area.

THE TRADING-AREA SELECTION PROCESS

To make the final selection of a trading area, the retailer must evaluate the alternatives in accordance with each of the following criteria, referred to as a "minimum
threshold:"

1. a stated minimum population having the desired demographic characteristics (such as 10,000 persons)
2. a stated minimum sales volume (such as $300,000/year)
3. a stated minimum daily traffic count (such as 5,000 vehicles/day)

If a trading area does not meet at least one or a certain combination of these minimums, the retailer excludes it from further consideration.

SUMMARY

A retail trading area is the area from which the retailer attracts all or most of its
customers. The size, shape, and internal structure of a trading area depend upon
several factors. Trading-area size is directly related to (1) the type and size of the
retailer's operation, (2) the number, size, and type of neighboring stores, (3) the
nature and actions of competing stores, and (4) the character of the transportation
network. The shape of a trading area is determined, in part, by the effects of the
local network of transportation; by physical, social, and political barriers; and by the
location of competitors. The internal structure of trading areas reflects the relative
ability of either a single retailer or a cluster of retailers to attract customers from
various distances or customer-source regions. Three internal trading-area structures
are general, composite, and proportional.

379

The trading-area problem is how to identify, evaluate, and select trading-area alternatives. Retailers can identify potential trading areas by using spotting techniques and quantitative procedures. The retailer determines the value of each trading area by determining first its gross and then its net adequacy. To refine the net adequacy further, it then assesses the future growth potential of each area. Gross adequacy is defined as a measure of the trading area's total capacity to consume. This consumption capacity is a function of both residential (those who live inside the trading area) and nonresidential (those who live outside the trading area) consumers. Residential consumption is measured by population/demographic and household/residential-unit factors. The number and type of nonresidential units within a trading area are used to measure nonresidential consumption. Total trading-area sales can be estimated using either the corollary data method or the per capita sales method.

Net adequacy is the level of support a given retailer can expect to attract from the trading area. The expectations of a retailer must depend upon the relationship between a trading area's capacity to consume and its capacity to retail. Through a competitive audit, the retailer can ascertain within reliable limits the trading area's capacity to retail. The retailer can obtain an estimate of the amount of sales that it can expect to derive from the trading area by dividing the trading area's capacity to consume by its capacity to retail, using either the total sales method or sales per square foot method. Before selecting which trading area alternatives to consider further, the retailer should determine the future growth potential of the area.

KEY TERMS AND CONCEPTS

retail trading area	spotting technique	corollary data method
general trading area	retail gravitation	per capita sales method
composite trading area	break-even point	competitive audit
proportional trading area	trading-area adequacy	outshopper analysis
primary trading zone	gross adequacy	total sales method
secondary trading zone	net adequacy	sales per square foot method
fringe trading zone	trading-area potential	

REVIEW QUESTIONS

1. What are the two characteristics common to most trading-area definitions?
2. What are the three purposes of any trading-area analysis?
3. How do the retailer's operations affect the size of a trading area?
4. Which factors have an impact on the shape of a retail trading area? Briefly explain each factor.
5. How are composite retail trading areas structured?

6. How much business can a retailer expect to receive from the secondary zone of a proportional trading area?
7. Describe the limitation associated with the license plate survey method of identifying trading areas.
8. How is Converse's break-even point formula expressed? Define each part of the expression.
9. What are the components of trading-area adequacy? Define each.

10. What determines a trading area's capacity to consume? Describe each factor.
11. How might a retailer assess the impact of "outsiders" on a trading area's capacity to consume?
12. Describe the per capita sales method for estimating trading-area sales.
13. What two methods are used to gain a clearer picture of the competitive environment of a trading area? Briefly describe each method.
14. Develop a demographic profile of the typical out-shopper.
15. Describe the sales per square foot method of estimating a retailer's share of the total sales within a trading area.
16. What should a retailer consider when assessing the growth potential of a trading area?
17. On what basis might a retailer make a final selection of a trading area?

ENDNOTES

1. William Applebaum and S. B. Cohen, "The Dynamics of Store Trading Areas and Market Equilibrium," *Annals of the Association of American Geographers* 51 (1961): 15.
2. Victor Gruen and Larry Smith, *Shopping Towns U.S.A.* (New York: Reinhold, 1960), 278.
3. Applebaum and Cohen, "The Dynamics of Store Trading Areas and Market Equilibrium," 14.
4. D. L. Huff, "Defining and Estimating a Trading Area," *Journal of Marketing* 28 (1964): 38.
5. Committee on Definitions of the American Marketing Association, *Marketing Definitions: A Glossary of Marketing Terms* (Chicago: American Marketing Association, 1960), 196–207.
6. See Ross L. Davies, *Marketing Geography* (Corbridge, Northumberland, England: Retailing and Planning Associates, 1976), 200–202.
7. Paul D. Converse, *Retail Trade Areas in Illinois,* Business Study No. 4 (Urbana, IL: University of Illinois, 1946), 30–31.

8. C. Samuel Craig, Avijit Ghosh, and Sara McLafferty, "Models of the Retail Location Process: A Review," *Journal of Retailing* 60 (Spring 1984): 15.
9. Huff, "Defining and Estimating a Trading Area," 34.
10. Richard L. Nelson, *The Selection of Retail Locations* (New York: F. W. Dodge, 1958), 181.
11. Dale M. Lewison and Ray Robins, "A Model for Evaluating the Adequacy of a Retail Trading Area," *Proceedings: Small Business Administration Directors Institute,* 1980.
12. Ibid.
13. Ibid., 186.
14. Rom J. Markin, Jr., *Retailing Management,* 2d ed. (New York: Macmillan, 1971), 170; Fred D. Reynolds and William R. Darden, "International Patronage: A Psychographic Study of Consumer Outshoppers," *Journal of Marketing* 36 (October 1972): 50–54.

RELATED READINGS

Belk, Leland L., and Newman, Larry M. "The Influence of Area Characteristics on Intermarket Patronage." *Developments in Marketing Science, Proceedings.* J. C. Rogers, III, ed. (Academy of Marketing Science 1983), 317–22.

Black, William C.; Ostlund, Lyman E.; and Westbrook, Robert A. "Spatial Demand Models in an Intrabrand Context." *Journal of Marketing* 49 (Summer 1985), 106–13.

Carusone, Peter S. "The Hierarchy of Priorities for Smaller-City CBD's." *Developments in Marketing Science, Proceedings.* N. K. Malhotra, ed. (Academy of Marketing Science 1985), 202–5.

Clithero, Joseph B., and Levenson, Lawrence A. "Urban

Renewal Projects Pull Up Short of Revitalizing Downtown Retailing when They Only Entail Brick and Mortar." *Marketing News* (February 1985), 23.

Dove, Rhonda W. "Retail Store Selection and the Older Shopper." *Marketing Comes of Age, Proceedings.* David M. Klein and Allen E. Smith, eds. (Southern Marketing Association 1984), 75–77.

Ghosh, Avijit, and McLafferty, Shara L. "Locating Stores in Uncertain Environments: A Scenario Planning Approach." *Journal of Retailing* 58 (Winter 1982), 5–22.

Hawes, Jon M., and Lumpkin, James R. "Understanding the Outshopper." *Journal of the Academy of Marketing Science* 12 (Fall 1984), 200–217.

———. "Winning the Battle for Intermarket Patronage." *1985 Proceedings*. J. C. Crawford and B. C. Garland, eds. (Southwestern Marketing Association 1985), 196–200.

Houston, Franklin S., and Stanton, John. "Evaluating Retail Trade Areas for Convenience Stores." *Journal of Retailing* 60 (Spring 1984), 124–36.

Ingene, Charles A., and Lusch, Robert F. "Market Selection Decisions for Department Stores." *Journal of Retailing* 56 (Fall 1980), 21–40.

Lewison, Dale M.; Willenborg, John F.; and Pitts, Robert E. "Trade Area Attributes, Consumer Patronage Behavior, and Retail Sales—A Recursive Model." *Contemporary Marketing Thought, 1977 Educators' Proceedings*. B. A. Greenberg and D. N. Bellenger, eds. (American Marketing Association 1977), 308–11.

Lewison, Dale M., and Zerbst, Robert A. "Trade Area Mix and Intensity Concepts for Evaluating Retail Site Alternatives." *Annals of Regional Science* 11 (July 1977), 86–96.

Lord, J. Dennis, and Mesimer, Douglas B. "Trade Area, Land Use Mix, and Diurnal Shifts in Store Patronage Patterns." *Akron Business and Economic Review* 13 (Fall 1982), 17–22.

Nevin, John R., and Houston, Michael J. "Image as a Component of Attraction to Intraurban Shopping Areas." *Journal of Retailing* 56 (Spring 1980), 77–93.

Olsen, Janeen E., and Granzin, Kent L. "Consumer Logistics: The Location Subsystem." *Developments in Marketing Science, Proceedings*. N. K. Malhotra, ed. (Academy of Marketing Science 1985), 21–25.

Papadopoulos, N. G. "Consumer Outshopping Research: Review and Extension." *Journal of Retailing* 56 (Winter 1980), 41–58.

Reindenbach, R. Eric; Cooper, M. Bixby; and Harrison, Mary Carolyn. "A Factor Analytic Comparison of Out Shopping Behavior in Larger Retail Trade Areas." *Journal of the Academy of Marketing Science* 12 (Winter - Spring 1984), 145–58.

Sewall, Murphy A.; Stanley, Thomas J.; and Danko, William. "Predictive Validation of Gravity Model Forecasting of Retailer Sales Potential." *AMA Educators' Proceedings*. R. W. Belk et al, eds. (American Marketing Association 1984), 76–79.

Stanley, Thomas J., and Korgaonkar, Pradeep. "Explaining Retail Trade in the Urban Environment." *AMA Educators' Proceedings*. R. W. Belk et al, eds. (American Marketing Association 1984), 381–84.

Wee, Chow-Hou, and Pearce, Michael R. "Retail Gravitational Models: A Review with Implications for Further Research." *Developments in Marketing Science, Proceedings*. J. D. Lindquist, ed. (Academy of Marketing Science 1984), 300–305.

Weisbrod, Glen E.; Parcells, Robert J.; and Kern, Clifford. "A Disaggregate Model for Predicting Shopping Area Market Attraction." *Journal of Retailing* 60 (Spring 1984), 65–83.

PART FIVE
Retail Mix Management: Implementing the Retailing Mix

Outline

THE SITE-IDENTIFICATION PROCESS

The Isolated Site
The Unplanned Clustered Site
The Planned Clustered Site

THE SITE-EVALUATION PROCESS

Principles of Site Evaluation
Methods of Site Evaluation

THE SITE-SELECTION PROCESS

Objectives

■ Delineate and describe the four major ingredients of the retail mix

■ Classify and characterize the various types of site alternatives

■ Identify and use the five principles of site evaluation to assess the value of alternative sites

■ Describe and apply the basic method of retail site evaluation

■ Make a final site-selection decision through the process of elimination

14
The Retail Site

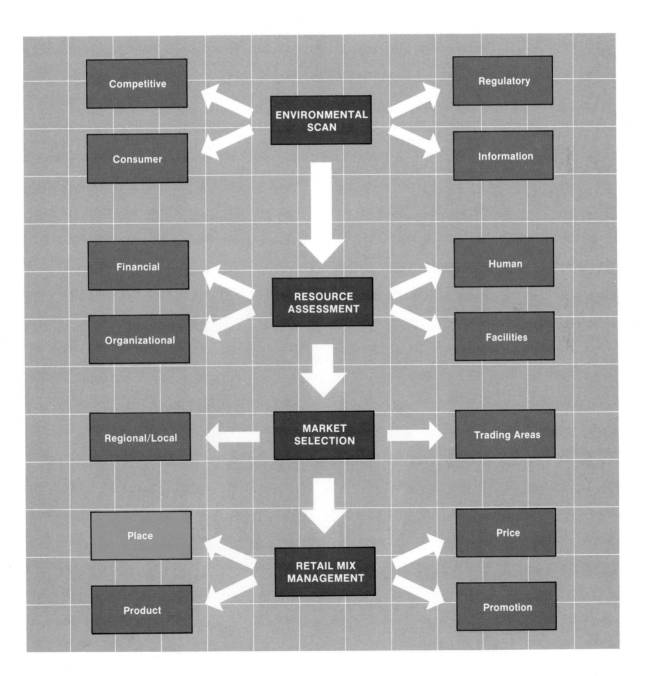

A primary concern of retail managers is the effective management of the four major ingredients of the **retail mix**, commonly referred to as the 4 Ps of marketing: *place, product, price,* and *promotion.* Figure 14–1 illustrates the major ingredients of the retail mix and describes the decisions associated with each ingredient. Management must creatively combine the four ingredients into a successful merchandising mix consistent with expectations and needs of the firm's targeted consumers. The retail mix presents the decisions over which the retail manager can exercise the most control. As markets and their environments change, the 4 Ps can be adjusted to meet new challenges. The next 11 chapters are devoted to the study of place, product, price, and promotion decisions. This chapter covers decisions involving selection of the right site.

A **retail site** is *the actual physical location from which the retailer operates a retail business.* Numerous specialists in the retailing field have commented that a retailer's site is one of the principal tools in obtaining and maintaining a competitive advantage through "spatial monopoly."[1]

Using a behavioral approach, Gruen suggests that a given site is unique because its "positional qualities" serve a particular trading-area consumer in a manner that no other site can match.[2] Obviously, competing sites also are uniquely situated. Therefore, the *retailer's site problem* is how to identify, evaluate, and select the best available site alternative to serve profitably the needs of an identified trading-area consumer (see Figure 14–2).

THE SITE-IDENTIFICATION PROCESS

The first step in appraising retail site locations is to identify all potential site alternatives. The number of site alternatives within any given trading area can range from an extremely limited choice to a very large selection (see Figure 14–3). Before at-

FIGURE 14–1
Ingredients of the retail mix

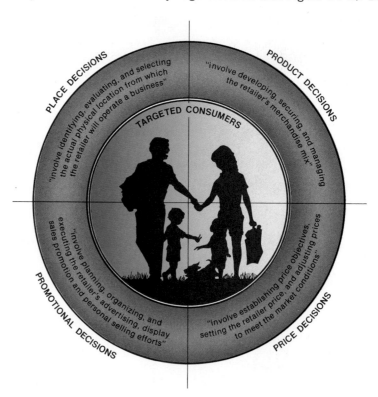

PLACE DECISIONS "involve identifying, evaluating, and selecting the actual physical location from which the retailer will operate a business"

PRODUCT DECISIONS "involve developing, securing, and managing the retailer's merchandise mix"

TARGETED CONSUMERS

PROMOTIONAL DECISIONS "involve planning, organizing, and executing the retailer's advertising, display sales promotion and personal selling efforts"

PRICE DECISIONS "involve establishing price objectives, setting the retailer price, and adjusting prices to meet the market conditions."

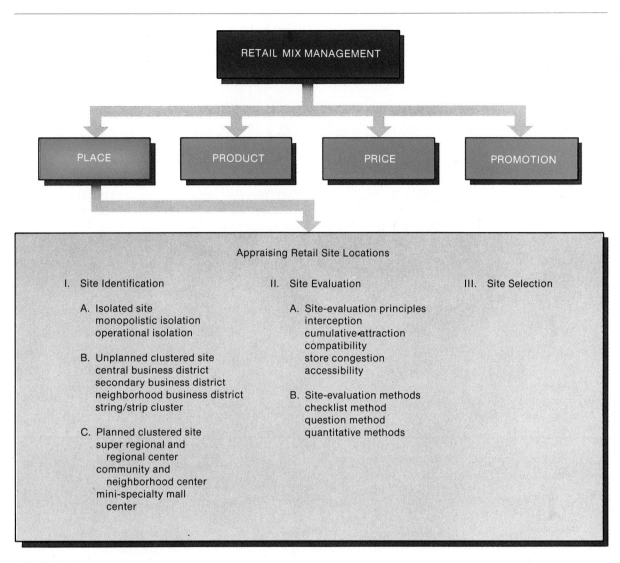

FIGURE 14–2
Appraising retail site locations

tempting any formal evaluation, the retailer should screen the alternatives by asking three questions:

1. Is the site available for rent or purchase **(availability)**?
2. Are the site and facilities of a suitable size and structure **(suitability)**?
3. Is the asking rental rate or selling price within the retailer's operating budget **(acceptability)**?

To be considered for further evaluation, a site alternative must meet all three screening criteria: it must be available, suitable, and acceptable.

Retail sites can be classified as either isolated or clustered. **Isolated sites** are *retail locations geographically separated from other retailing sites*. Isolated sites, however, can be located next to other forms of economic and social activity. **Clustered sites** are *retail locations that are either next to each other or in close proximity*.

387

From a shopping perspective, a cluster is two or more closely located retailers capable of sharing customers with minimal effort. Retail clusters are of two types: unplanned and planned. An *unplanned retail cluster* is the result of a natural evolutionary process. A *planned retail cluster* is the result of a planning process.

The Isolated Site

One site alternative is to "go it alone" by selecting an absolute location that is isolated from other retailers. The degree of physical isolation can range from being "around the corner and down the block" to "far out on the outskirts of town." In relative location terms, an isolated site is situated so that it will not normally share consumer traffic with other retailers; however, its relative location offers certain advantages in attracting customers from other sources of business. Generally, the retailer that selects an isolated site is seeking to gain either a monopolistic or an operational advantage.

FIGURE 14–3
Fast-foods stalk locations

When the Navy's submarine-tender U.S.S.L.Y. Spear heads out to sea, it carries a Baskin-Robbins ice cream shop on board.

That's hardly the usual site for a fast-food restaurant, but the industry's growth is making traditional locations harder to find and more expensive to acquire.

The maturing fast-food business' market-share struggle that has forced chains to adopt harder advertising and marketing tactics is spilling over into the fight for sales.

As a result, the major fast-food chains are looking at unusual unit designs and some new markets in an effort to maximize brand visibility and sales growth.

Placing fast-food units on military bases is only one of the options chains are pursuing. The first of 70 planned Burger Kings inside Woolworth stores opened in New York in time for Thanksgiving. A McDonald's soon will appear in Montreal's Central Station train depot.

Hospitals, colleges, museums and bus stations are now also on the list of alternate expansion vehicles being considered. But with 2 million Americans in uniform, the armed forces heads the list as a market too good to ignore.

When Burger King opened the first military unit last year at the U.S. Navy Exchange at Pearl Harbor, it was considered an oddity and a publicity gimmick. That store did $2 million in sales in its first year, compared with Burger King's systemwide average of about $850,000, and competitors are fighting for the chance to construct oddities of their own. . . . Less expansion of suburban areas minimized the number of prime traditional locations.

One positive result has been to make restaurant site selection a more sophisticated and serious undertaking.

"Prior to 1977, commitment to accurate site selection by the industry was weak," . . . "The philosophy often was to build down the street from McDonald's, figuring that if the location is good enough for them, it's good enough for us."

McDonald's real-estate expertise still is admired widely and is a major factor in the chain's success. As it explores a wide variety of alternatives to traditional street-corner sites, competitors still are inclined to follow. McDonald's this year will exceed its annual goal of 500 new stores by being flexible enough to adapt to any location that is both available and promising.

Thus there is the McSnack unit at the Ridgedale Center shopping mall in Minnetonka, Minn. With only 400 sq. ft. of space, there's no room for grill equipment so no hamburgers are available. Even so, McDonald's executives recently told securities analysts that the little store is doing $500,000 in annual sales with a profit margin comparable to a full-size store.

FIGURE 14–3, *continued*

In contrast to McSnack is the chain's 7,000th store, opened last year in Falls Church, Va. Situated on a 1.4-acre site, the 128-seat unit has two dining rooms in its three modules, connected by glass-enclosed corridors. Annual sales are projected to be half again as much as McDonald's $1.1 million average.

Other companies see different potential in those few large sites available. The saturation problem has led several companies that began as franchises to become franchisors of their own restaurant concepts.

The newest trend is for these companies to turn large properties into multiconcept locations. Itasca, Ill.-based Chart House is considering linking expansion of its franchised Burger Kings with two of the chains it owns by coupling one of its hamburger restaurants with a Luther's Bar-B-Que and Godfather's Pizza on a single site.

Nashville-based Shoney's Inc. (a Big Boy licensee that also owns the Captain D's seafood and Famous Recipe fried-chicken chains) and W. R. Grace & Co.'s fast-food division (Del Taco and other chains) are looking at similar setups.

That configuration has built-in cost-efficiencies and is easier than finding three separate locations in a tight real-estate market, but . . . "That setup may sound good, but a good location for a pizza restaurant may be a terrible one for a different concept," . . .

In addition to the Woolworth locations, Burger King has franchise agreements that will put its stores on major toll roads (operated by Howard Johnson Co.) and highways (run by Truckstops of America). Greyhound Corp. operates 26 franchises in selected bus terminals. Others are open in student unions at Boston's Northeastern University and Triton College in River Grove, Ill.

There's a McDonald's in Ohio University in Athens, O., and one in Lexington Vocational Technical High School in Lexington, Mass. Big Mac also is the first to crack the potentially lucrative healthcare market with a unit in Philadelphia's Children's Hospital

As a gentle tweek, there's a McDonald's at the airport in Burger King's headquarters city of Miami. There are Golden Arches on a riverboat beneath St. Louis' arch and a store in the Toronto Zoo.

But Burger King may have the last word in unusual locations.

Its Columbus, O., franchise last summer unveiled the Burger Bus, a completely mobile, full-menu Burger King on wheels. Company officials said they are monitoring the bus' success with an eye to expanding the concept.

Source: Scott Hume, "Fast-Foods Stalk Locations." Reprinted with permission of *Advertising Age*, 28 Nov. 1983. Copyright Crain Communications Inc.

Monopolistic Isolation

Monopolistic isolation is *a site affording a retailer a uniquely convenient and accessible location to serve consumers.* A monopolistically isolated site is isolated from competing retail sites, but uniquely situated for traffic-generating activities. Examples are a convenience-food store in a residential area, a neighborhood bar, a local service station, and a cafeteria located in an office complex. A familiar example of monopolistic isolation to students is the local campus bookstore.

Operational Isolation

Some retailers prefer to locate in isolated areas because they think it gives them greater flexibility in operating a retail business. A retailer that uses such an **operational isolation** strategy can achieve flexibility in a number of areas.

Site geography. Site alternatives that meet the size, shape, and terrain requirements of the retailer's operation constitute site geography. A home-improvement center, for example, normally requires a large, flat site to accommodate large showrooms and storage facilities.

Transportation network. Some site alternatives have transportation networks that generate good consumer traffic and also have good supply connections. A large warehouse-showroom retailer might consider locating the store at the junction of two major highway systems where customer traffic is high. However, it should also consider whether there is an adjacent railroad spur to handle large numbers of heavy, bulky products efficiently.

Type of facilities. Certain site alternatives permit the installation of facilities that are conducive to the retailer's operations. The architectural motif of the store, the store's internal layout, fixturing, and atmosphere, as well as supporting facilities such as parking and signing, are all important considerations to any retailer. Most clustered locations have numerous facility restrictions, whereas isolation permits great freedom in facility design.

Operating methods. Some sites offer the retailer freedom of operation and avoidance of group rules commonly found in shopping centers. Such restrictions include store operating hours, external displays, and cooperative advertising programs.

Operating costs. A site must give the retailer the opportunity to operate within its business' cost constraints. The low-margin/high-turnover retailer (e.g., discount houses) needs to keep operating expenses low in order to offer discount prices. An isolated site can have low rental costs that help hold prices down.

Along with its advantages, an isolationist strategy has several disadvantages. First, the retailer must attract and hold its own customers. The shopping and specialty retailer that uses an isolationist strategy could encounter serious problems, since these consumers prefer either to compare brands or are one-stop shoppers. A second disadvantage is that retailers usually must design and build their own facilities. Only the largest retail organizations have the human and financial resources to engage in such activities. Third, the isolated retailer cannot share operating costs with neighboring establishments. Clustered locations allow retailers the opportunity to share certain common ground costs such as maintenance, security, lighting, and snow and garbage removal.

The Unplanned Clustered Site

Prior to widespread urban planning and zoning laws, "unplanned" retailing clusters sprang up, many of which still exist today. In cities where local zoning ordinances are not strictly enforced, they continue to form. Unplanned retailing clusters are often part of larger unplanned business districts where retailers can be either clustered together or scattered with no discernible pattern. While they come in all sizes, shapes, and patterns, there are four general types of unplanned clusters: the central business district, the secondary business district, the neighborhood business district, and the string-strip shopping cluster.

Central Business District

The **central business district (CBD)** was, and in many cities still is, the single most important retailing cluster. However, since World War II the CBD has declined in its role as the city's principal place to shop. Among the commonly cited reasons for the CBD's decline are

- the migration of middle- and upper-income consumers to the suburbs
- the development of fast, accessible intracity transportation networks, which allow people to live anywhere in the city and still work in the CBD

- the general congestion in the CBD and its effects on free movement and accessibility
- environmental pollution (air, noise, etc.) and its physiological effects
- the general decay of the physical facilities in many downtown areas and its psychological effect
- the high crime rates in and around the CBD
- the problems associated with the influx of low-income and ethnic groups into the areas immediately surrounding the CBD

Despite all of its problems and numerous predictions of its extinction, the CBD and the retailing clusters within it have survived. In fact, some cities are experiencing a renaissance. Revitalized CBDs have resulted from

- converting streets to pedestrian malls
- modernizing physical facilities
- reducing traffic congestion by using one-way streets and modern traffic-control devices
- constructing new middle- and upper-income residential complexes
- renovating low-income residential areas
- organizing commercial businesses to develop and promote the downtown area

Whereas some CBD revitalization projects have been extremely successful, others have failed. Successful revitalization projects include the Nicollet Mall in Minneapolis, Ghirardelli Square in San Francisco, Faneuil Hall Marketplace in Boston, and the Gallery at Market Street East in Philadelphia. The key to successful revitalization projects is not so much the development of new and existing facilities, but the creation of a safe and pleasant shopping atmosphere. The developers of the revitalization projects for Boston's Faneuil Hall Marketplace and Philadelphia's Gallery demonstrate why it is necessary to create the right atmospherics (see Figure 14–4).

What are the advantages and disadvantages of shopping in the central business district (CBD)?

Creating The Right Atmospherics For The CBD

The idea in simplest terms is to make shopping fun, a form of entertainment that can compete with other recreational activities for people's leisure time. To achieve this end . . . a "lighthearted, colorful, intensely human shopping environment," an immovable feast of small chain stores, single-item boutiques and specialty food services is presented in the upbeat architecture of skylighted plaza, uninterrupted sight lines and plenty of public amenities—fountains, trees, benches, etc.

In the case of Philadelphia [Gallery]—two department stores anchor the assemblage—as the typical suburban mall—adding major retailer presence to the otherwise single-item proprietorships. In Boston [Faneuil Hall Marketplace] . . . their absence intensifies the emphasis on a variety of specialty fare. Overall, however, the effect is the same: an atmosphere of continuous variety, conviviality, and, above all, comfort; a place where people will come to pass the time as well as make a purchase.

Source: Junius Ellis, "Jim Rouse: Nobody Builds 'em Better," *Sky* (Los Angeles: East West Network, December 1978), 47.

Malls Breathe New Life Into Cities

Americans may buy their jeans and socks at the local shopping center, but when it comes to the new and novel—high-fashion clothes, fine chocolates and unusual gift items—there's no place like the city or, more specifically, the urban retail mall.

Across the country, the urban mall is emerging as a significant retail opportunity of the 1980s. Frequently boasting an array of tony shops targeted to the upscale resident, tourist and local office worker, these shopping enclaves are designed to provide consumers with an unusual shopping experience. The ambiance is as important as the merchandise mix.

Tenants frequently are selected on the basis of their merchandising style and marketing sophistication, with mall developers and managers assuming responsibility for the theatrics—special events, entertainment, floral shows and the like. All of this often occurs in a restored or renovated building or area that, not too long ago, was the victim of decay.

The excitement of the city mall has spread to virtually every major metropolis. There's Water Tower Place in Chicago; South Street Seaport, Citicorp and, this fall, Herald Center in New York; Portside in Toledo; Grand Avenue in Milwaukee; Dallas Galleria in Dallas; Nicollet Mall in Minneapolis, and Waterside in Norfolk, VA., to name a few. More are in the planning stages for such cities as Albuquerque, Miami, Seattle and Richmond, VA.

In many instances, the rebirth of downtown shopping is simply a matter of good business sense. The city is, after all, where many urbanites as well as suburbanites work and, very often, play.

"The highest grossing stores are in downtown because there's a multiplicity of markets there—resident, workers, visitor, businessman. It's market piled upon market."

"The expressways that were built to haul people into the city for their white-collar jobs are making it more accessible for them to return to the city for entertainment. There's more parking now, more lighting, and it's safer," . . .

At the same time, there's also a return to living in the city, particularly among foreigners, single people and the affluent. "Singles and foreigners tend to be in the city and, as a result, there are a number of exclusive communities there," . . .

"Those people must be served better with convenient, upscale retail centers."

Source: Cara S. Troyer, "Malls Breathe New Life into Cities." Reprinted with permission of *Advertising Age,* 9 Aug. 1984. Copyright Crain Communications Inc.

FIGURE 14–4
Revitalization of the CBD

Secondary Business Districts

Most medium- and large-size cities have one or more **secondary business districts (SBD),** *located at the intersections of major traffic arteries.* In some cases, these SBDs were originally the downtown areas of cities that were later incorporated into larger cities. In other cases, they represent the natural evolution of a retailing cluster to meet the convenience shopping needs of adjacent neighborhoods. As the name implies, these clusters are secondary to central business districts. They are similar to CBDs except they are much smaller. A typical SBD generally varies from 10 to 30 stores, radiating from one or more major intersections along primary traffic arteries.

The typical store mix of an SBD includes one or two branch department stores (or some other mass merchandiser) that serve as the principal consumer attraction; several specialty, shopping, and convenience goods retailers; and various service establishments including hair-care, dry cleaning, laundry, insurance, and real estate services. Often one or more large, nonretailing generators (e.g., hospital, office complex, university, manufacturing plant) are in the immediate vicinity of an SBD. These nonretailing establishments are often important nonresidential sources of business.

Neighborhood Business Districts

The **neighborhood business district (NBD)** is *a small retailing cluster that serves primarily one or two residential areas.* The NBD generally contains four to five stores, usually including some combination of food and drug stores, gasoline service stations, neighborhood bars, self-service laundries, barber shops, beauty shops, and small, general-merchandise stores. The most common structural arrangement for the NBD is the "four-corners" layout, with a retailer situated on each corner. In some cases additional stores extend to midblock along one or two of the streets. Although the four-corners layout is generally associated with secondary and residential streets, these streets represent the major "feeder" into the adjacent residential neighborhoods. For the convenience retailer that wants to serve a particular neighborhood, the NBD is a logical alternative.

String/Strip Cluster

The **string/strip cluster** *develops along a major thoroughfare and depends upon the consumption activity of people who travel these busy thoroughfares.* The size of the

What are the positional strengths of this type of shopping cluster?

string (or strip) is directly related to the average volume of traffic along a thorough-fare. Some stretch for miles along the heavily traveled arteries leading into and out of a CBD, whereas others are limited to one or two blocks along streets carrying a lower density of traffic. Examples of long strips are those with new and used car lots, rows of mobile home dealerships, strings of home-furnishings outlets, and a strand of side-by-side fast-food restaurants.

The positional strengths of the string/strip cluster are their ability to

- intercept consumers as they travel from one place to another
- expose consumers to the retailer's operations
- attract consumers on impulse
- provide lower rents than central and secondary business districts

The Planned Clustered Site

Over the last several decades, the growth of suburban populations has provided retailers with the opportunity to meet the needs of the suburban shopper. Originally, the basic problem was to develop an institution that could satisfy the shopping needs of a geographically dispersed market. The most common solution was and still is a one-stop shopping institution such as a planned shopping center. Through careful planning, a developer could offer a merchandise mix (products, services, prices) to meet most customer needs for convenience, shopping, and specialty goods.

A planned shopping center is "a group of commercial establishments planned, developed, owned, and managed as a unit related in location, size, and type of shops to the trade area the unit serves."[3] Shopping centers vary in nature according to their tenants and the size of the markets they serve. On the basis of type and size, shopping centers are classified as regional, community, neighborhood, and specialty centers.

The Super Regional and Regional Center

Regional shopping centers serve regional markets varying in size according to the type of transportation network serving the center, the location of competing centers and unplanned business districts, the willingness of consumers to travel various distances to shop, and the tenant mix. The Urban Land Institute identifies two types of regional shopping centers: a **super regional shopping center** is *built around at least three and often four major department stores;* a **regional shopping center** is *built around one or two full-line department stores.*[4] The typical size of each center ranges from 400,000 to 600,000 square feet of gross leasable area (GLA) for the regional center to 750,000 to 1,000,000 square feet of GLA for the super regional center.[5]

The regional and super regional centers provide consumers an extensive assortment of convenience, shopping, and specialty goods as well as numerous personal and professional services and recreational facilities. This extensive assortment is achieved through a balanced tenancy of some 50–150 individual stores.

Shopping centers are designed in a variety of shapes and arrangements. A given configuration must conform to a site's terrain and the tenants' space requirements, as well as provide ease of customer movement. While any number of configurations are possible, Figure 14–5 illustrates four basic shopping center configurations. The "I" plan is the simplest and most commonly used regional shopping center configuration (see Figure 14–5a). Although the "I" plan is efficient for retailer

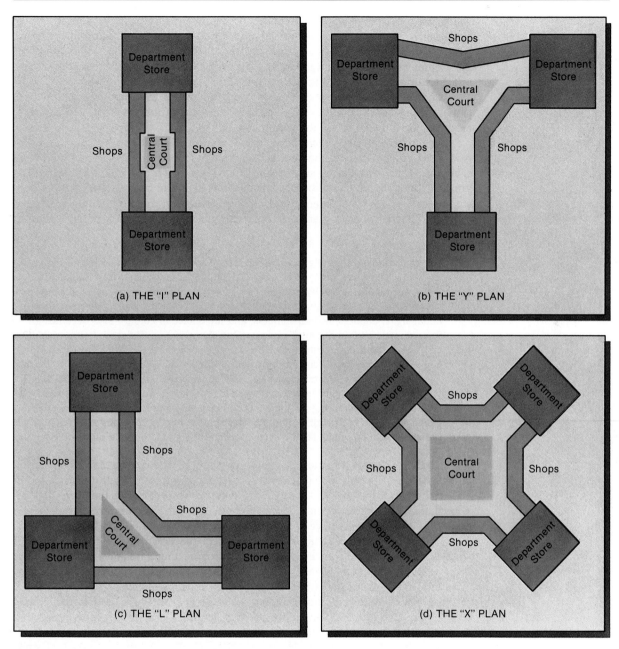

FIGURE 14–5
Shopping center configurations

space requirements and customer movement, it does not create an interesting and exciting shopping environment.

For regional and super regional centers containing three or more major anchors, retailers can use either the "Y" plan (see Figure 14–5b) or the "L" plan (see

Figure 14–5c). Examples of a modified "Y" plan include the TownEast Shopping Center in Mesquite, Texas, near Dallas; the Pompano Fashion Square in Pompano Beach, Florida; and the Santa Anita Fashion Park in Arcadia, California. Tysons Corner Center in Fairfax County, Virginia, and the North Park Mall in Dallas, Texas, represent modifications of the basic "L" plan.

The "X" plan serves as the basic configuration for the four-anchor, super regional center (see Figure 14–5d). The best example of this configuration is Crossroads Center in Oklahoma City.

Regardless of the configuration, a key feature of most super regional and regional shopping centers is the central court. Some super regional centers also have several smaller secondary courts, each displaying its own character and decor. The importance of courts lies in their image-creating role. The central court is what consumers remember most often and most vividly. Hence, in recent years, more and more emphasis has been placed on court design. As one shopping center specialist writes:

> . . .concentrate on excellence in the design of courts—on such various exciting features as glass space-frame domes, special lighting fixtures, sculptural fountains, landscaped areas, specially-designed staircases, escalators, glass-enclosed elevators (for multi-level centers) and important art work. The design of the graphics—directional signs, banners, central symbols, and the choice of colors—also becomes an important element in the total impact on the shopper . . . The main court, in addition to serving as an exciting place for the shopper to sit, relax, and meet friends, could also be designed for functional and profitable uses. In order to provide for this flexibility, permanent installations (i.e., fountains, plantings, artwork) should be placed so as to allow for large open areas for special events—concerts, auto and boat (as well as other large equipment) displays, art shows, and community programs. The idea of providing amphitheater-type seating in the main court adds to the possibilities of arranging festive events for both the young and the older shopper.[6]

The third design consideration is the planning of mall areas. Mall areas are the traffic arteries of the shopping center; as such, they must facilitate the movement and exchange of customers throughout the entire complex. The length and width of mall areas are prime considerations in planning for this movement and exchange process. "Where the distance from one major store to another is long (over 700 feet), there are both physical and psychological reactions to the 'tunnel' effect."[7] Several design features are employed to overcome these negative reactions. The most common one is a "break" in the mall approximately midway between major attractions. The central court is the most common midway break; however, if the distance between the central court and each department store is too long, additional breaks may be required. Secondary court areas and slight angles in the mall that require shoppers to make short turns before seeing the remainder of the mall can be extremely effective in reducing the tunnel effect. Also, by using a series of small storefront setbacks starting at each end of the mall, the mall will appear shorter and wider.[8]

In addition to customer movement and exchange, mall areas should facilitate customer shopping. "Generally the design of the malls and arcades leading to the main courts should strive for an intimate character and subdued atmosphere. The purpose is to have the shopper's eye attracted to the store displays."[9] Store fronts should be designed to afford the consumer some privacy for "window shopping" without being hassled by passing pedestrian traffic. On the other hand, some mall designs have incorporated "kiosks" to create the happy and busy atmosphere of an

What are the advantages of a kiosk?

open marketplace. These freestanding booths with highly specialized product lines (greeting cards, cutlery items, T-shirts, candy) and services (minibanks, snack bars, utility cashiers) add a new dimension to the shopping atmosphere of the mall and contribute substantially to the mall's profitability.

Community and Neighborhood Centers

Community and neighborhood shopping centers serve the market areas that their names suggest. The **neighborhood shopping center** *obtains its customers from one or a few neighborhoods within its immediate vicinity.* Its trading area can be roughly defined as the area within a five-minute drive of the center, containing anywhere from 7,000 to 50,000 potential customers. The **community shopping center** *serves a composite of many neighborhoods within a 10- to 15-minute drive from the shopping center.* The number of potential customers within its trading area ranges from 20,000 to 100,000. In smaller cities, the community shopping center serves an entire city and often competes with the downtown area.

The size of the market areas for each of these centers is primarily a function of the number of stores in the center and its tenant mix. The neighborhood center usually contains 5–15 stores, with a supermarket as the principal tenant. Comprising largely convenience goods retailers, the neighborhood center sells products that meet the daily living needs of its local area. With a gross leasable area (GLA) ranging from 25,000 to 100,000 square feet, the neighborhood center frequently includes a hardware store, drug store, and various personal-service retailers, such as beauty and barber shops.[10]

The community center is considerably larger and more diverse in its mix of tenants than the neighborhood center. Containing from 10 to 30 retail establishments with a total GLA of 75,000–300,000 square feet, the community center offers a wide range of shopping goods and convenience goods. The community center is likely to be anchored by one or more mass merchandising stores, the most common being junior department stores, discount stores, and discount department stores. Large supermarkets and variety stores also play an important role in attracting consumers to the community center.

The Mini-Specialty Shopping Center

The **mini-specialty shopping center** *essentially is a miniature regional mall.* Offering many of the same features as regional malls, these centers range in size from 100,000 to 300,000 square feet with 15–30 specialty stores, boutiques, and service retailers. The largest store usually does not exceed 25,000 square feet. Most mini-specialty malls are enclosed malls with a common architectural motif and decor. Discoveries, Inc., located in a middle-upper-class neighborhood in Oklahoma City, is an example of this type of mall. Discoveries is

> a collection of small specialty shops combined under one roof, where the shopper might come and have lunch or dinner. The building also offers child care services to encourage longer stays by the mother. A prime concern was to create a casual, noncommercial atmosphere. No advertising by any of the tenants is allowed, either within the building or on the exterior. All shops use identical lettering next to or above their doorways. . . All corridors and public areas are used to display paintings and art works. These are handled by an art dealer and instructor who has her studio within the building. The dress shop provides modeling during the noon lunch period within the Tea Room.[11]

A similar mini-specialty mall theme is found in the Quadrangle in Dallas, Texas.

This section has covered several ways to describe sites. The identification process is the first step in appraising site alternatives. At this point, we turn our attention to the second step, the site-evaluation process.

THE SITE-EVALUATION PROCESS

For any type of retailer, a number of potentially successful site alternatives exists. Unfortunately, an even greater number of unsuccessful alternatives also exists. Hence, retailers must carefully *evaluate* each alternative on the basis of several criteria. A common mistake many retailers make is to use a "site typology" approach to evaluate site alternatives. This approach assumes that the evaluator stops with the identification process, then simply selects the most appropriate type of site within a general site class. Although the isolated and clustered (planned and unplanned) locations discussed in the previous section have their advantages as site alternatives, the retailer would be mistaken in assuming that by selecting a particular type of location, all the advantages normally associated with the location type automatically would accrue to the retailer's site. Each site has its own position qualities and whether a site can reap the full advantages of a particular class of site depends upon individual circumstances. Retailers must therefore evaluate the positional qualities of *each* individual, unique site.

The following sections discuss the site-evaluation process in two phases. The first section explains several principles of site evaluation and how retailers use them to assess the value of alternative sites. The second looks at several methods retailers use to evaluate alternative site locations.

Principles of Site Evaluation

Several consumer-oriented location principles can aid retailers in evaluating site alternatives. While there are no standard criteria by which all sites can be judged, the following location principles provide the necessary framework for developing practical solutions to the problem of retail site evaluation. These location principles are

(a)

(b)

A specialty mall center

(1) interception, (2) cumulative attraction, (3) compatibility, (4) store congestion, and (5) accessibility.

Principle of Interception

The principle of **interception** *covers positional qualities of a site that determine its ability to "intercept" consumers as they travel from one place to another.* Interception has two distinct elements: first, a "source region" from which consumers are drawn; second, a "terminal region" or consumer destination, a region to which consumers are drawn. Examples of source and terminal regions are residential areas, office complexes, industrial plants, business districts, and shopping centers. Any point between source and terminal regions can be considered a point of interception. In considering the interceptor qualities of a site, the evaluator has both an identification and an evaluation problem. The identification problem consists of determining (1) the location of source and terminal regions, (2) the lines connecting those regions, and (3) appropriate points (sites) along the connection line. The evaluation problem is one of measuring the magnitude and quality of these regions, lines, and points. Thus, the evaluator's problem is how to determine whether a site is an efficient "intervening opportunity" between known source and terminal regions.

A different perspective of the interception principle is often expressed as the "concept of location vulnerability." In this case, the evaluator's job is to determine the source of a competitor's business and then locate a site that intercepts the competitor's customer flow. If such a location exists, the firm's competitor is vulnerable in a locational sense, at least with respect to one or more source regions.

It is difficult to measure the interceptor qualities of a site. The difficulty arises because of the numerous potential source and terminal regions, connecting lines, and interceptor points (sites) along these lines of movement. Location specialists often use traffic volume as a surrogate measurement of interception. They assume that a site on a high-volume traffic artery is a good point of interception. This assumption may prove to be reasonable after the evaluator conducts a traffic study and determines not only the volume of traffic but also its quality and character.

399

Principle of Cumulative Attraction

According to the principle of **cumulative attraction,** *a cluster of similar and complementary retailing activities will generally have greater drawing power than dispersed and isolated stores engaging in the same retailing activities.*[12] Retail-location literature often refers to the cumulative attraction effects of the familiar "rows," "cities," and "alleys." In many large cities, certain types of retailing establishments tend to cluster in specific areas. Examples are the familiar automobile rows, mobile home cities, and restaurant alleys. The evaluator's problem in this case is how to determine whether the retail operation can benefit from the cumulative drawing power of a site's immediate environment.

Principle of Compatibility

Retail **compatibility** refers to the *"degree to which two businesses interchange customers."*[13] As a rule, *the greater the compatibility between businesses located in close proximity, the greater the interchange of customers and the greater the sales volume of each compatible business.*

Compatibility between retailers occurs when their merchandising mixes are complementary. An example of retailer compatibility based on complementary product mixes is where an apparel shop, shoe store, and jewelry store are located very close to one another. If there are several apparel, shoe, and jewelry stores located in the same cluster, all the better! They are not only complementary, they also provide a healthy competitive situation that satisfies the customers' need for comparison shopping and thus provide greater customer interchange for the retailer.

A high degree of compatibility is more likely to occur when the pricing structures of neighboring businesses are complementary. Other things being equal, there will be a greater interchange of customers between one high-margin retailer and another than between a high-margin and a low-margin retailer. For example, a high-margin specialty retailer cannot expect to prosper by locating an operation in a community shopping center anchored by a budget supermarket and a discount store. Since the large majority of customers who shop at these low-margin stores are economy-minded, they are highly unlikely to make good prospects for the specialty shop.

Equally important in site evaluation is to determine whether neighboring businesses are compatible. For example, an exclusive dress shop would be incompatible with a pet shop because of the odor and noise produced by the pets. Other businesses that are incompatible are a funeral home and an eating establishment, a beauty parlor and an auto repair shop, and a bowling alley and a fur shop.

Principle of Store Congestion

At some point, the advantages of cumulative attraction and compatibility end, and the problems of site congestion begin. The principle of **store congestion** *states that as locations become more saturated with stores, other business activities, and people, they become less attractive to additional shopping traffic.* This phenomenon is due to the limited mobility of people and cars in the area. Retailers should have learned this lesson from the original congested central business districts. While the excitement of the crowd can be a positive factor, the aggravation of a mob can be a limiting factor discouraging customers from visiting the site. Thus, in the site-evaluation process, the retailer should estimate at what point the volume of vehicle and foot traffic would limit business, both in the present and in the near future.

Principle of Accessibility

The principle of accessibility is perhaps the most basic of all the retail site-evaluation principles. As expressed by one specialist, "the accessibility of a store, whether isolated or one of a group, is a practical basis for appraising a site's potentiality. An inaccessible site would be of no value to even the most astute of merchants."[14] According to the principle of **accessibility,** *the more easily potential consumers can approach, enter, traverse, and exit a site, the more likely they will visit the site to shop.* Greater site accessibility means greater likelihood of customer visits (shopping), which means greater likelihood of higher sales volume. Any major hindrance in any one of the four components of accessibility limits consumer traffic and sales.

Accessibility is a function of both physical and psychological dimensions. The physical dimensions of accessibility are tangible site attributes that either facilitate or hinder the actual physical movement of potential consumers onto, through, or out of a site. Psychological dimensions of accessibility include how potential customers *perceive* the ease of movement toward and away from a site. If consumers believe that it is difficult, dangerous, or inconvenient to enter a site, then a psychological barrier has been created equal to any physical barrier. Retailers should consider both real and apparent barriers to accessibility.

Number of traffic arteries. The number of traffic arteries adjacent to a site has a profound effect on the consumer's ability to approach and enter the site. Other things being equal, a corner site that is approachable from two traffic arteries is more accessible than a site served by a single traffic artery. Traffic arteries are not all equal, though. Major thoroughfares provide greater accessibility to trading areas than secondary/feeder or side streets. Because their function is to provide access for local traffic, side streets are of less value to retailers. Furthermore, side streets are only wide enough to move limited amounts of local traffic before severe congestion problems occur.

Number of traffic lanes. The more lanes in a traffic artery, the more accessible a site located on this artery is. Multiple-lane arteries are the consumer's first choice in selecting routes for most planned shopping trips. However, multiple lanes often reduce the consumer's access into a site, especially with left turns. Given some drivers' hesitancy to turn left across traffic, wide roads create a consumer psychological barrier, especially when consumers must cross two or more lanes of oncoming traffic. In essence, multiple lanes increase consumers' perceived risks.

Directional flow of traffic arteries. The accessibility of any site is enhanced if the site is directly accessible from all possible directions. Any reduction in the number of directions from which the site can be approached would have an adverse effect on accessibility. Usually, several traffic arteries adjacent to the site enhance accessibility. The location analyst should examine local maps to determine which directional biases exist.

Number of intersections. The number of intersections in the site's general vicinity has both positive and negative effects on accessibility. A large number of intersections offers consumers a greater number of ways to approach a site, but it may also reduce accessibility because of slower speeds and the consumers' increased risk of an accident. Where intersections are plentiful, the role of traffic-control devices (such as traffic lights and stop signs) becomes critical.

Configuration of intersections. Consumers generally perceive a site located on a three-corner or four-corner intersection as very accessible. The reason for this perception is that three- and four-corner intersections are fairly standard; consumers are familiar with them and how to negotiate them. Where more than four corners exist at an intersection, consumers are often confused by this "unstandardized" configuration. This "zone of confusion" exists across the entire intersection and presents the potential consumer with numerous conflict situations.

Type of median. The type of median associated with each of the site's adjacent traffic arteries strongly influences accessibility. Some medians are crossable, while others are not. Generally, crossable medians increase a site's accessibility, although in varying degrees. Medians that provide a "crossover lane" are more encouraging to potential consumers attempting site entry than those without a crossover lane. Crossable medians that force consumers to wait in a traffic lane until crossover is possible create a perceived danger. The driver often has to put up with horn honkers and has the fear of being "stuck out there." This situation results in a psychological deterrent to the site's accessibility.

Uncrossable medians are both a physical and psychological barrier to site entry. Elevated and depressed medians serve to physically separate traffic, but they also serve to separate traffic in a psychological sense. Potential consumers traveling on the right side of an uncrossable median will tend to feel isolated from left-side locations and become more aware of right-side locations, where access is substantially easier.

How do uncrossable medians affect a site's accessibility?

Speed limit on traffic arteries.   The speed limit on a traffic artery influences a site's accessibility, since it determines the amount of time potential customers have in which to make a decision about entering a site. Expert opinions vary over what constitutes an ideal speed limit. The limit must be high enough to encourage consumers to use the route, but low enough to allow them a safe and easy approach to the site. Most experts believe a speed limit between 25 and 40 mph is best.

Number and type of traffic-control devices.   Several different devices are used to control traffic. The most common are traffic lights, stop signs, rule signs, and guidance lines. In terms of accessibility, *traffic lights* have enormous effect at crossovers because of the protection left-turn arrows allow. Traffic lights may be more important for their psychological value than for their physical value. Consumers perceive that retail sites with controlled crossovers are more accessible. Sites with "free left turn" lights are extremely important to site accessibility.

Stop signs are another major accessibility improvement. Stop signs can increase accessibility in two ways. First, the chances of creating consumer awareness of the retailer's location and product offering are higher if traffic "stoppers" force consumers to halt and look around. Second, stop signs help to space the flow of traffic. Psychologically, these breaks in traffic are extremely important to the potential customer attempting to cross over from a left-hand lane.

Traffic rule signs, in addition to speed limit signs, also influence the accessibility of a site. Traffic signs prohibiting U-turns and left turns can reduce site accessibility.

Finally, one effective way to reduce traffic confusion and to increase the actual and perceived safety and ease of entering a site is to employ *guidance lines* (turn- and through-arrows and traffic lines) to direct traffic. The use of guidance lines is especially important at intersection locations. Any means of traffic guidance that tells the consumer how and where to go will enhance accessibility.

Size and shape of site.   The size of the proposed site should be large enough to facilitate all four components of accessibility. Sufficient space should be available to allow ease of parking as well as turning and backing without interfering with consumers who are entering and exiting the site. The shape of the site also can affect accessibility. The wider the site, the greater the exposure to passing traffic, thereby increasing consumer awareness of the retailer's location and activities. Finally, a site should be deep enough to allow ease of entry without interference from exiting traffic or other on-site traffic activities.

Methods of Site Evaluation

Analysts use several methods to evaluate retail site alternatives.[15] Some of these methods are subjective, verbal descriptions of a site's worth, while others provide objective, quantitative measurements. The subjective methods lack the qualities for good scientific decision making, while the latter methods require specialized skills and equipment. Certain methods, however, incorporate both simplicity and objectivity without the need for specialized training or equipment. Two such methods of site evaluation are the checklist method and the question method.

The Checklist Method

The **checklist method** *provides the evaluator with a set of procedural steps to follow in arriving at a subjective, yet quantitative, expression of a site's value.* First, the evaluator enumerates the general factors that are usually considered in any site evaluation. A typical list of factors would include all or most of the site-evaluation principles previously discussed: interception, cumulative attraction, compatibility, and accessibility. Second, for each general factor, several attribute measurements are identified that reflect the location needs of the proposed retail operation. For example, interception, which is a key location attribute for most convenience retailers, can be divided into the volume and quality of vehicular and pedestrian traffic.

Third, each location attribute receives a subjective weight based on its relative importance to a particular type of retailer. One widely used weighting system assigns 3 to very important, 2 to moderately important, 1 to slightly important, and 0 to unimportant attributes. The fourth step is to rate each site alternative in terms of each location attribute. While any number of rating scales can be constructed, one possible rating might be a scale ranging from 1 to 10, with 1 being very poor and 10 being very superior. To illustrate, a site alternative located on a major thoroughfare with a high volume of traffic throughout the day might be rated a 9 or a 10; another site alternative located on a traffic artery characterized by high volumes of traffic only during the morning and evening rush hours could be rated either a 5 or a 6.

Step five involves the calculation of a weighted rating for each attribute for each site alternative. The weighted rating is obtained by multiplying each attribute rating by its weight. Sixth, the weighted ratings for all attributes are summed to produce an overall rating for each site alternative. Finally, the last step is to rank all evaluated alternatives in order of their overall ratings. Figure 14–6 illustrates the use of the checklist method for evaluating one site alternative for a fast-food restaurant. If, for example, the numerical value of 236 is the highest of all evaluated alternatives, then from the standpoint of site considerations this alternative would be rated as the retailer's first choice.

The checklist method has the advantages of being (1) easy to understand, (2) simple to construct, and (3) easy to use. In addition, it gives considerable weight to the opinions of location experts who know the firm and its locational requirements.[16] Nevertheless, the checklist method, like any method, has its drawbacks.

> The list of location criteria is based to a large degree on the decision maker's intuitive judgment of the importance of these items. The decision maker using this method must consider the interactive effects of traffic flow . . . as well as other variables associated with potential sites. Intuition can easily be overtaxed in situations where multiple site decisions in highly complex markets have to be made.[17]

The Question Method

Whereas the checklist method requires the analyst to construct a list of factors and attributes to consider in making the site evaluation, the **question method** is *a predesigned set of questions the evaluator must answer.* To use it, the evaluator answers each question on the question list and makes a final judgment based on each site alternative's value to the proposed operation. Mertes provides an exceptionally good set of questions that many retail analysts use in evaluating site locations (see Figure 14–7, p. 406). The question method has the same advantages and disadvantages of the checklist method.

Quantitative Methods

Although beyond the scope of this book, several quantitative models can be used in evaluating retailer sites. Two of these are analog models and regression analysis.

FIGURE 14–6
The checklist method

Evaluation Factor	Rating	Weight	Weighted Rating
Interception			
Volume of vehicular traffic	8	3	24
Quality of vehicular traffic	8	3	24
Volume of pedestrian traffic	3	3	9
Quality of pedestrian traffic	2	3	6
Cumulative attraction			
Number of attractors	4	1	4
Degree of attraction	5	1	5
Compatibility			
Type of compatibility	6	2	12
Degree of compatibility	7	1	7
Accessibility			
Number of traffic arteries	8	3	24
Number of traffic lanes	10	3	30
Directional flow of traffic	7	2	14
Number of intersections	7	2	14
Configuration of intersections	4	3	12
Type of medians	2	3	6
Speed limits of traffic arteries	5	3	15
Number/type of traffic-control devices	6	2	12
Size and shape of site	6	3	18
Overall site rating			236

*For definitions of evaluation factors, see the text discussion of site-evaluation criteria.

Analog models *make sales projections for new stores based on the sales perfor-mance of existing stores.* For the chain retailer, the evaluation problem can be ap-proached by finding the best "match" between the site characteristics of new site alternatives and those of a successful existing site. This matching process is usually quantified into a statistical model.

Ease of implementation is the principal advantage of an analog approach; however, this model suffers from two important drawbacks. "One problem is that the results are dependent on the particular stores chosen as analogs and therefore rely heavily on the analyst's ability to make judicious selection of analogous stores. . . . The second, and perhaps more important difficulty, is that the method does not directly consider the competitive environment in evaluating the sites. The competitive situation is brought into consideration only through the selection of an-alog stores."[18]

Regression models are a more rigorous approach to the problem of site lo-cation; hence, they offer certain advantages over checklist, question, and analog approaches. First, a regression model allows "systematic consideration of both trad-ing area factors as well as site-specific elements in a single framework. Further, regression models allow the analyst to identify the factors that are associated with various levels of revenues from stores at different sites."[19] The basic multiple regression model used in analyzing determinants of retail performance is expressed as a linear function of location (L), store attributes (S), market attributes (M), price (P), and competition (C):

$$Y = f(L,S,M,P,C)$$

THE QUESTION METHOD

1. Who is the shopping center developer?
2. How long has he been in the business of developing real estate?
3. What are his financial resources?
4. With whom has he arranged for the financing of the center?
5. What is his reputation for integrity?
6. Who performed the economic analysis? Does the report cover both favorable and unfavorable factors?
7. What experience has the economic consultant had?
8. Has an architectural firm been retained to plan the center?
9. Has the architect designed other centers? Have they been successful from a retailing standpoint?
10. Who will build the center? The developer? An experienced contractor? An inexperienced contractor?
11. Has the developer had experience with other centers?
12. What is, or will be, the quality of management for the center?
13. Will the management have merchandising and promotion experience? (Some developers are large retailers rather than real estate operators.)
14. What percent of the leases have been signed? Are they on a contingent basis?
15. Has every facet of the lease been carefully studied?
16. Is the ratio of parking area to selling area 3-to-1 or more?
17. Has sufficient space (300 square feet) been assigned to each car?
18. Is the parking space designed so that the shopper does not walk more than 300 to 350 feet from the farthest spot to the store?
19. What is the angle of parking space? (Ninety degrees provides the best capacity and circulation.)
20. What is the planned or actual car turnover? (3.3 cars per parking space per day is the average.)
21. Is the number of total spaces adequate for the planned business volume? (Too many spaces make the center look dead; too few openly invite competition around the center.)
22. Does the parking scheme distribute the cars so as to favor no one area?
23. Is there an adequate number of ingress/egress roads in proper relationship with the arrangement of parking spaces?
24. For the larger centers, a ring road is preferable. Is this the case?
25. Is the site large enough for the type of center?
26. Is the size sufficiently dominant to forestall the construction of similar shopping centers nearby?
27. Is the center of regular shape? If not, does the location of the buildings minimize the disadvantages of the site's shape?
28. Is the site sufficiently deep? (A depth of at least 400 feet is preferred; if less, the center may look like a strip development.)
29. Is the site level? Is it on well-drained land?
30. Does the center face north and/or east?
31. Can the center be seen from a distance?
32. Are any structures, such as a service station, located in the parking area? (If so, do they impede the site's visibility?)
33. Is the site a complete unit? (A road should not pass through the site.)
34. Are the buildings set far enough back on the site that the entire area may be seen?
35. Are all the stores readily accessible to each other, with none having an advantage?

Source: John Mertes, "Site Opportunities for the Smaller Retailer," *Journal of Retailing* 39(3)[Fall 1963], 44.

FIGURE 14–7
The question method

THE SITE-SELECTION PROCESS

The final selection of a retail site is essentially a process of elimination. Through an analysis of regional and local markets, an assessment of retail trading areas, and an appraisal of retail site locations, the range of choices has been narrowed down to site alternatives consistent with the firm's objectives, operations, and future expectations. If markets, trading areas, and sites have all been carefully evaluated, the retailer should be able to arrive at the final location decision. Normally, the retailer will not select the optimal location; rather, it will select a compromise location that possesses most of the desirable attributes.

In the end, no steps, procedures, or models can totally quantify the final site-selection process. Nevertheless, with the data generated and the analysis completed in the market-, trading-area, and site-evaluation process, the retailer has sufficient information to make a good site selection.

SUMMARY

To appraise retail site locations, the location analyst must determine each site's ability to interact with its trading area. The retailer's problem is how to identify, evaluate, and select a good site location.

The site-identification process is the first step in appraising retail site locations. After identifying all potential site alternatives, the evaluator then can initially screen each alternative in terms of its availability, suitability, and acceptability. Retail site alternatives can be classified as either isolated or clustered. Isolated sites are retail locations geographically separated from other retail sites; they normally will not share customers with other retailers. The retailer that selects an isolated site is seeking to gain either a monopolistic or an operational advantage.

Clustered sites are retail locations that are geographically adjacent to each other or in close proximity; normally they are capable of sharing customers with minimal effort on the part of the customer. Two types of clustered sites exist. The first, an unplanned retail cluster, is one that results from the natural evolutionary process of urban growth. It includes central business districts, secondary business districts, neighborhood business districts, and string/strip clusters. The second is the planned retail cluster. As the name implies, it results from a planning process, and includes such planned retailing clusters as regional, community, neighborhood, and mini-specialty shopping centers.

The second step in appraising retail site locations is the site-evaluation process. This step involves understanding and employing site-evaluation principles and site-evaluation methods. Several principles used in the evaluation process are interception, cumulative attraction, compatibility, store congestion, and accessibility. The checklist and question methods provide the basic framework for making both subjective and objective evaluations of retail site alternatives.

The final step in site appraisal is the site-selection process. The process of elimination narrows the range of choices to site alternatives that are consistent with the firm's objectives, operations, and future expectations. Essentially, the task of site selection becomes one of selecting the best location from several acceptable alternatives.

KEY TERMS AND CONCEPTS

retail mix	price decisions	availability
place decisions	promotion decisions	suitability
product decisions	retail site	acceptability

isolated sites

clustered sites

monopolistic isolation

operational isolation

central business district

secondary business district

neighborhood business district

string/strip cluster

super regional shopping center

regional shopping center

neighborhood shopping center

community shopping center

mini-specialty shopping center

interception

cumulative attraction

compatibility

store congestion

accessibility

checklist method

question method

analog method

regression method

REVIEW QUESTIONS

1. What ingredients make up the retail mix? Briefly describe the decisions associated with each ingredient.
2. What three questions should the retailer ask in conducting an initial screening of site alternatives?
3. Why would a retailer select an isolated site?
4. What is the key to successfully revitalizing the central business district?
5. Compare and contrast the secondary and neighborhood business districts.
6. What are the positional strengths of the string/strip retailing cluster?
7. What distinguishes a super regional from a regional shopping center?
8. Describe the four basic shopping center configurations.
9. How might a shopping center developer overcome the "tunnel" effect?
10. Compare and contrast a community and neighborhood shopping center.

11. What is a mini-specialty mall center?
12. Describe the site-evaluation principle of interception.
13. Why is cumulative attraction important?
14. How does the principle of compatibility affect the evaluation of a retail site?
15. Describe the role of traffic arteries and lanes in determining the accessibility of a site.
16. What role do the number and configuration of intersections play in creating an accessible site?
17. How do the number and type of traffic-control devices influence the accessibility of a retail site?
18. What are the seven steps of the checklist method of retail site evaluation?
19. Describe the two quantitative methods of retail site evaluation.

ENDNOTES

1. John E. Mertes, "A Retail Structural Theory for Site Analysis," *Journal of Retailing* (Summer 1974): 20.
2. N. J. Gruen and C. Gruen, "A Behavioral Approach to Determining Optimum Location for the Retail Firm," *Land Economics* 43 (1967): 320.
3. Steering Committee for the Study, *Dollars and Cents of Shopping Centers* (Washington: The Urban Land Institute, 1978), 294.

4. Ibid.
5. Ibid.
6. Louis G. Redstone, *New Dimensions in Shopping Centers and Stores* (McGraw-Hill, 1973), 51, 68. Used by permission.
7. Ibid., 68.
8. Ibid.
9. Ibid.

10. Ibid., 5.
11. Ibid., 154.
12. See Richard L. Nelson, *The Selection of Retail Locations* (New York: F. W. Dodge, 1958), 58–64.
13. Ibid., 66.
14. Mertes, "A Retail Structural Theory for Site Analysis," 24–25.
15. Dale M. Lewison and Nelson Nunnally, "Retail Site Evaluation and Selection—New Models or Same Old Approaches," *Economic and Business Perspectives* (Martin, TN: University of Tennessee Press, 1979), 15–22.
16. J. L. Goldstucker, D. N. Gellenger, T. J. Stanley, and Ruth L. Otte, *New Developments in Retail Trading Area Analysis and Site Selection* (Atlanta: Publishing Services Division, College of Business Administration, Georgia State University, 1978), 66–67.
17. Thomas J. Stanley and Murphy A. Sewall, "Image Inputs to a Probabilistic Model: Predicting Retail Potential," *Journal of Marketing* 40 (July 1976): 48.
18. C. Samuel Craig, Avijit Grosh, and Sara McLafferty, "Models of the Retail Location Process: A Review," *Journal of Retailing* 60 (Spring 1984): 21.
19. Ibid.

RELATED READINGS

Achabal, Dale; Gorr, Wilpen L.; and Mahajan, Vijay. "Multiloc: A Multiple Store Location Decision Model." *Journal of Retailing* 58 (Summer 1982), 5–25.

Gill, James D., and Evans, Kenneth R. "Shopping Center Patronage Motives of Shopping Orientation Groups." *1985 AMA Educators' Proceedings.* R. F. Lusch et al, eds. (American Marketing Association 1985), 202–8.

Goodchild, Michael F. "ILACS: A Location-Allocation Model for Retail Site Selection." *Journal of Retailing* 60 (Spring 1984), 84–100.

Hawes, Jon M., and Lewison, Dale M. "Retail Site Evaluation: An Examination of the Principle of Accessibility." *AMA Educators' Proceedings.* R. W. Belk et al, eds. (American Marketing Association 1984), 280–84.

Lewison, Dale M.; DeLozier, W. Wayne; and Robbins, Ray B. "Assessing the Accessibility of Retail Sites." *Survival and Growth in the 1980's, Proceedings.* R. D. Lewis, ed. (Southwestern Small Business Institute Association 1981), 139–48.

Peterson, Eric C. "Recipes for New Sites." *Stores* (March 1985), 70–72.

_____. "Targeting the Market." *Stores* (July 1985), 62–65.

"Shopping Centers Will Be America's Towns of Tomorrow." *Marketing News* (November 28, 1980), 1, 11.

Spalding, Lewis A. "Good Sites." *Stores* (January 1982), 55–56, 59, 63, 65.

Taylor, Ronald D. "Multiple Regression Analysis as a Retail Site Selection Method: An Empirical Review." *Developments in Marketing Science, Proceedings.* V. V. Bellur, ed. (Academy of Marketing Science 1981), 184–87.

Thompson, John S. *Site Selection.* (New York: Chain Store Publishing Corporation, 1982)

Vitaska, Charles R. "Consumer Perceptions of Shopping Centers—A Preliminary Typology." *Evolving Marketing Thought for 1980, Proceedings.* J. H. Summey and R. D. Taylor, eds. (Southern Marketing Association 1980), 72–75.

Wee, Chow-Hou. "Complexity of Shopping Area Image: Its Factor Analytic Structure in Relation to the Effects of Familiarity and Size of the Area." *Developments in Marketing Science, Proceedings.* N. K. Malhotra, ed. (Academy of Marketing Science 1985), 196–201.

Outline

THE MERCHANDISING PROCESS

THE PRODUCT MIX

Total-Product Concept
Product-Mix Concept
Product-Mix Decisions

PRODUCT EVALUATION

Product Considerations
Market Considerations
Supply Considerations

PRODUCT INFORMATION

Internal Sources
External Sources

PRODUCT-MIX STRATEGIES

Narrow Variety/Shallow Assortment
Wide Variety/Shallow Assortment
Narrow Variety/Deep Assortment
Wide Variety/Deep Assortment

PRODUCT-MIX TRENDS

Shotgun Merchandising
Rifle Merchandising

Objectives

■ Understand tactics used in developing a merchandise mix

■ Recognize retailers' need to market all of a product's dimensions

■ Understand and make the "which" and "how many" product decisions

■ Evaluate new and existing products and their impact on merchandising decisions

■ Acquire and evaluate sources of product information

■ Define and describe the various types of product-mix strategies

■ Discuss major emerging trends in the development of product mixes

15
The Product Mix

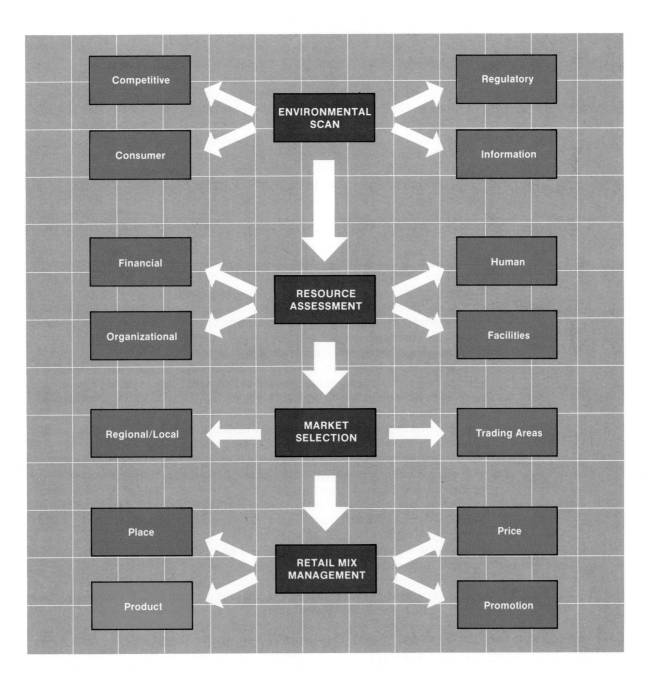

As identified in Chapter 1, the retailer's problem is how to find the "right blend" of marketing ingredients that satisfy the needs of the target market. The "right blend" is the best combination of the right product, at the right time, in the right quantities, at the right price, with the right appeal. The focus of discussion in this and the next five chapters is the *offering of the right product in the right quantities* within the context of the right place, time, price, and appeal.

THE MERCHANDISING PROCESS

Consumers patronize a particular retail outlet for many different reasons—its convenient locations, friendly personnel, desirable prices, and pleasant shopping atmosphere. The patronage reason common to all customers for visiting a particular store, however, is the expectation of finding a product or a set of products that will fulfill some present or future need. In a general sense, fulfilling customer product expectations is what retail merchandising is all about.

Merchandising is *the process of developing, securing, and managing the merchandise mix to meet the marketing objectives of the firm.* The *merchandise mix* refers to the retailer's total offering, be it goods or services or both. The *merchandising process,* as illustrated in Figure 15–1, consists of three stages. The first stage is developing the merchandise mix, which is composed of the product mix and the service mix. The retailer's concern here is to determine "what" and "how many" products and services to offer consumers. Next, the retailer must secure the products. Stage two deals with this problem of buying and procuring the merchandise mix. In this stage, the retailer determines "from where," "when," and "how" to get products into the store. The final stage in the merchandising process is the managing of the merchandise mix. To ensure efficient, profitable operations, the retailer must plan and control the merchandise mix.

Predetermined organizational objectives should direct the retailer's merchandising efforts. While numerous specific objectives can be identified, two overall objectives are used in guiding the merchandising process: (1) customer satisfaction through market segmentation and (2) firm profitability through operational efficiency. In other words, in developing, securing, and managing the merchandise mix, the retailer must consider both the customer's needs and the requirements for a profitable operation.

Developing the merchandise mix is a means for the retailer to segment the market and appeal to a select group of consumers. Just as the retail-location decision can segment a market geographically, merchandise-mix decisions can segment markets demographically and by behavioral dimensions. By buying, stocking, and selling a select combination of products and by offering a certain level of services, the retailer can appeal to consumers of a particular age, sex, occupation, race, or income level, as well as to other demographic groupings. Likewise, the retailer can develop the merchandise mix to appeal to certain *life-styles*—the "swinger," the "sophisticate," the "homebody"—or to certain *buyer-behavior patterns*—the brand-loyal consumer, the style-conscious consumer, the quality-minded consumer. Careful development of the merchandise mix can allow the retailer to establish and maintain a differential advantage over competitors in serving the needs of a target market or markets.

Equally important in the merchandising process is ensuring the profitability of the firm. To accomplish the second objective, the retailer must efficiently develop, secure, and control the merchandising process. The retailer should include in its mix, products that contribute to the total profitability of the mix. For example, some of the products the retailer stocks and sells may not be very profitable, but they contribute greatly to the total profitability of the mix by generating additional customer traffic and additional profitable sales of other products in the mix. Also, the

FIGURE 15–1
The merchandising
process

CHAPTER 15
THE PRODUCT MIX

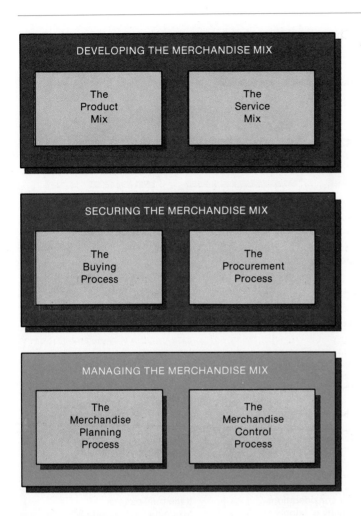

retailer's customer-service levels must not only meet the customers' needs but also be affordable to the retailer.

To ensure profitable operations, the retailer must use a merchandise budget in which sales, stocks, reductions, purchases, markups, and margins are carefully planned. The final attempt to manage profitability is to control product inventories. One of the fastest ways "to end up in the red" is to mismanage the "backroom" operations.

The entire merchandising process is examined in this and the next five chapters. The remainder of this chapter describes factors affecting the retailer's product mix. Figure 15–2 illustrates the retailer's main concerns in developing the product mix. Chapter 16 discusses the retailer's service mix. The problems in securing the merchandise mix and their solutions are handled in Chapter 17. The procurement process, the merchandise-planning process, and the merchandise-control process are treated in Chapters 18, 19, and 20, respectively.

To develop the product mix the retailer must first understand what a product really is. The product is not simply some item of merchandise that has certain physical and functional attributes; it is something much more complex. Before we discuss the concept of the product mix, let's first examine the "total-product concept."

THE PRODUCT MIX

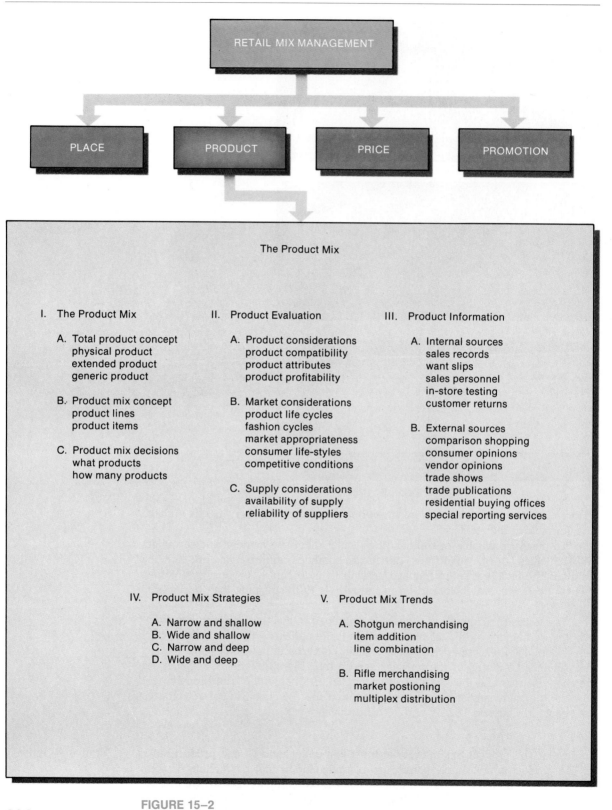

FIGURE 15–2
Developing and managing the product mix

Total-Product Concept

The **total-product concept** *recognizes that a product is more than just the tangible object offered for sale.* The retailer that sells "things" will soon discover that it has no one to sell them to. To be successful, the retailer must act on the premise that a product is more than just the functional and aesthetic features of the physical product; instead, it incorporates the various service features and psychological benefits conveyed by the product. In essence, the total-product concept acknowledges the need for retailers to market every one of a product's dimensions. The relationship among the many facets of a product is illustrated in Figure 15–3. As shown, the total-product concept is the sum of all physical, extended, and generic products.

The Physical Product

The **physical product** *encompasses both the functional and aesthetic features of a product.* A product's functional features include the tangible elements of size, shape, and weight, together with the chemical and/or biological makeup of the product. Functional features are extremely important because they determine to a large extent how well the product will actually perform the functions it was designed to accomplish. If a product cannot clean and polish, or brighten and freshen, or cool and heat—in short, if it can't perform the basic function it was designed to do— then all other aspects of the product are severely diminished. The aesthetic features of a product are elements that appeal to the consumer's five senses. If a product does not look, smell, feel, sound, and/or taste "right," its merchandising qualities have been substantially reduced or eliminated. Consumers have strong preconceived ideas about how a product should look, smell, feel, sound, and taste.

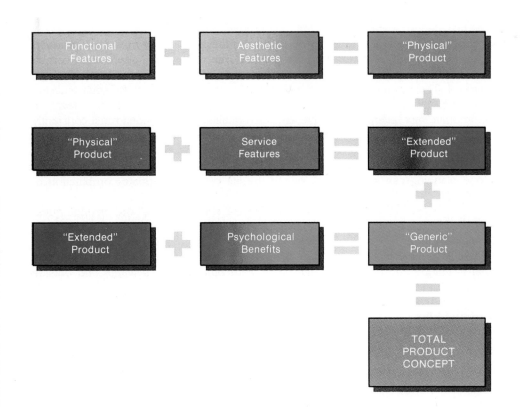

FIGURE 15–3
The total-product concept

The Extended Product

The **extended product** *surrounds the physical product with the whole set of service features provided as a conditional part of the sale.* Service features are "extras" that might include delivery, alterations, installation, repairs, warranties, returns, adjustments, wrapping, telephone and mail ordering, or any other service that consumers want for purchase satisfaction. A retailer must determine which service features are *required* for the purchase decision and which are simply *desired* by the customer as an added product dimension. These requirements and desires then are incorporated into the retailer's product/service mix.

The Generic Product

The final product in the total-product concept is the generic product. When consumers buy products, they are seeking something more than the physical and extended product: they expect to benefit in some way from the purchase.[1] The **generic product** is defined as *the extended product (functional, aesthetic, and service features) plus the expected psychological benefits that consumers derive from buying, using, and possessing the product.* As discussed in Chapter 4, consumers buy products to be beautiful, safe, thin, comfortable, and noticed, or to gain prestige, recognition, security, independence, love, or a host of other benefits. Retailers that recognize that a product's psychological endowments are as important as, if not more important than, the product itself will have considerably more to sell to their customer than just a physical product. People don't want lawn and garden tools; they want nice-looking lawns and gardens their families can play on and their neighbors can admire. To paraphrase Charles Revson of Revlon Cosmetics: We manufacture cosmetics; in the store, women seek hope and the promise of beauty.

Product-Mix Concept

The first step in operationalizing the total-product concept is to develop the retailer's product mix. The **product-mix concept** refers to *the full range or mixture of products the retailer offers to consumers.* The product mix represents "appropriate combinations" of products to meet the specific needs of one or more identified target markets. The number of appropriate mixes is nearly unlimited. As such, success often depends on whether the retailer can identify and operationalize a *new and appropriate mix.* Even large, well-established retailing organizations must constantly seek ways to improve and update their mix of products. In making product-mix decisions, the retailer must also recognize the degree of perishability of many products. What is an appropriate mix today might not be an appropriate mix tomorrow. Good planning can substantially extend the life of an appropriate combination of products.

If the product mix represents "appropriate combinations," the obvious question becomes "appropriate combinations of what?" The answer is "appropriate combinations of product lines and product items." A **product line** is *any grouping of related products.* A **product item** refers to *a specific product within a product line that is unique and clearly distinguishable from other products within and outside the product line.*

Product Lines

Based on type and degree of relationship, product lines are often subdivided to facilitate the retailer's planning of a product mix. Products can be related in terms of (1) satisfying a particular need (e.g., health or beauty aids); (2) being used together (e.g., pieces of living room furniture); or (3) being purchased or used by a similar customer group (e.g., women's, men's, or children's wearing apparel). The degree to which products are related also can vary greatly from being very closely related to very remotely related. Using type and degree of relationship, we will illustrate one way that product lines might be classified to facilitate the retailer's development of a product mix. It should be noted that there is no singly accepted and used method of subdividing product lines, nor is there common terminology for subdivisions. For our illustration we subdivide the product line into three groupings: merchandise group, merchandise class, and merchandise category.

A **merchandise group** is *a broadly related line of products that retailers and consumers associate together according to end use.* Examples of merchandise groups include such wide product combinations as furniture, appliances, home furnishings, housewares, wearing apparel, sporting goods, food products, personal-care products, and automotive products. Single-line retailers often are identified on the basis of these broad product groupings (e.g., hardware store, clothing store). Mass merchandisers frequently use merchandise groups to identify operating divisions.

A **merchandise class** is *a closely related line of products within a merchandise group.* At this level, the particular consumer need, usage pattern, or behavior is more clearly distinguished. By subdividing merchandise groups into merchandise classes, the retailer can refine the product mix. Merchandise classes often correspond to the operating departments of a traditional department store and serve as a way to identify many specialty retailers (e.g., men's, women's, or children's wearing apparel).

A **merchandise category** is *a specific line of products within a merchandise class, for example, sport and dress shirts within men's wearing apparel, lipstick and eye shadow within cosmetics, and sofas and end tables within living room furniture.* This subdivision is important because within merchandise categories, products are directly comparable and substitutable. It is the level within a product line at which consumer *comparison shopping* occurs.

An example of the three subdivisions (merchandise groups, classes, and categories) of a product is illustrated in Figure 15–4. As shown, subdividing a product line is essentially a refinement process. This refinement is useful in simplifying the retailer's problem of how to develop a product mix for a number of reasons:

- It enables the retailer to develop product lines more precisely suited to the needs of a target market.
- It permits better planning of the type and amount of space each line requires, as well as the fixturing necessary to display the merchandise properly. In addition, store layouts based on well-defined product lines simplify the customer's in-store search process, thereby enhancing the chances that the customer will make a purchase.
- Product-line refinement contributes to the operational efficiency of the store. Well-defined product lines help to promote the ease of planning, executing, and controlling the store's buying, stocking, and selling activities.
- Clearly defined product lines aid the retailer in its efforts to establish and maintain a unique and consistent store image. (Author's note: Although product lines can be subdivided into various groups, classes, and categories of merchandise, for the sake of brevity in the discussions to follow, our usage will be limited to the term *product line* unless otherwise specified.)

417

Is this a merchandise group, class, or category? Why is product classification important?

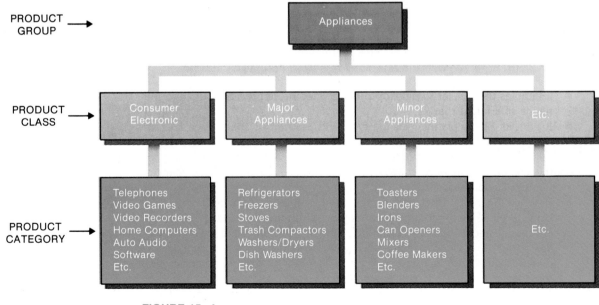

FIGURE 15–4
Product-line subdivisions

Product Items

Within a product line, a **product item** *is distinguishable by its brand, style, size, color, material, price, or any combination of these factors.* A *brand* is a distinctive grouping of products identified by a name, a term, a design, a symbol, or any combination of these markings. Used to identify the products of a particular manufacturer or seller, brand is a common criterion in distinguishing both product lines and product items within those lines. *Style* refers to the characteristic or distinctive form, outline, or shape a product item possesses.[2] As a unique mode of expression or presentation, style can be the principal criterion consumers use to distinguish one product item from another (e.g., clothing). Products also come in various sizes. *Size* can refer to the actual size of the product (e.g., 42-Long or X-Large) or to the size of the package in which the product comes (e.g., family size, 12-ounce bottle). The physical magnitude, extent, and bulk of a product are not only distinguishing features that influence the consumer's purchase decision—they are also important factors in the retailer's decision to buy, stock, display, and shelve the product. *Colors, materials,* and *prices* are also important features in distinguishing one product item from another. The potential combinations of these features are virtually limitless in light of the large selection of brands, styles, sizes, colors, materials, and price lines available to most retailers.

Product-Mix Decisions

In developing the product mix the retailer faces two basic decisions: "Which product lines and items?" and "How many product lines and items?" An examination of Figure 15–5 reveals that retailers must make both decisions with respect to the merchandising activities of buying, stocking, and selling. Product-mix decisions should not be based on a single activity. A product is only "right" when it is "right" for *all three activities.* If a product is easy to sell but creates extremely difficult buying and stocking problems, the retailer should seriously question whether to include it in the product mix! Obviously, any product can create some problems in one or more of these activities, so the retailer must determine whether these problems are surmountable. If so, then it must consider the relative costs and benefits that would result from including that product in the mix.

Which Products?

No simple criteria determine whether a product line or item should be part of the product mix. The retailer must judge each product on its own merits relative to its particular situation. In considering the "which products" decision, the retailer should ask the following questions:

1. Is the product consistent with our current and proposed product mix?
2. Is it consistent with the store image we want to portray?
3. Will the product be appropriate to existing target markets or will it require the development and cultivation of new market segments?

FIGURE 15–5
Product-mix decisions

What	Product Lines	Are to Be Bought?
How Many	Product Items	Are to Be Stocked?
		Are to Be Sold?

4. What level of sales support does the product require in terms of personal selling, advertising, and sales promotions?
5. What is the existing market potential and what growth potential does the product possess?
6. How susceptible is the product to demand cycles and the actions of competitors?
7. Does the product require new fixturing or specialized storage facilities or can it be properly displayed and stored with existing fixtures and facilities?

Which products to include in the mix will vary depending upon whether the retailer is starting a new business and creating a new product mix or is currently in business and adjusting an existing product mix. In creating a new product mix, the retailer must decide whether to include or exclude products. Adjusting an existing product mix concerns decisions of adding and dropping products. How retailers make these decisions follows.

How Many Products?

The number of different product lines and items a retailer should include in the product mix constitutes another basic problem. The retailer should ask and attempt to answer the following basic questions to help make the "how many products" decision.

1. Should we carry several product lines or specialize in one or a few lines?
2. How broad a selection (brands, styles, sizes) should we offer in each line?
3. How many different price lines should we offer?
4. Do we want a broad or limited market appeal?
5. Are there strong consumer preferences for certain brands and styles? If so, what are they?
6. What are the cyclical demand patterns (product, fashion, seasonal cycles) associated with the various product items?
7. What effect does an extensive or limited product offering have on inventory control and investment?

The "how many products" decision is two-dimensional, requiring decisions on both product variety and product assortment. **Product variety** is *the number of different product lines the retailer stocks in the store.* The retailer can engage in variety strategies ranging from a narrow variety of one or a few product lines to a wide variety encompassing a large number of product lines. **Product assortment** refers to *the number of different product items that the retailer stocks within a particular product line.* Assortment strategies vary from shallow assortments of one or a few product items within each line to deep assortments having a large selection of product items within each line. The dimensions of the "how many products" decision are illustrated in Figure 15–6. These variety and assortment strategies can be used to create a myriad of product mixes. Before discussing these product-mix strategies (combinations of variety and assortment strategies), however, we will examine the various criteria and sources of information retailers use in evaluating which products and how many they should include in their product mix.

PRODUCT EVALUATION

Retailers continually are besieged with a barrage of "new" and "improved" products. Each of these products must be evaluated before any product-mix decision can be made. Some require a more extensive evaluation than others. Retailers use

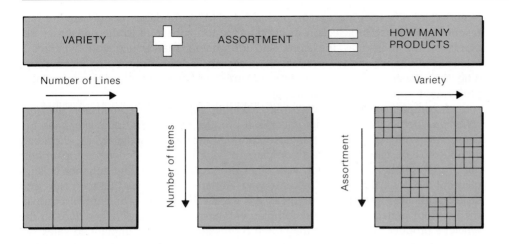

FIGURE 15–6
How many products?

VARIETY ✚ ASSORTMENT ═ HOW MANY PRODUCTS

Number of Lines

Variety

Number of Items

Assortment

three sets of criteria to aid them in making which and how many products decisions: product, market, and supply considerations.

Product Considerations

Product considerations are those criteria directly concerned with the characteristics of the product itself. The three product considerations are product compatibility, product attributes, and product profitability.

Product Compatibility

In developing a product mix, the retailer should consider **product compatibility—** *the nature of the relationship between various product lines and between various product items within them.* Based on the type of compatibility, retailers classify products as (1) substitutes, (2) complements, and (3) unrelated. The degree of product compatibility ranges from a perfect to a general relationship.

A **substitute** is *a product consumers use for the same general purpose as another product;* it has the same basic functional attributes and meets the same basic consumer needs. A *perfect substitute* is a product consumers perceive as essentially the same as another product. In this case, the consumer is totally indifferent about the product bought and used. A *general substitute* is a product consumers perceive as different from another product but that serves the same general purpose (e.g., Stove Top Stuffing instead of potatoes).

In deciding which products to sell, the retailer usually should avoid perfect substitutes. They divert sales from other products without adding anything in return. From the consumer's viewpoint, perfect substitutes do not even add the element of choice because a choice situation is unimportant. In addition, perfect substitutes complicate the problems of inventory control and increase the retailer's handling costs. General substitutes present a different situation. For the homemaker whose family is tired of potatoes, the availability of a general substitute (dressing or rice) might preserve a lost sale (potatoes). General substitutes represent an increase in the selection a retailer offers consumers. As such, they can increase total sales.

Sales representatives continually are contacting retailers to carry their "new/me-too" products. In deciding on how many products, the retailer must realize that many "new" products offered by manufacturers are often nothing more than "me-too" substitutes that add little, if anything, to the store's total sales. With lower-priced substitutes, the retailer's sales conceivably could be reduced. Whether a dif-

421

ferent brand name, product color, package design, or modified product feature represents an increase in selection or another me-too substitute to the consumer depends on the individual, the store, and the general market situation. Whereas a selection of various me-too products is necessary for consumer comparison shopping, the retailer should review the product mix periodically to avoid an unprofitable proliferation of me-too merchandising.

A **complement** is *a product that is bought and used in conjunction with another product.* A *perfect complement* is a product consumers must purchase because their original product purchase cannot function immediately or effectively without it (e.g., film is a perfect complement to a camera). *General complements* are products sold in conjunction with other products because they enhance or supplement the original purchase in some way. Apparel accessories that are color- and style-coordinated with a suit or dress are excellent examples of general complements. Both perfect and general complements are *highly desirable* additions to the retailer's product mix because they often represent additional, unplanned sales beyond the original, planned purchase. Also, consumers tend to be less sensitive about the price of complements; hence, retailers often sell them at above-average markups. As a rule, the depth of assortment for complements is rather extensive and the chances for additional sales increase when consumers have a great selection.

Unrelated products are neither substitutes nor complements, but retailers seriously consider them for their product mix since they represent potential additional sales, theoretically at low risk and a reasonable profit. Some impulse goods fit this description. Normally, unrelated products are not stocked in depth; rather, retailers often follow a strategy of "creaming," stocking and selling only the best-selling items. Sometimes unrelated products are simply added to the existing product mix, other times unrelated products are combined to create new product mixes. The process of item additions and line combinations will be discussed later in this chapter.

Product Attributes

The attributes of the product itself strongly influence which and how many products retailers stock. Four **product attributes** that retailers consider are *product bulk, standardization, service requirements,* and *required selling method.*

Product bulk is the weight or size of a product in relation to its value. Bulky products usually require substantial space, both on the sales floor and in the stockroom, and often require special handling. If only limited space is available, the retailer may have to forego stocking bulky products or limit the depth of selection for such products. Furniture, appliances, lawn and garden equipment, and some home-improvement products are all examples. In addition, many bulky products typically are low in sales per square foot of floor space. In fact, some retailers have found that the space these bulky items occupy should be (and has been) turned over to more productive merchandise with higher per-square-foot sales. Many major department stores have either eliminated or reduced their selection and amount of space they devote to these products.

Product standardization is the second product attribute retailers should consider in evaluating product attributes. Generally, standardized products fit into the retailer's routine operating procedures, whereas unstandardized products often require special buying, stocking, and handling. Few products offer enough potential to the retailer to justify developing specialized merchandising skills. Unless the supplier is willing to make certain adjustments or provide considerable support, unstandardized products should be excluded from the product mix. An exception would be the retailer that specializes in the unusual; in such cases, unstandardized products can enhance the store's image.

Because products vary noticeably with respect to *required service levels,* retailers should evaluate each product individually. If a required customer service (e.g., home delivery, home repair, or long-term credit) is *not* part of the retailer's normal service offering, the retailer should seriously consider the product's service requirements before adding the product to the product line. It is seldom possible for a retailer to add a new service for a new product line and expect that line to be profitable.

Required selling methods are particular selling skills needed to sell a product. For some products the retailer must use a personal selling approach, while others can be sold on a self-service basis. Generally, self-service retailers should not sell merchandise that requires personal selling. Likewise, the upscale retailer that stocks too many self-service items risks the prestige and product-quality image of the store. When the retailer's product mix includes products requiring personal selling, they should be stocked in sufficient depth to give salespeople something to sell. Where both self-service and personal-selling products are stocked, new products should be evaluated on the basis of whether they fit with existing products in each category.

Product Profitability

In determining the merits of a product, **product profitability** is one of the most important and complex criteria retailers use, since it can be expressed and measured in so many different ways. As examples, profit can be expressed on a per-unit basis or on the basis of several units (e.g., an order quantity); it can be calculated on the basis of time (e.g., per month) or space (e.g., per square foot); or it can be computed as a return on the retailer's investment. Profitability was discussed in Chapter 7. It is sufficient to state here that each product should make some contribution to profit; that contribution can be direct in the sense of per-unit profit or indirect by creating customer traffic and additional sales on other products.

Market Considerations

Market considerations are criteria retailers use to evaluate a product according to its compatibility with the retailer's markets and customers. All products have demand

What type of product is being sold—a perfect complement or a general complement?

(a)   (b)

cycles and patterns. These cycles have implications for the retailer's decisions on which and how many products to stock. We briefly describe two of these cycles: the product life cycle and the fashion cycle.

Product Life Cycle

Products pass through several stages in their lifetime, each identified by its sales-performance characteristics. This series of stages is called the **product life cycle (PLC)**.[3] By knowing what stage a product is in, the retailer has useful information for judging both the existing and future sales potential of the product. Also, this information suggests a particular retailing strategy, depending on the PLC stage. The four stages of the product life cycle are *introduction, growth, maturity,* and *decline.* Figure 15–7 illustrates one basic shape of the PLC as defined by sales-performance levels.

In the *introductory stage,* products are characterized by low sales and losses, high risk, and high costs. In many cases, products never make it out of the introductory stage. Thus, the retailer's risks are high. On the other hand, where manufacturers invest heavily in advertising to gain consumer awareness and acceptance and offer liberal returns and adjustments, the retailer's risk is substantially reduced. For many retailers, new products are essential to their avant garde image. In such cases the necessary merchandising skill is to select only introductory products that are truly innovative. Another consideration for retailers is that the manufacturer may decide to limit the distribution of the product to a few *exclusive* or several *selective* outlets. Faced with this situation the retailer must decide to get in now or be shut out permanently. If the retailer stocks introductory products, it should limit the selection to a few key items until the primary demand for the product has been established. "Most of the really successful new products have been just slightly ahead of their time. . . . They've caught the leading edge of a trend. But if they're too far ahead, they're not well understood and if they're too different, they require a habit change. To be a real success a product should be both better and different—a lot better and a little different."[4]

Almost without exception, the most desirable products for retailers are those in the *growth stage.* Products in the growth stage are characterized by accelerating sales, highest profit levels of any stage in the PLC, limited competitors in the market, and lower relative costs and risk. To satisfy the growing number of customers, retailers usually stock an extensive assortment of growth products.

In the *maturity stage,* sales increase at a decreasing rate and finally begin to level off. Characteristics of this stage are (1) the market is highly competitive; (2) prices and margins fall; (3) advertising is more intense; and (4) profits are lower.

FIGURE 15–7
The product life cycle

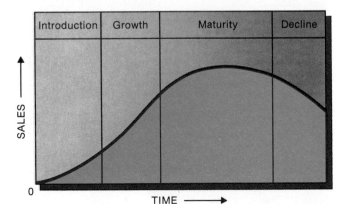

Most retailers should include or continue to include mature products in their product mix, since consumers expect most stores to carry them.

As a rule, retailers do not include *declining products* in their product mix. Normally, retailers drop these products if they have not done so already, Products in the decline stage are high-risk items for retailers. The stage is characterized by rapidly declining sales and profits (or losses), and little, if any, manufacturer support in promotion. Retailers that continue to stock declining products should only do so in limited quantities and assortments and only if demand is sufficient to yield a reasonable profit.

Fashion Cycle

Like the product life cycle, the **fashion cycle** is *a conceptualization of the "life of a fashion."* A fashion is "a concept of what is currently appropriate"[5] and represents the currently prevailing style. Fashion is a reflection of a society's cultural, social, and economic environment at one particular point. As one fashion expert writes, "Fashion trends reflect the changes in what a culture is thinking, feeling, and doing, both in work and recreation; how an era is behaving morally; and how stable or successful a country is financially."[6] For retailers, fashions represent great opportunities but also substantial risks. Fashionable products include

- high-margin items that can provide above-average profits
- shopping and specialty goods for which consumers will spend time, money, and effort to find
- products that enhance the retailer's general image and help generate consumer traffic
- a means of distinguishing a retailer's operation from competitors'

Fashion-conscious consumers are

- oriented toward the social world
- gregarious and likeable
- active participants in society
- self-assertive, competitive, and venturesome
- attention seekers and self-confident
- aesthetic-, power-, and status-oriented individuals[7]

Although fashion products present a considerable opportunity to retailers, they are also very risky. This risk is due to the high uncertainty surrounding both consumers' *level* of acceptance and the *duration* of their acceptance of the fashion. One management tool retailers use to reduce the risks of including fashion products in their product mix is the *fashion cycle.* During its lifetime, a fashion passes through three stages: introduction, acceptance, and decline. From its beginning in the introductory stage to its obsolescence in the decline stage, the fashion innovation struggles to obtain customer acceptance and customer adoptions.

Customer acceptance of fashion varies significantly according to the level of acceptance (as measured by sales) and the duration of that acceptance (as measured by weeks, months, years). Based on these two acceptance factors, four types of fashion cycles occur: the flop, fad, ford, and classic (see Figure 15–8). A **flop** is *a fashion cycle rejected by all consumer segments almost immediately.* Other than for a few fashion innovators who try and then discard the fashion, a flop gains neither a significant level nor duration of acceptance. Flops are fashion items most retailers hope to avoid; they not only represent financial losses resulting from obsolete merchandise, they also tend to tarnish the retailer's image as a fashion leader.

FIGURE 15–8
Types of fashion cycles

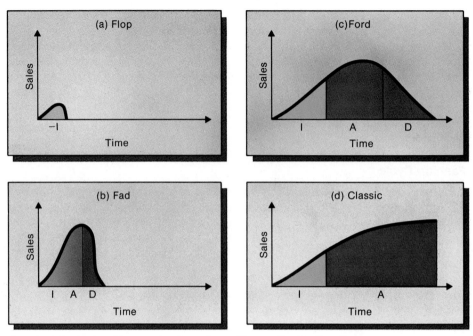

Key: I = Introductory Stage   A = Acceptance Stage   D = Decline Stage

For fashion retailers some flops are inevitable—they are the realization of the risks that go with fashion merchandising. In men's fashions the no-lapel sportcoat and the Nehru jacket represent two past flops.

A **fad** is *a fashion that obtains a relatively high level of customer acceptance for a short time.* It is quickly accepted, but rejected with the same quickness (see Figure 15–9). Typically, the lifetime of a fad ranges from a few weeks to several months. Fads are both extremely profitable and extremely risky. Because a relatively large number of these items can be sold at substantial markups (consumers are somewhat price insensitive) in a short period of time, fads are very profitable. They are also highly risky, however, because of the short duration of the cycle. For most fads, the retailer must stock the item at the introductory or early part of the fad cycle.

A *best-seller in fashion merchandising is referred to as a* **ford.** A ford is also referred to as a "runner" or "hot item." Fords gain wide customer acceptance over extended periods of time. Because of their wide acceptance, long-term salability, and stable demand, fords are usually produced by many different manufacturers in a variety of price lines.[8] For the same reasons, nearly every retailer must include fords in the product mix or suffer loss of profits and loss of a fashion image. The miniskirt is an excellent example of a ford, lasting from 1965 to 1971. Men's leisure suits are another example of a ford.

The "classic look," the "classic cut," and the "classic shape" all describe a style trend that endures for several years (see Figure 15–10). The **classic** fashion *has both a high level and a long duration of acceptance.* Although a classic might undergo minor changes, it essentially looks the same. The classic, even more than the ford, is an absolute must in the retailer's product mix. The retailer's decision relative to the classic is not whether to stock it, but rather which price line to stock from which supplier with which product features. The pantsuit, introduced as a fashionable women's garment in 1966, retains a high level of acceptance in almost all market segments. It has become a classic fashion because it fits the needs and lifestyles of the modern woman, especially the working woman.

FIGURE 15–9
Great fads of our time

CHAPTER 15
THE PRODUCT MIX

How many do you remember? How many
did you own? How long did
you keep them?

Shmoos
Rubik's Cubes
Hula Hoops
Nehru jackets
Running
Pet Rocks
Puka beads
Love beads
Indian glass beads
3-D movies
The Lindy
Skateboards
Ankle bracelets
Coonskin caps
Telephone booth packing
Flubber (from the Disney flick
   The Absent-Minded Professor)
Slime (mutant son of Flubber)
Nautilus
Super Balls
Dickies
Clackers
Zoot suits
E.T.
Disco

Source: Adapted from Stephen Fried, "Summer Madness," *Philadelphia* August 1983, p. 122.

FIGURE 15–10
Trend or fad?
Guidelines for assess-
ing trends and fads

- A new product is more likely to be a trend if it is consistent with the consumer's basic values and lifestyles. New products which produce value and lifestyle conflicts are more likely to be a fad!
- A new product is more likely to be a trend if it promotes a voluntary change in behavior that is derived from customer satisfaction. Products which force a behavioral change (e.g., adoption of inexpensive products during tough economic times) tend to be more fadish in nature.
- A new product stands a better chance of becoming a trend if it can be modified or expressed in different ways by different people. Fads are more rigid (e.g., exaggerated, extreme, and impractical hairstyles).
- A new product is more likely to be a trend if it is based on a good underlying theme (e.g., physical fitness). Fadish products are often based on a specific manifestation or expression of a basic theme (e.g., fadish diet). Specific manifestations come and go and often are replaced by other expressions of a basic theme.
- A new product is more likely to be a trend if it is supported by new developments in related areas (e.g., nutrition, physical fitness, nonsmoking, and stress reduction). If a new product stands alone, it is more likely to be a fad.

Source: Adapted from "Distinguishing Fads from Trends with 6 Research Guidelines," *Marketing News,* 21 January 1983, 3, 15.

What are fashionable products? Who buys them?

Market Appropriateness

Retailers should evaluate new-product candidates on their chances for success in the marketplace, that is, how well the new product matches the consumption and buying needs of the retailer's targeted consumers. Several characteristics serve as good indicators of how well a product might be received by the retailer's current and potential customers, including

- *relative advantage*—the extent to which the new product is perceived to be better than existing products. A product that offers clear-cut advantages or provides a more satisfying benefit package is more likely to attract the interest and patronage of the store's customers.
- *affinity*—the extent to which the new product is consistent with the consumer's current buying and usage behavior. Products that require noticeable behavioral modification are often viewed by consumers as being incompatible with their needs. A product that is consistent with the consumer's beliefs, values, and experiences is more likely to gain customer acceptance and a faster and higher rate of adoptions.
- *trialability*—the extent to which a new product can be tested on a trial basis. All new-product purchases involve some risk to the purchaser. Anything that reduces the risk substantially improves the chances for initial and subsequent purchases. A product that can be physically divided into small quantities and given as free samples or sold in the trial sizes benefits from good trialability. If divisibility is not possible, demonstrations and guarantees can be used to reduce perceived risks.
- *observability*—the extent to which a new product's favorable attributes can be seen by the consumer. If a product's relative advantages are easily visible to the consumer and can be easily described to others, the new product's probability of market success is greatly enhanced.
- *complexity*—the extent to which a new product can be easily understood or used. Products that require the consumer to invest a considerable amount of time and effort to reap any benefits will involve greater selling efforts and a slower rate of consumer adoptions.

These five product characteristics provide additional criteria by which the retailer can judge the market appropriateness of a given product line or item.

Life-Styles

As discussed in Chapter 4, life-style is a pattern of living shaped by psychological influences, social experiences, and demographic makeup. By knowing the activities, interest, and opinions of targeted consumers, retailers are better able to select products that are consistent with both the consumer's life-style and the retailer's image. *Developing product lines in accord with consumer living patterns is referred to as* **life-style merchandising**.[9] This method of product evaluation requires the retailer to

1. identify target markets based on consumers' life-styles and their product, place, promotion, and price preferences
2. determine which life-style markets are consistent with the retailer's image and mode of doing business
3. evaluate which and how many products to carry based on their ability to satisfy certain life-style markets

Many fashion retailers go to trade shows and producer markets looking for merchandise suited for their targeted consumers' life-style. One illustration of how re-

(a)

(b)

Are these fashion items flops, fads, fords, or classics?

tailers can characterize consumers' life-styles appears in Figure 15–11. By using this life-style scheme and ones like it, retailers can select, purchase, and stock merchandise that matches their target consumers' life-styles.

Competitive Conditions

To decide which products to include in or exclude from the product mix, the retailer must consider the competitive conditions under which the product is available to the retailer. Two aspects of competitive conditions are the type and degree of competition. The type of competition refers to the question of whether the product is available to direct or indirect competitors. A **direct competitor** is *one whose merchandising program is about the same as another retailer's.* An **indirect competitor** is *one whose merchandising program is noticeably different from that of a retailer of similar products.*

If the product is available to direct competitors, then the product has no "distinctive" advantage to any retailer. In some cases, however, it might help a retailer to establish that the store's image is on par with its competitors' and therefore promote comparison shopping. Where the product is available to indirect competitors, a retailer that adopts the product might either help or hurt the store's image. If upscale, indirect competitors stock the product, the retailer's image can be enhanced, but if downscale, indirect competitors stock the product, the retailer's image could be damaged.

429

FIGURE 15–11
Life-style merchandising

"The Perfectionist"
- Age: 25–45
- Size: Misses 4–14
- A woman who is *first* in a fashion trend; has the most advanced taste of all customers—the "Fashion Leader."
- Active; worldly; career-oriented; involved; free-spirited; energy abounding.
- Inherently understands fashion . . . incorporates fashion into every aspect of her lifestyle.
- Uniqueness and individuality are her two main concerns—she depends on clothes as a means of self-expression.
- She is governed by her emotions. When in an adventurous mood, she seeks the most advanced fashions . . . always avant-garde, nonconforming, often impractical. When in a classic mood, her taste level is pure, clean, and sophisticated.
- She combines a mix of fashion looks to cover her variety of emotional and active lifestyle needs.
- She is extremely conscious of her body; chooses clothes to complement her figure.
- Demands and appreciates quality.
- Impressed by designers who style for her contemporary lifestyle.
- Not necessarily price conscious; buys what she desires.
- She is influenced by her surroundings when shopping.
- Does not respond well to markdowns or price promotions.
- Needs little salespeople attention.
- Expects new arrivals often.
- Buys impulsively.
- Loyal to a store wherever she feels her *mood runs free.*

"The Updated"
- Age: 25–60
- Size: Misses 4–16
- Desires fashion after it has been modified from its pure, advanced stages. Very often *this season's updated styles were last season's perfectionist styles.*
- Demands smart-looking items; stylish, yet not extreme.
- Working girl or woman; housewife; mother.
- Desires clothes that are functional additions to her wardrobe—multipurpose.
- Desires high degree of quality, practicality, and value for the price.

- Not necessarily label conscious.
- Will buy regular stock markdowns; responds only moderately to price promotions.
- Loyal to store that separates her look, supports her type, and puts her look together for her.
- Fastest-growing misses customer type.

"The Young Affluent"
- Age: 25–50
- Size: Misses 4–14
- Career woman, wife.
- Leads active social life; involved.
- Often attracted to designer labels.
- Ruled by current designer trends.
- Respects fine merchandise.
- Demands quality.
- Is an investment buyer; designer wardrobe builder.
- Taste level similar to updated customer, but not price conscious.

"The Traditionalist"
- Age: 26–65
- Size: Misses 8–20
- The conformist . . . likes fashion only after it is accepted.
- Less career-oriented; more job-oriented. Oftentimes office worker, teacher, housewife.
- Does not react to, or desire, fashion extremes.
- Extremely label conscious—loyal to those she has worn and liked in the past.
- Price conscious; quality aware.
- Very practical; demands ease of care.
- Very insecure about fashion in general—must have fashion put together for her.
- Fashion influenced by peers.
- Loyal to stores and professional salespeople who service her needs.
- Responds exceptionally well to price promotions and markdowns.
- Replacement customer; conservative taste.

"The Establishment"
- Age: 45 +
- Size: Misses 8–20
- Older, refined woman—dignified.
- Active in community; holds prestigious position.
- An investment buyer; wardrobe builder.
- Loves fine workmanship, fabrics, and detail.
- Concerned with quality and value.
- Appreciates designer merchandise.
- Limitless buying ability.
- Seeks clothes that fill her needs.

Source: M. M. Cohn, Little Rock, AK.

The degree of competition refers to the number of competitors that are or will be stocking the product. Competitive conditions can be either **exclusive** (no competitors), **selective** (few competitors), or **intensive** (many competitors). For many retailers, exclusive rights to a product offer several advantages. First, they help build an exclusive image by distinguishing the retailer's product mix from the competitors' mixes. Second, they permit the retailer greater freedom in merchandising products, since it can worry less about what competitors are doing.

Suppliers, however, do not grant exclusive rights to their products without expecting something in return. Therefore, retailers must have a clear understanding with their suppliers of the requirements they must meet to handle the product exclusively.

For retailers, selective competition is generally not as desirable as an exclusive arrangement. For those that want some limit on competition but still need comparable products to facilitate customer comparison shopping, a selective arrangement is the best alternative. If intense competition exists, retailers normally have little incentive to stock the product. However, retailers are often "forced" to carry intensively distributed products because they are so readily available in competitive outlets and consumers expect them to be in stock.

The retailer's typical assortment strategy varies with competitive conditions. For exclusive products, retailers should carry a deep assortment of product items. For selective products, retailers should carry a limited assortment of the merchandise. And, for intensively distributed products, retailers must resort to one of two strategies: (1) stock only the best-selling items to satisfy customers whose preferred item is not available and who will accept a substitute, or (2) stock a deep assortment to satisfy most customers and thereby create a store image of "complete selection."

Supply Considerations

In evaluating what and how many products should be included in the product mix, the retailer should examine not only market conditions but also supply considerations. Two such considerations are the **availability** and the **reliability of the supplier**.

Availability of Supply

Before making a decision to stock a product, the retailer should study the product's availability. Four basic questions the retailer should ask are

1. Is the product readily available through the retailer's normal channels of distribution?
2. Are alternative backup sources of supply available?
3. Will the product be available on a continuing basis?
4. What are the terms and conditions of sale under which the product is available?

Ideally, for the retailer to make a positive decision on a product candidate, the product should be available from normal channels, with sufficient alternative supply sources, and under terms and conditions consistent with the sales and profit potential of the product.

Reliability of Supplier

In deciding whether to include a product in the product mix, a retailer should also evaluate the supplier. The ease of getting the product into the store at the *right time,* in the *right quantities*, and in *good condition* is a necessary consideration. Some criteria a retailer can use to describe a supplier's reliability include (1) shipping on time, (2) filling orders adequately, (3) maintaining adequate stocks (avoiding stock-outs), and (4) adjusting orders to meet the retailer's changing needs. These criteria are useful to retailers in making their "supplier" decision. Later buying and procurement chapters (Chapters 17 and 18) provide further detail on how retailers can choose the right supplier.

A number of excellent sources of product information can aid retailers in making product-mix decisions. Internal sources include sales records, want books and slips, sales personnel, in-store testing, and customer returns. External sources are comparison shopping, consumer opinions and behavior, vendors, trade shows, trade publications, residential buying offices, and special reporting services.

Internal Sources

Sales Records

The most widely used internal source of product information must be the store's past sales for various product lines and items. Past sales records are especially useful in making decisions about staple merchandise. Due to the regularity of demand for staples, past demand often is the key to predicting future demand. On the other hand, the cyclical demand patterns for fashion goods limit the usefulness of past sales in estimating future demand (see Chapter 19). For fashion goods, the past may very well be the past and have little to do with what consumers want in the future. Although past sales data are useful in many situations, they are of limited or no use for new products.

Want Books and Slips

Another method for determining what customers want is to record their inquiries about (1) products the retailer does not stock, and (2) products the retailer carries but that currently are out of stock. Salespeople can systematically record these inquiries in want books or want slips. **Want books** and **slips** range from simple blank notebooks and slips of paper to printed books and forms. Regardless of their composition, want books and slips must be filled out in enough detail to identify the product clearly and to be of use to the merchandise buyer.

Sales Personnel

Sales personnel are an excellent source of information. Because they have more direct contact with consumers than anyone else in the firm, salespeople are in a position to observe why and how consumers buy. Reports from sales personnel must be viewed with caution, though, since they are subjective and tend to reflect the salesperson's own biases and preferences. Nevertheless, if properly encouraged, salespeople can provide the retail manager with information on how existing products are selling and on which products might sell in the future.

In-Store Testing

Retailers frequently use test marketing within their stores to judge customer wants. Products are pretested by stocking a sample order and observing customer responses. If the product stimulates no interest, the retailer can dispose of the merchandise with minimal losses. If the product sells in sufficient quantities over a short period of time, the retailer can reorder a much larger quantity of the merchandise. For in-store testing to be valid, the test product must be supported by a total merchandising effort. As one expert writes, ". . . a pre-test requires sufficient stock, assortment, display, and employee excitement. If you starve the item by insufficient breadth and depth or if you are not prepared to push it by window displays, interior displays, and sales personnel, do not bother with it at all. Unless you treat it fairly, the results are bound to be disappointing."[10]

Customer Returns

Sometimes it is as important to find out what customers do not want as it is to find out what they do want. Store data on products customers return or require adjustment for provide the retailer with valuable information on the product mix. For the data to be useful, however, the retailer must try to discover the reasons customers returned the merchandise (see Chapter 16).

External Sources

Comparison Shopping

A good outside source of information on what consumers want is what other stores sell them. Through **comparison shopping** at both competing and noncompeting stores, a retailer can often discover missed product opportunities. The retailer can also inspect the merchandising techniques that competitors are using to move certain products successfully. The retailer who makes comparative checks should examine the competitor's window displays, store displays, advertisements, promotions, featured products, prices, quantities on shelves, and product appeals. Some retailers go further by hiring people to pose as customers to discover what methods and appeals competitive salespeople are using in merchandising their products. By learning how competitors think, the retailer can distinguish between what promotions are used to promote fast movers and which are used to move "dogs."

For "complete" information on what competitors are doing, many retailers use the "three-level comparison shopping" strategy. Under this strategy, retailers shop at stores operating above, at, and below their own targeted market. By shopping at all three levels, the retailer obtains information on what products customers might want in the near future (above), what products they are currently buying (at), and what products are dated (below). This strategy provides information to many retailers on the products they should *add* in the near future and those they should quickly *delete* from their product mix.

Consumer Opinions and Behavior

Perhaps the most effective methods for determining consumer preferences are to ask them and to observe them. By asking consumers their opinions and observing their behavior, the retailer obtains first-hand information on what products consumers want and when, where, how, and why they want them. Three commonly used methods for soliciting consumer opinions and observing consumer behavior are consumer surveys, consumer panels, and consumer counts (see Chapter 6).

Vendors

Being in contact daily with large numbers of retailers, vendors and their representatives have a wide range of experiences upon which to base their product opinions. They are thus excellent sources of product information for retailers, though retailers must be wary of their reliability. In an attempt to sell their products, some vendors

433

shade the truth. On the other hand, most vendors recognize that repeat business is the only way to stay in business, and the only way to obtain repeat business is to develop strong relationships with retailers based on trust. To stick a retailer with a "dog" is not an act that builds trust. As a rule, vendor information is accurate in a general sense; however, the retailer should recognize that vendor representatives often become overly enthusiastic about their own products.

Trade Shows

Trade shows are *occasions when manufacturers get together to exhibit their merchandise in one place.* Trade shows range from exhibitions of a particular line of products to general merchandise displays. These events allow retailers to comparison shop, talk to various vendor representatives, and inspect displayed merchandise. They also provide retailers an opportunity to talk about their experiences with various products, vendors, and merchandising programs. Additionally, trade-show programs usually feature guest speakers on a wide range of topics that often are informative to the participating retailers. Since a trade show promotes getting caught up in the excitement, though, a retailer may want to wait until returning to the store before placing any orders.

Trade Publications

Trade publications are good sources of information for two reasons: (1) they provide basic trade information, and (2) they contain numerous advertisements of interest to the retailer. Trade publications consist of feature articles and special reports on topics including new products, industry trends, merchandising tips, current developments, and legal and environmental issues. Trade publications of a specialized nature include *Chain Store Age Executive, American Druggist, Discount Merchandiser, Department Store Management, Hardware Retailer, Progressive Grocer,* and

What are the advantages of trade shows as sources of product information?

Women's Wear Daily, to name just a few. Additional features of trade publications are manufacturers' advertisements, which are often highly informative and directed toward retailers, not consumers.

Residential Buying Offices

Many retailers either rely on independent residential buyers or establish their own **residential buying offices** in major producer markets. In the apparel industry, for example, major producer markets (domestic) are New York, Dallas, and Los Angeles. By having a representative in producer areas, the retailer keeps abreast of which products are available and which new products are in the offering (see Chapter 17).

Special Reporting Services

Retailers subscribe to numerous **special reporting services**. Frequently, these services offer information on certain product lines and merchandising activities (e.g., advertising, store displays, and facings). They provide retailers with information on a periodic basis (daily, weekly, monthly) in the form of newspapers, special reports, or flash reports. The cost of these services can be substantial; moreover, depending on the reporting, the information can be dated. Nevertheless, they do provide the retailer with a "feel" for what is going on in its area of interest.

The basic objective in planning product-mix strategies is to offer consumers an optimum number of product lines and an optimum number of product items within each line. The optimum number of lines and items a retailer should carry varies with the type and extent of the market served. Also, the retailer's operating capabilities affect its optimum strategy. Several different optimal strategies are possible, depending upon the retailer's circumstances. Retailers can develop strategic plans for their product mix by studying various combinations of product varieties and product assortments. Figure 15–12 (p. 436) illustrates the four basic variety- and assortment-combination strategies—(1) narrow variety/shallow assortment, (2) wide variety/shallow assortment, (3) narrow variety/deep assortment, and (4) wide variety/deep assortment. These four combination strategies provide an excellent reference for retailers in creating product-mix strategies.

**PRODUCT-MIX
STRATEGIES**

Narrow Variety/Shallow Assortment

Retailers that select a **narrow variety/shallow assortment strategy** *offer consumers the most limited product selection (lines and items) of any of the combination strategies.* Retail operations characterized by narrow variety/shallow assortment are unconventional types. Vending machines that hold only two or three choices of soft drinks, door-to-door sales representatives who sell only one product line with a limited number of product features, and the newsstand that offers only one or two newspapers are examples of retail institutions that use the narrow variety/shallow assortment strategy. The key to merchandising this limited product-mix strategy successfully is *place and time conveniences.* Because it offers a very limited choice of products, the narrow variety/shallow assortment retailer must make its offering readily available where and when consumers want it. Consumers will not spend much time, money, or effort to look for such a limited offering. Generally, the narrow variety/shallow assortment strategy suffers from a poor image and little, if any, customer loyalty other than that generated by convenience. A limited product mix,

FIGURE 15–12
Product-mix strategies

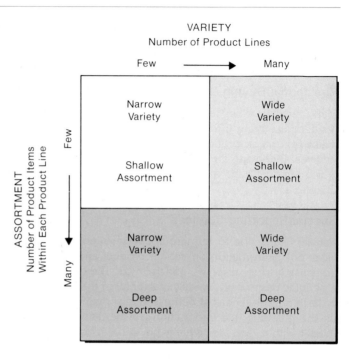

however, does create certain benefits: it simplifies operations, it makes inventory control problems insignificant, and it minimizes facility requirements. A major benefit is the retailer's small investment in inventories.

Wide Variety/Shallow Assortment

The basic philosophy behind the **wide variety/shallow assortment strategy** is *"stock a little of everything."* Using this strategy, the retailer offers a wide selection of different product lines, but limits the selection of brands, styles, sizes, and so on within each line. Most variety stores (five and dime stores), general stores, and some discount houses follow this product-mix philosophy. A wide and shallow product mix offers the advantages of appealing to a broad market, satisfying the consumer in terms of product availability if not product selection, promoting one-stop shopping, and permitting reasonable control over inventories. The disadvantages of this product-mix strategy are lost sales and customers disappointed by the lack of selection within lines, low inventory turnover rate on slow-moving product lines, weak store image, and limited store loyalty.

A paradox of sorts can occur within the wide variety/narrow assortment strategy. A retailer that wants to project a prestige image might choose to stock many different high-priced product lines but limit the selection within each line to one or two unique items—originals or limited editions. A similar paradox is the antique retailer that sells products ranging from household furnishings to automotive accessories, with each product item being unique in some aspect.

Narrow Variety/Deep Assortment

The "specialty" philosophy characterizes the **narrow variety/deep assortment strategy.** Some retailers try to appeal to a select group of consumers by offering only one or a few product lines with an excellent selection within each line. Specialty retailers can benefit greatly from their specialist image (see Figure 15–13). By offering a specialized mix of products supported by specialized personnel, the narrow

FIGURE 15–13
The specialty-store
philosophy

A first-time father rushes into the shop during his lunch hour, eagerly grabs Early Games for Young Children, forks over $30 for the software, and leaves. His child's age? Barely 2. "I don't know if he'll get anything out of it," shrugs Tom Byrom, 37, a San Francisco savings and loan executive. "But I have an IBM PC at home, so why not? Anything to keep him happy."

The Ultimate Baby Store?

There is a rush of equally indulgent new parents to My Child's Destiny, a specialty store off San Francisco's fashionable Union Square. Laid out in a series of boutiques that feature everything from clothes and haircuts to books and computers, the store should run up $7.5 million in retail and mail-order sales by the time its first year ends in June, says owner Roy L. Raymond, 37. He hopes to make My Child's Destiny—with its toddler-height counters, low handrails, and free diapers in the restrooms—the ultimate baby store.

The Selective Inventory

One secret to the store's success is what it does not carry. There are no sex-stereotyped toys on the shelves. Each book in the 600-title, oak-shelved "library" is screened for violence, and all violent playthings are banned. Raymond carries clothes with natural fibers only and has the city's widest selection of European shoes for his largely upscale clientele. They are the kind of customers Raymond hopes can appreciate what could be his favorite toy in the store: Talking Computer, imported from France.

Source: Pamela Ellis-Simons, "A Boutique Born to Be the Ultimate Baby Store," *Business Week*, 22 April 1985, 65.

variety/deep assortment retailer can develop a distinct store image and a loyal customer following. Additional advantages to the retailer include

- rare sales losses due to an inadequate selection of brands, styles, sizes, colors, and materials
- greater likelihood of a high level of repeat shopping
- greater specialization in the buying, managing, and selling of a limited line of products
- good economies of scale in ordering large quantities of the same product

The principal limitation of a specialty strategy is that successful operations *depend solely upon a single or limited line of products*. This strategy of "putting all the eggs in one basket" creates a high risk for the retailer, which sells in a very limited market. If adverse conditions occur in the market area, then the specialty retailer suffers the most.

Wide Variety/Deep Assortment

The full-line department store best typifies the **wide variety/deep assortment strategy.** One-stop shopping is the basic philosophy of this all-inclusive product-mix strategy. A large number of product lines with supporting depth in each line allow the retailer to make a broad market appeal while satisfying most of the product needs of specific target markets. Very few sales are lost as a result of an inadequate variety or assortment. Generally, satisfied customers develop store loyalty, leading to a high level of repeat shopping. Although retailers generally regard a wide variety/deep assortment strategy as the most desirable strategy from the viewpoint of selling, they also recognize the problems they must encounter in the store operations. The most common problems are (1) the high level of investment in inventory necessary to support such a diverse product mix; (2) the low stock-turnover rate associated with many marginal product lines; and (3) the amount of space, fixtures, and equipment the retailer must have to merchandise properly such a wide range of products.

PRODUCT-MIX TRENDS

To survive in the contemporary world of retailing, product mixes must be adapted rapidly and creatively to the dynamics of the marketplace. Future winners in the field of retailing will be those that can best identify consumers' emerging unsatisfied needs and develop innovative product-mix strategies to satisfy them.

Two emerging product-mix trends of particular interest are shotgun merchandising and rifle merchandising.

Shotgun Merchandising

Shotgun merchandising is *the marketing strategy of broadening the retail offering to meet the expanding needs of consumers.* By expanding the number of product options, retailers try to increase the size of their total market by appealing to several submarkets. In this strategy, the retailer attempts to satisfy the specific needs of several individual market segments. In diversifying the product mix, the shotgun merchandiser is attempting to develop a general-purpose mix that will satisfy the product needs of most consumers "pretty well." A retailer can either add new product items or combine major product lines to develop a general-purpose mix.

Item Addition

Item addition *involves adding to one retailer's traditional product lines the more desirable product items normally associated with another type of retailer.* Book, magazine, cosmetic, and apparel racks are item additions to the supermarket's primary product offerings. In the retailing industry, item addition is often referred to as *cherry picking,* because the product item additions are ones retailers consider the cream of the crop—the best of the product line. Characteristics of these product items are (1) low risk due to reasonably sure sales, (2) relatively high turnover rates, (3) adequate margins for respectable profits, (4) minimal personal selling effort, (5) routine ordering and stocking procedures, and (6) relatively low per-unit prices with high levels of impulse and unplanned purchasing.

Retailers use the item-addition strategy on both a permanent and a temporary basis. Frequently, retailers add products on a trial basis to determine how well customers will receive them and whether the product additions provide sufficient profits with minimal operating difficulties. Rax Restaurants, for instance, by adding wine and beer to its menu, tried to appeal to a more upscale audience.[11] If these conditions are met, the retailer will add the product on a permanent basis. In other instances some retailers engage in an item-addition strategy on a seasonal basis. During Christmas, for example, retailers add "hot items" as potential gift selections, although during other times of the year they would not stock these items.

Line Combination

Line combination is the second strategy that shotgun merchandisers use to develop a general-purpose mix. In this strategy, *the retailer combines two or more broad product lines into the store operation.* The principle behind combining major merchandise lines is to provide consumers with a one-stop shopping opportunity for a wide range of products and therefore satisfy several needs under one roof. An example of a retail organization that uses the line-combination strategy is the superstore. The superstore combines many of the standard product lines of the supermarket, drug store, variety store, and hardware store. With consumers demanding more and more convenience and with the soaring price of gasoline, superstores could be the wave of the future.

In addition to diversified product lines, the shotgun merchandiser also varies the place, price, and promotional elements of the merchandising mix. By incorporating supermarket and warehouse methods of operation into large yet modest facilities, the shotgun merchandiser can offer nationally branded merchandise below usual market prices. Although standard promotional appeals are used, the shotgun merchandiser has the added opportunity to appeal to consumers on the basis of a complete shopping environment—product value with time and place convenience.

Rifle Merchandising

Rifle merchandising is *a strategy of targeting a product offering to a select group of customers.* Although the number of product lines is very selective—often only one or two lines—there is a large assortment of product items within each line. In essence, the rifle merchandiser employs a penetration strategy, concentrating product options within limited lines to serve "all" of the individual needs of a given market segment for a particular line of products. By concentrating on a limited line, the rifle merchandiser develops a specific-purpose mix that will satisfy very well all of the targeted consumers' specific needs for a given product. In creating specific-purpose mixes, the rifle merchandiser uses one of two marketing strategies: either market positioning or multiplex distribution.

Market Positioning

Market positioning is *the strategy of creating a "position" for a store and its product mix in the minds of consumers by relating it to other stores and their mixture of products.* By specializing in certain product lines and by offering a choice within those lines, the rifle retailer hopes to establish a market niche and a particular market image in the consumer's mind. This image-creating process leads the rifle merchandiser to program its entire operation so that the consumer will perceive it as occupying a unique position within a particular product category (see Figure 15–14). By focusing on certain product lines and developing highly complementary price, place, and promotional strategies, the rifle merchandiser attempts to achieve "classification dominance" within those product lines.[12] Classification dominance refers to the retailing approach of carrying a tremendously wide assortment of merchandise with great depth in each line. In effect, this approach positions the store in the minds of consumers as one that "has it all" in a particular class of merchandise. Baskin-Robbins Ice Cream Shops, National Shirt Shops, Radio Shacks, Dunkin' Donut Shops, and McDonald Restaurants are all examples of multiunit retailers that have pursued a limited-line market-positioning policy. Rifle merchandisers have used successfully the market-positioning strategy for a variety of product lines including sporting goods, formal wear, home-decorating services, real estate services, entertainment, and personal-care products.

Multiplex Distribution

"No single retailing approach is likely to be sufficient in the future simply because markets are diverging more and more with respect to wants, needs, and buying power. Therefore, a single way of doing business is unlikely to appeal to all market segments."[13]

FIGURE 15–14

The corporate level: A market-positioning strategy

It used to be a dingy basement where shoppers rummaged through piles of bargain-priced clothes. But six months ago, Carson Pirie Scott & Co. transformed the 40,000-sq. ft. room into a colorful, mirrored space more befitting an exclusive shop in Beverly Hills than an 81-year-old department store in downtown Chicago. The new store-within-a-store is called Corporate Level, and it represents a bold attempt by Carson's to recapture the cream of the shopping masses—professional women who have fled department stores in search of high-quality merchandise and service.

Targeting the Career Woman

Carson's is not alone in its quest for the woman executive, who generally spends more on clothes than average shoppers. Many retailers provide wardrobe consultants for working women, and some have departments that sell "career" clothes. But Carson's approach is being heralded as one of the most comprehensive. . . .

Tailoring the Producer-Service Mix

What makes Corporate Level different is that almost everything a customer needs is in one place. Designer outfits are steps away from shoes and accessories. And a woman not only can buy clothes but have her shoes repaired and her hair styled, drop off dry cleaning, make photocopies, and eat a meal. For $50 annually, she gets an extra package of services that allows her to cash checks, reserve a meeting room, and use a fashion consultant.

Source: Jo Ellen Daily, "One-Stop Shopping for the Woman on the Go," *Business Week,* 18 March 1985, 116.

An extension of the market-positioning strategy is the **multiplex distribution strategy**. In the last decade, rifle merchandisers have begun to operate multiple types of outlets with individual product mixes serving multiple market segments.

This strategy is called multiplex distribution. In multiplex distribution, *the rifle merchandiser is aiming at a number of different target markets.* This specialized type of merchandiser accomplishes the task of serving several target markets using a "free-form" organization that permits it to develop a specialized product mix for each market segment. Operating under the assumption that no one individual store can please all consumers, the multiplex retailer simply develops individual product mixes positioned to meet the needs of a given market segment. J. C. Penney has been one of the leading proponents of the free-form organization. Currently, the firm operates full-line department stores, limited-line soft-goods stores, insurance centers, discount stores, catalog desks and stores, and several foreign retail operations. The Limited also employs the free-form concept of multiplex distribution (see Figure 15–15, p. 442).

SUMMARY

Offering the right product in the right quantities in the right place at the right time at the right price and with the right appeal constitutes the merchandising process. The three stages of the merchandising process are developing the merchandise mix (product and service mix), securing the merchandising mix (buying and procurement process), and managing the merchandise mix (planning and controlling process).

In developing a product mix, the retailer must first understand the total-product concept. The total product is the sum of the product's functional, aesthetic, and

(Opposite page)   Rifle merchandising is the strategy of targeting products to a select group of consumers. (Courtesy of Carson Pirie Scott & Co.)

Never before. Ever. Has there been anything like it. We devoted an entire floor in our State Street store to the Corporate Level. And we built a single objective into every square inch: serving you, the working woman. Saving you hours and days of precious time by putting all your needs in one place, on one level. Fashion, food, beauty and beyond! Everything from alterations to vacations—and a personal wardrobe consultant to help you every step of the way!

The Limited, Inc. is a growth company focused exclusively on women's apparel. The Company's primary business is to provide fashion, quality, and value to the American woman through multiple retail formats:

☐ LIMITED STORES. There are 500 Limited stores in over 125 major markets throughout the United States. Limited stores sell medium-priced fashion apparel tailored to the tastes and lifestyles of fashion-conscious contemporary women 20 to 40 years of age. The majority of Limited stores are located in regional shopping centers with the remainder in key downtown locations.

☐ LIMITED EXPRESS. Distinguished by a unique store design and merchandise selection, Limited Express stores offer an exciting assortment of popular-priced sportswear and accessories designed to appeal primarily to fashion-forward women 15 to 25 years of age. Currently there are 45 Limited Express stores located in regional shopping centers in California, Texas, and the Midwest.

☐ LANE BRYANT. Lane Bryant is the nation's leading retailer of women's special-size apparel. The 223 Lane Bryant stores specialize in the sale of medium-priced fashion, basic, and intimate apparel designed to appeal to the special-size woman, with particular emphasis on those over 25 years of age. The stores are located in regional shopping centers throughout the United States.

☐ BRYLANE MAIL ORDER. The nation's foremost catalogue retailer of women's special-size apparel

and shoes, Brylane Mail Order publishes five catalogues, each directed to a specific special-size customer. The catalogues include *Lane Bryant, Roaman's, Tall Collection, Nancy's Choice,* and *LB For Short.*

☐ VICTORIA'S SECRET. Through retail stores and a nationally distributed mail order catalogue, Victoria's Secret offers European and American designer lingerie for the fashionable contemporary woman 25 to 45 years of age. The 12 stores are located in the San Francisco, Boston, Columbus, Dallas, Chicago, and New York metropolitan areas.

☐ SIZES UNLIMITED. This newly-established division is an off-price retailer of women's special-size apparel. Composed of Sizes Unlimited and Smart Size stores, the division offers nationally known brand and private label merchandise designed to appeal primarily to women 25 to 50 years of age. The 77 stores are located in smaller shopping centers throughout the East and Midwest.

☐ MAST INDUSTRIES. Mast Industries is a large, international supplier of moderate-priced apparel for fashion-conscious women. The Commercial Division employs a worldwide network of 150 contract production facilities to produce merchandise against specific orders from retailers, wholesalers, and manufacturers. Through sales offices in New York and Los Angeles, as well as a field sales force, the Wholesale Division supplies a wide variety of apparel products to department and specialty stores throughout the United States.

Source: Roger D. Blackwell and W. Wayne Talarzyk, "Lifestyle Retailing: Competitive Strategies," *Journal of Retailing* 59 (Winter 1983): 14.

FIGURE 15–15

The Limited, Inc.: A multiple-distribution retail organization

service features plus the psychological benefits the customer expects from buying and using the product. A retailer's product mix refers to the full range of products it offers to the consumer. The product mix represents "appropriate combinations" of products designed to meet the specific needs of one or more identified, target markets. It is composed of product lines (any grouping of related products) and product items (specific products within a product line that are clearly distinguishable). Product lines can be subclassified into merchandise groups, classes, and categories. Product items are different brands of products, differentiated by brand name, style, size, color, material, and price.

Product-mix decisions revolve around two separate but related decisions—which and how many products to stock. The decision of which products to stock depends on whether the retailer is starting a new business and thus creating a new product mix or is currently in business and adjusting the existing product mix. Deciding how many products concerns developing product variety (number of different products to stock) and product assortment (number of different product items to stock in each product line).

Retailers use several criteria deciding which and how many products to carry. These criteria are product compatibility, product attributes, product profitability, product life cycles, fashion cycles, product appropriateness, and competitive conditions. The retailer must also consider the availability of needed products and the reliability of the suppliers.

In evaluating the merits of a product, the retailer can consult several available sources of information. Internal sources consist of sales records, want books and slips, sales personnel, in-store testing, and customer returns. External sources of information are comparison shopping, consumer opinions and behavior, vendors, trade shows, trade publications, residential buying offices, and special reporting services.

In developing product-mix strategies, a retailer can use one of four variety/assortment strategies: narrow variety/shallow assortment, wide variety/shallow assortment, narrow variety/deep assortment, and wide variety/deep assortment. Correct selection of a product-mix strategy depends upon the retailer's current or proposed variety/assortment situation.

Retailers are responding to the changing marketplace by employing either a shotgun or a rifle approach to merchandising. The shotgun merchandiser appeals to a combination of market segments by broadening its product lines through either product-item addition or product-line combination. The rifle merchandiser appeals to a target-market segment by using either a market-positioning strategy or a multiplex distribution system.

KEY TERMS AND CONCEPTS

merchandising	product substitute	observability
total-product concept	product complement	complexibility
physical product	unrelated products	life-style merchandising
extended product	product attributes	direct and indirect competitors
generic product	product profitability	exclusive, selective, and intensive competitive conditions
product-mix concept	product life cycle	
product line	fashion cycle	availability of supply
product item	flop	reliability of supplier
merchandise group	fad	want books and slips
merchandise class	ford	in-store testing
merchandise category	classic	comparison shopping
product variety	relative advantage	trade shows
product assortment	affinity	residential buying offices
product compatibility	trialability	special reporting services

narrow variety/shallow
assortment strategy

wide variety/shallow assortment
strategy

narrow variety/deep assortment
strategy

wide variety/deep assortment
strategy

shotgun merchandising

item addition

line combination

rifle merchandising

market positioning

multiplex distribution

REVIEW QUESTIONS

1. What are the principal tasks to be accomplished within the merchandising process?
2. What is the total-product concept? Briefly describe each of the concept's components.
3. How do product lines differ from product items?
4. What are the two basic decisions faced by the retailer in developing the product mix?
5. Define product variety. How does it differ from product assortment?
6. Identify and describe the three basic classes of products based on product compatibility. Which of these classes of products should be included in the retailer's product mix?
7. How do the product attributes of bulk and standardization influence the retailer's decisions of which and how many products should be stocked?
8. What should the retailer's stocking strategy be for products in each of the four stages of the product life cycle?
9. Develop a profile of a fashion-conscious consumer.
10. Describe each of the four fashion cycles and discuss what the retailer's stock position should be relative to each cycle.

11. Which five product characteristics are used in evaluating new product offerings relative to their market appropriateness?
12. What is life-style merchandising?
13. What are the internal sources of product information?
14. Describe the three-level comparison shopping strategy for gathering product information.
15. What are the four basic variety- and assortment-combination strategies used in developing a retail product mix? Briefly describe each strategy.
16. What are the most common problems associated with using a wide variety/deep assortment product-mix strategy?
17. Compare and contrast the strategies of shotgun and rifle merchandising.
18. List the characteristics of the typical product-item addition.
19. How can retailers develop a market position for their stores and product mixes?
20. What is multiplex distribution?

ENDNOTES

1. See Kenneth E. Miller and Kent L. Granzin, "Simultaneous Loyalty and Benefit Segmentation of Retail Store Customers," *Journal of Retailing* 55 (Spring, 1979): 47–60.
2. Mabel D. Erwin and Lila A. Kinchen, *Clothing for Moderns* (New York: Macmillan, 1969).
3. David R. Rink and John E. Swan, "Product Life Cycle Research: A Literature Review," *Journal of Business Research* 7 (September 1979): 219–42.
4. Anna Sobezynski, "New Product Success Can Be All in the Timing," *Advertising Age,* 3 May 1984, M15.

5. Alfred H. Daniels, "Fashion Merchandising," in *Inside the Fashion Business,* ed. J. A. Jarnow and Beatrice Judelle (New York: John Wiley and Sons, 1974).
6. Kathryn M. Greenwood and Mary F. Murphy, *Fashion Innovation and Marketing* (New York: Macmillan, 1978), 57–58.
7. Miriam Tatzel, "Skill and Motivation in Clothes Shopping: Fashion-Conscious, Independent, and Apathetic Consumers," *Journal of Retailing* 58 (Winter, 1982): 91–92.

8. Ibid., 56.
9. See Elizabeth A. Richards and Stephen S. Sturman, "Life-Style Segmentation in Apparel Marketing," *Journal of Marketing* 41 (October, 1977): 89–91.
10. Greenwood and Murphy, *Fashion Innovation and Marketing*, 73.
11. Noel Wical, "Rax Chain to Feature Beer, Wine, Garden Decor," *Advertising Age,* 6 June 1983, 52MW.

12. See Louis W. Stern and Adel El-Ansary, *Marketing Channels* (Englewood Cliffs, NJ: Prentice-Hall, 1977), 50–52.
13. Jagdish N. Sheth, "Emerging Trends for the Retailing Industry," *Journal of Retailing* 59 (Fall, 1983): 14.

RELATED READINGS

Blackwell, Roger D. "Successful Retailers of 80's Will Cater to Specific Lifestyle Segments." *Marketing News* (March 7, 1980), 3.

Chick, Leslie S., and Byrd Joseph. "General Merchandise Retailing." *Retail Control* (October 1982), 49–57.

Douglas, Susan P., and Soloman, Michael R. "Clothing the Female Executive: Fashion or Fortune?" *AMA Educators' Proceedings.* P. E. Murphy et al, eds. (American Marketing Association 1983), 127–32.

Dunkin, Amy. "No-Frills Products: An Idea Whose Time Has Gone." *Business Week* (June 17, 1985), 64–65.

"The Halston-Penney Liaison: A Couple to Watch." *Stores* (August 1983), 26–27.

"J. C. Penney Goes after Affluent Shoppers." *The Wall Street Journal* (February 15, 1983), 33.

Jocoby, Jacob, and Olson, Jerry C. *Perceived Quality: How Consumers View Stores and Merchandise.* (Lexington, Mass.: Lexington Books, 1984)

King, Charles W., and Ring, Lawrence J. "Market Positioning across Retail Fashion Institutions: A Comparative Analysis of Store Types." *Journal of Retailing* 56 (Spring 1980), 37–55.

Levitt, Theodore. "Marketing Success through Differentiation—Of Anything." *Harvard Business Review* 58 (January - February 1980), 83–91.

Lumpkin, James R., and McConkey, C. William. "Identifying Determinants of Store Choice of Fashion Shoppers." *Akron Business and Economic Review* 15 (Winter 1984), 30–35.

Mangone, Dominic M. "How to Measure Merchandise Profitability." *Retail Control* (October 1984), 11–20.

Manners, George E., and Stone, Louis H. "Target Return Applications for Individual Product Lines in Merchandising Firms." *Developments in Marketing Science, Proceedings.* N. K. Malhotra, ed. (Academy of Marketing Science 1985), 187–90.

Marx, Thomas G. "The Economies of Single- and Multi-Line Retail Automobile Dealerships." *Journal of Marketing* 44 (Spring 1980), 29–35.

Pessemier, Edgar A. "Store Image and Positioning." *Journal of Retailing* 56 (Spring 1980), 94–106.

"Safeway Jilts 'The Family of Four' to Woo 'The Jogging Generation'." *Business Week* (November 21, 1983), 93–99.

Smith, Michael F., and Hunt, James M. "Commodity-Dominant versus Service-Dominant Retailers: Consumer Perceptions and Implications." *Marketing Comes of Age, Proceedings.* David M. Klein and Allen E. Smith, eds. (Southern Marketing Association 1984), 134–37.

Solan, Pat. "Fast Fashion: Hot Retail Arena." *Advertising Age* (August 12, 1985), 1, 73.

Solomon, Michael R. *The Psychology of Fashion.* (Lexington, Mass.: Lexington Books, 1985)

"Taking the Risk out of Fashion." *Chain Store Age* (April 1980), 51–52.

Troxell, Mary. *Fashion Merchandising,* 3rd ed. (New York: McGraw-Hill Book Co., 1981)

Wingate, Isabel; Gillespie, Karen; and Anderson, Mary. *Know Your Merchandise,* 5th ed. (New York: McGraw-Hill Book Co., 1984)

Outline

TYPES OF RETAIL SERVICES

THE RETAIL-SERVICE PROBLEM

Retail-Service Levels
Retail-Service Objectives
Retail-Service Determinants

THE RETAIL-SERVICE MIX

Store Hours
Consumer Credit
Delivery Service
Alterations and Repairs
Wrapping
Customer Complaints

Objectives

■ Comprehend the need to support the product mix with adequate customer services

■ Differentiate among consumer expectations for various service types and levels

■ Identify the principal objectives in providing customer services and discuss the factors that determine level of services required to meet those objectives

■ Name the major components of the service mix and explain how each component enhances the retailer's product mix and facilitates consumers' purchase decision making

The Service Mix

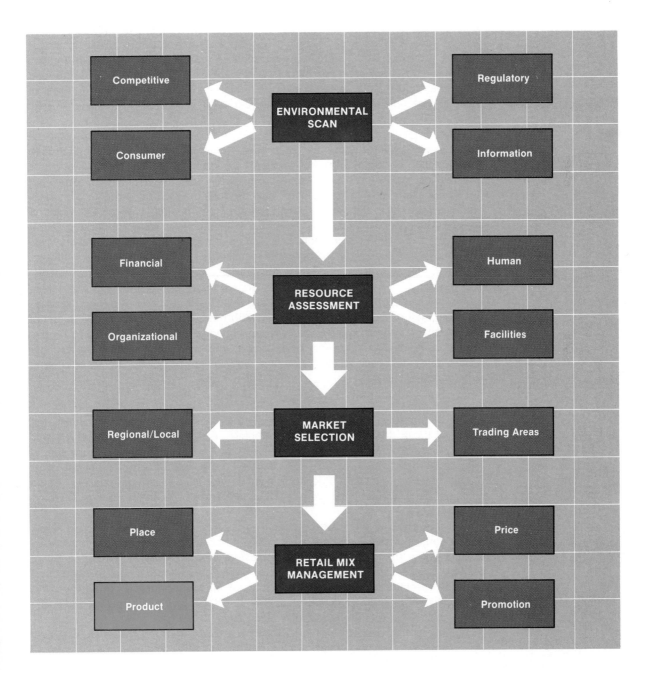

Often overlooked in the retailer's merchandise mix is the service mix. As discussed in the previous chapter, consumers buy more than a physical product. In fact, consumers expect the retailer to perform certain services before, during, and after the sale. These services often are as important as, if not more important than, the product itself. This chapter describes the role of the service mix in the retailer's total merchandise mix.

TYPES OF RETAIL SERVICES

The term *retail services* encompasses a wide variety of activities.[1] Retailers offer either primary services or complementary services. **Primary-service** retailers *concentrate on rendering services to consumers and typically sell physical products as supplements to these services.* Service is their reason for being in business. Examples of service retailers are banking, insurance, and real estate firms; firms that provide recreational and entertainment services; personal-care specialists ranging from hair stylists to health-spa owners; and establishments that provide home and auto repair and maintenance services. Retailers can obtain information on most of these service retailers from the "Selected Services" section of the *Census of Business.*

Many retailers *view the services they offer as secondary or supplementary to the physical products they sell.* These **complementary services** are neither their main function nor the reason these retailers are in business. Essentially, consumers and retailers consider supplementary services as "fringe benefits" that some, but not all, retailers offer in addition to their product mixes. Supplementary services enhance the retailer's merchandising program by providing "extras." Examples of supplementary services are delivery, credit, wrapping and packaging, parking, return privileges, installation, maintenance, repairs, alterations, some consulting services, and a host of other operations that only supplement the retailer's business format.

The following sections address the retailer's fundamental problem of offering supplementary services. Figure 16–1 outlines the major concerns with developing and implementing a supplementary service mix. The marketing of primary services involves most of the problems associated with marketing products; hence, many of the merchandising techniques discussed in previous chapters and those to be discussed in chapters to follow can be applied to primary-service retailing. As a matter of fact, primary-service retailers also face the problem of developing an offering of supplementary services.

THE RETAIL-SERVICE PROBLEM

The basic problems retailers face in developing their service mix are essentially the same as those they encounter in developing their product mix. The service-mix decision entails determining "which services" and "how many services" they should offer consumers. Thus, retailers must decide on the level of services that will complement their product mix. Prior to making service-level decisions, retailers should consider the relative importance of each service and its role in the consumer's buying process.

Based on relative importance, services can be classified as essential, expected, and optional. **Essential services** are *basic and necessary to a particular retail operation.* Without them, it is unlikely that the retailer could survive. While the list of essential services varies from one type of operation to another, the following services are essential to most retailers: (1) maintaining store hours, (2) providing parking facilities, (3) handling customer complaints, (4) supplying information and assistance, and (5) furnishing product display facilities.

Expected services are *not essential for the retailer to operate, but are expected by consumers.* Delivery, credit, and alterations are three services that consumers expect appliance, furniture, and clothing retailers, respectively, to provide. **Optional**

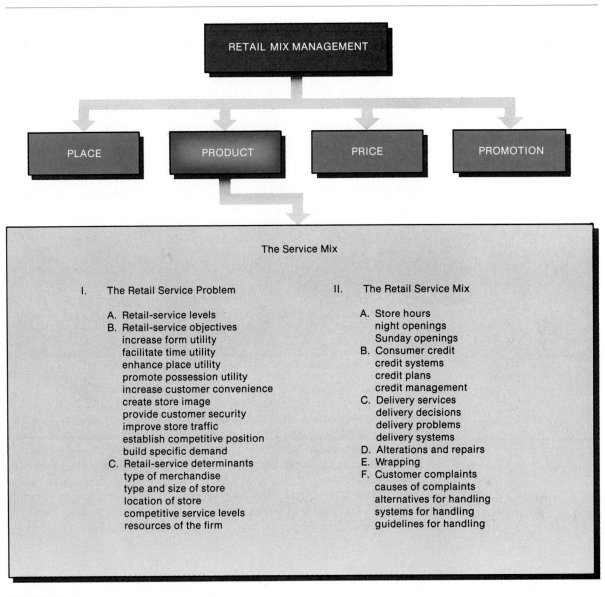

RETAIL MIX MANAGEMENT

PLACE

PRODUCT

PRICE

PROMOTION

The Service Mix

I.   The Retail Service Problem

A. Retail-service levels
B. Retail-service objectives
   increase form utility
   facilitate time utility
   enhance place utility
   promote possession utility
   increase customer convenience
   create store image
   provide customer security
   improve store traffic
   establish competitive position
   build specific demand
C. Retail-service determinants
   type of merchandise
   type and size of store
   location of store
   competitive service levels
   resources of the firm

II.   The Retail Service Mix

A. Store hours
   night openings
   Sunday openings
B. Consumer credit
   credit systems
   credit plans
   credit management
C. Delivery services
   delivery decisions
   delivery problems
   delivery systems
D. Alterations and repairs
E. Wrapping
F. Customer complaints
   causes of complaints
   alternatives for handling
   systems for handling
   guidelines for handling

FIGURE 16–1
Developing and implementing the service mix

services are *neither necessary to the retailer's operation nor expected by the retailer's customers.* Although not as important as essential and expected services, optional services can help a retailer develop a unique service offering and thereby distinguish itself. For example, "Rich's in Atlanta is offering automobile leasing. . .open and closed leasing contracts are available and financing is arranged . . . Woodward & Lothrop has gone into the apartment-finding business in Washington, D.C., and environs . . . Marshall Field has a corporate gift service."[2]

Retail-Service Levels

A **service level** is *the extent to which a retailer will provide consumers with "extra" help in purchasing a product.* The level of service is a function of the type and number of services the retailer provides and the terms and conditions under which

449

FIGURE 16–2
The low end of the ser-
vice continuum

The stores are drafty when the weather is cold and stuffy when it is hot. Customers have to find dollies and grappling hooks and then wrestle refrigerators, desks, and other heavy items to the checkout line themselves. There are no home deliveries. Credit cards are not accepted, and shoppers even pay a membership fee for the privilege of spending their money. But no one seems to mind. "Everything is so cheap. It's an experience to go there," says Camilla P. Wenrick, who works for a San Diego real estate developer.

Members-Only Warehouse Clubs

Wenrick is talking about warehouse clubs, a booming phenomenon that is blurring the distinction between retailing and wholesaling. These huge stores offer rock-bottom prices on everything from dishwashers and stoves to canned goods and TV dinners. These cash-and-carry clubs are open to members only, offer no amenities, and do little advertising, but they typically sell merchandise at 20% to 40% below supermarket and discount-store prices.

$4 Billion Sales

The idea has attracted a dozen companies—including such heavyweights as Zayre, Wal-Mart, and Pay 'n Save—which are expected to record close to $4 billion in sales this year. Most stores opened their doors only within the past two years. Even so, warehouse clubs can now be found in about half of the 100 largest markets in the country, and even faster growth is projected.

Source: "Boom Times in a Bargain-Hunter's Paradise," *Business Week,* 11 March 1985, 116.

they are provided. A retailer's service level can range along a continuum from a low to a high service level. A low-service-level retailer offers only services that are essential to its operation (see Figure 16–2). Although these services are typically essential to the consumer's purchase of the product, some retailers even assess a separate charge for them. At the other end of the continuum, high-service-level retailers offer consumers expected and optional services. At this level, retailers offer all essential and expected services free of charge; optional services might entail a separate assessment.

Retail-Service Objectives

Increasing Form Utility

Retailers often receive products from suppliers that require final adjustments and assembly, since production runs are set for standardized models, sizes, and product features. To put the product in a more desirable form, retailers offer a wide range of services. Some of the retailer's services are automatically and routinely applied to the product, whereas others are handled by the consumer. A few form-creating services retailers offer include altering and tailoring for clothing products, installing appliances and home furnishings, engraving and personalizing jewelry, and assembling lawn and garden equipment.

Facilitating Time Utility

Time is important in merchandising any product. The retailer that adds time utility to a product enhances its total value. For some consumers the right time is now; they want immediate gratification. Consumer credit and extended store hours are two services that retailers offer to create time utility.

Other consumers are more concerned with saving time. For these consumers,

450

retailers can add time utility to their product mix by accepting telephone and mail orders or by providing carryout services. Layaway services also add time utility by permitting the consumer to reserve a purchase for some future time when payment is more convenient. Finally, storage service (e.g., for furs) provides consumers with safe places to keep merchandise for future use, thereby adding time utility.

Enhancing Place Utility

Services also play an important role in the creation of place utility. The best way for retailers to add place utility to their product mix is through convenient locations. Delivery services also form an essential part of some retailers' total product. Without home deliveries, most bulky products (e.g., furniture and appliances) would have no value to consumers who have no means to transport them. Some retailers offer catering services to enhance the place value of their products. Window and in-store displays also create place utility by highlighting product price specials in locations where consumers are sure to find them.

Promoting Possession Utility

Possession utility is the satisfaction consumers receive from owning and using a product. To promote possession utility, retailers must provide consumers with information to facilitate the exchange of ownership process. Personal selling, fashion shows, information booths, complaint desks, bridal registries, and consultants are some of the informational services that retailers offer. In the Boston area, the Wm. Filene's & Sons Co., a division of Federated Department Stores, is using touch-sensitive video terminals in its consumer information service mix: "Designed as a customer self-operated aid, the system serves three purposes: bridal registry, seasonal gift registry, and gift suggestions. Information (a bride's color scheme or silverware pattern, for example) stored in Filene's data-processing system can be retrieved by touching a certain area of the video screen. Some responses are supplied on computer printout."[3] Additionally, retailers provide credit, cash, personal checks, and tender itemized receipts (an itemized list of products purchased by name or brand model, size, per-unit price, number of items purchased, date and time of purchase, and basic store information).

Increasing Customer Convenience

Many of the services just cited are instrumental in the retailer's efforts to increase customers' convenience. Additional services that provide customer convenience and comfort include packaging, bagging, free parking, restaurants, snack bars, restrooms, lounges, parcel checking, push carts, water fountains, and complimentary coffee. Any service that helps customers get into the store, travel around the store, and stay in the store not only enhances customers' convenience but also increases the likelihood of planned purchases as well as additional, *unplanned* purchases.

Creating a Store Image

The retailer's service offering can contribute to or detract from the image consumers have of a store. By using the service mix, a retailer can pursue one of several image strategies. By offering a *full range of services,* the retailer can promote the image of being a full-service store with quality merchandise and prestige prices. Conversely, the retailer can choose to offer only services that are essential to the exchange process, thereby creating a no-frills, low-price image. The retailer can select either of these approaches or any number of image strategies between the two extremes.

Providing Customer Security

Services also are used to provide the customer with personal security and product security. Restroom attendants, properly lighted stores and parking facilities, and security guards all enhance the customer's feeling of a safe and secure environment. Perhaps of equal importance to most customers is product security, provided by such services as warranties, return privileges, allowances, and maintenance contracts.

Improving Store Traffic

Any service can potentially increase the number of customers attracted to the store. Retailers frequently incorporate into their mix services that are essentially unrelated to their principal business, used solely to generate additional traffic through their stores. For example, some stores provide (1) rooms for public and private meetings, (2) space for various types of exhibits, (3) rental services for products that might not be related to their product mix, (4) post office, utility bill collection, and entertainment ticket facilities, (5) license bureaus, and (6) various types of professional services (e.g., tax, health, and personal care). All these services tend to draw customers into the store who might not otherwise be attracted. The exposure the store receives, together with impulse and convenience purchases that result from this additional traffic, can more than justify the use of the space and other resources devoted to such services.

Establishing Competitive Position

Retailers can use services to establish either competitive parity or to create a competitive edge. To remain competitive, retailers offer many services because they are either essential to the retailer's operation, competitors offer them, or customers expect them. To gain a competitive edge, some retailers offer services that are not essential to their operations nor expected by consumers. If the retailer can develop a distinctive service mix, the competitive benefits can be long lasting and reasonably difficult to imitate.

Building Specific Demand

While most services contribute either directly or indirectly to the total demand, retailers often build demand for a particular product line or item by offering services that focus the consumers' attention on that product. By conducting a cooking course, for example, a retailer can direct consumers' attention toward cookware and related product lines. Also, with the tremendous increase in the number of "do it yourselfers," some home centers offer instructional services and classes on how to repair plumbing, hang a light fixture, and so on in order to promote related product lines.

Retail-Service Determinants

Several factors enter into the decision about what service level to offer consumers. Guided by the previously discussed service objectives, the retailer should consider at least the following five determinants: type of merchandise, type and size of store, location of the store, service levels of competitors, and resources of the firm.

Type of Merchandise

The type of merchandise a retailer carries dictates to some extent the services that consumers expect and desire. The physical and psychological attributes of a product

What service objectives might be met by offering an on-site store cooking course?

CHAPTER 16
THE SERVICE MIX

are perhaps the two most important determinants of what the retailer's service level should be. For example, home delivery and installation are services that consumers expect when they buy furniture and appliance products. The bulky nature of such products makes these necessary services for most consumers. Additionally, in buying appliances and many other mechanical products, most consumers look for the availability of repair services before making a purchase decision. Warranties and maintenance contracts also are services that most retailers offer with these types of merchandise to reduce consumers' perceived risk.

Another example of how the type of merchandise affects a retailer's service level is in the high-fashion apparel industry. In this industry, consumers normally *expect* (1) sales personnel to aid in the selection and evaluation of the garment relative to the customer's needs, (2) comfortable, secure fitting rooms, (3) expert alteration and tailoring services, (4) several credit plans and check-cashing privileges for the convenience of the "cashless" consumer, and (5) quality packaging in first-class garment boxes and bags. In addition to these *expected* services, the high-fashion goods retailer might also enhance its merchandise offering by providing certain *desired* services such as fashion shows, personal consulting services, and garment storage.

Type and Size of Store

Consumers tend to associate certain services with specific types of retail operations. Consumers generally expect department stores to be full-service retailers, whereas they perceive the discounter as either a cash-and-carry retailer or at most a limited-service retailer. Consumers expect lawn and garden shops to provide information on when and how to care for plants, jewelry stores to repair watches and appraise jewelry, and supermarkets to provide shopping carts, check cashing, bagging, and carryout service. Also, consumers look for a higher level of services from prestige or status-conscious stores than from stores that appeal to the mass market. Thus, before establishing a service level, the retailer should ask the question, "Given my *type* of operation, which services do customers normally expect to receive and which might they like to receive?"

The physical *size* of a store also influences what service level is feasible. To be offered effectively, some services require substantial space. The type and number of services that a small retailer with limited space can offer must be restricted to those that are essential to the operation or at least those that can be provided with a minimal spatial commitment.

Location of Store

Where a store is located can influence the types of services a retailer should offer. Depending on the store's location, the retailer should consider services that (1) *overcome a locational deficiency,* (2) *fit into a locational surrounding,* and (3) *intensify a locational advantage.* For example, retailers located in the central business districts of major metropolitan areas have included several services to overcome the deficiencies associated with their locations. Downtown locations often lack adequate on-site parking facilities; as a service to their customers, many such retailers arrange for free parking at public and private facilities.

Additionally, many suburban shopping centers have extended their shopping hours (evening and Sunday openings) to accommodate the work schedules of their customers. Both of these are examples of how retailers can overcome location deficiencies.

To illustrate how a retailer's service levels are influenced by the retailer's locational setting, consider the service requirements of some specialty shopping centers. If a retailer elects to locate a store in a center where quality-oriented, high-service-level retailers operate, then normally it will have to offer a similar level of service. Otherwise, the operation will not appeal to the type of customer attracted to the cluster.

And, finally, an example of a service included in a service mix enhancing a locational advantage might be a quality lakeside restaurant providing complementary pre- or post-dinner cruises aboard a paddleboat.

Competitive Service Levels

Many retailers prefer to engage in *nonprice competition.* Competing with service levels is one form of nonprice competition. Unfortunately, this kind of competition creates a dilemma for the retailer. If one retailer exceeds its competitors' service levels, then the additional costs incurred lead to higher operating margins and therefore make it more vulnerable to price competition. On the other hand, if the retailer offers services below that of other retailers, it is not competitive in the area of services. As a general rule, the retailer should offer a service level comparable to that of competing operations of a similar type.

Resources of the Firm

Services require resources. Each service must be based on adequate facilities and equipment, trained personnel, and sufficient capital investment. In addition to having adequate resources, the retailer must decide whether a service offering is worth the resources necessary to making the service available. The key question is, "Are there better alternative uses?" For example, delivery services require storage and loading facilities, delivery trucks, stockroom clerks, and truck drivers. To justify the investment, the retailer must determine that consumers need this service and that any resulting sales volume more than offsets the investment.

The retailer's service mix includes all those nonproduct "extras" that retailers offer to consumers to enhance the merchandise mix and to facilitate purchases. The major components of the service mix include store hours, credit plans, delivery, alterations and repairs, wrapping, and customer complaints.

THE RETAIL-SERVICE MIX

Store Hours

In today's market, the retailer does not work an eight-to-five job. Because of changing consumer life-styles, increasing competitive conditions, various legal restrictions, and additional operational requirements, retailers must provide store hours that are convenient to the customers in the areas in which they operate. While consumers do not view store hours as a service in the same sense as delivery, alteration, and repair services, store hours are critical in creating the time utility that most consumers need.

Evening Hours

Evening hours from Monday through Saturday have become commonplace for most supermarkets and other retailers of necessity goods. Likewise, for many mass merchandisers operating in community and regional shopping centers, evening hours have become an expected service. The duration of hours ranges from all night to an eight, nine, or ten o'clock closing. In part, night openings are the retailer's response to changing life-styles of consumers who find it more convenient and enjoyable to shop at night. Although night openings help meet the objective of satisfying the customers, that increased customer satisfaction is not necessarily accomplished at a profit. Evening hours not only increase the cost of doing business (labor, utilities), but also increase personnel problems (individuals who do not want to work at night) and security risks (as exemplified by the number of night robberies at convenience-food stores).

Sunday Hours

The issue of **Sunday hours** is similar to night hours in all respects except for the social, religious, and legal restrictions imposed in some parts of the country. Many state and local governments have enacted laws, often referred to as blue laws, that determine (1) whether Sunday openings are allowed, (2) what types of products can be sold on Sundays (necessities versus nonnecessities), and (3) when and how many hours stores can be open (e.g., from 1 to 6 P.M.). In addition to legal restrictions, retailers should consider the effect Sunday hours have on their stores' images.

455

In some small communities, a retailer's image could be damaged by a Sunday opening. Social and religious beliefs may forbid working on Sundays. Ultimately, the retailer's decision on store hours depends upon local market conditions.

Consumer Credit

"Charge it!" "Buy now, pay later!" "Easy terms available!" "Only $10 down and $10 a month!" "Financing is available!" "Four years to pay!" These notices proclaim that credit has become a basic way of life for many U.S. consumers. For a substantial majority, credit has become either an essential or an expected part of the retailer's service mix. For most retailers, the question is not whether to offer credit, but what type of credit to offer.

Consumers view credit both positively and negatively. Consumers perceive that the advantages of using credit include (1) increased ease and convenience of shopping, (2) establishment of credit ratings, (3) increase in current buying power without readily available funds, (4) security of not having to carry cash, (5) ease and convenience of returning and exchanging merchandise, (6) ease in maintaining purchase and payment records, (7) expedience in ordering by telephone and mail, (8) status of having and using credit, (9) identification of the customer as being a regular, and (10) inclusion on the retailer's mailing list for special promotions.[4]

The negative feelings consumers have concerning credit include (1) credit encourages indebtedness by making buying too easy, (2) credit costs money and therefore increases the price of goods for both the credit user and nonuser, (3) credit is dangerous because credit cards can be lost and mistakes can be made in billing credit accounts, (4) credit is the rich person's service and working people are better off by waiting until they can pay cash, and (5) credit limits comparison shopping to the more expensive stores that offer credit.[5]

Consumers' views of credit depend to a certain extent on their social class. In a study of credit card usage, researchers found that lower classes used their credit cards for installment purchases, restricted their use of credit cards to the purchase of durable and necessity goods, and tended to search for retailers that honored their particular credit cards. In contrast, the researchers learned that upper-class consumers view the use of credit cards more as a convenience, use credit cards in making luxury-goods purchases, and do not seek out stores that accept their particular credit cards.[6]

Credit Systems

The retailer can elect to use one of several different credit systems: in-house credit, third-party credit, and private-label credit.

In-house credit system. An **in-house credit system** is *owned, operated, and managed by the retail firm.* Retailers offer credit services for a variety of reasons, including (1) consumers expect the service, (2) the retailer's store image will be enhanced, (3) many consumers cannot afford the retailer's assortment of merchandise unless they are offered credit, (4) competitors offer credit arrangements, and (5) market and economic conditions dictate the need for credit. Offering an in-store credit plan has advantages and disadvantages for most retailers. Advantages include the following:

- *Customer attraction.* Stores that offer credit services tend to attract customers who are more interested in product quality, store reputation, and service offerings and less interested in prices.

- *Customer loyalty.* Credit-granting stores more easily build repeat business, since credit customers tend to be more loyal than cash customers.
- *Customer good will.* Credit-granting stores generally have a more personal relationship with their customers and therefore become the first place the customer shops for a particular purchase.
- *Increased sales.* Credit services increase total sales volume because credit customers tend to buy more goods and pay higher prices than customers who do not use credit.
- *Sales stabilization.* Credit sales are more evenly spread throughout the month, whereas cash sales correspond more closely with those times immediately following paydays.
- *Market information.* Credit applications provide considerable amounts of information (age, sex, income, occupation, etc.) on the credit consumer; credit records can reveal a history of what, when, and where (which department) the customer bought.
- *Promotional effort.* Because credit customers are known to be customers of the store, they are an excellent foundation upon which to build a mailing or telephone list for special promotions; additionally, the monthly statement credit customers receive is an effective vehicle for promotional literature.

In addition to these advantages, retailers realize the disadvantages associated with offering credit services. The most commonly cited disadvantages are those related to increased costs. They are

- *Higher operating expenses.* These result from the additional facilities, personnel, equipment, and communications expenses necessary to provide credit services.
- *Costs of fees and commissions.* Such fees are paid to outside credit agencies that provide part or all of the retailer's credit services.
- *Tied-up funds.* Capital is diverted to accounts receivable, thereby forcing the retailer to borrow working capital.
- *Bad debts.* Losses from uncollectables are part of the risk of providing credit services.

These additional costs are acceptable to the retailer if they can be covered by offsetting revenues. Some retailers realize a substantial profit from their charges for credit services. Sears, for example, makes substantial profits on its retail credit operations.

Third-party credit system. As an alternative to offering in-store credit services, *many retailers accept one or more of the credit cards issued by outside institutions.* Retailers often refer to these cards as **third-party** cards. The most common types of credit cards are those issued by banks (MasterCard and Visa) and entertainment-card companies (American Express, Diner's Club, and Carte Blanche). Gasoline companies also issue credit cards that consumers can use at stations carrying their brands.

The major advantages retailers gain from accepting third-party cards are (1) they do not have the problems of establishing and maintaining a credit department; (2) they are relieved of the unpleasant tasks of investigating credit applications, billing customers, and pursuing collections; (3) they can offer credit to consumers who otherwise would not qualify (e.g., out-of-town consumers) and thereby make sales they might have lost; and (4) they can maintain a steady cash flow, since financial institutions convert credit card sales quickly and regularly into cash minus agreed-upon service charges. The retailer does, however, have certain responsibilities in accepting and processing credit card sales. They include filling out sales drafts properly, cooperating with financial institutions in identifying expired and stolen cards, obtaining authorization for charges over certain purchase ceilings, and submitting sales drafts to the credit agency within an agreed-upon time.

The chief disadvantages for retailers that accept credit cards are the costs of the service and the depersonalization of their relationship with customers. The rates credit agencies charge retailers vary with the retailer's potential credit sales volume and several market and competitive conditions. Since the rate is negotiable, the retailer should make every effort to obtain the best possible terms. Depersonalization comes in the form of reduced store loyalty (the customer can shop anywhere the credit card is accepted) and consumers' lost feeling of "belonging" to a store in which they have a personal account.

Private-label system. A **private-label credit system** is *one that retailers offer under their name but that a bank operates and manages.* The retail firm realizes most of the benefits associated with in-house credit systems while avoiding many of the problems associated with credit management. Typically, the cost of this type of system is comparable to most in-house systems. The retailer that has had difficulty in turning its credit operation into a profit center should consider a private-label system.

Credit Plans

Depending on the type of credit system employed, one or more of three different types of credit plans will be available to the consumer: the open account, the installment plan, and revolving credit. The retailer's decision about which and how many types of credit plans to offer depends on the customer's need for a particular type of credit balanced against the retailer's need for cash for operating expenses.

Open account. Often referred to as the "regular charge" or "open book credit," the **open-account credit** plan *allows customers to buy merchandise and to pay for it within a specific time period without charges or interest.* Usually, the customer is expected to pay the full amount within 30 days of the billing date, although some retailers extend the due date to either 60 or 90 days to promote special occasions or to distinguish their credit services from the 30-day services their competitors offer. This **deferred billing** *is often used during the Christmas season as a sales promotion tool and as an incentive to finalize the sale of a major purchase* (e.g., the appliance dealer who offers "90 days same as cash"). Beyond the due date, if full payment is not received, the retailer can assess a finance charge. The retailer usually grants an open account without requiring the customer to make a down payment or to put up collateral to secure the purchase. Given the free nature of the service and its lack of formal security, retailers generally reduce both credit costs and risks by limiting open-account credit to customers who have established records of good credit.

Installment credit. For most customers, purchasing large-ticket items such as automobiles, furniture, and appliances would be impossible if they could not make small down payments and spread their additional payments over several months or years. The **installment-credit** plan *allows consumers to pay their total purchase price (less down payment) in equal installment payments over a specified time period.* Usually, equal installment payments are due monthly, although weekly and quarterly payments are optional. Retailers prefer to receive a down payment on installment purchases that equals or exceeds the initial depreciation of the product. Some retailers require only a minimal down payment or no down payment in order to make the sale.

Installment-credit arrangements are legal contracts between retailers and consumers. The terms and conditions of contracts include the total amount of each payment, the number of payments, and the dates the payments are due. In addition, the contract specifies the financial charges being assessed (interest, service, insurance) and the penalties for late or nonpayment. Retailers carry installment accounts in one of three ways: conditional sales agreements, chattel mortgages, and lease agreements. In the **conditional sales agreement,** *the title of the goods passes to the consumer conditional upon full payment.* The retailer can repossess the product and obtain a judgment against the consumer for any lost product value and expenses resulting from the repossession. Retailers prefer the conditional sales contract since it gives them the most protection from loss.

In a **chattel mortgage agreement,** *the title passes to the customer when the contract is signed, but the product is secured by a lien against it for the unpaid balance.* **Lease agreements** are *contracts in which the customer rents a product in the present with the option to buy in the future.* Consumers usually pay periodic rent, which is applied toward the purchase price. Since federal and state governments regulate installment-credit contracts, the retailer should consult with a lawyer to ensure that it is satisfying all legal requirements (legal implications concerning credit are discussed in Chapter 5).

Revolving credit. Revolving credit incorporates some of the features of both the open-account and installment plans. Several variations of revolving credit plans are used. The two most common ones are the fixed-term and the option-term plans. The **fixed-term revolving credit** plan *requires the customer to pay a fixed amount on any unpaid balance at regularly scheduled intervals (usually monthly) until the amount is paid in full.* Under this plan, customers have a credit limit, such as $500, and may make credit purchases up to this limit as long as they continue to pay the agreed-upon fixed payment (e.g., $50) each month. People who use fixed-term revolving accounts are usually charged a finance charge (e.g., 1.5 percent per month, or 18 percent annually) on the unpaid balance.

Option-term revolving credit *provides customers with basically two payment options. They can either pay the full amount of the bill within a specified number of days (typically 30) and avoid any finance charges or they can make at least a minimum payment and be assessed finance charges on the unpaid balance.* As with the fixed-term account, a credit line is established and customers are free to make purchases up to the established limits.

Credit Management

If a retailer decides to offer in-store credit as part of the service mix, then it must develop a credit-management system. Credit management involves a wide range of activities that are beyond the scope of this text. Two activities are essential to successful credit management: (1) forming sound policies for granting credit and (2) determining good procedures for collecting credit accounts.

Granting credit. In granting credit to individuals, retailers should first request that applicants complete a credit application. Credit applications are essential tools for collecting necessary information to evaluate the credit applicant. Whether the retailer personally investigates the applicant or uses one of the many credit bureaus, it should evaluate each individual on the basis of the **three "C's" of credit**: character, capacity, and capital.

Character in a credit sense refers to attributes that distinguish one individual from another in meeting obligations. Desirable traits include maturity and honesty—characteristics that indicate the applicant's willingness to accept responsibility (to pay bills) regardless of the circumstances. To make this evaluation, the retailer can use personal interviews, reference checks, and the applicants's credit history.

Capacity is the measure of an individual's earning power and ability to pay. A credit applicant's income is not only important in deciding whether to extend credit, but also in determining how much credit to extend. The third indication of an individual's credit worthiness is *capital* (i.e., the applicant's tangible assets). The accumulation of capital suggests that the applicant is capable of managing financial affairs. It also provides the retailer with something substantial if it must sue the customer for nonpayment.

A more sophisticated system for screening credit applications involves the use of a **credit-scoring system**. The procedures for developing a credit-scoring system follow.

- *Identifying*—an examination of good and bad credit accounts to identify characteristics associated with individuals who are good or poor credit risks. Figure 16–3 is one list of general characteristics that might be used in developing a credit-scoring system.
- *Weighting*—the weighting of each characteristic (by assigning point values) based on its ability to discriminate between good and poor credit risks.
- *Scoring*—the evaluation of credit applications by summing the points received on the various application characteristics to arrive at a total score.
- *Accepting/Rejecting*—accepting or rejecting a credit application based on a minimum point score.
- *Limiting*—setting a credit limit based on the total points assigned to the application; the higher the score, the higher the credit limit.[7]

Credit collections. Most credit accounts are handled through a routine, efficient billing system without any collection problems. When credit-collection problems (such as slow payment, nonpayment, or incorrect payment) occur, the retailer must have the necessary policies and procedures to handle them. Any credit-collection procedure entails several basic steps. First, credit accounts must be *reviewed* periodically and routinely to identify delinquent accounts. The immediate identification of delinquent accounts is critical because the more overdue the account becomes, the harder it is to collect.

Second, the retailer should make every effort to *determine the reason* for the delinquency. If the customer faces unexpected financial problems, the retailer should strive to reach some type of mutually agreeable arrangement. Such arrangements not only satisfy the debt, they also preserve the debtor as a customer. On the other hand, if the customer has no intention of repaying the debt or is a poor manager of finances, the retailer should initiate actions to settle the account. It can either require the consumer to make payments with penalties on a definite time schedule, or it can turn the account over to a collection agency. Eventually, the retailer realizes that some customers are *no longer desirable* as either credit customers or cash customers (typically, a customer whose account is far overdue will avoid the store and take cash business elsewhere). Thus, in general, credit-collection methods must be flexible enough to meet specific situations.

FIGURE 16–3
Characteristics used in developing credit-scoring systems

Telephone at home	Bank savings account
Own/rent living accommodations	Bank checking account
Age	Zip code of residence
Time at home address	Age of automobile
Industry in which employed	Make and model of automobile
Time with employer	Geographic area of United States
Time with previous employer	Finance company reference
Type of employment	Debt-to-income ratio
Number of dependents	Monthly rent/mortgage payment
Types of credit reference	Family size
Income	Telephone area code
Savings and loan references	Location of relatives
Trade-union membership	Number of children
Age difference between man and wife	Number of other dependents
Telephone at work	Ownership of life insurance
Length of product being purchased	Width of product being purchased
First letter of last name	

Source: Noel Capon, "Credit Scoring Systems: A Critical Analysis," *Journal of Marketing* 46 (Spring, 1982): 85.

Delivery Service

Offering delivery service is one of the most controversial issues in developing a service mix. In general, delivery service is difficult to plan, execute, and control. Before delivery service is included in the service mix, the retailer must have a clear understanding of when to offer it, what problems it entails, under which terms and conditions it can be offered, and what type of delivery system is most appropriate to the retailer's operation.

Delivery-Service Decision

Numerous circumstances justify including delivery services in the service mix. First, as previously stated, delivery is practically indispensable in retailing such bulky products as furniture and appliances. For similar reasons—plus the additional problems of their untidy nature—building materials, lawn products (trees and shrubs), and many farm and garden products require optional delivery service. Second, in large urban areas where customers traveling by public transportation are greatly inconvenienced by taking purchases with them, delivery is often necessary. Third, retailers that actively solicit telephone and mail orders must provide home-delivery services. A customer who makes purchases by telephone or mail frequently does so to avoid the hassle of going to the store.

Fourth, delivery services for emergency goods, such as prescription drugs, are perceived by consumers as a valuable addition to the retailer's service mix. For many elderly people and shut-ins, delivery services are the only way they can shop; for them it is an *essential* service. Fifth, for retailers engaged in institutional sales

461

(such as schools and hospitals), sales frequently are made and prices quoted on the basis of delivering the product to the institution's facilities. Sixth, some retailers have a prestige image to protect and therefore must include delivery services in their merchandise mix. The status-oriented consumer in many cases expects home delivery. It would hardly be appropriate to ask a woman who has just purchased a $5,000 mink coat to lug it with her if she asks to have it delivered to her home!

Finally, delivery services can be used to develop a competitive advantage by providing extra time and place convenience. Domino's Pizza, Inc., has built a 2,000-unit chain based on the firm's unique selling proposition: "The pizza will be delivered hot in 30 minutes or it's free of charge to the consumer."[8] Currently, Domino's is testing BakeUps (pizza dough topped with a western omelette or a cream cheese, apple, blueberry, and strudel mixture) as a home-delivery breakfast. Domino's will deliver the BakeUps with 24 ounces of coffee and that morning's *USA Today* newspaper for $4.95.[9] Believing that home delivery will be the next home run for the fast-food business, Godfather's Pizza and Burger King are also testing home-delivery services.[10]

Delivery-Service Problems

The problems associated with delivery service are substantial. One of the most difficult problems is *immediacy of delivery*. When consumers purchase a product, they want immediate possession with delivery either the same day or within a short period of time. Not receiving a purchase on time causes considerable customer dissatisfaction and order cancellations. It is virtually impossible for the retailer to provide immediate delivery without increasing costs. To send a delivery truck half-empty or to reroute a truck to deliver one package is an efficient use of neither equipment nor personnel.

A second major problem involves "not at homes." Delivery personnel often face the recurring problem of what to do when the *customer is not at home*. In such cases the delivery person can (1) leave the package on the doorstep, creating potential security and weather problems; (2) leave a note asking for further instruction, which inconveniences the customer and the retailer; (3) leave the package with a neighbor, which inconveniences the neighbor and causes a potential security problem; or (4) call back, which causes inconvenience to the delivery person and thereby increases delivery costs. Some retailers attempt to reduce this problem by telephoning the customer before delivery.

A third problem in offering delivery services is the *variations in demand* for the services. The day-to-day, week-to-week, and month-to-month fluctuations in demand for delivery services seriously undermine management planning for these services. During low-demand periods, personnel, equipment, and facilities are underutilized. During periods of high demand, the retailer has insufficient delivery capacity to handle the demand. To be always ready to handle peak delivery times will be cost prohibitive. Additional problems associated with delivery services include damage in transit, inaccurate deliveries, and problems of security.

Delivery-Service System

In developing a home-delivery system, retailers can elect to use either an in-store system, an independent system, or a combination of the two. Each system has its advantages and disadvantages.

In-store systems. In-store delivery systems *can be either wholly owned and operated by an individual store (private store systems) or partially owned and operated with other stores (cooperative store systems).* Private in-store systems offer numerous advantages. Of all the delivery systems, they give the retailer the greatest level of control over delivery operations and the greatest degree of flexibility in adjusting services to customer needs. Using the private system, the retailer can personalize delivery vehicles with its name, slogan, and other messages. Personalization has prestige value for both the store and the customer (a prestige retailer's delivery truck in the customer's driveway can be seen by all the neighbors). Finally, in a private system, the delivery personnel work for the retailer. Properly trained delivery personnel can provide the retailer with feedback from present customers (complaints and messages) and prospects for new sales opportunities (maintenance contracts). Unfortunately, private systems are the most expensive to establish and maintain. Many retailers simply cannot afford to operate their own private delivery system.

Independent systems. Independent delivery systems are *owned and operated independently from the retailer.* They offer their services either on a contractual basis (consolidated systems) or on an open-to-the-general-public basis (parcel post and express services). Consolidated systems are independent firms that, for a fee, will deliver a store's packages. The fee depends upon the number, size, weight, and handling characteristics of the packages. The typical consolidated operation of an independent system is to pick up the store's packages on a regularly scheduled basis, take the packages to a central facility where they are sorted to facilitate efficient routing, and deliver the packages to customers on a specific time schedule. In addition, most consolidated delivery firms perform C.O.D. functions, make call backs, and assume full liability for packages that are either damaged or lost. The major limitations that retailers experience in using consolidated services are lack of control over delivery time and inability to monitor the behavior of personnel making the delivery.

Express services and parcel post serve the needs of the general public. As an alternative, retailers resort to these systems when the delivery destination lies outside of their delivery-system area.

Alterations and Repairs

Alterations and repairs are offered by many retailers, both as a supplement to the sale of products and as an income-producing service. Consumers expect retailers of expensive clothing to provide alteration services, and retailers of appliances, television sets, automobiles, and other durable goods to provide repair services. Traditionally, retailers offered alteration services as part of the sales price of the garment. In recent years, however, retailers have experimented with various types of alteration charges ranging from no charge for minor alterations to partial or full charge for major alterations. To facilitate product-related alterations and to justify their investment in workroom facilities, equipment, and personnel, some retailers have established income-producing tailoring operations. For repairs on durable goods, retailers usually charge customers according to the terms and conditions of product warranties and established store policies. Normally, consumers bear no charge (or at most a minimum charge) for repairs on products still under warranty or that occur within a prescribed period after the purchase date. After the warranty or policy date expires, the retailer charges the consumer for repairs on a profit-making basis.

To increase their income from repair services, many chain retailers (such as Sears) offer maintenance contracts on a fixed-fee basis.[11] In addition to creating revenues, maintenance contracts also aid retailers in fully utilizing their repair and service departments.

The retailer that deems it necessary to provide alteration or repair services has two operation alternatives: in-store and out-of-store services. By offering in-store alteration and repair services, the retailer has all of the advantages associated with direct control of such activities. However, this alternative also presents numerous management problems and requires substantial capital investments.

Out-of-store alterations are subcontracted to private-service retailers specializing in tailoring services. Retailers normally use authorized, local repair services, factory repair services, and other subcontracted private-service firms to do out-of-store repairs. The disadvantages for retailers that use out-of-store repair services are lack of control, customer inconvenience, and longer service time.

Wrapping

As part of the retailer's service, U.S. consumers expect their purchases to be wrapped. To meet this consumer need, retailers must decide on the type of wrapping service(s) they will offer and where these wrapping services will be performed.

The three basic types of wrapping services retailers perform are bagging or sacking, store wrap, and gift wrap. Most consumers expect retailers to place their purchases in a bag even when their purchases are prepackaged products. **Bagging** *serves the following purposes: (1) it facilitates handling (especially when multiple purchases are involved); (2) it protects purchases from inclement weather; and (3) it preserves the privacy of the customer purchase.* The importance of providing adequate bagging is illustrated by our own experiences with improperly bagged merchandise—the crushed cookies under the half gallon of milk, the sack that breaks in the middle of the driveway, and the bag of canned goods that weighs a ton! Proper bagging takes into account the size, shape, weight, and strength of the bag and the goods that go into it.

Store wrap is *the wrapping of customers' purchases in a standard (color and design) wrapping paper or box.* Most department and specialty stores offer this service free of charge. Store wrap is not only an additional service for many retailers, but also a way to supplement their stores' advertising programs. The retailer that incorporates its prestige name with store wrap can provide additional purchase incentives for customers who either seek a prestige gift or want their gift receivers to know that the present came from a prestige store.

Gift wraps *normally incorporate additional wrapping features such as bows and ribbons to distinguish them clearly from store wraps.* Due to increased costs of materials and labor, the customer normally is charged an additional fee for gift-wrapping services.

Wrapping services are handled on either a departmental or a centralized basis. **Department wrapping** is *performed by either the salesperson who makes the sale or the department cashier and wrapper.* The advantages of having the salesperson wrap the merchandise are its convenience for the customer, the opportunity for the salesperson to make an extra sale, and the enhancement of the store's image through personalized service. Disadvantages of department wrapping are that salespeople must leave their primary job of selling and that salespeople normally do not excel at gift wrapping. In many stores, **centralized wrapping** is performed at one central location. In many large stores, however, centralized wrapping occurs on each floor. Although this type of wrapping is more cost-efficient than department wrapping, it does represent an inconvenience for customers, who must find the wrapping desk and may have to wait in line.

Customer Complaints

In 1962, President John F. Kennedy identified four basic consumer rights: "the right to safety, the right to be informed, the right to choose, and the right to be heard." Two of these rights, the rights to be heard and to be informed, are key factors in the customer-complaint process. Customers expect to be informed of all of the retailer's operating policies that affect their patronage, and they expect to be heard when they have a complaint to register. Whether one views consumer complaints as a consumer right or a retail service is unimportant; what is important is that consumer complaints must be handled if the retailer is to satisfy customers and keep them coming back.

While customer complaints typically are viewed negatively, especially if they are excessive in number, they also can be viewed positively. First, a customer who complains gives the retailer a chance to *identify and correct a problem.* Many customers simply switch to a different store as a silent complaint. Second, customer complaints serve as a major *source of information* regarding the retailer's products, services, and other merchandising activities. In developing the necessary service apparatus to handle customer complaints, the retailer should first identify the causes

Should a retailer offer gift wrapping services?

of complaints, then develop the appropriate methods, systems, and steps for handling and reducing complaints.

Causes of Complaints

Most customer complaints result from one of three general causes: product-related, service-related, and customer-related difficulties. Product-related causes include the following:

1. *poor-quality products*—inferior workmanship and materials that cause fading or bleeding colors, shrinking or stretching fabrics, and rusting or tarnishing metals
2. *damaged products*—merchandise that is chipped, stained, soiled, ripped, spoiled, or scratched
3. *incorrect products*—merchandise that is either mislabeled according to size and price or mismatched in terms of color and style
4. *insufficient selection*—out-of-stock merchandise, discontinued merchandise, limited-line merchandise, and new merchandise

Service-related causes involve customer dissatisfaction with sales personnel and services such as checkout, delivery, workroom, and customer accounts. Complaints about sales personnel usually center around the salesperson's (1) *disposition* (indifferent, discourteous, unfriendly, pushy), (2) *incompetence* (lack of product knowledge, poor selling skills, lack of familiarity with store policies), (3) *dishonesty* (unfulfilled promises, false information, additional charges, incorrect change), or (4) *selling methods* (overselling customers by selling them too much of an item or by trading them up to a product they cannot afford). Customer complaints concerning delivery services include late, lost, and incorrect deliveries and untidy and unpleasant delivery personnel. Improper alterations, lengthy delays, and overcharges are the chief causes of complaints stemming from workroom services. Finally, improper handling of accounts irritates customers. Errors in billing, receipt of a bill after it has already been paid, delays in receiving account statements, and monthly literature are some of the more irksome problems.

Customers make mistakes; sometimes they are intentional, sometimes they are not. Customer mistakes are also a cause of customer-related complaints. For example, customers may purchase a product thinking it will match or fit another product they own. If it does not, they may want to return it. If the retailer does not issue a refund, then the customer surely will complain. A "change of mind" is another customer-related cause of complaint. Customers often change their minds because they later think the product is not really the style, quality, price, or color they wanted. To most consumers, these are legitimate reasons for returning goods and they expect the retailer to make an exchange or give a refund. To question the customer's motives is an invitation to further customer complaints. Finally, the retailer faces the habitual complainer.[12] This person is always dissatisfied and will always complain about something. The retailer should handle the habitual complainers courteously, but they often are not worth the retailer's time and trouble and the retailer should consider a policy of encouraging them to shop elsewhere.

Alternatives for Handling Complaints

The retailer has several alternatives in handling consumer complaints. They include offering returns and refunds, making product adjustments, price adjustments, and service adjustments, and practicing good customer relations. The appropriate alternative often depends on the nature of the consumer complaint.

Returns and refunds. Policies on returning merchandise range from "no returns" or "all sales final" to "satisfaction guaranteed or your money back." If the retailer has a no-return policy, it should make that policy clear to all customers by either posting signs, printing the policy on sales slips, verbal statements by salespeople, or a combination of these means.

Retailers that guarantee satisfaction must decide whether to refund the customer's money in the form of cash or as a credit slip. Some retailers prefer to give cash refunds because they feel this policy creates greater customer satisfaction, relieves the store of further obligation, and frees store personnel to perform more productive work. Proponents of the credit-slip refund believe this method is better because it maintains contact with the customer and ensures a future sale and at least part of the profit from the original sale. They also think credit slips are more appropriate for people who receive the merchandise as a gift, since their customer chose to give a more personalized gift of merchandise than cash. As with the no-return policy, retailers should inform customers of any conditions or restrictions on returning merchandise and receiving refunds before the purchase is made.

Product adjustments. Retailers can correct product-related complaints by one or more product adjustments. Complaints about incorrect products can easily be handled by allowing customers to exchange the incorrect product for a correct one. Most retailers have a very fair exchange policy provided the customer has not abused the product. By offering to clean, repair, alter, or exchange products, retailers can satisfy most customers' complaints about damaged products.

One way to handle consumer complaints about poor-quality products is to substitute a higher-quality product for the poor-quality product. This policy is especially appropriate when the product sold was, in fact, of lower quality than the price suggested, or when the retailer wants to protect a quality product and store image. Finally, complaints concerning insufficient selection can be handled by either (1) agreeing to stock the product, (2) explaining why the product cannot be stocked, then offering an appropriate substitute, or (3) directing the customer to a store that stocks the desired product.

Price adjustments. In granting price adjustments to consumers, retailers can either give an allowance or a discount on the purchase price of the product. Since it is not always possible to exchange or adjust a product that has been damaged, the retailer often can satisfy customers by reducing the price of the product to compensate them for the damages. Price adjustments also can include free merchandise and discount coupons. When the retailer is obviously at fault, price adjustments are generally the most effective way to show the customer that the store is making an extra effort to correct the problem.

Service adjustments. Retailers use service adjustments in much the same way as price adjustments. When a customer complains about any of the retailer's services, the retailer should handle the problem by making the appropriate adjustment. For example, if a consumer says that a garment alteration is unsatisfactory, the retailer should make the additional alteration free of charge and, in many cases, should deliver the garment to the customer's home at the retailer's expense. Another example might be an error in billing that shows the customer paid a bill late. Any late charges or interest penalties the retailer would normally charge should be dropped.

Customer relations. Some situations generate customer complaints for which none of the preceding adjustments are appropriate. A rude salesperson is one example. In such cases, the customer may just want to be heard or to "blow off steam." Whether the complaint is justified or not, good customer relations dictate the retailer listen carefully and politely, reassure the customer, and apologize for the situation. Who knows? The individual might be a very good customer who simply had a bad day and was set off by a minor incident. By allowing the customer to register the complaint and by handling that complaint professionally, the retailer keeps a good customer.

Systems for Handling Complaints

Customer complaints usually are handled in small stores by the owner or manager of the store. In large stores, however, a system for handling customer complaints must be developed. Three alternative systems are the centralized system, the decentralized system, and a combination system.

Centralized complaint system. *All customer complaints are referred to a central office or complaint desk under a* **centralized complaint system.** This arrangement allows the retailer to utilize personnel who are trained in the art of handling people. Also, in using this system the retailer can implement a more uniform policy in handling complaints and making adjustments. When the customer's complaint involves a particular sales department or its personnel, a centralized system has the additional advantage of appearing more impartial to the complaining customer. It also allows the store's management to receive more accurate information on complaints than if a particular department or its personnel handled and reported the complaint itself. Additional benefits of a centralized complaint system are (1) complaints are handled in private and not aired in public, and (2) complaint records can be standardized, analyzed, and used by management to correct the causes of complaints.

Shortcomings associated with central complaint systems focus on the fact that most customers prefer to deal with the department or salesperson from which they made their original purchase. Customers know where to find the department or salesperson, and the circumstances surrounding the complaint are most likely to be understood by both parties.

Decentralized complaint system. A **decentralized complaint system** *handles customer complaints at the department level.* Departmental salespersons usually handle minor complaints and adjustments while the department manager is responsible for major complaints. Although customers generally prefer this type of system, it has its disadvantages. First, there can be considerable variation in how complaints are handled within and between departments. Second, many complaints are not reported to central management, and much of what is reported is biased. Third, commissioned salespersons are reluctant to make certain adjustments if it affects their commissions and they are more interested in selling than in spending time handling complaints. Finally, most departmental personnel are not trained to handle complaints or to make adjustments.

Combination system. In an attempt to gain the advantages of both the centralized and decentralized systems, many retailers employ a combination of the two. Customers with complaints go directly to the department involved, where most adjustments are made. When major adjustments are necessary or when the customer is

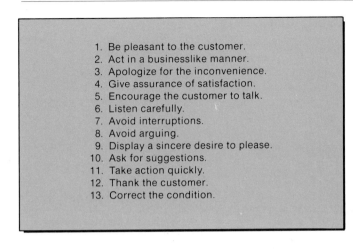

1. Be pleasant to the customer.
2. Act in a businesslike manner.
3. Apologize for the inconvenience.
4. Give assurance of satisfaction.
5. Encourage the customer to talk.
6. Listen carefully.
7. Avoid interruptions.
8. Avoid arguing.
9. Display a sincere desire to please.
10. Ask for suggestions.
11. Take action quickly.
12. Thank the customer.
13. Correct the condition.

dissatisfied with the department adjustment, complaining customers are directed to a central complaint office.

Guidelines for Handling Complaints

How a store handles a customer's complaint can, in many cases, be more important to the customer than the actual adjustment. Many retailers have found that if they display an immediate and sincere willingness to be fair, the customer will reciprocate by being willing to accept any reasonable adjustment. There are no absolute rules or steps for handling all complaints and all customers. The general guidelines presented in Figure 16–4 representing some "do's" and "don'ts" for handling customer complaints are appropriate to most situations.

SUMMARY

Retailers offer services under two sets of circumstances. Primary services are offered as part of the principal business function. Complementary services are services that retailers offer in conjunction with or as a supplement to a basic product mix. The basic problems in developing a service mix are which and how many services to offer.

Services can be classified according to their relative importance to the consumer. Essential services are basic and necessary to a particular retail operation. Expected services are not absolutely essential for operating reasons, but are necessary for customer patronage reasons—the consumer expects them to be available. Optional services are neither necessary to the retailer's operation nor expected by the retailer's customers. They include all other services that distinguish the retailer's service mix.

The service mix can be developed to meet any number of objectives. Some of the more common service objectives are to (1) increase form utility, (2) facilitate time utility, (3) enhance place utility, (4) promote possession utility, (5) increase consumer convenience, (6) create a desirable store image, (7) provide customer security, (8) increase store traffic, (9) establish a competitive position, and (10) build demand. In deciding what level of service to offer, the retailer considers the type of merchandise, the type and size of the store, the location of the store, the service level of competitors, and the resources of the firm.

The retailer's service mix can incorporate any number of services. Services basic to most retailing operations include store hours, credit, delivery, alterations and repairs, wrapping, and customer complaints.

KEY TERMS AND CONCEPTS

primary services

complementary services

essential services

expected services

optional services

service level

evening hours

Sunday hours

in-house credit system

third-party credit system

private-label credit system

open-account credit

deferred billing

installment credit

conditional sales agreement

chattel mortgage agreement

lease agreement

fixed-term revolving credit

option-term revolving credit

three C's of credit

credit-scoring system

in-store delivery system

independent delivery system

bagging

store wrap

gift wrap

department wrapping system

centralized wrapping system

centralized complaint system

decentralized complaint system

REVIEW QUESTIONS

1. Distinguish between a primary-service retailer and one that offers complementary services.
2. How are services classified? Describe the three classes of services and their relationship to the retailer's operation. Provide examples of each type of service.
3. Which services might the retailer offer to increase form utility?
4. Which services might the retailer offer to promote possession utility?
5. How might the retailer build specific demand through a service mix?
6. How does store location influence the retailer's service mix?
7. What are the advantages to consumers of using credit?
8. What are the two chief disadvantages for retailers that accept third-party credit cards?
9. How does a private-label credit system differ from in-store and third-party systems?
10. Briefly describe the three types of credit plans.
11. What are the three C's of credit? Describe each.
12. Outline the basic procedures for establishing a credit-scoring system.
13. What problems face the retailer that develops and operates a home-delivery system?
14. Compare the advantages and disadvantages of in-store and out-of-store systems for providing alteration and repair services.
15. Characterize the three basic types of wrapping services.
16. Identify the major product-, service-, and customer-related causes of complaints.
17. What are the alternative methods for handling customer complaints?

ENDNOTES

1. See Duane L. Davis, Joseph P. Guiltinan, and Wesley H. Jones, "Service Characteristics, Consumer Search, and the Classification of Retail Services," *Journal of Retailing* 55 (Fall, 1979): 3–23.
2. "Retailers Expand Old Services, Add New Ones to Attract Customers," *Stores* (October, 1984), 52–53.
3. "Touch-sensitive video terminals in store, hotel, banks, trade shows," *Marketing News,* 26 November 1982, 8.
4. See William H. Bolen, *Contemporary Retailing* (Englewood Cliffs, NJ: Prentice-Hall, 1978), 391–92; *The Buyer's Manual,* rev. ed. (New York: National Retail Merchants Association, 1965), 372.
5. Bolen, *Contemporary Retailing,* 392.

6. Lee H. Mathews and John W. Slocum, Jr., "Social Class and Commercial Bank Credit Card Usage," *Journal of Marketing* 33 (January, 1969): 71–78.

7. See Noel Capon, "Credit Scoring Systems: A Critical Analysis," *Journal of Marketing* 46 (Spring, 1982): 82–91.

8. Bernie Whalen, "People-Oriented Marketing Delivers a Lot of Dough," *Marketing News,* 16 March 1984, 4.

9. Katie Byand, "1 Burger, Hold the Mayo, and Bring It to the House," *Akron Beacon Journal,* 14 January 1985, C3.

10. Scott Hume, "Godfather's Aims to Home Delivery Market," *Advertising Age,* 7 May 1984, 28.

11. See Michael Perry and Arnon Perry, "Service Contract Compared to Warranty as a Means to Reduce Consumer's Risk," *Journal of Retailing* 52 (Summer, 1976): 33–40.

12. See Noel B. Zabriskie, "Fraud by Consumers," *Journal of Retailing* 48 (Winter, 1972): 27.

RELATED READINGS

Abend, Jules. "Collections: Making 'em Pay." *Stores* (April 1985), 32–38, 40.

Adams, Ronald J., and Mays, Carole T. "Some Correlates of Consumer Dissatisfaction with Retail Complaint Handling Performance." *Developments in Marketing Science, Proceedings.* V. V. Bellur, ed. (Academy of Marketing Science 1981), 267–70.

Bates, Albert D., and Didion, Jamie G. "Special Services Can Personalize Retail Environment." *Marketing News* (April 12, 1985), 13.

Barnes, Nora Ganim. "The Seventh Day: Extended Hours for Shoppers." *Developments in Marketing Science, Proceedings.* J. D. Lindquist, ed. (Academy of Marketing Science 1984), 311–16.

Bearden, William O., and Teel, Jesse E. "An Investigation of Personal Influence on Consumer Complaining." *Journal of Retailing* 56 (Fall 1980), 3–20.

Czepiel, John A.; Solomon, Michael R.; and Surprenant, Carol F. *The Service Encounter.* (Lexington, Mass.: Lexington Books, 1984)

Gill, R. B. "Debit Card at POS?—J. C. Penney's View." *Retail Control* (April - May 1984), 2–9.

Hoy, Mariea G., and Fisk, Raymond P. "Older Consumers and Services: Implications for Marketers." *1985 AMA Educators' Proceedings.* R. F. Lusch et al, eds. (American Marketing Association 1985), 50–55.

Hutchens, Stephen P. "All Sales Final: Can Merchandise Return Policies Be a Deterrent to Patronage?" *1985 Proceedings.* J. C. Crawford and B. C. Garland, eds. (Southwestern Marketing Association 1985), 181–83.

Jay, Lonny J. "The Value of Credit Marketing: A Senior Management Approach and Perspective." *Retail Control* (January 1984), 34–44.

Judd, L. Lynn. "Hours Open and Full-Time/Part-Time Employee Decision Areas: Do These Operating Factors Along with Competitive Situation Affect Small Retailer Success?" *Developments in Marketing Science, Proceedings.* J. D. Lindquist, ed. (Academy of Marketing Science 1984), 317–21.

Kernkraut, Steven J. "Using Bad Credit Models to Improve Credit Management." *Retail Control* (December 1983), 26–46.

Krentler, Kathleen A., and Guiltinan, Joseph P. "Strategies for Tangibilizing Retail Services: An Assessment." *Journal of the Academy of Marketing Science* 12 (Fall 1984), 77–92.

Morey, Richard C. "Measuring the Impact of Service Level on Retail Sales." *Journal of Retailing* 56 (Summer 1980), 81–90.

Rosen, Stuart M. "New Moves towards a Cashless Society—Overview of EFT in the United States." *Retail Control* (April - May 1984), 10–21.

Upah, Gregory D. "Mass Marketing in Services Retailing: A Review and Synthesis of Major Methods." *Journal of Retailing* 56 (Fall 1980), 59–76.

Viedenberg, Harrie, and Wee, Chow-Hou. "Retailer Controllable Sources of Customer Dissatisfaction: The Importance of After-Sales Service." *Developments in Marketing Science, Proceedings.* J. D. Lindquist, ed. (Academy of Marketing Science 1984). 294–99.

Whalen, Bernie. "Retail Customer Service: Marketing's Last Frontier." *Marketing News* (March 15, 1985), 16, 18.

Outline

ORGANIZING THE BUYING PROCESS

Formality
Centrality
Specialization

THE BUYING PROCESS

IDENTIFYING SOURCES OF SUPPLY

The Raw-Resource Producer
The Final Manufacturer
The Wholesaling Intermediary
The Resident Buying Office

SURVEYING SOURCES OF SUPPLY

The Buying Plan
The Resource File

CONTACTING SOURCES OF SUPPLY

Vendor-Initiated Contacts
Retailer-Initiated Contacts

EVALUATING SOURCES OF SUPPLY

Evaluation Criteria
Evaluation Methods

NEGOTIATING WITH SOURCES OF SUPPLY

Negotiating the Price
Negotiating the Service

BUYING FROM SOURCES OF SUPPLY

Buying Strategies
Buying Methods

Objectives

- Discuss the various ways in which the retailer can organize for the buying process

- Identify alternative sources of supply and channel options for procuring the product mix

- Explain the methods and procedures for initiating and maintaining supply contacts

- Discuss the criteria for evaluating and methods for negotiating with sources of supply

- Discuss the strategies for deciding how many sources of supply should be used in securing merchandise

- Describe the buying methods used in the actual purchasing of merchandise

17
The Buying Process

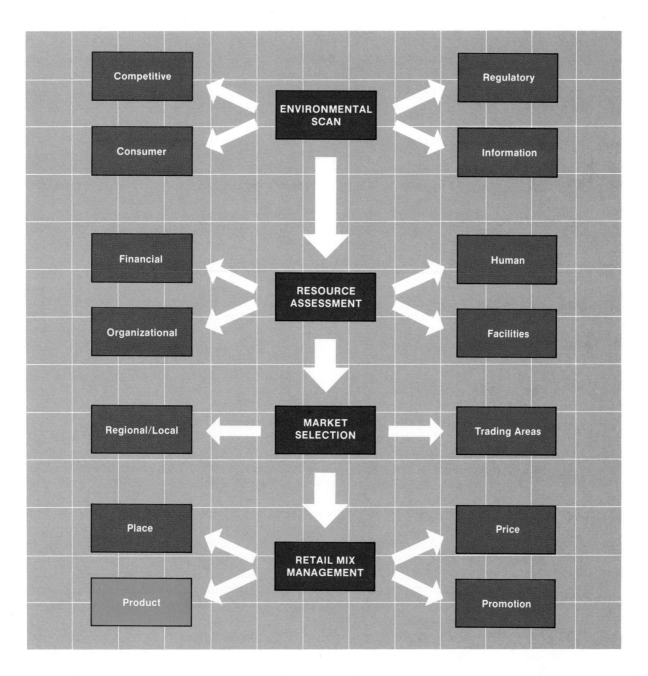

The first stage in the merchandising process is developing the product mix and the service mix (discussed in Chapters 15 and 16). The second stage is to secure the merchandise mix, which includes the buying process and the procurement process. The buying process is the focus for discussion in this chapter, while the following chapter takes up the procurement process. Before examining the buying process, we should examine the various ways in which the retailer can organize for the buying process.

ORGANIZING THE BUYING PROCESS

To complete the buying task in an efficient and timely manner, a retailer must establish a buying organization. In developing a buying organization, the retailer should decide upon how formal, centralized, and specialized the organization should be.[1]

Formality

The first decision the retailer should make is how formal the buying structure should be. A **formal buying organization** *has a separate department or division to handle the buying function and related merchandising activities.* Used by large retailers, the formal structure presents a clear definition of the department's authority and permits greater utilization of personnel trained in the buying process. Formal buying structures, however, are generally more costly to establish and to maintain. **Informal buying organizations** *incorporate the buying process into the existing organizational structure, where the task of buying is handled by existing store personnel.* Because of their lower costs and greater flexibility, informal buying organizations are used mainly by smaller retailers. Shortcomings of informal buying structures include the lack of clearly defined authorities and responsibilities and the lack of coordination between various buying activities and personnel.

Centrality

Centrality is not an organizational issue for the single-unit retailer, but for the multiunit retailer, the decision to handle the buying process with either a centralized or decentralized structure is an extremely important issue. In **centralized buying,** *the retailer gives a central office the authority and responsibility to buy merchandise, rather than leaving the decision to each individual store in the multiunit chain.* With a central buying office, the retailer can take advantage of discount structures through volume purchases, coordinate and control the buying process for the entire chain, use full-time buying specialists, gain preferred treatment from suppliers, and maintain a consistent customer image of the store's merchandise and quality. On the other hand, central buying hinders adapting to local market needs. Additional problems include information lags, time delays, and poor morale because of the distance between the buying office and the local units and the formal nature of the buying organization.

Decentralized buying is *structured and conducted at the local level.* Each store or group of stores within a certain geographic market is responsible for the buying process. Adaptability to local market needs is the major advantage in this type of buying organization. Lack of control, inconsistency between stores, and loss of some economies of scale in purchasing are the main shortcomings of buying structures developed around local autonomy. In determining its needs, a retailing organization must weigh the advantages and disadvantages of centralized versus decentralized buying.

474

Specialization

The final consideration in establishing the buying organization is specialization. Some retailers prefer an organizational structure in which *each buyer specializes in one or a few related merchandise lines*—**specialized buying**. Other retailers find it necessary to have a *few buyers secure all of the retailer's lines of merchandise*—**generalized buying**. Large retailers with a wide variety/deep assortment product mix (e.g., a department store) generally prefer specialization, while smaller retailers with narrowly defined product mixes like the generalized approach to buying. Higher costs are the principal disadvantage of specialized buying, whereas lower costs are the primary benefit of generalized buying. In turn, increased buying skills and product and market knowledge are associated with specialization, while less-developed skills and less knowledge are found in a generalized buying organization.

THE BUYING PROCESS

The buying process is the retailer's first step in getting merchandise into the store. Primary concerns are determining (1) what sources of supply are available and under what terms and conditions; (2) how to contact and evaluate various suppliers; and (3) how, when, and where to negotiate with and buy from alternative supply sources. In the buying process, a retailer should follow, in sequence, the six steps identified in Figure 17–1 (p. 476), which provide the structure for this chapter on the buying process.

IDENTIFYING SOURCES OF SUPPLY

The first step in the retailer's buying process is identifying the available sources of supply. From these sources, the retailer must decide which channel to use in procuring each merchandise line. In some cases, a direct channel to the manufacturer or original producer (e.g., farmer) is preferred. In other cases, an indirect or extended supply channel using one or more intermediaries—often referred to as *middlemen*—is desirable. Specifically, the retailer can select from any one or a combination of the following sources of supply:

- raw-resource producers
- manufacturers
- intermediaries
- resident buying offices

Each of these sources is discussed in the following sections.

The Raw-Resource Producer

Under certain circumstances, the retailer may elect to obtain supplies directly from the raw-resource producer. Food retailers are the most common example of retailing organizations that use this type of direct channel. Large food retailing chains (e.g., Safeway) frequently bypass traditional supply sources in their efforts to secure fresh fruits and vegetables and to obtain raw materials for their private-label brands. Both large and small food retailers often secure stocks of some specialty food items (e.g., ethnic foods) directly from local producers. In many cases, these local producers are the only available sources of supply. Buying food products directly from the raw-resource producer offers a retailer the advantages of increased speed and reduced handling. Both are important in the distribution of food products if these perishables are to reach the store fresh and with minimal damage. Other products

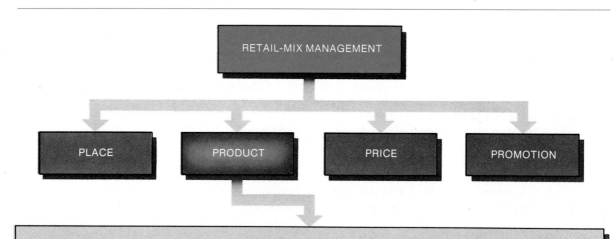

The Buying Process

I. Identifying Sources of Supply

   A. Raw-resource producers
   B. Manufacturers
   C. Wholesaling intermediaries
      merchant intermediaries
      agent intermediaries
      contractual intermediaries
   D. Resident buying offices

II. Surveying Sources of Supply
   A. The buying plan
   B. The resource file

III. Contacting Sources of Supply

   A. Vendor-initiated contracts
      store visits
      telephone and mail
   B. Retailer-initiated contracts
      central market visits
      resident buying offices
      merchandise shows
      telephone and mail

IV. Evaluating Sources of Supply

   A. Evaluation criteria
      merchandise criteria
      distribution criteria
      price criteria
      promotional criteria
      service criteria
   B. Evaluation methods
      weighted-rating method
      most-important method
      minimum cut-off method

V. Negotiating with Sources of Supply

   A. Negotiating the price
      the list price
      discounts and allowances
      transportation and handling
   B. Negotiating the service

VI. Buying from Sources of Supply

   A. Buying strategies
   B. Buying methods

FIGURE 17–1
Developing and implementing the buying process

retailers buy directly from raw-resource producers include lumber, some construction materials, and other bulky materials that incur extra expense if handled by additional intermediaries.

The Final Manufacturer

Before the advent of large-scale retailing, most retailers had to use wholesalers to secure their stocks, since they could not buy in large enough quantities to deal directly with manufacturers. In recent times, large retailing organizations have emerged that have the volume to consider direct purchasing from manufacturers. Today, manufacturers maintain different policies regarding direct sales to retailers. Some refuse to sell to retailers under any circumstances; others sell to any retailer who can buy in sufficient quantities to make the transaction profitable.

Where direct buying is available and feasible, several advantages can accrue to the retailer. Obtaining *fresher products* is often cited as one benefit of buying directly from the manufacturer. Merchandise procured from the manufacturer is frequently packaged and shipped directly from the production line. By avoiding wholesale storage and handling, the retailer receives the merchandise in a fresher condition.

Quicker delivery is the second benefit that retailers derive from making direct purchases. Direct channels of distribution are generally faster than indirect channels in processing initial orders, whereas wholesalers are usually faster on fill-in orders. For highly perishable fashion and fad items, direct purchases are almost a necessity.

The third advantage of using the manufacturer as a source of supply is *lower price*. By eliminating the wholesaler and taking on the intermediary's functions, the retailer may reduce certain costs and realize savings. For this reason, the large retail organization can buy large quantities of merchandise at discount. Fourthly, manufacturers can provide retailers *more information* about their product lines than wholesalers do, since manufacturers' salespersons specialize in selling only their products, whereas wholesalers' salespersons sell product lines of several manufacturers.

The fifth advantage of the manufacturer-to-retailer channel is *better adjustment*. Direct relationships between manufacturers and retailers lead both to more lenient adjustment policies and to quicker adjustment responses on products that have been returned by the retailer's customers. Most adjustment negotiations can be conducted more efficiently by face-to-face meetings than by going through third parties (wholesalers). Finally, direct purchases permit the retailer to order and secure goods made to its *specifications*. Many large chain operations (e.g., Penney's and Sears) have a large percentage of their goods made to their specifications and identified with their names. The retailer trying to develop a product line tailored to the needs of specific target markets may see specification buying as the best alternative in meeting those needs. Small retailing organizations also engage in specification buying for a limited number of product items to create a unique or specialized image.

The Wholesaling Intermediary

The third alternative source of supply is wholesaling intermediaries that position themselves in the distribution channel between the manufacturer and the retailer. Their role in facilitating the transfer of goods between manufacturers and retailers varies, depending upon the nature of their operations as well as the functions and services they are willing to provide. Most intermediaries do not provide the full range of wholesaling functions—buying, selling, breaking bulk, assortment creation, stocking, delivery services, credit extension, information and consultation, and title transfer (see Figure 17–2). Instead, they tend to specialize in one or a limited number of these functions. Based on the number and type of functions, wholesaling intermediaries fall into several groups. Figure 17–3 identifies these groups of wholesalers. The retailer's selection of one of these types depends upon its specific needs.

477

Buying tasks. Wholesalers act as purchase agents when they anticipate the merchandise needs of retailers and their customers. By locating appropriate sources of supply and securing merchandise that is suitable to the retailer's needs, the wholesaler greatly enhances the retailer's buying and procurement processes.

Selling tasks. Wholesalers help simplify buying procedures by having salespersons calling at the retailer's place of business. Wholesaling intermediaries help reduce the retailer's cost of securing goods by: (1) eliminating some trips to the market, and (2) assuming some of the responsibilities (e.g., order follow-up, self-stocking), for getting the merchandise onto the retailer's displays.

Credit-extending tasks. Many wholesaling intermediaries finance part or all of a retailer's inventory. The most common credit extension is the setting of the date when the net price of an invoice is due in full. By providing 30, 45, 60, or more days to pay an invoice without charges, the wholesaler is in effect financing the retailer's inventory. Consignment and memorandum selling wherein the retailer does not pay for the merchandise until it is sold is still another form of extending credit. In addition, many wholesalers make available to retailers short-, intermediate-, and long-term loans that can be used as working and fixed capital.

Informing tasks. Marketing research and source information are two important functions provided by the wholesaler. Many large wholesaling operations engage in an ongoing effort to determine marketplace needs and conditions. By passing this information on, retailers have reference points for examining their market performances and adjusting their marketing programs. On the source side, the wholesaler's unique position within the channel allows him to provide useful information of products, manufacturer's programs, supply sources, and activities of competitors.

Consulting tasks. Wholesalers provide their customers with a host of various advisory services. The more common consultant services deal with accounting, advertising, personnel training, financial and legal advice, location analysis, inventory control, and facilities planning.

Title-transferring tasks. Free-and-clear title to products is essential to the exchange process. Merchant wholesalers that own the goods they deal in assume the responsibility for transfer of payments and the management of title exchange. Agent wholesalers that do not take title to the goods facilitate the exchange of title by providing or arranging for the services necessary to the title-exchange process.

Bulk-breaking tasks. A quantity gap occurs between manufacturer's need to produce and sell in larger quantities and the retailer's need to buy in smaller quantities. Wholesaling intermediaries help bridge this quantity gap by: (1) buying in car- or truck-load quantities, (2) performing break-in bulk activities, and (3) selling smaller quantities (e.g., case lots) to retailers. This bulk-breaking function helps reduce the cost of doing business by reducing inventory carrying and handling costs.

Assortment-creating tasks. An assortment gap exists between manufacturers that need (manufacturing economies of scale) to provide and sell a limited line of identical or nearly identical products and retailers that must offer the consumer a wider selection of products. Wholesalers can fill this gap by buying the limited product lines and items of many different manufacturers and combining these lines and items into appropriate assortments. The retailer's quest for either mass- or target-market appeal is greatly enhanced by the availability of diversified product assortments.

Stocking tasks. Retailers often have limited stockroom space and inventory investment capital. Wholesalers provide an invaluable service by reducing the space and capital needed for retail stock. This reduces the need for facilities and inventory carrying costs for the retailer. The local nature of wholesalers also enhances the time and place availability of products for restocking purposes.

Delivery tasks. Quick and frequent deliveries by the wholesaler help avoid or replenish stockout conditions that result in lost sales. A timely delivery system is one service a wholesaler provides that aids the retailer in holding down in-store inventories that are required to meet customer expectations. Reliable deliveries are also an integral part in reducing safety stock and the risk and investment associated with such stock.

FIGURE 17–2
Wholesaling functions

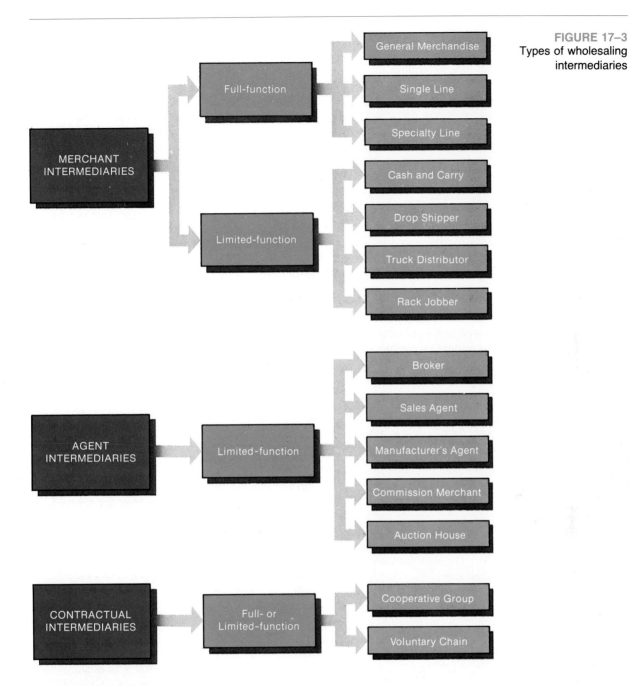

FIGURE 17–3
Types of wholesaling
intermediaries

MERCHANT INTERMEDIARIES

- Full-function
  - General Merchandise
  - Single Line
  - Specialty Line
- Limited-function
  - Cash and Carry
  - Drop Shipper
  - Truck Distributor
  - Rack Jobber

AGENT INTERMEDIARIES

- Limited-function
  - Broker
  - Sales Agent
  - Manufacturer's Agent
  - Commission Merchant
  - Auction House

CONTRACTUAL INTERMEDIARIES

- Full- or Limited-function
  - Cooperative Group
  - Voluntary Chain

Merchant Intermediaries

Merchant intermediaries are *wholesalers that are directly involved in the purchase and sale of goods as they move through the channel of distribution*. What distinguishes merchant intermediaries from agent intermediaries is that merchants take title to the goods they deal in, while agents do not assume ownership. As illustrated in Figure 17–3, merchant intermediaries can be classified as full-function and limited-function operations. For many small and medium-size retailers that do not have the volume of sales to buy directly from the manufacturer, merchant intermediaries represent the most important source of supply.

479

Full function. Full-function merchant intermediaries *generally perform a full range of wholesaling functions.* Based on the width of their product lines, three types of full-function merchant intermediaries can be identified. The **general-merchandise wholesaler** *handles a number of different and often unrelated product lines with no one product line being dominant.* Typically, the product lines are nonperishable, staple goods, including hardware, household durables, personal-care products, and electrical, plumbing, and automotive supplies. **Single-line wholesalers** *limit their activities to one general product line* (e.g., either hardware, drugs, groceries, or dry goods), while **specialty-line wholesalers** *restrict their activities to one specialty line within a general line of products* (e.g., frozen foods).

Limited function. As the name implies, limited-function merchant intermediaries *limit their activities to certain wholesaling functions,* in the belief that many retailers are only interested in having those functions provided and do not want to pay for services that are neither needed nor used.

Based on the functions they perform, several types of limited-function merchant intermediaries exist. The **cash-and-carry wholesaler,** for example, is *the discount supermarket of the wholesaling industry* because the retailer must (1) go to the wholesaler's place of business, (2) select and assemble the order, (3) check out at a central station, (4) pay cash for the assembled order, and (5) load and transport the order. Staple groceries, hardware, and variety goods are the most commonly stocked product lines of the cash-and-carry wholesaler.

Drop shippers are *wholesaling operators that normally distribute bulky products, such as lumber and building materials, that are expensive to transport and handle.* The drop shipper operates out of an office, takes retail orders by phone or mail, passes the orders on to the producer, and arranges to have the order shipped directly to the retailer.

The third type of limited-function intermediary is the **truck distributor,** which *essentially operates its business out of a truck.* By carrying inventory on the truck, the driver/salesperson can travel an established sales route and perform the sales and delivery functions almost simultaneously. Truck distributors are important sources of supply for many fast-moving perishable food products (e.g., produce, bakery, and dairy products). They are also important in distributing some specialty items in the hardware and variety-goods lines.

The **rack jobber,** another limited-function intermediary, *operates in much the same manner as the truck distributor, but the rack jobber usually furnishes the racks or shelves for displaying merchandise.* In addition, they "are responsible for maintaining fully stocked racks, building attractive displays, and price marking the merchandise. In essence, the retailer merely furnishes floor or shelf space and then collects the money as the customers go through the checkout stands."[2]

This display is associated with which type of limited-function merchant wholesaler?

Agent Intermediaries

Agent intermediaries *specialize in buying and selling merchandise for others.* They facilitate the exchange process between manufacturers and retailers by bringing them together. The two distinguishing characteristics of agent intermediaries are (1) they do not take title to the goods they deal in and (2) they normally provide only a limited number of functions. Also, agent intermediaries usually work on a commission basis, may have either an intermittent or continuous working relationship with clients, and normally do not represent both the buyer and seller in the same transaction. See Figure 17–4.

FIGURE 17–4
The gray market

At Bi-Rite Photo, a tiny camera store typical of many others in midtown Manhattan, a Nikon motor drive costs either $230 or $165. The body of an Olympus OM-4 costs $325 or $290. And a Minolta X-700 can be yours for $189 or $150.

You can choose your price: The higher one if you want a product imported by the "official" distributor or the lower one if you don't mind a gray-market item the store obtained from an "unauthorized" distributor.

To Warranty or Not to Warranty

Why pay more? Perhaps because official products come with a manufacturer's guarantee. Or perhaps it just somehow seems like the right thing to do. "I guess [such purchasers] think they're patriots or something," shrugs Bi-Rite owner Ely Steinfeld.

The Gray Network

A growing army of retailers like Steinfeld, along with an international network of gray distributors, are trying to turn top-price consumers into a dying breed. . . . Perhaps the most successful gray-market retailer is New York's 47 St. Photo, started as a dime-a-dozen camera discounter in 1966. . . . So strong is the influence of retailers such as 47 St. that most camera stores now "cannot exist without stocking gray," says Bi-Rite's Steinfeld. He predicts that gray imports will continue to grab market share and shelf space, regardless of the dollar's strength and opposition from manufacturers.

Source: *Business Week;* 15 April 1985; pp. 86–87.

. . . and the serpentine pipeline

As a light snow dusted the grimy streets of Seventh Avenue, Barry Brandt readied himself for his daily assault on the city's garment district. Dressed in a short, casual jacket, he braved the cold with a quiet determination that heightened as he turned onto Broadway. . . .

In less than an hour, Brandt completed a crucial series of tasks that would enable hundreds of shoppers to get hold of name-brand clothing at prices heavily discounted from those at department stores.

On this particular morning, Brandt's shopping list was mindboggling. He spent $30,000 for 2,500 garments. Not bad, considering the buy worked out to only $12 per garment, 40 percent less than the regular wholesale price. This savings would eventually be passed on to consumers.

Such shrewd deals are all part of the serpentine pipeline that feeds the nation's growing number of off-price apparel stores. Thanks to Brandt and countless other buyers, a dazzling array of apparel is finding its way to market at heavily discounted prices.

When discounters cannot buy name-brand goods directly from manufacturers, they turn to several sources. There are independent businesses like Manhattan-based Brandt Buying Service, a three-person office specializing in off-price buys. Then there are "jobbers," middlemen who take merchandise that manufacturers or major department stores cannot sell, unloading it on other stores or on consumers directly.

Nestled deeper in the underground network of suppliers are "diverters"—shadowy, yet by most accounts highly dependable and trustworthy operators who assemble millions of dollars worth of hard-to-get name-brand goods for discounters while keeping their tracks well covered.

Most clothing manufacturers know these buyers are funneling goods into the controversial off-price pipeline, but they apparently have no objection as long as buyers don't disclose where they got their merchandise. Indiscreet buyers risk trouble with their sources.

Source: Nancy Yoshihara, "Tide of Off-Price Apparel Swells Via Semi-Secret Pipeline," *The State/Columbia, SC,* 19 February 1984, 26.

Brokers are *agent intermediaries whose primary function is to bring prospective buyers and sellers together to complete a transaction. Information* is the broker's stock-in-trade. Seasonal products (food) and unusual products (technical products or used goods) for which general market information is lacking are the most common product lines handled by a broker.

Sales agents are *agent intermediaries that assume the entire marketing function for a manufacturer.* In effect, the sales agent becomes the manufacturer's marketing department. The sales agent is found predominately in such industries as textiles, home furnishings, canned foods, apparel, and metals.

The **manufacturers' agent** is *essentially the sales organization for several manufacturers within a prescribed market territory.* Normally they carry complementary product lines from several manufacturers as opposed to product lines that compete directly. Manufacturers' agents can be valuable sources of supply for such product lines as furniture and home furnishings, electrical and plumbing products, construction equipment and supplies, dry goods, apparel, and accessories.

Commission merchants *can be an important source of supply for retailers interested in securing certain types of dry goods and agricultural products* (e.g., fruits and vegetables). The typical commission-house operator takes physical possession of goods, provides storage and handling, and acts as the selling agent for the producer.

The last agent intermediary is the **auction house.** The principal function of the auction house is *to provide a place where producers and retailers can meet and complete a sales transaction.* By providing the physical facilities for producers to display their products and retailers to inspect them, the auction house plays an important role in the wholesaling of used cars and agricultural products.

Contractual Intermediaries

To combat the numerous competitive advantages of large chain organizations, many small retailers have entered into contractual arrangements with wholesalers. Typically, the retailer agrees to purchase a certain amount of merchandise from the wholesaler in return for considerations. Lower prices are the most important considerations, although these contractual arrangements often spell out other services that the wholesaler will supply (e.g., merchandising and promotional services). These lower prices are made possible by the fact that the wholesaler has several retailers under contract, thereby permitting the wholesaler to realize economies of scale similar to those it receives in selling to chain organizations.

The two types of contractual intermediaries are cooperative groups and voluntary chains. The **cooperative group** is *a wholesaling organization owned by the participating retailers and from which they receive patronage refunds (therefore lower prices) based on how much each cooperative member buys from the wholesaler.* The **voluntary chain** is *a wholesale operation owned and operated by an independent wholesaler and that retailers may voluntarily join.* Western Auto and Independent Grocers' Alliance (IGA) are examples of voluntary chains. Some contractual intermediaries operate as full-function wholesalers, whereas others limit the functions they provide. Super Valu Stores, Inc., the nation's largest wholesaler, calls itself a "retail support company." The most important form of support is helping retailers expand their business through bigger, more competitive stores. Super Valu offers independent retailers advantages only chains are supposed to have: low prices, up-to-date stores, good locations, and sophisticated operations. To aid retailers, Super Valu employs retail counselors who patrol stores, detect trouble spots, and offer advice. For particular problems, retailers can call on specialists.[3]

The Resident Buying Office

Resident buying offices are *organizations specializing in the buying function and located in major wholesaling and producing markets.* Their central-market location puts the resident buyer in an excellent position to serve as the retailer's "eyes and ears" on supply conditions. The principal services resident buyers offer are information and buyer assistance. They provide information on (1) the availability of products; (2) the reliability of suppliers; (3) the present and future market and supply trends; and (4) the special deals, prices, promotions, and services that various suppliers offer. Buyer-assistance services include locating sources of supply, making initial contact with suppliers, aiding in sales negotiations by using their clout as representatives of several retailers, arranging delivery and payment schedules, and following up on orders to ensure the fast and timely arrival of merchandise at the retailer's store.

The two general types of buying offices are the **store-owned** buying office and the **independent** buying office. Figure 17–5 identifies and characterizes each of these resident buyers. Although resident buying offices are most commonly associated with the central apparel markets of New York, Dallas, and Los Angeles, other central markets are also populated with resident buyers. Because High Point, North Carolina, for example, is the capital of the U.S. furniture industry, several resident buying offices are located there.

FIGURE 17–5
Types of resident buyers

Store-owned resident buying offices	Private	Owned and operated by and for an individual out-of-town retailer
		Decreasing in importance due to the lack of economies of scale in buying
	Associated	Owned and operated by and for a group of out-of-town retailers
		Increasing in importance due to the potential economies of scale in buying
	Chain	Owned and operated by and for retail chains and department-store ownership groups
		Offers advice and information to individual stores in the chain and to the chain's central buying office
Independent resident buying offices	Salaried	Owned and operated by an independent for clients that typically sign a one-year contract
		Larger retailers are usually charged a fee equal to about 0.5 percent of the retailer's annual sales, while smaller retailers are charged a minimum flat fee
	Merchandise broker	Owned and operated by an independent for both retailers and producers
		The producer pays the commission (3 to 5 percent on net sales) rather than the retailer

Source: Adapted from William R. Davidson, Alton F. Doody, and Daniel J. Sweeney, *Retailing Management,* 4th ed. (New York: Ronald Press, 1975), 386–87.

The retailer should have some method for determining which sources of supply are most appropriate to its operation. Many retail buyers are deluged with merchandise offerings from potential supply sources. Thus, the retailer must develop an initial screening procedure to identify sources that might best suit the operation's needs. In devising an initial screening procedure, the retailer should use a *buying plan* and a *resource file.*

The Buying Plan

A buying plan is essential if the retail buyer is to accomplish the task of securing the desired merchandise. To avoid such basic mistakes as buying the wrong merchandise and overbuying and underbuying a merchandise line, the retailer should have a clear idea of "what type" of merchandise to buy. The marketplace presents a tremendous assortment of merchandise of different qualities, styles, and prices from different vendors. Therefore, prior to contacting supply sources and engaging in the buying process, the buyer should formulate some guidelines covering what quality, style, and price lines are consistent with the store's image and its customers' needs. A good buying plan establishes the guidelines not only for merchandise but also for the terms and conditions under which that merchandise is acceptable. See Chapter 18 for a more detailed discussion.

The Resource File

To facilitate preparing for the buying process, the retailer should establish and maintain a resource file on all potential merchandise suppliers. The resource file should contain a sufficient amount of information to allow the buyer to conduct the initial screening of suppliers. Those who do not comply with the retailer's buying plan guidelines can be eliminated immediately from further consideration. Some resource files also provide an overall rating of the supplier's past performance. To facilitate easy access to resource files, retailers often cross-reference by firm and merchandise lines. The files themselves range from standard file folders to four-by-six-inch reference cards.

The third step in the buying process is to make contact with the potential sources of supply. Although most retailers have preferred sources of supply, and some suppliers may be eliminated during the survey step of the buying process, each retailer should strive to maintain as many supply-source contacts as possible. Such contacts are not only alternative sources of supply buy also valuable sources of information. Contacts for a potential sales transaction can be initiated by either the vendor or the retailer.

Vendor-Initiated Contacts

Vendor-initiated contacts include store visits by sales representatives and telephone and mail-order solicitations.

Store Visits

Sales calls at the retailer's place of business represent the most common method of selling staple merchandise. Store visits are also used to sell some fashion goods to medium-size and small retailers, which usually lack the resources to go to the market. From the retailer's viewpoint, store visits by supplier representatives offer the benefits of (1) saving time and money traveling to the market, (2) avoiding the strenuous market-search process, (3) allowing easy in-store access to inventory and sales records for reference purposes, and (4) permitting consultation with other store personnel before placing an order.

The primary limitations of store visits are that the retailer does not have the opportunity to (1) simultaneously compare the merchandise lines of several producers and (2) gain a "feel" for what is going on in the industry through the interaction that occurs with other retailers and vendors at trade shows and central markets.

Telephone and Mail

For some vendors, telephone and mail are popular methods of contacting retailers. These vendors use telephone and mail contacts to prospect for customers, to make appointments for store visits, to follow up on orders, and to check on the needs of existing accounts. Some vendors prefer telephone contacts because of the personal, two-way nature of the telephone. Others make extensive use of the mail to accomplish specific contact objectives. For example, vendors send catalogs to retailers to provide them with sources of information for comparing their merchandise offerings with those of competitive suppliers. Another advantage is that the retailer can avoid lengthy conversations when the vendor's offer is made by telephone or mail, as opposed to when it is made through a store visit.

Retailer-Initiated Contacts

Like vendors, retailers sometimes make initial contacts for products they need. Visiting central markets, using resident buying offices, attending merchandise shows, and making telephone and mail inquiries are the four ways that retailers seek vendors' products and services.

Central-Market Visits

A central market is a geographic area or city that is a dominant source of supply for a particular type of merchandise. Within these central markets are concentrated the selling offices and merchandise showrooms of a large number of suppliers (see Figure 17–6). In one visit the retailer can review and compare the merchandise offerings of several suppliers. Frequently, suppliers help retailers in their review and comparison process by setting up permanent displays in a central facility. The furniture mart in Chicago and the apparel mart in Dallas are examples of these types of facilities. Retailers visiting central markets have opportunities to inspect the merchandise personally, to make contacts with a wide variety of suppliers, and to interact with and exchange ideas with suppliers and other retailers. Generally, the frequency with which buyers take trips to central markets depends upon (1) the *type of merchandise* they wish to secure (fashion goods usually require multiple trips, whereas a single annual trip is usually enough for most staple goods); (2) the *retailer's inventory policies* (low levels of inventory and high rates of turnover usually mean that the retailer must make several trips to the central market); and (3) the *use of resident buying offices* (having a representative in the market reduces the retailer's need for frequent visits).

Resident Buying Offices

Associated with central markets are the resident buying offices discussed previously. These offices allow contacts with existing suppliers to be maintained on a continuing basis while the retailer prospects for and makes contact with new supply alternatives.

485

Merchandise Shows

Merchandise shows or trade fairs are periodic displays of the merchandise lines of many suppliers in one place at one time. Usually, a group of suppliers gets together and stages a show at a hotel or some other central facility such as a merchandise mart or convention facility. Typically, merchandise shows feature a general type of merchandise (e.g., toys, furniture, or some type of wearing apparel); however, multiline showings are also common. Merchandise showings can be either national, regional, or local in scope. The advantages and disadvantages of merchandise shows are basically the same as those of central markets, and the skills and procedures for successful buying are the same for merchandise shows as for market trips.

Telephone and Mail

Retailers use telephone and mail contacts to make initial inquiries on the availability of particular types of merchandise and to place last-minute orders, reorders, and orders for fill-in merchandise. When the retailer is familiar with the supplier and the merchandise, telephone and mail contacts are very efficient and relatively safe. However, telephone and mail orders to unknown suppliers can be quite risky, since

FIGURE 17–6

The regional apparel center

Hard times have encouraged the growth of a new wholesale vehicle—the regional apparel center—although this has not yet signaled the demise of Seventh Avenue.

As Peg Canter, buyer-service representative for the Atlanta Apparel Center points out, "Larger stores that have enough volume need both the regional centers as well as New York. You get the feel first in New York. It's enough to stand on Seventh Avenue and see what everyone's wearing, and you know what to buy."

But regional centers have grown dramatically in response to the economic crunch that made week-long buying sprees to New York very expensive. The four major apparel centers in the country are eager to prove their efficacy to national fashion purveyors.

Los Angeles: California has always been thought of as having a unique style. Arthur Winters, a professor at New York's Fashion Institute of Technology, attributes this California school of fashion more to Californians' individualized life styles rather than to a distinct regional style of dress. During the past few years the California Mart, in Los Angeles, has been doubling its attendance, according to Karen Witynski, the mart's director of communications.

Like Seventh Ave., the mart is open every day, with five weekends a year earmarked for major market activity. The mart, which has 2,000 permanent showrooms, draws buyers mainly from the Southwest, the whole of California and Washington and Oregon.

Various incentives are offered to buyers to attend the mart.

Among them are rebates on air fare, gasoline, free meals, and other amenities. The California Mart is promoted via newsletters, market directories and a calendar of events. The mart also publishes a buyers' registration, which is helpful to manufacturers for use as a mailing list.

Dallas: The *grande dame* of apparel centers will be 20 years old next year. Its impressive 10,000 lines attract 100,000 buyers each year to its five annual markets. The mart spends $17 million yearly on promotion.

Dallas also capitalizes on the rivalry said to exist between the California and New York markets by carrying lines a Californian would go to New York for and vice versa. The Texas metropolis has added incentive to shake off a Texas chic image by demonstrating that Dallas folk can be as fashionable, or more fashionable than anybody else.

FIGURE 17–6, *continued*

Chicago: The midwestern capital, once a very important apparel center, is attempting to regain some lost ground. In fact, Chicago boasts of having the largest design community outside of New York and promotes its local designers at its mart.

The opening of Chicago's Apparel Mart seven years ago "acted as a catalyst to unite retailers, designers and manufacturers," says Dorothy Fuller, the Apparel Center's fashion director. "Eighteen or so companies have started up business since the Apparel Center opened because they had a viable marketplace."

The mart's 4,000 lines are frequented by national chains such as I. Magnin that use local budgets for mart shopping sprees. Fashion is now the fifth largest industry in Chicago, says Ms. Fuller, generating more than $1 billion a year.

Atlanta: The Sunbelt boom was well under way when Atlanta's Apparel Mart fortuitously opened its doors in 1979. A total of 18,000 buyers frequent the mart's 1,000 showrooms. Many of them arrive by automobile from surrounding states.

According to Peg Canter, the only known buyer-service representative out of all the marts in the country, the Atlanta Mart, like the others, is particularly appealing to the small retailer, though larger department stores are beginning to appreciate the mart's cost- and time-effectiveness.

Besides publishing brochures and direct mail pieces, the Atlanta Mart sends leasing agents to New York weekly in order to attract showroom occupancy. It also advertises in *Women's Wear Daily* and other trade publications. As a result, the center is now 97% leased.

Peg Canter, in her work as a mart-retailer-manufacturer liaison, is bothered by one aspect of the manufacturer-retailer relationship—the manufacturers' inappreciation of the small retailer. "The foundation of all retail is the small specialty store," she says. "It's the most profitable part of the business for the manufacturers, but they tend to be shortsighted sometimes in favor of the department store. Yet department stores are too demanding. They want markdown money, returns, co-op advertising, all things the independent retailer pays for. If they didn't have the independent retailer to foot those bills, where would they be? The strength of the regional markets is to me a sign that they've realized this."

Source: "Opportunity Calls beyond Seventh Avenue," Reprinted with permission of *Advertising Age,* 5 September 1983. Copyright Crain Communications Inc.

the retailer is unable to inspect the merchandise and to determine how reliable the supplier is in meeting delivery dates and sales terms. In addition, retailers often use telephone and mail orders to place small orders, resulting in higher per-unit transportation and handling costs. Regardless of these disadvantages, telephone and mail contacts offer the small, geographically isolated retailer an opportunity to establish and maintain relationships with a wide variety of suppliers.

Once the retailer has identified and contacted several sources of supply, it must then evaluate each supplier to determine how consistent their operating characteristics are with its needs. In this third step of the buying process, the retailer must use evaluation criteria and methods that rank the relative capabilities of each supply alternative to serve its needs.

EVALUATING
SOURCES OF
SUPPLY

Evaluation Criteria

A retailer can use several criteria in evaluating potential suppliers. They are merchandise criteria, distribution criteria, price criteria, promotion criteria, and service criteria.

Merchandise Criteria

The first consideration in evaluating alternative sources of supply is the merchandise the supplier offers. The suitability, availability, and adaptability of the suppliers' merchandise lines are three factors retailers commonly use as merchandise criteria. *Suitability* refers to how well the merchandise fits the needs of the retailer's customers and the store's image. Suitability can be judged on the basis of such assortment factors as brand, style, and price, as well as individual factors such as uniqueness, originality, and durability. Suitable merchandise is also judged according to aesthetics (e.g., fabric, color, and print) and quality (e.g., construction, fit, and crafting).[4]

If the retailer deems the merchandise suitable, then its *availability* becomes the next criterion to consider. In determining availability, the buyer must first find out whether the supplier will accept an order. If so, will the merchandise be available in the appropriate quantities, sizes, styles, and colors? Merchandise availability may in fact be based on the size of the retailer's order. For example, many suppliers establish minimum quantities that retailers must order to purchase merchandise from them.

The third merchandise criterion a retailer should use is *adaptability*—the supplier's willingness to make necessary changes in the product to meet the needs of the retailer and its customers. Adaptability might involve (1) producing products to the retailer's specifications, (2) placing the retailer's private label on the product, and (3) adjusting production (color, sizes, styles) to take advantage of fast-moving items or incorporating new trends into existing merchandise lines.

Distribution Criteria

Delays in delivery are of great concern to all retailers. An important evaluation criterion, therefore, is how well suppliers perform their *distribution* and *delivery* functions. The supplier's past performance record is usually a good indication of future performance. Also of interest to most retailers is the degree of *exclusiveness* that the supplier offers in particular lines of merchandise. Most retailers prefer some degree of exclusiveness and therefore want to determine whether the product is offered on an exclusive (one retailer per market), selective (few retailers per market), or intensive (many retailers per market) basis. For some retailers and products (specialty stores and goods), exclusiveness is an important criterion; for other stores and products (discounters and convenience goods), exclusiveness is of little importance.

Additional distribution and delivery policies that the retailer should consider for potential suppliers are (1) whether delivery services are offered, (2) terms and conditions of the delivery service, (3) order size and assortment constraints, (4) initial order–processing time, (5) reorder processing time, and (6) ease and flexibility of placing an order. Among the more important distribution criteria retailers should use are the percentages of (1) customer orders filled, (2) customer orders filled accurately, (3) items out of stock, (4) customer orders that arrive in good condition, and (5) customer orders filled within a certain time.[5]

Price Criteria

Price criteria center around two considerations: the price to the consumer and the price to the retailer. Regarding the price to the consumer, the major issues the retailer should evaluate are price appropriateness and price maintenance. As previously discussed, the retail selling price must be appropriate to the retailer's target market. Price *appropriateness* should be measured in terms of value (i.e., offering the consumer the best quality at the best price). This price/quality relationship can include any number of price/quality combinations. For the prestige retailer, price appropriateness is offering consumers top-quality merchandise at a prestige price; for the discounter, acceptable quality at the lowest price constitutes price appropriateness.

Price *maintenance* is the supplier's policy of maintaining the retail selling price at or above a certain level. Some suppliers insist that their customers (retailers) sell their merchandise at the suggested retail price. For the high-volume discounter that relies heavily on price appeal substantiated by price comparisons, price-maintenance policies are simply unacceptable in most cases.

The second group of price considerations concerns the price the retailer must pay for the merchandise. Perhaps the most important consideration is whether the price will permit the retailer to take a markup sufficient to cover expenses, make a profit, and still be competitive in the marketplace. Price negotiation and how it affects the retailer's evaluation of suppliers will be discussed shortly.

Promotional Criteria

Many merchandise lines require a considerable amount of promotional support to be successfully marketed. Therefore, the *type* and *amount* of promotional assistance the retailer can expect from a supplier are important evaluation criteria. Promotional assistance assumes many different forms, including advertising allowances, cooperative advertising, in-store demonstrations, free display materials, and various consumer inducements such as premiums, coupons, contests, and samples. Also, the extent to which the supplier supports the sale of merchandise through national and/or local advertising is an important factor retailers should consider. Some suppliers are willing and able to supply their customers with advertising art as well as layout copy suggestions. For many small and medium-size retailers, such assistance can strongly influence their decision in selecting suppliers. Ultimately, the essential question for the retailer is, "Does the supplier help me sell?"

Service Criteria

In addition to the various types of merchandise, distribution, price, and promotional supports already discussed, some suppliers will provide some or all of the following supplementary services:

- financing and credit services
- return privileges
- warranty and repair services
- sales force training
- accounting services
- inventory planning and control
- prepackaging, prelabeling, and preticketing
- markdown insurance
- display units, fixtures, and signs
- store facilities design services

The extent to which the retailer might consider some of these services in evaluating supply sources depends on its need for them. While any one of these services can help the retailer reduce either operating expenses or the capital investment required to operate the business, they also make the retailer more dependent on the supplier furnishing the service. Care must be taken to determine what strings are attached.

489

Evaluation Methods

To evaluate alternative sources of supply effectively, retailers must systematically assess each source using objective methods. Three such methods are the weighted-rating method, the single-most-important criterion method, and the minimum-cutoff method.

The Weighted-Rating Method

The **weighted-rating method** is *a procedure for evaluating supply alternatives by assigning weighted values to each of a set of evaluation criteria.* Although several weighted-rating procedures have been devised, the "decision matrix approach to vendor selection" developed by John S. Berens, a description of which follows, illustrates the method.[6]

Step 1: Criteria selection. This step entails selecting criteria to evaluate sources of supply (see preceding discussion of criteria) that are most relevant to the retailer and its relationship to potential suppliers.

Step 2: Criteria weighting. At this stage, predetermined weights (or levels of importance) are assigned to each evaluation criterion. Frequently, this weighting process is accomplished by simply rank-ordering all of the criteria from the most important to the least important and assigning the highest value to the criterion deemed most important and subsequent lower values to those deemed less important.

Step 3: Supplier selection. This is a procedure for choosing which potential suppliers to include in the evaluation.

Step 4: Supplier rating. In this step, each of the selected suppliers is rated on the basis of each evaluation criterion. By comparing each supplier with all other suppliers for each criterion, the retailer can assign a minimal rating for each supplier.

Step 5: Weighted rating. Each supplier's rating is multiplied on each evaluation criterion (step 4) by the criterion weight (step 2) to obtain the weighted rating for each supplier. To obtain the overall weighted rating for each supplier, simply add the weighted rating on each criterion for each supplier.

In using this method, the retailer starts by selecting the source that received the highest weighted rating and attempts to secure the necessary commitments from that supplier. If more than one source is needed or if the highest-rated source is not available, the retailer simply proceeds down the weighted-rating list until all the needed supply sources are secured. Figure 17–7 illustrates Berens' weighted-rating method.

The Single-Most-Important Criterion Method

As the name implies, some retailers evaluate and select suppliers on the basis of the **single-most-important criterion**. This method is similar to the weighted-rating method in that the retailer completes the criteria-selection, criteria-weighting, and supplier-selection steps just described. Suppliers are then compared and one is judged superior according to the single-most-important criterion. If no supplier is judged superior on the basis of the most-important criterion, then the evaluation

	Criteria Weight (Step 2)	Supplier A		Supplier B		Supplier C		Supplier D		Supplier E	
Criterion 1: Supplier Can Fill Reorders	6	3	18	2	12	4	24	1	6	0	0
Criterion 2: Markup Is Adequate	4	2	8	4	16	3	12	0	0	1	4
Criterion 3: Customers Ask for the Line	1	1	1	2	2	4	4	3	3	0	0
Criterion 4: Supplier's Line Has Significant Changes from Season to Season	2	3	6	4	8	2	4	1	2	0	0
Criterion 5: Supplier's Line Contributes to Fashion Leadership	5	2	10	1	5	0	0	3	15	4	20
Criterion 6: Supplier's Line is Cut to Fit Customers Well	2	1	2	0	0	3	6	4	8	2	4
Criterion 7: Supplier Advertises Line in Local Media	1	0	0	1	1	2	2	4	4	3	3
Supplier TOTAL SCORES			45		44		52		38		31

FIGURE 17–7
The decision matrix approach to supplier selection (source: John S. Berens, "A Decision Matrix Approach to Supplier Selection," *Journal of Retailing*, Volume 47, No. 4 (Winter 1971–1972); 52)

procedure continues to the second-most-important criterion, the third, and so on, until one supplier emerges as superior.

The Minimum-Cutoff Method

The **minimum-cutoff method** *recognizes that it is not always possible to determine precisely the importance of each criterion.* However, it is usually possible to establish some minimum standard or cutoff point for each evaluation criterion. Using this method, the retailer (1) selects the criteria to be included in the evaluation, (2) establishes a minimum-cutoff standard for each criterion, (3) compares each supplier to the minimum cutoff on each criterion, (4) eliminates all suppliers that fall below the minimum-cutoff standard on any criterion, and (5) chooses among suppliers that have exceeded the minimum cutoff on all criteria. This method can be combined with the single-most-important criterion method to produce an even more exacting supplier-evaluation technique.

The fourth step in the buying process is active negotiation with suppliers that have been identified in the evaluation step as potentially suitable sources. In negotiation, various issues of concern to both the retailer and the supplier are discussed. In the retailer/supplier relationship, the two most common issues subject to negotiation are *price* and *service.*

NEGOTIATING
WITH SOURCES
OF SUPPLY

Negotiating the Price

In contrast to the fixed prices that the final consumer encounters on most products at the retailer's store, the price the retailer pays for the same merchandise is, in most cases, subject to negotiation. While any number of factors could conceivably influence the price the retailer pays, three factors play dominant roles: (1) list price, (2) discount and allowance terms, and (3) transportation and handling terms.

The Starting Point: List Price

Price negotiations usually start with the supplier's basic price list. For administrative convenience, *most suppliers establish their pricing structures around basic* **list prices** that they use for an extended time period. By adjusting their list prices upward or downward using various types of "add-ons" and "discounts," suppliers can avoid publishing frequently revised price lists while at the same time make necessary price accommodations for individual retail customers.

As the starting point for negotiation, the basic list price *is a crucial element in estimating what a supplier's "final" price will be to the retailer.* Since some suppliers publish what are, in effect, inflated list prices, substantial differences in the final price can result because of large variations in discounts and allowances as well as transportation and handling terms.

Discount and Allowance Terms

The final selling price to the retailer is the difference between the supplier's list price and the negotiated discounts and allowances. The principal types of discounts are trade, quantity, seasonal and cash discounts, and promotional allowances.

Trade discounts. A trade discount is a form of compensation that the buyer may receive for performing certain services (functions) for the supplier. Also referred to as a functional discount, the trade discount is usually used by the supplier selling merchandise through catalogs and is based on a quoted list price. Using the trade-discount method, the supplier offers one price to all potential buyers. The supplier makes price changes simply by adjusting the amount of the trade discount offered to any given buyer. The size of the trade discount the supplier allows depends on the type, quantity, and quality of the services the potential buyer is willing to provide. Therefore, variations in trade discounts are legally justifiable on the basis of the different costs associated with doing business with different buyers. If the buyer is instrumental in helping the supplier realize certain savings, part of those savings are passed along to the buyer in the form of larger trade discounts.

Trade discounts come in one of two forms: single and chain. The **single trade discount** *is expressed as a single percentage adjustment (e.g., 50 percent) to the supplier's list price.* For example, a product with a list price of $200 less a 40 percent trade discount (which would amount to an $80 trade discount) would cost the retailer $120 ($200 × .40 = $80; $200 − $80 = $120). A trade discount can also be calculated using a chain of discounts. *Expressed as a series of percentages (e.g., 40 percent, 20 percent, 10 percent), the* **chain trade discount** *is applied to the list price in successive order.* The first percentage discount is calculated on the original list price, the second percentage discount is calculated on the value resulting from the first calculation, and so on until each percentage discount is taken into account. For example, a product listed at $300 less a 40/20/10 percent discount would cost the retailer $129.60, since altogether that would represent a discount of

56.8 percent. To illustrate this calculation of a chain trade discount, consider the following:

$$
\begin{array}{rl}
\text{list price} = & \$300.00 \quad (\$300 \times 40\% = \$120) \\
& \underline{-120.00} \\
& 180.000 \quad (\$180 \times 20\% = \$36) \\
& \underline{-\ 36.00} \\
& 144.00 \quad (\$144 \times 10\% = \$14.40) \\
& \underline{-\ 14.40} \\
\text{retailer's price} = & \$129.60
\end{array}
$$

The purpose for expressing the trade discount in the form of a chain is to facilitate the process of offering different discounts to different buyers. The buyer that performs many services for the supplier receives the entire discount chain (40 percent, 20 percent, 10 percent), while the buyer that performs a limited number of services is offered only part of the chain (40 percent, 20 percent, or possibly simply 40 percent).

Quantity discounts. Suppliers offer quantity discounts to retailers as an inducement to buy large quantities of merchandise. Large order quantities can help to reduce the supplier's selling, handling, billing, transporting, and inventory costs. These cost savings are, in part, passed along to the buyer in the form of quantity discounts. Quantity discounts for the retailer represent an additional way to reduce the price of the merchandise. However, buying large quantities normally increases the retailer's operating expenses, ties up operating capital, and creates additional inventory-control problems. Also, the retail buyer must be aware of the potential risk of overbuying and then having to mark down the overstocked merchandise. Thus, the retailer must carefully evaluate the trade-offs of the relative costs and benefits resulting from quantity discounts; otherwise, the big deal might soon turn into obsolete merchandise.

Quantity discounts can be expressed and calculated in several different ways. They can be based on either the dollar value of the total order or on the number of units (or cases) in the order. Quantity discounts can also be handled as a percentage reduction from list price or simply expressed in some form of a schedule with unit or dollar sales corresponding to a particular dollar discount amount. A different approach to quoting quantity discounts is to quote a carload or truckload price. Any order less than a carload or a truckload is adjusted by a system of "add-ons." For example, a retailer placing a less-than-carload order is quoted the carload unit price, plus a certain percentage (e.g., 6 percent) of that price as an add-on. Given the numerous methods for calculating quantity discounts, the retailer should take the time to verify exactly what type and how much of a quantity discount the supplier is offering.

Three types of quantity discounts—noncumulative, cumulative, and free merchandise—are commonly used. A **noncumulative quantity discount** *is based on a single order or shipment.* The supplier uses this type of discount to encourage the retailer to increase the size of a given order. The bigger the order, the bigger the absolute discount. *Quantity discounts that apply to several orders or shipments placed with the supplier over an extended period (usually a year) are referred to as* **cumulative discounts.** Not only do these discounts apply to several orders, but usually the amount of the discount increases as the total (accumulated) order size increases. The supplier's purpose for applying cumulative discounts is to encourage return trade by reducing the price of merchandise on subsequent orders. *Free merchandise* is also a form of quantity discount. The "13" dozen, whereby the supplier offers one free dozen for every 12 dozen the retailer orders, is a common means by which the retailer receives free merchandise instead of either a price reduction or a cash payment.

Seasonal discounts. Seasonal discounts are *price reductions given to buyers who are willing to order, receive, and pay for goods during the "off season."* To even out production throughout the year, many manufacturers of seasonal goods will offer seasonal discounts. For example, a retailer will be granted a seasonal discount on Christmas merchandise if it accepts early delivery in spring as opposed to in the fall. Although the retailer can realize a savings in the cost of the merchandise by taking seasonal discounts, these savings must be viewed in light of (1) additional inventory costs and problems, (2) increased risks resulting from price changes, style changes, and merchandise depreciation, and (3) restricted use of investment capital already tied up in the merchandise.

Cash discounts. A **cash discount** is *one given for making prompt payment.* To encourage retailers to pay their bills before the due date, the supplier sometimes permits the retailer to deduct a certain percentage discount from the net invoice price. In negotiating cash discounts and related payment terms, the retailer needs to consider three factors: the net invoice price, the discount amount, and the dating terms.

The first consideration in negotiating cash discounts is to establish what constitutes the net invoice price. As the base for calculating cash discounts, the net invoice price is crucial in determining the dollar amount of the discount. The **net invoice price** is *the net value of the invoice or the total invoice minus all other discounts (trade, quantity, seasonal, etc.).* An exception may occur when the supplier allows the transportation charges to be included in the net invoice figure. Depending on trade practices, the inclusion of transportation charges may be open for negotiation. If so, it is obviously to the retailer's advantage to have them included.

The second factor the retailer must consider is the **discount amount**. While a 2 percent cash discount is common in many trades, the rate ranges from no cash discounts to whatever the supplier is willing to allow. In some industry trades, the amount of the cash discount is standardized, and both the retailer and supplier are generally bound by these trade standards. In other trades, the cash discount amount is totally negotiable. Some retailers insist upon a cash discount and will automatically deduct a standard discount if payment is made within a specific time period (usually 10 days). They take the discount regardless of the terms expressed in the supplier's invoice.

Dating terms are as significant in negotiating cash discounts and payment conditions as the net invoice price and the discount amount. The importance of dating terms is that they (1) determine the cash discount period or the amount of time the retailer has to take advantage of the cash discount and (2) provide the invoice due date or the amount of time the retailer has to pay the net invoice price in full. Ten days is the most common cash discount period, while 30 days from the dating of the invoice is a fairly standard invoice due date. However, both cash-discount periods and invoice due dates vary depending on the particular situation and on the ability of the retailer to negotiate dating terms.

Two general classes of dating terms exist: immediate and future. Sometimes suppliers insist on **immediate dating**, *allowing no time for the cash discount or extra* time for the invoice payment. Prepayment and cash on delivery (COD) are two examples of immediate dating. **Prepayment dating** *means that the retailer must make payment when the order is placed.* Suppliers use prepayment terms when two circumstances occur simultaneously: (1) the retailer is either unknown or unreliable (bad credit rating), and (2) the merchandise is customized or highly perishable. **Cash on delivery** terms are *enforced when the retailer is either unknown or unreliable, but when the merchandise can be easily sold if returned to the supplier.*

Future dating is *the practice of allowing the retailer more time to take advantage of the cash discount or to pay the net amount of the invoice.* In essence, it encourages the retailer to delay payment and helps in the short-term financing of inventory. Figure 17–8 describes several types of future dating.

One additional negotiating issue regarding cash discounts is *anticipation* or an extra cash discount for paying the net invoice *before the expiration of the cash-discount period.* It is an amount the retailer may take in addition to the cash discount. The amount of anticipation will depend on the number of days the invoice is paid prior to the last day of the discount period. For example, if the retailer pays the invoice on the fourth day of a 10-day cash-discount period, the retailer is entitled to deduct six days of anticipation at a previously agreed-upon daily discount rate. Anticipation is utilized extensively by large retailers as well as by those with surplus cash available.

Most experts would recommend that retailers take every cash discount available, since most cash discounts yield an equivalent annual interest rate far in excess of the yield produced by most other investments. Also, the yield on most cash discounts is more than enough to cover the interest on funds borrowed to meet the time requirement of the cash-discount period.

Promotional allowances. To gain the retailer's cooperation in promotional activities, the supplier will frequently offer the retailer a promotional allowance. **Promo-**

FUTURE DATING TERMS	SELECTED EXAMPLES	EXPLANATION OF EXAMPLES	
		Cash Discount Terms	Net Invoice Terms
Net	Net, 30	no cash discount allowed	net amount due within 30 days of invoice date
Date of Invoice (DOI)	2/10, net 30	2-percent discount within 10 days of invoice date	net amount due within 30 days of invoice date
End of Month (EOM)	2/10, net 60, EOM	2-percent discount within 20 days of the first day of the month following the invoice date	net amount due within 60 days of the first day of the month following the invoice date
Receipt of Goods (ROG)	4/10, net 45, ROG	4-percent discount within 10 days after receiving the goods at the retailer's place of business	net amount due within 45 days after receiving the goods at the retailer's place of business
Extra	3/10-60 extra, net 90	3-percent discount within 70 days of invoice date	net amount due within 90 days of invoice date

FIGURE 17–8
Types of future-dating terms

tional allowances, *which reduce the price retailers pay suppliers for merchandise, include advertising allowances, preferred selling space, free display materials, and merchandise deals.*[7] *Advertising allowances* are discounts retailers earn by advertising the supplier's products in the local media. In essence, the retailer assumes part or all of the supplier's local advertising function and is compensated by the supplier for money spent and services performed in the form of an advertising allowance. *Preferred selling space,* whereby "the retail buyer will offer preferred selling space to the vendor and in return will be granted an allowance from the regular price,"[8] might include (1) a freestanding display in a high-traffic aisle, (2) an end-of-aisle display, (3) a high-exposure area near a checkout counter, or (4) a special window display. In some cases, the more preferred the selling space, the greater the allowance. Retailers also use *free display materials* in the form of counter, window, and floor displays, signs, banners, and shelf strips, as well as various types of giveaways. These materials help to increase sales, reduce selling costs, and earn the retailer allowances from suppliers. Promotional allowances also can take the form of *merchandise deals* in which free merchandise is substituted for monetary allowances as compensation for performing promotional functions. As with all other discounts, promotional allowances must be judged on a cost/benefit basis.

Transportation and Handling Terms

The retailer's actual laid-in cost of merchandise also depends on which party assumes the transportation charges and handling responsibilities. In negotiating transportation and handling terms, the retailer must consider all of the following issues: Who pays transportation charges? Who bears transportation charges? Where does the *title exchange hands*? Who is responsible for filing *claims*? The payer and the bearer of transportation charges may or may not be the same person. For example, to facilitate delivery speed, the supplier may pay transportation charges when the goods are loaded at the factory; however, these charges may be charged back to the retailer on the invoice. In such cases the retailer ultimately bears the cost of transportation. Equally important is the point at which the title to the merchandise is transferred from the supplier to the retailer. The party that has title while the goods are in transit is responsible for bearing any insurance costs that might be needed above the liability of the carrier to cover loss. Where title exchange occurs also influences the party that is responsible for filing and collecting any damage claims against the carrier. Damage claims not only can be expensive to collect in some cases, but can also occupy a considerable amount of the retailer's time. Figure 17–9 illustrates the six most commonly expressed transportation and handling terms. However, as a note of caution, transportation terms are characterized by a variety of expressions (e.g., the terms *plant* or *factory* are often substituted for *origin*, whereas *store* or *retailer* can be used instead of *destination*). Therefore, retailers should not hesitate to clarify any expression they do not fully understand.

Negotiating the Service

In addition to price, the various types and levels of services that the supplier provides also are subject to negotiation. In some cases a service is fairly standard with only minor adjustments allowed; in other cases, certain services are totally negotiable. The previous discussion on evaluating sources of supply identified 10 different supplier services. In negotiating for services, the retailer must realize that although services may be available, it may not receive some or any of them unless it actively seeks them as part of the buying process. The terms and conditions for any of these 10 services must be detailed before the purchase if the retailer expects the supplier to provide them.

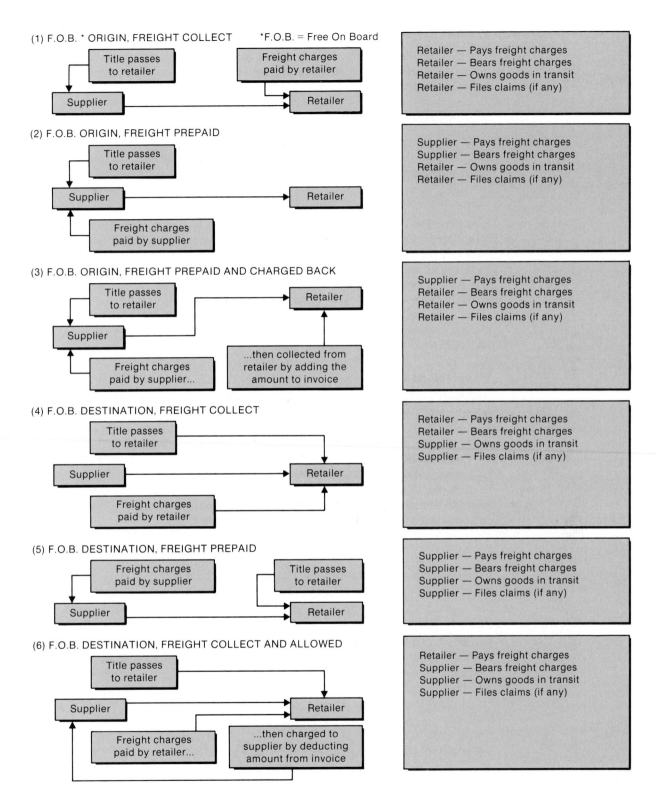

FIGURE 17–9

Transportation terms and conditions (source: Adapted from Murray Krieger, *Practical Merchandising Math for Everyday Use* [New York: National Retail Merchants Association, 1980], 4)

The final step in the retailer's buying process is the actual purchase of the merchandise. Two issues to consider are buying strategies and buying methods retailers use in the process.

Buying Strategies

In deciding how many different sources of supply to use in securing the store's merchandise, the retailer can elect to pursue one of two buying strategies: concentrated or dispersed.

Concentrated Buying

A **concentration strategy** is *one in which the retailer decides to use a limited number of suppliers, believing it leads to lower total costs and preferential treatment.* By concentrating purchases, the retailer can lower the laid-in cost of the merchandise by taking advantage of quantity discounts and lower transportation rates. Additionally, it can lower operating expenses, since ordering, receiving, and processing of merchandise are more efficient with fewer suppliers. Equally important, many retailers believe that if they become a preferred customer by concentrating their purchases, they can expect to receive special considerations for merchandise and supplier services.

Dispersed Buying

Proponents of the **dispersion strategy** of buying believe that concentrated buying is "concentrated risk," since it is dangerous to "put all your eggs in a few baskets." By *spreading orders over many suppliers,* these retailers believe they can (1) obtain a greater variety of merchandise, (2) be made aware of "hot" items, (3) ensure backup sources of supply, and (4) promote competitive services from different supply sources. The decision to use a concentration or a dispersion strategy is one retailers must make in light of their individual situation. Generally, retailers of staple merchandise tend to concentrate their purchases, whereas retailers of fashion merchandise usually elect to use a less-concentrated approach.

Buying Methods

Retailers use several buying methods, depending upon their circumstances. They include regular, consignment, memorandum, approval, and specification buying.

Regular Buying

Retailers use regular buying to secure the vast majority of their merchandise lines. **Regular buying** *involves the systematic cutting and issuing of purchase orders and reorders.* The entire buying process is conducted in conjunction with the merchandise budget and the inventory-control process. Purchases are mechanical and automatic. Most staple goods and many fashion goods can be handled by this method.

Consignment Buying

Consignment buying is *an arrangement whereby the supplier retains ownership of the merchandise shipped to the retailer,* and the retailer (1) displays the merchandise, (2) sells it to the final consumer, (3) deducts an agreed-upon percentage commission, and (4) remits the remainder to the supplier. Merchandise not sold within a prescribed time is returned to the supplier. This method of buying is usually used by the retailer when the merchandise is expensive, new, or of such a high-risk nature that the extent and duration of demand for it is relatively unknown.

Memorandum Buying

Memorandum buying is *essentially a variation of consignment buying. The main difference is that the title to the merchandise exchanges hands when it is shipped to the retailer.* The retailer retains the right to return to the supplier any unsold merchandise and to pay for the merchandise after it has been sold. The retailer's purpose for assuming title is to gain more control in setting the selling price to the final consumer.

Approval Buying

When merchandise is shipped to the retailer's store before the final purchase decision has been made, the retailer is buying on approval. Before the retailer can sell the merchandise it must secure ownership. **Approval buying** *allows the retailer to inspect the merchandise before making the purchase decision and to postpone any purchase until physical possession has been secured.* Postponing possession can result in lower inventory carrying costs, more time to take advantage of cash discounts, and more time to prepare a merchandising program for the goods.

Specification Buying

Many large retail organizations want to buy some of their merchandise made to their specifications. Their specifications can range from minor changes in existing lines of merchandise to complete specifications covering raw materials, design, quality, labeling, and packaging. Through **specification buying,** *the retailer can acquire merchandise that is unique and distinctive from that of competitors and that is thus personalized.* Usually, specification buying involves considerable negotiation between retailer and supplier, and ordering lead times are quite long.

SUMMARY

The buying process is the first stage in the retailer's efforts to get merchandise into the store. It involves the six steps of identifying, surveying, contacting, evaluating, negotiating with, and buying from sources of supply.

The first step of identifying sources of supply is establishing what type of channel to use in procuring each merchandise line. The retailer has several options in selecting sources of supply, including various types of raw-resource producers, manufacturers, intermediaries, and resident buying offices.

The second step, surveying sources of supply, involves determining which sources of supply are most appropriate for the retailer's operation. It provides a means by which an initial screening of supply sources can be made. The surveying step requires the retailer to develop and maintain a buying plan and a resource file.

Contacting sources of supply is the third step in the buying process. Contacts can be initiated by either the vendor or the retailer. Vendor-initiated contacts include store visits by vendor salespersons or mail and telephone solicitations. Retailers contact sources of supply by visiting central markets, using resident buying offices, attending merchandise shows, and making telephone and mail inquiries.

The fourth step in the buying process is the evaluation of various alternative suppliers. Suppliers can be evaluated on the basis of (1) the suitability, availability, and adaptability of the merchandise they offer; (2) the exclusiveness and policies associated with the supplier's distribution system; (3) the appropriateness of the supplier's price and policies regarding price maintenance; (4) the type and amount of promotional assistance; and (5) the type and amount of supplementary services. Three methods used in evaluating supply sources include the weighted-rating method, the single-most-important criterion method, and the minimum-cutoff method.

Negotiating with sources of supply is the fifth step in the buying process. Negotiation involves discussing various issues of concern to both the retailer and the supplier. The two most common issues subject to negotiation are price and service. Price negotiations start with the supplier's list price and those discounts and allowances taken to adjust the list price. The most common price adjustments are trade, quantity, seasonal, and cash discounts, along with promotional allowances. Also of concern are various transportation and handling terms that affect the retailer's laid-in cost of the new merchandise.

The final step in the buying process is actual purchase of the merchandise from several suppliers, using various buying methods. The retailer can elect to concentrate purchases with a few suppliers or disperse them among many suppliers. In the actual buying process, the retailer can buy merchandise using a regular, consignment, memorandum, approval, or specification method of buying.

KEY TERMS AND CONCEPTS

formal buying organization

informal buying organization

centralized buying

decentralized buying

specialized buying

generalized buying

merchant intermediaries

full-function merchant
  intermediaries

general-merchandise wholesaler

single-line wholesaler

specialty-line wholesaler

limited-function merchant
  intermediaries

cash-and-carry wholesaler

drop shipper

truck distributor

rack jobber

agent intermediary

broker

sales agent

manufacturers' agent

commission merchant

auction house

contractual intermediary

cooperative group

voluntary chain

resident buying office

store-owned buying office

independent buying office

weighted-rating method

single-most-important criterion
  method

minimum-cutoff method

list price

single trade discount

chain trade discount

noncumulative quantity discount

cumulative quantity discount

seasonal discount

cash discount

net invoice price

discount amount

dating terms

immediate dating

prepayment dating

cash on delivery

future dating

promotional allowances

concentration strategy

dispersion strategy

regular buying

consignment buying

memorandum buying

approval buying

specification buying

REVIEW QUESTIONS

1. How formal should the retailer's buying organization be?
2. What are the relative strengths and weaknesses of a centralized buying organization?
3. Why might the retailer consider buying directly from the manufacturer?
4. How are full-function merchant wholesalers distinguished from one another?
5. Identify and describe the four types of limited-function merchant wholesalers.
6. What is the principal difference between an agent intermediary and a merchant intermediary?
7. What are the two types of contractual intermediaries? How do they differ?
8. What type of information and buyer assistance services does the resident buying office provide?
9. From the retailer's viewpoint, what are the benefits of having vendor sales representatives make store visits?
10. What is a merchandise show?
11. How can the retailer evaluate the merchandise offered by a given supplier? Identify and discuss the criteria used in making such evaluations.
12. What distribution and delivery policies and standards should the retailer consider when evaluating a particular supplier?
13. Describe the minimum-cutoff method of supplier evaluation.
14. What is the starting point for price negotiations between retailers and suppliers?
15. What would be the retailer's price if a product had a list price of $40 and a trade discount structure of 30/20/5?
16. How does a cumulative quantity discount differ from a noncumulative discount?
17. What are the two general classes of dating terms? Discuss each class.
18. What are promotional allowances? Describe their four common forms.
19. What issues should the retailer consider when negotiating transportation and handling terms?
20. What are the two buying-strategy options open to the retailer when deciding how many different souces of supply should be used in securing the store's merchandise?
21. Identify and briefly describe the five buying methods a retailer might use.

ENDNOTES

1. See Barry Berman and Joel R. Evans, *Retail Management—A Strategic Approach* (New York: Macmillan, 1979), 292.
2. William J. Stanton, *Fundamentals of Marketing* (New York: McGraw-Hill, 1978), 346.
3. Bill Saporito, "Super Valu Does Two Things Well," *Fortune*, 18 April 1983, 114.
4. Elizabeth C. Hirschman, "An Exploratory Comparison of Decision Criteria Used by Retail Buyers," in R. F. Lusch and W. R. Darden, eds., *Retail Patronage Theory* (Norman, OK: Center for Economic and Management Research, The University of Oklahoma, 1981), 3.
5. Louis W. Stern and Adel I. El-Ansary, *Marketing Channels* (Englewood Cliffs, NJ: Prentice-Hall, 1977), 143.
6. John S. Berens, "A Decision Matrix Approach to Supplier Selection," *Journal of Retailing* 47 (Winter, 1971): 52.
7. Maryanne Smith Bohlinger, *Merchandise Buying Principles and Applications* (Dubuque, IA: William C. Brown, 1977), 436.
8. Ibid., 439.

RELATED READINGS

Brown, James R.; Lusch, Robert F.; and Muehling, Darrel D. "Conflict and Power-Dependence Relations in Retailer-Supplier Channels." *Journal of Retailing* 59 (Winter 1983), 53–80.

Dilts, Jeffrey C. "A Cross-Channel Comparison of Channel Conflict." *1985 AMA Educators' Proceedings*. R. F. Lusch et al, eds. (American Marketing Association 1985), 166–71.

Ernst, Robert L. "Distribution Channel Detente Benefits Suppliers, Retailers, and Consumers." *Marketing News* (March 7, 1980), 19–20.

Hutt, Michael D. "The Retail Buying Committee: A Look at Cohesiveness and Leadership." *Journal of Retailing* 55 (Winter 1979), 87–97.

Johnson, Jean L.; Koenig, Harold F.; and Brown, James R. "The Bases of Marketing Channel Power: An Exploration and Confirmation of Their Underlying Dimensions." *1985 AMA Educators' Proceedings.* R. F. Lusch et al, eds. (American Marketing Association 1985), 160–65.

Levy, Michael, and van Breda, Michael. "A Financial Perspective on the Shift of Marketing Functions." *Journal of Retailing* 60 (Winter 1984), 23–42.

Martin, Claude R. "Normative Model for Department Store Buying." *Evolving Marketing Thought for 1980, Proceedings.* J. H. Summey and R. D. Taylor, eds. (Southern Marketing Association 1980), 499–501.

"Planning Systems Put Buyers in Their Place—The Market." *Chain Store Age Executive* (July 1985), 93–94.

"Retail Distribution." *Forbes* (January 17, 1980), 176–82.

Smith, Rick, and Chavie, Rick. "More Effective Buying Using State-of-the-Art Techniques." *Retail Control* (August 1984), 42–49.

Warner, Robert. "How a Buyer Can Increase Productivity." *Chain Store Age* (February 1981), 27.

Woodside, Arch G. "Reseller Buying Behavior: Some Questions and Tentative Answers." *Evolving Marketing Thought for 1980, Proceedings.* J. H. Summey and R. D. Taylor, eds. (Southern Marketing Association 1980), 492–96.

Outline

Objectives

- Identify all of the activities involved with physically getting the merchandise into the store and onto the shelves

- Describe the necessary procedures for placing and writing a purchase order and ensuring that each order is properly processed

- Design and explain an effective in-store system for receiving, checking, marking, and stocking incoming merchandise

- Discuss the procedures for processing suppliers' invoices and returning defective merchandise

18
The Procurement Process

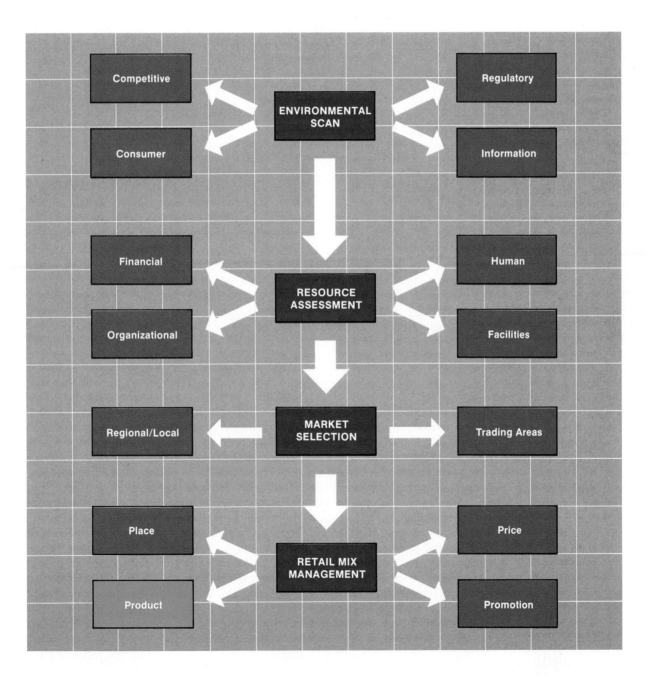

O nce the retail buyer has completed the buying process of identifying, surveying, contacting, evaluating, negotiating, and buying, the next stage in securing the merchandise mix is the procurement process. The **procurement process** *involves all of the activities of physically getting the merchandise into the store
and onto the shelves.*

**THE
PROCUREMENT
PROCESS**

In securing merchandise, too many retailers focus on the buying process and fail to
devote sufficient time and attention to the actual procurement of that merchandise.
Being basically a "backroom" operation, the procurement process lacks the glamour
and excitement of buying. While this might explain the lack of attention procurement
receives, it does not justify that neglect. Close control and supervision of the procurement process are as important to the retailer's profit picture as is careful buying.
If the buyer is to secure the merchandise desired in the way intended, procedures
for controlling procurement must be developed and maintained. The four basic
steps in the procurement process are illustrated in Figure 18–1. In chronological
order, they are ordering and following up, receiving and checking, marking and
stocking, and paying and returning.

**ORDERING AND
FOLLOWING UP**

The first step in physically procuring the retailer's merchandise is to place a purchase order and then follow up on that purchase order to ensure it is properly and
efficiently processed. Order placement and follow-up activities provide the focus for
the following discussion.

Ordering

When ordering merchandise, the buyer often faces a variety of circumstances that
determine which of many different types of orders must be placed. Ordering procedures might involve placing orders (1) with different suppliers at different levels
in the channel of distribution; (2) at different times to accommodate past, present,
and future needs; (3) for either regular or special merchandise; and (4) with complete or partial specification of terms and conditions of sale. Figure 18–2 identifies
and briefly describes seven different types of orders.

Manual Purchase-Order System

Retailers can place merchandise orders in either oral or written form. Because oral
agreements in some states are legally binding only up to some stated limit and are
subject to vastly different interpretations, retailers should have them accurately transcribed into written form at the earliest possible time. Orders placed by telephone
or in person (such as at central markets or at merchandise shows) are a convenient
means of establishing the initial agreement; however, most retailers believe it is
necessary to follow up oral agreements with written orders to prevent any future
misunderstandings.

When placing a written order, the buyer can use a form provided by the supplier or one provided by the retailer. It is generally recommended—for several reasons—that retailers use their own forms whenever possible. First, since the written
order form can become a legally binding contract between the retailer and the supplier, the retailer should have *total familiarity* with the form. While written forms that
suppliers provide are often quite similar, they are sometimes organized along different formats that could be confusing to the buyer. Second, a standard form developed by the retailer provides both the *exact information needed* and the *number
of copies necessary* for efficient order processing. Third, by using the retailer's stan-

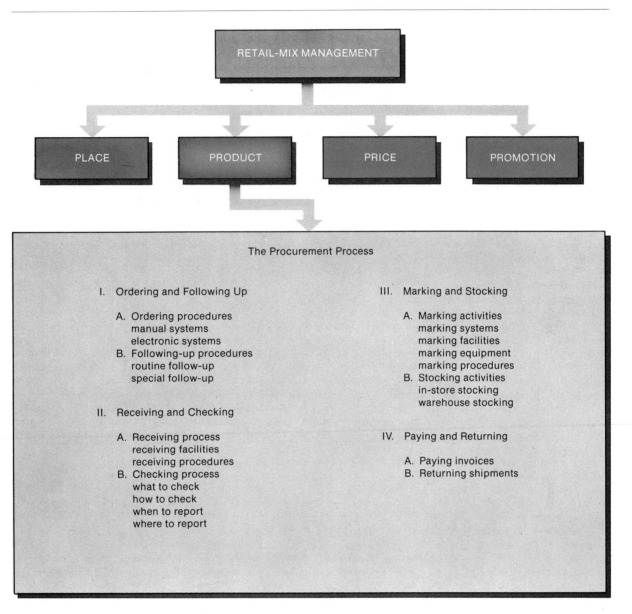

FIGURE 18–1
Structuring and implementing the procurement process

dard order form, the problems associated with *processing* suppliers' forms in their multitude of shapes, sizes, and colors can be avoided. Finally, when the retailer uses a form it has developed, it *protects itself* from any legally binding conditions that might be printed on the suppliers's order form or that might have been overlooked in signing the order.

The order form requires careful preparation because it contains all the details of a particular business transaction. While most order forms vary in format, they contain essentially the same information. The **order form,** as a legally binding contract when signed by both parties, *specifies the terms and conditions under which the transaction is to be conducted.* These terms and conditions usually are stated on both the front and back of the order form.

507

Regular orders:	Orders placed by the buyer directly with the vendor. Involves ordering regular stock items with complete specifications as to terms and conditions of sale and delivery.
Reorders:	Orders placed with existing supplier for previously purchased goods, usually under terms and conditions specified by the original order.
Advance orders:	Orders placed in advance of both the normal buying season and the immediate needs of the retailer. Involves ordering regular stock items in anticipation of receiving preferred treatment.
Back orders:	Orders placed by the buyer for merchandise that was ordered but not received on time. Involves orders that the supplier intends to ship as soon as goods are available.
Blanket orders:	Orders placed with suppliers for merchandise for all or part of a season. Involves ordering merchandise without specifying such assortment details as sizes, colors, and styles and such delivery details as when and how much to ship. Requisitions against the blanket order will be placed as the need for the merchandise arises.
Open orders:	Orders placed with central market representatives (e.g. resident buyers) to be filled by whatever supplier the representative considers best suited to fill the order.
Special orders:	Orders placed with suppliers for merchandise not normally carried in stock or for specially manufactured merchandise. May involve specification buying.

FIGURE 18–2
Types of orders

The front of the order form usually contains the following standard information:

- *retailer description*—the complete name and address of the retailer together with the names and telephone numbers of persons to be contacted should a problem occur
- *supplier description*—the complete name and address of the supplier together with the names and telephone numbers of persons to be contacted should a problem occur
- *order number*—a serial number used for filing the order and for future reference
- *store and department number*—a number assigned to each store (multiunit operations) and department, used to identify the store and/or department for which the merchandise is being secured
- *order date*—the date that the order was sent or placed with the supplier; important in determining the time it takes a supplier to process an order
- *delivery date*—the date the order is to be shipped; it is important because the retailer can refuse to accept any merchandise shipped before that date and it prevents the supplier from shifting the burden of inventory to the retailer before the retailer is ready to assume the responsibility
- *cancellation date*—the date after which the retailer reserves the right to cancel any merchandise that has not been received, preventing the sup-

plier from unloading unwanted merchandise onto the retailer late in the selling season

- *discount terms*—a complete listing and description of all negotiated discounts that apply to the order
- *transportation terms*—a complete description of all shipping and handling terms including transportation charges, methods and modes of transportation, place of delivery, handling and insurance arrangements, methods of labeling, packaging requirements, and so on
- *merchandise description*—a complete description of the merchandise including class, style, color, unit price, total price, order quantities, and other information serving to identify the merchandise
- *miscellaneous information*—a complete description of any additional requirements in terms of ticketing information, instructions for receiving, checking, and marking merchandise, reorder agreements, invoicing arrangements, and so on
- *authorized signatures*—the signatures of individuals authorized to place an order; usually the signature of either the store buyer, merchandise manager, or both is required

The back side of the retailer's order form usually contains a standardized statement of the general conditions under which the supplier will be held legally responsible if it accepts the retailer's order.

An equally important issue in writing the order is the distribution of order copies. The size and complexity of the retailer's organization will determine the number of copies the retailer should make and distribute. In large retail organizations it is not unusual for seven copies to be distributed. Two copies are sent to the supplier, which retains one for its files and uses the other to acknowledge the retailer's order by returning it. A third copy goes to the accounting department to inform it of the purchase and to check payments issued when the supplier's invoice is received. A fourth copy is sent to the receiving department so it can inspect incoming merchandise. The store or department for which the merchandise was ordered receives the fifth copy to help in planning a merchandise program. The sixth and seventh copies of the purchase order are retained by the buyer and the merchandise manager, who use them for follow-up purposes and as a working document in the open-order file. Small retail organizations normally make only three copies: one for the supplier and two for internal store accounting and processing purposes.

Electronic Purchase-Order System

Several technological developments for improving purchase-order management via computer linkages have emerged during the last several years; one of these is the development of the **electronic purchase-order (EPO) system**.[1] Retail managers now have a variety of options for structuring their EPO system. Figure 18–3 illustrates the most common structures retailers and vendors use in exchanging electronic purchase-order and invoice data.[2] The options follow.

- *Mail linkages*—purchase-order and invoice data are transcribed onto magnetic tape or diskettes and transmitted between retailers and vendors via the mail. This is a practical option for a large volume of information when time is not a critical element.
- *Telephone linkages*—purchase-order and invoice data are communicated between the retailer's computer and the vendor's computer via the tele-

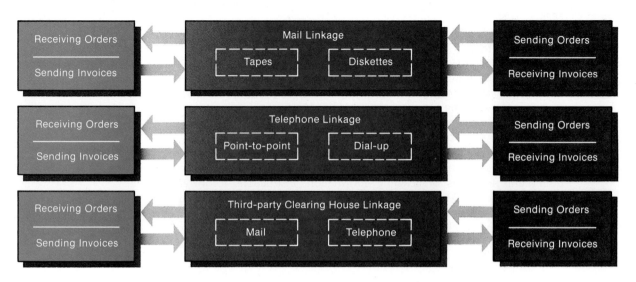

FIGURE 18–3
Electronic purchase-order systems

phone. The *point-to-point* option involves arranging transmission schedules and common protocols to allow direct computer-to-computer interchange of data. The *dial-up* option involves the storage of retailer orders and vendor invoices in on-line files and allowing each party to have dial-up access to these files. K Mart's dial-up system works something like this: (1) store manager electronically sends purchase orders to K Mart headquarters, (2) store order is "homogenized" in the ordering system, (3) consolidated purchase orders for each store are available each morning, and (4) each vendor has an assigned path and time slot for calling K Mart headquarters to obtain orders.[3]

■ *Third-party clearing houses*—a third-party data-processing company makes arrangements to (1) receive orders and invoices, (2) sort them by addressees, (3) store them on-line, and (4) allow subsequent access by authorized addressees. This method would allow the use of a standardized machine language to establish a bridge for common communication, thereby eliminating the need for separate and distinct methodologies among various vendors and retailers. The May Co.–Haggar experiment with an EPO system utilized the clearinghouse approach.[4]

To the retailer, the advantages of the EPO system include more effective management of inventory, more effective open-to-buy systems, and reduction of ordering lead times, thereby improving in-stock positions and stock turnovers while reducing inventory carrying costs.

Following Up

The retailer that wants to be sure that the right order is received in the right place at the right time will develop follow-up procedures. Following up an order is also necessary to make a purchase contract legally binding. In most cases, the original copy of the purchase order, which is sent to the supplier, constitutes a legal *offer to buy*. No purchase contract exists, however, until the seller *accepts* the buyer's offer.[5] Therefore, the first step in following up an order is to determine whether the supplier has accepted the order to do so. The retailer should maintain adequate records, including the supplier's formal notification of acceptance for each order. Suppliers usually notify the retailer of their acceptance by returning the acknowledgment copy of the order form or by using their own acceptance forms. Follow-up procedures also include checking the supplier's acceptance form to determine whether the supplier has made any changes in the order. Such changes could legally bind the retailer unless they "materially alter the intent of the offer or unless the buyer files a written objection to their inclusion."[6] Retailers use both routine and special procedures in following up an order.

Routine Follow-Up

Routine follow-up procedures are *used to check for order acceptance and discrepancies between the retailer's original order and the supplier's acceptance.* Various types of filing systems are used to "flag" purchase orders that have not been checked. The buyer manually or electronically reviews the files frequently to determine which orders require additional attention. Routine procedures also are used to check on the progress of orders for merchandise that are considered either extremely important or overdue. Once these important or overdue orders are identified, the buyer contacts the supplier to check on the status of the order. Depending upon the circumstances, the buyer will routinely send either a postcard, a personal letter, or a telegram. If the circumstances are urgent, a telephone call might be used.

Special Follow-Up

Special follow-up procedures are *used if the importance of the order merits them.* These special procedures usually involve the use of a field expediter (e.g., resident buyer) who makes a personal visit to the supplier. Such personal visits generally are seen as the strongest method available for putting pressure on the supplier to meet its obligations.

Once the order has been placed and received, the retailer must efficiently process incoming shipments to ensure their timely arrival on the sales floor. Figure 18–4 illustrates the tasks associated with in-store handling of incoming merchandise shipments.

Receiving is *the actual physical exchange of goods between the retailer and the supplier's transporting agent.* It is the point at which the retailer takes physical possession of the goods. **Checking** is *the process of determining whether the supplier has shipped what the retailer ordered and whether what was shipped has arrived in good condition.*

RECEIVING AND CHECKING

Receiving Process

Retailers receive their merchandise in a variety of ways. The nature of the retailer's business along with the retailer's physical facilities dictates to a large extent how goods are brought into the store (see Figure 18–5). Large stores usually require more elaborate receiving facilities and procedures than do small stores. Merchandise that is either large and bulky or that is ordered in large quantities needs a greater amount of space within the receiving center. Also, high-value merchandise must have greater control and security than low-value merchandise. Whatever the retailer's particular situation, receiving facilities and procedures should be designed to meet the store's individual needs.

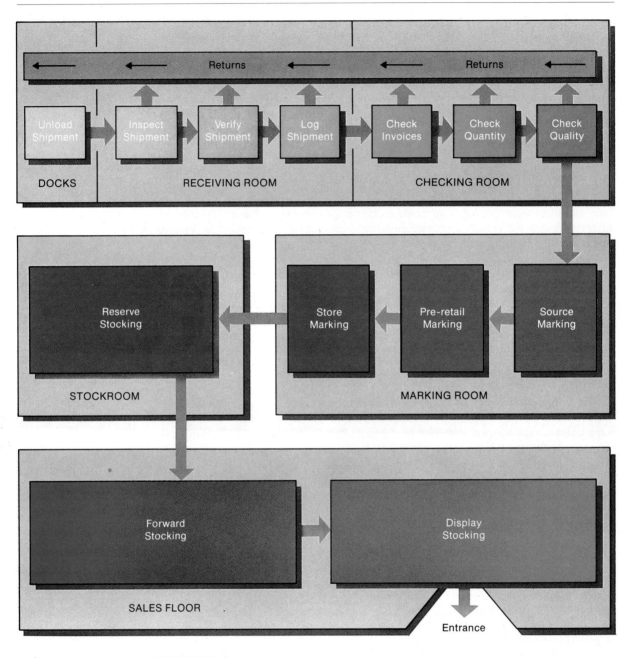

FIGURE 18–4
The in-store merchandise-handling process

Receiving Facilities

Retailers can receive their merchandise shipments through either the front door (customer entrance) or the back door. Generally, the retailer should avoid front-door receiving for a number of reasons. First, it interferes with the smooth flow of customer traffic. Second, receiving, checking, and stocking areas usually are located in remote areas in the back of the store. Third, the front door and the sales floor are not designed to accommodate receiving activities, so there is an increased like-

After a buyer at Boston-headquartered Filene's writes out an order it gets initialled approval by a dmm, if up to $50,000; by a gmm, if between $50,000 and $100,000; and by a front office executive if for more.

Upon approval, the order, which bears the buyer's "due in store" time—a window spread of ten days for domestic goods—is given to a computer clerk for typing.

One of several print-outs goes to Donald F. Ralph, director of transportation logistics, at the Natick distribution center 12 miles west on Interstate 90 (Mass. Pike). A week's batch of these is computer summarized for Ralph, becoming his RAM (Receiving and Marking) report. This gives him preliminary cues for staffing his receiving and processing area in days ahead.

Then RAM gets daily fine-tuning.

Right outside Ralph's office, his traffic supervisor, Mark Piaget, spends a quarter hour each noontime at an IBM 3101 computer keyboard. By entry password and a five letter codeword meaning "shipping inquiry" he reaches, in succession, headquarters mainframes of the five national surface carriers among a total of nine that Filene's routinely uses. (There were 30 carriers as recently as 1982.)

Within a few seconds, back from each carrier headquarters will come, on screen and printed out, a listing of all loads headed for Natick. It will show trailer numbers, vendors, carton or garment counts, weights, and in-transit truck locations at time of inquiry.

With these five computered reports, plus four more gathered by phone from regional carriers, Ralph or an assistant is set to match information with the RAM report. They are ready to have employee calls balanced with work loads to order preticketing, to alert the promotion department, and to make any other preparations necessary.

Ralph will even know exactly what the freight pay-out will be. And he will always know there will be no need for subsequent audit, because Filene's has contracts with each carrier at a simplified Freight of All Kinds (FAK) tariff.

Ralph explains, "The standard New York-to-Boston hundredweight charge for lampshades is $11. For most apparel it is $8.50. For cosmetics it is $7. Our contract-arranged rate with Ryder/P.I.E. is a simplified $8 for any and all goods."

Ralph mentions Ryder/P.I.E. particularly because he credits that carrier for initiating the program of vendor-carrier-retailer liaisons fully described in the accompanying article—a program he claims is an important step toward a paperless, minimal error, cost-effective system.

"From the standpoints of service and rates, every one of our nine carriers deserves four stars," he says, "but Ryder/P.I.E. is the first really to close the loop connecting our vendors and ourselves—to provide management-information for the traffic function."

Some 93% of Filene's incoming freight is by highway, including a 7% chunk by United Parcel Service; 7% is by air through Boston's international airport.

Ironically, one of Ryder/P.I.E.'s competitors is the Wm. Filene's Sons Co. itself!

The $450 million volume department store has a fleet of 100 trailers and 20 tractors used primarily for serving its 14 upstairs and its 15 famous automatic-markdown Basement stores from their respective distribution centers.

But Filene's is owned by Federated Department Stores, and since there are some 400 Federated vendors in Filene's trading area, a back-haul trucking tactic has very naturally developed to serve not only Filene's, but other Federated stores. Runs are mainly from vendors to New York City shippers/consolidators, "and we're pretty decent with our family members in rate negotiations," says Ralph.

All but bulk-shipped imports are pre-allotted to Filene's individual upstairs store as they come into the Natick center. But virtually everything for the Basement stores get post-allotted in their two centers, one for fashions, another for the balance. A substantial amount of this basement inflow is opportunistically purchased overstock from other retailers, Filene's Basement being one of the nation's most notable pioneer off-pricers (1909-founded).

Testifying to the advantages of post-allotment for big-volume retailers is Filene's aim to switch Natick to that policy, starting this fall.

Another goal, says Ralph, is to make freight payments electronically, immediately upon receipt of goods—a week ahead of due date, thus being in position to earn anticipatory interest from the float.

Source: "At Filene's: Closing the Gap with Vendors," *Stores* (April, 1984), 57.

FIGURE 18–5

At Filene's: Closing the gap with vendors

lihood of damaged shipping cartons as well as the sales floor display fixtures. Additionally, it creates problems in trying to maintain a clean sales floor. Finally, receiving shipments through the front door is simply inconsistent with many retailers' store images.

Regardless of how the merchandise is brought into the store or how small the store, adequate space should be set aside for receiving merchandise. The typical back-door receiving operation consists of an unloading area and a receiving area. The area devoted to the unloading of merchandise should permit easy maneuverability and facilitate careful handling. For large stores, unloading docks must be large enough to allow forklift trucks to handle bulky merchandise and quantity shipments that arrive on pallets. Large unloading docks also are useful for sorting and organizing incoming shipments before they are moved to the receiving area. Equally important is the *height* of the unloading dock. Merchandise that must be thrown up or down from a delivery vehicle increases the amount of work to unload a truck as well as the chances of damaging the incoming merchandise. The door(s) leading from the unloading area to the receiving area should be designed to facilitate easy access. Large overhead doors should be designed to be out of the way, to handle any type of unloading device, and to permit two-way traffic. In addition to forklift trucks, some retailers have installed such mechanical unloading devices as chutes, roller conveyors, and overhead conveyor systems to facilitate the unloading process.

The receiving area usually is located adjacent to the unloading area on the store's ground floor. It should be large enough to permit easy maneuverability, to allow inspection of incoming shipments, and to act as a holding area for merchandise awaiting transfer to the checking room. The layout of the receiving room should be designed to facilitate the inspection of incoming packages and cartons. The receiving room typically is equipped with tables (stationary and portable) and conveyor systems for inspecting small packages and cartons. Holding bins of various types and sizes also are employed as temporary storage facilities for shipments awaiting further processing. For large cartons and bulk shipments, the retailer should allow enough floor space in the receiving area for the shipment to be spread out and inspected.

Receiving Procedures

The responsibility for receiving merchandise in large stores usually is delegated to a full-time receiving clerk who is held accountable for any errors in receiving goods and documenting the receipt. Receiving responsibilities in small stores often are assumed by either the store manager, assistant manager, or one of the sales personnel. In addition to the responsibility of controlling incoming merchandise, the receiving department also must control the flow of outgoing merchandise to the sales floor. Store sales personnel should not be allowed to remove merchandise from the receiving room until it has been properly processed. Proper processing normally involves the three basic activities of inspecting, verifying, and logging incoming shipments.

Inspecting shipments. Standard procedures for inspecting incoming merchandise involve several activities. First, all incoming shipments are placed so that each package (box or carton) in the shipment is clearly visible. Next, a visual inspection of the exterior of each package is conducted to determine whether the package has been damaged (crushed, punctured) or opened (broken seal). If a package has been badly damaged or opened, the receiving clerk should refuse to accept the shipment unless the carrier's employee agrees to serve as a witness to the visual inspection of the contents inside the package. Packages that are slightly damaged may be accepted, but before signing for the shipment, the receiving clerk should make a notation of the damage on all transportation and receiving documents. These notations will facilitate the processing of any future damage or loss claims by both the store and the supplier.

Verifying shipments. The receiving clerk should make several verifications after the shipment has been inspected for visual damage. First, the clerk must verify that the shipment was ordered. This step is accomplished by consulting the receiving department's file of purchase orders or a log (schedule) of incoming shipments. Most retailers require suppliers to mark each package with the purchase-order number. Second, the completeness of the shipment must be verified. Sometimes suppliers will ship only partial orders. In such cases, the retailer may or may not decide to accept shipment depending upon its needs at the time. Third, the receiving clerk should verify that the actual makeup of the shipment is the same as that described on the bill of lading. The number of cartons in the shipment and the weight of each carton should also be checked to see if they correspond to the bill of lading. Fourth, freight charges sometimes are verified by comparing the total weight of the shipment with various rate schedules. Finally, additional verification might include recording the name and address of the supplier and the carrier, the name of the person making the delivery, and the delivery date.

Logging shipments. To facilitate and organize the processing of incoming shipments, each shipment is logged in a receiving record and assigned a receiving number. The **receiving record** *and number follow the shipment through the checking, marking, and stocking steps of the procurement process and serve as a quick reference should problems occur.* The accounting department also uses the record to verify shipment before invoices are paid. Further, the record can be used as a source of identification if the merchandise must be returned. The information logged in the receiving record includes (1) the purchase-order number, (2) the supplier's name and address, (3) the number of invoices, (4) the number of packages in the shipment, (5) the name and address of the carrier, (6) the delivery date, (7) the condition of the shipment, (8) the weight of the shipment, (9) transportation charges, and (10) identification of the department for which the merchandise was ordered.

Checking Process

After inspecting, verifying, and logging the shipment, the retailer must check the merchandise contained in the shipment. While the checking of the merchandise can be conducted in the receiving room, most retailers prefer to have a separate area or room (if space permits) in which to accomplish this task. Checking involves opening each package, removing the merchandise, and examining the package's contents. Given the nature of these activities and the chances for damaging or losing merchandise, a separate, spacious, protected checking area is quite desirable. Accessibility to the receiving area and to the marking and stocking rooms must be considered in locating the checking room. The ideal layout locates all these rooms in a straight line—receiving to checking to marking to stocking.

What to Check

The retailer can make three checks to ensure it has received what it ordered: an invoice, a quantity, and a quality check. *The retailer compares the invoice with the purchase order in the* **invoice check**. The invoice is the supplier's bill and is the document that itemizes particulars of the shipment in terms of merchandise assortment, quantity, and price. It also identifies the terms of the sale, delivery terms, and the amount due for payment. Checking personnel must determine whether there is an exact match between the retailer's purchase order and the supplier's invoice.

During the **quantity check,** *the checking personnel unpack and sort each package to check the actual physical contents of each package against the purchase order, the invoice, or both.* Essentially, the checker sorts each package by style, size, and color (or other assortment factors) and makes a physical count to determine whether the package contains the same number of units as are listed on the invoice and purchase order. Any shortages, overages, or substitutions are noted and reported to the buyer or merchandise manager. It is not an uncommon practice for some suppliers to ship substitute merchandise if they are out of the merchandise that was ordered. Equally common are honest mistakes by the supplier in filling the order—shipping the wrong assortment of styles, sizes, and colors is to be expected on occasion. The retailer should not tolerate many incorrect shipments, though; instead, it should begin to look for alternative suppliers.

The third check is the **quality check,** which *actually involves two separate checks.* First, the merchandise is examined for any damage that is obviously the result of shipping. Such damage is the responsibility of the carrier and the insurer of the shipment. The second check is for imperfections in the merchandise and for lesser-quality merchandise than the retailer ordered. Regular checking personnel can detect merchandise that has either been damaged in shipment or has obvious imperfections (cracked, stained, scratched, torn). However, the detection of lower-than-ordered quality creates problems. Usually if checking personnel suspect that merchandise might be of lower quality than what was ordered, they should inform either the buyer or the merchandise manager, who makes the final determination on the quality.

How to Check

The retailer can use any one of four methods to check the quantity of incoming shipments. They are the direct check, the blind check, the semiblind check, and the combination check. With the **direct check** system, *the retailer checks off from the invoice, which lists all of the ordered and shipped items, each group of items as they are counted.* If the invoice is not available and the merchandise is needed on the sales floor, the retailer can make a direct check against the purchase order to verify the quantity. Speed and simplicity are the principal advantages of the direct check. The **blind check** is *a procedure in which the checker lists and describes each merchandise group on a blank form and then counts and records the number of items in each group.* The checker may also record any additional information deemed pertinent. Next, the buyer, merchandise manager, or some other knowledgeable person compares the checker's list and descriptions with the invoice or purchase order to determine whether any discrepancies exist. Generally, the blind method is the most accurate for checking incoming shipments, but it is also the most expensive due to the additional time and labor involved.

The **semiblind check** is *a checking technique that provides the checker with a list and description of each merchandise group in the shipment but not the quantities for each group.* The checker must physically count and record the number of items in each merchandise group. The semiblind method has the advantages of being both reasonably fast and accurate. The **combination method** is *simply using* *the direct check method when the supplier's invoice is available and the blind or semiblind check method when the retailer does not have the supplier's invoice.*

When to Report

It is extremely important that the retailer promptly report any damages or discrepancies to the appropriate person upon completion of the checking process. The retailer must report or return unwanted merchandise immediately to receive prompt and fair adjustments. The longer these goods are left in the store, the more difficult receiving satisfactory adjustments on claims becomes. When damages or losses result from shipment, the retailer should quickly notify all concerned parties.

Where to Report

The retailer should immediately notify the appropriate supplier when discrepancies occur between (1) the supplier's invoice and the retailer's purchase order, (2) the supplier's invoice and the quantity check, or (3) the quality ordered and the quality received. Merchandise adjustments and return privileges and procedures will be discussed later in this chapter. To ensure a timely response, the retailer should immediately notify the carrier and insurer of the shipment. Finally, the buyer, merchandise manager, department manager, and the accounting office should be notified of any problem shipment so that they can adjust their plans accordingly.

Marking is *affixing to merchandise the information necessary for stocking, controlling, and selling.* Customers want information on the price, size, and color of merchandise before they are willing to buy, and the retailer needs to know when and from where the merchandise was secured, its cost, and where it goes in order to maintain proper inventory and record controls. **Stocking** *includes all of the activities associated with in-store and between-store distribution of merchandise.* Stocking may involve moving merchandise to the sales floor for display or to the reserve or stocking rooms for storage.

MARKING AND STOCKING

Marking Activities

The facilities, equipment, procedures, and personnel used in marking merchandise should be tailored to the volume and type of merchandise to be marked. Small, hand- and mechanically operated marking systems usually are sufficient for most small retail operations. More sophisticated mechanical and electronic systems are more appropriate for large retailing organizations with sufficient merchandise volume to justify the expense. Regardless of which system is installed, developing and maintaining controlled marking procedures are necessary for several reasons. First, well-marked merchandise is necessary for customer selection. Customers need informative, easy-to-read tags to make their merchandise selections without the aid of the store's sales personnel. Unmarked or poorly marked merchandise often discourages the customer from considering the merchandise beyond an initial inspection. Well-marked merchandise is especially important to the self-service and self-selection retailer, where sales floor assistance may not always be readily available to the customer. Second, clearly and informatively marked merchandise also can aid in the selling activities of store personnel. Tags and tickets containing information on size, color, style, and supplier can be useful to the salesperson trying to provide the level of assistance the customer expects. They also are useful in aiding sales personnel in stocking and organizing sales floor displays. Third, well-marked merchandise aids sales personnel in handling returns and adjustments. Sales personnel can more easily find the proper place on the sales floor to put returned merchandise when the merchandise is marked with the correct information.

Marking procedures also can aid store personnel in deciding whether to accept returned merchandise. Sometimes customers bring merchandise to a store for a refund or an exchange when, in fact, the merchandise was purchased from a different store carrying different brands at different prices. Some customers intentionally do this to obtain a higher cash refund than the price they paid at another store; others do so innocently and unintentionally.

Finally, good marking procedures permit better inventory control. One of the first steps a retailer should take in organizing a stock and record-control system is to ensure that all incoming merchandise is properly marked. The value of well-marked merchandise is enormous when taking both book and physical inventory.

Marking Systems

Physically marking merchandise can be handled in a number of ways. The three most common marking systems are source marking, preretailing, and store marking. **Source marking** is *the system by which the retailer authorizes the manufacturer or supplier to mark the merchandise before it is shipped to the store.* The merchandise is marked either with preprinted tickets sent to the supplier by the retailer or with tickets printed by the manufacturer based on information supplied by the retailer. Source marking reduces both in-store marking expenses and the time it takes the retailer to get the merchandise onto the sales floor. When a standard tag code and format are used, the retailer can make very effective use of electronic data processing equipment. Used on a wide range of staple goods and some fashion goods, source marking can be offered as a service with a separate charge or as a free service. If a supplier offers marking services free of charge to one of its customers, the Robinson-Patman Act requires that all competing retailers be informed of the service and allowed to take advantage of it under similar circumstances.

Preretailing is *a retail buying practice of deciding upon the selling price of merchandise before it is purchased and recording that price on the store's copy of the purchase order* so that the store's "markers" can put the selling price on the merchandise as soon as it comes through the doors. Store personnel who are responsible for marking merchandise can do so upon its arrival without having to contact the store buyer, since the price is on the store's purchase order. Sometimes the store buyer is away at trade shows or performing other duties and cannot be reached. Without preretailing, marking personnel at some stores would leave the merchandise unmarked because of lack of instructions, and the merchandise would remain off the sales floor for an extended period. Preretailing also forces the buyer to consider the price before the merchandise is ordered and carefully consider an adequate markup.

Store marking is *the practice of having store personnel mark all merchandise after the store has received it.* It also is used to complete the marking process initiated in the preretailing system. When using store marking, the retailer must invest in marking facilities and equipment and establish marking procedures. An example of store marking occurs when supermarket "stock personnel" use hand-held markers to stamp prices on canned goods in the aisles.

Marking Facilities

Merchandise should be marked before it reaches the sales floor. To use sales personnel to mark merchandise on the sales floor is not only more costly but also sometimes creates additional problems such as sidestepping the stockers cited in the preceding example. The most common problems associated with marking merchandise on the sales floor are (1) a greater frequency of errors, slower performance, and poorer-quality work due to the distractions that normally occur with sales floor activities; (2) a lack of security for marking tags and equipment left unsupervised, thereby affording unscrupulous customers the opportunity to alter the price of previously marked merchandise; (3) a loss of sales because sales personnel were busy marking merchandise; (4) a messy-appearing sales floor; (5) the interference with a smooth customer traffic flow due to the marking activities.

Marking Equipment

Marking merchandise can be accomplished through the use of hand, mechanical, and electronic equipment. The size and nature of the retailer's operation often determine which type of equipment is most appropriate.

Hand marking. Hand marking involves the use of grease pencils, ink stamps, and pens. The desired information is marked directly on either the merchandise or its package, or on a gummed label, string tag, or pin ticket attached to the merchandise. Hand marking is the least desirable method of marking merchandise because it (1) is more time consuming, (2) results in more marking errors, and (3) lacks permanency and neatness. Further, price security is jeopardized, since grease and ink markings can be blotted out, smeared, and easily changed.

Mechanical marking. Mechanical equipment is capable of producing tags and tickets in both printed (human-readable language) and punched (machine-readable language) forms. Marking machines offer the advantages of fewer errors, faster speed, greater permanency, more legibility, and a higher level of price security than hand marking. Also, more information can be placed on smaller tags using mechanical as opposed to hand marking, and some mechanical marking devices allow the operator to attach the tag to the merchandise automatically, thereby reducing labor costs.

Electronic marking. Recent technological advancements in electronic (computer-controlled) equipment have generated a wave of new marking procedures that are compatible with various **point-of-sale (POS)** systems. Electronic marking devices can code prices onto tickets and tags that can be quickly and automatically read and processed by optical scanning equipment or optical character recognition (OCR) systems. Optical scanners usually are employed at checkout counters, where they read all information on the ticket or tag and transmit that information to the store's computer system for further processing (e.g., for inventory control and accounting records). While the checkout counter wand is the most common type of optical scanner used in general merchandise retailing, fixed-slot scanners (checkout counters with built-in laser beams that read tags as the merchandise is passed over the beam) are the predominant system used in the supermarket industry.

Marking Procedures

In making decisions on marking systems, facilities, and equipment, the retailer must decide what and how much information to place on the tag, where and how to attach the tag to the merchandise, and when to use bulk marking.

Coding merchandise tags. Most retailers want more than just price information on their merchandise tags. The most common information they want, in addition to the retail price, is

- size
- color
- style
- department identification number
- supplier identification number
- merchandise class identification number
- merchandise receiving date
- merchandise stocking date (sales floor)
- cost of the merchandise

The retail price, along with the size, color, and style of the merchandise, should be placed on the tag in such a manner that the customer can easily identify this information. The department, supplier, and the merchandise class most frequently are identified by means of the National Retail Merchants Association's classification system. The last three informational requirements (receiving date, stocking date, and cost of the merchandise) are placed on the tag in coded form to disguise such information from the customers. In marking merchandise, retailers can choose to use either a standardized or customized system.

With the installation of optical scanners, many retailers have elected to use a standardized marking system. These universal vendor marking (UVM) systems involve coding merchandise tags with a machine-readable code that is sponsored by one or more trade associations. The National Retail Merchants Association sponsors the **optical character recognition-font A (OCR-A)** code which is equally human and machine readable. Figure 18–6 illustrates the OCR-A. The second standardized code in common use is the **universal product code (UPC)**. Used largely within the supermarket industry, the UPC is *a bar code system that identifies both the product and the manufacturer.* Currently, the retail industry is attempting to develop standards for placing both OCR-A and UPC on the same ticket, thereby creating one universal marking system.

Many retailers have their own customized marking system. Receiving and stocking dates, for example, are coded using a transformation of the date by addition, subtraction, multiplication, or division. A receiving date of 10–12–80 could be transformed to 40–42–110 by adding 30 to the month, day, and year. Reversing their position (to 110–42–40) can further disguise the dates.

Two types of cost codes are commonly used: word and symbol codes. **Word cost codes** *use a 10-letter word or words in which no letter is repeated.* Some popular word codes are MAKE PROFIT, MONEY TALKS, and REPUBLICAN. Each letter in the word code is assigned a single-digit number. For example,

$$\begin{array}{cccccccccc} M & O & N & E & Y & & T & A & L & K & S \\ 1 & 2 & 3 & 4 & 5 & & 6 & 7 & 8 & 9 & 0 \end{array}$$

To use such a cost code, the retailer would code EYES on the price tag for a merchandise item that costs $45.40. **Symbol cost codes** *use easy-to-recognize symbols as direct substitutes for numbers.* One such system of symbols is[7]

$$\begin{array}{c|c|c} 1 & 2 & 3 \\ \hline 4 & 5 & 6 \\ \hline 7 & 8 & 9 \end{array}$$

$$X = 0$$

Simply stated, OCR-A is a type style equally as readable as that used in the publishing of this text with one important unique characteristic—it is also completely acceptable to computer controlled reading devices, commonly called "wands" or "scanners." Here is a sample of OCR-A—the characters used in the NRMA voluntary identification standard:

A C D M N P R U X Y

1 2 3 4 5 6 7 8 9 0

$ > . / "

Acknowledging that it is easily read, here is how it can be formatted to provide in-store marking:

C10422 012

P46301314

M45 196

16½ x 36

>$15.00

Human and computer interpretation of this is relatively easy: the "C," "P," and "M" are used to identify each of the data components in merchandise description.

- The "C" line—covers Department 104, Class 22, and Season Code 012 (12th week in 1980)
- The "P" line—Vendor (or House) number 463, Style 01314
- The "M" line—Color Code 45 represents light blue, Size Code 196 represents Shirt Size 16½ x 36.
- The actual shirt size is printed for the customer's convenience in a non-OCR-A style of print.
- The price is printed in OCR-A for both human reading and machine processing.

This illustration indicates the identification for merchandise to the finest level of detail—generally referred to as SKU, or stockkeeping unit, level. Within the OCR-A standard there is complete flexibility in the level of marking detail, in addition to full SKU:

- Department, class, and price
- Department, class, vendor, stock number (or style), and price
- Department, class, vendor, stock (or style), color, and price
- Department, class, vendor, stock (or style), size, and price

Source: National Retail Merchants Association, "OCR-A Marking System: Its Application as Today's Marking Technology," *Receiving, Marking, and Handling Merchandise* (New York: NRMA, 1981), 64.

FIGURE 18–6
What is OCR-A?

The same merchandise item costing the retailer $45.40 would be coded as X. The main limitations of symbol codes are that they take longer to write than either letters or numbers, and the marker is usually less familiar with such symbols and thus prone to make mistakes. Whatever coding device is used for disguising date and cost information, it should be in human- and machine-readable forms.

Attaching merchandise tags.   Price tags can be attached to merchandise in a variety of ways and places. Price tags are attached by strings, pins, snaps, gummed labels, and heat seals. To prevent price tag switching, retailers should attach tags so that customers cannot easily remove them without damaging or destroying the tag. At the same time, the tag must be attached so that store personnel can remove it at the point of sale without damaging the merchandise. Visibility and consistency are the key considerations in deciding where to place the tags on the merchandise. With merchandise marked in the same place, both customers and store employees can readily locate the tag. Such visibility and consistency prevent the unnecessary opening of packages, maintain cleaner and neater displays, and reduce wear and tear on merchandise.

Re-marking merchandise tags.   Re-marking merchandise often becomes necessary due to damage, obsolescence, or an increase in the wholesale price. Whatever the reasons for re-marking, the retailer must accomplish this task with the same care as the original marking. In re-marking merchandise, the retailer should set strict policies on how markdowns are to be shown. Some retailers manually re-mark merchandise on the sales floor by crossing out the old price and adding the new price to the ticket. While this policy permits the customer to identify the price as a reduced price, it also identifies the merchandise as being somewhat undesirable, at least at the former price. Manual re-marking also increases the opportunity for consumer fraud—the retailer that re-marks with a red ballpoint pen is inviting some customers to do a little re-marking of their own. Other retailers prefer to send the merchandise back to the marking room for re-marking and to replace the old price tag with a new one. The use of the marking room for re-marking provides both greater security and greater accuracy. The use of new price tags for merchandise that has been marked down offers the retailer the opportunity to sell the merchandise at a lower price without the negative connotation of its being inferior merchandise.

In re-marking merchandise to reflect price increases, retailers should remove the old price tag and replace it with a new one. Covering up the price simply invites the customer to have a peek at the old price. It also is an invitation to remove the new tag. More important, all customers will be somewhat dissatisfied with the merchandise and the store knowing that they had to pay a higher price. Some customers may even refuse to buy the merchandise solely because of the increase. Equally important is the detrimental effect that visible price increases can have on the store's image.

Bulk marking.   Retailers frequently elect to use bulk marking on merchandise that is characterized by low unit value, high turnover, and suitabile size and shape for bin, rack, or table displays. Individual marking is too expensive for many hardware items, variety goods, candies, and toiletries. **Bulk marking** *involves simply placing similar merchandise with the same price in a display and attaching one price card to the display.* It can save time in marking and speed the delivery of merchandise to the sales floor.

Stocking Activities

Once the merchandise has been marked, the retailer must decide where to stock the merchandise. The retailer can utilize an in-store or warehouse stocking plan or some combination of the two plans.

In-Store Stocking

The primary goal in stocking for many retailers is to move the merchandise as close as possible to its selling point. To accomplish this goal, most retailers follow the policy of **in-store stocking,** *maximizing the amount of display and forward stock and minimizing the amount of stock in reserve.* **Display stock** *is stock placed on various display fixtures that customers can directly examine.* **Forward stock** *is backup stock that is temporarily stored on the sales floor near its selling department.*

What are the advantages of this type of in-store stocking fixture?

Forward stock may be carried in perimeter storage areas around the department or in drawers or cupboards beneath the sales floor display fixtures. **Reserve stock** is *backup stock held in reserve, usually in a central stockroom.* Because reserve stocks frequently create access problems for sales personnel, most retailers prefer to limit the amount of stock in these areas. Reserve stocks usually are converted to forward or display stocks as quickly as possible.

Warehouse Stocking

Warehouse stocking is often used in addition to or in place of in-store display, forward, and reserve stocking. For certain types of merchandise or under certain operating conditions, warehouse stocking is necessary or at least more efficient. Bulky products such as furniture and appliances usually require warehouse stocking, since the retailer must limit the amount of display stock on the sales floor. Forward stocking is generally prohibitive for such products. Disassembled products that retailers sell in their cartons are usually picked up by the consumer at a warehouse delivery door or are delivered to the customer's home by the retailer. Seasonal products typically are held in warehouses until the appropriate selling season.

Many retailers find it desirable to use central warehouse and distribution centers that serve several stores because of the operating conditions associated with chain store operations. The receiving, checking, marking, and stocking functions are initially accomplished at these regional facilities, then the merchandise is distributed to individual stores. These central facilities often are more efficient based on the economies of scale that large retailers can realize in ordering, transporting, and processing incoming merchandise and in using modern, expensive facilities and equipment. A recent development in the use of central facilities is to place less emphasis on storage and more emphasis on distribution. In essence, the overall goal of these central facilities is to keep the merchandise moving in the right direction to where it is needed. Many retailers can keep merchandise storage costs to a minimum using this policy.

523

Regardless of where stocking occurs, three elements are necessary to ensure its success: *accessibility, security,* and *controllability.* Stocks must be accessible to authorized personnel to maintain the flow of merchandise to the final consumer. While strict policies and procedures are necessary to ensure the security of the merchandise, these policies and procedures should not be unduly cumbersome. When temporary stockouts occur on the sales floor, sales personnel should be able to replenish display stocks from either forward or reserve stocks with minimal time and effort. Otherwise, a strong temptation exists for sales personnel to inform customers that the shortage is permanent.

Security and controllability go hand in hand. To avoid unacceptable shrinkage levels, merchandise must be secured from customer theft, employee pilferage, damage from dirt, dust, and the elements, and misplacement. Essentially, security involves limited access to the merchandise, good housekeeping, and careful maintenance of records.

PAYING AND RETURNING

Paying Invoices

Paying *involves the procedures for processing and settling suppliers' invoices.* In large organizations, the accounting department is responsible for making payments. The owner, manager, or bookkeeper in small retail establishments assumes the responsibilities of rendering payments. Most retailers prefer to pay invoices after they have received and checked the merchandise. This preference is especially strong when the retailer is dealing with an unknown supplier or suppliers whose return and adjustment policies on damaged merchandise and incorrect shipments are either restrictive or unknown. Sometimes invoices must be paid prior to receiving and checking to take full advantage of cash discounts that were negotiated.

Returning Shipments

Returns *occur when a retailer does not accept all or part of a merchandise shipment and sends some or all of the merchandise back to the supplier.* In returning merchandise to the supplier, the retailer must carefully determine whether it has legitimate reasons for the returns. Unfair returns along with unfair cancellations are two key causes of friction between suppliers and retailers. As discussed previously, good supplier relationships are critical to successful retailing operations. Unfairly returning merchandise jeopardizes good relationships between the supplier and the retailer.

When returns are justified, retailers should use their own return forms. The retailer typically fills the form out in triplicate and sends the original copy to the supplier with the returned merchandise. The buyer retains the second copy, and the accounting department holds the third copy. It is, however, a good idea to contact the supplier before processing the return form and returning the merchandise. Most suppliers have their own return procedures, and retailers can save a considerable amount of time and effort if they work out prior agreements on returns. Depending on the nature of the complaint and the reason for the return, the supplier may elect either to credit the retailer's account, ship replacement merchandise, or refuse to make an adjustment on the grounds that the return is unfair. Discussing the return prior to any action could save both parties considerable handling and transportation costs as well as unnecessary effort.

SUMMARY

The procurement process includes all of the physical operations associated with getting the merchandise into the store and onto the shelves. The four basic steps in procurement are ordering and following up, receiving and checking, marking and stocking, and paying and returning.

Retailers must develop the necessary procedures for ordering merchandise—in either oral or written form—and for following up on those orders, which is necessary to make a purchase contract legally binding. Receiving is the physical exchange of goods between the retailer and the supplier's transporting agent. Retailers must plan facilities and procedures for receiving, inspecting, verifying, and logging incoming shipments. Checking is the process of determining whether the supplier has shipped what the retailer ordered and whether it has arrived in good condition. Personnel are trained to know what and how to check merchandise and when and where to report any problems.

Marking is affixing to the merchandise the information necessary for stocking, controlling, and selling the merchandise. Marking systems retailers use include source marking, preretailing, and store marking. Retailers must decide what and how much information to place on merchandise tags, where and how to attach tags to merchandise, and how to re-mark merchandise. Stocking includes the activities associated with in-store and between-store distribution of merchandise. The primary goal of stocking is to move the merchandise as close as possible to its selling point.

Paying involves the procedures for processing and settling the supplier's invoice. Returning merchandise becomes necessary when a legitimate reason exists for not accepting the supplier's shipment.

KEY TERMS AND CONCEPTS

procurement process

order form

electronic purchase-order system (EPO)

routine follow-up

special follow-up

receiving

checking

receiving record

invoice check

quantity check

quality check

direct check

blind check

semiblind check

combination check

marking

stocking

source marking

preretailing

store marking

point-of-sale (POS)

optical character recognition-font A (OCR-A)

universal product code (UPC)

word cost codes

symbol cost codes

bulk marking

in-store stocking

display stock

forward stock

reserve stock

warehouse stocking

paying

returns

REVIEW QUESTIONS

1. Why would you recommend that retailers use their own purchase-order form?
2. What options do retailers have in structuring their electronic purchase-order system?
3. What is the strongest follow-up method available to the retailer for putting pressure on suppliers to meet their obligations?
4. Why should the retailer avoid front-door receiving?
5. What are the three basic activities normally associated with proper receiving procedures? Describe each activity.
6. The retailer makes three checks to see that it has received what was ordered. What are the three checks?
7. How might the retailer check quantities of incoming shipments?
8. What are the three most common marking systems? Briefly describe each system.
9. Why is hand marking the least desirable method of marking merchandise?
10. What are the two most commonly used standardized marking systems for coding merchandise tags?
11. Using the word code REPUBLICAN, what is the cost of a merchandise item with the code of BANE?
12. When is bulk marking used?
13. What options does the retailer have for in-store stocking? Describe each option.
14. What three guidelines should be used when developing a stocking plan?
15. When should the retailer pay invoices?

ENDNOTES

1. See Jules Abend, "Computer Links," *Stores* (June, 1984), 75.
2. See National Retail Merchants Association, "The Future—Electronic Purchase Order and Invoice," *Receiving, Marking, and Merchandise Handling* (New York: NRMA, 1981), 71–78.
3. See "At K-Mart: Nearly 200 Vendors Now on a Direct Electronic Purchase Order System: How It Is Working," *Stores* (May, 1981), 50–52.
4. Abend, "Computer Links," 75.
5. Lamar Lee, Jr., and Donald W. Dobler, *Purchasing and Materials Management: Text and Cases* (New York: McGraw-Hill, 1979), 420.
6. Ibid.
7. John W. Wingate, Elmer O. Schaller, and F. Leonard Miller, *Retail Merchandise Management* (Englewood Cliffs, NJ: Prentice-Hall, 1972), 154.

RELATED READINGS

Corr, Fitzhugh L. "Scanners in Marketing Research: Paradise (Almost)." *Marketing News* (January 4, 1985), 1, 15.

Fox, Harold W. "Scanners in Supermarkets: Past, Present, and Prospects." *1984 Proceedings.* J. R. Lumpkin and J. C. Crawford, eds. (Southwestern Marketing Association 1984), 56–59.

Harris, Brian F., and Mills, Michael K. "The Impact of Item Price Removal on Grocery Shopping Behavior." *Journal of Retailing* 56 (Winter 1980), 73–93.

Hollander, Stanley C. "Merchandise Shortages and Retail Policies." *Business Topics* (Summer 1978), 27–33.

Jackson, Gary B., and Racer, Miriam J. "Shopper Attitude Related to the Use of the Electronic Scanner in Grocery Stores." *1985 Proceedings.* J. C. Crawford and B. C. Garland, eds. (Southwestern Marketing Association 1985), 189–91.

Joseph, Anthony. "Centralized versus Store-Controlled Merchandise Replenishment." *Retail Control* (April - May 1985), 2–21.

Langrehr, Frederick W., and Langrehr, Virginia B. "Shoppers' Acceptance of Item Price Removal: A Trend and Store Type Analysis." *AMA Educators' Proceedings.* P. E. Murphy et al, eds. (American Marketing Association 1983), 231–34.

Moore, Robert D. "Distribute or Drop Ship? A Continuing Struggle." *Retail Control* (November 1982), 9–15.

Pommer, Michael D.; Berkowitz, Eric N.; and Walton, John R. "UPC Scanning: An Assessment of Shopping Response to Technological Change." *Journal of Retailing* 56 (Summer 1980), 25–44.

Schulz, David P. "Just-in-Time Systems." *Stores* (April 1985), 28–31.

Woodruff, Robert A. "Merchandise Processing Systems." *Retail Control* (September 1982), 2–11.

Outline

THE MERCHANDISE-MANAGEMENT PROCESS

MERCHANDISE PLANNING

DOLLAR PLANNING: MERCHANDISE BUDGETS

Planning Sales
Planning Stock Levels
Planning Reductions
Planning Purchases
Planning Profit Margins

UNIT PLANNING: MERCHANDISE LISTS

Basic Stock List
Model Stock List
Never-Out List

Objectives

- Discuss the need for merchandise planning as an essential tool in ensuring that both the customer's merchandise needs and the retailer's financial requirements are satisfied

- Plan an acceptable balance between merchandise inventories and sales

- Devise and use a merchandise budget in the dollar planning of the retailer's investment in merchandise inventory

- Devise and use a merchandise list in the unit planning of the retailer's merchandise assortment and support

19
The Merchandise-Planning Process

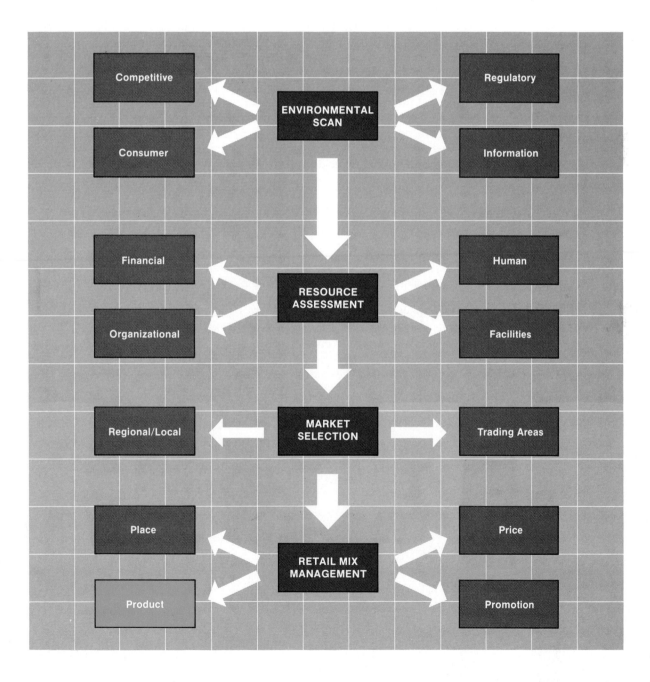

The previous four chapters examined the first two stages in the merchandising process, developing and securing the merchandise mix. The third stage of the merchandising process concerns managing the merchandise mix, which Chapters 19 and 20 discuss. For reasons of organizational simplicity, merchandise management will be examined after the basic activities associated with developing and securing the merchandise mix are identified. In practice, however, managing the merchandise mix coincides with its development and securement.

THE MERCHANDISE-MANAGEMENT PROCESS

A sound policy for managing merchandise is essential if the retailer is to offer the right product in the right place at the right time in the right quantities and at the right price. The basic ingredients of the merchandise-management process are illustrated in Figure 19–1. As portrayed, **merchandise management** *focuses on planning and controlling the retailer's merchandise inventories.* **Merchandise planning** *consists of establishing objectives and devising plans for obtaining those objectives.* The planning process normally includes both dollar planning in terms of merchandise budgets and unit planning in terms of merchandise lists. **Merchandise control** *involves designing dollar and unit inventory information and analysis systems for collecting, recording, analyzing, and using merchandise data to determine whether the stated objectives have been achieved.* In summary, planning is the process of establishing performance guidelines, while control is the process of checking on how well management is following those guidelines. The remainder of this chapter is devoted to the merchandise-planning process; the next chapter carefully examines the topic of merchandise control.

MERCHANDISE PLANNING

The overall objective of merchandise planning is to satisfy both the customer's merchandise needs and the retailer's financial requirements. To accomplish that objective, the retailer must devise merchandise plans that create an acceptable balance between merchandise inventories and sales. This inventory-to-sales balance requires the retailer to plan each merchandise category carefully with respect to (1) inventory investment, (2) inventory assortment, and (3) inventory support.

    Inventory investment involves *planning the total dollar investment in merchandise inventory so that the firm can realize its financial objectives.* **Inventory assortment** is *planning the number of different product items (brand, style, size,*

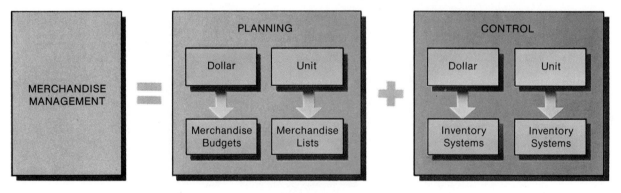

FIGURE 19–1
The merchandise-management process

color, material, and price combinations) the retailer should stock within a particular product line, and determining whether this assortment is adequate to meet the merchandise-selection needs of the firm's targeted consumers. **Inventory support** refers to planning the number of units the retailer should have on hand for each product item to meet sales estimates (e.g., stocking 100 six-packs of Coca-Cola in the 12-ounce can). By carefully planning the investment, assortment, and support aspects of merchandise inventories, the retailer can take a major step toward the merchandising objective of "customer satisfaction at a profit."

Both dollar and unit planning are essential if the retailer expects to balance inventory investment, assortment, and support. Inventory investment is the focus for dollar planning, whereas unit planning centers on the retailer's inventory assortment and support. Figure 19–2 illustrates the major concerns in the development and implementation of the retailer's merchandise-planning process.

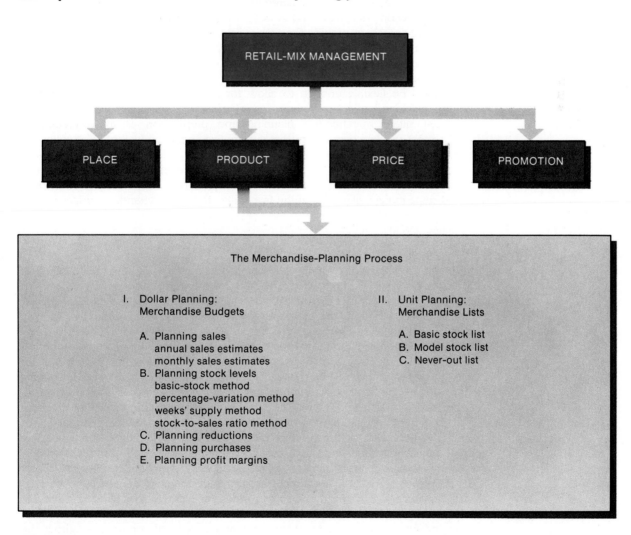

FIGURE 19–2
Developing and implementing the merchandise-planning process

Dollar planning is *largely a financial-management tool that retailers use to plan the amount of total value (dollars) inventory they should carry.* It answers the inventory question of how much the retailer should invest in merchandise during any specified period. Dollar planning is accomplished through the use of a **merchandise budget**—*a financial plan for managing merchandise inventory investments.* The merchandise budget consists of the following five stages:

1. planning sales
2. planning stock levels
3. planning reductions
4. planning purchases
5. planning profit margins

Certain areas must be considered in the merchandise budget for it to succeed as a plan of action. The merchandise budget should (1) be planned well in advance of the selling season to provide time for revisions; (2) be kept simple enough to be easily understood and followed by managers, yet complete enough to ensure adequate operational guidelines; (3) represent the combined judgment of both buyers and sales personnel; (4) cover a time period for which reliable estimates are feasible; and (5) be flexible enough to allow for necessary adjustments to changing market conditions.[1]

To facilitate merchandise planning and preparation of the merchandise budget, most retailers use a form that summarizes basic budgetary information for a given merchandise grouping during a specified time period. Figure 19–3 illustrates a commonly used form for preparing the retailer's merchandise budget. Let's now discuss how the retailer can obtain the necessary information to complete this form, and examine individually each of the five stages in the merchandise budget.

Planning Sales

The starting point in developing the merchandise budget is sales planning. It is absolutely necessary to forecast future sales for the budgetary process to work in planning the retailer's investment in merchandise inventory. If future sales are incorrectly estimated during this initial stage, then all other aspects of the merchandise budget (stock levels, reductions, purchases, profit margins) will reflect this initial error and will require the retailer to adjust the budget throughout its application.

Prior to making sales estimates, the retailer must select the control unit for which these projections will be made. The **control unit** is *the merchandise grouping that serves as the basic reporting unit for various types of information* (e.g., past, current, and future sales). The retailer can elect to estimate future sales for an entire store, for a merchandise division or department, or for an individual product line or item. The discussion of the product mix in Chapter 15 identified three possible control units: merchandise groups (broadly related lines of products that often correspond with operating divisions, such as appliances), merchandise classes (closely related lines of products that often correspond with operating departments, such as small appliances), and merchandise categories (specific lines of products that are directly comparable and substitutable, such as blenders). To increase accuracy in estimating future sales and to obtain a greater degree of control throughout the entire budgetary process, retailers generally prefer narrowly defined control units. Therefore, using merchandise categories as the basic control unit is recommended

FIGURE 19–3

A commonly used form
for preparing a mer-
chandise budget

| SIX-MONTH MERCHANDISE BUDGET | | | | | | | | | |

Date _____   Department _____

		Aug.	Sept.	Oct.	Nov.	Dec.	Jan.	Total
Sales	Last Year							
	Planned							
	Adjusted							
	Actual							
BOM Stock Levels	Last Year							
	Planned							
	Adjusted							
	Actual							
Reductions	Last Year							
	Planned							
	Adjusted							
	Actual							
Purchases	Last Year							
	Planned							
	Adjusted							
	Actual							
Initial Markup %	Last Year							
	Planned							
	Adjusted							
	Actual							

because it is generally much easier to aggregate information (summing merchandise categories into merchandise classes and groups) than it is to disaggregate information (breaking down merchandise groups into classes and categories). Also, the retailer is in a better position to pinpoint future merchandise opportunities as well as existing operational problems by using narrowly defined control units. Once the control unit has been established, the retailer can proceed to make annual, seasonal, and monthly sales estimates.

Annual Sales Estimates

An examination of the retailer's past sales records is the starting point for making sales forecasts for each merchandise category (control unit). By plotting the actual

533

sales for each control unit over the last few years, the retailer can identify past sales patterns and gain some insight into possible future sales trends. This type of approach to sales estimates is generally referred to as time-series forecasting. It represents a simple, inexpensive, and widely used method for obtaining reasonably reliable estimates of sales in the near future. Time-series forecasting is generally quite appropriate for staple merchandise, somewhat less appropriate for fashionable merchandise (those fashions in a ford or classic life cycle), and totally inappropriate for faddish merchandise.

For purposes of illustration, Figure 19–4 presents a department store's six-year sales experience (1981–1986) with automatic-drip coffee makers and electric blenders. As illustrated, past sales for these two merchandise categories reveal some interesting patterns. While both have experienced sales increases, the amount and stability of those increases are noticeably different. The store's past blender sales reveal a small yet steady increase in dollar sales. Looking at changes in the percentage increase in sales per year, we see that sales are increasing but at a decreasing rate. These figures suggest that the blender is in the maturity stage of its product life cycle and that sales are fairly stable and predictable, at least in the near future. The past sales pattern for coffee makers shows both large and small dollar and percentage increases, together with drastic changes from one year to the next. Viewing the overall pattern of coffee maker sales, the retailer could conclude that this product has passed through the growth stage of its product life cycle and done so fairly erratically at that. (Look at the percentage increase in sales. Sales increasing at an increasing rate are indicative of a product in the growth stage of the product life cycle.) In 1986, however, sales of coffee makers began to show increasing sales at a decreasing rate—a possible sign that the product is entering its maturity stage. Thus, because of the erratic changes in the rate of sales of coffee makers and the data's suggestion that the product *might* be entering its maturity stage, the retailer's 1987 sales estimates for coffee makers are very likely to be much less accurate than sales estimates for blenders.

Annual sales estimates for each merchandise category are made largely using judgmental or qualitative methods. Two such methods are the fixed and variable adjustment procedures.

FIGURE 19–4

Five-year sales record for automatic-drip coffee makers and electric blenders

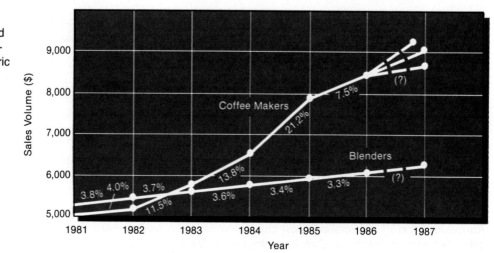

Fixed adjustment method. With the fixed adjustment method, the retailer adjusts last year's sales by some fixed percentage to estimate the coming year's sales. The direction (plus or minus) and the size (the exact percentage) of the adjustment are based on the retailer's past sales experience with each merchandise category. For example, based on the past sales trend for electric blenders (as illustrated in Figure 19–4), the department store's forecaster might well expect a 3.2 percent increase in sales for 1987 in the absence of any other extenuating circumstances that might strongly influence the sale of blenders. The fixed adjustment method usually works reasonably well in estimating future sales if a clear and stable sales trend has been established. When past sales patterns are erratic, however, a fixed percentage adjustment is totally inappropriate.

Equally inappropriate is the "beat last year's sales" approach in calculating next year's sales estimates. Some retailers simply estimate future sales using a fixed percentage (e.g., 4, 6, 8 percent) that will yield sales estimates above last year's sales performance. This approach does not recognize that various merchandise categories are in different stages of their product life cycles. While some are in the growth stage (accelerated sales growth), others may be in the maturity (declining sales growth) or decline (decreased sales) stages of the cycle. Beating last year's sales may be an appropriate sales goal for the store as a whole, but it is not an appropriate sales-estimating method for an individual category of merchandise.

Variable adjustment method. The second method for estimating annual sales is the variable adjustment method. The forecaster using this method usually starts with an examination of the past sales history of the merchandise category just as with the fixed adjustment method. Based on the sales history, the forecaster determines a percentage change (e.g., 6 percent) that appears reasonable. The figure is then adjusted upward or downward by a degree that depends on the nature of the merchandise and its exposure and sensitivity to environmental influences. The retailer making these adjustments might consider the following external environmental factors: (1) the general prosperity of local and national markets; (2) the rate of inflation; (3) the chances for recessionary developments; (4) discernible trends in the growth or decline in the size of the target market population; (5) changes in the demographic makeup of the population (e.g., age, income, family structure, etc.); (6) developing legal and/or social restrictions; (7) changing patterns of competition (e.g., type, size, and merchandising strategies); and (8) changing consumer preferences and life-styles. Internal factors to consider in adjusting annual sales estimates include (1) changes in the amount and location of shelf or floor space devoted to the merchandise category; (2) changes in the amount and type of planned promotional support; and (3) changes in basic operating policies (e.g., longer store hours or higher levels of service).

In summary, the **annual sales estimate** for a particular merchandise category *equals the previous year's sales plus or minus a fixed or variable percentage adjustment.* The adjustment factor is largely a blend of forecaster judgment, experience, and analytical skill. In the case of the variable adjustment method, the forecaster must carefully weigh the impact of environmental factors upon sales forecasts for particular merchandise categories.

Monthly Sales Estimates

Retail planning periods typically are based on one-month or several-month periods. For example, some retailers estimate sales for products for the three-month winter season or the six-month fall/winter season. The best operational estimate for budgetary planning purposes is **monthly sales estimates.** Estimating monthly sales involves three steps: (1) making annual sales estimates; (2) determining estimated monthly sales; and (3) adjusting monthly sales estimates using a monthly sales index. To facilitate our discussion of how to make monthly sales estimates, Figure 19–5 provides a hypothetical example. It illustrates the past sales history by month and year of men's and women's watches for the jewelry department of Selmer's Department Store. We shall use the data in this table as the basis for discussing the three steps in estimating monthly sales.

Step 1: Making annual sales estimates. In making monthly sales estimates, the forecaster starts with annual sales estimates. The previous discussion outlined methods for estimating annual sales. In our hypothetical example (Figure 19–5), the annual sales increases in men's and women's watches have ranged between 1.2 and 3.8 percent. Let's assume, based on past sales trends and various internal and external environmental factors, the forecaster determines that a 2.86 percent increase in sales is a reasonable expectation for the upcoming year (1987). By multiplying 175,000 (1986 sales) by .0286, the forecaster estimates a sales increase of $5,000 (rounded). The estimated 1987 sales for men's and women's watches then would be $175,000 plus $5,000, or $180,000.

Step 2: Determining average estimated monthly sales. The second step in estimating monthly sales is to allocate the annual sales estimate derived in step 1 on a monthly basis. One way to make this allocation is to determine *average estimated*

FIGURE 19–5

Monthly and annual sales records for men's and women's watches (jewelry department, Selmer's Department Store)

Period	1982 Sales ($)	1983 Sales ($)	1984 Sales ($)	1985 Sales ($)	1986 Sales ($)	Total Sales (1982-1986) ($)
MONTHLY						
Jan.	3,000	2,000	5,000	4,000	3,000	17,000
Feb.	4,000	2,000	5,000	3,000	4,000	18,000
Mar.	6,000	7,000	5,000	8,000	8,000	34,000
Apr.	6,000	8,000	7,000	6,000	8,000	35,000
May	22,000	27,000	23,000	22,000	25,000	119,000
June	26,000	25,000	28,000	27,000	30,000	136,000
July	8,000	7,000	5,000	6,000	7,000	33,000
Aug.	7,000	9,000	5,000	7,000	8,000	36,000
Sept.	11,000	14,000	9,000	11,000	8,000	53,000
Oct.	9,000	6,000	11,000	9,000	9,000	44,000
Nov.	20,000	19,000	23,000	24,000	23,000	109,000
Dec.	38,000	40,000	42,000	44,000	42,000	206,000
ANNUAL						
Total	160,000	166,000	168,000	171,000	175,000	840,000
% Increase	—	3.8	1.2	1.8	2.4	—

monthly sales by dividing the annual sales estimate by the number of months in a year (12). In our watch example, the 1987 estimated annual sales of $180,000 are divided by 12 to arrive at average estimated monthly sales of $15,000. This figure would be a reasonably reliable estimate of monthly sales if we could assume that sales of men's and women's watches were evenly distributed over the 12 months of the year. Brief examination of the past monthly sales patterns, however, reveals considerable variation among months in the sale of watches. For example, the monthly sales data in Figure 19–5 make it clear that the sale of watches is highly seasonal. The peak sales occur during the May/June and November/December sales periods that correspond to the gift-giving occasions of high school and college graduation and Christmas, respectively. Some type of adjustment therefore must be made to accommodate these monthly sales fluctuations.

Step 3: Adjusting average estimated monthly sales. Average estimated monthly sales are adjusted using a *monthly sales index* based on past monthly sales records. The purpose of this adjustment is to obtain a *planned monthly sales figure* that is the final estimate of each month's sales that the retailer will use throughout the budgetary process. By indexing past monthly sales, the forecaster can establish a sales norm for an "average month" by which all other monthly sales can be judged. The average month is represented by an index value of 100. Any month with an index below 100 represents monthly sales below the norm. Above-average sales are represented by index values in excess of 100. For example, a monthly sales index of 76 indicates that sales for that month are 24 (100 − 76) percent below the average. An index value of 181 denotes an above-average sales performance of 81 (181 − 100) percent.

The forecaster must make several calculations to obtain the monthly sales index. The calculation involves the sequential determination of (1) past average monthly sales, (2) past average annual sales, (3) an average month's sales, and then (4) the monthly sales index. Once the monthly sales index has been determined, it is used to forecast planned monthly sales. To show how these calculations are made, Figure 19–6 continues with the watch example from Figure 19–5.

The sequential formulas for calculating the monthly sales index are shown in Figure 19–7, together with the formula for calculating planned monthly sales. Let's examine these procedures.

The first task is to determine *past average monthly sales;* that is, to figure the average sales performance for each month over the last several years—the sales period. This sales period can range from 2 to 20 years or more, depending upon the availability of sales records and the number of years the forecaster deems relevant to current and future sales trends. For our purposes, the sales period in Figure 19–6 covers the five-year period from 1982 through 1986. Figure 19–7a outlines the procedures for calculating past average monthly sales. Using Figure 19–6 figures,

$$\text{past average monthly sales for January} = \frac{\$17,000}{5} = \$3,400$$

In our watch example, past average monthly sales for each month are presented in Figure 19–6.

The second task is to calculate *past average annual sales.* In this step the forecaster computes the average annual sales performance for men's and women's watches over the sales period. The procedure used in calculating past average

Monthly Sales Period	Past Total Monthly Sales (1982-1986) ($)[1]	Past Average Monthly Sales (1982-1986) ($)	An Average Month's Sales (1982-1986) ($)	Monthly Sales Index[2]	Average Estimated Monthly Sales (1987) ($)[3]	Planned Monthly Sales (1987) ($)
Jan.	17,000	3,400	14,000	24	15,000	3,600
Feb.	18,000	3,600	14,000	26	15,000	3,900
Mar.	34,000	6,800	14,000	49	15,000	7,350
Apr.	35,000	7,000	14,000	50	15,000	7,500
May	119,000	23,800	14,000	170	15,000	25,500
June	136,000	27,200	14,000	194	15,000	29,100
July	33,000	6,600	14,000	47	15,000	7,050
Aug.	36,000	7,200	14,000	51	15,000	7,650
Sept.	53,000	10,600	14,000	76	15,000	11,400
Oct.	44,000	8,800	14,000	63	15,000	9,450
Nov.	109,000	25,400	14,000	181	15,000	27,150
Dec.	206,000	41,400	14,000	296	15,000	44,400
Annual Sales Period	Past Total Annual Sales (1982-1986) ($)	Past Average Annual Sales (1982-1986) ($)	An Average Month's Sales (1982-1986) ($)		Annual Sales Estimate (1987)	
	840,000	168,000	14,000	—	180,000	—

[1]Obtained from Figure 19-5.
[2]Rounded to nearest whole number.
[3]Obtained from Step 2.

annual sales is shown in Figure 19–7b. Again, using Figure 19–6 figures,

$$\text{past average annual sales for 1981–1986} = \frac{\$840,000}{5} = \$168,000$$

The third task is to determine an *average month's sales;* that is, what an average month's sales were during the sales record period. In our watch example, an average month's sales were $14,000. This value was determined using the formula in Figure 19–7c. According to Figure 19–6,

$$\text{an average month's sales for 1981–1986} = \frac{\$168,000}{12} = \$14,000$$

The fourth task is to determine the *monthly sales index* for each month of the year. The monthly sales index for a given month is defined as the past average monthly sales for that month divided by an average month's sales for the period, multiplied by 100 (see Figure 19–7d). For example,

$$\text{monthly sales index for January} = \frac{\$3,400}{\$14,000} \times 100 = 24.28$$

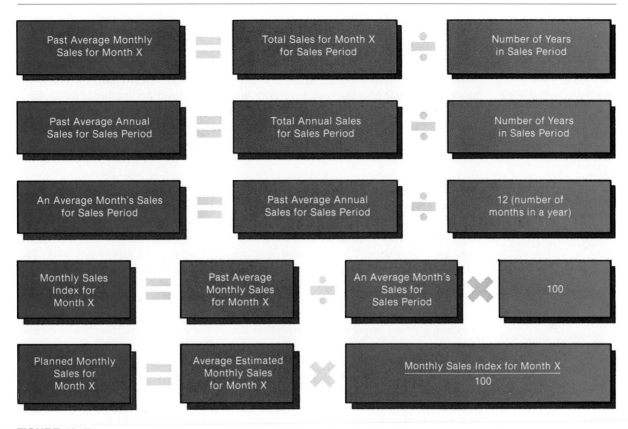

FIGURE 19–7
Formulas for calculating the monthly sales index and planned monthly sales

The index figure just calculated can be interpreted in two ways. The index number for January (approximately 24) indicates that expected January sales for watches at Selmer's are approximately 24 percent of the norm or, put another way, 76 percent below average monthly sales. This figure (24.28, rounded) and those for the remaining months are shown in column five of Figure 19–6.

Once the monthly sales index has been calculated, it can be used to adjust the average estimated monthly sales (see step 2) to obtain the final sales figure the retailer will use in the budgetary planning process: *planned monthly sales.* To accomplish this final adjustment, the forecaster divides the monthly sales index by 100 and multiplies this figure by the average estimated monthly sales. Calculating procedures are shown in Figure 19–7e.

$$\text{planned monthly sales for January} = \$15,000 \times \frac{24}{100} = \$3,600$$

The planned monthly sales figure is the best estimate of each month's sales for the upcoming year based on sales records and internal and external environmental considerations. Having determined a reliable estimate of each month's future sales, the retailer must then plan for the necessary stock levels to support those estimates—planned monthly sales.

Planning Stock Levels

The second stage in developing a merchandise budget involves planning appropriate stock levels for a specific sales period. Ideally the retailer's stock plan should (1) meet sales expectations, (2) avoid out-of-stock conditions, (3) guard against overstock conditions, and (4) keep inventory investment at an acceptable level. While it is extremely difficult to devise a plan to achieve all of these objectives, four methods can serve the retailer in planning stock requirements. They are the basic stock method, the percentage variation method, the week's supply method, and the stock-to-sales ratio method.

The Basic Stock Method

The **basic stock method** is *designed to meet sales expectations and avoid out-of-stock conditions by beginning each month with stock levels that equal the estimated sales for that month plus an additional basic stock amount that serves as a "cushion" or "safety stock" in the event that actual sales exceed estimated sales.* The safety stock also protects the retailer against stockouts if future shipments of merchandise are delayed or arrive damaged and must be returned to the vendor. On the negative side, safety stock means that the retailer has a larger investment in inventory and increased inventory carrying costs. Retailers that use the basic stock method want to ensure minimum stock levels for a particular merchandise category. Generally, retailers that operate stores and departments with low inventory turnover are most likely to use this method.

The basic stock method involves calculating the beginning-of-the-month stock (BOM stock) for each month of the sales period. The BOM stock is computed by adding a basic stock amount to each of the planned monthly sales as determined in the sales planning stage of the budgetary process. For example, let's assume that the department manager for the jewelry department of Selmer's Department Store is in the process of planning stocks for the upcoming Christmas season (October, November, and December). Using the basic stock method, the department manager would plan the BOM stock for each of the three months (sales period) using the procedures outlined in Figure 19–8.

To illustrate the use of the basic stock method, we continue to use the watch example introduced in the previous sales-planning discussion. Figure 19–9 reconstructs the three-month Christmas sales period of October, November, and December. Based on past sales records, the retailer knows that the turnover rate (number of times the average stock on hand is sold during a given time period) for watches during this three-month sales period has averaged about two. Using the information in Figure 19–9, BOM stock is determined for the month of October in the following manner:

$$\text{average monthly sales for October, November, December} = \$81,000 \div 3 = \$27,000$$

$$\text{average stock for October, November, December} = \$81,000 \div 2 = \$40,500$$

$$\text{basic stock} = \$40,500 - \$27,000 = \$13,500$$

$$\text{BOM stock for October} = \$9,450 + \$13,500 = \$22,950$$

As shown, a basic or safety stock of $13,500 is added to each month's planned sales to arrive at the BOM stock. The BOM stocks for November and December are shown in Figure 19–9. When actual sales either exceed or fall short of planned sales

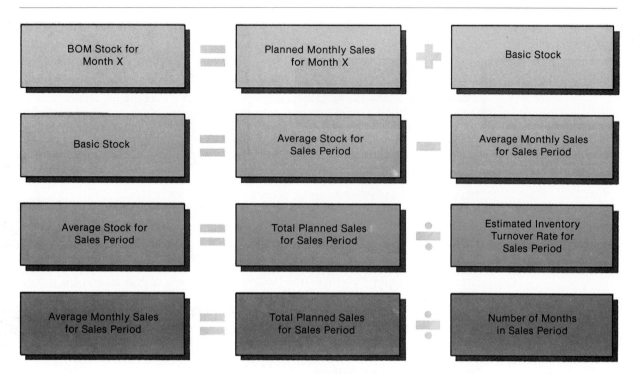

FIGURE 19-8
The basic stock method for determining BOM stock

FIGURE 19-9
BOM stock for men's
and women's watches
(jewelry department,
Selmer's Department
Store)

Sales Period	Planned Monthly Sales ($)[1]	BOM Stock Using Basic Stock Method ($)	BOM Stock Using Percentage Variation Method ($)
Oct.	9,450	22,500	27,337.50
Nov.	27,150	40,650	40,905.00
Dec.	44,400	57,900	53,460.00
Total	81,000	—	—

[1]Obtained from Figure 19-6.

FIGURE 19-9
BOM stock for men's
and women's watches
(jewelry department,
Selmer's Department
Store)

for a given month, the retailer can easily adjust the amount of overage or shortfall to bring the next month's BOM stock back to its calculated level (in this case, $13,500).

The Percentage Variation Method

The **percentage variation method** *uses a procedure that attempts to adjust stock levels in accordance with actual variations in sales.* With this method, BOM stock is increased or decreased from average stock for the sales period by one-half of the percentage variation in planned monthly sales for that month from the average monthly sales for the sales period. The calculating procedures for the percentage variation method are shown in Figure 19-10.

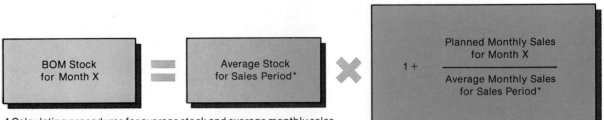

* Calculating procedures for average stock and average monthly sales were reviewed in the previous discussion of the basic stock method.

FIGURE 19–10
The percentage variation method for determining BOM stock

$$\text{BOM stock for October} = \$40,500 \times \frac{1}{2}\left(1 + \frac{\$9,450}{\$27,000}\right) = \$27,337.50$$

The BOM stocks for November and December have been calculated and are shown along with the October BOM stock in Figure 19–9.

Retailers prefer to use the percentage variation method with merchandise categories characterized by a high turnover rate (usually exceeding six times per year) because it results in less stock fluctuation than if the basic stock method were used.

The Week's Supply Method

The **week's supply method** is *a stocking plan that determines stock levels in direct proportion to sales.* Serving as a means to plan stocks on a weekly basis, this method uses a desired annual stock turnover rate to establish the amount of stock necessary to cover a predetermined number of weeks. If the manager of Selmer's jewelry department thinks an annual stock turnover rate of eight is both desirable and feasible, determining stock for the start of the Christmas sales period (October) would be done as shown in Figure 19–11. Using the data in Figure 19–9,

FIGURE 19–11
The week's supply method of determining BOM stock

$$\text{number of weeks to be stocked} = 52 \div 8 = 6.5 \text{ weeks}$$

$$\text{average weekly sales} = \$180,000 \div 52 = \$3,462$$

$$\text{BOM stock for October} = \$3,462 \times 6.5 = \$22,503$$

Having determined the number of weeks' supply to be stocked (6.5 weeks) and the average weekly sales ($3,462), stock levels can be replenished frequently and regularly (e.g., weekly or biweekly) before stock shortages occur. The principal limitation of this method is that during weeks with a slow stock turn (below annual rate), there will be an excessive accumulation of stock. Therefore, this method is most appropriate for retailers whose merchandise categories show stable sales and stable stock turnover rates.

The Stock-to-Sales Ratio Method

The **stock-to-sales ratio method** is another method retailers use to determine BOM levels. *The assumption behind this method is that the retailer should maintain a certain ratio of goods on hand to planned monthly sales.* This ratio could be 2 to 1, 3 to 1, or any other appropriate relationship. A stock-to-sales ratio of 2 to 1 means the planned monthly sales of $5,000 would require $10,000 of stock. The key to using this method is finding a dependable stock-to-sales ratio. The best source for this ratio is the retailer's own past records, providing they have been kept in sufficient detail over a reasonable length of time. Stock-to-sales ratios also can be obtained from various trade sources, such as the National Retail Merchants Association's publication *Department Merchandising and Operating Results of Department and Specialty Stores.*

To illustrate this method, let's assume that past sales records for Selmer's jewelry department reveal that a 2 to 1 stock-to-sales ratio is desirable. Based on the planned monthly sales cited in Figure 19–9, the BOM stock for October would be calculated as shown in Figure 19–12.

$$\text{BOM stock for October} = \$9,450 \times 2 = \$18,900$$

Using the same procedures, the BOM stock for November would be $54,000, while December's BOM stock would be $88,800.

Planning Reductions

The third stage in developing the merchandise budget is planning of reductions. **Retail reductions** *can be defined as "the allowance for the difference between the original retail value of merchandise and the actual final sales value of the merchan-*

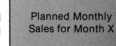 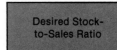

| BOM Stock for Month X | = | Planned Monthly Sales for Month X | × | Desired Stock-to-Sales Ratio |

FIGURE 19–12
The stock-to-sales ratio method of determining BOM stock

dise."[2] This difference is the result of three factors: markdowns, discounts, and shortages. **Markdowns** are *reductions in the original retail price for the purpose of stimulating the sale of merchandise.* **Discounts** are *reductions in the original retail price that are granted to store employees as special fringe benefits and to special customers (e.g., clergy, senior citizens, disadvantaged consumers) in recognition of their special status.* **Shortages** are *reductions in the total value of the retailer's inventory as a result of shoplifting, pilfering, and merchandise being damaged and misplaced.* Markdowns will be discussed fully as a pricing strategy in Chapter 21. Employee discounts were discussed in Chapter 9 in conjunction with employee compensation. The problems of shoplifting and pilfering were discussed in Chapter 11, and stock shortages will receive additional treatment in the next chapter.

Planning reductions is necessary for several reasons. First, the major purpose of the merchandise budget is to outline the retailer's total dollar investment in inventory. Therefore, any occurrence that might reduce the value of that inventory should be accounted for if the retailer is to have an accurate inventory investment picture. Second, the merchandise budget calls for an estimate of stock levels in dollar amounts. So, without reduction planning, the retailer's proposed stock levels might be inadequate to meet expected sales levels. Finally, reduction planning is necessary if the retailer is to plan future purchases accurately. An estimate of reductions is a key input variable into the planned-purchases formula.

Planning reductions essentially involves making a percentage-of-sales (dollars) estimate for each of the three major reduction factors: markdowns, discounts, and shortages. These percentage estimates are either made on the basis of past experience or obtained from trade sources. To be consistent with sales and stock-level planning, reduction estimates should be made in retail dollars on a monthly basis for a particular merchandise category. Continuing our watch example, if the retailer's past records reveal that for the month of October men's and women's watches experienced average monthly markdowns of 6 percent and discounts and shortages averaged 1.5 percent and 2.5 percent, respectively, then the total planned reductions for October would be 10 percent of planned monthly sales, or $945 (see Figure 19–9). Having determined a monthly estimate of reductions, the retailer can proceed to plan purchases.

Planning Purchases

Planning purchases constitutes the fourth stage in developing a merchandise budget. In this stage, the retailer plans the dollar amount of merchandise that it must purchase for a given time period (e.g., a month or a season) in light of planned sales and reductions for that period as well as the planned stock levels at the beginning of the period and the desired stock levels at the end of the period. (The ending stock is usually equal to the beginning stock for the next period.) The format for calculating planned purchases for a monthly planning period is as follows:

$$
\begin{aligned}
&\text{planned monthly sales}\\
+\;&\text{planned monthly reductions}\\
+\;&\text{desired end-of-the-month stock}\\
\hline
=\;&\text{total stock needs for the month}\\
-\;&\text{planned beginning-of-the-month stock}\\
\hline
=\;&\text{planned monthly purchases}
\end{aligned}
$$

For illustration purposes, let's assume that the manager of Selmer's jewelry department is planning the October purchases of men's and women's watches. From our previous discussions we have the following information concerning October: (1) planned monthly sales estimated at $9,450 (see Figure 19–9); (2) planned monthly reductions estimated at 10 percent of sales of $945; (3) desired end-of-the-month stock of $40,650 (the beginning-of-the-month stock for November—see Figure 19–9); (4) planned beginning-of-the-month stock of $22,500 (see Figure 19–9). Given this information, the planned purchases for the month of October are

planned monthly sales	$ 9,450
+ planned monthly reductions	945
+ desired end-of-the-month stock	40,650
= total stock needs for the month	$51,045
− planned beginning-of-the-month stock	22,500
= planned monthly purchases	$28,545

The planned monthly purchases of $28,545 were computed in terms of retail prices. To find out what the manager must spend in terms of cost prices, the retailer must multiply the retail value ($28,545) by the cost equivalent (the percentage of the retail price that is the manager's cost). For example, if merchandise costs are 60 percent of the retail price, then the manager can plan to make purchases totaling $17,127 at cost prices ($28,545 × .60).

The planned monthly purchase value represents the retailer's additional merchandise needs for that month. It tells the retailer how much merchandise must be purchased and made available during that month. It does *not* tell the retailer when those purchases should be made. Order-processing requirements, delivery schedules, and other considerations demand that some of the planned purchases for a month may have to be ordered far in advance. The timing of purchases depends on a number of internal (retailer) and external (supplier) conditions. Purchase-order timing will be discussed more fully in the next chapter.

Planning Profit Margins

An integral part of developing the merchandise budget is to allow for a reasonable profit by ensuring an adequate dollar **gross margin**—*the difference between cost of goods sold and net sales.* To be adequate, the retailer's dollar gross margin must be sufficient to cover the operating expenses associated with buying, stocking, and selling the merchandise, as well as producing an acceptable operating profit. The procedures for determining dollar gross margin and operating profit are as follows:

	net sales (dollars)
−	cost of goods sold (dollars)
=	gross margin (dollars)
−	operating expenses (dollars)
=	operating profit (dollars)

The retailer attempts to achieve an adequate gross margin and operating profit by planning an **initial markup percentage**—*the percentage difference between the cost of the merchandise and its original retail price*—that will cover expenses, profits, and reductions. The formula for calculating the initial markup percentage is shown in Figure 19–13.

Sales and reduction estimates are obtained from the sales and reduction planning stages of the merchandise budget. Expense estimates are based on past experience as revealed by expense records. Once sales, reduction, and expense estimates have been made, the retailer can then establish a realistic profit objective. To

facilitate easy planning, reductions, expenses, and profits are estimated as a *percentage of sales.* For example, in planning the required initial markup percentage on men's and women's watches for the coming year (1987), the manager of Selmer's jewelry department has estimated total annual sales of $180,000, reductions at 10 percent of sales or $18,000, and anticipated expenses at 20 percent of sales or $36,000. Further, assuming that the manager desires a profit objective of 12 percent of sales or $21,600, which is considered both feasible and acceptable, the manager calculates the required initial markup on watches:

$$\frac{\text{required initial}}{\text{markup percentage}} = \frac{\$36{,}000 + \$21{,}600 + \$18{,}000}{\$180{,}000 + \$18{,}000} = 38.2\%$$

The same formula can be used when expenses, profits, reductions, and sales are expressed in percentage terms (sales equal 100 percent). For example,

$$\frac{\text{required initial}}{\text{markup percentage}} = \frac{20\% + 12\% + 10\%}{100\% + 10\%} = 38.2\%$$

This required initial markup percentage represents an overall average for a merchandise category (e.g., watches). As long as this category average is maintained, the actual initial markup on any individual merchandise item (a watch of a particular brand, style, and price) may vary from this average to adjust to different demand conditions, competitive circumstances, and other external and internal merchandising factors. A more in-depth discussion of markup and gross margin appears in Chapter 21.

In summary, the merchandise budget is the sequential dollar planning of sales, stock levels, reductions, purchases, and profit margins. By carefully planning the dollar investment in merchandise inventory, the retailer is developing a blueprint of what must be accomplished to realize a desired profit and other financial goals. The retailer's merchandise budget also sets the financial standards by which actual performance can be measured.

UNIT PLANNING: MERCHANDISE LISTS

Unit planning is an operational management tool retailers use to plan the merchandise assortment and support. It is directed at determining the amount of inventory the retailer should carry by items and by units. It answers the inventory questions of how many product items (assortment) and how many units of each item (support) the retailer should stock. Unit planning involves the use of several *merchandise lists*—a set of operational plans for managing the retailer's total selection of merchandise. Based on the type of merchandise the retailer carries, one or more of the following three merchandise lists will apply.

1. basic stock list—for planning staple merchandise
2. model stock list—for planning fashion merchandise
3. never-out list—for planning key items and best sellers

Merchandise lists essentially are representations of the "ideal" stock for meeting the consumer's merchandise needs in terms of assortment and support.

Basic Stock List

The **basic stock list** is *a planning instrument retailers use to determine the assortment and support for staple merchandise.* **Staples** are *product items for which sales are either very stable or highly variable but very predictable.* In either case, the retailer's estimates of the required assortment of merchandise items and the number of support units for each item can be made with a relatively high degree of accuracy. Thus, in planning for staple merchandise, the retailer can develop a very specific stocking plan. The basic stock list is a schedule or listing of "stock-keeping units" (SKU) for staple merchandise. A **stock-keeping unit** is *either a "single item of merchandise or a group of items for which separate sales and stock records are kept."*[3] In the basic stock list, each SKU is usually identified in very precise terms. A retailer can use the following product characteristics to distinguish clearly a stock-keeping unit of staple merchandise: (1) brand name, (2) style or model number, (3) product or package size, (4) product color or material, (5) retail and/or cost price of the product, and (6) manufacturer's name and identification number. In addition to a complete listing of stock-keeping units, the basic stock list also contains a detailed description of the stock position for each SKU by stock levels (merchandise support, or the total number of units). Also, this description of stock support normally identifies (1) a minimum stock level to be on hand, (2) the actual stock on hand, (3) the amount of stock on order, (4) planned sales, and (5) actual sales. Stock support information is recorded on a standardized form at regular and frequent intervals (e.g., quarterly or monthly). Figure 19–14 (p. 548) illustrates one of several possible forms for recording the information contained in a basic stock list.

The importance of carefully maintaining a basic stock list cannot be overstated. Most merchandise departments, including those that are fashion oriented, contain at least some product items that are basic staples. Examples are black nylon socks and white cotton briefs in the men's wear department. Given the "essential" character of staple merchandise in the consumer's buying behavior patterns, close supervision over the stock position of staples is absolutely necessary. The simple fact that consumers expect an adequate supply of staple merchandise makes it all the more important to have an adequate supply. Many staple items have no totally satisfactory substitutes for many consumers. A stockout of a particular staple will force the consumer to look elsewhere for the item. By not being able to meet the consumer's need for a basic staple, the retailer not only loses the sale but also damages the store's assortment image and strains the customer's good will. Additionally, the customer, in the process of looking elsewhere, may decide to switch to a competitor whose stock of staples is well maintained.

Model Stock List

Stock planning for fashion merchandise is accomplished through use of the **model stock list**—*a schedule or listing of stock-keeping units for fashion merchandise.* The model stock list differs from the basic stock list because it defines each SKU in general rather than precise terms. Commonly used criteria in identifying a model stock-keeping unit are *general price lines* ("better dresses" at $100, $150, and $200 or "moderate dresses" at $40, $60, and $80); *distribution of sizes* (misses 8, 10, 12, 14, and 16); *certain basic colors* (black cocktail dresses or navy-blue blazers);

547

Stock Keeping Unit		Vendor Description			Merchandise Description					Price		Stock Description				
Number	Name	Manuf. Name	Manuf. I.D.	Brand	Style/ Model	Material	Color	Size		R	C		Quarters			
													1	2	3	4
												MS				
												PS				
												AS				
												OH				
												OO				
												MS				
												PS				
												AS				
												OH				
												OO				
												MS				
												PS				
												AS				
												OH				
												OO				
												MS				
												PS				
												AS				
												OH				
												OO				

Key: R = Retail Price   PS = Planned Sales   OH = Stock on Hand
      C = Cost Price   AS = Actual Sales   OO = Stock on Order
   MS = Minimum Stock

FIGURE 19–14
A basic stock list form

general style features (long and short sleeve dresses or crew neck, v-neck, and turtleneck sweaters); and *product materials* (wool, cotton, and polyester dresses). The basis for the more general character of each SKU in a model stock plan is the transience of fashion merchandise, which represents only the currently prevailing style. The likelihood of style changes within a short period and the high probability that market demand (sales) will fluctuate considerably within any selling season require a more general approach to stock planning. If the model stock list calls for 300 "better dresses" equally distributed among the $100, $150, and $200 price lines, the retailer is still free to adapt to specific fashion trends that are currently stylish. In the initial planning of model stock lists, desired support quantities for each stock-keeping unit are established on the basis of past sales experience. The exact distribution of those quantities among the various assortment features (e.g., colors, styles, and materials) is left to the buyer's judgment about what is and will be appropriate for the store's customers. In essence, the model stock list provides general guidelines on the size and composition of an ideal stock of fashion merchandise, without specifying the exact nature of the merchandise assortment or support.

The form used in planning the model stock list differs somewhat from the basic stock list form. First, the vendor description is usually absent or abbreviated. Second, the merchandise description is more generalized. Finally, the stock description is frequently more detailed, breaking down each season (quarter) into desired stock levels at various times within the season: beginning of the season, seasonal peak, and end of the season.

Never-Out List

The **never-out list** is *a specially created list of merchandise items that are identified as key items or best sellers for which the retailer wants extra protection against the possibility of a stockout.* Due to the high level of demand for these items, many retailers establish rigid stock requirements. For example, a retailer might specify that 99 percent of all items on the never-out list must be on hand and on display at all times. Stockouts of these key items result in permanent loss of sales. Typically, the consumer will simply not wait to purchase best sellers. Never-out lists can include fast-selling staples, key seasonal items, and best-selling fashion merchandise. The integrity of the never-out list is preserved through regular and frequent revision. The importance of the never-out list is underscored by the fact that many chain organizations expect individual store managers to have a near-perfect record in maintaining the stock levels for merchandise on the list. Even a moderate number of stockouts of merchandise on the list is considered an indication of poor management.

SUMMARY

Establishing merchandise objectives and devising tactics for obtaining these objectives constitute the focal point for the merchandise-planning process. The planning process normally includes both dollar planning, in terms of merchandise budgets, and unit planning, as accomplished through the use of merchandise lists. Satisfying consumers' needs and ensuring retailers' profits are the principal reasons for planning the merchandise mix. The retailer must carefully plan inventory investment (the total dollar amount invested in merchandise), inventory assortment (the number of different products stocked within a particular product line), and inventory support (the number of units to be stocked for each product item).

Dollar planning is accomplished through the use of a merchandise budget—a financial plan for managing merchandise inventory investments—that requires the retailer to consider (1) sales, (2) stock levels, (3) reductions, (4) purchases, and (5) profit margins. The retailer uses unit planning to determine the amount of inventory to carry in terms of items (assortment) and units (support). A merchandise list—a set of operational plans for managing the retailer's total selection of merchandise—is used in unit planning. Based on the type of merchandise the retailer carries, one or more of the following lists are appropriate: basic stock list (for planning staple merchandise), model stock list (for planning fashion merchandise), and never-out list (for planning key items and best sellers).

549

KEY TERMS AND CONCEPTS

merchandise management	annual sales estimates	shortages
merchandise planning	monthly sales estimates	gross margin
merchandise control	basic stock method	initial markup percentage
inventory investment	percentage variation method	basic stock list
inventory assortment	week's supply method	staples
inventory support	stock-to-sales ratio method	stock-keeping unit
dollar planning	retail reductions	model stock list
merchandise budget	markdowns	never-out list
control unit	discounts	

REVIEW QUESTIONS

1. Distinguish among the three concepts of inventory investment, assortment, and support.
2. What is a merchandise budget? Identify the five stages in developing a merchandise budget.
3. Why do the authors recommend the use of merchandise categories as the basic control unit in making sales estimates?
4. How does the variable adjustment method differ from the fixed adjustment method of estimating annual sales?
5. David Ostrem is the manager of the Shoe Shack and is responsible for making sales estimates and placing orders for new stock. Because of seasonality of sales, David is required to make monthly sales estimates. Given an annual sales estimate of $9000 for 1987 and the past sales record for children's dress shoes (see sales record), calculate the planned monthly sales for 1987—the final sales figure David will use in the budgetary planning process.

The Shoe Shack
monthly sales record*
children's dress shoes

	1982	1983	1984	1985	1986
Jan.	400	400	500	600	600
Feb.	300	400	400	500	700
March	300	400	500	600	800
April	800	800	900	1000	1200
May	700	700	800	800	800
June	400	500	600	500	700
July	200	300	300	500	700
Aug.	600	600	600	700	800
Sept.	900	1100	1400	1500	1800
Oct.	500	700	600	700	800
Nov.	400	500	500	600	700
Dec.	700	800	900	1000	1200

*Rounded to the nearest hundred.

6. Gina Lewis is the department manager of the "better dresses" department. Having estimated planned monthly sales for the upcoming year, Gina must now plan the appropriate stock levels for the fall season. To obtain a better idea of the stock that will be needed, Gina has decided to calculate BOM stock for each month using both basic stock and percentage variation methods. Using an estimated inventory turnover rate of two, calculate the BOM stock for each month using both methods.

Planned Monthly Sales

August	$32,000
September	$18,000
October	$10,000

7. A hardware retailer estimates its total annual sales for plumbing equipment to be $72,000 and hopes to achieve an annual stock turnover rate of six. Using the week's supply method, calculate the BOM stock for January.

8. What are retail reductions? Identify and describe the cause of retail reductions.

9. How are planned monthly purchases determined?

10. Given the following information, calculate the required initial markup percentage:

    1. sales $240,000
    2. expenses .... 22 percent of sales
    3. reductions .... 8 percent of sales
    4. desired profit .... 14 percent of sales

11. What is an SKU? How are SKUs distinguished from one another?

12. Basic stock lists are used as a planning instrument for what type of merchandise?

13. What is a model stock list? What criteria are used in identifying a model stock-keeping unit?

14. What are never-out lists used for?

ENDNOTES

1. See Maryanne S. Bohlinger, *Merchandise Buying—Principles and Applications* (Dubuque, IA: William C. Brown, 1977), 283.

2. Ibid., 296.

3. John W. Wingate, Elmer O. Schaller, and F. Leonard Miller, *Retail Merchandise Management* (Englewood Cliffs, NJ: Prentice-Hall, 1972), 4.

RELATED READINGS

Abend, Jules. "New AIM." *Stores* (March 1982), 54–59.

———. "PCs, Easier Software." *Stores* (August 1985), 25–30.

Bernstein, Joseph E. "Inventory Shortage and the 'Back Burner'." *Retail Control* (December 1984), 50–57.

Joseph, Anthony M. "Inventory Planning and Control for Improved Profitability." *Retail Control* (October 1984), 21–39.

Lesser, Jack A., and Schwartz, Martin L. "The Effect of Stock-Out on Retail Store Customers." *Marketing Comes of Age, Proceedings.* David M. Klein and Allen E. Smith, eds. (Southern Marketing Association 1984), 142–45.

McGinnis, Michael A.; Gable, Myron; and Madden, R. Burt. "Improving the Profitability of Retail Merchandising Decisions—Revisited." *Journal of the Academy of Marketing Science* 12 (Winter - Spring 1984), 49–57.

Schary, Philip B., and Christopher, Martin. "The Anatomy of a Stock-Out." *Journal of Retailing* 55 (Summer 1979), 59–70.

Shipp, Ralph D., Jr. *Retail Merchandising*, 2nd ed. (Boston: Houghton Mifflin Co., 1985)

Staples, William, and Swerdlow, Robert. "Planning and Budgeting for Effective Retail Merchandise Management." *Journal of Small Business Management* (January 1978), 1–6.

Wilson, Cyrus C., and Haueisen, William D. "Retail Information Systems Can Help Provide Profits Needed for Growth." *Marketing News* (March 7, 1980), 4, 14–15.

Outline

INVENTORY-INFORMATION SYSTEMS

Inventory Information
Inventory Systems
Inventory Valuation

INVENTORY-ANALYSIS SYSTEM

Stock Turnover
Return on Inventory Investment
Open-to-Buy

Objectives

- Describe the need for merchandise control in maintaining a planned balance between the retailer's merchandise inventory and sales

- Outline the method for collecting and procedures for processing merchandise data

- Discuss the methods and procedures for valuing the retailer's inventories

- Explain the methods and procedures for evaluating past merchandising performances

- Identify the methods and procedures for making future merchandise decisions

20
The Merchandise-Control Process

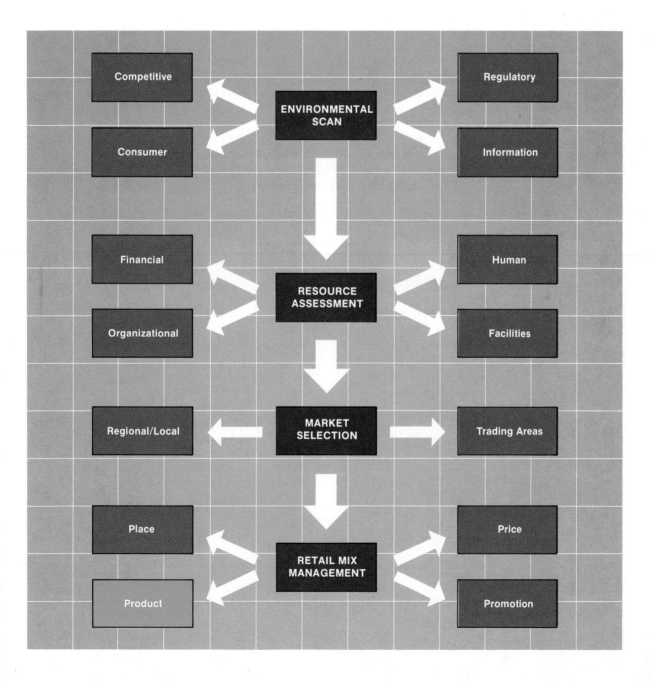

M erchandise control complements merchandise planning. It is the process of designing and maintaining inventory systems for controlling the planned balance between the retailer's merchandise inventory and sales. As illustrated in Figure 20–1, merchandise control can be viewed as the sum of two types of inventory systems: an inventory-information system and an inventory-analysis system. The **inventory-information system** is *the set of methods and procedures for collecting and processing merchandise data pertinent to the planning and control of merchandise inventories.* The **inventory-analysis system** *includes methods for evaluating the retailer's past merchandising performance and decision-making tools for controlling future merchandising activities.* As with merchandise planning, merchandise control must use the retailer's inventory information and analysis systems to control inventory investment as well as inventory assortment and support.

The retailer's merchandise controls must be capable of supplementing the basic merchandising decisions of buying, stocking, and selling. A well-conceived merchandise-control system can aid in the merchandise decision-making process by providing essential information and analysis on both the right amount (dollars) and the right quantity (units) to buy, stock, and sell. It also provides a better position

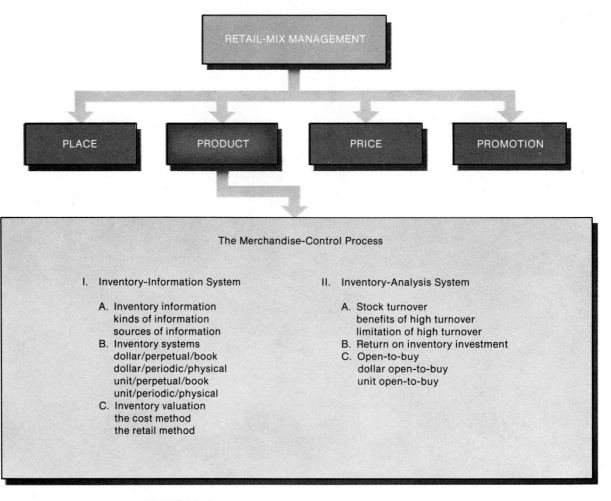

The Merchandise-Control Process

I. Inventory-Information System

A. Inventory information
    kinds of information
    sources of information
B. Inventory systems
    dollar/perpetual/book
    dollar/periodic/physical
    unit/perpetual/book
    unit/periodic/physical
C. Inventory valuation
    the cost method
    the retail method

II. Inventory-Analysis System

A. Stock turnover
    benefits of high turnover
    limitation of high turnover
B. Return on inventory investment
C. Open-to-buy
    dollar open-to-buy
    unit open-to-buy

FIGURE 20–1
Developing and implementing the merchandise-control process

to (1) prevent stockouts, which result in lower profits due to lost sales and reduced store loyalty because of customer dissatisfaction, and (2) avoid overstocks, which lower profits because of higher inventory carrying costs and greater risks of mark-downs.

Our discussion of merchandise control starts with how merchandise data are collected and processed. It then examines the methods and tools for evaluating and using merchandise data.

If retailers are to control their inventories effectively, they must have an efficient means of obtaining information on the past and current status of those inventories. An adequate inventory-information system is a prerequisite to planning and controlling future merchandising activities. Before examining the major types of inventory-information systems, let's consider the kinds of information that retailers need in controlling inventories and where (sources) they can obtain that information.

Inventory Information

Kinds of Information

Merchandise investment and merchandise assortment and support are the principal elements the retailer wants to control. To complement merchandise planning, the retailer's inventory-information system must be capable of providing both dollar control and unit control. **Dollar control** *considers the "value" of merchandise and attempts to identify the dollar amount of investment in merchandise.* The use of dollar control requires the retailer to collect, record, and analyze merchandise data in terms of dollars. **Unit control** *deals not with dollars, but with the number of different product items (assortment) and the number of units stocked within each item (support).* It is the number of physical units (sales, purchases, and stock levels) recorded and analyzed. Both dollar and unit control are essential for the retailer who needs investment information for profit control and assortment information for stock control.

Sources of Information

The retailer's source of inventory information is the inventory system. Inventory systems differ depending on when (perpetually or periodically) inventory is taken and how (book or physical) it is taken. Based on these two factors, inventory procedures can be classified either as perpetual book inventory systems or periodic physical inventory systems.

A **perpetual book inventory** *refers to a system whereby inventory is taken and information is gathered on a continuous or ongoing basis using various accounting records to compute stock on hand at any given time.* The purchase, sales, and markdown figures needed to calculate stock on hand are derived from internal accounting records that must be kept current if the computed book inventory is to reflect correctly the retailer's true stock position. In summary, a perpetual book inventory represents an up-to-the-minute, -day, or -week accounting system in which all transactions affecting inventory are considered either as they occur or shortly thereafter. Its major advantage is that the retailer can determine stock on hand as required by operating conditions and the need for inventory information.

A **periodic physical inventory** *refers to a system in which stock information is gathered on an intermittent basis (usually once or twice a year) using an actual physical count and inspection of the merchandise items to compute sales for the period since the last physical inventory.* The use of a periodic physical inventory system is limited by the time-consuming process of making an actual, physical count of each merchandise item and by the fact that most retailers have faster, easier, and more time-saving methods for obtaining sales information. Nevertheless, a physical inventory must be taken at least once a year for income tax reporting purposes. A physical count of the retailer's inventory also is necessary to determine stock shortages (book inventory minus physical inventory). Finally, for the small retailer that can afford neither the electronic data-processing equipment nor the accounting personnel to maintain a sophisticated accounting system, a periodic physical inventory is the only alternative.

Inventory Systems

The major types of inventory-information systems used in merchandise control are (1) dollar/perpetual/book, (2) dollar/perpetual/physical, (3) unit/perpetual/book, and (4) unit/periodic/physical. These four systems are based on the kinds of information the retailer needs and the methods and the sources for obtaining that information. Let's examine these systems.

Dollar/Perpetual/Book

Dollar control using a **perpetual book inventory** system *provides the retailer with continuous information on the amount of inventory (dollars) that should be on hand at any given time as determined by internal accounting records.* The basic procedures for calculating a perpetual book inventory in dollars are as follows:

$$
\begin{array}{l}
 \text{beginning stock on hand} \\
+\ \text{purchases} \\
\hline
=\ \text{total stock handled} \\
-\ \text{sales} \\
-\ \text{markdowns} \\
\hline
=\ \text{ending stock on hand}
\end{array}
$$

Dollar control systems express values either in terms of retail prices or cost prices. The various accounting methods for inventory valuation will be discussed later in this chapter. To simplify our discussions of dollar control, we shall consider all values at retail price.

In the preceding formulation, the beginning stock-on-hand value is the ending stock-on-hand value from the preceding accounting period. Merchandise data concerning purchases, sales, and markdowns are obtained from the appropriate internal accounting records. The computed ending stock on hand is the dollar value of the retailer's inventory, provided no shortages have occurred as a result of customer shoplifting, employee pilfering, or other causes that would reduce the value of the merchandise on hand. To determine actual stock shortages, the retailer would have to check the book inventory by taking a physical inventory. Many retailers use an estimated shortage percentage (e.g., 2%) based on past experience to adjust the ending stock-on-hand value perpetually. A final adjustment is then made at the end of the season or year by conducting a physical count and valuation of the merchandise.

The primary limitation in using a perpetual book inventory for controlling dollar investment in merchandise is the need to obtain accurate and timely merchandise information. A complete up-to-the-minute information system capable of reporting all relevant transactions (purchases, sales, and markdowns) as they occur is necessary. While this limitation creates few problems for large retailers that can afford and justify the expenses associated with sophisticated information-reporting systems, the expenses involved in establishing and maintaining such systems often are prohibitive for the small retailer. On a more promising note, the increasing capabilities and decreasing prices of minicomputers are making the perpetual book inventory system a reality for many small and medium-size retailers.

Dollar/Periodic/Physical

A **periodic physical inventory** system for dollar control *provides the retailer with periodic information on the amount of inventory (dollars) actually on hand at a given time as determined by a physical count and valuation of the merchandise.* It permits the retailer to compute the dollar amount of sales that have occurred since the last physical count. The use of a periodic physical inventory system for dollar control requires a less complex system for reporting merchandise information. However, it provides information on a less timely basis and of a less useful nature. A periodic physical inventory usually is computed at designated intervals (monthly, quarterly, or semiannually) using the following basic procedure:

$$
\begin{array}{rl}
& \text{beginning stock on hand} \\
+ & \text{purchases} \\
\hline
= & \text{total stock handled} \\
- & \text{ending stock on hand} \\
\hline
= & \text{sales and markdowns} \\
- & \text{markdowns} \\
\hline
= & \text{sales}
\end{array}
$$

The beginning stock on hand is the value of the ending stock on hand brought forward from the previous accounting period. Internal purchases and markdown records are used to determine the dollar amount of purchases and markdowns since the last accounting. The ending stock-on-hand figure is derived from a physical count and valuation of the merchandise inventory. The sales figure is computed as shown and incorporates the value of whatever shortages have occurred.

Most retailers have easier and more timely means by which they can obtain sales information; however, as previously stated, the periodic physical inventory system can be used to determine sales figures for merchandise groupings that are not part of the sales reporting system.

In summary, both perpetual book and periodic physical systems of dollar control can be used at all operating levels. While small retailers tend to calculate the dollar amount of investment in merchandise for the store as a whole, large retailers make these same calculations for departments (jewelry), merchandise categories (watches), and price lines ($79.95). Obviously, the use of dollar control at each of these more refined levels provides the retailer with more detailed information concerning its inventory investment position and a greater ability to identify potential investment problems and opportunities.

Unit/Perpetual/Book

A perpetual book inventory system for unit control—**a unit/perpetual/book system**—*involves continuous recording of all transactions (e.g., number of units sold or purchased) which changes the unit status of the retailer's merchandise inventory.* Under such a system, each unit transaction is posted as it occurs or shortly thereafter (e.g., on a daily basis). Perpetual unit control provides the retailer with a running total of the number of units of a given type that are flowing into and out of the store or department. It helps the retailer continuously control the balance between units on hand and unit sales. In other words, this system allows the retailer to develop and maintain the required merchandise assortment and support necessary to meet consumers' selection expectations. Perpetual unit control systems are maintained manually or through the use of various automatic recording systems.

Manual systems. A manual system of perpetual unit control is maintained by the retailer's accounting personnel, who continuously record merchandise data on standard forms. Figure 20–2 illustrates one such form, as well as the basic information needed to maintain a daily perpetual book inventory in units. To determine stock on hand, the accountant simply adds the number of units received during the accounting period and subtracts the number of units sold during the accounting period. For example, to determine the ending stock on hand for October 9 (see Figure 20–2):

beginning stock on hand (from Oct. 7):	8 units
+ units received (Oct. 9):	+ 12 units
= total stock on hand:	20 units
− units sold (Oct. 9):	− 1 unit
= ending stock on hand (Oct. 9):	= 19 units

In this example, the beginning stock on hand is the ending stock on hand for October 7. The number of units received into stock is obtained from records furnished by the receiving department or clerk. Information on the number of units sold can be gathered using a number of manual systems, such as (1) *point-of-sale tallies* (sales personnel keep track of the number of units sold by making a tally mark on a merchandise list after each sale); (2) *price-ticket stubs* (sales personnel remove information stubs from price tickets when the merchandise is sold and collect, sort, and tally the number of units sold); and (3) *cash-register stubs* (sales personnel remove information stubs from receipts before giving them to customers; these stubs are then used to determine the number of units sold).

Automatic systems. Automatic systems of perpetual unit control accomplish the same tasks as manual systems except they are a faster, more timely, and more accurate means of obtaining inventory information. The use of computer-based electronic data-processing equipment allows the retailer to convert automatically merchandise data on sales, purchases, and stocks into useful information for planning and controlling merchandise assortment and support. Several automatic systems are available, including tag, card, and point-of-sale systems. A *tag system* uses prepunched merchandise tags containing basic assortment information that are attached to each merchandise item. These tags are collected when the item is sold and sent to a data processing facility where the information is fed into the computer. *Card systems* are similar to tag systems, except sales personnel record assortment information directly onto punch cards or scanner cards, which are then fed into the data processing system and used for unit control purposes. *Point-of-sale (POS) systems* use cash registers or terminals capable of transmitting assortment information (e.g., style, price, color, material) directly to the central data processing facility as the sale is being recorded. A number of different methods can be used to record sales and assortment information in a point-of-sale system. Two of the more commonly used methods are (1) *optical scanners,* which read codes (e.g., Universal

Merchandise Item: 12-Inch Portable T.V., G.E., Model 71			
Date	Merchandise Received	Merchandise Sold	Stock on Hand
10-2			10
10-3	10	0	20
10-4	0	1	19
10-5	0	4	15
10-6	0	2	13
10-7	0	5	8
10-9	12	1	19
10-10	0	2	17
10-11	0	3	14
10-12	0	4	10
10-13	0	0	10
10-14	0	0	10
10-16	0	2	8
10-17	0	1	7
10-18	10	0	17
10-19	0	3	14
10-20			
10-21			
10-23			
10-24			
10-25			
10-26			
10-27			
10-28			
10-30			
10-31			

Product Code) that have been premarked or imprinted on the merchandise item or package, and (2) *terminal keys,* which transmit data directly to the computer when sales personnel depress them.

Both manual and automatic perpetual book inventory systems are used in unit control to obtain information regarding the assortment and support status of the retailer's inventory. Manual systems are generally used to control assortment and support of merchandise items characterized by a high unit value and a short selling season (e.g., men's and women's wearing apparel and accessories). The use of manual systems for fashionable merchandise is considered appropriate because sales can be easily recorded by number of units and unit reorders. Manual systems are not practical for small, fast-selling staples for which rapid turnover would prohibit a timely and accurate record of sales, purchases, and stocks. With the advent of automatic systems, however, perpetual book inventory systems are becoming a realistic alternative for controlling the assortment and support for such staple items.

Unit/Periodic/Physical

Unit control also can be achieved by *making a periodic physical check on the status of the retailer's inventory*—**unit/periodical/physical inventory.** For example, the department manager may be assigned the responsibility of monitoring the stock levels for all merchandise items within the department at regular intervals. Stock levels are monitored using either a visual inspection or a physical count.

Visual inspection. In visually inspecting the stock levels, stock-control personnel visually examine the stock of each item to determine whether sales have depleted the stock to the point of reordering. Several stock-control methods can determine at a glance the general condition of the stock. For example, display or storage bins can be divided into quarters, with each quarter having the capacity to hold a certain number of units. When a designated number of quarters (e.g., two) are empty, the person responsible for stock control reorders merchandise to refill the bin. Another example of visual stock control is placing merchandise (e.g., hardware items) on a sequentially numbered pegboard (e.g., 1–25). When the stock reaches a certain level, say 10, then 15 units are reordered. Visual inspection is a reasonably appropriate inventory-information system for staple merchandise of low unit value that the retailer can quickly obtain from suppliers. While visual-inspection systems are easier and less expensive to establish and maintain than physical-count systems, their major weakness is that they do not provide information on the *rate of sales* for individual items.

Physical count. The second method of monitoring stock levels and determining unit sales is a physical count—the process of actually counting and recording the number of units on hand at regular intervals. Using a periodic physical count, the retailer attempts to determine the number of units sold since the last physical count by adding purchases during the intervening period to the beginning stock on hand and then subtracting the ending stock on hand obtained from the current physical count. For example, to determine monthly unit sales for a merchandise item in which the retailer began the month with 300 units on hand, purchased 80 units during the month, and ended the month with 190 units (as determined by physical count), the following computations are necessary:

beginning monthly stock on hand:	300 units
+ monthly purchases:	+ 80 units
= total stock handled during the month:	= 380 units
− ending monthly stock on hand:	− 190 units
= monthly sales (including shortages):	= 190 units

A physical counting system is considerably more time-consuming and expensive than the visual-inspection method. However, the retailer can collect sales information for a given specific period and determine the relationship between sales and stocks at the time of the physical count. A stock-counting system also is generally used for staple goods of a low per-unit value.

Inventory Valuation

A major financial concern of every retailer is determining the actual worth of the inventory on hand. How the retailer establishes the value of its inventory can have a profound effect on the outcome of various financial statements (e.g., the income statement and the balance sheet). Knowing the true value of inventories is also an essential element in sound financial planning and control. Retailers can value their inventories at cost (what they paid for the merchandise) or at retail (what they can sell the merchandise for). This section examines the cost and retail methods of inventory and reviews the relative strengths and weaknesses of each method.

The Cost Method

Small retailers generally prefer the **cost method of inventory valuation** because it is easy to understand, easy to implement, and requires a limited amount of record keeping. In using the cost approach, *the retailer simply values merchandise inventory at the original cost to the store each time a physical inventory is taken.* One of two procedures is typically used in computing the cost value of merchandise items. First, the original cost can be coded on the price tag or merchandise container using either a word or symbol code (see the discussion of marking procedures in Chapter 18). When taking physical inventory, the retailer records the cost and the number of units for each merchandise item. Multiplying the two yields the total cost value for each type of item.

The second procedure retailers use is to imprint a serialized reference number on each price tag corresponding to an itemized merchandise stock-control list containing the per-unit cost of each item. Again, the retailer can compute total cost values by multiplying the number of units obtained during the physical count by the per-unit cost as shown on the control sheet.

A major problem in using the cost method occurs when the retailer procures various shipments at different times during inflationary periods. If the wholesale price of an inventory item remained constant, the retailer's costs for various shipments of the same product would be identical. Unfortunately, constant wholesale prices are the exception, while fluctuating wholesale prices are typically the rule. While the rate of inflation can vary significantly, the mere fact that inflation exists creates a problem (the extent of the problem depends on the rate of inflation), with different shipments of identical products being purchased at different wholesale prices (i.e., cost to retailer). The retailer then must decide which cost value to use. FIFO (first-in, first-out) and LIFO (last-in, first-out) are two *inventory costing methods* used to resolve this dilemma.

The FIFO method. Using the **FIFO method,** *the retailer assumes that merchandise items are sold in the order in which they are purchased;* that is, older stock is sold before newer stock that was purchased at a later date. When the FIFO method is used, the cost of the oldest units in stock determines the retailer's cost of goods sold. From an operational viewpoint of maintaining the freshness of merchandise in stock, FIFO makes good sense and is the operating practice of most retailers. From a financial accounting viewpoint, however, during inflationary periods the FIFO method results in an overstatement of profits, thereby increasing the firm's tax liability (see Figure 20–3).

The LIFO method. "Under **LIFO** —the last-in, first-out method—*recent acquisition costs are used to price inventory (even though in actuality, the inventory bought last is not sold first).*"[1] Under this method, the cost of the newest units in stock determines the retailer's cost of goods sold. During a rising market (increasing wholesale prices), using the LIFO method will result in tax savings due to lower gross profits (see Figure 20–3). In order for LIFO to be advantageous to the firm, the following conditions are appropriate: "high inflation, a level of markdowns that does not exceed the benefits of inflation, and rising inventory costs."[2] To determine the savings from using LIFO, the retailer can use the formula shown in Figure 20–4. The ending inventory value is obtained from the retailer's inventory system

What would you call a technique that enabled a small business to reduce its tax bill and increase its cash flow without any additional investment? Unbelievable? Too good to be true?

Accountants would call this method LIFO—last in, first out—one of two methods of valuing inventory. LIFO values business inventory based on the cost of the last item placed into stock. The other method of evaluation, FIFO—first in, first out—places a value on inventory based on the cost of the first item placed in stock. During inflationary times, the last items purchased are more expensive, and under LIFO these items are assumed to be sold first. In effect, this method eliminates the inflation rate from the inventory's value.

The use of LIFO to value inventory results in lower "paper" profits, which in turn reduces the firm's taxable income. The business (or its owner) pays less income tax and net cash flow is greatly improved. But, since reported profits are lower, the small firm's ability to borrow money and attract investors also is lessened. However, a recent IRS ruling overcomes this disadvantage. The IRS will allow a business to show the value of its inventory under both the LIFO and FIFO methods. In effect, the owner can use LIFO for tax purposes and FIFO for reporting purposes.

To calculate the savings from using LIFO, the firm simply takes its ending inventory, multiplies it by the rate of inflation, and multiplies the result by the marginal tax rate.* For example, suppose a firm has 10,000 units in inventory that cost $3.00 each at the beginning of the year and $5.00 at the year end. Sales revenue was $70,000. The following table compares the income tax savings gained by using the LIFO technique to value inventory.

	FIFO	LIFO
sales revenue	$70,000	$70,000
cost of goods sold	30,000	50,000
gross profit	40,000	20,000
income tax*	$ 8,000	$ 4,000

Income tax savings = $8,000 − $4,000 = $4,000

*Marginal tax rate = 20%

Clearly, LIFO can improve the typical small firm's financial position. The rules on converting to LIFO are very confusing, and the assistance of a professional is required to decipher them. The benefits of switching to LIFO are worth the effort. In fact, tax expert John Klug calls LIFO "one of the greatest weapons in the artillery of the business taxpayer."

Adapted from "LIFO Saves." Reprinted with permission, INC. magazine, (Jan. 1981). Copyright © 1981 by INC. Publishing Company, 38 Commercial Wharf, Boston MA. 02110.

FIGURE 20–3
LIFO versus FIFO

FIGURE 20–4
Computing savings
from using LIFO

(discussed earlier), while the rate of inflation is determined using one or more price indexes. "Almost all large-volume department stores and many discount, specialty and drug chains use the Department Store Inventory Price Indexes established by the Bureau of Labor Statistics as an indication of inflation" (see Figure 20–5).[3] The marginal tax rate is computed by the accounting department using tax tables prepared by the Internal Revenue Service.

Although the cost method is simple to use, it does have several disadvantages. First, a cost valuation of inventory requires a physical count of the merchandise, and the need to count and decode prices is both time-consuming and costly. Second, using the cost method does not provide a book inventory of what merchandise ought to be on hand. Therefore, the retailer has no means to determine shortages. Remember, shortages equal book inventory minus physical inventory.

FIGURE 20–5
Department store inventory price indexes— July 1983

	Percentage Change to July 1983 from	
	January 1983	July 1982
I. Piece goods	2.7	1.8
II. Domestics and draperies	2.6	3.2
III. Women's and children's shoes	−1.2	−2.3
IV. Men's and boys' shoes	1.0	0.1
V. Infants' wear	2.4	4.0
VI. Women's underwear	3.3	3.9
VII. Women's and girls' hosiery	1.9	3.6
VIII. Women's and girls' accessories	1.2	5.0
IX. Women's outerwear and girls' wear	4.2	2.9
X. Men's clothing	2.4	3.6
XI. Men's furnishings	−0.2	2.1
XII. Boys' clothing and furnishings	3.2	3.6
XIII. Jewelry	2.4	2.6
XIV. Notions	1.4	2.7
XV. Toilet articles and drugs	6.4	9.7
XVI. Furniture and bedding	2.2	1.2
XVII. Floor coverings	0.9	1.5
XVIII. Housewares	1.9	2.0
XIX. Major appliances	2.0	1.0
XX. Radio and television	−1.2	−2.7
Groups I–XV: Soft goods	2.9	3.7
Groups XVI–XX: Durable goods	1.6	1.2
Store total	2.5	3.0

Source: Bureau of Labor Statistics, U.S. Department of Labor, "LIFO Survey Shows It's Here to Stay," *Chain Store Age Executive* (January, 1984), 33.

Finally, the cost method is often untimely, since physical inventory is usually taken only once or twice a year. As a result, the retailer cannot prepare weekly, monthly, and quarterly financial statements. Semiannual or annual financial statements are inadequate for effective planning and control for many retailers. The disadvantages of the cost method can be largely overcome if the retailer elects to employ the retail method of inventory valuation.

The Retail Method

The **retail method of inventory valuation** *allows the retailer to estimate the cost value of an ending inventory for a particular accounting period without taking a physical inventory.* Essentially, the retail method is a book inventory system whereby the cost value for each group of related merchandise (e.g., a department) is based on its retail value (selling price). By determining the percentage relationship between the total cost and the total retail value of the merchandise available for sale during an accounting period, the retailer can obtain a reliable estimate of the ending inventory value at cost. To use the retail method, the retailer must make the following calculations: (1) the total merchandise available for sale, (2) the cost complement, (3) the total retail deductions, and (4) the ending inventory at retail and cost values.

Total merchandise available. The total merchandise available for sale is illustrated in the following example:

	Cost	Retail
beginning inventory:	$120,000	$200,000
+ net purchases:	80,000	140,000
+ additional markons:	——	2,000
+ freight charges:	4,000	——
= total merchandise available:	$204,000	$342,000

As shown, beginning inventory and purchase figures are kept both at cost and at retail values. The beginning inventory is the ending inventory brought forward from the previous accounting period. It is obtained from the stock ledger that the retailer's accounting department maintains. Net purchases represent all purchases the retailer made during the accounting period minus any returns to the vendor. A purchase journal is used to record all purchase transactions. Any additional markons taken since setting the original retail price are added to the retail value of the inventory to reflect the market value of the merchandise. A price-change journal is maintained to keep track of additional markons as well as markdowns and other changes in the original retail selling price. Finally, freight charges are added to portray the true cost of the merchandise correctly. These charges are obtained from the purchase journal.

Cost complement. The cost complement is the average relationship of cost to retail value for all merchandise available for sale during an accounting period. In essence, it is the complement of the cumulative markup percentage. The cost complement is computed as follows:

$$\text{cost complement} = \frac{\text{cost value of inventory}}{\text{retail value of inventory}}$$

Using the previous example in which the value of the total merchandise available for sale equaled $204,000 at cost and $342,000 at retail,

$$\text{cost complement} = \frac{\$204,000}{\$342,000} = .5965$$

In this example, the retailer's merchandise cost is, on the average, equal to 59.65 percent of the retail value of the merchandise.

Retail deductions. The third step in using the retail method is to determine the total merchandise available for sale. Retail deductions include merchandise that has been sold, marked down, discounted, stolen, and lost. Total retail deductions are obtained by summing all of the deductions, reducing the retail value of the merchandise that was available for sale. To continue our illustration,

sales for period:	$160,000
+ markdowns:	30,000
+ discounts:	10,000
+ shortages (estimated):	2,000
= total retail deductions	$202,000

The sales figure for the accounting period represents both cash and credit sales and is obtained from the retailer's sales journal. The amount of markdowns taken during the accounting period and the amount of the discounts granted to employees and special customers can be secured from the price-change journal. Because shortages due to shoplifting, employee pilfering, and lost merchandise cannot be determined without a physical inventory, the retailer usually estimates the shortage figure on past experience.

Ending inventory value. The final step in implementing the retail method is to determine the value of ending inventory at retail and at cost. The retail value of ending inventory is computed by subtracting total retail deductions from total merchandise available for sale at retail. In our example,

total merchandise available at retail:	$342,000
− total retail deductions:	202,000
= ending inventory at retail:	$140,000

The cost value of ending inventory is calculated by multiplying the ending inventory at retail by the cost complement in the following manner:

$$\text{ending inventory at cost} = \text{ending inventory at retail} \times \text{cost complement}$$

$$\text{ending inventory at cost} = \$140,000 \times .5965 = \$83,510$$

While the figure $83,510 is only an estimate of the true cost value of the ending inventory, it is sufficiently reliable to allow the retailer to estimate both the cost of goods sold and gross margin for the accounting period. To complete our example:

total merchandise available at retail:	$204,000
− ending inventory at retail:	83,510
= cost of goods sold:	$120,490
sales for the period:	$160,000
− cost of goods sold:	120,490
= gross margin:	$ 39,150

Although the retail method has the disadvantages of requiring the retailer to keep more records (stock ledger and sales, purchases, and price-change journals) and using averages to estimate cost values, its advantages are numerous. The retail method forces the retailer to "think retail," in that both retail and cost figures are highlighted by the method. Second, frequent and regular calculations of various financial and operating statements are possible due to the availability of cost and retail information; these statements are essential to good financial planning and control and allow the retailer to adjust more quickly to changing market conditions. Third, when the retail method is used, physical inventories are taken in retail prices, thereby eliminating the costly, time-consuming job of decoding cost prices. Recording physical inventory in retail prices greatly simplifies the process and encourages a more frequent physical count of stock. Fourth, the retail method facilitates planning and control on a departmental basis. Sales, purchases, inventories, and price-change information are recorded by department. This information can be used to evaluate each department's performance. Fifth, by providing a book figure on what inventory should be on hand, the retail method allows the retailer to determine shortages each time a physical inventory is taken. Sixth, the retail method facilitates planning for insurance coverage and collecting insurance claims by providing an up-to-date valuation of the retailer's inventory.

Given the many advantages of the retail method of inventory valuation, it is not surprising that it is used extensively by large departmentalized and chain store retailers to gain tighter control over their various operating units.

INVENTORY-ANALYSIS SYSTEM

Inventory information is only useful when it provides the retailer with insights into past mistakes and with foresight for future planning. Merchandise data collected and processed by the inventory-information system can be used to evaluate past performances and to plan future actions. A determination of stock turnover and return on inventory investment are the principal methods for evaluating the retailer's past performance in controlling merchandise inventories. The dollar and unit open-to-buy methods are two of the more important tools for controlling future merchandising activities.

Stock Turnover

Stock turnover is *the rate at which the retailer depletes and replenishes stock.* Specifically, stock turnover is defined as the number of times during a specific time period that the average stock on hand is sold, generally on an annual basis.

Stock turnover rates can be calculated in both dollars (at retail or at cost) and units. The formulas used to figure stock turnover rates are shown in Figure 20–6. Data on net sales, cost of goods sold, and number of units sold are obtained from the inventory-information system (previously discussed). **Average stock** on hand for any time period is *defined as the sum of the stock on hand at the beginning of the period, at each intervening period, and at the end of the period divided by the number of stock listings.* For example, the average stock at retail for the summer season of June, July, and August would be calculated as follows:

June 1:	$ 60,000
July 1:	40,000
August 1:	50,000
August 31:	35,000
total inventory:	$185,000

$$\text{average stock} = \frac{\text{total inventory}}{\text{number of listings}}$$

$$\text{average stock} \atop \text{(June–August)} = \frac{\$185,000}{4} = \$46,250$$

If the net sales (retail dollars) for the three-month summer season were $220,000, then the stock turnover rate at retail would be

$$\text{stock turnover} \atop \text{at retail} = \frac{\text{net sales}}{\text{average stock on hand}}$$

$$\text{stock turnover} \atop {\text{at retail} \atop \text{(June–August)}} = \frac{\$220,000}{\$46,250} = 4.76$$

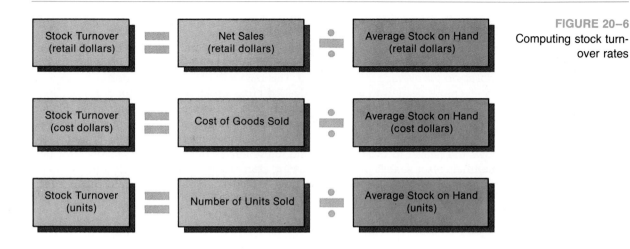

FIGURE 20–6
Computing stock turn-
over rates

Benefits of High Turnover

High stock turnover rates generally reflect good merchandise planning and control. Several benefits accrue to retailers with a high rate of stock turnover. They include (1) *fresher merchandise* (with a rapid stock turnover there is more frequent replacement of merchandise and, therefore, a continuous flow of new and fresh merchandise into the store); (2) *fewer markdowns and less depreciation* (a fast stock turnover is associated with a faster rate of sales and, therefore, reduced losses resulting from style or fashion obsolescence and soiled or damaged merchandise); (3) *lower expense* (a quick stock turnover helps to reduce inventories and, therefore, reduce such inventory expenses as interest and insurance payments, storage costs, and taxes on inventory, as well as helping to reduce selling promotional costs, since a new and fresh selection of merchandise tends to more easily sell itself); (4) *greater sales* (a rapid stock turnover allows the retailer to adjust its merchandise assortment in accordance with the changing needs of the target market and, therefore, generate more customer interest and a greater sales volume); and (5) *higher returns* (a rapid stock turnover resulting in an increase in sales and a corresponding decrease in stocks will generate a higher return on inventory investment; hence, a more productive and efficient use of the retailer's capital).

Increasing the rate of stock turnover requires the retailer to control the size and content of its inventory. In exercising this control, it must carefully balance inventory investment for greater profit with inventory assortment and support for adequate customer selection. Strategies retailers commonly use to increase stock turnover include (1) limiting the merchandise assortment to the most popular brands, styles, sizes, colors, and price lines; (2) reducing the merchandise support by maintaining a minimum reserve or safety stock; (3) clearing out slow-moving stock through price reductions; and (4) increasing the promotional effort in an attempt to increase sales.

Limitations of High Turnover

A high rate of stock turnover is not without its problems. Excessively high stock turns could mean that the retailer is buying in too-small quantities. If so, then the retailer is (1) not taking full advantage of available quantity discounts; (2) adding to its cost of transportation and handling; and (3) increasing accounting costs by processing too many orders. Another potential problem with high stock turnover is the danger of losing sales because of stockouts.

Return on Inventory Investment

The second method for evaluating the retailer's past performance in controlling merchandise inventories is **return on inventory investment**—*the ratio of gross margin dollars to the average stock on hand.* This ratio tells the retailer the dollar investment in inventory needed to achieve a desired gross profit (gross margin dollars).[4] Specifically, return on inventory investment can be expressed as shown in Figure 20–7. Essentially, return on inventory investment concerns the relationship between stock turnover and profitability. The importance of this ratio is that it allows the retailer to evaluate past and future effects of turnover on a store's (or department's) profitability. Before initiating plans to increase the stock turnover rate, the retailer should first determine how a higher stock turnover rate might affect profitability.

Open-to-Buy

Open-to-buy (OTB) is one of the retailer's most important tools in controlling future merchandise inventories. This tool helps the retailer decide how much to buy. As the name implies, **open-to-buy** is *the amount of new merchandise the retailer can buy during a specific time period without exceeding the planned purchases for that period.* Open-to-buy represents the difference between what the retailer plans to buy and what it has already bought—planned purchases minus purchase commitments. Open-to-buy is used for both dollar and unit control. Dollar open-to-buy sets a financial constraint on the retailer's buying activities, while unit open-to-buy controls assortment and support in the buying process.

Open-to-buy is a versatile control tool. The retailer can use it to control purchase activities on a daily, weekly, or monthly basis. Also, OTB can help control purchases of any classification or subclassification of merchandise. As a control tool, it allows the retailer to allocate purchases so stocks are maintained at predetermined levels by either the merchandise budget (dollar planning and control) or a merchandise list (unit planning and control).

Dollar Open-to-Buy

Dollar OTB is used to determine the amount of money the retailer has to spend for new merchandise at any given time. It can be calculated and recorded at both retail and cost prices. To calculate **dollar OTB at retail** prices for any day of a monthly period, *the buyer starts with planned monthly purchases and subtracts purchase commitments already made during the month.* Figure 20–8 shows the procedural steps for determining dollar OTB at retail. To obtain **dollar OTB at cost,** the buyer

FIGURE 20–7
Computing return on inventory investment

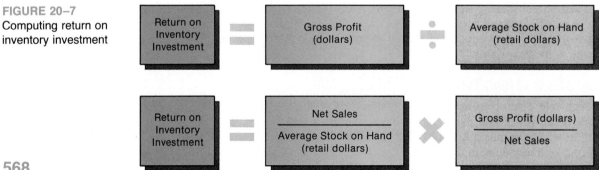

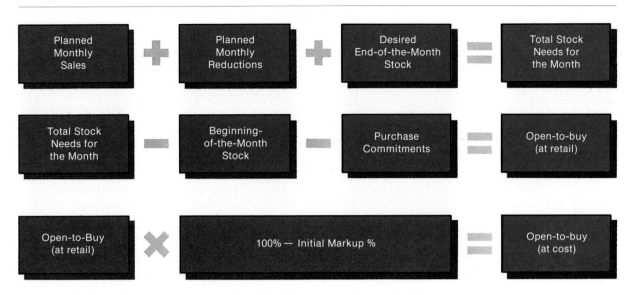

FIGURE 20–8
Computing dollar open-to-buy at retail (top) and open-to-buy at cost (bottom)

simply multiplies OTB at retail by the complement of the initial markup percentage. Figure 20–8 illustrates the formula for determining OTB at cost.

To illustrate, a buyer for a women's apparel department is planning a trip to the market on April 15. Before leaving on the trip, the buyer wants to know how much she can buy without exceeding the budget. An examination of the merchandise budget for April reveals that planned sales for the month were $70,000, while reductions (shortages, markdowns, and discounts) were $4,000. Inventory records reveal that the store started the month with $60,000 worth of inventory and plans call for an ending inventory of $50,000. A review of purchase orders indicates that the department has made purchase commitments of $14,000 since the beginning of the month. Given an initial markup percentage of 50 percent on retail, the buyer calculates the dollar open-to-buy to be $50,000 at retail and $25,000 at cost. These figures were obtained by first calculating planned purchases for April ($70,000 + $4,000 + $50,000 − $60,000 = $64,000), then subtracting all purchase commitments ($14,000) made through the 15th of the month. Figure 20–9 illustrates a form for calculating a weekly dollar OTB using a slightly different format, one commonly used by small retailing organizations for computing their OTB position regularly and frequently.

Unit Open-to-Buy

For the retailer engaged in unit control, unit OTB is a successful and necessary tool in preventing stockouts and overstocking. Unit OTB is most frequently used to control inventories of staple merchandise. This method lends itself to formal and systematic procedures for reordering merchandise the sales trends of which are well established and predictable. **Unit open-to-buy** calculations *involve two steps: (1) determining maximum inventory and (2) computing the unit OTB quantity.*

Step 1: Determine maximum inventory. **Maximum inventory** is *the number of merchandise units the retailer needs to cover expected sales during the reorder and*

The Boutique
Dollar Open-to-buy

Department _____   Week Ending _____

1. Physical inventory on hand this Monday	
2. On order this Monday	
3. Total inventory and on order (lines 1 plus 2)	
4. Planned sales this week (Monday thru Saturday)	
5. Planned closing physical inventory at end of this week (Saturday)	
6. Planned on order at end of this week	
7. Planned total closing inventory and on order at end of this week (lines 5 plus 6)	
8. Planned total closing inventory and on order and planned sales for this week ending Saturday (lines 7 plus 4)	
9. Open to buy for this week (lines 8 minus 3)	

delivery periods plus a safety stock for either unexpected sales or problems in securing the merchandise. The formula for determining maximum inventory is shown in Figure 20–10.

As an illustration, a hardware retailer reorders a staple item of merchandise every six weeks with the expectation that it will take three weeks before the merchandise is delivered. Based on past experience, the hardware retailer expects to sell approximately 40 units a week and considers a two-week safety stock necessary. The maximum inventory for the merchandise is 440 units. It is calculated as follows:

$$MI = (6 \text{ weeks} + 3 \text{ weeks}) \times 40 \text{ units} + 80 \text{ units}$$
$$= (9 \text{ weeks}) \times 40 \text{ units} + 80 \text{ units}$$
$$= 360 \text{ units} + 80 \text{ units}$$
$$= 440 \text{ units}$$

Therefore, the hardware retailer must stock 440 units to cover the reorder period and delivery period and to ensure a safety stock capable of covering two weeks' sales if the reorder is delayed or sales are higher than expected.

Step 2: Compute unit open-to-buy. Maximum inventory represents the number of merchandise units the retailer is open-to-buy if it had no stock on hand (SOH) or stock on order (SOO). Unit open-to-buy is defined as maximum inventory minus stock on hand and stock on order. The computation formula is as shown in Figure 20–10. Suppose our hardware dealer determines that it had 210 units on hand (obtained from the inventory-information system) and 90 units on order (obtained from purchase orders). Then,

$$\text{open-to-buy} = 440 - (210 + 90) \text{ (or 140 units)}$$

The systematic nature of unit open-to-buy permits easy computerization of this control tool. Figure 20–11 illustrates a computerized unit open-to-buy report for a casual dress department. As seen in this figure, unit control of assortment and support is maintained along price lines (e.g., $12.00, $18.00, etc.) and sizes (e.g., missy and juniors).

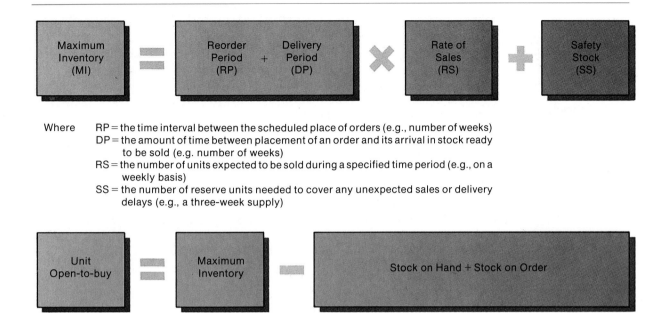

Where RP = the time interval between the scheduled place of orders (e.g., number of weeks)
DP = the amount of time between placement of an order and its arrival in stock ready
to be sold (e.g. number of weeks)
RS = the number of units expected to be sold during a specified time period (e.g., on a
weekly basis)
SS = the number of reserve units needed to cover any unexpected sales or delivery
delays (e.g., a three-week supply)

FIGURE 20–10
Computing unit open-to-buy

		EOM	Feb.			Anticipated	Planned	Open to		On Order			Open-
	Price	Inv.	on	Available	Planned	Mark	2/28	Receive				June	to-buy
Code	Range	1/31	Order	for Sale	Sales	Downs	Inv.	Feb.	March	April	May	July	Mar-July
700	14.00	771	100	871	500	40	750	419	300	800	1000	100	2885
702	18.00	621	85	706	425	30	900	649	500	1000	250	0	2625
704	22.00	1412	210	1622	800	70	1500	748	200	1400	1400	50	3410
706	26.00	3201	610	3811	1600	120	3000	909	800	800	0	0	4310
707	30.00	2120	350	2470	1000	80	2500	1110	1000	750	500	0	4820
708	35.00	1409	300	1709	600	50	1200	141	150	150	100	100	2530
TOTAL MISSY		9534	1655	11189	4925	390	8850	3976	2950	4900	3250	250	20580
710	14.00	494	500	994	700	50	1050	806	1000	1000	500	500	3405
712	18.00	1464	1000	2464	1000	80	1500	116	850	850	550	550	4460
714	22.00	2026	800	2826	1100	100	1700	74	1500	1200	700	0	4795
716	26.00	2251	100	2351	850	70	1500	69	1000	200	100	0	3820
TOTAL JUNIOR		6235	2400	8635	3650	300	5750	1065	4350	3250	1850	1050	17280
TOTAL CASUAL		15769	4055	19824	8575	690	15600	5041	7300	8150	5100	1300	37860

UNIT OPEN-TO-BUY REPORT
WEEK ENDING FEB. 21
Dept. 42 Casual Dresses

FIGURE 20–11
Unit open-to-buy report (source: Mary D. Troxell, *Fashion Merchandising,* 2d ed. [New
York: Gregg Division, McGraw-Hill, 1976], 283)

Merchandise control involves designing dollar- and unit-inventory information and
analysis systems for collecting, recording, analyzing, and using merchandise data to
control the planned balance between the retailer's merchandise inventory and sales.

Merchandise control is the necessary complement to merchandise planning (see Chapter 18).

An inventory-information system is a set of methods and procedures for collecting and processing merchandise data that are pertinent to planning and controlling merchandise inventories. Depending on the kind of information needed and the available sources of that information, the retailer can elect to use a (1) dollar/perpetual/book system, (2) dollar/periodic/physical system, (3) unit/perpetual/book system, or (4) unit/periodic/physical system. An essential element in dollar control is knowing the true value of inventories. The two methods of inventory valuation are the cost method and the retail method. The cost method is simpler to use, while the retail method provides more timely and useful information.

The inventory-analysis system includes methods for evaluating the retailer's past merchandising performance as well as the decision-making tools available for controlling future merchandising activities. Stock turnover analysis and return on inventory investment ratios are used to evaluate the retailer's past performance. Dollar and unit open-to-buy are key methods of controlling future inventories.

KEY TERMS AND CONCEPTS

inventory-information system

inventory-analysis system

dollar control

unit control

perpetual book inventory

periodic physical inventory

dollar/perpetual/book system

dollar/periodic/physical system

unit/perpetual/book system

unit/periodic/physical system

cost method of inventory valuation

first-in, first-out method of costing inventories

last-in, first-out method of costing inventories

retail method of inventory valuation

stock turnover at retail

stock turnover at cost

stock turnover in units

average stock

return on inventory investment

open-to-buy

dollar open-to-buy at retail

dollar open-to-buy at cost

unit open-to-buy

maximum inventory

REVIEW QUESTIONS

1. Describe the concerns of dollar and unit control.
2. What distinguishes perpetual book inventory from periodic physical inventory?
3. How is a dollar/perpetual/book inventory determined?

4. What is the purpose of a dollar/periodic/physical inventory system?
5. What types of manual and automatic systems are used to gather information on the number of units sold?

6. How are stock levels monitored in a unit/periodic/physical inventory system? Briefly describe each method.
7. What are the two procedures used in calculating the cost value of merchandise items?
8. Describe the FIFO and LIFO methods of costing inventories.
9. What are the disadvantages of the cost method of inventory valuation?
10. Using the retail method of inventory valuation, how does the retailer obtain a reliable estimate of the ending inventory value at cost?
11. What is the cost-complement factor in the retail method of inventory valuation?
12. List the advantages of using the retail method of inventory valuation.
13. How are dollar (at retail and at cost) and unit stock turnover rates computed?
14. What are the benefits and limitations of high stock turnover rates?
15. Why is the return on inventory investment ratio important?
16. What is open-to-buy?
17. What are the procedural steps for determining dollar open-to-buy?
18. What is maximum inventory? How is it computed? What role does it have in determining unit open-to-buy?

ENDNOTES

1. "LIFO Survey Shows It's Here to Stay," *Chain Store Age Executive* (January, 1984), 32.
2. Ibid.
3. Ibid.
4. See Daniel J. Sweeney, "Improving the Profitability of Retail Merchandising Decisions," *Journal of Marketing* 37 (January, 1973): 60–68.

RELATED READINGS

Berlin, Peter D. "Using Retail Method of Inventory to Reduce Shrinkage." *Retail Control* (March 1984), 41–45.

Brame, Ken. "Merchandise Unit Control for Better Profitability." *Retail Control* (September 1984), 41–46.

Bunton, B. James, and Sycamore, Robert J. "What's Wrong with the Retail Method?" *Retail Control* (November 1982), 35–56.

Congdon, Robert J. "What's the Best Way to Capture Item Numbers?" *Retail Control* (December 1983), 13–18.

Fink, Michael M. "On-Line Big Ticket System at Wickes Furniture." *Retail Control* (December 1984), 32–49.

Gilberg, Mitchell. "Create Open-to-Buy Plans the Easy Way." *Retail Control* (December 1984), 21–31.

Greco, Alan J. "The Integration of Short and Long Range Planning for Retailers through Expanded Point-of-Sale Based Information Systems." *Developments in Marketing Science, Proceedings.* J. D. Lindquist, ed. (Academy of Marketing Science 1984), 348.

Lake, Marjorie A. "Strategies for Spreading OTB Timing!" *Stores* (April 1982), 19–23.

Levy, Michael, and Ingene, Charles A. "Using Residual Income Analysis (RIA) to Make Merchandising Decisions." *Retail Control* (January 1985), 27–41.

Mason, J. Berry, and Mayer, Morris L. "Retail Merchandise Information Systems for the 1980's." *Journal of Retailing* 56 (Spring 1980), 36–76.

Paxton, Daniel. "GMROI: The Axis of Retail Profit Planning." *Retail Control* (November 1983), 2–24.

Rothman, Marian Burk. "Expanding the Concept of Inventory Management." *Stores* (June 1979), 55–62.

Outline

SETTING THE RETAIL PRICE

Price-Setting Objectives
Price-Setting Determinants
Price-Setting Methods
Price-Setting Policies

ADJUSTING THE RETAIL PRICE

Discount Adjustments
Markon Adjustments
Markdown Adjustments
Markdown Strategies
Markdown Control

Objectives

■ Set specific, measurable price objectives consistent with the needs of both the consumer and the retailer

■ Assess the impact of demand, competition, cost, product, and legal considerations on the retailer's price-setting activities

■ Describe the methods by which retailers set their prices

■ Differentiate the numerous policies supplementing and modifying retail price-setting methods

■ Explain the need to adapt prices to the changing external and internal environmental conditions of the retail firm

■ Distinguish among the three basic types of price adjustments

■ Identify the reasons why price markdowns are necessary and explain the factors determining when and how much of a price markdown should be taken

■ Develop and implement markdown pricing and control strategies

21
The Retail Price

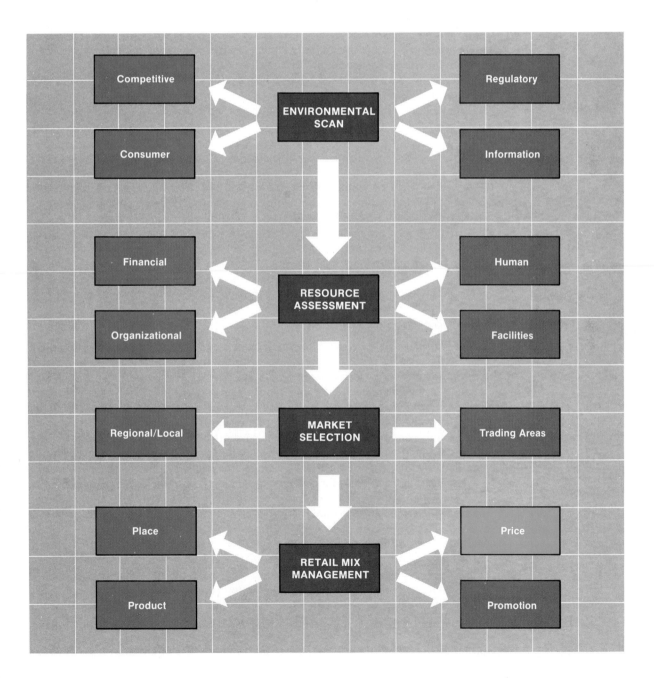

The right price is one consumers are willing and able to pay and retailers are willing to accept in exchange for merchandise and services. It is the price that allows the retailer to make a fair profit while providing the consumer with value satisfaction before, during, and after the sale. From the consumer's viewpoint, price can act as a forceful attraction or as an absolute repellent in the consumer's store-selection process. It can also serve as either an incentive or a deterrent in the consumer's decision to buy. Some consumers consider price the most important criterion in selecting stores and products; other consumers are far less sensitive to price. Retailers view prices in terms of (1) profitability, or how much they will have left after covering the merchandise cost and operating expenses; (2) sales volume, or how many merchandise units they can sell at various prices; (3) consumer traffic, or how many consumers they can attract to the store using various price levels or strategies; and (4) store image, or what type of image they will project to consumers through different price levels, policies, and strategies.

This chapter will examine price-setting objectives, determinants, methods, and policies as well as the various means of adjusting retail prices: discounts, markons, and markdowns. Figure 21–1 illustrates the pricing concerns of the retail manager.

SETTING THE RETAIL PRICE

Price-Setting Objectives

In any decision-making process, the decision maker should establish objectives. Price setting is no exception. Before the retailer can effectively establish prices consistent both with the firm's requirements and the consumer's expectations, it should set specific, measurable objectives based on well-thought-out pricing guidelines.

Retail price objectives are generally categorized in three groups: sales objectives, profit objectives, and competitive objectives. Some retailers make pricing decisions based on a single objective (e.g., increased sales volume); others strive to achieve a balance among all three objectives (e.g., a competitive price that will generate sales growth at a reasonable profit).

Sales Objectives

Retailers usually state sales objectives in terms of either sales volume or market share. The primary reason that retailers set **sales-volume objectives** is *to achieve future sales growth or to maintain current sales levels.* Sales growth in the form of "beating last year's sales" by some percentage is a common objective for many retailers. How appropriate this kind of pricing objective is ultimately depends on its effect on profits. Retailers can set prices to increase dollar sales volume, but if those prices fail to generate sufficient revenues to more than offset additional costs, the net result could be reduced profit levels. Before setting a volume-oriented price objective, the retailer should carefully evaluate the market's potential response. Otherwise, the higher net sales figure might be attained, but at a lower total profit.

Market-share objectives are *price-setting goals that retailers set to increase or maintain their share of the total market.* Many retailers prefer market-share objectives to sales objectives because the former represent a relative measure of how well they are performing in the market compared to competitors. Put another way, market share is a measure of the retailer's sales position relative to all competitors in the same trading area, in terms of percentage share of total sales for that trading area. When total sales within a trading area are expanding or contracting, the retailer's market share is a better reflection of what the store has accomplished than a total sales measurement.

In using *market-share growth* as the principal objective in setting prices, the retailer must realize that any increase in percentage share of the market must come

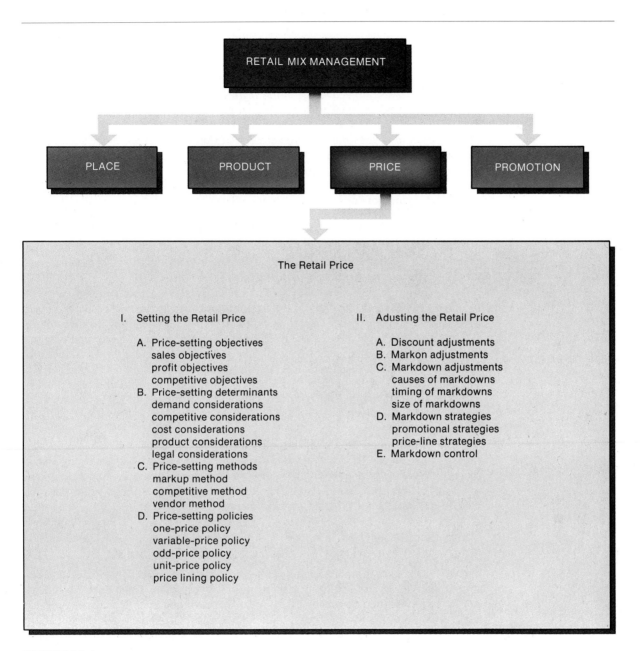

FIGURE 21–1
Setting and adjusting the retail price

at the expense of one or more of its competitors. Therefore, some type of aggressive action and retaliatory pricing actions should be anticipated from competitors seeking to protect their share of the market. As a pricing objective, market-share growth may be a more desirable goal for a new and expanding product market than an older one, since many competitors in the former situation are more interested in increasing their sales than market share. For mature and stable product markets, however, *market-share maintenance* is generally the more accepted pricing objective. Price-cutting activities in mature markets will force competitors to meet the new price, lowering profit margins for all concerned.

Profit Objectives

Profit maximization and target return on investment and on net sales are the three most-cited profit objectives that retailers use to guide their price-setting decisions. **Profit-maximization objectives** *seek the highest possible profit through pricing and other merchandising activities.* In practice, a profit-maximization objective has several limitations. First, a retailer might have to maximize profits at the expense of other members of the channel (wholesalers and manufacturers). If so, such activities will lead to conflict within the marketing channel, possibly jeopardizing the retailer's source of supply and substantially damaging the cooperative spirit necessary for distribution efficiencies. Second, for many people profit maximization has negative connotations of "price gouging" and excessive profits. Damage to the retailer's image and the chances of government intervention make profit-maximization efforts a risky policy. Third, if the retailer were to achieve excessive profits, it is very likely that additional competitors would be attracted into the trade area. Finally, because of inability to obtain perfect information, the retailer can never know if maximum profit objectives have been achieved.

Target return objectives are *profit objectives retailers commonly use for guiding their price-setting decisions.* Target returns are usually expressed as a certain percentage return on either capital investment or net sales. *Return on investment* (ROI) is a ratio of profits to capital investments (facilities, fixtures, equipment, inventory, etc.). ROI is a measure of how efficient a retailer is in using its investment to generate profits. As an example, the retailer may wish to earn a target return of 10, 15, or 20 percent. A 15 percent return simply means that the retailer wants to earn a net profit of 15 percent for every dollar of capital invested. A 15 percent ROI means the investment is working harder (i.e., more efficiently) than it would be at a 10 percent ROI.

Return on net sales (ROS) is the percentage value derived by dividing dollar profit by net sales. To achieve this targeted return, retailers set prices by using markup percentages large enough to cover all appropriate operating expenses (payroll, rent, utilities, professional services, etc.), plus the desired dollar profit per unit needed to generate the targeted percentage return on net sales.

Competitive Objectives

Competitive price objectives also take several forms, including *(1) meeting competition, (2) preventing competition,* and *(3) nonprice competition.* Some retailers simply play follow the leader in their price-setting activities. Their price objectives can be best described as meeting their major competitor's price. For some product lines, certain retailers within a given trade area act as price leaders. The price followers simply adjust their prices accordingly. Other retailers take preventing competition as their pricing objective. In preventive pricing, retailers usually set their prices at levels low enough to discourage additional competitors from entering the market. Finally, some retailers prefer to avoid price competition. Instead, they would rather compete on the basis of better product or service offerings, better locations and facilities, greater promotional efforts, or any other merchandising activities except price.

Price-Setting Determinants

Each retailer faces several considerations in trying to establish a selling price that will both sell the merchandise and offer a profitable return. In setting prices, the

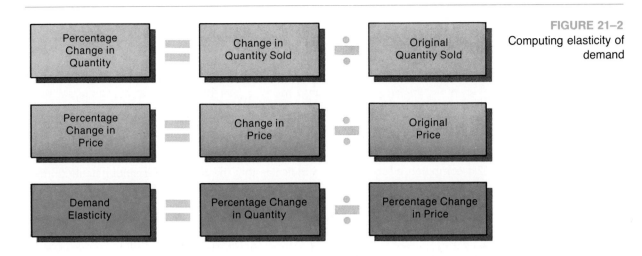

FIGURE 21–2
Computing elasticity of
demand

retailer should examine demand, competitive, cost, product, and legal considerations.

Demand Considerations

In setting a price, retailers should consider not only economic costs but noneconomic factors as well. Consumers' perceptions of and reactions to different prices must be taken into account before making price-setting decisions. By studying their target market's consuming behavior, retailers often can find circumstances in which they can "use price to communicate status, snob appeal, 'quality,' low purchase risk, or economy."[1] Other consumers, or even the same consumers under different purchase conditions, more closely reflect the law of demand. These consumers will buy more products at lower prices than at higher prices. "Psychological" pricing has little or no effect on that purchase behavior. Regardless of the price set, the retailer must always consider the effects of different price levels on consumer demand. This effect is called elasticity of demand.

Price elasticity of demand is *a measure of the effect a price change has on consumer demand (i.e., the number of units sold).* Demand elasticity describes the relationship between a percentage change in price and a percentage change in quantity sold. The formulas used in computing demand elasticity are shown in Figure 21–2. A demand elasticity greater than 1 is referred to as *elastic demand*—a condition in which a change in price strongly influences consumer demand. *Inelastic demand* occurs when a change in price has little or no influence on consumer demand. A demand elasticity of less than 1 represents an inelastic situation. A demand elasticity of 1 represents *unitary elasticity* whereby changes in price are offset exactly by changes in demand.

A good way to remember the difference between elastic demand and inelastic demand is to consider the consumer's degree of *sensitivity* to the price change. Inelastic demand means that consumers are relatively insensitive to the change in price, whereas under elastic demand conditions they are sensitive to price changes.

To illustrate how price elasticity of demand can be calculated, consider the following example. Suppose a restaurant raised its price for a sirloin steak dinner from $10 to $14 and experienced a sharp drop in orders for the sirloin dinner, from 800 to 400 in the first month. The elasticity of demand for this menu item is computed as follows:

$$\text{percentage change in quantity} = \frac{400}{800} = 50\%$$

$$\text{percentage change in price} = \frac{4}{10} = 40\%$$

$$\text{demand elasticity} = \frac{50\%}{40\%} = 1.25$$

The computed elasticity of 1.25 indicates that the demand for sirloin steak dinners is elastic. A $4 increase in price had a major effect on consumer demand (50% decrease) for this particular menu item.

In some cases, changing the price of a merchandise item will not only change the demand for that item, it also will change the demand for a different merchandise item. *Cross-elasticity of demand* occurs when a change in the price of one product results in a change in demand for another product. For example, the demand for a complementary product (e.g., film) may decrease as a result of increased prices and reduced demand for the product it complements (e.g., cameras). A different result can occur between "substitute" products. In this situation, cross-elasticity of demand might produce an increased demand for tea as the price of coffee rises. The price/demand interplay between products must be watched closely by retailers if they are to avoid costly pricing errors.

While it would be virtually impossible to make a formal determination of the price elasticity of demand for each merchandise line carried, the retailer should develop a "feel" for which products are highly sensitive to changes in price. Knowing whether a product is generally elastic, inelastic, or unitary in demand is one of several important factors a retailer must understand in setting a retail price in harmony with the target market's demand.

Competitive Considerations

A retailer does not operate in a vacuum and certainly cannot set prices as though no one else exists. Therefore, it is imperative that the retailer consider the pricing actions of competitors in setting prices. By reviewing the past and current pricing strategies of competitors, the retailer can determine whether its prices are in line with the competitors that are most likely sources for consumer price comparisons. While prices need not equal those of competitors, the retailer should provide consumers with a price difference within an acceptable range. In their minds, consumers will accept and justify some price differential among competitive retail stores because of differences in service, location, and product-mix factors.

An equally important reason for examining competitors' price strategies is to determine what reactions the retailer might expect from competitors in response to its own price-setting activities. Undue price competition among retailers in the form of pricing "wars" usually does not benefit any of the parties. In setting prices, retailers must realize that price competition is one of the least distinctive forms of competition. Price cuts by the retailer can be instantaneously offset by competitors that easily match the lower price. Given the relative brevity of price competition (because of the high likelihood of precipitating price reprisals), retailers must consider the alternative forms of competition (product, service, promotion, and so on) before engaging in aggressive price-setting activities that could have a serious negative impact on their profitability. To increase sales at the expense of profits is not a wise pricing strategy, at least not over the long run.

The freedom a retailer enjoys in setting prices depends on its estimate of its competitive position. If a retailer judges its competitive position as strong because of a distinctive retail mix, highly loyal consumers, or a unique store image, then the retailer has greater freedom in price-setting decisions. On the other hand, me-too retailers that lack distinctiveness in the nonprice areas of their operations are restricted to a me-too pricing strategy.

Finally, the retailer must recognize that the competitor's price is more important for some merchandise items than for others. In particular, the competitor's price is an important consideration for two different product groups. First, the retailer must closely consider products that *consumers purchase frequently* and the *supplier distributes intensively* since consumers can easily make price comparisons. Second, for products with high unit value—big-ticket items—retailers need to seriously consider competitors' prices. For these kinds of products the retailer can set prices below, with, or above those of competitors, depending upon the type of price image desired.

Cost Considerations

A major determinant in any price-setting decision is the cost the retailer must pay for merchandise. In defining the retailer's merchandise cost, it is not only important to include the actual cost of the merchandise, but also all costs incurred in getting the merchandise into the store and in preparing the merchandise for sale. Retailers determine merchandise costs by following the procedure outlined in Figure 21–3. By calculating merchandise cost in this way, the retailer has a more accurate picture of the true cost of the merchandise. For many retailers, merchandise cost is both a reference and starting point for price-setting decisions. Their approach to the pricing problem is a cost-oriented approach in which they set the retail selling price of a product at a level high enough to cover not only the cost of the merchandise, but also the fixed and variable expenses associated with merchandising the product plus an additional profit margin.

Product Considerations

Retailers should not make price-setting decisions without considering the characteristics of the product. Different products have the ability to command different prices at different times and in different locations. In setting the retail price, the retailer must consider these differences. While it would be impossible to discuss the effects

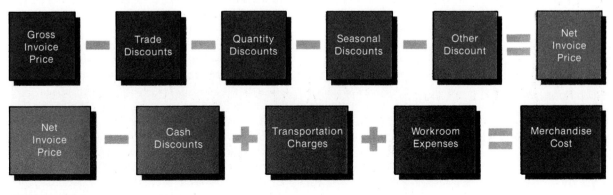

FIGURE 21–3
Determining merchandise cost

of all the varied product characteristics on price setting, some selected examples should illustrate their importance.

Retailers must consider *product perishability* and its associated risks in pricing a product. Perishable products often require higher initial prices to cover markdowns that are necessary as the product loses its marketability. Product perishability takes several forms:

- *physical perishability*—a loss of marketability due to physical damage or deterioration of the product
- *style or fashion perishability*—a loss of marketability as a result of style, fashion, or model obsolescence, as in being "out of style" or "the old model"
- *seasonal perishability*—a loss of marketability because the product is out of season
- *competitive perishability*—a loss of marketability as a result of the aggressive actions of competitors, such as a pricing war

Whatever form product perishability takes, the initial and subsequent impact on the retail price of the product can be substantial. It is also worth noting that a retailer might decide to set a lower initial price on some highly perishable products to move them out before a loss in marketability occurs. For example, a retailer might place a low price on a quart of fresh strawberries during the strawberry-picking season.

Product quality, be it perceived or real, is another major product determinant the retailer should examine before setting a price. Depending on the price/quality image the retailer wants to project, one of several possible pricing strategies can be used. Figure 21–4 illustrates nine possible pricing strategies based on product quality. From this figure, we can see that the retailer can assume quite a number of roles in offering a particular product-quality level at various price levels.

Product uniqueness is a characteristic that retailers can use to realize a premium price for the product. Consumers who seek something different tend to be insensitive to price in their buying behavior and are therefore willing to pay higher prices for products that exhibit originality.

Legal Considerations

Price-setting decisions are subject to a number of legal constraints. According to law, any pricing activity that any governmental agency considers to be a present or probable restraint on trade or an unfair trade practice can be illegal. Price setting is

FIGURE 21–4

Product-quality considerations in price-setting decisions (source: Phillip Kotler, *Principles of Marketing* [Englewood Cliffs, NJ: Prentice-Hall, 1980], 402)

	PRODUCT PRICE		
PRODUCT QUALITY	High	Medium	Low
High	Premium Strategy	Penetration Strategy	Superbargain Strategy
Medium	Overpricing Strategy	Average-Quality Strategy	Bargain Strategy
Low	Hit-and-run Strategy	Shoddy-Goods Strategy	Cheap-Goods Strategy

perhaps the most regulated aspect of the retailer's business. The legalities of pricing were discussed in Chapter 5.

Price-Setting Methods

Price-setting decisions are both an art and a science. A policy of setting low prices might well produce high sales volumes, but inadequate profit margins. High prices usually allow for excellent profit margins; however, before those profits can be realized, the merchandise must be sold. Knowing when a price is too high or too low is an art that comes with the experience of being in the business. Nevertheless, certain price-setting methods blend the art of experience with the science of retail mathematics.[2]

Markup Method of Pricing

Markup is the difference between the cost of the merchandise and its retail price. Although markup appears to be a relatively simple concept, it incorporates a number of complex relationships expressed in a variety of ways. Before examining each of these relationships and expressions in detail, let's review the basic dimensions of markup. First, markup can be determined and expressed in terms of either *dollars* or as a *percentage* of either the cost of the merchandise or its retail price. Second, when markup is determined on a single item of merchandise, it is called an *individual markup*. A *cumulative markup* refers to the markup on more than one merchandise item. Third, markups can be viewed in terms of what was originally planned (the initial markup) or in terms of what was actually realized (the maintained markup). Finally, markup can be adjusted by cash discounts and workroom expenses to determine gross margin.

Dollar markup. **Dollar markup** is *a cost-oriented approach to setting retail prices wherein the retailer adds a dollar amount to the cost of the merchandise that is large enough to cover related operating expenses and to provide a given dollar profit.* The basic dollar relationships between merchandise cost, retail price, and markup are best expressed as follows:

$$retail = cost + markup$$
$$cost = retail - markup$$
$$markup = retail - cost$$

Using these formulas, the retailer can solve any dollar markup problem. Dollar markup is used most frequently for big-ticket items. For example, the owner of a jewelry store that has paid $3,000 for a diamond ring and prices it at $4,000 is just as likely to think in terms of a $1,000 markup as a 25 percent markup on retail or a 33-1/3 percent markup on cost. In addition, many retailers prefer dollar markups because they think they represent a "hard" as opposed to a "relative" number. Dollar values simply appear more real. Dollar markup can be deceptive when one compares different lines of merchandise.

Percentage markups. **Percentage markups** are *usually calculated to facilitate the process of setting prices and to permit comparisons between merchandise lines and departments.* In calculating percentage markups the retailer must first determine the markup base. Markups can be calculated on the cost of the merchandise or on the retail selling price. The formulas for calculating percentage markup are illustrated in Figure 21–5. As an illustration, suppose a hardware retailer pays $80 for a power lawnmower that sells at retail for $150. The retailer's percentage markup on cost

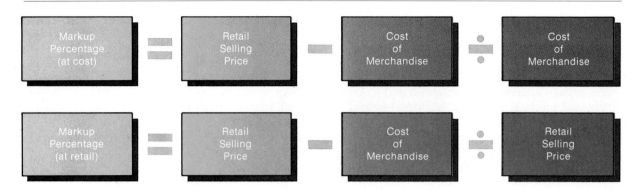

FIGURE 21–5
Determining markup percentage (at cost or at retail)

would be 87.5 percent, whereas on retail it is 46.7 percent. The calculations are as follows:

$$\text{markup percentage at cost} = \frac{\$150 - \$80}{\$80} = 87.5\%$$

$$\text{markup percentage at retail} = \frac{\$150 - \$80}{\$150} = 46.7\%$$

In practice, retailers prefer to compute markups on the retail base for several reasons:

- *psychological reasons*—a retail-based markup is always smaller than a cost-based markup; therefore, it is more acceptable to consumers who desire smaller markups
- *comparison reasons*—a retail-based markup facilitates comparisons between store operations and trade statistics because trade-association statistics generally are reported by percentage of net sales. Also, markup on retail is more consistent with internal expresssions of financial operating ratios that are computed as a percentage of net sales.
- *inventory reasons*—markup on retail is consistent with the retail method of inventory (which was discussed in Chapter 20)
- *emphasis reasons*—a retail-based markup encourages the retailer to think in terms of retail prices and their resulting profits.

Given its popularity, retail-based markups will serve as the focus for the remaining discussion of markups.

Cumulative markups. In daily operations, retailers find it useful to use a cumulative markup on a group of merchandise items (e.g., a product line). This cumulative markup cannot be computed by averaging the individual markups on each merchandise item in the group. Instead, *the retailer must calculate* **cumulative markup** *based on the weight each item contributes to the total markup of all the items in the merchandise group.* To illustrate, the buyer for the men's department of a large specialty store wants to determine the cumulative markup on a stock of men's summer suits. A check of inventory and purchase records for the month of June reveals that the month started with an inventory costing $20,000 that retails for $40,000. Additional purchases costing $16,000 and retailing for $30,000 were added since the beginning of the month. The total cost and retail value of the merchandise is

	Cost	Retail
beginning stock:	$20,000	$40,000
additional purchases:	+ 16,000	+ 30,000
total stock:	$36,000	$70,000

The cumulative markup percentage at retail is computed as

$$\text{markup percentage at retail} = \frac{\text{retail (\$)} - \text{cost (\$)}}{\text{retail (\$)}}$$

$$= \frac{\$70,000 - \$36,000}{\$70,000} = 48.6\%$$

Using the cumulative markup percentage, the retailer can adjust markup plans throughout the merchandising season.

Up to this point, we have discussed markup in general terms as the difference between the cost of merchandise and its retail price. However, it is now necessary to distinguish among three forms of markup: the initial markup, the maintained markup, and the gross margin.

Initial and maintained markups. The **initial markup** *refers to the difference between merchandise cost and the original retail price.* Stated differently, it represents the first markup placed on a merchandise item. Rarely, however, does the retailer receive the initial markup for each item within a merchandise line because of the retail reductions that decrease the original retail price set for the merchandise item. As previously discussed, retail reductions take the form of shortages resulting from merchandise that is either lost or stolen, discounts granted to employees and special customers, and markdowns that sometimes become necessary to sell merchandise that has lost some of its marketability.

A **maintained markup** is *the difference between gross merchandise cost and the actual selling price of the merchandise.* Stated differently, maintained markup equals initial markup minus all retail reductions. The difference between the initial markup and the maintained markup is that the former is what the retailer originally hoped to receive, whereas the latter is what the retailer actually received.

Although retailers do not usually expect to gain the full initial markup on merchandise sales, they still need to use initial markup as a profit-margin planning tool. By carefully planning the initial markup, the retailer establishes a benchmark for achieving an acceptable profit after covering store operating expenses and retail reductions.

The **initial markup percentage** is the key element in guiding the retailer's price-setting decisions. Essentially, it is a pricing strategy that establishes the initial markup percentage—and therefore the retail price—to achieve a specified target profit. The basic formula retailers use to calculate the initial markup percentage is shown in Figure 21–6.

As shown, the initial markup percentage equals the sum of the operating expenses, operating profit, alterations cost, and retail reduction, divided by the sum of the net sales and retail reduction. As previously stated, the initial markup must be large enough to cover store operating expenses and retail reductions as well as to provide a profit and to cover any alteration costs. Alteration costs are added because they represent a legitimate expense that the retailer incurs in the process of making

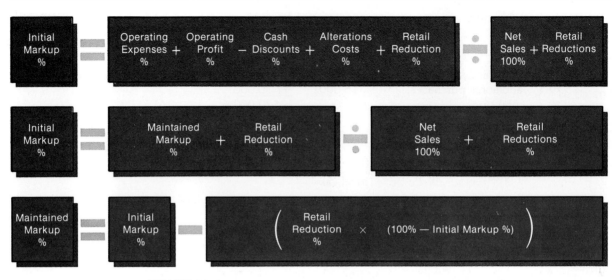

FIGURE 21–6
Computing the initial and maintained markup percentage

the merchandise more marketable. As the word implies, alteration is any change the retailer must make in the product to sell it in its final form. Examples are alterations in trousers, sport coats, assembling products that manufacturers send in parts, and so forth.

As a brief illustration of the initial markup percentage formula, take a look at the following problem. A sporting goods retailer wants to know what the initial markup percentage should be on a new line of tennis rackets. Planning records reveal the following figures: (1) estimated operating expenses of 28 percent, (2) planned operating profit of 12 percent, (3) estimated alteration cost (e.g., stringing rackets) of 4 percent, (4) expected shortages of 2 percent, (5) planned markdowns of 4 percent, and (6) estimated employee discounts of 1 percent. Using the preceding formula, the initial markup percentage should be

$$\frac{\text{initial}}{\text{markup \%}} = \frac{28\% + 12\% + 4\% + 7\%}{100\% + 7\%}$$

$$= \frac{51}{107} = 47.7\%$$

To determine the actual percentage markup realized once the foregoing computations have been completed, the retailer can use the maintained markup percentage formula expressed in Figure 21–6. For example, if the retailer had originally planned for an initial markup of 40 percent, and retail reductions amounting to 8 percent actually occurred, then

$$\frac{\text{maintained}}{\text{markup \%}} = .40 - [.08(1.00 - .40)]$$

$$= .352 \text{ or } 35.2\%$$

The retail reduction percentage is adjusted because it was based on net sales, while the initial markup percentage was based on the original retail price.

Gross margin. Gross margin *refers to the difference between net sales and total merchandise costs.* As such, it is closely related to maintained markup (net sales minus gross merchandise costs). The differences between gross margin and maintained markup or between total merchandise cost and gross merchandise costs are adjustments for cash discounts and alteration costs. This difference can be illustrated as follows:

$$\frac{\text{gross}}{\text{margin}} = \frac{\text{maintained}}{\text{markup}} + \frac{\text{cash}}{\text{discounts}} - \frac{\text{alteration}}{\text{costs}}$$

$$\frac{\text{maintained}}{\text{markup}} = \frac{\text{gross}}{\text{margin}} - \frac{\text{cash}}{\text{discounts}} + \frac{\text{alteration}}{\text{costs}}$$

If there were no cash discounts or alteration costs, then gross margin would equal maintained markup.

Competitive Pricing Method

With the competitive pricing method, the retailer sets retail prices in relation to competitors' prices. It is largely a judgmental price-setting method whereby the retailer uses competitive prices as reference points for price-setting decisions. Competitive price setting is popular among some retailers because it is simple to administer. A list of trade-area competitors and their merchandise prices is essentially all a retailer needs to make pricing decisions. The basic decision rules associated with this pricing procedure are to price either below, at, or above competitors' price levels. In most cases, it is not a question of being a high- or a low-price retailer; rather, the decision is to select the relative position of being higher or lower in price when compared to competitors. Figure 21–7 (p. 588) illustrates the relative price positions of types of retailers.

Pricing below competition. One price-setting alternative is to establish price levels below those of competitors. Mass merchandisers, such as discounters, engage in pricing strategies that attempt to undersell competitors. Pricing below competition is a price-setting policy aimed at generating large dollar revenues to achieve a desired dollar target return. In other words, these retailers practice a low-price/high-volume/high-turnover pricing strategy.

For the lower-price retailer to succeed at selling merchandise at low prices and still generate sufficient profit margins, certain merchandising strategies must be used. To price below competition, the retailer must not only secure merchandise at a lower cost, it must also keep operating expenses as low as possible. The lower-price retailer usually stocks and sells "presold" or "self sold" merchandise, thereby reducing advertising and personal selling expenses. Typically, these retailers sell name brands at the lowest prices to build traffic and to promote a low-price image. For many standard items, low-price retailers stock private brands that consumers cannot easily compare with other retailers' private brands and on which they can receive high margins at the lower prices. Additionally, these retailers keep their service offerings at the minimum levels necessary to sell the merchandise. Any nonessential services they offer carry a separate, additional charge. Their physical facilities are spartan and project an austere image. In addition, the structure of the store's management organization is generally flat (the number and specialization of managers are minimal and general). The profit strategy of the retailer that elects to price below competition, generally speaking, is to keep expenses low to keep prices

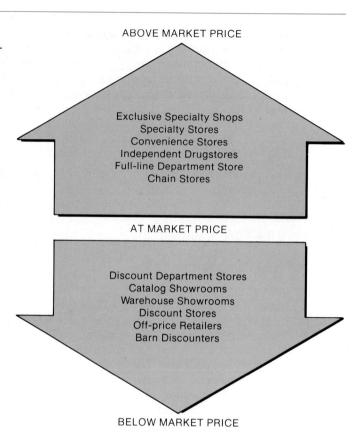

FIGURE 21–7
The relative price position of retailers

ABOVE MARKET PRICE

Exclusive Specialty Shops
Specialty Stores
Convenience Stores
Independent Drugstores
Full-line Department Store
Chain Stores

AT MARKET PRICE

Discount Department Stores
Catalog Showrooms
Warehouse Showrooms
Discount Stores
Off-price Retailers
Barn Discounters

BELOW MARKET PRICE

low. This, in turn, attracts consumers and generates a profitable sales level through rapid inventory turnover rates.

Pricing below competition is not without its risks. This aggressive price-setting strategy often leads to pricing wars that put considerable strain on the profitability of all competing retailers within the trading area. Also, retailers that rely primarily on price competition as their principal merchandising strategy find that if that strategy fails, they cannot very easily reposition themselves against the higher-priced retailers that have a variety of competitive weapons (e.g., assortment, service, and selective promotional strategies).

Pricing with competition. The second alternative method of competitive price setting open to the retailer is to sell a merchandise item at the "going" or traditional price within the store's general trading area. Pricing on par with competition implies that the retailer has, in general, elected to de-emphasize the price factor as a major merchandising tool. Instead, it has decided to compete on a location, product, service, and promotion basis. Competitive price parity does not necessarily imply that the retailer matches every price exactly. Usually this policy involves setting prices that are within an acceptable range of the competitive standard. Small price discrepancies either go unnoticed by consumers or are accepted by them, especially if they reflect proportional variances in service levels.

Although competitive pricing is a relatively safe and simple method of establishing the retail selling price, the retailer must monitor the competitive situation to avoid missing a pricing opportunity. If a competitor makes a small price reduction in key merchandise that another retailer is offering, and that retailer does not make an equivalent price reduction, the second retailer stands to lose considerable sales volume and profit. As a result, price parity among retailers is a common practice that does not "rock the boat."

Pricing above competition.   Some retailers attempt to differentiate themselves by setting prices above the going trade-area price. The profit strategy of the higher-priced retailer is the opposite of that of the lower-priced retailer. Although the higher-priced stores do not expect to achieve the turnover rates of their lower-priced competitors, they do expect their products to cover variable selling expenses and to make a fair contribution to the store's fixed operating expenses. At the same time, the higher-priced retailer expects its products to make a substantially *greater per-unit profit* than the lower-priced retailer's products.

Strategically, if the retailer decides to set prices above those of competitors, then it must include several of the following consumer benefits: (1) many free services, (2) higher quality merchandise, (3) exclusive merchandise, (4) personalized sales attention, (5) plusher shopping atmosphere, (6) full-staffed stores in all functional areas of store operations, (7) prestige image, (8) superconvenient locations, and (9) longer store hours. In other words, the retailer of higher-priced merchandise must provide consumers with a *total product* having functional, aesthetic, and service features that give consumers the psychological benefits they expect from buying, using, and possessing the product. Many exclusive specialty shops and some department stores engage in price-setting strategies that establish prices above those of less-prestigious competitors.

Vendor Pricing Method

A third price-setting alternative available to the retailer is to let the manufacturer or wholesaler determine the retail price. This type of price setting assumes the form of a "suggested retail price." Vendors suggest retail prices by either supplying the retailer with a price list, printing the price on the package, or affixing a price tag to the merchandise. While the retailer is not legally required to use the suggested retail price, many retailers think that for certain products it represents a fair estimate of the going market price. For retailers who are part of a highly integrated marketing channel of distribution, the suggested retail price is often a key element in the *total* marketing strategy for that channel. Therefore, the retailer is expected to abide by it.

Some manufacturers believe they have a vested interest in trying to maintain retail prices for their products at or above certain levels or within a set range of prices. For products consumers view as having a strong price/quality relationship, maintaining price is essential to the product's image as a quality piece of merchandise. Also, price maintenance creates a reasonable price consistency among similar retail outlets within a trading area. If a consumer purchases one of the manufacturer's products in one retail outlet for $20 and soon discovers that the same product is available at another outlet for $15, that consumer is very likely to be dissatisfied with the product regardless of how well it performs. Finally, if the manufacturer permits certain retailers to reduce prices below certain levels, other high-margin retailers may decide to eliminate the product from their merchandise assortment.

While the vendor method of setting prices does relieve the retailer of that difficult task, its use is not appropriate for many products and many retailers. As guidelines for retailers, the vendor's suggested price is not appropriate when (1) it fails to provide a sufficient margin to cover merchandise costs, store operating expenses, and an adequate profit; (2) it fails to stimulate sufficient sales; (3) it simply is not competitive with merchandise of a similar quality; or (4) it fails to provide the retailer's customers with the value they deserve.

Price-Setting Policies

Retailers are also guided by a number of price-setting policies that supplement and modify the price-setting methods discussed in the previous section. For example, a retailer may set prices by using the markup method. The established retail price (e.g., $40) is then modified to accommodate an odd pricing policy (e.g., $39.95). This section discusses several price-setting policies: the one-price policy, the variable-price policy, the multiple-price policy, odd pricing, unit pricing, and price lining.

One-Price Policy

Most U.S. retailers follow a **one-price policy,** charging *all customers the same price for the same product under similar circumstances.* In contrast to many foreign consumers, most U.S. consumers are accustomed to paying the established price marked on the merchandise. Price "haggling" or "bargaining" is usually limited to big-ticket items such as automobiles and appliances and to used merchandise for which the value of the merchandise is subject to negotiation. Bargaining over the price for big-ticket items often centers on the allowance the customer can receive for a trade-in. The use of a trade-in allowance gives the retailer the opportunity to "wheel and deal" to make a sale, while still maintaining a basic one-price policy.

A one-price policy has its advantages. First, it greatly facilitates the speed at which each transaction can be made. Second, a one-price policy helps to simplify the retailer's various accounting records. Third, it substantially reduces the retailer's need for sales personnel and makes a self-service strategy possible. The major weakness in the one-price policy is a lack of flexibility; that is, it does not allow the retailer to readily adjust prices to the customer's purchase motives (e.g., economy).

Variable-Price Policy

A **variable-price policy** *allows the customer to negotiate the final selling price.* The best bargainers receive the lowest prices. Retailers that use variable pricing deal in merchandise with one or more of the following characteristics: (1) high initial markups, (2) need for personal selling, (3) unstandardized or specialized product features, (4) service requirements, and (5) infrequent purchase rates. While variable pricing gives the retailer price flexibility and increases its ability to adjust to the consumer's purchase motivations, it can increase the retailer's labor costs, selling time, and dissatisfaction among any customers who were unable to negotiate the same low price as some customers.

Multiple-Price Policy

A **multiple-price policy** *attempts to increase both unit and dollar sales volume.* Using this pricing strategy, the retailer gives customers a discount for making quantity purchases. That is, the retailer offers consumers a reduced price if they are willing to purchase several units at the multiple-unit price. For example, the retailer can price a can of peas at $.50 each or three for $1.37. In this example, consumers can save $.13 by taking advantage of the retailer's multiple-unit pricing policy. Essentially, multiple-unit pricing is a form of psychological pricing, in that many consumers have been conditioned to expect a bargain price if they buy in multiple quantities.

The ethics of multiple-unit pricing have received considerable attention from consumer groups in recent years. The attention has been directed at retailers that use two practices: (1) *deceptive multiple-unit prices,* the practice of either implying a substantial savings (e.g., $.50 each or two for $.99), or no savings at all (e.g.,

*How might the retailer
misuse this type of
price-setting policy?*

CHAPTER 21
THE RETAIL PRICE

$.49 each or two for $.98); and (2) *phony multiple-unit prices,* advertising a multiple-unit price of three for $.98 when the individual price is $.29. These deceptions are based on the recognition that consumers naturally assume that multiple-unit prices represent a savings.

Retailers commonly use multiple-unit pricing with products purchased on a regular, frequent basis, and characterized by a low per-unit price. Supermarkets, for example, use multiple pricing to stimulate sales for such basic staples as canned goods, paper products, and soft drinks. Multiple-unit pricing is also used occasionally to clear out merchandise that has lost some of its marketability. A clothing store might price men's suits at 2 for $199 (regularly $150 each) during its end-of-season sale.

Odd-Pricing Policy

Odd pricing is *the strategy of setting prices that end in odd numbers (e.g., $.49, $1.99, $9.95, and $29.50).* By setting prices below even-dollar amounts, the retailer is using the psychological ploy that consumers perceive odd prices as substantially below even prices (e.g., $2.95 is perceived to be considerably less than $3.00).[3] The theory is that a $2.95 price will make consumers think in terms of $2.00 rather than $3.00. With increased state sales tax rates, however, the usefulness of the odd-pricing strategy has diminished. Many consumers have now been conditioned to think in terms of the next dollar value. Nevertheless, odd pricing continues as a major pricing policy for many retailers.

The strategy of odd pricing varies with the general price level of the product involved. Products with low per-unit prices (under $5) are odd priced at one or two cents below an even price (e.g., $.49, $1.99, and $3.98). As the per-unit price increases, products are priced at odd values that represent a greater reduction from even prices. For example, products ranging in price from $10 to $20 tend to be odd priced at $9.95 or $19.95—a five-cent differential. Nine- and five-dollar odd endings are common among big-ticket items (e.g., $199 and $495). While nine and five are the most common odd-price endings, retailers also use three and seven to project a bargain-price image.

What is the psychology involved with odd pricing?

Unit-Pricing Policy

Given the multiplicity of package sizes and shapes together with the diversity of price tags and product labels, many consumers cannot determine which purchase is the best value for their money. As a result, some retailers have initiated a unit-pricing system to eliminate that uncertainty.[4] **Unit pricing** is *the retailing practice of posting prices on a per-unit-measurement basis.* By stating the price per ounce, pound, quart, or yard for each brand, the retailer helps the consumer make price comparisons among products of different sizes, shapes, and quantities.

The general procedure retailers use in posting unit prices is to place per-unit price tags on shelf facings either directly above or below the product. Maintaining a unit price system usually means that the retailer will incur additional time, labor, equipment, and material expenses. Some stores have initiated unit-pricing systems in anticipation of possible legislation. In other cases, stores have been required by legislative action to install unit pricing. For the most part, unit pricing is used by retailers of food goods, drug products, beauty aids, and other similar products.

Price-Lining Policy

The objective of a **price-lining** policy is *to direct retail prices at a targeted consumer group.*[5] To accomplish this objective, the retailer must perform two tasks. First, the retailer must identify the appropriate pricing zone for each targeted consumer group. A **pricing zone** is *a range of prices that appeals to a particular group of consumers either for demographic reasons* (e.g., income or occupation), *psychographic reasons* (e.g., life-style or personality), *product usage reasons* (e.g., heavy or light users), or *product benefit reasons* (e.g., economy, function, or sociability). Usually, retailers identify price zones in broad terms. For example, the economy price range, the intermediate or family price range, and the prestige or luxury price range are typical consumer categories for price lining. While most retailers tend to focus on one broadly defined price range, some retailers try to cover more than one range (e.g., middle-to-high), but rarely try to appeal to all three ranges. Attempting to cover the entire price range would defeat the target-marketing objective of a price-lining strategy.

Pricing lines are *specific pricing points established within pricing zones.* For example, assume a specialty store retailer has identified three pricing zones for men's suits. They are (1) the low-range suit (under $100), (2) the middle-range suit ($100–$200), and (3) the high-range suit (above $200). Also suppose the retailer has targeted the middle-price range consumer as the one to whom it wishes to appeal. Then, the retailer might establish price lines at $119.95, $159.95, and $189.95. The use of price lines is commonly associated with shopping goods and in particular with wearing apparel.

A price-lining policy has several advantages for both the consumer and the retailer. For the consumer, the advantages are (1) it facilitates comparison among merchandise items; and (2) it reduces shopping confusion and frustration and aids the consumer in making purchase decisions. For the retailer, price lining (1) simplifies the personal selling effort, (2) makes advertising and sales promotion more effective, (3) increases the chances of trading up the customer to the next price, (4) creates an image of good merchandise depth and support, and (5) simplifies the buying process, since the buyer secures only merchandise that can be profitably priced at a given pricing point.

A price-lining policy also creates some difficulties. If the retailer does not carefully establish pricing points, it is likely to project an image of inadequate merchandise assortment to consumers and therefore eliminate customers who are either above or below the price lines they seek. A second potential problem is that retailers find it extremely difficult to reduce one line without reducing all lines. To do so is to destroy the carefully planned spread between all price lines. Price lining also makes it easier for competitors to develop successful competitive-pricing strategies. A limited number of price lines might well aid competitors in planning counter-price strategies. Finally, during times of rising costs, it is difficult to maintain price lines without reducing product quality.

ADJUSTING THE RETAIL PRICE

Price adjustments are one means whereby the retailer can adapt to changing external and internal environmental conditions. Retailers often find it necessary to make either upward or downward adjustments in their prices. These price movements are essential if the retailer expects to accomplish the dual goals of meeting customers' price expectations and preserving acceptable profit margins. This section examines the three basic types of adjustment: discounts, markons, and markdowns.

Discount Adjustments

In our previous discussion on developing the merchandise budget (see Chapter 19), we examined the role of markdowns, discounts, and shortages in planning retail reductions. **Discounts** *were defined as reductions in the original retail price, granted to store employees as special fringe benefits and to special customers* (e.g., clergy, senior citizens, and some disadvantaged consumers) *in recognition of their special circumstances.* Regardless of the reason for granting the discount, each discount given represents a downward adjustment in the retailer's price, and as such has a direct impact upon the retailer's profit margins.

Employee discounts are a customary privilege in many retail organizations. They represent a supplementary means of compensating employees and are frequently used as a motivational tool. The extent of the employee discount varies considerably from one retail organization to another. However, a 10–20 percent discount is quite common.

Customer discounts are granted to special consumer segments for a number of reasons. Drug stores frequently give "golden agers" discounts to customers over the age of 65. Many retailers grant charitable organizations a discount from the original selling price. Sales to other business or professional organizations are often made at a discount price.

Markon Adjustments

Retailers use the term "markon" in a variety of ways. However, for our purposes, **markon** *refers to markups taken after the initial selling price has been established.* In essence, a markon represents an additional markup and an upward adjustment in the initial selling price. These upward adjustments are needed to cover increases in wholesale prices and operating expenses as well as to correct consumers' quality perceptions of merchandise. When consumers believe the quality of a product is questionable due to its low price, retailers can sometimes correct this misconception by increasing the price, thereby taking advantage of what is commonly referred to as the perceived price/quality relationship. Retailers also take additional markons when the demand for the merchandise item is high and consumer price sensitivity for the item is low.

Markdown Adjustments

A **markdown** is *a downward adjustment in the original selling price of a merchandise item.* A markdown represents the difference between what the merchandise was originally valued at and what it is actually sold for. Markdowns, together with shortages and employee/customer discounts, are the *three major factors* retailers consider in planning retail reductions (see Chapter 19). Retailers use both dollars and percentages to express markdowns. "All men's slacks reduced $5!" is a typical dollar markdown expression. Per-unit **markdown percentages** are *computed as a percentage of the reduced selling price or as a percentage of the original selling price.* The latter expression is generally referred to as the off-retail markdown percentage.

The formula used in computing per-unit markdowns as a percentage of the reduced price is shown in Figure 21–8. For example, a dress originally priced at $30 is reduced to $20; the markdown as a percentage of the reduced price would be ($30 − $10)/$20 or 50 percent. This procedure is generally preferred for expressing reduced prices.

The off-retail markdown percentage formula is also shown in Figure 21–8. Using the same dress example, the off-retail markdown percentage would be 33-1/3 percent or ($30 − $20)/$30.

Causes of Markdowns

Retailers must take markdowns for a number of reasons. In some cases, the causes of markdowns are beyond the control of the retailer. These causes generally are the result of unforeseen shifts in consumer expectations and unexpected changes in the retail market environment. In other cases, markdowns are caused by errors in the retailer's judgment. The causes for these markdowns are either fully or partially

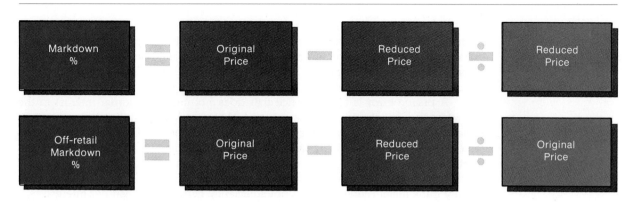

FIGURE 21–8
Determining markdown percentage

controllable if the retailer will initiate the necessary corrective actions. Markdown causes can be categorized as buying-, selling-, and operational-related causes.

Buying-related causes. Many markdowns result from errors that retailers make in buying or procuring merchandise. Price reductions are often necessary to adjust for errors in the assortment, support, and quality of merchandise the retailer purchased, as well as for mistakes in the timing of purchases and the selection of suppliers.

Assortment errors occur when the retailer buys brands, styles, models, sizes, colors, and materials that do not match what consumers want to buy. Assortment errors are serious not only because they necessitate markdowns, but also because they can require major price reductions to move the merchandise. Very attractive prices are typically the only means of selling merchandise that the consumer really does not want. Even then, some items may not be sold.

Support errors are quantity errors that result when the retailer buys too much merchandise. By overbuying and overstocking certain merchandise items, the retailer ties up capital that could be invested in more profitable merchandise. In addition, the retailer frequently faces cash-flow problems when too much money is tied up in overstocked merchandise items. Support errors occur when the retailer fails to plan sales, stocks, and purchases adequately or fails to execute the plans outlined on the merchandise budget and merchandise list.

Timing errors occur when retailers secure merchandise at the wrong time; they fail to match retail inventories with what their consumers want when they want it. In these cases, markdowns become necessary, since the retailer faces surplus merchandise at the end of a selling season. Reordering at the height of a selling season and late shipments are two common causes for surplus merchandise.

Misjudging the quality of merchandise that consumers expect is another reason retailers take markdowns. To move merchandise with unacceptable materials or workmanship, retailers must reduce prices.

The final buying-related cause of markdowns is the retailer's *selection of suppliers.* Two of the more common supplier-related mistakes are "failing to develop a close working relationship with key resources whose advice can help avoid mistakes" and "overdepending on a few pet resources with a high proportion of stock invested in their mistakes."[6] Additionally, the retailer should evaluate the service-performance levels of each supplier. Late shipments, incorrect shipments, and damaged shipments all contribute to the retailer's need to take price reductions.

595

Selling-related causes. Even buying and securing the right merchandise in the right quantity at the right time are not enough to avoid unplanned price reductions; retailers must also control their selling activities. Selling-related causes of markdowns include errors in pricing, attempts to stimulate sales or to gain competitive price parity, and various policies and practices relating to the sale of merchandise.

A *pricing error* is any set price that does not create customer interest in the merchandise. Initial prices can be set too high or too low. High prices result in lost sales because consumers' perceptions of value are not satisfied. Low prices result in customer concern over the quality of the merchandise. In either case, price adjustments are needed to match customers' perceptions of value and quality. Also, additional markdowns on merchandise that has already been reduced may be necessary if the initial markdown has not sufficiently generated consumer interest.

Markdowns are frequently used by retailers as devices to *stimulate sales*. This purposeful reduction of prices may be employed to attract additional consumer traffic into the store, to introduce a new line of merchandise, to boost customer interest during a slack sales period, to reduce inventories on slow-moving merchandise, or for a host of other reasons. Sales-stimulation markdowns can take the form of loss or low-price leaders, special or promotional prices, a multiunit pricing scheme, or the use of coupons and premiums.

In some cases, retailers use markdowns to achieve *competitive parity*. Direct and indirect competitors that sell the same (or similar) merchandise at lower prices have a comparative shopping advantage over other retailers in their trading areas. The lack of price competitiveness may or may not be the retailer's fault. For example, the lack of competitive prices can occur as a result of (1) unforeseen decreases in wholesale prices after the retailer has placed the initial order; (2) the lack of buying power, occurring when a competitor's size simply does not allow quantity discounts; and (3) miscalculations of consumers' price sensitivity. Regardless of the reasons, retailers take the markdowns to achieve competitive price parity when they cannot justify the price differential on the basis of additional customer services, unique store-image characteristics, or general convenience factors such as time and place utility.

Selling policies also can create conditions that lead to markdowns. First a policy of "aggressive selling" (e.g., trading the customer up to higher-priced merchandise, selling the customer more than is desired, making false or misleading claims about product performance) can lead to an above-average rate of merchandise returns. By the time the merchandise makes it back to the sales floor, it may be late in the selling season. Hence, the retailer must reduce prices to clear the merchandise out by the end of the season. Second, some retailers engage in "umbrella merchandising"—the stocking of a limited number of high-fashion merchandise items, such as designer clothing and limited editions, to display merchandise that creates or enhances the store's contemporary image. This promotional merchandise is often stocked with the retailer's knowledge that much of it will require drastic price reductions to be sold. Third, a policy of "assortment maintenance"—the image-building policy of carrying a complete selection until late into the selling season—will require markdowns in the form of clearance sales. Finally, a selling policy of encouraging customers to take home merchandise supported by a liberal return policy increases the likelihood of taking markdowns.

Operationally related causes. In the day-to-day operations of a retail store, both internal and external circumstances arise that create the need for some type of corrective action in the form of a price reduction. Two such circumstances are market shifts and distressed merchandise.

Market shifts are changes in demand levels for a particular merchandise line. Faddish and fashion merchandise often have fast and sometimes unexpected changes in both the level and duration of customer acceptance. Introduction of a new product or a new brand can have unsettling effects on the demand for existing products already in stock. The demand for seasonal merchandise is highly dependent on having near-average climatic conditions. A mild winter, for example, can seriously reduce the demand for winter sporting equipment.

By its very nature, *distressed merchandise* requires price reductions. Merchandise that becomes damaged, dirty, or shopworn needs to be marked down to compensate the purchaser for the obvious reduction in value. Odd lots (e.g., where one or more pieces of a set are missing) also require markdowns.

Timing of Markdowns

An important issue that every retailer must consider is *when* to take markdowns. Opinions differ on the subject. Some retailers prefer to take early markdowns, while others feel that a policy of late markdowns is the more profitable strategy. Several factors strongly influence the timing of markdowns, including

1. The type of merchandise under consideration—staple, fashion, faddish, or seasonal goods
2. The kind of store image the retailer is trying to project—economy, prestige, contemporary, etc.
3. The length of the selling season
4. The nature of the target consumer—highly sensitive to price or largely indifferent to price
5. The size of the initial markup
6. The availability of selling and storage space—hence, the need to free up space, for new, incoming merchandise
7. The retailer's sales-promotion policies—frequent and continuous use of "minisales" or infrequent use of "big event" sales

The following discussion presents some of the relative advantages and disadvantages of taking early and late markdowns.

Early markdowns. **Early markdowns** *reduce the selling price of a merchandise item when either of the following conditions is present: (1) there is a notable slack in the rate of sales for that item or (2) the item has been in stock for a specific time period (e.g., six weeks).* Proponents of early markdowns cite a number of advantages, enumerated here.

1. *Fresher stock:* Early markdowns help make room for new merchandise by weeding out slow movers, thereby freeing investment capital and selling and storage space.
2. *Smaller markdowns:* Early markdowns reduce the size of the markdown required to sell the merchandise because some demand for the item still exists, and because the chances of the item's becoming shopworn are substantially reduced.
3. *Reduced selling expenses:* Early markdowns promote rapid clearance of merchandise without the additional advertising and personal selling expenses that are normally associated with major sale promotion campaigns.

4. *Increased customer traffic:* Early markdowns encourage customers to take advantage of reduced prices (both advertised and unadvertised specials) because of the continuous availability of marked-down merchandise.

5. *Reduced selling risks:* Early markdowns permit sufficient time to take a second and possibly a third price reduction in one selling season if they become necessary to move the merchandise.

6. *Heightened market appropriateness:* Early markdowns prevent repetitive showing of dated merchandise at regular prices. Market appropriateness is extremely important in selling fashion merchandise. Many fashion-oriented consumers are willing to buy only new arrivals at full prices, and they expect a continuous influx of new merchandise. Other fashion-oriented consumers are willing to buy fashion merchandise that is well along in the fashion cycle only if the price has been reduced.

Early markdowns are most frequently used by large department stores and medium-priced specialty retailers who are very promotion oriented.

Some retailers have an early-markdown policy that takes markdowns on a routine basis. These **automatic markdown** policies *reduce prices by a fixed percentage at regular intervals.* Automatic markdowns are generally taken without regard to how well the merchandise is selling. A principal proponent of the automatic-markdown policy is the bargain-basement department of Filene's Department Store in Boston. Its typical fixed schedule of markdowns is 25 percent after 12 days, 50 percent after 18 days, and 75 percent after 24 days. Any merchandise remaining after 30 selling days is disposed of by giving it to charitable organizations.

Late markdowns. **Late markdowns** *maintain the original selling price until late in the selling season, at which time a major clearance sale is held.* A policy of taking late markdowns is most commonly associated with smaller specialty retailers and the more prestige- or status-oriented stores. Late-markdown advocates stress the following advantages of such a policy:

1. *They preserve exclusive image.* Late markdowns help prestige retailers preserve their store image of high quality and exclusiveness by not mixing sale-priced goods with regular-priced merchandise and by not mixing regular, prestige-oriented customers with bargain-seekers during the normal course of the selling season. Typically, the only time this mixing of merchandise and customers occurs to any extent is during the one or two major clearance sales.

2. *They encourage creative selling.* Late markdowns allow sufficient time for the retailer to experiment with different selling approaches. By displaying the merchandise in different places and ways, the retailer can often influence the demand for that item. The use of different sales approaches can also be initiated to determine their effects on sales.

3. *They allow "late bloomers."* Late markdowns allow each merchandise line a trial sales period of sufficient duration to realize the line's full potential. Some lines of merchandise simply take longer to catch on. Given the needed customer exposure, however, these items can gain wide acceptance at regular retail prices.

4. *They reduce purchase postponement.* Late markdowns discourage customers from waiting until the merchandise item is placed on sale before making a purchase.

5. *They create the "big event."* Late markdowns allow the retailer to accumulate large quantities of regularly stocked merchandise for a major clearance sale. Due to its infrequency and the fact that the clearance sale incorporates regularly stocked merchandise, the potential promotional impact is great enough to create the "big event."

Retailers can use several compromise markdown strategies. For example, some retailers take early markdowns on certain merchandise lines (e.g., highly seasonal items) and late markdowns on other lines (e.g., staple merchandise). Other retailers schedule clearance sales for the last selling day of each month. The advantages of monthly clearance sales are that they force the retailer to make a frequent and regular review of its stock position and they generate consumer traffic during what is normally a slow-selling period (end-of-month). Lack of flexibility is the most frequently cited limitation of the monthly clearance sale.

Size of Markdowns

The purpose of a markdown is to increase the customer's incentive to buy the merchandise. The size of each markdown, therefore, should be large enough to attract customers' attention and induce them to buy. At the same time, unnecessarily deep markdowns will adversely affect the retailer's profit margins. There are no hard and fast rules for determining the size of a markdown. Some retailers believe in making the first "bath" count; that is, they take deep initial markdowns, thereby reducing the need for later, more drastic markdowns. Other retailers think taking several shallow markdowns is the best approach to clearing merchandise with the least-negative impact on profit margins. There are, however, several general considerations that the retailer should take into account when determining the size of the discount. Chief among them are

- type of merchandise
- price of the merchandise
- time of the selling season

The degree of physical, fashion, or seasonal perishability will strongly influence the size of the markdown. Highly perishable merchandise (e.g., a particular fashion near the end of its fashion cycle or a seasonal product approaching the end of the season) typically requires substantial markdowns as part of the clearance effort. Capturing customer interest in merchandise that is, by contrast, relatively unperishable can usually be accomplished with less drastic markdowns. Fashionable and seasonal items often require initial markdowns of 25–50 percent, whereas 10–15 percent markdowns on staple merchandise usually are sufficient to create customer interest.

The original retail selling price of the merchandise will strongly influence the size of the markdown needed to generate customer interest. For example, a $5 markdown on a $100 item would hardly be sufficient to attract additional buyers. On the other hand, that same $5 markdown on a $20 item is perhaps more than enough to clear the item out of stock. On average, the retailer must reduce the price at least 15 percent to create customer attention. In some cases, a much larger markdown is needed to induce the customer to buy.

The amount of markdown the retailer takes also depends on the time in the selling season. Early in the selling season the retailer can take smaller markdowns with the knowledge that if the merchandise fails to sell at the reduced price, there is still time to take additional markdowns. A policy of late markdowns usually means the retailer must take deep markdowns to stimulate sales.

Several additional factors could determine the size of the markdown. For example, the need for substantial markdowns often depends on the number of units in stock that require clearance, the need for space (storage and selling), and the need for investment capital. A retailer faced with a drastically overstocked position may decide that the only way to correct the situation is to take drastic markdowns. A continuous flow of incoming merchandise means that the retailer must have adequate storage and selling space. Faced with the choice of either drastically reducing prices on old merchandise for clearance purposes or keeping new merchandise off the sales floor, the retailer ultimately decides to clear the floor of old merchandise. Finally, old merchandise represents a major source of funds for many retailers. To gain the immediate use of these funds, the retailer will need to take substantial markdowns.

Markdown Strategies

Retailers utilize a number of pricing strategies that incorporate markdowns either directly or indirectly. Clearance sales are examples of direct markdowns. Indirect price reductions are best exemplified by the retailer's use of coupons, premiums, and trading stamps. The following discussion examines some of the more common pricing strategies that either directly or indirectly incorporate the markdown concept.

Promotional Pricing Strategies

All promotional pricing strategies have a least one thing in common: they are designed to draw consumers into the store where, it is hoped, they will purchase not only reduced merchandise but also regularly priced merchandise. To this end, retailers use a variety of promotional pricing strategies. Typical are sale prices, prices with coupons and premiums, leader prices, and special-purchase prices.

Sale prices. "Sales" are an everyday occurrence in most retail markets. Retailers cite a variety of reasons for holding sales, such as clearances, liquidations, and closeouts. Retailers also use several different occasions for conducting a sale: seasonal sales, either spring, summer, fall, or winter, and anniversary sales; before-, during-, and after-holiday sales, including Christmas, Easter, Memorial Day, Fourth-of-July, Labor Day, and Thanksgiving sales. Some retailers conduct sales that are either brand-specific, or not specifically oriented toward any particular product or brand.

The actual markdown or price reduction is expressed in a variety of ways. Reduced sale prices are expressed as either (1) a certain dollar or percentage value "off" the original selling price, (2) a multiple-unit price (e.g., three for $9.97), or (3) a fraction of the original selling price. Montgomery Ward's advertised Money-Saver Sale illustrates all three expressions (see Figure 21–9).

Coupons. Coupons are sales promotion devices involving redeemable cards (e.g., direct mail) or cut-outs (e.g., newspapers) that allow the customer to purchase specific merchandise at a reduced price. Although coupons issued by the manufacturer represent a reduced price for the consumer, they do not represent a markdown for the retailer, since the manufacturer reimburses the retailer for any payments made to customers. However, coupons issued by the retailer *do* represent markdowns, since the retailer bears the cost of the difference between the original and reduced

FIGURE 21–9
Price-reduction
expressions

CHAPTER 21
THE RETAIL PRICE

Money-saver

sale

1/3 off.

Hurry! Dress shirts priced for a sellout.

3 for 9⁹⁷
Reg. 4.99 each.

Polyester/cotton broadcloth with smaller collar, short sleeves, 2 pockets. Machine wash, little or no ironing. Stock up on classic white and light colors. In 14½-17.

1/2 price.

Casual shirts in the new natural textures.

5⁹⁷ each
Reg. $12 each.

Terry knits. Pullovers of machine-wash cotton/polyester. Solids: S,M,L,XL. **Homespun look.** Epaulets and fashion pockets. Polyester/cotton: washable. S,M,L,XL.

**WHY PASS UP A GOOD BUY?
USE CHARG-ALL CREDIT**

MONTGOMERY WARD

selling price. Coupon prices are expressed in a variety of ways: percentage-off pricing, fractional pricing, multiple-unit pricing, and conditional pricing (e.g., buy one, get one free).

Premiums.   Premiums include free merchandise or merchandise that has been drastically reduced. Retailers normally offer premiums to consumers after they have completed some requirement (such as test driving an automobile, filling out a form, or buying a certain dollar amount of merchandise). In a general sense, the cost of premiums to the retailer represents an indirect markdown.

Leader pricing.   **Leader pricing** is *the strategy of selling key merchandise items below their normal markup and in some cases even below the retailer's merchandise costs (negative markup).* As with other promotional prices, the main objective of leader pricing is to attract consumers to the store in the hope that they also will purchase other merchandise that has normal markups. While leader merchandise contributes very little profit on a per-unit basis, its indirect contribution to total dollar profit can be substantial if the retailer makes anticipated additional sales on high-profit items. To be effective, leader merchandise should include well-known (frequently national brands), widely used items priced low enough to attract most income groups and be easily recognized as a bargain. In addition, price leaders should not be stocked in large quantities or directly compete with other merchandise in the retailer's assortment. Supermarkets, in their weekly advertised specials, often use meat, dairy, and bakery products as leader merchandise.

Does this sales promotion device represent a markdown for the retailer?

Leader pricing strategies differ depending upon the extent of the markdown and the retailer's purpose in attracting the potential customer. Three types of leader pricing strategies exist: low-leaders, loss-leaders, and bait-leaders.

Low-leaders are *prices set below the customary selling price but above the retailer's actual cost of the merchandise.* Customer attraction is the principal objective of the low-leader strategy. Low-leaders also generate some gross profit, thereby contributing to the retailer's operating expenses and possibly to the retailer's operating profit.

Loss-leaders are *prices reduced to or below the retailer's cost of the merchandise.* Such drastic price cuts aim to improve substantially the store's customer traffic. To be profitable, the sales of regular-priced merchandise must be great enough to more than offset the losses generated by the sale of loss-leaders. The extensive use of loss-leader pricing by some retailers has generated considerable criticism by those who maintain that it is basically an unfair trade practice with the intent to injure competition. In response to these criticisms, many states have enacted "unfair trade practice acts" establishing a floor below which retailers cannot reduce their prices. This floor is usually established as the retailer's invoice cost of goods or the invoice cost plus some minimum markup, such as 5 percent (see Chapter 5).

A **bait-leader** is *an extremely attractive advertised price on merchandise that the retailer does not intend to sell.* As the name implies, the attractive advertised price is "bait" to get the customer into the store. Having accomplished this, the retailer attempts to switch the customer from the merchandise featured in the advertisement to merchandise priced at full markup; hence, the common description for this pricing strategy—"bait and switch." Retailers use a number of ploys to switch the customer to more expensive merchandise. In the first step, called the trade-off, the retailer tries to disinterest the customer in the advertised bait merchandise. The trade-off can be handled in several ways, including (1) *persuasion,* convincing the customers that the bait merchandise is of extremely inferior quality and represents a poor value even at the sharply reduced price; (2) *refusal,* refusing to sell the merchandise on the ground that it is unsafe, unhealthy, or unsupported (e.g., warranties) by either the retailer or the manufacturer; and (3) *stockouts,* informing the customer that the advertised merchandise was in very short supply and all units were sold prior to the customer's visit. The second task is trading up the customer to more expensive merchandise by stressing the higher quality of the substitute merchandise, the better services the customer will receive (delivery, installation, wrapping, repairs, etc.), the easy availability of credit, and any other appeal that is judged to be effective in convincing the baited customer.

The legal nature of "bait and switch" is somewhat fuzzy. It is usually considered an unfair trade practice (deceptive pricing), however, if the retailer absolutely refuses to sell the advertised merchandise. In any case, many retailers believe that this pricing strategy is not only an unethical and misleading business practice, but a short-sighted selling strategy that eventually leads to customer dissatisfaction and the loss of return trade.

Special-purchase pricing. A **special-purchase price** is *a low advertised price on merchandise that the retailer has purchased at reduced prices.* Because these promotional prices are initially set below the retailer's customary price for such merchandise, indirectly they represent a markdown pricing strategy. The purpose for special-purchase pricing is the same as for most promotional pricing: customer traffic generation. The legalities of *first* establishing a going market price is the most commonly cited reason for not directly advertising special purchases as being reduced in price. Special-purchase pricing is most often associated with large chain-store retailers that enjoy buying economies of scale.

Price-Line Adjustment Strategies

For the retailer whose original price-setting strategies included the use of pricing zones (a range of prices) and pricing lines (at specific pricing points), markdown adjustments create a slightly different price-reduction problem. Essentially, two general problems exist. First, the retailer must determine the *amount of the markdown*; then, the *public nature of the markdown*.

Shallow markdowns usually involve reducing the price of a merchandise item from one pricing point within a pricing zone to a lower pricing point within the same zone. Shallow markdowns are adequate only "when the supply to be cleared is small and when it is believed that the same people who rejected it at the original price will find it a good value at the reduced price."[7] Deep markdowns are taken by moving a merchandise line from a pricing point in one zone to a pricing point in a lower pricing zone. Deep markdowns become necessary when the retailer considers the merchandise inappropriate for the targeted customer within the original pricing zone, but possibly suited to the value expectations of the targeted customers within a lower pricing zone.

The second issue the retailer must consider in making price-line adjustments is whether to inform the customer that a markdown adjustment has been made. The retailer may decide to simply drop a merchandise item from one price point to a lower pricing point without informing the customers of the markdown condition of the item. This task is usually performed by replacing the old price tag with a new price. On the other hand, the retailer may choose to inform the public of the reduced price when only a few merchandise units are involved or when the negative impact (e.g., reduced quality perception) created by the markdown is thought to be outweighed by the positive aspects of the reduction (e.g., its promotion value).

When the retailer believes it is beneficial for the customer to know about the price reduction, it can communicate this information in two ways: re-mark the old price tag so that the reduction is shown on the original tag, or elect to mark the merchandise down to an "off" pricing point. For example, a merchandise item can be reduced from its original pricing point of $29.95 to $24.00 rather than to the next lower pricing point of $19.95. In this case, consumers perceive the even-ending pricing point as a reduced price.

Markdown Control

Some markdowns are inevitable. They are the natural result of risks retailers must assume in going into business. An extremely low markdown percentage could indicate that the retailer is not assuming sufficient risks to take advantage of emerging market opportunities. On the other hand, excessive markdowns are often indicative of poor planning and control procedures. Chapters 19 and 20 discussed the criteria and methods for managing the merchandise mix. By carefully planning sales, stock levels, purchases, and profit margins, the retailer can control to a reasonable extent both the amount and the timing of markdowns. To facilitate the control of markdowns, many retailers require their buyers to maintain records on the causes or reasons markdowns were taken on a particular merchandise item. Careful analysis of these causes allows the retailer to take corrective action when unnecessary and excessive markdowns are detected.

SUMMARY

Retailers view prices in terms of their ability to generate profits, sales, and consumer traffic, as well as how they affect the store's image. In setting retail prices, the retailer can elect to be guided by profit, sales, or competitive objectives. A number of factors influence the retailer's price-setting decisions, including demand, competitive, cost, product, and legal considerations.

Retail price-setting methods include those that are cost-oriented (markups), competition-oriented, and vendor-oriented. Retailers often use a number of different pricing policies in refining their price-setting tactics; for example, retailers can use a one-price policy, a variable-price policy, a multiple-unit policy, odd pricing, unit pricing, and price lining in providing a guideline for their stores' prices.

Price adjustments are adaptive mechanisms that retailers use in their efforts to accommodate changing market conditions and operating requirements. Both upward and downward adjustments are needed from time to time to adapt to the dynamic retailing environment. Three types of price adjustments are common among retailers: discounts, markons, and markdowns. Discounts are reductions in the original selling price that are given to store employees and to special customer groups. Markons refer to additional markups on merchandise, taken after the initial markup and the establishment of the initial selling price. Markdowns represent a downward movement in prices and are often necessary to clear certain merchandise items from inventory.

The three general causes for markdowns are buying-related (e.g., assortment, support, and timing errors as well as misjudgment of merchandise quality and problems associated with suppliers), selling-related (e.g., attempts to stimulate sales, to achieve competitive parity, and to correct improper selling policies), and operational-related (e.g., market shifts and distressed merchandise). Some retailers prefer to take early markdowns, while others believe late markdowns are more profitable. The size of the markdown depends on the type of merchandise, the price of the merchandise item, and the time in the selling season. Markdown pricing strategies include promotional strategies (sales, coupons, premiums, price leaders, and special-purchase prices) and price-line adjustment tactics. Finally, to avoid excessive and unnecessary markdowns, the retailer must establish markdown control policies.

KEY TERMS AND CONCEPTS

sales-volume objectives	maintained markup	unit pricing
market-share objectives	initial markup percentage	price lining
profit-maximization objectives	gross margin	pricing zone
target return objectives	pricing below competition	pricing line
competitive price objectives	pricing with competition	discounts
price elasticity of demand	pricing above competition	markons
dollar markup	one-price policy	markdowns
percentage markup	variable-price policy	markdown percentage
cumulative markup	multiple-price policy	off-retail markdown percentage
initial markup	odd pricing	early markdowns

automated markdown   low-leader   special-purchase pricing

late markdowns   loss-leader   markdown control

leader pricing   bait-leader

REVIEW QUESTIONS

1. When might the retailer prefer a market share–maintenance objective over a market share–growth objective?
2. Why might profit maximization be an inappropriate pricing objective?
3. How are the two target return-pricing objectives expressed? Explain each expression.
4. What does price elasticity of demand measure? What are the three types of demand elasticity?
5. From a product perspective, when are competitive price levels a more important pricing consideration?
6. How are merchandising costs determined?
7. Identify and discuss the several forms of product perishability.
8. Identify the formulas for calculating percentage markup at retail and at cost. Why do most retailers prefer markups based on retail?
9. Compare and contrast the initial and maintained markups.
10. Which merchandising strategies are essential to a successful below-competition pricing strategy?
11. When is the vendor's suggested selling price not appropriate?
12. What are the strengths and weaknesses of a one-price policy?
13. What are pricing zones and pricing lines?
14. What are the advantages to the consumer and to the retailer of a price-lining policy?
15. Who receives discount adjustments and why do they receive them?
16. What is a markon? When are they applied?
17. Describe the two methods for computing markdowns.
18. Briefly describe the four selling-related causes of markdowns.
19. What are the advantages of early markdowns?
20. What size markdown should the retailer take?
21. Describe the typical promotional pricing strategies used by the retailer.
22. Distinguish among low-, loss-, and bait-leaders.
23. How are shallow and deep markdowns taken within and between price lines?

ENDNOTES

1. M. Wayne DeLozier and Arch G. Woodside, "Pricing and Marketing Communications: The Noneconomic Factors," *Journal of the Academy of Marketing Science* 4 (Fall, 1976): 814–24.
2. See Marvin A. Jolson, "A Diagrammatic Model for Merchandising Calculation," *Journal of Retailing* 51 (Fall, 1975): 13–22.
3. See Zarrel V. Lambert, "Perceived Prices as Related to Odd and Even Price Endings," *Journal of Retailing* 51 (Fall, 1975): 13–22.
4. See Bruce F. McElroy and David A. Aaker, "Unit Pricing Six Years after Introduction," *Journal of Retailing* 55 (Fall, 1979): 44–57.
5. See Richard J. Hise and Myron Gable, "Analyzing Retailer Price-Lining Policies," *Proceedings: Southern Marketing Association,* H. W. Nash and D. P. Robin, eds. (1977), 39–41.
6. John W. Eingate, Elmer O. Schaller, and F. Leonard Miller, *Retail Merchandise Management* (Englewood Cliffs, NJ: Prentice-Hall, 1972), 131.
7. Ibid., 140.

RELATED READINGS

Aaker, David A., and Ford, Gary T. "Unit Pricing Ten Years Later: A Replication." *Journal of Marketing* 47 (Winter 1983), 118–22.

Berkowitz, Eric N., and Walton, John R. "Information Needs for Comparative Pricing Decisions." *AMA Educators' Proceedings*. P. E. Murphy et al, eds. (American Marketing Association 1983), 241–45.

Blattberg, Robert C.; Epen, Gary D.; and Lieberman, Joshua. "A Theoretical and Empirical Evaluation of Price Deals for Consumer Nondurables." *Journal of Marketing* 45 (Winter 1981), 116–29.

Carlson, Phillip G. "Fashion Retailing: The Sensitivity of Rate of Sale to Markdown." *Journal of Retailing* 59 (Spring 1983), 67–78.

————. "Fashion Retailing: Reorder Window and Markdown Threshold." *Retail Control* (September 1983), 52–57.

Dawson, Lyndon E., and Mayer, Morris L. "Changing Perspectives on Resale Price Maintenance: A New Philosophy on an Old Marketing Practice." *Marketing Comes of Age, Proceedings*. David M. Klein and Allen E. Smith, eds. (Southern Marketing Association 1984), 201–4.

Frazier, Robert M. "Reducing Markdowns for Increased Profitability." *Retail Control* (March 1985), 2–26.

Grant, R. M. "On Cash Discounts to Retail Customers: Further Evidence." *Journal of Marketing* 49 (Winter 1985), 145–46.

Halsband, Albert. "Implementing a Price Change Management System." *Retail Control* (April - May 1984), 22–43.

Riesz, Peter C. "Price versus Quality in the Market-place—1961–1975." *Journal of Retailing* 54 (Winter 1978), 15–28.

Roth, Stanley, Sr. "The Debate over Resale Price Maintenance." *Retail Control* (April - May 1985), 48–57.

Sewall, Murphy A., and Goldstein, Michael H. "The Comparative Advertising Controversy: Consumer Perceptions of Catalog Showroom Reference Prices." *Journal of Marketing* 43 (Summer 1979), 85–92.

Whalen, Bernard F. "Strategic Mix of Odd, Even Prices Can Lead to Increased Retail Profits." *Marketing News* (March 7, 1980), 24.

Outline

RETAIL PROMOTIONS

The Communication Process
The Promotion Mix

RETAIL ADVERTISING

Understanding How Advertising Works
Identifying Types of Advertising
Developing an Advertising Strategy

PLANNING THE ADVERTISING FUNCTION

Determining Advertising Objectives
Developing Advertising Budgets

ORGANIZING THE ADVERTISING FUNCTION

Establishing Advertising Departments
Using Outside Advertising Specialists

EXECUTING THE ADVERTISING FUNCTION

Creating Retail Advertisements
Selecting Advertising Media

CONTROLLING THE ADVERTISING FUNCTION

Objectives

- Describe the communication process and discuss its impact on the retail promotions

- Identify and define the five major components of the retailer's promotion mix

- Discern the role of retail advertising in attracting, informing, and motivating consumers

- Specify and analyze the components necessary for planning a successful retail advertising program

- Delineate the organizational structures and the advertising functions necessary for effectively accomplishing an advertising program

- Discuss the instruments and methodologies used in evaluating advertising effectiveness

22
Retail Advertising

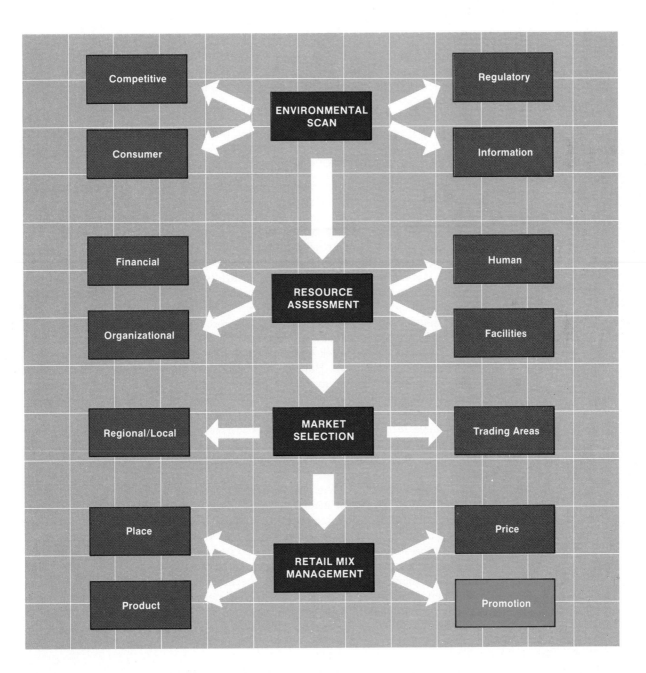

U nlike most other businesses, retailers do not generally take their product to market. Instead, they rely on consumers to take the initiative of visiting their stores or placing an order by phone or mail. Most consumers will not take this initiative unless they are in some way motivated to do so. Before consumers will visit a particular store, however, they must be aware of its existence, know its location, and have some idea of what is available inside. Before they visit or place an order, they also may want information about prices they must pay, the terms of sale they can expect, services available, store hours, and so forth. In addition, consumers need to be persuaded that a given retailer's offering is most suited to their needs. Effective retailers supply this information and persuasion, generally through their retail promotional efforts.

RETAIL PROMOTIONS

The fourth element in the retail mix is promotion. **Promotion** *involves both providing the consumer information regarding the retailer's store and its product/service offering and influencing consumer perceptions, attitudes, and behavior toward the store and what it has to offer.* As implied in the definition, promotion is both an informative and a persuasive communication process; therefore, it is useful to view the retailer's promotional efforts from the standpoint of the communication process.

The Communication Process

The **communication process** *involves transmitting meaningful messages between senders (i.e., retailers) and receivers (i.e., target consumers).* Figure 22–1 illustrates the communication process and its various participants (senders and receivers), processes (encoding and decoding), and acts (transmission and feedback). Let's review the workings of this basic communication model.

The *source* of the communication process is the **sender** —*a retailer that wants to inform or persuade a select group of consumers* (**receivers**) *about the benefits of an idea (e.g., lower prices, quality merchandise, high fashion, fast service, or contemporary image).* To be communicated effectively, the message must be **encoded** into *messages using signs and symbols* (e.g., words, displays, pictures, or gestures) that (1) promote understanding of the idea, (2) attract attention of intended audiences, (3) stimulate needs felt by intended audiences, and (4) suggest a course of action for need satisfaction. Having developed an effective message, the sender must then select the most appropriate communication channel or *medium* (e.g., salespeople, newspapers, magazines, radio, television, direct mail, in-store displays, and sales promotions) for **transmitting** the message to consumers targeted as the most suitable *recipients* of the message. The receiver or target audience is the intended *destination* of the sender's message and the *object* of the sender's promotional efforts (e.g., creating awareness, generating interest, and initiating behavioral change).

With the reception of the message, the receiver **decodes** it and interprets its meaning either correctly or incorrectly depending on how well the message was encoded and the decoder's experience and skill with the communication process. Once the decoding process has been completed, the receiver may or may not react (e.g., visit the store, phone in an order, or do nothing). The nature of the receiver's *response* or lack of it is then communicated back to the sender as **feedback.** The information gained through the feedback mechanism is vital in developing and encoding new ideas for future promotions. A final element in the communication process is **noise,** *anything that occurs during the communication process that distracts senders or receivers, interferes with the encoding and decoding activity, or interrupts the transmission or feedback process* (see Figure 22–1). As we shall see, an under-

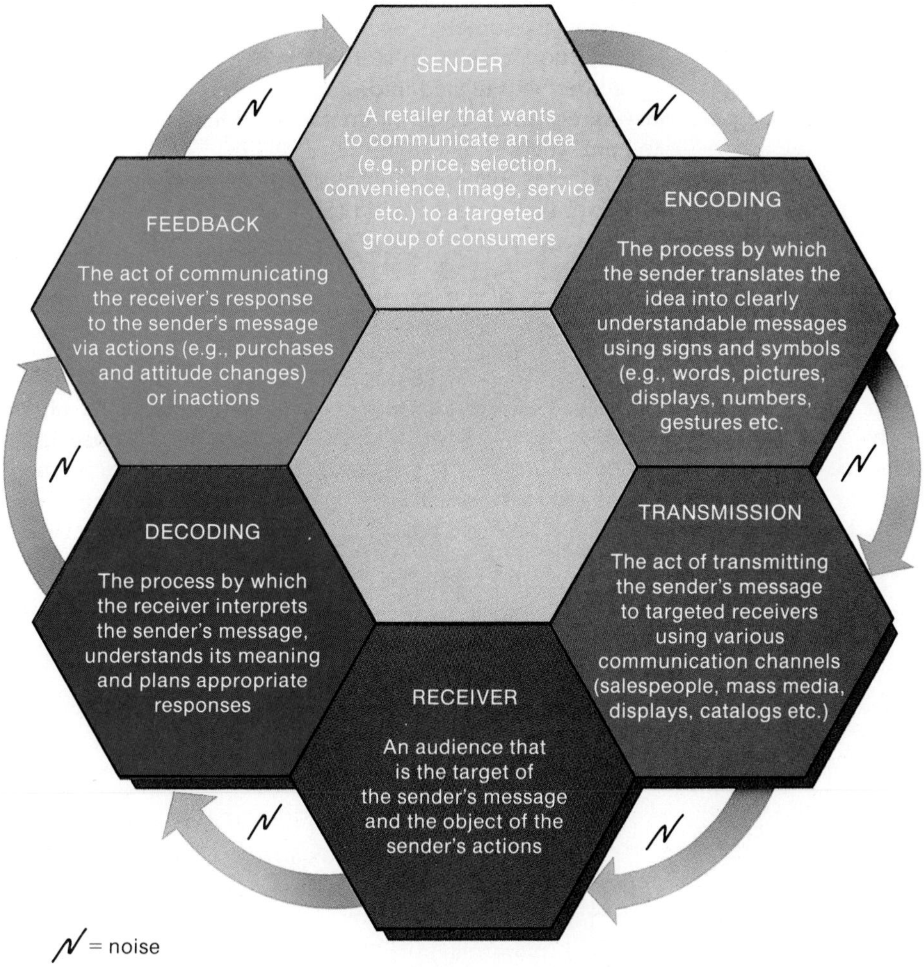

FIGURE 22–1
The communication
process

SENDER

A retailer that wants
to communicate an idea
(e.g., price, selection,
convenience, image, service
etc.) to a targeted
group of consumers

ENCODING

The process by which
the sender translates the
idea into clearly
understandable messages
using signs and symbols
(e.g., words, pictures,
displays, numbers,
gestures etc.

FEEDBACK

The act of communicating
the receiver's response
to the sender's message
via actions (e.g., purchases
and attitude changes)
or inactions

TRANSMISSION

The act of transmitting
the sender's message
to targeted receivers
using various
communication channels
(salespeople, mass media,
displays, catalogs etc.)

DECODING

The process by which
the receiver interprets
the sender's message,
understands its meaning
and plans appropriate
responses

RECEIVER

An audience that
is the target of
the sender's message
and the object of the
sender's actions

$\mathcal{N}$ = noise

standing and appreciation of the communication process is vital to the development
and implementation of effective retail promotions.

The Promotion Mix

The retailer's promotion mix comprises various combinations of the five basic promotional elements: advertising, personal selling, store displays, sales promotions,
and publicity. This section briefly defines and characterizes each type of promotion.
The remainder of this chapter is devoted to an in-depth look at the advertising
function, Chapter 23 presents on extensive discussion of personal selling, and
Chapter 24 fully examines the issues surrounding store displays, sales promotions,
and publicity.

In developing and implementing the promotion mix, retailers utilize some
combination of the elements that follow to inform consumers about their stores,
merchandise, services, or ideas and to persuade them to accept their point of view
or to direct them toward desirable courses of action.

■ **advertising**—indirect, nonpersonal communication carried by a mass medium and paid for by an identified retailer

611

■ **personal selling**—direct, face-to-face communication between a retail salesperson and a retail consumer

■ **store displays**—direct, nonpersonal in-store presentations and exhibitions of merchandise together with related information

■ **sales promotions**—direct and indirect nonpersonal inducements that offer an extra value to consumers

■ **publicity**—indirect, nonpersonal communication (positive or negative) carried by a mass medium that is neither paid for nor credited to an identified sponsor

Figure 22–2 presents a comparison of the general characteristics of each type of promotion.

RETAIL ADVERTISING

Retail advertising includes all paid forms of nonpersonal communications about stores, merchandise, service, or ideas by an identified retailer. Its purpose is to influence favorably consumers' attitudes and perceptions about the store, its merchandise, its activities, and to induce sales directly or indirectly. Advertising is described as a *paid* form of communication to distinguish it from publicity. Advertising

PROMOTION TYPE / CHARACTERISTIC	ADVERTISING	PERSONAL SELLING	STORE DISPLAY	SALES PROMOTION	PUBLICITY
MODE OF COMMUNICATION	Indirect Nonpersonal	Direct Face-to-face	Direct Nonpersonal	Indirect Nonpersonal	Indirect Nonpersonal
REGULARITY OF ACTIVITY	Regular	Regular	Regular	Irregular	Irregular
FLEXIBILITY OF MESSAGE	Unvarying Uniform	Personalized Tailored	Unvarying Uniform	Unvarying Uniform	Beyond Retailer's Control
DIRECTNESS OF FEEDBACK	Indirect Feedback	Direct Feedback	Indirect Feedback	Indirect Feedback	Indirect Feedback
CONTROL OF MESSAGE CONTENT	Controllable	Controllable	Controllable	Controllable	Uncontrollable
IDENTITY OF SPONSOR	Identified	Identified	Identified	Unidentified	Identified
COST PER CONTACT	Low to Moderate	High	Varies	Varies	No Cost

FIGURE 22–2

Characteristic profile of types of promotion (source: Adapted from William Zikmund and Michael d'Amico, *Marketing* [New York: John Wiley and Sons, 1984], 494)

is nonpersonal because the message is delivered through the public medium to many consumers simultaneously. This distinguishes advertising from personal selling (see Figure 22–2).

Understanding How Advertising Works

For most retailers, advertising is the principal tool to establish a store image and generate customer traffic. Since it is also an important expense, retailers must commit their time, effort, and thought in carefully managing their advertising programs and expenditures. Unfortunately, however, many retailers fail to develop comprehensive advertising plans. Instead, they advertise sporadically to promote sales, or they rely solely on media representatives to plan their advertising for them.

Some retailers do attempt to develop an advertising plan, but make crucial mistakes by failing to set objectives, or by using rule-of-thumb formulas for allocating budgets, or by advertising the wrong things in the wrong way. The famous retailer John Wanamaker reportedly once said, "I know that half of my advertising is wasted, but the problem is I don't know which half." Many retailers would undoubtedly agree. The retailer that fails to develop a comprehensive advertising strategy and control it effectively not only wastes money, but also puts itself at a disadvantage with competitors that do advertise more carefully.

Many retailers are quite skeptical of advertising. Unlike John Wanamaker, they think that not half but all of their advertising just "doesn't work." When questioned about this feeling, a retailer is likely to respond, "I tried it once, and I got no results." This generally means the retailer noticed no additional store traffic or sales after the advertising.

When well planned and well done, however, advertising does work. Almost anyone who has ever placed a classified ad in a newspaper can attest to that. So why did our skeptical retailer not see results? Many explanations are possible. First, the retailer's location, prices, or merchandise might have been poorly selected. Advertising cannot offset an otherwise poor marketing effort. Second, changes in the retailer's environment—inflation, unemployment, bad weather, or competitors' activities—may have offset the effects of the advertising. Third, advertising may have been poorly planned, poorly executed, aimed at the wrong market, or simply inadequate. Advertising, like any other business activity, must be well planned, executed, and timed. Moreover, retail advertising's effects are manifested *over time*, not immediately, unless the retailer is promoting some specific reason to buy now, such as a "sale." Small wonder, then, that our skeptical retailer "tried once and got no results."

How Advertising Affects Consumers

Consumers go through a series of steps, at varying rates, before they are motivated to accept something such as a store or a product and to take the action to patronize the business or buy the product they have accepted. Communications theorists have proposed several models of this personal "adoption" process, most of which are similar. The one presented here is known as **DAGMAR** (Defining Advertising Goals for Measured Advertising Results). As developed by Russell Colley, *the model describes a sequence of steps through which prospective customers move from total unawareness of the store and its offering to store patronage and purchase (action).* These steps are shown in Figure 22–3.

As the illustration depicts, several steps intervene between unawareness and store selection (or purchase behavior). Through advertising, the retailer can help

| Unawareness | Awareness | Comprehension | Conviction | Action |

FIGURE 22–3

The DAGMAR consumer-adoption model (source: Adapted from Russell H. Colley, *Defining Advertising Goals for Measured Advertising Results* [New York: Association for National Advertisers, Inc., 1961], 46–69)

consumers move to *awareness* of the store and its offerings; to *comprehension* or understanding of the store and its image, price structure, services, and so on; to *conviction* or favorable attitudes toward the store. Advertising cannot accomplish this process alone. Other aspects of the retailer's marketing mix also play important roles in moving customers through this behavioral sequence. Advertising does play a strong role, however, particularly in the awareness and comprehension steps.

How Advertising Affects Entire Markets

Advertising affects a large number of people simultaneously with a single message because of the mass media it uses. Although it is itself a mass form of communications (and is therefore impersonal), *the ultimate effects of advertising are often magnified by personal communications among consumers.* This phenomenon, known as the **two-step flow of communications,** is illustrated in Figure 22–4.

FIGURE 22–4

Two-step flow model of communications

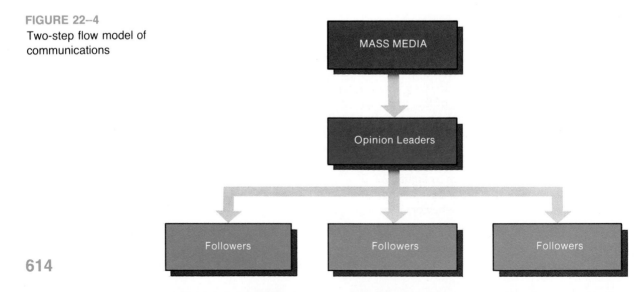

The first step in the process is the communications flow from the media to opinion leaders. **Opinion leaders,** you will recall from our discussion in Chapter 4, *are persons whose attitudes, opinions, preferences, and actions affect others.* The second step in the process is word-of-mouth communications from opinion leaders to others (followers) in the groups. This communication may take place through personal conversations (a "fashionable" woman tells her friends where she bought her new dress) or through nonverbal personal communications (the friends notice the label on her dress). Regardless of how the second step takes place, it is crucial to the influence advertising has on consumers.

An obvious implication of the two-step flow theory is that retail advertising should reach opinion leaders. Unfortunately, this is not an easy task, since opinion leaders are not easy to locate. First, opinion leadership is a matter of degree, not an absolute that people either have or do not have. Second, opinion leaders often use the same mass media as opinion followers, making it difficult and costly to reach them selectively. Third, opinion leaders may not be different demographically from opinion followers; therefore, they are difficult to define as a marketing segment. Finally, opinion leaders are rarely if ever opinion leaders for more than one type of product or store. In many cases, they are simply more interested in a product or store or more expert on the subject than opinion followers.

None of this means, however, that the retailer cannot attempt to locate opinion leaders and direct advertising toward them. Through observation, a retailer may be able to locate opinion leaders. For example, a women's fashion retailer may read in the newspaper the names of the sponsors and participants in style shows put on by a women's club, then write or call these potential opinion leaders and invite them to select some merchandise. If they are satisfied, the retailer would ask them to "pass the word." A sporting goods retailer may read about successful hunters or fishers in the sports section, invite them to the store, allow them to sample the merchandise, and ask them to spread the word. In neither case is it illegal to pass along a commission for business steered one's way—this is a common practice among automobile dealers.

Other methods of working with opinion leaders include the following:

- create opinion leaders out of certain persons by supplying them with free merchandise and information
- work through influential persons in the community such as disc jockeys, television personalities, and class presidents
- create advertising that depicts persons having conversations about one's store or products
- develop advertising that is of "conversational value"

Identifying Types of Advertising

Retail advertising has two basic purposes: to get customers into the store and to contribute to the store's image. The first purpose is immediate: today's advertising brings buyers into the store tomorrow, tomorrow's advertising brings them the next day, and so on. To accomplish this, the store must give buyers some specific reason to come to the store now. Retailers also want long-run, or delayed, results from advertising. They want customers to know "who" the store is in relation to competitors and the community as a whole. They also want customers to be favorably inclined to shop at the store because of their image. Accordingly, retailers undertake two basic kinds of advertising: product and institutional.

Product Advertising

Product advertising *presents specific merchandise for sale and urges customers to come to the store immediately to buy.* This indirect form of advertising helps to create and maintain the store's reputation through its merchandise. Product advertising themes center around promoting merchandise that is new, exclusive, and of superior quality and design, as well as themes relating to complete assortments and merchandise events. Announcements of sales, special promotions, or other immediate-purpose advertising are also forms of product advertising. (See advertisement on facing page.)

Institutional Advertising

Institutional advertising *sells the store generally as an enjoyable place to shop.* Through institutional advertising, the store helps to establish its image as a fashion leader, price leader, leader in offering wide merchandise selection, superior service, or quality, or whatever image the store chooses to cultivate. In reality, practically all of the store's product advertising should communicate its institutional image as well. The art, copy, typography, and logotype of product advertising all help to convey the store's image. (See advertisement on page 619.) These components of advertisements are discussed in a subsequent section.

Cooperative Advertising

Another way a retailer might undertake product advertising economically is to take advantage of **cooperative advertising**. In cooperative advertising, *manufacturers prepare print and broadcast advertising material of their own products and allow the retailer to insert its store name and address in the ad.* Then the manufacturer and retailer split the cost of media space or time to run the ad. Usually the cost split is 50/50, although these percentages vary. Some manufacturers also make direct-mail advertising of their products available to retailers to distribute to their customers. Sometimes this material is free to the retailer; at other times the manufacturer charges a nominal fee. (See advertisement on page 621.)

Developing an Advertising Strategy

Like all other retail mix operations, advertising, to be effective, must be done within the framework of an overall plan. A comprehensive advertising program, like any other well-managed project, must be systematically planned, organized, executed, and controlled. In other words, the retailer must (1) determine what it wishes to accomplish with advertising, (2) establish the organizational structure necessary for objective implementation, (3) develop a means for reaching these objectives, and (4) measure the degree to which it met those objectives. At the minimum, a retailer's advertising strategy should consist of the components shown in Figure 22–5.

PLANNING THE ADVERTISING FUNCTION

Planning the advertising function involves (1) a statement of objectives (the specific results the retailer expects to achieve from advertising), and (2) development of a budget (the determination and allocation of money to accomplish the objectives).

Determining Advertising Objectives

Objectives—statements of results the retailer wishes to achieve—are the most essential requirement for effective advertising planning. Effective planning is next to impossible without desired end results toward which to plan.

(Opposite page)   A product line advertisement. (Courtesy of J.C. Penney Company)

HALSTON III™

A total look.
Because there's nothing more
beautiful than a confident woman.

You're looking smarter than ever.
JCPenney

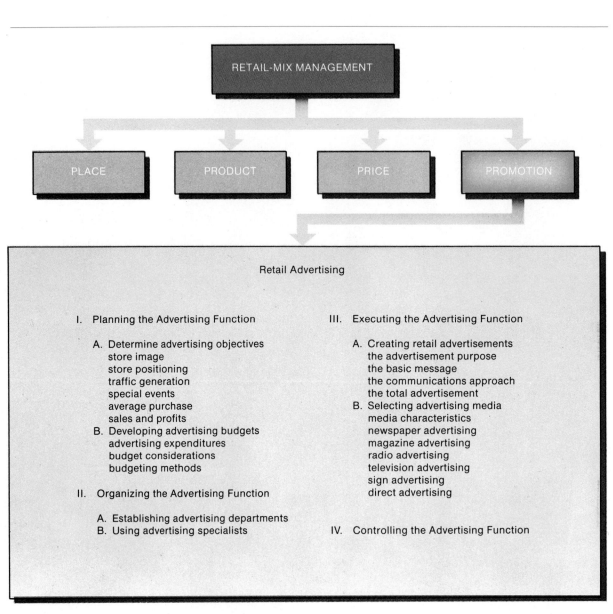

RETAIL-MIX MANAGEMENT

PLACE   PRODUCT   PRICE   PROMOTION

Retail Advertising

I. Planning the Advertising Function

    A. Determine advertising objectives
       store image
       store positioning
       traffic generation
       special events
       average purchase
       sales and profits
    B. Developing advertising budgets
       advertising expenditures
       budget considerations
       budgeting methods

II. Organizing the Advertising Function

    A. Establishing advertising departments
    B. Using advertising specialists

III. Executing the Advertising Function

    A. Creating retail advertisements
       the advertisement purpose
       the basic message
       the communications approach
       the total advertisement
    B. Selecting advertising media
       media characteristics
       newspaper advertising
       magazine advertising
       radio advertising
       television advertising
       sign advertising
       direct advertising

IV. Controlling the Advertising Function

FIGURE 22–5
Developing and implementing the advertising function

(Opposite page)   Creating an institutional image. (Courtesy of Goldwaters)

Goldwaters

TROPICAL FEVER: CATCH IT!

Bold, fiery accents to instantly ignite your fashion wardrobe. Our colors are so hot — only your summer whites and neutrals can cool them.

Explore new color routes! Take our sizzling palm fronds accented with white beads and you've arrived with style. Necklace 16.50; earrings 10.00; bright bangle to mix, match or stack 10.00; from the innovative and exciting Tropical Tradewinds collection by Van Allen.

Drench your wardrobe with festively colored cocoa chips. You'll never dream of trading the 32" necklace 56.00; drop earrings 18.00; easy-fit elasticized bracelet 22.50; a carnival of color from the Mardi Gras collection by Miriam Haskell. *Goldwaters Fashion Jewelry*

Nature of Advertising Objectives

All retailers should have two basic types of objectives for their advertising effort. The first type consists of the broad, overall aims—the *policy objectives*—of the institution, such as achieving a high level of sales or profits over a sustained period of time while at the same time promoting the total image of the institution for its excellent service, matchless value, and so on. These objectives serve as a basic policy guide to resolve potential conflicts.

The second type of objectives, *operational objectives,* consists of the more specific, measurable results expected of advertising efforts.[1] These goals must be established for specific time periods, for particular products, for the store as a whole, or for specific advertising campaigns. Many retailers fail to establish these specific goals.

Ideally, advertising goals should be specific, measurable, and realistic. A goal is specific when it spells out precisely the results expected from advertising, and it is measurable when it is expressed quantitatively. Useful objectives, for example, would be

- to increase each month's sales in the sportswear department this year by 15 percent over the corresponding month last year
- to increase by 20 percent from January 3 to December 20 the number of household heads with incomes over $25,000 in this city who respond with our store name when asked "Which is the first store in town in which you would shop for the best quality sportswear?"
- to increase by 10 percent over last year's average the number of purchases made in this store this year

Each of these advertising objectives not only provides specific targets toward which retail advertisers might work, they are expressed in numbers that the retailer can measure.

Types of Advertising Objectives

Store image. To acquire and keep regular customers, every store needs to be thought of as unique in some manner by its target market. The retailer may wish to establish an image by size (large), merchandise specialization (Early American furniture store), clientele ("designer" lines for "discriminating" shoppers), fashion leadership or merchandise quality (always presenting fashion "news"), or by price levels (not being undersold on products with well-known prices). An example of a measurable store image objective is "By December, at least 30 percent of the people in our market area will answer with our store's name when asked, "At which store would you expect to find the latest fashions?"

Store positioning. Positioning is a term advertisers use to refer to attempts to get the market to think of the store in a certain manner in relation to its competition. Wendy's now-famous television ad "Where's the beef?" was a very successful commercial that positioned Wendy's as the restaurant with the very large burger, one with more beef than the competitive products offered by McDonald's (Big Mac) or Burger King (The Whopper).[2] A supermarket, for example, may wish to be thought

(Opposite page)   Cooperative advertisements benefit both the retailer and the manufacturer. (Courtesy of Lazarus and Timberland)

of as the store with the city's highest quality meat and produce. This niche in the consumer's mind is established not only with effective meat and produce merchandising but also with relentless advertising. This objective might be stated measurably and specifically as "By December, at least 32 percent of a representative sample of city residents will name our store when asked 'At which store would you expect to find the best meat and produce?'" One family-owned supermarket has used the advertisement "Homemade Is Always Best" to position itself against its main competition—a clutch of new fast-food chain stores. Each of their full-page, four-color newspaper ads is targeted against a different chain product—hamburger, pizza, fried chicken, beef sandwich—and carries the "Homemade is always best" theme.

Traffic generation. Traffic refers to the number of people who visit the store and the frequency with which they visit. In general, the more consumers who visit the store, the greater the store's sales. Retailers can generate traffic in many ways. One of the surest methods is to provide customers with a special purpose for visiting; this can be achieved through sales, "theme" promotions (such as bridal seminars), special-merchandise showings, demonstrations, and so forth, each of which must be advertised. The retailer can measure the results of its efforts to produce traffic by actually counting the number of people who enter the store or by assuming that an increase in the store's sales reflects an increase in the amount of traffic. Therefore, an indirect method for measuring traffic increases is to measure the increase in the average *number* of daily purchases, regardless of their size, over a specified period.

Special events. As previously discussed, one method of increasing store traffic is by promoting special events to give customers particular reasons for visiting the store. These sales-promotional events are planned in advance, oriented around some theme, and coordinated through merchandising, store decoration, and advertising. One of retailing's most famous special events is Dallas' Nieman-Marcus' annual "Fortnight," a two-week fall happening featuring a unique theme; for example, the store might create an exotic atmosphere of some foreign country complete with displays and sales of rare and exclusive merchandise. The event induces many customers to visit the store out of curiosity. Many of those so persuaded make purchases totally unrelated to the special advertised event. Measurable objectives might be evaluated by head counts or average number of purchases made during the course of the promotion. (See advertisement on facing page.)

Increasing average purchases. Most advertising objectives are indiscriminate; that is, they concern a target market consisting of both present and potential customers. Many retailers feel, however, that the most fruitful method for expanding sales is to induce present customers to buy more. Retailers can identify present customers through charge account records, by asking them to register, by recording names and addresses from personalized checks, and in other ways. Such people have already demonstrated a measure of favor toward the store by buying, so concentrated efforts to induce them to buy more may be one of the greatest potential payoffs to advertising. Most retailers attempt to accomplish this objective by direct-mail invitations to sales or by new-merchandise showings. This objective can be quantitatively stated as follows: "This year we will increase the average amount of purchases by our charge-account customers by 10 percent."

(Opposite page)   A special event advertisement. (Courtesy of Neiman-Marcus/Dallas)

A GERMAN FORTNIGHT

OCTOBER 17-NOVEMBER 5. CELEBRATING 300 YEARS OF GERMAN IMMIGRATION IN NORTH AMERICA.

Succumb to the outrageous luxury of Baden-Baden. ■ Where Napoleon III and the Kaiser along with their courts summered and "took the cure" — the legendary waters of the river Oos. ■■ We've recaptured the famous spa in Cosmetics. ■ With its own Lancaster Beauty Farm with lotions, scrubs, masques and massage creams to cleanse and purify body and facial skin. ■ And Ralph Lauren makeup artists to make a healthy glow more glowing. ■■ Ah, what wonders these waters work. ■ Complimentary makeovers by Ralph Lauren and Lancaster teams, daily. ■■■ Lancaster facials, 30.00. Make your appointment: 741-6911, ext. 2101, First Floor, Downtown.

Neiman-Marcus

Sales and profits. Advertising is, of course, intended to contribute to expanded sales. Therefore, some retailers express advertising in terms of either sales or profits; for example, "This year we will expand total store sales (or the sales of some particular department or line) by 15 percent." the major limitation of such a broad sales objective for advertising is that many factors affect sales besides advertising. For example, prices, quality of merchandise, effectiveness of promotion, general economic conditions, and competition are just a few among many factors influencing a store's sales performance. Thus, it is not recommended that retailers state advertising objectives in terms of either sales or profits, since advertising alone should not shoulder the burden of achieving a desired sales level.

Developing Advertising Budgets

Executing the advertising campaign requires spending money. Therefore, determining the advertising appropriation is the next step in developing a comprehensive advertising plan. Although many retailers use the terms "appropriation" and "budget" synonymously, *appropriation* refers to the total expenditure for advertising undertaken in a time period, whereas *budget* refers to the allocation of this total expenditure across departments, merchandise lines, advertising media, and planning periods such as weeks, months, and seasons.

Advertising Expenditures

Before the retailer can properly make an advertising appropriation, it must first determine which expenditures are advertising expenditures and which are not. Most retailers consider the following to be advertising expenses: (1) space and time costs in print and broadcast media; (2) advertising-department salaries and travel and entertainment expenses; (3) cost of advertising consultants; (4) advertising research services; (5) media costs for contests, premiums, and sampling promotions; (6) direct-mail advertising to consumers; and (7) storage of advertising materials. Other expenditures that some retailers include as advertising expenses are catalogs, advertising office supplies, point-of-sale materials, window display installation services, consumer contest awards, product tags, signs on company-owned vehicles, public relations, and other consultants. Whichever expenses are included under advertising expenditures, the retailer should avoid including so many classes of expenditures that it depletes the allowance for media expenditures and other activities directly related to advertising.

Retail accounting methods treat advertising as an expense item on the income statement, and it is accepted as such by the Internal Revenue Service. The retailer should also think of advertising as an *investment,* however, even though it will not appear in the firm's capital budget.[3] While it is true that most of the retailer's advertising is used to meet short-range objectives and produce immediate sales, the retailer must remember that advertising also has long-term, cumulative effects in building consumer patronage and good will. The retailer that thinks of advertising as an investment expenditure rather than as an expense is less likely to try to keep the expense at a minimum, which is management's natural reaction to any expense item.

Budget Considerations

Budgeting, as defined here, refers to the process of dividing the total advertising appropriation into its various components; in other words, splitting up the advertising "pie." In how many ways must the retailer budget its advertising appropriation? At a minimum, the retailer should allocate the budget across either department or merchandise lines, among advertising media, and through time-planning periods.[4]

Departments and merchandise lines. At different times, the store will want to feature different items in its product line and de-emphasize the promotion of others. A women's clothing store will feature coats at certain times and swimwear at other times. Some stores choose to promote high-markup, low-turnover items heavily and de-emphasize lower-markup, higher-turnover items. Others may elect either to introduce a new line or achieve a higher market penetration in a given line. Whatever the store's goals are for its merchandise lines and departments, different goals require different levels of expenditures for advertising. The retailer's advertising budget should reflect these differences.

Media. Retailers can select from among several different advertising media, depending upon their objectives and strategies. Some media give retailers discounts for signing long-term contracts. For example, a retailer can buy more newspaper space with a given dollar by making a yearly "space contract" with the newspaper rather than buying the same space over a year on an issue-by-issue basis. It is therefore important for the retailer to determine how much of the total advertising appropriation it intends to devote to each of the media to make those expenditures more efficient.

Time periods. Most retailers advertise more at certain times and less at others. Some choose to advertise extensively before and during heavy buying periods, while others attempt to offset slack periods with heavier advertising. Some retailers, such as clothing stores, have definite sales seasons, while others, such as supermarkets, experience less seasonal variation in sales. Retailers that expect to advertise according to a time pattern should therefore develop an advertising budget for time periods. Most retailers develop quarterly and monthly advertising budgets, but others develop extremely short-run budgets such as two-week intervals. When these time allocations are made, the store manager knows how much must be spent to advertise certain merchandise in certain media during a certain time period.

Budgeting Methods

Retailers use many methods to determine their advertising budgets. These range in sophistication from little more than guesswork to highly sophisticated techniques. The methods described here appear in ascending order of sophistication.

Educated-guess method. Some small sole proprietors *use their intuition and practical experience to develop an advertising budget.* The retailer simply takes a look at last year's sales and advertising expenditures, determines what it hopes to accomplish this year, considers other expenditures needed, and thinks up an amount to spend on advertising next year. This method is a little better than no method at all, since more sophisticated methods are available that are not much more difficult to use.

Percentage-of-sales method. One of the most widely used methods of determining the advertising appropriation is the percentage-of-sales method. In developing a budget with this method, the retailer *takes a predetermined percentage of either last year's sales or estimated sales for the coming year to calculate how much to spend on advertising.* The percentage figure the retailer uses is based on either the "traditional" figure the company has taken in the past, personal "insight," or an industry average. Once the retailer has determined the total advertising budget, it is then allocated according to sales by departments, merchandise lines, and time periods.

The percentage-of-sales method is popular among retailers because it is simple to use. Unfortunately, it has no logical tie-in with achieving advertising objectives. Moreover, the percentage-of-sales method fails to consider changes in population, competitive activity, and other environmental factors that affect every business. Thus, although this method has widespread appeal because it is easy to understand and to apply, it is a questionable way to set advertising budgets.

Competitive parity method. Some retailers *set their advertising appropriation at the amount they estimate their most important competitors are spending.* By monitoring the amount of advertising Retailer B is doing and estimating its costs, Retailer A may determine its appropriation and even allocate the appropriation across time periods, media, and merchandise in the same proportions as B.

There are three basic problems with this method. First, Retailer A is using an estimate of the amount Retailer B has spent in the *past* to estimate how much to spend in the *future.* In general, little relationship could be expected between how much one store spent for advertising *last* year and how much another should spend *next* year. Second, Retailer B may not allocate its total promotional dollars in the same manner as A. B may de-emphasize advertising and emphasize in-store personal selling. If A bases its advertising appropriation on B's expenditures, it may underadvertise without compensating for B's in-store effort. Third, A has no way of knowing whether B's allocation method is appropriate for B, much less for A, and B's advertising expenditures certainly bear little direct relation to A's sales, profit objectives, market position, or share of the market. Therefore, this method has drawbacks that, under most conditions, make it undesirable to use.

Objective and task method. One of the most logical methods of advertising appropriation and budgeting is the **objective and task method**. *Retailers using this method follow a basic four-step process:*

1. establish the objectives for advertising
2. determine the type and amounts of advertising necessary to accomplish these objectives
3. determine the overall cost of the advertisement
4. schedule the advertisements day by day

The last step allows for budgeting the total appropriation across media, product lines, and time periods.

As discussed earlier in this chapter, advertising *objectives* should be specific and measurable. As an example, assume that one of the retailer's advertising objectives is the following: "By November 30 of this year, 50 percent of all women in our trading area who are 25 or older and who have household incomes over $25,000 will give our store name when asked 'Which store in town sells the best women's coats?' " To reach this objective, the retailer must perform certain *tasks,* such as producing advertisements, selecting the media needed to reach the stated target market, determining how many ads to run in each medium selected, and when (time of month, week, day) to run these ads. After establishing all of the tasks necessary to meet the objective(s), the retailer adds the costs to perform each task. This sum is the retailer's advertising budget.

Quite often the retailer will find that the advertising budget derived is more than the company can afford. In these cases, the retailer must revise its objectives downward and reformulate the tasks necessary to meet the new objectives.

The objective and task budgeting method offers several strengths. First, advertising expenditures are based on specifically stated objectives, not on "guess-timates" or competitors' advertising expenditures. Second, this method forces the retailer into *planning* an advertising strategy and become a part of it. Third, it helps the retailer to create criteria against which to measure performance.

Although this budgeting method has several strengths, it is not without its weaknesses. First, the question arises whether the retailer's objectives are sound ones worth achieving. If the expenditures to achieve the objectives reduce long-run profits, these objectives would be of questionable value. Sometimes, however, management feels that the psychological benefits outweigh profit motives. Second, it is difficult for retailers and their media consultants to determine the best combination of media, reach, and frequency to attain their objectives. Even with these weaknesses, the objective and task method is a sound and practical advertising budgeting approach for retailers.

ORGANIZING THE ADVERTISING FUNCTION

The day-to-day advertising functions retailers perform include deciding which products to promote, developing copy and artwork, and scheduling and placing their ads in the media. How the store is organized to execute these functions depends on the size of the store and the funds available for specialized personnel to perform the functions.

Establishing Advertising Departments

In small sole proprietorships and partnerships, the owner-manager or one of the partners must handle the advertising function. With so many other store duties to perform, it is unlikely that this person will be an expert in advertising production. Thus, the main function is to establish advertising objectives, appropriations, and budgets and to work with outside advertising specialists, usually freelancers, representatives of media, and advertising agencies. Representatives of newspapers, radio, and television can and will produce finished print and broadcast advertising and offer advice on media placement and scheduling. These same services also are provided by advertising agency account representatives, although many small stores do not work with agencies except, perhaps, for special events and seasonal promotions.

Some large stores have small advertising departments with an advertising manager who supervises a few artists, copywriters, and production specialists. The manager usually is responsible for establishing objectives, appropriations, budgets, and scheduling and for working with store merchandise managers and other managers to determine what will be promoted and how. This is usually the person who interacts with outside specialists in agencies and the media. Since most retailers advertise primarily in newspapers, the artists and copywriters spend most of their time developing newspaper copy. The production specialists arrange for the advertisements to be either engraved or made camera-ready for newspaper printing. Broadcast advertising usually is produced with the help of agencies or personnel of the television and radio stations.

Very large stores are likely to have a complete advertising and sales-promotion department. A **sales-promotion director** *usually is responsible for supervising and coordinating the activities of an advertising manager, a display manager, and a special events, publicity, or public relations coordinator.* The **advertising manager** *performs all the advertising activities described and supervises an art director, copy chief, and production manager.* The **sales-promotion manager** *works with merchandise managers in developing and coordinating advertising, promotion, and displays with sales and special promotions.* Even in the largest stores, in-house advertising production is likely to be print oriented; however, large stores often use the services of an advertising agency for broadcast production and scheduling.

Using Outside Advertising Specialists

Freelancers, advertising agencies, and media representatives are the three principal advertising specialists available to the retailer. An **advertising freelancer** *might be an artist, copywriter, or photographer who produces advertising on a part-time basis for small retailers.* Freelancers usually operate alone, but in some cases have a small staff, charge a fee or an hourly rate for work, and either work on their own premises or at the retailer's store.

Media representatives are *the employees of newspapers and radio or television stations whose principal job is to sell advertising space and time.* These specialists also can arrange to produce the retailer's advertisements. Usually, newspapers do not charge for production and take compensation only for the space they sell. Radio stations normally do not charge for production, only for time, but they will charge the retailer a production fee for the tapes they make if the tapes are broadcast on other stations. Television stations generally charge a fee for producing commercials in addition to the air time the retailer uses.

Although **advertising agencies** produce the majority of national advertising, most retailers do not use them. There are two reasons for this. First, agencies receive *most* of their compensation from the media from which they buy time and space, not from their clients. Media offer a discount, usually 15 percent, to agencies for the time and space they buy for their clients. However, most media offer local advertisers a substantially lower rate which is not "commissionable." Therefore, agencies must place the retailer's advertising either at "national" rates to make a commission or at local ("retail") rates, charging the retailer a fee—usually 15 percent—for production.

EXECUTING THE ADVERTISING FUNCTION

Few retailers become directly involved in creating advertising. Nonetheless, all must be able to distinguish good, effective advertising from poor, ineffective advertising. Actually, "creating" advertising is the responsibility of "creative" advertising personnel: artists, copywriters, and others who work for the store, agency, or media. Since a full discussion of "creativity" and creating advertising is beyond the scope of this chapter, the reader is referred to any standard advertising text for detail. This section introduces the basic process of creating advertising. For the sake of simplicity, the discussion is limited to creating newspaper advertising, the most common kind of retail advertising.

Creating Retail Advertisements

There are as many processes for creating ads as there are creators of ads. In general, though, the creator of an advertisement must take into account the following steps in developing an effective ad:

1. determine the purpose of the advertisement
2. decide upon the basic message
3. select the communications approach
4. develop the total advertisement, part by part

The Purpose of the Advertisement

An individual advertisement can have one or more purposes, such as promoting the store as a whole, making customers aware of a special event, focusing on a single product, or highlighting several products. Regardless of the retailer's purpose for a single advertisement, all advertising has some degree of "institutional" content as well. To achieve the double benefit of special-purpose advertising and institutional advertising, the retailer should select a special theme, product, or combination of products to feature, but always maintain the same style in advertisements.

Other purposes also must be considered: Is the advertising intended to elicit an immediate response? If so, perhaps direct action ("Come in today") should be suggested. Is the advertisement part of a campaign with a unified theme? If so, the message must be coordinated with that theme.

The Basic Message

In persuasive communications such as advertising, two basic elements are *what is said* and *how it is said*—substance and style. Too many advertisers concentrate on style and forget about substance, but the substance must be clearly specified before advertising can be effective. Stipulating the basic **advertisement message** is *determining what to say*. Most retail advertising messages are quite simple: "Ours is a high-fashion store"; "Our women's coats are of highest quality"; "Our meat selection is the best in town"; "Our stereophonic equipment is now on sale"; and so forth. But the message should not be pulled out of thin air. Instead, it should be based on the target customer's wants and needs and the ability of what is being advertised to *satisfy* those wants and needs. The combination of these two is the advertising *appeal.* If, for example, the advertiser thinks that its target customers are concerned not with the quality of a coat but with its social acceptability, then the basic appeal of the message should be "Fashionable women wear this coat," not "This coat will last for five years." In both of these messages, it should be noted, the basic message stresses the *benefit* consumers derive from buying, and not the *features* of the coat from which they derive the benefit. Although the retailer's advertisement can point out that a coat has a double-stitched lining (a product feature), the resulting benefit (the lining is unlikely to separate from the coat) is the basic message the retailer should stress.

In determining what to say, the retailer must decide whether to advertise a single product or several products in the same advertisement. While it is obviously more cost efficient to promote several products in a single advertisement, the retailer might find it is more profitable to emphasize one product, especially during a particular season of the year. If the retailer advertises an assortment of *related goods,* however, its advertisement is likely to be even more effective than advertising a single product. Men's sport coats, slacks, and shoes can be advertised very effectively together, since collectively they represent an ensemble worn together. The promotion of many products in a supermarket ad also is effective, since shoppers are interested in the total price they must pay for the items. But a furniture store advertising sofas and bedroom suites in the same space would be less effective than advertising each singularly, since the products are unrelated. Thus, a retailer must carefully plan what to say and how to say it, both of which depend on the target market's needs and the retailer's ability to satisfy those needs.

The Communication Approach

In determining the **communications approach,** *the advertiser turns its attention from what it is saying to how it is saying it.* Most messages can be communicated effectively using either a rational approach or an emotional approach. The *rational* approach uses facts, narrative, and logical reasoning to persuade the consumer. The *emotional* approach appeals to the consumer's sense of aesthetics, ego, or feelings. For example, a tire dealer may effectively use a rational approach in promoting snow tires ("You can get there on time—even if you wake up to snow") or it may arouse a husband's fear and protective instincts by depicting a solemn wife and two wide-eyed children under the headline, "Are you sure they'll get home tonight?" Both approaches can be effective; however, advertising practitioners believe that the emotional approach is more effective.

The Total Advertisement

After the retailer has determined the message and approach, it must then develop the total advertisement. The **total advertisement** *consists of several components: headline, illustration, copy, logotype or "signature," and layout (the visual arrangement).* Although each of these components has a specific purpose, they work together to accomplish the ad's basic purpose: *to motivate the consumer to action.* It is worthwhile here to reiterate the phases of the consumer's mental adoption process outlined earlier in this chapter: moving from nonawareness through awareness, comprehension, conviction, and motivation.

The layout, illustration, and headline of the advertisement all work to capture the consumer's attention and to create *awareness.* As discussed previously, the elements of size, novelty, contrast, and color help to capture a consumer's attention. Every advertisement should incorporate one or more of these attention-getting elements.

Layout. The principal purpose of an ad's **layout** is *to capture consumers' attention and guide them through all parts of the advertisement.* Several other layout considerations merit attention. For example, one old advertising rule of thumb is that the principal focal point of the layout should occur five-eighths from the top. Also, sparse illustrations with lots of white space suggest quality and prestige, whereas cluttered ads suggest discounting and a price appeal. These guidelines are two among many that retailers use to develop effective advertising layouts.

Headline. The **headline** of an ad *performs several functions besides getting attention.* It should motivate the reader to review the remainder of the ad by *providing news* ("Blatt's Biggest Sale Ever!"), *selecting readers* ("Now You Can Get Organized"), and *arousing curiosity* ("Color TV for a Dollar a Day? Want to Know More?"). In general, the more original or unique the headline, the better. However, the headline must be coordinated with the remainder of the advertisement's basic message. In fact, the headline condenses the basic advertising message, telling the reader essentially what is to come.

Illustration. **Illustrations** *help to build consumer comprehension.* The most common illustration is a drawing or a photograph of the product. The illustration can depict the product alone, isolate certain product features or details, show the product in context (such as illustrating a sofa in a completely furnished living room), depict the product in use, or illustrate how a consumer can derive a benefit from the product. Any of these approaches can be effective, depending on the purpose of the advertisement. An illustration of a man playing golf, for example, might be quite effective in illustrating the benefits of a lawn-care service.

Copy. The **copy**—*what is actually said in the advertisement*—helps to develop consumer comprehension, conviction, and action. In brief, good advertising copy should be simple and readable, yet vivid in word selection; it should be conversational in tone, interesting, enthusiastic, informative, point out benefits, and suggest action. Effective copy can be either brief or lengthy; however, the chance that anyone will read long copy is remote. Only the most interested person will spend the time and effort to study an advertisement with a lot of copy.

Logotype. The **logotype,** or "logo" in common usage, is *the store's distinctive "signature" that appears in all advertising* (see Figure 22–6). It is usually coordinated with the store's sign, with its point-of-purchase advertising, labels, shopping bags, and so forth. Done in a distinctive style, script, or type, it identifies the store in the consumer's mind in much the same way that a trademark identifies a product or company. The store's logo should be designed carefully, since it may have a significant impact upon consumers. A two-year-old child, for example, may instantly recognize a Sears store or Sears advertising by the logo, although the child cannot read the word "Sears."

Most retailers use the same logo for all their advertising, although some stores will vary their logos depending on the products they advertise. A logo is effective when it suggests the store's "character" or the nature of the retailer's merchandise. For example, a women's sportswear store might use a "lazy" script for a logotype, whereas an early-American furniture store would choose an antique type of script. A good logo communicates the store's personality and product offerings.

Selecting Advertising Media

The retailer's advertising message must be carried to the market by some communications vehicle. These vehicles are called advertising *media.* The retailer can select from among *print media,* such as newspapers, shopping publications, and magazines; *broadcast media,* such as radio and television; *sign media,* such as outdoor and transit; and *miscellaneous media,* including point-of-purchase media and advertising specialties, such as calendars or ashtrays. The retailer can also choose to become its own medium and use direct advertising to the consumer through mailed or hand-delivered letters, circulars, and catalogs.

Selecting advertising media is not an easy task. The retailer must choose the medium or media that will do the best job of communicating the advertising message to the greatest number of consumers in the retailer's target market at the

FIGURE 22–6
The family of logos for the May Department Stores Co.

lowest cost. To accomplish these tasks, large retailers usually employ several media over a given time. To select the best media for their purposes, retailers must first understand the strengths and weaknesses of each medium.

Media Characteristics

Retailers must consider many characteristics in choosing advertising media. Some media are costly, some are inexpensive; some communicate a given message well, others poorly; some present the message continuously, others are instantaneous.

Communication effectiveness *refers to a medium's ability to deliver the impact the retailer desires to the target market.* Print media show consumers pictures and words they can see and read. With radio, consumers can only listen to the advertiser's message, whereas with television they can both see and hear the retailer's communication. The print media are generally thought to be effective with the intelligent audience, whereas the broadcast media are more effective with the less intelligent audience. Newspapers and radio stimulate quick attention to a retailer's current offering, whereas television and magazines create long-term images in the consumer's mind. Depending on its purposes, the retailer can choose to advertise in the print media, the broadcast media, or a combination of both. A combination is preferred by retailers that wish to develop a long-term store image as well as stimulate quick sales.

Geographic selectivity is *a medium's ability to "home in" on a specific geographic area such as a city and its surrounding area.* This is an important media characteristic to a retailer, since most customers live in the local area. A medium that delivers the message to many people outside the retailer's market has a high degree of "wastage" circulation, viewership, or listenership, since these people are unlikely to buy from that retailer. Of the major media, local newspapers, local radio stations, and local television stations offer the retailer reasonably good geographic selectivity.

Audience selectivity *refers to the medium's ability to present the message to a certain target audience within a population.* Most magazines appeal to people with special interests, such as antique collectors, golfers, and electronics hobbyists. Radio stations also have a high degree of audience selectivity. Because of a station's programming format (e.g., country and western music, classical music, rock), it can appeal to distinct groups of consumers. Television can also be highly selective when individual programs are considered. People who watch "Monday Night Football" are different from those who watch "Days of Our Lives." Newspapers, on the other hand, do not have a selective audience. They appeal to groups with a wide array of interests and socioeconomic profiles. Audience selectivity can be increased if ads are placed in strategic locations *within* a newspaper (for example, an ad for a sporting goods store in the sports section).

Flexibility *refers to the number of different "things" the advertiser can do in the medium.* Direct mail, for example, allows the advertiser to enclose money, coupons, pencils, postage-paid envelopes—in fact, practically anything, limited only by the advertiser's ingenuity. Radio, on the other hand, can provide words, music, and sound, but nothing more.

Impact *refers to how well a medium stimulates particular behavioral responses within the target market.* For example, television and magazines are better than other media in building store images, whereas newspapers and the yellow pages of a telephone directory are better at bringing about immediate purchase behavior.

Prestige is *the amount of status consumers attach to a medium.* In general, consumers attribute more prestige to advertising in print media than broadcast media. Naturally, the prestige of print media varies with the individual publication (e.g., the *New Yorker* versus *Mad* magazine). Broadcast media are thought to be less prestigious in general because of the typically "lowbrow" nature of programming in most broadcast media.

Immediacy is *the medium's ability to present a timely or newsworthy message.* Radio announcements, for example, can be prepared today and aired tomorrow, whereas magazines require one to three months' notice in advance of the issue date. Newspapers also need very little lead time (usually 24 hours) to place a retailer's ad. For example, a snow or ice storm can hit a city one day, knocking out electrical power, and retailers can advertise oil-burning lamps and butane-burning stoves the next day. A medium's ability to deliver a retailer's message *immediately* helps the retailer when external events present instant opportunities to the business.

Life *means the length of time the announcement continues to "sell."* Broadcast announcements are gone in an instant and must be repeated to be effective. But a newspaper ad may "live" for several hours while people read the paper. Ads in magazines, which people read leisurely, may continue to "live" for several weeks, since consumers leave them in their homes and re-expose themselves to them over a long period of time.

Coverage *refers to the percentage of a given market that a medium reaches.* A newspaper might be read by 70–90 percent of adults in a certain city, whereas only a fraction of the same market may be reached by a "hard rock" FM radio station. Although coverage is often an important criterion in reaching a market, it must be considered in light of audience selectivity.

Cost *should be viewed in both absolute and relative terms.* An *absolute cost* is the amount of money a retailer must pay to run an advertisement in a medium. For example, the cost of a full-page ad in a newspaper might be $2,000 for one day. The *relative cost* of an advertisement is the number of dollars the retailer spends to reach a specific number of people. For example, if the full-page ad in the newspaper mentioned reaches 300,000 people, then the relative cost is $6.67 per 1,000 readers. If, on the other hand, the retailer spent $250 on a radio ad, it would have spent much less money in absolute terms; however, if the message was heard by only 25,000 people, then the relative cost would be $10.00 per 1,000 people reached. Therefore, retailers should compare relative costs as well as absolute costs in selecting media. Once again, audience selectivity and "wastage" should be among criteria considered in making final media selections.

Frequency *refers to the number of times the same viewer or reader may be exposed to the same advertisement.* A consumer might pass an outdoor poster twice daily for 90 days, whereas a radio spot might be broadcast a dozen times before a person hears it once. Similarly, consumers are likely to read newspapers only once per day, but see a magazine ad in the same issue several times.

Newspaper Advertising

Newspapers have always made up the bulk of the retailer's advertising, probably because the local nature of newspapers fits the retailer's desire for geographic coverage, prestige, and immediacy. In addition, newspapers are a "participative" medium that people read in part for its advertising. In fact, many consumers use newspapers as a shopping guide. As mentioned earlier, retailers can gain some measure of audience selectivity by advertising in specific sections of the paper such as the sports, society, and financial sections. The cost of newspaper advertising is neither the highest nor the lowest of the advertising media available to retailers.

By size and format, newspapers are classified as either standard or tabloid. Most large newspapers are standard; that is, they are about 23.5 inches deep and

8 columns wide, with each column about 2 inches wide. Tabloid newspapers are smaller "booklet" papers of 5 columns wide by about 14 inches deep, or about half the size of standard newspapers. The New York *Daily News* is an example of a tabloid newspaper.

Newspapers also are classified as dailies and weeklies. Some "dailies," however, are published only four to six days a week, and some "weeklies" are published two or three times per week. Additionally, newspapers may be metropolitan, community, or shopping newspapers. Metropolitan newspapers are circulated over an entire metropolitan area (e.g., the *New York Times*), whereas community newspapers are published for a portion of a city or a suburb (e.g., *Newsday*, the Long Island newspaper). Shopping newspapers are comprised mostly of retail advertising and classified advertising.

Newspapers sell two kinds of advertising space: *classified* and *display*. Classified advertising is placed in a special section and is used only by certain kinds of retailers, such as automobile dealers. Most retailers, however, use display advertising, which is spread throughout the newspaper. The basic unit of space the retailer buys from the newspaper is *agate line* (or "line" in common use). An agate line is one column wide and 1/14 of an inch deep. Fourteen lines of space thus equal one *column inch*, the basic space unit for smaller papers. (The width of a column is not a factor in calculating newspaper space.) One full page of advertising equals about 2,400 lines or approximately 172 column inches, depending upon the size of the paper.

Newspapers publish their rates on *rate cards* that they make available to customers. A retailer that buys newspaper space one time with no stipulations would pay the paper's *open rate*. However, few retailers actually pay the open rate, since the cost of newspaper space generally decreases with the quantity bought and increases as the retailer improves the "quality" of its advertising by specifying a particular position in the paper or by using color.

Most retailers that advertise regularly make *space contracts* with the newspaper. In the contract, the retailer agrees to use a certain amount of space over the year and pay a certain amount per line that is lower than the paper's open rate for the same space. The lower rate is simply a quantity discount. A retailer that advertises heavily in a newspaper can receive up to 40 percent off the open rate in a large space contract. If at the end of the year it becomes apparent that the store will not use the amount of space for which it contracted, the paper will "short rate" the retailer, charging it more for subsequent space so that the retailer averages the normal rate for the total space used during the year. If the retailer uses more space than it contracted for, the paper will give it a rebate at the end of the year. This rebate represents a lower rate for more space used.

Unless otherwise specified by the retailer, newspaper rates are "R.O.P." (run of the paper), meaning the paper will put the ad wherever it sees fit in composing the paper. This is not necessarily undesirable, since newspapers, like other businesses, want to satisfy their customers. Therefore, they do the best they can to make up an attractive paper and place advertising where it fits best. However, a retailer can specify a position in the paper if it is willing to pay a premium called a *position charge*. The retailer can then specify the first three pages, the sports, society, or financial section, or even a specific page. Some retailers even rent a certain space permanently. In ROP, newspapers generally place larger ads closer to the front of a section and smaller ads nearer the back.

Most newspapers can print in color, and color advertising is becoming more common. Needless to say, the retailer pays more for color, and the more color used, the more the retailer pays. Many newspapers also are capable of inserting preprinted color advertisements.

Newspaper rate structures are determined by the circulation: the greater the circulation, the higher the rates, and vice versa. The paid and unpaid circulation of a paper is audited by the Audit Bureau of Circulations, which publishes a report of circulations throughout the paper's city and its retail trading zone, the area beyond the city proper for which the city is a trade center. To compare newspapers' advertising rates, which vary widely, advertisers commonly use a calculation called the *milline rate*, which is the paper's cost of getting a line of advertising to a million people. The formula for the milline rate is

$$\text{milline rate} = \frac{\text{line rate x } 1,000,000}{\text{circulation}}$$

Magazine Advertising

Few retailers advertise in consumer magazines. Although magazines do offer a high degree of prestige, audience slectivity, and impact (if used correctly), they generally lack geographic selectivity, which is what the vast majority of retailers require. Since magazines' advertising rates, like newspapers', are based on their total circulation, a retailer must pay for wasted circulation outside its trading area if it places an ad. Thus, a Kansas City retailer that advertises in a nationally circulated magazine pays to advertise not only to Kansas City residents, but also to readers in Maine and Louisiana. To offset this disadvantage, many magazines publish regional editions (same editorial matter, different advertising) for certain geographic areas (e.g., Southwest) and major cities (e.g., New York).

Magazines also require a considerable period of time between the publication date and the date advertising materials must be available. Therefore, they do not accommodate the immediate-response advertising that makes up the majority of retail business. Most retailers that use magazines are either nationwide chains or stores with branches in several cities within a closely confined area.

Magazine space is usually bought in pages and fractions, such as half page, one-third page, or two-thirds page. Generally, the only premium positions are inside the front cover, the inside and outside of the back cover, opposite the table of contents, and the center spread. Magazine rates, like newspaper rates, are based on circulations, and the rate structures, circulations, facts of publication, and publication requirements are published in *Standard Rate and Data Service*. Magazines' rates are compared by a calculation known as CPM (cost per thousand). As briefly described earlier, it is computed as follows:

$$\text{CPM} = \frac{\text{cost of page x } 1,000}{\text{circulation}}$$

If a full-page black and white advertisement in a magazine costs $5,000 and the circulation is 750,000, then CPM = $5,000 x 1,000/750,000 = $6.67. As with newspapers, one magazine may have a higher cost per page but a lower CPM than another, depending on their relative circulations.

Radio Advertising

Americans own about five radio receivers per household, and American retailers have used radio extensively almost since its inception. Among its advantages are low cost and a high degree of geographic and audience selectivity. Although radio broadcasters claim otherwise, sound alone is not a very good communications medium. Therefore, advertisers should stick with a simple message, make it easy to remember (hence the radio "jingle"), and repeat the message frequently.

635

Like other media advertising rates, radio rates are based on audience sizes. *Coverage* is the geographic area over which the station's signal can be heard, while *audience* refers to the number of people who actually listen.

Some 50,000-watt "clear channel" radio stations broadcast over a very large geographic area, including many areas outside the retailer's market area. *Regional* stations cover smaller geographic areas that are much larger than a typical city. *Local* stations, 1,000 watts or less, broadcast a signal that will not carry further than about 25 miles. In these instances, most listeners are clearly in the retailer's market area.

As mentioned earlier, radio stations appeal to highly specialized audiences because of their programming: rock and roll stations, easy-listening stations, classical music stations, all-news stations, or talk-show stations (see Figure 22–7). Moreover, radio listeners are much more station-loyal than television viewers, who switch freely from one channel to another. Radio is particularly important to drivers, who have their radios tuned in about 62 percent of their "drive time," 7 to 9 A.M. and 4 to 6 P.M.

Radio advertising is sold as either *network* radio (buying from several stations that air joint programming) or *spot* radio (bought from individual stations). Since most retailers want to advertise in one city only, most buy spot radio announcements. Stations divide their total air time into classes, usually labeled as AAA, AA, A, B, and C, with the best time being early morning (6 to 10 A.M.) and late afternoon (3 to 7 P.M.). Generally, the fewest people listen at night, so this time is the cheapest. Spot announcements usually are sold in 1-minute, 30-second, and 10-second periods for a certain number of repetitions (e.g., 15 times, 50 times, 150 times). Retailers often buy weekly "package plans" that involve a number of repetitions of a message of a certain duration over a certain time class. For example, retailers can select twenty 30-second announcements in class AA time for a week. They also can buy joint sponsorship of certain programs, such as the daily stock market report. *Standard Rate and Data Service* lists radio stations' packages and rates and describes their programming.

Radio rates are based on audience size. Estimates of the number and characteristics of listeners at certain times of the day are made by companies like The Pulse, Inc., and American Research Bureau. These statistics are sold to radio stations, which in turn make them available to potential advertisers. The retailer, as an advertiser, can write its own radio copy and have the station "produce" it—provide the announcer and develop a musical background and whatever sound effects are needed. Normally the station does not charge for this service if the retailer runs the message on the producing station.

Television Advertising

Television is the most glamorous and conspicuous advertising medium in this country. Reputed to reach about 99 percent of all U.S. homes, this medium garners a large amount of advertising dollars, but not from retailers.

Although television is an excellent communications medium, its high cost constraints eliminate all but the largest retailers from using it regularly. Moreover, the preparation of television commercials requires expertise not usually found in the advertising departments of stores, so most retailers depend on advertising agencies to produce and place their television commercials. Television stations will also produce commercials for a fee.

Like radio time, television time is sold as network or spot time. Unlike radio, the majority of television programming originates from the networks. Since most retailers' markets are localized, only the largest nationwide chains can buy network

	All	Station managers	Program directors	Sales personnel
Adult contemporary	34%	36%	35%	30%
Rock/AOR	9	6	11	10
Beautiful music	1	2	1	
Big band	1	1	1	
Black				2
Classical				2
Country	16	16	15	17
Easy rock	1		1	
Jazz			1	
Mellow music			1	
MOR	1	1	1	2
Music of your life	2	2	2	2
News	1	2		
News/talk	5	3	5	6
Oldies/nostalgia	1		2	
Personality	2	2	1	4
Service radio				2
Talk	1	2	1	
Top 40	2	2	4	2
Urban contemporary	1	1	1	4
Dependent of market	2	4	1	
No answer	18	21	16	15

FIGURE 22–7
Radio executives predict the hottest formats (source: "New Tools, New Tunes," *Advertising Age*, 11 July 1983, M11 and Ted Bolten Associates and Mc-Gavren Guild Radio/"Radio Trends: Insiders Looking Out," a 1982 study based on response of 314 radio executives of stations represented by Mc-Gavren Guild)

television time. Most retailers buy spot announcements from local stations. In contrast to the number of radio stations, only a few television stations operate in most cities.

Television time rate structures and the measurements of audience size on which rates are based are quite complex. A complete discussion is beyond the scope of this text; the reader is referred to any standard advertising text. In general, television stations divide their time into classes based on the size of their audience at a given time. The larger the audience, the higher the cost of advertising time. *Prime time,* when most people watch television, is 7:30 to 11 P.M. on the east and west coasts and 6:30 to 10 P.M. in the middle of the country. *Fringe time* is the hours immediately preceding and following prime time. *Daytime* and *late nighttime,* the least expensive times, are when the fewest people watch television. Therefore, advertising rates are lowest during the times with few viewers and highest during prime time, which normally attracts the most viewers.

Local stations sell spot announcements in and around programming at certain times, as well as packages of announcements much like radio packages. As in almost all media, television stations allow advertisers a quantity discount. The greater the number of repetitions the advertiser buys, the lower the cost per repetition. The retailer can buy 1-minute, 30-second, and 10-second spots (or combinations of these), or it may buy partial sponsorship of the station's local programming.

The sizes of local television audiences for local stations are measured by firms such as the A. C. Nielsen Company and the American Research Bureau. These companies use diaries, electronic recording devices, and interviews to estimate the number of people in the station's market area watching various television programs. With these figures, station managers can compute a CPM figure in much the same manner that newspapers compute their CPMs. Television and radio stations have a special problem, however. Viewership and listenership figures vary with the same program on a day-to-day and week-to-week basis and also vary from one program to another. Thus, for any one program, it is sensible to use an average audience size. A way to calculate CPM (cost per thousand) for a television station is shown here:

$$CPM = \frac{\text{average cost of a minute's advertising} \times 1{,}000}{\text{average audience size}}$$

Sign Advertising

Retailers make extensive use of outdoor advertising media, especially posters, bulletins, and spectaculars. Using these signs, retailers can gain impact, coverage, frequency, geographic selectivity, and a long life for a relatively low CPM. However, outdoor signs are good for presenting only a short reminder message, perhaps the store name, an illustration, and a few words of copy.

Outdoor signs are owned or leased by local "plant operators" that install the advertisers' messages and are responsible for maintaining the signs and the surrounding areas. The three basic outdoor signs are the 30-sheet, 12- by 25-foot *poster* that most people call a "billboard," *painted bulletins,* and outdoor *spectaculars.* Painted bulletins are signs approximately 14 by 48 feet upon which the advertising message is actually painted in sections by an artist working from a miniature. By painting the advertisement in sections, the advertiser can remove the message and take it to another location. Outdoor spectaculars are nonstandardized, custommade signs that use elaborate lighting, falling water, rising steam, billowing smoke, and other techniques to attract consumers' attention. Although these signs have higher attention value, they are quite costly to produce.

Outdoor signs usually are bought in "showings" for periods of time of 90 days and up. A number 100 showing is a number of signs sufficient for a daily exposure of the message to a population equal to that of the market area. Other showing sizes are number 75s, 50s, 25s, and 150s. A showing size of 75, for example, means that the number of signs will expose the advertiser's message to 75 percent of the market area. The number of signs in a showing is not fixed. Fewer signs are needed if they are exposed to heavy traffic, whereas more signs are needed if they are exposed to light-traffic areas. The Traffic Audit Bureau, Inc. audits, by markets, the "circulation" of posters and bulletins (the amount of traffic passing by), and publishes the results in *The Audited Circulation Values of Outdoor Advertising.* The

What are the advantages and disadvantages of this type of advertising?

medium's prices are based on these circulation figures. The CPM of outdoor advertising can be computed as follows:

$$CPM = \frac{\text{rental of all showings bought per month x 1,000}}{\text{number of cars passing by in a month x average number of passengers in the car (the ''auto load factor'')}}$$

Transit advertising includes car cards, exterior displays, and station posters. *Car cards* are the posters (usually 11" by 28") displayed on interior wall racks in buses, subway trains, and the cars of rapid transit systems. *Exterior displays,* which vary in size, are the advertisements shown on the outside of buses, cars, and taxis. *Station posters* are the signs displayed in the interiors of subway, railroad, and rapid-transit stations.

Advertisers buy transit advertising from transit-advertising companies, also known as *operators,* which function much the same way as outdoor plant operators. Car cards normally are sold in *runs.* A full run is two cards in every bus, car, and so forth in the market. Half runs and quarter runs are also possible. The rate structure in transit advertising is similar to that of outdoor advertising, since it is based on the volume of traffic passing through bus and train routes. The rates for exterior or traveling displays and station posters are not standardized, but, as for outdoor showings, are based on the number of people who view them. Cost per thousand for transit advertising is calculated in the same manner as for outdoor media. Like outdoor advertising, transit advertising is also very inexpensive.

Direct Advertising

Direct advertising is a medium retailers use extensively to communicate their product offerings to a select group of consumers. In direct advertising, the retailer creates its own advertisement and distributes it directly to consumers either through the mail or through the personal distribution of circulars, handbills, and other printed matter. Although direct advertising is expensive in terms of cost per thousand, it is the most selective medium, since the ads are read only by people the retailer selects. It also is a personal form of advertising and extremely flexible. Direct advertising can include pictures, letters, records, pencils, coins, coupons, premiums, samples, and any other gifts the retailer chooses to include.

Retailers may choose to distribute direct advertising to their charge customers or other known or potential customers, or they may buy a mailing list from "mailing-list houses" which sell them for a certain charge per thousand names. The variety of these lists is astonishing, ranging from magazine subscribers to professional groups to hobbyists to owners of certain products. The retailer never sees these lists. Instead, advertising pieces are sent to the mailing-list house, which addresses and mails them. Some retailers prepare their own direct advertising, whereas others choose agencies to prepare it and arrange for distribution. The cost of direct-mail advertising is also measured by the cost-per-thousand criterion, as follows:

$$CPM = \frac{\text{cost of preparing and distributing advertising x 1,000}}{\text{total number of recipients}}$$

Unlike with most other advertising media, the effectiveness of direct advertising can be directly measured if the advertisement calls for a response or an order. By dividing the total sales resulting from customer responses to direct advertising by the total cost of preparing and distributing the direct-advertising materials, the retailer can establish a measure of the cost per sale or response for this promotion.

CONTROLLING THE ADVERTISING FUNCTION

To establish some measure of control over its advertising effort, the retailer must evaluate the effects of advertising. To do this, the retailer must first establish specific, measurable advertising objectives (discussed at the beginning of this chapter). Additionally, it must either acquire or develop instruments and methodologies that determine whether those objectives were met. As stated earlier, advertising objectives can be stated in terms of either sales or communications levels. Because sales are affected by factors both internal and external to the retailer's operations, meaningful measurements of the retailer's **advertising effectiveness** are difficult to make, especially in the long run. Short-run advertising objectives can be measured in a broad way, however, if we assume very few things change in the short run (one day to a week). If noticeable changes do occur in this short run, then the retailer must temper its evaluation of advertising effectiveness in light of this information or consider the evaluation a failure. Given that external and internal factors remain relatively stable, the retailer can make a gross measurement of its advertising's sales effectiveness in two ways.

1. For all advertising messages designed to stimulate immediate sales (such as coupons, half-price sales, etc.), the retailer can measure dollar sales

increases, increases in number of purchases, increases in store traffic, and so on against those for a comparable period of time (e.g., last year at the same time or last week).

2. For any direct-advertising campaign, the retailer can measure in-store and out-of-store inquiries, sales increases, or traffic increases.

Increases in sales, consumer traffic, and number of purchases are all important success measurements for advertising. An even more appropriate measurement of the success of a retail promotion, though, is to compare the gross profits from additional sales generated by the promotion to the cost of the promotion.[5] One method for obtaining this measurement is shown in Figure 22-8.

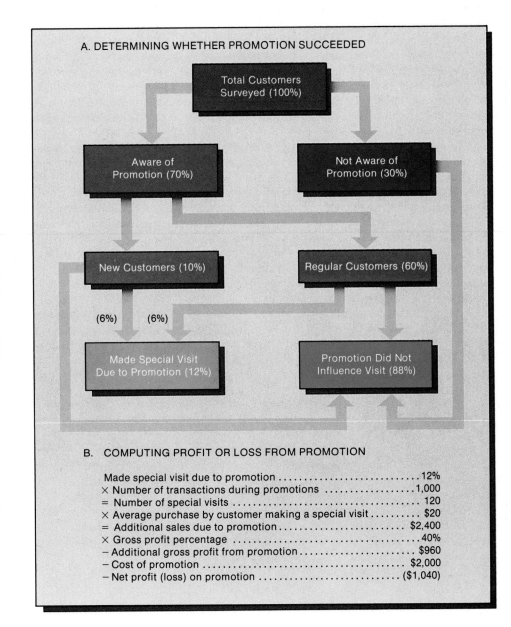

A. DETERMINING WHETHER PROMOTION SUCCEEDED

Total Customers Surveyed (100%)

Aware of Promotion (70%)

Not Aware of Promotion (30%)

New Customers (10%)

Regular Customers (60%)

(6%) (6%)

Made Special Visit Due to Promotion (12%)

Promotion Did Not Influence Visit (88%)

B. COMPUTING PROFIT OR LOSS FROM PROMOTION

Made special visit due to promotion 12%
× Number of transactions during promotions 1,000
= Number of special visits 120
× Average purchase by customer making a special visit $20
= Additional sales due to promotion $2,400
× Gross profit percentage 40%
− Additional gross profit from promotion $960
− Cost of promotion $2,000
− Net profit (loss) on promotion . . . . ($1,040)

FIGURE 22-8
The effectiveness of advertising (source: Irwin Broh, "Measure Success of Promotions with In-Store Customer Surveys," *Marketing News*, 13 May 1983, 17)

Advertising designed to achieve communications objectives should be measured over the long run. Changes in customer awareness, attitudes, perceptions, and behavioral intentions toward the store should be measured either by using personal interviews or mail surveys. In this case, the retailer must use both pretest and posttest measurement to establish any possible change in consumers' opinions of the store. A detailed explanation of research instruments and methodologies for increasing advertising effectiveness is beyond the scope of this book. Students who have an interest in this subject should study the related readings indicated at the end of this chapter.

SUMMARY

Promotion is the fourth element in the retail mix. It involves providing consumers information about the retailer's store and its offering and influencing their perceptions, attitudes, and behavior. Promotion is also closely related to the communication process, since transmitting meaningful messages through the retailer's promotion mix involves five major components: advertising, personal selling, store displays, sales promotion, and publicity. Managing the retail advertising function consists of planning, organizing, executing, and controlling advertising strategies. Advertising works for the retailer by prompting individual consumers to move through the adoption process and by stimulating the two-step flow of mass communications.

In developing advertising plans, the retailer sets advertising objectives, identifies the types of advertising it must do, and develops advertising appropriations and budgets. Effective advertising objectives are specific and measurable and can be related to either sales or communications effects.

Retail advertising takes the form of product advertising, institutional advertising, or some combination of the two. The advertising appropriation is the total amount a retailer spends on advertising, whereas the budget is the allocation of this appropriation across departments or across merchandise lines, time periods, and advertising media. Advertising appropriation and budgeting methods include the educated-guess method, the percentage-of-sales method, the competitive parity method, and the objective and task method.

Organizing and executing the advertising function depends heavily on store size and the funds available to spend on advertising. Small stores rely heavily on outside advertising specialists, whereas large stores normally have a sales promotion and advertising manager to supervise artists, copywriters, publicity directors, and display managers. In addition, this manager works with store merchandise managers and outside advertising specialists.

Executing the advertising function consists of creating advertisements and selecting advertising media. In creating advertisements, the retailer must determine the purpose of the advertisement, create the basic message, develop the communications approach, and finalize the total advertisement. In print advertising, the total advertisement consists of layout, headline, illustration, copy, and logotype. The advertising media retailers use are newspapers, consumer magazines, radio, television, sign media, direct advertising, and numerous other miscellaneous media.

Advertising control, the job of evaluating the effectiveness of advertising, consists of determining what to measure and how to measure it. The retailer may choose either sales or communications measures of advertising effectiveness and may measure effectiveness by numerous methods.

KEY TERMS AND CONCEPTS

promotion

communication process

senders

encoding

transmission

receivers

decoding

feedback

noise

advertising

personal selling

store displays

sales promotion

publicity

DAGMAR

two-step flow of
communications

opinion leaders

product advertising

institutional advertising

cooperative advertising

advertising budgets

educated-guess method

percentage-of-sales method

competitive parity method

objective and task method

sales-promotion director

advertising manager

sales-promotion manager

advertising freelancer

media representative

advertising agencies

advertisement message

communications approach

total advertisement

layout

headline

illustration

copy

logotype

communication effectiveness

geographic selectivity

audience selectivity

flexibility

impact

prestige

immediacy

life

coverage

cost

frequency

newspaper advertising

magazine advertising

radio advertising

television advertising

sign advertising

direct advertising

advertising effectiveness

REVIEW QUESTIONS

1. What are the purposes of retail promotion?
2. Identify and briefly describe the various participants, processes, and acts of the communication process.
3. What are the five elements of the promotion mix? Define each element.
4. How does advertising affect consumers? How does it affect markets?
5. How is product advertising different from institutional advertising?
6. What is the purpose of an advertising objective aimed at store positioning?
7. Why might the retailer view advertising as an investment instead of as an operating expense?
8. What considerations should the retailer take into account when allocating advertising budgets?
9. What are the basic problems associated with using the competitive parity method of determining advertising budgets?
10. Describe the four-step objective and task method of determining the retailer's advertising budget.
11. Do retailers make extensive use of advertising agencies? Why or why not?

12. In developing the basic advertising message, the retailer is concerned with which two issues?
13. Which two general communication approaches are used in conveying the retailer's message?
14. What are the five components of a total advertisement? Define each component.
15. Which media characteristics do retailers consider when selecting the most appropriate types of media for communicating with their consumers?
16. Newspapers sell two kinds of advertising space. What are they? How is newspaper space measured?
17. Explain the following newspaper advertising concepts: open rate, space contract, ROP, and position charge.
18. How are newspaper rate structures determined?
19. Identify the positive and negative aspects of magazine advertising from the retailer's viewpoint.
20. How is radio advertising sold?
21. From the retailer's perspective, what are the positive and negative characteristics of television advertising?
22. What are the three types of outdoor advertising? Describe each type.

ENDNOTES

1. Russell H. Colley, *Defining Advertising Goals for Measured Advertising Results* (New York: Association for National Advertisers, Inc., 1961), 49–69.
2. David Kettlewell, "Positioning, Not Sales, is Real Value of Wendy's Ad," *Format* (June, 1984), 1.
3. Joel Dean, "Does Advertising Belong in the Capital Budget?" *Journal of Marketing* 30 (October, 1966): 15.
4. Much of this discussion is based on Shirley F. Milton, *Advertising for Modern Retailers* (New York: Fairchild, 1974), 62–67.
5. Irwin Broh, "Measure Success of Promotions with In-Store Customer Surveys," *Marketing News*, 13 May 1983, 17.

RELATED READINGS

Bearden, William O.; Lichtenstein, Donald R.; and Teel, Jesse E. "Comparison Price, Coupon, and Brand Effects on Consumers, Reactions to Retail Newspaper Advertisements." *Journal of Retailing* 60 (Summer 1984), 11–34.

Childers, Terry L., and Houston, Michael J. "Conditions for a Picture-Superiority Effect on Consumer Memory." *Journal of Consumer Research* (September 1984), 643–54.

Dunn, S. Watson, and Barban, Arnold M. *Advertising: Its Role in Modern Marketing*, 6th ed. (New York: The Dryden Press, 1985)

Engel, James; Warshaw, Martin; and Kinnear, Thomas. *Promotional Strategy*, 5th ed. (Homewood, Ill.: Richard D. Irwin, 1983)

Farris, Paul W., and Albion, Mark S. "The Impact of Advertising on the Price of Consumer Products." *Journal of Marketing* 44 (Summer 1980), 17–35.

George, Richard J., and Lord, John B. "Supermarket Promotional Strategies: What's Hot and What's Not." *Developments in Marketing Science, Proceedings*. N. K. Malhotra, ed. (Academy of Marketing Science 1985), 299–302.

Green, Paul E.; Mahajan, Vijay; Goldberg, Stephen M.; and Kedia, Pradeep K. "A Decision Support System for Developing Retail Promotional Strategy." *Journal of Retailing* 59 (Fall 1983), 116–43.

Kincaid, William M. *Promotion: Products, Services, and Ideas*, 2nd ed. (Columbus: Charles E. Merrill Publishing Co., 1983)

Mason, J. B., and Wilkerson, J. B. "Addendum: Are Supermarket Advertisements Designed to Deceive Consumers?" *Journal of Advertising* 7 (Winter 1978), 56–59.

Mizerski, Richard W.; White, J. Dennis; and Hunt, Jame B. "The Use of Emotion in Advertising." *AMA Educa-*

tors' *Proceedings.* R. W. Belk et al, eds. (American Marketing Association 1984), 244–48.

Moriarty, Mark. "Feature Advertising—Price Interaction Effects in the Retail Environment." *Journal of Retailing* 59 (Summer 1983), 80–98.

"Outdoor Is In! By the Boards." *Stores* (May 1982), 57–65.

Percy, Larry, and Woodside, Arch G. *Advertising and Consumer Psychology.* (Lexington, Mass.: Lexington Books, 1983)

Rust, Roland T. *Advertising Media Models: A Practical Guide.* (Lexington, Mass.: Lexington Books, 1985)

Shimp, Terence A., and DeLozier, M. Wayne. *Promotion Management and Marketing Communications.* (New York: The Dryden Press, 1986)

Teel, Jesse E., and Bearden, William O. "A Media Planning Algorithm for Retail Advertisers." *Journal of Retailing* 56 (Winter 1980), 23–29.

Young, Robert F., and Greyser, Stephen A. *Managing Cooperative Advertising: A Strategic Approach.* (Lexington, Mass.: D. C. Heath Co., 1983)

Outline

THE EFFECTIVE SALESPERSON

Physical Traits
Personality Traits
Individual Skills
Message-Presentation Skills
The "Super" Salesperson

THE RETAIL SELLING PROCESS

Preparing for Customers
Prospecting for Customers
Contacting the Customer
Presenting the Merchandise
Handling Objections
Closing the Sale

RETAIL SALES MANAGEMENT

Objectives

- Explain why the basis for personal selling is good communications

- Identify the traits and skills of a good salesperson

- Name and discuss the seven steps of the retail selling process

- Describe procedures for training, motivating, and evaluating salespeople

23

Personal Selling

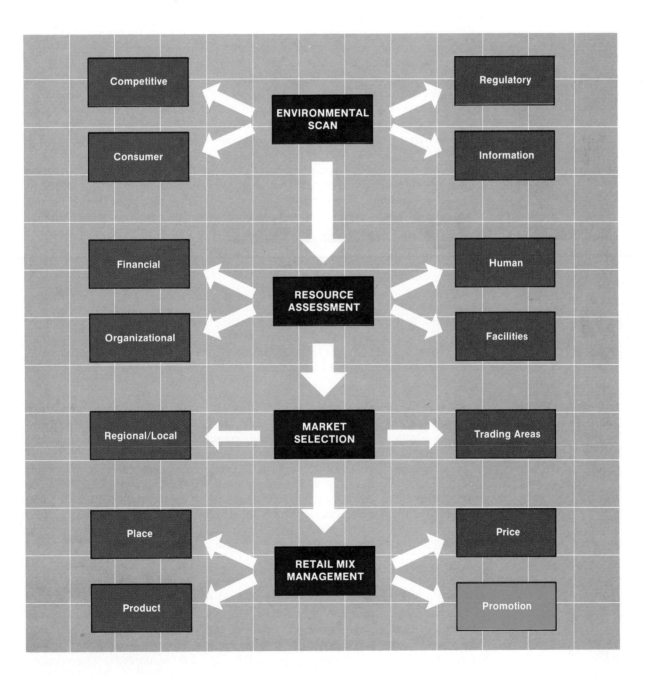

"In a product's long journey from the producer to the customer, the last two feet are the most important. That 'last two feet' is the distance across the sales counter."[1] Retail selling is a special kind of selling whereby the customer comes to the store with a general or specific need in mind. The retail salesperson must close the sale while the customer is still in the store; otherwise, the sale might be lost forever.[2]

Personal selling is, perhaps, the most important element in the store image–creating process. Salespeople are usually the first people in the store to interact with customers on a face-to-face basis. Thus, their influence on how consumers perceive a store is tremendous. One writer observed, for example, "in the case of department stores, clerks are mentioned more often than any other image-creating factor."[3] In research conducted on women's clothing stores, knowledgeability and friendliness of salespeople were critical factors in determining store choice.[4] In sum, salespeople are a significant factor either in enhancing or in detracting from the consumer's total impressions of a retail store.

This chapter covers personal selling as a communication process, the characteristics of a good salesperson, the steps in the retail selling process, how to train salespeople, and how to evaluate their performance. The issues and concerns associated with managing the retailer's personal selling efforts are shown in Figure 23–1.

The basis for *all* personal selling is personal communications. Communications is *not* something you do *to* somebody, *but* something you do *with* somebody. **Personal communications** is *the process of exchanging ideas and meanings with other people.* Although one person is listening, even that person is active, not passive, in every communications situation. Figure 23–2 shows the basic elements of the communications interaction between a customer and a salesperson.

The model also illustrates that both the customer and salesperson are simultaneously sending and receiving information. The transmission and reception of information comes in many forms, such as words, objects, fragrances, colors, gestures, appearances, music, voice qualities (e.g., emotionally irritated, elated), to name but a few modes. With all of these channels of communications occurring at the same time, a good salesperson must be a good listener and observer and adapt quickly to each moment in the selling situation. These and other communications factors are carefully discussed throughout this chapter.

THE EFFECTIVE SALESPERSON

Whether a salesperson is an "order getter" or an "order taker," certain qualities or characteristics are needed to be effective. **Order getters** *must be aggressive salespeople to obtain sales.* They must persuade customers that what they are selling is best for them. **Order takers** *simply comply with customers' requests for certain types of merchandise.* The more difficult job (and more rewarding) of the two is order getting. Although most of the characteristics described in this section apply more to the order getter, they also are traits that order takers should have to be successful in their work. Characteristics of an effective salesperson fall into four categories: physical traits, personality traits, individual skills, and message-presentation skills. This section addresses each of these categories.

Physical Traits

Although a fine line may exist between physical traits, such as personal grooming and hygiene, and personality traits, they are sufficiently different to discuss separately. Clean clothing, shined shoes, clean, well-groomed hair, clean teeth and fresh breath, a well-shaven, clean-smelling body, and a nice smile are essential. Of course, these physical features can quickly be negated by an unpleasant personality.

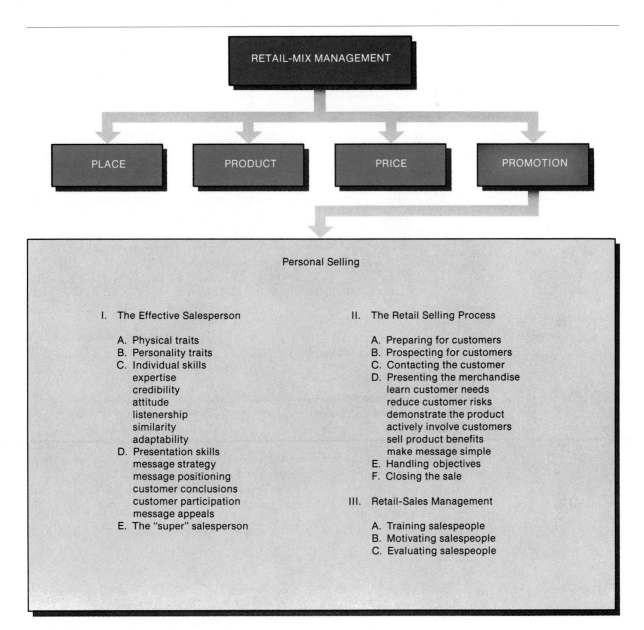

FIGURE 23–1
Developing and managing the personal selling effort

These traits will not be elaborated upon since every person is aware of them. Obviously, personal grooming and hygiene are extremely important ingredients in good personal selling.

Personality Traits

Personality traits are individual characteristics people learn over a lifetime. They become an inherent part of a person through prior learning.

Good salespeople have developed the personality traits of sociability, curiosity, imagination, creativity, enthusiasm, sincerity, ambition, and reliability. Good salespeople get along with people, want to know, want to try new ways, want to do

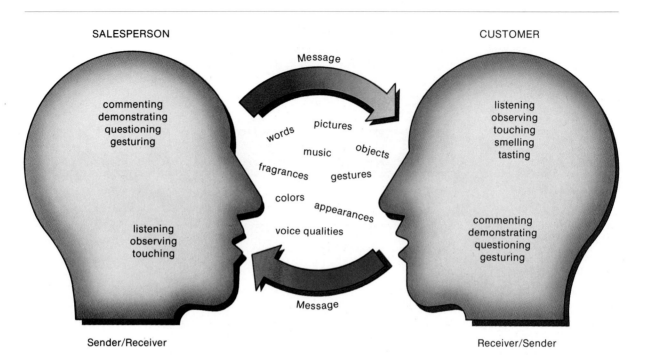

SALESPERSON   CUSTOMER

Message

commenting   listening
demonstrating   observing
questioning   words   pictures   touching
gesturing   objects   smelling
                            music   tasting
                      fragrances   gestures
                       colors
                              appearances   commenting
listening   voice qualities   demonstrating
observing   questioning
touching   gesturing

Message

Sender/Receiver   Receiver/Sender

FIGURE 23–2

A communications model of the customer-salesperson interaction (a partial adaptation from Robert F. Spohn and Robert Y. Allen, *Retailing* [Reston, VA: Reston Publishing, 1977], 236)

something different, have great interest in their work, are honest about their work and dealings with others, want to achieve certain self-imposed objectives, and state the truth about the product they sell. These personal characteristics separate the good salesperson from the poor salesperson.

Individual Skills

Individual selling skills can be developed if one is willing to work on them. Again, it can be difficult to separate individual skills from personality traits over time.

Based on research, several skills an individual can acquire are (1) perceived expertise, (2) perceived credibility, (3) positive attitude, (4) good listenership, (5) salesperson-customer similarity, (6) adaptability. At this point we will take a closer look at these skills.

Expertise

Salespeople whom customers *perceive* as expert have a much greater chance of making a sale than salespeople whom customers perceive as having less expertise. People who are high in expertise are those who are more qualified than others to speak on a particular topic. Salespeople with special education or training, information, and knowledge to talk about the product they sell have the expertise to be effective at their job. However, the key word in this discussion is *perceived*. No matter how expert the salesperson is, selling effectiveness depends upon whether the customer *perceives* the person as an expert. To illustrate, two researchers set up an in-the-field experiment in a music store to determine the effects of salesperson expertise versus nonexpertise on the sale of a cleaning kit for eight-track tape decks. In making the sales presentation, one salesperson demonstrated a high level of product knowledge by describing technical features of using the cleaning kit. In the nonexpert portion of the study, the salesperson admitted to not knowing how "this thing" worked, but said it is supposed to help the tape player somehow. The researchers found that the expert presentation produced significantly higher sales than the nonexpert presentation.[5] This study and others suggest that expertise must be communicated to each customer to effectively increase sales.

Credibility

Similarly, how effective a salesperson will be in making a sale depends in part upon how *credible* the customer perceives the person to be. The more credible a salesperson is perceived to be, the more sales are likely to be made. A credible salesperson is believable, trustworthy, and honest in dealing with customers. Research in this area shows strong evidence of the persuasive powers of people who are perceived as credible.

Attitude

A salesperson is more effective with a positive rather than a negative attitude toward himself or herself, the message (and product), and the customer. A positive attitude toward oneself means self-confidence, not arrogance. Successful salespeople have confidence in their abilities to do their job.

A salesperson also must have a positive attitude toward the product and what is said about it. If the salesperson does not believe in the product, why should the customer? Finally, a salesperson must have a positive attitude toward customers. This attitude is shown by paying careful atttention to what the customer is saying, showing respect for the customer, and not "talking down" to the customer. Customers can quickly notice a salesperson's positive attitude toward them and react favorably to it.

Listening Skills

Listening skills are overlooked too often by salespeople. Some sales clerks are so busy talking and listening to themselves that they fail to listen to their customers. Failure to be a good listener often leads to lost sales. If they do not listen carefully, salespeople cannot determine customers' needs, wants, or preferences. Good listening skills not only improve the salesperson's chances of making a sale, but also can provide feedback through the salesperson to top management about changes that might be made in store policies, merchandise lines carried, and a variety of other aspects of store operations. Figure 23–3 presents some guidelines for developing good listening skills.

Similarity

"People are persuaded more by a communicator they perceive to be similar to themselves," one expert pointed out. Salespersons who can discover quickly a similarity that exists between them and a customer can capitalize on this common characteristic to enhance their chances of making the sale. A salesperson can detect similarities by asking questions, listening, and observing. For example, if the customer is accompanied by children and the salesperson is a parent, the subject can be brought up in conversation. Or, if through conversation one learns that the customer is a student, professor, or staff member at the local university, the salesperson should mention the fact—if it is true—that he or she buys season tickets to all the games, attends the plays, supports the university, or whatever. The more specific the similarities, the better. *Perceived similarity* can be based on personality,

FIGURE 23–3

1. Do not only listen to the words themselves, but also watch carefully for nonverbal cues to the real intentions of the customer.
2. Practice being interested in what customers have to say. Remember you are not always the most interesting person around.
3. Be sensitive to the customer's personal pronouns, such as "I", "we", "you", "us" and "our". These are cues to things that really interest the customer.
4. Do not be distracted by peculiarities in the speech of the customer.
5. Establish eye contact with customer.
6. Ask clarifying questions to test your understanding of a message.
7. Shut up and listen when the customer wants to talk.
8. Relax. Try not to give the customer the impression that you are just waiting to jump in and start talking.
9. Do not assume you understand the customer's problem or need. Keep listening while they keep talking.
10. Listen for ideas, not just words.

Source: Ronald B. Marks, *Personal Selling*, 2d ed. (Boston: Allyn and Bacon, Inc., 1985), 130–31.

dress, race, skin color, religion, politics, interests, group affiliations, and many more attributes. Clever salespersons quickly determine these similarities between themselves and their customers and use them in casual talk.

To illustrate, in the study mentioned earlier on the sale of eight-track cleaners at the music store, the sales clerks were instructed to observe the kind of music the customer was buying and comment that they, too, enjoyed that kind of music (classical, rock, or whatever). Under this condition of similarity (enjoy same music), sales-clerks were able to sell significantly more tape cleaners at the checkout counter than when they said they preferred a different type of music (dissimilar condition).[6] In another study, researchers found that retail salespersons could be more effective in selling merchandise when they and their customers were similar along any one or more of the following dimensions: height, age, political preference, sex, race, and nationality.[7] The simple rule here is to either show or express some similarity between salespersons and their customers.

Adaptability

Good salespeople can adapt to differences in customer types. Figure 23–4 shows the types of customers that salespeople will encounter and provides suggestions for how they should react to each customer type. Salespeople must learn to identify these customer types and adapt accordingly, without losing their own identity.

Message-Presentation Skills

Through training, salespeople can develop skills in message presentation that will help them become more persuasive and increase sales.

Message Strategy

Salespeople can present merchandise to customers either by explaining only the strengths and benefits of the product (one-sided message) or by describing the strengths as well as the weaknesses of the product (two-sided message). Although it might sound strange to tell customers the weaknesses in a product (or the strength of competitors' products), this strategy works under certain circumstances.

FIGURE 23–4

Customer types and what salespersons should say or do

Basic Types of Customer	Basic Characteristic	Secondary Characteristic	Other Characteristics	What Salesperson Should Say or Do
Arguer	Takes issue with each statement of salesperson	Disbelieves claims, tries to catch salesperson in error	Cautious, slow to decide	Demonstrate; show product knowledge; use "Yes, but . . ."
Chip on shoulder	Definitely in a bad mood	Indignation; angry at slight provocation	Acts as if being deliberately baited	Avoid argument; stick to basic facts; show good assortment
Decisive	Knows what is wanted	Customer confident choice is right	Not interested in another opinion—respects sales person's brevity	Win sale—not argument; sell self; tactfully inject opinion
Doubting Thomas	Doesn't trust sales talk	Hates to be managed	Arrives at decision cautiously	Back up merchandise statements by manufacturers' tags, labels; demonstrate merchandise; let customer handle merchandise
Fact-finder	Interested in factual information—detailed	Alert to sales person's errors in description	Looks for actual tags and labels	Emphasize label and manufacturer's facts; volunteer care information
Hesitant	Ill at ease—sensitive	Shopping at unaccustomed price range	Unsure of own judgment	Make customer comfortable; use friendliness and respect
Impulsive	Quick to decide or select	Impatience	Liable to break off sale abruptly	Close rapidly; avoid oversell, overtalk; note key points
Look around	Little ability to make own decisions	Anxious—fearful of making a mistake	Wants sales person's aid in decision—wants adviser—wants to do "right thing"	Emphasize merits of product and service, "zeroing" in on customer-expressed needs and doubts
Procrastinator	I'll wait 'til tomorrow	Lacks confidence in own judgment	Insecure	Reinforce customers' judgments
Silent	Not talking—but thinking!	Appears indifferent but truly listening	Appears nonchalant	Ask direct questions—straightforward approach
Think it over	Refers to need to consult someone	Looking for another adviser	Not sure of own uncertainty	Get agreement on small points; draw out opinions; use points agreed upon for close

Source: C. Winston Borgen, *Learning Experiences in Retailing* (Santa Monica, CA: Goodyear Publishing), 293.

When consumers are not knowledgeable about the product, however, the general rule is to present them with a one-sided message. That is, to be more persuasive and produce more sales, it is better to tell them only about the benefits, advantages, and strengths of the product. Because of their lack of product knowledge, they are unable to comprehend the weaknesses in the product and would be confused if you tried to explain them. Therefore, to this audience, *sell only the strong points of the product.*

On the other hand, if the salesperson is presenting a product to a customer who is very knowledgeable about the product, the best strategy is either to explain the strengths of the product as well as its weaknesses or to describe both the product's strengths and the competing products' strengths. Since they are knowledgeable about the product, they will have already recognized the weakness in your merchandise or the strengths of other retailers' products. Therefore, do not insult their product knowledge or intelligence. Instead, admit to *minor* weaknesses in your brand or *minor* strengths in those of your competitors. Your customers will respect you for your honesty and you will be more credible to them. When using the two-sided message, always remember that *your* merchandise "wins." That is, there are fewer weaknesses in your merchandise or fewer strengths in your competitors' brands. By first determining your customer's knowledge level, you can use this selling skill to produce good results.

Message Positioning

In selling merchandise, salespeople should place their strongest selling points at the beginning (the opening) and the end (the closing) of the message, *never* in the middle. Psychologists tell us that people remember the beginning and ending of a message better than the middle. Therefore, salespeople should always capture the customer's attention with strong points of the merchandise at the beginning of the sales presentation and summarize those points in the closing.

Customer Conclusions

The general selling rule is to draw a conclusion in the sales presentation, summarizing reasons the product is right for the customer. Unfortunately, many customers cannot add together the logical statements made as to why they should purchase the merchandise. Therefore, the salesperson should do it for them by quickly summarizing major points and telling them (in conclusion) why they should buy. The exception to this rule is when one encounters highly intelligent people who can easily draw conclusions for themselves. In this situation, to draw a conclusion is to insult the intelligence of the prospective buyer.

Customer Participation

Are salespersons more effective simply by describing the advantage of a product to a customer, or will they succeed more often by describing these same advantages while the customer is using the product? The answer to this question is that salespeople are more likely to sell a product when they can get the prospective buyer to try the product as they are explaining its benefits. For example, a person who sells vacuum cleaners in a department store will be more successful by sprinkling dirt, hair, and other materials on a carpet and having the customer actually use the vacuum cleaner to clean the carpet. "Feel the powerful suction of this model. See how easily it picks up dirt and hair," the sales clerk might say as the customer is moving the appliance back and forth over the carpet. Psychologists tell us that *active participation* not only helps consumers learn the benefits of a product, but also helps persuade them to purchase the product. In retail selling, the rule is to let customers touch, feel, smell, taste, and hear the product. Get them to take a test drive, taste the sausage, smell the ham, feel the power as they maneuver the dials, play the video game, see how the diamond ring looks on their hand. Customers' active involvement and participation with the product in the store is a powerful selling technique. It is perhaps the most effective way to present the "message" to them.

Message Appeals

All people have emotions. The "heart" often rules the mind. In presenting a sales message to customers, salespeople must recognize and use the emotions of their customers to good advantage. We all would like to believe we buy products on a purely rational and logical basis, but usually we do not. Instead, we purchase most products largely on an emotional basis. To ourselves we say, "Doesn't this dress look nice on me?" "This car is sexy (therefore, it makes me sexy)," or "Won't my husband think I'm a good cook if I use this brand of product!" Given these emotional aspects of purchase behavior, salespeople should acquire the skill of describing their merchandise in emotional terms. To develop this skill, salespeople should

- "use highly affective (emotional) language to describe a situation"; that is, they should use highly emotional language to report the facts
- "associate proposed ideas with other popular or unpopular ideas"
- "associate ideas with visual or nonverbal stimuli that might arouse emotions"; that is, present ideas, displays, merchandise, and so on that depict emotionally charged scenes
- ". . . display nonverbal emotional cues"; that is, exhibit body and hand movements, facial expressions, and vocal characteristics consistent with the sales message[8]

The "Super" Salesperson

Several studies have been conducted to determine what makes a "super" salesperson. While these characteristics could have been discussed under the headings of personality traits or individual skills, their importance merits special attention.

Through his experience and study of what makes a good salesperson, Robert McMurry feels that the "super" salesperson possesses the following characteristics:

1. *has a compulsive need to win*—must make the sale as a conquest over the customer
2. *holds the affection of others*—because the super salesperson feels unloved and unwanted, he or she must "buy" the affection and attention of others
3. *has great empathy toward others*—very sensitive to how others feel and can react to minor changes in what customers say and do
4. *has a high level of energy*—a self-starter with a high level of drive who might be described as a "workaholic"
5. *has tremendous self-confidence*—believes in himself or herself and ability to make the sale; this self-confidence, however, is often a compensation for suppressed feelings of inadequacy and insecurity
6. *has a continuous desire for money*—has a high level of aspiration for material things in life and loves to show off; this requires money
7. *has a well-developed and disciplined habit of industry*—feels uncomfortable when not working
8. *considers each objective and obstacle as a challenge*—is very competitive and experiences the "thrill" of victory in overcoming consumer objections and resistance in closing the sale

McMurry believes that a person must have these characteristics (particularly the last five) to be a super salesperson.[9]

In a seven-year research project, Mayer and Greenberg investigated the characteristics of the super salesperson and found two essential qualities: *empathy* and *ego drive*. Further, they concluded that a good salesperson has both qualities and that they act synergistically, each reinforcing the other.[10] These studies suggest to the retailer characteristics to look for in hiring good salespeople as well as ideas for training current salespeople.

The ideas discussed in this section are most relevant to the sales job of "order getting." Order getters use creative selling approaches to sell the product, the store, and themselves. These people are responsible for creating sales through persuasive communications. "Order takers," on the other hand, simply comply with the requests of their customers. Examples of order takers are gasoline attendants and counter persons at fast-food restaurants. While they have little room for creative selling, order takers can increase sales through minimal suggestive selling, such as "Would you like french fries with your order?" Examples of order getters are salespeople in jewelry stores, clothing stores, and appliance stores and encyclopedia and insurance salespeople. People who work in order-getting sales jobs must use their imaginative selling approaches and utilize the concepts discussed in this section. Because of the skills required of order getters, they receive higher financial compensation than order takers.

THE RETAIL SELLING PROCESS

Several basic steps occur in every selling situation. The length of time that a salesperson takes in each step depends upon the product being sold, the customer, and the selling situation. The seven steps of the retail selling process appear in Figure 23–5.

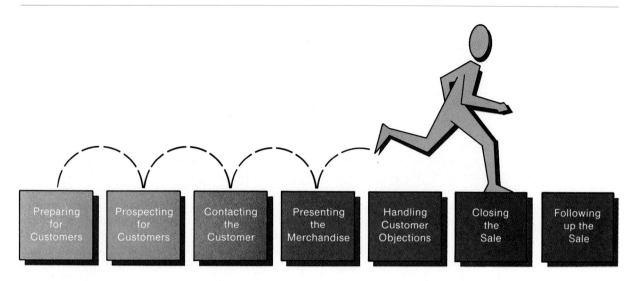

FIGURE 23–5
The seven steps of the retail selling process

Preparing for Customers

Preparing for the customer is the first step in the selling process. In this stage, the salesperson does the *preliminary* work necessary for effective interaction with the customer. This stage can be subdivided into two parts: long-run preparation and short-run preparation.

In long-run preparation, the salesperson learns store policies and procedures and gains knowledge about the merchandise. These learning activities include store operating procedures, return policies, store guarantees, how to operate merchandise the store (or department) sells, and what warranties the manufacturer of the merchandise offers customers, to name but a few. Short-term preparations are daily and weekly activities, including learning what merchandise is currently in stock, which items are on sale, any changes in store policies and operating procedures that have occurred, changes that have occurred in new styles, fashions, models of merchandise, and dozens of other day-to-day store happenings.

In both the short and long run, store management and the salesperson share in the responsibility to prepare for meeting customers. Management must continually inform salespeople in a prompt, clear way about store operating policies and procedures. Salespeople must constantly update themselves on changes in merchandise, manufacturers' policies relating to the merchandise, and the store's literature and sales aids. For either party to fail in these responsibilities could mean lost sales.

Prospecting for Customers

Prospecting is the search process of finding people who are *willing to buy* the merchandise a store has to offer and are *able to pay* for that merchandise. Salespeople learn through experience how to spot good prospects. Good prospects generally display more intense interest in the merchandise than poor prospects who are "just browsing." A variety of behavioral cues set the good prospects apart from the poor prospects. For example, having several bags of merchandise from other stores is often a clue to a shopper's interest in making additional purchases.

Prospecting is particularly important when the store is full of customers. An alert salesperson will single out prime prospects and not waste time with browsers. When the store is not busy, salespeople should attend to everyone, including weak prospects. Doing this builds possible future business and enhances the store's image of concern for its customers.

Contacting the Customer

Initial impressions are important determinants in successfully making a sale. A nice, warm smile and an appearance of genuine interest in customers and their needs are parts of a good initial impression. Additionally, at the beginning of the contact, the salesperson should make an opening comment that quickly captures the attention and arouses the interest of the buyer. Further, the first words should be positive and should stimulate any needs that the customer might be displaying. For example, a woman might be looking at a blouse she is holding up; the salesperson might open by saying, "That blouse certainly would look nice on you. Would you like to try it on?" This opening compliments the woman's taste in clothing, stimulates her need to "look nice," and requests her to take an *action* (try it on). A simple "May I help you?" is a routine, worn-out phrase that almost invites the customer to turn the salesperson's request down.

Openings should be *original* and appropriate to the situation. Consider the following examples of customer situations and potential salesperson responses.

Situation 1: Customer looking at a home video game.

- *preferred opening:* Salesperson: "Press this button here like this (salesperson turns game on), and the game's all set to go. Why don't you try your luck?"
- *nonpreferred opening:* Salesperson: "Do you need some help in how to operate this thing?" Customer: (Gads, he thinks I'm stupid or something.) "No, I was just looking."

Situation 2: Woman looking at a coat in an exclusive, high-fashion women's clothing store.

- *preferred opening:* "That's 100-percent mink. Please let me help you on with it to see how it looks and feels."
- *Nonpreferred opening:* "Want some help?" Customer: (She thinks I don't know how to put on a coat!) "No, thank you."

Situation 3: Shopper looking at a telephone in a phone center store.

- *preferred opening:* "That phone will make a call for you if simply one button is pressed. Look how easy it is to operate."
- *nonpreferred opening:* "Are you interested in a phone?"

In summary, the opening statement a salesperson makes at the point of initial contact can determine whether conversation will continue and, therefore, whether the sale can be made. A good opening should attract the customer's attention, arouse interest, stimulate a customer need, and be original to the situation. A poor opening is generally one that the customer can answer with a yes or no. In a selling situation, a good beginning is usually necessary for a happy ending (the sale).

Presenting the Merchandise

Once initial contact has been made, the salesperson is in a position to present the merchandise and the sales message. How the salesperson should present the merchandise depends upon the customer. Since customers are not identical, neither should the salesperson's presentations be identical; instead, they should be tailored to the individual person and the current circumstances. Some basic guidelines can help the salesperson make a good presentation. However, one must remember that salespeople must continually exercise their creativity to adapt to customers and to the particular circumstances.

Learn the Customer's Needs and Wants

To know what merchandise to show the customer, the salesperson must learn what the customer needs and wants. Asking key questions and listening attentively help the salesperson to determine what merchandise the store has that might meet those needs and wants. This is the merchandise the salesperson shows first.

At this point, the salesperson must closely observe the customer's *reactions* to each piece of merchandise shown. Through observation, the salesperson attempts to determine the customer's level of product interest; that is, whether the product is a "must have," "should have," or "would be nice to have" item. This initial presentation must also be used to determine whether to try to trade up the customer. In **trading up,** *the salesperson attempts either to sell higher-quality, higher-priced merchandise or to sell a larger quantity than the customer originally intended to buy.* The salesperson might believe that the customer would be better satisfied with either more durable, stronger, lighter, heavier, bigger, or softer materials. The salesperson might also think the customer needs a larger quantity to complete the job or to save money. Trading up is neither immoral nor unethical in and of itself. Instead, it depends on the salesperson's motives. Since customer need satisfaction is a goal of the retailer (as was discussed under the topic of the marketing concept), then determining customer needs and wants is a logical first step in presenting and selling merchandise.

Reduce Customers' Perceived Risk

When customers buy products, they run the risk that the product might not perform correctly, might fall apart or break down, might embarrass them in a social setting (your "gold" necklace chain turns your neck green), or might be unsafe (it might injure their children or blow up in their face). These concerns are particularly strong for high-cost items. For example, refrigerators, washers, cars, sets of tires, houses, and television sets represent substantial outlays of money and therefore risk. Perceived risk can be in the form of financial risk, physical risk, or social risk. Therefore, products with high perceived risk need to be accompanied by assurances of satisfactory performance. In these instances, a salesperson should stress the manufacturer's warranty, the retailer's money-back guarantee, the retailer's in-house repair facilities ("You won't have to send this watch back to Switzerland for six months to have it repaired."), the dependable brand name, and so on. This selling situation might also be an opportunity for the salesperson to trade up the customer to higher-quality merchandise to reduce perceived risk and thus make the sale.

Demonstrate the Product

Some products lend themselves to demonstration more than others, but virtually all products can be demonstrated somehow. Demonstrating the merchandise means that the customer sees the product in action. Through demonstration, the customer can see the features, benefits, and possible advantages of the product. While demonstrating the product, the salesperson should point out the unique features and benefits of the merchandise to *reinforce* what the customer is seeing. Many times a product can sell itself, particularly if the salesperson helps a little. Additionally, demonstrations can help some customers to reduce their perceived risk in purchasing the product.

Actively Involve the Customer

Get customers actively involved with the product! Have them touch, smell, taste, hear, and feel it. "Push the accelerator and feel the power, *experience* its smooth ride, *listen* to the quietness of its engine and the outside air, *touch* the soft velour seats," a car salesperson might say while the customer is actually using, controlling, and experiencing the product.

Chances of persuading customers to buy a product improve greatly when they actively interact with the product. A good salesperson will point out how the product affects the customer's five senses ("Smell the manly scent of this cologne." "Taste the rich flavor of this coffee." "Feel the softness of this sweater.") The more senses a salesperson can stimulate within the customer, the greater the chance of a sale.

Sell Product Benefits, Not the Product

This guideline has been alluded to in the last several pages, but not specifically stated. It is deserving of separate attention. "In the factory we produce cosmetics; in the store we sell the promise and hope of beauty!" We don't sell the steak, we sell the sizzle." What all manufacturers, retailers, and salespeople must realize is that "we" don't sell physical products, but the physical, social, and psychological *benefits* they provide consumers. People don't buy lawn mowers, they buy trim lawns. People don't buy 1/4″ drill bits, they buy 1/4″ holes. Customers buy, in effect, the end result (the benefit), not the product for the product's sake. Therefore, salespeople in presenting their merchandise should sell benefits. Encyclopedia sales representatives learned this idea a long time ago ("We provide your children with *educational* materials, not encyclopedias. Don't you think your child's education is important?").

Make the Message Simple

Too often salespeople present merchandise by using *technical* terms and phrases that the average customer does not understand. As a result, many customers are frightened off or confused and a sale is lost. Good salespeople present the product message in words that are clear and understandable to the customer. The salesperson must be ready to adapt quickly to the level of understanding and sophistication of each consumer. In some cases, the salesperson must use analogies and speak in a simple language. For other customers, the salesperson might engage in technical conversation. The sales-message level should be geared to the customer's product-knowledge level. Therefore a "golden" rule is to *communicate the message at the customer's level of understanding and knowledge.* Salespeople should not talk "above their customers' heads," nor insult their intelligence by speaking too simply.

These guidelines for presenting the merchandise should enhance the salesperson's persuasiveness and increase the chances of a sale. In every case, the salesperson *must adapt* to each customer as an individual with unique needs, problems, knowledge levels, and circumstances. *Adaptability* is a key to sales success.

Handling Objections

Consumers who do not purchase the product immediately after the merchandise presentation are likely to have perceived "stumbling blocks," objections to buying the product. A salesperson must anticipate objections and know how to handle each type. Figure 23–6 summarizes techniques of handling customer objections. Customer objections come in five forms: product, price, place (store), timing, and salesperson.

Method	When to Use	How to Use
Head-on	With objections arising from incorrect information	Salespeople directly, but politely, deny the truth of the objection; to avoid alienating prospects, it is helpful to offer proof
Indirect denial	With objections arising from incorrect information	Salespeople never directly tell prospects that they are wrong, but still manage to correct the mistaken impression
Compensation	With valid objections, but where compensating factors are present	Salespeople agree with prospects initially, but then proceed to point out factors that outweigh or compensate for the objection (for this reason, it is often called the "yes, but" technique)
"Feel, felt, found"	With emotional objections, especially when prospects have retreated from their adult ego states, and when the prospect fails to see the value of a particular feature and benefit	Salespeople express their understanding for how prospects feel, indicate that they are okay since others have also felt that way, but have found their fears to be without substance
Boomerang	When the objection can be turned into a positive factor	Salespeople take the objection and turn it into a reason for buying
Forestalling	With any type of objection	From prior experience, salespeople anticipate an objection and incorporate an answer into the presentation itself, hoping to forestall the objection from ever coming up

FIGURE 23–6
Summary of objection-handling techniques

Source: Ronald B. Marks, *Personal Selling* (Boston: Allyn and Bacon, Inc., 1985), 326.

Some consumers think the *product* is just not right for them. It is too big, too small, too heavy, too light, does not look right on them, is too simple, too complex, or one of a host of other objections. If the consumer has talked to the salesperson up to this point, there is generally some interest in the merchandise. Therefore, the customer can still be sold by overcoming the objections. The salesperson must be *creative* and *adaptable* in handling objections. If the customer says "This doesn't look right on me," it probably means "My friends (family, coworkers, boss, etc.) wouldn't like it." The creative salesperson could counter with reasons why the customer's reference groups might well approve of this merchandise. This approach reinforces the customer's self-image and gives supporting approval from others for making the purchase.

In other cases, customers might object to the product by saying they are not sure it will perform as it should. In this situation, the salesperson should reiterate the proven record of the product, its warranties, and store guarantees. The customer must be reassured that the product's benefits are genuine and that it will perform as stated. Each product objection requires a unique solution.

Price is a common customer objection that takes two forms. First, the customer really wants the product but doesn't have the cash to pay for it. In this case, the salesperson can emphasize the easy credit terms the store has available for customers ("For only $10 a month, you can buy this washing machine."). In other cases the customer does not consider the product worth the price. In these situations, the salesperson must emphasize the product value. The salesperson can talk about competitors' prices being about the same, even though their products do not have comparable features, warranties, guarantees, etc. However, all these claims *must be true!* Otherwise, the salesperson might make the sale but lose a customer for life.

Customers might not like the *store* itself. An advertisement or a display caught their eye, they came into the store and saw something they liked, but they usually don't shop in this store or "a store like this" and therefore feel uncomfortable buying here. To meet this form of objection, the salesperson must assure customers of the integrity of the store, its management, and its merchandise.

Putting the purchase off (*timing*) is another objection that salespeople frequently encounter. In these cases, customers might not know exactly *why* they don't want to buy now; they just don't. Customers usually use the "timing" objection to conceal their real objections. Thus, this form of objection is difficult for salespeople to handle, since they do not understand its underlying motives. Handling this objection is "groping in the dark." Nevertheless, the salesperson can emphasize the need to buy *today* ("The sale ends today at this extraordinarily low price." "There are only a few left in stock." "People have flocked into the store to get this item—we cannot guarantee it will be here tomorrow."). Any statement indicating the urgency to buy *now* can overcome this objection. But, remember, any statements must be true. Otherwise, a store may lose a customer permanently.

One last objection a customer might have is to the *salesperson*. Shifty eyes, long hair, short hair, conservative dress, wild dress, garlic on the breath, or any number of other "faults" may turn away a customer. The customer simply says "I don't like dealing with this 'character.'" Whatever the reason, the salesperson is often unlikely to detect this objection. If detection occurs, the customer's attention should be directed to the product, its benefits, its advantages, its need-fulfilling capacities, or the sale should be turned over to another salesperson. The latter could be a painful decision, but one that makes a sale for the store and one for which the other salesperson might reciprocate in the future.

Closing the Sale

Closing the sale is the "natural" conclusion to the selling process. The salesperson has prepared to meet the customer, has greeted the customer, has presented the merchandise, and has handled customer objections (if any). Now the salesperson is at the point to suggest that the customer make the purchase. *Timing* in the closing stage, however, is critical. Customers often provide verbal or physical (body language) cues that suggest they might be ready to make a purchase. Figure 23–7 identifies several examples of physical and verbal cues for spotting closing opportunities. In timing the closing, the salesperson must adapt to the individual customer and circumstances. Some customers do not want to be rushed into making the final decision. Other customers don't want to wait too long to have the salesperson begin to close. Still other customers either do not know how to make the decision or just won't make the decision without help. In the latter situation, the salesperson must *tell* them to make the purchase. They want to be told. These people need someone to make the decision for them. In some instances, customers have a friend or relative with them. A salesperson who detects that the customer's companion likes the product might ask how the companion likes the product ("How do you think the dress looks on Ms. Jones?").

In other cases, customers definitely make up their own minds and don't want to be pushed into a decision. In dealing with this type of customer, the salesperson can remind customers of their need and of how the merchandise meets that need, restate the advantages and benefits of the merchandise, and explain why they must buy now and not put off the decision.

Skilled salespeople have developed several closing techniques that move the customer closer to the purchase decision. For example, after the customer has examined several pieces of merchandise, the salesperson can usually determine the one or two merchandise items the customer prefers. To avoid confusing the customer and to aid in the final decision, the salesperson should put away the less-preferred items. If the customer has tried on seven rings, the five or six least-preferred rings should be put back in their cases. "I can tell this is the one you really

FIGURE 23–7
Spotting closing cues

Physical cues provided by customers

1. The customer closely reexamines the merchandise under consideration.
2. The customer reaches for his billfold or opens her purse.
3. The customer samples the product for the second or third time.
4. The customer is nodding in agreement as the terms and conditions of sale are explained.
5. The customer is smiling and appears excited as he or she admires the merchandise.
6. The customer intensely studies the service contract.

Verbal cues provided by customers

1. The customer asks "Do you offer free home delivery?"
2. The customer remarks "I always wanted a pair of Porsche sunglasses."
3. The customer inquires "Do you have this item in red?"
4. The customer states "This ring is a real bargain."
5. The customer exclaims "I feel like a million bucks in this outfit!"
6. The customer requests "Can you complete the installation by Friday?"

---

like the most," the salesperson might say. "May I wrap this for you?" "Will this be cash or charge?" Figure 23–8 identifies seven of the more commonly used closing techniques.

Another aspect of closing a sale is to *show customers other merchandise that complements the item they are going to buy.* This technique is called **suggestive selling**. For example, if the customer is buying a sport coat, the salesperson can suggest a shirt and tie that are a "perfect" match for the coat. If the customer has decided on a sofa and matching chair for the den, the salesperson might suggest end tables and lamps that complement the ensemble. Suggestive selling is a service to customers who might not have thought of purchasing complementary items to enhance the appearance or use of their intended purchase. Also, the store and the salesperson can make additional sales. Both customers and salespeople can benefit

Technique	Definition	Example
Direct close	The salesperson asks the customer directly for the order	"Can I write this order up for you?"
Assumptive close	The salesperson assumes the customer is going to buy and proceeds with completing the sales transaction	"Would you like to have this gift wrapped?"
Alternative close	The salesperson asks the customer to make a choice in which either alternative is favorable to the retailer	"Will this be cash or charge?"
Summary/agreement close	The salesperson closes by summarizing the major features, benefits, and advantages of the product and obtains an affirmative agreement from the customer on each point	"This dishwasher has the features you were looking for"—YES "You want free home delivery"—YES "It is in your price range"—YES "Let's write up the sale."
Balance-sheet close	The salesperson starts by listing the advantages and disadvantages of making the purchase and closes by pointing out how the advantages outweigh the disadvantages	"This dishwasher is on sale; it has all the features you asked for, you have 90 days to pay for it without any financial charges, and we will deliver it free. Even though we can not deliver it until next week, now is the time to buy."
Emotional close	The salesperson attempts to close the sale by appealing to the customer's emotions (love, fear, acceptance, recognition)	"The safety of your children could well depend on this smoke alarm. Now is the time to get it installed."
Standing-room-only close	The salesperson tries to get the customer to act immediately by stressing that the offer is limited	"The sale ends today." "This is the last one we have in stock."

FIGURE 23–8
Types of closing techniques

from suggestive selling when the additional items represent true benefits for the customer.

Next, the salesperson must perform several *administrative* tasks in closing the sale. These tasks include ringing up the sale on the cash register, checking the accuracy of the address and other parts of the check that the customer might use to make the purchase, verifying the customer's credit card, and boxing, bagging, or wrapping the merchandise.

Finally, closing the sale is not complete until the salesperson has said thank you, asked the customer to come back, and has said good-bye. These comments appear to be, and perhaps are, routine; however, most customers expect them and appreciate them. Of most importance is that the salesperson be sincere in these expressions. Customers can tell if the salesperson appreciates their business, really wants to be of service to them in the future, and genuinely wishes they have a good day. This phase in closing the sale is called *developing good will.* Repeat business depends upon it!

A good salesperson continues to sell the customer *after* the sale. The sale is not over once the customer has walked out the door. Sure, the customer has the merchandise and the store has the customer's money. However, the customer's satisfaction might not be complete. Many customers are happy about their purchases at the time they bought them. But later they begin to suffer doubt about the wisdom of their buying decision. This "doubt" phase usually affects consumers who have made a substantial investment of time, effort, and money. Examples of substantial investments are purchases of furniture, major appliances, cars, expensive jewelry, houses, and some clothing. During this phase, customers might have regrets, might not be wholly satisfied with the purchase, and might never return to the store (lost future business). Therefore, a salesperson should follow up the sale by assuring customers that they made the right decision, that the merchandise is of good quality, that their friends and relatives will approve, and that the retail store and manufacturer back the merchandise.

Salespeople have three principal ways to follow up the sale: (1) write a letter to the customer, (2) telephone the customer, and (3) make a personal visit to the customer. For most salespeople a personal visit is out of the question since it would involve so much time away from work. An exception is the real estate agent who is usually on the road anyway and can survey the neighborhood while traveling to and from the customer's new home.

Thus, with certain exceptions, the telephone and the letter are the best options for following up a sale. Of these two, which is more effective in reducing a customer's postpurchase doubt? The answer seems to be the letter. In a study comparing the two methods, one researcher found that customers receiving a letter after their purchase "experienced less [doubt], had more favorable attitudes toward the store, and had higher intentions of purchase."[11] Additionally, the researcher learned that telephone calls were not only ineffective, but even counterproductive. That is, customers who were called felt *greater doubt,* had *less favorable* attitudes toward the store, and were *less likely* to buy merchandise at that store in the future! The reasons for the negative effects of the telephone call were (1) customers were suspicious about the salesperson's motives for the call ("That salesman is trying to get me to buy something else"); (2) customers had had unpleasant experiences with previous salespeople who called on the telephone to sell them something they didn't want in the first place; and (3) the telephone caught the customer at a bad time (in the shower, changing the baby's diaper, having an important conversation with a friend). Letters, on the other hand, can be taken from the mailbox and read at a time convenient to the customer. Therefore, the rule on sales follow-up is to send the customer a letter.

RETAIL SALES MANAGEMENT

Managing sales personnel involves three factors: (1) training, (2) motivation, and (3) evaluation. Retailers who take the time either to train or have others train their salespeople are making a wise investment. Well-trained salespeople have acquired the skills to produce for themselves and for their employer.

The key to motivating sales personnel is to understand the underlying needs each salesperson has and then provide the specific support and reward that each salesperson requires to achieve the company's and their own goals. Retailers often fail to recognize that each salesperson is different and therefore should be motivated in a different way. Thus, the person in charge of managing sales personnel must learn what benefits each salesperson. Some are motivated by money, others by recognition, others by advancement and the possibility of achieving higher status, and still others by the intricacy of the work itself. Although all of these motives can be important to every individual to varying degrees, usually one holds the key to success. Once the sales manager has discovered the key to what inspires a particular individual, then the manager can move that person toward achieving personal and store goals.

Another management task is to evaluate the performance of sales personnel. Evaluation is a form of control. When sales personnel are evaluated, management has information on the progress of each employee and the progress of the store toward its goals. Equally important, the employees have feedback on how well they are performing their jobs.

The specifics of training, motivation, and evaluating retail personnel were discussed fully in Chapter 9; the reader is referred to that discussion.

SUMMARY

Personal selling can be viewed as a communication process between the salesperson and a customer. Communication is a two-way process in which both members actively exchange ideas and meanings. The characteristics of a good salesperson generally can be divided into physical traits, personality traits, individual skills, and message-presentation skills.

The steps in the retail selling process are (1) preparing for the customer, (2) prospecting for customers, (3) contacting the customer, (4) presenting the merchandise, (5) handling objections, (6) closing the sale, and (7) following up the sale. A good salesperson prepares well for the sale even before greeting the customer, then throughout the sale adapts to each customer and set of store circumstances as they exist at the time.

In retail sales management, three essential ingredients for success are knowing how to train, motivate, and evaluate salespeople. Every training program should spell out the content of the program and the training process. The sales manager must examine employee needs individually to determine the key that motivates each salesperson.

In all, salespeople are perhaps the retailer's most valuable asset. They interact face-to-face with customers to make the sale and to project the kind of image the retailer desires. Thus, an investment in salespeople is a wise decision.

KEY TERMS AND CONCEPTS

personal selling

personal communications

order getter

order taker

physical traits

personality traits

individual selling skills

perceived expertise

perceived credibility

positive attitude

listening skills

salesperson-customer similarity

adaptability of salesperson

message-presentation skills

trading up

head-on method

indirect denial method

compensation method

feel, felt, found method

boomerang method

forestalling method

direct close technique

assumptive close technique

alternative close technique

summary/agreement close technique

balance-sheet close technique

emotional close technique

standing-room-only close technique

suggestive selling

REVIEW QUESTIONS

1. How are personal selling and personal communications related?
2. What are some of the personality traits of a good salesperson?
3. Describe the role of salesperson expertise and credibility in the selling process.
4. How can a salesperson improve listening skills?
5. How does salesperson-customer similarity affect the selling process?
6. When should a salesperson use a one-sided sales message? When should a two-sided sales message be used?
7. Where should the strongest selling points be positioned within a sales message?
8. Should the salesperson draw conclusions for the customer? Are there any exceptions?
9. How can salespeople integrate emotional terms into a sales presentation?
10. What are the characteristics of a super salesperson?

11. In prospecting for customers, what should the salesperson determine?
12. Describe the sales practice of trading up the customer.
13. Which three forms of perceived risk are part of each customer purchase? How might the retail salesperson reduce these risks?
14. What should the retail salesperson sell?
15. What are the most commonly used methods for handling customer objections? Provide an original (nontextbook) example of each technique.
16. When should a salesperson attempt to close a sale?
17. Describe the various types of closing techniques available to the salesperson. Provide an original example of each technique.
18. What is the best option for following up a sale? Why?

667

ENDNOTES

1. David L. Kurtz, H. Robert Dodge, and Jay E. Klop-maker, *Professional Selling,* 4th ed. (Plano, TX: Business Publications, Inc., 1985), 365.
2. See Ronald B. Marks, *Personal Selling,* 2d ed. (Boston: Allyn and Bacon, Inc., 1985), 374.
3. Pierre Martineau, "The Personality of the Retail Store," *Harvard Business Review* 36 (January–February, 1958): 50–51.
4. See Ronald B. Marks, "Operationalizing the Concept of Store Image," *Journal of Retailing* 52 (Fall, 1976): 37.
5. Arch G. Woodside and J. William Davenport, "The Effect of Salesman Similarity and Expertise on Consumer Purchasing Behavior," *Journal of Marketing Research* 11 (May, 1974): 198–202.
6. Ibid.
7. Gilbert A. Churchill, Robert H. Collins, and William A. Strang, "Should Retail Salespersons Be Similar to Their Customers?" *Journal of Retailing* 51 (Fall, 1975): 29–42.
8. E. P. Bettinghaus, *Persuasive Communications* (New York: Holt, Rinehart and Winston, 1973): 160–61.
9. Robert N. McMurry, "The Mystique of Super Salesmanship," *Harvard Business Review* (March–April, 1961): 113–22.
10. David Mayer and Herbert M. Greenberg, "What Makes a Good Salesman?" *Harvard Business Review* (July–August, 1964): 119–25.
11. Shelby D. Hunt, "Post-Transaction Communications and Dissonance Reduction," *Journal of Marketing* 34 (July, 1970): 50.

RELATED READINGS

Avila, Ramon. "Predicting Salesperson Success Using Personal and Personality Characteristics: A Theoretical Framework." *Developments in Marketing Science, Proceedings.* N. K. Malhotra, ed. (Academy of Marketing Science 1985), 242–46.

Dubinsky, Alan J., and Howe, Vince. "Empirical Dimensionality of the Retail Sales Job." *AMA Educators' Proceedings.* R. W. Belk et al, eds. (American Marketing Association 1984), 158–61.

Dubinsky, Alan J., and Mattson, Bruce E. "Determinants of Retail Sales—People's Role Conflict and Ambiguity." *Developments in Marketing Science, Proceedings.* V. V. Bellur, ed. (Academy of Marketing Science 1981), 148–52.

Farah, John J. "What Makes a Good Salesperson?" *Developments in Marketing Science, Proceedings.* J. C. Rogers, III, ed. (Academy of Marketing Science 1983), 334–38.

Futrell, Charles. *ABC's of Selling.* (Homewood, Ill.: Richard D. Irwin, 1985)

————. *Fundamentals of Selling.* (Homewood, Ill.: Richard D. Irwin, 1984)

Ford, Neil M.; Churchill, Gilbert A., Jr.; and Walker, Orville C., Jr. *Sales Force Performance.* (Lexington, Mass.: Lexington Books, 1984)

Jocoby, Jacob, and Craig, C. Samuel. *Personal Selling: Theory, Research, and Practice.* (Lexington, Mass.: Lexington Books, 1984)

Levy, Michael, and Dubinsky, Alan J. "Identifying and Addressing Retail Salespeople's Ethical Problems: A Method and Application." *Journal of Retailing* 59 (Spring 1983), 46–66.

Molly, John T. "Clothes: Your First and Last Sales Tool." *Marketing Times* 28 (March - April 1981), 28–34.

Pederson, Carlton A.; Wright, Milburn D.; and Weitz, Barton A. *Selling: Principles and Methods,* 8th ed. (Homewood, Ill.: Richard D. Irwin, 1984)

Skinner, Steven J.; Dubinsky, Alan J.; and Donnelly, James H., Jr. "The Use of Social Bases of Power in Retail Sales." *Journal of Personal Selling & Sales Management* 4 (November 1984), 48–56.

Weitz, Barton A. "Effectiveness in Sales Interaction: A Contingency Framework." *Journal of Marketing* 45 (Winter 1981), 85–103.

Outline

Objectives

- Discuss the unique contribution of retail displays, sales promotions, and publicity in communicating the retailer's merchandising messages to the consumer

- Plan and construct an effective in-store display

- List many innovative sales-promotion tools and describe how they attract customers and stimulate purchases

- Explain how to plan favorable publicity and manage unplanned publicity

Retail Displays, Sales Promotions, and Publicity

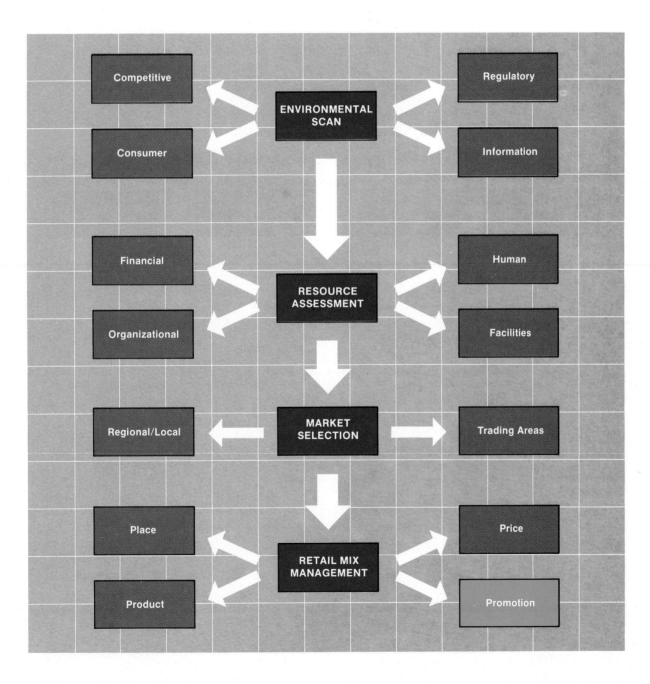

To supplement the advertising program, the retailer must offer in-store promotional support, provide special purchase inducements, and capitalize on public events that affect the store and its personnel. This chapter examines the role of retail displays, sales promotions, and publicity as part of the retailer's total promotional effort. Figure 24–1 portrays the issues to be discussed in this chapter.

RETAIL DISPLAYS

Retail advertising may attract consumers to the store, but the retailer's displays are largely responsible for making the sale after the consumer is in the store. Retail displays are nonpersonal, in-store presentations and exhibitions of merchandise together with related information. In practice, retail displays are used to (1) maximize product exposure, (2) enhance product appearance, (3) stimulate product interest,

RETAIL-MIX MANAGEMENT

PLACE   PRODUCT   PRICE   PROMOTION

Retail Displays, Sales Promotion, and Publicity

I. Retail Displays

    A. Types of displays
    B. Display elements
    C. Display content
    D. Display arrangements

II. Sales Promotion

    A. Coupons
    B. Sampling
    C. Premiums
    D. Trading stamps
    E. Contests and sweepstakes
    F. Specialties
    G. Tie-ins

III. Publicity

    A. What is publicity?
    B. Kinds of publicity
    C. Developing a publicity store
    D. Advantages of publicity
    E. Objectives of publicity

FIGURE 24–1

Developing and implementing retail displays, sales promotions, and publicity campaigns

(4) exhibit product information, (5) facilitate sales transactions, (6) ensure product security, (7) provide product storage, (8) remind customers of planned purchases, and (9) generate additional sales of impulse items. "Merchandise displays must gain the attention of consumers, provide proper balance, be constructed in proper proportion, be hard-hitting, and convey their message quickly. The consumer only spends an average of 11 seconds observing a display."[1] In addition, retail displays are essential ingredients in creating the shopping atmospherics of the store, since a store's sight, sound, touch, taste, and scent appeals are to a large extent the result of in-store displays. (The reader is referred to the section on creating store image and buying atmosphere in Chapter 10.) The present discussion examines the various types of interior displays and their content and arrangements.

Types of Displays

Store interiors are largely the sums of all the displays designed to sell the retailer's merchandise. While retail displays can be classified in a variety of ways, we shall identify four general types of displays: selection, special, point-of-purchase, and audiovisual.

Selection Displays

Nearly all the merchandise of retailers that rely on self-service and self-selection selling is presented to the consumer in the form of **selection displays.** *These mass displays typically occupy rows of stationary aisle and wall units (shelves, counters, tables, racks, and bins) designed to expose the consumer to the retailer's complete assortment of merchandise.* Selection display units are generally "open" to promote merchandise inspection. Their primary functions are to provide customer access to the store's merchandise and to facilitate self-service sales transactions. As a rule, retailers use selection displays to exhibit their normal, everyday assortments of convenience and shopping goods. To be effective, selection displays should present the merchandise in (1) logical selling or usage groupings, (2) a simple, well-organized arrangement, (3) a clean, neat condition, (4) an attractive, informative setting, and (5) a safe, secure state. Customer convenience and operational efficiency are the watchwords for good selection displays.

Special Displays

A **special display** is, as the name implies, *a notable presentation of merchandise designed to attract special attention and make a lasting impression upon the consumer.* Special displays use highly desirable in-store locations, special display equipment or fixtures, and distinctive merchandise.

By placing special displays in highly desirable locations within the store, the retailer ensures maximum exposure for the display and its merchandise. End-of-aisles, counter tops, checkout stands, store entrances and exits, and free-standing units in high-traffic areas are all preferred locations for gaining special attention from shoppers.

By using unique combinations of display equipment (counters, tables, racks, shelves, bins, mobiles) and display fixtures (stands, easels, millinery heads, forms, set pieces), the retailer can create a dramatic setting that will attract consumer attention and build shopper interest. The choice of display equipment and fixtures will depend on the merchandise to be displayed, the amount of space available for the display, and the effect sought in the display.

While store location and display equipment and fixtures are extremely important in constructing a special display, the key to successful display merchandising is

673

the merchandise itself. Special displays highlight merchandise that is capable of attracting customers into the store, building the store's image, improving the store's sales volume, or increasing its net profits. Therefore, special displays are reserved for advertised, best-selling, high-margin, and high-fashion merchandise, together with product items that are suited to impulse and complementary buying behavior. Also, in selecting merchandise for special displays, the items selected should lend themselves to good display techniques—capable of creating a favorable sight, sound, taste, touch, or scent appeal.

Point-of-Purchase Displays

A **point-of-purchase (POP) display** is a particular type of special display. We have chosen to treat it separately because of its importance and because of its popularity with manufacturers.

Retailers make heavy use of point-of-purchase materials in their stores to stimulate immediate purchase behavior. Point-of-purchase is usually the last chance retailers have to tell their customers about the store's merchandise.

Because of the rapid growth in self-service stores in the United States, POP materials are becoming a more important element in the retailer's total communications effort. According to one study, 64.8 percent of supermarket purchases were unplanned, underscoring the value of POP materials in activating customers' unplanned purchases.[2]

Point-of-purchase promotion includes such items as counter displays, window displays, shelf extenders, grocery-cart ads, floor-stand displays, dumpbins, end-aisle stands, banners, shelf talkers, clocks, counter cards, and video-screen displays. Some of these materials are permanent fixtures, such as the Schlitz revolving clock, whereas others are temporary, such as counter cards. Regardless of the kinds of materials the retailer uses, they must attract customer *attention and interest*, reinforce the store's creative theme, and fit in with the store's interior decoration.

Is this an effective use of special display?

In recent years, retailers have begun to "program" their on-site promotions. The idea is to stage a sequence of steps that lead the prospective customer from some point outside the store to the ultimate point of making a purchase decision.

Grocers have been particularly active in using POP materials to increase their sales. Promotional materials such as handbills, bag stuffers, and window signs remind shoppers of what they saw advertised in the local newspapers. Counter decorations include hanging dummy products, manufacturers' signs, and price signs. To draw customers' attention to special sales, some retailers use in-store microphones to gain customer attention and create customer interest in the store's merchandise. K Mart, for example, announces its "blue light specials" over a public-address system. Each department in the K Mart store is supposed to announce a "special sale" on an item in its department for 15 minutes each day. The purpose of this form of promotion is to keep customers in the store to "shop around." K Mart's experience has been that people will "hang around all day" to get a "blue light special." Thus, such point-of-purchase promotion not only increases store traffic but *maintains* it for longer periods of time.

Because of space limitations, retailers must carefully select the POP materials they use. One expert said "The key is to make point-of-purchase promotional materials *more* communicative and less decorative. By tying the messages more directly to television and print advertising, sales promotion can be made more effective and less of an independent communications medium."[3]

Consumer-durable selling seems to follow this pattern:

1. Increasingly, more consumer durables are sold in mass-merchandise outlets. Thus, sales clerks have become less important in selling these products, while point-of-purchase materials have become more important. So, customers must be given materials that show the value of products where no salesperson-customer interaction is involved.
2. Because mass retailers are putting severe restrictions on POP displays, requiring them to be small, sophisticated, tasteful, and contribute to store profit.
3. Retailers expect POP materials to be up-to-date. Retailers should expect that manufacturers will provide them with materials that are both timely and model-related. The POP materials should be related to current consumer needs.
4. Specialty retailers expect special point-of-purchase items. These POP materials should inform the small but sophisticated market of the specialty retailer and must be oriented to quality and service.[4]

The importance of point-of-purchase advertising to retailers becomes clear when one realizes that expenditures in POP grew at an average rate of 10 percent each year during the middle 1970s, reaching 36 percent in 1979. The toiletries and cosmetics industries saw the greatest growth in POP; sales in those areas rose by 88 percent.[5]

Point-of-purchase materials undoubtedly are very valuable tools to retailers in stimulating sales, but retailers must recognize that POP materials must be coordinated with their product displays as well as with other promotional and marketing tools such as advertising, publicity, and pricing to have maximum impact.

Audiovisual Displays

Marketers have been very innovative in developing additional display tools. In particular, they have learned to apply current technology to stimulate consumer pur-

How do audiovisual displays aid the consumer?

chases. For example, retailers now use **visual merchandising, audio merchandising,** and **audiovisual merchandising** to sell their products. All of these display approaches use technology to "speak" to and "show" the consumer available merchandise. These devices include *shelf talkers* (tape recordings describing the merchandise audibly), rear-screen projections (slide projectors that present wide-screen, color pictures of the merchandise and its use), and audiovisual displays (a combination of sound and video tape or slides to present the product's story). As technology changes, so will sales promotions.

Display Elements

To communicate effectively the desired message, the retailer must carefully consider and plan each element of a display. Display elements include the merchandise, use of shelf display areas or window display, props, colors, background materials, lighting, and signs.[6] In creating attention-getting displays, the retailer must consider the contrast, repetition, motion, harmony, balance, rhythm, and proportion of each display (see Figure 24–2).

Display Content

Display content is the type and amount of merchandise to be set off in a particular special display. Cluttered displays of unrelated merchandise attract little attention and prove to be ineffective in stimulating customer interest. To ensure good display content, many retailers have confined their efforts to one of three groupings.

Unit groupings of merchandise *are used to highlight a separate category of product items (e.g., shoes, shirts, cocktail dresses, or handbags).* Unit groupings contain merchandise that is almost identical (e.g., five black leather handbags of different sizes) or closely related (e.g., three red leather handbags and five brown suede bags). **Related groupings** of merchandise are *ensemble displays presenting accessory items along with the featured merchandise.* For example, a mannequin is dressed in a matching sportswear outfit with sporting accessories (e.g., tennis racket and bag). The principal idea behind the inclusion of accessory items is to remind the customer of a need for more than the featured item—in other words, to use suggestive selling. In using either unit or related groupings of merchandise, the display should contain an odd number of product items. Consumers perceive an odd number of items as more intriguing; hence, the items are capable of attract-

Display elements must be evaluated to determine how well and if they attract and hold the attention of passersby.

Contrast is one way to attract attention. Contrast is achieved by using different colors, lighting, form (size and shape), lettering, or textures.

Repetition attracts consumer attention by duplicating an object to reinforce and strengthen the impression. By displaying 20 tennis rackets, the image is created of a store with a wide assortment of merchandise in that category.

Physical motion is a powerful attention getter, as is dominance. If an item is much larger than other items in a display, it will be the dominant item and will draw attention to the entire display.

Once attention has been harnessed, the next step is to direct that attention to the intended message. Harmony and graduation frequently are used to accomplish this.

Harmony refers to the unification of merchandise, lighting, props, shelf space, and showcards to create a pleasing effect. Balance, emphasis, rhythm, and proportion work to focus attention on the central point.

Formal balanced displays in which one side is duplicated by the other tend to produce feelings of dignity, neatness, and order. Informally balanced displays in which one side does not exactly match the other tend to generate excitement and are less stuffy.

Rhythm refers to the eye's path after initial contact with the display. The objective is to hold the eye until the entire display is seen.

Design specialists use vertical lines to create the image of height, strength, and dignity. Horizontal lines connote calmness, width, and sophistication; diagonal lines create action, and curved lines suggest continuity and femininity.

Proportion concerns the relative sizes of the display's various objects. Attention can be directed to the desired focal point by arranging items in a graduated pattern from the small to the large.

The proportion concept also involves the positioning of objects in patterns. Popular display patterns include pyramids, steps, zigzags, repetition, and mass.

The image of height and formality is created with pyramids, while the zigzag is a popular method of displaying clothing to create an aura of excitement.

Repetition arrangements are used primarily in shelf merchandising situations. Merchandise items are placed equidistant from one another in a straight, horizontal line.

The mass arrangement is the placement of a large quantity of merchandise in either neatly stacked lines or in jumbled dump bins to convey the image of a sale item.

Source: Ray Marquardt, "Merchandise Displays Are Most Effective When Marketing, Artistic Factors Combine," *Marketing News,* 16 August 1983, 3.

FIGURE 24–2
Developing an attractive display

ing more attention and creating a more dramatic setting. Where an even number of merchandise items are to be displayed (e.g., a set of eight stem glasses), it is recommended that one item be set apart from the rest or differentiated in some other way (e.g., elevated).

Theme groupings *display merchandise according to a central theme or setting.* Themes help provide a focus in planning displays. They are useful vehicles around which the five sensory appeals can be employed. The number of possible display themes is unlimited. For example, there are product themes ("Shoes complete the appearance"), seasonal themes ("Swing into spring"), patronage themes ("Cheaper by the dozen"), usage themes ("Mealtime magic"), occasion themes ("Along the bridal path"), color themes ("Pastel softness"), life-style themes ("The swinging singles set"), holiday themes ("Santa approved"), as well as themes based on historical events, current events, and special events.

What is the purpose of ensemble displays?

Display Arrangement

Display arrangement is organizing display merchandise into interesting, pleasing, and stimulating patterns. A haphazard arrangement of merchandise items within a display can substantially reduce its effectiveness. While selection displays are simply arranged in some well-organized fashion, special-display merchandise is frequently presented using one of four definite arrangement patterns: the pyramid, zig-zag, step, or fan arrangement. Figure 24–3 illustrates these patterns.

Pyramid arrangements are *triangular displays of merchandise in either vertical (stacked) or horizontal (unstacked) form.* "The pyramid begins at a large or broad base and progresses up to an apex, or point, at the highest level."[7] The vertical pyramid can be either two or three dimensional and is well suited to displaying boxed and canned merchandise; it also represents an efficient use of space. The base of a horizontal pyramid is placed in the rear of the display, thereby achieving the proper visual perspective. Where different-sized merchandise items are being displayed, larger items are positioned at the base, while the smallest item occupies the apex. Figure 24–3a illustrates the use of pedestal displayers arranged in pyramid fashion—an effective arrangement for window, counter, and table displays.

Zig-zag arrangements are *modified pyramids that zig and zag their way to the apex of the display.* No two display levels are at the same height. This arrangement is less monotonous than the pyramid; it is perceived to be more fluid and graceful, and perhaps more feminine. A zig-zag pattern of pedestal displayers (such as the one shown in Figure 24–3b) would be especially appropriate for displaying women's jewelry, cosmetics, small apparel items, and shoes.

Step arrangements are *essentially that: a series of steps.* "Step arrangements lead the eye in a direct line; they begin at a low point on one side of a display area and progress directly to a higher point on the opposite side of that area."[8] Typically, step displays are constructed so that the base of each step increases in area (see Figure 24–3c); this increased base area is used for displaying accessory items, while the steps are used for the featured merchandise. The step arrangement is well suited to displaying a wide variety of merchandise.

Fan arrangements *spread up and out from a small base, thereby directing the viewer's eyes upward and outward.* Figure 24–3d illustrates this inverted-pyramid arrangement using displayers hanging from the ceiling. The fan pattern is used to display merchandise ranging from clothing goods to sporting goods.

SALES PROMOTION

The importance of sales promotion in business is evident, considering that expenditures in this area exceed $40 billion per year. Moreover, sales-promotion expenditures have been increasing rapidly. Not surprisingly, studies of this retailing tool are gaining in popularity.

Sales promotion includes such a wide variety of tools that it is not easy to define. Generally speaking, sales promotion is a "catch all" term describing all promotional activities except advertising, personal selling, and publicity. More specifically, **sales promotion** is *any direct inducement offering an extra value or incentive to consumers to stimulate quick and immediate purchase behavior.* This broad definition of sales promotion is necessary, since so many innovative techniques developed each year fall outside strict definitions of advertising, personal selling, and publicity. These sales-promotion tools are described individually in the following sections.

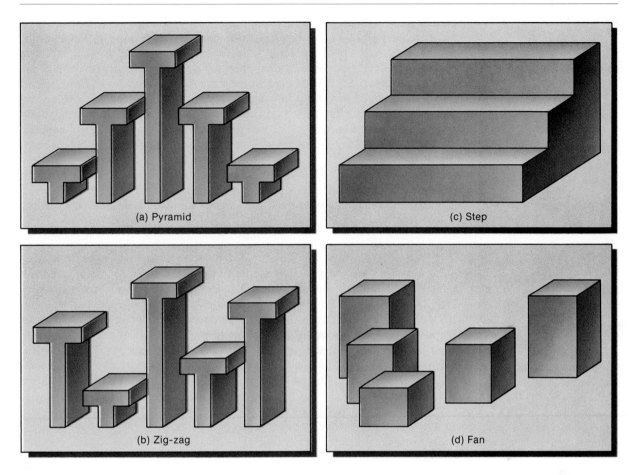

FIGURE 24–3
A gallery of display arrangements

Coupons

When presented to retailers, coupons give consumers a price reduction on specific kinds of merchandise. Coupons are delivered to potential customers through newspapers, magazines, mail, on and in packages, and door-to-door.

Couponing *aids retailers by attracting customers to the store.* Shoppers come into the store to purchase the "bargain" but usually end up buying other merchandise as well. Retailers should grasp several principles about coupons:

- couponing is best used with products that are in the introductory or trial stages of their life cycle
- couponing is best used for products that are purchased frequently
- by selectively choosing target customers who are most likely to use coupons, the retailer can efficiently produce in-store traffic[9]

Although couponing has its advantages, it also has its problems. First, everyone has gotten into the act. With more than 120 billion coupons distributed in 1984,

679

it becomes more difficult to gain customer attention and to get "one up" on competitors. A second problem is in coupon distribution. In-pack coupons, for example, only create repurchases by current users, not new users, which is a major objective in couponing.[10] One study has shown that 47 percent of frequent coupon redeemers use coupons for brands they would have bought anyway.[11] Third, misredemption (illegal redemption) is a major problem. Safeguards are curbing this activity, however.[11] Fourth, the use of complex coupons (e.g., self-destruct, sticky, multiple purchase, and size-specification coupons) adds significantly to handling time at checkout counters and often such coupons are misunderstood by consumers.[13]

Finally, it is interesting to note that "strangely enough, coupons work best with older, more affluent, better educated, urban consumers and married consumers rather than with consumers who need the savings more—the less affluent, young, single, and less educated."[14]

Sampling

Sampling is *another sales-promotion method that retailers use to create customer purchasing on a full-time basis.* Sampling places the product in the customers' hands so that they can use it on a trial basis. Trial use involves active participation, which can quickly lead to a customer purchase decision. However the retailer must realize that only some products should be sampled. The kinds of products retailers can sample have *low unit cost, are small in size,* and *are subject to high repeat sales.* Supermarkets hand out samples of sausage; bakeries provide sample pastries; Hickory Farms places cheese and crackers at convenient points throughout its stores so that customers can sample them. Sampling is generally quite expensive, but it does give customers direct experience and involvement with the product and thus is a powerful tool to induce purchases.

Premiums

Premiums are *units of merchandise that retailers offer customers at a substantially reduced price or, in some cases, free. Merchandise that is substantially reduced in price is usually a* **self-liquidating premium.** A self-liquidating premium is merchandise for which customers pay just enough to cover the retailer's out-of-pocket cost for the item. In the cosmetic industry, such self-liquidating premiums as gifts-with-purchases (g-w-p) and purchases-with-purchases (p-w-p) are used extensively as sales generators.

The purpose of premiums is to create immediate purchases. In some instances, premiums can generate sustained sales. For example, Burger King offered "Jedi" drinking glasses for $.49 each time a customer purchased a medium or large Coke. The customer had to make several trips to Burger King to get a full set of glasses because a different glass was available each week for four weeks.[15]

Premiums create excitement and enthusiasm in consumers. They also create a savings for the customer averaging about 50 percent of the regular retail price for the item. Retailers can generate tremendous store traffic and increase sales by occasionally offering customers a premium. The long-term benefits of premium offers are familiarizing the customer with the store's offering, making customers aware that the store exists, and developing a customer's habit to shop at the store. There are shortcomings to the use of premiums, however. For example, premiums "diminish the importance of the product and give consumers a reason to pay more attention to what they get, rather than the product itself."[16]

Trading Stamps

Founded by Sperry and Hutchinson (S&H) in 1896, the trading-stamp industry has moved through a highly cyclical pattern from great popularity to near disaster. The latest surge in the use of trading stamps came in the early 1950s, rising to a peak in the mid-to-late 1960s. By the early 1970s, trading-stamp usage had declined dramatically. The biggest users of trading stamps were and still are supermarkets. With the high rate of inflation and the growing number of discount food stores, however, supermarkets began to discontinue the use of trading stamps, emphasizing low prices in their advertising instead. Also, with the energy crunch of 1974–75, another major user of trading stamps, gasoline stations, discontinued the practice of issuing them.

The primary reason that retailers adopt the use of trading stamps is to differentiate the store's total offering. Retailers that are first to adopt stamps at the beginning of the upswing of their promotional cycle profit the most. At this stage, retailers can attract new customers to their stores and maintain a loyal following. As more and more retailers adopt trading stamps, however, the advantage of the early users is neutralized. At the peak of the cycle, virtually every store issues stamps and no one has an advantage. At that point, the strategy usually changes to "no stamps, but lower prices."

Smart retailers will watch carefully the cyclical pattern of trading stamps and reintroduce them into their operations early in the new upswing. These retailers reap the major benefits of using trading stamps.[17]

Contests and Sweepstakes

Contests and sweepstakes are ways of attracting attention to a retailer's store and generating excitement. **Contests** *require the entrant to solve a puzzle correctly, write the last line of a jingle, suggest a name for a product or store, or perform some other task to win the prize.* Contests have proven to be an effective way to stimulate short-term sales at both the local and national level.

Sweepstakes are *like contests, except that they do not require a demonstration of skill.* Instead, the entrant must simply fill out a sweepstakes card to be eligible to win. Sweepstakes involve pure chance and a minimal effort for the entrants. Because of the relaxation in the "games of chance" laws, more retailers are using sweepstakes in their sales-promotion programs.

> The growth and variety of sweepstakes are endless. There is the *"straight" sweepstakes, where the winning entry blank is pulled out of a crowded drum of hopefuls. And the "matching" sweepstakes, where numbers or symbols are matched to a preselected number or symbol.*
> Then there is the *"instant win" (rub-off or wash-off) variety of sweepstakes—* the hottest item right now. And let us not forget the *"programmed learning" type of sweepstakes, where the entrant is required to give back some information from a label, package or advertisement, with winners chosen from the "correct" entries.*[18]

Contests and sweepstakes should be coordinated with advertising for maximum impact. One writer points out the method: "By holding six sweepstakes simultaneously, with cash, boat, van, car, and travel prizes they attract the broadest range of interests to their ad."[19] These kinds of prizes can develop interest in a retailer's store and stimulate sales over the short and the long run, but the retailer must be willing to take the risk of investing heavily for these payoffs.

681

Specialties

Specialties are *useful devices to attract an awareness of and interest in the retailer's store.* Pens, pencils, calendars, key cases, matchbooks, and T-shirts bearing the retailer's name or slogan are examples of specialty items. Normally, these items are presented to customers as gifts to show appreciation and build good will. They also promote a long-term relationship with customers.

In developing specialty items, retailers can be as creative as they wish. Successful specialty items match current fads and interests. Retailers can place their names on frisbees, kites, decks of cards, trash cans, or any object they can imagine.

Tie-ins

Sales-promotion **tie-ins** are another approach retailers use to attract attention to their stores' offerings. McDonald's, for example, tied-in with Paramount Pictures to offer Star Trek meals—"children's meals in boxes with Star Trek designs on the outside and space-age plastic toys inside."[20] Such tie-ins can be beneficial to both parties. In this case McDonald's was "hitchhiking" on the potential success of the movie, Star Trek. Tie-ins can generate excitement, enthusiasm, and sales if the tie-in is successful. If the tie-in (such as a movie) bombs, though, the retailer can suffer.

Tie-ins assume a variety of forms. Besides a tie-in with an entertainment event, tie-ins can occur in conjunction with national holidays, special occasions, sporting events, local celebrations, annual conventions, unusual events, and other products, to name but a few ways. The purpose of tie-ins is to capitalize on the excitement generated by momentary trends or events. They are by definition transient: How many people today would buy a coffee mug with a bicentennial decal (1776–1976) on it?

Tie-ins of complementary merchandise have several advantages and disadvantages. Advantages of such tie-ins include

- *increased awareness*—by promoting two or more compatible pieces of merchandise, the retailer can attract more attention than promoting a single piece of merchandise
- *increased readership*—readership of advertising sales-promotion literature will increase, particularly if there is a logical tie-in between the merchandise
- *reinforced image*—where there are natural "go togethers," the image of the store's merchandise can be reinforced because of the combined benefits the consumer will derive from using both pieces of merchandise together
- *cross brand trial*—if customers are loyal to one brand of a store's merchandise, they are likely to try the complementary merchandise because of the "promotional marriage"
- *cost efficiency*—retailers can save money by promoting tie-ins; that is, two or more pieces of merchandise can be promoted together, achieving a synergistic effect

Before deciding to tie-in, the retailer must consider several pertinent questions. Are there seasonal preferences for the merchandise, and do they coincide? If timing matches—great! If not, it would be a mistake to make the tie-in. Are the target consumers the same for the tie-in merchandise? If not, the promotion would probably not be cost effective. Does the tie-in merchandise share similar promotion ideas (themes)? If not, the tie-in probably will not work.[21]

Any sales-promotion approach is limited only by the imagination of the retailer. In New Orleans, a jewelry retailer created a $1,000,000 "town" in the store. Aucoin Hart Jewelers built a miniature town called "Caratville" to attract shoppers to the store during the Christmas season. The six-by-eight-foot village included several homes, a church, and a railroad. The village was constructed of $1,000,000 worth of rubies, diamonds, emeralds, and gold. (What a sight! What an attraction!) With this extravaganza, Hart's Jewelers coordinated its unique sales promotion with advertising to produce a total impact on potential customers.[22]

As we can see from these illustrations, sales promotion is limited only by a retailer's imagination. Sales promotion is ever-changing and will continue to change as long as technology and the human mind continue to develop.

The Future of Sales Promotion

"In the 1970s inflation hit the consumer's pocketbook hard, especially in the grocery store. Knowing this fact, business helped consumers through a variety of sales promotion incentives,"[23] particularly through coupons and cents-off promotions. During the 1970s the focus of sales promotion was on developing efficient ways to use promotion techniques through existing delivery vehicles, such as newspapers, magazines, Sunday supplements, and direct mail.

Some of the innovations in coupon delivery developed in the 1970s were the "instant" coupon, which is affixed to the package and can be redeemed immediately, and the use of high-value refunds to induce brand trial purchases. Also, manufacturer-retailer tie-ins on sweepstakes exploded in the 1970s. These tie-ins were accomplished through rub-off devices, matching devices, and instant winner devices that many retailers (especially supermarkets) used to generate customer interest in their store and its merchandise.

In the 1980s electronic-technology communications will continue to replace the traditional sales-promotion delivery systems. With the rapidly expanding number of "TV channels, FM waves, satellite-to-earth broadcasting, cable TV, home computers, home retrieval systems, two-way TV and home video recording," consumers will have unusual in-home opportunities to bank, to shop, to visit the library, and to see friends, all without leaving their homes![24]

Although the basic sales-promotion devices will not change, the delivery of these devices will.

> For instance, coupons, refunds, premiums, and other promotion offers now delivered in media and by mail may, in the future, be offered over the airwaves via the TV screen.
>
> All consumers may have to do is press a button and have the offer of their choice delivered to their home via an electronic printout receptacle hooked up to the home TV screen.
>
> Stores might even run Best Food Day ads on TV. Again, the consumer could push a button and receive a printout of the store's ad right in their living room. Or they may store their Best Food Day information-promotion offers, features and pricing data in a computer bank.[25]

Additionally, in the 1980s, vending machines could add moving displays, film strips, and sound promotions since vending machines already have electric hookups. Some soft-drink machines already "talk" to consumers.

The remainder of the 1980s will be a challenging era for retailers. Only the innovative, creative, and imaginative retailer that takes advantage of technological change will survive. It will be an exciting period for everyone: manufacturers, retailers, and consumers.

683

Publicity is an often-overlooked part of the retailer's total promotional message. The reason retailers often fail to use publicity is that they do not consider it a part of their promotional mix. They believe publicity is something that just happens and is out of their control. However, retailers can generate publicity favorable to their stores if they carefully plan their news events (see Figure 24–4). This section describes what publicity is, the kinds of publicity, how to develop a publicity story, the distinctive advantages of publicity, and the objectives of publicity.

What Is Publicity?

Publicity is "any form of non-paid commercially significant news or editorial comment about ideas, products, or institutions."[26] Publicity can either be good news about a retailer or bad news. Naturally, retailers want the media to pick up good news about their stores, but that is not always the case. A newspaper headline announcing "Two J. B. Mason's Store Employees Arrested for Pilfering" might cast a dark shadow over the integrity of the store in many customers' minds. On the other hand, a headline that reads "J. B. Mason's Sponsors Telethon for Crippled Children" makes a positive impression on the community.

FIGURE 24–4
What makes an event "special"?

Special events don't necessarily equal participating in an auto show or sponsoring a rock tour—not all sponsorships are special events. As might be expected, the line between special events and other promotion techniques can be fuzzy. But, there are distinct characteristics common to all promotions that fall under the classification of special events:

- A special event is in most cases a leisure pursuit, either sports or something that fits within the broad definition of the arts.
- It involves some form of public participation on the part of the audience—attending a fest, competing in a triathlon—as opposed to seeing an ad or reading about a product.
- Unlike ad campaigns, which may run as long as they are effective, special events occur within a prescribed time frame and have a definite opening and closing.
- An event is independently legitimate; it can stand on its own merits apart from any sponsor. Furthermore, the event does not form part of the primary commercial function of the sponsoring body (but there is usually some link between the sponsoring organization and the event). In other words, horse races are not special events because they are the chief business of their sponsor, the track authority. So too, for sweepstakes, coupons and premiums. While they may be nifty promotions, they are created exclusively to step up direct sales of their sponsor's product and can not stand alone.

On the other hand, the New York City Marathon is a special event because it is an entity apart from sponsor Manufacturers Hanover Trust, and running is not the chief function of the bank.

- The sponsoring body of a special event expects a return on its investment. While foundations often support charitable and civic ventures, they rarely sponsor a special event.
- The bulk of publicity derived from a special event happens spontaneously, usually within an editorial, not an advertising, context. This is quite different from advertising where mentions are specifically placed and paid for.

Source: Reprinted with permission of *Advertising Age*, 18 April 1983. Copyright Crain Communications Inc.

Although publicity is "free," it usually is not. This statement sounds like a contradiction, but it is not. Publicity is "free" in the sense that media such as newspapers and television report newsworthy items about a company without charging the company a fee, as they would if it were an advertisement. Many retailers, particularly large ones, hire staff publicists who write favorable stories for release to the media. These people are paid to do this job. The supplies and other expenses associated with the job also cost the company money. Therefore, publicity is not totally free. Additionally, all retailers are subject to bad publicity, which can affect sales. Lost sales resulting from customer ill will from bad publicity are an *opportunity cost*. An opportunity cost is money (sales) a company loses that it otherwise normally would have made. (There are many other causes of opportunity costs besides bad publicity.) In sum, even though publicity does bear a cost, the prudent retailer will attempt to generate favorable publicity, which can lead to increased sales and a good reputation.

Kinds of Publicity

Publicity can be either planned or unplanned. With **planned publicity,** *the retailer exercises some control over the news item.* With **unplanned publicity,** *the retailer can suffer irreparable damage to its reputation and financial posture.*

A retail firm has some measure of control over its publicity through press releases, press conferences, photographs, letters to the editor, editorials, and special events. Large retailers, for example, will typically send out dozens of news releases about their stores and activities. Further, large retailers use press conferences to describe major new events that might be of interest to the public. Pictures and drawings are useful devices for showing store-expansion plans, new equipment to better serve customers, and so forth; these are generally newsworthy items that bring attention to the retailer. Each of these approaches to gaining favorable publicity is subject to the whim of the news media, since they select what they consider to be newsworthy. The media have space or time to fill, though, and persistence and continual dissemination of releases to the media can increase the likelihood of favorable coverage by the media.

Developing a Publicity Story

To develop a publicity story, the retailer first must identify the *kinds* of stories the media accepts and the *criteria* they use to make their decisions. This step gives retailers basic ideas on which to develop stories.

Stories that depict new and unusual events, store innovations, improvements in working conditions, new store openings, and stories that are *currently* important to the public often attract the interest of the news media. Additionally, publicity *must* be newsworthy, must be somewhat unusual, must appeal to a broad cross section of the public, and must be truthful. Furthermore, publicity stories are more effective if they are dramatic or emotional and use photographs and illustrations to show action or human interest.

Advantages of Publicity

Publicity has at least three advantages over other methods that retailers use to communicate with their customers. First, the public perceives news stories as having higher *credibility* than either advertising, personal selling, or sales promotion, which people view as "sales" methods intended to persuade them to buy. People see news stories as factual, objective, and more truthful than the other promotion tools retailers use because the stories "originated" from the media, not from the retailers.

Second, consumers are more likely to read thoroughly a news item about a retailer than they would an advertisement about the same store. People glance at advertisements; they read the news. Third, publicity usually is presented in a highly dramatic way. It captures the attention and emotions of its readers (or viewers). These are all distinct advantages publicity has in communicating messages about retail stores.

Objectives of Publicity

As with advertising, the objectives of publicity are to make consumers aware of the retail store and its merchandise, to make a favorable store impression in the minds of potential and current consumers, and ultimately to generate interest in the store, and to increase store traffic, and sales. Through careful planning, retailers can create and disseminate many news stories favorable to their stores with the hope and expectation that some proportion of those stories will be picked up by the media.

Good publicity can instill in consumers confidence and trust in the store and help to build a lasting, favorable store reputation. Publicity is a powerful communications tool that retailers should not neglect in developing their total promotional program.

SUMMARY

Retail displays, sales promotions, and publicity are very effective promotional tools for helping retailers achieve their objectives. They stimulate quick customer action to purchase, and they influence customer attitudes toward and images about the store and its merchandise.

As in-store presentations of the retailer's merchandise, retail displays assume a key role in creating a shopping atmosphere and enhancing the consumer's buying mood. Depending on the objectives to be achieved, retailers use a variety of methods to present their merchandise, including selection, special, point-of-purchase, and audiovisual displays. To ensure effective displays, retailers plan merchandise exhibits by controlling their content (unit, related, and theme groupings) and arrangements (pyramid, zig-zag, step, and fan patterns).

Coupons, sampling, premiums, trading stamps, contests, sweepstakes, specialties, and tie-ins are among the many devices that retailers use to communicate with customers about their store and their merchandise. Sales-promotion approaches are limited only by the imagination of the retailer. With the ever-exploding technology of our day, businesses are creating increasingly large numbers of sales-promotion tools to stimulate customer interest in their merchandise.

Publicity is another important part of a retailer's promotion program. Good publicity can bring attention to a retailer and its merchandise and help build a good store reputation and sales. Bad publicity can ruin a retailer. Therefore, a retailer must learn how to control the publicity the store gets.

Retailers can obtain good publicity by preparing press releases, press conferences, photographs, letters to the editor, editorials, and by staging special events. Bad publicity can be avoided by developing and implementing policies preventing employees, suppliers, government agencies, and others from adversely affecting the retailer's business.

In developing a publicity story, the retailer should identify the kind of stories that media are willing to accept and the criteria they use to judge them. Good publicity stories should be of current interest to the public, be newsworthy, use photographs and illustrations, be emotional or dramatic, have human interest, be truthful, and show action.

Publicity's major strength over other promotional tools is its perceived credibility. Because it appears in the newspaper, on television, or through some other medium, most consumers view the information as factual and unbiased. Therefore, publicity attracts attention and is generally viewed as believable.

KEY TERMS AND CONCEPTS

selection display

special display

point-of-purchase display

visual merchandising

audio merchandising

audiovisual display

unit groupings

related groupings

theme groupings

pyramid arrangements

zig-zag arrangements

step arrangements

fan arrangements

sales promotion

couponing

sampling

premiums

self-liquidating premiums

trading stamps

contests

sweepstakes

specialties

tie-ins

planned publicity

unplanned publicity

REVIEW QUESTIONS

1. What merchandising objectives might be achieved through the use of in-store displays?
2. What is the primary function of a selection display?
3. Special displays should be reserved for what type of merchandise?
4. Identify the types of items used in constructing a point-of-purchase display.
5. What display elements should the retailer consider in creating attention-getting displays? Briefly explain each element.
6. Describe the three types of display content. Provide an example of each type.
7. Which four arrangement patterns are used in constructing a store display? Describe each arrangement.

8. What is a sales promotion?
9. What problems face the retailer that utilizes coupons as part of a sales-promotion program?
10. What is the primary purpose of sampling?
11. How does a self-liquidating premium work?
12. What is the difference between a contest and a sweepstakes?
13. Describe the four types of sweepstakes that retailers use.
14. What are the advantages of using tie-in promotions of complementary merchandise?
15. How might the retailer exercise some control over its publicity?
16. What three advantages does publicity have over other forms of promotions?

ENDNOTES

1. Ray Marquardt, "Merchandise Displays Are Most Effective When Marketing, Artistic Factors Are Combined," *Marketing News,* 19 August 1983, 3.

2. Kevin Higgins, "In-Store Merchandising Is Attracting More Marketing Dollars with Last Word in Sales," *Marketing News,* 19 August 1983, 1.

3. Cameron S. Foote, "Space Limitations Put Squeeze on P.O.P. Promotional Material," *Advertising Age,* 4 February 1980, S5.

4. Ibid.

5. "P.O.P. Both Efficient and Timely," *Advertising Age,* 10 March 1980, S5.

6. Marquardt, "Merchandise Displays," 3.

7. See Kenneth Mills and Judith Paul, *Visual Merchandising* (Englewood Cliffs, NJ: Prentice-Hall, Inc., 1983).

8. Ibid.

9. "Couponing Grows, Gives Boost to New Products, Repeat Purchases, Kenyon & Eckhardt Study Shows," *Advertising Age,* 12 February 1962, 63–68.

10. Kevin Higgins, "Couponing's Growth Is Easy to Understand," *Advertising Age,* 28 September 1984, 12.

11. Marji Simon, "Survey Probes Strengths, Weaknesses of Promotions," *Marketing News,* 8 June 1984, 4.

12. See Dorothy Cohen, "Couponing and Sampling Can Entail Numerous Legal Problems," *Marketing News,* 28 September 1984, 14; Kevin Higgins, "UPC Codes Represent Newest Method of Combating Coupon Misredemption," *Marketing News,* 28 September 1984, 75; Nancy Giges, "New Coupon Trap Set," *Advertising Age,* 30 May 1983, 1.

13. P. Rajan Varadarajan, "Issue of Efficient Coupon Handling and Processing Pits Manufacturers Against Retailers, Coupon Clearinghouses," *Marketing News,* 28 September 1984, 13.

14. William A. Robinson, "What Are Promos' Weak, Strong Points?" *Advertising Age,* 7 April 1980, 54.

15. Scott Hume, "Burger King Drinks to the Jedi," *Advertising Age,* 22 August 1983, M11.

16. Cara S. Trager, "Promotions Blemish Cosmetics Industry," *Advertising Age,* 10 May 1984, 22.

17. See Louis E. Boone, James C. Johnson, and George P. Ferry, "Trading Stamps: Their Role in Today's Marketplace," *Journal of the Academy of Marketing Science* 6 (Spring, 1979): 70–78. Also see the classic article by Fred C. Allvine, "The Future of Trading Stamps and Games," *Journal of Marketing* 33 (January, 1969).

18. Eileen Norris, "Everyone Will Grab at a Chance to Win," *Advertising Age,* 22 August 1983, 10.

19. Robinson, "What Are Promos' Weak, Strong Points?"

20. "McDonald's Plans Next Film Tie," *Advertising Age,* 11 February 1980, 44.

21. Al Kaufman, "Tie-in Promotions: How to Make Them Successful," *Advertising Age,* 19 November 1979, 54, 56.

22. "La. Jeweler Creates Holiday 'Caratville,'" *Advertising Age,* December 1979, 34BS.

23. Ed Meyer, "Life Styles Hold Key to the 1980's," *Advertising Age,* 28 January 1980, 47.

24. Ibid.

25. Ibid.

26. James F. Engel, Hugh G. Wales, and Martin R. Warshaw, *Promotional Strategy* (Homewood, IL: Richard D. Irwin, 1971), 3.

"Display Makers Serve Two Masters." *Marketing News* (December 7, 1984), 15, 19.

George, Richard J., and Lord, John B. "Alternative Retailer Couponing Strategies: Consumer Reactions and Marketing Implications." *Developments in Marketing Science, Proceedings.* J. D. Lindquist, ed. (Academy of Marketing Science 1984), 306–10.

Higgins, Kevin. "Couponing's Growth Is Easy to Understand: It Works." *Marketing News* (September 28, 1984), 12–13.

Kopp, Robert J. "Premiums Provide Great Impact, But Little Glamour." *Marketing News* (June 7, 1985), 12, 14.

Marlow, Nancy D., and Marlow, Edward K. "Coupons: A Review of the Literature." *Marketing Comes of Age, Proceedings.* David M. Klein and Allen E. Smith, eds. (Southern Marketing Association 1984), 149–52.

Moore, H. Frazier, and Kalupa, Frank B. *Public Relations: Principles, Cases, and Problems,* 9th ed. (Homewood, Ill.: Richard D. Irwin, 1985)

Pegler, Martin M. *The Language of Store Planning and Display.* (New York: Fairchild Books, 1984)

————. *Visual Merchandising and Display.* (New York: Fairchild Books, 1984)

Reiling, Lynn. "Video Shock Gives Retailer Low-Cost Promotional Boost." *Marketing News* (February 1, 1985), 22, 24.

Reibstein, David J., and Traver, Phyllis A. "Factors Affecting Coupon Redemption Rates." *Journal of Marketing* 46 (Fall 1982), 102–13.

Roth, Laszlo. *Display Design.* (Englewood Cliffs: Prentice-Hall, 1980)

Seitel, Fraser P. *The Practice of Public Relations.* (Columbus: Charles E. Merrill Publishing Co., 1984)

Spalding, Lewis A. "Taped for Success." *Stores* (May 1985), 23–24, 29–30, 32.

PART SIX
Retail Careers: Evaluating Employment Opportunities

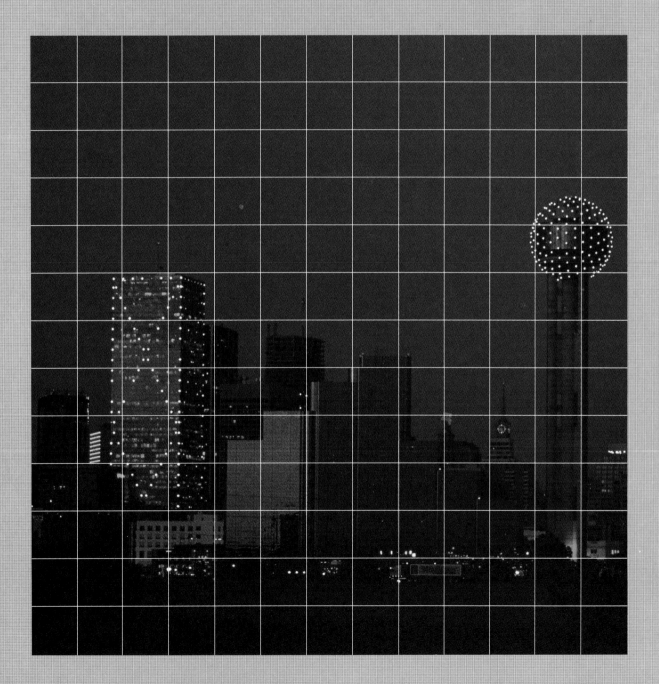

Outline

RETAILER ATTRIBUTES AND PERSONALITIES

The People Pleaser
The Risk Taker
The Problem Solver
The Decision Maker
The Retail Entrepreneur

EMPLOYMENT ASPECTS OF A RETAILING CAREER

Employment Security
Employee Compensation
Working Conditions
Career Advancement
Job Satisfaction

EMPLOYEE OPPORTUNITIES

Making a Personal Assessment
Securing a Retail Position

OWNERSHIP OPPORTUNITIES

Objectives

- Distinguish personal attributes and personality traits essential to the successful retailer

- Judge the opportunities associated with a retailing career

- Assess one's own personal strengths and weaknesses as applicable to the retailing field

- Plan a successful employment-search process

- Decide whether one is the kind of person who can successfully start and run an independent retail business

25
Retailing Careers

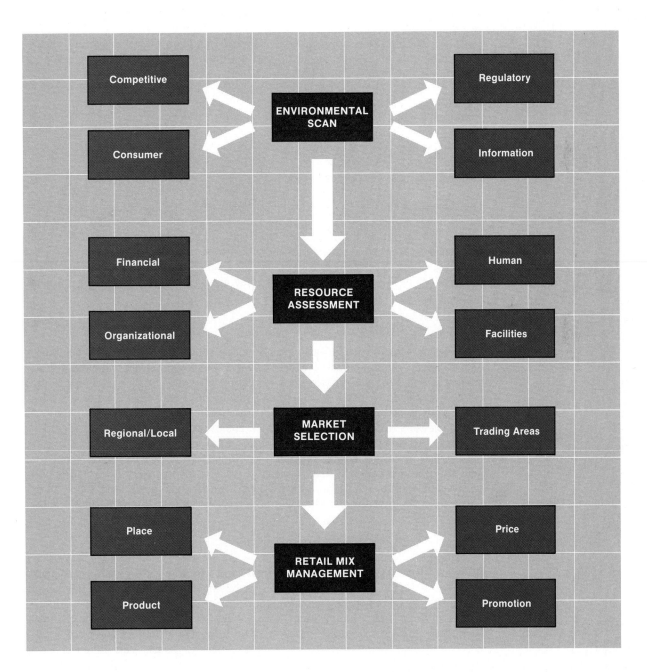

So you want to consider being a retailer? Or at least you might want to consider entering the retailing field. This chapter provides a glimpse of what it is like to be in retailing. You will discover some of the joys and, yes, also some of the frustrations involved in the retailing field. You will learn that people must possess special characteristics to be successful retailers. You will read about employment opportunities, ownership opportunities, employment features in a retailing career, and the personal attributes of retailers. Once you have read this chapter, you decide. Is retailing for you?

RETAILER ATTRIBUTES AND PERSONALITIES

Whether a neophyte or a veteran, an independent entrepreneur or a chain store employee, the retailer must have a *mind for marketing* to succeed in the marketplace. Although there is no universally accepted definition of the "marketing mind," some attributes are generally considered essential for success. For example, the marketing mind must be

> creative, yet scientific;
> imaginative, yet practical;
> outgoing, yet reserved;
> respectful, yet questioning;
> emotional, yet controlled;
> courageous, yet prudent.

The key to success is to evoke each of these attributes at the appropriate time. While they are difficult, if not impossible, to measure, these personality characteristics tend to surface in the successful marketing-minded retailer. Some of the more successful retailer personality types include the people pleaser, the risk taker, the problem solver, the decision maker, and the retail entrepreneur. Although these personalities are not mutually exclusive, they are discussed individually to facilitate understanding.

The People Pleaser

The retailer is in the people business. No other type of business deals so directly with so many people in such a variety of ways. Successful retailers have a genuine interest in and general liking for *people*. "People pleasing" retailers can "read" their customers' minds, guess their wants and needs, anticipate their likes and dislikes, understand their hopes and fears, and adapt to their customers' viewpoints. As people pleasers, retailers can talk with their customers in a common language. That is to say, successful merchandising is largely a matter of good communications.

Finally, people-pleasing retailers can appreciate their customers, empathize with them and recognize their motives. Thus, people pleasers are retailers who understand people, recognize their problems, know their goals, and try to satisfy their needs. To be a successful retailer, a person must be able and willing to please people.

The Risk Taker

Risks are an inherent part of any business, and retailing is no exception. Perhaps the greatest single risk that retailers face is buying merchandise, since they might not be able to sell what they have bought or they might have to sell their merchandise at lower prices than expected. There are also risks in deciding where to locate, how many and which markets to serve, how extensive a product line to offer, and which and how many services to provide. Since no retailer can either precisely determine what the customer wants or provide everything that all competitors are doing better, risks are simply unavoidable in retailing. The risk taker not only is willing to assume the inherent chances in going into business, but is able to tell a good merchandising risk from a bad one. In addition, the successful risk taker can reduce risk by gathering and analyzing pertinent information.

The Problem Solver

The marketing-minded retailer not only *understands* marketing-problem situations, but *enjoys* solving them. As discussed in Chapter 1, retailing is one big problem: how to satisfy customers at a profit. Therefore, the retailer must have the capacity, determination, and stamina to overcome all the barriers associated with any problem-solving situation. A typical retail operation faces a great diversity of problems, ranging from the physical problems of getting the merchandise into the store and onto the shelves to the mental and emotional problems of handling dissatisfied and vocal customers. Regardless of the situation, the retailer must be prepared to solve not only routine problems, but also unusual ones. What's more, the retailer should enjoy it!

The Decision Maker

The number of managerial decisions a retailer faces can be quite large and the range of possible choices in each decision can be equally broad. Retailers must make daily decisions about locations, facilities, merchandise, prices, promotions, and service. In addition, they make periodic decisions about staff, suppliers, and investors. Not everyone is willing or able to make these decisions under the pressure of time constraints and with limited knowledge of the marketplace. To the marketing-minded decision maker, making choices under adverse and uncertain conditions is natural. The decision maker must understand and adapt daily to a changing marketplace. Such a person's strength lies in the ability and desire to make moment-by-moment and year-by-year decisions on a continual basis. People pleaser, risk taker, problem solver, and decision maker: *the successful retailer must be all these and more.*

The Retail Entrepreneur

A retail entrepreneur organizes, manages, and assumes the responsibilities of running a retail business. Although the term **entrepreneur** *is generally used in reference to an individual, the concept of entrepreneurship is actually appropriate to all retail organizations,* since entrepreneural skills are needed in all successful retailing careers. Like most skills, entrepreneurship exists in degrees. No single measurement is appropriate for all individuals and no one test measures all of the attributes a retailer needs to be successful in retailing. However, two psychologists have developed what they deem indicators of what makes a successful retailing entrepreneur. A summary of this test of entrepreneurial mental skills and attitudes is shown in Figure 25–1.

The entrepreneurial skills of people-pleasing, decision-making, problem-solving, and risk-taking people, together with the abilities for organizing and managing, can be acquired in part either in a formal learning situation such as a college classroom or in an informal learning situation such as a work setting. Most people learn these entrepreneurial skills in both ways.

The ideas in this book should have built upon and expanded whatever entrepreneurial skills you have and given you new insights into the world of retailing and the entrepreneurial spirit that people need to launch prosperous retailing careers.

Your psychological makeup can play a strong role in making your business a success or a failure. Here are some questions based on ideas supplied by Richard Boyatzis and David Winter, two psychologists who have studied the entrepreneurial character. The questions are designed to reveal whether you have entrepreneurial attitudes. Even if no answer fits your feelings precisely, choose the one that comes closest. (The answers to these questions are provided in the chapter summary.)

1. If you have a free evening, would you most likely (a) watch TV, (b) visit a friend, (c) work on a hobby?
2. In your daydreams, would you most likely appear as (a) a millionaire floating on a yacht, (b) a detective who has solved a difficult case, (c) a politician giving an election night victory speech?
3. To exercise, would you rather (a) join an athletic club, (b) join a neighborhood team, (c) do some jogging at your own pace?
4. When asked to work with others on a team, which would you anticipate with most pleasure? (a) Other people coming up with good ideas, (b) cooperating with others, (c) getting other people to do what you want.
5. Which game would you rather play? (a) Monopoly, (b) roulette, (c) bingo.
6. Your employer asks you to take over a company project that is failing. Would you tell him that you will (a) take it, (b) won't take it because you're up to your gills in work, (c) give him an answer in a couple of days when you have more information?
7. In school, were you more likely to choose courses emphasizing (a) fieldwork, (b) papers, (c) exams?
8. In buying a refrigerator, would you (a) stay with an established, well-known brand, (b) ask your friends what they bought, (c) compare thoroughly the advantages of different brands?
9. While on a business trip in Europe, you are late for an appointment with a client in a neighboring town. Your train has been delayed indefinitely. Would you (a) rent a car to get there, (b) wait for the next scheduled train, (c) reschedule the appointment?
10. Do you believe people you know who have succeeded in business (a) have connections, (b) are more clever than you are, (c) are about the same as you but maybe work a little harder?
11. An employee who is your friend is not doing his job. Would you (a) take him out for a drink, hint broadly that things are not going right and hope he gets the message, (b) leave him alone and hope he straightens out, (c) give him a strong warning and fire him if he doesn't shape up?
12. You come home to spend a relaxing evening and find that your toilet has just overflowed. Would you (a) study your home repair book to see if you can fix it yourself, (b) persuade a handy friend to fix it for you, (c) call a plumber?
13. Do you enjoy playing cards most when you (a) play with good friends, (b) play with people who challenge you, (c) play for high stakes?
14. You operate a small office-cleaning business. A close friend and competitor suddenly dies of a heart attack. Would you (a) reassure his wife that you will never try to take away any customers, (b) propose a merger, (c) go to your former competitor's customers and offer them a better deal?

Source: Marlys Harris, "The Entrepreneur—Do You Have What It Takes?" *Money* 7 (March, 1978), 52.

FIGURE 25–1
Testing the entrepreneurial you

EMPLOYMENT ASPECTS OF A RETAILING CAREER

In judging the career opportunities in different fields of endeavor, a person should investigate the employment features for each career path. This discussion examines several key aspects of a retailing career. Specifically, it examines employment security, employee compensation, working conditions, career advancement, and job satisfaction.

Employment Security

Employment in the retail sector offers the capable individual a very high level of job security. Several factors account for this security. First, while all economic sectors suffer during a recession, the decline in retail employment is notably less than employment losses in either the manufacturing or wholesaling sectors of the economy. Even during recessionary periods, consumers continue to buy. However, they do become more selective in making their purchases. Second, the large number of employment opportunities in retailing creates a high level of job mobility. Generally, increased mobility results in increased job security. Simply put, the greater the demand for an employee's services by outside concerns, the greater the perceived value of that employee to the current employer. The net result is greater employment security.

The third factor accounting for the high level of job security in retailing is "transferability of skills." Good merchandising skills can easily be transferred from one department within the firm to another, from one type of retailer to a different retailing operation, and even from retailing firms to wholesaling and manufacturing companies. Essentially, this transferability of skills is an extension of the mobility factor. Since it increases the number of employment opportunities, it thereby increases present job security.

Employee Compensation

Retail salaries vary considerably. They range from minimum wage for lower-echelon, part-time employees to competitive salaries for upper-echelon managers. In the past, starting salaries and benefits for management trainees were below-market relative to other business fields. Recently, the gap in starting salaries between retailing and other industries has been closing rapidly and has closed for larger retailing organizations. Even when starting retail salaries are somewhat lower than those in other industries, the multitude of managerial levels within most retailing organizations and thus the opportunities for rapid advancement can often result in a higher salary for the retail manager in just a few years. Equally important is the fact that retailing is a geographically dispersed industry in which a large number of middle- and upper-level managerial positions offer very attractive salaries and benefits. Also, for the prospective employee with limited formal education, entry to higher-salaried positions in retailing is not education-oriented but productivity-oriented (e.g., based on the ability to generate profits or sales). Finally, there is the opportunity for self-employment. The potential returns for individuals owning and operating their own business are discussed later in this chapter.

Working Conditions

The working conditions surrounding retail employment have their pluses and minuses. On the plus side, the retail employee enjoys the benefits of a variety of work assignments, a number of pleasant work environments, and a host of people-oriented work relationships.

If "variety is the spice of life," then the prospective employee should find a retailing career very attractive. The variety of work assignments associated with retailing stems from two factors. First, the retail business is highly dynamic because of continuously changing economic conditions, the regular changes in merchandising seasons, and the attraction of new and old customers. Each of these conditions fosters new and interesting challenges for the retail employee. Second, the natural progression in the training of retail management personnel requires that the employee gain experience with all aspects of business. Typically, retail training programs involve experiences with merchandising (e.g., buying and selling responsibilities), operations management (e.g., inventory planning and control responsibilities), sales promotion (e.g., advertising and retail display responsibilities), and personnel management (e.g., recruiting and training store personnel) Figure 25–2 illustrates these programs.

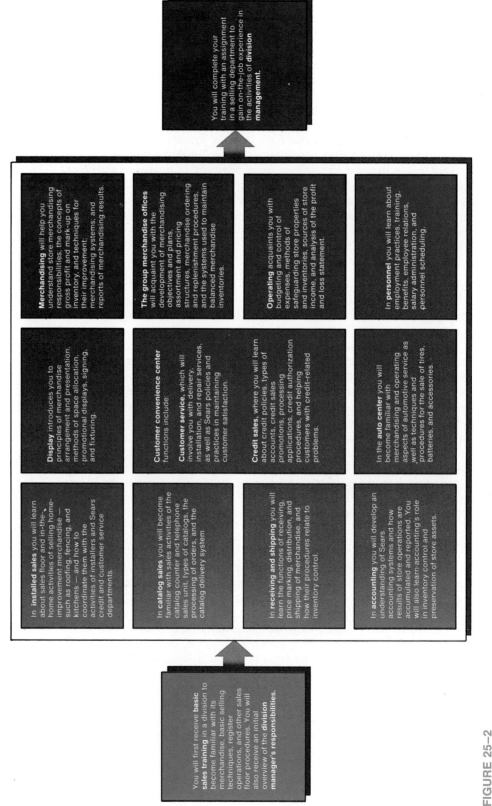

You will first receive **basic sales training** in a division to become familiar with its merchandise, basic selling techniques, register operations, and other sales floor procedures. You will also receive an initial overview of the **division manager's responsibilities.**

In **installed sales** you will learn about sales floor and in-the-home activities of selling home-improvement merchandise — such as roofing, fencing, and kitchens — and how to coordinate them with the activities of installers and Sears credit and customer service departments

In **catalog sales** you will become familiar with sales activities of the catalog counter and telephone sales unit, types of catalogs, the processing of orders, and the catalog delivery system

In **receiving and shipping** you will learn the functions of receiving, price marking, distribution, and shipping of merchandise, and how their procedures relate to inventory control.

In **accounting** you will develop an understanding of Sears accounting systems and how results of store operations are accumulated and reported. You will also learn accounting's role in inventory control and preservation of store assets.

Display introduces you to principles of merchandise arrangement and presentation, methods of space allocation, promotional displays, signing, and fixturing.

Customer convenience center functions include:

Customer service, which will involve you with delivery, installation, and repair services, as well as Sears policies and practices in maintaining customer satisfaction.

Credit sales, where you will learn about credit policies, types of accounts, credit sales promotions, processing applications, credit authorization procedures, and helping customers with credit-related problems.

In the **auto center** you will become familiar with merchandising and operating aspects of automotive service as well as techniques and procedures for the sale of tires, batteries, and accessories.

Merchandising will help you understand store merchandising responsibilities; the concepts of gross profit and mark-up on inventory, and techniques for their improvement; merchandising systems; and reports of merchandising results.

The group merchandise offices will acquaint you with the development of merchandising objectives and plans, assortment and pricing structures, merchandise ordering and replenishment procedures, and the systems used to maintain balanced merchandise inventories.

Operating acquaints you with budgeting and control of expenses, methods of safeguarding store properties and inventories, sources of store income, and analysis of the profit and loss statement.

In **personnel** you will learn about employment practices, training, benefits, employee relations, salary administration, and personnel scheduling.

You will complete your training with an assignment in a selling department to gain on-the-job experience in the activities of **division management.**

FIGURE 25–2

Retailing: A variety of work experiences—the Sears model (source: *Retail Management Careers,* Sears Merchandise Group, company brochure, 9)

The pleasant work environment for the typical retail employee is the result of the retailer's efforts at creating a *buying atmosphere* for the store. When contrasted with the sterile atmosphere of most offices, the opportunity to work in an exciting and stimulating physical store environment is a definite plus of retail employment.

For many individuals, the "action is where the people are." Given the people-oriented nature of the retailing business, individuals who crave action should find a retailing career very rewarding. Personal interactions with customers, suppliers, and other store personnel on a continuous basis can provide the action-oriented person with a wide variety of challenging situations.

The most commonly cited minuses of a retailing career concern working hours. Of particular concern are the questions of how long and when employees work. While lower-echelon positions have a "normal" work week of 40 hours, the aspiring management trainee should expect to work considerably longer. However, when compared to the hours expected at lower-level managerial positions in other businesses, the retail manager's work week is reasonable. The longer retail store hours of recent years have resulted in increased supervision during nonstandard working times. Because of these extended hours, both management and nonmanagement personnel are expected to work off-hours (such as evenings), off-days (such as weekends), and some off-times (such as holidays).

Career Advancement

The opportunities for rapid advancement are numerous in retailing as a result of several interacting factors: the number of retail establishments, the diversity of retailing positions, and the number of managerial levels. The number of retail establishments is both large and expanding. As a result, managerial positions abound. For the ambitious and talented individual, finding potential positions for career advancement is not difficult. Equally important in finding a career environment where rapid advancement is possible is a job market characterized by a diversity of positions. In retailing there is enough diversity to allow all individuals to seek out and foster a career niche best suited to their talents (see Figure 25–3). Additionally, upward mobility need not be hampered by getting locked into a particular type of job that suits neither the talents nor the aspirations of the individual.

The third factor contributing to an accelerated rate of advancement in retailing is the large number of managerial levels in the typical retail organization. Consider for example the managerial levels that might be found in a department store chain: assistant department manager, department manager, assistant merchandise and/or promotions manager, assistant store manager, store manager, and upward into the various district, regional, and national managerial positions. The aspiring retail manager does not have to wait for a chance at the one big career break. By making small yet steady career advancements, the retail manager exercises greater control over future opportunities and realizes greater satisfaction from current job responsibilities.

Consider a final note. Retailing careers offer women some of the best opportunities for professional advancement in the business world. These opportunities are due in part to women's power as the majority of customers at many stores. The belief that women managers have both a greater understanding of the needs of women shoppers and a greater capability for developing meaningful relationships with this group of customers has created a career path for women in retailing that can definitely be characterized by rapid advancement.

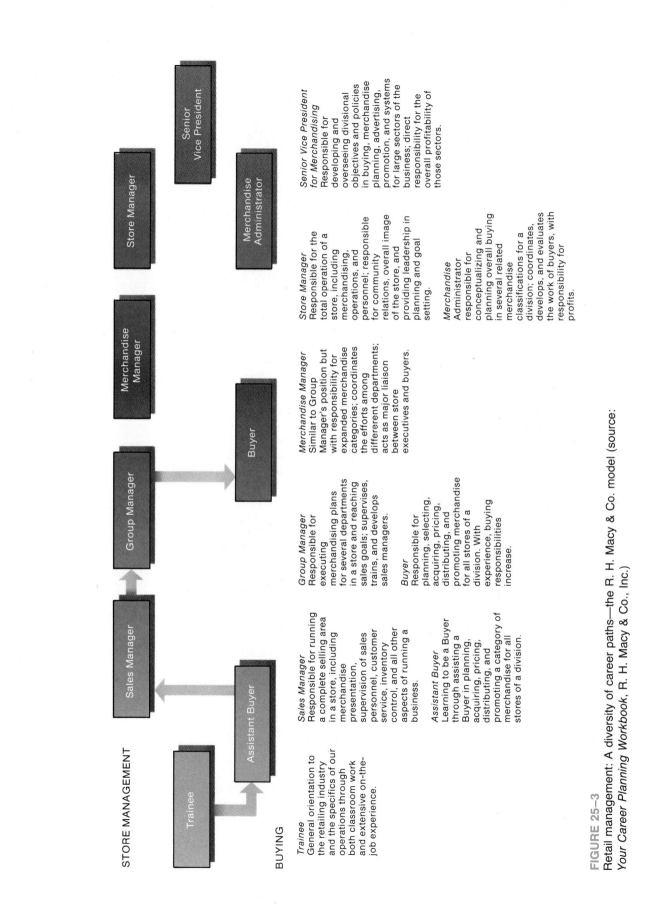

STORE MANAGEMENT

BUYING

Trainee
General orientation to the retailing industry and the specifics of our operations through both classroom work and extensive on-the-job experience.

Sales Manager
Responsible for running a complete selling area in a store, including merchandise presentation, supervision of sales personnel, customer service, inventory control, and all other aspects of running a business.

Assistant Buyer
Learning to be a Buyer through assisting a Buyer in planning, acquiring, pricing, distributing, and promoting a category of merchandise for all stores of a division.

Group Manager
Responsible for executing merchandising plans for several departments in a store and reaching sales goals; supervises, trains, and develops sales managers.

Buyer
Responsible for planning, selecting, acquiring, pricing, distributing, and promoting merchandise for all stores of a division. With experience, buying responsibilities increase.

Merchandise Manager
Similar to Group Manager's position but with responsibility for expanded merchandise categories; coordinates the efforts among different departments; acts as major liaison between store executives and buyers.

Store Manager
Responsible for the total operation of a store, including merchandising, operations, and personnel; responsible for community relations, overall image of the store, and providing leadership in planning and goal setting.

Merchandise Administrator
responsible for conceptualizing and planning overall buying in several related merchandise classifications for a division; coordinates, develops, and evaluates the work of buyers, with responsibility for profits.

Senior Vice President for Merchandising
Responsible for developing and overseeing divisional objectives and policies in buying, merchandise planning, advertising, promotion, and systems for large sectors of the business; direct responsibility for the overall profitability of those sectors.

FIGURE 25–3

Retail management: A diversity of career paths—the R. H. Macy & Co. model (source: *Your Career Planning Workbook*, R. H. Macy & Co., Inc.)

Job Satisfaction

Many aspects of a retailing career can provide job satisfaction. Some of the aspects already mentioned are the diversity of job responsibilities, the potential for rapid advancement, the opportunity to work with people, the challenge of an ever-changing environment, and a competitive level of compensation. Others are the freedom to use one's own initiative, the quick recognition of one's abilities, and the continuous opportunities to demonstrate leadership.

The nature of the operating and merchandising activities of a retail store gives employees and managers a considerable degree of independence. For motivated individuals, the opportunity to use their own initiative in assuming responsibilities and making meaningful decisions is very rewarding and tends to promote considerable job satisfaction. For people who want the freedom to "do their thing," retailing careers provide many opportunities. Most store managers, for example, are largely responsible for "running their own show." Their responsibilities extend to all facets of the business: merchandising, operations, personnel, promotions, and finance. Retail buyers, for instance, have considerable freedom. As expressed by one department manager, "Self-actualization reaches an apex when you are a buyer."[1]

Retailing offers people ample opportunity to demonstrate their talents and abilities and have those talents and abilities recognized. Most people need feedback on their performance before they can make a judgment on how satisfied they are with their performance. Where else can an individual get a daily rating of job performance? In large retailing organizations, sales, expense, and profit figures are computed daily using electronic data processing systems for each operating unit. In smaller retailing organizations, the relative sales and profit positions of various operating units are usually known through more informal means. In either case, this timely feedback affords career-minded people the opportunity to demonstrate their abilities and to communicate their successes to their superiors who are directly responsible for career advancements.

The opportunity to assume a leadership role is a key factor in realizing job satisfaction for some individuals. The people-intensive nature of retailing offers unlimited occasions for leadership-minded people to "stand out" rather than "fit in."

Finally, job satisfaction for many people is related at least in part to the status or image of their field of endeavor within the general business community. In the past, retailing has often been viewed as occupying one of the lower rungs of the business status ladder. In recent years, however, as retailers have become a dominant force in the marketing and distribution of goods, their status within the business community has risen considerably. As one observer of the business scene writes:

> Regarding the social stigma of retailing, it seems to me that as retailing organizations have grown, the place of companies such as Sears, Jewel, K-Mart, and Federated has risen in the constellation of business organization, and as that has occurred, the stigma of being a retailer has declined. . . . as retailers have grown and competition increased, the need for analytical work is more highly recognized by retailing management than it might have been a dozen years ago. In other words, positioning the piece goods department at Bloomingdale's may require some of the same skills as positioning Tang at General Foods.[2]

Successful retailing requires the same professional skills as any other business, a fact that is now widely recognized throughout the business community.

Employment choices are among the most important decisions people make. They represent long-term commitments that have profound effects on their professional lives, personal lives, family lives, and general life-styles. Therefore, it behooves prospective employees to approach their choices of employment with the utmost preparation. The first step in planning for employment is to assess one's personal strengths and weaknesses, hopes and aspirations, as well as audit one's career goals and objectives. In other words, each prospective employee needs to make a life audit and a career audit before engaging in an employment search.

Making a Personal Assessment

The Life Audit

For some very understandable reasons, no one has your best interest at heart as much as you do. No one can know and understand you or your abilities, interests, and aspirations as well as you. Unfortunately, many individuals do not really know themselves well because they have never taken the time to stop and assess what it is they want and expect out of their lives. A **life audit** is *an attempt by individuals to seek insight into their true feelings about their own abilities and aspirations*. A form of self-analysis, it involves simply answering truthfully a series of questions centering around one's expectations of life. No prescribed set of questions is included in every life audit; however, the questions cited here are a small sampling of those suggested by Dr. Donald P. Crane as being enlightening in any self-analysis.

1. What do I do well?
2. What do I dislike doing?
3. What do I want (or need) to do better?
4. What long-term aspirations (regarding my personal life. . .) do I have?
5. What are my most positive personal traits?
6. What are my most negative personal traits?[3]

In addition, a life audit should include questions regarding family issues, personal values, general attitudes, basic beliefs, and personal goals and objectives. A life audit gives people better understanding of themselves and whether they might be successful and happy in the world of retailing.

The Career Audit

In starting and maintaining a successful career, we need to develop career plans that include necessary strategies and tactics for success. *Before developing meaningful career strategies and tactics, however, we should conduct a* **career audit**. Figure 25–4 illustrates a career audit. It identifies a set of 20 questions that many executive recruiters believe will aid in discovering oneself and one's career aspirations. These questions are not only useful in developing initial career plans, they also can serve as guidelines to help continually evaluate career assets and liabilities.

Once both a life and a career audit have been made, the final step in making a personal assessment is to identify life and career goals. To promote clarity and permit future reference, you should write these goals down and file them in a secure place. Although your life and career goals will undergo many modifications throughout your life and career, the act of specifying your goals in written form will force you to carefully assess what you want out of your life and your career.

FIGURE 25–4
Twenty questions to
ask in making a career
audit

1. Do I work better in a large or small corporation?
2. How important is geographic location to me? To my family?
3. Am I a loner, or do I work better as a member of a group?
4. Am I more comfortable following than leading?
5. Do I analyze better than I execute?
6. Am I an innovator?
7. Do I work more successfully under pressure?
8. Am I a good planner?
9. Am I a good listener?
10. Do I think well on my feet?
11. Do I express myself well orally? In writing?
12. What characteristics do I admire in others?
13. Which function of my job do I perform most effectively?
14. Which do I perform least effectively?
15. What do I enjoy doing most?
16. In the past six months, what accomplishment has most satisfied me? Which has been the most difficult?
17. What have I done to correct my shortcomings?
18. What level of responsibility do I aspire to in five years?
19. What should I be earning then?
20. How will I achieve these levels?

Source: Robert Ankerson, "Marketing a New Product," *MBA: Master In Business Administration* (October, 1975), 28.

Securing a Retail Position

Once you have completed making a personal assessment of yourself, you are then ready to proceed with *securing a retail position*—the **employment-search process.** Since employment opportunities in retailing are both numerous and varied, the strategies and tactics employed in searching for a retail position must be both systematic and comprehensive. This discussion covers the basics of identifying prospective employers, obtaining a personal interview, preparing for a personal interview, and taking a personal interview.

Identifying Prospective Employers

Prospective employer identification is a four-step process whereby the prospective employee (you) attempts to organize opportunities. The four steps include listing employment criteria, ranking employment criteria, scaling employment preferences, and matching job preferences with prospective employers.

Step 1: Listing employment criteria. In the initial stages of the employment-search process, you must determine the general conditions under which you are willing to accept a job. While the particulars of any job (e.g., salary) are determined during actual employment negotiation, you may have certain preconditions regarding employment. Some of the more common preconditions are related to location, organization, and position. For personal, professional, and many other reasons, you may prefer or need to work in a particular part of the country or in a particular state or city. Any preconditions regarding the kind of organization for which you are willing to work should also be listed. Representative organizational preconditions might include the size of the firm, the type of organization (e.g., independent vs. chain

703

organization), and the nature of the operation (e.g., department, specialty, or discount organization). Finally, a list of any preconditions regarding employment positions you are either willing or not willing to accept needs to be included. For example, you should consider your interest (or lack of interest) in accepting a position in such areas as merchandising, operations management, sales promotion, or personnel. In summary, identify any criteria you consider important to you as preconditions for employment.

Step 2: Ranking employment criteria. Typically, not all of the criteria identified in Step 1 will be of equal importance to you. Therefore, Step 2 of the prospective employer-identification process requires that you rank each of the employment criteria according to their importance. Some criteria you may judge to be extremely important or essential (e.g., for family reasons you must find a job in the greater Chicago area); others you might treat as preferences but not absolutely essential (e.g., you prefer to work in the merchandising area for a large department store). Finally, you might view other criteria as not being all that important, although, in your opinion, they are a definite plus (e.g., the opportunity to work in a particular merchandising department—women's apparel). By going through this process of ranking employment criteria, you develop a concrete means of judging employment opportunities.

Step 3: Scaling employment preferences. Your third step in identifying prospective employers is to develop a preference scale of employment opportunities. This step requires developing general job descriptions for three preference levels: first, second, and third. For example, your most-preferred job description might be an assistant manager of a women's apparel department in a major Chicago metro-area department store, preferably somewhere in the northwest part of the city. On the other end of the scale, your least-preferred job description might be the same type of job in the Milwaukee area. Once you have developed two or three general job descriptions for each of the three preference levels, you will be ready to proceed with the final stage of the employer-identification process.

Step 4: Matching job preferences with prospective employers. Now that you have listed, ranked, and scaled your employment preferences, the final step in the employer-identification process is to match those preferences with prospective employers. This matching process consists of compiling a list of jobs and screening that list of prospective employers according to your scaled preferences.

In compiling a **jobs list,** *it will be to your benefit to explore all possible sources.* Your campus placement office is the logical starting point. For many students, it represents one of the most fruitful sources for good leads for potential employment. It also provides a number of services (e.g., setting up personal interviews) that can greatly facilitate your employment-search process. By checking with your placement office frequently and regularly, you will be able to keep your jobs list updated. While your school placement service is one of your best sources, you should not limit your search by using it exclusively. You also need to develop some method for systematically checking the employment sections of local and national newspapers as well as trade and professional journals, magazines, and newspapers. In recent years, federal equal employment opportunity requirements have made these publications a good source for locating employment opportunities. Commercial employment agencies are still another source. Before making any commitments to one of these agencies, however, be sure you fully understand the services they provide and the conditions and terms under which those services are provided. You can obtain additional job leads by sending inquiries to the personnel departments of retail firms that you believe have the potential for offering the type of employment you desire. Finally, some of the best leads to employment opportunities come through personal contacts. Your professors, friends, relatives, and social and professional acquaintances often provide an inside track to such opportunities. Further, their information and support can be extremely useful in getting you on this inside track. You have probably made the effort to develop personal contacts by engaging in extracurricular activities of both a social and professional nature. If not, start immediately. It's never too late!

Screening a jobs list is a fairly routine procedure if you have carefully completed the previous step in the employment-search process—scaling employment preferences. Jobs-list screening involves (1) reducing your jobs list to employment opportunities that meet your minimum requirements for employment, and then (2) rank ordering the remaining jobs on the list according to your employment preferences. The result of this screening process is a list of available and acceptable employment opportunities, rank ordered from the most desirable to the least desirable. As your employment-search process continues, you will need to revise your list continually.

Obtaining a Personal Interview

Retailers use personal interviews as a way to question and observe job applicants in a face-to-face situation. Most retailers consider interviews essential in hiring prospective employees. For lower-echelon positions, one short interview with the store's personnel manager is usually all that is necessary for consideration for a job. By contacting the personnel department and completing an application form, qualified applicants will normally be granted a personal interview.

The personal-interview process for most managerial positions is much more involved. Typically, it involves a series of personal interviews with various managers at different levels. While it is necessary to be successful at each of these interviews, getting the *initial* interview is the most crucial step because without it nothing else happens.

Obtaining the initial interview can be quite simple or it can be extremely difficult. The method you use in getting the first interview depends on the circumstances surrounding the job (e.g., type and level of the position) and the employment practices of the firm (e.g., where and how they recruit). In obtaining the initial interview with retailing firms, you can use one of several methods. They include (1) obtaining an on-campus interview schedule from your school placement office and scheduling an interview time and place through that office, (2) contacting the store's personnel office and making arrangements for the initial interview, (3) asking personal contacts to set up a personal interview, and (4) writing brief letters and making telephone calls and personal visits to one or more of the firm's managers to discuss possible employment opportunities. If you choose to use the last method, you should expect some difficulty in getting to the right person. Your persistence can also help you to land the job you want. Also, the practice you obtain from unsuccessful attempts will improve your skills at making the right contacts. Once you have arranged a personal interview, you must carefully prepare for your interview to increase your chances for success.

Preparing for a Personal Interview

A lack of preparation is perhaps the most common error that applicants make in the personal-interview process. It is foolish for anyone to spend several years in college preparing for a career and then fail to spend several hours preparing for the key interview that could very well launch a career with the right firm. Preparing for a personal interview involves getting to know something about the firm interviewing you and helping the firm in its efforts to get to know you.

Before entering a personal interview, you should do some research on the firm. Your ability to talk knowledgeably about the firm and its activities will pay substantial dividends during the actual interview. Not only will it make a favorable impression upon the interviewer, it will allow you both to answer and ask questions within a meaningful context. Your information search on the firm should help you to discuss the firm's organizational structure, market positions, merchandising strategies, financial positions, and future prospects. Examining various trade magazines, industrial directories, and other reference books can provide a good general picture of the firm and its operations.

Helping the firm to know you involves preparing a résumé, which should include (1) a brief statement of personal data (e.g., name, address, telephone number, marital status, date of birth, health status, and physical condition); (2) a brief outline of educational experience (i.e., type of degree, name of school, date of graduation, major and minor fields of study, class ranking, scholarships, honors, awards, and extracurricular activities); (3) a short history of work experience (i.e., a list of jobs, position and responsibilities, names of employers, and dates of employment); and (4) a summary of other activities, interests, and skills that support your professional credentials. Also, you might wish to include a list of references and a short statement of your career objectives. In preparing a résumé, a number of guidelines are helpful.

1. *Be concise.* The purpose of a résumé is to stimulate the interviewer's interest and not to tell your life story. A one-page résumé is usually sufficient to create this interest. If interviewers want to know more, they will ask for more information and clarification.
2. *Be factual.* Experienced interviewers will recognize résumé "puffery" and will generally take a dim view of it. A statement of a few real accomplishments is received much more favorably than a list of artificial ones.
3. *Be professional.* A well-organized, neatly produced résumé is an excellent "scene setter" for your personal interview. A poorly organized résumé with confusing layout, typewriting errors, misspellings, and blurred or messy copying make a definite statement about your abilities to organize and to produce good work.

As a final note, you must recognize that it is your responsibility to establish and verify the time and place for each interview. Missing or being late to an interview is rarely excusable, regardless of the reason. Therefore, you should plan for unforeseen delays to ensure getting to your interview on time.

Taking a Personal Interview

The interview situation will vary considerably, depending on the interviewer's personal preferences. Some interview situations are very formal and conducted under a structured question-and-answer format. Other interview situations are very informal and conducted without any apparent structure. Figure 25–5 (pp. 708–9) outlines the typical stages and topics covered during the initial interview process. In either case, your ability to read the interview situation and to react accordingly will determine your success. No absolute rules apply in taking a personal interview, but the guidelines that follow are useful in most interview situations.

1. *Dress appropriately.* The job or position for which you are interviewing will provide you with cues on how to dress. Do not overdress or underdress for the occasion. For example, for management-level positions, you should

wear a suit or sport coat or a dress or pants suit that is stylish, yet not faddish.

2. *Be prepared for openers.* Many interviewers like to open their interviews with broad questions such as (a) "What do you expect out of life?" (b) "Why do you want to work for our firm?" (c) "Where do you want to be in your career 10 years from now?" or (d) "What do you think you can do for our company?" A list of additional questions commonly asked during the personal-interview process is shown in Figure 25–6 (pp. 709–10). Providing good answers to these questions can be difficult. However, if you have made the life and career audits suggested earlier in this chapter, you should be able to formulate interesting and informative answers to such questions.

3. *Be relaxed.* Interviewers expect a reasonable amount of nervousness. However, an undue amount of nervousness could well suggest to the interviewer that you are unable to handle pressure situations. Avoid nervous gestures. On the other hand, avoid being so relaxed or "laid back" that you give the impression of being disinterested in the interview or the job.

4. *Listen carefully.* Let the interviewer guide the interview, at least during the initial stages. Interviewers provide cues as to how they want to conduct their interview and what they want to talk about. Good listening skills are noticed by an interviewer. Also, by listening carefully you will be able to fully understand the nature of the questions asked and therefore make better responses. A source of irritation for many interviewers is an answer that does not match the question!

5. *Ask questions.* If you want a job with the interviewer's company, you should be able to show your interest by asking intelligent questions about the firm. Three or four standard questions about the company's operations are sufficient to show your interest and to allow you to make standard comparisons between various firms with which you have interviewed.

6. *Be informative.* You should answer the interviewer's questions fully and quickly, but avoid talking too much or too fast. Most of the interviewer's questions will require more than a yes or no answer. However, you should avoid telling your life story, boasting about your accomplishments, and complaining about your problems. Where appropriate, support your answers with as much factual information as possible.

7. *Be somewhat aggressive.* It is better to be perceived as a little too aggressive than too passive. Interviewers usually view a reasonable amount of aggressiveness favorably. However, the over-aggressiveness might raise questions in the interviewer's mind as to how well you might fit in and work with others. In terms of aggressiveness, the right impression to portray might be that you are a "mover," but not a "shaker."

8. *Be honest.* Answer questions as truthfully as you can. Interviewers recognize that everyone has strengths and weaknesses. A frank admission of a weakness you have adds credibility to the statements you make about your strengths. Admitting a weakness also makes you appear more trustworthy in the eyes of the interviewer. Additionally, honest answers help you to avoid making contradictory statements—a failing that is sure to make the interviewer question your professionalism, sincerity, and honesty.

Following these guidelines greatly improves one's chances for a successful interview. One last point: If you can make the interviewer feel comfortable and at ease, then you have gone a long way toward getting a second interview and possibly a position with that company.

FIGURE 25–5

Stages and topics covered during the initial interview (stages 2 and 3 are the most important parts of the interview)

Stages	Interviewer Topics	Interviewer Looks for
1. First impressions	Introduction and greeting Small talk about traffic conditions, the weather, the record of the basketball team	Firm handshake, eye contact Appearance and dress appropriate to the business, not campus, setting
2. Your record	*Education* Reasons for choice of school and major Grades: effort required for them Special areas of interest Courses enjoyed most and least, reasons Special achievements, toughest problems Value of education as career preparation Reaction to teachers High school record, SAT scores *Work Experience* Nature of jobs held Why undertaken Level of responsibility reached Duties liked most and least Supervisory experience Relations with others *Activities and Interests* Role in extracurricular, athletic, community, and social service activities Personal interests—hobbies, cultural interests, sports	Intellectual abilities Breadth and depth of knowledge Relevance of course work to career interests Special or general interest Value placed on achievement Willingness to work hard Relation between ability and achievement Reaction to authority Ability to cope with problems Sensible use of resources (time, energy, money) High energy level, vitality, enthusiasm Leadership ability; interest in responsibility Willingness to follow directions Ability to get along with others Seriousness of purpose Ability to motivate oneself, to make things happen Positive "can do" attitude Diversity of interests Awareness of world outside the laboratory Social conscience; good citizenship
3. Your career goals	Type of work desired Immediate objectives Long-term objectives Interest in this company Other companies being considered Desire for further education/training Geographical preferences and limitations Attitude toward relocation Health factors that might affect job performance	Realistic knowledge of strengths and weaknesses Preparation for employment Knowledge of opportunities Seriousness of purpose; career-oriented rather than job-oriented Knowledge of the company Real interest in the company Work interests in line with talents Company's chance to get and keep you
4. The company	Company opportunities Where you might fit Current and future projects Major divisions and departments Training programs, educational and other benefits	Informed and relevant questions Indications of interest in answers Appropriate but not undue interest in salary or benefits

FIGURE 25–5, *continued*

Stages	Interviewer Topics	Interviewer Looks for
5. Conclusion	Further steps you should take (application form, transcript, references) Further steps company will take, outline how application handled, to which departments it will be sent, time of notification of decision Cordial farewell	Candidate's attention to information as a sign of continued interest

Source: Reprinted with permission from *Peterson's Business and Management Jobs 1985,* © 1984 by Peterson's Guides, Inc., P.O. Box 2123, Princeton, New Jersey 08540. 1986 edition available at bookstores or direct from the publisher.

The Endicott Survey, published by the Placement Center of Northwestern University, periodically updates its original list of questions most commonly asked of college graduates at interviews. Variations of that list have appeared in many publications.

1. What are your long-range and short-range goals and objectives, when and why did you establish these goals, and how are you preparing yourself to achieve them?
2. What specific goals, other than those related to your occupation, have you established for yourself for the next 10 years?
3. What do you see yourself doing five years from now?
4. What do you really want to do in life?
5. What are your long-range career objectives?
6. How do you plan to achieve your career goals?
7. What are the most important rewards you expect in your career?
8. What do you expect to be earning in five years?
9. Why did you choose the career for which you are preparing?
10. Which is more important to you, the money or the type of job?
11. What do you consider to be your greatest strengths and weaknesses?
12. How would you describe yourself?
13. How do you think a friend or a professor who knows you well would describe you?
14. What motivates you to put forth your greatest effort?
15. How has your education prepared you for a career?
16. Why should I hire you?
17. What qualifications do you have that make you think that you will be successful?
18. How do you determine or evaluate success?
19. What do you think it takes to be successful in a company like ours?
20. In what ways do you think you can make a contribution to our company?
21. What qualities should a successful manager possess?
22. Describe the relationship that should exist between a supervisor and subordinates.
23. What two or three accomplishments have given you the most satisfaction? Why?

FIGURE 25–6

Fifty questions most commonly asked at interviews

709

FIGURE 25-6,
continued

24. Describe your most rewarding college experience.
25. If you were hiring a graduate for this position, what qualities would you look for?
26. Why did you select your college or university?
27. What led you to choose your field of major study?
28. What academic subjects did you like best? Least?
29. Do you enjoy doing independent research?
30. If you could do so, would you plan your academic study differently?
31. What changes would you make in your college or university?
32. Do you think that your grades are a good indication of your academic achievement?
33. What have you learned from participation in extracurricular activities?
34. Do you have plans for continued study? (Graduate students may be asked: Why did you decide to pursue an advanced degree?)
35. In what kind of work environment are you most comfortable?
36. How do you work under pressure?
37. In what part-time or summer jobs have you been most interested? Why?
38. How would you describe the ideal job for you following graduation?
39. Why did you decide to seek a position with this company?
40. What do you know about our company?
41. What two or three things are most important to you in your job?
42. Are you seeking employment in a company of a certain size? Why?
43. What criteria are you using to evaluate the company for which you hope to work?
44. Do you have a geographical preference? Why?
45. Will you relocate? Does relocation bother you?
46. Are you willing to travel?
47. Are you willing to spend at least six months as a trainee?
48. Why do you think you might like to live in the community in which our company is located?
49. What major problem have you encountered and how did you deal with it?
50. What have you learned from your mistakes?

Source: Reprinted with permission from *Peterson's Business and Management Jobs, 1985,* © 1984 by Peterson's Guides, Inc., P.O. Box 2123, Princeton, New Jersey 08540. 1986 edition available at bookstores or direct from the publisher.

OWNERSHIP OPPORTUNITIES

Regardless of their income, many people who work for others live a hand-to-mouth, paycheck-to-paycheck existence. According to one old adage, the only way to get ahead is to get other people to work for you or to get money working for you. The basic idea expressed in this saying is that income and perhaps job satisfaction are limited when you work for someone else. To many people, self-employment is the answer to a better income, more independence, a more rewarding career, and an improved life-style. Many people think that going into business for themselves is the only way they can fully realize their hopes and aspirations. These individuals are willing to assume the considerable burdens and risks of owning and operating their own businesses to have a chance at realizing their personal, career, and life goals.

The 24 preceding chapters have fully discussed the factors necessary for a successful retail operation. With that background in mind, consider the question of whether *you* are the kind of person who could succeed as an independent retailer. To help answer this question we offer a self-evaluation test, Figure 25-7 (pp. 711-12), that should provide you with some insight into whether you have the personal attributes to become an independent retailer.

If, after having taken the self-evaluation test (see Figure 25–7), you decide that you have what it takes to be an independent retailer, three options are open to you: (1) start a new business, (2) buy an existing business, and (3) secure a franchise. Each option has its advantages and disadvantages, which you should fully explore. To aid you, Figure 25–8 (pp. 712–13) compares the issues surrounding the decision to start a new business or buy an existing one. The principal concerns associated with securing a franchise are outlined in Figure 25–9 (pp. 713–14).

FIGURE 25–7
Do you have what it takes to be an independent retailer?

Under each question, check the answer that says what you feel or comes closest to it. Be honest with yourself.

Are you a self-starter?
- ☐ I do things on my own. Nobody has to tell me to get going.
- ☐ If someone gets me started, I keep going all right.
- ☐ Easy does it, man. I don't put myself out until I have to.

How do you feel about other people?
- ☐ I like people. I can get along with just about anybody.
- ☐ I have plenty of friends—I don't need anyone else.
- ☐ Most people bug me.

Can you lead others?
- ☐ I can get most people to go along when I start something.
- ☐ I can give the orders if someone tells me what we should do.
- ☐ I let someone else get things moving. Then I go along if I feel like it.

Can you take responsibility?
- ☐ I like to take charge of things and see them through.
- ☐ I'll take over if I have to, but I'd rather let someone else be responsible.
- ☐ There's always some eager beaver around wanting to show how smart he is. I say let him.

How good an organizer are you?
- ☐ I like to have a plan before I start. I'm usually the one to get things lined up when the gang wants to do something.
- ☐ I do all right unless things get too goofed up. Then I cop out.
- ☐ You get all set and then something comes along and blows the whole bag. So I just take things as they come.

How good a worker are you?
- ☐ I can keep going as long as I need to. I don't mind working hard for something I want.
- ☐ I'll work hard for a while, but when I've had enough, that's it, man!
- ☐ I can't see that hard work gets you anywhere.

Can you make decisions?
- ☐ I can make up my mind in a hurry if I have to. It usually turns out O.K., too.
- ☐ I can if I have plenty of time. If I have to make up my mind fast, I think later I should have decided the other way.
- ☐ I don't like to be the one who has to decide things. I'd probably blow it.

Can people trust what you say?
- ☐ You bet they can. I don't say things I don't mean.
- ☐ I try to be on the level most of the time, but sometimes I just say what's easiest.
- ☐ What's the sweat if the other fellow doesn't know the difference?

FIGURE 25–7,
continued

Can you stick with it?
☐ If I make up my mind to do something, I don't let *anything* stop me.
☐ I usually finish what I start—if it doesn't get fouled up.
☐ If it doesn't go right away, I turn off. Why beat your brains out?

How good is your health?
☐ Man, I *never* run down!
☐ I have enough energy for most things I want to do.
☐ I run out of juice sooner than most of my friends seem to.

Now count the checks you made.
How many checks are there beside the *first* answer to each question? _____
How many checks are there beside the *second* answer to each question? _____
How many checks are there beside the *third* answer to each question? _____

     If most of your checks are beside the first answer, you probably have what it takes to run a business. If not, you're likely to have more trouble than you can handle by yourself. Better find a partner who is strong on the points you're weak on. If many checks are beside the third answer, not even a good partner will be able to shore you up.

Source: *Checklist for Going into Business,* Small Marketers Aids No. 71, Small Business Administration (October, 1976), 4–5.

FIGURE 25–8
To start or buy?

     Should I start my own business from scratch or should I purchase an existing business? These are the two alternatives facing the potential small business manager. If the business is started fresh, there are these advantages:

1. You can create a business in your own image. The business is not a made-over version of someone else's place, but it is formed the way you think it should be.
2. You do not run the risk of purchasing a business with a poor reputation that you would inherit.
3. The concept you have for the business is so unusual that only a new business is possible.

     The creation of a new business also has some substantial drawbacks. Some of the disadvantages include:

1. Too small a market for your product or service.
2. High cost of new equipment.
3. Lack of a source of advice on how things are done and who can be trusted.
4. Lack of name recognition. It may take a long time to persuade customers to give your business a try.

     Buying an existing business also has advantages and disadvantages. The major advantages are:

1. A successful business may provide the buyer with an immediate source of income.
2. An existing business may already be in the best location.
3. An existing business already has employees who are trained and suppliers who have established ties to the business.
4. Equipment is already installed and the productive capacity of the business is known.
5. Inventories are in place, and suppliers have extended trade credit which can be continued.
6. There is no loss of momentum. The business is already operating.
7. You have the opportunity to obtain advice and counsel from the previous owner.
8. Often, you can purchase the business you want at a price much lower than the cost of starting the same business from scratch.

Purchasing an existing business can have some real drawbacks, such as the following:

1. You can be misled, and end up with a business that is a "dog."
2. The business could have been so poorly managed by the previous owner that you inherit a great deal of ill will.
3. A poorly managed business may have employees who are unsuited to the business or poorly trained.
4. The location of the business may have become, or is becoming, unsuitable.
5. The equipment may have been poorly maintained or even be obsolete.
6. Change can be difficult to introduce in an established business.
7. Inventory may be out of date, damaged, or obsolete.
8. You can pay too much for the business.

To avoid buying a business that cannot be made profitable, investigate six critical areas:

1. Why does the owner wish to sell? Look for the real reason and do not simply accept what you are told.
2. Determine the physical condition of the business. Consider the building and its location.
3. Conduct a thorough analysis of the market for your products or services. Who are your present and potential customers? You cannot know too much about your customers. Conduct an equally thorough analysis of your competitors, both direct and indirect. How do they operate and why do customers prefer them?
4. Consider all of the legal factors which might constrain the expansion and growth of the business. Become familiar with zoning restrictions.
5. Identify the actual owner of the business and all liens that might exist.
6. Using the material covered in previous chapters, analyze the financial condition of the business.

The business can be evaluated on the basis of its assets, its future earnings, or a combination of both. Don't confuse the value of a business with its price. Price is determined through negotiation. The bargaining zone represents that area within which agreement can be reached.

Source: Norman M. Scarborough and Thomas W. Zimmerer, *Effective Small Business Management* (Columbus: Charles E. Merrill Publishing Co., 1984), 130–31.

The Franchisor and the Franchise

1. Is the potential market for the product or service adequate to support your franchise? Will the prices you charge be in line with the market?
2. Is the market's population growing, remaining static, or shrinking? Is the demand for your product or service growing, remaining static, or shrinking?
3. Is the product or service safe and reputable?
4. What will the competition, direct or indirect, be in your sales territory? Do any other franchisees operate in this general area?
5. Is the franchise international, national, regional, or local in scope? Does it involve full- or part-time involvement?
6. How many years has the franchisor been in operation? Does it have a sound reputation for honest dealings with franchisees?
7. How many franchise outlets now exist? How many will there be a year from now? How many outlets are company-owned?
8. How many franchisees have failed? Why?
9. What services and assistance will the franchisor provide? Training programs? Advertising assistance? Financial aid? Are these one-time programs or are they continuous in nature?
10. Will the firm perform a location analysis to help you find a suitable site?

FIGURE 25–9

A retail franchise: Is it for you?

FIGURE 25–9,
continued

11. Will the franchisor offer you exclusive distribution rights for the length of the agreement, or may it sell to other franchises in this area?

12. What facilities and equipment are required for the franchise? Who pays for construction? Is there a lease agreement?

13. What is the total cost of the franchise? What are the initial capital requirements? Will the franchisor provide financial assistance? Of what nature? What is the interest rate? Is the franchisor financially sound enough to fulfill all its promises?

14. How much is the franchise fee? **Exactly** what does it cover? Are there any continuing fees? What additional fees are there?

15. Does the franchisor provide an estimate of expenses and income? Are they reasonable for your particular area? Are they sufficiently documented?

16. Does the franchisor offer a written contract which covers all the details of the agreement? Have your attorney and your accountant studied its terms and approved it? Do **you** understand the implications of the contract?

17. What is the length of the franchise agreement? Under what circumstances can it be terminated? If you terminate the contract, what are the costs to you? What are the terms and costs of renewal?

18. Are you allowed to sell the franchise to a third party? If so, will you receive the proceeds?

19. Is there a national advertising program? How is it financed? What media are used? What help is provided for local advertising?

The Franchisee—You

20. Are you qualified to operate a franchise successfully? Do you have adequate drive, skills, experience, education, patience, and financial capacity? Are you prepared to work hard?

21. Are you willing to sacrifice some autonomy in operating a business to own a franchise?

22. Can you tolerate the financial risk?

23. Are you genuinely interested in the product or service you will be selling?

24. Has the franchisor investigated your background thoroughly enough to decide you are qualified to operate the franchise?

25. What can this franchisor do for you that you cannot do for yourself?

Source: Norman M. Scarborough and Thomas W. Zimmerer, *Effective Small Business Management* (Columbus: Charles E. Merrill Publishing Co., 1984), 101–2.

SUMMARY

Successful retailers have a "mind for marketing." They like people and enjoy working with them; they understand the risks associated with any business enterprise and are willing to assume those risks; they are challenged by problems and enjoy solving them; and they are willing to make decisions and to accept the responsibility that goes with making them. These people-pleasing, risk-taking, problem-solving, and decision-making personality traits are best summed up in the skills of the retail entrepreneur.

Figure 25–1 provided insight into some of the indicators of entrepreneurial attitudes (Author's note: The best answers to these questions are (1) c, (2) b, (3) c, (4) a, (5) a, (6) c, (7) a, (8) c, (9) a, (10) c, (11) c, (12) a, (13) b, and (14) c. Score one point for each correct answer. Questions 1, 2, 3, 7, 9, and 12 suggest whether you are a realistic problem solver who can run a business without constant help from others. Questions 5, 6, and 8 probe whether you take calculated risks and seek information before you act. Questions 4, 10, 13, and 14 show whether you, like the classic entrepreneur, find other people satisfying when they help fulfill your need to win. Question 11 reveals whether you take responsibility for your destiny—and your business. If you score between 11 and 14 points, you could have a good chance to succeed. If you score from 7 to 10 points, you'd better have a superb business idea or a lot of money to help you out. If you score 7 or less, stay where you are.[4])

The employment aspects of a retailing career involve (1) above-average employment security; (2) competitive compensation in managerial positions and below-average compensation in lower-echelon positions; (3) a variety of work assignments; (4) pleasant work environment; (5) opportunities for rapid advancement; and (6) the satisfaction of using one's own initiative, the quick recognition of one's abilities, and the opportunity to demonstrate leadership. In sum, retailing is a field offering each individual the opportunity to achieve his or her potential within a stimulating and enjoyable work environment.

Employment opportunities in retailing are both numerous and diverse. However, finding a retail position requires preparation and planning. Prior to the employment-search process, each individual needs to make a personal assessment, a life and career audit. These audits are useful in identifying personal and professional strengths and weaknesses as well as clarifying one's hopes and aspirations. The audits also provide direction for developing personal and professional goals and objectives.

The employment-search process consists of identifying prospective employers and obtaining, preparing for, and taking personal interviews. To identify possible employers, prospective employees should list and then rank their employment criteria, scale their employment preferences, and match their job preferences with prospective employers.

A number of methods are used in getting a personal interview. They include contacting either the school placement office or the store's personnel office, using personal contacts to set up interviews, and writing letters and making phone calls or personal visits to the appropriate store managers. Prior to taking an interview, the applicant should prepare a résumé and conduct research on the firm granting the interview.

Finally, common sense is the best rule for taking a personal interview. There are, however, several guidelines that are useful when taking an interview. Dress appropriately, be prepared for openers, be relaxed, listen carefully, ask questions, be informative, be somewhat aggressive, and be honest.

Thousands of people each year start a retail business, hoping to realize personal and professional goals that cannot be achieved by working for someone else. Some people have what it takes to own and operate their own business successfully, whereas others probably do not. Figure 25–9 is a self-evaluation test that provides some insight into whether an individual has what it takes. (If you have not already taken the test, do so now.) Your instructor can guide discussion on the answers you have given and provide insights into your probable success at operating a business of your own.

715

KEY TERMS AND CONCEPTS

people pleaser	entrepreneur	employment criteria
risk taker	life audit	employment preferences
problem solver	career audit	jobs list
decision maker	employment-search process	personal-interview process

REVIEW QUESTIONS

1. What are the essential attributes of a successful marketing mind?
2. What are the characteristics of a people pleaser?
3. Describe the factors that account for the relatively high level of job security within the retail-management field.
4. Why might a retailing career be described in terms of the old adage "variety is the spice of life"?
5. Why are there numerous opportunities for rapid career advancement in the field of retailing?
6. What is a life audit?
7. Describe briefly the four steps in identifying prospective employers.
8. What are the various options open to the prospective employee in obtaining an initial interview with a retail firm?
9. What information should be included on your résumé?
10. What are the eight guidelines to be followed when taking a personal interview?
11. What are the advantages and disadvantages of starting your own business from scratch?

ENDNOTES

1. Andres Mann, "Inside Federated Department Stores," *MBA* (November, 1974), 54.
2. Jonathan Maslow, "The Case for Retailing," *MBA* (December, 1974), 40.
3. Donald P. Crane, "An Experimental Program in Career Planning," *Collegiate News and Views* 30 (Winter, 1976): 6.
4. Marlys Harris, "The Entrepreneur—Do You Have What It Takes?" *Money,* March, 1978, 52.

RELATED READINGS

Cohen, William A. "A Tentative Model for Student Self-Marketing." *1985 AMA Educators' Proceedings.* R. F. Lusch et al, eds. (American Marketing Association 1985), 110–13.

Donaghy, William C. *The Interview—Skills and Applications.* (Glenview, Ill.: Scott, Foresman & Company, 1984)

Einhorn, Lois J.; Bradley, Patricia H.; and Baird, John E. *Effective Employment Interviewing—Unlocking Human Potential.* (Glenview, Ill.: Scott, Foresman & Company, 1982)

Frisbie, Gil A., and Petroshius, Susan M. "Career Perceptions and Influencing Factors on Business Students' Choice of Major." *1985 AMA Educators' Proceedings.* R. F. Lusch et al, eds. (American Marketing Association 1985), 99–104.

Gaedeke, Ralph, and Tootelian, Dennis. *Small Business Management.* (Glenview, Ill.: Scott, Foresman & Company, 1984)

Goldgehn, Leslie A., and Soares, Eric. "Marketing Our Students: An Emphasis on Communication Skills." *1985 AMA Educators' Proceedings.* R. F. Lusch et al, eds. (American Marketing Association 1985), 105–9.

Levitt, Julie G. *Your Career: How to Make It Happen.* (Cincinnati: South-Western Publishing Co., 1985)

Olm, Kenneth, and Eddy, George G. *Entrepreneurship and Venture Management.* (Columbus: Charles E. Merrill Publishing Co., 1985)

Stevenson, Howard H.; Roberts, Michael J.; and Grousbeck, H. Irving. *New Business Ventures and the Entrepreneurs,* 2nd ed. (Homewood, Ill.: Richard D. Irwin, 1985)

CASES

CASE 1

Ray's Super

Jeffrey Dilts, The University of Akron

BACKGROUND

"We can't make money on groceries," Ray Henry said, reacting to the recent price war that had turned the grocery business upside down. Henry is a manager of a moderate-size (20,000 square feet) supermarket operation located in a middle- to upper-income suburban area of the community. Until recently, the operation had managed to generate a reasonable return. New competition had begun to squeeze profits, however.

The area's economy was recovering from a recession that had reduced the population by seven percent due to job layoffs. Decreased volume placed greater importance on price competition. "Almost every trick of the trade was employed," Henry said, "including double and triple coupon redemptions." As a result, increases in area food prices were substantially below the national norm.

In the face of high labor costs, grocery chains attempted to negotiate wage concessions to improve profitability. Unsuccessful in this endeavor, National Groceries pulled out of the market, closing eight stores—including three large-scale super stores that had opened during the past two years.

Sav-More, a regional grocery wholesale operation, responded by opening three of the former National super stores and converting five of its existing area stores to a super discount warehouse format. An "Every Day Low Prices" policy on all items replaced weekly specials and double- and triple-coupon promotions. Sav-More advertising claimed price cuts on approximately 8,000 items, with the biggest cuts in packaged foods and paper goods.

Competitors, for the most part, responded in kind by cutting prices across the board. Overnight, the cost of a basket of 30 commonly purchased items had been reduced by an average of $7.89 in a majority of area stores.

CURRENT SITUATION

Very concerned with the turn of events, Henry noted that, "If this continues, I won't be able to stay in business." He suspected that the average purchase made in his store had declined, due largely to a reduction in volume for packaged goods. Revenues generated by perimeter departments, such as the deli and produce, appeared to be maintaining their previous levels.

Henry was not at a loss for alternatives; his personnel had recommended various solutions. He had to determine which action would help maintain customer patronage and build sales.

Mike Walle, assistant manager and part owner, had suggested an immediate price cut across the board to regain volume. Alf Dunlap, produce manager, disagreed because he thought such action would adversely affect profitability. Based on his previous management experience with a national chain, Dunlap argued that the size of the present store was not sufficient to generate the volumes necessary to be profitable at the lower margins suggested. Alternatively, he recommended that the operation build upon its strengths in perishables and personal service.

Ray Nader, head butcher, agreed that the operation could differentiate itself from competitors by employing service departments. "The main attraction of warehouse operations is price, not service," he commented. Accordingly, he recommended expanding the service areas to include a specialty fish department, based on customer suggestions. "The margin on specialty items and perishables can make up for the volume lost on low-margin packaged groceries," Nader pointed out.

ASSIGNMENT

☐ Evaluate the alternatives described in this situation. Under what conditions would one alternative be more appropriate than another?

☐ What action would you recommend that Ray Henry take? Explain.

CASE 2

Aubrey Creations, Inc.

Jon Hawes, The University of Akron

BACKGROUND

Aubrey Creations, founded in 1978, sells a line of fashion jewelry (most items under $50) through the party-plan method. To attract a base of customers who are more likely to make repeat purchases, Aubrey McDonald developed an extensive line of exceptionally high-quality skin-care products. The Aubrey Beauty Collection was introduced in 1981. Prices currently range from as low as $1.95 for a single item to $111.75 for the Total Look Collection.

Total revenues for Aubrey Creations during the last year were under $10 million. Operations have been almost entirely limited to the United States and approximately 2,000 sales consultants were involved in selling these products through the party-plan method. The company recently increased its recruitment efforts for sales consultants. Many of the leading members of this industry belong to the Direct Selling Association, a trade organization that (among other activities) enforces a strict code of ethical business conduct. Aubrey Creations, Inc. is a very active member of this organization.

CURRENT SITUATION

Aubrey McDonald, founder and CEO of Aubrey Creations, has "an opportunity." As for all firms in the direct-selling industry, sales revenues for Aubrey Creations tend to flatten when the economy picks up. Recent improvements in the economy have created this "opportunity" and Aubrey is searching for ways to overcome this recent decline in sales.

There is a very simple explanation for the inverse relationship between sales revenues of firms in the direct-selling industry and GNP. More than in any other field, business in the direct-selling industry depends upon the number and the intensity levels of salespeople. Few customers actively search for the products of direct-selling companies. These types of sales often require a great deal of personal selling effort to *persuade* people

to make a purchase. Consequently, when a direct-selling organization's sales force is reduced in number and/or the existing sales force becomes less active, revenues usually decline.

During periods of reduced overall economic activity, the sales forces of direct-selling companies often grow dramatically as people attempt to supplement family income by working in this field. When the economy improves, however, people often return to full-time employment in other industries or reduce the intensity of their sales efforts in direct-selling organizations.

At Aubrey, sales consultants arrange with hosts to sponsor parties in their homes. The host receives free products for encouraging 10–15 friends to attend the party, often referred to as the "show" or "booking." Sales consultants seldom attempt to sell both the jewelry and skin-care product lines at a particular party. The central event of a skin-care booking involves a complete makeover (at no charge) for one of the guests.

Besides selling products, sales consultants are also involved in building a sales organization. They recruit people to work in their sales organization and receive a commission for all of the sales made by these recruits.

Sales consultants earn income based on the level of their sales and the sales of their recruits. Incomes vary widely, but a few consultants made over $100,000 in 1985. In addition, Aubrey Creations sponsors several incentive programs to reward sales consultants who reach a certain level of sales. The top prize is a new Cadillac. Many other rewards, incentives, contests, and recognition are also provided. The highlight of each year is a national conference.

ASSIGNMENT

☐ Outline a plan of action to minimize the negative sales effects of an improving economic climate for Aubrey Creations.

Tri-State Audio-Video

Joseph McCafferty, The University of Akron

BACKGROUND

Brett Barta, owner and operator of Tri-State Audio-Video, has enjoyed considerable success as an independent retailer of consumer electronics. The mainstay of Tri-State's product mix has been high-quality stereos and television sets. Using value (quality products at reasonable prices) as the principal merchandising strategy, Barta has expanded his operation to include four outlets in the tri-state market area: two stores in south-central Michigan and two stores in northeast Indiana. Current expansion plans include opening new Tri-State Audio-Video outlets in northwest Ohio.

CURRENT SITUATION

Barta has a 10 o'clock appointment with his attorney, K. L. Kovach. A number of issues have surfaced recently that necessitated some sound legal advice. Of primary concern to Barta is his potential liability stemming from manufacturers' warranties; in other words, he wants to determine his responsibility under the Magnuson-Moss Warranty Act. Currently, Tri-State offers no warranties on any items sold. With manufacturers' warranties, Tri-State acts strictly as an intermediary between its customers and the producer. When a customer buys a product from Tri-State and brings it back within the time period allowed by the manufacturer's warranty, Barta's policy is to make sure the product gets back to the manufacturer and to make sure the customer is satisfied with whatever adjustment the manufacturer makes. To date, Barta has never been asked to refund a customer's money because the manufacturer was unable to repair or refused to replace the defective product. Upon reflection, this liability issue has never been much of a problem in the past because he had always dealt with well-known manufacturers that have a quality reputation to protect.

Today's visit concerns Barta's plans to sell compact disk players, one of the hottest items on the market. His new concern with warranty liability arose because none of his current suppliers market a compact disk player and the only available supplier is a relatively new company called Compact Disk Corporation (CDC). CDC has offered Barta an exclusive dealership for the tri-state area. Barta is worried over a recent article in a west coast newspaper citing various problems consumers are having with CDC's products and CDC's inability to provide quick and satisfactory repairs.

To facilitate the discussion with his lawyer, Barta brought along all of the literature he had received from CDC. Of particular interest was the CDC warranty statement. As described in the literature, CDC offered a "Full 90 Day Warranty," which guarantees the CDC compact disk player will not have defects in materials or workmanship for 90 days from date of original purchase. CDC will repair or replace the defective part free of charge if the defective product is delivered prepaid to CDC Service Division, 435 Johns Ave, Surfside, California. The full warranty statement also included a clause stating that CDC will not be responsible for any "consequential or incidental" damages. In addition to the full warranty, CDC also offers a "limited warranty" on defects in the product's turntable. This warranty simply states that coverage begins 90 days after the original purchase and lasts for one year after original purchase. It also states that no "consequential or incidental" damages are recoverable from the manufacturer under this warranty. To benefit from the warranty, the customer had to send the turntable to the manufacturer in California. The last paragraph in CDC's warranty states that after 90 days from purchase, there are no implied warranties of merchantability or fitness. After a brief discussion, Kovach advised Barta not to sign any contract with CDC until he received Kovach's written assessment of Tri-State's liability exposure.

ASSIGNMENT

☐ Assume the role of K. L. Kovach. What possible role could state laws play in determining the applicability of consumer warranties in light of the Magnuson-Moss Warranty Act? What parts of CDC's warranty would be disallowed by the Magnuson-Moss Warranty Act and what might be Barta's potential liability under this warranty? Prepare a written report.

Is It Bait and Switch—Or Is It Trading Up?

Joseph McCafferty, The University of Akron

BACKGROUND

The morning edition of the *Cleveland Gazette* carried two sales advertisements featuring special promotions on color television sets. Prough Home Centers, a chain of home appliance stores with 84 outlets in 14 states, ran an advertisement featuring repossessed color televisions (see Figure 1). The second advertisement (see Figure 2) was placed by The World of Entertainment, a specialty electronics store chain with outlets in eight states; it featured deep discounting of new, brand-name color televisions.

CURRENT SITUATION

The Johnsons' Experience

Dave and Carol Johnson, a newly wed couple, had been holding off purchasing a new color television until the right sale came along. The Prough Home Center ad caught Dave's attention. The price of $99.95 seemed almost to good to be true. Since the Johnson's lived only six blocks from the nearest outlet, they decided to check out what specific items were available. While Carol reminded Dave that the advertisement did specify "repossessed" color televisions, Dave dismissed Carol's comment, saying "At $99.95, who cares! So long as we can get a couple of good years of trouble-free service out of it, I'll be happy."

Upon entering the store, the Johnsons were met by Kathy O'Brian, a top performer in the store's sales department. Dave told O'Brian they had seen Prough's newspaper advertisement and expressed an interest in seeing which sets were available. Kathy informed the Johnsons that although the used sets were in good working order, many of the models had nicks and scratches and the lower-priced sets were generally

---

PROUGH HOME CENTERS
"The Professionals In Home Appliances"
Saturday Only
Repossessed, Repaired, Resold
COLOR TELEVISIONS
At Rock Bottom Prices
Starting at $99.95
LIKE NEW

FIGURE 1

THE WORLD OF ENTERTAINMENT
Proudly Presents
NEW, NAME BRAND, FAMILY SIZE
COLOR TELEVISIONS
$279.95
"We Buy Straight From The Factory"
DON'T MISS THIS DEAL
SALE ENDS SOON

FIGURE 2

---

smaller portable models with even more wear and tear. To support her statement, Kathy explained that the set advertised for $99.95 was a 12-inch, two-year-old model. Dave replied that he expected as much but would still like to see the selection of used sets.

As they started to the back of the store where the used sets were on display, O'Brian stopped them at a 14-inch Sony with remote control. "You know," she said, "this is the best set in the store. It's also the best value. This color portable comes complete with remote control and automatic tuning. The regular price on this Sony is $499 but it is currently on sale for $399, terms are 90 days same as cash. In addition, Sony has a great limited warranty, so you would not have to worry about any major repair bills. I really think this set offers excellent value. You really should consider taking advantage of this offer." As a commissioned salesperson, Kathy stood to benefit financially from the sale of a more expensive set.

"We really would like to look at the used sets if we could," Dave said.

"Sure," O'Brian replied. "I just wanted to show you an opportunity to make a real value purchase. Personally, I feel the smart buy is a new set because there is very little risk with such a purchase."

"What risk?" Carol asked.

"Well, as you would expect, the manufacturer's warranties are no longer in force on the used sets," O'Brian replied. "And the store's guarantee is limited to 30 days." Seeing that this final clincher had sold the Johnsons, O'Brian hurriedly started writing up the sales contract on the new Sony.

The Criss' Experience

The same day across town, Betty Criss was skimming the *Cleveland Gazette*. The sales promotion advertisement by The World of Entertainment caught Betty's eye.

Betty and her husband, Dick, had been watching television on a portable set for a long time and she thought the time had come to get a big 24-inch console television. When Betty saw The World's offer of "family size" color televisions for "$279.95" she knew that the time to buy a new color television had come. Dick Criss expressed some concern about this "almost too good to be true deal" but agreed to accompany Betty to the local outlet in Leipply Square.

Betty walked confidently into The World of Entertainment that night and expressed her interest in the color television console she had seen advertised. Bob Sproat, department manager, led Betty and Dick to a 19-inch color portable. "This is it! This is as family size as you can get," Sproat said. "We've been having trouble with the picture on this one all day, so let's see if I can get one in for you now."

Much to Sproat's delight, Betty's face shriveled at the sight of this family size portable. The truth was that The World of Entertainment had none of these sets in stock at the moment and the earliest Sproat could get one with an immediate order was 60 days, if he was lucky. He sensed an excellent opportunity to unload one of the many big console sets in stock. "This portable set has a very limited manufacturer's warranty and the store's guarantee is limited to 30 days. You've already seen the tough time I've had getting a clear picture. This particular model has already given us nothing but trouble. I doubt that it would last more than a couple of years, if that long."

Sproat stepped around the set on sale to a big color console on display in an adjacent setting. Betty's face lit up. Bob kicked his sales pitch into high gear. "Look at this beautiful console. It's got a great finish and would complement the decor of any home. The manufacturer's warranty is excellent and we have a full service department to support the warranty. It's a bit more in price than the one on sale, but look at how much more you're getting. At this price, I think we can even throw in a remote control. Personally, I would hate to see you get stuck with that other trouble maker when I can let you walk out of here today with this set." After extolling all of the big console's virtues, Sproat tried once again to get a clear picture on the portable, but without success.

As Betty and Dick stared at the fuzzy picture, Bob whipped out a sales contract and started filling in the necessary information. Within 20 minutes, Betty and Dick were driving home with a new 24-inch console in the back of the station wagon. "I thought he said he would deliver this thing," Dick said. "For $625.95 you would think he would at least have it delivered."

"He would have," Betty replied, "but they wouldn't be able to deliver it until the end of next week."

ASSIGNMENT

☐ Discuss the legal implications concerning the two sales experiences. What remedies might each family attempt, if any?

☐ Discuss the moral and ethical implications of the advertising and selling techniques employed by each retailer. Look at the transaction from both sides. Do retailers and consumers really deal at arm's length (with equal knowledge of the product and its value)?

CASE 5

The Family Shoe Shop

Dale M. Lewison, The University of Akron

BACKGROUND

The Family Shoe Shop is an independently owned and operated shoe store located in a large regional shopping center. R. P. Evans, the proprietor, has organized the store around three departments: 1,800 square feet of selling space are devoted to men's shoes, 1,600 square feet for women's shoes, and 1,200 square feet for the children's department.

CURRENT SITUATION

Each year Evans faces the task of completing the store's annual income statement. With this year's gross sales totaling $250,000, Evans hopes that he will end the year with a greater operating profit than last year's $39,800. An examination of the current year's sales records shows that it took 8,450 sales transactions and an average investment in inventory of $88,000 to generate the

$250,000 figure. Further examination of various records provides Evans with the following information: (1) the store opened the year with $48,000 of inventory; (2) the beginning inventory was supplemented throughout the year by net purchases of $112,000; (3) the year ended with an inventory on hand conservatively valued at $36,000; (4) workroom costs of $1,000 were incurred in getting the products ready for sale, and $4,000 was spent on transportation charges in getting the products to the store; and (5) the store earned a $2,000 cash discount by paying for the goods as soon as the invoice was received.

One figure that greatly disturbed Evans was the $1,100 in goods returned by customers. In addition, he had to make allowances totaling $250 for damaged merchandise.

Another of Evans' major concerns is operating expenses. After a concerted effort to control this year's operating expenses, he hopes that a lower expense figure will substantially improve his profit picture. Records kept by natural divisions reveal the following expenses:

Payroll	$26,000
Advertising	3,000
Taxes	1,700
Supplies	900

Services purchased	$ 500
Unclassified	100
Travel	350
Communications	550
Insurance	2,600
Pensions	1,100
Depreciation	1,450
Professional services	3,500
Donations	250
Bad debts	400
Equipment	600
Real property rentals	36,000

In addition to these operating expenses, Evans is very concerned about the $2,500 interest payments to the First Republic Bank. Something will have to be done to reduce the principal on that business loan. If nothing else works out, at least the income from the candy machine increased 100% from $75 last year to $150 this year.

ASSIGNMENT

☐ Given the information in the case, lend Evans a hand by developing a complete income statement.

CASE 6

Diamond Jim's

J. B. Wilkinson, The University of Akron

BACKGROUND

The recent acquisition of Diamond Jim's by Merchandise Amalgamated had thrown the jewelry store into a state of turmoil. Before the acquisition, Diamond Jim's had been an independent jewelry store owned and operated by Jim Weatherbee, who promptly retired after the transition period. As part of a retail conglomerate, the new management of Diamond Jim's was involved in preparing the jewelry store's first strategic plan. A situation analysis had been requested by the planning staff at Merchandise Amalgamated for the purpose of negotiating Diamond Jim's strategic role in the Merchandise Amalgamated "portfolio" and specifying objectives. The next phase would be strategy formulation.

According to the strategic format, a situation analysis identifies internal and external (environmental) constraints that must be considered in making strategic choices for an SBU (strategic business unit). An overall assessment of the firm's strengths and weaknesses must be included in the analysis of internal constraints. Merchandise Amalgamated considered financial strength and performance to be necessary components of this assessment. Competitive comparisons were encouraged.

CURRENT SITUATION

Allison Green, newly appointed assistant manager of Diamond Jim's, had assembled data from Jewelers of America, Inc., to compare the financial performance of Diamond Jim's to "high-performance" jewelry stores (Figures 1–3). Her assignment was to identify financial strengths and weaknesses of Diamond Jim's as well as to pinpoint performance problems. Although this type of analysis was only a small component of the situation analysis, it was thought to be an important consideration when formulating the retail strategy.

	Diamond Jim's	High-performance Jeweler
Net sales	100.0%	100.0%
Cost of sales	51.1	44.0
Gross profit	48.9	56.0
Operating expenses		
Payroll	24.9	28.1
Occupancy	6.0	7.0
Promotion	4.8	6.1
All other	9.9	8.5
Total operating expenses	45.6	49.7
Net profit	3.3	6.3

FIGURE 1
Operating statements for Diamond Jim's (3,100,000 sales/year) and a high-performance jeweler (1,500,000–5,000,000 sales/year)

	Percent of Sales		Sales Increase/Decrease	
	DJ	HPJ	DJ	HPJ
Total sales	100.0%	100.0%	+5.4%	+28.0%
Diamonds and colored stones	38.3	54.9	+8.2	+29.0
Watches	9.2	14.3	+7.0	+36.1
Karat gold and cultured pearls	18.5	29.6	+6.5	+25.5
All other merchandise and repairs	34.0	1.2	+4.5	n.a.

FIGURE 2
Sales analysis for Diamond Jim's and a high-performance jeweler (1,500,000–5,000,000 sales/year)

	Inventory Turnover (times)		Gross Profit (% of sales)	
	DJ	HPJ	DJ	HPJ
Total sales	2.00×	2.00×	48.9%	56.0%
Diamonds and colored stones	2.50×	2.06×	50.2%	56.0%
Watches	1.50×	1.80×	43.6%	54.4%
Karat gold and cultured pearls	1.09×	2.02×	52.5%	56.5%
All other merchandise and repairs	2.07×	1.14×	46.9%	62.7%

FIGURE 3
Inventory analysis for Diamond Jim's and a high-performance jeweler (1,500,000–5,000,000 sales/year).

Total sales: Total sales at retail less returns and allowances and sales taxes. Includes repair sales.

Gross profit: Percentage of sales dollar that remains after deducting cost of merchandise sold (FIFO basis). Reaching an adequate gross profit level is a matter of merchandise mix, initial markup percentages, markdowns, and competitive position. It is also a matter of management's attitude and smart buying.

Payroll: Includes all salaries paid, payroll taxes, worker's compensation insurance, health, medical, and life insurance for employees. Excludes withdrawals by owners.

Occupancy: All rents paid and other leasing costs such as area maintenance. Includes all utility expense (except telephone), taxes and insurance on building, as well as depreciation on furniture and fixtures. If own building, this category includes mortgage interest, taxes, upkeep, and depreciation.

Promotion: All expense for advertising or promotion. Also includes costs for window and interior displays, direct mail, and special promotions.

All other: Expenses not included in above categories such as telephone, bad debts, credit and collection expense, E.D.P. expense, donations, interest charges, professional services, and travel.

Inventory turnover: Computed by averaging starting and closing inventory figures (at cost) and dividing this figure into cost of sales. Indicates how often inventory at cost "turns" or is sold. Is a measure of merchandise productivity.

ASSIGNMENT

☐ Assume the role of Allison Green and prepare a report that will satisfactorily complete her assignment. Consider the following issues:

1. What are the major operating problems of Diamond Jim's? What are its principal strengths and weaknesses?
2. What strategy changes do you recommend based on your financial analysis?

CASE 7

The Jones Boycott: A Community Complains about Personnel Policies

Gary B. Frank, The University of Akron

Larry Mason turned to George Paul and said, "This is getting serious, George!"

Paul nodded decisively. "Yes, I think it's time for us to call in the lawyers on this, Larry. I don't know if we are right or wrong; I'm not even sure if it matters. In my mind there are at least two issues we must consider: legal and ethical. In any case, you will have to continue to manage the West Side store somehow, even if Reverend Jones makes good on his threat of a boycott. I'm sorry,

Larry, that we didn't take this matter seriously enough two months ago when this whole mess got started."

BACKGROUND

The "mess" that George Paul was bemoaning began as a complaint by the Reverend Thadeous S. Jones to Larry Mason, manager of the West Side Market. Specifically, the Reverend Jones had first called on Larry Mason after one of his parishoners, Aaron Washington, had talked to the Reverend about his failure in getting a job at the store. When Washington had applied, one of the assistant managers had told him not to bother filling out an application. The assistant manager had responded as he did because the store had just filled the last of its vacant positions, but his choice of words was unfortunate. Washington took the statement to mean that he was not welcome to apply since he was black.

It was the assistant manager's day off when the Reverend Jones arrived at the store, and Mason had no idea what had happened. After listening to the complaint, Mason replied, "I'm sure there was some mistake by Mr. Washington. We're an equal opportunity employer, we have many black employees, and we've never discouraged blacks from applying at any of our stores."

The Reverend Jones had looked around and then said: "Yes. Well I see that a couple of your baggers are black, but that's all I see. Mr. Washington is a qualified butcher, a man with a family to support, and I guess you thought he was probably too old to bag groceries for you."

This confrontation might have been resolved at that point, but the Reverend Jones' sarcasm had not been lost on Mason, and he had had a bad day already. He concluded the conversation by saying, "Reverend Jones, we're a good employer. We stand by our record. And I'm sorry if that doesn't suit you."

The next Sunday the Reverend talked at length from his pulpit about the need of his congregation to support employers that provide meaningful and dignified jobs to the members of the community—and to walk an extra block to shop at stores where the owners weren't just "trying to make a dollar off of our people."

That statement may have been unfair as applied to West Side Market but it did echo the concerns of many of the congregation. The west side was the older section of town that had been largely abandoned by whites as they moved to the suburbs. For 30 years the west side had been predominately black; however, the tone of the community had started to change in the last six or eight years.

"Gentrification" had hit the west side as young, urban professionals rediscovered the magnificent older homes of the district and the convenience of the sector's proximity to both the central business district and the riverside bars and clubs. These young professionals had an impact on the business mix of the area as trendy bars and health clubs started to displace older businesses. For many of the black businesspeople on the verge of retirement, the ability to sell out at the highest prices in memory was viewed as a godsend; but for others in the community, fear of losing employment made these changes unwelcome.

In this climate, the West Side Market became the unwitting center of community tension. The West Side Market had taken over and remodeled a market that had been vacant for four years. The new store did not displace anyone, and the competition that it provided the single existing food market had resulted in lower food prices in the neighborhood. But in the heat of the current social controversy, the beneficial impact of the West Side Market was largely ignored. The situation escalated as community rallies were held by the Reverend Jones. The news media covered these events, and in the course of two months the West Side Market's hiring practices became an open topic of community discussion.

So, as George Paul discussed these events with Mason, he had good cause for concern. Opening the new store had extended him financially, but his initial projections had been that the store would break even within a couple of years. However, an organized boycott, even for a few weeks, would force him to close the store, with ruinous losses.

CURRENT SITUATION

A very disturbed store owner, George Paul met with his lawyer, Justin Stanhope. After hearing the facts, Stanhope responded: "George, you're my friend and I hate to see you in a bind, but I have to warn you that your problem may be more than community relations. I'm somewhat surprised that you haven't already had a call from the Equal Employment Opportunity Commission. But I've dealt with the Reverend Jones before and I know that he has strong feelings about community self-help. So, maybe the Reverend Jones has done you a favor that neither you nor he recognizes yet. Reverend Jones pulls a lot of weight in that community and you made a mistake in not meeting with him before this got so far out of hand. At the same time, I think that he can be a reasonable man. He's intelligent and he truly cares for his community. If you can get him cooled off, you might be able to discuss this whole affair more rationally. As to whether you do have a legal problem, I can't answer you yet. We need more facts to go on."

At this point, Paul jumped back into the conversation. "Justin, you know that I'm always willing to call in the legal eagles when I'm in over my head. At the same time, I know from past experience what you folks charge. What with opening the new store, I am in a real cash bind. Is there anything I can do to help put together these facts?"

"Well, George, I did give a speech a while back to the Small Business Association that covered some of the problems in equal employment opportunity law. If you like, I'll have my secretary run off a copy for you. After you have gone through it, give me a call. I should caution you, though, that the speech was very general and the law in this area changes rapidly."

Paul took the speech home that night and settled down in his den to read it carefully. The text of this speech is shown in Figure 1.

After reading the speech, Paul called the manager of the West Side store. "Larry, we need to get together tomorrow morning. Meet me at 9:00 in my office. I've got some material that I want you to read—and it's going to mean that you will have to do a bunch of digging through your personnel files."

Equal employment and the law (presented to the Small Business Association by Justin Stanhope)

I'm pleased to be here this afternoon, and I believe the subject you have asked me to cover is a timely one. At one time only major corporations seemed to have to worry about equal opportunity employment, but that is no longer the case. The impact of the law is being felt by increasing numbers of small firms. Both the public and employees are far more knowledgeable about their rights. And fewer employees feel disloyal if they pursue those rights.

Most of you try to be fair in all aspects of your employment practices. As businesspeople you know that "fairness" is just good business practice. You recognize that if you limit employment to one class of people, you miss out on good potential employees. And you recognize that the morale of your current employees will be adversely affected if you act in a capricious, arbitrary, or discriminatory fashion. So I know that all of you try to follow a "Golden Rule" policy in the way you treat employees and applicants. However, despite your best intentions, you can inadvertently violate the law if you don't understand it. This is especially the case in the area of equal employment opportunity law.

So, today I'm going to give you a brief overview of the law and the associated administrative process. Since our time is limited, I will focus on Title VII of the Civil Rights Act of 1964, although you should be aware that there are numerous other pieces of antidiscrimination law.

The thrust of Title VII is put forth in Section 703 where it states that it shall be unlawful for an employer ". . . to limit, segregate or classify his employees in any way which would deprive or tend to deprive any individual of employment opportunities or otherwise adversely affect his status as an employee because of such individual's race, color, religion, sex or national origin."

That's a fairly simple statement, but note how far reaching it is in terms of your employment practices. It affects recruiting, hiring, performance appraisal, promotions, job transfers, and indeed all of your personnel policies and actions.

As businesspeople you wish to comply with the law, but in the early days after enactment, what constituted discrimination was often unclear. And employers often wondered what their defense would be if faced by a discrimination charge. Today, even though we see a continuing case-by-case development and interpretation of the law, business does have some general guides to follow. In 1978, the major federal equal employment opportunity enforcement agencies jointly issued the Federal Uniform Guidelines on Employee Selection Procedures. These guides are significant to you for three reasons:

1. They apply across most of the federal statutes and executive orders that may affect you.
2. They give an operational definition of employment discrimination so that you can monitor whether you are likely to have broken the law.
3. They lay out the defenses you have if you are the target of an EEO action.

We will talk about the latter two points at some length; but first, you must recognize that the law has never said that you must hire or retain unqualified employees. What Title VII does say is that if you are not able to identify qualified employees, you can't make your personnel decisions based upon race, sex, religion, or national origin.

Now, with regard to an operational or working definition of discrimination, the 1978 guides established what is known as the 4/5ths or 80% rule. Previous case law had developed the concept of adverse impact to define discrimination. Under the concept of adverse impact, if the effect of your employment practices led to disproportionate selection of a group, you had discriminated. But the employer did not know how equally balanced its labor force had to be to protect itself from a discrimination charge. Now, under the 80% rule, the employer has an advance guide to what constitutes adverse impact, and therefore this allows the employer to self-monitor actions. Slide 1 will show you how this works.

	Applied	Slide 1 Hired	Percentage Selected
Blacks	42	4	9.5%
Whites	215	35	16.3%

Highest Rate	16.3%
Times 80%	× .8%
Level below which adverse impact is demonstrated:	12.04%

To use the 80% rule in adverse-impact analysis, we need to identify applicant groups and have historic information on numbers applying and selected. We identify the group with the highest selection rate and multiply that rate by .8. If the selection rate for any other group is less than the result—here less than 12%—there is demonstrated adverse impact and the employer is held to have discriminated. The burden of proof to justify his actions then falls on the employer. You should note two facts:

1. The illustration we used was simplified. You would have a more complex analysis by the time you had included whites, blacks, American Indians, Asians, and Hispanics, cross categorized by male or female. Moreover, almost any identifiable group might claim protected status.
2. You are under a strong record-keeping requirement. The legitimacy of your selection procedure will depend on the outcome of the adverse-impact analysis. If you don't have records, there is a strong presumption of adverse impact.

At this point, assuming you have done adverse-impact analysis and have found that you have violated the 80% rule, you may choose to change your selection policies, or you may be ordered to change them. However, if you feel your selection methods are justified, the 1978 Uniform Guides tell you how to defend what you have done. The guides discuss multiple validation methods, but the process essentially amounts to a demonstration that the standards you have used are job related and are justified by business necessity.

Remember, the law does not require you to hire or maintain unqualified people. The law does require that an employer have the burden of proof to show that these qualifications are necessary for the job if they result in adverse impact.

The actual validation methodologies are quite complex and beyond the limits of our time today. I do caution you, though, that it is very difficult to validate procedures after you are the target of an EEO suit. In that case, your only hope is if you had previously conducted a full job analysis that identified the knowledge, skills, and abilities that each job required, and your selection procedures were based on these critical work behaviors.

If you are unable to justify your practices, you may be forced to modify your policies. You also may be liable for hefty back-pay settlements. The good news is that most cases are settled out of court through compromise. Due to limited resources, the EEOC has been forced to rely on voluntary compliance and negotiated settlements. If a charge is brought to the EEOC, it will make at least two attempts to get a voluntary settlement between you and the parties who have brought the charge. If that fails, it is still unlikely the EEOC will carry the suit against you unless your case is very blatant, involves large numbers, or covers new legal ground—the commission doesn't have the personnel to press every case. And, the affected employees or applicants are not likely to sue by themselves unless they can get backing from some outside group such as the American Civil Liberties Union.

Even though this is the case, it is not something you want to risk because you can't tell in advance which cases the EEOC will press all the way to court. Consequently, your best course of action is to mount a pre-emptive defense in depth. By this, I mean that you should build into your personnel policies protective measures such as:

1. Conduct job analyses of your positions.
2. From the job analyses, construct selection procedures that are based on critical job behaviors.
3. Monitor the outcome, and if you find that you are getting close to the 80% limit, change your policies.
4. Finally, federal enforcement agencies are increasingly taking a "holistic" approach in that they watch for good-faith efforts on behalf of the employer. So you should try to communicate in every way possible to your employees and job applicants that you are an equal opportunity employer, and follow through with actions that back your words.

If you do all this, it still won't totally protect you from individual charges of discrimination, but it will go a long way in preventing a class action, and that is a significant accomplishment.

The next morning while Mason was in his office, Paul called Stanhope. "Justin, I read your speech. I'm going to have the West Side manager pull together the figures for adverse-impact analysis. But we're at somewhat of a loss. We could analyze things six ways to Sunday, and we need some direction."

"Well, George, you're right. If you do get hit with an EEOC charge, they will probably go on a fishing expedition that covers all of your personnel policies. If that does happen, we will need to present your best case—and that may mean breaking the data down by store, or trying to lump all the stores together if that gives us better bottom line figures. But don't get carried away yet. For now, you aren't facing a charge and what you want to do is placate Reverend Jones. After we have gone through our own analysis of your personnel records, it may be helpful to lay the facts before Reverend Jones. For the analysis, I suggest you focus on the West Side Market's hiring data, and break it down into supervisory/nonsupervisory by male/female, and racial categories. Also, don't accuse me of trying to drum up business, but we might want to set up a review of all of your personnel policies just in case your problem worsens."

"Justin, I think you're right. I had no idea this EEOC stuff was so far reaching. It is time to take a close look at our personnel policies. But one question, how can we validate our personnel policies?"

"George, you're jumping the gun. Don't worry about that yet. Let's see what develops. And get me that data as soon as you can."

Within several days, Larry collected the personnel data on the store's first four months of operation, organized them into the suggested categories, and sent the result to Justin Stanhope's office. These data are shown in Figure 2.

ASSIGNMENT

☐ Advise George Paul on the following issues:

1. From a legal perspective, does he have basis for concern? Support your answer with a detailed analysis of the data presented.
2. How should George Paul resolve the problem (what specific actions do you recommend)?
3. What are the ethical issues in this case? How should these issues be resolved? Is there a conflict between the "most ethical" course of action and the objectives of West Side Market?

FIGURE 2

Hiring data: West Side Market

Position	Current Employees				Applicants			
	Black		White		Black		White	
	M	F	M	F	M	F	M	F
Supervisory								
Store Manager			1		2		7	2
Asst. Mgr. (Produce Mgr.)			1		1		5	
Asst. Mgr. (Stockperson)			1		2		6	
Butcher			1		3		5	
Deli and bakery		1					4	3
Nonsupervisory								
Meat cutters	2		3		6		12	2
Stockers	1		3		12	4	25	4
Produce	1		2		5	1	12	
Deli and bakery		3		2	3	12	1	8
Checkers		3		4		17		14
Baggers	4	1	2		24	6	20	5

730

Fallis Foods: Investigating an Innovative Store Layout

Charles R. Patton, Pan American University
Dale M. Lewison, The University of Akron

BACKGROUND

Steve Fallis has a right to be proud. As the owner and manager of the largest independent supermarket in Hopkinsville, Indiana, Fallis has enjoyed remarkable success over the last 10 years. As of last year, Fallis Foods had captured a 21% market share. Given that there are six supermarkets in the greater Hopkinsville area, he has been quite pleased with his store's performance. Nevertheless, Fallis has no intention of resting on his laurels. For Fallis Foods to maintain its current share of the food market and have any chance of improving its market share will require considerable forward planning effort. In Fallis' mind, innovation is a major ingredient in any successful plan for the future.

In recent weeks, he has been giving a great deal of thought to making some innovative changes in the store's layout; specifically, assembling product lines into more natural groupings and locating these natural groupings within a concentrated area of the store. Bakery products, for example, are currently assembled into a number of different groupings scattered throughout the store. In the past, Fallis Foods has followed the conventional wisdom of displaying bakery products using the grouping and locating practices of competitive supermarkets. Fallis thinks, however, that regrouping bakery products into one large group and placing it at a single location could well provide the store's customers with a more convenient shopping experience; it could also provide Fallis Foods with a distinctive merchandising practice and possibly a small but significant competitive advantage.

CURRENT SITUATION

Come Monday morning, Fallis decided to audit the store's current practices in merchandising bakery products. Armed with a blueprint of the store's layout (see Figure 1, p. 732) and a clipboard, he proceeded to collect the following information on the in-store groupings and locations of bakery products:

1. *In-store bakery shop*—a separate in-store bakery, installed at considerable expense two years ago, that carries a full line of freshly baked breads, rolls, cakes, pies, donuts, pastries, cookies, and other specialty bakery items. This department has above-average markups and operating expenses. It requires several full-time employees (bakers and salesclerks). Strict supervision is necessary to avoid too many "stales" that must be sold at reduced prices or given away to charity (see location A in Figure 1).

2. *Commercial bakery goods*—a full gondola of commercially baked breads, rolls, and pastries delivered by national and regional vendors (bakeries) that provide the full range of services normally associated with such rack jobbers. They stock the shelves, price the merchandise, accept returns of "stales," and provide other inventory control functions. This section is a carbon copy of the commercial bakery goods section found in most supermarkets. This section is known to have a high traffic count and is located at some distance from the store's "scratch" bakery shop (see location B in Figure 1).

3. *Frozen bakery products*—a growing line of bakery products are those displayed in the open, chest-type frozen-food cabinets. This assortment of frozen bakery products includes mostly nationally advertised, brand-name items (e.g., Sara Lee, Morton, and Rich's). While the assortment emphasis is on dessert items and pastries, there are several brands of frozen bread and roll dough that require baking by the consumer (see location C in Figure 1).

4. *Commercial cookies*—a large section of one gondola is devoted to packaged cookies. This product line is dominated by a few large national brands (e.g., Keebler, Nabisco, Duncan Hines, and Archway). To date, cookies baked by the store's bakery have had limited success competing against these long-established commercial products (see location D in Figure 1).

5. *Commercial cake mixes*—a large section of one gondola is devoted to commercial cake mixes (e.g., Duncan Hines, Betty Crocker, and Pillsbury). These are well-established product lines that offer considerable variety of flavors. To promote complementary sales, cake frostings are located adjacent to the cake mixes (see location E in Figure 1).

6. *Commercial muffin, biscuit, and bread mixes*—a six-foot section of one gondola is stocked with muffin,

FIGURE 1
Store layout blueprint:
Fallis Foods

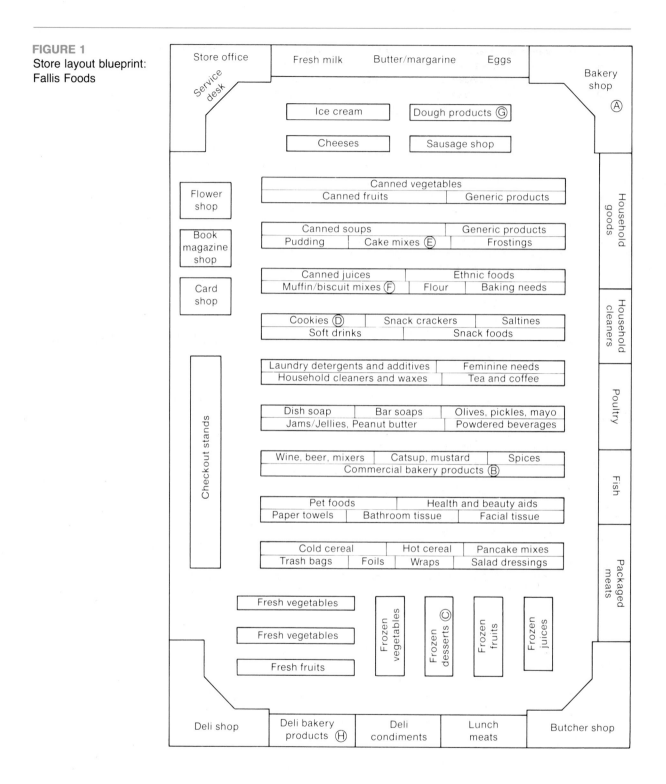

biscuit, and homemade bread mixes. Many local competitors place all "mixes" together; however, Fallis Foods has traditionally followed customer belief that muffin, biscuit, and bread mixes are more commonly associated with flour (see location F in Figure 1).

7. *Refrigerated dough products*—a large, open, chest-type refrigerator is used to display a complete selection of refrigerated dough products. Items within this product line include preformed pie crusts, breakfast pastries, bread dough, refrigerated desserts, and biscuit and roll doughs (see location G in Figure 1).

8. *Deli bakery products*—to complement the store's complete deli department, a small wall display is devoted to deli bakery products, such as specialty breads and rolls (see location H in Figure 1).

Having completed the audit and a review of its findings, Fallis had arrived at several tentative conclusions. First, the store offered an extensive selection of bakery products. Until now, he never realized the extent of the variety and assortment of products currently being stocked in the various bakery departments. The total number of possible choices facing the customer is almost staggering. Fallis wondered whether this extensive selection was necessary. Did it meet customers' need for selection or did it simply confuse them? Thinking about this issue, Fallis developed a hypothetical shopping scenario that he thought might be a fairly typical experience (see Figure 2, p. 734). The more he thought about it, the more he believed that there was a high likelihood of overkill in the selection of bakery goods currently being offered in his store.

Fallis also thought the bakery goods category appeared to have considerable duplication, perhaps too much. For example, is it necessary to stock both frozen and refrigerated pie crusts? Do customers perceive these two items to be different, and if so, is that difference important? Also, are all the various product brands and package sizes necessary? For Fallis, this issue of duplication needed close attention.

The final conclusion Fallis made centered on the issue of multiple locations for bakery products. The seven or eight current locations certainly must have some negative implications as far as customer convenience is concerned. For example, the several widely scattered locations must hinder the customer's ability to make price, brand, quality, and other relevant comparisons without considerable backtracking through the store. Multiple locations also hinder customers from finding the particular item they are looking for. In sum, it could confuse and irritate the customer.

Each of these tentative conclusions seems to support Fallis' contention that a more efficient, effective way to merchandise bakery products would be to regroup and relocate all such goods into one concentrated bakery department. The more he thought about the idea, the more he liked it. Before making any final decisions or drawing up any final plans, however, Fallis decided to contact Spatial Interactions, Inc (SII), a consulting firm that specializes in the spatial problems associated with retailing operations (e.g., retail location and store layout and design). After discussing the idea at some length with Wayne Duff, President of SII, Fallis was convinced that an in-depth study of all the issues surrounding his idea was essential before proceeding with any direct action. He provided Duff with a copy of the audit and the blueprint of the store's layout. He also agreed to cooperate with SII researchers assigned to the project. Fallis spent the next few hours discussing with Duff the particulars of the study. They agreed on a limited study that would

1. Identify the pros and cons of regrouping all bakery products into one concentrated location within the store. The pro and con statements should be made from two perspectives: (a) retail merchandising and operations and (b) consumer buying behavior.

2. Make a recommendation based on the pro and con statements as to what course of action would be most advisable for Fallis Foods (to be supported by a complete rationale statement).

3. Develop a store layout and design plan for remodeling the store that would incorporate a concentrated bakery-products section. The plan should also consider the regrouping and relocating of other product categories (e.g., beverages) and any recommendations related to this issue. (Note: this plan is to be developed regardless of the recommendation presented.)

ASSIGNMENT

☐ Assume the role of George Raymer, Project Research Director for SII. Duff has assigned the Fallis Foods project to you. A comprehensive report, complete with supporting graphics, is due within two months.

Driving home from work, Rita Thomas realized that she did not have any dessert to serve after the evening meal. Since Harold really appreciated having dessert, Rita decided to pop in at Fallis Foods to pick up something. Pie seemed like a good idea. Upon entering the store, Rita proceeded to travel around the store in her normal counter-clockwise pattern. Deciding to investigate all the possibilities, Rita made the following stops and was faced with the following choices:

Stop 1: Frozen-food case (location C in Figure 1)
    Choice 1: Frozen 8-inch pies, six varieties, mostly nationally advertised brands, must be thawed before eating.
    Choice 2: Frozen 9-inch pies, three varieties, local and regional brands, must be baked before serving.
    Choice 3: Frozen 5-inch pies (two to three servings), four varieties, must be baked before serving.
    Choice 4: Frozen individual pie pieces, individually wrapped, three varieties, must be thawed and warmed before serving.
    Choice 5: Frozen pie crusts, individual and multiple packs, three sizes (tart 4-inch, standard 8-inch, and family 9-inch), must be thawed, filled, and baked before serving.

Stop 2: Commercial bakery-goods section (location B in Figure 1)
    Choice 1: Prepackaged pies, baked by local and regional bakeries, standard 8-inch size, one day old, seven varieties, lowest prices, ready-to-eat.
    Choice 2: Prepackaged pies, national brands, individual sizes, four varieties, ready-to-eat.
    Choice 3: 8-count box of pie-like product called Little Debbie, individual servings that are individually wrapped, one variety, ready-to-eat.

Stop 3: Commercial cake mixes (location E in Figure 1)
    Choice 1: Packaged pie crust mixes, requiring additional ingredients, must be mixed and formed into pie crust, very reasonable.
    Choice 2: Packaged pie filling mixes, requiring preparation, nine varieties.

Stop 4: In-store bakery shop (location A in Figure 1)
    Choice 1: Freshly baked pies, five varieties, baked on premises, standard 8-inch size, more expensive, ready-to-eat.
    Choice 2: Freshly baked tarts, three varieties, baked on premises, individual servings, quite expensive, ready-to-eat.

Stop 5: Refrigerated dough products (location G in Figure 1)
    Choice 1: Refrigerated pie crusts, ready-to-use, require filling, may or may not be baked, standard 8-inch size, pie dough and graham cracker base.
    Choice 2: Refrigerated pie dough, must be rolled out and shaped, requires baking.

Stop 6: Canned goods section (see Figure 1)
    Choice 1 Canned pie fillings, six varieties, ready-to-use, very inexpensive.

Having made her whirlwind tour of the store, Rita was somewhat exhausted from all the rushing about, and even more confused at all the choices. Her original intention was to simply buy a pie for tonight's dessert, but the problem is which pie in what form and flavor and at what price?

FIGURE 2
A shopping scenario

Southwestern Supermarkets: Responding to an Extortion Threat

Jon Hawes, The University of Akron
George Glisan, Illinois State University

BACKGROUND

It was a telephone call that Mike Kelly really didn't want to take. It was 11:00 A.M. and he had been busy helping unload a shipment of frozen food. Nevertheless, the caller was insistent so Mike took the call.

"People are going to die," the voice on the other end of the line said.

"What?" Kelly said in disbelief. "Is this some type of a crank call?"

"No. People are going to die unless you give us $60,000. We have poisoned the food in three Southwestern stores in Waco, and unless you give us the money, your customers are going to die from poison. We will get back to you with details when you deliver the money. Talk to your boss about the money, but you had better not call the police!"

Kelly was dumbfounded. Needless to say, in his four years as manager of a Southwestern Supermarket, he had never before dealt with a similar situation. He took a moment to collect his thoughts, then called his boss as the extortionist had demanded. Bill Bault, vice president of sales, took the news calmly. Bault said he would be in the store within the hour and that Kelly should keep the matter secret until he arrived.

Bault immediately called George Powell, president of the chain of 152 supermarkets to inform him of the situation. Powell told him to go to the store and do his best to ensure the safety of Southwestern's customers. The resources of the chain were placed at Bault's disposal, he told him.

Bault went to the store and asked Kelly to repeat everything he could remember from the phone call. He asked Kelly if any of the store employees had recently been fired or if he could think of anyone else who might have a reason to make such a threat. Kelly drew a blank. As far as he knew, the six Southwestern Supermarkets located in Waco were highly respected members of the business community and enjoyed very good relations with the public. No one had been fired from his store within the past six months.

At 12:30 P.M. the extortionist called. This time he talked with Bault and again stated that people were going to die unless Southwestern Supermarkets complied with his demands. This time, however, the extortionist informed Bault that no one had been exposed to the poison yet. In fact, he said there would be no danger for the next two days.

Bault then called Powell and they discussed the latest developments. The president authorized Bault to pay the $60,000 but said that the police should be brought into the situation.

Bill then called the police and several nonuniformed detectives were dispatched to the store. When the extortionist called back at 3:45 P.M., Bill told him that Southwestern was willing to pay the $60,000, but that the police would handle delivery of the cash. After a brief outburst of rage, the extortionist hung up. He called back, however, and the negotiations continued over the next 36 hours. Several brief telephone conversations were conducted—the extortionist would hang up each time after a couple of minutes for fear of the call being traced. Ultimately, the arrangements were finalized. In the meantime, the police had been examining food in Southwestern's Waco stores for any signs of foul play. No evidence of poisoning was found.

The police delivered the money at 1:00 P.M., two days after Kelly had received the first call from the extortionist. Even though the extortionist's demands were followed, the money was still in the designated location at 5:00 A.M. the next morning. This was unexpected and caused the police and Southwestern executives great concern.

CURRENT SITUATION

The two-day period of safety originally promised by the extortionist had now passed. What should Southwestern do? The executives conferred and decided to close all six Southwestern Supermarkets in Waco immediately. Virtually all stock except for canned goods was taken to the city dump under armed guard. More than 1.3 million pounds of groceries were plowed into the landfill.

The company quickly began restocking the shelves of the six Waco stores and reopened four days later. Sales soon reached normal levels and customer reaction was reported to be extremely favorable.

ASSIGNMENT

☐ Assume that you were part of Southwestern's management team. What would have been your reaction to this extortion threat? Would you have informed the police? Would you have kept the stores open during the negotiations? Would you have agreed to pay the $60,000? When the extortionist failed to retrieve the money, would you have dumped the goods of all six local stores? Justify your solutions to each of these issues.

CASE 10

Jacobson's Dilemma: Location of a "Fancy" Restaurant

J. B. Wilkinson, The University of Akron

BACKGROUND

Up to now, George Jacobson had felt pretty good about all his decisions and activities in starting his own restaurant. Jacobson had been a military chef in the officers' mess at Fort Belvoir but had recently retired after 22 years in the service. Too young at 45 to simply "take it easy," Jacobson had decided to start a restaurant in Smithville, a central city in a three-county SMSA. The restaurant was positioned as a plush, moderately expensive lunch and dinner and cocktail bar type of restaurant featuring continental cuisine. Two shopping center locations were under consideration: Pinnacle Plaza and Hidden Valley Shopping Mall. Both of the intramall locations were comparable in terms of size/space, rent, and traffic, but Jacobson suspected that the shopping centers might differ considerably in terms of their trading area characteristics.

CURRENT SITUATION

Having spent the last three weeks collecting and organizing data on each retail center and its trading area, Jacobson believes he is ready to evaluate each center's potential as a location for a fancy restaurant. The data he has compiled concern the locational attributes of each center, the population and income characteristics of surrounding census tracts, and the retail tenant mix found within the city and each of its major retailing centers.

Location Characteristics

Figure 1 shows the location of both shopping malls in Smithville. Pinnacle Plaza (MRC 1) draws Smithville shoppers primarily from the area north of U.S. Route 72 (Census Tracts 2.01, 2.02, 3.01, 3.02, 4.01, 4.02, 5.01, 5.02, 5.03, 6.01, 6.02, 7.01, 7.02, 8, 11, and 13), while Hidden Valley (MRC 3) attracts Smithville shoppers primarily from areas south of State Route 1 (Census Tracts 19.01, 19.02, 19.03, 20, 21, 22, 23, 24, 25.01, 25.02, 26, 27.01, 27.02, 28.01, 28.02, 29.01, and 29.02). In addition, Pinnacle Plaza attracts shoppers from northern areas outside Smithville. Mountain View (pop. 30,000) is 40 miles north of Smithville on State Route 52; Pikesville (pop. 10,000) is 20 miles north on Moutain Pike; and Jolson (pop. 15,000) is 25 miles north on U.S. Route 254. The mountainous areas to the east of Smithville are relatively unpopulated; however, Hidden Valley attracts shoppers from southern areas outside Smithville, notably Dover (pop. 30,000), which is 25 miles southwest of Smithville on State Route 1, and Marshall (pop. 25,000), which is 15 miles away on U.S. Route 254.

Population/Income Characteristics

Table 1 (pp. 738–40) contains selected population and income characteristics for all census tracts that comprise each of the shopping centers' primary drawing areas.

Major Retail Center Characteristics

The retail store mix characteristics of the major retail centers (i.e., Pinnacle Plaza and Hidden Valley), the central business district of Smithville, the City of Smithville, and the Smithville SMSA are shown in Table 2 (p. 741), which also indicates the number of competitors.

Additional Information

Additional information collected by George Jacobson included the following:

1. Approximately 8% of family median income is spent on dining out (*Expenditure Patterns of the American Family*).

2. Average sales per eating and drinking place in the United States were $172,000, with approximately 5.0 eating and drinking places per 1,000 households in the United States in 1977 (*U.S. Bureau of the Census* and *Census of Retail Trade, 1977*).
3. Pinnacle Plaza had approximately 16,000 sq. ft. of floor space allocated to eating and drinking establishments. The eating and drinking establishments in Hidden Valley occupied approximately 55,000 sq. ft. (estimated by Jacobson).
4. The number of eating and drinking establishments in the market areas of Pinnacle Plaza and Hidden Valley was 100 and 94, respectively (estimated by Jacobson).

ASSIGNMENT

☐ Assume the role of a consultant and advise George Jacobson. Which location do you recommend as the preferred site for his restaurant? Provide Jacobson with a complete justification for your recommendation.

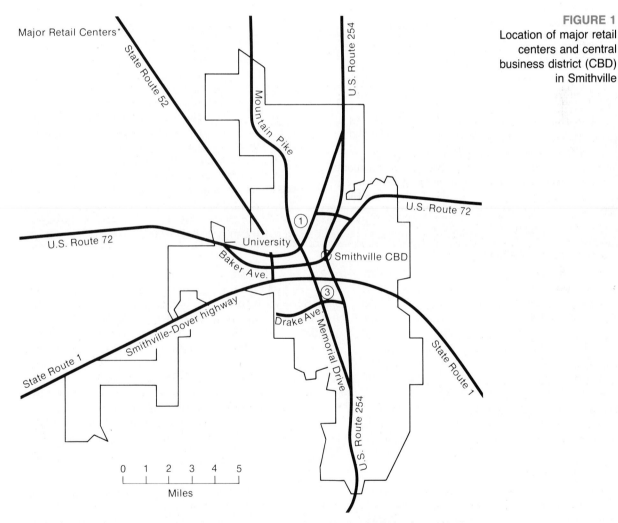

FIGURE 1
Location of major retail centers and central business district (CBD) in Smithville

*Concentration of retail stores (located inside the MSA but outside the CBD) having at least $5 million in retail sales and at least 10 retail establishments, one of which was classified as a department store (SIC 531).

TABLE 1

Population/income characteristics for selected census tracts, Smithville SMSA, 1980

	SMSA	Smithville City	Tract 2.01	Tract 2.02	Tract 3.01	Tract 3.02
AGE						
Total persons	308,593	142,513	821	4,255	5,313	4,335
3 and 4 years	8,274	3,572	21	83	172	147
16 yrs and over	230,134	107,383	624	3,588	3,741	2,944
18 yrs and over	217,498	101,377	590	3,433	3,482	2,718
21 yrs and over	198,327	92,294	527	2,242	3,148	2,478
60 yrs and over	38,970	15,076	120	273	387	241
62 yrs and over	33,840	12,844	100	229	314	205
Median	29.1	28.9	26.7	21.4	25.9	25.1
INCOME in 1979						
Households	106,369	50,790	292	854	1,601	1,228
Median	$15,472	$17,843	$11,023	$16,741	$16,542	$17,476
Mean	18,678	21,424	16,716	17,899	19,419	18,501
Families	84,881	38,746	238	743	1,405	1,101
Median	$17,565	$20,920	$11,989	$16,956	$17,181	$17,816
Mean	20,739	24,179	18,810	18,236	20,110	19,054
Per capita income	$6,488	$7,661	$6,055	$3,921	$5,789	$5,284

	Tract 4.01	Tract 4.02	Tract 5.01	Tract 5.02	Tract 5.03	Tract 6.01	Tract 6.02
AGE							
Total persons	813	3,970	2,401	3,291	2,409	1,917	2,716
3 and 4 years	27	124	69	105	73	31	55
16 yrs and over	538	2,724	1,685	2,263	1,704	1,438	2,058
18 yrs and over	492	2,519	1,552	2,110	1,577	1,329	1,921
21 yrs and over	453	2,296	1,401	1,887	1,437	1,192	1,749
60 yrs and over	26	214	121	163	130	132	228
62 yrs and over	21	168	95	139	108	101	203
Median	26.4	27.1	25.2	26.9	29.7	29.7	30.3
INCOME in 1979							
Households	224	1,167	698	970	737	591	928
Median	$22,262	$21,427	$22,917	$15,794	$19,480	$23,995	$22,567
Mean	21,789	23,367	24,088	17,270	22,309	25,411	21,905
Families	203	1,053	665	843	649	534	825
Median	$22,841	$22,361	$24,063	$16,599	$19,234	$24,750	$23,511
Mean	22,284	24,211	24,695	17,956	21,738	26,440	22,944
Per capita income	$5,582	$6,888	$6,952	$5,211	$6,757	$7,431	$7,484

	Tract 7.01	Tract 7.02	Tract 8	Tract 11	Tract 13	Tract 19.01	Tract 19.02
AGE							
Total persons	4,136	2,095	2,858	1,950	4,130	3,105	820
3 and 4 years	117	54	78	67	77	64	16
16 yrs and over	3,057	1,615	2,176	1,346	3,333	2,378	600
18 yrs and over	2,885	1,540	2,076	1,260	3,209	2,213	543
21 yrs and over	2,612	1,437	1,930	1,156	2,856	2,100	510
60 yrs and over	254	401	421	353	280	412	53
62 yrs and over	201	373	373	314	218	335	38
Median	25.8	31.3	28.9	26.6	26.7	37.9	37.2
INCOME in 1979							
Households	1,447	847	1,126	602	1,729	1,076	249
Median	$16,865	$11,911	$11,458	$6,463	$17,899	$31,303	$40,510
Mean	18,333	14,316	13,347	8,490	19,003	38,551	42,356
Families	1,124	523	755	433	993	925	249
Median	$18,289	$17,557	$12,392	$7,262	$20,040	$35,428	$40,510
Mean	20,079	18,269	14,744	9,604	21,617	42,738	42,356
Per capita income	$6,332	$5,873	$5,245	$2,742	$8,067	$13,652	$12,573

	Tract 19.03	Tract 20	Tract 21	Tract 22	Tract 23	Tract 24	Tract 25.01
AGE							
Total persons	2,084	2,555	5,207	2,961	5,793	5,011	2,125
3 and 4 years	24	50	192	96	141	156	67
16 yrs and over	1,630	2,207	3,896	2,357	4,451	3,766	1,679
18 yrs and over	1,494	2,151	3,728	2,291	4,255	3,606	1,626
21 yrs and over	1,406	2,051	3,406	2,103	3,870	3,143	1,445
60 yrs and over	240	675	1,039	378	617	239	171
62 yrs and over	178	582	942	336	511	185	142
Median	40.8	43.2	28.0	27.5	28.1	24.8	25.6
INCOME in 1979							
Households	713	1,197	2,133	1,182	2,209	2,014	1,054
Median	$44,430	$16,720	$7,339	$13,921	$14,857	$13,187	$11,217
Mean	48,089	17,735	8,939	16,446	16,644	14,861	14,056
Families	665	825	1,322	768	1,593	1,389	541
Median	$44,430	$16,720	$ 9,855	$15,211	$16,632	$15,578	$12,792
Mean	50,245	20,697	10,345	17,510	18,533	16,510	15,620
Per capita income	$16,262	$8,304	$3,693	$6,617	$6,425	$5,994	$7,116

	Tract 25.02	Tract 26	Tract 27.01	Tract 27.02	Tract 28.01	Tract 28.02	Tract 29.01
AGE							
Total persons	1,886	4,513	2,021	7,111	3,469	1,953	7,154
3 and 4 years	52	65	26	156	72	75	179
16 yrs and over	1,490	3,714	1,633	5,265	2,606	1,403	4,993
18 yrs and over	1,430	3,546	1,525	4,872	2,483	1,323	4,586
21 yrs and over	1,331	3,338	1,420	4,552	2,293	1,221	4,262
60 yrs and over	96	736	242	496	245	92	311
62 yrs and over	69	641	184	391	192	69	241
Median	26.2	37.8	43.7	32.8	29.5	27.9	31.2
INCOME in 1979							
Households	882	1,915	642	2,442	1,341	674	2,140
Median	$15,745	$22,789	$38,125	$32,167	$23,260	$23,351	$30,607
Mean	18,189	26,480	38,404	35,217	24,504	25,510	32,549
Families	523	1,294	599	2,061	917	569	2,006
Median	$15,993	$27,753	$39,489	$34,769	$29,275	$25,474	$31,073
Mean	15,886	31,292	40,016	38,500	29,242	27,489	33,214
Per capita income	$8,494	$11,223	$12,718	$12,008	$9,588	$8,563	$9,609

	Tract 29.02
AGE	
Total persons	3,908
3 and 4 years	126
16 yrs and over	2,674
18 yrs and over	2,505
21 yrs and over	2,339
60 yrs and over	125
62 yrs and over	109
Median	28.5
INCOME in 1979	
Households	1,172
Median	$26,654
Mean	27,211
Familes	1,068
Median	$27,165
Mean	27,882
Per capita income	$8,376

TABLE 2
Characteristics of major retail centers and central business district in the Smithville SMSA, 1977

SIC Code	Kind of Business	Standard Metropolitan Statistical Area	City	Central Business District	Major Retail Centers	
					No. 1	No. 3
	Retail stores					
	Number	2,574	1,208	158	48	77
	Sales (1,000)	941,530	(D)	111,086	43,221	66,452
54, 58, 591	Convenience goods stores					
	Number	810	379	35	10	20
	Sales (1,000)	(D)	(D)	8,562	8,269	10,245
53, 56, 57 594	Shopping goods stores					
	Number	726	375	73	33	40
	Sales (1,000)	239,539	(D)	43,066	34,095	36,511
52, 55, 59 ex. 591, 4, 6	All other stores					
	Number	1,038	454	50	5	17
	Sales (1,000)	(D)	(D)	59,458	857	19,696
58	Eating and drinking places					
	Number	332	214	20	4	13
	Sales (1,000)	69,875	53,303	5,203	(D)	(D)

CASE 11

Clemente Cleaners

Dale M. Lewison, The University of Akron
Charles R. Patton, Pan American University

BACKGROUND

Clemente Cleaners has occupied the same location on the northwest corner of Johnston Avenue and Oak Park Boulevard for the last 27 years. Bart Clemente, owner and operator of Clemente Cleaners, originally selected the site because he thought it represented a convenient stop for customers commuting between Walnut Valley, a large suburb, and the central business district of Omaha. Customers could drop off their cleaning on the way to work and pick it up on the way home. The selection of the Johnston Avenue site proved to be one of the best business decisions Clemente ever made. For 25 years, Clemente Cleaners serviced the commuting public and he enjoyed the benefits of a very successful business.

Two years ago, the Metro Traffic Engineering Department made a complete study of the numerous traffic problems that commuters were experiencing during their weekday work trips to and from the central city. After considerable deliberation, a decision was made to convert two of the major traffic arteries into one-way streets. Washington Avenue was designated a one-way westbound artery leading into the central business district, while Johnston Avenue was designated an eastbound traffic artery out of the city (Figure 1).

While the realignment of traffic arteries represented the end of numerous traffic problems, it also represented the beginning of a substantial decline in revenues for Clemente Cleaners. Although the present store remained reasonably profitable, many of Clemente's long-time commuter customers found it more convenient to go elsewhere.

Many of Clemente's customers from Walnut Valley had frequently commented on how satisfied they were with Clemente Cleaners and expressed their potential support should he decide to open a second conveniently located outlet in Walnut Valley. Unfortunately, good locations are hard to find in Walnut Valley, but after a 10-month search, Clemente has found a Madison Avenue site he thinks might be appropriate (see Figure 2).

From his service records, Clemente has determined that a large number of his former customers live within one mile of the site; most of these customers would have to pass the site on their shopping trips to Walnut Valley Mall and Eastland Shopping Center. Walnut Valley Mall is a large regional center anchored by Sears, J. C. Penney, and two large local department stores. A large discount store and a catalog showroom are the principal tenants of Eastland Shopping Center. In Clemente's mind, there is no question that the site's trading area contains sufficient business potential to support his proposed business venture. What troubled him was the site itself. While the existing building was adequate for his needs, he would have to share the parking lot (eight parking spaces) with Robert's Florist. In addition, Clemente was somewhat concerned with the site's accessibility.

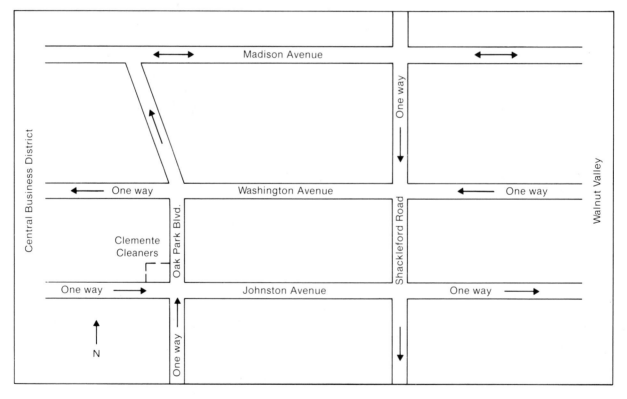

FIGURE 1
New traffic artery pattern

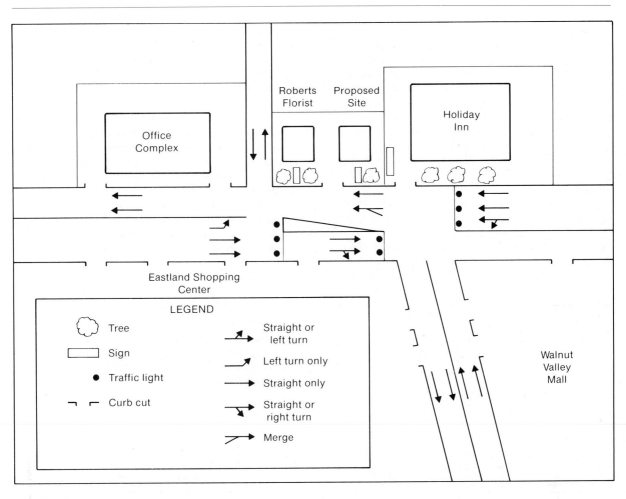

FIGURE 2
The proposed Madison Avenue site

CURRENT SITUATION

Clemente's option on the site expires at the end of the month. Hence, he must make a decision soon. Having limited experience in site analysis, Clemente has decided to engage the services of Professor Kristopher Michael, head of the marketing department at the local state university. Michael has agreed to investigate the site accessibility issue and to make appropriate recommendations. He has also agreed to address the issue of whether Clemente should exercise the rent, lease, or buy clause of his option.

ASSIGNMENT

☐ Assume the role of Professor Kristopher Michael. First, prepare a written report on the pros and cons of the site's accessibility. Make whatever recommendations you think are appropriate regarding the site's accessibility. Second, prepare a report on the pros and cons of renting, leasing, and buying a location and make a recommendation to Clemente regarding this issue. Be sure to provide adequate support and rationale for all of your recommendations.

CASE 12

Lockner's Department Store: The Role of a Toy Department

George Prough, The University of Akron
Dale M. Lewison, The University of Akron

INTRODUCTION

For the last 40 years, Lockner's Department Store has been recognized as one of the leading retail merchandisers in the midwestern city of Plains, Iowa (1985 population: 175,000). The area is expected to continue above-average population growth for the next 20 years. During the last four decades, Lockner's has built a reputation as an upscale retailer of quality merchandise. By carefully designing the firm's total merchandising program, Lockner's management has generally been successful in appealing to both middle- and upper-class consumers. Over the last five years sales and profit objectives for most merchandise departments have been met or exceeded. The one exception to this is the toy department. For Bill Lockner, founder and president of the store, this situation is simply unacceptable.

LOCKNER'S MERCHANDISING STRATEGY

The Product/Service Mixes

Good quality, high style, and an excellent variety of brand-name merchandise have been hallmarks of the firm's product mix. To help differentiate its product mix from competitive product offerings, Lockner's has featured a number of top-quality private labels in several different product lines. Also, a variety of specialty and imported goods not commonly found in competitive stores has been an integral part of Lockner's product strategy. To enhance its image as an upscale, full-line department store and as a one-stop shopping store, Lockner's carries a deep assortment of brands, models, styles, and colors for most product lines.

Excellent service is another key ingredient in the store's merchandising program. Lockner's offers a complete service mix with a variety of credit, delivery, and wrapping plans, and alterations, repair, and layaway services. All essential and expected services are provided free of charge or at some minimal fee in a limited number of cases.

The Promotional/Place Mixes

Lockner's promotional strategy is directed at enhancing the store's prestige image. To do so, local newspaper advertisements focus on appeals stressing product selection and quality, service offerings, and shopping atmosphere.

Product advertisements featuring a few carefully selected items are used to inform customers of new and special merchandise. The store also runs numerous institutional advertisements that attempt to communicate the message that "Lockner's is *the* place to shop." Once a customer has been attracted to the store, considerable attention is given to capitalizing on the traffic, through the use of such promotional tools as attractive and accessible displays, special effects, and promotional demonstrations.

The store is located on the newly opened Hub Mall, an open-air pedestrian mall in downtown Plains. The area features many renovated or new specialty and more fashion-oriented shops. Lockner's was completely renovated inside and out at the same time as the mall. Both the area and the store are accessible to the area's population and offer a very pleasurable and exciting shopping environment not found anywhere nearby.

THE TOY INDUSTRY

Estimates show sales in the toy industry to be somewhere in the neighborhood of $2 billion annually. Department stores typically sell about 13% of all toys, games, and hobby items. However, sales in department stores indicate that they sell a higher than average share of dolls and educational and scientific toys.

Toys are product items with interesting life cycles; both the level and duration of consumer acceptance can vary substantially from one toy line to another. Toys range from being very fadish product items whose life expectancy is very short (several months) to classics like Monopoly and Scrabble that remain popular for decades. Frequently, the general nature of the life cycle for a particular new toy can be explained by the toy's origin. Currently, many new toy ideas originate in popular movies or television programs; hence, the life expectancy depends on the level and duration of popularity for these entertainment vehicles. For instance, Strawberry Shortcake products once enjoyed tremendous success, but since the demise of the television program, the popularity of these products has declined considerably. In contrast, Star Wars toys have enjoyed tremendous popularity for several years and sales are expected to continue at fairly substantial levels as a result of plans to continue sequels into the 1990s.

Technologically and socially the toy industry has undergone considerable change during the last few decades. On the technological front, toys have evolved dramatically from the corn husk dolls of the 17th century. Today, computer technology has had a major impact on toys and games in the sense that many computer games and software for home computers have broadened the appeal of such "toys" to all age groups. The old rule that toys appeal only to young children no longer applies.

In addition, today's computer and board games offer people the opportunity to exercise their analytical prowess by making key decisions that affect the outcome of the game. For all age groups, the trend appears to be away from passive games of chance to more active games of skill and decision making.

Socially, toys have evolved with the social values and moods of the country. As exemplified by the Fisher Price line of toys, educational values are often pre-eminent for parents shopping for toys for their younger children. Today, motives for purchasing toys include not only entertainment value but the belief that toys can play an important role in the mental, physical, and creative development of children. Contemporary social values are also reflected in the type of toys purchased for children. In past years, dolls only cried "Mama"; today dolls have more extensive vocabularies, are often anatomically correct, and are capable of a number of biological functions. Further, as the roles of men and women are becoming redefined, so too are toys and toy buying. Boys are increasingly accepting dolls (Star Wars figures, G.I. Joe figures, He-Man figures, Cabbage Patch dolls, etc.) and girls are increasingly becoming active in sports.

The toy industry is a highly competitive business. Of the estimated 125,000 different toy items produced each year, approximately 12,000 achieve a high level of customer acceptance. Of the 12,000 that do gain wide acceptance, only a few will return to the same level of public acceptance the following year. Thus, knowing what is and what is not a hot item is vital to survival in the toy industry.

Product offerings are planned by toy manufacturers in April and production levels are set at that time. Product competition takes several forms. Toy manufacturers compete for the rights to produce toy items that are expected to succeed (e.g., Star Wars toys), for the development of new products, and for the development of additional product features and options for existing toys. Manufacturers' representatives, printed materials, and trade shows are the major promotional vehicles used to obtain orders from wholesalers and retailers. Orders for toys are accepted from April through August, and they are filled on a first come, first served basis. Because the manufacturer produces a preset number of a given toy,

it is essential that wholesalers and retailers place orders for "hot" items early. Advertising is vitally important on both the local and national level. To create product awareness and to promote product and brand preference, toy manufacturers advertise heavily on television during Saturday mornings and on other programs directed toward children. At the local level, manufacturers and retailers often run cooperative newspaper or other local advertising to inform customers about which stores have the product and what their prices may be.

Clearly the major target market for toys is the youth market. Children with allowances and some with babysitting, yardwork, and other income represent a strong economic force. In addition, children play an "influencer" role in the family. Demand for a particular toy depends heavily upon the ability of children to influence parents to purchase that item. A number of research studies show that

1. children are strongly influenced by television commercials; in three out of four cases, toys preferred had recently been seen on television
2. peer groups are strong influences of toy preference for many children (this influence occurs in the form of the "two-step flow of communication"—television advertisements to playmates or peers who buy the product and then influence their friends to buy it, too)
3. younger children attempt to influence parental purchasing more frequently than do older children
4. the frequency of parents giving in to a child's requests for a particular toy increases with the age of the child
5. parents are preferred twice as much as peers as a source of product information even by adolescent children
6. mothers are the general purchasing agent for most families; hence, they are a majority of the actual toy purchasers

MIKE ROGERS' SITUATION

It is February of 1986 and Mike Rogers, toy department manager for Lockner's Department Store, is contemplating the role played by the toy department in the firm's overall merchandising strategy. Currently, the toy department is used as a seasonal "leader" department, that is, its primary function is to attract consumers into the store during the Christmas season by offering an excellent selection of popular toys at very competitive prices. During the rest of the year, the toy department is largely neglected both by Lockner's management and by Lockner's customers. At these times, Lockner's stocks seasonal toys plus a variety of the most popular toys, and prices are kept competitive.

Lockner's toy stock during the nonholiday seasons consists primarily of the most popular toys and dolls. Rogers has never bought many board games, European specialty toys, specialty and collectable dolls, or the more extraordinary toys. Instead, he has chosen to stay with the basics except for the seasonal promotions.

Recently Rogers has been wondering whether a new role for the toy department might be worth considering. Rogers believes it would be appropriate to review the department's whole situation with the idea of identifying strategy alternatives and making possible recommendations for a new merchandising role for the toy department.

ASSIGNMENT

☐ What options are available for 1986–1987?
☐ Identify the merchandising role you would adopt for Lockner's toy department and justify your selection.

CASE 13

Showcase Gallery

Jeffrey Dilts, The University of Akron

BACKGROUND

Frank Smith had just finalized a deal for a store facility that would become the future "Showcase Gallery." Smith had always wanted to open his own furniture store in the community and had the opportunity to do so when the previous owner of a home furnishings store retired. The investment involved a 14,000-square-foot facility located in a growing, high-income suburban area. He had been able to finance the venture through previous savings and investments by his family.

Smith has a working knowledge of the furniture trade, having been employed for 11 years as a manufacturer's representative in the industry. He brought to the venture a knowledge of case goods and upholstery and experience in interior design—a level of knowledge not commonly found among retail personnel.

The opportunity to work for himself, to be his own boss, had always been a dream. Consequently, he placed great importance upon operational autonomy. Having experienced the other half of the dealer-supplier relationship, however, Smith recognized that his autonomy may have to be tempered somewhat to achieve benefits possible only through mutual cooperation.

CURRENT SITUATION

With the purchase of the retail facility, Smith first needed to decide which type of dealer-supplier arrangement would be most appropriate for his needs and the firm's future success. He had three alternatives: conventional arrangements, programmed merchandising, and business format franchising. As he examined each option, Smith realized that his decision not only would have significance in developing trade relations but also could have a major impact on his performance as a dealer. Before making the final decision, Frank mentally reviewed the implications of each dealer-supplier arrangement.

Conventional Arrangement

With a conventional arrangement, Smith would typically deal with many suppliers. Since the highly fragmented furniture industry consists of many dealers and manufacturers, dependence of any one firm upon another was accordingly low. Consequently, a conventional arrangement tended to involve a relatively less enduring, loosely aligned relationship. Frank had observed that dealers were often suspicious of suppliers and did not cooperate fully for fear of being locked into a given relationship.

Despite the potential problems, some dealers thought that this arrangement gave them greater operational flexibility in serving their customers. They were not confined to particular styles or price points offered by a given manufacturer; instead, they were able to adapt quickly to the changing needs of the community by using a large number of suppliers to provide an appropriate product assortment, one that would have broad appeal to various customer groups.

Programmed Merchandising

Programmed merchandising arrangements represent a second alternative. This type of relationship would require Smith to establish several formal or implied licensing agreements with a select number of primary suppliers. These supplier-developed arrangements are tailor-made programs designed to generate greater dealer commitment for one or more of the supplier's product lines. To encourage strong dealer commitment, the supplier offers selected retailers such customized programs as in-store merchandising assistance, advertising allowances, discount structures, and sales promotional support.

In return for the right to handle the supplier's merchandise line and to benefit from the privileges of the supplier's programs, Smith would be expected to limit his involvement with competitive products and to commit significant resources in support of each of the supplier's merchandise lines. Support requirements include maintaining a minimum level of inventory investment in each of the supplier's lines of merchandise and committing a minimum amount of floor space to permanent display of the supplier's products. Smith would also be expected to cooperate in such supplier-initiated programs as factory-authorized sales and other special sales promotions.

Business Format Franchise

Colony House, a business format franchise, is the third alternative that Frank investigated in some depth. This option involves a tightly knit dealer-supplier arrangement in which Colony House (the franchisor) would provide Frank (the franchisee) with a patterned way of doing business. A total store concept is provided by Colony House. This concept includes a plan for store layout and design, a complete line of merchandise, a comprehensive merchandising program, and a detailed operations manual. Colony House's total store concept is highly coordinated to achieve a sharply focused image that appeals to a targeted group of consumers. Product assortments include early and traditional American furniture

and home accessory items. In contrast to the industry's frequent style changes, Colony's continuity of established merchandise lines enables customers to purchase coordinated furniture pieces over an extended period of time.

The initial investment for a standard 12,000-square-foot operation would be approximately $250,000. Since Frank already has an existing facility, Colony House would require that he alter the exterior and interior of the building to make it consistent with the Colony House image. In return, Colony would provide architectural plans, training, and merchandising backup. Although no franchise fee was required, an annual fee (5% of sales) will be charged for promotional support.

Colony House believes that strong commitment is necessary for the formulated concept to succeed. Consequently, it screens retail applicants closely to determine their compatibility with Colony House. Each applicant's background, personality, and business philosophy are reviewed. Franchisees, although independent businesses, are expected to adhere very closely to Colony's recommendations regarding store operations and merchandising.

ASSIGNMENT

- [ ] Outline the advantages and disadvantages of each supplier-dealer arrangement.
- [ ] Recommend the most suitable supplier-dealer arrangement for Frank Smith. Provide the rationale for your recommendation.
- [ ] Advise Smith on how your recommendation will influence his trade relations and store performance.

CASE 14

J. Rogers Department Stores Company

Dale M. Lewison, The University of Akron
Jon Hawes, The University of Akron

BACKGROUND

Rogers' Emporium was established in 1907 by John Rogers. The foundation for the firm's present-day image as one of the leading retail merchandisers in the southwestern United States is based on the founder's early recognition of the potential market demand for upscale merchandise that emerged during the oil boom years. As old "J. R." used to say, "give the customers what they want, but always make a profit." This guiding principle has always served as the basic merchandising and

operating policy for the firm and has given it a national reputation as a unique and profitable merchandiser of a wide variety of unusual and everyday products and services.

The firm was reorganized into J. Rogers Department Stores Company in 1952. Its success has been attributed largely to its adherence to the policy of "gross margin maintenance." It is and always has been the company's operating goal to obtain an overall 40 percent gross margin for each of its stores. The following gross margin objectives were established for each of the store's general merchandise categories: 50 percent for wearing apparel, 60 percent for accessories, 30 percent for household goods, 30 percent for household furnishings, 40 percent for consumer electronics, and 40 percent for sporting goods.

Currently, the J. Rogers Department Stores Company operates three full-line department stores at Great Plains Mall, Parkside Mall, and Southland Mall. By March of this year the company's new store in Dixieland Mall will be open and in full operation. As with the three current stores, the new outlet will be a full-service department store appealing to the area's middle- and upper-class consumers.

As the GMM (general merchandise manager) for the last five years, Louis Stouch has been directly responsible for overseeing most of the major buying decisions for all three stores. During his tenure as GMM, Louis' track record has been outstanding as judged by the criterion of achieving the expected 40 percent overall gross margin. In each of the major merchandise categories and for most of the individual product lines, expected gross margins were realized. One of the more important exceptions has been Great Western Clothing Company's line of men's suits, The Naturals. Gross margins realized on The Naturals have varied considerably, and unsatis-

factory performance levels have characterized this product line in three of the last five years. A review of Great Western's other product lines carried by J. Rogers, however, revealed a sales and gross margin performance meeting or exceeding the firm's expectations. This latter fact would suggest the need to maintain good relationships with the Great Western Clothing Company.

CURRENT SITUATION

With the rapidly approaching summer buying season, Stouch must make an immediate decision whether to continue to carry The Naturals line of men's suits. He has already received next year's proposed merchandising program for The Naturals (see Figures 1 and 2) from Sharon Neidert, national sales manager for Great Western Clothing Company. Before making any decision regarding The Naturals, a comprehensive comparative analysis between last year's merchandising program (Figure 3, p. 750) and the new proposed program seemed in order. Having skimmed the new program, Stouch noticed a number of significant changes; perhaps these changes might be sufficient to ensure the 50 percent gross margin expectations that have not always

---

Mr. Louis Stouch
General Merchandise Manager
J. Rogers Department Stores
400 East Plains Ave
Dallas, Texas 78041

Dear Mr. Stouch:

A new season is upon us and we at Great Western Clothing Company are excited about our new merchandising program for The Naturals. The new program entails numerous changes, and we believe these changes will provide you with the opportunity to realize a substantial increase in unit sales at profitable levels. With the opening of your new store and the quantity discount structure of the new merchandising program, we think it would be in your best interest to place a unit order in excess of 300 units. Our sales representative, Jeb Works, will be calling upon you shortly to finalize your order. As always, we are looking forward to working with you and your organization.

Sincerely,

Sharon Neidert
National Sales Manager
Great Western Clothing Company

FIGURE 1

Product class	Men's apparel
Product line	"The Naturals"—mix and match suits
Product items	The summer "Naturals" are available as separate pieces and can be sold in any coat/slack combination (mix and match). Solid and patterned coats are available in standard sizes 30–48 and long sizes 40–48. Slacks are available in standard waist sizes. A standard length allows the slack to be altered to the customer's dimensions.

Merchandising program

List price	Coat: $90 Slack: $30
Discount structure	
Trade (chain)	Coat: 30%, 15%, 10% Slack: 25%, 10%, 5%
Quantity (noncumulative)	Coat: 0% per unit—1–99 units 1% per unit—100–199 units 4% per unit—200–299 units 8% per unit—300 or more units Slack: 0% per unit—1–199 units 1% per unit—200–299 units 4% per unit—300 or more units
Cash	2/10, n 30
Promotional allowance	Coat: 0% per unit—1–199 units .5% per unit—200–299 units 1.5% per unit—300 or more units Slack: 0% per unit—1–299 units 1% per unit—300 or more units
Shipping terms	FOB origin, freight prepaid
Reorder delivery time	2–3 weeks
Minimum reorder quantity	1 dozen

FIGURE 2

Year 2 merchandising program for The Naturals, Great Western Clothing Company

been realized in the past. Pressed for time, he decided to ask the assistant GMM, Cheryl Nader, to conduct the comparative analysis and to recommend possible courses of action.

ASSIGNMENT

☐ Assume the role of Cheryl Nader and develop a comprehensive comparative analysis report for each year of The Naturals merchandising program. Having discussed the project with Louis Stouch, you

have agreed to include within the report the following items:

1. A determination of the realized gross margin for the first year's program. (Sales records will show that 190 units were ordered and sold. Expense records will show that the average transportation cost per unit is 4 percent of list price, the average transit insurance cost per unit is 1 percent of list price, and the average alteration cost per unit is 1 percent of list price.)

2. A determination of the expected gross margin for the second year's program at various estimated unit sales levels (e.g., 175, 200, 250, and 300 units).

FIGURE 3

Year 1 merchandising program for The Naturals, Great Western Clothing Company

3. A statement of the advantages and disadvantages of the first year's program as compared to the second year's program.

4. A description of the alternative courses of action that are open to the company regarding the 1986 program.

5. A recommendation and justification of which alternative the company should pursue.

CASE 15

Itty-bitty Baby Boutique

J. B. Wilkinson, The University of Akron

BACKGROUND

Recent changes in the federal tax law authorized by the Economic Recovery Act of 1981 prompted many trade journals to publish articles about the new regulations that simplify the last in, first out (LIFO) method of inventory valuation used by retailers. Consequently, Millie Marie Baker, owner of Itty-bitty Baby Boutique, was rethinking her use of the "traditional" retail method of inventory valuation that estimates ending inventory at lower of cost or market (LCM).

Early in June of 1982, Baker consulted Bill Truly, senior auditor for B. S. Cheatum & Co., for an opinion. His response is shown in Figure 1.

☐ Advise Baker based on Truly's comments. Should she switch to dollar-value LIFO? Why? Why not?

FIGURE 1
Memorandum describing LIFO uses

B. S. Cheatum & Co.

MEMORANDUM

Date: July 5, 1982

TO: Ms. Millie Marie Baker, Owner
Itty-bitty Baby Boutique

FROM: Bill Truly, Senior Auditor
B. S. Cheatum & Co.

RE: Possible LIFO Election

Your request for a formal comparison of current inventory valuation procedures to an appropriate dollar-value LIFO method for Itty-bitty Baby Boutique has received careful consideration. Because Itty-bitty is a specialty store that carries a full line of infant apparel and some baby furniture and equipment, we believe that use of the Department Store Inventory Price Index for "Infants' Wear" will be acceptable to the IRS. The comparison shown below is premised on this assumption.

To demonstrate the value of dollar-value LIFO to your business, we reconstructed your 1981 income statement as it would have been if dollar-value LIFO had been elected for that year. Schedule 1 is a simplified version of your 1981 income statement. Schedule 2 explains determination of 1981 ending inventory under the retail method, lower of cost or market inventory valuation model. Schedule 3 illustrates the calculations necessary to estimate ending inventory under dollar-value LIFO using 1981 data. Notice that the cost ratio used to reduce the inventory increment to cost is based on purchases and is the complement of the net markon percentage—cumulative markon less markdowns expressed as a percentage of retail. The relevant BLS Department Store Inventory Price Indexes for Infants' Wear are shown below.

<u>Infants' Wear</u>

	Price Index (Jan. 1941 = 100)	Percent Change from Jan. 19XX to Jan. 19XX + 1
Jan. 1980	378.8	
Jan. 1981	420.7	11.1
Jan. 1982	444.7	5.7

In this illustration, your base year would begin Jan. 1, 1981. Consequently, the Jan. 1981 price index represents 100.0, and the adjusted price index for any year ended December 31, 19XX is found by dividing the following January index by the Jan. 1981 index. The adjusted price index for the year ended December 31, 1981 is 105.7 (444.7/420.7) and is used to determine the 1981 ending inventory in base year retail dollars.

Notice that the retail value of ending inventory that was found for the LCM model is reduced to base year cost (at retail) by dividing with the adjusted LIFO price index (105.7/100). An incremental inventory layer occurs if ending inventory at base year cost exceeds the previous year's ending inventory at base year cost. A decrement occurs if ending inventory at base year cost is less than the previous year's ending inventory at base year cost. When a decrement occurs, previous inventory layers must be liquidated in reverse order. Increments or decrements are first determined with base year retail dollars and then converted to relevant current-year retail dollars by the appropriate LIFO price index and then adjusted to cost using the cost ratio. Ending inventory is the sum of base year inventory at base year cost and the increments, if any, at current relevant year costs.

For the year ended December 31, 1981, ending inventory under the "traditional" retail method, LCM, was $370,000. Ending inventory at LIFO cost would have been $351,328. It follows that cost of sales is $1,080,000 under the LCM model and $1,098,672 under dollar-value LIFO. However, LIFO is a cost method. If you had elected LIFO for the year ended December 31, 1981, the beginning inventory would have had to be restated to cost. The $350,000 beginning inventory is stated at lower of cost or market. We estimate that a positive adjustment of $68,800 would have been required. This adjustment would reduce the LIFO cost of sales to $1,029,872. Thus, gross margin would have been $770,128 under LIFO. At a marginal tax rate of 50%, your tax bill would have been $25,064 more under dollar-value LIFO.

It is difficult to project what your 1982 dollar-value LIFO experience might be. We do estimate that you would have to restate 1982 beginning inventory to cost. That adjustment is likely to be around $74,000. Also, we are concerned about your expected markdowns as a percent of sales. The LCM model allows you to reduce ending inventory to lower of cost or market. Dollar-value LIFO only removes the effects of inflation. Which is best for you? Do you expect high markdowns as a percent of sales in the future? Another consideration is your ability to correctly predict sales and plan for inventory levels sufficient to prevent decrements. Inventory decrements under LIFO cause older costs (lower costs in periods of inflation) to enter the calculation of cost of sales. As a result, most businesses control inventory levels carefully to prevent liquidation of previous inventory layers.

We advise you to consider this decision carefully. Expected price level changes, inventory levels, and markdowns are important factors in estimating the financial advantage of electing dollar-value LIFO.

Please let us know your decision as soon as possible.

Schedule 1: 1981 Income Data for Itty-bitty Baby Boutique

Net sales	$1,800,000
less cost of sales (1)	1,080,000
Gross profit	720,000
less operating expense	666,000
Operating profit	$ 54,000

Notes:
(1) Cost of sales is computed as follows: Beginning inventory (at cost) + Purchases (at cost) − Ending inventory (at cost). Ending inventory for Itty-bitty was valued at lower of cost or market using the retail method. These computations are shown in Schedule 2.

Schedule 2: Determination of 1981 Ending Inventory Using Retail Method, LCM Model

	At Cost	At Retail	Cost Ratio
Inventory, Jan. 1, 1981	$ 350,000	$ 698,000	
Purchases	1,100,000	2,200,000	
Net additional markups		2,000	
Total (incl. beginning inv.)	$1,450,000	$ 2,900,000	.50
Deduct:			
Sales		(1,800,000)	
Net markdowns		(360,000)	
Ending inventory at LCM	$ 370,000 (1)	$ 740,000	

Notes:
(1) Ending inventory at LCM was found by reducing ending inventory at retail to cost through application of the cost ratio. The cost ratio for the LCM model is computed by dividing total merchandise available for sale at cost by total merchandise available for sale at retail before markdowns.

Schedule 3: Determination of 1981 Ending Inventory Using the Dollar-Value LIFO Method

Steps:
1. Price index for the year ended December 31, 1981 (Jan. 1, 1981 = 100) is 105.7.

2. Computation of cost ratio and ending inventory at retail.

	At Cost	At Retail	Cost Ratio
Inventory, Jan. 1, 1981	$ 350,000	$ 698,000	
Purchases	1,100,000	2,200,000	
Net additional markups		2,000	
Net markdowns		(360,000)	
Total (excl. beginning inv.)	1,100,000	1,842,000	.60
Total (incl. beginning inv.)	1,450,000	2,540,000	
Deduct:			
Sales		(1,800,000)	
Ending inventory at retail		$ 740,000	
Ending inventory at cost	$ 444,000		

3. Computation of ending inventory at LIFO cost.

	At Cost	At Retail
Ending inventory at retail deflated to base year retail $		$ 700,095 (1)
Base layer: At base yr. cost	$ 350,000	
At base yr. retail		(698,000)
Increment (or decrement) at base-year retail		2,095
Increment (or decrement) at current-year retail		2,214 (2)

CASE 16

Dude's Duds: Pricing a New Product Line

Jon Hawes, The University of Akron

BACKGROUND

Dude's Duds is a large, well-known clothing store chain with more than 400 retail outlets located throughout the United States and Canada. Appealing to teenagers and young aduls, Dude's success is based largely on the firm's ability to market faddish and fashionable merchandise at reasonable, competitive prices. While Dude's Duds stocks a limited selection of national manufacturers' brands (e.g., Levi's and Haggar) to enhance its store image and to generate consumer traffic, the vast majority of each outlet's merchandise consists of the firm's own private retailer brands. To ensure a reliable source of supply for their private labels, Dude's Duds purchased the Fashion-Plus Clothing Company (FPCC) in 1978. At the time of the takeover, FPCC was a well-established national manufacturer of high quality, fashionable apparel. FPCC's product mix consisted of a wide line of both men's and women's wearing apparel.

CURRENT SITUATION

The recent increase in the popularity and acceptance of western wearing apparel by many diverse consumer groups throughout all market areas of the country prompted Ralph West, general merchandise manager for Dude's Duds, to investigate the possibility of adding a new line of men's western-style shirts. Preliminary results of that investigation led West to conclude that such a line would appeal to the consumer group the firm identified as the "swingers"—a consumer market segment that wants faddish and stylish clothing of good quality but whose discretionary income requires moder-

ate prices. To West, adding a new line of men's western shirts would make good merchandising sense, but the production staff at Fashion-Plus will ultimately decide whether the new line is feasible given the price, cost, and profit constraints under which it must produce the product.

While Fashion-Plus is a wholly owned subsidiary of Dude's Duds, Inc., FPCC's management is responsible for making all production decisions. To determine the feasibility of new product lines, Bill Morris, manager for new product development, must collect the necessary information to make a cost and break-even analysis, to project expected profits, and to recommend a suggested retail price as well as a manufacturer's price (the price that Fashion-Plus should charge Dude's Duds). Having spent the last two weeks collecting data, Morris believes he now has the necessary information to make the required evaluations of the new western shirt project. Before proceeding with his analysis, he reviews the following information he has collected:

1. Several competitors have introduced similar lines of men's western shirts. Market research indicates that these lines are selling at a brisk pace at competitive retail stores for the following prices:

Retail Selling Price	Number of Times Observed
$14.00	2
15.00	7
16.00	5
17.00	3

2. Dude's Duds will apply a 40% initial markup on the retail selling price of shirts.
3. Production costs for the new shirts are estimated to be

Cloth	$2.20 per shirt
Buttons	.05 per shirt
Thread	.05 per shirt
Direct labor	20 minutes per shirt
Shipping weight	2 pounds per packaged shirt

4. Basic marketing costs for introducing the new line of shirts are estimated to be $300,000 the first year if a penetration pricing policy is used or $340,000 if a skimming pricing policy is employed.

5. A large company, FPCC has 15 production facilities strategically located throughout the United States. Last year, the average round-trip distance from FPCC production facilities to Dude's Duds outlets was 225 miles. Current plans are to produce the new line of shirts at each of FPCC's production facilities.

6. An examination of FPCC's annual report reveals the following information:

Managerial salaries	$1,500,000
Rent and utilities expense	1,200,000
Transportation costs	
(1,250,000 miles)	750,000
Depreciation on plant and	
equipment	1,300,000
Other overhead	2,000,000
Direct labor costs	
(2,000,000 hours)	8,000,000

Total company sales	45,000,000
Average order size	1,000 pounds

7. The Kurt Behrens Market Research Corporation was hired to develop a sales forecast for the new line of western shirts. Their research findings estimate that if a skimming pricing policy were used, Dude's Duds could expect to sell approximately 110,000–130,000 shirts. Under a penetration-type pricing policy, the Behrens organization estimates a unit sales volume of approximately 130,000–150,000 shirts.

ASSIGNMENT

☐ Assume that Bill Morris was unexpectedly called out of town and he has asked you to prepare the analysis and written report on the feasibility of the project, then make a recommendation for the pricing strategy he should use. At a minimum, your analysis should include a cost analysis (variable cost per shirt, fixed cost allocation for the line, and total cost per shirt), a break-even analysis in units and dollars, a determination of the manufacturer's price and suggested retail price, and a statement of expected profit the company can derive from the new line.

CASE 17

Campbell Clothiers

Kenneth Mast, The University of Akron
Dale M. Lewison, The University of Akron

BACKGROUND

Campbell Clothiers is a local chain of specialty stores that offers an extensive selection of men's and women's sporting and casual apparel and accessories. By appealing to the upscale tastes of middle- and upper-class consumers for fashionable casual and sporting apparel, Gabe and Sandy Campbell have successfully expanded their operation to include nine stores in northeastern Ohio. The success of Campbell Clothiers can be attributed to a number of merchandising factors. Campbell's is known for its unique offering of high-quality product lines, plush yet exciting store atmospherics, friendly and competent salespeople, and image-building promotions. Campbell's tends to limit its product selection to middle and upper pricing lines and points; however, the store's January and July clearance sales have almost become a legend in the local area as a value-packed sales promotion. While each of these factors has been an important ingredient in Campbell's successful merchandising blend, the store's management team believes the most important overall success ingredient is the organization's commitment to maintaining and cultivating its image of exclusivity. At Campbell Clothiers, exclusive means being unique, selective, different, tasteful, and distinctive in all of its merchandising activities.

CURRENT SITUATION

The morning had started peacefully for Jacqueline Theiss, sales promotion manager for Campbell Clothiers. As usual it did not stay that way. Campbell's new sportswear buyer, Kris Kovach, burst into Theiss' office:

Kris: Jacqueline, I just heard that Michizuki cancelled its sponsorship of the Super Bowl of Golf. This is a great opportunity to promote our new line of men's and women's sportswear by Outdoor World! A 20 percent off sale would really draw in customer traffic.

Jacqueline: What makes you think that?

Kris: Surely, WWTV is going to have to unload a lot of local air time in a hurry. If we act fast I know we can get some prime time slots at bargain rates. A sale this early in the season would really attract some attention.

Jacqueline: Where do you propose we get the money for this unexpected blessing? Not to mention the fact that two weeks is hardly enough time to plan, schedule, shoot, and edit a commercial.

Kris: You must have some money stuck away somewhere. And, I have already checked with Outdoor World and they have several canned commercials available for a small fee. All we would have to do is to add our sales promotional message and store identification to the end of the film.

Jacqueline: Assuming we can find the money—which is a big assumption—and these canned commercials are available and acceptable, is it worthwhile to spend this type of money on this particular product line?

Kris: You bet it is! Outdoor World is a well known national brand, it offers something for both men and women, and we have sufficient stock in all of our stores to support this type of sales promotion effort.

Jacqueline: Well, Kris, I have a meeting in five minutes. Let me think about it and I will get back to you with a decision by tomorrow afternoon.

Kris: OK, but we need to act quickly or we will lose this opportunity. I would really appreciate your support on this; it can be a successful campaign.

After her 10 o'clock meeting and lunch, Theiss contacted her account representative at WWTV and learned that Michizuki had in fact cancelled its sponsorship of the Super Bowl of Golf. Theiss was offered a 30 percent discount off the rate book price for local spots during the tournament. The minimum number of 30-second spots was six: four spots on Saturday and two spots on Sunday. In a quick mental calculation, Theiss determined the total minimum cost would be approximately $30,000 for air time. She indicated her interest in the spots and informed the account representative that she would make a decision within 24 hours.

The considerable time constraints surrounding the decision and numerous other pressing business matters led Theiss to seek help from Tyler Smith, the advertising manager for Campbell Clothiers. In the lengthy discussion that ensued, Theiss identified several key issues.

1. The $30,000 minimum price tag for air time would consume about 40 percent of Campbell's reserve advertising budget set aside each year for unexpected situations. It would leave a $45,000 reserve for the remainder of the year. This assumes that the expected $5,000 needed for producing the commercial and paying the fees asked by Outdoor World could be found elsewhere.

2. Kris Kovach has already spent most of her entire promotional budget and an examination of her promotional expenditures revealed inadequate support of the Outdoor World line of sportswear. Through luncheon and grapevine conversations, Theiss discovered that the line was not selling as well as had been expected and that Kovach was feeling a great deal of heat from the general merchandise manager.

3. While the Super Bowl of Golf is the single most important local sporting event during the year, its appeal is still limited to a rather select group of customers.

4. WWTV is a satellite station affiliate of the national network that has broadcasting rights to the Super Bowl of Golf. WWTV is a UHF station whose broadcast signal provides only partial coverage of the company's nine store trading areas. Specifically, WWTV provides 100 percent coverage of five store trading areas, 50 percent coverage of two store trading areas, and little or no coverage for two trading areas.

With the key issues of concern being identified, Tyler agreed to drop everything and to study the entire situation. He thought that by noon tomorrow he could recommend possible alternative courses of action.

ASSIGNMENT

☐ Assume Tyler Smith's role. Write a report outlining the various alternative courses of action. Recommend which alternative action the company should pursue and provide a complete justification for your recommendation.

Sweatmate Ltd.

George Prough, The University of Akron

BACKGROUND

Janet McGill has been working for the last 10 months as advertising director for Sweatmate Ltd., a manufacturer of home exercise equipment. Sweatmate's overall marketing efforts have been reasonably successful, resulting in a market share of about 6% of the home exercise equipment market. Industry experts say that Sweatmate's success is largely due to its product line, which they say is certainly above average in all respects. The company's products are sold through department stores, sports specialty stores, and discount stores. No sales effort is being directed at health spas or recreation and fitness centers, nor is any planned for some time.

CURRENT SITUATION

Part of McGill's efforts during the last 10 months have involved analyzing the existing advertising program. The national advertising seemed fine. Sweatmate was running magazine ads in some of the better known sport and fitness publications aimed at the household market. Brand awareness was about at the levels expected, roughly the same as that for most other competitors in the same market position as Sweatmate.

The more McGill looked, however, the more it became clear to her that some problems existed with the local and store advertising. About five years ago, John Occhino, her predecessor, had begun a cooperative advertising program. The program encouraged stores to develop ads featuring Sweatmate products either as the entire ad or as a portion of the ad. Sweatmate would then reimburse the store for 50% of the media costs associated directly with the Sweatmate products. Thus if the store spent $250 on the advertisement and the Sweatmate products' section of the ad occupied half the space or time of the ad, Sweatmate would reimburse the store $125. In addition, Sweatmate would send stores camera-ready copies of line drawings of the products as well as the Sweatmate trademarked logo for use in the newspaper ads. A store would then use these and develop its own ad, either in the store's advertising department, with the store's ad agency, or with the retail advertising department of the local newspaper. The maximum annual reimbursement allowance was 5% of the store's purchases from Sweatmate during that year.

In looking through the cooperative advertising files, McGill found that mainly larger stores took advantage of the program. Many had their own advertising departments or made extensive use of local advertising, especially newspapers. Because of that, very few of the ads looked alike or coincided in timing with Sweatmate's national advertising. The ads lacked consistency because Sweatmate's customers, the stores, controlled them.

ONE RETAILER'S PERSPECTIVE

McGill also found several letters from some of the smaller retailers complaining about the advertising program. She knew that the current system might not be used by small stores that had no advertising departments, no ad agency, and no large budget. McGill decided to pull one of these letters and determine the small retailer's view of the program.

She found the file of Baker's Sports Shop, a sporting goods store in Salem, Indiana. Included in the file was correspondence with Jon Baker, owner of the store. The correspondence indicated that Baker had tried to use the existing cooperative program but found it unsatisfactory.

Baker's letters indicated that in his small market no major stores existed to promote Sweatmate products. As a result, local awareness of the brand was quite limited. His budget was not large enough to give Sweatmate products the kind of visibility needed to build brand awareness, so Baker did very little in the way of using, let alone featuring, Sweatmate products in the store's advertising. In addition, Baker sometimes had found the artwork provided by Sweatmate to be the wrong size (Sweatmate required ads to be a prescribed minimum size).

Another complaint Baker voiced was that Sweatmate, in requiring the ad to be done by the stores, provided very little real assistance to those stores. He wanted more help. Baker believed that if Sweatmate could provide complete ads (artwork plus copy) for use by the stores, then his store would be better able to sell Sweatmate products. Brand awareness could be built up, and the stores and the products would do better.

A POSSIBLE SOLUTION

McGill thought she knew what Baker wanted. A quick phone call to Baker's Sports Shop confirmed this. He wanted completed newspaper ads with a place at the bottom of the ad for imprinting the names of the local dealers that carried Sweatmate products. The ad would be product rather than store oriented; it would give local dealers a chance to place their name, address, store hours, and similar information in an allotted space in the ad; and the stores would need to do little or no work in getting such an ad placed locally. McGill and Baker also discussed the possibility of a total media cooperative effort, using radio, Yellow Pages, outdoor, and whatever other advertising possibilities came to mind. In all these efforts, the stores cooperating would pay a minimal fee for their involvement in the cooperative activity.

McGill wasn't sure what to do next. The annual marketing and advertising plans were due soon. The old system of letting the customers control the retail advertising for Sweatmate worked very well, but only in portions of the total retail spectrum. A dealer-controlled system might offer some benefits in traditionally neglected areas. McGill had two weeks for her decision.

ASSIGNMENT

- [ ] What are the benefits and costs of customer-controlled and dealer-controlled cooperative advertising programs?
- [ ] What do you recommend that McGill do?

NAME INDEX

SUBJECT INDEX